P9-CMF-609

AN AMERICAN ANTHOLOGY

1787-1900

SELECTIONS ILLUSTRATING THE EDITOR'S CRITICAL REVIEW OF AMERICAN POETRY IN THE NINETEENTH CENTURY

EDITED BY

EDMUND CLARENCE STEDMAN

AUTHOR OF "POETS OF AMERICA," "VICTORIAN POETS," ETC.
AND EDITOR OF "A VICTORIAN ANTHOLOGY"

BOSTON AND NEW YORK
HOUGHTON MIFFLIN COMPANY
The Riverside Press Cambridge

COPYRIGHT NOTICE

I

MESSRS. D. APPLETON & CO., New York. — *W. C. Bryant:* Works — "Thanatopsis," "To a Waterfowl," "Oh, Fairest of the Rural Maids," "A Forest Hymn," "June," "The Past," "The Evening Wind," "To a Fringed Gentian," "The Hunter of the Prairies," "The Battle-Field," "An Evening Revery," "The Antiquity of Freedom," "America," "The Planting of the Apple Tree," "The May Sun sheds an Amber Light," "The Conqueror's Grave," "The Poet," "My Autumn Walk," "The Death of Slavery," "In Memory of John Lothrop Motley," "The Flood of Years;" *Abraham Coles:* "Dies Iræ;" *G. W. Doane:* Writings — "Evening," "Robin Redbreast;" *F. G. Halleck:* Writings — "Marco Bozzaris," "On the Death of J. R. Drake," "Alnwick Castle," "Burns," "Red Jacket;" *F. L. Stanton:* Songs of the Soil — "The Mocking Bird," "A Little Way."

MESSRS. WM. E. ASHMALL & CO., Arlington, N. J. — *Frances D. Swift Tatnall:* "Art Thou the Same?"

MESSRS. RICHARD G. BADGER & CO., Boston. — *Edwin Arlington Robinson:* The Children of the Night.

MESSRS. A. S. BARNES & CO., New York. — *Ray Palmer:* Poetical Works.

MESSRS BENZIGER BROTHERS, New York. — *Edmund Hill, C. P.:* Passion Flowers; *M. F. Egan:* Songs and Sonnets.

THE BOWEN-MERRILL COMPANY, Indianapolis. — *J. W. Riley:* Neighborly Poems, — Afterwhiles, — Rhymes of Childhood, — Flying Islands of the Night, — Armazindy (copyrighted by Mr. Riley); *F. L. Stanton:* Comes One with a Song (copyrighted by the Bowen-Merrill Co.).

BRENTANOS, New York. — *J. H. Boner:* Whispering Pines; *L. E. Mitchell:* Sylvian; *Tracy Robinson:* Song of the Palm.

THE CENTURY COMPANY, New York. — *C. E. Carryl:* The Admiral's Caravan, — Davy and the Goblin; *R. W. Gilder:* Five Books of Song, — In Palestine; *Oliver Herford:* Artful Antics; *R. U. Johnson:* Songs of Liberty, — The Winter Hour; *S. W. Mitchell:* Collected Poems; *J. W. Riley:* Poems Here at Home; *Irwin Russell:* Poems. From "The Century Magazine" and "St. Nicholas," — *J. K. Bangs:* "The Little Elf;" *John Bennett:* Songs from "Master Skylark;" *J. H. Boner:* "Poe's Cottage at Fordham;" *R. R. Bowker:* "Thomas à Kempis;" *Alice W. Brotherton:* "My Enemy;" *Alice L. Bunner:* "Immutabilis;" *Virginia W. Cloud:* "Care;" *W. D. Ellwanger:* "To Jessie's Dancing Feet;" *W. H. Hayne:* "Moonlight Song;" *Mary T. Higginson:* "Inheritance;" *T. W. Higginson:* "Such Stuff as Dreams;" *Mildred Howells:* "Romance;" *J. H. Ingham:* "Genesis;" *Tudor Jenks:* "Afternoon Tea;" *Mrs. R. H. Lathrop:* "Give me not Tears;" *Julie M. Lippmann:* "Love and Life," "Stone Walls;" *Agnes L. Carter Mason:* "Whenever a Little Child is Born;" *W. T. Meredith:* "Farragut;" *Harriet Monroe:* "A Farewell;" *Harriet S. Morgridge:* "Mother Goose Sonnets;" *Laura E. Richards:* "Where Helen Sits;" *A. B. Saxton:* "The First Step;" *C. W. Stoddard:* "Albatross;" *Edith M. Thomas:* "Breath of Hampstead Heath;" *W. H. Thompson:* "High Tide at Gettysburg," "Come Love or Death;" *L. F. Tooker:* "The Last Fight," "His Quest;" *Ella Wheeler Wilcox:* "Recrimination;" *R. B. Wilson:* "Such is the Death the Soldier dies;" *G. E. Woodberry:* "On a Portrait of Columbus," "America to England;" *William Young:* "Judith."

The Robert Clarke Company, Cincinnati. — *W. D. Gallagher:* Miami Woods; *W. H. Lytle:* Poems; *J. J. Piatt:* Odes in Ohio; *G. D. Prentice:* Poems; *W. H. Venable:* Melodies of the Heart, — The Last Flight.

Messrs. Henry T. Coates & Co., Philadelphia. — *Ethel Lynn Beers:* All Quiet along the Potomac, and Other Poems; *C. F. Hoffman:* Poems; *D. L. Proudfit:* Mask and Domino; *E. W. Watson:* Songs of Flying Hours.

The Columbia Monthly, New York. — *G. S. Hellman:* "Coleridge," "The Hudson."

The Cosmopolitan, Irvington, N. Y. — *Robert Bridges:* "The Unillumined Verge;" *W. H. Hayne:* "An Autumn Breeze," "The Yule Log."

The Criterion, New York. — *John Bennett:* "Her Answer;" *Rupert Hughes:* "For Decoration Day;" *Tudor Jenks:* "The Spirit of the Maine;" *Wilbur Underwood:* "The Cattle of his Hand."

Messrs. Thomas Y. Crowell & Co., New York. — *Sarah K. Bolton:* The Inevitable, and Other Poems; *N. H. Dole:* The Hawthorne Tree, and Other Poems; *E. F. Fenollosa:* East and West.

Mr. Joseph George Cupples, Boston. — *H. B. Carpenter:* A Poet's Last Songs.

Messrs. De Wolfe, Fiske & Co., Boston. — *Sarah P. McLean Greene:* Towhead.

The Dial, Chicago. — *C. L. Moore:* "To England."

Messrs. Dodd, Mead & Co., New York. — *P. L. Dunbar:* Lyrics of Lowly Life, — Lyrics of the Hearthside; *Ernest McGaffey:* Poems; *H. T. Peck:* Greystone and Porphyry. From "The Bookman," — *William Young:* "Philomel to Corydon."

The R. R. Donnelly & Sons Company, Chicago. — *Francis Brooks:* Poems; *Wallace Rice and Barrett Eastman:* Under the Stars, and Other Verses; *Wallace Rice:* The Flying Sands.

The Doubleday and McClure Company, New York. — *Martha G. Dickinson:* Within the Hedge; *Edwin Markham:* The Man with the Hoe, and Other Poems; *Howard Weeden:* Bandanna Ballads.

Messrs. E. P. Dutton & Co., New York. — *May Riley Smith:* Sometime, and Other Poems.

East and West, New York. — *Beatrix D. Lloyd:* "Night Wind;" *Alice Duer Miller:* "Song."

Mr. George H. Ellis, Boston. — *M. J. Savage:* Poems.

Messrs. Dana Estes & Co., Boston. — *Lloyd Mifflin:* At the Gates of Song.

Messrs. Funk & Wagnalls, New York. — *Richard Realf:* Poems.

Messrs. Harper & Brothers, New York. — *J. K. Bangs:* Cobwebs from a Library Corner — "To a Withered Rose," "May 30, 1893;" *Wallace Bruce:* Wayside Poems — "Two Argosies;" *William Allen Butler:* Nothing to Wear, and Other Poems; *Will Carleton:* Farm Ballads — "Out of the Old House, Nancy;" *G. W. Carryl:* Fables for the Frivolous — "The Sycophantic Fox;" *G. W. Curtis:* "Ebb and Flow;" *Cora Fabbri:* Lyrics — "White Roses;" *W. D. Howells:* Stops of Various Quills — "From Generation to Generation," "Change," "If," "Hope," "Vision," "Judgment Day," "What shall it Profit;" *Herman Melville:* Battle Pieces — "The College Colonel," "The Eagle of the Blue," "On the Slain at Chickamauga," "An Uninscribed Monument;" *W. A. Muhlenberg:* Works — "I Would not Live Alway," "Heaven's Magnificence;" *Margaret E. Sangster:* On the Road Home, — Easter Bells — "Whittier," "Awakening;" *Alice A. Sewall James:* Ode to Girlhood, and Other Poems — "Sinfonia Eroica," "The Butterfly," "Processional;" *Lew Wallace:* Song from "Ben Hur." From "Harper's Magazine" and "Harper's Weekly," — *Anna C. Brackett:* "In Hades;" *G. W. Carryl:* "When the Great Gray Ships come in;" *Virginia W. Cloud:* "An Old Street;" *George Cooper:* "Only One;" *J. B. Gilder:* "The Parting of the Ways;" *Hildegarde Hawthorne:* "A Song," "My Rose;" *W. H. Hayne:* "Exiles;" *Walter Malone:* "October in Tennessee;" *G. E. Montgomery:* "A Dead Soldier;" *R. K. Munkittrick:* "A Bulb;" *N. G. Shepherd:* "Roll-Call;" *R. H. Stoddard:* "The Lover;" *Princess Troubetskoy:* "A Mood," "Before the Rain," "A Sonnet;" *Mary E. Wilkins:* "Now is the Cherry in Bloom;" *G. E. Woodberry:* "Love's Rosary."

Messrs. Henry Holt & Co., New York. — *H. A. Beers:* The Ways of Yale; *C. L. Moore:* Book of Day Dreams; *R. K. Weeks:* Poems; *Theodore Winthrop:* Poems.

Messrs. Houghton, Mifflin & Co., Boston. — *T. B. Aldrich:* Poetical Works; *George Arnold:* Poems; *Arlo Bates:* Under the Beech Tree; *Gertrude Bloede:* Beyond the Shadow; *Alice Brown:* The Road to Castaly; *Alice and Phoebe Cary:* Poems; *Florence E. Coates:* Poems; *Helen G. Cone:* The Ride to the Lady; *Ina Coolbrith:* Songs from the Golden Gate; *Ellen M. Hutchinson Cortissoz:* Songs and Lyrics; *C. P. Cranch:* The Bird and the Bell; *Margaret Deland:* The Old Garden; *R. W. Emerson:* Poetical Works; *Annie Fields:* Under the Olive, — The Singing Shepherd; *J. T. Fields:* Ballads and Other Verses; *Louise G.*

Guiney: The Martyr's Idyl, — A Roadside Harp, — The White Sail, — In England and Yesterday; *J. C. Harris:* Uncle Remus and His Friends; *F. Bret Harte:* Poetical Works; *John Hay:* Poems; *T. W. Higginson:* Outdoor Studies; *O. W. Holmes:* Poetical Works; *Julia Ward Howe:* From Sunset Ridge; *W. D. Howells:* Poems; *Lucy Larcom:* Poetical Works; *Rose Hawthorne Lathrop:* Along the Shore; *Emma Lazarus:* Poems; *H. W. Longfellow:* Poetical Works; *J. R. Lowell:* Poetical Works; *Frances L. Mace:* Under Pine and Palm; *Caroline A. Mason:* The Lost Ring; *Emma H. Nason:* The Tower with Legends and Lyrics; *T. W. Parsons:* Poems; *Nora Perry:* After the Ball, — New Songs and Ballads; *Edna D. Proctor:* Song of the Ancient People; *Lizette W. Reese:* A Handful of Lavender, — A Quiet Road; *J. J. Roche:* Ballads of Blue Water; *J. O. Sargent:* Horatian Echoes; *Clinton Scollard:* Songs of Sunrise Lands; *Eliza Scudder:* Hymns and Sonnets; *F. D. Sherman:* Lyrics for a Lute, — Little-Folk Lyrics; *E. R. Sill:* The Hermitage, — Hermione; *Harriet P. Spofford:* Poems; *E. C. Stedman:* Poetical Works, — Poems Now First Collected; *Elizabeth Stoddard:* Poems; *W. W. Story:* Poetical Works; *Harriet B. Stowe:* Religious Studies; *Bayard Taylor:* Poetical Works; *Celia Thaxter:* Poetical Works; *W. R. Thayer:* Poems; "The *Edith M. Thomas:* Fair Shadow Land, — Lyrics and Sonnets, — A New Year's Masque — "The Inverted Torch;" *Maurice Thompson:* Poems; *H. D. Thoreau:* Letters; *Henry Timrod:* Poems; *J. T. Trowbridge:* The Vagabonds, and Other Poems; *Elizabeth S. Phelps Ward:* Songs of the Silent World; *C. H. Webb:* Vagrom Verse; *C. G. Whiting:* The Saunterer; *J. G. Whittier:* Poetical Works; *Forceythe Willson:* The Old Sergeant; *G. E. Woodberry:* The North Shore Watch, and Other Poems.

THE INDEPENDENT, New York. — *W. H. Hayne:* "A Cyclone at Sea;" *Sarah P. McLean Greene:* "The Lamp;" *Maurice Thompson:* "The Lion's Cub."

MR. P. J. KENEDY, New York. — Father Ryan's Poems.

THE LADIES' HOME JOURNAL, Philadelphia. — *Virginia W. Cloud:* "The Mother's Song."

MR. EDWIN RUTHVEN LAMSON, Boston. — *Ednah P. Clarke:* An Opal.

MESSRS. LEE & SHEPARD. — *S. W. Foss:* Dreams in Homespun.

MRS. FRANK LESLIE. — *E. A. U. Valentine:* "The Spirit of the Wheat."

THE J. B. LIPPINCOTT COMPANY, Philadelphia. — *L. J. Block:* Dramatic Sketches and Poems; *G. H. Boker:* Plays and Poems; *Robert Loveman:* His Poems; *H. S. Morris:* Madonna and Other Poems; *Henry Peterson:* Poems; *Edward Pollock:* Poems; *Margaret J. Preston:* Old Songs and New; *C. F. Richardson:* The Cross; *T. B. Read:* Poetical Works; *F. O. Ticknor:* Poems; *A. B. Paine:* "The Little Child."

MESSRS. LITTLE, BROWN & CO., Boston. — *A. B. Alcott:* Sonnets & Canzonets; *J. W. Chadwick:* A Book of Poems, — In Nazareth Town; *W. E. Channing:* Poems, — Thoreau: the Poet Naturalist; *Emily Dickinson:* Poems, 1st, 2d, and 3d series; *Mary M. Fenollosa:* Out of the Nest; *Gertrude Hall:* Allegretto, — Age of Fairy Gold; *Helen F. Jackson:* Verses, Sonnets, and Lyrics; *Louise Chandler Moulton:* Swallow Flights, — In the Garden of Dreams, — At the Wind's Will; *Margaret J. Preston:* Cartoons; *Laura E. Richards:* In My Nursery; *C. F. Richardson:* The End of the Beginning; *Susan Marr Spalding:* The Wings of Icarus; *Lilian Whiting:* From Dreamland Sent; *Sarah C. Woolsey:* Verses, — A Few More Verses.

MESSRS. LONGMANS, GREEN, & CO., New York. — *J. J. Piatt:* Idyls and Lyrics of the Ohio Valley, — Little New World Idyls; *Sarah M. B. Piatt:* Poems, — An Enchanted Castle.

LOTHROP PUBLISHING COMPANY, Boston. — *J. B. Bensel:* In the King's Garden; *Mary B. Dodge:* The Gray Masque; *P. H. Hayne:* Poems. From "Wide Awake," — *Clara D. Bates:* "Thistle Down;" *Henrietta R. Eliot:* "Why it was Cold in May."

MESSRS. LUCKHARDT & BELDER, New York. — *W. H. Gardner:* "When Love Comes Knocking."

THE MACMILLAN COMPANY, New York. — *Hamlin Garland:* The Trail of the Goldseekers, 1899, — Prairie Songs; *Ella Higginson:* When the Birds go North again, 1898; *Sophie Jewett:* The Pilgrim, and Other Poems, 1896; *William Winter:* Wanderers, 1892, — Brown Heath and Blue Bells, 1895; *G. E. Woodberry:* Wild Eden, 1899.

MESSRS. MAYNARD, MERRILL & CO., New York. — "Yale Verse."

THE MORNINGSIDE, New York. — *John Erskine:* "The Song;" *Jeannette B. Gillespy:* "Forgiven," — "A Valentine."

MESSRS. JOHN P. MORTON & CO., Louisville. — *Madison Cawein:* The Garden of Dreams.

MR. DAVID MCKAY, Philadelphia. — *D. L. Dawson:* The Seeker of the Marshes, and Other Poems.

MR. CHARLES WELLS MOULTON, Buffalo. — *Augusta C. Bristol:* The Web of Life; *J. B. Kenyon:* At the Gate of Dreams; *H. L. Koopman:* Orestes, and Other Poems; *Walter Malone:* Songs of Dusk and Dawn.

THE NEW ENGLAND PUBLISHING CO., Boston. — *Hezekiah Butterworth:* Songs of History.

MESSRS. G. P. PUTNAM'S SONS, New York. — *L. J. Block:* The New World; *Madison Cawein:* Myth and Romance, — Intimations of the Beautiful; *C. H. Crandall:* Wayside Music; *Danske Dandridge:* Joy, and Other Poems; *Elaine Goodale Eastman:* Apple Blossoms; *Arthur Grissom:* Beaux and Belles; *Grace D. Litchfield:* Mimosa Leaves; *J. H. Morse:* Summer Haven Songs; *Joseph O'Connor:* Poems; *Frederick Peterson:* In the Shade of Ygdrasil; *R. C. Rogers:* The Wind in the Clearing, — For the King; *Alice Wellington Rollins:* The Ring of Amethyst; *John Lancaster Spalding:* America, and Other Poems, — The Poet's Praise; *H. J. Stockard:* Fugitive Lines; *S. H. Thayer:* Songs of Sleepy Hollow.

THE A. D. F. RANDOLPH COMPANY, New York. — *Elisabeth G. Crane:* Sylva; *S. W. Duffield:* Warp and Woof; *Harriet M. Kimball:* Poems; *Mary A. Mason:* With the Seasons; *A. D. F. Randolph:* Hopefully Waiting, and Other Verses; *Katrina Trask:* Sonnets and Lyrics.

MR. GEORGE H. RICHMOND, New York. — *Caroline Duer and Alice Duer Miller:* Poems.

MESSRS. ROGERS & EASTMAN, Cleveland. — *Amy E. Leigh:* "If I but Knew."

MESSRS. J. N. ROSENBERG & J. M. PROSKAUER, New York. — "Columbia Verse."

THE ROYCROFTERS, East Aurora. — *L. H. Foote:* On the Heights. From "The Philistine," — *Irving Browne:* "At Shakespeare's Grave;" *J. J. Rooney:* "The Rahat," "A Beam of Light."

RUDDER PUBLISHING COMPANY, New York. — *T. F. Day:* Songs of Sea and Sail.

MR. R. H. RUSSELL, New York. — *R. B. Wilson:* The Shadows of the Trees.

G. SCHIRMER, New York. — *Peyton Van Rensselaer:* "At Twilight;" *Harry B. Smith:* "The Armorer's Song," "Song of the Turnkey."

MESSRS. CHARLES SCRIBNER'S SONS, New York. — *Anne R. Aldrich:* Songs about Life, Love and Death; *H. H. Boyesen:* Idyls of Norway; *H. C. Bunner:* Poems; *Charles de Kay:* Hesperus; *Mary Mapes Dodge:* Along the Way; *Julia C. R. Dorr:* Poems; *Eugene Field:* Writings; *Oliver Herford:* The Bashful Earthquake; *J. G. Holland:* Poetical Writings; *Sidney Lanier:* Poems; *G. P. Lathrop:* Dreams and Days; *G. C. Lodge:* Songs of the Wave; *C. H. Luders:* The Dead Nymph; *E. S. Martin:* Little Brother of the Rich; *Ernest McGaffey:* Poems of Gun and Rod; *G. P. Morris:* Poems; *F. J. O'Brien:* Poems and Stories; *T. N. Page:* Befo' de War; *Edith M. Thomas:* A Winter Swallow; *W. C. Wilkinson:* Poems; *W. B. Wright:* The Brook. From "Scribner's Magazine," — *Alice L. Bunner:* "Separation;" *Arthur Colton:* "A Song with a Discord," "To Faustine;" *Mrs. Margaret G. George Davidson:* "Moritura;" *Mildred Howells:* "A Moral in Sevres;" *Marguerite Merington:* "Hey Nonny No;" *Mrs. Miller:* "Stevenson's Birthday;" *J. H. Morse:* "The Wild Geese," "His Statement of the Case;" *Lizette W. Reese:* "Tears;" *V. T. Sutphen:* "Deep Waters;" *Marie van Vorst:* "Sing Again;" *Edith Wharton:* "Experience."

MESSRS. SMALL, MAYNARD & CO., Boston. — *Herbert Bates:* Songs of Exile; *James Buckham:* The Heart of Life; *Richard Burton:* Dumb in June, — Memorial Day, — Lyrics of Brotherhood; *Grace E. Channing Stetson:* Sea Drift; *J. V. Cheney:* Out of the Silence; *Zitella Cocke:* A Doric Reed; *Stephen Crane:* The Black Riders; *Ernest Crosby:* Plain Talk; *Richard Hovey:* Songs from Vagabondia, — Birth of Galahad, — Taliesin, — Along the Trail; *M. A. D. Howe:* Shadows; *William Lindsey:* Apples of Istakhar; *Josephine P. Peabody:* The Wayfarers; *Lilla Cabot Perry:* Impressions; *P. H. Savage:* First Poems, — Poems; *Evaleen Stein:* One Way to the Woods; *Charlotte P. Stetson:* In this Our World; *Father Tabb:* Poems, — Lyrics, — Child Verse; *F. R. Torrence:* The House of a Hundred Lights; *Walt Whitman:* Leaves of Grass.

THE FREDERICK A. STOKES COMPANY, New York. — *G. A. Baker:* Point Lace and Diamonds; *J. V. Cheney:* Thistle Drift, — Wood Blooms; *Stephen Crane:* War is Kind; *Mary B. C. Hansbrough:* Lyrics of Love and Nature; *W. H. Hayne:* Sylvan Lyrics; *Walter Learned:* Between Times; *S. M. Peck:* Cap and Bells, — Rings and Love Knots, — Rhymes and Roses; *F. D. Sherman:* Madrigals and Catches.

MESSRS. HERBERT S. STONE & CO., Chicago. — *Mary M. Adams:* The Choir Visible; *F. F. Browne:* Volunteer Grain; *Helen Hay:* Some Verses; *R. K. Munkittrick:* The Acrobatic Muse; *George Santayana:* Sonnets, and Other Poems. From "The Chap Book," — *John Bennett:* "God Bless You, Dear, To-Day;" *Julian Hawthorne:* "Were-Wolf;" *Beatrix D. Lloyd:* "Love and Time;" *J. W. Palmer:* "The Fight at San Jacinto."

THE CLAYTON F. SUMMY CO., Chicago. — *Theron Brown:* "His Majesty."

MR. JAMES H. WEST, Boston. — *J. W. Chadwick:* Power and Use.

THE WHITAKER AND RAY COMPANY, San Francisco, Cal. — *Herbert Bashford:* Songs from Puget Sea; *Joaquin Miller:* Complete Poetical Works.

THE WHITE-SMITH MUSIC PUBLISHING COMPANY, Boston. — *R. H. Buck:* "Kentucky Babe;" *Hattie Whitney:* "A Little Dutch Garden."

Mr. Thomas Whittaker, New York. — *C. F. Johnson:* What can I do for Brady, and Other Verse.

Messrs. M. Witmark & Sons, New York. — *E. D. Barker:* "Go Sleep My Honey."

Mr. Willis Woodward, New York. — *Hattie Starr:* "Little Alabama Coon."

The Youth's Companion, Boston. — *O. F. Adams:* "On a Grave in Christchurch, Hants;" *H. H. Bennett:* "The Flag Goes By."

II

All rights on poems in this work accredited to any one of the authors whose names are subjoined, — except in those cases already specifically mentioned in the preceding section of this copyright notice, — are vested in the said author, — or in his or her legal representatives, as noted within parentheses, — and are reserved by the holder or holders of the copyright.

Publishers of "AN AMERICAN ANTHOLOGY."

1900

Henry Abbey; John Albee; Anne R. Aldrich (Mrs. Helen M. Reeve Aldrich); Elizabeth Akers Allen; O. C. Auringer; Charlotte F. Bates; Katharine L. Bates; H. A. Beers; Joel Benton; R. M. Bell; C. L. Betts; Ambrose Bierce; H. A. Blood; Mary E. Bradley (Heirs of); Mary G. Brainard; John Burroughs; Mary F. Butts; G. W. Cable; Amelia W. Carpenter; R. W. Chambers; J. I. C. Clarke; T. M. Coan; T. S. Collier; Rose Terry Cooke (Rollin H. Cooke); W. A. Croffut; Mary K. Dallas (Miss Kyle); R. E. Day; Grace A. Dennen; Mary A. DeVere; C. M. Dickinson; Margaret E. Easter; Elaine Goodale Eastman; A. W. Eaton; G. T. Elliot; E. W. Ellsworth; Julia N. Finch; Maybury Fleming; Margaret W. Fuller; W. P. Garrison; Dora R. Goodale; A. C. Gordon; G. F. Gouraud; David Gray (David Gray, Jr.); Homer Greene; E. E. Hale; A. S. Hardy; W. W. Harney; T. L. Harris; Clarence Hawkes; J. R. Hayes; J. L. Heaton; H. W. Herbert (Mrs. Margaret H. Mather); Chauncey Hickox; Mary Thacher Higginson; C. L. Hildreth (Mrs. Hildreth); George Horton; Winifred Howells (William D. Howells); Edward Howland (Marie Howland); W. R. Huntington; Lawrence Hutton; J. J. Ingalls; J. H. Ingham; J. H. Jackson; Margaret T. Janvier; Rossiter Johnson; D. S. Jordan; Charles A. Keeler; J. B. Kenyon; Frederick Keppel; Hannah P. Kimball; F. L. Knowles; H. L. Koopman; Wilbur Larremore; W. C. Lawton; Walter Learned; Julie M. Lippmann; Albert Mathews; Brander Matthews; W. G. McCabe; L. E. Mitchell; Harriet Monroe; G. E. Montgomery (Mrs. Mary C. Montgomery); R. H. Newell; J. B. O'Reilly (James F. Murphy, executor and trustee); S. D. Osborne; Ray Palmer (Dr. Charles Ray Palmer); Caroline W. Fellowes Paradise; W. M. Payne; George Pellew (Mr. Henry Pellew); Arthur Peterson; C. H. Phelps; Elisabeth Pullen; J. R. Randall; J. E. Rankin; Annie D. Robinson; E. A. Robinson; Lucy Robinson; J. J. Rooney; Bertha B. Runkle; F. S. Saltus (F. H. Saltus); F. B. Sanborn; Frank Sewall; Milicent W. Shinn; D. B. Sickels; H. B. Smith; Harriet P. Spofford; Annie R. Stillman; C. W. Stoddard; Maurice Thompson; Vance Thompson; G. A. Townsend; Horace L. Traubel; Annie E. Trumbull; Clarence Urmy; W. H. Ward; E. F. Ware; L. D. Warner; J. E. Wayland; G. M. Whicher; E. L. White; E. R. White; William Young.

To

CYRUS OSBORNE BAKER

INTRODUCTION

The reader will comprehend at once that this book was not designed as a Treasury of imperishable American poems. To make a rigidly eclectic volume would be a diversion, and sometimes I have thought to spend a few evenings in obtaining two thirds of it from pieces named in the critical essays to which the present exhibit is supplementary. In fact, more than one projector of a handbook upon the lines of Palgrave's little classic has adopted the plan suggested, and has paid a like compliment to the texts revised by the editors of "A Library of American Literature."

But no "Treasury," however well conceived, would forestall the purpose of this compilation. It has been made, as indicated upon the title-page, in illustration of my review of the poets and poetry of our own land. It was undertaken after frequent suggestions from readers of "Poets of America," and bears to that volume the relation borne by "A Victorian Anthology" to "Victorian Poets." The companion anthologies, British and American, are meant to contain the choicest and most typical examples of the poetry of the English tongue during the years which they cover. The effective rise of American poetry was coincident with that of the Anglo-Victorian. It has been easy to show a preliminary movement, by fairly representing the modicum of verse, that has more than a traditional value, earlier than Bryant's and not antedating the Republic. Again, as the foreign volume was enlarged by the inclusion of work produced since the "Jubilee Year," so this one extends beyond the course surveyed in 1885, and to the present time. This should make it, in a sense, the breviary of our national poetic legacies from the nineteenth century to the twentieth. Now that it is finished, it seems, to the compiler at least, to afford a view of the successive lyrical motives and results of our first hundred years of song, from which the critic or historian may derive conclusions and possibly extend his lines into the future.

When entering upon my task, I cheerfully assumed that it would be less difficult than the one preceding it; for I had traversed much of this home-field in prose essays, and once again, — aided by the fine judgment of a colleague, —

while examining the whole range of American literature before 1890. Many poets, however, then not essential to our purpose, are quoted here. More space has been available in a work devoted to verse alone. Other things being equal, I naturally have endeavored, though repeating lyrics established by beauty or association, to make fresh selections. While verse of late has decreased its vogue as compared with that of imaginative prose, yet never has so much of it, good and bad, been issued here as within the present decade; never before were there so many rhythmical aspirants whose volumes have found publishers willing to bring them out attractively, and never have these tasteful ventures had more assurance of a certain, if limited, distribution. The time required for some acquaintance with them has not seemed to me misspent; yet the work of selection was slight compared with that of obtaining privileges from authors and book-houses, insuring correctness of texts and biographical data, and mastering the countless other details of this presentation. My forbearing publishers have derived little comfort from its successive postponements in consequence of these exigencies and of the editor's ill health. The delay, however, has rounded up more evenly my criticism and illustration of English poetry, carrying to the century's end this last volume of a series so long ago projected.

The anthologist well may follow the worker in mosaic or stained-glass, to better his general effects. Humble bits, low in color, have values of juxtaposition, and often bring out to full advantage his more striking material. The representation of a leading poet is to be considered by itself, and it is a pleasure to obtain for it a prelude and an epilogue, and otherwise to secure a just variety of mood and range. I have allotted many pages to the chiefs reviewed at chapter-length in "Poets of America," yet even as to these space is not a sure indication of the compiler's own feeling. An inclusion of nearly all the effective lyrics of Poe, and of enough of Emerson to show his translunary spirit at full height, still left each of these antipodal bards within smaller confines than are given to Longfellow, — the people's "artist of the beautiful" through half a century of steadfast production, or to Whittier — the born balladist, whose manner and purport could not be set forth compactly. Similar disproportions may appear in citation from poets less known, the effort being to utilize matter best suited to the general design. Time is the test of all traditions, even those of one's own propagating. We still canonize as our truest poets men who rose to eminence when poetry overtopped other literary interests, and whose lives were devoted to its production Yet there was an innocent tyranny in the extension of the prerogative accorded to the "elder poets" throughout the best days of a worshipful younger generation. The genius of new-comers might have been more compulsive if less overshadowed, and if less subject to the restrictions of an inauspicious period — that of the years immediately before and after the Civil War. Their output I have exhibited somewhat freely, as seemed the due of both the living and the dead. To the latter it may be the last tribute by one of their own kith and kin; to all, a tribute justly theirs whose choice it was to pursue an art upon which they had been bred and from its chiefs had learned beauty, reverence, aspiration, — but which they practised almost to alien ears. Not only their colleagues, but those that should have been their listeners, had perished, North and South. To the older members of this circle, — those born in the twenties, and thus falling within the closing division of the First Period, — even too little space has been allotted: the facts being that not until the Second Period was reached could an estimate be formed of the paging required for the entire book, and that then the selections already in type could not be readjusted.

A veteran author, Dr. English, recalls an assurance to the editor of American compilations famous in the day of Poe and the "Literati," that "his sins," much as he had incurred the wrath of the excluded, "were not of omission but of commission." Dr. Griswold performed an historical if not a critical service; he had a measure of conscience withal, else Poe would not have chosen him for a literary executor. But if this anthology were modelled upon his "Poets and Poetry of America" it would occupy a shelf of volumes. I have not hesitated to use any fortunate poem, howsoever unpromising its source. A ruby is a ruby, on the forehead of a Joss or found in the garment of a pilgrim. Here and there are included verses by masterful personages not writers by profession, and the texts of hymns, patriotic lyrics, and other memorabilia that have quality. As befits an anthology, selections mostly are confined to poems in their entirety, but the aim is to represent a poet variously and at his best; sometimes this cannot be achieved otherwise than by extracts from long poems, — by episodes, or other passages effective in themselves. The reader will find but a few extended Odes other than Lowell's Commemoration Ode and Stoddard's majestic monody on Lincoln, either of which it would be criminal here to truncate. In the foreign compendium there was little to present in the dramatic form, and that not often of a high order; from this volume dramatic dialogue — regretfully in cases like those of Boker and Taylor — is excluded altogether, with the exception of an essential specimen in the prefatory division; but lyrical interludes from dramas are not infrequent. As to sonnets, one often finds them the most serviceable expression of a minor poet. The sonnets of two or three Americans take rank with the best of their time, but I have tried to avoid those of the everyday grade. Finally, whatsoever a poet's standing or the class of selections, my tests are those of merit and anthological value, and the result should be judged accordingly. There is no reception more distrustful, not to say cynical, than that awarded nowadays to a presentment of the artistic effort of one's own time and people. An editor must look upon this as in the nature of things, happy if he can persuade his readers to use their own glasses somewhat objectively. With regard to a foreign field personal and local equations have less force, and to this no doubt I owe the good fortune that thus far little exception has been taken to the selection and range of material used for "A Victorian Anthology."

This brings to mind a departure in the following pages from the divisional arrangement of the last-named compilation. Essaying almost every method of setting forth our own poets, I found it impossible to follow the one which before had worked so aptly. A chronological system proved to be not merely the best, but seemingly the only one, applicable to my new needs.

The ease wherewith the British record permitted a classified arrangement was a pleasure to the orderly mind. It crystallized into groups, each animated by a master, or made distinct by the fraternization of poets with tastes in common. Whether this betokened an advanced or a provincial condition may be debatable, and the test of any "set" doubtless involves the measure of self-consciousness. Surveying the formative portion of the Victorian era it was easy to find the Roisterers, the Poets of Quality, the several flocks of English, Scottish, and Irish minstrels, the Rhapsodists, the Humanitarians, all preceding the composite idyllic school — that with Tennyson at its head. With and after Tennyson came the renaissance of the Preraphaelites, and also new balladists, song-writers, a few dramatists, the makers of verse-a-la-mode, and so on to the time's end. From all this, distinct in the receding past, it was possible to map out a cartograph as logical as the prose survey which it illustrates. But when the latter-day versemakers were reached, an effort to assort them had to be foregone, and not so much from lack of perspective as because, with few exceptions, they revealed more traits in common than in differentiation. It would be too much to expect that subsequent to the Victorian prime and the going out of its chief luminaries there should not be an interval of twilight — with its scattered stars, the Hespers of the past, the Phosphors of a day to come. The earlier groups were discernible, and reviewed by me, in their full activity; at present, when prose fiction, instead of verse, is the characteristic imaginative product, it is not hard to point out its various orders and working-guilds.

A derogatory inference need not be drawn from the failure of attempts to classify the early and later singers of our own land. Poetry led other forms of our literature during at least forty years, — say from 1835 to 1875. Nevertheless, like many observers, I found scarcely a group, except that inspired by the Transcendental movement, of more import than an occasional band such as the little set of "Croakers" when New York was in its 'teens. With the exception of Poe, the *dii majores*, as they have been termed, alike were interpreters of nature, sentiment, patriotism, religion, conviction, though each obtained mark by giving accentuated expression to one or two of these fundamental American notes. With the added exceptions of Whitman and Lanier, and of Lowell in his dialect satire, the leaders' methods and motives have had much in common, and the names excepted were not initiative of "schools." There were a few exemplars, chiefly outside of New England, of the instinct for poetry as an expression of beauty, and of feeling rather than of the convictions which so readily begat didacticism; yet for decades the choir of minor poets have pursued their art in the spirit of the leaders and have availed themselves of the same measures and diction.

Variances of the kind arising from conditions of locality and atmosphere have always been apparent. An approach can be made to a natural arrangement by geographical division somewhat upon the lines of Mr. Piatt's illustrated quarto, in which the lyrics and idylls of the Eastern States, the Middle, the Southern, the regions of the Middle West and the Pacific Slope, are successively exhibited. Until of late, however, the population and literature of the country were so restricted to the Atlantic seaboard that this method excites a sense of disproportion none the less unpleasing for its fidelity to the record. Thus by a process of exclusion the one satisfactory order proved to be the chronological; this being of the greater value since national evolution is more fully reflected in the poetry of

America than in that of countries, further advanced in the arts, wherein lyrical expression has derived importance from its literary worth rather than from its might as the voice of the people. If it is difficult to assort our poets of any one time into classes it chances that they are significantly classified by generations. The arrangement of this volume thus depends upon its time-divisions, of which the sequence can be traced by a glance at the preliminary Table of Contents.

Colonial verse, howsoever witty, learned, and godly, is beyond the purview; and well it may be, if only in obeisance to the distich of that rare old colonist, Nathaniel Ward, who tells us in "The Simple Cobbler of Agawam," that

"Poetry 's a gift wherein but few excel;
He doth very ill that doth not passing well."

Those who wish glimpses of life in New England after the forefathers were measurably adjusted to new conditions, may acquaint themselves with the lively eclogues of our first native poet, Ben Tompson. They will find nothing else so clever until — a hundred years later — they come upon the verse of Mistress Warren, the measures grave and gay of Francis Hopkinson, the sturdy humor of Trumbull and his fellow-wits. Barlow's "Columbiad" certainly belonged to neither an Homeric nor an Augustan age. Contemporary with its begetter was a true poet, one of nature's lyrists, who had the temperament of a Landor and was much what the Warwick classicist might have been if bred, afar from Oxford, to the life of a pioneer and revolutionist, spending his vital surplusage in action, bellicose journalism, and new-world verse. A few of Freneau's selecter songs and ballads long have been a part of literature, and with additions constitute my first gleanings of what was genuinely poetic in the years before Bryant earned his title as the father of American song. In that preliminary stage, an acting-drama began with Tyler and Dunlap and should have made better progress in the half-century ensuing. A dialect-ballad of the time, "The Country-Lovers," by Fessenden of New Hampshire, though unsuited to this Anthology, is a composition from which Lowell seems to have precipitated the native gold of "The Courtin'." Apart from these I think that sufficient, if not all, of what the opening years have to show of poetic value or association may be found in the selections from Freneau and others earlier than the First Lyrical Period, — a period which Pierpont, despite his birth-record, is entitled to lead off, considering the date of his first publications and the relation of his muse to an heroic future.

Accepting the advent of Bryant and Pierpont as the outset of a home minstrelsy which never since has failed of maintenance, our course hitherto divides itself readily into two periods, with the Civil War as a transitional rest between. The First ends with that national metamorphosis of which the impassioned verse of a few writers, giving no uncertain sound, was the prophecy and inspiration. The antecedent struggle was so absorbing that any conception of poetry as an art to be pursued for its own sake was at best not current; yet beauty was not infrequent in the strain of even the anti-slavery bards, and meanwhile one American singer was giving it his entire allegiance. Before reverting to these antebellum conditions, it should be noted that a Second Period began with the war olympiad, lasting to a date that enables a compiler to distinguish its stronger representatives until the beginning of the century's final decade. To complete the survey I add a liberal aftermath of verse produced in these last ten years; for it seems worth while to favor a rather inclusive chartage of the tendencies, even the minor currents and eddies, which the poetry of our younger writers reveals to those who care for it. As to omitted names, I reflect that their bearers well may trust to anthologists of the future, rather than to have lines embalmed here for which in later days they may not care to be held to account.

The sub-divisions of each of the lyrical periods, — covering, as to the First Period, three terms of about fifteen years each, and as to the Second, three of ten years each, represent literary generations, some of which so overlap one another as to be in a sense contemporary. Finally, the "Additional Selections" at the end of every sub-division, and succeeding the preliminary and supplementary pages, are for the most part chronologically ordered as concerns any specific group of poems. These addenda have afforded a serviceable means of preserving notable "single poems," and of paying attention to not a few unpretentious writers who, while uttering true notes, have obeyed Wordsworth's injunction to shine in their places and "be content."

Here I wish to set down a few conclusions, not so much in regard to the interest of the whole compilation as to its value in any summary of the later poetry of our English tongue.

When I told a New York publisher — a University man, whose judgment is well entitled to respect — that I had this book in mind as the final number of a series and as a companion to the British volume, he replied off-hand: "You cannot make it half so good as the other : we have n't the material." This I was not ready to dispute, yet was aware of having entertained a feeling, since writing "Poets of America," that if a native anthology must yield to the foreign one in wealth of choice production, it might prove to be, from an equally vital point of view, the more significant of the two. Now having ended my labor, that feeling has become a belief which possibly may be shared by others willing to consider the grounds of its formation.

In demurring to what certainly is a general impression, the first inquiry must be : What then constitutes the significance of a body of rhythmical literature as found in either of these anthologies, each restricted to its own territory, and both cast in the same epoch and language ? Undoubtedly, and first of all, the essential quality of its material as poetry ; next to this, its quality as an expression and interpretation of the time itself. In many an era the second factor may afford a surer means of estimate than the first, inasmuch as the purely literary result may be nothing rarer than what the world already has possessed, nor greatly differing from it ; nevertheless, it may be the voice of a time, of a generation, of a people, — all of extraordinary import to the world's future. A new constructive standard was set by Tennyson, with increase rather than reduction of intellectual power, but shortly before the art of the laureate and his school there was little to choose in technical matters between English and American rhythmists, Landor always excepted. Since the Georgian hey-day, imagination of the creative order scarcely has been dominant, nor is it so in any composite and idyllic era. Our own poetry excels as a recognizable voice in utterance of the emotions of a people. The storm and stress of youth have been upon us, and the nation has not lacked its lyric cry ; meanwhile the typical sentiments of piety, domesticity, freedom, have made our less impassioned verse at least sincere. One who underrates the significance of our literature, prose or verse, as both the expression and the stimulant of national feeling, as of import in the past and to the future of America, and therefore of the world, is deficient in that critical insight which can judge even of its own day unwarped by personal taste or deference to public impression. He shuts his eyes to the fact that at times, notably throughout the years resulting in the Civil War, this literature has been a "force." Its verse until the dominance of prose fiction — well into the seventies, let us say — formed the staple of current reading ; and fortunate it was — while pirated foreign writings, sold cheaply everywhere, handicapped the evolution of a native prose school — that the books of the "elder

American poets" lay on the centre-tables of our households and were read with zest by young and old. They were not the fosterers of new-world liberty and aspiration solely; beyond this, in the case of Longfellow for example, the legends read between the lines made his verse as welcome in Great Britain as among his own country-folk. The criterion of poetry is not its instant vogue with the ill-informed classes; yet when it is the utterance of an ardent people, as in the works of Longfellow, Bryant, Emerson, Lowell, Whittier, it once more assumes its ancient and rightful place as the art originative of belief and deed. Emerson presented such a union of spiritual and civic insight with dithyrambic genius as may not be seen again. His thought is now congenital throughout vast reaches, among new peoples scarcely conscious of its derivation. The transcendentalists, as a whole, for all their lapses into didacticism, made and left an impress. Longfellow and his pupils, for their part, excited for our people the old-world sense of beauty and romance, until they sought for a beauty of their own and developed a new literary manner — touched by that of the motherland, yet with a difference; the counterpart of that "national likeness" so elusive, yet so instantly recognized when chanced upon abroad. In Bryant, often pronounced cold and granitic by readers bred to the copious-worded verse of modern times, is found the large imagination that befits a progenitor. It was stirred, as that of no future American can be, by his observation of primeval nature. He saw her virgin mountains, rivers, forests, prairies, broadly; and his vocabulary, scant and doric as it was, proved sufficient — in fact the best — for nature's elemental bard. His master may have been Wordsworth, but the difference between the two is that of the prairie and the moor, Ontario and Windermere, the Hudson and the Wye. From "Thanatopsis" in his youth to "The Flood of Years" in his hoary age, Bryant was conscious of the overstress of Nature unmodified by human occupation and training. It is not surprising that Whitman — though it was from Emerson he learned to follow his own genius — so often expressed himself as in sympathy with Bryant, above other American poets, on the imaginative side. The elemental quality of the two is what makes them akin; what differentiates them is not alone their styles, but the advance of Whitman's generation from the homogeneous to the heterogeneous. The younger minstrel, to use his own phrase, also saw things *en masse;* but in his day and vision the synthesis of the new world was that of populous hordes surging here and there in the currents of democracy. Bryant is the poet of the ages, Whitman of the generations. The æsthetic note of poetry was restored by Longfellow, in his Vergilian office, and by Edgar Poe with surer magic and endurance. Has any singer of our time more demonstrably affected the rhythmical methods of various lands than Poe with his few but haunting paradigms? He gave a saving grace of melody and illusion to French classicism, to English didactics, — to the romance of Europe from Italy to Scandinavia. It is now pretty clear, notwithstanding the popularity of Longfellow in his day, that Emerson, Poe, and Whitman were those of our poets from whom the old world had most to learn; such is the worth, let the young writer note, of seeking inspiration from within, instead of copying the exquisite achievements of masters to whom we all resort for edification, — that is, for our own delight, which is not the chief end of the artist's throes. Our three most individual minstrels are now the most alive, resembling one another only in having each possessed the genius that originates. Years from now, it will be matter of fact that their influences were as lasting as those of any poets of this century.

The polemic work of Whittier, Lowell, and their allies, illustrates the applied force of lyrical expression. Their poetry of agitation scarcely found a counterpart on the Southern side until the four-years' conflict began; yet any study of the causes and conduct of that war confirms our respect for Fletcher's sage who cared to make the ballads of a nation rather than its laws. His saying never applies more shrewdly than at the stage of a nation's formation when the slightest deflection must needs be the equivalent of a vast arc in the circle of its futurity. It is strange to realize that the young now view the Civil War from a distance almost equal to that between their seniors' childhood and the war of 1812 — the veterans of which we watched with kindly humor when their lessening remnant still kept up its musty commemorations. Our youth know the immeasurably larger scope of the mid-century struggle; they cannot understand from the echo of its trumpetings the music of a time when one half of a people fought for a moral sentiment, — the other, for a birthright which pride would not forego. Even the motherland, though gaining a fresh view from that convulsion and its outcome, formed no adequate understanding of her progeny over sea. Years go by, and the oceans are held in common, and the world is learning that our past foretokened a new domain in art, letters, and accomplishment, of which we have barely touched the border. Making every allowance for the *gratia hospitum*, a recent visitor, William Archer, need not fear to stand by what he had the perception to discover and the courage to declare. In his judgment, "the whole world will one day come to hold Vicksburg and Gettysburg names of larger historic import than Waterloo or Sedan." If this be so, the significance of a literature of all kinds that led up to the "sudden making" of those "splendid names" is not to be gainsaid. Mr. Howells aptly has pointed out that war does not often add to great art or poetry, but the white heat of lyric utterance has preceded many a campaign, and never more effectively than in the years before our fight for what Mr. Archer calls "the preservation of the national idea." Therefore an American does not seem to me a laudable reader who does not estimate the following presentation in the full light of all that his country has been, is, and is to be.

Time has not clouded, but cleared, the lenses through which our neophytes regard those distant movements so fully in accord with the modern spirit as Poe's renaissance of art for beauty's sake, and Whitman's revolt against social and literary traditions. The academic vantage no less held its own with Parsons and Holmes as maintainers, — the former our purest classicist, and a translator equalled only by Bayard Taylor. The stately elegance of Parsons limited his audience, yet perfected the strength of his ode "On a Bust of Dante," than which no finer lyric ennobles this collection. Holmes's grace, humor, contemporaneousness, brought him into favor again and again, and the closing days of a sparkling career were the most zestful for the acknowledged master of new "architects of airy rhyme" on each side of the Atlantic. In Lowell, the many-sided, the best equipped, and withal the most spontaneous, of these worthies, their traits were combined. Never was there a singer at once so learned and so unstudied; no other American took the range that lies between the truth and feeling of his dialect verse and the height of his national odes.

This is not a critical Introduction, and the writer need not dwell upon the shortcomings of our still famous matin choir. These were discussed in commentaries that differ very little from what they would be if written now, though after this farther lapse of time I might not enter upon such judgments with the glow and interest of the earlier years, when those hoar and laurelled heads still shone benignantly above us.

Along the century's midway, a group of somewhat younger poets appeared, whose places of birth or settlement rendered them less subject to the homiletic mood which even Lowell recognized as his own besetting drawback. Taylor, Boker, Stoddard, Read, Story, and their allies, wrote poetry for the sheer love of it. They did much beautiful work, with a cosmopolitan and artistic bent, making it a part of the varied industry of men of letters; in fact, they were creating a civic Arcadia of their own, — but then came the tempest that sent poets and preachers alike to the storm-cellars, and certainly made roundelays seem inapposite as the "pleasing of a lute." Yet my expositions of the then current writers, taken with the sheaf of popular war-songs, Northern and Southern, bound up in a single section, prove that the fury of the fight called forth inspiring strains. Some of these were as quickly caught up by the public as were the best known efforts of the laureate of Anglo-Saxon expansion in a recent day. On the whole, the stern and dreadful war for the Union produced its due share of the lays of heroism and endeavor. But then, as oftentimes, pieces that outrivalled others were wont to have the temporal quality that does not make for an abiding place among the little classics of absolute song.

As the country slowly emerged from the shadow, its elder bards hung up their clarions, and betook themselves to the music of contentment and peace. Their heirs apparent were few and scattered; encouragement was small during years of reconstruction, and without the stimulus of a literary "market;" yet the exhibit in the first division of the post-bellum period shows that song had a share in the awakening of new emotional and æsthetic expression. Fifteen or twenty years more, and a resort to letters as a means of subsistence was well under way, — and like a late spring, vigorous when once it came. Poets, in spite of the proverb, sing best when fed by wage or inheritance. The progress of American journals, magazines, and the book-trade coincided with a wider extension of readers than we had known before. Such a condition may not foster the creative originality that comes at the price of blood and tears, but it has resulted in a hopeful prelude to whatsoever masterwork the next era has in store. The taste, charm, and not infrequent elevation of the verse contained in the three divisions of the second portion of this compilation render that portion, in its own way, a fit companion to the series preceding it. One must forego tradition to recognize this; in the Hall of Letters, as in Congress and wherever a levelling-up movement has prevailed, talent is less conspicuous by isolation than of old. The main distinction between the two Periods is a matter of dynamics; the second has had less to do with public tendencies and events. It has had none the less a force of its own: that of the beauty and enlightenment which shape the ground for larger offices hereafter, by devotees possibly no more gifted than their forbears, yet farther up the altar steps. In its consistency, tested by what went before, it stands comparison as reasonably as the product of the later Victorian artificers, when gauged by that of Tennyson, Arnold, the Brownings, and their colleagues.

It is not my province to specify the chief writers of this Period, so many of whom are still with us. As the country has grown, the Eastern song-belt has widened, and other divisions have found voice. The middle West quickly had poets to depict its broad and plenteous security; and more lately very original notes have come from territory bordering upon the Western Lakes. The Pacific coast and the national steppes and ranges as yet scarcely have found adequate utterance, though not without a few open-air minstrels. Dialect and folk-lore verse represents the new South; its abundant talent has been concerned otherwise with prose romance; yet the song of one woman, in a border State, equals in beauty that of any recent lyrist. American poets still inherit longevity. Since the premature death of the thrice-lamented Taylor — at a moment when he was ready to begin the life of Goethe which none could doubt would be a consummate work — a few others have gone that should have died hereafter. Sill was a sweet and wise diviner, of a type with Clough and Arnold. O'Reilly is zealously remembered, both the poet and the man. In Emma Lazarus a star went out, the western beacon of her oriental race. When Sidney Lanier died, not only the South that bore him, but the country and our English rhythm underwent the loss of a rare being — one who was seeking out the absolute harmony, and whose experiments, incipient as they were, were along the pathways of discovery. Eugene Field's departure lessened our laughter, wit, and tears. In the present year, Hovey, whom the new century seemed just ready to place among its choristers, was forbidden to outlive the completion of the intensely lyrical "Taliesin," his melodious swan-song.

To end this retrospect, it may be said that the imaginative faculty, of which both the metrical and the prose inventions alike were termed poetry by the ancients, has not lain dormant in the century's last quarter; although certain conditions, recognized in the opening chapter of "Victorian Poets" as close at hand, have obtained beyond doubt. The rhythm of verse is less essayed than that of prose — now the vehicle of our most favored craftsmen. Already books are written to show how an evolution of the novel has succeeded to that of the poem, which is true — and in what wise prose fiction is the higher form of literature, which is not yet proved. The novelist has outsped the poet in absorbing a new ideality conditioned by the advance of science; again, he has cleverly adjusted his work to the facilities and drawbacks of modern journalism. It is not strange that there should be a distaste for poetic illusion in an era when economics, no longer the dismal science, becomes a more fascinating study than letters, while its teachers have their fill of undergraduate hero-worship. At last a change is perceptible at the universities, a strengthening in the faculties of English, a literary appetite that grows by what it feeds on. Letters, and that consensus of poetry and science foreseen by Wordsworth, may well be taken into account in any vaticination of the early future. Meanwhile, what do we have? Here as abroad — and even if for the moment there appears no one of those excepted masters who of themselves re-create their age — there continues an exercise of the poet's art by many whose trick of song persists under all conditions. Our afterglow is not discouraging. We have a twilight interval, with minor voices and their tentative modes and tones; still, the dusk is not silent, and rest and shadow with music between the dawns are a part of the liturgy of life, no less than passion and achievement.

The reader will hardly fail to observe special phases of the middle and later portions of this compilation. In my reviews of the home-school a tribute was paid to the high quality of the verse proffered by our countrywomen. This brought out a witticism to the effect that such recognition would savor less of gallantry if more than a page or two, in so large a volume, had been reserved for expatiation upon the tuneful sisterhood. That book was composed of essays upon a group of elder poets, among whom no woman chanced to figure. A single chapter embraced a swift characterization of the choir at large, and in this our female poets obtained proportional attention as aforesaid. The tribute was honest, and must be rendered by any one who knows the field. A succession of rarely endowed women-singers, that began — not to go back to the time of Maria Brooks — near the middle of the century, still continues unbroken. Much of their song has been exquisite, some of it strong as sweet; indeed, a notable portion of our treasure-trove would be missing if their space in the present volume were otherwise filled. Not that by force of numbers and excellence women bear off the chief trophies of poetry, prose fiction, and the other arts; thus far the sex's achievements, in a time half seriously styled "the woman's age," are still more evident elsewhere. It cannot yet be said of the Parnassian temple, as of the Church, that it would have no parishioners, and the service no participants, if it were not for women. The work of their brother poets is not emasculate, and will not be while grace and tenderness fail to make men cowards, and beauty remains the flower of strength. Yet for assurance of the fact that their contribution to the song of America is remarkable, and even more so than it has been — leaving out the work of Elizabeth Browning — to that of Great Britain, one need only examine its representation in this anthology. I am not so adventurous as to mention names, but am confident that none will be ungrateful for my liberal selections from the verse upon the quality of which the foregoing statement must stand or fall.

Poetry being a rhythmical expression of emotion and ideality, its practice as a kind of artistic finesse is rightly deprecated, though even this may be approved in the young composer unconsciously gaining his mastery of technique. Our recent verse has been subjected to criticism as void of true passion, nice but fickle in expression, and having nothing compulsive to express. An international journal declares that "our poets are not thinking of what they shall say, for that lies close at hand, but of how they shall say it." On the whole, I suspect this to be more true abroad than here: our own metrists, if the less dexterous, are not without motive. There was said to be a lack of vigorous lyrics on the occasion of our war with Spain. The world-changing results of the war will find their artistic equivalent at sudden times when the observer, like Keats's watcher of the skies, sees the "new planet swim into his ken" — or at least finds this old planet made anew. Anglo-Saxon expansion or imperialism, call it as we will, has inspired one British poet, yet he is so much more racial than national that America claims a share in him. As for our poetry of the Spanish war, I think that sufficient will be found in my closing pages to indicate that our quickstep was enlivened by a reasonable measure of prosody. The Civil War was a different matter — preceded by years of excitement, and at last waged with gigantic conflicts and countless tragic interludes, until every home was desolate, North or South. Men and women still survive who — with Brownell, Willson, and others of the dead — made songs and ballads that, as I have said, were known the world over. Why should these veteran celebrants decline upon lesser themes, or not stand aside and let the juniors have their chance? The latter had scarcely tuned their strings when the Spanish fight was over. Still more to the point is the fact that poets of all time have been on the side of revolt. Our own, however patriotic, when there was so little of tragedy and the tug of war to endure, felt no exultation in chanting a feeble enemy's deathsong.

In any intermediary lyrical period its effect upon the listener is apt to be one of experiment and vacillation. It is true that much correct verse is written without inspiration, and as an act of taste. The makers seem artists, rather than poets: they work in the spirit of the graver and decorator; even as idyllists their appeal is to the bodily eye; they are over-careful of the look of words, and not only of their little pictures, but of the frames that contain them, — book-cover, margin, paper, adornment. That lyrical compositions should go forth in attractive guise is delectable, but not the one thing needful for the true poet, whose strength lies in that which distinguishes him from other artists, not in what is common to all. While making a fair presentation of the new modes and tendencies of the now somewhat timorous art of song, a guess at what may come out of them is far more difficult than were the prognostications of thirty years ago. Each phase has its own little grace or effect, like those of the conglomerate modern piano-music. Among those less rational than others I class attempts to introduce values absolutely exotic. The contention for a broad freedom in the chief of arts is sound. It may prove all things, and that which is good will stay. Owing to our farther remove from the European continent, foreign methods are essayed with us less sedulously than by the British minor poets. Both they and we were successful in a passing adoption of the "French forms," which, pertaining to construction chiefly, are common to various literatures. In attempting to follow the Gallic cadences and linguistic effects our kinsmen were bound to fail. Our own craftsmen even less have been able to capture graces quite inseparable from the specific rhythm, color, diction, that constitute the highly sensuous beauty of the modern French school. A painter, sculptor, or architect — his medium of expression being a universal one — can utilize foreign methods, if at a loss for something of his own. But there has not been an English-speaking captive to the bewitchment of the French rhythm and symbolism who has not achieved far less than if he had held fast to the resources of his native tongue. Literatures lend things of worth to one another, but only as auxiliaries and by gradual stages. Between the free carol of the English lyric, from the Elizabethan to the Victorian, and the noble variations of English blank verse in its every age and vogue, our poets have liberties enow, and will rarely go afield except under suspicion of reinforcing barren invention with a novel garniture. The technique of the lyrical Symbolists, for instance, is at best a means rather than an end. Though pertinent to the French language and spirit, it is apt, even in France and Belgium, to substitute

poetic material for creative design. That very language is so constituted that we cannot transmute its essential genius; those who think otherwise do not think in French, and even an imperfect appreciation of the tongue, and of its graces and limitations, should better inform them. Titles also are misleading: every poet is a symbolist in the radical sense, but not for the sake of the symbol. The glory of English poetry lies in its imagination and in its strength of thought and feeling. Deliberate artifices chill the force of spontaneity; but at the worst we have the certainty of their automatic correction by repeated failures.

Even as concerns the homely, slighted shepherd's trade, there is a gain in having our escape from provincialism indicated by distrust of inapt models, and through an appeal to our own constituency rather than to the outer world. The intermingling of peoples has qualified Binney Wallace's saying that "a foreign nation is a kind of contemporaneous posterity." The question as to a British or American production now must be, What is the verdict of the English-speaking world? To that vast jury the United States now contributes the largest contingent of intelligent members. Our poets who sing for their own countrymen will not go far wrong, whether or not they bear in mind the quest for "local color," — as to which it can be averred that our elder group honestly expressed the nature, life, sentiment, of its seacoast habitat, the oldest and therefore most American portion of this country. Younger settlements have fallen into line, with new and unmistakable qualities of diction, character, atmosphere. Our kinsmen, in their pursuit of local color, more or less deceive themselves; with all its human zest, it is but a secondary value in art, though work surcharged with it is often good of its kind, while higher efforts are likely to fall short. When found, we sometimes fail to recognize it, or care no more for it than for those provincial newspapers which are so racy to native readers and so tedious to the sojourner. What foreigners really long for is something radically new and creative. In any case, praise or dispraise from abroad is now of less import than the judgment of that land in which a work is produced. The method and spirit peculiar to a region make for "an addition to literature," but a work conveying them must have the universal cast to be enduring, though its author waits the longer for recognition. But this was always so; the artist gains his earliest satisfaction from the comprehension of his own guild. Time and his measure of worth may do the rest for him.

A public indifference to the higher forms of poetry is none the less hard to bear. A collective edition of an admired poet's lifework, with not a line in its volumes that is not melodious, or elegant, or imaginative, or all combined, and to which he has applied his mature and fastidious standards, appears without being made the subject of gratulation or extended review. A fresh and noble lyric, of some established order, gains small attention, while fetching trifles are taken up by the press. If a fair equivalent of the "Ode to a Nightingale" were now to come into print, a reviewer of the magazine containing it doubtless might content himself with saying: "There is also a poem by Mr. ——." But this, after all, in its stolid fashion may betoken a preference for something revelatory of the infinite unexplored domain of poetic values; a sense that we have a sufficiency of verse which, however fine, is conformed to typical masterpieces; a desire for variants in creative beauty to stimulate us until they each, in turn, shall also pass into an academic grade.

In offering this final volume of a series that has diverted me from projects more in the humor of the hour, I feel a touch of that depression which follows a long task, and almost ask whether it has been worth completion. Would not the labor have been better expended, for example, upon criticism of our prose fiction? The muse sits neglected, if not forspent, in the hemicycle of the arts:—

> "Dark Science broods in Fancy's hermitage,
> The rainbow fades,—and hushed they say is Song
> With those high bards who lingering charmed the age
> Ere one by one they joined the statued throng."

Yet after this verification of my early forecast, why should not the subsidiary prediction — that of poesy's return to dignity and favor — no less prove true? As it is, having gone too far to change for other roads, I followed the course whether lighted by the setting or the rising sun. Concerning the nature and survival of poetry much is said in view of the apparent condition. Song is conceded to be the language of youth, the voice of primitive races, — whence an inference that its service in the English tongue is near an end. But surely poetry is more than the analogue of even those folk-songs to which composers recur in aftertime and out of them frame masterpieces. Its function is continuous with the rhythm to which emotion, age after age, must resort for a supreme delivery, — the vibration that not only delights the soul of infancy, but quavers along the heights of reason and intelligence.

If the word "lost" can be applied to any one of the arts, it is to poetry last of all. Not so long ago it was linked with sculpture, now the crowning triumph of a world's exposition. We must be slow to claim for any century supereminence as the poetic age. Our own country, to return, has not been that of a primitive people, colonial or under the republic; and among all peoples once emerged from childhood modes of expression shift in use and favor, and there are many rounds of youth, prime, and decadence. Spring comes and goes and comes again, while each season has its own invention or restoration. The new enlightenment must be taken above all into account. The world is too interwelded to afford many more examples of a decline like Spain's, — in whose case the comment that a nation of lute-players could never whip a nation of machinists was not a cynicism but a study in ethnology. Her lustration probably was essential to a new departure; while as for America, she has indeed her brawn and force, but is only entering upon her song, nor does a brood of minor poets imply that she has passed a climacteric. It will be long before our people need fear even the springtime enervation of their instinctive sense of beauty, now more in evidence with every year.

More likely they have not yet completed a single round, inasmuch as there has been thus far so little of the indubitably dramatic in our rhythmical production. The poetic drama more than once has marked a culmination of imaginative literature. Constructively, it is the highest form of poetry, because it includes all others metrical or recitative; psychologically, still the highest, going beyond the epic presentment of external life and action: not only rendering deeds, but setting bare the workings of the soul. I believe that, later than Shakespeare's day, the height of utterance in his mode and tongue is not of the past, but still to be attained by us. Thus poetry is indeed the spirit and voice of youth, but the thought of sages, and of every age. Our own will have its speech again, and as much more quickly than after former periods of disuse as the processes of action and reaction speed swiftlier than of old. To one bred to look before and after this talk of atrophy seems childish, when he bears in mind what lifeless stretches preceded the Miltonic and the Georgian outbursts. A pause, a rest, has been indicated, at this time especially innocuous and the safeguard against cloying; meantime our new-fledged genius has not been listless, but testing the wing in fields outside the lyric hedgerows. In the near future the world, and surely its alertest and most aspiring country, will not lack for poets. Whatsoever the prognosis, one thing is to be gained from a compilation of the songs of many: this or that singer may be humble, an everyday personage among his fellows, but in his verse we have that better part of nature which overtops the evil in us all, and by the potency of which a race looks forward that else would straggle to the rear.

Compact Biographical Notes upon all the poets represented, as in "A Victorian Anthology," follow the main text of this book. They have been prepared by various hands, and revised by the editor — occasionally with a brief comment upon some name too recent to be found in the critical volume, "Poets of America."

For texts I have depended upon my own shelves, the public libraries, and the private stores of Mr. R. H. Stoddard and other colleagues. Acknowledgment is made to Mr. C. Alexander Nelson, of Columbia University, and to Mr. Robert Bridges, for repeated courtesies. Important aid has been derived from the Librarian of Brown University, Mr. Harry Lyman Koopman, and from the Harris-Anthony collection of American poetry within his charge. There is an enviable opportunity for the friends of this notable collection to place it beyond rivalry by filling in many of its gaps, and by making copious additions from the output of the last twenty years.

Throughout two years occupied with the main portion of the compilation, a time of frequent disability, I have owed much to the unstinted and competent service of Miss Ella M. Boult, B. L., who has been in every sense my assistant-editor, — not only as to matters of routine, but in the exercise of literary judgment. In correspondence, proof-reading, and textual revision, Miss Laura Stedman has been a zealous subordinate, and has paid special attention to the Biographical Notes. Many of the latter have been written by Miss Lucy C. Bull (now Mrs. Robinson) and Miss Beatrix D. Lloyd. At the inception of my task, I was aided by Miss Mary Stuart McKinney and Miss Louise Boynton, A. B. Miss McKinney, who had previous experience in connection with the Victorian Anthology, was the valued assistant-editor of the opening division of the present collection.

The attention of compilers and others is directed to the list of proprietary books and writings, under the copyright notices which follow the title-page. This anthology could not be issued without the friendly coöperation of American publishers, and pains has been taken to conserve their rights by legal specification at the outset, and in some instances by notices elsewhere. Where it has been doubtful whether rights exist, and, if so, under what ownership, the editor relies upon the indulgence of all concerned. My thanks are due to living authors, and to the heirs of the dead, for placing works at my disposal without restriction as to the character or extent of citations. The verse of one American writer, now living abroad, has been omitted at his own request. One or two Canadian poets, whose residence and service are now on this side of the border, are justly in such favor that I would seek to represent them here were not their songs and ballads already a choice portion of a Colonial division in the British compilation. E. C. S.

Lawrence Park, Bronxville, New York,
August, 1900.

TABLE OF CONTENTS

I. EARLY YEARS OF THE NATION

(THE QUARTER-CENTURY PRECEDING BRYANT AND HIS CONTEMPORARIES)

II. FIRST LYRICAL PERIOD

(in three divisions)

DIVISION I

(Pierpont, Halleck, Bryant, Drake, Mrs. Brooks, and Others)

Additional Selections

(VARIOUS POEMS BELONGING TO THIS DIVISION)

DIVISION II

(Emerson, Longfellow, Whittier, Poe, Holmes, and Others)

Ralph Waldo Emerson

Sarah Helen Whitman

William Lloyd Garrison

Nathaniel Parker Willis

William Gilmore Simms

Ralph Hoyt

Charles Fenno Hoffman

Henry Wadsworth Longfellow

Elizabeth Oakes Smith

John Greenleaf Whittier

William Davis Gallagher

Edgar Allan Poe

Samuel Francis Smith

Ray Palmer

Oliver Wendell Holmes

Frances Anne Kemble

Albert Pike

DIVISION III

(Lowell, Story, Whitman, Mrs. Howe, Parsons, Boker, Brownell, Read, the Stoddards, Taylor, Mrs. Dorr, Mrs. Cooke, Mrs. Preston, and Others)

James Russell Lowell

William Wetmore Story

Julia Ward Howe

Walt Whitman

Thomas Dunn English

Josiah Gilbert Holland

Herman Melville

Thomas William Parsons

William Wilberforce Lord

Henry Howard Brownell

Theodore O'Hara

Maria White Lowell

Thomas Buchanan Read

Francis Orrery Ticknor

Samuel Johnson

Erastus Wolcott Ellsworth

Elizabeth Stoddard

Thomas Lake Harris

George Henry Boker

John Randolph Thompson

James Matthew Legare

Thomas Wentworth Higginson

Charles Godfrey Leland

Bayard Taylor

Julia Caroline Ripley Dorr

John Williamson Palmer

Richard Henry Stoddard

Margaret Junkin Preston

Stephen Collins Foster

Rose Terry Cooke

Additional Selections

(various poems belonging to this division)

I

II

III

IV

III. SECOND LYRICAL PERIOD

(IN THREE DIVISIONS)

DIVISION I

(MITCHELL, TIMROD, HAYNE, MRS. JACKSON, MISS DICKINSON, STEDMAN, THE PIATTS, MRS. SPOFFORD, MRS. MOULTON, WINTER, ALDRICH, HOWELLS, HAY, HARTE, SILL, MILLER, LANIER, AND OTHERS)

Mary Ashley Townsend

John Albee

Edmund Clarence Stedman

Tracy Robinson

Charles Henry Webb

Richard Realf

George Arnold

Frances Louisa Bushnell

Annie Fields

Harriet McEwen Kimball

John James Piatt

Harriet Prescott Spofford

Louise Chandler Moulton

John Lancaster Spalding

Henry Bernard Carpenter

Robert Kelley Weeks

John White Chadwick

George Alfred Townsend

Edward Rowland Sill

William Gordon McCabe

Titus Munson Coan

Nora Perry

James Herbert Morse

Joaquin Miller

Joseph O'Connor

Charles Goodrich Whiting

Charles Edward Carryl

Sidney Lanier

DIVISION II

(Gilder, O'Reilly, Maurice Thompson, Father Tabb, Emma Lazarus, Mrs. Cortissoz, Edith Thomas, Eugene Field, Bates, Markham, Whitcomb Riley, Ina Coolbrith, R. U. Johnson, and Others)

Ina Coolbrith

Lloyd Mifflin

James Jeffrey Roche

Alice Wellington Rollins

Alice Williams Brotherton

Walter Learned

Henry Augustin Beers

Arthur Sherburne Hardy

William Young

Will Henry Thompson

Charles De Kay

Edward King

Hjalmar Hjorth Boyesen

Joel Chandler Harris

John Vance Cheney

O. C. Auringer

Emma Lazarus

Charles Leonard Moore

Edith Matilda Thomas

Samuel Minturn Peck

Arthur Wentworth Hamilton Eaton

Additional Selections

(various poems belonging to this division)

I

II

III

IV

V

VI

DIVISION III

(WOODBERRY, BUNNER, MRS. PULLEN, MISS REESE, H. S. MORRIS, MISS CONE, BURTON, SHERMAN, GARLAND, MISS MONROE, MISS GUINEY, AND OTHERS)

Robert Mowry Bell

Frank Dempster Sherman

John Hall Ingham

Harry Lyman Koopman

Oscar Fay Adams

Hamlin Garland

Virginia Woodward Cloud

Clinton Scollard

Harriet Monroe

Charlotte Perkins Stetson

Louise Imogen Guiney

Lilla Cabot Perry

Hannah Parker Kimball

Albert Bigelow Paine

Ernest McGaffey

Katrina Trask

Additional Selections

(VARIOUS POEMS BELONGING TO THIS DIVISION)

I

II

III

IV

IV. CLOSE OF THE CENTURY

(TYPICAL POETS AND POETRY OF THE FINAL YEARS)

IV. CLOSE OF THE CENTURY

(TYPICAL POETS AND POETRY OF THE FINAL YEARS)

Amélie Troubetzkoy

Gertrude Hall

Elaine Goodale Eastman

Winifred Howells

Richard Hovey

Julie Mathilde Lippmann

Mark A. De Wolfe Howe

Madison Cawein

John Bennett

Edward Lucas White

Martha Gilbert Dickinson

Walter Malone

John Jerome Rooney

Anne Reeve Aldrich

Herbert Bates

John Russell Hayes

Dora Read Goodale

Joseph Russell Taylor

Arthur Colton

Philip Henry Savage

Barrett Eastman

William Vaughn Moody

Frederic Lawrence Knowles

Edwin Arlington Robinson

Caroline Duer

Alice Duer Miller

Edward A. U. Valentine

Alice Archer (S.) James

Stephen Crane

Herbert Bashford

Rupert Hughes

Paul Laurence Dunbar

I

EARLY YEARS OF THE NATION

(THE QUARTER CENTURY PRECEDING BRYANT AND HIS CONTEMPORARIES)

FRENEAU'S EARLIER COLLECTIONS OF HIS POEMS: 1786–95
BRYANT'S "THANATOPSIS" IN "NORTH AMERICAN REVIEW": 1816

PRELUDE

I SAW the constellated matin choir
Then when they sang together in the dawn, —
The morning stars of this first rounded day
Hesperian, hundred-houred, that ending leaves
Youth's fillet still upon the New World's brow;
Then when they sang together, — sang for joy
Of mount and wood and cataract, and stretch
Of keen-aired vasty reaches happy-homed, —
I heard the stately hymning, saw their light
Resolve in flame that evil long inwrought
With what was else the goodliest demain
Of freedom warded by the ancient sea;
So sang they, rose they, to meridian,
And westering down the firmament led on
Cluster and train of younger celebrants
That beaconed as they might, by adverse skies
Shrouded, but stayed not nor discomfited, —
Of whom how many, and how dear, alas,
The voices stilled mid-orbit, stars eclipsed
Long ere the hour of setting; yet in turn
Others oncoming shine, nor fail to chant
New anthems, yet not alien, for the time
Goes not out darkling nor of music mute
To the next age, — that quickened now awaits
Their heralding, their more impassioned song.

E. C. S.

EARLY YEARS OF THE NATION

(THE QUARTER-CENTURY PRECEDING BRYANT AND HIS CONTEMPORARIES)

Philip Freneau

EUTAW SPRINGS

At Eutaw Springs the valiant died:
  Their limbs with dust are covered o'er;
Weep on, ye springs, your tearful tide;
  How many heroes are no more!

If in this wreck of ruin they
  Can yet be thought to claim a tear,
O smite thy gentle breast, and say
  The friends of freedom slumber here!

Thou, who shalt trace this bloody plain,
  If goodness rules thy generous breast,
Sigh for the wasted rural reign;
  Sigh for the shepherds sunk to rest!

Stranger, their humble groves adorn;
  You too may fall, and ask a tear:
'T is not the beauty of the morn
  That proves the evening shall be clear.

They saw their injured country's woe,
  The flaming town, the wasted field;
Then rushed to meet the insulting foe;
  They took the spear — but left the shield.

Led by thy conquering standards, Greene,
  The Britons they compelled to fly:
None distant viewed the fatal plain,
  None grieved in such a cause to die —

But, like the Parthians famed of old,
  Who, flying, still their arrows threw,
These routed Britons, full as bold,
  Retreated, and retreating slew.

Now rest in peace our patriot band;
  Though far from nature's limits thrown,
We trust they find a happier land,
  A brighter Phœbus of their own.

EPITAPH, FROM "THE FADING ROSE"

Here — for they could not help but die —
The daughters of the Rose-Bush lie:
Here rest, interred without a stone,
What dear Lucinda gave to none, —
What forward beau, or curious belle,
Could hardly touch, and rarely smell.

Dear Rose! of all the blooming kind
You had a happier place assigned,
And nearer grew to all that 's fair,
And more engaged Lucinda's care,
Than ever courting, coaxing swain,
Or ever all who love, shall gain.

SONG OF THYRSIS

IN "FEMALE FRAILTY"

The turtle on yon withered bough,
That lately mourned her murdered mate,
Has found another comrade now —
Such changes all await!
Again her drooping plume is drest,
Again she 's willing to be blest
And takes her lover to her nest.

If nature has decreed it so
With all above, and all below,
Let us like them forget our woe,
And not be killed with sorrow.
If I should quit your arms to-night
And chance to die before 't was light,
I would advise you — and you might —
Love again to-morrow.

THE WILD HONEYSUCKLE

Fair flower, that dost so comely grow,
Hid in this silent, dull retreat,
Untouched thy honied blossoms blow,
Unseen thy little branches greet:
No roving foot shall crush thee here,
No busy hand provoke a tear.

By Nature's self in white arrayed,
She bade thee shun the vulgar eye,
And planted here the guardian shade,
And sent soft waters murmuring by;
Thus quietly thy summer goes,
Thy days declining to repose.

Smit with those charms, that must decay,
I grieve to see your future doom;
They died — nor were those flowers more gay,
The flowers that did in Eden bloom;
Unpitying frosts and Autumn's power
Shall leave no vestige of this flower.

From morning suns and evening dews
At first thy little being came;
If nothing once, you nothing lose,
For when you die you are the same;
The space between is but an hour,
The frail duration of a flower.

THE INDIAN BURYING-GROUND

In spite of all the learned have said,
I still my old opinion keep;
The posture that we give the dead
Points out the soul's eternal sleep.

Not so the ancients of these lands; —
The Indian, when from life released,
Again is seated with his friends,
And shares again the joyous feast.

His imaged birds, and painted bowl,
And venison, for a journey dressed,
Bespeak the nature of the soul,
Activity, that wants no rest.

His bow for action ready bent,
And arrows with a head of stone,
Can only mean that life is spent,
And not the old ideas gone.

Thou, stranger, that shalt come this way,
No fraud upon the dead commit, —
Observe the swelling turf, and say,
They do not lie, but here they sit.

Here still a lofty rock remains,
On which the curious eye may trace
(Now wasted half by wearing rains)
The fancies of a ruder race.

Here still an aged elm aspires,
Beneath whose far projecting shade
(And which the shepherd still admires)
The children of the forest played.

There oft a restless Indian queen
(Pale Shebah with her braided hair),
And many a barbarous form is seen
To chide the man that lingers there.

By midnight moons, o'er moistening dews,
In habit for the chase arrayed,
The hunter still the deer pursues,
The hunter and the deer — a shade!

And long shall timorous Fancy see
The painted chief, and pointed spear,
And Reason's self shall bow the knee
To shadows and delusions here.

DEATH'S EPITAPH

FROM "THE HOUSE OF NIGHT"

Death in this tomb his weary bones hath laid,
Sick of dominion o'er the human kind;
Behold what devastations he hath made,
Survey the millions by his arm confined.

"Six thousand years has sovereign sway been mine,
None but myself can real glory claim;

Great Regent of the world I reigned alone,
And princes trembled when my mandate came.

"Vast and unmatched throughout the world, my fame
Takes place of gods, and asks no mortal date —
No: by myself, and by the heavens, I swear
Not Alexander's name is half so great.

"Nor swords nor darts my prowess could withstand,
All quit their arms, and bowed to my decree, —
Even mighty Julius died beneath my hand,
For slaves and Cæsars were the same to me!"

Traveller, wouldst thou his noblest trophies seek,
Search in no narrow spot obscure for those;
The sea profound, the surface of all land,
Is moulded with the myriads of his foes.

THE PARTING GLASS

THE man that joins in life's career
And hopes to find some comfort here,
To rise above this earthly mass, —
The only way 's to drink his glass.

But still, on this uncertain stage
Where hopes and fears the soul engage,
And while, amid the joyous band,
Unheeded flows the measured sand,
Forget not as the moments pass
That time shall bring the parting glass!

In spite of all the mirth I 've heard,
This is the glass I always feared,
The glass that would the rest destroy,
The farewell cup, the close of joy.

With you, whom reason taught to think,
I could for ages sit and drink;
But with the fool, the sot, the ass,
I haste to take the parting glass.

The luckless wight, that still delays
His draught of joys to future days,
Delays too long — for then, alas!
Old age steps up, and — breaks the glass!

The nymph who boasts no borrowed charms,
Whose sprightly wit my fancy warms, —
What though she tends this country inn,
And mixes wine, and deals out gin?
With such a kind, obliging lass,
I sigh to take the parting glass.

With him who always talks of gain
(Dull Momus, of the plodding train),
The wretch who thrives by others' woes,
And carries grief where'er he goes, —
With people of this knavish class
The first is still my parting glass.

With those that drink before they dine,
With him that apes the grunting swine,
Who fills his page with low abuse,
And strives to act the gabbling goose
Turned out by fate to feed on grass —
Boy, give me quick, the parting glass.

The man whose friendship is sincere,
Who knows no guilt, and feels no fear, —
It would require a heart of brass
With him to take the parting glass.

With him who quaffs his pot of ale,
Who holds to all an even scale,
Who hates a knave in each disguise,
And fears him not — whate'er his size —
With him, well pleased my days to pass,
May heaven forbid the Parting Glass!

ON THE RUINS OF A COUNTRY INN

WHERE now these mingled ruins lie
A temple once to Bacchus rose,
Beneath whose roof, aspiring high,
Full many a guest forgot his woes.

No more this dome, by tempests torn,
Affords a social safe retreat;
But ravens here, with eye forlorn,
And clustering bats henceforth will meet.

The Priestess of this ruined shrine,
Unable to survive the stroke,
Presents no more the ruddy wine, —
Her glasses gone, her china broke.

The friendly Host, whose social hand
Accosted strangers at the door,

Has left at length his wonted stand,
And greets the weary guest no more.

Old creeping Time, that brings decay,
Might yet have spared these mouldering walls,
Alike beneath whose potent sway
A temple or a tavern falls.

Is this the place where mirth and joy,
Coy nymphs, and sprightly lads were found?
Indeed! no more the nymphs are coy,
No more the flowing bowls go round.

Is this the place where festive song
Deceived the wintry hours away?
No more the swains the tune prolong,
No more the maidens join the lay.

Is this the place where Nancy slept
In downy beds of blue and green?
Dame Nature here no vigils kept,
No cold unfeeling guards were seen.

'T is gone! — and Nancy tempts no more;
Deep, unrelenting silence reigns;
Of all that pleased, that charmed before,
The tottering chimney scarce remains.

Ye tyrant winds, whose ruffian blast
Through doors and windows blew too strong,
And all the roof to ruin cast, —
The roof that sheltered us so long, —

Your wrath appeased, I pray be kind
If Mopsus should the dome renew,
That we again may quaff his wine,
Again collect our jovial crew.

ON A TRAVELLING SPECULATOR

On scent of game from town to town he flew,
The soldier's curse pursued him on his way;
Care in his eye, and anguish on his brow,
He seemed a sea-hawk watching for his prey.

With soothing words the widow's mite he gained,
With piercing glance watched misery's dark abode,
Filched paper scraps while yet a scrap remained,
Bought where he must, and cheated where he could;

Vast loads amassed of scrip, and who knows what;
Potosi's wealth seemed lodged within his clutch, —
But wealth has wings (he knew) and instant bought
The prancing steed, gay harness, and gilt coach.

One Sunday morn to church we saw him ride
In glittering state — alack! and who but he —
The following week, with Madam at his side,
To routs they drove — and drank Imperial tea!

In cards and fun the livelong day they spent,
With songs and smut prolonged the midnight feast, —
If plays were had, to plays they constant went,
Where Madam's top-knot rose a foot at least.

Three weeks, and more, thus passed in airs of state,
The fourth beheld the mighty bubble fail, —
And he, who countless millions owned so late,
Stopped short — and closed his triumphs in a jail.

THE SCURRILOUS SCRIBE

His soul extracted from the public sink,
For discord born he splasht around his ink;
In scandal foremost, as by scandal fed,
He hourly rakes the ashes of the dead.

Secure from him no traveller walks the streets,
His malice sees a foe in all he meets;
With dark design he treads his daily rounds,
Kills where he can, and, where he cannot, wounds.

Nature to him her stings of rancor gave
To shed, unseen, the venom of a knave;
She gave him cunning, every treacherous art,
She gave him all things but an upright heart;

And one thing more — she gave him but the pen,
No power to hurt, not even the brass of men,
Whose breasts though furies with their passions rule
Yet laugh at satire, pointed by a fool.

Was there no world but ours to give you room?
No Patagonia, for your savage home,
No region, where antarctic oceans roll,
No icy island, neighboring to the pole?

By dark suspicion led, you aim at all
Who will not to your sceptred idol fall;
To work their ruin, every baseness try,
First envy, next abuse us, then belie.

Such is your stretch! and thus awhile go on!
Your shafts rebound, and yet have injured none.
Hurt whom they will, let who will injured be,
The sons of smut and scandal hurt not me.

TO A CATY-DID

In a branch of willow hid
Sings the evening Caty-did:
From the lofty locust bough
Feeding on a drop of dew,
In her suit of green arrayed
Hear her singing in the shade —
Caty-did, Caty-did, Caty-did!

While upon a leaf you tread,
Or repose your little head
On your sheet of shadows laid,
All the day you nothing said:
Half the night your cheery tongue
Revelled out its little song, —
Nothing else but Caty-did.

From your lodging on the leaf
Did you utter joy or grief?
Did you only mean to say,
I have had my summer's day,
And am passing, soon, away
To the grave of Caty-did:
Poor, unhappy Caty-did!

But you would have uttered more
Had you known of nature's power;
From the world when you retreat,
And a leaf's your winding sheet,
Long before your spirit fled,
Who can tell but nature said, —
Live again, my Caty-did!
Live, and chatter Caty-did.

Tell me, what did Caty do?
Did she mean to trouble you?
Why was Caty not forbid
To trouble little Caty-did?
Wrong, indeed, at you to fling,
Hurting no one while you sing, —
Caty-did! Caty-did! Caty-did!

Why continue to complain?
Caty tells me she again
Will not give you plague or pain;
Caty says you may be hid,
Caty will not go to bed
While you sing us Caty-did, —
Caty-did! Caty-did! Caty-did!

But, while singing, you forgot
To tell us what did Caty *not:*
Caty did not think of cold,
Flocks retiring to the fold,
Winter with his wrinkles old;
Winter, that yourself foretold
When you gave us Caty-did.

Stay serenely on your nest;
Caty now will do her best,
All she can, to make you blest;
But you want no human aid, —
Nature, when she formed you, said,
"Independent you are made,
My dear little Caty-did:
Soon yourself must disappear
With the verdure of the year,"
And to go, we know not where,
With your song of Caty-did.

TO A HONEY BEE

Thou, born to sip the lake or spring,
Or quaff the waters of the stream,

Why hither come, on vagrant wing?
  Does Bacchus tempting seem, —
    Did he for you this glass prepare?
    Will I admit you to a share?

Did storms harass or foes perplex,
  Did wasps or king-birds bring dismay, —
Did wars distress, or labors vex,
  Or did you miss your way?
    A better seat you could not take
    Than on the margin of this lake.

Welcome! — I hail you to my glass:
  All welcome here you find;
Here let the cloud of trouble pass,
  Here be all care resigned.
    This fluid never fails to please,
    And drown the griefs of men or bees.

What forced you here we cannot know,
  And you will scarcely tell,
But cheery we would have you go
  And bid a glad farewell:
    On lighter wings we bid you fly, —
    Your dart will now all foes defy.

Yet take not, oh! too deep a drink,
  And in this ocean die;
Here bigger bees than you might sink,
  Even bees full six feet high.
    Like Pharaoh, then, you would be said
    To perish in a sea of red.

Do as you please, your will is mine;
  Enjoy it without fear,
And your grave will be this glass of wine,
  Your epitaph — a tear;
    Go, take your seat in Charon's boat;
    We 'll tell the hive, you died afloat.

PLATO TO THEON

The grandeur of this earthly round,
  Where Theon would forever be,
Is but a name, is but a sound —
  Mere emptiness and vanity.

Give me the stars, give me the skies,
  Give me the heaven's remotest sphere,
Above these gloomy scenes to rise
  Of desolation and despair.

These native fires that warmed the mind,
  Now languid grown, too dimly glow;
Joy has to grief the heart resigned,
  And love itself is changed to woe.

The joys of wine are all you boast, —
  These for a moment damp your pain;
The gleam is o'er, the charm is lost,
  And darkness clouds the soul again.

Then seek no more for bliss below,
  Where real bliss can ne'er be found;
Aspire where sweeter blossoms blow
  And fairer flowers bedeck the ground;

Where plants of life the plains invest,
  And green eternal crowns the year;
The little god within your breast
  Is weary of his mansion here.

Like Phosphor, sent before the day,
  His height meridian to regain, —
The dawn arrives — he must not stay
  To shiver on a frozen plain.

Life's journey past, for death prepare, —
  'T is but the freedom of the mind;
Jove made us mortal — his we are;
  To Jove, dear Theon, be resigned.

Author Unfound[1]

THE YANKEE MAN-OF-WAR

'T is of a gallant Yankee ship that flew the stripes and stars,
And the whistling wind from the west-nor'-west blew through the pitch-pine spars;
With her starboard tacks aboard, my boys, she hung upon the gale;
On an autumn night we raised the light on the old Head of Kinsale.

It was a clear and cloudless night, and the wind blew steady and strong,

[1] See Biographical Note, p. 778.

As gayly over the sparkling deep our good ship bowled along;
With the foaming seas beneath her bow the fiery waves she spread,
And bending low her bosom of snow, she buried her lee cat-head.

There was no talk of short'ning sail by him who walked the poop,
And under the press of her pond'ring jib, the boom bent like a hoop!
And the groaning water-ways, told the strain that held her stout main-tack,
But he only laughed as he glanced aloft at a white and silvery track.

The mid-tide meets in the Channel waves that flow from shore to shore,
And the mist hung heavy upon the land from Featherstone to Dunmore,
And that sterling light in Tusker Rock where the old bell tolls each hour,
And the beacon light that shone so bright was quench'd on Waterford Tower.

What looms upon our starboard bow? What hangs upon the breeze?
'T is time our good ship hauled her wind abreast the old Saltees,
For by her ponderous press of sail and by her consorts four
We saw our morning visitor was a British man-of-war.

Up spake our noble Captain then, as a shot ahead of us past —
"Haul snug your flowing courses! lay your topsail to the mast!"
Those Englishmen gave three loud hurrahs from the deck of their covered ark,
And we answered back by a solid broadside from the decks of our patriot bark.

"Out booms! out booms!" our skipper cried, "out booms and give her sheet,"
And the swiftest keel that was ever launched shot ahead of the British fleet,
And amidst a thundering shower of shot, with stun'-sails hoisting away,
Down the North Channel Paul Jones did steer just at the break of day.

Timothy Dwight

THE SMOOTH DIVINE

THERE smiled the smooth Divine, unused to wound
The sinner's heart with hell's alarming sound.
No terrors on his gentle tongue attend;
No grating truths the nicest ear offend.
That strange new-birth, that methodistic grace,
Nor in his heart nor sermons found a place.
Plato's fine tales he clumsily retold,
Trite, fireside, moral seesaws, dull as old, —
His Christ and Bible placed at good remove,
Guilt hell-deserving, and forgiving love.
'T was best, he said, mankind should cease to sin:
Good fame required it; so did peace within.
Their honors, well he knew, would ne'er be driven;
But hoped they still would please to go to heaven.
Each week he paid his visitation dues;
Coaxed, jested, laughed; rehearsed the private news;
Smoked with each goody, thought her cheese excelled;
Her pipe he lighted, and her baby held.
Or placed in some great town, with lacquered shoes,
Trim wig, and trimmer gown, and glistening hose,
He bowed, talked politics, learned manners mild,
Most meekly questioned, and most smoothly smiled;
At rich men's jests laughed loud, their stories praised,
Their wives' new patterns gazed, and gazed, and gazed;

Most daintily on pampered turkeys dined,
Nor shrunk with fasting, nor with study pined:
Yet from their churches saw his brethren driven,
Who thundered truth, and spoke the voice of heaven,
Chilled trembling guilt in Satan's headlong path,
Charmed the feet back, and roused the ear of death.
"Let fools," he cried, "starve on, while prudent I
Snug in my nest shall live, and snug shall die."

LOVE TO THE CHURCH

I LOVE thy kingdom, Lord,
The house of thine abode,
The church our blest Redeemer saved
With his own precious blood.

I love thy church, O God!
Her walls before thee stand,
Dear as the apple of thine eye,
And graven on thy hand.

If e'er to bless thy sons
My voice or hands deny,
These hands let useful skill forsake,
This voice in silence die.

For her my tears shall fall,
For her my prayers ascend;
To her my cares and toils be given
Till toils and cares shall end.

Beyond my highest joy
I prize her heavenly ways,
Her sweet communion, solemn vows,
Her hymns of love and praise.

Jesus, thou friend divine,
Our Saviour and our King,
Thy hand from every snare and foe
Shall great deliverance bring.

Sure as thy truth shall last,
To Zion shall be given
The brightest glories earth can yield,
And brighter bliss of heaven.

St. George Tucker

DAYS OF MY YOUTH

DAYS of my youth,
Ye have glided away;
Hairs of my youth,
Ye are frosted and gray;
Eyes of my youth,
Your keen sight is no more;
Cheeks of my youth,
Ye are furrowed all o'er;
Strength of my youth,
All your vigor is gone;
Thoughts of my youth,
Your gay visions are flown.

Days of my youth,
I wish not your recall;
Hairs of my youth,
I'm content ye should fall;
Eyes of my youth,
You much evil have seen;
Cheeks of my youth,
Bathed in tears have you been;
Thoughts of my youth,
You have led me astray;
Strength of my youth,
Why lament your decay?

Days of my age,
Ye will shortly be past;
Pains of my age,
Yet awhile ye can last;
Joys of my age,
In true wisdom delight;
Eyes of my age,
Be religion your light;
Thoughts of my age,
Dread ye not the cold sod;
Hopes of my age,
Be ye fixed on your God.

St. John Honeywood

DARBY AND JOAN

I

When Darby saw the setting sun,
He swung his scythe, and home he run,
Sat down, drank off his quart, and said,
"My work is done, I 'll go to bed."
"My work is done!" retorted Joan,
"My work is done! your constant tone;
But hapless woman ne'er can say,
'My work is done,' till judgment day.
You men can sleep all night, but we
Must toil." — "Whose fault is that?" quoth he.
"I know your meaning," Joan replied,
"But, Sir, my tongue shall not be tied;
I will go on, and let you know
What work poor women have to do:
First, in the morning, though we feel
As sick as drunkards when they reel, —
Yes, feel such pains in back and head
As would confine you men to bed,
We ply the brush, we wield the broom,
We air the beds, and right the room;
The cows must next be milked — and then
We get the breakfast for the men.
Ere this is done, with whimpering cries,
And bristly hair, the children rise;
These must be dressed, and dosed with rue,
And fed — and all because of you:
We next" — Here Darby scratched his head,
And stole off grumbling to his bed;
And only said, as on she run,
"Zounds! woman's clack is never done."

II

At early dawn, ere Phœbus rose,
Old Joan resumed her tale of woes;
When Darby thus — "I 'll end the strife,
Be you the man and I the wife:
Take you the scythe and mow, while I
Will all your boasted cares supply."
"Content," quoth Joan, "give me my stint."
This Darby did, and out she went.
Old Darby rose and seized the broom
And whirled the dirt about the room:
Which having done, he scarce knew how,
He hied to milk the brindled cow.
The brindled cow whisked round her tail
In Darby's eyes, and kicked the pail.
The clown, perplexed with grief and pain,
Swore he 'd ne'er try to milk again:
When turning round, in sad amaze,
He saw his cottage in a blaze:
For as he chanced to brush the room,
In careless haste, he fired the broom.
The fire at last subdued, he swore
The broom and he would meet no more.
Pressed by misfortune, and perplext,
Darby prepared for breakfast next;
But what to get he scarcely knew —
The bread was spent, the butter too.
His hands bedaubed with paste and flour,
Old Darby labored full an hour:
But, luckless wight! thou couldst not make
The bread take form of loaf or cake.
As every door wide open stood,
In pushed the sow in quest of food;
And, stumbling onwards, with her snout
O'erset the churn — the cream ran out.
As Darby turned the sow to beat,
The slippery cream betrayed his feet;
He caught the bread trough in his fall,
And down came Darby, trough, and all.
The children, wakened by the clatter,
Start up, and cry, "Oh! what 's the matter?"
Old Jowler barked, and Tabby mewed,
And hapless Darby bawled aloud,
"Return, my Joan, as heretofore,
I 'll play the housewife's part no more:
Since now, by sad experience taught,
Compared to thine my work is naught;
Henceforth, as business calls, I 'll take,
Content, the plough, the scythe, the rake,
And never more transgress the line
Our fates have marked, while thou art mine.
Then Joan, return, as heretofore,
I 'll vex thy honest soul no more;
Let 's each our proper task attend —
Forgive the past, and strive to mend."

Alexander Wilson

THE FISHERMAN'S HYMN

THE osprey sails above the sound,
The geese are gone, the gulls are flying;
The herring shoals swarm thick around,
The nets are launched, the boats are plying;
Yo ho, my hearts! let 's seek the deep,
Raise high the song, and cheerily wish her,
Still as the bending net we sweep,
"God bless the fish-hawk and the fisher!"

She brings us fish — she brings us spring,
Good times, fair weather, warmth, and plenty,
Fine stores of shad, trout, herring, ling,
Sheepshead and drum, and old-wives dainty.
Yo ho, my hearts! let 's seek the deep,
Ply every oar, and cheerily wish her,
Still as the bending net we sweep,
"God bless the fish-hawk and the fisher!"

She rears her young on yonder tree,
She leaves her faithful mate to mind 'em;
Like us, for fish, she sails to sea,
And, plunging, shows us where to find 'em.
Yo ho, my hearts! let 's seek the deep,
Ply every oar, and cheerily wish her,
While the slow bending net we sweep,
"God bless the fish-hawk and the fisher!"

THE BLUE-BIRD

WHEN winter's cold tempests and snows are no more,
Green meadows and brown-furrowed fields reappearing,
The fishermen hauling their shad to the shore,
And cloud-cleaving geese to the Lakes are a-steering;
When first the lone butterfly flits on the wing;
When red glow the maples, so fresh and so pleasing,
Oh then comes the blue-bird, the herald of spring!
And hails with his warblings the charms of the season.

Then loud-piping frogs make the marshes to ring;
Then warm glows the sunshine, and fine is the weather;
The blue woodland flowers just beginning to spring,
And spicewood and sassafras budding together:
Oh then to your gardens, ye housewives, repair!
Your walks border up; sow and plant at your leisure;
The blue-bird will chant from his box such an air
That all your hard toils will seem truly a pleasure.

He flits through the orchards, he visits each tree,
The red-flowering peach and the apple's sweet blossoms;
He snaps up destroyers wherever they be,
And seizes the caitiffs that lurk in their bosoms;
He drags the vile grub from the corn he devours,
The worm from their webs where they riot and welter;
His song and his services freely are ours,
And all that he asks is in summer a shelter.

The ploughman is pleased when he gleans in his train,
Now searching the furrows, now mounting to cheer him;
The gardener delights in his sweet simple strain,
And leans on his spade to survey and to hear him;
The slow-lingering schoolboys forget they 'll be chid,
While gazing intent as he warbles before 'em
In mantle of sky-blue, and bosom so red,
That each little loiterer seems to adore him.

When all the gay scenes of the summer are o'er,
And autumn slow enters so silent and sallow,
And millions of warblers, that charmed us before,
Have fled in the train of the sun-seeking swallow,
The blue-bird forsaken, yet true to his home,
Still lingers, and looks for a milder to-morrow,
Till, forced by the horrors of winter to roam,
He sings his adieu in a lone note of sorrow.

While spring's lovely season, serene, dewy, warm,
The green face of earth, and the pure blue of heaven,
Or love's native music, have influence to charm,
Or sympathy's glow to our feelings is given,
Still dear to each bosom the blue-bird shall be;
His voice like the thrillings of hope is a treasure;
For, through bleakest storms if a calm he but see,
He comes to remind us of sunshine and pleasure!

John Quincy Adams

TO SALLY

THE man in righteousness arrayed,
A pure and blameless liver,
Needs not the keen Toledo blade,
Nor venom-freighted quiver.
What though he wind his toilsome way
O'er regions wild and weary —
Through Zara's burning desert stray,
Or Asia's jungles dreary:

What though he plough the billowy deep
By lunar light, or solar,
Meet the resistless Simoon's sweep,
Or iceberg circumpolar!
In bog or quagmire deep and dank
His foot shall never settle;
He mounts the summit of Mont Blanc,
Or Popocatapetl.

On Chimborazo's breathless height
He treads o'er burning lava;
Or snuffs the Bohan Upas blight,
The deathful plant of Java.
Through every peril he shall pass,
By Virtue's shield protected;
And still by Truth's unerring glass
His path shall be directed.

Else wherefore was it, Thursday last,
While strolling down the valley,
Defenceless, musing as I passed
A canzonet to Sally,
A wolf, with mouth-protruding snout,
Forth from the thicket bounded —
I clapped my hands and raised a shout —
He heard — and fled — confounded.

Tangier nor Tunis never bred
An animal more crabbed;
Nor Fez, dry-nurse of lions, fed
A monster half so rabid;
Nor Ararat so fierce a beast
Has seen since days of Noah;
Nor stronger, eager for a feast,
The fell constrictor boa.

Oh! place me where the solar beam
Has scorched all verdure vernal;
Or on the polar verge extreme,
Blocked up with ice eternal —
Still shall my voice's tender lays
Of love remain unbroken;
And still my charming Sally praise,
Sweet smiling and sweet spoken.

THE LIP AND THE HEART

ONE day between the Lip and the Heart
A wordless strife arose,
Which was expertest in the art
His purpose to disclose.

The Lip called forth the vassal Tongue,
And made him vouch — a lie!
The slave his servile anthem sung,
And braved the listening sky.

The Heart to speak in vain essayed,
  Nor could his purpose reach —
His will nor voice nor tongue obeyed,
  His silence was his speech.

Mark thou their difference, child of earth!
  While each performs his part,
Not all the lip can speak is worth
  The silence of the heart.

Joseph Hopkinson

HAIL COLUMBIA

Hail, Columbia! happy land!
Hail, ye heroes! heaven-born band!
  Who fought and bled in Freedom's cause,
  Who fought and bled in Freedom's cause,
And when the storm of war was gone,
Enjoyed the peace your valor won.
  Let independence be our boast,
  Ever mindful what it cost;
  Ever grateful for the prize,
  Let its altar reach the skies.

    Firm, united, let us be,
    Rallying round our Liberty;
    As a band of brothers joined,
    Peace and safety we shall find.

Immortal patriots! rise once more:
Defend your rights, defend your shore:
  Let no rude foe, with impious hand,
  Let no rude foe, with impious hand,
Invade the shrine where sacred lies
Of toil and blood the well-earned prize.
  While offering peace sincere and just,
  In Heaven we place a manly trust,
  That truth and justice will prevail,
  And every scheme of bondage fail.

    Firm, united, etc.

Sound, sound, the trump of Fame!
Let Washington's great name
  Ring through the world with loud applause,
  Ring through the world with loud applause;
Let every clime to Freedom dear,
Listen with a joyful ear.
  With equal skill, and godlike power,
  He governed in the fearful hour
  Of horrid war; or guides, with ease,
  The happier times of honest peace.

    Firm, united, etc.

Behold the chief who now commands,
Once more to serve his country, stands —
  The rock on which the storm will beat,
  The rock on which the storm will beat;
But, armed in virtue firm and true,
His hopes are fixed on Heaven and you.
  When hope was sinking in dismay,
  And glooms obscured Columbia's day,
  His steady mind, from changes free,
  Resolved on death or liberty.

    Firm, united, let us be,
    Rallying round our Liberty;
    As a band of brothers joined,
    Peace and safety we shall find.

John Shaw

SONG

Who has robbed the ocean cave,
  To tinge thy lips with coral hue?
Who from India's distant wave
  For thee those pearly treasures drew?
    Who, from yonder orient sky,
    Stole the morning of thine eye?

Thousand charms, thy form to deck,
  From sea, and earth, and air are torn;
Roses bloom upon thy cheek,
  On thy breath their fragrance borne.
    Guard thy bosom from the day,
    Lest thy snows should melt away.

But one charm remains behind,
Which mute earth can ne'er impart;
Nor in ocean wilt thou find,
Nor in the circling air, a heart.
Fairest! wouldst thou perfect be,
Take, oh take that heart from me.

SLEIGHING SONG

WHEN calm is the night, and the stars shine bright,
The sleigh glides smooth and cheerily;
And mirth and jest abound,
While all is still around,
Save the horses' trampling sound,
And the horse-bells tinkling merrily.

But when the drifting snow in the traveller's face shall blow,
And hail is driving drearily,
And the wind is shrill and loud,
Then no sleigh shall stir abroad,
Nor along the beaten road
Shall the horse-bells tinkle merrily.

But to-night the skies are clear, and we have not to fear
That the time should linger wearily;
For good-humor has a charm
Even winter to disarm,
And our cloaks shall wrap us warm,
And the bells shall tinkle merrily.

Clement Clarke Moore

A VISIT FROM ST. NICHOLAS

'T WAS the night before Christmas, when all through the house
Not a creature was stirring, not even a mouse;
The stockings were hung by the chimney with care,
In hopes that ST. NICHOLAS soon would be there;
The children were nestled all snug in their beds,
While visions of sugar-plums danced in their heads;
And mamma in her 'kerchief, and I in my cap,
Had just settled our brains for a long winter's nap,
When out on the lawn there arose such a clatter,
I sprang from the bed to see what was the matter.
Away to the window I flew like a flash,
Tore open the shutters and threw up the sash.
The moon on the breast of the new-fallen snow
Gave the lustre of mid-day to objects below,
When, what to my wondering eyes should appear,
But a miniature sleigh, and eight tiny reindeer,
With a little old driver, so lively and quick,
I knew in a moment it must be St. Nick.
More rapid than eagles his coursers they came,
And he whistled, and shouted, and called them by name;
"Now, *Dasher!* now, *Dancer!* now, *Prancer* and *Vixen!*
On, *Comet!* on, *Cupid!* on, *Donder* and *Blitzen!*
To the top of the porch! to the top of the wall!
Now dash away! dash away! dash away all!"
As dry leaves that before the wild hurricane fly,
When they meet with an obstacle, mount to the sky;
So up to the house-top the coursers they flew,
With the sleigh full of Toys, and St. Nicholas too.
And then, in a twinkling, I heard on the roof
The prancing and pawing of each little hoof.
As I drew in my head, and was turning around,
Down the chimney St. Nicholas came with a bound.
He was dressed all in fur, from his head to his foot,

And his clothes were all tarnished with ashes and soot;
A bundle of Toys he had flung on his back,
And he looked like a pedler just opening his pack.
His eyes — how they twinkled! his dimples how merry!
His cheeks were like roses, his nose like a cherry!
His droll little mouth was drawn up like a bow,
And the beard of his chin was as white as the snow;
The stump of a pipe he held tight in his teeth,
And the smoke it encircled his head like a wreath;
He had a broad face and a little round belly,
That shook when he laughed, like a bowlful of jelly.
He was chubby and plump, a right jolly old elf,
And I laughed when I saw him, in spite of myself;
A wink of his eye and a twist of his head,
Soon gave me to know I had nothing to dread;
He spoke not a word, but went straight to his work,
And filled all the stockings; then turned with a jerk,
And laying his finger aside of his nose,
And giving a nod, up the chimney he rose;
He sprang to his sleigh, to his team gave a whistle,
And away they all flew like the down of a thistle.
But I heard him exclaim, ere he drove out of sight,
"*Happy Christmas to all, and to all a good-night.*"

Francis Scott Key

THE STAR-SPANGLED BANNER

O SAY, can you see, by the dawn's early light,
  What so proudly we hailed at the twilight's last gleaming —
Whose broad stripes and bright stars, through the clouds of the fight,
  O'er the ramparts we watched were so gallantly streaming!
And the rocket's red glare, the bombs bursting in air,
Gave proof through the night that our flag was still there;
O! say, does that star-spangled banner yet wave
O'er the land of the free, and the home of the brave?

On that shore dimly seen through the mists of the deep,
  Where the foe's haughty host in dread silence reposes,
What is that which the breeze, o'er the towering steep,
  As it fitfully blows, now conceals, now discloses?
Now it catches the gleam of the morning's first beam,
In full glory reflected now shines on the stream;
'T is the star-spangled banner; O long may it wave
O'er the land of the free, and the home of the brave!

And where is that band who so vauntingly swore
  That the havoc of war and the battle's confusion
A home and a country should leave us no more?
  Their blood has washed out their foul footsteps' pollution.
No refuge could save the hireling and slave
From the terror of flight, or the gloom of the grave;
And the star-spangled banner in triumph doth wave

O'er the land of the free, and the home of the brave.

O! thus be it ever, when freemen shall stand
Between their loved homes and the war's desolation!
Blest with victory and peace, may the heav'n-rescued land
Praise the power that hath made and preserved us a nation.
Then conquer we must, when our cause it is just,
And this be our motto — "*In God is our trust:*"
And the star-spangled banner in triumph shall wave
O'er the land of the free, and the home of the brave.

James Kirke Paulding

THE OLD MAN'S CAROUSAL

DRINK! drink! to whom shall we drink?
To a friend or a mistress? Come, let me think!
To those who are absent, or those who are here?
To the dead that we loved, or the living still dear?
Alas! when I look, I find none of the last!
The present is barren, — let 's drink to the past!

Come! here 's to the girl with a voice sweet and low,
The eye all of fire and the bosom of snow,
Who erewhile, in the days of my youth that are fled,
Once slept on my bosom, and pillowed my head!
Would you know where to find such a delicate prize?
Go seek in yon church-yard, for there she lies.

And here 's to the friend, the one friend of my youth,
With a head full of genius, a heart full of truth,
Who traveled with me in the sunshine of life,
And stood by my side in its peace and its strife!
Would you know where to seek for a blessing so rare?
Go drag the lone sea, you may find him there.

And here 's to a brace of twin cherubs of mine,
With hearts like their mother's, as pure as this wine,
Who came but to see the first act of the play,
Grew tired of the scene, and then both went away.
Would you know where this brace of bright cherubs have hied?
Go seek them in heaven, for there they abide.

A bumper, my boys! to a gray-headed pair,
Who watched o'er my childhood with tenderest care.
God bless them, and keep them, and may they look down
On the head of their son, without tear, sigh, or frown!
Would you know whom I drink to? go seek 'mid the dead,
You will find both their names on the stone at their head.

And here 's — but alas! the good wine is no more,
The bottle is emptied of all its bright store;
Like those we have toasted, its spirit is fled,
And nothing is left of the light that it shed.
Then, a bumper of tears, boys! the banquet here ends.
With a health to our dead, since we 've no living friends.

Washington Allston

AMERICA TO GREAT BRITAIN

All hail! thou noble land,
Our Fathers' native soil!
Oh, stretch thy mighty hand,
Gigantic grown by toil,
O'er the vast Atlantic wave to our shore!
For thou with magic might
Canst reach to where the light
Of Phœbus travels bright
The world o'er!

The Genius of our clime,
From his pine-embattled steep,
Shall hail the guest sublime;
While the Tritons of the deep
With their conchs the kindred league shall proclaim.
Then let the world combine,—
O'er the main our naval line
Like the milky-way shall shine
Bright in fame!

Though ages long have past
Since our Fathers left their home,
Their pilot in the blast,
O'er untravelled seas to roam,
Yet lives the blood of England in our veins!
And shall we not proclaim
That blood of honest fame
Which no tyranny can tame
By its chains?

While the language free and bold
Which the bard of Avon sung,
In which our Milton told
How the vault of heaven rung
When Satan, blasted, fell with his host;—
While this, with reverence meet,
Ten thousand echoes greet,
From rock to rock repeat
Round our coast;—

While the manners, while the arts,
That mould a nation's soul,
Still cling around our hearts,—
Between let Ocean roll,
Our joint communion breaking with the Sun:
Yet still from either beach
The voice of blood shall reach,
More audible than speech,
"We are One."

ROSALIE

"O pour upon my soul again
That sad, unearthly strain,
That seems from other worlds to plain;
Thus falling, falling from afar,
As if some melancholy star
Had mingled with her light her sighs,
And dropped them from the skies!

"No,—never came from aught below
This melody of woe,
That makes my heart to overflow,
As from a thousand gushing springs
Unknown before; that with it brings
This nameless light,—if light it be,—
That veils the world I see.

"For all I see around me wears
The hue of other spheres;
And something blent of smiles and tears
Comes from the very air I breathe.
O, nothing, sure, the stars beneath
Can mould a sadness like to this,—
So like angelic bliss."

So, at that dreamy hour of day,
When the last lingering ray
Stops on the highest cloud to play,—
So thought the gentle Rosalie,
As on her maiden reverie
First fell the strain of him who stole
In music to her soul.

ON THE LATE S. T. COLERIDGE

And thou art gone, most loved, most honored friend!
No, nevermore thy gentle voice shall blend
With air of Earth its pure ideal tones,
Binding in one, as with harmonious zones,
The heart and intellect. And I no more
Shall with thee gaze on that unfathomed deep,
The Human Soul,—as when, pushed off the shore,
Thy mystic bark would through the darkness sweep,
Itself the while so bright! For oft we seemed
As on some starless sea,—all dark above,

All dark below, — yet, onward as we drove,
To plough up light that ever round us streamed.

But he who mourns is not as one bereft
Of all he loved: thy living Truths are left.

Thomas Hastings

THE LATTER DAY

Hail to the brightness of Zion's glad morning;
Joy to the lands that in darkness have lain;
Hushed be the accents of sorrow and mourning;
Zion in triumph begins her mild reign!

Hail to the brightness of Zion's glad morning,
Long by the prophets of Israel foretold;
Hail to the millions from bondage returning;
Gentiles and Jews the blest vision behold!

Lo, in the desert rich flowers are springing;
Streams ever copious are gliding along;
Loud from the mountain-tops echoes are ringing;
Wastes rise in verdure, and mingle in song.

See, from all lands, from the isles of the ocean,
Praise to Jehovah ascending on high;
Fallen are the engines of war and commotion;
Shouts of salvation are rending the sky!

IN SORROW

Gently, Lord, oh, gently lead us,
Pilgrims in this vale of tears,
Through the trials yet decreed us,
Till our last great change appears.
When temptation's darts assail us,
When in devious paths we stray,
Let thy goodness never fail us,
Lead us in thy perfect way.

In the hour of pain and anguish,
In the hour when death draws near,
Suffer not our hearts to languish,
Suffer not our souls to fear;
And, when mortal life is ended,
Bid us in thine arms to rest,
Till, by angel bands attended,
We awake among the blest.

EXHORTATION

Child of sin and sorrow,
Filled with dismay,
Wait not for to-morrow,
Yield thee to-day.
Heaven bids thee come
While yet there 's room:
Child of sin and sorrow!
Hear and obey.

Child of sin and sorrow,
Why wilt thou die?
Come whilst thou canst borrow
Help from on high:
Grieve not that love
Which from above,
Child of sin and sorrow,
Would bring thee nigh.

Child of sin and sorrow,
Thy moments glide
Like the flitting arrow,
Or the rushing tide;
Ere time is o'er,
Heaven's grace implore:
Child of sin and sorrow,
In Christ confide.

Samuel Woodworth

THE BUCKET

How dear to this heart are the scenes of my childhood,
When fond recollection presents them to view!
The orchard, the meadow, the deep-tangled wild-wood,
And every loved spot which my infancy knew!
The wide-spreading pond, and the mill that stood by it,
The bridge, and the rock where the cataract fell,
The cot of my father, the dairy-house nigh it,
And e'en the rude bucket that hung in the well —
The old oaken bucket, the iron-bound bucket,
The moss-covered bucket which hung in the well.

That moss-covered vessel I hailed as a treasure,
For often at noon, when returned from the field,
I found it the source of an exquisite pleasure,
The purest and sweetest that nature can yield.
How ardent I seized it, with hands that were glowing,
And quick to the white-pebbled bottom it fell;
Then soon, with the emblem of truth overflowing,
And dripping with coolness, it rose from the well —
The old oaken bucket, the iron-bound bucket,
The moss-covered bucket arose from the well.

How sweet from the green mossy brim to receive it,
As poised on the curb it inclined to my lips!
Not a full blushing goblet could tempt me to leave it,
The brightest that beauty or revelry sips.
And now, far removed from the loved habitation,
The tear of regret will intrusively swell,
As fancy reverts to my father's plantation,
And sighs for the bucket that hangs in the well —
The old oaken bucket, the iron-bound bucket,
The moss-covered bucket that hangs in the well!

LOVES SHE LIKE ME?

O SAY, my flattering heart,
Loves she like me?
Is her's thy counterpart,
Throbs it like thee?
Does she remember yet
The spot where first we met,
Which I shall ne'er forget,
Loves she like me?

Soft echoes still repeat
"Loves she like me?"
When on that mossy seat,
Beneath the tree,
I wake my amorous lay
While lambkins round me play,
And whispering zephyrs say,
Loves she like me?

On her I think by day,
Loves she like me?
With her in dreams I stray
O'er mead and lea.
My hopes of earthly bliss
Are all comprised in this,
To share her nuptial kiss, —
Loves she like me?

Does absence give her pain?
Loves she like me?
And does she thus arraign
Fortune's decree?
Does she my name repeat?
Will she with rapture greet
The hour that sees us meet?
Loves she like me?

Richard Henry Dana

THE LITTLE BEACH-BIRD

Thou little bird, thou dweller by the sea,
Why takest thou its melancholy voice,
And with that boding cry
Why o'er the waves dost fly?
O, rather, bird, with me
Through the fair land rejoice!

Thy flitting form comes ghostly dim and pale,
As driven by a beating storm at sea;
Thy cry is weak and scared,
As if thy mates had shared
The doom of us: Thy wail, —
What doth it bring to me?

Thou call'st along the sand, and haunt'st the surge,
Restless and sad; as if, in strange accord
With the motion and the roar
Of waves that drive to shore,
One spirit did ye urge —
The Mystery — the Word.

Of thousands, thou, both sepulchre and pall,
Old Ocean! A requiem o'er the dead
From out thy gloomy cells
A tale of mourning tells, —
Tells of man's woe and fall,
His sinless glory fled.

Then turn thee, little bird, and take thy flight
Where the complaining sea shall sadness bring
Thy spirit never more;
Come, quit with me the shore,
And on the meadows light
Where birds for gladness sing!

IMMORTALITY

And do our loves all perish with our frames?
Do those that took their root and put forth buds,
And their soft leaves unfolded in the warmth
Of mutual hearts, grow up and live in beauty,
Then fade and fall, like fair, unconscious flowers?
Are thoughts and passions that to the tongue give speech,
And make it send forth winning harmonies, —
That to the cheek do give its living glow,
And vision in the eye the soul intense
With that for which there is no utterance —
Are these the body's accidents? — no more? —
To live in it, and when that dies, go out
Like the burnt taper's flame?

O, listen, man!
A voice within us speaks the startling word,
"Man, thou shalt never die!" Celestial voices
Hymn it around our souls: according harps,
By angel fingers touched when the mild stars
Of morning sang together, sound forth still
The song of our great immortality:
Thick clustering orbs, and this our fair domain,
The tall, dark mountains, and the deep-toned seas,
Join in this solemn, universal song.

O, listen ye, our spirits; drink it in
From all the air! 'T is in the gentle moonlight;
'T is floating in day's setting glories; Night,
Wrapt in her sable robe, with silent step
Comes to our bed and breathes it in our ears:
Night, and the dawn, bright day, and thoughtful eve,
All time, all bounds, the limitless expanse,
As one vast mystic instrument, are touched
By an unseen, living Hand; the conscious chords
Quiver with joy in this great jubilee;
The dying hear it, and as sounds of earth
Grow dull and distant, wake their passing souls
To mingle in this heavenly harmony.

THE CHANTING CHERUBS — A GROUP BY GREENOUGH

WHENCE come ye, Cherubs? from the moon?
Or from a shining star?
Ye sure are sent, a blessed boon,
From kinder worlds afar;
For, while I look, my heart is all delight:
Earth has no creatures half so pure and bright.

From moon nor star we hither flew;
The moon doth wane away, —
The stars they pale at morning dew;
We 're children of the day;
Nor change, nor night, was ever ours to bear;
Eternal light, and love, and joy, we share.

Then, sons of light, from Heaven above
Some blessed news ye bring.
Come ye to chant eternal love
And tell how angels sing,
And in your breathing, conscious forms to show
How purer forms above live, breathe, and glow?

Our parent is a human mind;
His winged thoughts are we;
To sun nor stars are we confined:
We pierce the deepest sea.
Moved by a brother's call, our Father bade
Us light on earth, and here our flight is stayed.

THE MOSS SUPPLICATETH FOR THE POET

THOUGH I am humble, slight me not,
But love me for the Poet's sake;
Forget me not till he 's forgot,
For care or slight with him I take.

For oft he passed the blossoms by
And turned to me with kindly look;
Left flaunting flowers and open sky,
And wooed me by the shady brook.

And like the brook his voice was low:
So soft, so sad the words he spoke,
That with the stream they seemed to flow;
They told me that his heart was broke.

They said the world he fain would shun,
And seek the still and twilight wood, —
His spirit, weary of the sun,
In humblest things found chiefest good;

That I was of a lowly frame,
And far more constant than the flower,
Which, vain with many a boastful name,
But fluttered out its idle hour;

That I was kind to old decay,
And wrapped it softly round in green, —
On naked root, and trunk of gray,
Spread out a garniture and screen.

They said that he was withering fast,
Without a sheltering friend like me;
That on his manhood fell a blast,
And left him bare, like yonder tree;

That spring would clothe his boughs no more,
Nor ring his boughs with song of bird, —
Sounds like the melancholy shore
Alone were through his branches heard.

Methought, as then he stood to trace
The withered stems, there stole a tear,
That I could read in his sad face —
Brothers! our sorrows make us near.

And then he stretched him all along,
And laid his head upon my breast,
Listening the water's peaceful song:
How glad was I to tend his rest!

Then happier grew his soothed soul;
He turned and watched the sunlight play
Upon my face, as in it stole,
Whispering, "Above is brighter day!"

He praised my varied hues, — the green,
The silver hoar, the golden, brown;
Said, Lovelier hues were never seen;
Then gently pressed my tender down.

And where I sent up little shoots,
He called them trees, in fond conceit:
Like silly lovers in their suits
He talked, his care awhile to cheat.

I said, I'd deck me in the dews,
Could I but chase away his care,
And clothe me in a thousand hues,
To bring him joys that I might share.

He answered, earth no blessing had
To cure his lone and aching heart;
That I was one, when he was sad,
Oft stole him from his pain, in part.

But e'en from thee, he said, I go
To meet the world, its care and strife,
No more to watch this quiet flow,
Or spend with thee a gentle life.

And yet the brook is gliding on,
And I, without a care, at rest,
While he to toiling life is gone;
Nor finds his head a faithful breast.

Deal gently with him, world! I pray;
Ye cares! like softened shadows come;
His spirit, well-nigh worn away,
Asks with ye but awhile a home.

O, may I live, and when he dies
Be at his feet a humble sod;
O, may I lay me where he lies,
To die when he awakes in God!

Sarah Josepha Hale

ALICE RAY

The birds their love-notes warble
Among the blossomed trees;
The flowers are sighing forth their sweets
To wooing honey-bees;
The glad brook o'er a pebbly floor
Goes dancing on its way,—
But not a thing is so like spring
As happy Alice Ray.

An only child was Alice,
And, like the blest above,
The gentle maid had ever breathed
An atmosphere of love;
Her father's smile like sunshine came,
Like dew her mother's kiss;
Their love and goodness made her home,
Like heaven, the place of bliss.

Beneath such tender training,
The joyous child had sprung,
Like one bright flower, in wild-wood bower,
And gladness round her flung;
And all who met her blessed her,
And turned again to pray
That grief and care might ever spare
The happy Alice Ray.

The gift that made her charming
Was not from Venus caught;
Nor was it, Pallas-like, derived
From majesty of thought;
Her heathful cheek was tinged with brown,
Her hair without a curl—

But then her eyes were love-lit stars,
Her teeth as pure as pearl.

And when in merry laughter
Her sweet, clear voice was heard,
It welled from out her happy heart
Like carol of a bird;
And all who heard were moved to smiles,
As at some mirthful lay,
And to the stranger's look replied,
"'T is that dear Alice Ray."

And so she came, like sunbeams
That bring the April green;
As type of nature's royalty,
They called her "Woodburn's queen!"
A sweet, heart-lifting cheerfulness,
Like spring-time of the year,
Seemed ever on her steps to wait,—
No wonder she was dear.

Her world was ever joyous—
She thought of grief and pain
As giants in the olden time,
That ne'er would come again;
The seasons all had charms for her,
She welcomed each with joy,—
The charm that in her spirit lived
No changes could destroy.

Her heart was like a fountain,
The waters always sweet,—
Her pony in the pasture,
The kitten at her feet,

The ruffling bird of Juno, and
The wren in the old wall,
Each knew her loving carefulness,
And came at her soft call.

Her love made all things lovely,
For in the heart must live
The feeling that imparts the charm, —
We gain by what we give.

THE WATCHER

The night was dark and fearful,
The blast swept wailing by;
A watcher, pale and tearful,
Looked forth with anxious eye:
How wistfully she gazes —
No gleam of morn is there!
And then her heart upraises
Its agony of prayer.

Within that dwelling lonely,
Where want and darkness reign,
Her precious child, her only,
Lay moaning in his pain;
And death alone can free him —
She feels that this must be:
"But oh! for morn to see him
Smile once again on me!"

A hundred lights are glancing
In yonder mansion fair,
And merry feet are dancing —
They heed not morning there:
Oh, young and lovely creatures,
One lamp, from out your store,
Would give that poor boy's features
To her fond gaze once more!

The morning sun is shining —
She heedeth not its ray;
Beside her dead reclining,
That pale, dead mother lay!
A smile her lip was wreathing,
A smile of hope and love,
As though she still were breathing —
"There 's light for us above!"

James Abraham Hillhouse[1]

THE DEMON-LOVER

FROM "HADAD"

SCENE. — The terraced roof of ABSALOM'S house, by night; adorned with vases of flowers, and fragrant shrubs; an awning spread over part of it. TAMAR and HADAD.

Tam. No, no, I well remember — proofs, you said,
Unknown to Moses.
Had. Well, my love, thou knowest
I 've been a traveller in various climes;
Trod Ethiopia's scorching sands, and scaled
The snow-clad mountains; trusted to the deep;
Traversed the fragrant islands of the sea,
And with the Wise conversed of many nations.
Tam. I know thou hast.
Had. Of all mine eyes have seen,
The greatest, wisest, and most wonderful,
Is that dread sage, the Ancient of the Mountain.
Tam. Who?
Had. None knows his lineage, age, or name: his locks
Are like the snows of Caucasus; his eyes
Beam with the wisdom of collected ages.
In green, unbroken years, he sees, 't is said,
The generations pass, like autumn fruits,
Garnered, consumed, and springing fresh to life,
Again to perish, while he views the sun,
The seasons roll, in rapt serenity,
And high communion with celestial powers.
Some say 't is Shem, our father, some say Enoch,
And some Melchizedek.
Tam. I've heard a tale
Like this, but ne'er believed it.
Had. I have proved it. —
Through perils dire, dangers most imminent,
Seven days and nights 'midst rocks and wildernesses,
And boreal snows, and never-thawing ice,
Where not a bird, a beast, a living thing,

[1] See BIOGRAPHICAL NOTE, p. 799.

Save the far-soaring vulture comes, I dared
My desperate way, resolved to know, or perish.
Tam. Rash, rash adventurer!
Had. On the highest peak
Of stormy Caucasus, there blooms a spot
On which perpetual sunbeams play, where flowers
And verdure never die; and there he dwells.
Tam. But didst thou see him?
Had. Never did I view
Such awful majesty: his reverend locks
Hung like a silver mantle to his feet,
His raiment glistered saintly white, his brow
Rose like the gate of Paradise, his mouth
Was musical as its bright guardians' songs.
Tam. What did he tell thee? Oh! what wisdom fell
From lips so hallowed?
Had. Whether he possess
The Tetragrammaton, — the powerful Name
Inscribed on Moses' rod, by which he wrought
Unheard of wonders, which constrains the Heavens
To part with blessings, shakes the earth, and rules
The strongest Spirits; or if God hath given
A delegated power, I cannot tell.
But 't was from him I learned their fate, their fall,
Who, erewhile, wore resplendent crowns in Heaven;
Now, scattered through the earth, the air, the sea.
Them he compels to answer, and from them
Has drawn what Moses, nor no mortal ear,
Has ever heard.
Tam. But did he tell it thee?
Had. He told me much, — more than I dare reveal;
For with a dreadful oath he sealed my lips.
Tam. But canst thou tell me nothing? — Why unfold
So much, if I must hear no more?
Had. You bade
Explain my words, almost reproached me, sweet,
For what by accident escaped me.
Tam. Ah!
A little — something tell me, — sure, not all
Were words inhibited.
Had. Then, promise never,
Never to utter of this conference
A breath to mortal.
Tam. Solemnly I vow.
Had. Even then, 't is little I can say, compared
With all the marvels he related.
Tam. Come,
I'm breathless. — Tell me how they sinn'd, how fell.
Had. Their Prince involved them in his ruin.
Tam. What black offence on his devoted head
Drew such dire punishment?
Had. The wish to be
As the All-Perfect.
Tam. Arrogating that
Peculiar to his Maker! — awful crime!
But what their doom? their place of punishment?
Had. Above, about, beneath; earth, sea, and air;
Their habitations various as their minds,
Employments, and desires.
Tam. But are they round us, Hadad? — not confined
In penal chains and darkness?
Had. So he said;
And so your holy books infer. What saith
Your Prophet? what the Prince of Uz?
Tam. I shudder,
Lest some dark Minister be near us now.
Had. You wrong them. They are bright Intelligences,
Robbed of some native splendor, and cast down,
'T is true, from Heaven; but not deformed, and foul,
Revengeful, malice-working Fiends, as fools
Suppose. They dwell, like Princes, in the clouds;
Sun their bright pinions in the middle sky;
Or arch their palaces beneath the hills,
With stones inestimable studded so,
That sun or stars were useless there.
Tam. Good heavens!
Had. He bade me look on rugged Caucasus,
Crag piled on crag beyond the utmost ken
Naked, and wild, as if creation's ruins
Were heaped in one immeasurable chain
Of barren mountains, beaten by the storms
Of everlasting winter. But within

Are glorious palaces, and domes of light,
Irradiate halls, and crystal colonnades,
Blazing with lustre past the noontide beam,
Or, with a milder beauty, mimicking
The mystic signs of changeful Mazzaroth.
Tam. Unheard of wonders!
Had. There they dwell, and muse,
And wander; Beings beautiful, immortal,
Minds vast as heaven, capacious as the sky;
Whose thoughts connect past, present, and to come,
And glow with light intense, imperishable.
So in the sparry chambers of the Sea
And Air-Pavilions, upper Tabernacles,
They study Nature's secrets, and enjoy
No poor dominion.
Tam. Are they beautiful,
And powerful far beyond the human race?
Had. Man's feeble heart cannot conceive it. When
The Sage described them, fiery eloquence
Broke from his lips, his bosom heaved, his eyes
Grew bright and mystical; moved by the theme,
Like one who feels a deity within.
Tam. Wondrous! — What intercourse have they with men?
Had. Sometimes they deign to intermix with man,
But oft with woman.
Tam. Ha! with woman?
Had. She
Attracts them with her gentler virtues, soft,
And beautiful, and heavenly, like themselves.
They have been known to love her with a passion
Stronger than human.
Tam. That surpasses all
You yet have told me.
Had. This the Sage affirms;
And Moses, darkly.
Tam. How do they appear? —
How love? —
Had. Sometimes 't is spiritual, signified
By beatific dreams, or more distinct
And glorious apparition. — They *have* stooped
To animate a human form, and love
Like mortals.
Tam. Frightful to be so beloved!
Frightful! who could endure the horrid thought?
Had. [*After a pause.*] But why contemn a Spirit's love? so high,
So glorious, if he haply deigned? —
Tam. Forswear
My Maker! love a Demon!
Had. No — Oh, no, —
My thoughts but wandered — Oft, alas! they wander.
Tam. Why dost thou speak so sadly now? — And lo!
Thine eyes are fixed again upon Arcturus.
Thus ever, when thy drooping spirits ebb,
Thou gazest on that star. Hath it the power
To cause or cure thy melancholy mood? —
[*He appears lost in thought.*
Tell me, — ascrib'st thou influence to the stars?
Had. [*Starting.*] The stars! — What know'st thou of the stars?
Tam. I know that they were made to rule the night.
Had. Like palace lamps! Thou echoest well thy grandsire! —
Woman! The stars are living, glorious,
Amazing, infinite! —
Tam. Speak not so wildly.
I know them numberless, resplendent, set
As symbols of the countless, countless years
That make eternity.
Had. Thou speak'st the word —
O, had ye proved — like those Great Sufferers, —
Shot, once for all, the gulf, — felt myriad ages
Only the prelude, — could ye scan the void
With eyes as searching as its torments, —
Then — then — mightst thou pronounce it feelingly!
Tam. What ails thee, Hadad? — Draw me not so close.
Had. Tamar! I need thy love — more than thy love —
Tam. Thy cheek is wet with tears —
Nay, let us part —
'T is late. I cannot, must not linger. —
[*Breaks from him, and exit.*
Had. Loved and abhorred! — Still, still accursed! —
[*He paces, twice or thrice, up and down with passionate gestures; then turns his face to the sky, and stands a moment in silence.*
O! where,
In the illimitable space, in what

Profound of untried misery, when all
His worlds, his rolling orbs of light, that fill
With life and beauty yonder infinite,
Their radiant journey run, forever set,
Where, where, in what abyss shall I be groaning? [*Exit.*

Richard Henry Wilde

STANZAS

My life is like the summer rose,
That opens to the morning sky,
But, ere the shades of evening close,
Is scattered on the ground — to die!
Yet on the rose's humble bed
The sweetest dews of night are shed,
As if she wept the waste to see —
But none shall weep a tear for me!

My life is like the autumn leaf
That trembles in the moon's pale ray:
Its hold is frail — its date is brief,
Restless — and soon to pass away!
Yet, ere that leaf shall fall and fade,
The parent tree will mourn its shade,
The winds bewail the leafless tree —
But none shall breathe a sigh for me!

My life is like the prints, which feet
Have left on Tampa's desert strand;
Soon as the rising tide shall beat,
All trace will vanish from the sand;
Yet, as if grieving to efface
All vestige of the human race,
On that lone shore loud moans the sea —
But none, alas! shall mourn for me!

A FAREWELL TO AMERICA

Farewell, my more than fatherland!
Home of my heart and friends, adieu!
Lingering beside some foreign strand,
How oft shall I remember you!
How often, o'er the waters blue,
Send back a sigh to those I leave,
The loving and beloved few,
Who grieve for me, — for whom I grieve!

We part! — no matter how we part,
There are some thoughts we utter not,
Deep treasured in our inmost heart,
Never revealed, and ne'er forgot!
Why murmur at the common lot?
We part! — I speak not of the pain, —
But when shall I each lovely spot
And each loved face behold again?

It must be months, — it may be years, —
It may — but no! — I will not fill
Fond hearts with gloom, — fond eyes with tears,
"Curious to shape uncertain ill."
Though humble, — few and far, — yet, still
Those hearts and eyes are ever dear;
Theirs is the love no time can chill,
The truth no chance or change can sear!

All I have seen, and all I see,
Only endears them more and more;
Friends cool, hopes fade, and hours flee,
Affection lives when all is o'er!
Farewell, my more than native shore!
I do not seek or hope to find,
Roam where I will, what I deplore
To leave with them and thee behind!

TO THE MOCKING-BIRD

Winged mimic of the woods! thou motley fool!
Who shall thy gay buffoonery describe?
Thine ever ready notes of ridicule
Pursue thy fellows still with jest and gibe.
Wit, sophist, songster, Yorick of thy tribe,
Thou sportive satirist of Nature's school,
To thee the palm of scoffing we ascribe,
Arch-mocker and mad Abbot of Misrule!
For such thou art by day — but all night long
Thou pourest a soft, sweet, pensive, solemn strain,
As if thou didst in this thy moonlight song
Like to the melancholy Jacques complain,
Musing on falsehood, folly, vice, and wrong,
And sighing for thy motley coat again.

Additional Selections

(CHOSEN FROM AMERICAN VERSE OF THE TIME)

ON SNOW-FLAKES MELTING ON HIS LADY'S BREAST

To kiss my Celia's fairer breast,
The snow forsakes its native skies,
But proving an unwelcome guest,
It grieves, dissolves in tears, and dies.

Its touch, like mine, but serves to wake
Through all her frame a death-like chill, —
Its tears, like those I shed, to make
That icy bosom colder still.

I blame her not; from Celia's eyes
A common fate beholders proved —
Each swain, each fair one, weeps and dies, —
With envy these, and those with love!

WILLIAM MARTIN JOHNSON

ON THE DEATH OF MY SON CHARLES

My son, thou wast my heart's delight,
Thy morn of life was gay and cheery;
That morn has rushed to sudden night,
Thy father's house is sad and dreary.

I held thee on my knee, my son!
And kissed thee laughing, kissed thee weeping;
But ah! thy little day is done,
Thou 'rt with thy angel sister sleeping.

The staff, on which my years should lean,
Is broken, ere those years come o'er me;
My funeral rites thou shouldst have seen,
But thou art in the tomb before me.

Thou rear'st to me no filial stone,
No parent's grave with tears beholdest;
Thou art my ancestor, my son!
And stand'st in Heaven's account the oldest.

On earth my lot was soonest cast,
Thy generation after mine,
Thou hast thy predecessor past;
Earlier eternity is thine.

I should have set before thine eyes
The road to Heaven, and showed it clear;
But thou untaught spring'st to the skies,
And leav'st thy teacher lingering here.

Sweet Seraph, I would learn of thee,
And hasten to partake thy bliss!
And oh! to thy world welcome me,
As first I welcomed thee to this.

Dear Angel, thou art safe in heaven;
No prayers for thee need more be made;
Oh! let thy prayers for those be given
Who oft have blessed thy infant head.

My father! I beheld thee born,
And led thy tottering steps with care;
Before me risen to Heaven's bright morn,
My son! my father! guide me there.

DANIEL WEBSTER

PRIVATE DEVOTION

I love to steal awhile away
From every cumbering care,
And spend the hours of setting day
In humble, grateful prayer.

I love, in solitude, to shed
The penitential tear;
And all His promises to plead,
When none but God can hear.

I love to think on mercies past,
And future good implore;
And all my cares and sorrows cast
On Him whom I adore.

I love, by faith, to take a view
Of brighter scenes in heaven;
The prospect doth my strength renew,
While here by tempests driven.

Thus, when life's toilsome day is o'er,
May its departing ray
Be calm as this impressive hour,
And lead to endless day.

PHOEBE HINSDALE BROWN

HYMN FOR THE DEDICATION OF A CHURCH

WHERE ancient forests round us spread,
Where bends the cataract's ocean-fall,
On the lone mountain's silent head,
There are thy temples, God of all!

Beneath the dark-blue, midnight arch,
Whence myriad suns pour down their rays,
Where planets trace their ceaseless march,
Father! we worship as we gaze.

The tombs thine altars are; for there,
When earthly loves and hopes have fled,
To thee ascends the spirit's prayer,
Thou God of the immortal dead.

All space is holy; for all space
Is filled by thee; but human thought
Burns clearer in some chosen place,
Where thy own words of love are taught.

Here be they taught; and may we know
That faith thy servants knew of old;
Which onward bears through weal and woe,
Till Death the gates of heaven unfold!

Nor we alone; may those whose brow
Shows yet no trace of human cares,
Hereafter stand where we do now,
And raise to thee still holier prayers!

ANDREWS NORTON

ROCKED IN THE CRADLE OF THE DEEP

ROCKED in the cradle of the deep
I lay me down in peace to sleep;
Secure I rest upon the wave,
For thou, O Lord! hast power to save.
I know thou wilt not slight my call,
For Thou dost mark the sparrow's fall;
And calm and peaceful shall I sleep,
Rocked in the cradle of the deep.

When in the dead of night I lie
And gaze upon the trackless sky,
The star-bespangled heavenly scroll,
The boundless waters as they roll, —
I feel thy wondrous power to save
From perils of the stormy wave:
Rocked in the cradle of the deep,
I calmly rest and soundly sleep.

And such the trust that still were mine,
Though stormy winds swept o'er the brine,
Or though the tempest's fiery breath
Roused me from sleep to wreck and death.
In ocean cave, still safe with Thee
The germ of immortality!
And calm and peaceful shall I sleep,
Rocked in the cradle of the deep.

EMMA HART WILLARD

THE SOUL'S DEFIANCE

I SAID to Sorrow's awful storm,
That beat against my breast,
Rage on — thou may'st destroy this form,
And lay it low at rest;
But still the spirit that now brooks
Thy tempest, raging high,
Undaunted on its fury looks
With steadfast eye.

I said to Penury's meagre train,
Come on — your threats I brave;
My last poor life-drop you may drain,
And crush me to the grave;
Yet still the spirit that endures
Shall mock your force the while,
And meet each cold, cold grasp of yours
With bitter smile.

I said to cold Neglect and Scorn,
Pass on — I heed you not;

Ye may pursue me till my form
And being are forgot;
Yet still the spirit, which you see
Undaunted by your wiles,
Draws from its own nobility
Its high-born smiles.

I said to Friendship's menaced blow,
Strike deep — my heart shall bear;
Thou canst but add one bitter woe
To those already there;
Yet still the spirit that sustains
This last severe distress
Shall smile upon its keenest pains,
And scorn redress.

I said to Death's uplifted dart,
Aim sure — oh, why delay?
Thou wilt not find a fearful heart —
A weak, reluctant prey;
For still the spirit, firm and free,
Unruffled by this last dismay,
Wrapt in its own eternity,
Shall pass away.

LAVINIA STODDARD

A NAME IN THE SAND

ALONE I walked the ocean strand;
A pearly shell was in my hand:
I stooped and wrote upon the sand
My name — the year — the day.
As onward from the spot I passed,
One lingering look behind I cast;
A wave came rolling high and fast,
And washed my lines away.

And so, methought, 't will shortly be
With every mark on earth from me:
A wave of dark oblivion's sea
Will sweep across the place
Where I have trod the sandy shore
Of time, and been, to be no more,
Of me — my day — the name I bore,
To leave nor track nor trace.

And yet, with Him who counts the sands
And holds the waters in his hands,
I know a lasting record stands
Inscribed against my name,
Of all this mortal part has wrought,
Of all this thinking soul has thought,
And from these fleeting moments caught
For glory or for shame.

HANNAH FLAGG GOULD

MY BRIGANTINE[1]

MY brigantine!
Just in thy mould and beauteous in thy form,
Gentle in roll and buoyant on the surge,
Light as the sea-fowl rocking in the storm,
In breeze and gale thy onward course we urge,
My water-queen!

Lady of mine!
More light and swift than thou none thread the sea,
With surer keel or steadier on its path;
We brave each waste of ocean-mystery
And laugh to hear the howling tempest's wrath,
For we are thine!

My brigantine!
Trust to the mystic power that points thy way,
Trust to the eye that pierces from afar,
Trust the red meteors that around thee play,
And, fearless, trust the Sea-Green Lady's Star,
Thou bark divine!

JAMES FENIMORE COOPER

[1] See BIOGRAPHICAL NOTE, p. 787.

II

FIRST LYRICAL PERIOD

(IN THREE DIVISIONS)

FROM THE OUTSET OF PIERPONT, BRYANT, AND THEIR ASSOCIATES, TO THE INTERVAL OF THE CIVIL WAR

1816–1860

1

Pierpont's "Airs of Palestine": Baltimore, 1816
Bryant's "Thanatopsis": North Amer. Review, Sept. 1817; "Poems" ("The Ages," etc.): Cambridge, 1821
Halleck and Drake's "The Croakers": N. Y. Evening Post, 1819
Mrs. Brooks's "Judith," etc.: Boston, 1820; "Zophiel": London, 1833
Pinkney's "Poems": Baltimore, 1825

2

Emerson's "Nature": Boston, 1836; "Poems": Boston, 1846
Whittier's "Mogg Megone": Boston, 1836; "Poems": Philadelphia, 1838
Longfellow's "Voices of the Night": Cambridge, 1839
Poe's "Tamerlane," etc.: Boston, 1827; "Al Aaraaf," etc.: Baltimore, 1829
Holmes's "Poems": Boston, 1836

3

Lowell's "A Year's Life": Boston, 1841; "Poems": Boston, 1844
Mrs. Howe's "Passion Flowers": Boston, 1854
Whitman's "Leaves of Grass": Brooklyn, 1855
Boker's "Calaynos, A Tragedy": Philadelphia, 1848
Taylor's "Ximena": Philadelphia, 1844; "Rhymes of Travel": New York, 1849
Stoddard's "Poems": Boston, 1852; "Songs of Summer": Boston, 1856

FIRST LYRICAL PERIOD

(IN THREE DIVISIONS)

DIVISION I

(PIERPONT, HALLECK, BRYANT, DRAKE, MRS. BROOKS, AND OTHERS)

John Pierpont

THE FUGITIVE SLAVE'S APOSTROPHE TO THE NORTH STAR

Star of the North! though night winds drift
The fleecy drapery of the sky
Between thy lamp and me, I lift,
Yea, lift with hope, my sleepless eye
To the blue heights wherein thou dwellest,
And of a land of freedom tellest.

Star of the North! while blazing day
Pours round me its full tide of light,
And hides thy pale but faithful ray,
I, too, lie hid, and long for night:
For night; — I dare not walk at noon,
Nor dare I trust the faithless moon, —

Nor faithless man, whose burning lust
For gold hath riveted my chain;
Nor other leader can I trust,
But thee, of even the starry train;
For, all the host around thee burning,
Like faithless man, keep turning, turning.

I may not follow where they go:
Star of the North, I look to thee
While on I press; for well I know
Thy light and truth shall set me free; —
Thy light, that no poor slave deceiveth;
Thy truth, that all my soul believeth.

They of the East beheld the star
That over Bethlehem's manger glowed;
With joy they hailed it from afar,
And followed where it marked the road,
Till, where its rays directly fell,
They found the Hope of Israel.

Wise were the men who followed thus
The star that sets man free from sin!
Star of the North! thou art to us, —
Who 're slaves because we wear a skin
Dark as is night's protecting wing, —
Thou art to us a holy thing.

And we are wise to follow thee!
I trust thy steady light alone:
Star of the North! thou seem'st to me
To burn before the Almighty's throne,
To guide me, through these forests dim
And vast, to liberty and Him.

Thy beam is on the glassy breast
Of the still spring, upon whose brink
I lay my weary limbs to rest,
And bow my parching lips to drink.
Guide of the friendless negro's way,
I bless thee for this quiet ray!

In the dark top of southern pines
I nestled, when the driver's horn
Called to the field, in lengthening lines,
My fellows at the break of morn.
And there I lay, till thy sweet face
Looked in upon "my hiding-place."

The tangled cane-brake, — where I crept
For shelter from the heat of noon,
And where, while others toiled, I slept
Till wakened by the rising moon, —
As its stalks felt the night wind free,
Gave me to catch a glimpse of thee.

Star of the North! in bright array
  The constellations round thee sweep,
Each holding on its nightly way,
  Rising, or sinking in the deep,
And, as it hangs in mid-heaven flaming,
The homage of some nation claiming.

This nation to the Eagle cowers;
  Fit ensign! she 's a bird of spoil;
Like worships like! for each devours
  The earnings of another's toil.
I 've felt her talons and her beak,
And now the gentler Lion seek.

The Lion at the Virgin's feet
  Crouches, and lays his mighty paw
Into her lap! — an emblem meet
  Of England's Queen and English law: —
Queen, that hath made her Islands free!
Law, that holds out its shield to me!

Star of the North! upon that shield
  Thou shinest! — O, forever shine!
The negro from the cotton-field
  Shall then beneath its orb recline,
And feed the Lion couched before it,
Nor heed the Eagle screaming o'er it!

WARREN'S ADDRESS TO THE AMERICAN SOLDIERS

STAND! the ground 's your own, my braves!
Will ye give it up to slaves?
Will ye look for greener graves?
  Hope ye mercy still?
What 's the mercy despots feel?
Hear it in that battle-peal!
Read it on yon bristling steel!
  Ask it, — ye who will.

Fear ye foes who kill for hire?
Will ye to your homes retire?
Look behind you! they 're a-fire!
  And, before you, see
Who have done it! — From the vale
On they come! — And will ye quail? —
Leaden rain and iron hail
  Let their welcome be!

In the God of battles trust!
Die we may, — and die we must;
But, O, where can dust to dust
  Be consigned so well,
As where Heaven its dews shall shed
On the martyred patriot's bed,
And the rocks shall raise their head,
  Of his deeds to tell!

THE BALLOT

A WEAPON that comes down as still
  As snowflakes fall upon the sod;
But executes a freeman's will,
  As lightning does the will of God.

THE EXILE AT REST

HIS falchion flashed along the Nile;
  His hosts he led through Alpine snows;
O'er Moscow's towers, that shook the while,
  His eagle flag unrolled, — and froze.

Here sleeps he now, alone; — not one
  Of all the kings whose crowns he gave,
Nor sire, nor brother, wife, nor son,
  Hath ever seen or sought his grave.

Here sleeps he now, alone; — the star,
  That led him on from crown to crown,
Hath sunk; — the nations from afar
  Gazed, as it faded and went down.

He sleeps alone; — the mountain cloud
  That night hangs round him, and the breath
Of morning scatters, is the shroud
  That wraps his martial form in death.

High is his couch; — the ocean flood
  Far, far below by storms is curled,
As round him heaved, while high he stood,
  A stormy and inconstant world.

Hark! Comes there from the Pyramids,
  And from Siberia's waste of snow,
And Europe's fields, a voice that bids
  The world be awed to mourn him? — No; —

The only, the perpetual dirge,
  That 's heard here, is the sea-bird's cry,
The mournful murmur of the surge,
  The cloud's deep voice, the wind's low sigh.

THE PILGRIM FATHERS

The Pilgrim Fathers, — where are they?
The waves that brought them o'er
Still roll in the bay, and throw their spray
As they break along the shore;
Still roll in the bay, as they rolled that day
When the Mayflower moored below,
When the sea around was black with storms,
And white the shore with snow.

The mists that wrapped the Pilgrim's sleep
Still brood upon the tide;
And his rocks yet keep their watch by the deep
To stay its waves of pride.
But the snow-white sail that he gave to the gale,
When the heavens looked dark, is gone, —
As an angel's wing through an opening cloud
Is seen, and then withdrawn.

The pilgrim exile, — sainted name!
The hill whose icy brow
Rejoiced, when he came, in the morning's flame,
In the morning's flame burns now.
And the moon's cold light, as it lay that night
On the hillside and the sea,
Still lies where he laid his houseless head, —
But the Pilgrim! where is he?

The Pilgrim Fathers are at rest:
When summer's throned on high,
And the world's warm breast is in verdure drest,
Go, stand on the hill where they lie.
The earliest ray of the golden day
On that hallowed spot is cast;
And the evening sun, as he leaves the world,
Looks kindly on that spot last.

The Pilgrim spirit has not fled:
It walks in noon's broad light;
And it watches the bed of the glorious dead,
With the holy stars by night.
It watches the bed of the brave who have bled,
And still guard this ice-bound shore,
Till the waves of the bay, where the Mayflower lay,
Shall foam and freeze no more.

MY CHILD

I cannot make him dead!
His fair sunshiny head
Is ever bounding round my study-chair;
Yet, when my eyes, now dim
With tears, I turn to him,
The vision vanishes — he is not there!

I walk my parlor floor,
And through the open door
I hear a footfall on the chamber stair;
I'm stepping toward the hall
To give the boy a call;
And then bethink me that — he is not there!

I thread the crowded street;
A satchelled lad I meet,
With the same beaming eyes and colored hair:
And, as he's running by,
Follow him with my eye,
Scarcely believing that — he is not there!

I know his face is hid
Under the coffin-lid;
Closed are his eyes; cold is his forehead fair;
My hand that marble felt;
O'er it in prayer I knelt;
Yet my heart whispers that — he is not there!

I cannot make him dead!
When passing by the bed,
So long watched over with parental care,
My spirit and my eye
Seek it inquiringly,
Before the thought comes that — he is not there!

When, at the cool, gray break
Of day, from sleep I wake,
With my first breathing of the morning air
My soul goes up, with joy,
To Him who gave my boy,
Then comes the sad thought that — he is not there!

When at the day's calm close,
Before we seek repose,
I'm with his mother, offering up our prayer,

Whate'er I may be saying,
I am, in spirit, praying
For our boy's spirit, though — he is not there!

Not there! Where, then, is he?
The form I used to see
Was but the raiment that he used to wear;
The grave, that now doth press
Upon that cast-off dress,
Is but his wardrobe locked; — *he* is not there!

He lives! In all the past
He lives; nor, to the last,
Of seeing him again will I despair;
In dreams I see him now;
And, on his angel brow,
I see it written, "Thou shalt see me *there!*"

Yes, we all live to God!
Father, thy chastening rod
So help us, thine afflicted ones, to bear,
That, in the spirit-land,
Meeting at thy right hand,
'T will be our heaven to find that — he is there!

Fitz-Greene Halleck

MARCO BOZZARIS

At midnight, in his guarded tent,
The Turk was dreaming of the hour
When Greece, her knee in suppliance bent,
Should tremble at his power:
In dreams, through camp and court, he bore
The trophies of a conqueror;
In dreams his song of triumph heard;
Then wore his monarch's signet ring:
Then pressed that monarch's throne — a king;
As wild his thoughts, and gay of wing,
As Eden's garden bird.

At midnight, in the forest shades,
Bozzaris ranged his Suliote band,
True as the steel of their tried blades,
Heroes in heart and hand.
There had the Persian's thousands stood,
There had the glad earth drunk their blood
On old Platæa's day;
And now there breathed that haunted air
The sons of sires who conquered there,
With arm to strike and soul to dare,
As quick, as far as they.

An hour passed on — the Turk awoke;
That bright dream was his last;
He woke — to hear his sentries shriek,
"To arms! they come! the Greek! the Greek!"
He woke — to die midst flame, and smoke,
And shout, and groan, and sabre-stroke,
And death-shots falling thick and fast
As lightnings from the mountain-cloud;
And heard, with voice as trumpet loud,
Bozzaris cheer his band:
"Strike — till the last armed foe expires;
Strike — for your altars and your fires;
Strike — for the green graves of your sires;
God — and your native land!"

They fought — like brave men, long and well;
They piled that ground with Moslem slain,
They conquered — but Bozzaris fell,
Bleeding at every vein.
His few surviving comrades saw
His smile when rang their proud hurrah,
And the red field was won;
Then saw in death his eyelids close
Calmly, as to a night's repose,
Like flowers at set of sun.

Come to the bridal-chamber, Death!
Come to the mother's, when she feels,
For the first time, her first-born's breath;
Come when the blessed seals
That close the pestilence are broke,
And crowded cities wail its stroke;
Come in consumption's ghastly form,
The earthquake shock, the ocean storm;
Come when the heart beats high and warm
With banquet-song, and dance, and wine;
And thou art terrible — the tear,
The groan, the knell, the pall, the bier,
And all we know, or dream, or fear
Of agony are thine.

But to the hero, when his sword
Has won the battle for the free,
Thy voice sounds like a prophet's word;
And in its hollow tones are heard
The thanks of millions yet to be.
Come, when his task of fame is wrought —
Come, with her laurel-leaf, blood-bought —
Come in her crowning hour — and then
Thy sunken eye's unearthly light
To him is welcome as the sight
Of sky and stars to prisoned men;
Thy grasp is welcome as the hand
Of brother in a foreign land;
Thy summons welcome as the cry
That told the Indian isles were nigh
To the world-seeking Genoese,
When the land wind, from woods of palm,
And orange-groves, and fields of balm,
Blew o'er the Haytian seas.

Bozzaris! with the storied brave
Greece nurtured in her glory's time,
Rest thee — there is no prouder grave,
Even in her own proud clime.
She wore no funeral-weeds for thee,
Nor bade the dark hearse wave its plume
Like torn branch from death's leafless tree
In sorrow's pomp and pageantry,
The heartless luxury of the tomb;
But she remembers thee as one
Long loved and for a season gone;
For thee her poet's lyre is wreathed,
Her marble wrought, her music breathed;
For thee she rings the birthday bells;
Of thee her babe's first lisping tells;
For thine her evening prayer is said
At palace-couch and cottage-bed;
Her soldier, closing with the foe,
Gives for thy sake a deadlier blow;
His plighted maiden, when she fears
For him the joy of her young years,
Thinks of thy fate, and checks her tears;
And she, the mother of thy boys,
Though in her eye and faded cheek
Is read the grief she will not speak,
The memory of her buried joys,
And even she who gave thee birth,
Will, by their pilgrim-circled hearth,
Talk of thy doom without a sigh;
For thou art Freedom's now, and Fame's:
One of the few, the immortal names,
That were not born to die.

ON THE DEATH OF JOSEPH RODMAN DRAKE

Green be the turf above thee,
Friend of my better days!
None knew thee but to love thee,
Nor named thee but to praise.

Tears fell when thou wert dying,
From eyes unused to weep,
And long, where thou art lying,
Will tears the cold turf steep.

When hearts, whose truth was proven,
Like thine, are laid in earth,
There should a wreath be woven
To tell the world their worth;

And I who woke each morrow
To clasp thy hand in mine,
Who shared thy joy and sorrow,
Whose weal and woe were thine;

It should be mine to braid it
Around thy faded brow,
But I 've in vain essayed it,
And feel I cannot now.

While memory bids me weep thee,
Nor thoughts nor words are free, —
The grief is fixed too deeply
That mourns a man like thee.

ALNWICK CASTLE

Home of the Percys' high-born race,
Home of their beautiful and brave,
Alike their birth and burial-place,
Their cradle and their grave!
Still sternly o'er the castle gate
Their house's Lion stands in state,
As in his proud departed hours;
And warriors frown in stone on high,
And feudal banners flout the sky
Above his princely towers.

A gentle hill its side inclines,
Lovely in England's fadeless green,
To meet the quiet stream which winds
Through this romantic scene
As silently and sweetly still,
As when at evening on that hill,
While summer's wind blew soft and low,
Seated by gallant Hotspur's side,

His Katherine was a happy bride
  A thousand years ago.

Gaze on the Abbey's ruined pile:
  Does not the succoring ivy, keeping
Her watch around it, seem to smile,
  As o'er a loved one sleeping?
One solitary turret gray
  Still tells, in melancholy glory,
The legend of the Cheviot day,
  The Percys' proudest border story.
That day its roof was triumph's arch;
  Then rang from isle to pictured dome
The light step of the soldier's march,
  The music of the trump and drum;
And babe and sire, the old, the young,
And the monk's hymn and minstrel's song,
And woman's pure kiss, sweet and long,
  Welcomed her warrior home.

Wild roses by the Abbey towers
  Are gay in their young bud and bloom;
They were born of a race of funeral-flowers
That garlanded, in long-gone hours,
  A templar's knightly tomb.
He died, the sword in his mailed hand,
On the holiest spot of the Blessed land,
  Where the Cross was damped with his dying breath,
When blood ran free as festal wine,
And the sainted air of Palestine
  Was thick with the darts of death.

Wise with the lore of centuries,
What tales, if there "be tongues in trees,"
  Those giant oaks could tell,
Of beings born and buried here;
Tales of the peasant and the peer,
Tales of the bridal and the bier,
  The welcome and farewell,
Since on their boughs the startled bird
First, in her twilight slumbers, heard
  The Norman's curfew-bell!

I wandered through the lofty halls
  Trod by the Percys of old fame,
And traced upon the chapel walls
  Each high heroic name, —
From him who once his standard set
Where now, o'er mosque and minaret,
  Glitter the Sultan's crescent moons,
To him who, when a younger son,
Fought for King George at Lexington,
  A major of dragoons.

That last half stanza — it has dashed
  From my warm lips the sparkling cup;
The light that o'er my eyebeam flashed,
  The power that bore my spirit up
Above this bank-note world — is gone;
And Alnwick 's but a market town,
And this, alas! its market day,
And beasts and borderers throng the way;
Oxen and bleating lambs in lots,
Northumbrian boors and plaided Scots,
  Men in the coal and cattle line;
From Teviot's bard and hero land,
From royal Berwick's beach of sand,
From Wooller, Morpeth, Hexham, and
  Newcastle-upon-Tyne.

These are not the romantic times
So beautiful in Spenser's rhymes,
  So dazzling to the dreaming boy:
Ours are the days of fact, not fable,
Of knights, but not of the round table,
  Of Bailie Jarvie, not Rob Roy:
'T is what "our President" Monroe
  Has called "the era of good feeling":
The Highlander, the bitterest foe
To modern laws, has felt their blow,
Consented to be taxed, and vote,
And put on pantaloons and coat,
  And leave off cattle-stealing:
Lord Stafford mines for coal and salt,
The Duke of Norfolk deals in malt,
  The Douglas in red herrings;
And noble name and cultured land,
Palace, and park, and vassal-band,
Are powerless to the notes of hand
  Of Rothschild or the Barings.

The age of bargaining, said Burke,
Has come: to-day the turbaned Turk
(Sleep, Richard of the lion heart!
Sleep on, nor from your cerements start)
  Is England's friend and fast ally;
The Moslem tramples on the Greek,
  And on the Cross and altar-stone,
  And Christendom looks tamely on,
And hears the Christian maiden shriek,
  And sees the Christian father die;
And not a sabre-blow is given
For Greece and fame, for faith and heaven,
  By Europe's craven chivalry.

You 'll ask if yet the Percy lives
  In the armed pomp of feudal state?
The present representatives
  Of Hotspur and his "gentle Kate"

Are some half-dozen serving-men
In the drab coat of William Penn;
  A chambermaid, whose lip and eye,
And cheek, and brown hair, bright and curling,
  Spoke Nature's aristocracy;
And one, half groom, half seneschal,
Who bowed me through court, bower, and hall,
From donjon-keep to turret wall,
For ten-and-sixpence sterling.

BURNS

TO A ROSE, BROUGHT FROM NEAR ALLOWAY KIRK, IN AYRSHIRE, IN THE AUTUMN OF 1822

WILD Rose of Alloway! my thanks;
  Thou 'mindst me of that autumn noon
When first we met upon "the banks
  And braes of bonny Doon."

Like thine, beneath the thorn-tree's bough,
  My sunny hour was glad and brief;
We 've crossed the winter sea, and thou
  Art withered — flower and leaf.

And will not thy death-doom be mine —
  The doom of all things wrought of clay —
And withered my life's leaf like thine,
  Wild rose of Alloway?

Not so his memory, — for his sake
  My bosom bore thee far and long,
His — who a humbler flower could make
  Immortal as his song.

The memory of Burns — a name
  That calls, when brimmed her festal cup,
A nation's glory and her shame,
  In silent sadness up.

A nation's glory — be the rest
  Forgot — she 's canonized his mind;
And it is joy to speak the best
  We may of human kind.

I 've stood beside the cottage-bed
  Where the Bard-peasant first drew breath;
A straw-thatched roof above his head,
  A straw-wrought couch beneath.

And I have stood beside the pile,
  His monument — that tells to Heaven
The homage of earth's proudest isle
  To that Bard-peasant given!

Bid thy thoughts hover o'er that spot,
  Boy-minstrel, in thy dreaming hour;
And know, however low his lot,
  A Poet's pride and power:

The pride that lifted Burns from earth,
  The power that gave a child of song
Ascendency o'er rank and birth,
  The rich, the brave, the strong;

And if despondency weigh down
  Thy spirit's fluttering pinions then,
Despair — thy name is written on
  The roll of common men.

There have been loftier themes than his,
  And longer scrolls, and louder lyres,
And lays lit up with Poesy's
  Purer and holier fires:

Yet read the names that know not death;
  Few nobler ones than Burns are there;
And few have won a greener wreath
  Than that which binds his hair.

His is that language of the heart,
  In which the answering heart would speak, —
Thought, word, that bids the warm tear start,
  Or the smile light the cheek;

And his that music, to whose tone
  The common pulse of man keeps time,
In cot or castle's mirth or moan,
  In cold or sunny clime.

And who hath heard his song, nor knelt
  Before its spell with willing knee,
And listened, and believed, and felt
  The Poet's mastery

O'er the mind's sea, in calm and storm,
  O'er the heart's sunshine and its showers,
O'er Passion's moments bright and warm,
  O'er Reason's dark, cold hours;

On fields where brave men "die or do,"
  In halls where rings the banquet's mirth,

Where mourners weep, where lovers woo,
From throne to cottage-hearth ?

What sweet tears dim the eye unshed,
What wild vows falter on the tongue,
When "Scots wha hae wi' Wallace bled,"
Or "Auld Lang Syne" is sung !

Pure hopes, that lift the soul above,
Come with his Cotter's hymn of praise,
And dreams of youth, and truth, and love,
With "Logan's" banks and braes.

And when he breathes his master-lay
Of Alloway's witch-haunted wall,
All passions in our frames of clay
Come thronging at his call.

Imagination's world of air,
And our own world, its gloom and glee,
Wit, pathos, poetry, are there,
And death's sublimity.

And Burns — though brief the race he ran,
Though rough and dark the path he trod,
Lived — died — in form and soul a Man,
The image of his God.

Through care, and pain, and want, and woe,
With wounds that only death could heal,
Tortures — the poor alone can know,
The proud alone can feel;

He kept his honesty and truth,
His independent tongue and pen,
And moved, in manhood as in youth,
Pride of his fellow-men.

Strong sense, deep feeling, passions strong,
A hate of tyrant and of knave,
A love of right, a scorn of wrong,
Of coward and of slave;

A kind, true heart, a spirit high,
That could not fear and would not bow,
Were written in his manly eye
And on his manly brow.

Praise to the bard ! his words are driven,
Like flower-seeds by the far winds sown,
Where'er, beneath the sky of heaven,
The birds of fame have flown.

Praise to the man ! a nation stood
Beside his coffin with wet eyes,
Her brave, her beautiful, her good,
As when a loved one dies.

And still, as on his funeral-day,
Men stand his cold earth-couch around,
With the mute homage that we pay
To consecrated ground.

And consecrated ground it is,
The last, the hallowed home of one
Who lives upon all memories,
Though with the buried gone.

Such graves as his are pilgrim-shrines,
Shrines to no code nor creed confined —
The Delphian vales, the Palestines,
The Meccas of the mind.

Sages with wisdom's garland wreathed,
Crowned kings, and mitred priests of power,
And warriors with their bright swords sheathed,
The mightiest of the hour;

And lowlier names, whose humble home
Is lit by fortune's dimmer star,
Are there — o'er wave and mountain come,
From countries near and far;

Pilgrims whose wandering feet have pressed
The Switzer's snow, the Arab's sand,
Or trod the piled leaves of the West,
My own green forest-land.

All ask the cottage of his birth,
Gaze on the scenes he loved and sung,
And gather feelings not of earth
His fields and streams among.

They linger by the Doon's low trees,
And pastoral Nith, and wooded Ayr,
And round thy sepulchres, Dumfries !
The poet's tomb is there.

But what to them the sculptor's art,
His funeral columns, wreaths and urns ?
Wear they not graven on the heart
The name of Robert Burns ?

RED JACKET

COOPER, whose name is with his country's woven,
First in her files, her PIONEER of mind —

A wanderer now in other climes, has proven
His love for the young land he left behind;

And throned her in the senate-hall of nations,
Robed like the deluge rainbow, heaven-wrought;
Magnificent as his own mind's creations,
And beautiful as its green world of thought:

And, faithful to the Act of Congress, quoted
As law authority, it passed *nem. con.*,
He writes that we are, as ourselves have voted,
The most enlightened people ever known;

That all our week is happy as a Sunday
In Paris, full of song, and dance, and laugh;
And that, from Orleans to the Bay of Fundy,
There 's not a bailiff or an epitaph;

And furthermore — in fifty years, or sooner,
We shall export our poetry and wine;
And our brave fleet, eight frigates and a schooner,
Will sweep the seas from Zembla to the Line.

If he were with me, King of Tuscarora!
Gazing, as I, upon thy portrait now,
In all its medalled, fringed, and beaded glory,
Its eye's dark beauty, and its thoughtful brow —

Its brow, half martial and half diplomatic,
Its eye upsoaring like an eagle's wings —
Well might he boast that we, the Democratic,
Outrival Europe, even in our kings!

For thou wast monarch born. Tradition's pages
Tell not the planting of thy parent tree,
But that the forest tribes have bent for ages
To thee, and to thy sires, the subject knee.

Thy name is princely — if no poet's magic
Could make RED JACKET grace an English rhyme,
Though some one with a genius for the tragic
Hath introduced it in a pantomime —

Yet it is music in the language spoken
Of thine own land, and on her herald-roll;
As bravely fought for, and as proud a token
As Cœur de Lion's of a warrior's soul.

Thy garb — though Austria's bosom-star would frighten
That medal pale, as diamonds the dark mine,
And George the Fourth wore, at his court at Brighton,
A more becoming evening dress than thine;

Yet 't is a brave one, scorning wind and weather
And fitted for thy couch, on field and flood,
As Rob Roy's tartan for the Highland heather,
Or forest green for England's Robin Hood.

Is strength a monarch's merit, like a whaler's?
Thou art as tall, as sinewy, and as strong
As earth's first kings — the Argo's gallant sailors,
Heroes in history and gods in song.

Is beauty? — Thine has with thy youth departed;
But the love-legends of thy manhood's years,
And she who perished, young and broken-hearted,
Are — but I rhyme for smiles and not for tears.

Is eloquence? — Her spell is thine that reaches
The heart, and makes the wisest head its sport;
And there 's one rare, strange virtue in thy speeches,
The secret of their mastery — they are short.

The monarch mind, the mystery of commanding,
The birth-hour gift, the art Napoleon,

Of winning, fettering, moulding, wielding, banding
 The hearts of millions till they move as one:

Thou hast it. At thy bidding men have crowded
 The road to death as to a festival;
And minstrels, at their sepulchres, have shrouded
 With banner-folds of glory the dark pall.

Who will believe? Not I — for in deceiving
 Lies the dear charm of life's delightful dream;
I cannot spare the luxury of believing
 That all things beautiful are what they seem;

Who will believe that, with a smile whose blessing
 Would, like the Patriarch's, soothe a dying hour,
With voice as low, as gentle, and caressing,
 As e'er won maiden's lip in moonlit bower;

With look like patient Job's eschewing evil;
 With motions graceful as a bird's in air;
Thou art, in sober truth, the veriest devil
 That e'er clinched fingers in a captive's hair!

That in thy breast there springs a poison fountain
 Deadlier than that where bathes the Upas-tree;
And in thy wrath a nursing cat-o'-mountain
 Is calm as her babe's sleep compared with thee!

And underneath that face, like summer ocean's,
 Its lip as moveless, and its cheek as clear,
Slumbers a whirlwind of the heart's emotions,
 Love, hatred, pride, hope, sorrow — all save fear.

Love — for thy land, as if she were thy daughter,
 Her pipe in peace, her tomahawk in wars;
Hatred — of missionaries and cold water;
 Pride — in thy rifle-trophies and thy scars;

Hope — that thy wrongs may be by the Great Spirit
 Remembered and revenged when thou art gone;
Sorrow — that none are left thee to inherit
 Thy name, thy fame, thy passions, and thy throne!

Joseph Rodman Drake

FROM "THE CULPRIT FAY"

THE FAY'S SENTENCE

THE monarch sat on his judgment-seat,
 On his brow the crown imperial shone,
The prisoner Fay was at his feet,
 And his peers were ranged around the throne.
He waved his sceptre in the air;
 He looked around and calmly spoke;
His brow was grave and his eye severe,
 But his voice in a softened accent broke:

"Fairy! Fairy! list and mark,
 Thou hast broke thine elfin chain,
Thy flame-wood lamp is quenched and dark,
 And thy wings are dyed with a deadly stain —
Thou hast sullied thine elfin purity
In the glance of a mortal maiden's eye,
Thou hast scorned our dread decree,
And thou shouldst pay the forfeit high,
But well I know her sinless mind
Is pure as the angel forms above,
Gentle and meek, and chaste and kind,
Such as a spirit well might love;
Fairy! had she spot or taint,
Bitter had been thy punishment.
Tied to the hornet's shardy wings;
Tossed on the pricks of nettle's stings;
Or seven long ages doomed to dwell

With the lazy worm in the walnut-shell;
Or every night to writhe and bleed
Beneath the tread of the centipede;
Or bound in a cobweb dungeon dim,
Your jailer a spider huge and grim,
Amid the carrion bodies to lie,
Of the worm, and the bug, and the murdered fly;
These it had been your lot to bear,
Had a stain been found on the earthly fair.
Now list, and mark our mild decree —
Fairy, this your doom must be :

"Thou shalt seek the beach of sand
Where the water bounds the elfin land,
Thou shalt watch the oozy brine
Till the sturgeon leaps in the bright moonshine,
Then dart the glistening arch below,
And catch a drop from his silver bow.
The water-sprites will wield their arms
And dash around, with roar and rave,
And vain are the woodland spirits' charms,
They are the imps that rule the wave.
Yet trust thee in thy single might, —
If thy heart be pure and thy spirit right,
Thou shalt win the warlock fight.

"If the spray-bead gem be won,
The stain of thy wing is washed away,
But another errand must be done
Ere thy crime be lost for aye;
Thy flame-wood lamp is quenched and dark,
Thou must re-illumine its spark.
Mount thy steed and spur him high
To the heaven's blue canopy;
And when thou seest a shooting star,
Follow it fast, and follow it far —
The last faint spark of its burning train
Shall light the elfin lamp again.
Thou hast heard our sentence, Fay;
Hence ! to the water-side, away !"

THE FIRST QUEST

The goblin marked his monarch well;
He spake not, but he bowed him low,
Then plucked a crimson colon-bell,
And turned him round in act to go.
The way is long, he cannot fly,
His soilëd wing has lost its power,
And he winds adown the mountain high,
For many a sore and weary hour,
Through dreary beds of tangled fern,
Through groves of nightshade dark and dern,
Over the grass and through the brake,
Where toils the ant and sleeps the snake ;
Now o'er the violet's azure flush
He skips along in lightsome mood;
And now he thrids the bramble bush,
Till its points are dyed in fairy blood.
He has leapt the bog, he has pierced the brier,
He has swum the brook, and waded the mire,
Till his spirits sank, and his limbs grew weak,
And the red waxed fainter in his cheek.
He had fallen to the ground outright,
For rugged and dim was his onward track,
But there came a spotted toad in sight,
And he laughed as he jumped upon her back;
He bridled her mouth with a silk-weed twist;
He lashed her sides with an osier thong;
And now through evening's dewy mist,
With leap and spring they bound along,
Till the mountain's magic verge is past,
And the beach of sand is reached at last.

Soft and pale is the moony beam,
Moveless still the glassy stream,
The wave is clear, the beach is bright
With snowy shells and sparkling stones;
The shore-surge comes in ripples light,
In murmurings faint and distant moans;
And ever afar in the silence deep
Is heard the splash of the sturgeon's leap,
And the bend of his graceful bow is seen —
A glittering arch of silver sheen,
Spanning the wave of burnished blue,
And dripping with gems of the river dew.

The elfin cast a glance around,
As he lighted down from his courser toad,
Then round his breast his wings he wound,
And close to the river's brink he strode;
He sprang on a rock, he breathed a prayer,
Above his head his arms he threw,
Then tossed a tiny curve in air,
And headlong plunged in the waters blue.

Up sprung the spirits of the waves,
From sea-silk beds in their coral caves;

With snail-plate armor snatched in haste,
They speed their way through the liquid waste;
Some are rapidly borne along
On the mailëd shrimp or the prickly prong,
Some on the blood-red leeches glide,
Some on the stony star-fish ride,
Some on the back of the lancing squab,
Some on the sideling soldier-crab,
And some on the jellied quarl, that flings
At once a thousand streamy stings, —
They cut the wave with the living oar
And hurry on to the moonlight shore,
To guard their realms and chase away
The footsteps of the invading Fay.

Fearlessly he skims along,
His hope is high, and his limbs are strong,
He spreads his arms like the swallow's wing,
And throws his feet with a frog-like fling;
His locks of gold on the waters shine,
At his breast the tiny foam-beads rise,
His back gleams bright above the brine,
And the wake-line foam behind him lies.
But the water-sprites are gathering near
To check his course along the tide;
Their warriors come in swift career
And hem him round on every side;
On his thigh the leech has fixed his hold,
The quarl's long arms are round him rolled,
The prickly prong has pierced his skin,
And the squab has thrown his javelin,
The gritty star has rubbed him raw,
And the crab has struck with his giant claw;
He howls with rage, and he shrieks with pain,
He strikes around, but his blows are vain;
Hopeless is the unequal fight,
Fairy ! naught is left but flight.

He turned him round and fled amain
With hurry and dash to the beach again;
He twisted over from side to side,
And laid his cheek to the cleaving tide.
The strokes of his plunging arms are fleet,
And with all his might he flings his feet,
But the water-sprites are round him still,
To cross his path and work him ill.
They bade the wave before him rise;
They flung the sea-fire in his eyes,
And they stunned his ears with the scallop stroke,
With the porpoise heave and the drum-fish croak.
Oh ! but a weary wight was he
When he reached the foot of the dog-wood tree;
— Gashed and wounded, and stiff and sore,
He laid him down on the sandy shore;
He blessed the force of the charmëd line,
And he banned the water-goblins' spite,
For he saw around in the sweet moonshine,
Their little wee faces above the brine,
Giggling and laughing with all their might
At the piteous hap of the Fairy wight.

THE SECOND QUEST

Up, Fairy ! quit thy chick-weed bower,
The cricket has called the second hour,
Twice again, and the lark will rise
To kiss the streaking of the skies —
Up ! thy charmëd armor don,
Thou 'lt need it ere the night be gone.

He put his acorn helmet on;
It was plumed of the silk of the thistle down;
The corselet plate that guarded his breast
Was once the wild bee's golden vest;
His cloak, of a thousand mingled dyes,
Was formed of the wings of butterflies;
His shield was the shell of a lady-bug queen,
Studs of gold on a ground of green;
And the quivering lance, which he brandished bright,
Was the sting of a wasp he had slain in fight.
Swift he bestrode his fire-fly steed;
He bared his blade of the bent grass blue;
He drove his spurs of the cockle seed,
And away like a glance of thought he flew,
To skim the heavens and follow far
The fiery trail of the rocket-star.

The moth-fly, as he shot in air,
Crept under the leaf, and hid her there;
The katy-did forgot its lay,
The prowling gnat fled fast away,
The fell mosquito checked his drone
And folded his wings till the Fay was gone,
And the wily beetle dropped his head,
And fell on the ground as if he were dead;
They crouched them close in the darksome shade,
They quaked all o'er with awe and fear,

For they had felt the blue-bent blade,
And writhed at the prick of the elfin spear;
Many a time on a summer's night,
When the sky was clear and the moon was bright,
They had been roused from the haunted ground,
By the yelp and bay of the fairy hound;
They had heard the tiny bugle horn,
They had heard the twang of the maize-silk string,
When the vine-twig bows were tightly drawn,
And the nettle shaft through air was borne,
Feathered with down of the hum-bird's wing.
And now they deemed the courier ouphe
Some hunter sprite of the elfin ground;
And they watched till they saw him mount the roof
That canopies the world around;
Then glad they left their covert lair,
And freaked about in the midnight air.

Up to the vaulted firmament
His path the fire-fly courser bent,
And at every gallop on the wind,
He flung a glittering spark behind;
He flies like a feather in the blast
Till the first light cloud in heaven is past,
But the shapes of air have begun their work,
And a drizzly mist is round him cast,
He cannot see through the mantle murk,
He shivers with cold, but he urges fast,
Through storm and darkness, sleet and shade;
He lashes his steed and spurs amain,
For shadowy hands have twitched the rein,
And flame-shot tongues around him played,
And near him many a fiendish eye
Glared with a fell malignity,
And yells of rage, and shrieks of fear,
Came screaming on his startled ear.

His wings are wet around his breast,
The plume hangs dripping from his crest,
His eyes are blurred with the lightning's glare,
And his ears are stunned with the thunder's blare,
But he gave a shout, and his blade he drew,
He thrust before and he struck behind,
Till he pierced their cloudy bodies through,
And gashed their shadowy limbs of wind;
Howling the misty spectres flew,—
They rend the air with frightful cries,
For he has gained the welkin blue,
And the land of clouds beneath him lies.

Up to the cope careering swift
In breathless motion fast,
Fleet as the swallow cuts the drift,
Or the sea-roc rides the blast,
The sapphire sheet of eve is shot,
The spherëd moon is past,
The earth but seems a tiny blot
On a sheet of azure cast.
O! it was sweet in the clear moonlight,
To tread the starry plain of even,
To meet the thousand eyes of night,
And feel the cooling breath of heaven!
But the Elfin made no stop or stay
Till he came to the bank of the milky-way;
Then he checked his courser's foot,
And watched for the glimpse of the planet-shoot.

ELFIN SONG

Ouphe and goblin! imp and sprite!
Elf of eve! and starry Fay!
Ye that love the moon's soft light,
Hither — hither wend your way;
Twine ye in a jocund ring,
Sing and trip it merrily,
Hand to hand, and wing to wing,
Round the wild witch-hazel tree.

Hail the wanderer again,
With dance and song, and lute and lyre.
Pure his wing and strong his chain,
And doubly bright his fairy fire.
Twine ye in an airy round,
Brush the dew and print the lea;
Skip and gambol, hop and bound,
Round the wild witch-hazel tree.

The beetle guards our holy ground,
He flies about the haunted place,
And if mortal there be found,
He hums in his ears and flaps his face;
The leaf-harp sounds our roundelay,
The owlet's eyes our lanterns be;
Thus we sing, and dance, and play,
Round the wild witch-hazel tree.

THE AMERICAN FLAG

When Freedom from her mountain height
Unfurled her standard to the air,
She tore the azure robe of night,
And set the stars of glory there.
She mingled with its gorgeous dyes
The milky baldric of the skies,
And striped its pure celestial white
With streakings of the morning light;
Then from his mansion in the sun
She called her eagle bearer down,
And gave into his mighty hand
The symbol of her chosen land.

Majestic monarch of the cloud,
Who rear'st aloft thy regal form,
To hear the tempest trumpings loud
And see the lightning lances driven,
When strive the warriors of the storm,
And rolls the thunder-drum of heaven,
Child of the sun! to thee 't is given
To guard the banner of the free,
To hover in the sulphur smoke,
To ward away the battle stroke,
And bid its blendings shine afar,
Like rainbows on the cloud of war,
The harbingers of victory!

Flag of the brave! thy folds shall fly,
The sign of hope and triumph high,
When speaks the signal trumpet tone,
And the long line comes gleaming on.
Ere yet the life-blood, warm and wet,
Has dimmed the glistening bayonet,
Each soldier eye shall brightly turn
To where thy sky-born glories burn,
And, as his springing steps advance,
Catch war and vengeance from the glance.
And when the cannon-mouthings loud
Heave in wild wreaths the battle shroud,
And gory sabres rise and fall
Like shoots of flame on midnight's pall,
Then shall thy meteor glances glow,
And cowering foes shall shrink beneath
Each gallant arm that strikes below
That lovely messenger of death.

Flag of the seas! on ocean wave
Thy stars shall glitter o'er the brave;
When death, careering on the gale,
Sweeps darkly round the bellied sail,
And frighted waves rush wildly back
Before the broadside's reeling rack,
Each dying wanderer of the sea
Shall look at once to heaven and thee,
And smile to see thy splendors fly
In triumph o'er his closing eye.

Flag of the free heart's hope and home!
By angel hands to valor given;
Thy stars have lit the welkin dome,
And all thy hues were born in heaven.
Forever float that standard sheet!
Where breathes the foe but falls before us,
With Freedom's soil beneath our feet,
And Freedom's banner streaming o'er us?

"The Croakers"

(HALLECK AND DRAKE)

THE NATIONAL PAINTINGS

COL. TRUMBULL'S "THE DECLARATION OF INDEPENDENCE"

Awake, ye forms of verse divine!
Painting! descend on canvas wing, —
And hover o'er my head, Design!
Your son, your glorious son, I sing;
At Trumbull's name I break my sloth,
To load him with poetic riches:
The Titian of a table-cloth!
The Guido of a pair of breeches!

Come, star-eyed maid, Equality!
In thine adorer's praise I revel;
Who brings, so fierce his love to thee,
All forms and faces to a level:
Old, young, great, small, the grave, the gay,
Each man might swear the next his brother,
And there they stand in dread array,
To fire their votes at one another.

How bright their buttons shine! how straight
Their coat-flaps fall in plaited grace!

How smooth the hair on every pate!
How vacant each immortal face!
And then the tints, the shade, the flush,
(I wrong them with a strain too humble),
Not mighty Sherred's strength of brush
Can match thy glowing hues, my Trumbull!

Go on, great painter! dare be dull —
No longer after Nature dangle;
Call rectilinear beautiful;
Find grace and freedom in an angle;
Pour on the red, the green, the yellow,
"Paint till a horse may mire upon it,"
And, while I've strength to write or bellow,
I'll sound your praises in a sonnet.

JOSEPH RODMAN DRAKE

THE MAN WHO FRETS AT WORLDLY STRIFE

THE man who frets at worldly strife
Grows sallow, sour, and thin;
Give us the lad whose happy life
Is one perpetual grin:
He, Midas-like, turns all to gold, —
He smiles when others sigh,
Enjoys alike the hot and cold,
And laughs through wet and dry.

There's fun in everything we meet, —
The greatest, worst, and best;
Existence is a merry treat,
And every speech a jest:
Be 't ours to watch the crowds that pass
Where Mirth's gay banner waves;
To show fools through a quizzing-glass,
And bastinade the knaves.

The serious world will scold and ban,
In clamor loud and hard,
To hear Meigs called a Congressman,
And Paulding styled a bard;
But, come what may, the man's in luck
Who turns it all to glee,
And laughing, cries, with honest Puck,
"Good Lord! what fools ye be."

JOSEPH RODMAN DRAKE

ODE TO FORTUNE

FAIR lady with the bandaged eye!
I'll pardon all thy scurvy tricks,
So thou wilt cut me, and deny
Alike thy kisses and thy kicks:
I'm quite contented as I am,
Have cash to keep my duns at bay,
Can choose between beefsteaks and ham,
And drink Madeira every day.

My station is the middle rank,
My fortune — just a competence —
Ten thousand in the Franklin Bank,
And twenty in the six per cents;
No amorous chains my heart enthrall,
I neither borrow, lend, nor sell;
Fearless I roam the City Hall,
And bite my thumb at Sheriff Bell.

The horse that twice a week I ride
At Mother Dawson's eats his fill;
My books at Goodrich's abide,
My country-seat is Weehawk hill;
My morning lounge is Eastburn's shop,
At Poppleton's I take my lunch,
Niblo prepares my mutton-chop,
And Jennings makes my whiskey-punch.

When merry, I the hours amuse
By squibbing Bucktails, Guards, and Balls,
And when I'm troubled with the blues
Damn Clinton and abuse canals:
Then, Fortune, since I ask no prize,
At least preserve me from thy frown!
The man who don't attempt to rise
'T were cruelty to tumble down.

HALLECK AND DRAKE

Lydia Huntley Sigourney

COLUMBUS

ST. STEPHEN'S cloistered hall was proud
In learning's pomp that day,
For there a robed and stately crowd
Pressed on in long array.
A mariner with simple chart
Confronts that conclave high,

While strong ambition stirs his heart,
And burning thoughts of wonder part
  From lip and sparkling eye.

What hath he said? With frowning face,
  In whispered tones they speak,
And lines upon their tablets trace,
  Which flush each ashen cheek;
The Inquisition's mystic doom
  Sits on their brows severe,
And bursting forth in visioned gloom,
Sad heresy from burning tomb
  Groans on the startled ear.

Courage, thou Genoese! Old Time
  Thy splendid dream shall crown;
Yon Western Hemisphere sublime,
  Where unshorn forests frown,
The awful Andes' cloud-wrapt brow,
  The Indian hunter's bow,
Bold streams untamed by helm or prow,
And rocks of gold and diamonds, thou
  To thankless Spain shalt show.

Courage, World-finder! Thou hast need!
  In Fates' unfolding scroll,
Dark woes and ingrate wrongs I read,
  That rack the noble soul.
On! on! Creation's secrets probe,
  Then drink thy cup of scorn,
And wrapped in fallen Cæsar's robe,
Sleep like that master of the globe,
  All glorious, — yet forlorn.

THE INDIAN'S WELCOME TO THE PILGRIM FATHERS

Above them spread a stranger sky;
  Around, the sterile plain;
The rock-bound coast rose frowning nigh;
  Beyond, — the wrathful main:
Chill remnants of the wintry snow
  Still choked the encumbered soil,
Yet forth those Pilgrim Fathers go
  To mark their future toil.

'Mid yonder vale their corn must rise
  In summer's ripening pride,
And there the church-spire woo the skies
  Its sister-school beside.
Perchance mid England's velvet green
  Some tender thought reposed,
Though nought upon their stoic mien
  Such soft regret disclosed.

When sudden from the forest wide
  A red-browed chieftain came,
With towering form, and haughty stride,
  And eye like kindling flame:
No wrath he breathed, no conflict sought,
  To no dark ambush drew,
But simply to the Old World brought
  The welcome of the New.

That welcome was a blast and ban
  Upon thy race unborn;
Was there no seer, — thou fated Man! —
  Thy lavish zeal to warn?
Thou in thy fearless faith didst hail
  A weak, invading band,
But who shall heed thy children's wail
  Swept from their native land?

Thou gav'st the riches of thy streams,
  The lordship o'er thy waves,
The region of thine infant dreams
  And of thy father's graves, —
But who to yon proud mansions, piled
  With wealth of earth and sea,
Poor outcast from thy forest wild,
  Say, who shall welcome thee?

THE RETURN OF NAPOLEON FROM ST. HELENA

Ho! City of the gay!
  Paris! what festal rite
Doth call thy thronging million forth,
  All eager for the sight?
Thy soldiers line the streets
  In fixed and stern array,
With buckled helm and bayonet,
  As on the battle-day.

By square, and fountain side,
  Heads in dense masses rise,
And tower and battlement and tree
  Are studded thick with eyes.
Comes there some conqueror home
  In triumph from the fight,
With spoil and captives in his train,
  The trophies of his might?

The Arc de Triomphe glows!
  A martial host is nigh;
France pours in long succession forth
  Her pomp of chivalry.
No clarion marks their way,
  No victor trump is blown;

Why march they on so silently,
  Told by their tread alone?

Behold, in glittering show,
  A gorgeous car of state!
The white-plumed steeds, in cloth of gold,
  Bow down beneath its weight;
And the noble war-horse, led
  Caparisoned along,
Seems fiercely for his lord to ask,
  As his red eye scans the throng.

Who rideth on yon car?
  The incense flameth high,—
Comes there some demi-god of old?
  No answer!—No reply!
Who rideth on yon car?—
  No shout his minions raise,
But by a lofty chapel dome
  The muffled hero stays.

A king is standing there,
  And with uncovered head
Receives him in the name of France:
  Receiveth whom?—The dead!
Was he not buried deep
  In island-cavern drear,
Girt by the sounding ocean surge?
  How came that sleeper here?

Was there no rest for him
  Beneath a peaceful pall,
That thus he brake his stony tomb,
  Ere the strong angel's call?
Hark! hark! the requiem swells,
  A deep, soul-thrilling strain!
An echo, never to be heard
  By mortal ear again.

A requiem for the chief,
  Whose fiat millions slew,—
The soaring eagle of the Alps,
  The crushed at Waterloo:—
The banished who returned,
  The dead who rose again,
And rode in his shroud the billows proud
  To the sunny banks of Seine.

They laid him there in state,
  That warrior strong and bold,—
The imperial crown, with jewels bright,
  Upon his ashes cold,
While round those columns proud
  The blazoned banners wave,
That on a hundred fields he won
  With the heart's-blood of the brave;

And sternly there kept guard
  His veterans scarred and old,
Whose wounds of Lodi's cleaving bridge
  Or purple Leipsic told.
Yes, there, with arms reversed,
  Slow pacing, night and day,
Close watch beside the coffin kept
  Those veterans grim and gray.

A cloud is on their brow,—
  Is it sorrow for the dead,
Or memory of the fearful strife
  Where their country's legions fled?
Of Borodino's blood?
  Of Beresina's wail?
The horrors of that dire retreat,
  Which turned old History pale?

A cloud is on their brow,—
  Is it sorrow for the dead,
Or a shuddering at the wintry shaft
  By Russian tempests sped?
Where countless mounds of snow
  Marked the poor conscripts' grave,
And, pierced by frost and famine, sank
  The bravest of the brave.

A thousand trembling lamps
  The gathered darkness mock,
And velvet drapes his hearse, who died
  On bare Helena's rock;
And from the altar near,
  A never-ceasing hymn
Is lifted by the chanting priests
  Beside the taper dim.

Mysterious one, and proud!
  In the land where shadows reign,
Hast thou met the flocking ghosts of those
  Who at thy nod were slain?
Oh, when the cry of that spectral host
  Like a rushing blast shall be,
What will thine answer be to them?
  And what thy God's to thee?

Charles Sprague

FROM "CURIOSITY"

THE NEWS

THE news ! our morning, noon, and evening cry,
Day unto day repeats it till we die.
For this the cit, the critic, and the fop,
Dally the hour away in Tonsor's shop;
For this the gossip takes her daily route,
And wears your threshold and your patience out;
For this we leave the parson in the lurch,
And pause to prattle on the way to church;
Even when some coffined friend we gather round,
We ask, "What news?" then lay him in the ground;
To this the breakfast owes its sweetest zest,
For this the dinner cools, the bed remains unpressed.
What gives each tale of scandal to the street,
The kitchen's wonder, and the parlor's treat?
See the pert housemaid to the keyhole fly,
When husband storms, wife frets, or lovers sigh;
See Tom ransack your pockets for each note,
And read your secrets while he cleans your coat;
See, yes, to listen see even madam deign,
When the smug seamstress pours her ready strain;
This wings the lie that malice breeds in fear, —
No tongue so vile but finds a kindred ear;
Swift flies each tale of laughter, shame, or folly,
Caught by Paul Pry and carried home to Polly;
On this each foul calumniator leans,
And nods and hints the villany he means:
Full well he knows what latent wildfire lies
In the close whisper and the dark surmise;
A muffled word, a wordless wink has woke
A warmer throb than if a Dexter spoke;
And he, o'er Everett's periods who would nod,
To track a secret, half the town has trod.

O thou, from whose rank breath nor sex can save,
Nor sacred virtue, nor the powerless grave, —
Felon unwhipped! than whom in yonder cells
Full many a groaning wretch less guilty dwells,
Blush — if of honest blood a drop remains
To steal its lonely way along thy veins,
Blush — if the bronze, long hardened on thy cheek,
Has left a spot where that poor drop can speak;
Blush to be branded with the slanderer's name,
And, though thou dreadst not sin, at least dread shame.
We hear, indeed, but shudder while we hear
The insidious falsehood and the heartless jeer;
For each dark libel that thou lickest to shape,
Thou mayest from law but not from scorn escape;
The pointed finger, cold, averted eye,
Insulted virtue's hiss — thou canst not fly.

FICTION

Look now, directed by yon candle's blaze,
Where the false shutter half its trust betrays —
Mark that fair girl reclining in her bed,
Its curtain round her polished shoulders spread:
Dark midnight reigns, the storm is up in power;
What keeps her waking in that dreary hour?
See where the volume on her pillow lies —
Claims Radcliffe or Chapone those frequent sighs?
'T is some wild legend — now her kind eye fills,
And now cold terror every fibre chills;
Still she reads on — in fiction's labyrinth lost,
Of tyrant fathers, and of true love crossed;
Of clanking fetters, low, mysterious groans,
Blood-crusted daggers, and uncoffined bones,

Pale, gliding ghosts, with fingers dropping gore,
And blue flames dancing round a dungeon door; —
Still she reads on — even though to read she fears,
And in each key-hole moan strange voices hears,
While every shadow that withdraws her look
Glares in her face, the goblin of her book;
Still o'er the leaves her craving eye is cast,
On all she feasts, yet hungers for the last;
Counts what remains, now sighs there are no more,
And now even those half tempted to skip o'er;
At length, the bad all killed, the good all pleased,
Her thirsting Curiosity appeased,
She shuts the dear, dear book, that made her weep,
Puts out her light, and turns away to sleep.

THE WINGED WORSHIPPERS

GAY, guiltless pair,
What seek ye from the fields of heaven?
Ye have no need of prayer,
Ye have no sins to be forgiven.

Why perch ye here,
Where mortals to their Maker bend?
Can your pure spirits fear
The God ye never could offend?

Ye never knew
The crimes for which we come to weep.
Penance is not for you,
Blessed wanderers of the upper deep.

To you 't is given
To wake sweet Nature's untaught lays,
Beneath the arch of heaven
To chirp away a life of praise.

Then spread each wing,
Far, far above, o'er lakes and lands,
And join the choirs that sing
In yon blue dome not reared with hands.

Or, if ye stay
To note the consecrated hour,
Teach me the airy way,
And let me try your envied power.

Above the crowd,
On upward wings could I but fly,
I 'd bathe in yon bright cloud,
And seek the stars that gem the sky.

'T were Heaven indeed
Through fields of trackless light to soar,
On nature's charms to feed,
And Nature's own great God adore.

THE BROTHERS

WE are but two— the others sleep
Through death's untroubled night;
We are but two — O, let us keep
The link that binds us bright.

Heart leaps to heart — the sacred flood
That warms us is the same;
That good old man — his honest blood
Alike we fondly claim.

We in one mother's arms were locked —
Long be her love repaid;
In the same cradle we were rocked,
Round the same hearth we played.

Our boyish sports were all the same,
Each little joy and woe; —
Let manhood keep alive the flame,
Lit up so long ago.

We are but two — be that the band
To hold us till we die;
Shoulder to shoulder let us stand,
Till side by side we lie.

John Neal

MEN OF THE NORTH

Men of the North, look up!
There 's a tumult in your sky;
A troubled glory surging out,
Great shadows hurrying by.

Your strength — where is it now?
Your quivers — are they spent?
Your arrows in the rust of death,
Your fathers' bows unbent?

Men of the North, awake!
Ye 're called to from the deep;
Trumpets in every breeze —
Yet there ye lie asleep.

A stir in every tree;
A shout from every wave;
A challenging on every side;
A moan from every grave:

A battle in the sky;
Ships thundering through the air —
Jehovah on the march —
Men of the North, to prayer!

Now, now — in all your strength;
There 's that before your way,
Above, about you, and below,
Like armies in array.

Lift up your eyes, and see
The changes overhead;
Now hold your breath and hear
The mustering of the dead.

See how the midnight air
With bright commotion burns,
Thronging with giant shapes,
Banner and spear by turns.

The sea-fog driving in,
Solemnly and swift,
The moon afraid — stars dropping out —
The very skies adrift;

The Everlasting God,
Our Father — Lord of Love —
With cherubim and seraphim
All gathering above;

Their stormy plumage lighted up
As forth to war they go;
The shadow of the Universe,
Upon our haughty foe!

MUSIC OF THE NIGHT

There are harps that complain to the presence of night,
To the presence of night alone —
In a near and unchangeable tone —
Like winds, full of sound, that go whispering by,
As if some immortal had stooped from the sky,
And breathed out a blessing — and flown!

Yes! harps that complain to the breezes of night,
To the breezes of night alone;
Growing fainter and fainter, as ruddy and bright
The sun rolls aloft in his drapery of light,
Like a conqueror, shaking his brilliant hair
And flourishing robe, on the edge of the air!
Burning crimson and gold
On the clouds that unfold,
Breaking onward in flame, while an ocean divides
On his right and his left. So the Thunderer rides,
When he cuts a bright path through the heaving tides,
Rolling on, and erect, in a charioting throne!

Yes! strings that lie still in the gushing of day,
That awake, all alive, to the breezes of night;
There are hautboys and flutes too, forever at play
When the evening is near, and the sun is away,
Breathing out the still hymn of delight;
These strings by invisible fingers are played —

By spirits, unseen and unknown,
But thick as the stars, all this music is made;
And these flutes, alone,
In one sweet dreamy tone,
Are ever blown,
Forever and forever.
The live-long night ye hear the sound,
Like distant waters flowing round
In ringing caves, while heaven is sweet
With crowding tunes, like halls
Where fountain-music falls,
And rival minstrels meet.

William Cullen Bryant

THANATOPSIS

To him who in the love of Nature holds
Communion with her visible forms, she speaks
A various language; for his gayer hours
She has a voice of gladness, and a smile
And eloquence of beauty, and she glides
Into his darker musings, with a mild
And healing sympathy, that steals away
Their sharpness, ere he is aware. When thoughts
Of the last bitter hour come like a blight
Over thy spirit, and sad images
Of the stern agony, and shroud, and pall,
And breathless darkness, and the narrow house,
Make thee to shudder and grow sick at heart;—
Go forth, under the open sky, and list
To Nature's teachings, while from all around —
Earth and her waters, and the depths of air —
Comes a still voice:—

Yet a few days, and thee
The all-beholding sun shall see no more
In all his course; nor yet in the cold ground,
Where thy pale form was laid with many tears,
Nor in the embrace of ocean, shall exist
Thy image. Earth, that nourished thee, shall claim
Thy growth, to be resolved to earth again,
And, lost each human trace, surrendering up
Thine individual being, shalt thou go
To mix forever with the elements,
To be a brother to the insensible rock
And to the sluggish clod, which the rude swain
Turns with his share, and treads upon. The oak
Shall send his roots abroad, and pierce thy mould.

Yet not to thine eternal resting-place
Shalt thou retire alone, nor couldst thou wish
Couch more magnificent. Thou shalt lie down
With patriarchs of the infant world — with kings,
The powerful of the earth — the wise, the good,
Fair forms, and hoary seers of ages past,
All in one mighty sepulchre. The hills
Rock-ribbed and ancient as the sun, — the vales
Stretching in pensive quietness between;
The venerable woods — rivers that move
In majesty, and the complaining brooks
That make the meadows green; and, poured round all,
Old Ocean's gray and melancholy waste, —
Are but the solemn decorations all
Of the great tomb of man. The golden sun,
The planets, all the infinite host of heaven,
Are shining on the sad abodes of death
Through the still lapse of ages. All that tread
The globe are but a handful to the tribes
That slumber in its bosom. — Take the wings
Of morning, pierce the Barcan wilderness,
Or lose thyself in the continuous woods
Where rolls the Oregon, and hears no sound,
Save his own dashings — yet the dead are there;
And millions in those solitudes, since first
The flight of years began, have laid them down

In their last sleep — the dead reign there alone.
So shalt thou rest, and what if thou withdraw
In silence from the living, and no friend
Take note of thy departure? All that breathe
Will share thy destiny. The gay will laugh
When thou art gone, the solemn brood of care
Plod on, and each one as before will chase
His favorite phantom; yet all these shall leave
Their mirth and their employments, and shall come
And make their bed with thee. As the long train
Of ages glides away, the sons of men—
The youth in life's fresh spring, and he who goes
In the full strength of years, matron and maid,
The speechless babe, and the gray-headed man—
Shall one by one be gathered to thy side,
By those, who in their turn shall follow them.

So live, that when thy summons comes to join
The innumerable caravan, which moves
To that mysterious realm, where each shall take
His chamber in the silent halls of death,
Thou go not, like the quarry-slave at night,
Scourged to his dungeon, but, sustained and soothed
By an unfaltering trust, approach thy grave
Like one who wraps the drapery of his couch
About him, and lies down to pleasant dreams.

TO A WATERFOWL

WHITHER, midst falling dew,
While glow the heavens with the last steps of day,
Far, through their rosy depths, dost thou pursue
Thy solitary way?

Vainly the fowler's eye
Might mark thy distant flight to do thee wrong,
As, darkly painted on the crimson sky,
Thy figure floats along.

Seek'st thou the plashy brink
Of weedy lake, or marge of river wide,
Or where the rocking billows rise and sink
On the chafed ocean side?

There is a Power whose care
Teaches thy way along that pathless coast—
The desert and illimitable air—
Lone wandering, but not lost.

All day thy wings have fanned,
At that far height, the cold, thin atmosphere,
Yet stoop not, weary, to the welcome land,
Though the dark night is near.

And soon that toil shall end;
Soon shalt thou find a summer home, and rest,
And scream among thy fellows; reeds shall bend,
Soon, o'er thy sheltered nest.

Thou 'rt gone! the abyss of heaven
Hath swallowed up thy form; yet on my heart
Deeply hath sunk the lesson thou hast given,
And shall not soon depart.

He, who, from zone to zone,
Guides through the boundless sky thy certain flight,
In the long way that I must tread alone
Will lead my steps aright.

O FAIREST OF THE RURAL MAIDS

O FAIREST of the rural maids!
Thy birth was in the forest shades;
Green boughs, and glimpses of the sky,
Were all that met thine infant eye.

Thy sports, thy wanderings, when a child,
Were ever in the sylvan wild;
And all the beauty of the place
Is in thy heart and on thy face.

The twilight of the trees and rocks
Is in the light shade of thy locks;

Thy step is as the wind, that weaves
Its playful way among the leaves.

Thine eyes are springs, in whose serene
And silent waters heaven is seen;
Their lashes are the herbs that look
On their young figures in the brook.

The forest depths, by foot unprest,
Are not more sinless than thy breast;
The holy peace, that fills the air
Of those calm solitudes, is there.

A FOREST HYMN

THE groves were God's first temples. Ere man learned
To hew the shaft, and lay the architrave,
And spread the roof above them — ere he framed
The lofty vault, to gather and roll back
The sound of anthems; in the darkling wood,
Amid the cool and silence, he knelt down,
And offered to the Mightiest solemn thanks
And supplication. For his simple heart
Might not resist the sacred influence
Which, from the stilly twilight of the place,
And from the gray old trunks that high in heaven
Mingled their mossy boughs, and from the sound
Of the invisible breath that swayed at once
All their green tops, stole over him, and bowed
His spirit with the thought of boundless power
And inaccessible majesty. Ah, why
Should we, in the world's riper years, neglect
God's ancient sanctuaries, and adore
Only among the crowd, and under roofs
That our frail hands have raised? Let me, at least,
Here in the shadow of this aged wood,
Offer one hymn — thrice happy, if it find
Acceptance in His ear.

Father, thy hand
Hath reared these venerable columns, thou
Didst weave this verdant roof. Thou didst look down
Upon the naked earth, and, forthwith, rose
All these fair ranks of trees. They in thy sun
Budded, and shook their green leaves in thy breeze,
And shot toward heaven. The century-living crow,
Whose birth was in their tops, grew old and died
Among their branches, till, at last, they stood,
As now they stand, massy, and tall, and dark,
Fit shrine for humble worshipper to hold
Communion with his Maker. These dim vaults,
These winding aisles, of human pomp or pride
Report not. No fantastic carvings show
The boast of our vain race to change the form
Of thy fair works. But thou art here — thou fill'st
The solitude. Thou art in the soft winds
That run along the summit of these trees
In music; thou art in the cooler breath
That from the inmost darkness of the place
Comes, scarcely felt; the barky trunks, the ground,
The fresh moist ground, are all instinct with thee.
Here is continual worship; — Nature, here,
In the tranquillity that thou dost love,
Enjoys thy presence. Noiselessly, around,
From perch to perch, the solitary bird
Passes; and yon clear spring, that, midst its herbs,
Wells softly forth and wandering steeps the roots
Of half the mighty forest, tells no tale
Of all the good it does. Thou hast not left
Thyself without a witness, in the shades,
Of thy perfections. Grandeur, strength, and grace
Are here to speak of thee. This mighty oak —
By whose immovable stem I stand and seem
Almost annihilated — not a prince
In all that proud old world beyond the deep
E'er wore his crown as loftily as he
Wears the green coronal of leaves with which
Thy hand has graced him. Nestled at his root
Is beauty, such as blooms not in the glare

Of the broad sun, that delicate forest flower,
With scented breath and look so like a smile,
Seems, as it issues from the shapeless mould,
An emanation of the indwelling Life,
A visible token of the upholding Love,
That are the soul of this great universe.

My heart is awed within me when I think
Of the great miracle that still goes on,
In silence, round me — the perpetual work
Of thy creation, finished, yet renewed
Forever. Written on thy works I read
The lesson of thy own eternity.
Lo! all grow old and die — but see again,
How on the faltering footsteps of decay
Youth presses — ever gay and beautiful youth
In all its beautiful forms. These lofty trees
Wave not less proudly that their ancestors
Moulder beneath them. Oh, there is not lost
One of earth's charms: upon her bosom yet,
After the flight of untold centuries,
The freshness of her far beginning lies
And yet shall lie. Life mocks the idle hate
Of his arch enemy Death — yea, seats himself
Upon the tyrant's throne, — the sepulchre,
And of the triumphs of his ghastly foe
Makes his own nourishment. For he came forth
From thine own bosom, and shall have no end.

There have been holy men who hid themselves
Deep in the woody wilderness, and gave
Their lives to thought and prayer, till they outlived
The generation born with them, nor seemed
Less aged than the hoary trees and rocks
Around them; — and there have been holy men
Who deemed it were not well to pass life thus.
But let me often to these solitudes
Retire, and in thy presence reassure
My feeble virtue. Here its enemies,
The passions, at thy plainer footsteps shrink
And tremble and are still. O God! when thou
Dost scare the world with tempests, set on fire
The heavens with falling thunder-bolts, or fill,
With all the waters of the firmament,
The swift dark whirlwind that uproots the woods
And drowns the villages; when, at thy call,
Uprises the great deep and throws himself
Upon the continent, and overwhelms
Its cities — who forgets not, at the sight
Of these tremendous tokens of thy power,
His pride, and lays his strifes and follies by?
Oh, from these sterner aspects of thy face
Spare me and mine, nor let us need the wrath
Of the mad unchained elements to teach
Who rules them. Be it ours to meditate,
In these calm shades, thy milder majesty,
And to the beautiful order of thy works
Learn to conform the order of our lives.

JUNE

I GAZED upon the glorious sky
And the green mountains round,
And thought that when I came to lie
At rest within the ground,
'T were pleasant that, in flowery June,
When brooks send up a cheerful tune,
And groves a joyous sound,
The sexton's hand, my grave to make,
The rich, green mountain-turf should break.

A cell within the frozen mould,
A coffin borne through sleet,
And icy clods above it rolled,
While fierce the tempests beat —
Away! — I will not think of these —
Blue be the sky and soft the breeze,
Earth green beneath the feet,
And be the damp mould gently pressed
Into my narrow place of rest.

There through the long, long summer hours,
The golden light should lie,
And thick young herbs and groups of flowers
Stand in their beauty by.
The oriole should build and tell
His love-tale close beside my cell;
The idle butterfly
Should rest him there, and there be heard
The housewife bee and humming-bird.

And what if cheerful shouts at noon
Come, from the village sent,
Or songs of maids, beneath the moon
With fairy laughter blent?
And what if, in the evening light,
Betrothëd lovers walk in sight
Of my low monument?
I would the lovely scene around
Might know no sadder sight nor sound.

I know that I no more should see
The season's glorious show,
Nor would its brightness shine for me,
Nor its wild music flow;
But if, around my place of sleep,
The friends I love should come to weep,
They might not haste to go.
Soft airs, and song, and light, and bloom
Should keep them lingering by my tomb.

These to their softened hearts should bear
The thought of what has been,
And speak of one who cannot share
The gladness of the scene;
Whose part, in all the pomp that fills
The circuit of the summer hills,
Is that his grave is green;
And deeply would their hearts rejoice
To hear again his living voice.

THE DEATH OF THE FLOWERS

THE melancholy days are come, the saddest of the year,
Of wailing winds, and naked woods, and meadows brown and sere.
Heaped in the hollows of the grove, the autumn leaves lie dead;
They rustle to the eddying gust, and to the rabbit's tread.
The robin and the wren are flown, and from the shrubs the jay,
And from the wood-top calls the crow through all the gloomy day.

Where are the flowers, the fair young flowers, that lately sprang and stood
In brighter light and softer airs, a beauteous sisterhood?
Alas! they all are in their graves, the gentle race of flowers
Are lying in their lowly beds, with the fair and good of ours.
The rain is falling where they lie, but the cold November rain
Calls not from out the gloomy earth the lovely ones again.

The wind-flower and the violet, they perished long ago,
And the brier-rose and the orchis died amid the summer glow;
But on the hill the golden-rod, and the aster in the wood,
And the yellow sun-flower by the brook, in autumn beauty stood,
Till fell the frost from the clear cold heaven, as falls the plague on men,
And the brightness of their smile was gone, from upland, glade, and glen.

And now, when comes the calm mild day, as still such days will come,
To call the squirrel and the bee from out their winter home;
When the sound of dropping nuts is heard, though all the trees are still,
And twinkle in the smoky light the waters of the rill,
The south wind searches for the flowers whose fragrance late he bore,
And sighs to find them in the wood and by the stream no more.

And then I think of one who in her youthful beauty died,
The fair meek blossom that grew up and faded by my side.
In the cold moist earth we laid her, when the forest cast the leaf,
And we wept that one so lovely should have a life so brief:
Yet not unmeet it was that one like that young friend of ours,
So gentle and so beautiful, should perish with the flowers.

THE PAST

THOU unrelenting Past!
Strong are the barriers round thy dark domain,
And fetters, sure and fast,
Hold all that enter thy unbreathing reign.

Far in thy realm withdrawn
Old empires sit in sullenness and gloom,

And glorious ages gone
Lie deep within the shadow of thy womb.

Childhood, with all its mirth,
Youth, Manhood, Age that draws us to the ground,
And last, Man's Life on earth,
Glide to thy dim dominions, and are bound.

Thou hast my better years;
Thou hast my earlier friends, the good, the kind,
Yielded to thee with tears —
The venerable form, the exalted mind.

My spirit yearns to bring
The lost ones back — yearns with desire intense,
And struggles hard to wring
Thy bolts apart, and pluck thy captives thence.

In vain; thy gates deny
All passage save to those who hence depart;
Nor to the streaming eye
Thou giv'st them back — nor to the broken heart.

In thy abysses hide
Beauty and excellence unknown; to thee
Earth's wonder and her pride
Are gathered, as the waters to the sea;

Labors of good to man,
Unpublished charity, unbroken faith,
Love, that midst grief began,
And grew with years, and faltered not in death.

Full many a mighty name
Lurks in thy depths, unuttered, unrevered;
With thee are silent fame,
Forgotten arts, and wisdom disappeared.

Thine for a space are they —
Yet shalt thou yield thy treasures up at last:
Thy gates shall yet give way,
Thy bolts shall fall, inexorable Past!

All that of good and fair
Has gone into thy womb from earliest time,
Shall then come forth to wear
The glory and the beauty of its prime.

They have not perished — no!
Kind words, remembered voices once so sweet,
Smiles, radiant long ago,
And features, the great soul's apparent seat.

All shall come back; each tie
Of pure affection shall be knit again;
Alone shall Evil die,
And Sorrow dwell a prisoner in thy reign.

And then shall I behold
Him, by whose kind paternal side I sprung,
And her, who, still and cold,
Fills the next grave — the beautiful and young.

THE EVENING WIND

SPIRIT that breathest through my lattice, thou
That cool'st the twilight of the sultry day,
Gratefully flows thy freshness round my brow;
Thou hast been out upon the deep at play,
Riding all day the wild blue waves till now,
Roughening their crests, and scattering high their spray,
And swelling the white sail. I welcome thee
To the scorched land, thou wanderer of the sea!

Nor I alone; a thousand bosoms round
Inhale thee in the fulness of delight;
And languid forms rise up, and pulses bound
Livelier, at coming of the wind of night;
And, languishing to hear thy grateful sound,
Lies the vast inland stretched beyond the sight.
Go forth into the gathering shade; go forth,
God's blessing breathed upon the fainting earth!

Go, rock the little wood-bird in his nest,
Curl the still waters, bright with stars, and rouse
The wide old wood from his majestic rest,
Summoning from the innumerable boughs

The strange, deep harmonies that haunt his breast;
Pleasant shall be thy way where meekly bows
The shutting flower, and darkling waters pass,
And where the o'ershadowing branches sweep the grass.

The faint old man shall lean his silver head
To feel thee; thou shalt kiss the child asleep,
And dry the moistened curls that overspread
His temples, while his breathing grows more deep;
And they who stand about the sick man's bed
Shall joy to listen to thy distant sweep,
And softly part his curtains to allow
Thy visit, grateful to his burning brow.

Go — but the circle of eternal change,
Which is the life of Nature, shall restore,
With sounds and scents from all thy mighty range,
Thee to thy birthplace of the deep once more;
Sweet odors in the sea-air, sweet and strange,
Shall tell the home-sick mariner of the shore;
And, listening to thy murmur, he shall deem
He hears the rustling leaf and running stream.

TO THE FRINGED GENTIAN

THOU blossom bright with autumn dew,
And colored with the heaven's own blue,
That openest when the quiet light
Succeeds the keen and frosty night,

Thou comest not when violets lean
O'er wandering brooks and springs unseen,
Or columbines, in purple dressed,
Nod o'er the ground-bird's hidden nest.

Thou waitest late and com'st alone,
When woods are bare and birds are flown,
And frost and shortening days portend
The aged year is near his end.

Then doth thy sweet and quiet eye
Look through its fringes to the sky,
Blue — blue — as if that sky let fall
A flower from its cerulean wall.

I would that thus, when I shall see
The hour of death draw near to me,
Hope, blossoming within my heart,
May look to heaven as I depart.

THE HUNTER OF THE PRAIRIES

AY, this is freedom! — these pure skies
Were never stained with village smoke:
The fragrant wind, that through them flies,
Is breathed from wastes by plough unbroke.
Here, with my rifle and my steed,
And her who left the world for me,
I plant me, where the red deer feed
In the green desert — and am free.

For here the fair savannas know
No barriers in the bloomy grass;
Wherever breeze of heaven may blow,
Or beam of heaven may glance, I pass.
In pastures, measureless as air,
The bison is my noble game;
The bounding elk, whose antlers tear
The branches, falls before my aim.

Mine are the river-fowl that scream
From the long stripe of waving sedge;
The bear, that marks my weapon's gleam,
Hides vainly in the forest's edge;
In vain the she-wolf stands at bay;
The brinded catamount, that lies
High in the boughs to watch his prey,
Even in the act of springing, dies.

With what free growth the elm and plane
Fling their huge arms across my way,
Gray, old, and cumbered with a train
Of vines, as huge, and old, and gray!
Free stray the lucid streams, and find
No taint in these fresh lawns and shades;
Free spring the flowers that scent the wind
Where never scythe has swept the glades

Alone the Fire, when frost-winds sere
The heavy herbage of the ground,
Gathers his annual harvest here,
With roaring like the battle's sound,

And hurrying flames that sweep the plain,
  And smoke-streams gushing up the sky;
I meet the flames with flames again,
  And at my door they cower and die.

Here, from dim woods, the aged past
  Speaks solemnly; and I behold
The boundless future in the vast
  And lonely river, seaward rolled.
Who feeds its founts with rain and dew?
  Who moves, I ask, its gliding mass,
And trains the bordering vines, whose blue
  Bright clusters tempt me as I pass?

Broad are these streams — my steed obeys,
  Plunges, and bears me through the tide.
Wide are these woods — I tread the maze
  Of giant stems, nor ask a guide.
I hunt till day's last glimmer dies
  O'er woody vale and glassy height;
And kind the voice and glad the eyes
  That welcome my return at night.

THE BATTLE-FIELD

ONCE this soft turf, this rivulet's sands,
  Were trampled by a hurrying crowd,
And fiery hearts and armëd hands
  Encountered in the battle-cloud.

Ah! never shall the land forget
  How gushed the life-blood of her brave —
Gushed, warm with hope and courage yet,
  Upon the soil they fought to save.

Now all is calm, and fresh, and still;
  Alone the chirp of flitting bird,
And talk of children on the hill,
  And bell of wandering kine are heard.

No solemn host goes trailing by
  The black-mouthed gun and staggering wain;
Men start not at the battle-cry,
  Oh, be it never heard again!

Soon rested those who fought; but thou
  Who minglest in the harder strife
For truths which men receive not now,
  Thy warfare only ends with life.

A friendless warfare! lingering long
  Through weary day and weary year,
A wild and many-weaponed throng
  Hang on thy front, and flank, and rear.

Yet nerve thy spirit to the proof,
  And blench not at thy chosen lot.
The timid good may stand aloof,
  The sage may frown — yet faint thou not.

Nor heed the shaft too surely cast,
  The foul and hissing bolt of scorn;
For with thy side shall dwell, at last,
  The victory of endurance born.

Truth, crushed to earth, shall rise again;
  The eternal years of God are hers;
But Error, wounded, writhes in pain,
  And dies among his worshippers.

Yea, though thou lie upon the dust,
  When they who helped thee flee in fear,
Die full of hope and manly trust,
  Like those who fell in battle here.

Another hand thy sword shall wield,
  Another hand the standard wave,
Till from the trumpet's mouth is pealed
  The blast of triumph o'er thy grave.

FROM "AN EVENING REVERY"

O THOU great Movement of the Universe,
Or Change, or Flight of Time — for ye are one!
That bearest, silently, this visible scene
Into night's shadow and the streaming rays
Of starlight, whither art thou bearing me?
I feel the mighty current sweep me on,
Yet know not whither. Man foretells afar
The courses of the stars; the very hour
He knows when they shall darken or grow bright;
Yet doth the eclipse of Sorrow and of Death
Come unforewarned. Who next, of those I love,
Shall pass from life, or, sadder yet, shall fall
From virtue? Strife with foes, or bitterer strife
With friends, or shame and general scorn of men —
Which who can bear? — or the fierce rack of pain —

Lie they within my path? Or shall the years
Push me, with soft and inoffensive pace,
Into the stilly twilight of my age?
Or do the portals of another life
Even now, while I am glorying in my strength,
Impend around me? Oh, beyond that bourne,
In the vast cycle of being which begins
At that dread threshold, with what fairer forms
Shall the great law of change and progress clothe
Its workings? Gently — so have good men taught —
Gently, and without grief, the old shall glide
Into the new; the eternal flow of things,
Like a bright river of the fields of heaven,
Shall journey onward in perpetual peace.

THE ANTIQUITY OF FREEDOM

HERE are old trees, tall oaks, and gnarlëd pines,
That stream with gray-green mosses; here the ground
Was never trenched by spade, and flowers spring up
Unsown, and die ungathered. It is sweet
To linger here, among the flitting birds
And leaping squirrels, wandering brooks, and winds
That shake the leaves, and scatter, as they pass,
A fragrance from the cedars, thickly set
With pale blue berries. In these peaceful shades —
Peaceful, unpruned, immeasurably old —
My thoughts go up the long dim path of years,
Back to the earliest days of liberty.

O FREEDOM! thou art not, as poets dream,
A fair young girl, with light and delicate limbs,
And wavy tresses gushing from the cap
With which the Roman master crowned his slave
When he took off the gyves. A bearded man,
Armed to the teeth, art thou; one mailëd hand
Grasps the broad shield, and one the sword; thy brow,
Glorious in beauty though it be, is scarred
With tokens of old wars; thy massive limbs
Are strong with struggling. Power at thee has launched
His bolts, and with his lightnings smitten thee;
They could not quench the life thou hast from heaven;
Merciless Power has dug thy dungeon deep,
And his swart armorers, by a thousand fires,
Have forged thy chain; yet, while he deems thee bound,
The links are shivered, and the prison walls
Fall outward; terribly thou springest forth,
As springs the flame above a burning pile,
And shoutest to the nations, who return
Thy shoutings, while the pale oppressor flies.

Thy birthright was not given by human hands:
Thou wert twin-born with man. In pleasant fields,
While yet our race was few, thou sat'st with him,
To tend the quiet flock and watch the stars,
And teach the reed to utter simple airs.
Thou by his side, amid the tangled wood,
Didst war upon the panther and the wolf,
His only foes; and thou with him didst draw
The earliest furrow on the mountain's side,
Soft with the deluge. Tyranny himself,
Thy enemy, although of reverend look,
Hoary with many years, and far obeyed,
Is later born than thou; and as he meets
The grave defiance of thine elder eye,
The usurper trembles in his fastnesses.

Thou shalt wax stronger with the lapse of years,
But he shall fade into a feebler age —
Feebler, yet subtler. He shall weave his snares,
And spring them on thy careless steps, and clap
His withered hands, and from their ambush call
His hordes to fall upon thee. He shall send
Quaint maskers, wearing fair and gallant forms
To catch thy gaze, and uttering graceful words

To charm thy ear; while his sly imps, by stealth,
Twine round thee threads of steel, light thread on thread,
That grow to fetters; or bind down thy arms
With chains concealed in chaplets. Oh! not yet
Mayst thou unbrace thy corselet, nor lay by
Thy sword; nor yet, O Freedom! close thy lids
In slumber; for thine enemy never sleeps,
And thou must watch and combat till the day
Of the new earth and heaven. But wouldst thou rest
Awhile from tumult and the frauds of men,
These old and friendly solitudes invite
Thy visit. They, while yet the forest trees
Were young upon the unviolated earth,
And yet the moss-stains on the rock were new,
Beheld thy glorious childhood, and rejoiced.

AMERICA

Oh mother of a mighty race,
Yet lovely in thy youthful grace!
The elder dames, thy haughty peers,
Admire and hate thy blooming years.
With words of shame
And taunts of scorn they join thy name.

For on thy cheeks the glow is spread
That tints thy morning hills with red;
Thy step — the wild deer's rustling feet
Within thy woods are not more fleet;
Thy hopeful eye
Is bright as thine own sunny sky.

Ay, let them rail — those haughty ones,
While safe thou dwellest with thy sons.
They do not know how loved thou art,
How many a fond and fearless heart
Would rise to throw
Its life between thee and the foe.

They know not, in their hate and pride,
What virtues with thy children bide;
How true, how good, thy graceful maids
Make bright, like flowers, the valley shades;
What generous men
Spring, like thine oaks, by hill and glen; —
What cordial welcomes greet the guest
By thy lone rivers of the West;
How faith is kept, and truth revered,
And man is loved, and God is feared,
In woodland homes,
And where the ocean border foams.

There 's freedom at thy gates and rest
For Earth's down-trodden and opprest,
A shelter for the hunted head,
For the starved laborer toil and bread.
Power, at thy bounds,
Stops and calls back his baffled hounds.

Oh, fair young mother! on thy brow
Shall sit a nobler grace than now.
Deep in the brightness of the skies
The thronging years in glory rise,
And, as they fleet,
Drop strength and riches at thy feet.

Thine eye, with every coming hour,
Shall brighten, and thy form shall tower;
And when thy sisters, elder born,
Would brand thy name with words of scorn,
Before thine eye,
Upon their lips the taunt shall die.

THE PLANTING OF THE APPLE-TREE

Come, let us plant the apple-tree.
Cleave the tough greensward with the spade;
Wide let its hollow bed be made;
There gently lay the roots, and there
Sift the dark mould with kindly care,
And press it o'er them tenderly,
As, round the sleeping infant's feet,
We softly fold the cradle-sheet;
So plant we the apple-tree.

What plant we in this apple-tree?
Buds, which the breath of summer days
Shall lengthen into leafy sprays;
Boughs where the thrush, with crimson breast,
Shall haunt and sing and hide her nest;
We plant, upon the sunny lea,
A shadow for the noontide hour,
A shelter from the summer shower,
When we plant the apple-tree.

What plant we in this apple-tree?
Sweets for a hundred flowery springs

To load the May-wind's restless wings,
When, from the orchard row, he pours
Its fragrance through our open doors;
A world of blossoms for the bee,
Flowers for the sick girl's silent room,
For the glad infant sprigs of bloom,
We plant with the apple-tree.

What plant we in this apple-tree?
Fruits that shall swell in sunny June,
And redden in the August noon,
And drop, when gentle airs come by,
That fan the blue September sky,
While children come, with cries of glee,
And seek them where the fragrant grass
Betrays their bed to those who pass,
At the foot of the apple-tree.

And when, above this apple-tree,
The winter stars are quivering bright,
And winds go howling through the night,
Girls, whose young eyes o'erflow with mirth,
Shall peel its fruit by cottage-hearth,
And guests in prouder homes shall see,
Heaped with the grape of Cintra's vine
And golden orange of the line,
The fruit of the apple-tree.

The fruitage of this apple-tree
Winds and our flag of stripe and star
Shall bear to coasts that lie afar,
Where men shall wonder at the view,
And ask in what fair groves they grew;
And sojourners beyond the sea
Shall think of childhood's careless day,
And long, long hours of summer play,
In the shade of the apple-tree.

Each year shall give this apple-tree
A broader flush of roseate bloom,
A deeper maze of verdurous gloom,
And loosen, when the frost-clouds lower,
The crisp brown leaves in thicker shower.
The years shall come and pass, but we
Shall hear no longer, where we lie,
The summer's songs, the autumn's sigh,
In the boughs of the apple-tree.

And time shall waste this apple-tree.
Oh, when its aged branches throw
Thin shadows on the ground below,
Shall fraud and force and iron will
Oppress the weak and helpless still?
What shall the tasks of mercy be,
Amid the toils, the strifes, the tears
Of those who live when length of years
Is wasting this little apple-tree?

"Who planted this old apple-tree?"
The children of that distant day
Thus to some aged man shall say;
And, gazing on its mossy stem,
The gray-haired man shall answer them:
"A poet of the land was he,
Born in the rude but good old times;
'T is said he made some quaint old rhymes,
On planting the apple-tree."

THE MAY SUN SHEDS AN AMBER LIGHT

THE May sun sheds an amber light
On new-leaved woods and lawns between;
But she who, with a smile more bright,
Welcomed and watched the springing green,
Is in her grave,
Low in her grave.

The fair white blossoms of the wood
In groups beside the pathway stand;
But one, the gentle and the good,
Who cropped them with a fairer hand,
Is in her grave,
Low in her grave.

Upon the woodland's morning airs
The small birds' mingled notes are flung;
But she, whose voice, more sweet than theirs,
Once bade me listen while they sung,
Is in her grave,
Low in her grave.

That music of the early year
Brings tears of anguish to my eyes;
My heart aches when the flowers appear;
For then I think of her who lies
Within her grave,
Low in her grave.

THE CONQUEROR'S GRAVE

WITHIN this lowly grave a Conqueror lies,
And yet the monument proclaims it not,
Nor round the sleeper's name hath chisel wrought
The emblems of a fame that never dies,—

Ivy and amaranth, in a graceful sheaf,
Twined with the laurel's fair, imperial leaf.
A simple name alone,
To the great world unknown,
Is graven here, and wild-flowers, rising round,
Meek meadow-sweet and violets of the ground,
Lean lovingly against the humble stone.

Here, in the quiet earth, they laid apart
No man of iron mould and bloody hands,
Who sought to wreak upon the cowering lands
The passions that consumed his restless heart;
But one of tender spirit and delicate frame,
Gentlest, in mien and mind,
Of gentle womankind,
Timidly shrinking from the breath of blame:
One in whose eyes the smile of kindness made
Its haunts, like flowers by sunny brooks in May,
Yet, at the thought of others' pain, a shade
Of sweeter sadness chased the smile away.

Nor deem that when the hand that moulders here
Was raised in menace, realms were chilled with fear,
And armies mustered at the sign, as when
Clouds rise on clouds before the rainy East—
Gray captains leading bands of veteran men
And fiery youths to be the vulture's feast.
Not thus were waged the mighty wars that gave
The victory to her who fills this grave:
Alone her task was wrought,
Alone the battle fought;
Through that long strife her constant hope was stayed
On God alone, nor looked for other aid.

She met the hosts of Sorrow with a look
That altered not beneath the frown they wore,
And soon the lowering brood were tamed, and took,
Meekly, her gentle rule, and frowned no more.
Her soft hand put aside the assaults of wrath,
And calmly broke in twain
The fiery shafts of pain,
And rent the nets of passion from her path.
By that victorious hand despair was slain.
With love she vanquished hate and overcame
Evil with good, in her Great Master's name.

Her glory is not of this shadowy state,
Glory that with the fleeting season dies;
But when she entered at the sapphire gate
What joy was radiant in celestial eyes!
How heaven's bright depths with sounding welcomes rung,
And flowers of heaven by shining hands were flung!
And He who, long before,
Pain, scorn, and sorrow bore,
The Mighty Sufferer, with aspect sweet,
Smiled on the timid stranger from his seat;
He who returning, glorious, from the grave,
Dragged Death, disarmed, in chains, a crouching slave.

See, as I linger here, the sun grows low;
Cool airs are murmuring that the night is near.
Oh, gentle sleeper, from thy grave I go
Consoled though sad, in hope and yet in fear.
Brief is the time, I know,
The warfare scarce begun;
Yet all may win the triumphs thou hast won.
Still flows the fount whose waters strengthened thee,
The victors' names are yet too few to fill
Heaven's mighty roll; the glorious armory,
That ministered to thee, is open still.

THE POET

Thou, who wouldst wear the name
Of poet mid thy brethren of mankind,
And clothe in words of flame
Thoughts that shall live within the general mind!
Deem not the framing of a deathless lay
The pastime of a drowsy summer day.

But gather all thy powers,
And wreak them on the verse that thou dost weave,
And in thy lonely hours,
At silent morning or at wakeful eve,
While the warm current tingles through thy veins,
Set forth the burning words in fluent strains.

No smooth array of phrase,
Artfully sought and ordered though it be,
Which the cold rhymer lays
Upon his page with languid industry,
Can wake the listless pulse to livelier speed,
Or fill with sudden tears the eyes that read.

The secret wouldst thou know
To touch the heart or fire the blood at will?
Let thine own eyes o'erflow;
Let thy lips quiver with the passionate thrill;
Seize the great thought, ere yet its power be past,
And bind, in words, the fleet emotion fast.

Then should thy verse appear
Halting and harsh, and all unaptly wrought,
Touch the crude line with fear,
Save in the moment of impassioned thought;
Then summon back the original glow, and mend
The strain with rapture that with fire was penned.

Yet let no empty gust
Of passion find an utterance in thy lay,
A blast that whirls the dust
Along the howling street and dies away;
But feelings of calm power and mighty sweep,
Like currents journeying through the windless deep.

Seek'st thou, in living lays,
To limn the beauty of the earth and sky?
Before thine inner gaze
Let all that beauty in clear vision lie;
Look on it with exceeding love, and write
The words inspired by wonder and delight.

Of tempests wouldst thou sing,
Or tell of battles — make thyself a part
Of the great tumult; cling
To the tossed wreck with terror in thy heart;
Scale, with the assaulting host, the rampart's height,
And strike and struggle in the thickest fight.

So shalt thou frame a lay
That haply may endure from age to age,
And they who read shall say:
"What witchery hangs upon this poet's page!
What art is his the written spells to find
That sway from mood to mood the willing mind!"

MY AUTUMN WALK

On woodlands ruddy with autumn
The amber sunshine lies;
I look on the beauty round me,
And tears come into my eyes.

For the wind that sweeps the meadows
Blows out of the far Southwest,
Where our gallant men are fighting,
And the gallant dead are at rest.

The golden-rod is leaning,
And the purple aster waves,
In a breeze from the land of battles,
A breath from the land of graves.

Full fast the leaves are dropping
Before that wandering breath;
As fast, on the field of battle,
Our brethren fall in death.

Beautiful over my pathway
The forest spoils are shed;
They are spotting the grassy hillocks
With purple and gold and red.

Beautiful is the death-sleep
Of those who bravely fight
In their country's holy quarrel,
And perish for the Right.

But who shall comfort the living,
The light of whose homes is gone:
The bride that, early widowed,
Lives broken-hearted on;

The matron whose sons are lying
 In graves on a distant shore;
The maiden, whose promised husband
 Comes back from the war no more?

I look on the peaceful dwellings
 Whose windows glimmer in sight,
With croft and garden and orchard,
 That bask in the mellow light;

And I know that, when our couriers
 With news of victory come,
They will bring a bitter message
 Of hopeless grief to some.

Again I turn to the woodlands,
 And shudder as I see
The mock-grape's blood-red banner
 Hung out on the cedar-tree;

And I think of days of slaughter,
 And the night-sky red with flames,
On the Chattahoochee's meadows,
 And the wasted banks of the James.

Oh, for the fresh spring-season,
 When the groves are in their prime,
And far away in the future
 Is the frosty autumn-time!

Oh, for that better season,
 When the pride of the foe shall yield,
And the hosts of God and Freedom
 March back from the well-won field;

And the matron shall clasp her first-born
 With tears of joy and pride;
And the scarred and war-worn lover
 Shall claim his promised bride!

The leaves are swept from the branches;
 But the living buds are there,
With folded flower and foliage,
 To sprout in a kinder air.

Roslyn, October, 1864.

THE DEATH OF SLAVERY

O thou great Wrong, that, through the slow-paced years,
Didst hold thy millions fettered, and didst wield
The scourge that drove the laborer to the field,
And turn a stony gaze on human tears,
 Thy cruel reign is o'er;
 Thy bondmen crouch no more
In terror at the menace of thine eye;
 For He who marks the bounds of guilty power,
Long-suffering, hath heard the captive's cry,
 And touched his shackles at the appointed hour,
And lo! they fall, and he whose limbs they galled
Stands in his native manhood, disenthralled.

A shout of joy from the redeemed is sent;
 Ten thousand hamlets swell the hymn of thanks;
 Our rivers roll exulting, and their banks
Send up hosannas to the firmament!
 Fields where the bondman's toil
 No more shall trench the soil,
Seem now to bask in a serener day;
 The meadow-birds sing sweeter, and the airs
Of heaven with more caressing softness play,
 Welcoming man to liberty like theirs.
A glory clothes the land from sea to sea,
For the great land and all its coasts are free.

Within that land wert thou enthroned of late,
 And they by whom the nation's laws were made,
 And they who filled its judgment-seats, obeyed
Thy mandate, rigid as the will of Fate.
 Fierce men at thy right hand,
 With gesture of command,
Gave forth the word that none might dare gainsay;
 And grave and reverend ones, who loved thee not,
Shrank from thy presence, and in blank dismay
 Choked down, unuttered, the rebellious thought;
While meaner cowards, mingling with thy train,
Proved, from the book of God, thy right to reign.

Great as thou wert, and feared from shore to shore,
 The wrath of Heaven o'ertook thee in thy pride;

Thou sitt'st a ghastly shadow; by thy side
Thy once strong arms hang nerveless evermore.
And they who quailed but now
Before thy lowering brow,
Devote thy memory to scorn and shame,
And scoff at the pale, powerless thing thou art.
And they who ruled in thine imperial name,
Subdued, and standing sullenly apart,
Scowl at the hands that overthrew thy reign,
And shattered at a blow the prisoner's chain.

Well was thy doom deserved; thou didst not spare
Life's tenderest ties, but cruelly didst part
Husband and wife, and from the mother's heart
Didst wrest her children, deaf to shriek and prayer;
Thy inner lair became
The haunt of guilty shame;
Thy lash dropped blood; the murderer, at thy side,
Showed his red hands, nor feared the vengeance due.
Thou didst sow earth with crimes, and, far and wide,
A harvest of uncounted miseries grew,
Until the measure of thy sins at last
Was full, and then the avenging bolt was cast!

Go now, accursed of God, and take thy place
With hateful memories of the elder time,
With many a wasting plague, and nameless crime,
And bloody war that thinned the human race;
With the Black Death, whose way
Through wailing cities lay,
Worship of Moloch, tyrannies that built
The Pyramids, and cruel creeds that taught
To avenge a fancied guilt by deeper guilt —
Death at the stake to those that held them not.
Lo! the foul phantoms, silent in the gloom
Of the flown ages, part to yield thee room.

I see the better years that hasten by
Carry thee back into that shadowy past,
Where, in the dusty spaces, void and vast,
The graves of those whom thou hast murdered lie.
The slave-pen, through whose door
Thy victims pass no more,
Is there, and there shall the grim block remain
At which the slave was sold; while at thy feet
Scourges and engines of restraint and pain
Moulder and rust by thine eternal seat.
There, mid the symbols that proclaim thy crimes,
Dwell thou, a warning to the coming times.

IN MEMORY OF JOHN LOTHROP MOTLEY

SLEEP, Motley, with the great of ancient days,
Who wrote for all the years that yet shall be!
Sleep with Herodotus, whose name and praise
Have reached the isles of earth's remotest sea;
Sleep, while, defiant of the slow decays
Of time, thy glorious writings speak for thee,
And in the answering heart of millions raise
The generous zeal for Right and Liberty.
And should the day o'ertake us when, at last,
The silence — that, ere yet a human pen
Had traced the slenderest record of the past,
Hushed the primeval languages of men —
Upon our English tongue its spell shall cast,
Thy memory shall perish only then.

THE FLOOD OF YEARS

A MIGHTY Hand, from an exhaustless Urn,
Pours forth the never-ending Flood of Years,
Among the nations. How the rushing waves
Bear all before them! On their foremost edge,
And there alone, is Life. The Present there

Tosses and foams, and fills the air with roar
Of mingled noises. There are they who toil,
And they who strive, and they who feast, and they
Who hurry to and fro. The sturdy swain —
Woodman and delver with the spade — is there,
And busy artisan beside his bench,
And pallid student with his written roll.
A moment on the mounting billow seen,
The flood sweeps over them and they are gone.
There groups of revellers whose brows are twined
With roses, ride the topmost swell awhile,
And as they raise their flowing cups and touch
The clinking brim to brim, are whirled beneath
The waves and disappear. I hear the jar
Of beaten drums, and thunders that break forth
From cannon, where the advancing billow sends
Up to the sight long files of armëd men,
That hurry to the charge through flame and smoke.
The torrent bears them under, whelmed and hid,
Slayer and slain, in heaps of bloody foam.
Down go the steed and rider, the plumed chief
Sinks with his followers; the head that wears
The imperial diadem goes down beside
The felon's with cropped ear and branded cheek.
A funeral-train — the torrent sweeps away
Bearers and bier and mourners. By the bed
Of one who dies men gather sorrowing,
And women weep aloud; the flood rolls on;
The wail is stifled and the sobbing group
Borne under. Hark to that shrill, sudden shout,
The cry of an applauding multitude,
Swayed by some loud-voiced orator who wields
The living mass as if he were its soul!
The waters choke the shout and all is still.
Lo! next a kneeling crowd, and one who spreads
The hands in prayer — the engulfing wave o'ertakes
And swallows them and him. A sculptor wields
The chisel, and the stricken marble grows
To beauty; at his easel, eager-eyed,
A painter stands, and sunshine at his touch
Gathers upon his canvas, and life glows;
A poet, as he paces to and fro,
Murmurs his sounding lines. Awhile they ride
The advancing billow, till its tossing crest
Strikes them and flings them under, while their tasks
Are yet unfinished. See a mother smile
On her young babe that smiles to her again;
The torrent wrests it from her arms; she shrieks
And weeps, and midst her tears is carried down.
A beam like that of moonlight turns the spray
To glistening pearls; two lovers, hand in hand,
Rise on the billowy swell and fondly look
Into each other's eyes. The rushing flood
Flings them apart: the youth goes down; the maid
With hands outstretched in vain, and streaming eyes,
Waits for the next high wave to follow him.
An aged man succeeds; his bending form
Sinks slowly. Mingling with the sullen stream
Gleam the white locks, and then are seen no more.

Lo! wider grows the stream — a sea-like flood
Saps earth's walled cities; massive palaces
Crumble before it; fortresses and towers
Dissolve in the swift waters; populous realms
Swept by the torrent see their ancient tribes
Engulfed and lost; their very languages
Stifled, and never to be uttered more.

I pause and turn my eyes, and looking back
Where that tumultuous flood has been, I see
The silent ocean of the Past, a waste
Of waters weltering over graves, its shores
Strewn with the wreck of fleets where mast and hull
Drop away piecemeal; battlemented walls
Frown idly, green with moss, and temples stand

Unroofed, forsaken by the worshipper.
There lie memorial stones, whence time has gnawed
The graven legends, thrones of kings o'erturned,
The broken altars of forgotten gods,
Foundations of old cities and long streets
Where never fall of human foot is heard,
On all the desolate pavement. I behold
Dim glimmerings of lost jewels, far within
The sleeping waters, diamond, sardonyx,
Ruby and topaz, pearl and chrysolite,
Once glittering at the banquet on fair brows
That long ago were dust; and all around
Strewn on the surface of that silent sea
Are withering bridal wreaths, and glossy locks
Shorn from dear brows by loving hands, and scrolls
O'erwritten, haply with fond words of love
And vows of friendship, and fair pages flung
Fresh from the printer's engine. There they lie
A moment, and then sink away from sight.
I look, and the quick tears are in my eyes,
For I behold in every one of these
A blighted hope, a separate history
Of human sorrows, telling of dear ties
Suddenly broken, dreams of happiness
Dissolved in air, and happy days too brief
That sorrowfully ended, and I think
How painfully must the poor heart have beat
In bosoms without number, as the blow
Was struck that slew their hope and broke their peace.
Sadly I turn and look before, where yet
The Flood must pass, and I behold a mist
Where swarm dissolving forms, the brood of Hope,
Divinely fair, that rest on banks of flowers,
Or wander among rainbows, fading soon
And reappearing, haply giving place
To forms of grisly aspect such as Fear
Shapes from the idle air — where serpents lift
The head to strike, and skeletons stretch forth
The bony arm in menace. Further on
A belt of darkness seems to bar the way
Long, low, and distant, where the Life to come
Touches the Life that is. The Flood of Years
Rolls toward it near and nearer. It must pass
That dismal barrier. What is there beyond?
Hear what the wise and good have said. Beyond
That belt of darkness, still the Years roll on
More gently, but with not less mighty sweep.
They gather up again and softly bear
All the sweet lives that late were overwhelmed
And lost to sight, all that in them was good,
Noble, and truly great, and worthy of love —
The lives of infants and ingenuous youths,
Sages and saintly women who have made
Their households happy; all are raised and borne
By that great current in its onward sweep,
Wandering and rippling with caressing waves
Around green islands with the breath
Of flowers that never wither. So they pass
From stage to stage along the shining course
Of that bright river, broadening like a sea.
As its smooth eddies curl along their way
They bring old friends together; hands are clasped
In joy unspeakable; the mother's arms
Again are folded round the child she loved
And lost. Old sorrows are forgotten now,
Or but remembered to make sweet the hour
That overpays them; wounded hearts that bled
Or broke are healed forever. In the room
Of this grief-shadowed present there shall be
A Present in whose reign no grief shall gnaw
The heart, and never shall a tender tie
Be broken; in whose reign the eternal Change
That waits on growth and action shall proceed
With everlasting Concord hand in hand.

James Gates Percival

ELEGIAC

O, IT is great for our country to die, where ranks are contending!
Bright is the wreath of our fame; glory awaits us for aye,—
Glory, that never is dim, shining on with light never ending,—
Glory that never shall fade, never, O never, away!

O, it is sweet for our country to die! How softly reposes
Warrior youth on his bier, wet by the tears of his love,
Wet by a mother's warm tears. They crown him with garlands of roses,
Weep, and then joyously turn, bright where he triumphs above.

Not to the shades shall the youth descend, who for country hath perished;
Hebe awaits him in heaven, welcomes him there with her smile;
There, at the banquet divine, the patriot spirit is cherished;
Gods love the young who ascend pure from the funeral pile.

Not to Elysian fields, by the still, oblivious river;
Not to the isles of the blest, over the blue, rolling sea;
But on Olympian heights shall dwell the devoted forever;
There shall assemble the good, there the wise, valiant, and free.

O, then, how great for our country to die, in the front rank to perish,
Firm with our breast to the foe, victory's shout in our ear!
Long they our statues shall crown, in songs our memory cherish;
We shall look forth from our heaven, pleased the sweet music to hear.

THE CORAL GROVE

DEEP in the wave is a coral grove,
Where the purple mullet and gold-fish rove,
Where the sea-flower spreads its leaves of blue,
That never are wet with falling dew,
But in bright and changeful beauty shine,
Far down in the green and glassy brine.
The floor is of sand like the mountain drift
And the pearl-shells spangle the flinty snow;
From coral rocks the sea-plants lift
Their boughs, where the tides and billows flow;
The water is calm and still below,
For the winds and waves are absent there,
And the sands are bright as the stars that glow
In the motionless fields of upper air:
There with its waving blade of green,
The sea-flag streams through the silent water,
And the crimson leaf of the dulse is seen
To blush, like a banner bathed in slaughter:
There with a light and easy motion,
The fan-coral sweeps through the clear, deep sea;
And the yellow and scarlet tufts of ocean
Are bending like corn on the upland lea:
And life, in rare and beautiful forms,
Is sporting amid those bowers of stone,
And is safe, when the wrathful spirit of storms
Has made the top of the wave his own:
And when the ship from his fury flies,
Where the myriad voices of ocean roar,
When the wind-god frowns in the murky skies,
And demons are waiting the wreck on shore;
Then far below, in the peaceful sea,
The purple mullet and gold-fish rove,
Where the waters murmur tranquilly,
Through the bending twigs of the coral grove.

NEW ENGLAND

HAIL to the land whereon we tread,
Our fondest boast!
The sepulchre of mighty dead,
The truest hearts that ever bled,
Who sleep on glory's brightest bed,
A fearless host:

No slave is here; — our unchained feet
Walk freely, as the waves that beat
Our coast.

Our fathers crossed the ocean's wave
To seek this shore;
They left behind the coward slave
To welter in his living grave;
With hearts unbent, high, steady, brave,
They sternly bore
Such toils as meaner souls had quelled;
But souls like these, such toils impelled
To soar.

Hail to the morn when first they stood
On Bunker's height!
And fearless stemmed the invading flood,
And wrote our dearest rights in blood,
And mowed in ranks the hireling brood,
In desperate fight:
O, 't was a proud, exulting day,
For even our fallen fortunes lay
In light.

There is no other land like thee,
No dearer shore;
Thou art the shelter of the free;
The home, the port of liberty
Thou hast been, and shalt ever be,
Till time is o'er.
Ere I forget to think upon
My land, shall mother curse the son
She bore.

Thou art the firm, unshaken rock,
On which we rest;
And rising from thy hardy stock,
Thy sons the tyrant's frown shall mock,
And slavery's galling chains unlock,
And free the oppressed:
All who the wreath of freedom twine
Beneath the shadow of the vine
Are blessed.

We love thy rude and rocky shore,
And here we stand:
Let foreign navies hasten o'er,
And on our heads their fury pour,
And peal their cannon's loudest roar,
And storm our land:
They still shall find, our lives are given
To die for home; — and leant on Heaven
Our hand.

Maria Gowen Brooks

("MARIA DEL OCCIDENTE")

FROM "ZOPHIËL"

PALACE OF THE GNOMES

HIGH towered the palace and its massive pile,
Made dubious if of nature or of art,
So wild and so uncouth; yet, all the while,
Shaped to strange grace in every varying part.

And groves adorned it, green in hue, and bright
As icicles about a laurel-tree;
And danced about their twigs a wondrous light;
Whence came that light so far beneath the sea?

Zophiël looked up to know, and to his view
The vault scarce seemed less vast than that of day;
No rocky roof was seen, a tender blue
Appeared, as of the sky, and clouds about it play;

And, in the midst, an orb looked as 't were meant
To shame the sun; it mimicked him so well.
But ah! no quickening, grateful warmth it sent;
Cold as the rock beneath, the paly radiance fell.

Within, from thousand lamps the lustre strays,
Reflected back from gems about the wall;

And from twelve dolphin shapes a fountain plays,
Just in the centre of the spacious hall:

But whether in the sunbeam formed to sport,
These shapes once lived in suppleness and pride,
And then, to decorate this wondrous court,
Were stolen from the waves and petrified,

Or, moulded by some imitative Gnome,
And scaled all o'er with gems, they were but stone,
Casting their showers and rainbows 'neath the dome,
To man or angel's eye might not be known.

No snowy fleece in these sad realms was found,
Nor silken ball, by maiden loved so well;
But ranged in lightest garniture around,
In seemly folds a shining tapestry fell.

And fibres of asbestos, bleached in fire,
And all with pearls and sparkling gems o'er-flecked,
Of that strange court composed the rich attire,
And such the cold, fair form of sad Tahathyam decked.

Of marble white the table they surround,
And reddest coral decked each curious couch,
Which softly yielding to their forms was found,
And of a surface smooth and wooing to the touch.

Of sunny gold and silver, like the moon,
Here was no lack; but if the veins of earth,
Torn open by man's weaker race, so soon
Supplied the alluring hoard, or here had birth

That baffling, maddening, fascinating art,
Half told by Sprite most mischievous, that he
Might laugh to see men toil, then not impart,
The guests left unenquired: — 't is still a mystery.

Here were no flowers, but a sweet odor breathed,
Of amber pure, a glistening coronal,
Of various-colored gems, each brow enwreathed,
In form of garland, for the festival.

THE RESPITE

The banquet-cups, of many a hue and shape,
Bossed o'er with gems, were beautiful to view;
But, for the madness of the vaunted grape,
Their only draught was a pure limpid dew,

To Spirits sweet; but these half-mortal lips
Longed for the streams that once on earth they quaffed;
And, half in shame, Tahathyam coldly sips
And craves excuses for the temperate draught.

"Man tastes," he said, "the grape's sweet blood that streams
To steep his heart when pained; when sorrowing he
In wild delirium drowns the sense, and dreams
Of bliss arise, to cheat his misery."

Nor with their dews were any mingling sweets
Save those, to mortal lip, of poison fell;
No murmuring bee was heard in these retreats,
The mineral clod alone supplied their hydromel.

The Spirits while they sat, in social guise,
Pledging each goblet with an answering kiss,
Marked many a Gnome conceal his bursting sighs;
And thought death happier than a life like this.

But they had music; at one ample side
Of the vast area of that sparkling hall,
Fringed round with gems that all the rest outvied,
In form of canopy, was seen to fall

The stony tapestry, over what at first
An altar to some deity appeared;

But it had cost full many a year to adjust
The limpid crystal tubes that 'neath upreared

Their different gleaming lengths; and so complete
Their wondrous rangement, that a tuneful Gnome
Drew from them sounds more varied, clear, and sweet,
Than ever yet had rung in any earthly dome.

Loud, shrilly, liquid, soft, — at that quick touch
Such modulation wooed his angel ears
That Zophiël wondered, started from his couch,
And thought upon the music of the spheres.

SONG OF EGLA

Day in melting purple dying,
Blossoms all around me sighing,
Fragrance from the lilies straying,
Zephyr with my ringlets playing,
Ye but waken my distress:
I am sick of loneliness.

Thou to whom I love to hearken,
Come ere night around me darken:
Though thy softness but deceive me,
Say thou 'rt true, and I 'll believe thee.
Veil, if ill, thy soul's intent:
Let me think it innocent!

Save thy toiling, spare thy treasure:
All I ask is friendship's pleasure:
Let the shining ore lie darkling;
Bring no gem in lustre sparkling;
Gifts and gold are nought to me:
I would only look on thee;

Tell to thee the high-wrought feeling,
Ecstasy but in revealing;
Paint to thee the deep sensation,
Rapture in participation,
Yet but torture, if comprest
In a lone unfriended breast.

Absent still? Ah, come and bless me!
Let these eyes again caress thee.
Once, in caution, I could fly thee.
Now I nothing could deny thee.
In a look if death there be,
Come, and I will gaze on thee!

FAREWELL TO CUBA

Adieu, fair isle! I love thy bowers,
I love thy dark-eyed daughters there;
The cool pomegranate's scarlet flowers
Look brighter in their jetty hair.

They praised my forehead's stainless white;
And when I thirsted, gave a draught
From the full clustering cocoa's height,
And smiling, blessed me as I quaffed.

Well pleased, the kind return I gave,
And, clasped in their embraces' twine,
Felt the soft breeze like Lethe's wave
Becalm this beating heart of mine.

Why will my heart so wildly beat?
Say, Seraphs, is my lot too blest,
That thus a fitful, feverish heat
Must rifle me of health and rest?

Alas! I fear my native snows —
A clime too cold, a heart too warm —
Alternate chills — alternate glows —
Too fiercely threat my flower-like form.

The orange-tree has fruit and flowers;
The grenadilla, in its bloom,
Hangs o'er its high, luxuriant bowers,
Like fringes from a Tyrian loom.

When the white coffee-blossoms swell,
The fair moon full, the evening long
I love to hear the warbling bell,
And sun-burnt peasant's wayward song.

Drive gently on, dark muleteer,
And the light seguidilla frame;
Fain would I listen still, to hear
At every close thy mistress' name.

Adieu, fair isle! the waving palm
Is pencilled on thy purest sky;
Warm sleeps the bay, the air is balm,
And, soothed to languor, scarce a sigh

Escapes for those I love so well,
  For those I 've loved and left so long;
On me their fondest musings dwell,
  To them alone my sighs belong.

On, on, my bark! blow, southern breeze!
  No longer would I lingering stay;
'T were better far to die with these
  Than live in pleasure far away.

William Augustus Muhlenberg

I WOULD NOT LIVE ALWAY

I WOULD not live alway — live alway below!
Oh no, I 'll not linger when bidden to go:
The days of our pilgrimage granted us here
Are enough for life's woes, full enough for its cheer:
Would I shrink from the path which the prophets of God,
Apostles, and martyrs, so joyfully trod?
Like a spirit unblest, o'er the earth would I roam,
While brethren and friends are all hastening home?

I would not live alway: I ask not to stay
Where storm after storm rises dark o'er the way;
Where seeking for rest we but hover around,
Like the patriarch's bird, and no resting is found;
Where Hope, when she paints her gay bow in the air,
Leaves its brilliance to fade in the night of despair,
And joy's fleeting angel ne'er sheds a glad ray,
Save the gleam of the plumage that bears him away.

I would not live alway — thus fettered by sin,
Temptation without and corruption within;
In a moment of strength if I sever the chain,
Scarce the victory 's mine, ere I 'm captive again;
E'en the rapture of pardon is mingled with fears,
And the cup of thanksgiving with penitent tears:
The festival trump calls for jubilant songs,
But my spirit her own *miserere* prolongs.

I would not live alway — no, welcome the tomb,
Since Jesus hath lain there I dread not its gloom;
Where he deigned to sleep, I'll too bow my head,
All peaceful to slumber on that hallowed bed.
Then the glorious daybreak, to follow that night,
The orient gleam of the angels of light,
With their clarion call for the sleepers to rise
And chant forth their matins, away to the skies.

Who, who would live alway? away from his God,
Away from yon heaven, that blissful abode,
Where the rivers of pleasure flow o'er the bright plains,
And the noontide of glory eternally reigns;
Where the saints of all ages in harmony meet,
Their Saviour and brethren transported to greet,
While the songs of salvation exultingly roll
And the smile of the Lord is the feast of the soul.

That heavenly music! what is it I hear?
The notes of the harpers ring sweet in mine ear!
And see, soft unfolding those portals of gold,
The King all arrayed in his beauty behold!
Oh give me, oh give me, the wings of a dove,
To adore him — be near him — enwrapt with his love;
I but wait for the summons, I list for the word —
Alleluia — Amen — evermore with the Lord!

HEAVEN'S MAGNIFICENCE

Since o'er thy footstool here below
Such radiant gems are strown,
Oh, what magnificence must glow,
My God, about thy throne!
So brilliant here these drops of light,
There the full ocean rolls, how bright!

If night's blue curtain of the sky,
With thousand stars inwrought,
Hung like a royal canopy
With glittering diamonds fraught,
Be, Lord, thy temple's outer veil,
What splendor at the shrine must dwell!

The dazzling sun at noontide hour,
Forth from his flaming vase
Flinging o'er earth the golden shower
Till vale and mountain blaze,
But shows, O Lord, one beam of thine:
What, then, the day where thou dost shine!

Ah, how shall these dim eyes endure
That noon of living rays!
Or how my spirit, so impure,
Upon thy brightness gaze!
Anoint, O Lord, anoint my sight,
And robe me for that world of light.

John Gardiner Calkins Brainard

MR. MERRY'S LAMENT FOR "LONG TOM"

Thy cruise is over now,
Thou art anchored by the shore,
And never more shalt thou
Hear the storm around thee roar;
Death has shaken out the sands of thy glass.
Now around thee sports the whale,
And the porpoise snuffs the gale,
And the night-winds wake their wail,
As they pass.

The sea-grass round thy bier
Shall bend beneath the tide,
Nor tell the breakers near
Where thy manly limbs abide;
But the granite rock thy tombstone shall be.
Though the edges of thy grave
Are the combings of the wave —
Yet unheeded they shall rave
Over thee.

At the piping of all hands,
When the judgment signal's spread —
When the islands, and the lands,
And the seas give up their dead,
And the south and the north shall come;
When the sinner is dismayed,
And the just man is afraid,
Then heaven be thy aid,
Poor Tom.

THE DEEP

There's beauty in the deep:
The wave is bluer than the sky;
And though the lights shine bright on high,
More softly do the sea-gems glow
That sparkle in the depths below;
The rainbow's tints are only made
When on the waters they are laid,
And Sun and Moon most sweetly shine
Upon the ocean's level brine.
There's beauty in the deep.

There's music in the deep:
It is not in the surf's rough roar,
Nor in the whispering, shelly shore —
They are but earthly sounds, that tell
How little of the sea-nymph's shell,
That sends its loud, clear note abroad,
Or winds its softness through the flood,
Echoes through groves with coral gay,
And dies, on spongy banks, away.
There's music in the deep.

There's quiet in the deep:
Above, let tides and tempests rave,
And earth-born whirlwinds wake the wave;
Above, let care and fear contend
With sin and sorrow to the end:
Here, far beneath the tainted foam
That frets above our peaceful home,
We dream in joy, and wake in love,
Nor know the rage that yells above.
There's quiet in the deep.

EPITHALAMIUM

I saw two clouds at morning,
  Tinged with the rising sun,
And in the dawn they floated on,
  And mingled into one:
I thought that morning cloud was blest,
It moved so sweetly to the west.

I saw two summer currents
  Flow smoothly to their meeting,
And join their course, with silent force,
  In peace each other greeting:
Calm was their course through banks of
    green,
While dimpling eddies played between.

Such be your gentle motion,
  Till life's last pulse shall beat;
Like summer's beam, and summer's stream,
  Float on, in joy, to meet
A calmer sea, where storms shall cease —
A purer sky, where all is peace.

George Washington Doane

EVENING

Softly now the light of day
Fades upon my sight away;
Free from care, from labor free,
Lord, I would commune with Thee:

Thou, whose all-pervading eye,
  Naught escapes, without, within,
Pardon each infirmity,
  Open fault and secret sin.

Soon, for me, the light of day
Shall forever pass away;
Then, from sin and sorrow free,
Take me, Lord, to dwell with Thee:

Thou, who, sinless, yet hast known
  All of man's infirmity;
Then from Thine eternal throne,
  Jesus, look with pitying eye.

ROBIN REDBREAST

Sweet Robin, I have heard them say
That thou wert there upon the day
The Christ was crowned in cruel scorn
And bore away one bleeding thorn, —
That so the blush upon thy breast,
In shameful sorrow, was impressed;
And thence thy genial sympathy
With our redeemed humanity.

Sweet Robin, would that I might be
Bathed in my Saviour's blood, like thee;
Bear in my breast, whate'er the loss,
The bleeding blazon of the cross;
Live ever, with thy loving mind,
In fellowship with human kind;
And take my pattern still from thee,
In gentleness and constancy.

William Bourne Oliver Peabody[1]

LAMENT OF ANASTASIUS

It was but yesterday, my love, thy little
    heart beat high,
And I had scorned the warning voice that
    told me thou must die;
I saw thee move with active bound, with
    spirits light and free,
And infant grace and beauty gave their
    glorious charm to thee.

Upon the dewy field I saw thine early foot-
    steps fly,
Unfettered as the matin bird that cleaves
    the radiant sky;
And often as the sunrise gale blew back
    thy shining hair,
Thy cheek displayed the red-rose tinge
    that health had painted there.

[1] See Biographical Note, p. 814.

Then, withered as my heart had been, I
could not but rejoice
To hear upon the morning wind the music
of thy voice,
Now echoing in the careless laugh, now
melting down to tears:
'T was like the sounds I used to hear in
old and happier years.

Thanks for that memory to thee, my lovely
little boy!
'T is all remains of former bliss that care
cannot destroy;
I listened, as the mariner suspends the outbound oar
To taste the farewell gale that blows from
off his native shore.

I loved thee, and my heart was blessed; but
ere the day was spent,
I saw thy light and graceful form in drooping illness bent,
And shuddered as I cast a look upon the
fainting head,
For all the glow of health was gone, and
life was almost fled.

One glance upon thy marble brow made
known that hope was vain;
I knew the swiftly wasting lamp would
never light again;
Thy cheek was pale, thy snow-white lips
were gently thrown apart,
And life in every passing breath seemed
gushing from the heart.

And, when I could not keep the tear from
gathering in my eye,
Thy little hand pressed gently mine in token
of reply;
To ask one more exchange of love thy look
was upward cast,
And in that long and burning kiss thy
happy spirit passed.

I trusted I should not have lived to bid
farewell to thee,
And nature in my heart declares it ought
not so to be;
I hoped that thou within the grave my
weary head should lay,
And live beloved, when I was gone, for
many a happy day.

With trembling hand I vainly tried thy
dying eyes to close,
And how I envied in that hour thy calm
and deep repose!
For I was left alone on earth, with pain and
grief oppress'd;
And thou wert with the sainted, where the
weary are at rest.

Yes! I am left alone on earth; but I will
not repine
Because a spirit loved so well is earlier
blessed than mine:
My fate may darken as it will, I shall not
much deplore,
Since thou art where the ills of life can
never reach thee more.

Amos Bronson Alcott

CHANNING

CHANNING! my Mentor whilst my thought
was young,
And I the votary of fair liberty, —
How hung I then upon thy glowing tongue,
And thought of love and truth as one with
thee!
Thou wast the inspirer of a nobler life,
When I with error waged unequal strife,
And from its coils thy teaching set me free.
Be ye, his followers, to his leading true,
Nor privilege covet, nor the wider sway;
But hold right onward in his loftier way,
As best becomes, and is his rightful due.
If learning 's yours, — gifts God doth least
esteem, —
Beyond all gifts was his transcendent view;
O realize his Pentecostal dream!

EMERSON

MISFORTUNE to have lived not knowing
thee!
'T were not high living, nor to noblest end,
Who, dwelling near, learned not sincerity,
Rich friendship's ornament that still doth
lend

To life its consequence and propriety.
Thy fellowship was my culture, noble friend:
By the hand thou took'st me, and did'st condescend
To bring me straightway into thy fair guild;
And life-long hath it been high compliment
By that to have been known, and thy friend styled,
Given to rare thought and to good learning bent;
Whilst in my straits an angel on me smiled.
Permit me, then, thus honored, still to be
A scholar in thy university.

MARGARET FULLER

THOU, Sibyl rapt! whose sympathetic soul
Infused the myst'ries thy tongue failed to tell;
Though from thy lips the marvellous accents fell,
And weird wise meanings o'er the senses stole,
Through those rare cadences, with winsome spell;
Yet even in such refrainings of thy vôice
There struggled up a wailing undertone,
That spoke thee victim of the Sisters' choice, —
Charming all others, dwelling still alone.
They left thee thus disconsolate to roam,
And scorned thy dear, devoted life to spare.
Around the storm-tost vessel sinking there
The wild waves chant thy dirge and welcome home;
Survives alone thy sex's valiant plea,
And the great heart that loved the brave and free.

THOREAU

WHO nearer Nature's life would truly come
Must nearest come to him of whom I speak;
He all kinds knew, — the vocal and the dumb;
Masterful in genius was he, and unique,
Patient, sagacious, tender, frolicsome.
This Concord Pan would oft his whistle take,
And forth from wood and fen, field, hill, and lake,
Trooping around him in their several guise,
The shy inhabitants their haunts forsake:
Then he, like Æsop, man would satirize,
Hold up the image wild to clearest view
Of undiscerning manhood's puzzled eyes,
And mocking say, "Lo! mirrors here for you:
Be true as these, if ye would be more wise."

HAWTHORNE

ROMANCER, far more coy than that coy sex!
Perchance some stroke of magic thee befell,
Ere thy baronial keep the Muse did vex,
Nor grant deliverance from enchanted spell,
But tease thee all the while and sore perplex,
Till thou that wizard tale shouldst fairly tell,
Better than poets in thy own clear prose.
Painter of sin in its deep scarlet dyes,
Thy doomsday pencil Justice doth expose,
Hearing and judging at the dread assize;
New England's guilt blazoning before all eyes,
No other chronicler than thee she chose.
Magician deathless! dost thou vigil keep,
Whilst 'neath our pines thou feignest deathlike sleep?

BARTOL

POET of the Pulpit, whose full-chorded lyre
Startles the churches from their slumbers late,
Discoursing music, mixed with lofty ire
At wrangling factions in the restless state,
Till tingles with thy note each listening ear, —
Then household charities by the friendly fire
Of home, soothe all to fellowship and good cheer!
No sin escapes thy fervent eloquence,
Yet, touching with compassion the true word,
Thou leavest the trembling culprit's dark offence
To the mediation of his gracious Lord.
To noble thought and deep dost thou dispense
Due meed of praise, strict in thy just award.
Can other pulpits with this preacher cope?
I glory in thy genius, and take hope!

WENDELL PHILLIPS

PEOPLE'S Attorney, servant of the Right!
Pleader for all shades of the solar ray,
Complexions dusky, yellow, red, or white;
Who, in thy country's and thy time's despite,
Hast only questioned, What will Duty say?
And followed swiftly in her narrow way:
Tipped is thy tongue with golden eloquence,
All honeyed accents fall from off thy lips,—
Each eager listener his full measure sips,
Yet runs to waste the sparkling opulence,—
The scorn of bigots, and the worldling's flout.
If Time long held thy merit in suspense,
Hastening repentant now, with pen devout,
Impartial History dare not leave thee out.

GARRISON

FREEDOM'S first champion in our fettered land!
Nor politician nor base citizen
Could gibbet thee, nor silence, nor withstand.
Thy trenchant and emancipating pen
The patriot Lincoln snatched with steady hand,
Writing his name and thine on parchment white,
'Midst war's resistless and ensanguined flood;
Then held that proclamation high in sight
Before his fratricidal countrymen,—
"Freedom henceforth throughout the land for all,"—
And sealed the instrument with his own blood,
Bowing his mighty strength for slavery's fall;
Whilst thou, stanch friend of largest liberty,
Survived, — its ruin and our peace to see.

Theodore Dwight Woolsey

THE ECLIPSE OF FAITH

THE shapes that frowned before the eyes
  Of the early world have fled,
And all the life of earth and skies,
  Of streams and seas, is dead.

Forgotten is the Titan's fame,
  The dread Chimæra now
Is but a mild innocuous flame
  Upon a mountain's brow,
Around whose warmth its strawberry red
The arbutus hangs and goatherds tread.

And now has Typho spent his rage,
  The Sirens now no more
Entice the song-struck mariner
  To give his voyage o'er.
The sailor past Messina hies,
And scorns the den where Scylla lies.

Leda's twin sons no more are seen
  In battle's hottest press,
Nor shine the wind-tost waves between
  To seamen in distress.

The muse is but the poet's soul,
  That looked towards Helicon,
And for its living thought divine
  Raised up a mountain throne.

But ah! is nought save fable slain
  In this new realm of thought?
Or has the shaft Primeval Truth
  And Truth's great Author sought?

Yes, wisdom now is built on sense;
  We measure and we weigh,
We break and join, make rare and dense,
  And reason God away.

The wise have probed this wondrous world,
  And searched the stars, and find
All curious facts and laws revealed,
  But not Almighty mind.

From thinking dust we mould the spheres,
  And shape earth's wondrous frame:
If God had slept a million years,
  All things would be the same.

O give me back a world of life,
  Something to love and trust,
Something to quench my inward strife
  And lift me from the dust.

I cannot live with nature dead,
  Mid laws and causes blind;
Powerless on earth, or overhead,
  To trace the all-guiding mind;

Then boast that I have found the keys
  That time and space unlock,
That snatch from heaven its mysteries,
  Its fear from the earthquake shock.

Better the instinct of the brute
  That feels its God afar,
Than reason, to his praises mute,
  Talking with every star.

Better the thousand deities
  That swarmed in Greece of yore,
Than thought that scorns all mysteries
  And dares all depths to explore.

Better is childhood's thoughtless trust
  Than manhood's daring scorn;
The fear that creeps along the dust
  Than doubt in hearts forlorn.

And knowledge, if it cost so dear,
  If such be reason's day,
I 'll lose the pearl without a tear,
  And grope my star-lit way.

And be the toils of wisdom curst
  If such the meed we earn ;
If freezing pride and doubt are nurst,
  And faith forbid to burn.

Albert Gorton Greene

THE BARON'S LAST BANQUET

O'ER a low couch the setting sun had
  thrown its latest ray,
Where in his last strong agony a dying
  warrior lay,
The stern old Baron Rudiger, whose frame
  had ne'er been bent
By wasting pain, till time and toil its iron
  strength had spent.

"They come around me here, and say my
  days of life are o'er,
That I shall mount my noble steed and
  lead my band no more;
They come, and to my beard they dare to
  tell me now, that I,
Their own liege lord and master born, —
  that I, ha ! ha ! must die.

"And what is death ? I 've dared him oft
  before the Paynim spear, —
Think ye he 's entered at my gate, has
  come to seek me here ?
I 've met him, faced him, scorned him,
  when the fight was raging hot, —
I 'll try his might — I 'll brave his power;
  defy, and fear him not.

"Ho ! sound the tocsin from my tower, and
  fire the culverin, —
Bid each retainer arm with speed, — call
  every vassal in,
Up with my banner on the wall, — the banquet board prepare;
Throw wide the portal of my hall, and
  bring my armor there !"

An hundred hands were busy then — the
  banquet forth was spread —
And rung the heavy oaken floor with many
  a martial tread,
While from the rich, dark tracery along
  the vaulted wall,
Lights gleamed on harness, plume, and
  spear, o'er the proud old Gothic
  hall.

Fast hurrying through the outer gate the
  mailed retainers poured,
On through the portal's frowning arch, and
  thronged around the board.
While at its head, within his dark, carved
  oaken chair of state,
Armed cap-a-pie, stern Rudiger, with
  girded falchion, sate.

"Fill every beaker up, my men, pour forth
the cheering wine;
There 's life and strength in every drop, —
thanksgiving to the vine!
Are ye all there, my vassals true? — mine
eyes are waxing dim;
Fill round, my tried and fearless ones, each
goblet to the brim.

"You 're there, but yet I see ye not.
Draw forth each trusty sword
And let me hear your faithful steel clash
once around my board;
I hear it faintly: — Louder yet! — What
clogs my heavy breath?
Up all, and shout for Rudiger, 'Defiance
unto Death!'"

Bowl rang to bowl — steel clang to steel —
and rose a deafening cry
That made the torches flare around, and
shook the flags on high: —
"Ho! cravens, do ye fear him? — Slaves,
traitors! have ye flown?
Ho! cowards, have ye left me to meet him
here alone!

"But I defy him: — let him come!" Down
rang the massy cup,
While from its sheath the ready blade came
flashing half way up;
And with the black and heavy plumes
scarce trembling on his head,
There in his dark, carved oaken chair Old
Rudiger sat, — dead.

Edward Coate Pinkney

A HEALTH

I FILL this cup to one made up
Of loveliness alone,
A woman, of her gentle sex
The seeming paragon;
To whom the better elements
And kindly stars have given
A form so fair, that, like the air,
'T is less of earth than heaven.

Her every tone is music's own,
Like those of morning birds,
And something more than melody
Dwells ever in her words;
The coinage of her heart are they,
And from her lips each flows
As one may see the burdened bee
Forth issue from the rose.

Affections are as thoughts to her,
The measures of her hours;
Her feelings have the fragrancy,
The freshness of young flowers;
And lovely passions, changing oft,
So fill her, she appears
The image of themselves by turns, —
The idol of past years!

Of her bright face one glance will trace
A picture on the brain,
And of her voice in echoing hearts
A sound must long remain;
But memory, such as mine of her,
So very much endears,
When death is nigh my latest sigh
Will not be life's, but hers.

I fill this cup to one made up
Of loveliness alone,
A woman, of her gentle sex
The seeming paragon —
Her health! and would on earth there
stood
Some more of such a frame,
That life might be all poetry,
And weariness a name.

SONG

WE break the glass, whose sacred wine
To some beloved health we drain,
Lest future pledges, less divine,
Should e'er the hallowed toy profane;
And thus I broke a heart that poured
Its tide of feelings out for thee,
In draught, by after-times deplored,
Yet dear to memory.

But still the old, impassioned ways
And habits of my mind remain,

And still unhappy light displays
  Thine image chambered in my brain,
And still it looks as when the hours
  Went by like flights of singing birds,
Or that soft chain of spoken flowers
  And airy gems, — thy words.

A SERENADE

Look out upon the stars, my love,
  And shame them with thine eyes,
On which, than on the lights above,
  There hang more destinies.
Night's beauty is the harmony
  Of blending shades and light;
Then, lady, up, — look out, and be
  A sister to the night!

Sleep not! thine image wakes for aye
  Within my watching breast:
Sleep not! from her soft sleep should fly
  Who robs all hearts of rest.
Nay, lady, from thy slumbers break,
  And make this darkness gay
With looks, whose brightness well might make
  Of darker nights a day.

VOTIVE SONG

I burn no incense, hang no wreath,
  On this thine early tomb:
Such cannot cheer the place of death,
  But only mock its gloom.
Here odorous smoke and breathing flower
  No grateful influence shed;
They lose their perfume and their power,
  When offered to the dead.

And if, as is the Afghaun's creed,
  The spirit may return,
A disembodied sense to feed,
  On fragrance, near its urn, —
It is enough that she, whom thou
  Didst love in living years,
Sits desolate beside it now,
  And fall these heavy tears.

George Pope Morris

WOODMAN, SPARE THAT TREE!

Woodman, spare that tree!
  Touch not a single bough!
In youth it sheltered me,
  And I 'll protect it now.
'T was my forefather's hand
  That placed it near his cot;
There, woodman, let it stand,
  Thy axe shall harm it not.

That old familiar tree,
  Whose glory and renown
Are spread o'er land and sea —
  And wouldst thou hew it down?
Woodman, forbear thy stroke!
  Cut not its earth-bound ties;
Oh, spare that aged oak
  Now towering to the skies!

When but an idle boy,
  I sought its grateful shade;
In all their gushing joy
  Here, too, my sisters played.
My mother kissed me here;
  My father pressed my hand —
Forgive this foolish tear,
  But let that old oak stand.

My heart-strings round thee cling,
  Close as thy bark, old friend!
Here shall the wild-bird sing,
  And still thy branches bend.
Old tree! the storm still brave!
  And, woodman, leave the spot;
While I 've a hand to save,
  Thy axe shall harm it not.

WE WERE BOYS TOGETHER

We were boys together,
  And never can forget
The school-house near the heather,
  In childhood where we met;
The humble home to memory dear,
  Its sorrows and its joys;

Where woke the transient smile or tear,
  When you and I were boys.

We were youths together,
  And castles built in air,
Your heart was like a feather,
  And mine weighed down with care;
To you came wealth with manhood's prime,
  To me it brought alloys —
Foreshadowed in the primrose time,
  When you and I were boys.

We 're old men together:
  The friends we loved of yore,
With leaves of autumn weather,
  Are gone forevermore.
How blest to age the impulse given,
  The hope time ne'er destroys,
Which led our thoughts from earth to heaven
  When you and I were boys!

NEAR THE LAKE

NEAR the lake where drooped the willow,
    Long time ago!
Where the rock threw back the billow,
    Brighter than snow,
Dwelt a maid, beloved and cherished
    By high and low;
But with autumn's leaf she perished,
    Long time ago!

Rock and tree and flowing water,
    Long time ago!
Bee and bird and blossom taught her
    Love's spell to know.
While to my fond words she listened,
    Murmuring low,
Tenderly her dove-eyes glistened,
    Long time ago!

Mingled were our hearts forever,
    Long time ago!
Can I now forget her? — Never!
    No — lost one — no!
To her grave these tears are given,
    Ever to flow:
She 's the star I missed from heaven,
    Long time ago!

MY MOTHER'S BIBLE

THIS book is all that 's left me now!
  Tears will unbidden start, —
With faltering lip and throbbing brow
  I press it to my heart.
For many generations past,
  Here is our family tree;
My mother's hands this Bible clasped,
  She, dying, gave it me.

Ah! well do I remember those
  Whose names these records bear;
Who round the hearth-stone used to close
  After the evening prayer,
And speak of what these pages said,
  In tones my heart would thrill!
Though they are with the silent dead,
  Here are they living still.

My father read this holy book
  To brothers, sisters dear;
How calm was my poor mother's look
  Who leaned God's word to hear!
Her angel face — I see it yet!
  What vivid memories come!
Again that little group is met
  Within the halls of home!

Thou truest friend man ever knew,
  Thy constancy I 've tried;
Where all were false I found thee true,
  My counsellor and guide.
The mines of earth no treasures give
  That could this volume buy:
In teaching me the way to live,
  It taught me how to die.

WHERE HUDSON'S WAVE

WHERE Hudson's wave o'er silvery sands
  Winds through the hills afar,
Old Cronest like a monarch stands,
  Crowned with a single star!
And there, amid the billowy swells
  Of rock-ribbed, cloud-capped earth,
My fair and gentle Ida dwells,
  A nymph of mountain-birth.

The snow-flake that the cliff receives,
The diamonds of the showers,
Spring's tender blossoms, buds, and leaves,
The sisterhood of flowers,
Morn's early beam, eve's balmy breeze,
Her purity define;
Yet Ida 's dearer far than these
To this fond breast of mine.

My heart is on the hills. The shades
Of night are on my brow:
Ye pleasant haunts and quiet glades,
My soul is with you now!
I bless the star-crowned highlands where
My Ida's footsteps roam:
O for a falcon's wing to bear
Me onward to my home!

JEANNIE MARSH

Jeannie Marsh of Cherry Valley,
At whose call the muses rally;
Of all the nine none so divine
As Jeannie Marsh of Cherry Valley.
She minds me of her native scenes,
Where she was born among the cherries;
Of peaches, plums, and nectarines,
Pears, apricots, and ripe strawberries.

Jeannie Marsh of Cherry Valley,
In whose name the muses rally;
Of all the nine none so divine
As Jeannie Marsh of Cherry Valley.
A sylvan nymph of queenly grace,
A goddess she in form and feature;
The sweet expression of the place,
A dimple in the smile of nature.

George Denison Prentice

MEMORIES

Once more, once more, my Mary dear,
I sit by that lone stream,
Where first within thy timid ear
I breathed love's burning dream.
The birds we loved still tell their tale
Of music, on each spray,
And still the wild-rose decks the vale —
But thou art far away.

In vain thy vanished form I seek,
By wood and stream and dell,
And tears of anguish bathe my cheek
Where tears of rapture fell;
And yet beneath these wild-wood bowers
Dear thoughts my soul employ,
For in the memories of past hours
There is a mournful joy.

Upon the air thy gentle words
Around me seemed to thrill,
Like sounds upon the wind-harp's chords
When all the winds are still,
Or like the low and soul-like swell
Of that wild spirit-tone,
Which haunts the hollow of the bell
When its sad chime is done.

I seem to hear thee speak my name
In sweet low murmurs now;
I seem to feel thy breath of flame
Upon my cheek and brow;
On my cold lips I feel thy kiss,
Thy heart to mine is laid —
Alas, that such a dream of bliss
Like other dreams must fade!

NEW ENGLAND

FOR A CELEBRATION IN KENTUCKY OF THE LANDING OF THE PILGRIMS

Clime of the brave! the high heart's home,
Laved by the wild and stormy sea!
Thy children, in this far-off land,
Devote to-day their hearts to thee;
Our thoughts, despite of space and time,
To-day are in our native clime,
Where passed our sinless years, and where
Our infant heads first bowed in prayer.

Stern land! we love thy woods and rocks,
Thy rushing streams, thy winter glooms,
And Memory, like a pilgrim gray,
Kneels at thy temples and thy tombs:

The thoughts of these, where'er we dwell,
Come o'er us like a holy spell,
A star to light our path of tears,
A rainbow on the sky of years.

Above thy cold and rocky breast
The tempest sweeps, the night-wind wails,
But Virtue, Peace, and Love, like birds
Are nestled mid thy hills and vales;
And Glory, o'er each plain and glen,
Walks with thy free and iron men,
And lights her sacred beacon still
On Bennington and Bunker Hill.

Additional Selections

(VARIOUS POEMS BELONGING TO THIS DIVISION)

HOME, SWEET HOME!

MID pleasures and palaces though we may roam,
Be it ever so humble, there 's no place like home;
A charm from the sky seems to hallow us there,
Which, seek through the world, is ne'er met with elsewhere.
Home, Home, sweet, sweet Home!
There 's no place like Home! there 's no place like Home!

An exile from home, splendor dazzles in vain;
O, give me my lowly thatched cottage again!
The birds singing gayly, that came at my call, —
Give me them, — and the peace of mind, dearer than all!
Home, Home, sweet, sweet Home!
There 's no place like Home! there 's no place like Home!

How sweet 't is to sit 'neath a fond father's smile,
And the cares of a mother to soothe and beguile!
Let others delight mid new pleasures to roam,
But give me, oh, give me, the pleasures of home!
Home! Home! sweet, sweet Home!
There 's no place like Home! there 's no place like Home!

To thee I 'll return, overburdened with care;
The heart's dearest solace will smile on me there;
No more from that cottage again will I roam;
Be it ever so humble, there 's no place like home.
Home! Home! sweet, sweet Home!
There 's no place like Home! there 's no place like Home!

JOHN HOWARD PAYNE

EXHORTATION TO PRAYER

NOT on a prayerless bed, not on a prayerless bed
Compose thy weary limbs to rest;
For they alone are blest
With balmy sleep
Whom angels keep;
Nor, though by care oppress,
Or anxious sorrow,
Or thought in many a coil perplexed
For coming morrow,
Lay not thy head
On prayerless bed.

For who can tell, when sleep thine eyes shall close,
That earthly cares and woes
To thee may e'er return?
Arouse, my soul!
Slumber control,
And let thy lamp burn brightly;
So shall thine eyes discern
Things pure and sightly;
Taught by the Spirit, learn

Never on prayerless bed
To lay thine unblest head.

Hast thou no pining want, or wish, or care,
That calls for holy prayer?
Has thy day been so bright
That in its flight
There is no trace of sorrow?
And thou art sure to-morrow
Will be like this, and more
Abundant? Dost thou yet lay up thy store
And still make plans for more?
Thou fool! this very night
Thy soul may wing its flight.

Hast thou no being than myself more dear,
That ploughs the ocean deep,
And when storms sweep
The wintry, lowering sky,
For whom thou wak'st and weepest?
Oh, when thy pangs are deepest,
Seek then the covenant ark of prayer;
For He that slumbereth not is there —
His ear is open to thy cry.
Oh, then, on prayerless bed
Lay not thy thoughtless head.

Arouse thee, weary soul, nor yield to slumber,
Till in communion blest
With the elect ye rest —
Those souls of countless number;
And with them raise
The note of praise,
Reaching from earth to heaven —
Chosen, redeemed, forgiven;
So lay thy happy head,
Prayer-crowned, on blessed bed.

MARGARET MERCER

FORGIVENESS OF SINS A JOY UNKNOWN TO ANGELS

TREMBLING before thine awful throne,
O Lord! in dust my sins I own:
Justice and Mercy for my life
Contend! — Oh, smile, and heal the strife!

The Saviour smiles! Upon my soul
New tides of hope tumultuous roll:
His voice proclaims my pardon found,
Seraphic transport wings the sound!

Earth has a joy unknown in heaven, —
The new-born peace of sin forgiven!
Tears of such pure and deep delight,
Ye angels! never dimmed your sight.

Ye saw of old on chaos rise
The beauteous pillars of the skies;
Ye know where morn exulting springs,
And evening folds her drooping wings.

Bright heralds of the Eternal Will,
Abroad his errands ye fulfil;
Or, throned in floods of beamy day,
Symphonious in his presence play.

Loud is the song, — the heavenly plain
Is shaken with the choral strain;
And dying echoes, floating far,
Draw music from each chiming star.

But I amid your choirs shall shine,
And all your knowledge shall be mine;
Ye on your harps must lean to hear
A secret chord that mine will bear!

AUGUSTUS LUCAS HILLHOUSE

THE CROSSED SWORDS[1]

SWORDS crossed, — but not in strife!
The chiefs who drew them, parted by the space
Of two proud countries' quarrel, face to face
Ne'er stood for death or life.

Swords crossed that never met
While nerve was in the hands that wielded them;
Hands better destined a fair family stem
On these free shores to set.

Kept crossed by gentlest bands!
Emblems no more of battle, but of peace;
And proof how loves can grow and wars can cease,
Their once stern symbol stands.

It smiled first on the array
Of marshalled books and friendliest companies;
And here a history among histories,
It still shall smile for aye.

[1] See BIOGRAPHICAL NOTE, p. 793.

See that thou memory keep
Of him the firm commander; and that other,
The stainless judge; and him our peerless brother, —
All fallen now asleep.

Yet more: a lesson teach,
To cheer the patriot-soldier in his course,
That Right shall triumph still o'er insolent Force:
That be your silent speech.

Oh, be prophetic too!
And may those nations twain, as sign and seal
Of endless amity, hang up their steel
As we these weapons do!

The archives of the Past,
So smeared with blots of hate and bloody wrong,
Pining for peace, and sick to wait so long,
Hail this meek cross at last.

NATHANIEL LANGDON FROTHINGHAM

LAKE SUPERIOR

"FATHER of lakes!" thy waters bend
Beyond the eagle's utmost view,
When, throned in heaven, he sees thee send
Back to the sky its world of blue.

Boundless and deep, the forests weave
Their twilight shade thy borders o'er,
And threatening cliffs, like giants, heave
Their rugged forms along thy shore.

Pale silence, mid thy hollow caves,
With listening ear, in sadness broods;
Or startled echo, o'er thy waves,
Sends the hoarse wolf-notes of thy woods.

Nor can the light canoes, that glide
Across thy breast like things of air,
Chase from thy lone and level tide
The spell of stillness deepening there.

Yet round this waste of wood and wave,
Unheard, unseen, a spirit lives,
That, breathing o'er each rock and cave,
To all a wild, strange aspect gives.

The thunder-riven oak, that flings
Its grisly arms athwart the sky,
A sudden, startling image brings
To the lone traveller's kindled eye.

The gnarled and braided boughs, that show
Their dim forms in the forest shade,
Like wrestling serpents seem, and throw
Fantastic horrors through the glade.

The very echoes round this shore
Have caught a strange and gibbering tone;
For they have told the war-whoop o'er,
Till the wild chorus is their own.

Wave of the wilderness, adieu!
Adieu, ye rocks, ye wilds, ye woods!
Roll on, thou element of blue,
And fill these awful solitudes!

Thou hast no tale to tell of man;
God is thy theme. Ye sounding caves,
Whisper of him whose mighty plan
Deems as a bubble all your waves!

SAMUEL GRISWOLD GOODRICH

THE HOUR OF PEACEFUL REST

THERE is an hour of peaceful rest
To mourning wanderers given;
There is a joy for souls distrest,
A balm for every wounded breast,
'T is found alone in heaven.

There is a soft, a downy bed,
Far from these shades of even —
A couch for weary mortals spread,
Where they may rest the aching head,
And find repose, in heaven.

There is a home for weary souls
By sin and sorrow driven;
When tossed on life's tempestuous shoals,
Where storms arise, and ocean rolls,
And all is drear but heaven.

There faith lifts up her cheerful eye,
To brighter prospects given;
And views the tempest passing by,
The evening shadows quickly fly,
And all serene in heaven.

There fragrant flowers immortal bloom,
And joys supreme are given;
There rays divine disperse the gloom:
Beyond the confines of the tomb
Appears the dawn of heaven.

WILLIAM BINGHAM TAPPAN

SONG OF THE ELFIN STEERSMAN

ONE elf, I trow, is diving now
  For the small pearl; and one,
The honey-bee for his bag he
  Goes chasing in the sun;
And one, the knave, has pilfered from
  The nautilus his boat,
And takes his idle pastime where
  The water-lilies float.

And some the mote, for the gold of his coat,
  By the light of the will-o'-wisp follow;
And others, they trip where the alders dip
  Their leaves in the watery hollow;
And one is with the firefly's lamp
  Lighting his love to bed:
Sprites, away! elf and fay,
  And see them hither sped.

Haste! hither whip them with this end
  Of spider's web — anon
The ghost will have fled to his grave-bed,
  And the bat winked in the sun.
Haste! for the ship, till the moon dip
  Her horn, I did but borrow;
And crowing cocks are fairy clocks,
  That mind us of to-morrow.

The summer moon will soon go down,
  And the day-star dim her horn,
O blow, then, blow, till not a wave
  Leap from the deep unshorn!
Blow, sweep their white tops into mist,
  As merrily we roam,
Till the wide sea one bright sheet be,
  One sheet of fire and foam.

Blow, till the sea a bubble be,
  And toss it to the sky, —
Till the sands we tread of the ocean-bed,
  As the summer fountains dry.
The upper shelves are ours, my elves,
  Are ours, and soon the nether
With sea-flowers we shall sprinkled see,
  And pearls like dew-drops gather.

The summer moon will soon go down,
  And then our course is up;
Our frigate then the cockle-shell,
  Our boat the bean-flower cup.
Sprites away! elf and fay,
  From thicket, lake, and hollow;
The blind bat, look! flits to his nook,
  And we must quickly follow.

Ha! here they come, skimming the foam,
  A gallant crew. But list!
I hear the crow of the cock — O blow,
  Till the sea-foam drift like mist.
Fairies, haste! flood and blast
  Quickly bring, and stay
The moon's horn — look! to his nook
  The blind bat flits — away!

GEORGE HILL

THE DAUGHTER OF MENDOZA

O LEND to me, sweet nightingale,
  Your music by the fountain,
And lend to me your cadences,
  O river of the mountain!
That I may sing my gay brunette,
A diamond spark in coral set,
Gem for a prince's coronet —
  The daughter of Mendoza.

How brilliant is the morning star,
  The evening star how tender, —
The light of both is in her eyes,
  Their softness and their splendor.
But for the lash that shades their light
They were too dazzling for the sight,
And when she shuts them, all is night —
  The daughter of Mendoza.

O ever bright and beauteous one,
  Bewildering and beguiling,
The lute is in thy silvery tones,
  The rainbow in thy smiling;
And thine is, too, o'er hill and dell,
The bounding of the young gazelle,
The arrow's flight and ocean's swell —
  Sweet daughter of Mendoza!

What though, perchance, we no more
    meet, —
  What though too soon we sever?
Thy form will float like emerald light
  Before my vision ever.
For who can see and then forget
The glories of my gay brunette —
Thou art too bright a star to set,
  Sweet daughter of Mendoza!

MIRABEAU BONAPARTE LAMAR

THE GREEN ISLE OF LOVERS

They say that, afar in the land of the west,
Where the bright golden sun sinks in glory to rest,
Mid ferns where the hunter ne'er ventured to tread,
A fair lake unruffled and sparkling is spread;
Where, lost in his course, the rapt Indian discovers,
In distance seen dimly, the green Isle of Lovers.

There verdure fades never; immortal in bloom,
Soft waves the magnolia its groves of perfume;
And low bends the branch with rich fruitage depressed,
All glowing like gems in the crowns of the east;
There the bright eye of nature in mild glory hovers;
'T is the land of the sunbeam, — the green Isle of Lovers!

Sweet strains wildly float on the breezes that kiss
The calm-flowing lake round that region of bliss
Where, wreathing their garlands of amaranth, fair choirs
Glad measures still weave to the sound that inspires
The dance and the revel, mid forests that cover
On high with their shade the green Isle of the Lover.

But fierce as the snake, with his eyeballs of fire,
When his scales are all brilliant and glowing with ire,
Are the warriors to all save the maids of their isle,
Whose law is their will, and whose life is their smile;
From beauty there valor and strength are not rovers,
And peace reigns supreme in the green Isle of Lovers.

And he who has sought to set foot on its shore,
In mazes perplexed, has beheld it no more;
It fleets on the vision, deluding the view,
Its banks still retire as the hunters pursue;
O! who in this vain world of woe shall discover
The home undisturbed, the green Isle of the Lover!

ROBERT CHARLES SANDS

"THE LONELY BUGLE GRIEVES"[1]

FROM AN "ODE ON THE CELEBRATION OF THE BATTLE OF BUNKER HILL, JUNE 17, 1825"

The trump hath blown,
And now upon that reeking hill
Slaughter rides screaming on the vengeful ball;
While with terrific signal shrill,
The vultures, from their bloody eyries flown,
Hang o'er them like a pall.
Now deeper roll the maddening drums,
And the mingling host like ocean heaves:
While from the midst a horrid wailing comes,
And high above the fight the lonely bugle grieves!

GRENVILLE MELLEN

THE WORLD I AM PASSING THROUGH

Few, in the days of early youth,
Trusted like me in love and truth.
I 've learned sad lessons from the years;
But slowly, and with many tears;
For God made me to kindly view
The world that I was passing through.

How little did I once believe
That friendly tones could e'er deceive!
That kindness, and forbearance long,
Might meet ingratitude and wrong!
I could not help but kindly view
The world that I was passing through.

[1] See page 505.

And though I 've learned some souls are
base,
I would not, therefore, hate the race;
I still would bless my fellow men,
And trust them, though deceived again.
God help me still to kindly view
The world that I am passing through!

Through weary conflicts I have passed,
And struggled into rest at last;
Such rest as when the rack has broke
A joint, or nerve, at every stroke.
The wish survives to kindly view
The world that I am passing through.

From all that fate has brought to me
I strive to learn humility,
And trust in Him who rules above,
Whose universal law is love.
Thus only can I kindly view
The world that I am passing through.

When I approach the setting sun,
And feel my journey nearly done,
May earth be veiled in genial light,
And her last smile to me seem bright!
Help me till then to kindly view
The world that I am passing through!

And all who tempt a trusting heart
From faith and hope to drift apart, —
May they themselves be spared the pain
Of losing power to trust again!
God help us all to kindly view
The world that we are passing through!

LYDIA MARIA CHILD

EVENING HYMN

SLOWLY by God's hand unfurled,
Down around the weary world
Falls the darkness; oh, how still
Is the working of Thy will!

Mighty Maker! Here am I, —
Work in me as silently,
Veil the day's distracting sights,
Show me heaven's eternal lights.

From the darkened sky come forth
Countless stars, a wondrous birth!
So may gleams of glory dart
Through the dim abyss, my heart;

Living worlds to view be brought
In the boundless realms of thought,
High and infinite desires,
Burning like those upper fires.

Holy truth, eternal right,
Let them break upon my sight,
Let them shine unclouded, still,
And with light my being fill.

Thou art there. Oh, let me know,
Thou art here within me too;
Be the perfect peace of God
Here as there now shed abroad.

May my soul attunëd be
To that perfect harmony,
Which, beyond the power of sound,
Fills the universe around.

WILLIAM HENRY FURNESS

DIVISION II

(EMERSON, LONGFELLOW, WHITTIER, POE, HOLMES, AND OTHERS)

Ralph Waldo Emerson

EACH AND ALL

LITTLE thinks, in the field, yon red-cloaked
clown
Of thee from the hill-top looking down;
The heifer that lows in the upland farm,
Far-heard, lows not thine ear to charm;
The sexton, tolling his bell at noon,
Deems not that great Napoleon
Stops his horse, and lists with delight,
Whilst his files sweep round yon Alpine
height;
Nor knowest thou what argument
Thy life to thy neighbor's creed has lent.

All are needed by each one;
Nothing is fair or good alone.
I thought the sparrow's note from heaven,
Singing at dawn on the alder bough;
I brought him home, in his nest, at even;
He sings the song, but it cheers not now,
For I did not bring home the river and sky;
He sang to my ear, — they sang to my eye.
The delicate shells lay on the shore;
The bubbles of the latest wave
Fresh pearls to their enamel gave,
And the bellowing of the savage sea
Greeted their safe escape to me.
I wiped away the weeds and foam,
I fetched my sea-born treasures home;
But the poor, unsightly, noisome things
Had left their beauty on the shore
With the sun and the sand and the wild uproar.
The lover watched his graceful maid,
As mid the virgin train she strayed,
Nor knew her beauty's best attire
Was woven still by the snow-white choir.
At last she came to his hermitage,
Like the bird from the woodlands to the cage;
The gay enchantment was undone,
A gentle wife, but fairy none.
Then I said, "I covet truth;
Beauty is unripe childhood's cheat;
I leave it behind with the games of youth:"
As I spoke, beneath my feet
The ground-pine curled its pretty wreath,
Running over the club-moss burrs;
I inhaled the violet's breath;
Around me stood the oaks and firs;
Pine-cones and acorns lay on the ground;
Over me soared the eternal sky,
Full of light and of deity;
Again I saw, again I heard,
The rolling river, the morning bird;
Beauty through my senses stole;
I yielded myself to the perfect whole.

THE PROBLEM

I LIKE a church; I like a cowl;
I love a prophet of the soul;
And on my heart monastic aisles
Fall like sweet strains, or pensive smiles:
Yet not for all his faith can see
Would I that cowlëd churchman be.
Why should the vest on him allure,
Which I could not on me endure?

Not from a vain or shallow thought
His awful Jove young Phidias brought;
Never from lips of cunning fell
The thrilling Delphic oracle;
Out from the heart of nature rolled
The burdens of the Bible old;
The litanies of nations came,
Like the volcano's tongue of flame,
Up from the burning core below, —
The canticles of love and woe:
The hand that rounded Peter's dome
And groined the aisles of Christian Rome
Wrought in a sad sincerity;
Himself from God he could not free;
He builded better than he knew;
The conscious stone to beauty grew.

Knowst thou what wove yon woodbird's nest
Of leaves and feathers from her breast?
Or how the fish outbuilt her shell,
Painting with morn each annual cell?
Or how the sacred pine-tree adds
To her old leaves new myriads?
Such and so grew these holy piles,
Whilst love and terror laid the tiles.
Earth proudly wears the Parthenon,
As the best gem upon her zone,
And Morning opes with haste her lids
To gaze upon the Pyramids;
O'er England's abbeys bends the sky,
As on its friends, with kindred eye;
For out of Thought's interior sphere
These wonders rose to upper air;
And Nature gladly gave them place,
Adopted them into her race,
And granted them an equal date
With Andes and with Ararat.

These temples grew as grows the grass;
Art might obey, but not surpass.
The passive Master lent his hand
To the vast soul that o'er him planned;
And the same power that reared the shrine
Bestrode the tribes that knelt within.
Ever the fiery Pentecost
Girds with one flame the countless host,
Trances the heart through chanting choirs,
And through the priest the mind inspires.
The word unto the prophet spoken
Was writ on tables yet unbroken;
The word by seers or sibyls told,

In groves of oak, or fanes of gold,
Still floats upon the morning wind,
Still whispers to the willing mind.
One accent of the Holy Ghost
The heedless world hath never lost.
I know what say the fathers wise, —
The Book itself before me lies,
Old Chrysostom, best Augustine,
And he who blent both in his line,
The younger Golden Lips or mines,
Taylor, the Shakespeare of divines.
His words are music in my ear,
I see his cowlëd portrait dear;
And yet, for all his faith could see,
I would not the good bishop be.

THE RHODORA

ON BEING ASKED WHENCE IS THE FLOWER

In May, when sea-winds pierced our solitudes,
I found the fresh Rhodora in the woods,
Spreading its leafless blooms in a damp nook,
To please the desert and the sluggish brook.
The purple petals, fallen in the pool,
Made the black water with their beauty gay;
Here might the red-bird come his plumes to cool,
And court the flower that cheapens his array.
Rhodora! if the sages ask thee why
This charm is wasted on the earth and sky,
Tell them, dear, that if eyes were made for seeing,
Then Beauty is its own excuse for being:
Why thou wert there, O rival of the rose!
I never thought to ask, I never knew:
But, in my simple ignorance, suppose
The self-same Power that brought me there brought you.

THE HUMBLE-BEE

Burly, dozing humble-bee,
Where thou art is clime for me.
Let them sail for Porto Rique,
Far-off heats through seas to seek;
I will follow thee alone,
Thou animated torrid-zone!
Zigzag steerer, desert cheerer,
Let me chase thy waving lines;
Keep me nearer, me thy hearer,
Singing over shrubs and vines.

Insect lover of the sun,
Joy of thy dominion!
Sailor of the atmosphere;
Swimmer through the waves of air;
Voyager of light and noon;
Epicurean of June;
Wait, I prithee, till I come
Within earshot of thy hum, —
All without is martyrdom.

When the south wind, in May days,
With a net of shining haze
Silvers the horizon wall,
And with softness touching all,
Tints the human countenance
With the color of romance,
And infusing subtle heats,
Turns the sod to violets,
Thou, in sunny solitudes,
Rover of the underwoods,
The green silence dost displace
With thy mellow, breezy bass.

Hot midsummer's petted crone,
Sweet to me thy drowsy tone
Tells of countless sunny hours,
Long days, and solid banks of flowers;
Of gulfs of sweetness without bound
In Indian wildernesses found;
Of Syrian peace, immortal leisure,
Firmest cheer, and bird-like pleasure.

Aught unsavory or unclean
Hath my insect never seen;
But violets and bilberry bells,
Maple-sap and daffodels,
Grass with green flag half-mast high,
Succory to match the sky,
Columbine with horn of honey,
Scented fern and agrimony,
Clover, catchfly, adder's-tongue
And brier-roses, dwelt among;
All beside was unknown waste,
All was picture as he passed.

Wiser far than human seer,
Yellow-breeched philosopher
Seeing only what is fair,
Sipping only what is sweet,
Thou dost mock at fate and care,

Leave the chaff and take the wheat.
When the fierce northwestern blast
Cools sea and land so far and fast,
Thou already slumberest deep;
Woe and want thou canst outsleep;
Want and woe, which torture us,
Thy sleep makes ridiculous.

THE SNOW-STORM

ANNOUNCED by all the trumpets of the sky,
Arrives the snow, and, driving o'er the fields,
Seems nowhere to alight: the whited air
Hides hills and woods, the river, and the heaven,
And veils the farm-house at the garden's end.
The sled and traveller stopped, the courier's feet
Delayed, all friends shut out, the house-mates sit
Around the radiant fireplace, enclosed
In a tumultuous privacy of storm.

Come see the north wind's masonry.
Out of an unseen quarry evermore
Furnished with tile, the fierce artificer
Curves his white bastions with projected roof
Round every windward stake, or tree, or door.
Speeding, the myriad-handed, his wild work
So fanciful, so savage, naught cares he
For number or proportion. Mockingly,
On coop or kennel he hangs Parian wreaths;
A swan-like form invests the hidden thorn;
Fills up the farmer's lane from wall to wall,
Maugre the farmer's sighs; and at the gate
A tapering turret overtops the work.
And when his hours are numbered, and the world
Is all his own, retiring, as he were not,
Leaves, when the sun appears, astonished Art
To mimic in slow structures, stone by stone,
Built in an age, the mad wind's night-work,
The frolic architecture of the snow.

FORERUNNERS

LONG I followed happy guides,
I could never reach their sides;
Their step is forth, and, ere the day
Breaks up their leaguer, and aw-
Keen my sense, my heart was young,
Right good-will my sinews strung,
But no speed of mine avails
To hunt upon their shining trails.
On and away, their hasting feet
Make the morning proud and sweet;
Flowers they strew, — I catch the scent;
Or tone of silver instrument
Leaves on the wind melodious trace;
Yet I could never see their face.
On eastern hills I see their smokes,
Mixed with mist by distant lochs.
I met many travellers
Who the road had surely kept;
They saw not my fine revellers, —
These had crossed them while they slept.
Some had heard their fair report,
In the country or the court.
Fleetest couriers alive
Never yet could once arrive,
As they went or they returned,
At the house where these sojourned.
Sometimes their strong speed they slacken,
Though they are not overtaken;
In sleep their jubilant troop is near, —
I tuneful voices overhear;
It may be in wood or waste, —
At unawares 't is come and past.
Their near camp my spirit knows
By signs gracious as rainbows.
I thenceforward and long after,
Listen for their harp-like laughter
And carry in my heart, for days,
Peace that hallows rudest ways.

BRAHMA

IF the red slayer think he slays,
Or if the slain think he is slain,
They know not well the subtle ways
I keep, and pass, and turn again.

Far or forgot to me is near;
Shadow and sunlight are the same;
The vanished gods to me appear;
And one to me are shame and fame.

They reckon ill who leave me out;
When me they fly, I am the wings;
I am the doubter and the doubt,
And I the hymn the Brahmin sings.

The strong gods pine for my abode,
And pine in vain the sacred Seven;

But thou, meek lover of the good!
Find me, and turn thy back on heaven.

FORBEARANCE

Hast thou named all the birds without a gun?
Loved the wood-rose, and left it on its stalk?
At rich men's tables eaten bread and pulse?
Unarmed, faced danger with a heart of trust?
And loved so well a high behavior,
In man or maid, that thou from speech refrained,
Nobility more nobly to repay?
O, be my friend, and teach me to be thine!

CHARACTER

The sun set, but set not his hope:
Stars rose; his faith was earlier up:
Fixed on the enormous galaxy,
Deeper and older seemed his eye;
And matched his sufferance sublime
The taciturnity of time.
He spoke, and words more soft than rain
Brought the Age of Gold again:
His action won such reverence sweet
As hid all measure of the feat.

MERLIN

Thy trivial harp will never please
Or fill my craving ear;
Its chords should ring as blows the breeze,
Free, peremptory, clear.
No jingling serenader's art,
Nor tinkle of piano strings,
Can make the wild blood start
In its mystic springs.
The kingly bard
Must smite the chords rudely and hard,
As with hammer or with mace;
That they may render back
Artful thunder, which conveys
Secrets of the solar track,
Sparks of the supersolar blaze.
Merlin's blows are strokes of fate,
Chiming with the forest tone,
When boughs buffet boughs in the wood;
Chiming with the gasp and moan
Of the ice-imprisoned flood;
With the pulse of manly hearts;
With the voice of orators;
With the din of city arts;
With the cannonade of wars;
With the marches of the brave;
And prayers of might from martyrs cave.

Great is the art,
Great be the manners, of the bard.
He shall not his brain encumber
With the coil of rhythm and number;
But, leaving rule and pale forethought,
He shall aye climb
For his rhyme.
"Pass in, pass in," the angels say,
"Into the upper doors,
Nor count compartments of the floors,
But mount to paradise
By the stairway of surprise."

Blameless master of the games,
King of sport that never shames,
He shall daily joy dispense
Hid in song's sweet influence.
Forms more cheerly live and go,
What time the subtle mind
Sings aloud the tune whereto
Their pulses beat,
And march their feet,
And their members are combined.

By Sybarites beguiled,
He shall no task decline;
Merlin's mighty line
Extremes of nature reconciled,
Bereaved a tyrant of his will,
And made the lion mild.
Songs can the tempest still,
Scattered on the stormy air,
Mould the year to fair increase,
And bring in poetic peace.

He shall not seek to weave,
In weak, unhappy times,
Efficacious rhymes;
Wait his returning strength.
Bird that from the nadir's floor
To the zenith's top can soar, —
The soaring orbit of the muse exceeds that journey's length.
Nor profane affect to hit
Or compass that, by meddling wit,
Which only the propitious mind
Publishes when 't is inclined.

There are open hours
When the God's will sallies free,
And the dull idiot might see
The flowing fortunes of a thousand years;
Sudden, at unawares,
Self-moved, fly-to the doors,
Nor sword of angels could reveal
What they conceal.

FROM "WOODNOTES"

"THE HEART OF ALL THE SCENE"

'T WAS one of the charmëd days
When the genius of God doth flow,
The wind may alter twenty ways,
A tempest cannot blow;
It may blow north, it still is warm;
Or south, it still is clear;
Or east, it smells like a clover-farm;
Or west, no thunder fear.
The musing peasant lowly great
Beside the forest water sate;
The rope-like pineroots crosswise grown
Composed the network of his throne;
The wide lake, edged with sand and grass,
Was burnished to a floor of glass,
Painted with shadows green and proud
Of the tree and of the cloud.
He was the heart of all the scene;
On him the sun looked more serene;
To hill and cloud his face was known,—
It seemed the likeness of their own;
They knew by secret sympathy
The public child of earth and sky.
"You ask," he said, "what guide
Me through trackless thickets led,
Through thick-stemmed woodlands rough and wide.
I found the water's bed.
The watercourses were my guide;
I travelled grateful by their side,
Or through their channel dry;
They led me through the thicket damp,
Through brake and fern, the beavers' camp,
Through beds of granite cut my road,
And their resistless friendship showed:
The falling waters led me,
The foodful waters fed me,
And brought me to the lowest land,
Unerring to the ocean sand.
The moss upon the forest bark
Was pole-star when the night was dark;
The purple berries in the wood
Supplied me necessary food;
For Nature ever faithful is
To such as trust her faithfulness.
When the forest shall mislead me,
When the night and morning lie,
When sea and land refuse to feed me,
'T will be time enough to die;
Then will yet my mother yield
A pillow in her greenest field,
Nor the June flowers scorn to cover
The clay of their departed lover."

"THE UNDERSONG"

HEED the old oracles,
Ponder my spells;
Song wakes in my pinnacles
When the wind swells.
Soundeth the prophetic wind,
The shadows shake on the rock behind,
And the countless leaves of the pine are strings
Tuned to the lay the wood-god sings.
Hearken! Hearken!
If thou wouldst know the mystic song
Chanted when the sphere was young.
Aloft, abroad, the pæan swells;
O wise man! hear'st thou half it tells?
O wise man! hear'st thou the least part?
'T is the chronicle of art.
To the open air it sings
Sweet the genesis of things,
Of tendency through endless ages,
Of star-dust, and star-pilgrimages,
Of rounded worlds, of space and time,
Of the old flood's subsiding slime,
Of chemic matter, force and form,
Of poles and powers, cold, wet and warm:
The rushing metamorphosis
Dissolving all that fixture is,
Melts things that be to things that seem,
And solid nature to a dream.
O, listen to the undersong,
The ever old, the ever young;
And, far within those cadent pauses,
The chorus of the ancient Causes!
Delights the dreadful Destiny
To fling his voice into the tree,
And shock thy weak ear with a note
Breathed from the everlasting throat.
In music he repeats the pang
Whence the fair flock of Nature sprang.
O mortal! thy ears are stones;
These echoes are laden with tones

Which only the pure can hear;
Thou canst not catch what they recite
Of Fate and Will, of Want and Right,
Of man to come, of human life,
Of Death and Fortune, Growth and Strife.

"THE MIGHTY HEART"

COME learn with me the fatal song
Which knits the world in music strong;
Come lift thine eyes to lofty rhymes,
Of things with things, of times with times,
Primal chimes of sun and shade,
Of sound and echo, man and maid,
The land reflected in the flood,
Body with shadow still pursued.
For Nature beats in perfect tune,
And rounds with rhyme her every rune,
Whether she work in land or sea,
Or hide underground her alchemy.
Thou canst not wave thy staff in air,
Or dip thy paddle in the lake,
But it carves the bow of beauty there,
And the ripples in rhymes the oar forsake.
The wood is wiser far than thou;
The wood and wave each other know,
Not unrelated, unaffied,
But to each thought and thing allied,
Is perfect Nature's every part,
Rooted in the mighty Heart.
But thou, poor child! unbound, unrhymed,
Whence camest thou, misplaced, mistimed,
Whence, O thou orphan and defrauded?
Is thy land peeled, thy realm marauded?
Who thee divorced, deceived and left?
Thee of thy faith who hath bereft,
And torn the ensigns from thy brow,
And sunk the immortal eye so low?
Thy cheek too white, thy form too slender,
Thy gait too slow, thy habits tender
For royal man; — they thee confess
An exile from the wilderness, —
The hills where health with health agrees,
And the wise soul expels disease.
Hark! in thy ear I will tell the sign
By which thy hurt thou mayst divine.
When thou shalt climb the mountain cliff,
Or see the wide shore from thy skiff,
To thee the horizon shall express
But emptiness on emptiness;
There lives no man of Nature's worth
In the circle of the earth;
And to thine eye the vast skies fall,
Dire and satirical,
On clucking hens and prating fools,
On thieves, on drudges, and on dolls.
And thou shalt say to the Most High,
"Godhead! all this astronomy,
And fate and practice and invention,
Strong art and beautiful pretension,
This radiant pomp of sun and star,
Throes that were, and worlds that are,
Behold! were in vain and in vain;
It cannot be, — I will look again.
Surely now will the curtain rise,
And earth's fit tenant me surprise;
But the curtain doth not rise,
And Nature has miscarried wholly
Into failure, into folly."

Alas! thine is the bankruptcy,
Blessed Nature so to see.
Come, lay thee in my soothing shade,
And heal the hurts which sin has made.
I see thee in the crowd alone;
I will be thy companion.
Quit thy friends as the dead in doom,
And build to them a final tomb;
Let the starred shade that nightly falls
Still celebrate their funerals,
And the bell of beetle and of bee
Knell their melodious memory.
Behind thee leave thy merchandise,
Thy churches and thy charities;
And leave thy peacock wit behind;
Enough for thee the primal mind
That flows in streams, that breathes in wind;
Leave all thy pedant lore apart;
God hid the whole world in thy heart.

DAYS

DAUGHTERS of Time, the hypocritic Days,
Muffled and dumb like barefoot dervishes,
And marching single in an endless file,
Bring diadems and fagots in their hands.
To each they offer gifts after his will,
Bread, kingdoms, stars, and sky that holds them all.
I, in my pleachëd garden, watched the pomp,
Forgot my morning wishes, hastily
Took a few herbs and apples, and the Day
Turned and departed silent. I, too late,
Under her solemn fillet saw the scorn.

THE EARTH

OUR eyeless bark sails free,
Though with boom and spar
Andes, Alp, or Himmalee
Strikes never moon or star.

WAVES

ALL day the waves assailed the rock,
I heard no church-bell chime;
The sea-beat scorns the minster clock
And breaks the glass of Time.

TERMINUS

IT is time to be old,
To take in sail:
The god of bounds,
Who sets to seas a shore,
Came to me in his fatal rounds,
And said: "No more!
No farther shoot
Thy broad ambitious branches, and thy root.
Fancy departs: no more invent;
Contract thy firmament
To compass of a tent.
There 's not enough for this and that,
Make thy option which of two;
Economize the failing river,
Not the less revere the Giver,
Leave the many and hold the few.
Timely wise accept the terms,
Soften the fall with wary foot;
A little while
Still plan and smile,
And — fault of novel germs —
Mature the unfallen fruit.
Curse, if thou wilt, thy sires,
Bad husbands of their fires,
Who, when they gave thee breath,
Failed to bequeath
The needful sinew stark as once,
The Baresark marrow to thy bones,
But left a legacy of ebbing veins,
Inconstant heat and nerveless reins, —
Amid the Muses, left thee deaf and dumb,
Amid the gladiators, halt and numb."
As the bird trims her to the gale,
I trim myself to the storm of time,
I man the rudder, reef the sail,
Obey the voice at eve obeyed at prime:
"Lowly faithful, banish fear,
Right onward drive unharmed;
The port, well worth the cruise, is near,
And every wave is charmed."

THRENODY

THE south-wind brings
Life, sunshine, and desire,
And on every mount and meadow
Breathes aromatic fire;
But over the dead he has no power,
The lost, the lost, he cannot restore;
And, looking over the hills, I mourn
The darling who shall not return.

I see my empty house,
I see my trees repair their boughs;
And he, the wondrous child,
Whose silver warble wild
Outvalued every pulsing sound
Within the air's cerulean round, —
The hyacinthine boy, for whom
Morn well might break and April bloom,
The gracious boy, who did adorn
The world whereinto he was born,
And by his countenance repay
The favor of the loving Day, —
Has disappeared from the Day's eye;
Far and wide she cannot find him;
My hopes pursue, they cannot bind him.
Returned this day, the south-wind searches,
And finds young pines and budding birches;
But finds not the budding man;
Nature, who lost, cannot remake him;
Fate let him fall, Fate can't retake him;
Nature, Fate, men, him seek in vain.

And whither now, my truant wise and sweet,
O, whither tend thy feet?
I had the right, few days ago,
Thy steps to watch, thy place to know;
How have I forfeited the right?
Hast thou forgot me in a new delight?
I hearken for thy household cheer,
O eloquent child!
Whose voice, an equal messenger,
Conveyed thy meaning mild.
What though the pains and joys
Whereof it spoke were toys
Fitting his age and ken,
Yet fairest dames and bearded men,
Who heard the sweet request,
So gentle, wise, and grave,

Bended with joy to his behest,
And let the world's affairs go by,
Awhile to share his cordial game,
Or mend his wicker wagon-frame,
Still plotting how their hungry ear
That winsome voice again might hear;
For his lips could well pronounce
Words that were persuasions.

Gentlest guardians marked serene
His early hope, his liberal mien;
Took counsel from his guiding eyes
To make this wisdom earthly wise.
Ah, vainly do these eyes recall
The school-march, each day's festival,
When every morn my bosom glowed
To watch the convoy on the road;
The babe in willow wagon closed,
With rolling eyes and face composed;
With children forward and behind,
Like Cupids studiously inclined;
And he the chieftain paced beside,
The centre of the troop allied,
With sunny face of sweet repose,
To guard the babe from fancied foes.
The little captain innocent
Took the eye with him as he went,
Each village senior paused to scan
And speak the lovely caravan.
From the window I look out
To mark thy beautiful parade,
Stately marching in cap and coat
To some tune by fairies played;
A music heard by thee alone
To works as noble led thee on.

Now Love and Pride, alas ! in vain,
Up and down their glances strain.
The painted sled stands where it stood;
The kennel by the corded wood;
His gathered sticks to stanch the wall
Of the snow-tower, when snow should fall;
The ominous hole he dug in the sand,
And childhood's castles built or planned;
His daily haunts I well discern, —
The poultry-yard, the shed, the barn, —
And every inch of garden ground
Paced by the blessed feet around,
From the roadside to the brook
Whereinto he loved to look.
Step the meek fowls where erst they ranged;
The wintry garden lies unchanged;
The brook into the stream runs on;
But the deep-eyed boy is gone.

On that shaded day,
Dark with more clouds than tempests are,
When thou didst yield thy innocent breath
In birdlike heavings unto death,
Night came, and Nature had not thee;
I said, " We are mates in misery."
The morrow dawned with needless glow;
Each snowbird chirped, each fowl must crow;
Each tramper started; but the feet
Of the most beautiful and sweet
Of human youth had left the hill
And garden, — they were bound and still.
There 's not a sparrow or a wren,
There 's not a blade of autumn grain,
Which the four seasons do not tend
And tides of life and increase lend;
And every chick of every bird,
And weed and rock-moss is preferred.
O ostrich-like forgetfulness !
O loss of larger in the less !
Was there no star that could be sent,
No watcher in the firmament,
No angel from the countless host
That loiters round the crystal coast,
Could stoop to heal that only child,
Nature's sweet marvel undefiled,
And keep the blossom of the earth,
Which all her harvests were not worth ?
Not mine, — I never called thee mine,
But Nature's heir, — if I repine,
And seeing rashly torn and moved
Not what I made, but what I loved,
Grow early old with grief that thou
Must to the wastes of Nature go, —
'T is because a general hope
Was quenched, and all must doubt and grope.
For flattering planets seemed to say
This child should ills of ages stay,
By wondrous tongue, and guided pen,
Bring the flown Muses back to men.
Perchance not he but Nature ailed,
The world and not the infant failed.
It was not ripe yet to sustain
A genius of so fine a strain,
Who gazed upon the sun and moon
As if he came unto his own,
And, pregnant with his grander thought,
Brought the old order into doubt.
His beauty once their beauty tried;
They could not feed him, and he died,
And wandered backward as in scorn,
To wait an æon to be born.
Ill day which made this beauty waste,

Plight broken, this high face defaced!
Some went and came about the dead;
And some in books of solace read;
Some to their friends the tidings say;
Some went to write, some went to pray;
One tarried here, there hurried one;
But their heart abode with none.
Covetous death bereaved us all,
To aggrandize one funeral.
The eager fate which carried thee
Took the largest part of me:
For this losing is true dying;
This is lordly man's down-lying,
This his slow but sure reclining,
Star by star his world resigning.

O child of paradise,
Boy who made dear his father's home,
In whose deep eyes
Men read the welfare of the times to come,
I am too much bereft.
The world dishonored thou hast left.
O truth's and nature's costly lie!
O trusted broken prophecy!
O richest fortune sourly crossed!
Born for the future, to the future lost!
The deep Heart answered, "Weepest thou?
Worthier cause for passion wild
If I had not taken the child.
And deemest thou as those who pore,
With aged eyes, short way before,—
Think'st Beauty vanished from the coast
Of matter, and thy darling lost?
Taught he not thee—the man of eld,
Whose eyes within his eyes beheld
Heaven's numerous hierarchy span
The mystic gulf from God to man?
To be alone wilt thou begin
When worlds of lovers hem thee in?
To-morrow, when the masks shall fall
That dizen Nature's carnival,
The pure shall see by their own will,
Which overflowing Love shall fill,
'T is not within the force of fate
The fate-conjoined to separate.
But thou, my votary, weepest thou?
I gave thee sight—where is it now?
I taught thy heart beyond the reach
Of ritual, bible, or of speech;
Wrote in thy mind's transparent table,
As far as the incommunicable;
Taught thee each private sign to raise
Lit by the supersolar blaze.
Past utterance, and past belief,
And past the blasphemy of grief,
The mysteries of Nature's heart;
And though no Muse can these impart,
Throb thine with Nature's throbbing breast,
And all is clear from east to west.

"I came to thee as to a friend;
Dearest, to thee I did not send
Tutors, but a joyful eye,
Innocence that matched the sky,
Lovely locks, a form of wonder,
Laughter rich as woodland thunder,
That thou mightst entertain apart
The richest flowering of all art:
And, as the great all-loving Day
Through smallest chambers takes its way,
That thou mightst break thy daily bread
With prophet, savior and head;
That thou mightst cherish for thine own
The riches of sweet Mary's Son,
Boy-Rabbi, Israel's paragon.
And thoughtest thou such guest
Would in thy hall take up his rest?
Would rushing life forget her laws,
Fate's glowing revolution pause?
High omens ask diviner guess;
Not to be conned to tediousness.
And know my higher gifts unbind
The zone that girds the incarnate mind.
When the scanty shores are full
With Thought's perilous, whirling pool;
When frail Nature can no more,
Then the Spirit strikes the hour:
My servant Death, with solving rite,
Pours finite into infinite.
Wilt thou freeze love's tidal flow,
Whose streams through nature circling go?
Nail the wild star to its track
On the half-climbed zodiac?
Light is light which radiates,
Blood is blood which circulates,
Life is life which generates,
And many-seeming life is one,—
Wilt thou transfix and make it none?
Its onward force too starkly pent
In figure, bone, and lineament?
Wilt thou, uncalled, interrogate,
Talker! the unreplying Fate?
Nor see the genius of the whole
Ascendant in the private soul,
Beckon it when to go and come,
Self-announced its hour of doom?
Fair the soul's recess and shrine,
Magic-built to last a season;
Masterpiece of love benign,
Fairer that expansive reason

Whose omen 't is, and sign.
Wilt thou not hope thy heart to know
What rainbows teach, and sunsets show?
Verdict which accumulates
From lengthening scroll of human fates,
Voice of earth to earth returned,
Prayers of saints that inly burned, —
Saying, *What is excellent,*
As God lives, is permanent;
Hearts are dust, hearts' loves remain;
Heart's love will meet thee again.
Revere the Maker; fetch thine eye
Up to his style, and manners of the sky.
Not of adamant and gold
Built he heaven stark and cold;
No, but a nest of bending reeds,
Flowering grass and scented weeds;
Or like a traveller's fleeing tent,
Or bow above the tempest bent;
Built of tears and sacred flames,
And virtue reaching to its aims;
Built of furtherance and pursuing,
Not of spent deeds, but of doing.
Silent rushes the swift Lord
Through ruined systems still restored,
Broadsowing, bleak and void to bless,
Plants with worlds the wilderness;
Waters with tears of ancient sorrow
Apples of Eden ripe to-morrow.
House and tenant go to ground,
Lost in God, in Godhead found."

CONCORD HYMN

SUNG AT THE COMPLETION OF THE BATTLE MONUMENT, APRIL 19, 1836

By the rude bridge that arched the flood,
Their flag to April's breeze unfurled,
Here once the embattled farmers stood,
And fired the shot heard round the world.

The foe long since in silence slept;
Alike the conqueror silent sleeps;
And Time the ruined bridge has swept
Down the dark stream which seaward creeps.

On this green bank, by this soft stream,
We set to-day a votive stone;
That memory may their deed redeem,
When, like our sires, our sons are gone.

Spirit, that made those heroes dare
To die, and leave their children free,
Bid Time and Nature gently spare
The shaft we raise to them and thee.

ODE

SUNG IN THE TOWN HALL, CONCORD, JULY 4, 1857

O TENDERLY the haughty day
Fills his blue urn with fire;
One morn is in the mighty heaven,
And one in our desire.

The cannon booms from town to town,
Our pulses beat not less,
The joy-bells chime their tidings down,
Which children's voices bless.

For He that flung the broad blue fold
O'er-mantling land and sea,
One third part of the sky unrolled
For the banner of the free.

The men are ripe of Saxon kind
To build an equal state, —
To take the statute from the mind
And make of duty fate.

United States! the ages plead, —
Present and Past in under-song, —
Go put your creed into your deed,
Nor speak with double tongue.

For sea and land don't understand
Nor skies without a frown
See rights for which the one hand fights
By the other cloven down.

Be just at home; then write your scroll
Of honor o'er the sea,
And bid the broad Atlantic roll
A ferry of the free.

And henceforth there shall be no chain,
Save underneath the sea
The wires shall murmur through the main
Sweet songs of liberty.

The conscious stars accord above,
The waters wild below,
And under, through the cable wove,
Her fiery errands go.

For He that worketh high and wise,
Nor pauses in his plan,
Will take the sun out of the skies
Ere freedom out of man.

THE TEST

I HUNG my verses in the wind,
Time and tide their faults may find.
All were winnowed through and through,
Five lines lasted sound and true;
Five were smelted in a pot
Than the South more fierce and hot;
These the siroc could not melt,
Fire their fiercer flaming felt,
And the meaning was more white
Than July's meridian light.
Sunshine cannot bleach the snow,
Nor time unmake what poets know.
Have you eyes to find the five
Which five hundred did survive?

Sarah Helen Whitman

SONNETS

(FROM THE SERIES RELATING TO EDGAR ALLAN POE)

I

WHEN first I looked into thy glorious eyes,
And saw, with their unearthly beauty pained,
Heaven deepening within heaven, like the skies
Of autumn nights without a shadow stained,
I stood as one whom some strange dream enthralls;
For, far away in some lost life divine,
Some land which every glorious dream recalls,
A spirit looked on me with eyes like thine.
Even now, though death has veiled their starry light,
And closed their lids in his relentless night,—
As some strange dream, remembered in a dream,
Again I see, in sleep, their tender beam;
Unfading hopes their cloudless azure fill,
Heaven deepening within heaven, serene and still.

2

Oft since thine earthly eyes have closed on mine,
Our souls, dim-wandering in the hall of dreams,
Hold mystic converse on the life divine,
By the still music of immortal streams;
And oft thy spirit tells how souls, affied
By sovran destinies, no more can part,—
How death and hell are powerless to divide
Souls whose deep lives lie folded heart in heart.
And if, at times, some lingering shadow lies
Heavy upon my path, some haunting dread,
Then do I point thee to the harmonies
Of those calm heights whereto our souls arise
Through suffering,—the faith that doth approve
In death the deathless power and divine life of love.

3

On our lone pathway bloomed no earthly hopes:
Sorrow and death were near us, as we stood
Where the dim forest, from the upland slopes,
Swept darkly to the sea. The enchanted wood
Thrilled, as by some foreboding terror stirred;
And as the waves broke on the lonely shore,
In their low monotone, methought I heard
A solemn voice that sighed, "Ye meet no more."
There, while the level sunbeams seemed to burn
Through the long aisles of red, autumnal gloom,—
Where stately, storied cenotaphs inurn
Sweet human hopes, too fair on Earth to bloom,—

Was the bud reaped, whose petals pure and cold
Sleep on my heart till Heaven the flower unfold.

4

If thy sad heart, pining for human love,
In its earth solitude grew dark with fear,
Lest the high Sun of Heaven itself should prove
Powerless to save from that phantasmal sphere
Wherein thy spirit wandered, — if the flowers
That pressed around thy feet, seemed but to bloom
In lone Gethsemanes, through starless hours,
When all who loved had left thee to thy doom, —
Oh, yet believe that, in that hollow vale
Where thy soul lingers, waiting to attain
So much of Heaven's sweet grace as shall avail
To lift its burden of remorseful pain,
My soul shall meet thee, and its Heaven forego
Till God's great love, on both, one hope, one Heaven bestow.

William Lloyd Garrison

LIBERTY FOR ALL

THEY tell me, Liberty! that in thy name
I may not plead for all the human race;
That some are born to bondage and disgrace,
Some to a heritage of woe and shame,
And some to power supreme, and glorious fame:
With my whole soul I spurn the doctrine base,
And, as an equal brotherhood, embrace
All people, and for all fair freedom claim!
Know this, O man! whate'er thy earthly fate —
God never made a tyrant nor a slave:
Woe, then, to those who dare to desecrate
His glorious image! — for to all He gave
Eternal rights, which none may violate;
And, by a mighty hand, the oppressed He yet shall save!

FREEDOM FOR THE MIND

HIGH walls and huge the body may confine,
And iron grates obstruct the prisoner's gaze,
And massive bolts may baffle his design,
And vigilant keepers watch his devious ways:
Yet scorns the immortal mind this base control!
No chains can bind it, and no cell enclose:
Swifter than light, it flies from pole to pole,
And, in a flash, from earth to heaven it goes!
It leaps from mount to mount — from vale to vale
It wanders, plucking honeyed fruits and flowers;
It visits home, to hear the fireside tale,
Or in sweet converse pass the joyous hours.
'T is up before the sun, roaming afar,
And, in its watches, wearies every star!

Nathaniel Parker Willis

PARRHASIUS

THERE stood an unsold captive in the mart,
A gray-haired and majestical old man,
Chained to a pillar. It was almost night,
And the last seller from the place had gone,
And not a sound was heard but of a dog
Crunching beneath the stall a refuse bone,
Or the dull echo from the pavement rung.
As the faint captive changed his weary feet.
He had stood there since morning, and had borne

From every eye in Athens the cold gaze
Of curious scorn. The Jew had taunted him
For an Olynthian slave. The buyer came
And roughly struck his palm upon his breast,
And touched his unhealed wounds, and with a sneer
Passed on; and when, with weariness o'er-spent,
He bowed his head in a forgetful sleep,
The inhuman soldier smote him, and, with threats
Of torture to his children, summoned back
The ebbing blood into his pallid face.

'T was evening, and the half-descended sun
Tipped with a golden fire the many domes
Of Athens, and a yellow atmosphere
Lay rich and dusky in the shaded street
Through which the captive gazed. He had borne up
With a stout heart that long and weary day,
Haughtily patient of his many wrongs,
But now he was alone, and from his nerves
The needless strength departed, and he leaned
Prone on his massy chain, and let his thoughts
Throng on him as they would. Unmarked of him
Parrhasius at the nearest pillar stood,
Gazing upon his grief. The Athenian's cheek
Flushed as he measured with a painter's eye
The moving picture. The abandoned limbs,
Stained with the oozing blood, were laced with veins
Swollen to purple fulness; the gray hair,
Thin and disordered, hung about his eyes;
And as a thought of wilder bitterness
Rose in his memory, his lips grew white,
And the fast workings of his bloodless face
Told what a tooth of fire was at his heart.

The golden light into the painter's room
Streamed richly, and the hidden colors stole
From the dark pictures radiantly forth,
And in the soft and dewy atmosphere
Like forms and landscapes magical they lay.
The walls were hung with armor, and about
In the dim corners stood the sculptured forms
Of Cytheris, and Dian, and stern Jove,
And from the casement soberly away
Fell the grotesque long shadows, full and true,
And like a veil of filmy mellowness,
The lint-specks floated in the twilight air.
Parrhasius stood, gazing forgetfully
Upon his canvas. There Prometheus lay,
Chained to the cold rocks of Mount Caucasus —
The vulture at his vitals, and the links
Of the lame Lemnian festering in his flesh;
And, as the painter's mind felt through the dim,
Rapt mystery, and plucked the shadows forth
With its far reaching fancy, and with form
And color clad them, his fine, earnest eye
Flashed with a passionate fire, and the quick curl
Of his thin nostril, and his quivering lip
Were like the winged god's, breathing from his flight.

"Bring me the captive now!
My hand feels skilful, and the shadows lift
From my waked spirit airily and swift,
And I could paint the bow
Upon the bended heavens — around me play
Colors of such divinity to-day.

"Ha! bind him on his back!
Look! — as Prometheus in my picture here!
Quick — or he faints! — stand with the cordial near!
Now — bend him to the rack!
Press down the poisoned links into his flesh!
And tear agape that healing wound afresh!

"So — let him writhe! How long
Will he live thus? Quick, my good pencil, now!
What a fine agony works upon his brow!
Ha! gray-haired, and so strong!
How fearfully he stifles that short moan!
Gods! if I could but paint a dying groan!

"'Pity' thee! So I do!
I pity the dumb victim at the altar —
But does the robed priest for his pity falter?
I'd rack thee though I knew
A thousand lives were perishing in thine —
What were ten thousand to a fame like mine?

"'Hereafter!' Ay — hereafter!
A whip to keep a coward to his track!
What gave Death ever from his kingdom back
To check the skeptic's laughter?
Come from the grave to-morrow with that story,
And I may take some softer path to glory.

"No, no, old man! we die
Even as the flowers, and we shall breathe away
Our life upon the chance wind, even as they!
Strain well thy fainting eye —
For when that bloodshot quivering is o'er,
The light of heaven will never reach thee more.

"Yet there's a deathless name!
A spirit that the smothering vault shall spurn,
And like a steadfast planet mount and burn;
And though its crown of flame
Consumed my brain to ashes as it shone,
By all the fiery stars! I'd bind it on! —

"Ay — though it bid me rifle
My heart's last fount for its insatiate thirst —
Though every life-strung nerve be maddened first —
Though it should bid me stifle
The yearning in my throat for my sweet child,
And taunt its mother till my brain went wild —

"All — I would do it all —
Sooner than die, like a dull worm, to rot,
Thrust foully into earth to be forgot!
Oh heavens! — but I appall
Your heart, old man! forgive — ha! on your lives
Let him not faint! — rack him till he revives!

"Vain — vain — give o'er! His eye
Glazes apace. He does not feel you now —
Stand back! I'll paint the death-dew on his brow!
Gods! if he do not die
But for one moment — one — till I eclipse
Conception with the scorn of those calm lips!

"Shivering! Hark! he mutters
Brokenly now — that was a difficult breath —
Another? Wilt thou never come, oh Death!
Look! how his temple flutters!
Is his heart still? Aha! lift up his head!
He shudders — gasps — Jove help him! — so — he's dead."

How like a mounting devil in the heart
Rules the unreined ambition! Let it once
But play the monarch, and its haughty brow
Glows with a beauty that bewilders thought
And unthrones peace forever. Putting on
The very pomp of Lucifer, it turns
The heart to ashes, and with not a spring
Left in the bosom for the spirit's lip,
We look upon our splendor and forget
The thirst of which we perish! Yet hath life
Many a falser idol. There are hopes
Promising well; and love-touched dreams for some;
And passions, many a wild one; and fair schemes
For gold and pleasure — yet will only this
Balk not the soul — Ambition, only, gives,
Even of bitterness, a beaker full!
Friendship is but a slow-awaking dream,
Troubled at best; Love is a lamp unseen,
Burning to waste, or, if its light is found,
Nursed for an idle hour, then idly broken;
Gain is a grovelling care, and Folly tires,
And Quiet is a hunger never fed;

And from Love's very bosom, and from Gain,
Or Folly, or a Friend, or from Repose —
From all but keen Ambition — will the soul
Snatch the first moment of forgetfulness
To wander like a restless child away.
Oh, if there were not better hopes than these —
Were there no palm beyond a feverish fame —
If the proud wealth flung back upon the heart
Must canker in its coffers — if the links
Falsehood hath broken will unite no more —
If the deep yearning love, that hath not found
Its like in the cold world, must waste in tears —
If truth and fervor and devotedness,
Finding no worthy altar, must return
And die of their own fulness — if beyond
The grave there is no heaven in whose wide air
The spirit may find room, and in the love
Of whose bright habitants the lavish heart
May spend itself — what thrice-mocked fools are we!

UNSEEN SPIRITS

The shadows lay along Broadway,
'T was near the twilight-tide,
And slowly there a lady fair
Was walking in her pride.
Alone walked she; but, viewlessly,
Walked spirits at her side.

Peace charmed the street beneath her feet,
And Honor charmed the air;
And all astir looked kind on her,
And called her good as fair,
For all God ever gave to her
She kept with chary care.

She kept with care her beauties rare
From lovers warm and true,
For her heart was cold to all but gold,
And the rich came not to woo —
But honored well are charms to sell
If priests the selling do.

Now walking there was one more fair —
A slight girl, lily-pale;
And she had unseen company
To make the spirit quail:
'Twixt Want and Scorn she walked forlorn,
And nothing could avail.

No mercy now can clear her brow
For this world's peace to pray;
For, as love's wild prayer dissolved in air,
Her woman's heart gave way! —
But the sin forgiven by Christ in heaven
By man is cursed alway!

THE TORN HAT

There's something in a noble boy,
A brave, free-hearted, careless one,
With his unchecked, unbidden joy,
His dread of books and love of fun —
And in his clear and ready smile,
Unshaded by a thought of guile,
And unrepressed by sadness —
Which brings me to my childhood back,
As if I trod its very track,
And felt its very gladness.
And yet it is not in his play,
When every trace of thought is lost,
And not when you would call him gay,
That his bright presence thrills me most.
His shout may ring upon the hill,
His voice be echoed in the hall,
His merry laugh like music trill,
And I unheeding hear it all;
For, like the wrinkles on my brow,
I scarcely notice such things now.
But when, amid the earnest game,
He stops as if he music heard,
And, heedless of his shouted name
As of the carol of a bird,
Stands gazing on the empty air
As if some dream were passing there —
'T is then that on his face I look,
His beautiful but thoughtful face,
And, like a long-forgotten book,
Its sweet, familiar meaning trace,
Remembering a thousand things
Which passed me on those golden wings,
Which time has fettered now —
Things that came o'er me with a thrill,
And left me silent, sad, and still,
And threw upon my brow
A holier and a gentler cast,
That was too innocent to last.

'T is strange how thought upon a child
  Will, like a presence, sometime press;
And when his pulse is beating wild,
  And life itself is in excess —
When foot and hand, and ear and eye,
Are all with ardor straining high —
  How in his heart will spring
A feeling, whose mysterious thrall
Is stronger, sweeter far than all;
  And, on its silent wing,
How with the clouds he 'll float away,
As wandering and as lost as they!

TO GIULIA GRISI

When the rose is brightest,
  Its bloom will soonest die;
When burns the meteor brightest,
  'T will vanish from the sky.
If Death but wait until delight
  O'errun the heart like wine,
And break the cup when brimming quite,
I die — for thou hast poured to-night
  The last drop into mine.

William Gilmore Simms

THE SWAMP FOX

We follow where the Swamp Fox guides,
  His friends and merry men are we;
And when the troop of Tarleton rides,
  We burrow in the cypress tree.
The turfy hammock is our bed,
  Our home is in the red deer's den,
Our roof, the tree-top overhead,
  For we are wild and hunted men.

We fly by day and shun its light,
  But, prompt to strike the sudden blow,
We mount and start with early night,
  And through the forest track our foe.
And soon he hears our chargers leap,
  The flashing sabre blinds his eyes,
And ere he drives away his sleep,
  And rushes from his camp, he dies.

Free bridle-bit, good gallant steed,
  That will not ask a kind caress
To swim the Santee at our need,
  When on his heels the foemen press, —
The true heart and the ready hand,
  The spirit stubborn to be free,
The twisted bore, the smiting brand, —
  And we are Marion's men, you see.

Now light the fire and cook the meal,
  The last perhaps that we shall taste;
I hear the Swamp Fox round us steal,
  And that 's a sign we move in haste.
He whistles to the scouts, and hark!
  You hear his order calm and low.
Come, wave your torch across the dark,
  And let us see the boys that go.

We may not see their forms again,
  God help 'em, should they find the strife!
For they are strong and fearless men,
  And make no coward terms for life;
They 'll fight as long as Marion bids,
  And when he speaks the word to shy,
Then, not till then, they turn their steeds,
  Through thickening shade and swamp to fly.

Now stir the fire and lie at ease, —
  The scouts are gone, and on the brush
I see the Colonel bend his knee,
  To take his slumbers too. But hush!
He 's praying, comrades; 't is not strange;
  The man that 's fighting day by day
May well, when night comes, take a change,
  And down upon his knees to pray.

Break up that hoe-cake, boys, and hand
  The sly and silent jug that 's there;
I love not it should idly stand
  When Marion's men have need of cheer.
'T is seldom that our luck affords
  A stuff like this we just have quaffed,
And dry potatoes on our boards
  May always call for such a draught.

Now pile the brush and roll the log;
  Hard pillow, but a soldier's head
That 's half the time in brake and bog
  Must never think of softer bed.
The owl is hooting to the night,
  The cooter crawling o'er the bank,
And in that pond the flashing light
  Tells where the alligator sank.

What! 't is the signal! start so soon,
And through the Santee swamp so deep,
Without the aid of friendly moon,
And we, Heaven help us! half asleep!
But courage, comrades! Marion leads,
The Swamp Fox takes us out to-night;
So clear your swords and spur your steeds,
There 's goodly chance, I think, of fight.

We follow where the Swamp Fox guides,
We leave the swamp and cypress-tree,
Our spurs are in our coursers' sides,
And ready for the strife are we.
The Tory camp is now in sight,
And there he cowers within his den;
He hears our shouts, he dreads the fight,
He fears, and flies from Marion's men.

THE LOST PLEIAD

Not in the sky,
Where it was seen
So long in eminence of light serene,—
Nor on the white tops of the glistering wave,
Nor down in mansions of the hidden deep,
Though beautiful in green
And crystal, its great caves of mystery,—
Shall the bright watcher have
Her place, and, as of old, high station keep!

Gone! gone!
Oh! nevermore, to cheer
The mariner, who holds his course alone
On the Atlantic, through the weary night,
When the stars turn to watchers, and do sleep,
Shall it again appear,
With the sweet-loving certainty of light,
Down shining on the shut eyes of the deep!

The upward-looking shepherd on the hills
Of Chaldea, night-returning with his flocks,
He wonders why his beauty doth not blaze,
Gladding his gaze,—
And, from his dreary watch along the rocks,
Guiding him homeward o'er the perilous ways!
How stands he waiting still, in a sad maze,
Much wondering, while the drowsy silence fills
The sorrowful vault!—how lingers, in the hope that night
May yet renew the expected and sweet light,
So natural to his sight!

And lone,
Where, at the first, in smiling love she shone,
Brood the once happy circle of bright stars:
How should they dream, until her fate was known,
That they were ever confiscate to death?
That dark oblivion the pure beauty mars,
And, like the earth, its common bloom and breath,
That they should fall from high;
Their lights grow blasted by a touch, and die,
All their concerted springs of harmony
Snapt rudely, and the generous music gone!

Ah! still the strain
Of wailing sweetness fills the saddening sky;
The sister stars, lamenting in their pain
That one of the selectest ones must die,—
Must vanish, when most lovely, from the rest!
Alas! 't is ever thus the destiny.
Even Rapture's song hath evermore a tone
Of wailing, as for bliss too quickly gone.
The hope most precious is the soonest lost,
The flower most sweet is first to feel the frost.
Are not all short-lived things the loveliest?
And, like the pale star, shooting down the sky,
Look they not ever brightest, as they fly
From the lone sphere they blest!

THE DECAY OF A PEOPLE

This the true sign of ruin to a race—
It undertakes no march, and day by day
Drowses in camp, or, with the laggard's pace,
Walks sentry o'er possessions that decay;
Destined, with sensible waste, to fleet away;—
For the first secret of continued power
Is the continued conquest;—all our sway
Hath surety in the uses of the hour;
If that we waste, in vain walled town and lofty tower!

SONG IN MARCH

Now are the winds about us in their glee,
Tossing the slender tree;
Whirling the sands about his furious car,
March cometh from afar;

Breaks the sealed magic of old Winter's
dreams,
And rends his glassy streams;
Chafing with potent airs, he fiercely takes
Their fetters from the lakes,
And, with a power by queenly Spring sup-
plied,
Wakens the slumbering tide.

With a wild love he seeks young Summer's
charms
And clasps her to his arms;
Lifting his shield between, he drives away
Old Winter from his prey; —
The ancient tyrant whom he boldly braves,
Goes howling to his caves;
And, to his northern realm compelled to
fly,
Yields up the victory;
Melted are all his bands, o'erthrown his
towers,
And March comes bringing flowers.

Ralph Hoyt

OLD

By the wayside, on a mossy stone,
Sat a hoary pilgrim sadly musing;
Oft I marked him sitting there alone,
All the landscape like a page perusing;
Poor, unknown,
By the wayside, on a mossy stone.

Buckled knee and shoe, and broad-rimmed
hat,
Coat as ancient as the form 't was folding,
Silver buttons, queue, and crimped cravat,
Oaken staff his feeble hand upholding,
There he sat!
Buckled knee and shoe, and broad-rimmed
hat.

Seemed it pitiful he should sit there,
No one sympathizing, no one heeding,
None to love him for his thin gray hair,
And the furrows all so mutely pleading
Age and care;
Seemed it pitiful he should sit there.

It was summer, and we went to school,
Dapper country lads and little maidens,
Taught the motto of the "Dunce's Stool," —
Its grave import still my fancy ladens,
"Here 's a fool!"
It was summer, and we went to school.

Still, in sooth, our tasks we seldom tried,
Sportive pastime only worth our learning,
But we listened when the old man sighed,
And that lesson to our hearts went burn-
ing,
And we cried;
Still, in sooth, our tasks we seldom tried.

When the stranger seemed to mark our
play,
(Some of us were joyous, some sad-
hearted),
I remember well, — too well, — that day!
Oftentimes the tears unbidden started,
Would not stay, —
When the stranger seemed to mark our play.

When we cautiously adventured nigh
We could see his lip with anguish quiver:
Yet no word he uttered, but his eye
Seemed in mournful converse with the
river
Murmuring by,
When we cautiously adventured nigh.

One sweet spirit broke the silent spell, —
Ah, to me her name was always heaven!
She besought him all his grief to tell,
(I was then thirteen, and she eleven),
Isabel!
One sweet spirit broke the silent spell.

Softly asked she with a voice divine,
"Why so lonely hast thou wandered
hither;
Hast no home? — then come with me to
mine;
There 's our cottage, let me lead thee
thither;
Why repine?"
Softly asked she with a voice divine.

"Angel," said he sadly, "I am old:
Earthly hope no longer hath a morrow,
Yet why I sit here thou shalt be told;"
Then his eye betrayed a pearl of sor-
row, —

Down it rolled;
"Angel," said he sadly, "I am old!

"I have tottered here to look once more
On the pleasant scene where I delighted
In the careless, happy days of yore,
Ere the garden of my heart was blighted
To the core;
I have tottered here to look once more!

"All the picture now to me how dear!
E'en this gray old rock where I am seated
Seems a jewel worth my journey here;
Ah, that such a scene should be completed
With a tear!
All the picture now to me how dear!

"Old stone school-house! — it is still the same!
There 's the very step so oft I mounted;
There 's the window creaking in its frame,
And the notches that I cut and counted
For the game:
Old stone school-house! — it is still the same!

"In the cottage yonder I was born;
Long my happy home — that humble dwelling;
There the fields of clover, wheat, and corn,
There the spring with limpid nectar swelling;
Ah, forlorn!
In the cottage yonder I was born.

"Those two gateway sycamores you see
Then were planted, just so far asunder
That long well-pole from the path to free,
And the wagon to pass safely under;
Ninety-three!
Those two gateway sycamores you see.

"There 's the orchard where we used to climb
When my mates and I were boys together,
Thinking nothing of the flight of time,
Fearing naught but work and rainy weather;
Past its prime!
There 's the orchard where we used to climb!

"There the rude three-cornered chestnut rails,
Round the pasture where the flocks were grazing,
Where so sly I used to watch for quails
In the crops of buckwheat we were raising,
Traps and trails,
There the rude three-cornered chestnut rails.

"How in summer have I traced that stream,
There through mead and woodland sweetly gliding,
Luring simple trout with many a scheme
From the nooks where I have found them hiding;
All a dream!
How in summer have I traced that stream!

"There 's the mill that ground our yellow grain;
Pond and river still serenely flowing;
Cot, there nestling in the shaded lane,
Where the lily of my heart was blowing, —
Mary Jane!
There's the mill that ground our yellow grain!

"There 's the gate on which I used to swing,
Brook, and bridge, and barn, and old red stable:
But, alas! the morn shall no more bring
That dear group around my father's table;
Taken wing!
There 's the gate on which I used to swing!

"I am fleeing! — all I loved are fled;
Yon green meadow was our place for playing;
That old tree can tell of sweet things said,
When around it Jane and I were straying;
She is dead!
I am fleeing! — all I loved are fled!

"Yon white spire — a pencil on the sky,
Tracing silently life's changeful story,
So familiar to my dim old eye,
Points me to seven that are now in glory
There on high!
Yon white spire, a pencil on the sky.

"Oft the aisle of that old church we trod,
Guided thither by an angel mother,—
Now she sleeps beneath its sacred sod,
Sire and sisters, and my little brother;
Gone to God!
Oft the aisle of that old church we trod.

"There I heard of Wisdom's pleasant ways;
Bless the holy lesson! — but, ah, never
Shall I hear again those songs of praise,
Those sweet voices silent now forever!
Peaceful days!
There I heard of Wisdom's pleasant ways.

"There my Mary blest me with her hand,
When our souls drank in the nuptial blessing,
Ere she hastened to the spirit land:
Yonder turf her gentle bosom pressing:
Broken band!
There my Mary blest me with her hand.

"I have come to see that grave once more,
And the sacred place where we delighted,
Where we worshipped in the days of yore,
Ere the garden of my heart was blighted
To the core;
I have come to see that grave once more.

"Haply, ere the verdure there shall fade,
I, all withering with years, shall perish;
With my Mary may I there be laid,
Join forever — all the wish I cherish —
Her dear Shade! —
Haply, ere the verdure there shall fade."

"Angel," said he sadly, "I am old!
Earthly hope no longer hath a morrow;
Now why I sit here thou hast been told."
In his eye another pearl of sorrow,—
Down it rolled;
"Angel," said he sadly, "I am old!"

By the wayside, on a mossy stone,
Sat the hoary pilgrim, sadly musing;
Still I marked him sitting there alone,
All the landscape like a page perusing;
Poor, unknown,
By the wayside, on a mossy stone.

Charles Fenno Hoffman

SPARKLING AND BRIGHT

Sparkling and bright in liquid light,
Does the wine our goblets gleam in,
With hue as red as the rosy bed
Which a bee would choose to dream in.
Then fill to-night, with hearts as light,
To loves as gay and fleeting
As bubbles that swim on the beaker's brim,
And break on the lips while meeting.

Oh! if Mirth might arrest the flight
Of Time through Life's dominions,
We here a while would now beguile
The graybeard of his pinions,
To drink to-night, with hearts as light,
To loves as gay and fleeting
As bubbles that swim on the beaker's brim,
And break on the lips while meeting.

But since Delight can't tempt the wight,
Nor fond Regret delay him,
Nor Love himself can hold the elf,
Nor sober Friendship stay him,
We'll drink to-night, with hearts as light,
To loves as gay and fleeting
As bubbles that swim on the beaker's brim,
And break on the lips while meeting.

MONTEREY

We were not many — we who stood
Before the iron sleet that day —
Yet many a gallant spirit would
Give half his years if he then could
Have been with us at Monterey.

Now here, now there, the shot, it hailed
In deadly drifts of fiery spray,
Yet not a single soldier quailed
When wounded comrades round them wailed
Their dying shout at Monterey.

And on — still on our column kept
Through walls of flame its withering way;

Where fell the dead, the living stept,
Still charging on the guns which swept
The slippery streets of Monterey.

The foe himself recoiled aghast,
When, striking where he strongest lay,
We swooped his flanking batteries past,
And braving full their murderous blast,
Stormed home the towers of Monterey.

Our banners on those turrets wave,
And there our evening bugles play;
Where orange boughs above their grave
Keep green the memory of the brave
Who fought and fell at Monterey.

We are not many — we who pressed
Beside the brave who fell that day;
But who of us has not confessed
He 'd rather share their warrior rest,
Than not have been at Monterey?

THE MINT JULEP

'T IS said that the gods on Olympus of old
(And who the bright legend profanes with a doubt?)
One night, 'mid their revels, by Bacchus were told
That his last butt of nectar had somehow run out!

But determined to send round the goblet once more,
They sued to the fairer immortals for aid
In composing a draught which, till drinking were o'er,
Should cast every wine ever drank in the shade.

Grave Ceres herself blithely yielded her corn,
And the spirit that lives in each amber-hued grain,
And which first had its birth from the dew of the morn,
Was taught to steal out in bright dew-drops again.

Pomona, whose choicest of fruits on the board
Were scattered profusely in every one's reach,
When called on a tribute to cull from the hoard,
Expressed the mild juice of the delicate peach.

The liquids were mingled while Venus looked on
With glances so fraught with sweet magical power,
That the honey of Hybla, e'en when they were gone,
Has never been missed in the draught from that hour.

Flora, then, from her bosom of fragrancy, shook,
And with roseate fingers pressed down in the bowl,
All dripping and fresh as it came from the brook,
The herb whose aroma should flavor the whole.

The draught was delicious, and loud the acclaim,
Though something seemed wanting for all to bewail,
But Juleps the drink of immortals became,
When Jove himself added a handful of hail.

Henry Wadsworth Longfellow

HYMN TO THE NIGHT

I HEARD the trailing garments of the Night
Sweep through her marble halls!
I saw her sable skirts all fringed with light
From the celestial walls!

I felt her presence, by its spell of might,
Stoop o'er me from above;
The calm, majestic presence of the Night,
As of the one I love.

I heard the sounds of sorrow and delight,
The manifold, soft chimes,

That fill the haunted chambers of the Night,
  Like some old poet's rhymes.

From the cool cisterns of the midnight air
  My spirit drank repose;
The fountain of perpetual peace flows
  there, —
  From those deep cisterns flows.

O holy Night! from thee I learn to bear
  What man has borne before!
Thou layest thy finger on the lips of Care,
  And they complain no more.

Peace! Peace! Orestes-like I breathe this
  prayer!
  Descend with broad-winged flight,
The welcome, the thrice-prayed for, the
  most fair,
  The best-belovëd Night!

A PSALM OF LIFE

WHAT THE HEART OF THE YOUNG MAN SAID TO THE PSALMIST

TELL me not, in mournful numbers,
  Life is but an empty dream! —
For the soul is dead that slumbers,
  And things are not what they seem.

Life is real! Life is earnest!
  And the grave is not its goal;
Dust thou art, to dust returnest,
  Was not spoken of the soul.

Not enjoyment, and not sorrow,
  Is our destined end or way;
But to act, that each to-morrow
  Find us farther than to-day.

Art is long, and Time is fleeting,
  And our hearts, though stout and brave,
Still, like muffled drums, are beating
  Funeral marches to the grave.

In the world's broad field of battle,
  In the bivouac of Life,
Be not like dumb, driven cattle!
  Be a hero in the strife!

Trust no Future, howe'er pleasant!
  Let the dead Past bury its dead!
Act, — act in the living Present!
  Heart within, and God o'erhead!

Lives of great men all remind us
  We can make our lives sublime,
And, departing, leave behind us
  Footprints on the sands of time;

Footprints, that perhaps another,
  Sailing o'er life's solemn main,
A forlorn and shipwrecked brother,
  Seeing, shall take heart again.

Let us then, be up and doing,
  With a heart for any fate;
Still achieving, still pursuing,
  Learn to labor and to wait.

THE SKELETON IN ARMOR

"SPEAK! speak! thou fearful guest!
Who, with thy hollow breast
Still in rude armor drest,
  Comest to daunt me!
Wrapt not in Eastern balms,
But with thy fleshless palms
Stretched, as if asking alms,
  Why dost thou haunt me?"

Then from those cavernous eyes
Pale flashes seemed to rise,
As when the Northern skies
  Gleam in December;
And, like the water's flow
Under December's snow,
Came a dull voice of woe
  From the heart's chamber.

"I was a Viking old!
My deeds, though manifold,
No Skald in song has told,
  No Saga taught thee!
Take heed that in thy verse
Thou dost the tale rehearse,
Else dread a dead man's curse;
  For this I sought thee.

"Far in the Northern Land,
By the wild Baltic's strand,
I, with my childish hand,
  Tamed the gerfalcon;
And, with my skates fast-bound,
Skimmed the half-frozen Sound,
That the poor whimpering hound
  Trembled to walk on.

"Oft to his frozen lair
Tracked I the grisly bear,
While from my path the hare
Fled like a shadow;
Oft through the forest dark
Followed the were-wolf's bark,
Until the soaring lark
Sang from the meadow.

"But when I older grew,
Joining a corsair's crew,
O'er the dark sea I flew
With the marauders.
Wild was the life we led;
Many the souls that sped,
Many the hearts that bled,
By our stern orders.

"Many a wassail-bout
Wore the long Winter out;
Often our midnight shout
Set the cocks crowing,
As we the Berserk's tale
Measured in cups of ale,
Draining the oaken pail
Filled to o'erflowing.

"Once as I told in glee
Tales of the stormy sea,
Soft eyes did gaze on me,
Burning yet tender;
And as the white stars shine
On the dark Norway pine,
On that dark heart of mine
Fell their soft splendor.

"I wooed the blue-eyed maid,
Yielding, yet half afraid,
And in the forest's shade
Our vows were plighted.
Under its loosened vest
Fluttered her little breast,
Like birds within their nest
By the hawk frighted.

"Bright in her father's hall
Shields gleamed upon the wall,
Loud sang the minstrels all,
Chanting his glory;
When of old Hildebrand
I asked his daughter's hand,
Mute did the minstrels stand
To hear my story.

"While the brown ale he quaffed,
Loud then the champion laughed,
And as the wind-gusts waft
The sea-foam brightly,
So the loud laugh of scorn,
Out of those lips unshorn,
From the deep drinking-horn
Blew the foam lightly.

"She was a Prince's child,
I but a Viking wild,
And though she blushed and smiled,
I was discarded!
Should not the dove so white
Follow the sea-mew's flight?
Why did they leave that night
Her nest unguarded?

"Scarce had I put to sea,
Bearing the maid with me, —
Fairest of all was she
Among the Norsemen! —
When on the white sea-strand,
Waving his armëd hand,
Saw we old Hildebrand,
With twenty horsemen.

"Then launched they to the blast,
Bent like a reed each mast,
Yet we were gaining fast,
When the wind failed us;
And with a sudden flaw
Came round the gusty Skaw,
So that our foe we saw
Laugh as he hailed us.

"And as to catch the gale
Round veered the flapping sail,
'Death!' was the helmsman's hail,
'Death without quarter!'
Midships with iron keel
Struck we her ribs of steel;
Down her black hulk did reel
Through the black water!

"As with his wings aslant,
Sails the fierce cormorant,
Seeking some rocky haunt,
With his prey laden,
So toward the open main,
Beating to sea again,
Through the wild hurricane,
Bore I the maiden.

"Three weeks we westward bore,
And when the storm was o'er,
Cloud-like we saw the shore
Stretching to leeward;
There for my lady's bower
Built I the lofty tower,
Which, to this very hour,
Stands looking seaward.

"There lived we many years;
Time dried the maiden's tears;
She had forgot her fears,
She was a mother;
Death closed her mild blue eyes;
Under that tower she lies;
Ne'er shall the sun arise
On such another.

"Still grew my bosom then,
Still as a stagnant fen!
Hateful to me were men,
The sunlight hateful!
In the vast forest here,
Clad in my warlike gear,
Fell I upon my spear,
Oh, death was grateful!

"Thus, seamed with many scars,
Bursting these prison bars,
Up to its native stars
My soul ascended!
There from the flowing bowl
Deep drinks the warrior's soul,
Skoal! to the Northland! *skoal!*"
Thus the tale ended.

THE VILLAGE BLACKSMITH

Under a spreading chestnut-tree
The village smithy stands;
The smith, a mighty man is he,
With large and sinewy hands;
And the muscles of his brawny arms
Are strong as iron bands.

His hair is crisp, and black, and long,
His face is like the tan;
His brow is wet with honest sweat,
He earns whate'er he can,
And looks the whole world in the face,
For he owes not any man.

Week in, week out, from morn till night,
You can hear his bellows blow;
You can hear him swing his heavy sledge
With measured beat and slow,
Like a sexton ringing the village bell,
When the evening sun is low.

And children coming home from school
Look in at the open door;
They love to see the flaming forge,
And hear the bellows roar,
And catch the burning sparks that fly
Like chaff from a threshing-floor.

He goes on Sunday to the church,
And sits among his boys;
He hears the parson pray and preach,
He hears his daughter's voice,
Singing in the village choir,
And it makes his heart rejoice.

It sounds to him like her mother's voice,
Singing in Paradise!
He needs must think of her once more,
How in the grave she lies;
And with his hard, rough hand he wipes
A tear out of his eyes.

Toiling, — rejoicing, — sorrowing,
Onward through life he goes;
Each morning sees some task begin,
Each evening sees its close;
Something attempted, something done,
Has earned a night's repose.

Thanks, thanks to thee, my worthy friend,
For the lesson thou hast taught!
Thus at the flaming forge of life
Our fortunes must be wrought;
Thus on its sounding anvil shaped
Each burning deed and thought!

ENDYMION

The rising moon has hid the stars;
Her level rays, like golden bars,
Lie on the landscape green,
With shadows brown between.

And silver white the river gleams,
As if Diana, in her dreams,
Had dropt her silver bow
Upon the meadows low.

On such a tranquil night as this,
She woke Endymion with a kiss,

When, sleeping in the grove,
He dreamed not of her love.

Like Dian's kiss, unasked, unsought,
Love gives itself, but is not bought;
Nor voice, nor sound betrays
Its deep, impassioned gaze.

It comes, — the beautiful, the free,
The crown of all humanity, —
In silence and alone
To seek the elected one.

It lifts the boughs, whose shadows deep
Are Life's oblivion, the soul's sleep,
And kisses the closed eyes
Of him who slumbering lies.

O weary hearts! O slumbering eyes!
O drooping souls, whose destinies
Are fraught with fear and pain,
Ye shall be loved again!

No one is so accursed by fate,
No one so utterly desolate,
But some heart, though unknown,
Responds unto his own.

Responds, — as if with unseen wings
An angel touched its quivering strings;
And whispers, in its song,
"Where hast thou stayed so long?"

SERENADE FROM "THE SPANISH STUDENT"

STARS of the summer night!
Far in yon azure deeps,
Hide, hide your golden light!
She sleeps!
My lady sleeps!
Sleeps!

Moon of the summer night!
Far down yon western steeps,
Sink, sink in silver light!
She sleeps!
My lady sleeps!
Sleeps!

Wind of the summer night!
Where yonder woodbine creeps,
Fold, fold thy pinions light!
She sleeps!
My lady sleeps!
Sleeps!

Dreams of the summer night!
Tell her, her lover keeps
Watch! while in slumbers light
She sleeps!
My lady sleeps!
Sleeps!

THE ARROW AND THE SONG

I SHOT an arrow into the air,
It fell to earth, I knew not where;
For, so swiftly it flew, the sight
Could not follow it in its flight.

I breathed a song into the air,
It fell to earth, I knew not where;
For who has sight so keen and strong
That it can follow the flight of song?

Long, long afterward, in an oak
I found the arrow, still unbroke;
And the song, from beginning to end,
I found again in the heart of a friend.

DANTE

TUSCAN, that wanderest through the realms of gloom,
With thoughtful pace, and sad, majestic eyes,
Stern thoughts and awful from thy soul arise,
Like Farinata from his fiery tomb.
Thy sacred song is like the trump of doom;
Yet in thy heart what human sympathies,
What soft compassion glows, as in the skies
The tender stars their clouded lamps relume!
Methinks I see thee stand with pallid cheeks
By Fra Hilario in his diocese,
As up the convent-walls, in golden streaks,
The ascending sunbeams mark the day's decrease;
And, as he asks what there the stranger seeks,
Thy voice along the cloister whispers "Peace!"

CURFEW

SOLEMNLY, mournfully,
Dealing its dole,
The Curfew Bell
Is beginning to toll.

Cover the embers,
And put out the light;
Toil comes with the morning,
And rest with the night.

Dark grow the windows,
And quenched is the fire;
Sound fades into silence, —
All footsteps retire.

No voice in the chambers,
No sound in the hall!
Sleep and oblivion
Reign over all!

The book is completed,
And closed, like the day;
And the hand that has written it
Lays it away.

Dim grow its fancies;
Forgotten they lie;
Like coals in the ashes,
They darken and die.

Song sinks into silence,
The story is told,
The windows are darkened,
The hearth-stone is cold.

Darker and darker
The black shadows fall;
Sleep and oblivion
Reign over all.

FROM "EVANGELINE"

EVANGELINE IN ACADIE

SOMEWHAT apart from the village, and nearer the Basin of Minas,
Benedict Bellefontaine, the wealthiest farmer of Grand-Pré,
Dwelt on his goodly acres; and with him, directing his household,
Gentle Evangeline lived, his child, and the pride of the village.
Stalworth and stately in form was the man of seventy winters;
Hearty and hale was he, an oak that is covered with snowflakes;
White as the snow were his locks, and his cheeks as brown as the oak-leaves.
Fair was she to behold, that maiden of seventeen summers.
Black were her eyes as the berry that grows on the thorn by the wayside,
Black, yet how softly they gleamed beneath the brown shade of her tresses!
Sweet was her breath as the breath of kine that feed in the meadows.
When in the harvest heat she bore to the reapers at noontide
Flagons of home-brewed ale, ah! fair in sooth was the maiden.
Fairer was she when, on Sunday morn, while the bell from its turret
Sprinkled with holy sounds the air, as the priest with his hyssop
Sprinkles the congregation, and scatters blessings upon them,
Down the long street she passed, with her chaplet of beads and her missal,
Wearing her Norman cap, and her kirtle of blue, and the ear-rings,
Brought in the olden time from France, and since, as an heirloom,
Handed down from mother to child, through long generations.
But a celestial brightness — a more ethereal beauty —
Shone on her face and encircled her form, when, after confession,
Homeward serenely she walked with God's benediction upon her.
When she had passed, it seemed like the ceasing of exquisite music.

Firmly builded with rafters of oak, the house of the farmer
Stood on the side of a hill commanding the sea; and a shady
Sycamore grew by the door, with a woodbine wreathing around it.
Rudely carved was the porch, with seats beneath; and a footpath
Led through an orchard wide, and disappeared in the meadow.
Under the sycamore-tree were hives overhung by a penthouse,
Such as the traveller sees in regions remote by the roadside,

Built o'er a box for the poor, or the blessëd image of Mary.
Farther down, on the slope of the hill, was the well with its moss-grown
Bucket, fastened with iron, and near it a trough for the horses.
Shielding the house from storms, on the north, were the barns and the farm-yard.
There stood the broad-wheeled wains and the antique ploughs and the harrows;
There were the folds for the sheep; and there, in his feathered seraglio,
Strutted the lordly turkey, and crowed the cock, with the selfsame
Voice that in ages of old had startled the penitent Peter.
Bursting with hay were the barns, themselves a village. In each one
Far o'er the gable projected a roof of thatch; and a staircase,
Under the sheltering eaves, led up to the odorous corn-loft.
There too the dove-cot stood, with its meek and innocent inmates
Murmuring ever of love; while above in the variant breezes
Numberless noisy weathercocks rattled and sang of mutation.

ON THE ATCHAFALAYA

Water-lilies in myriads rocked on the slight undulations
Made by the passing oars, and, resplendent in beauty, the lotus
Lifted her golden crown above the heads of the boatmen.
Faint was the air with the odorous breath of magnolia blossoms,
And with the heat of noon; and numberless sylvan islands,
Fragrant and thickly embowered with blossoming hedges of roses,
Near to whose shores they glided along, invited to slumber.
Soon by the fairest of these their weary oars were suspended.
Under the boughs of Wachita willows, that grew by the margin,
Safely their boat was moored; and scattered about on the greensward,
Tired with their midnight toil, the weary travellers slumbered.
Over them vast and high extended the cope of a cedar.
Swinging from its great arms, the trumpet-flower and the grapevine
Hung their ladder of ropes aloft like the ladder of Jacob,
On whose pendulous stairs the angels ascending, descending,
Were the swift humming-birds, that flitted from blossom to blossom.
Such was the vision Evangeline saw as she slumbered beneath it.
Filled was her heart with love, and the dawn of an opening heaven
Lighted her soul in sleep with the glory of regions celestial.

. . . .

Softly the evening came. The sun from the western horizon
Like a magician extended his golden wand o'er the landscape;
Twinkling vapors arose; and sky and water and forest
Seemed all on fire at the touch, and melted and mingled together.
Hanging between two skies, a cloud with edges of silver,
Floated the boat, with its dripping oars, on the motionless water.
Filled was Evangeline's heart with inexpressible sweetness.
Touched by the magic spell, the sacred fountains of feeling
Glowed with the light of love, as the skies and waters around her.
Then from a neighboring thicket the mocking-bird, wildest of singers,
Swinging aloft on a willow spray that hung o'er the water,
Shook from his little throat such floods of delirious music,
That the whole air and the woods and the waves seemed silent to listen.
Plaintive at first were the tones and sad: then, soaring to madness,
Seemed they to follow or guide the revel of frenzied Bacchantes.
Single notes were then heard, in sorrowful, low lamentation;
Till, having gathered them all, he flung them abroad in derision,
As when, after a storm, a gust of wind through the tree-tops
Shakes down the rattling rain in a crystal shower on the branches.
With such a prelude as this, and hearts that throbbed with emotion,

Slowly they entered the Têche, where it flows through the green Opelousas,
And, through the amber air, above the crest of the woodland,
Saw the column of smoke that arose from a neighboring dwelling; —
Sounds of a horn they heard, and the distant lowing of cattle.

THE FINDING OF GABRIEL

Then it came to pass that a pestilence fell on the city,
Presaged by wondrous signs, and mostly by flocks of wild pigeons,
Darkening the sun in their flight, with naught in their craws but an acorn.
And, as the tides of the sea arise in the month of September,
Flooding some silver stream, till it spreads to a lake in the meadow,
So death flooded life, and, o'erflowing its natural margin,
Spread to a brackish lake, the silver stream of existence.
Wealth had no power to bribe, nor beauty to charm, the oppressor;
But all perished alike beneath the scourge of his anger; —
Only, alas! the poor, who had neither friends nor attendants,
Crept away to die in the almshouse, home of the homeless.
Then in the suburbs it stood, in the midst of meadows and woodlands; —
Now the city surrounds it; but still, with its gateway and wicket
Meek, in the midst of splendor, its humble walls seem to echo
Softly the words of the Lord: — "The poor ye always have with you."
Thither, by night and by day, came the Sister of Mercy. The dying
Looked up into her face, and thought, indeed, to behold there
Gleams of celestial light encircle her forehead with splendor,
Such as the artist paints o'er the brows of saints and apostles,
Or such as hangs by night o'er a city seen at a distance.
Unto their eyes it seemed the lamps of the city celestial,
Into whose shining gates erelong their spirits would enter.

Thus, on a Sabbath morn, through the streets, deserted and silent,
Wending her quiet way, she entered the door of the almshouse.
Sweet on the summer air was the odor of flowers in the garden;
And she paused on her way to gather the fairest among them,
That the dying once more might rejoice in their fragrance and beauty.
Then, as she mounted the stairs to the corridors, cooled by the east-wind,
Distant and soft on her ear fell the chimes from the belfry of Christ Church,
While intermingled with these, across the meadows were wafted
Sounds of psalms, that were sung by the Swedes in their church at Wicaco.
Soft as descending wings fell the calm of the hour on her spirit;
Something within her said, "At length thy trials are ended;"
And, with light in her looks, she entered the chambers of sickness.
Noiselessly moved about the assiduous, careful attendants,
Moistening the feverish lip, and the aching brow, and in silence
Closing the sightless eyes of the dead, and concealing their faces,
Where on their pallets they lay, like drifts of snow by the roadside.
Many a languid head, upraised as Evangeline entered,
Turned on its pillow of pain to gaze while she passed, for her presence
Fell on their hearts like a ray of the sun on the walls of a prison.
And, as she looked around, she saw how Death, the consoler,
Laying his hand upon many a heart, had healed it forever.
Many familiar forms had disappeared in the night-time;
Vacant their places were, or filled already by strangers.

Suddenly, as if arrested by fear or a feeling of wonder,
Still she stood, with her colorless lips apart, while a shudder
Ran through her frame, and, forgotten, the flowerets dropped from her fingers,

And from her eyes and cheeks the light and bloom of the morning.
Then there escaped from her lips a cry of such terrible anguish,
That the dying heard it, and started up from their pillows.
On the pallet before her was stretched the form of an old man.
Long, and thin, and gray were the locks that shaded his temples;
But, as he lay in the morning light, his face for a moment
Seemed to assume once more the forms of its earlier manhood;
So are wont to be changed the faces of those who are dying.
Hot and red on his lips still burned the flush of the fever,
As if life, like the Hebrew, with blood had besprinkled its portals,
That the Angel of Death might see the sign, and pass over.
Motionless, senseless, dying, he lay, and his spirit exhausted
Seemed to be sinking down through infinite depths in the darkness —
Darkness of slumber and death, forever sinking and sinking.
Then through those realms of shade, in multiplied reverberations,
Heard he that cry of pain, and through the hush that succeeded
Whispered a gentle voice, in accents tender and saintlike,
"Gabriel! O my beloved!" and died away into silence.
Then he beheld, in a dream, once more the home of his childhood;
Green Acadian meadows, with sylvan rivers among them,
Village, and mountain, and woodlands; and walking under their shadow,
As in the days of her youth, Evangeline rose in his vision.
Tears came into his eyes; and as slowly he lifted his eyelids,
Vanished the vision away, but Evangeline knelt by his bedside.
Vainly he strove to whisper her name, for the accents unuttered
Died on his lips, and their motion revealed what his tongue would have spoken.
Vainly he strove to rise; and Evangeline, kneeling beside him,
Kissed his dying lips, and laid his head on her bosom.
Sweet was the light of his eyes; but it suddenly sank into darkness,
As when a lamp is blown out by a gust of wind at a casement.

All was ended now, the hope, and the fear, and the sorrow,
All the aching of heart, the restless, unsatisfied longing,
All the dull, deep pain, and constant anguish of patience!
And, as she pressed once more the lifeless head to her bosom,
Meekly she bowed her own, and murmured, "Father, I thank thee!"

FROM "THE BUILDING OF THE SHIP"

THE REPUBLIC

THOU, too, sail on, O Ship of State!
Sail on, O UNION, strong and great!
Humanity with all its fears,
With all the hopes of future years,
Is hanging breathless on thy fate!
We know what Master laid thy keel,
What Workmen wrought thy ribs of steel,
Who made each mast, and sail, and rope,
What anvils rang, what hammers beat,
In what a forge and what a heat
Were shaped the anchors of thy hope!
Fear not each sudden sound and shock,
'T is of the wave and not the rock;
'T is but the flapping of the sail,
And not a rent made by the gale!
In spite of rock and tempest's roar,
In spite of false lights on the shore,
Sail on, nor fear to breast the sea!
Our hearts, our hopes, are all with thee,
Our hearts, our hopes, our prayers, our tears,
Our faith triumphant o'er our fears,
Are all with thee, — are all with thee!

FROM "THE SONG OF HIAWATHA"

THE DEATH OF MINNEHAHA

ALL day long roved Hiawatha
In that melancholy forest,
Through the shadow of whose thickets,

In the pleasant days of Summer,
Of that ne'er forgotten Summer,
He had brought his young wife homeward
From the land of the Dacotahs;
When the birds sang in the thickets,
And the streamlets laughed and glistened,
And the air was full of fragrance,
And the lovely Laughing Water
Said with voice that did not tremble,
"I will follow you, my husband!"
  In the wigwam with Nokomis,
With those gloomy guests that watched her,
With the Famine and the Fever,
She was lying, the Beloved,
She, the dying Minnehaha.
  "Hark!" she said; "I hear a rushing,
Hear a roaring and a rushing,
Hear the Falls of Minnehaha
Calling to me from a distance!"
"No, my child!" said old Nokomis,
"'T is the night-wind in the pine-trees!"
  "Look!" she said; "I see my father
Standing lonely at his doorway,
Beckoning to me from his wigwam
In the land of the Dacotahs!"
"No, my child!" said old Nokomis,
"'T is the smoke, that waves and beckons!"
  "Ah!" said she, "the eyes of Pauguk
Glare upon me in the darkness,
I can feel his icy fingers
Clasping mine amid the darkness!
Hiawatha! Hiawatha!"
  And the desolate Hiawatha,
Far away amid the forest,
Miles away among the mountains,
Heard that sudden cry of anguish,
Heard the voice of Minnehaha
Calling to him in the darkness,
"Hiawatha! Hiawatha!"
  Over snow-fields waste and pathless,
Under snow-encumbered branches,
Homeward hurried Hiawatha,
Empty-handed, heavy-hearted,
Heard Nokomis moaning, wailing:
"Wahonowin! Wahonowin!
Would that I had perished for you,
Would that I were dead as you are!
Wahonowin! Wahonowin!"
  And he rushed into the wigwam,
Saw the old Nokomis slowly
Rocking to and fro and moaning,
Saw his lovely Minnehaha
Lying dead and cold before him,
And his bursting heart within him
Uttered such a cry of anguish,
That the forest moaned and shuddered,
That the very stars in heaven
Shook and trembled with his anguish.
  Then he sat down, still and speechless,
On the bed of Minnehaha,
At the feet of Laughing Water,
At those willing feet, that never
More would lightly run to meet him,
Never more would lightly follow.
  With both hands his face he covered,
Seven long days and nights he sat there,
As if in a swoon he sat there,
Speechless, motionless, unconscious
Of the daylight or the darkness.
  Then they buried Minnehaha;
In the snow a grave they made her,
In the forest deep and darksome,
Underneath the moaning hemlocks;
Clothed her in her richest garments,
Wrapped her in her robes of ermine,
Covered her with snow, like ermine;
Thus they buried Minnehaha.
  And at night a fire was lighted,
On her grave four times was kindled,
For her soul upon its journey
To the Islands of the Blessed.
From his doorway Hiawatha
Saw it burning in the forest,
Lighting up the gloomy hemlocks;
From his sleepless bed uprising,
From the bed of Minnehaha,
Stood and watched it at the doorway,
That it might not be extinguished,
Might not leave her in the darkness.
  "Farewell!" said he, "Minnehaha!
Farewell, O my Laughing Water!
All my heart is buried with you,
All my thoughts go onward with you!
Come not back again to labor,
Come not back again to suffer,
Where the Famine and the Fever
Wear the heart and waste the body.
Soon my task will be completed,
Soon your footsteps I shall follow
To the Islands of the Blessed,
To the Kingdom of Ponemah,
To the Land of the Hereafter!"

THE WARDEN OF THE CINQUE PORTS

A MIST was driving down the British
    Channel,
  The day was just begun,

And through the window-panes, on floor and panel,
Streamed the red autumn sun.

It glanced on flowing flag and rippling pennon,
And the white sails of ships;
And, from the frowning rampart, the black cannon
Hailed it with feverish lips.

Sandwich and Romney, Hastings, Hithe, and Dover
Were all alert that day,
To see the French war-steamers speeding over,
When the fog cleared away.

Sullen and silent, and like couchant lions,
Their cannon, through the night,
Holding their breath, had watched, in grim defiance,
The sea-coast opposite.

And now they roared at drum-beat from their stations
On every citadel;
Each answering each, with morning salutations,
That all was well.

And down the coast, all taking up the burden,
Replied the distant forts,
As if to summon from his sleep the Warden
And Lord of the Cinque Ports.

Him shall no sunshine from the fields of azure,
No drum-beat from the wall,
No morning gun from the black fort's embrasure,
Awaken with its call!

No more, surveying with an eye impartial
The long line of the coast,
Shall the gaunt figure of the old Field Marshal
Be seen upon his post!

For in the night, unseen, a single warrior,
In sombre harness mailed,
Dreaded of man, and surnamed the Destroyer,
The rampart wall had scaled.

He passed into the chamber of the sleeper,
The dark and silent room,
And as he entered, darker grew, and deeper,
The silence and the gloom.

He did not pause to parley or dissemble,
But smote the Warden hoar;
Ah! what a blow! that made all England tremble
And groan from shore to shore.

Meanwhile, without, the surly cannon waited,
The sun rose bright o'erhead;
Nothing in Nature's aspect intimated
That a great man was dead.

MY LOST YOUTH

Often I think of the beautiful town
That is seated by the sea;
Often in thought go up and down
The pleasant streets of that dear old town,
And my youth comes back to me.
And a verse of a Lapland song
Is haunting my memory still:
"A boy's will is the wind's will,
And the thoughts of youth are long, long thoughts."

I can see the shadowy lines of its trees,
And catch, in sudden gleams,
The sheen of the far-surrounding seas,
And islands that were the Hesperides
Of all my boyish dreams.
And the burden of that old song,
It murmurs and whispers still:
"A boy's will is the wind's will,
And the thoughts of youth are long, long thoughts."

I remember the black wharves and the slips,
And the sea-tides tossing free;
And Spanish sailors with bearded lips,
And the beauty and mystery of the ships,
And the magic of the sea.
And the voice of that wayward song
Is singing and saying still:
"A boy's will is the wind's will,
And the thoughts of youth are long, long thoughts."

I remember the bulwarks by the shore,
And the fort upon the hill;

The sunrise gun, with its hollow roar,
The drum-beat repeated o'er and o'er,
And the bugle wild and shrill.
And the music of that old song
Throbs in my memory still:
"A boy's will is the wind's will,
And the thoughts of youth are long, long thoughts."

I remember the sea-fight far away,
How it thundered o'er the tide!
And the dead captains, as they lay
In their graves, o'erlooking the tranquil bay
Where they in battle died.
And the sound of that mournful song
Goes through me with a thrill:
"A boy's will is the wind's will,
And the thoughts of youth are long, long thoughts."

I can see the breezy dome of groves,
The shadows of Deering's Woods;
And the friendships old and the early loves
Come back with a Sabbath sound, as of doves
In quiet neighborhoods.
And the verse of that sweet old song,
It flutters and murmurs still:
"A boy's will is the wind's will,
And the thoughts of youth are long, long thoughts."

I remember the gleams and glooms that dart
Across the school-boy's brain;
The song and the silence in the heart,
That in part are prophecies, and in part
Are longings wild and vain.
And the voice of that fitful song
Sings on, and is never still:
"A boy's will is the wind's will,
And the thoughts of youth are long, long thoughts."

There are things of which I may not speak;
There are dreams that cannot die;
There are thoughts that make the strong heart weak,
And bring a pallor into the cheek,
And a mist before the eye.
And the words of that fatal song
Come over me like a chill:
"A boy's will is the wind's will,
And the thoughts of youth are long, long thoughts."

Strange to me now are the forms I meet
When I visit the dear old town;
But the native air is pure and sweet,
And the trees that o'ershadow each well-known street,
As they balance up and down,
Are singing the beautiful song,
Are sighing and whispering still:
"A boy's will is the wind's will,
And the thoughts of youth are long, long thoughts."

And Deering's Woods are fresh and fair,
And with joy that is almost pain
My heart goes back to wander there,
And among the dreams of the days that were,
I find my lost youth again.
And the strange and beautiful song,
The groves are repeating it still:
"A boy's will is the wind's will,
And the thoughts of youth are long, long thoughts."

THE CHILDREN'S HOUR

BETWEEN the dark and the daylight,
When the night is beginning to lower,
Comes a pause in the day's occupations,
That is known as the Children's Hour.

I hear in the chamber above me
The patter of little feet,
The sound of a door that is opened,
And voices soft and sweet.

From my study I see in the lamplight,
Descending the broad hall stair,
Grave Alice, and laughing Allegra,
And Edith with golden hair.

A whisper, and then a silence:
Yet I know by their merry eyes
They are plotting and planning together
To take me by surprise.

A sudden rush from the stairway,
A sudden raid from the hall!
By three doors left unguarded
They enter my castle wall!

They climb up into my turret
O'er the arms and back of my chair;

If I try to escape, they surround me;
They seem to be everywhere.

They almost devour me with kisses,
Their arms about me entwine,
Till I think of the Bishop of Bingen
In his Mouse-Tower on the Rhine!

Do you think, O blue-eyed banditti,
Because you have scaled the wall,
Such an old mustache as I am
Is not a match for you all!

I have you fast in my fortress,
And will not let you depart,
But put you down into the dungeon
In the round-tower of my heart.

And there will I keep you forever,
Yes, forever and a day,
Till the walls shall crumble to ruin,
And moulder in dust away.

THE CUMBERLAND

At anchor in Hampton Roads we lay,
On board of the Cumberland, sloop-of-war;
And at times from the fortress across the bay
The alarum of drums swept past,
Or a bugle blast
From the camp on the shore.

Then far away to the south uprose
A little feather of snow-white smoke,
And we knew that the iron ship of our foes
Was steadily steering its course
To try the force
Of our ribs of oak.

Down upon us heavily runs,
Silent and sullen, the floating fort;
Then comes a puff of smoke from her guns,
And leaps the terrible death,
With fiery breath,
From each open port.

We are not idle, but send her straight
Defiance back in a full broadside!
As hail rebounds from a roof of slate,
Rebounds our heavier hail
From each iron scale
Of the monster's hide.

"Strike your flag!" the rebel cries,
In his arrogant old plantation strain.
"Never!" our gallant Morris replies;
"It is better to sink than to yield!"
And the whole air pealed
With the cheers of our men.

Then, like a kraken huge and black,
She crushed our ribs in her iron grasp!
Down went the Cumberland all a wrack,
With a sudden shudder of death,
And the cannon's breath
For her dying gasp.

Next morn, as the sun rose over the bay,
Still floated our flag at the mainmast head.
Lord, how beautiful was Thy day!
Every waft of the air
Was a whisper of prayer,
Or a dirge for the dead.

Ho! brave hearts that went down in the seas!
Ye are at peace in the troubled stream;
Ho! brave land! with hearts like these,
Thy flag, that is rent in twain,
Shall be one again,
And without a seam!

THE BELLS OF LYNN

O curfew of the setting sun! O Bells of Lynn!
O requiem of the dying day! O Bells of Lynn!

From the dark belfries of yon cloud-cathedral wafted,
Your sounds aerial seem to float, O Bells of Lynn!

Borne on the evening wind across the crimson twilight,
O'er land and sea they rise and fall, O Bells of Lynn!

The fisherman in his boat, far out beyond the headland,
Listens, and leisurely rows ashore, O Bells of Lynn!

Over the shining sands the wandering cattle homeward

Follow each other at your call, O Bells of
Lynn!

The distant lighthouse hears, and with his
flaming signal
Answers you, passing the watchword on,
O Bells of Lynn!

And down the darkening coast run the tumultuous surges,
And clap their hands, and shout to you, O
Bells of Lynn!

Till from the shuddering sea, with your
wild incantations,
Ye summon up the spectral moon, O Bells
of Lynn!

And startled at the sight, like the weird
woman of Endor,
Ye cry aloud, and then are still, O Bells of
Lynn!

CHAUCER

An old man in a lodge within a park;
The chamber walls depicted all around
With portraitures of huntsman, hawk, and
hound,
And the hurt deer. He listeneth to the
lark,
Whose song comes with the sunshine
through the dark
Of painted glass in leaden lattice bound;
He listeneth and he laugheth at the sound,
Then writeth in a book like any clerk.
He is the poet of the dawn, who wrote
The Canterbury Tales, and his old age
Made beautiful with song; and as I read
I hear the crowing cock, I hear the note
Of lark and linnet, and from every page
Rise odors of ploughed field or flowery
mead.

MILTON

I pace the sounding sea-beach and behold
How the voluminous billows roll and run,
Upheaving and subsiding, while the sun
Shines through their sheeted emerald far
unrolled,
And the ninth wave, slow gathering fold by
fold
All its loose-flowing garments into one,
Plunges upon the shore, and floods the dun
Pale reach of sands, and changes them to
gold.
So in majestic cadence rise and fall
The mighty undulations of thy song,
O sightless bard, England's Mæonides!
And ever and anon, high over all
Uplifted, a ninth wave superb and strong
Floods all the soul with its melodious seas.

NATURE

As a fond mother, when the day is o'er,
Leads by the hand her little child to bed,
Half willing, half reluctant to be led,
And leave his broken playthings on the
floor,
Still gazing at them through the open door,
Nor wholly reassured and comforted
By promises of others in their stead,
Which, though more splendid, may not
please him more;
So Nature deals with us, and takes away
Our playthings one by one, and by the hand
Leads us to rest so gently, that we go
Scarce knowing if we wish to go or stay,
Being too full of sleep to understand
How far the unknown transcends the what
we know.

WAPENTAKE

TO ALFRED TENNYSON

Poet! I come to touch thy lance with
mine;
Not as a knight, who on the listed field
Of tourney touched his adversary's shield
In token of defiance, but in sign
Of homage to the mastery, which is thine,
In English song; nor will I keep concealed,
And voiceless as a rivulet frost-congealed,
My admiration for thy verse divine.
Not of the howling dervishes of song,
Who craze the brain with their delirious
dance,
Art thou, O sweet historian of the heart!
Therefore to thee the laurel-leaves belong,
To thee our love and our allegiance,
For thy allegiance to the poet's art.

A BALLAD OF THE FRENCH FLEET

OCTOBER, 1746

MR. THOMAS PRINCE *loquitur*

A FLEET with flags arrayed
Sailed from the port of Brest,
And the Admiral's ship displayed
The signal: "Steer southwest."
For this Admiral D'Anville
Had sworn by cross and crown
To ravage with fire and steel
Our helpless Boston Town.

There were rumors in the street,
In the houses there was fear
Of the coming of the fleet,
And the danger hovering near.
And while from mouth to mouth
Spread the tidings of dismay,
I stood in the Old South,
Saying humbly: "Let us pray!

"O Lord! we would not advise;
But if in thy Providence
A tempest should arise
To drive the French Fleet hence,
And scatter it far and wide,
Or sink it in the sea,
We should be satisfied,
And thine the glory be."

This was the prayer I made,
For my soul was all on flame,
And even as I prayed
The answering tempest came;
It came with a mighty power,
Shaking the windows and walls,
And tolling the bell in the tower,
As it tolls at funerals.

The lightning suddenly
Unsheathed its flaming sword,
And I cried: "Stand still, and see
The salvation of the Lord!"
The heavens were black with cloud,
The sea was white with hail,
And ever more fierce and loud
Blew the October gale.

The fleet it overtook,
And the broad sails in the van
Like the tents of Cushan shook,
Or the curtains of Midian.
Down on the reeling decks
Crashed the o'erwhelming seas;
Ah, never were there wrecks
So pitiful as these!

Like a potter's vessel broke
The great ships of the line;
They were carried away as a smoke,
Or sank like lead in the brine.
O Lord! before thy path
They vanished and ceased to be,
When thou didst walk in wrath
With thine horses through the sea!

JUGURTHA

How cold are thy baths, Apollo!
Cried the African monarch, the splendid,
As down to his death in the hollow
Dark dungeons of Rome he descended,
Uncrowned, unthroned, unattended;
How cold are thy baths, Apollo!

How cold are thy baths, Apollo!
Cried the Poet, unknown, unbefriended,
As the vision, that lured him to follow,
With the mist and the darkness blended,
And the dream of his life was ended;
How cold are thy baths, Apollo!

THE TIDE RISES, THE TIDE FALLS

THE tide rises, the tide falls,
The twilight darkens, the curlew calls;
Along the sea-sands damp and brown
The traveller hastens toward the town,
And the tide rises, the tide falls.

Darkness settles on roofs and walls,
But the sea, the sea in the darkness calls;
The little waves, with their soft, white hands,
Efface the footprints in the sands,
And the tide rises, the tide falls.

The morning breaks; the steeds in their stalls
Stamp and neigh, as the hostler calls;
The day returns, but nevermore
Returns the traveller to the shore,
And the tide rises, the tide falls.

MY BOOKS

Sadly as some old mediæval knight
Gazed at the arms he could no longer wield,
The sword two-handed and the shining shield
Suspended in the hall, and full in sight,
While secret longings for the lost delight
Of tourney or adventure in the field
Came over him, and tears but half concealed
Trembled and fell upon his beard of white,
So I behold these books upon their shelf,
My ornaments and arms of other days;
Not wholly useless, though no longer used,
For they remind me of my other self,
Younger and stronger, and the pleasant ways
In which I walked, now clouded and confused.

Elizabeth Oakes Smith

FROM "THE SINLESS CHILD"

Her ways were gentle while a babe,
With calm and tranquil eye,
That turned instinctively to seek
The blueness of the sky.
A holy smile was on her lip
Whenever sleep was there;
She slept, as sleeps the blossom, hushed
Amid the silent air.

And ere she left with tottling steps
The low-roofed cottage door,
The beetle and the cricket loved
The young child on the floor;
For every insect dwelt secure
Where little Eva played,
And piped for her its blithest song
When she in greenwood strayed.

With wing of gauze and mailëd coat
They gathered round her feet,
Rejoiced, as are all gladsome things,
A truthful soul to greet.
They taught her infant lips to sing
With them a hymn of praise,
The song that in the woods is heard,
Through the long summer days.

And everywhere the child was traced
By snatches of wild song
That marked her feet along the vale
Or hillside, fleet and strong.
She knew the haunts of every bird —
Where bloomed the sheltered flower,
So sheltered that the searching frost
Might scarcely find its bower.

No loneliness young Eva knew,
Though playmates she had none:
Such sweet companionship was hers,
She could not be alone;
For everything in earth or sky
Caressed the little child, —
The joyous bird upon the wing,
The blossom in the wild.

Much dwelt she on the green hill-side,
And under forest tree;
Beside the running, babbling brook,
Where lithe trout sported free.
She saw them dart, like stringëd gems,
Where the tangled roots were deep,
And learned that love forevermore
The heart will joyful keep.

She loved all simple flowers that spring
In grove or sunlit dell,
And of each streak and varied hue
Would pretty meanings tell.
For her a language was impressed
On every leaf that grew,
And lines revealing brighter worlds
That seraph fingers drew.

The opening bud that lightly swung
Upon the dewy air,
Moved in its very sportiveness
Beneath angelic care;
She saw that pearly fingers oped
Each curved and painted leaf,
And where the canker-worm had been
Were looks of angel grief.

Each tiny leaf became a scroll
Inscribed with holy truth,

A lesson that around the heart
  Should keep the dew of youth,
Bright missals from angelic throngs
  In every byway left: —
How were the earth of glory shorn,
  Were it of flowers bereft!

Young Eva said all noisome weeds
  Would pass from earth away,
When virtue in the human heart
  Held its predestined sway.
Exalted thoughts were always hers,
  Some deemed them strange and wild;
And hence, in all the hamlets round,
  Her name of Sinless Child.

THE DROWNED MARINER

A MARINER sat on the shrouds one night;
  The wind was piping free;
Now bright, now dimmed was the moonlight pale,
And the phosphor gleamed in the wake of the whale,
  As he floundered in the sea;
The scud was flying athwart the sky,
The gathering winds went whistling by,
And the wave as it towered, then fell in spray,
Looked an emerald wall in the moonlight ray.

The mariner swayed and rocked on the mast,
  But the tumult pleased him well;
Down the yawning wave his eye he cast,
And the monsters watched as they hurried past
  Or lightly rose and fell;
For their broad, damp fins were under the tide,
And they lashed as they passed the vessel's side,
And their filmy eyes, all huge and grim,
Glared fiercely up, and they glared at him.

Now freshens the gale, and the brave ship goes
  Like an uncurbed steed along;
A sheet of flame is the spray she throws,
As her gallant prow the water ploughs,
  But the ship is fleet and strong:
The topsails are reefed and the sails are furled,
And onward she sweeps o'er the watery world,
And dippeth her spars in the surging flood;
But there came no chill to the mariner's blood.

Wildly she rocks, but he swingeth at ease,
  And holds him by the shroud;
And as she careens to the crowding breeze,
The gaping deep the mariner sees,
  And the surging heareth loud.
Was that a face, looking up at him,
With its pallid cheek and its cold eyes dim?
Did it beckon him down? did it call his name?
Now rolleth the ship the way whence it came.

The mariner looked, and he saw with dread
  A face he knew too well;
And the cold eyes glared, the eyes of the dead,
And its long hair out on the wave was spread.
  Was there a tale to tell?
The stout ship rocked with a reeling speed,
And the mariner groaned, as well he need;
For, ever, down as she plunged on her side,
The dead face gleamed from the briny tide.

Bethink thee, mariner, well, of the past, —
  A voice calls loud for thee: —
There 's a stifled prayer, the first, the last; —
The plunging ship on her beam is cast, —
  Oh, where shall thy burial be?
Bethink thee of oaths that were lightly spoken,
Bethink thee of vows that were lightly broken,
Bethink thee of all that is dear to thee,
For thou art alone on the raging sea:

Alone in the dark, alone on the wave,
  To buffet the storm alone,
To struggle aghast at thy watery grave,
To struggle and feel there is none to save, —
  God shield thee, helpless one!
The stout limbs yield, for their strength is past,
The trembling hands on the deep are cast,
The white brow gleams a moment more,
Then slowly sinks — the struggle is o'er.

Down, down where the storm is hushed to sleep,
Where the sea its dirge shall swell,
Where the amber drops for thee shall weep,
And the rose-lipped shell her music keep,
There thou shalt slumber well.
The gem and the pearl lie heaped at thy side,
They fell from the neck of the beautiful bride,
From the strong man's hand, from the maiden's brow,
As they slowly sunk to the wave below.

A peopled home is the ocean bed;
The mother and child are there;
The fervent youth and the hoary head,
The maid, with her floating locks outspread,
The babe with its silken hair;
As the water moveth they lightly sway,
And the tranquil lights on their features play;
And there is each cherished and beautiful form,
Away from decay, and away from the storm.

John Greenleaf Whittier

PROEM

(WRITTEN TO INTRODUCE THE FIRST GENERAL COLLECTION OF HIS POEMS)

I LOVE the old melodious lays
Which softly melt the ages through,
The songs of Spenser's golden days,
Arcadian Sidney's silvery phrase,
Sprinkling our noon of time with freshest morning dew.

Yet, vainly in my quiet hours
To breathe their marvellous notes I try;
I feel them, as the leaves and flowers
In silence feel the dewy showers,
And drink with glad, still lips the blessing of the sky.

The rigor of a frozen clime,
The harshness of an untaught ear,
The jarring words of one whose rhyme
Beat often Labor's hurried time,
Or Duty's rugged march through storm and strife, are here.

Of mystic beauty, dreamy grace,
No rounded art the lack supplies;
Unskilled the subtle lines to trace,
Or softer shades of Nature's face,
I view her common forms with unanointed eyes.

Nor mine the seer-like power to show
The secrets of the heart and mind;
To drop the plummet-line below
Our common world of joy and woe,
A more intense despair or brighter hope to find.

Yet here at least an earnest sense
Of human right and weal is shown;
A hate of tyranny intense,
And hearty in its vehemence,
As if my brother's pain and sorrow were my own.

O Freedom! if to me belong
Nor mighty Milton's gift divine,
Nor Marvell's wit and graceful song,
Still with a love as deep and strong
As theirs, I lay, like them, my best gifts on thy shrine!

THE FAREWELL

OF A VIRGINIA SLAVE MOTHER TO HER DAUGHTERS SOLD INTO SOUTHERN BONDAGE

GONE, gone, — sold and gone,
To the rice-swamp dank and lone.
Where the slave-whip ceaseless swings,
Where the noisome insect stings,
Where the fever demon strews
Poison with the falling dews,
Where the sickly sunbeams glare
Through the hot and misty air;

Gone, gone, — sold and gone,
To the rice-swamp dank and lone,
From Virginia's hills and waters;
Woe is me, my stolen daughters!

Gone, gone, — sold and gone,
To the rice-swamp dank and lone.
There no mother's eye is near them,
There no mother's ear can hear them;
Never, when the torturing lash
Seams their back with many a gash,
Shall a mother's kindness bless them,
Or a mother's arms caress them.
Gone, gone, — sold and gone,
To the rice-swamp dank and lone,
From Virginia's hills and waters;
Woe is me, my stolen daughters!

Gone, gone, — sold and gone,
To the rice-swamp dank and lone.
O, when weary, sad, and slow,
From the fields at night they go,
Faint with toil, and racked with pain,
To their cheerless homes again,
There no brother's voice shall greet them;
There no father's welcome meet them.
Gone, gone, — sold and gone,
To the rice-swamp dank and lone,
From Virginia's hills and waters;
Woe is me, my stolen daughters!

Gone, gone, — sold and gone,
To the rice-swamp dank and lone.
From the tree whose shadow lay
On their childhood's place of play;
From the cool spring where they drank;
Rock, and hill, and rivulet bank;
From the solemn house of prayer,
And the holy counsels there;
Gone, gone, — sold and gone,
To the rice-swamp dank and lone,
From Virginia's hills and waters;
Woe is me, my stolen daughters!

Gone, gone, — sold and gone,
To the rice-swamp dank and lone;
Toiling through the weary day,
And at night the spoiler's prey.
Oh, that they had earlier died,
Sleeping calmly, side by side,
Where the tyrant's power is o'er,
And the fetter galls no more!
Gone, gone, — sold and gone,
To the rice-swamp dank and lone,
From Virginia's hills and waters;
Woe is me, my stolen daughters!

Gone, gone, — sold and gone,
To the rice-swamp dank and lone.
By the holy love He beareth;
By the bruisëd reed He spareth;
Oh, may He, to whom alone
All their cruel wrongs are known,
Still their hope and refuge prove,
With a more than mother's love.
Gone, gone, — sold and gone,
To the rice-swamp dank and lone,
From Virginia's hills and waters;
Woe is me, my stolen daughters!

ICHABOD

So fallen! so lost! the light withdrawn
Which once he wore!
The glory from his gray hairs gone
Forevermore!

Revile him not, the Tempter hath
A snare for all;
And pitying tears, not scorn and wrath,
Befit his fall!

Oh, dumb be passion's stormy rage,
When he who might
Have lighted up and led his age,
Falls back in night.

Scorn! would the angels laugh, to mark
A bright soul driven,
Fiend-goaded, down the endless dark,
From hope and heaven!

Let not the land once proud of him
Insult him now,
Nor brand with deeper shame his dim,
Dishonored brow.

But let its humbled sons, instead,
From sea to lake,
A long lament, as for the dead,
In sadness make.

Of all we loved and honored, naught
Save power remains;
A fallen angel's pride of thought,
Still strong in chains.

All else is gone; from those great eyes
The soul has fled:
When faith is lost, when honor dies,
The man is dead!

Then, pay the reverence of old days
To his dead fame;
Walk backward, with averted gaze,
And hide the shame!

ASTRÆA

"Jove means to settle
Astræa in her seat again,
And let down from his golden chain
An age of better metal."
BEN JONSON, 1615.

O POET rare and old!
Thy words are prophecies;
Forward the age of gold,
The new Saturnian lies.

The universal prayer
And hope are not in vain;
Rise, brothers! and prepare
The way for Saturn's reign.

Perish shall all which takes
From labor's board and can;
Perish shall all which makes
A spaniel of the man!

Free from its bonds the mind,
The body from the rod;
Broken all chains that bind
The image of our God.

Just men no longer pine
Behind their prison-bars;
Through the rent dungeon shine
The free sun and the stars.

Earth own, at last, untrod
By sect, or caste, or clan,
The fatherhood of God,
The brotherhood of man!

Fraud fail, craft perish, forth
The money-changers driven,
And God's will done on earth,
As now in heaven!

THE BAREFOOT BOY

BLESSINGS on thee, little man,
Barefoot boy, with cheek of tan!
With thy turned-up pantaloons,
And thy merry whistled tunes;
With thy red lip, redder still
Kissed by strawberries on the hill;
With the sunshine on thy face,
Through thy torn brim's jaunty grace;
From my heart I give thee joy, —
I was once a barefoot boy!
Prince thou art, — the grown-up man
Only is republican.
Let the million-dollared ride!
Barefoot, trudging at his side,
Thou hast more than he can buy
In the reach of ear and eye, —
Outward sunshine, inward joy:
Blessings on thee, barefoot boy!

Oh for boyhood's painless play,
Sleep that wakes in laughing day,
Health that mocks the doctor's rules,
Knowledge never learned of schools,
Of the wild bee's morning chase,
Of the wild flower's time and place,
Flight of fowl and habitude
Of the tenants of the wood;
How the tortoise bears his shell,
How the woodchuck digs his cell,
And the ground-mole sinks his well;
How the robin feeds her young,
How the oriole's nest is hung;
Where the whitest lilies blow,
Where the freshest berries grow,
Where the ground-nut trails its vine,
Where the wood-grape's clusters shine;
Of the black wasp's cunning way,
Mason of his walls of clay,
And the architectural plans
Of gray hornet artisans!
For, eschewing books and tasks,
Nature answers all he asks;
Hand in hand with her he walks,
Face to face with her he talks,
Part and parcel of her joy, —
Blessings on the barefoot boy!

Oh for boyhood's time of June,
Crowding years in one brief moon,
When all things I heard or saw,
Me, their master, waited for.

I was rich in flowers and trees,
Humming-birds and honey-bees;
For my sport the squirrel played,
Plied the snouted mole his spade;
For my taste the blackberry cone
Purpled over hedge and stone;
Laughed the brook for my delight
Through the day and through the night, —
Whispering at the garden wall,
Talked with me from fall to fall;
Mine the sand-rimmed pickerel pond,
Mine the walnut slopes beyond,
Mine, on bending orchard trees,
Apples of Hesperides!
Still as my horizon grew,
Larger grew my riches too;
All the world I saw or knew
Seemed a complex Chinese toy,
Fashioned for a barefoot boy!

Oh for festal dainties spread,
Like my bowl of milk and bread;
Pewter spoon and bowl of wood,
On the door-stone, gray and rude!
O'er me, like a regal tent,
Cloudy-ribbed, the sunset bent,
Purple-curtained, fringed with gold,
Looped in many a wind-swung fold;
While for music came the play
Of the pied frogs' orchestra;
And, to light the noisy choir,
Lit the fly his lamp of fire.
I was monarch: pomp and joy
Waited on the barefoot boy!

Cheerily, then, my little man,
Live and laugh, as boyhood can!
Though the flinty slopes be hard,
Stubble-speared the new-mown sward,
Every morn shall lead thee through
Fresh baptisms of the dew;
Every evening from thy feet
Shall the cool wind kiss the heat:
All too soon these feet must hide
In the prison cells of pride,
Lose the freedom of the sod,
Like a colt's for work be shod,
Made to tread the mills of toil,
Up and down in ceaseless moil:
Happy if their track be found
Never on forbidden ground;
Happy if they sink not in
Quick and treacherous sands of sin.
Ah! that thou couldst know thy joy,
Ere it passes, barefoot boy!

MAUD MULLER

Maud Muller on a summer's day
Raked the meadow sweet with hay.

Beneath her torn hat glowed the wealth
Of simple beauty and rustic health.

Singing, she wrought, and her merry glee
The mock-bird echoed from his tree.

But when she glanced to the far-off town,
White from its hill-slope looking down,

The sweet song died, and a vague unrest
And a nameless longing filled her breast, —

A wish that she hardly dared to own,
For something better than she had known.

The Judge rode slowly down the lane,
Smoothing his horse's chestnut mane.

He drew his bridle in the shade
Of the apple-trees, to greet the maid,

And asked a draught from the spring that flowed
Through the meadow across the road.

She stooped where the cool spring bubbled up,
And filled for him her small tin cup,

And blushed as she gave it, looking down
On her feet so bare, and her tattered gown.

"Thanks!" said the Judge; "a sweeter draught
From a fairer hand was never quaffed."

He spoke of the grass and flowers and trees,
Of the singing birds and the humming bees;

Then talked of the haying, and wondered whether
The cloud in the west would bring foul weather.

And Maud forgot her brier-torn gown
And her graceful ankles bare and brown;

And listened, while a pleased surprise
Looked from her long-lashed hazel eyes.

At last, like one who for delay
Seeks a vain excuse, he rode away.

Maud Muller looked and sighed: "Ah me!
That I the Judge's bride might be!

"He would dress me up in silks so fine,
And praise and toast me at his wine.

"My father should wear a broadcloth coat;
My brother should sail a painted boat.

"I'd dress my mother so grand and gay,
And the baby should have a new toy each day.

"And I'd feed the hungry and clothe the poor,
And all should bless me who left our door."

The Judge looked back as he climbed the hill,
And saw Maud Muller standing still.

"A form more fair, a face more sweet,
Ne'er hath it been my lot to meet.

"And her modest answer and graceful air
Show her wise and good as she is fair.

"Would she were mine, and I to-day,
Like her, a harvester of hay;

"No doubtful balance of rights and wrongs,
Nor weary lawyers with endless tongues,

"But low of cattle and song of birds,
And health and quiet and loving words."

But he thought of his sisters, proud and cold,
And his mother, vain of her rank and gold.

So, closing his heart, the Judge rode on,
And Maud was left in the field alone.

But the lawyers smiled that afternoon,
When he hummed in court an old love-tune;

And the young girl mused beside the well
Till the rain on the unraked clover fell.

He wedded a wife of richest dower,
Who lived for fashion, as he for power.

Yet oft, in his marble hearth's bright glow,
He watched a picture come and go;

And sweet Maud Muller's hazel eyes
Looked out in their innocent surprise.

Oft, when the wine in his glass was red,
He longed for the wayside well instead;

And closed his eyes on his garnished rooms
To dream of meadows and clover-blooms.

And the proud man sighed, with a secret pain,
"Ah, that I were free again!

"Free as when I rode that day,
Where the barefoot maiden raked her hay."

She wedded a man unlearned and poor,
And many children played round her door

But care and sorrow, and childbirth pain,
Left their traces on heart and brain.

And oft, when the summer sun shone hot
On the new-mown hay in the meadow lot,

And she heard the little spring brook fall
Over the roadside, through the wall,

In the shade of the apple-tree again
She saw a rider draw his rein;

And, gazing down with timid grace,
She felt his pleased eyes read her face.

Sometimes her narrow kitchen walls
Stretched away into stately halls;

The weary wheel to a spinet turned,
The tallow candle an astral burned,

And for him who sat by the chimney lug,
Dozing and grumbling o'er pipe and mug,

A manly form at her side she saw,
And joy was duty and love was law.

Then she took up her burden of life again,
Saying only, "It might have been."

Alas for maiden, alas for Judge,
For rich repiner and household drudge!

God pity them both! and pity us all,
Who vainly the dreams of youth recall.

For of all sad words of tongue or pen,
The saddest are these: "It might have been!"

Ah, well! for us all some sweet hope lies
Deeply buried from human eyes;

And, in the hereafter, angels may
Roll the stone from its grave away!

SKIPPER IRESON'S RIDE

Of all the rides since the birth of time,
Told in story or sung in rhyme, —
On Apuleius's Golden Ass,
Or one-eyed Calendar's horse of brass,
Witch astride of a human back,
Islam's prophet on Al-Borák, —
The strangest ride that ever was sped
Was Ireson's, out from Marblehead!
Old Floyd Ireson, for his hard heart,
Tarred and feathered and carried in a cart
By the women of Marblehead!

Body of turkey, head of owl,
Wings adroop like a rained-on fowl,
Feathered and ruffled in every part,
Skipper Ireson stood in the cart.
Scores of women, old and young,
Strong of muscle, and glib of tongue,
Pushed and pulled up the rocky lane,
Shouting and singing the shrill refrain:
"Here 's Flud Oirson, fur his horrd horrt,
Torr'd an' futherr'd an' corr'd in a corrt
By the women o' Morble'ead!"

Wrinkled scolds with hands on hips,
Girls in bloom of cheek and lips,
Wild-eyed, free-limbed, such as chase
Bacchus round some antique vase,
Brief of skirt, with ankles bare,
Loose of kerchief and loose of hair,
With conch-shells blowing and fish-horns' twang,
Over and over the Mænads sang:
"Here's Flud Oirson, fur his horrd horrt,
Torr'd an' futherr'd an' corr'd in a corrt
By the women o' Morble'ead!"

Small pity for him! — He sailed away
From a leaking ship in Chaleur Bay, —
Sailed away from a sinking wreck,
With his own town's-people on her deck!
"Lay by! lay by!" they called to him.
Back he answered, "Sink or swim!
Brag of your catch of fish again!"
And off he sailed through the fog and rain!
Old Floyd Ireson, for his hard heart,
Tarred and feathered and carried in a cart
By the women of Marblehead!

Fathoms deep in dark Chaleur
That wreck shall lie forevermore.
Mother and sister, wife and maid,
Looked from the rocks of Marblehead
Over the moaning and rainy sea, —
Looked for the coming that might not be!
What did the winds and the sea-birds say
Of the cruel captain who sailed away? —
Old Floyd Ireson, for his hard heart,
Tarred and feathered and carried in a cart
By the women of Marblehead.

Through the street, on either side,
Up flew windows, doors swung wide;
Sharp-tongued spinsters, old wives gray,
Treble lent the fish-horn's bray.
Sea-worn grandsires, cripple-bound,
Hulks of old sailors run aground,
Shook head, and fist, and hat, and cane,
And cracked with curses the hoarse refrain:
"Here 's Flud Oirson, fur his horrd horrt,
Torr'd an' futherr'd an' corr'd in a corrt
By the women o' Morble'ead!"

Sweetly along the Salem road
Bloom of orchard and lilac showed.
Little the wicked skipper knew
Of the fields so green and the sky so blue.
Riding there in his sorry trim,
Like an Indian idol glum and grim,
Scarcely he seemed the sound to hear
Of voices shouting, far and near:
"Here 's Flud Oirson, fur his horrd horrt,
Torr'd an' futherr'd an' corr'd in a corrt
By the women o' Morble'ead!"

"Hear me, neighbors!" at last he cried, —
"What to me is this noisy ride?
What is the shame that clothes the skin
To the nameless horror that lives within?
Waking or sleeping, I see a wreck,
And hear a cry from a reeling deck!

Hate me and curse me, — I only dread
The hand of God and the face of the dead!"
Said old Floyd Ireson, for his hard heart,
Tarred and feathered and carried in a cart
By the women of Marblehead!

Then the wife of the skipper lost at sea
Said, "God has touched him! why should we!"
Said an old wife mourning her only son,
"Cut the rogue's tether and let him run!"
So with soft relentings and rude excuse,
Half scorn, half pity, they cut him loose,
And gave him a cloak to hide him in,
And left him alone with his shame and sin.
Poor Floyd Ireson, for his hard heart,
Tarred and feathered and carried in a cart
By the women of Marblehead!

THE SWAN SONG OF PARSON AVERY

WHEN the reaper's task was ended, and the summer wearing late,
Parson Avery sailed from Newbury, with his wife and children eight,
Dropping down the river-harbor in the shallop "Watch and Wait."

Pleasantly lay the clearings in the mellow summer-morn,
With the newly planted orchards dropping their fruits first born,
And the home-roofs like brown islands amid a sea of corn.

Broad meadows reached out seaward the tided creeks between,
And hills rolled wave-like inland, with oaks and walnuts green:
A fairer home, a goodlier land, his eyes had never seen.

Yet away sailed Parson Avery, away where duty led,
And the voice of God seemed calling, to break the living bread
To the souls of fishers starving on the rocks of Marblehead.

All day they sailed: at nightfall the pleasant land-breeze died,
The blackening sky, at midnight, its starry lights denied,
And far and low the thunder of tempest prophesied!

Blotted out were all the coast-lines, gone were rock, and wood, and sand;
Grimly anxious stood the skipper with the rudder in his hand,
And questioned of the darkness what was sea and what was land.

And the preacher heard his dear ones, nestled round him, weeping sore:
"Never heed, my little children! Christ is walking on before
To the pleasant land of heaven, where the sea shall be no more."

All at once the great cloud parted, like a curtain drawn aside,
To let down the torch of lightning on the terror far and wide;
And the thunder and the whirlwind together smote the tide.

There was wailing in the shallop, woman's wail and man's despair,
A crash of breaking timbers on the rocks so sharp and bare,
And, through it all, the murmur of Father Avery's prayer.

From his struggle in the darkness with the wild waves and the blast,
On a rock, where every billow broke above him as it passed,
Alone, of all his household, the man of God was cast.

There a comrade heard him praying, in the pause of wave and wind:
"All my own have gone before me, and I linger just behind;
Not for life I ask, but only for the rest Thy ransomed find!

"In this night of death I challenge the promise of Thy word! —
Let me see the great salvation of which mine ears have heard! —
Let me pass from hence forgiven, through the grace of Christ, our Lord!

"In the baptism of these waters wash white my every sin,
And let me follow up to Thee my household and my kin!
Open the sea-gate of Thy heaven, and let me enter in!"

When the Christian sings his death-song, all the listening heavens draw near,
And the angels, leaning over the walls of crystal, hear
How the notes so faint and broken swell to music in God's ear.

The ear of God was open to His servant's last request;
As the strong wave swept him downward the sweet hymn upward pressed,
And the soul of Father Avery went, singing, to its rest.

There was wailing on the mainland, from the rocks of Marblehead;
In the stricken church of Newbury the notes of prayer were read;
And long, by board and hearthstone, the living mourned the dead.

And still the fishers outbound, or scudding from the squall,
With grave and reverent faces, the ancient tale recall,
When they see the white waves breaking on the Rock of Avery's Fall!

THE VANISHERS

Sweetest of all childlike dreams
In the simple Indian lore
Still to me the legend seems
Of the shapes who flit before.

Flitting, passing, seen and gone,
Never reached nor found at rest,
Baffling search, but beckoning on
To the Sunset of the Blest.

From the clefts of mountain rocks,
Through the dark of lowland firs,
Flash the eyes and flow the locks
Of the mystic Vanishers!

And the fisher in his skiff,
And the hunter on the moss,
Hear their call from cape and cliff,
See their hands the birch-leaves toss.

Wistful, longing, through the green
Twilight of the clustered pines,
In their faces rarely seen
Beauty more than mortal shines.

Fringed with gold their mantles flow
On the slopes of westering knolls;
In the wind they whisper low
Of the Sunset Land of Souls.

Doubt who may, O friend of mine!
Thou and I have seen them too;
On before with beck and sign
Still they glide, and we pursue.

More than clouds of purple trail
In the gold of setting day;
More than gleams of wing or sail
Beckon from the sea-mist gray.

Glimpses of immortal youth,
Gleams and glories seen and flown,
Far-heard voices sweet with truth,
Airs from viewless Eden blown;

Beauty that eludes our grasp,
Sweetness that transcends our taste,
Loving hands we may not clasp,
Shining feet that mock our haste;

Gentle eyes we closed below,
Tender voices heard once more,
Smile and call us, as they go
On and onward, still before.

Guided thus, O friend of mine!
Let us walk our little way,
Knowing by each beckoning sign
That we are not quite astray.

Chase we still, with baffled feet,
Smiling eye and waving hand,
Sought and seeker soon shall meet,
Lost and found, in Sunset Land!

THE ETERNAL GOODNESS

O friends! with whom my feet have trod
The quiet aisles of prayer,
Glad witness to your zeal for God
And love of man I bear.

I trace your lines of argument;
  Your logic linked and strong
I weigh as one who dreads dissent,
  And fears a doubt as wrong.

But still my human hands are weak
  To hold your iron creeds:
Against the words ye bid me speak
  My heart within me pleads.

Who fathoms the Eternal Thought?
  Who talks of scheme and plan?
The Lord is God! He needeth not
  The poor device of man.

I walk with bare, hushed feet the ground
  Ye tread with boldness shod;
I dare not fix with mete and bound
  The love and power of God.

Ye praise His justice; even such
  His pitying love I deem:
Ye seek a king; I fain would touch
  The robe that hath no seam.

Ye see the curse which overbroods
  A world of pain and loss;
I hear our Lord's beatitudes
  And prayer upon the cross.

More than your schoolmen teach, within
  Myself, alas! I know:
Too dark ye cannot paint the sin,
  Too small the merit show.

I bow my forehead to the dust,
  I veil mine eyes for shame,
And urge, in trembling self-distrust,
  A prayer without a claim.

I see the wrong that round me lies,
  I feel the guilt within;
I hear, with groan and travail-cries,
  The world confess its sin.

Yet, in the maddening maze of things,
  And tossed by storm and flood,
To one fixed trust my spirit clings;
  I know that God is good!

Not mine to look where cherubim
  And seraphs may not see,
But nothing can be good in Him
  Which evil is in me.

The wrong that pains my soul below
  I dare not throne above,
I know not of His hate, — I know
  His goodness and His love.

I dimly guess from blessings known
  Of greater out of sight,
And, with the chastened Psalmist, own
  His judgments too are right.

I long for household voices gone,
  For vanished smiles I long,
But God hath led my dear ones on,
  And He can do no wrong.

I know not what the future hath
  Of marvel or surprise,
Assured alone that life and death
  His mercy underlies.

And if my heart and flesh are weak
  To bear an untried pain,
The bruisèd reed He will not break,
  But strengthen and sustain.

No offering of my own I have,
  Nor works my faith to prove;
I can but give the gifts He gave,
  And plead His love for love.

And so beside the Silent Sea
  I wait the muffled oar;
No harm from Him can come to me
  On ocean or on shore.

I know not where His islands lift
  Their fronded palms in air;
I only know I cannot drift
  Beyond His love and care.

O brothers! if my faith is vain,
  If hopes like these betray,
Pray for me that my feet may gain
  The sure and safer way.

And Thou, O Lord! by whom are seen
  Thy creatures as they be,
Forgive me if too close I lean
  My human heart on Thee!

FROM "SNOW-BOUND"

THE WORLD TRANSFORMED

UNWARMED by any sunset light
The gray day darkened into night,
A night made hoary with the swarm
And whirl-dance of the blinding storm,
As zigzag, wavering to and fro,
Crossed and recrossed the wingëd snow:
And ere the early bedtime came
The white drift piled the window-frame,
And through the glass the clothes-line posts
Looked in like tall and sheeted ghosts.

So all night long the storm roared on:
The morning broke without a sun;
In tiny spherule traced with lines
Of Nature's geometric signs,
In starry flake, and pellicle,
All day the hoary meteor fell;
And, when the second morning shone,
We looked upon a world unknown,
On nothing we could call our own.
Around the glistening wonder bent
The blue walls of the firmament,
No cloud above, no earth below, —
A universe of sky and snow!
The old familiar sights of ours
Took marvellous shapes; strange domes and towers
Rose up where sty or corn-crib stood,
Or garden-wall, or belt of wood;
A smooth white mound the brush-pile showed,
A fenceless drift what once was road;
The bridle-post an old man sat
With loose-flung coat and high cocked hat;
The well-curb had a Chinese roof;
And even the long sweep, high aloof,
In its slant splendor, seemed to tell
Of Pisa's leaning miracle.

FIRELIGHT

Shut in from all the world without,
We sat the clean-winged hearth about,
Content to let the north-wind roar
In baffled rage at pane and door,
While the red logs before us beat
The frost-line back with tropic heat;
And ever, when a louder blast
Shook beam and rafter as it passed,
The merrier up its roaring draught
The great throat of the chimney laughed;
The house-dog on his paws outspread
Laid to the fire his drowsy head,
The cat's dark silhouette on the wall
A couchant tiger's seemed to fall;
And, for the winter fireside meet,
Between the andirons' straddling feet,
The mug of cider simmered slow,
The apples sputtered in a row,
And, close at hand, the basket stood
With nuts from brown October's wood.

What matter how the night behaved?
What matter how the north-wind raved?
Blow high, blow low, not all its snow
Could quench our hearth-fire's ruddy glow
O Time and Change! — with hair as gray
As was my sire's that winter day,
How strange it seems, with so much gone
Of life and love, to still live on!
Ah, brother! only I and thou
Are left of all that circle now, —
The dear home faces whereupon
That fitful firelight paled and shone.
Henceforward, listen as we will,
The voices of that hearth are still;
Look where we may, the wide earth o'er,
Those lighted faces smile no more.
We tread the paths their feet have worn,
  We sit beneath their orchard-trees,
  We hear, like them, the hum of bees
And rustle of the bladed corn;
We turn the pages that they read,
  Their written words we linger o'er,
But in the sun they cast no shade,
No voice is heard, no sign is made,
  No step is on the conscious floor!
Yet Love will dream, and Faith will trust,
(Since He who knows our need is just,)
That somehow, somewhere, meet we must.
Alas for him who never sees
The stars shine through his cypress-trees!
Who, hopeless, lays his dead away,
Nor looks to see the breaking day
Across the mournful marbles play!
Who hath not learned, in hours of faith,
  The truth to flesh and sense unknown,
That Life is ever lord of Death,
  And Love can never lose its own!

MOTHER

Our mother, while she turned her wheel
Or run the new-knit stocking-heel,
Told how the Indian hordes came down
At midnight on Cocheco town,

And how her own great-uncle bore
His cruel scalp-mark to fourscore.
Recalling, in her fitting phrase,
  So rich and picturesque and free,
  (The common unrhymed poetry
Of simple life and country ways,)
The story of her early days, —
She made us welcome to her home;
Old hearths grew wide to give us room;
We stole with her a frightened look
At the gray wizard's conjuring-book,
The fame whereof went far and wide
Through all the simple country-side;
We heard the hawks at twilight play,
The boat-horn on Piscataqua,
The loon's weird laughter far away;
We fished her little trout-brook, knew
What flowers in wood and meadow grew,
What sunny hillsides autumn-brown
She climbed to shake the ripe nuts down,
Saw where in sheltered cove and bay
The ducks' black squadron anchored lay,
And heard the wild geese calling loud
Beneath the gray November cloud.

SISTER

As one who held herself a part
Of all she saw, and let her heart
  Against the household bosom lean,
Upon the motley-braided mat
Our youngest and our dearest sat,
Lifting her large, sweet, asking eyes,
  Now bathed in the unfading green
And holy peace of Paradise.
Oh, looking from some heavenly hill,
  Or from the shade of saintly palms,
  Or silver reach of river calms,
Do those large eyes behold me still?
With me one little year ago: —
The chill weight of the winter snow
  For months upon her grave has lain;
And now, when summer south-winds blow
  And brier and harebell bloom again,
I tread the pleasant paths we trod,
I see the violet-sprinkled sod
Whereon she leaned, too frail and weak
The hillside flowers she loved to seek,
Yet following me where'er I went
With dark eyes full of love's content.
The birds are glad; the brier-rose fills
The air with sweetness; all the hills
Stretch green to June's unclouded sky;
But still I wait with ear and eye
For something gone which should be nigh,
A loss in all familiar things,
In flower that blooms, and bird that sings.
And yet, dear heart! remembering thee,
  Am I not richer than of old?
Safe in thy immortality,
  What change can reach the wealth I hold?
  What chance can mar the pearl and gold
Thy love hath left in trust with me?
And while in life's late afternoon,
  Where cool and long the shadows grow,
I walk to meet the night that soon
  Shall shape and shadow overflow,
I cannot feel that thou art far,
Since near at need the angels are;
And when the sunset gates unbar,
  Shall I not see thee waiting stand,
And, white against the evening star,
  The welcome of thy beckoning hand?

PROPHETESS

Another guest that winter night
Flashed back from lustrous eyes the light.
Unmarked by time, and yet not young,
The honeyed music of her tongue
And words of meekness scarcely told
A nature passionate and bold,
Strong, self-concentred, spurning guide,
Its milder features dwarfed beside
Her unbent will's majestic pride.
She sat among us, at the best,
A not unfeared, half-welcome guest,
Rebuking with her cultured phrase
Our homeliness of words and ways.
A certain pard-like, treacherous grace
Swayed the lithe limbs and dropped the lash,
Lent the white teeth their dazzling flash;
And under low brows, black with night,
Rayed out at times a dangerous light;
The sharp heat-lightnings of her face
  Presaging ill to him whom Fate
  Condemned to share her love or hate.
A woman tropical, intense
In thought and act, in soul and sense,
She blended in a like degree
The vixen and the devotee,
Revealing with each freak or feint
  The temper of Petruchio's Kate,
The raptures of Siena's saint.
Her tapering hand and rounded wrist
Had facile power to form a fist;
The warm, dark languish of her eyes
Was never safe from wrath's surprise

Brows saintly calm and lips devout
Knew every change of scowl and pout;
And the sweet voice had notes more high
And shrill for social battle-cry.

Since then what old cathedral town
Has missed her pilgrim staff and gown,
What convent-gate has held its lock
Against the challenge of her knock!
Through Smyrna's plague-hushed thoroughfares,
Up sea-set Malta's rocky stairs,
Gray olive slopes of hills that hem
Thy tombs and shrines, Jerusalem,
Or startling on her desert throne
The crazy Queen of Lebanon
With claims fantastic as her own,
Her tireless feet have held their way;
And still, unrestful, bowed, and gray,
She watches under Eastern skies,
With hope each day renewed and fresh,
The Lord's quick coming in the flesh,
Whereof she dreams and prophesies!

IN SCHOOL-DAYS

Still sits the school-house by the road,
A ragged beggar sunning;
Around it still the sumachs grow,
And blackberry vines are running.

Within, the master's desk is seen,
Deep scarred by raps official;
The warping floor, the battered seats,
The jack-knife's carved initial;

The charcoal frescos on its wall;
Its door's worn sill, betraying
The feet that, creeping slow to school,
Went storming out to playing!

Long years ago a winter sun
Shone over it at setting;
Lit up its western window-panes,
And low eaves' icy fretting.

It touched the tangled golden curls,
And brown eyes full of grieving,
Of one who still her steps delayed
When all the school were leaving.

For near her stood the little boy
Her childish favor singled:
His cap pulled low upon a face
Where pride and shame were mingled.

Pushing with restless feet the snow
To right and left, he lingered;—
As restlessly her tiny hands
The blue-checked apron fingered.

He saw her lift her eyes; he felt
The soft hand's light caressing,
And heard the tremble of her voice,
As if a fault confessing.

"I 'm sorry that I spelt the word:
I hate to go above you,
Because,"—the brown eyes lower fell,—
"Because, you see, I love you!"

Still memory to a gray-haired man
That sweet child-face is showing.
Dear girl! the grasses on her grave
Have forty years been growing!

He lives to learn, in life's hard school,
How few who pass above him
Lament their triumph and his loss,
Like her,—because they love him.

1870.

THE TWO ANGELS

God called the nearest angels who dwell with Him above:
The tenderest one was Pity, the dearest one was Love.

"Arise," He said, "my angels! a wail of woe and sin
Steals through the gates of heaven, and saddens all within.

"My harps take up the mournful strain that from a lost world swells,
The smoke of torment clouds the light and blights the asphodels.

"Fly downward to that under world, and on its souls of pain
Let Love drop smiles like sunshine, and Pity tears like rain!"

Two faces bowed before the Throne, veiled in their golden hair;
Four white wings lessened swiftly down the dark abyss of air.

The way was strange, the flight was long; at last the angels came
Where swung the lost and nether world, red-wrapped in rayless flame.

There Pity, shuddering, wept; but Love, with faith too strong for fear,
Took heart from God's almightiness and smiled a smile of cheer.

And lo! that tear of Pity quenched the flame whereon it fell,
And, with the sunshine of that smile, hope entered into hell!

Two unveiled faces full of joy looked upward to the Throne,
Four white wings folded at the feet of Him who sat thereon!

And deeper than the sound of seas, more soft than falling flake,
Amidst the hush of wing and song the Voice Eternal spake:

"Welcome, my angels! ye have brought a holier joy to heaven;
Henceforth its sweetest song shall be the song of sin forgiven!"

CENTENNIAL HYMN

Our fathers' God! from out whose hand
The centuries fall like grains of sand,
We meet to-day, united, free,
And loyal to our land and Thee,
To thank Thee for the era done,
And trust Thee for the opening one.

Here, where of old, by Thy design,
The fathers spake that word of Thine
Whose echo is the glad refrain
Of rended bolt and falling chain,
To grace our festal time, from all
The zones of earth our guests we call.

Be with us while the New World greets
The Old World thronging all its streets,
Unveiling all the triumphs won
By art or toil beneath the sun;
And unto common good ordain
This rivalship of hand and brain.

Thou, who hast here in concord furled
The war flags of a gathered world,
Beneath our Western skies fulfil
The Orient's mission of good-will,
And, freighted with love's Golden Fleece,
Send back its Argonauts of peace.

For art and labor met in truce,
For beauty made the bride of use,
We thank Thee; but, withal, we crave
The austere virtues strong to save,
The honor proof to place or gold,
The manhoood never bought nor sold!

Oh make Thou us, through centuries long,
In peace secure, in justice strong;
Around our gift of freedom draw
The safeguards of thy righteous law:
And, cast in some diviner mould,
Let the new cycle shame the old!
1876.

IN THE "OLD SOUTH"

She came and stood in the Old South Church
A wonder and a sign,
With a look the old-time sibyls wore,
Half-crazed and half-divine.

Save the mournful sackcloth about her wound,
Unclothed as the primal mother,
With limbs that trembled and eyes that blazed
With a fire she dare not smother.

Loose on her shoulders fell her hair,
With sprinkled ashes gray;
She stood in the broad aisle strange and weird
As a soul at the judgment day.

And the minister paused in his sermon's midst,
And the people held their breath,
For these were the words the maiden spoke
Through lips as the lips of death:

"Thus saith the Lord, with equal feet
All men my courts shall tread,
And priest and ruler no more shall eat
My people up like bread!

"Repent! repent! ere the Lord shall speak
  In thunder and breaking seals!
Let all souls worship Him in the way
  His light within reveals."

She shook the dust from her naked feet,
  And her sackcloth closer drew,
And into the porch of the awe-hushed church
  She passed like a ghost from view.

They whipped her away at the tail o' the cart
  Through half the streets of the town,
But the words she uttered that day nor fire
  Could burn nor water drown.

And now the aisles of the ancient church
  By equal feet are trod,
And the bell that swings in its belfry rings
  Freedom to worship God!

And now whenever a wrong is done
  It thrills the conscious walls;
The stone from the basement cries aloud
  And the beam from the timber calls.

There are steeple-houses on every hand,
  And pulpits that bless and ban,
And the Lord will not grudge the single church
  That is set apart for man.

For in two commandments are all the law
  And the prophets under the sun,
And the first is last and the last is first,
  And the twain are verily one.

So long as Boston shall Boston be,
  And her bay-tides rise and fall,
Shall freedom stand in the Old South Church
  And plead for the rights of all!

MULFORD

UNNOTED as the setting of a star
  He passed; and sect and party scarcely knew
  When from their midst a sage and seer withdrew
To fitter audience, where the great dead are
In God's republic of the heart and mind,
Leaving no purer, nobler soul behind.

AN AUTOGRAPH

I WRITE my name as one,
On sands by waves o'errun
Or winter's frosted pane,
Traces a record vain.

Oblivion's blankness claims
Wiser and better names,
And well my own may pass
As from the strand or glass.

Wash on, O waves of time!
Melt, noons, the frosty rime!
Welcome the shadow vast,
The silence that shall last!

When I and all who know
And love me vanish so,
What harm to them or me
Will the lost memory be?

If any words of mine,
Through right of life divine,
Remain, what matters it
Whose hand the message writ?

Why should the "crowner's quest"
Sit on my worst or best?
Why should the showman claim
The poor ghost of my name?

Yet, as when dies a sound
Its spectre lingers round,
Haply my spent life will
Leave some faint echo still.

A whisper giving breath
Of praise or blame to death,
Soothing or saddening such
As loved the living much.

Therefore with yearnings vain
And fond I still would fain
A kindly judgment seek,
A tender thought bespeak.

And, while my words are read,
Let this at least be said:
"Whate'er his life's defeatures,
He loved his fellow-creatures.

"If, of the Law's stone table,
To hold he scarce was able
The first great precept fast,
He kept for man the last.

"Through mortal lapse and dulness
What lacks the Eternal Fulness,
If still our weakness can
Love Him in loving man?

"Age brought him no despairing
Of the world's future faring;
In human nature still
He found more good than ill.

"To all who dumbly suffered,
His tongue and pen he offered;
His life was not his own,
Nor lived for self alone.

"Hater of din and riot
He lived in days unquiet;
And, lover of all beauty,
Trod the hard ways of duty.

"He meant no wrong to any,
He sought the good of many,
Yet knew both sin and folly, —
May God forgive him wholly!"

William Davis Gallagher

THE CARDINAL BIRD

A DAY and then a week passed by:
The redbird hanging from the sill
Sang not; and all were wondering why
It was so still —
When one bright morning, loud and clear,
Its whistle smote my drowsy ear,
Ten times repeated, till the sound
Filled every echoing niche around;
And all things earliest loved by me, —
The bird, the brook, the flower, the tree, —
Came back again, as thus I heard
The cardinal bird.

Where maple orchards towered aloft,
And spicewood bushes spread below,
Where skies were blue, and winds were soft,
I could but go —
For, opening through a wildering haze,
Appeared my restless childhood's days;
And truant feet and loitering mood
Soon found me in the same old wood
(Illusion's hour but seldom brings
So much the very form of things)
Where first I sought, and saw, and heard
The cardinal bird.

Then came green meadows, broad and bright,
Where dandelions, with wealth untold,
Gleamed on the young and eager sight
Like stars of gold;
And on the very meadow's edge,
Beneath the ragged blackberry hedge,
Mid mosses golden, gray and green,
The fresh young buttercups were seen,
And small spring-beauties, sent to be
The heralds of anemone:
All just as when I earliest heard
The cardinal bird.

Upon the gray old forest's rim
I snuffed the crab-tree's sweet perfume:
And farther, where the light was dim,
I saw the bloom
Of May-apples, beneath the tent
Of umbrel leaves above them bent;
Where oft was shifting light and shade
The blue-eyed ivy wildly strayed;
And Solomon's-seal, in graceful play,
Swung where the straggling sunlight lay:
The same as when I earliest heard
The cardinal bird.

And on the slope, above the rill
That wound among the sugar-trees,
I heard them at their labors still,
The murmuring bees:
Bold foragers! that come and go
Without permit from friend or foe;
In the tall tulip-trees o'erhead
On pollen greedily they fed,
And from low purple phlox, that grew
About my feet, sipped honey-dew: —
How like the scenes when first I heard
The cardinal bird!

How like! — and yet . . . The spell
grows weak: —
Ah, but I miss the sunny brow —
The sparkling eye — the ruddy cheek!
Where, where are now
The three who then beside me stood
Like sunbeams in the dusky wood?
Alas, I am alone! Since then,
They 've trod the weary ways of men:
One on the eve of manhood died;
Two in its flush of power and pride.
Their graves are green, where first we heard
The cardinal bird.

The redbird, from the window hung,
Not long my fancies thus beguiled:
Again in maple-groves it sung
Its wood-notes wild;
For, rousing with a tearful eye,
I gave it to the trees and sky!
I missed so much those brothers three,
Who walked youth's flowery ways with
me,
I could not, dared not but believe
It too had brothers, that would grieve
Till in old haunts again 't was heard, —
The cardinal bird.

AUTUMN IN THE WEST

The autumn time is with us. Its approach
Was heralded, not many days ago,
By hazy skies that veiled the brazen sun,
And sea-like murmurs from the rustling
corn,
And low-voiced brooks that wandered
drowsily
By pendent clusters of empurpling grapes
Swinging upon the vine. And now, 't is
here!
And what a change hath passed upon the
face
Of nature, where the waving forest spreads,
Then robed in deepest green! All through
the night
The subtle frost has plied its magic art;
And in the day the golden sun hath
wrought
True wonders; and the winds of morn and
even
Have touched with magic breath the
changing leaves.
And now, as wanders the dilating eye
Athwart the varied landscape, circling far,
What gorgeousness, what blazonry, what
pomp
Of colors bursts upon the ravished sight!
Here, where the poplar rears its yellow
crest,
A golden glory; yonder, where the oak
Stands monarch of the forest, and the
ash
Is girt with flame-like parasite, and broad
The dogwood spreads beneath, and, fringing
all,
The sumac blushes to the ground, a flood
Of deepest crimson; and afar, where looms
The gnarlëd gum, a cloud of bloodiest
red.

Out in the woods of autumn! I have
cast
Aside the shackles of the town, that vex
The fetterless soul, and come to hide my-
self,
Miami! in thy venerable shades.
Here where seclusion looks out on a
scene
Of matchless beauty, I will pause awhile,
And on this bank with varied mosses
crowned
Gently recline. Beneath me, silver-bright,
Glide the calm waters, with a plaintive
moan
For summer's parting glories. High o'er-
head,
Seeking the sedgy brinks of still lagoons
That bask in southern suns the winter
through,
Sails tireless the unerring waterfowl,
Screaming among the cloud-racks. Oft
from where,
In bushy covert hid, the partridge stands,
Bursts suddenly the whistle clear and
loud,
Far-echoing through the dim wood's fretted
aisles.
Deep murmurs from the trees, bending
with brown
And ripened mast, are interrupted oft
By sounds of dropping nuts; and warily
The turkey from the thicket comes, and
swift
As flies an arrow darts the pheasant down,
To batten on the autumn; and the air,
At times, is darkened by a sudden rush
Of myriad wings, as the wild pigeon
leads
His squadrons to the banquet. Far away,

Where tranquil groves on sunny slopes supply
Their liberal store of fruits, the merry laugh
Of children, and the truant school-boy's shout,
Ring on the air, as, from the hollows borne,
Nuts load their creaking carts, and lush pawpaws
Their motley baskets fill, with clustering grapes
And golden-sphered persimmons spread o'er all.

Edgar Allan Poe

TO HELEN

HELEN, thy beauty is to me
Like those Nicæan barks of yore,
That gently, o'er a perfumed sea,
The weary, wayworn wanderer bore
To his own native shore.

On desperate seas long wont to roam,
Thy hyacinth hair, thy classic face,
Thy Naiad airs, have brought me home
To the glory that was Greece
And the grandeur that was Rome.

Lo! in yon brilliant window-niche
How statue-like I see thee stand,
The agate lamp within thy hand!
Ah, Psyche, from the regions which
Are Holy Land!

THE RAVEN

ONCE upon a midnight dreary, while I pondered, weak and weary,
Over many a quaint and curious volume of forgotten lore, —
While I nodded, nearly napping, suddenly there came a tapping,
As of some one gently rapping, rapping at my chamber door.
"'T is some visitor," I muttered, "tapping at my chamber door:
Only this and nothing more."

Ah, distinctly I remember it was in the bleak December,
And each separate dying ember wrought its ghost upon the floor.
Eagerly I wished the morrow; — vainly I had sought to borrow
From my books surcease of sorrow — sorrow for the lost Lenore,
For the rare and radiant maiden whom the angels name Lenore:
Nameless here for evermore.

And the silken sad uncertain rustling of each purple curtain
Thrilled me — filled me with fantastic terrors never felt before;
So that now, to still the beating of my heart, I stood repeating
"'T is some visitor entreating entrance at my chamber door,
Some late visitor entreating entrance at my chamber door:
This it is and nothing more."

Presently my soul grew stronger; hesitating then no longer,
"Sir," said I, "or Madam, truly your forgiveness I implore;
But the fact is I was napping, and so gently you came rapping,
And so faintly you came tapping, tapping at my chamber door,
That I scarce was sure I heard you" — here I opened wide the door: —
Darkness there and nothing more.

Deep into that darkness peering, long I stood there wondering, fearing,
Doubting, dreaming dreams no mortals ever dared to dream before;
But the silence was unbroken, and the stillness gave no token,
And the only word there spoken was the whispered word, "Lenore?"
This I whispered, and an echo murmured back the word, "Lenore:"
Merely this and nothing more.

Back into the chamber turning, all my soul within me burning,
Soon again I heard a tapping somewhat louder than before.

"Surely," said I, "surely that is something at my window lattice;
Let me see, then, what thereat is, and this mystery explore;
Let my heart be still a moment and this mystery explore:
'T is the wind and nothing more."

Open here I flung the shutter, when, with many a flirt and flutter,
In there stepped a stately Raven of the saintly days of yore.
Not the least obeisance made he; not a minute stopped or stayed he;
But, with mien of lord or lady, perched above my chamber door,
Perched upon a bust of Pallas just above my chamber door:
Perched, and sat, and nothing more.

Then this ebony bird beguiling my sad fancy into smiling
By the grave and stern decorum of the countenance it wore, —
"Though thy crest be shorn and shaven, thou," I said, "art sure no craven,
Ghastly grim and ancient Raven wandering from the Nightly shore:
Tell me what thy lordly name is on the Night's Plutonian shore!"
Quoth the Raven, "Nevermore."

Much I marvelled this ungainly fowl to hear discourse so plainly,
Though its answer little meaning — little relevancy bore;
For we cannot help agreeing that no living human being
Ever yet was blessed with seeing bird above his chamber door,
Bird or beast upon the sculptured bust above his chamber door,
With such name as "Nevermore."

But the Raven, sitting lonely on the placid bust, spoke only
That one word, as if his soul in that one word he did outpour.
Nothing further then he uttered, not a feather then he fluttered,
Till I scarcely more than muttered, — "Other friends have flown before;
On the morrow *he* will leave me, as my Hopes have flown before."
Then the bird said, "Nevermore."

Startled at the stillness broken by reply so aptly spoken,
"Doubtless," said I, "what it utters is its only stock and store,
Caught from some unhappy master whom unmerciful Disaster
Followed fast and followed faster till his songs one burden bore:
Till the dirges of his Hope that melancholy burden bore
Of 'Never — nevermore.'"

But the Raven still beguiling all my fancy into smiling,
Straight I wheeled a cushioned seat in front of bird and bust and door;
Then, upon the velvet sinking, I betook myself to linking
Fancy unto fancy, thinking what this ominous bird of yore,
What this grim, ungainly, ghastly, gaunt, and ominous bird of yore
Meant in croaking "Nevermore."

This I sat engaged in guessing, but no syllable expressing
To the fowl whose fiery eyes now burned into my bosom's core;
This and more I sat divining, with my head at ease reclining
On the cushion's velvet lining that the lamp-light gloated o'er,
But whose velvet violet lining with the lamp-light gloating o'er
She shall press, ah, nevermore!

Then, methought, the air grew denser, perfumed from an unseen censer
Swung by seraphim whose foot-falls tinkled on the tufted floor.
"Wretch," I cried, "thy God hath lent thee — by these angels he hath sent thee
Respite — respite and nepenthe from thy memories of Lenore!
Quaff, oh quaff this kind nepenthe, and forget this lost Lenore!"
Quoth the Raven, "Nevermore."

"Prophet!" said I, "thing of evil! prophet still, if bird or devil!
Whether Tempter sent, or whether tempest tossed thee here ashore,
Desolate yet all undaunted, on this desert land enchanted —

On this home by Horror haunted — tell me truly, I implore:
Is there — *is* there balm in Gilead? — tell me — tell me, I implore!"
Quoth the Raven, "Nevermore."

"Prophet!" said I, "thing of evil — prophet still, if bird or devil!
By that Heaven that bends above us, by that God we both adore,
Tell this soul with sorrow laden if, within the distant Aidenn,
It shall clasp a sainted maiden whom the angels name Lenore:
Clasp a rare and radiant maiden whom the angels name Lenore!"
Quoth the Raven, "Nevermore."

"Be that word our sign of parting, bird or fiend!" I shrieked, upstarting:
"Get thee back into the tempest and the Night's Plutonian shore!
Leave no black plume as a token of that lie thy soul hath spoken!
Leave my loneliness unbroken! quit the bust above my door!
Take thy beak from out my heart, and take thy form from off my door!"
Quoth the Raven, "Nevermore."

And the Raven, never flitting, still is sitting, still is sitting
On the pallid bust of Pallas just above my chamber door;
And his eyes have all the seeming of a demon's that is dreaming,
And the lamp-light o'er him streaming throws his shadow on the floor:
And my soul from out that shadow that lies floating on the floor
Shall be lifted — nevermore!

THE SLEEPER

At midnight, in the month of June,
I stand beneath the mystic moon.
An opiate vapor, dewy, dim,
Exhales from out her golden rim,
And, softly dripping, drop by drop,
Upon the quiet mountain-top,
Steals drowsily and musically
Into the universal valley.
The rosemary nods upon the grave;
The lily lolls upon the wave;
Wrapping the fog about its breast,
The ruin moulders into rest;
Looking like Lethe, see! the lake
A conscious slumber seems to take,
And would not, for the world, awake.
All beauty sleeps! — and lo! where lies
Irene, with her destinies!

O lady bright! can it be right,
This window open to the night?
The wanton airs, from the tree-top,
Laughingly through the lattice drop;
The bodiless airs, a wizard rout,
Flit through thy chamber in and out,
And wave the curtain canopy
So fitfully, so fearfully,
Above the closed and fringëd lid
'Neath which thy slumb'ring soul lies hid,
That, o'er the floor and down the wall,
Like ghosts the shadows rise and fall.
O lady dear, hast thou no fear?
Why and what art thou dreaming here?
Sure thou art come o'er far-off seas,
A wonder to these garden trees!
Strange is thy pallor: strange thy dress:
Strange, above all, thy length of tress,
And this all solemn silentness!

The lady sleeps. Oh, may her sleep,
Which is enduring, so be deep!
Heaven have her in its sacred keep!
This chamber changed for one more holy,
This bed for one more melancholy,
I pray to God that she may lie
Forever with unopened eye,
While the pale sheeted ghosts go by.

My love, she sleeps. Oh, may her sleep,
As it is lasting, so be deep!
Soft may the worms about her creep!
Far in the forest, dim and old,
For her may some tall vault unfold:
Some vault that oft hath flung its black
And wingëd panels fluttering back,
Triumphant, o'er the crested palls
Of her grand family funerals:
Some sepulchre, remote, alone,
Against whose portal she hath thrown,
In childhood, many an idle stone:
Some tomb from out whose sounding door
She ne'er shall force an echo more,
Thrilling to think, poor child of sin,
It was the dead who groaned within!

LENORE

Ah, broken is the golden bowl! the spirit flown forever!
Let the bell toll! — a saintly soul floats on the Stygian river;
And, Guy De Vere, hast *thou* no tear? — weep now or nevermore!
See, on yon drear and rigid bier low lies thy love, Lenore!
Come, let the burial rite be read — the funeral song be sung:
An anthem for the queenliest dead that ever died so young,
A dirge for her the doubly dead in that she died so young.

"Wretches, ye loved her for her wealth and hated her for her pride,
And when she fell in feeble health, ye blessed her — that she died!
How *shall* the ritual, then, be read? the requiem how be sung
By you — by yours, the evil eye, — by yours, the slanderous tongue
That did to death the innocence that died, and died so young?"

Peccavimus; but rave not thus! and let a Sabbath song
Go up to God so solemnly the dead may feel no wrong.
The sweet Lenore hath gone before, with Hope that flew beside,
Leaving thee wild for the dear child that should have been thy bride:
For her, the fair and debonair, that now so lowly lies,
The life upon her yellow hair but not within her eyes;
The life still there, upon her hair — the death upon her eyes.

"Avaunt! avaunt! from fiends below, the indignant ghost is riven —
From Hell unto a high estate far up within the Heaven —
From grief and groan, to a golden throne, beside the King of Heaven!
Let no bell toll, then, — lest her soul, amid its hallowed mirth,
Should catch the note as it doth float up from the damnëd Earth!
And I! — to-night my heart is light! — no dirge will I upraise,
But waft the angel on her flight with a Pæan of old days!"

TO ONE IN PARADISE

Thou wast all that to me, love,
  For which my soul did pine:
A green isle in the sea, love,
  A fountain and a shrine
All wreathed with fairy fruits and flowers,
  And all the flowers were mine.

Ah, dream too bright to last!
  Ah, starry Hope, that didst arise
But to be overcast!
  A voice from out the Future cries,
"On! on!" — but o'er the Past
  (Dim gulf!) my spirit hovering lies
Mute, motionless, aghast.

For, alas! alas! with me
  The light of Life is o'er!
  No more — no more — no more —
(Such language holds the solemn sea
  To the sands upon the shore)
Shall bloom the thunder-blasted tree,
  Or the stricken eagle soar.

And all my days are trances,
  And all my nightly dreams
Are where thy gray eye glances,
  And where thy footstep gleams —
In what ethereal dances,
  By what eternal streams.

THE CITY IN THE SEA

Lo! Death has reared himself a throne
In a strange city lying alone
Far down within the dim West,
Where the good and the bad and the worst and the best
Have gone to their eternal rest.
There shrines and palaces and towers
(Time-eaten towers that tremble not)
Resemble nothing that is ours.
Around, by lifting winds forgot,
Resignedly beneath the sky
The melancholy waters lie.

No rays from the holy heaven come down
On the long night-time of that town;
But light from out the lurid sea
Streams up the turrets silently,
Gleams up the pinnacles far and free:
Up domes, up spires, up kingly halls,
Up fanes, up Babylon-like walls,
Up shadowy long-forgotten bowers
Of sculptured ivy and stone flowers,
Up many and many a marvellous shrine
Whose wreathëd friezes intertwine
The viol, the violet, and the vine.

Resignedly beneath the sky
The melancholy waters lie.
So blend the turrets and shadows there
That all seem pendulous in air,
While from a proud tower in the town
Death looks gigantically down.

There open fanes and gaping graves
Yawn level with the luminous waves;
But not the riches there that lie
In each idol's diamond eye, —
Not the gayly-jewelled dead,
Tempt the waters from their bed;
For no ripples curl, alas,
Along that wilderness of glass;
No swellings tell that winds may be
Upon some far-off happier sea;
No heavings hint that winds have been
On seas less hideously serene!

But lo, a stir is in the air!
The wave — there is a movement there!
As if the towers had thrust aside,
In slightly sinking, the dull tide;
As if their tops had feebly given
A void within the filmy Heaven!
The waves have now a redder glow,
The hours are breathing faint and low;
And when, amid no earthly moans,
Down, down that town shall settle hence,
Hell, rising from a thousand thrones,
Shall do it reverence.

ISRAFEL

And the angel Israfel, whose heart-strings are a lute, and who has the sweetest voice of all God's creatures. — KORAN.

In Heaven a spirit doth dwell
  Whose heart-strings are a lute;
None sing so wildly well
As the angel Israfel,
And the giddy stars (so legends tell),
Ceasing their hymns, attend the spell
  Of his voice, all mute.

Tottering above
  In her highest noon,
  The enamoured moon
Blushes with love,
  While, to listen, the red levin
  (With the rapid Pleiads, even,
  Which were seven)
  Pauses in Heaven.

And they say (the starry choir
  And the other listening things)
That Israfeli's fire
Is owing to that lyre
  By which he sits and sings,
The trembling living wire
  Of those unusual strings.

But the skies that angel trod,
  Where deep thoughts are a duty,
Where Love 's a grown-up God,
Where the Houri glances are
  Imbued with all the beauty
Which we worship in a star.

Therefore thou art not wrong,
  Israfeli, who despisest
An unimpassioned song;
To thee the laurels belong,
  Best bard, because the wisest:
Merrily live, and long!

The ecstasies above
  With thy burning measures suit:
Thy grief, thy joy, thy hate, thy love,
  With the fervor of thy lute:
  Well may the stars be mute!

Yes, Heaven is thine; but this
  Is a world of sweets and sours;
  Our flowers are merely — flowers,
And the shadow of thy perfect bliss
  Is the sunshine of ours.

If I could dwell
Where Israfel
  Hath dwelt, and he where I,
He might not sing so wildly well
  A mortal melody,
While a bolder note than this might swell
  From my lyre within the sky.

THE HAUNTED PALACE

In the greenest of our valleys
  By good angels tenanted,
Once a fair and stately palace —
  Radiant palace — reared its head.
In the monarch Thought's dominion,
  It stood there;
Never seraph spread a pinion
  Over fabric half so fair.

Banners yellow, glorious, golden,
  On its roof did float and flow
(This — all this — was in the olden
  Time long ago),
And every gentle air that dallied,
  In that sweet day,
Along the ramparts plumed and pallid,
  A wingëd odor went away.

Wanderers in that happy valley
  Through two luminous windows saw
Spirits moving musically,
  To a lute's well-tunëd law,
Round about a throne where, sitting,
  Porphyrogene,
In state his glory well befitting,
  The ruler of the realm was seen.

And all with pearl and ruby glowing
  Was the fair palace door,
Through which came flowing, flowing, flowing,
  And sparkling evermore,
A troop of Echoes, whose sweet duty
  Was but to sing,
In voices of surpassing beauty,
  The wit and wisdom of their king.

But evil things, in robes of sorrow,
  Assailed the monarch's high estate;
(Ah, let us mourn, for never morrow
  Shall dawn upon him desolate!)
And round about his home the glory
  That blushed and bloomed,
Is but a dim-remembered story
  Of the old time entombed.

And travellers now within that valley
  Through the red-litten windows see
Vast forms that move fantastically
  To a discordant melody;
While, like a ghastly rapid river,
  Through the pale door
A hideous throng rush out forever,
  And laugh — but smile no more.

THE CONQUEROR WORM

Lo! 't is a gala night
  Within the lonesome latter years.
An angel throng, bewinged, bedight
  In veils, and drowned in tears,
Sit in a theatre to see
  A play of hopes and fears,
While the orchestra breathes fitfully
  The music of the spheres.

Mimes, in the form of God on high,
  Mutter and mumble low,
And hither and thither fly;
  Mere puppets they, who come and go
At bidding of vast formless things
  That shift the scenery to and fro,
Flapping from out their condor wings
  Invisible Woe.

That motley drama — oh, be sure
  It shall not be forgot!
With its Phantom chased for evermore
  By a crowd that seize it not,
Through a circle that ever returneth in
  To the self-same spot;
And much of Madness, and more of Sin,
  And Horror the soul of the plot.

But see amid the mimic rout
  A crawling shape intrude:
A blood-red thing that writhes from out
  The scenic solitude!
It writhes — it writhes! — with mortal pangs
  The mimes become its food,
And seraphs sob at vermin fangs
  In human gore imbued.

Out — out are the lights — out all!
  And over each quivering form
The curtain, a funeral pall,
  Comes down with the rush of a storm,
While the angels, all pallid and wan,
  Uprising, unveiling, affirm
That the play is the tragedy, "Man,"
  And its hero, the Conqueror Worm.

THE BELLS

I

HEAR the sledges with the bells,
Silver bells!
What a world of merriment their melody foretells!
How they tinkle, tinkle, tinkle,
In the icy air of night!
While the stars, that oversprinkle
All the heavens, seem to twinkle
With a crystalline delight;
Keeping time, time, time,
In a sort of Runic rhyme,
To the tintinnabulation that so musically wells
From the bells, bells, bells, bells,
Bells, bells, bells —
From the jingling and the tinkling of the bells.

II

Hear the mellow wedding bells,
Golden bells!
What a world of happiness their harmony foretells!
Through the balmy air of night
How they ring out their delight!
From the molten-golden notes,
And all in tune,
What a liquid ditty floats
To the turtle-dove that listens, while she gloats
On the moon!
Oh, from out the sounding cells,
What a gush of euphony voluminously wells!
How it swells!
How it dwells
On the Future! how it tells
Of the rapture that impels
To the swinging and the ringing
Of the bells, bells, bells,
Of the bells, bells, bells, bells,
Bells, bells, bells —
To the rhyming and the chiming of the bells!

III

Hear the loud alarum bells,
Brazen bells!
What a tale of terror, now, their turbulency tells!
In the startled ear of night
How they scream out their affright!
Too much horrified to speak,
They can only shriek, shriek,
Out of tune,
In a clamorous appealing to the mercy of the fire,
In a mad expostulation with the deaf and frantic fire,
Leaping higher, higher, higher,
With a desperate desire,
And a resolute endeavor
Now — now to sit or never,
By the side of the pale-faced moon.
Oh, the bells, bells, bells!
What a tale their terror tells
Of Despair!
How they clang, and clash, and roar!
What a horror they outpour
On the bosom of the palpitating air!
Yet the ear it fully knows,
By the twanging
And the clanging,
How the danger ebbs and flows;
Yet the ear distinctly tells,
In the jangling
And the wrangling,
How the danger sinks and swells, —
By the sinking or the swelling in the anger of the bells,
Of the bells,
Of the bells, bells, bells, bells,
Bells, bells, bells —
In the clamor and the clangor of the bells!

IV

Hear the tolling of the bells,
Iron bells!
What a world of solemn thought their monody compels!
In the silence of the night
How we shiver with affright
At the melancholy menace of their tone!
For every sound that floats
From the rust within their throats
Is a groan.
And the people — ah, the people,
They that dwell up in the steeple,
All alone,
And who tolling, tolling, tolling,
In that muffled monotone,
Feel a glory in so rolling
On the human heart a stone —

They are neither man nor woman,
They are neither brute nor human,
They are Ghouls:
And their king it is who tolls;
And he rolls, rolls, rolls,
Rolls
A pæan from the bells;
And his merry bosom swells
With the pæan of the bells,
And he dances, and he yells:
Keeping time, time, time,
In a sort of Runic rhyme,
To the pæan of the bells,
Of the bells:
Keeping time, time, time,
In a sort of Runic rhyme,
To the throbbing of the bells,
Of the bells, bells, bells —
To the sobbing of the bells;
Keeping time, time, time,
As he knells, knells, knells,
In a happy Runic rhyme,
To the rolling of the bells,
Of the bells, bells, bells:
To the tolling of the bells,
Of the bells, bells, bells, bells,
Bells, bells, bells —
To the moaning and the groaning of the bells.

ANNABEL LEE

It was many and many a year ago,
In a kingdom by the sea,
That a maiden there lived whom you may know
By the name of Annabel Lee;
And this maiden she lived with no other thought
Than to love and be loved by me.

I was a child and she was a child,
In this kingdom by the sea,
But we loved with a love that was more than love,
I and my Annabel Lee;
With a love that the wingëd seraphs of heaven
Coveted her and me.

And this was the reason that, long ago,
In this kingdom by the sea,
A wind blew out of a cloud, chilling
My beautiful Annabel Lee;
So that her highborn kinsmen came
And bore her away from me,
To shut her up in a sepulchre
In this kingdom by the sea.

The angels, not half so happy in heaven,
Went envying her and me;
Yes! that was the reason (as all men know,
In this kingdom by the sea)
That the wind came out of the cloud by night,
Chilling and killing my Annabel Lee.

But our love it was stronger by far than the love
Of those who were older than we,
Of many far wiser than we;
And neither the angels in heaven above,
Nor the demons down under the sea,
Can ever dissever my soul from the soul
Of the beautiful Annabel Lee:

For the moon never beams, without bringing me dreams
Of the beautiful Annabel Lee;
And the stars never rise, but I feel the bright eyes
Of the beautiful Annabel Lee;
And so, all the night-tide, I lie down by the side
Of my darling — my darling — my life and my bride,
In her sepulchre there by the sea,
In her tomb by the sounding sea.

ULALUME

The skies they were ashen and sober;
The leaves they were crispëd and sere,
The leaves they were withering and sere;
It was night in the lonesome October
Of my most immemorial year;
It was hard by the dim lake of Auber,
In the misty mid region of Weir:
It was down by the dank tarn of Auber,
In the ghoul-haunted woodland of Weir.

Here once, through an alley Titanic
Of cypress, I roamed with my Soul —
Of cypress, with Psyche, my Soul.
These were days when my heart was volcanic

As the scoriac rivers that roll,
As the lavas that restlessly roll
Their sulphurous currents down Yaanek
In the ultimate climes of the pole,
That groan as they roll down Mount Yaanek
In the realms of the boreal pole.

Our talk had been serious and sober,
But our thoughts they were palsied and sere,
Our memories were treacherous and sere,
For we knew not the month was October,
And we marked not the night of the year,
(Ah, night of all nights in the year!)
We noted not the dim lake of Auber
(Though once we had journeyed down here),
Remembered not the dank tarn of Auber
Nor the ghoul-haunted woodland of Weir.

And now, as the night was senescent
And star-dials pointed to morn,
As the star-dials hinted of morn,
At the end of our path a liquescent
And nebulous lustre was born,
Out of which a miraculous crescent
Arose with a duplicate horn,
Astarte's bediamonded crescent
Distinct with its duplicate horn.

And I said — "She is warmer than Dian:
She rolls through an ether of sighs,
She revels in a region of sighs:
She has seen that the tears are not dry on
These cheeks, where the worm never dies,
And has come past the stars of the Lion
To point us the path to the skies,
To the Lethean peace of the skies:
Come up, in despite of the Lion,
To shine on us with her bright eyes:
Come up through the lair of the Lion,
With love in her luminous eyes."

But Psyche, uplifting her finger,
Said — "Sadly this star I mistrust,
Her pallor I strangely mistrust:
Oh, hasten! — oh, let us not linger!
Oh, fly! — let us fly! — for we must."
In terror she spoke, letting sink her
Wings until they trailed in the dust;
In agony sobbed, letting sink her
Plumes till they trailed in the dust,
Till they sorrowfully trailed in the dust.

I replied — "This is nothing but dreaming:
Let us on by this tremulous light!
Let us bathe in this crystalline light!
Its sibyllic splendor is beaming
With hope and in beauty to-night:
See, it flickers up the sky through the night!
Ah, we safely may trust to its gleaming,
And be sure it will lead us aright:
We safely may trust to a gleaming
That cannot but guide us aright,
Since it flickers up to Heaven through the night."

Thus I pacified Psyche and kissed her,
And tempted her out of her gloom,
And conquered her scruples and gloom;
And we passed to the end of the vista,
But were stopped by the door of a tomb,
By the door of a legended tomb;
And I said — "What is written, sweet sister,
On the door of this legended tomb?"
She replied — "Ulalume — Ulalume —
'T is the vault of thy lost Ulalume!"

Then my heart it grew ashen and sober
As the leaves that were crispèd and sere,
As the leaves that were withering and sere,
And I cried — "It was surely October
On this very night of last year
That I journeyed — I journeyed down here,
That I brought a dread burden down here:
On this night of all nights in the year,
Ah, what demon has tempted me here?
Well I know, now, this dim lake of Auber,
This misty mid region of Weir:
Well I know, now, this dank tarn of Auber,
This ghoul-haunted woodland of Weir."

Samuel Francis Smith

AMERICA

My country, 't is of thee,
Sweet land of liberty,
Of thee I sing;
Land where my fathers died,
Land of the pilgrims' pride,
From every mountain-side
Let freedom ring.

My native country, thee,
Land of the noble free, —
Thy name I love;
I love thy rocks and rills,
Thy woods and templed hills;
My heart with rapture thrills
Like that above.

Let music swell the breeze,
And ring from all the trees,
Sweet freedom's song;
Let mortal tongues awake,
Let all that breathe partake,
Let rocks their silence break, —
The sound prolong.

Our fathers' God, to Thee,
Author of liberty,
To Thee I sing;
Long may our land be bright
With freedom's holy light;
Protect us by thy might,
Great God our King.

1832.

Ray Palmer

FAITH

My faith looks up to Thee,
Thou Lamb of Calvary,
Saviour divine!
Now hear me while I pray,
Take all my guilt away,
O let me from this day
Be wholly Thine!

May Thy rich grace impart
Strength to my fainting heart,
My zeal inspire;
As Thou hast died for me,
O may my love for Thee
Pure, warm, and changeless be, —
A living fire!

While life's dark maze I tread,
And griefs around me spread,
Be Thou my guide;
Bid darkness turn to day,
Wipe sorrow's tears away,
Nor let me ever stray
From Thee aside.

When ends life's transient dream,
When death's cold, sullen stream
Shall o'er me roll;
Blest Saviour, then, in love,
Fear and distrust remove;
O bear me safe above,
A ransomed soul!

1830.

Oliver Wendell Holmes

OLD IRONSIDES

Ay, tear her tattered ensign down!
Long has it waved on high,
And many an eye has danced to see
That banner in the sky;
Beneath it rung the battle shout,
And burst the cannon's roar; —
The meteor of the ocean air
Shall sweep the clouds no more.

Her deck, once red with heroes' blood,
Where knelt the vanquished foe,
When winds were hurrying o'er the flood,
And waves were white below,

No more shall feel the victor's tread,
Or know the conquered knee;
The harpies of the shore shall pluck
The eagle of the sea!

O, better that her shattered hulk
Should sink beneath the wave;
Her thunders shook the mighty deep,
And there should be her grave;
Nail to the mast her holy flag,
Set every threadbare sail,
And give her to the god of storms,
The lightning and the gale!

THE LAST LEAF

I SAW him once before,
As he passed by the door,
And again
The pavement stones resound,
As he totters o'er the ground
With his cane.

They say that in his prime,
Ere the pruning-knife of Time
Cut him down,
Not a better man was found
By the Crier on his round
Through the town.

But now he walks the streets,
And he looks at all he meets
Sad and wan,
And he shakes his feeble head,
That it seems as if he said,
"They are gone."

The mossy marbles rest
On the lips that he has prest
In their bloom,
And the names he loved to hear
Have been carved for many a year
On the tomb.

My grandmamma has said —
Poor old lady, she is dead
Long ago —
That he had a Roman nose,
And his cheek was like a rose
In the snow;

But now his nose is thin,
And it rests upon his chin
Like a staff,
And a crook is in his back,
And a melancholy crack
In his laugh.

I know it is a sin
For me to sit and grin
At him here;
But the old three-cornered hat,
And the breeches, and all that,
Are so queer!

And if I should live to be
The last leaf upon the tree
In the spring,
Let them smile, as I do now,
At the old forsaken bough
Where I cling.

THE HEIGHT OF THE RIDICULOUS

I WROTE some lines once on a time
In wondrous merry mood,
And thought, as usual, men would say
They were exceeding good.

They were so queer, so very queer,
I laughed as I would die;
Albeit, in the general way,
A sober man am I.

I called my servant, and he came;
How kind it was of him
To mind a slender man like me,
He of the mighty limb.

"These to the printer," I exclaimed,
And, in my humorous way,
I added (as a trifling jest,)
"There 'll be the devil to pay."

He took the paper, and I watched,
And saw him peep within;
At the first line he read, his face
Was all upon the grin.

He read the next; the grin grew broad,
And shot from ear to ear;
He read the third; a chuckling noise
I now began to hear.

The fourth; he broke into a roar;
The fifth; his waistband split;

The sixth; he burst five buttons off,
  And tumbled in a fit.

Ten days and nights, with sleepless eye,
  I watched that wretched man,
And since, I never dare to write
  As funny as I can.

LA GRISETTE

Ah, Clemence! when I saw thee last
  Trip down the Rue de Seine,
And turning, when thy form had past,
  I said, "We meet again," —
I dreamed not in that idle glance
  Thy latest image came,
And only left to memory's trance
  A shadow and a name.

The few strange words my lips had taught
  Thy timid voice to speak,
Their gentler signs, which often brought
  Fresh roses to thy cheek,
The trailing of thy long loose hair
  Bent o'er my couch of pain,
All, all returned, more sweet, more fair;
  Oh, had we met again!

I walked where saint and virgin keep
  The vigil lights of Heaven,
I knew that thou hadst woes to weep,
  And sins to be forgiven;
I watched where Genevieve was laid,
  I knelt by Mary's shrine,
Beside me low, soft voices prayed;
  Alas! but where was thine?

And when the morning sun was bright,
  When wind and wave were calm,
And flamed, in thousand-tinted light,
  The rose of Notre Dame,
I wandered through the haunts of men,
  From Boulevard to Quai,
Till, frowning o'er Saint Etienne,
  The Pantheon's shadow lay.

In vain, in vain; we meet no more,
  Nor dream what fates befall;
And long upon the stranger's shore
  My voice on thee may call,
When years have clothed the line in moss
  That tells thy name and days,
And withered, on thy simple cross,
  The wreaths of Père-la-Chaise!

ON LENDING A PUNCH-BOWL

This ancient silver bowl of mine, it tells of
  good old times,
Of joyous days and jolly nights, and merry
  Christmas chimes;
They were a free and jovial race, but hon-
  est, brave, and true,
Who dipped their ladle in the punch when
  this old bowl was new.

A Spanish galleon brought the bar, — so
  runs the ancient tale;
'T was hammered by an Antwerp smith,
  whose arm was like a flail;
And now and then between the strokes, for
  fear his strength should fail,
He wiped his brow and quaffed a cup of
  good old Flemish ale.

'T was purchased by an English squire to
  please his loving dame,
Who saw the cherubs, and conceived a
  longing for the same;
And oft as on the ancient stock another
  twig was found,
'T was filled with caudle spiced and hot, and
  handed smoking round.

But, changing hands, it reached at length a
  Puritan divine,
Who used to follow Timothy, and take a
  little wine,
But hated punch and prelacy; and so it
  was, perhaps,
He went to Leyden, where he found con-
  venticles and schnapps.

And then, of course, you know what 's next:
  it left the Dutchman's shore
With those that in the Mayflower came, —
  a hundred souls and more, —
Along with all the furniture, to fill their
  new abodes, —
To judge by what is still on hand, at least
  a hundred loads.

'T was on a dreary winter's eve, the night
  was closing dim,
When brave Miles Standish took the bowl,
  and filled it to the brim;
The little Captain stood and stirred the
  posset with his sword,
And all his sturdy men-at-arms were ranged
  about the board.

He poured the fiery Hollands in, — the man that never feared, —
He took a long and solemn draught, and wiped his yellow beard;
And one by one the musketeers — the men that fought and prayed —
All drank as 't were their mother's milk, and not a man afraid.

That night, affrighted from his nest, the screaming eagle flew,
He heard the Pequot's ringing whoop, the soldier's wild halloo;
And there the sachem learned the rule he taught to kith and kin:
"Run from the white man when you find he smells of Hollands gin!"

A hundred years, and fifty more, had spread their leaves and snows,
A thousand rubs had flattened down each little cherub's nose,
When once again the bowl was filled, but not in mirth or joy, —
'T was mingled by a mother's hand to cheer her parting boy.

"Drink, John," she said, "'t will do you good, — poor child, you 'll never bear
This working in the dismal trench, out in the midnight air;
And if — God bless me! — you were hurt, 't would keep away the chill."
So John *did* drink, — and well he wrought that night at Bunker's Hill!

I tell you, there was generous warmth in good old English cheer;
I tell you, 't was a pleasant thought to bring its symbol here:
'T is but the fool that loves excess; hast thou a drunken soul?
Thy bane is in thy shallow skull, not in my silver bowl!

I love the memory of the past, — its pressed yet fragrant flowers,—
The moss that clothes its broken walls, the ivy on its towers;
Nay, this poor bauble it bequeathed, — my eyes grow moist and dim,
To think of all the vanished joys that danced around its brim.

Then fill a fair and honest cup, and bear it straight to me;
The goblet hallows all it holds, whate'er the liquid be;
And may the cherubs on its face protect me from the sin
That dooms one to those dreadful words, — "My dear, where *have* you been?"

AFTER A LECTURE ON KEATS

"Purpureos spargam flores."

THE wreath that star-crowned Shelley gave
Is lying on thy Roman grave,
Yet on its turf young April sets
Her store of slender violets;
Though all the Gods their garlands shower,
I too may bring one purple flower.
Alas! what blossom shall I bring,
That opens in my Northern spring?
The garden beds have all run wild,
So trim when I was yet a child;
Flat plantains and unseemly stalks
Have crept across the gravel walks;
The vines are dead, long, long ago,
The almond buds no longer blow.
No more upon its mound I see
The azure, plume-bound fleur-de-lis;
Where once the tulips used to show,
In straggling tufts the pansies grow;
The grass has quenched my white-rayed gem,
The flowering "Star of Bethlehem,"
Though its long blade of glossy green
And pallid stripe may still be seen.
Nature, who treads her nobles down,
And gives their birthright to the clown,
Has sown her base-born weedy things
Above the garden's queens and kings.
Yet one sweet flower of ancient race
Springs in the old familiar place.
When snows were melting down the vale,
And Earth unlaced her icy mail,
And March his stormy trumpet blew,
And tender green came peeping through,
I loved the earliest one to seek
That broke the soil with emerald beak,
And watch the trembling bells so blue
Spread on the column as it grew.
Meek child of earth! thou wilt not shame
The sweet, dead poet's holy name;

The God of music gave thee birth,
Called from the crimson-spotted earth,
Where, sobbing his young life away,
His own fair Hyacinthus lay.
The hyacinth my garden gave
Shall lie upon that Roman grave!

THE VOICELESS

We count the broken lyres that rest
Where the sweet wailing singers slumber,
But o'er their silent sister's breast
The wild-flowers who will stoop to number?
A few can touch the magic string,
And noisy Fame is proud to win them: —
Alas for those that never sing,
But die with all their music in them!

Nay, grieve not for the dead alone
Whose song has told their hearts' sad story, —
Weep for the voiceless, who have known
The cross without the crown of glory!
Not where Leucadian breezes sweep
O'er Sappho's memory-haunted billow,
But where the glistening night-dews weep
On nameless sorrow's churchyard pillow.

O hearts that break and give no sign
Save whitening lip and fading tresses,
Till Death pours out his longed-for wine
Slow-dropped from Misery's crushing presses, —
If singing breath or echoing chord
To every hidden pang were given,
What endless melodies were poured,
As sad as earth, as sweet as heaven!

THE LIVING TEMPLE

Not in the world of light alone,
Where God has built his blazing throne,
Nor yet alone in earth below,
With belted seas that come and go,
And endless isles of sunlit green,
Is all thy Maker's glory seen:
Look in upon thy wondrous frame, —
Eternal wisdom still the same!

The smooth, soft air with pulse-like waves
Flows murmuring through its hidden caves,
Whose streams of brightening purple rush,
Fired with a new and livelier blush,
While all their burden of decay
The ebbing current steals away,
And red with Nature's flame they start
From the warm fountains of the heart.

No rest that throbbing slave may ask,
Forever quivering o'er his task,
While far and wide a crimson jet
Leaps forth to fill the woven net
Which in unnumbered crossing tides
The flood of burning life divides,
Then, kindling each decaying part,
Creeps back to find the throbbing heart.

But warmed with that unchanging flame
Behold the outward moving frame,
Its living marbles jointed strong
With glistening band and silvery thong,
And linked to reason's guiding reins
By myriad rings in trembling chains,
Each graven with the threaded zone
Which claims it as the master's own.

See how yon beam of seeming white
Is braided out of seven-hued light,
Yet in those lucid globes no ray
By any chance shall break astray.
Hark how the rolling surge of sound,
Arches and spirals circling round,
Wakes the hushed spirit through thine ear
With music it is heaven to hear.

Then mark the cloven sphere that holds
All thought in its mysterious folds;
That feels sensation's faintest thrill,
And flashes forth the sovereign will;
Think on the stormy world that dwells
Locked in its dim and clustering cells!
The lightning gleams of power it sheds
Along its hollow glassy threads!

O Father! grant thy love divine
To make these mystic temples thine!
When wasting age and wearying strife
Have sapped the leaning walls of life,
When darkness gathers over all,
And the last tottering pillars fall,
Take the poor dust thy mercy warms,
And mould it into heavenly forms!

THE CHAMBERED NAUTILUS

THIS is the ship of pearl, which, poets feign,
Sails the unshadowed main, —
The venturous bark that flings
On the sweet summer wind its purpled wings
In gulfs enchanted, where the Siren sings,
And coral reefs lie bare,
Where the cold sea-maids rise to sun their streaming hair.

Its webs of living gauze no more unfurl;
Wrecked is the ship of pearl!
And every chambered cell,
Where its dim dreaming life was wont to dwell,
As the frail tenant shaped his growing shell,
Before thee lies revealed, —
Its irised ceiling rent, its sunless crypt unsealed!

Year after year beheld the silent toil
That spread his lustrous coil;
Still, as the spiral grew,
He left the past year's dwelling for the new,
Stole with soft step its shining archway through,
Built up its idle door,
Stretched in his last-found home, and knew the old no more.

Thanks for the heavenly message brought by thee,
Child of the wandering sea,
Cast from her lap, forlorn!
From thy dead lips a clearer note is born
Than ever Triton blew from wreathëd horn!
While on mine ear it rings,
Through the deep caves of thought I hear a voice that sings: —

Build thee more stately mansions, O my soul,
As the swift seasons roll!
Leave thy low-vaulted past!
Let each new temple, nobler than the last,
Shut thee from heaven with a dome more vast,
Till thou at length art free,
Leaving thine outgrown shell by life's unresting sea!

BILL AND JOE

COME, dear old comrade, you and I
Will steal an hour from days gone by,
The shining days when life was new,
And all was bright with morning dew,
The lusty days of long ago,
When you were Bill and I was Joe.

Your name may flaunt a titled trail
Proud as a cockerel's rainbow tail,
And mine as brief appendix wear
As Tam O'Shanter's luckless mare;
To-day, old friend, remember still
That I am Joe and you are Bill.

You 've won the great world's envied prize,
And grand you look in people's eyes,
With H O N. and LL. D.
In big brave letters, fair to see, —
Your fist, old fellow! off they go! —
How are you, Bill? How are you, Joe?

You 've worn the judge's ermined robe;
You 've taught your name to half the globe;
You 've sung mankind a deathless strain;
You 've made the dead past live again:
The world may call you what it will,
But you and I are Joe and Bill.

The chaffing young folks stare and say
"See those old buffers, bent and gray, —
They talk like fellows in their teens!
Mad, poor old boys! That 's what it means," —
And shake their heads; they little know
The throbbing hearts of Bill and Joe! —

How Bill forgets his hour of pride,
While Joe sits smiling at his side;
How Joe, in spite of time's disguise,
Finds the old schoolmate in his eyes, —
Those calm, stern eyes that melt and fill
As Joe looks fondly up at Bill.

Ah, pensive scholar, what is fame?
A fitful tongue of leaping flame;
A giddy whirlwind's fickle gust,
That lifts a pinch of mortal dust;
A few swift years, and who can show
Which dust was Bill and which was Joe?

The weary idol takes his stand,
Holds out his bruised and aching hand,

While gaping thousands come and go, —
How vain it seems, this empty show!
Till all at once his pulses thrill; —
'T is poor old Joe's "God bless you, Bill!"

And shall we breathe in happier spheres
The names that pleased our mortal ears,
In some sweet lull of harp and song
For earth-born spirits none too long,
Just whispering of the world below
Where this was Bill and that was Joe?

No matter; while our home is here
No sounding name is half so dear;
When fades at length our lingering day,
Who cares what pompous tombstones say?
Read on the hearts that love us still,
Hic jacet Joe. *Hic jacet* Bill.

UNDER THE VIOLETS

Her hands are cold; her face is white;
  No more her pulses come and go;
Her eyes are shut to life and light; —
  Fold the white vesture, snow on snow,
  And lay her where the violets blow.

But not beneath a graven stone,
  To plead for tears with alien eyes;
A slender cross of wood alone
  Shall say, that here a maiden lies
  In peace beneath the peaceful skies.

And gray old trees of hugest limb
  Shall wheel their circling shadows round
To make the scorching sunlight dim
  That drinks the greenness from the ground,
  And drop their dead leaves on her mound.

When o'er their boughs the squirrels run,
  And through their leaves the robins call,
And, ripening in the autumn sun,
  The acorns and the chestnuts fall,
  Doubt not that she will heed them all.

For her the morning choir shall sing
  Its matins from the branches high,
And every minstrel-voice of Spring,
  That trills beneath the April sky,
  Shall greet her with its earliest cry.

When, turning round their dial-track,
  Eastward the lengthening shadows pass,
Her little mourners, clad in black,
  The crickets, sliding through the grass,
  Shall pipe for her an evening mass.

At last the rootlets of the trees
  Shall find the prison where she lies,
And bear the buried dust they seize
  In leaves and blossoms to the skies.
  So may the soul that warmed it rise!

If any, born of kindlier blood,
  Should ask, What maiden lies below?
Say only this: A tender bud,
  That tried to blossom in the snow,
  Lies withered where the violets blow.

HYMN OF TRUST

O Love Divine, that stooped to share
  Our sharpest pang, our bitterest tear,
On Thee we cast each earth-born care,
  We smile at pain while Thou art near!

Though long the weary way we tread,
  And sorrow crown each lingering year,
No path we shun, no darkness dread,
  Our hearts still whispering, Thou art near!

When drooping pleasure turns to grief,
  And trembling faith is changed to fear,
The murmuring wind, the quivering leaf,
  Shall softly tell us, Thou art near!

On Thee we fling our burdening woe,
  O Love Divine, forever dear,
Content to suffer while we know,
  Living and dying, Thou art near!

EPILOGUE TO THE BREAKFAST-TABLE SERIES

AUTOCRAT — PROFESSOR — POET

At a Bookstore

Anno Domini 1972

A crazy bookcase, placed before
A low-price dealer's open door;
Therein arrayed in broken rows
A ragged crew of rhyme and prose,
The homeless vagrants, waifs, and strays
Whose low estate this line betrays

(Set forth the lesser birds to lime)
YOUR CHOICE AMONG THESE BOOKS 1 DIME!

Ho! dealer; for its motto's sake
This scarecrow from the shelf I take;
Three starveling volumes bound in one,
Its covers warping in the sun.
Methinks it hath a musty smell,
I like its flavor none too well,
But Yorick's brain was far from dull,
Though Hamlet pah! 'd, and dropped his skull.

Why, here comes rain! The sky grows dark, —
Was that the roll of thunder? Hark!
The shop affords a safe retreat,
A chair extends its welcome seat,
The tradesman has a civil look
(I 've paid, impromptu, for my book),
The clouds portend a sudden shower, —
I 'll read my purchase for an hour.

. . . .

What have I rescued from the shelf?
A Boswell, writing out himself!
For though he changes dress and name,
The man beneath is still the same,
Laughing or sad, by fits and starts,
One actor in a dozen parts,
And whatsoe'er the mask may be,
The voice assures us, *This is he.*

I say not this to cry him down;
I find my Shakespeare in his clown,
His rogues the selfsame parent own;
Nay! Satan talks in Milton's tone!
Where'er the ocean inlet strays,
The salt sea wave its source betrays;
Where'er the queen of summer blows,
She tells the zephyr, "I 'm the rose!"

And his is not the playwright's page;
His table does not ape the stage;
What matter if the figures seen
Are only shadows on a screen,
He finds in them his lurking thought,
And on their lips the words he sought,
Like one who sits before the keys
And plays a tune himself to please.

And was he noted in his day?
Read, flattered, honored? Who shall say?
Poor wreck of time the wave has cast
To find a peaceful shore at last,
Once glorying in thy gilded name
And freighted deep with hopes of fame,
Thy leaf is moistened with a tear,
The first for many a long, long year!

For be it more or less of art
That veils the lowliest human heart
Where passion throbs, where friendship glows,
Where pity's tender tribute flows,
Where love has lit its fragrant fire,
And sorrow quenched its vain desire,
For me the altar is divine,
Its flame, its ashes, — all are mine!

And thou, my brother, as I look
And see thee pictured in thy book,
Thy years on every page confessed
In shadows lengthening from the west,
Thy glance that wanders, as it sought
Some freshly opening flower of thought,
Thy hopeful nature, light and free,
I start to find myself in thee!

. . . .

Come, vagrant, outcast, wretch forlorn
In leather jerkin stained and torn,
Whose talk has filled my idle hour
And made me half forget the shower,
I 'll do at least as much for you,
Your coat I 'll patch, your gilt renew,
Read you — perhaps — some other time.
Not bad, my bargain! Price one dime!

DOROTHY Q.

A FAMILY PORTRAIT

GRANDMOTHER'S mother: her age, I guess,
Thirteen summers, or something less;
Girlish bust, but womanly air;
Smooth, square forehead with uprolled hair;
Lips that lover has never kissed;
Taper fingers and slender wrist;
Hanging sleeves of stiff brocade;
So they painted the little maid.

On her hand a parrot green
Sits unmoving and broods serene.
Hold up the canvas full in view, —
Look! there 's a rent the light shines through,

Dark with a century's fringe of dust, —
That was a Red-Coat's rapier-thrust!
Such is the tale the lady old,
Dorothy's daughter's daughter, told.

Who the painter was none may tell, —
One whose best was not over well;
Hard and dry, it must be confessed,
Flat as a rose that has long been pressed;
Yet in her cheek the hues are bright,
Dainty colors of red and white,
And in her slender shape are seen
Hint and promise of stately mien.

Look not on her with eyes of scorn, —
Dorothy Q. was a lady born!
Ay! since the galloping Normans came,
England's annals have known her name;
And still to the three-hilled rebel town
Dear is that ancient name's renown,
For many a civic wreath they won,
The youthful sire and the gray-haired son.

O Damsel Dorothy! Dorothy Q.!
Strange is the gift that I owe to you;
Such a gift as never a king
Save to daughter or son might bring, —
All my tenure of heart and hand,
All my title to house and land;
Mother and sister and child and wife
And joy and sorrow and death and life!

What if a hundred years ago
Those close-shut lips had answered No,
When forth the tremulous question came
That cost the maiden her Norman name,
And under the folds that look so still
The bodice swelled with the bosom's thrill?
Should I be I, or would it be
One tenth another, to nine tenths me?

Soft is the breath of a maiden's Yes:
Not the light gossamer stirs with less;
But never a cable that holds so fast
Through all the battles of wave and blast,
And never an echo of speech or song
That lives in the babbling air so long!
There were tones in the voice that whispered then
You may hear to-day in a hundred men.

O lady and lover, how faint and far
Your images hover, — and here we are,
Solid and stirring in flesh and bone, —
Edward's and Dorothy's — all their own, —
A goodly record for Time to show
Of a syllable spoken so long ago! —
Shall I bless you, Dorothy, or forgive
For the tender whisper that bade me live?

It shall be a blessing, my little maid!
I will heal the stab of the Red-Coat's blade,
And freshen the gold of the tarnished frame,
And gild with a rhyme your household name;
So you shall smile on us brave and bright
As first you greeted the morning's light,
And live untroubled by woes and fears
Through a second youth of a hundred years.

CACOËTHES SCRIBENDI

If all the trees in all the woods were men;
And each and every blade of grass a pen;
If every leaf on every shrub and tree
Turned to a sheet of foolscap; every sea
Were changed to ink, and all earth's living tribes
Had nothing else to do but act as scribes,
And for ten thousand ages, day and night,
The human race should write, and write, and write,
Till all the pens and paper were used up,
And the huge inkstand was an empty cup,
Still would the scribblers clustered round its brink
Call for more pens, more paper, and more ink.

THE STRONG HEROIC LINE

Friends of the Muse, to you of right belong
The first staid footsteps of my square-toed song;
Full well I know the strong heroic line
Has lost its fashion since I made it mine;
But there are tricks old singers will not learn,
And this grave measure still must serve my turn.
So the old bird resumes the selfsame note
His first young summer wakened in his throat;
The selfsame tune the old canary sings,
And all unchanged the bobolink's carol rings;

When the tired songsters of the day are still
The thrush repeats his long-remembered trill;
Age alters not the crow's persistent caw,
The Yankee's "Haow," the stammering Briton's "Haw;"
And so the hand that takes the lyre for you
Plays the old tune on strings that once were new.
Nor let the rhymester of the hour deride
The straight-backed measure with its stately stride:
It gave the mighty voice of Dryden scope;
It sheathed the steel-bright epigrams of Pope;
In Goldsmith's verse it learned a sweeter strain;
Byron and Campbell wore its clanking chain;
I smile to listen while the critic's scorn
Flouts the proud purple kings have nobly worn;
Bid each new rhymer try his dainty skill
And mould his frozen phrases as he will;
We thank the artist for his neat device;
The shape is pleasing, though the stuff is ice.

Fashions will change — the new costume allures,
Unfading still the better type endures;
While the slashed doublet of the cavalier
Gave the old knight the pomp of chanticleer,
Our last-hatched dandy with his glass and stick
Recalls the semblance of a new-born chick;
(To match the model he is aiming at
He ought to wear an eggshell for a hat).
Which of these objects would a painter choose,
And which Velasquez or Van Dyck refuse?

FROM "THE IRON GATE"

As on the gauzy wings of fancy flying
From some far orb I track our watery sphere,
Home of the struggling, suffering, doubting, dying,
The silvered globule seems a glistening tear.

But Nature lends her mirror of illusion
To win from saddening scenes our age-dimmed eyes,
And misty day-dreams blend in sweet confusion
The wintry landscape and the summer skies.

So when the iron portal shuts behind us,
And life forgets us in its noise and whirl,
Visions that shunned the glaring noonday find us,
And glimmering starlight shows the gates of pearl.

I come not here your morning hour to sadden,
A limping pilgrim, leaning on his staff, —
I, who have never deemed it sin to gladden
This vale of sorrows with a wholesome laugh.

If word of mine another's gloom has brightened,
Through my dumb lips the heaven-sent message came;
If hand of mine another's task has lightened,
It felt the guidance that it dares not claim.

But, O my gentle sisters, O my brothers,
These thick-sown snow-flakes hint of toil's release;
These feebler pulses bid me leave to others
The tasks once welcome; evening asks for peace.

Time claims his tribute; silence now is golden;
Let me not vex the too long suffering lyre;
Though to your love untiring still beholden,
The curfew tells me — cover up the fire.

Frances Anne Kemble[1]

LAMENT OF A MOCKING-BIRD

SILENCE instead of thy sweet song, my bird,
Which through the darkness of my winter days
Warbling of summer sunshine still was heard;
Mute is thy song, and vacant is thy place.

The spring comes back again, the fields rejoice,
Carols of gladness ring from every tree;
But I shall hear thy wild triumphant voice
No more: my summer song has died with thee.

What didst thou sing of, O my summer bird?
The broad, bright, brimming river, whose swift sweep
And whirling eddies by the home are heard,
Rushing, resistless, to the calling deep.

What didst thou sing of, thou melodious sprite?
Pine forests, with smooth russet carpets spread,
Where e'en at noonday dimly falls the light,
Through gloomy blue-green branches overhead.

What didst thou sing of, O thou jubilant soul?
Ever-fresh flowers and never-leafless trees,
Bending great ivory cups to the control
Of the soft swaying orange-scented breeze.

What didst thou sing of, thou embodied glee?
The wide wild marshes with their clashing reeds
And topaz-tinted channels, where the sea
Daily its tides of briny freshness leads.

What didst thou sing of, O thou wingèd voice?
Dark, bronze-leaved oaks, with silver mosses crowned,
Where thy free kindred live, love, and rejoice,
With wreaths of golden jasmine curtained round.

These didst thou sing of, spirit of delight!
From thy own radiant sky, thou quivering spark!
These thy sweet southern dreams of warmth and light,
Through the grim northern winter drear and dark.

Albert Pike

TO THE MOCKING-BIRD

THOU glorious mocker of the world! I hear
Thy many voices ringing through the glooms
Of these green solitudes; and all the clear,
Bright joyance of their song enthralls the ear,
And floods the heart. Over the spherëd tombs
Of vanished nations rolls thy music-tide:
No light from History's starlit page illumes
The memory of these nations; they have died:
None care for them but thou; and thou mayst sing
O'er me, perhaps, as now thy clear notes ring
Over their bones by whom thou once wast deified.

Glad scorner of all cities! Thou dost leave
The world's mad turmoil and incessant din,
Where none in others' honesty believe,
Where the old sigh, the young turn gray and grieve,
Where misery gnaws the maiden's heart within.

[1] See BIOGRAPHICAL NOTE, p. 804.

Thou fleest far into the dark green woods,
Where, with thy flood of music, thou canst win
Their heart to harmony, and where intrudes
No discord on thy melodies. Oh, where,
Among the sweet musicians of the air,
Is one so dear as thou to these old solitudes?

Ha! what a burst was that! The Æolian strain
Goes floating through the tangled passages
Of the still woods; and now it comes again,
A multitudinous melody, like a rain
Of glassy music under echoing trees,
Close by a ringing lake. It wraps the soul
With a bright harmony of happiness,
Even as a gem is wrapped when round it roll
Thin waves of crimson flame, till we become,
With the excess of perfect pleasure, dumb,
And pant like a swift runner clinging to the goal.

I cannot love the man who doth not love,
As men love light, the song of happy birds;
For the first visions that my boy-heart wove,
To fill its sleep with, were that I did rove
Through the fresh woods, what time the snowy herds
Of morning clouds shrunk from the advancing sun,
Into the depths of Heaven's blue heart, as words
From the poet's lips float gently, one by one,
And vanish in the human heart; and then
I revelled in such songs, and sorrowed, when,
With noon-heat overwrought, the music-gush was done.

I would, sweet bird, that I might live with thee,
Amid the eloquent grandeur of these shades,
Alone with Nature! — but it may not be:
I have to struggle with the stormy sea
Of human life until existence fades
Into death's darkness. Thou wilt sing and soar
Through the thick woods and shadow-chequered glades,
While pain and sorrow cast no dimness o'er
The brilliance of thy heart; but I must wear,
As now, my garments of regret and care,
As penitents of old their galling sackcloth wore.

Yet, why complain? What though fond hopes deferred
Have overshadowed Life's green paths with gloom?
Content's soft music is not all unheard:
There is a voice sweeter than thine, sweet bird,
To welcome me, within my humble home;
There is an eye, with love's devotion bright,
The darkness of existence to illume.
Then why complain? When Death shall cast his blight
Over the spirit, my cold bones shall rest
Beneath these trees; and from thy swelling breast
Over them pour thy song, like a rich flood of light.

THE WIDOWED HEART

Thou art lost to me forever! — I have lost thee, Isadore!
Thy head will never rest upon my loyal bosom more;
Thy tender eyes will never more look fondly into mine,
Nor thine arms around me lovingly and trustingly entwine, —
Thou art lost to me forever, Isadore!

Thou art dead and gone, dear loving wife, thy heart is still and cold,
And mine, benumbed with wretchedness, is prematurely old:
Of our whole world of love and joy thou wast the only light, —
A star, whose setting left behind, ah me! how dark a night! —
Thou art lost to me forever, Isadore!

The vines and flowers we planted, Love, I tend with anxious care,
And yet they droop and fade away, as though they wanted air:

They cannot live without thine eyes to feed
them with their light;
Since thy hands ceased to train them, Love,
they cannot grow aright; —
Thou art lost to them forever, Isadore!

Our little ones inquire of me, where is their
mother gone: —
What answer can I make to them, except
with tears alone?
For if I say "To Heaven," then the poor
things wish to learn
How far it is, and where, and when their
mother will return; —
Thou art lost to them forever, Isadore!

Our happy home has now become a lonely,
silent place;
Like Heaven without its stars it is, without thy blessed face:
Our little ones are still and sad; — none
love them now but I,
Except their mother's spirit, which I feel
is always nigh; —
Thou lovest us in Heaven, Isadore!

Their merry laugh is heard no more, they
neither run nor play,
But wander round like little ghosts, the
long, long summer-day:
The spider weaves his web across the windows at his will,
The flowers I gathered for thee last are on
the mantel still; —
Thou art lost to me forever, Isadore!

Restless I pace our lonely rooms, I play
our songs no more,
The garish sun shines flauntingly upon the
unswept floor;
The mocking-bird still sits and sings, O
melancholy strain!
For my heart is like an autumn cloud that
overflows with rain;
Thou art lost to me forever, Isadore!

Alas! how changed is all, dear wife, from
that sweet eve in spring,
When first my love for thee was told, and
thou to me didst cling,
Thy sweet eyes radiant through their tears,
pressing thy lips to mine,
In our old arbor, Dear, beneath the over-
arching vine; —
Those lips are cold forever, Isadore!

The moonlight struggled through the
leaves, and fell upon thy face,
So lovingly upturning there, with pure and
trustful gaze;
The southern breezes murmured through
the dark cloud of thy hair,
As like a happy child thou didst in my
arms nestle there; —
Death holds thee now forever, Isadore!

Thy love and faith so plighted then, with
mingled smile and tear,
Was never broken, Darling, while we dwelt
together here:
Nor bitter word, nor dark, cold look thou
ever gavest me —
Loving and trusting always, as I loved and
worshipped thee; —
Thou art lost to me forever, Isadore!

Thou wast my nurse in sickness, and my
comforter in health,
So gentle and so constant, when our love
was all our wealth:
Thy voice of music cheered me, Love, in
each despondent hour,
As Heaven's sweet honey-dew consoles the
bruised and broken flower; —
Thou art lost to me forever, Isadore!

Thou art gone from me forever; — I have
lost thee, Isadore!
And desolate and lonely I shall be forever
more:
Our children hold me, Darling, or I to God
should pray
To let me cast the burthen of this long,
dark life away,
And see thy face in Heaven, Isadore!

DIXIE

Southrons, hear your country call you!
Up, lest worse than death befall you!
To arms! To arms! To arms, in Dixie!
Lo! all the beacon-fires are lighted, —
Let all hearts be now united!
To arms! To arms! To arms, in Dixie!
Advance the flag of Dixie!
Hurrah! hurrah!
For Dixie's land we take our stand,
And live or die for Dixie!

To arms! To arms!
And conquer peace for Dixie!
To arms! To arms!
And conquer peace for Dixie!

Hear the Northern thunders mutter!
Northern flags in South winds flutter!
Send them back your fierce defiance!
Stamp upon the accursed alliance!

Fear no danger! Shun no labor!
Lift up rifle, pike, and sabre!
Shoulder pressing close to shoulder,
Let the odds make each heart bolder!

How the South's great heart rejoices
At your cannons' ringing voices!
For faith betrayed, and pledges broken,
Wrongs inflicted, insults spoken.

Strong as lions, swift as eagles,
Back to their kennels hunt these beagles!
Cut the unequal bonds asunder!
Let them hence each other plunder!

Swear upon your country's altar
Never to submit or falter,
Till the spoilers are defeated,
Till the Lord's work is completed.

Halt not till our Federation
Secures among earth's powers its station!
Then at peace, and crowned with glory,
Hear your children tell the story!

If the loved ones weep in sadness,
Victory soon shall bring them gladness, —
To arms!
Exultant pride soon banish sorrow,
Smiles chase tears away to-morrow.
To arms! To arms! To arms, in Dixie!
Advance the flag of Dixie!
Hurrah! hurrah!
For Dixie's land we take our stand,
And live or die for Dixie!
To arms! To arms!
And conquer peace for Dixie!
To arms! To arms!
And conquer peace for Dixie!

Theodore Parker

THE HIGHER GOOD

FATHER, I will not ask for wealth or fame,
Though once they would have joyed my carnal sense:
I shudder not to bear a hated name,
Wanting all wealth, myself my sole defence.
But give me, Lord, eyes to behold the truth;
A seeing sense that knows the eternal right;
A heart with pity filled, and gentlest ruth;
A manly faith that makes all darkness light:
Give me the power to labor for mankind;
Make me the mouth of such as cannot speak;
Eyes let me be to groping men and blind;
A conscience to the base; and to the weak
Let me be hands and feet; and to the foolish, mind;
And lead still further on such as thy kingdom seek.

JESUS

JESUS, there is no dearer name than thine
Which Time has blazoned on his mighty scroll;
No wreaths nor garlands ever did entwine
So fair a temple of so vast a soul.

There every virtue set his triumph-seal;
Wisdom, conjoined with strength and radiant grace,
In a sweet copy Heaven to reveal,
And stamp perfection on a mortal face.

Once on the earth wert thou, before men's eyes,
That did not half thy beauteous brightness see;
E'en as the emmet does not read the skies,
Nor our weak orbs look through immensity.

Elizabeth Clementine Kinney

TO THE BOY

WHO GOES DAILY PAST MY WINDOWS SINGING

Thou happiest thing alive,
Anomaly of earth!
If sound thy lineage give,
Thou art the natural birth
Of affluent Joy —
Thy mother's name was Mirth,
Thou little singing boy!

Thy star — it was a sun!
Thy time the month of May,
When streams to music run,
And birds sing all the day:
Nature did tune
Thy gushing voice by hers;
A fount in June
Not more the bosom stirs;
A freshness flows
Through every bubbling note, —
Sure Nature knows
The strains Art never wrote.

Where was the human curse,
When thou didst spring to life?
All feel it less, or worse,
In pain, in care, in strife.
Its dreadful word
Fell from the lips of Truth;
'T is but deferred,
Unconscious youth!
That curse on thee
Is sure some day to fall;
Alas, more heavily
If Manhood takes it all!

I will not think of this —
It robs me of my part
In thy outgushing bliss:
No! keep thy glad young heart
Turned toward the sun; —
What yet shall be,
None can foresee:
One thing is sure — that thou hast well begun!

Meantime shall others share,
Wild minstrel-boy,
As I, to lighten care,
The music of thy joy, —
Like scents of flowers,
Along life's wayside passed
In dreary hours, —
Too sweet to last;
Like touches soft
Of Nature, on those strings
Within us, jarred so oft
By earth's discordant things.

THE QUAKERESS BRIDE

No, not in the halls of the noble and proud,
Where Fashion assembles her glittering crowd,
Where all is in beauty and splendor arrayed,
Were the nuptials performed of the meek Quaker maid.

Nor yet in the temple those rites which she took, —
By the altar, the mitre-crowned bishop and book,
Where oft in her jewels stands proudly the bride,
Unawed by those vows which through life shall abide.

The building was humble, but sacred to One
Who heeds the deep worship that utters no tone;
Whose presence is not to the temple confined,
But dwells with the contrite and lowly of mind.

'T was there, all unveiled, save by modesty, stood
The Quakeress bride, in her white satin hood:
Her charms unadorned by the garland or gem,
Yet fair as the lily just plucked from its stem.

A tear glistened bright in her dark shaded eye,
And her bosom half uttered a tremulous sigh,

As the hand she had pledged was confidingly given,
And the low murmured words were recorded in heaven.

I 've been at the bridal where wealth spread the board,
Where the sparkling red wine in rich goblets was poured;
Where the priest in his surplice from ritual read,
And the solemn response was impressively said.

I 've seen the fond sire, in his thin locks of gray,
Give the pride of his heart to the bridegroom away;
While he brushed the big tear from his deep furrowed cheek,
And bowed the assent which his lips might not speak.

But in all the array of the costlier scene,
Naught seemed to my eye so sincere in its mien,
No language so fully the heart to resign,
As the Quakeress bride's — "*Until death I am thine!*"

THE BLIND PSALMIST

He sang the airs of olden times
In soft, low tones to sacred rhymes,
Devotional, but quaint;
His fingers touched the viol's strings,
And at their gentle vibratings
The glory of an angel's wings
Hung o'er that aged saint!

His thin, white locks, like silver threads
On which the sun its radiance sheds,
Or like the moonlit snow,
Seemed with a lustre half divine
Around his saintly brow to shine,
Till every scar, or time-worn line,
Was gilded with its glow.

His sightless balls to heaven upraised,
As with the spirit's eyes he gazed
On things invisible —
Reflecting some celestial light —
Were like a tranquil lake at night,
On which two mirrored planets bright
The concave's glory tell.

Thus, while the patriarchal saint
Devoutly sang to music quaint,
I saw old Homer rise
With buried centuries from the dead,
The laurel green upon his head,
As when the choir of bards he led,
With rapt, but blinded eyes!

And Scio's isle again looked green,
As when the poet there was seen,
And Greece was in her prime;
While Poesy with epic fire
Did once again the Bard inspire,
As when he swept his mighty lyre
To vibrate through all time.

The vision changed to Albion's shore:
I saw a sightless Bard once more
From dust of ages rise!
I heard the harp and deathless song
Of glorious Milton float along,
Like warblings from the birds that throng
His muse's Paradise!

And is it thus, when blindness brings
A veil before all outer things,
That visual spirits see
A world within, than this more bright,
Peopled with living forms of light,
And strewed with gems, as stars of night
Strew diamonds o'er the sea?

Then, reverend saint! though old and blind,
Thou with the quenchless orbs of mind
Canst natural sight o'erreach;
Upborne on Faith's triumphant wings,
Canst see unutterable things,
Which only through thy viol's strings,
And in thy songs, find speech.

A DREAM

'T was summer, and the spot a cool retreat —
Where curious eyes came not, nor footstep rude
Disturbed the lovers' chosen solitude:
Beneath an oak there was a mossy seat,

Where we reclined, while birds above us wooed
Their mates in songs voluptuously sweet.
A limpid brook went murmuring by our feet,
And all conspired to urge the tender mood.
Methought I touched the streamlet with a flower,
When from its bosom sprang a fountain clear,
Falling again in the translucent shower
Which made more green each blade of grass appear:
"This stream 's thy heart," I said; "Love's touch alone
Can change it to the fount which maketh green my own."

MOONLIGHT IN ITALY

THERE 's not a breath the dewy leaves to stir;
There 's not a cloud to spot the sapphire sky;
All Nature seems a silent worshipper:
While saintly Dian, with great, argent eye,
Looks down as lucid from the depths on high
As she to Earth were Heaven's interpreter;
Each twinkling little star shrinks back, too shy
Its lesser glory to obtrude by her
Who fills the concave and the world with light;
And ah! the human spirit must unite
In such a harmony of silent lays,
Or be the only discord in this night,
Which seems to pause for vocal lips to raise
The sense of worship into uttered praise.

Frances Sargent Osgood

TO SLEEP

COME to me, angel of the weary hearted!
Since they my loved ones, breathed upon by thee,
Unto thy realms unreal have departed,
I too may rest — even I: ah! haste to me.

I dare not bid thy darker, colder brother
With his more welcome offering appear,
For those sweet lips at morn will murmur, "Mother,"
And who shall soothe them if I be not near?

Bring me no dream, dear Sleep, though visions glowing
With hues of heaven thy wand enchanted shows;
I ask no glorious boon of thy bestowing,
Save that most true, most beautiful, — repose.

I have no heart to roam in realms of Faëry,
To follow Fancy at her elfin call:
I am too wretched — too soul-worn and weary;
Give me but rest, for rest to me is all.

Paint not the Future to my fainting spirit,
Though it were starred with glory like the skies;
There is no gift immortals may inherit,
That could rekindle hope in these cold eyes.

And for the Past — the fearful Past — ah! never
Be Memory's downcast gaze unveiled by thee:
Would thou couldst bring oblivion forever
Of all that is, that has been, and will be!

A DANCING GIRL

SHE comes — the spirit of the dance!
And but for those large, eloquent eyes,
Where passion speaks in every glance,
She 'd seem a wanderer from the skies.

So light that, gazing breathless there,
Lest the celestial dream should go,
You 'd think the music in the air
Waved the fair vision to and fro!

Or that the melody's sweet flow
Within the radiant creature played,

And those soft wreathing arms of snow
  And white sylph feet the music made.

Now gliding slow with dreamy grace,
  Her eyes beneath their lashes lost,
Now motionless, with lifted face,
  And small hands on her bosom crossed.

And now with flashing eyes she springs, —
  Her whole bright figure raised in air,
As if her soul had spread its wings
  And poised her one wild instant there!

She spoke not; but, so richly fraught
  With language are her glance and smile,
That, when the curtain fell, I thought
  She had been talking all the while.

ON SIVORI'S VIOLIN

A DRYAD'S home was once the tree
From which they carved this wondrous toy,
Who chanted lays of love and glee,
Till every leaflet thrilled with joy.

But when the tempest laid it low,
The exiled fay flew to and fro;
Till finding here her home once more,
She warbles wildly as before!

CALUMNY

A WHISPER woke the air,
  A soft, light tone, and low,
  Yet barbed with shame and woe.
Ah! might it only perish there,
  Nor farther go!

But no! a quick and eager ear
  Caught up the little, meaning sound;
Another voice has breathed it clear;
  And so it wandered round
From ear to lip, from lip to ear,
Until it reached a gentle heart
That throbbed from all the world apart
And that — it broke!

It was the only heart it found, —
  The only heart 't was meant to find,
    When first its accents woke.
  It reached that gentle heart at last,
    And that — it broke!

SONG

YOUR heart is a music-box, dearest!
  With exquisite tunes at command,
Of melody sweetest and clearest,
  If tried by a delicate hand;
But its workmanship, love, is so fine,
  At a single rude touch it would break;
Then, oh! be the magic key mine,
  Its fairy-like whispers to wake.
And there 's one little tune it can play,
  That I fancy all others above, —
You learned it of Cupid one day, —
  It begins with and ends with "I love!"
    "I love!"
  My heart echoes to it "I love!"

ON A DEAD POET

THE hand that swept the sounding lyre
  With more than mortal skill,
The lightning eye, the heart of fire,
  The fervent lip are still!
No more, in rapture or in woe,
  With melody to thrill,
    Ah, nevermore!

But angel hands shall bring him balm
  For every grief he knew,
And Heaven's soft harps his soul shall calm
  With music sweet and true,
And teach to him the holy charm
  Of Israfel anew,
    Forevermore!

Love's silver lyre he played so well
  Lies shattered on his tomb,
But still in air its music-spell
  Floats on through light and gloom;
And in the hearts where soft they fell,
  His words of beauty bloom
    Forevermore!

Alfred Billings Street

THE SETTLER

His echoing axe the settler swung
Amid the sea-like solitude,
And rushing, thundering, down were flung
The Titans of the wood;
Loud shrieked the eagle as he dashed
From out his mossy nest, which crashed
With its supporting bough,
And the first sunlight, leaping, flashed
On the wolf's haunt below.

Rude was the garb, and strong the frame
Of him who plied his ceaseless toil:
To form that garb, the wild-wood game
Contributed their spoil;
The soul that warmed that frame disdained
The tinsel, gaud, and glare, that reigned
Where men their crowds collect;
The simple fur, untrimmed, unstained,
This forest-tamer decked.

The paths which wound mid gorgeous trees,
The streams whose bright lips kissed their flowers,
The winds that swelled their harmonies
Through those sun-hiding bowers,
The temple vast — the green arcade,
The nestling vale — the grassy glade,
Dark cave and swampy lair, —
These scenes and sounds majestic, made
His world and pleasures, there.

His roof adorned a lovely spot,
Mid the black logs green glowed the grain,
And herbs and plants the woods knew not
Throve in the sun and rain.
The smoke-wreath curling o'er the dell,
The low — the bleat — the tinkling bell,
All made a landscape strange,
Which was the living chronicle
Of deeds that wrought the change.

The violet sprung at spring's first tinge,
The rose of summer spread its glow,
The maize hung on its autumn fringe,
Rude winter brought its snow;
And still the settler labored there,
His shout and whistle woke the air,
As cheerily he plied
His garden spade, or drove his share
Along the hillock's side.

He marked the fire-storm's blazing flood
Roaring and crackling on its path,
And scorching earth, and melting wood,
Beneath its greedy wrath;
He marked the rapid whirlwind shoot
Trampling the pine-tree with its foot,
And darkening thick the day
With streaming bough and severed root,
Hurled whizzing on its way.

His gaunt hound yelled, his rifle flashed,
The grim bear hushed its savage growl,
In blood and foam the panther gnashed
Its fangs, with dying howl;
The fleet deer ceased its flying bound,
Its snarling wolf-foe bit the ground,
And with its moaning cry
The beaver sank beneath the wound,
Its pond-built Venice by.

Humble the lot, yet his the race,
When Liberty sent forth her cry,
Who thronged in Conflict's deadliest place,
To fight — to bleed — to die!
Who cumbered Bunker's height of red,
By hope through weary years were led,
And witnessed Yorktown's sun
Blaze on a Nation's banner spread,
A Nation's freedom won.

THE LOON

Tameless in his stately pride, along the lake of islands,
Tireless speeds the lonely loon upon his diving track; —
Emerald and gold emblazon, satin-like, his shoulder,
Ebony and pearl inlay, mosaic-like, his back.
Sailing, thus sailing, thus sails the brindled loon,
When the wave rolls black with storm, or sleeps in summer noon.

Sailing through the islands, oft he lifts his loud bravura; —
Clarion-clear it rings, and round ethereal trumpets swell;
Upward looks the feeding deer, he sees the aiming hunter,
Up and then away, the loon has warned his comrade well.
Sailing, thus sailing, thus sails the brindled loon,
Pealing on the solitude his sounding bugle-tune.

Sacred is the loon with eye of wild and flashing crimson;
Eye that saw the Spirit Hah-wen-ne-yo through the air
Falling, faint a star — a shaft of light — a shape of splendor, —
Falling on the deep that closed that shining shape to bear.
Sailing, thus sailing, thus sailed the brindled loon,
With the grand shape falling all a-glitter from the moon.

Long before the eagle furls his pinion on the pine-top,
Long before the blue-bird gleams in sapphire through the glen,
Long before the lily blots the shoal with golden apples,
Leaves the loon his southern sun to sail the lake again.
Sailing, then sailing, then sails the brindled loon,
Leading with his shouting call the Spring's awakening croon.

Long after bitter chills have pierced the windy water,
Long after Autumn dies all dolphin-like away;
Long after coat of russet dons the deer for winter,
Plies the solitary loon his cold and curdled bay.
Sailing, there sailing, there sails the brindled loon,
Till in chains no more to him the lake yields watery boon.

Christopher Pearse Cranch

THE BOBOLINKS

When Nature had made all her birds,
With no more cares to think on,
She gave a rippling laugh, and out
There flew a Bobolinkon.

She laughed again; out flew a mate;
A breeze of Eden bore them
Across the fields of Paradise,
The sunrise reddening o'er them.

Incarnate sport and holiday,
They flew and sang forever;
Their souls through June were all in tune,
Their wings were weary never.

Their tribe, still drunk with air and light,
And perfume of the meadow,
Go reeling up and down the sky,
In sunshine and in shadow.

One springs from out the dew-wet grass;
Another follows after;
The morn is thrilling with their songs
And peals of fairy laughter.

From out the marshes and the brook,
They set the tall reeds swinging,
And meet and frolic in the air,
Half prattling and half singing.

When morning winds sweep meadow-lands
In green and russet billows,
And toss the lonely elm-tree's boughs,
And silver all the willows,

I see you buffeting the breeze,
Or with its motion swaying,
Your notes half drowned against the wind,
Or down the current playing.

When far away o'er grassy flats,
Where the thick wood commences,
The white-sleeved mowers look like specks
Beyond the zigzag fences,

And noon is hot, and barn-roofs gleam
White in the pale blue distance,
I hear the saucy minstrels still
In chattering persistence.

When Eve her domes of opal fire
Piles round the blue horizon,
Or thunder rolls from hill to hill
A Kyrie Eleison,

Still merriest of the merry birds,
Your sparkle is unfading, —
Pied harlequins of June, — no end
Of song and masquerading.

What cadences of bubbling mirth,
Too quick for bar and rhythm!
What ecstasies, too full to keep
Coherent measure with them!

O could I share, without champagne
Or muscadel, your frolic,
The glad delirium of your joy,
Your fun unapostolic,

Your drunken jargon through the fields,
Your bobolinkish gabble,
Your fine Anacreontic glee,
Your tipsy reveller's babble!

Nay, let me not profane such joy
With similes of folly;
No wine of earth could waken songs
So delicately jolly!

O boundless self-contentment, voiced
In flying air-born bubbles!
O joy that mocks our sad unrest,
And drowns our earth-born troubles!

Hope springs with you: I dread no more
Despondency and dulness;
For Good Supreme can never fail
That gives such perfect fulness.

The life that floods the happy fields
With song and light and color
Will shape our lives to richer states,
And heap our measures fuller.

STANZA FROM AN EARLY POEM

Thought is deeper than all speech,
Feeling deeper than all thought;
Souls to souls can never teach
What unto themselves was taught.

THE PINES AND THE SEA

Beyond the low marsh-meadows and the beach,
Seen through the hoary trunks of windy pines,
The long blue level of the ocean shines.
The distant surf, with hoarse, complaining speech,
Out from its sandy barrier seems to reach;
And while the sun behind the woods declines,
The moaning sea with sighing boughs combines,
And waves and pines make answer, each to each.
O melancholy soul, whom far and near,
In life, faith, hope, the same sad undertone
Pursues from thought to thought! thou needs must hear
An old refrain, too much, too long thine own:
'T is thy mortality infects thine ear;
The mournful strain was in thyself alone.

Jones Very

THE IDLER

I idle stand that I may find employ,
Such as my Master when He comes will give;
I cannot find in mine own work my joy,
But wait, although in waiting I must live;
My body shall not turn which way it will,
But stand till I the appointed road can find,
And journeying so his messages fulfil,
And do at every step the work designed.
Enough for me, still day by day to wait
Till Thou who formest me findest me too a task,

A cripple lying at the rich man's gate,
Content for the few crumbs I get to ask,
A laborer but in heart, while bound my hands
Hang idly down still waiting thy commands.

THE NEW WORLD

THE night that has no star lit up by God,
The day that round men shines who still are blind,
The earth their grave-turned feet for ages trod,
And sea swept over by His mighty wind, —
All these have passed away, the melting dream
That flitted o'er the sleeper's half-shut eye,
When touched by morning's golden-darting beam;
And he beholds around the earth and sky
That ever real stands, the rolling shores
And heaving billows of the boundless main,
That show, though time is past, no trace of years.
And earth restored he sees as his again,
The earth that fades not and the heavens that stand,
Their strong foundations laid by God's right hand.

THE OLD ROAD

THE road is left that once was trod
By man and heavy-laden beast;
And new ways opened, iron-shod,
That bind the land from west to east.

I asked of Him who all things knows
Why none who lived now passed that way:
Where rose the dust the grass now grows?
A still, low voice was heard to say,—

"Thou knowest not why I change the course
Of him who travels: learn to go,
Obey the Spirit's gentle force,
Nor ask thou where the stream may flow.

"Man shall not walk in his own ways,
For he is blind and cannot see;
But let him trust, and lengthened days
Shall lead his feet to heaven and Me.

"Then shall the grass the path grow o'er,
That his own wilfulness has trod;
And man nor beast shall pass it more,
But he shall walk with Me, his God."

YOURSELF

'T IS to yourself I speak; you cannot know
Him whom I call in speaking such a one,
For you beneath the earth lie buried low,
Which he, alone, as living walks upon.
You may at times have heard him speak to you,
And often wished perchance that you were he;
And I must ever wish that it were true,
For then you could hold fellowship with me:
But now you hear us talk as strangers, met
Above the room wherein you lie abed;
A word perhaps loud spoken you may get,
Or hear our feet when heavily they tread;
But he who speaks, or he who 's spoken to,
Must both remain as strangers still to you.

THE DEAD

I SEE them, — crowd on crowd they walk the earth,
Dry leafless trees no autumn wind laid bare;
And in their nakedness find cause for mirth,
And all unclad would winter's rudeness dare;
No sap doth through their clattering branches flow,
Whence springing leaves and blossoms bright appear:
Their hearts the living God have ceased to know
Who gives the springtime to the expectant year.
They mimic life, as if from Him to steal
His glow of health to paint the livid cheek;
They borrow words for thoughts they cannot feel,

That with a seeming heart their tongue may speak;
And in their show of life more dead they live
Than those that to the earth with many tears they give.

THE GIFTS OF GOD

The light that fills thy house at morn,
Thou canst not for thyself retain;
But all who with thee here are born,
It bids to share an equal gain.

The wind that blows thy ship along,
Her swelling sails cannot confine;
Alike to all the gales belong,
Nor canst thou claim a breath as thine.

The earth, the green out-spreading earth,
Why hast thou fenced it off from me?
Hadst thou than I a nobler birth,
Who callest thine a gift so free?

The wave, the blue encircling wave,
No chains can bind, no fetters hold;
Its thunders tell of Him who gave
What none can ever buy for gold.

Henry Beck Hirst

THE FRINGILLA MELODIA

Happy Song-sparrow, that on woodland side
Or by the meadow sits, and ceaseless sings
His mellow roundelay in russet pride,
Owning no care between his wings.

He has no tax to pay, nor work to do:
His round of life is ever a pleasant one;
For they are merry that may naught but woo
From yellow dawn till set of sun.

The verdant fields, the riverside, the road,
The cottage garden, and the orchard green,
When Spring with breezy footstep stirs abroad,
His modest mottled form have seen.

The cedar at the cottage door contains
His nest; the lilac by the walk as well,
From whence arise his silver-swelling strains,
That echo loudly down the dell.

And when at dewy eve the farmer lies
Before his door, his children all around,
From twig to twig the simple sparrow flies,
Frightened to hear their laughter's sound.

Or when the farm-boy with his shining spade,
Freshening the mould around the garden flowers,
Disturbs him, timid but not yet afraid,
He chirps about him there for hours.

And when, his labor o'er, the urchin leaves
The haunted spot, he seeks some lofty spray,
And there with ruffled throat, delighted, weaves,
Gushing with joy, his lovely lay.

Perchance, his nest discovered, children come,
And peer, with curious eyes, where lie the young
And callow brood, and then, with ceaseless hum,
He, shrew-like, scolds with double tongue.

A little while, and on the gravelled walk
The nestlings hop, or peer between the grass,
While he sits watching on some blossom stalk,
Lest danger might toward them pass.

He sees the cat with stealthy step, and form
Pressed closely to the ground, come creeping through
The whitewashed fence, and with a loud alarm
He flies; and they — they swift pursue.

So passes Summer; and when Autumn treads
 With sober step the yellowing woods and vales,
A mellower song the gentle sparrow sheds
 From orchard tree or garden pales.

And, as the nights grow cold and woodlands dim,
 He seeks, with many a kin, a warmer clime,
And perching there, along some river's rim,
 Fills up with song the solemn time.

But, with the sun of March, his little soul,
 Warm with the love of home, impels him where,
In bygone hours, he owned love's sweet control;
 And soon he breathes his native air.

And then again his merry song rings out,
 And meadow, orchard, valley, wood, and plain
Ring with his bridal notes, that seem to flout
 Dull echo with their silver strain.

And so his round of life runs ever on:
 Happy, contented, in his humble sphere
He lives, loves, sings, and, when the day is gone,
 Slumbers and dreams, devoid of fear.

THE FUNERAL OF TIME[1]

Lo! through a shadowy valley
 March with measured step and tread
A long array of Phantoms wan
 And pallid as the dead, —
 The white and waxen dead!
 With a crown on every head,
 And a torch in every hand
 To fright the sheeted ghosts away
 That guard its portals night and day,
 They seek the Shadow-Land.

On as the pale procession stalks,
 The clouds around divide,
Raising themselves in giant shapes,
 And gazing down in pride
 On the spectres as they glide
 Through the valley long and wide, —
 On the spectres all so pale
 In vestments whiter than the snow,
 As through the dim defile they go
 With melancholy wail.

On tramps the funeral file; and now
 The weeping ones have passed,
A throng succeeding, loftier
 And statelier than the last, —
 The Monarchs of the Past!
 And upon the solemn blast,
 Wave their plumes and pennons high,
 And loud their mournful marches sweep
 Up from the valley dark and deep
 To the over-arching sky.

And now the Cycle-buried years
 Stride on in stern array:
Before each band the Centuries,
 With beards of silver gray,
 The Marshals of the Day,
 In silence pass away;
 And behind them come the Hours
 And Minutes, who, as on they go,
 Are swinging steadily to and fro
 The incense round in showers.

Behold the bier, — the ebony bier, —
 On sinewy shoulders borne,
Of many a dim, forgotten Year
 From Primal Times forlorn.
 All weary and all worn,
 With their ancient garments torn
 And their beards as white as Lear's,
 Lo! how they tremble as they tread,
 Mourning above the marble dead,
 In agonies of tears!

How very wan the old man looks!
 As wasted and as pale
As some dim ghost of shadowy days
 In legendary tale.
 God give the sleeper hail!
 And the world hath much to wail
 That his ears no more may hear;
 For, with his palms across his breast,
 He lieth in eternal rest
 Along his stately bier.

[1] See BIOGRAPHICAL NOTE, p. 799.

How thin his hair! How white his beard!
How waxen-like his hands,
Which nevermore may turn the glass
That on his bosom stands,—
The glass whose solemn sands
Were won from Stygian strands!
For his weary work is done,
And he has reaped his latest field,
And none that scythe of his can wield
'Neath the dim, descending sun.

At last they reach the Shadow-Land,
And with an eldritch cry
The guardian ghost sweeps wailingly
Athwart the troubled sky,
Like meteors flashing by,
As asunder crashing fly,
With a wild and clangorous din,
The gates before the funeral train,
Filing along the dreary plain
And marching slowly in.

Lo! 't is a temple! and around
Tall ebony columns rise
Up from the withering earth, and bear
Aloft the shrivelling skies,
Where the tempest trembling sighs,
And the ghostly moonlight dies
'Neath a lurid comet's glare,
That over the mourners' plumèd heads
And on the Dead a lustre sheds
From its crimson floating hair!

The rites are read, the requiem sung;
And as the echoes die,
The Shadow Chaos rises
With a wild unearthly cry,—
A giant, to the sky!
His arms outstretched on high
Over Time that dead doth lie;
And with a voice that shakes the spheres,
He shouts to the mourners mad with fears,
"Depart! Lo! here am I!"

Down, showering fire, the comet sweeps;
Shivering the pillars fall;
And lightning-like the red flames rush,
A whirlwind, over all!
And Silence spreads her pall,
Like pinions over the hall,
Over the temple overthrown,
Over the dying and the unburied dead;
And, with a heavily-drooping head,
Sits, statue-like, alone!

Epes Sargent

A LIFE ON THE OCEAN WAVE

A LIFE on the ocean wave,
A home on the rolling deep,
Where the scattered waters rave,
And the winds their revels keep!
Like an eagle caged, I pine
On this dull, unchanging shore:
Oh! give me the flashing brine,
The spray and the tempest's roar!

Once more on the deck I stand
Of my own swift-gliding craft:
Set sail! farewell to the land!
The gale follows fair abaft.
We shoot through the sparkling foam
Like an ocean-bird set free;—
Like the ocean-bird, our home
We 'll find far out on the sea.

The land is no longer in view,
The clouds have begun to frown;
But with a stout vessel and crew,
We 'll say, Let the storm come down!
And the song of our hearts shall be,
While the winds and the waters rave,
A home on the rolling sea!
A life on the ocean wave!

THE HEART'S SUMMER

THE cold blast at the casement beats;
The window-panes are white;
The snow whirls through the empty streets;
It is a dreary night!
Sit down, old friend, the wine-cups wait;
Fill to o'erflowing, fill!

Though winter howleth at the gate,
  In our hearts 't is summer still!

For we full many summer joys
  And greenwood sports have shared,
When, free and ever-roving boys,
  The rocks, the streams, we dared;
And, as I looked upon thy face,
  Back, back o'er years of ill,
My heart flies to that happy place,
  Where it is summer still.

Yes, though like sere leaves on the ground,
  Our early hopes are strown,
And cherished flowers lie dead around,
  And singing birds are flown,
The verdure is not faded quite,
  Not mute all tones that thrill;
And seeing, hearing thee to-night,
  In my heart 't is summer still.

Fill up! The olden times come back
  With light and life once more;
We scan the Future's sunny track
  From Youth's enchanted shore;
The lost return: through fields of bloom
  We wander at our will;
Gone is the winter's angry gloom, —
  In our hearts 't is summer still.

Robert Traill Spence Lowell

THE BRAVE OLD SHIP, THE ORIENT

Woe for the brave ship Orient!
Woe for the old ship Orient!
For in broad, broad light, and with land in sight,
Where the waters bubbled white,
One great sharp shriek! One shudder of affright! —
And —
    down went the brave old ship, the Orient!

It was the fairest day in the merry month of May,
And sleepiness had settled on the seas;
And we had our white sail set, high up, and higher yet,
And our flag flashed and fluttered at its ease;
The cross of St. George, that in mountain and in gorge, —
On the hot and dusty plain, —
On the tiresome, trackless main, —
Conquering out, — conquering home again, —
Had flamed, the world over, on the breeze.
Ours was the far-famed Albion,
And she had her best look of might and beauty on,
As she swept across the seas that day.
The wind was fair and soft, both alow and aloft,
And we wore the even hours away.
The steadying sun heaved up as day drew on,
And there grew a long swell of the sea.
And, first in upper air, then under, everywhere,
From the topmost towering sail
Down, down to quarter-rail,
The wind began to breathe more free.
It was soon to breathe its last,
For a wild and bitter blast
Was the master of that stormy day to be.

"Ho! Hilloa! A sail!" was the topman's hail:
"A sail, hull-down upon our lee!"
Then with sea-glass to his eye,
And his gray locks blowing by,
The Admiral sought what she might be.
And from top, and from deck,
Was it ship? Was it wreck? A far-off, far-off speck,
Of a sudden we found upon our lee.

On the round waters wide, floated no thing beside,
But we and the stranger sail;
And a hazy sky, that threatened storm,
Came coating the heaven so blue and warm,
And ahead hung the portent of a gale:
A black bank hanging there
When the order came, to wear,
Was remembered, ever after, in the tale.

Across the long, slow swell
That scarcely rose and fell,

The wind began to blow out of the cloud;
And scarce an hour was gone ere the gale
was fairly on,
And through our strained rigging howled
aloud.
Before the stormy wind, that was madden-
ing behind,
We gathered in our canvas farthest spread.
Black clouds had started out
From the heavens all about,
And the welkin grew all black overhead.
But though stronger and more strong
The fierce gale rushed along,
The stranger brought her old wind in her
breast.
Up came the ship from the far-off sea
And on with the strong wind's breath rushed
we.
She grew to the eye, against the clouded
sky,
And eagerly her points and gear we guessed.
As we made her out, at last,
She was maimed in spar and mast
And she hugged the easy breeze for rest.

We could see the old wind fail
At the nearing of our gale;
We could see them lay their course with
the wind:
Still we neared and neared her fast,
Hurled on by our fierce blast,
With the seas tumbling headlong behind.
She had come out of some storm, and, in
many a busy swarm,
Her crew were refitting, as they might,
The wreck of upper spars
That had left their ugly scars,
As if the ship had come out of a fight.
We scanned her well, as we drifted by, —
A strange old ship, with her poop built
high,
And with quarter-galleries wide,
And a huge beaked prow, as no ships are
builded now,
And carvings all strange, beside.
A Byzantine bark, and a ship of name and
mark
Long years and generations ago;
Ere any mast or yard of ours was growing
hard
With the seasoning of long Norwegian
snow.
She was the brave old Orient,
The old imperial Orient,
Brought down from times afar,
Not such as our ships are,
But unchanged in hull and unchanged in
spar,
Since mighty ships of war were builded so.

Down her old black side poured the water
in a tide,
As they toiled to get the better of a leak.
We had got a signal set in the shrouds,
And our men through the storm looked on
in crowds: —
But for wind, we were near enough to
speak.
It seemed her sea and sky were in times
long, long gone by,
That we read in winter-evens about;
As if to other stars
She had reared her old-world spars,
And her hull had kept an old-time ocean
out.
We saw no signal fly, and her men scarce
lifted eye,
But toiled at the work that was to do:
It warmed our English blood
When across the stormy flood
We saw the old ship and her crew.
The glories and the memories of other days
agone
Seemed clinging to the old ship, as in
storm she labored on.
The old ship Orient!
The brave, imperial Orient!

All that stormy night through, our ship was
lying-to
Whenever we could keep her to the wind;
But late in the next day we gained a quiet
bay,
For the tempest had left us far behind.
So before the sunny town
Went our anchors splashing down;
Our sails we hung all out to the sun;
While airs from off the steep
Came playing at bo-peep
With our canvas, hour by hour, in their fun.
We leaned on boom or rail with many a
lazy tale
Of the work of the storm that had died;
And watched, with idle eyes,
Our floats, like summer flies,
Riding lazily about the ship's side.
Suddenly they cried, from the other deck,
That the Orient was gone to wreck!
That her hull lay high on a broken shore,
And the brave old ship would float no more.

But we heard a sadder tale, ere the night
came on,
And a truer tale, of the ship that was gone.
They had seen from the height,
As she came from yester-night,
While the storm had not gone by, and the
sea was running high,
A ship driving heavily to land;
A strange great ship (so she seemed to be
While she tumbled and rolled on the far-
off sea,
And strange when she toiled, near at hand),
But some ship of mark and fame,
Though crippled, then, and lame,
And that must have been gallantly manned.
So she came, driving fast;
They could tell her men, at last;
There were harbors down the coast on her
lee;
When, strangely, she broached to, —
Then, with her gallant crew,
Went headlong down into the sea.

That was the Orient,
The brave old Orient, —
Such a ship as nevermore will be.

THE AFTER-COMERS

Ex noto fictum carmen . . . .
. . . . licuit semperque licebit
signatum præsente nota producere [carmen].
HOR. A. P. 240, 58, 59.

THOSE earlier men that owned our earth
When land and sea and skies were newer,
Had they, by eldest's right of birth,
Sea stronger, greener land, sky bluer?
Had what they sang and drew more worth
That bards and painters then were fewer?

Their daisy, oak and rose were new;
Fresh runnels down their valleys babbled;
New were red lip, true eyes, fresh dew;
All dells, all shores, had not been rabbled;
Nor yet the rhyming lovers' crew
Tree-bark and casement-pane had scrab-
bled.

Feelings sprang fresh, to them, and thought;
Fresh things were hope, trust, faith, en-
deavor;
All things were new, wherein men wrought,
And so they had the lead, forever.
To move the world their frank hearts sought
Not even where to set their lever.

Then utterance, like thought, was young,
And, when these yearning two were mated,
What shapes of airy life were flung
Before the world as yet unsated!
Life was in hand; life was in tongue;
Life in whatever they created.

Must then the world to us be stale?
Must we be only after-comers?
Must wilted green and sunshine pale
Make mean all our dear springs and sum-
mers?
To those free lords of song and tale
Must we be only tricked-out mummers?

Oh, no! was ever life-blood cold?
Was wit e'er dull, when mirth was in it?
Or when will blushing love be old?
Or thrill of bobolink or linnet?
Are all our blossoms touched with mould?
Lurks not fresh bloom where we may win
it?

Yes! Life and strength forever *can*;
Life springs afresh through endless ages;
Nor on our true work falls a ban,
That it must halt, at shortened stages:
Throw man into it! man draws man
In canvas, stone, or written pages.

Henry Peterson[1]

FROM AN "ODE FOR DECORATION DAY"

O GALLANT brothers of the generous South,
Foes for a day and brothers for all
time!
I charge you by the memories of our
youth,
By Yorktown's field and Montezuma's
clime,
Hold our dead sacred — let them quietly
rest

[1] See BIOGRAPHICAL NOTE, p. 815.

In your unnumbered vales, where God
thought best.
Your vines and flowers learned long since
to forgive,
And o'er their graves a broidered mantle
weave:
Be you as kind as they are, and the word
Shall reach the Northland with each summer bird,
And thoughts as sweet as summer shall
awake
Responsive to your kindness, and shall make
Our peace the peace of brothers once again,
And banish utterly the days of pain.

And ye, O Northmen! be ye not outdone
In generous thought and deed.
We all do need forgiveness, every one;
And they that give shall find it in their
need.
Spare of your flowers to deck the stranger's
grave,
Who died for a lost cause: —
A soul more daring, resolute, and brave,
Ne'er won a world's applause.
A brave man's hatred pauses at the tomb.
For him some Southern home was robed in
gloom,
Some wife or mother looked with longing
eyes
Through the sad days and nights with tears
and sighs,
Hope slowly hardening into gaunt Despair.
Then let your foeman's grave remembrance
share:
Pity a higher charm to Valor lends,
And in the realms of Sorrow all are friends.

RINALDO

Bring me a cup of good red wine
To drink before I die;
Though earthly joys I must resign,
I 'll breathe no earthly sigh.

I 've lived a bold and robber life,
I 've had on earth my way,
For with the gun or with the knife,
I made mankind obey.

My mother's name, my father's race,
Though he was false, she true,
It matters not — they sleep in peace.
What more can I or you?

They sleep in peace, though swords flashed
wild
Around my infant head,
And I was left an orphan child,
An outcast's path to tread.

Men are but grapes upon the vine;
My vine was planted where
Nor hand did tend, nor warm sun shine,
And mildew filled the air.

I was a robber brave and bold.
I did not, in the mart,
Lie, cheat, and steal with purpose cold.
Mine was too frank a heart.

All men are robbers, — all who win,
And get more than their due;
Though solemn phrases veil the sin,
The thief's eye glances through.

The world denied me gold and land,
And love which all men crave;
I took the first with strong right hand,
The last I left a slave.

And though the tiger 's caged at length, —
Who made him such God knows, —
He can but fail who measures strength
Against a world of foes.

Then bring a cup of rich red wine
Before the bell tolls three,
For better men than I and mine
Have died upon the tree.

James Thomas Fields

WITH WORDSWORTH AT RYDAL

The grass hung wet on Rydal banks,
The golden day with pearls adorning,
When side by side with him we walked
To meet midway the summer morning.

The west wind took a softer breath,
The sun himself seemed brighter shining,
As through the porch the minstrel stepped,
His eye sweet Nature's look enshrining.

He passed along the dewy sward,
The linnet sang aloft, "Good morrow!"
He plucked a bud, the flower awoke
And smiled without one pang of sorrow.

He spoke of all that graced the scene
In tones that fell like music round us;
We felt the charm descend, nor strove
To break the rapturous spell that bound us.

We listened with mysterious awe,
Strange feeling mingling with our pleasure;
We heard that day prophetic words, —
High thoughts the heart must always treasure.

Great Nature's Priest! thy calm career,
Since that sweet morn, on earth has ended;
But who shall say thy mission died
When, winged for heaven, thy soul ascended?

COMMON SENSE

She came among the gathering crowd,
A maiden fair, without pretence,
And when they asked her humble name,
She whispered mildly, "Common Sense."

Her modest garb drew every eye,
Her ample cloak, her shoes of leather;
And, when they sneered, she simply said,
"I dress according to the weather."

They argued long, and reasoned loud,
In dubious Hindoo phrase mysterious,
While she, poor child, could not divine
Why girls so young should be so serious.

They knew the length of Plato's beard,
And how the scholars wrote in Saturn;
She studied authors not so deep,
And took the Bible for her pattern.

And so she said, "Excuse me, friends,
I find all have their proper places,
And *Common Sense* should stay at home
With cheerful hearts and smiling faces."

Henry David Thoreau

INSPIRATION

If with light head erect I sing,
Though all the Muses lend their force,
From my poor love of anything,
The verse is weak and shallow as its source.

But if with bended neck I grope
Listening behind me for my wit,
With faith superior to hope,
More anxious to keep back than forward it, —

Making my soul accomplice there
Unto the flame my heart hath lit,
Then will the verse forever wear, —
Time cannot bend the line which God has writ.

I hearing get, who had but ears,
And sight, who had but eyes before;
I moments live, who lived but years,
And truth discern, who knew but learning's lore.

Now chiefly is my natal hour,
And only now my prime of life;
Of manhood's strength it is the flower,
'T is peace's end, and war's beginning strife.

It comes in summer's broadest noon,
By a gray wall, or some chance place,
Unseasoning time, insulting June,
And vexing day with its presuming face.

I will not doubt the love untold
Which not my worth nor want hath bought,
Which wooed me young, and wooes me old,
And to this evening hath me brought.

THE FISHER'S BOY

My life is like a stroll upon the beach,
As near the ocean's edge as I can go;
My tardy steps its waves sometimes o'erreach,
Sometimes I stay to let them overflow.

My sole employment is, and scrupulous care,
To place my gains beyond the reach of tides, —
Each smoother pebble, and each shell more rare,
Which Ocean kindly to my hand confides.

I have but few companions on the shore:
They scorn the strand who sail upon the sea;
Yet oft I think the ocean they 've sailed o'er
Is deeper known upon the strand to me.

The middle sea contains no crimson dulse,
Its deeper waves cast up no pearls to view;
Along the shore my hand is on its pulse,
And I converse with many a shipwrecked crew.

SMOKE

Light-winged Smoke! Icarian bird,
Melting thy pinions in thy upward flight;
Lark without song, and messenger of dawn,
Circling above the hamlets as thy nest;
Or else, departing dream, and shadowy form
Of midnight vision, gathering up thy skirts;
By night star-veiling, and by day
Darkening the light and blotting out the sun;
Go thou, my incense, upward from this hearth,
And ask the gods to pardon this clear flame.

MIST

Low-anchored cloud,
Newfoundland air,
Fountain-head and source of rivers,
Dew-cloth, dream-drapery,
And napkin spread by fays;
Drifting meadow of the air,
Where bloom the daisied banks and violets,
And in whose fenny labyrinth
The bittern booms and heron wades;
Spirit of lakes and seas and rivers, —
Bear only perfumes and the scent
Of healing herbs to just men's fields.

Emily Chubbuck Judson

WATCHING

Sleep, love, sleep!
The dusty day is done.
Lo! from afar the freshening breezes sweep
Wide over groves of balm,
Down from the towering palm,
In at the open casement cooling run,
And round thy lowly bed,
Thy bed of pain,
Bathing thy patient head,
Like grateful showers of rain,
They come;
While the white curtains, waving to and fro,
Fan the sick air;
And pitying the shadows come and go,
With gentle human care,
Compassionate and dumb.

The dusty day is done,
The night begun;
While prayerful watch I keep,
Sleep, love, sleep!
Is there no magic in the touch
Of fingers thou dost love so much?
Fain would they scatter poppies o'er thee now;
Or, with its mute caress,
The tremulous lip some soft nepenthe press
Upon thy weary lid and aching brow;
While prayerful watch I keep,
Sleep, love, sleep!

On the pagoda spire
The bells are swinging,
Their little golden circlet in a flutter
With tales the wooing winds have dared to utter
Till all are ringing,
As if a choir
Of golden-nested birds in heaven were singing;

And with a lulling sound
The music floats around,
And drops like balm into the drowsy ear;
Commingling with the hum
Of the Sepoy's distant drum,
And lazy beetle ever droning near.
Sounds these of deepest silence born,
Like night made visible by morn;
So silent that I sometimes start
To hear the throbbings of my heart,
And watch, with shivering sense of pain,
To see thy pale lids lift again.

The lizard, with his mouse-like eyes,
Peeps from the mortise in surprise
At such strange quiet after day's harsh din;
Then boldly ventures out,
And looks about,
And with his hollow feet
Treads his small evening beat,
Darting upon his prey
In such a tricky, winsome sort of way,
His delicate marauding seems no sin.
And still the curtains swing,
But noiselessly;
The bells a melancholy murmur ring,
And tears were in the sky:
More heavily the shadows fall,
Like the black foldings of a pall
Where juts the rough beam from the wall;
The candles flare
With fresher gusts of air;
The beetle's drone
Turns to a dirge-like, solitary moan;
Night deepens, and I sit in cheerless doubt, alone.

MY BIRD

Ere last year's moon had left the sky,
A birdling sought my Indian nest,
And folded, O, so lovingly,
Her tiny wings upon my breast.

From morn till evening's purple tinge,
In winsome helplessness she lies,
Two rose-leaves, with a silken fringe,
Shut softly on her starry eyes.

There 's not in Ind a lovelier bird;
Broad earth owns not a happier nest;
O God, thou hast a fountain stirred,
Whose waters nevermore shall rest!

This beautiful, mysterious thing,
This seeming visitant from Heaven,
This bird with the immortal wing,
To me — to me, Thy hand has given.

The pulse first caught its tiny stroke,
The blood its crimson hue, from mine; —
This life, which I have dared invoke,
Henceforth is parallel with Thine.

A silent awe is in my room —
I tremble with delicious fear;
The future, with its light and gloom,
Time and Eternity, are here.

Doubts — hopes, in eager tumult rise;
Hear, O my God! one earnest prayer:
Room for my bird in Paradise,
And give her angel plumage there!

Arthur Cleveland Coxe

IONA

A MEMORIAL OF ST. COLUMBA

We gazed on Corryvrekin's whirl,
We sailed by Jura's shore,
Where sang of old the mermaid-girl,
Whose shell is heard no more;
We came to Fingal's pillared cave,
That minster in the sea,
And sang — while clapped its hands the wave
And worshipped even as we.

But when, at fair Iona's bound,
We leaped upon its soil,
I felt indeed 'twas holy ground, —
Too holy for such spoil;
For spoilers came in evil day,
Where once to Christ they prayed:
Alas! His Body — ta'en away,
We know not where 't was laid.

We strode above those ancient graves,
We worshipped by that Cross,
And where their snow-white manes the waves
Like troops of chargers toss,

We gazed upon the distant scene,
And thought how Columb came
To kindle here the Gospel's sheen,
And preach the Saviour's name:

Came where the rude marauding clan
Enforced him to an isle;
Came but to bless and not to ban,
To make the desert smile.
He made his island church a gem
That sparkled in the night,
Or like that Star of Bethlehem,
That bathes the world with light.

But look ! this isle that gems the deep —
One glance may all behold —
This was the shelter of his sheep,
This was Columba's fold.
Bishops were gold in days of yore,
For golden was their good,
But in their pastoral hands they bore
A shepherd's staff of wood.

Here elders and his deacons due
'Neath one blest roof they dwelt,
And, ere the bird of dawning crew,
They rose to pray, — and knelt:
Here, watching through the darker hours,
Vigil and fast they kept,
Like those, once hailed by heavenly powers,
While Herod drowsed and slept.

Thus gleaming like a pharos forth
To shed of Truth the flame,
A Patmos of the frozen North
Iona's isle became.
The isles that waited for God's Law
Mid all the highlands round,
That beacon as it blazed — they saw,
They sought the Light and found.

It shone upon those headlands hoar
That crest thy coasts, Argyle;
To watchers, far as Mona's shore,
It seemed a burning pile;
To peasant cots and fishers' skiffs
It brightened lands and seas ;
From Solway to Edina's cliffs,
And southward to the Tees.

Nay more ! For when, that day of bliss,
I sought Columba's bay,
Came one, as from the wilderness,
A thousand leagues away;
A bishop of Columba's kin,
As primitive as he,
Knelt pilgrim-like, those walls within,
The Saint of Tennessee.

Thrilled as with rapture strange and wild,
I saw him worship there;
And Otey, like a little child,
Outpoured his soul in prayer.
For oh ! to him came thoughts, I ween,
Of one who crossed the seas,
And brought from distant Aberdeen
Gifts of the old Culdees.

Great God, how marvellous the flame
A little spark may light !
What here was kindled first — the same
Makes far Atlantis bright:
Not Scotia's clans, nor Umbria's son
Alone that beacon blest,
It shines to-day o'er Oregon,
And glorifies our West.

Columbia from Columba claims
More than great Colon brought,
And long entwined those twins of names
Shall waken grateful thought;
And where the Cross is borne afar
To California's shore,
Columba's memory like a star
Shall brighten evermore.

William Ellery Channing

FROM "A POET'S HOPE"

Lady, there is a hope that all men have, —
Some mercy for their faults, a grassy place
To rest in, and a flower-strown, gentle grave;
Another hope which purifies our race,
That, when that fearful bourne forever past,
They may find rest, — and rest so long to last.

I seek it not, I ask no rest for ever,
My path is onward to the farthest shores, —

Upbear me in your arms, unceasing river,
That from the soul's clear fountain swiftly pours,
Motionless not, until the end is won,
Which now I feel hath scarcely felt the sun.

To feel, to know, to soar unlimited
Mid throngs of light-winged angels sweeping far,
And pore upon the realms unvisited
That tessellate the unseen, unthought star, —
To be the thing that now I feebly dream,
Flashing within my faintest, deepest gleam.

Ah! caverns of my soul! how thick your shade,
Where flows that life by which I faintly see: —
Wave your bright torches, for I need your aid,
Golden-eyed demons of my ancestry!
Your son though blinded hath a light within,
A heavenly fire which ye from suns did win.

And, lady, in thy hope my life will rise
Like the air-voyager, till I upbear
These heavy curtains of my filmy eyes
Into a lighter, more celestial air:
A mortal's hope shall bear me safely on,
Till I the higher region shall have won.

O Time! O Death! I clasp you in my arms,
For I can soothe an infinite cold sorrow,
And gaze contented on your icy charms
And that wild snow-pile which we call to-morrow;
Sweep on, O soft and azure-lidded sky,
Earth's waters to your gentle gaze reply.

I am not earth-born, though I here delay;
Hope's child, I summon infiniter powers,
And laugh to see the mild and sunny day
Smile on the shrunk and thin autumnal hours;
I laugh, for hope hath happy place with me, —
If my bark sinks, 'tis to another sea.

HYMN OF THE EARTH

My highway is unfeatured air,
My consorts are the sleepless Stars,
And men my giant arms upbear, —
My arms unstained and free from scars.

I rest forever on my way,
Rolling around the happy Sun;
My children love the sunny day,
But noon and night to me are one.

My heart has pulses like their own,
I am their Mother, and my veins,
Though built of the enduring stone,
Thrill as do theirs with godlike pains.

The forests and the mountains high,
The foaming ocean and the springs,
The plains, — O pleasant Company,
My voice through all your anthem rings!

Ye are so cheerful in your minds,
Content to smile, content to share:
My being in your chorus finds
The echo of the spheral air.

No leaf may fall, no pebble roll,
No drop of water lose the road;
The issues of the general Soul
Are mirrored in its round abode.

THE BARREN MOORS

On your bare rocks, O barren moors,
On your bare rocks I love to lie! —
They stand like crags upon the shores,
Or clouds upon a placid sky.

Across those spaces desolate
The fox pursues his lonely way,
Those solitudes can fairly sate
The passage of my loneliest day.

Like desert islands far at sea
Where not a ship can ever land,
Those dim uncertainties to me
For something veritable stand.

A serious place distinct from all
Which busy Life delights to feel, —
I stand in this deserted hall,
And thus the wounds of time conceal.

No friend's cold eye, or sad delay,
Shall vex me now where not a sound
Falls on the ear, and every day
Is soft as silence most profound.

No more upon these distant worlds
The agitating world can come,
A single pensive thought upholds
The arches of this dreamy home.

Within the sky above, one thought
Replies to you, O barren moors!
Between, I stand, a creature taught
To stand between two silent floors.

TEARS IN SPRING

(LAMENT FOR THOREAU)

THE swallow is flying over,
But he will not come to me;
He flits, my daring rover,
From land to land, from sea to sea;
Where hot Bermuda's reef
Its barrier lifts to fortify the shore,
Above the surf's wild roar
He darts as swiftly o'er, —
But he who heard his cry of spring
Hears that no more, heeds not his wing.

How bright the skies that dally
Along day's cheerful arch,
And paint the sunset valley!
How redly buds the larch!
Blackbirds are singing,
Clear hylas ringing,
Over the meadow the frogs proclaim
The coming of Spring to boy and dame,
But not to me, —
Nor thee!

And golden crowfoot 's shining near,
Spring everywhere that shoots 't is clear,
A wail in the wind is all I hear;
A voice of woe for a lover's loss,
A motto for a travelling cross, —
And yet it is mean to mourn for thee,
In the form of bird or blossom or bee.

Cold are the sods of the valley to-day
Where thou art sleeping,
That took thee back to thy native clay;
Cold, — if above thee the grass is peeping
And the patient sunlight creeping,
While the bluebird sits on the locust-bough
Whose shadow is painted across thy brow,
And carols his welcome so sad and sweet
To the Spring that comes and kisses his feet.

EDITH

EDITH, the silent stars are coldly gleaming,
The night wind moans, the leafless trees are still.
Edith, there is a life beyond this seeming,
So sleeps the ice-clad lake beneath thy hill.

So silent beats the pulse of thy pure heart,
So shines the thought of thy unquestioned eyes.
O life! why wert thou helpless in thy art?
O loveliness! why seem'st thou but surprise?

Edith, the streamlets laugh to leap again;
There is a spring to which life's pulses fly;
And hopes that are not all the sport of pain,
Like lustres in the veil of that gray eye.

They say the thankless stars have answering vision,
That courage sings from out the frost-bound ways;
Edith, I grant that olden time's decision —
Thy beauty paints with gold the icy rays.

As in the summer's heat her promise lies,
As in the autumn's seed his vintage hides,
Thus might I shape my moral from those eyes,
Glass of thy soul, where innocence abides.

Edith, thy nature breathes of answered praying;
If thou dost live, then not my grief is vain;
Beyond the nerves of woe, beyond delaying,
Thy sweetness stills to rest the winter's pain.

Mary Elizabeth (Hewitt) Stebbins

THE SUNFLOWER TO THE SUN

Hymettus' bees are out on filmy wing,
Dim Phosphor slowly fades adown the west,
And Earth awakes. Shine on me, O my king!
For I with dew am laden and oppressed.

Long through the misty hours of morning gray
The flowers have watched to hail thee from yon sea!
Sad Asphodel, that pines to meet thy ray,
And Juno's roses, pale for love of thee.

Perchance thou dalliest with the Morning Hour,
Whose blush is reddening now the eastern wave;
Or to the cloud forever leavest thy flower,
Wiled by the glance white-footed Thetis gave.

I was a proud Chaldean monarch's child!
Euphrates' waters told me I was fair, —
And thou, Thessalia's shepherd, on me smiled,
And likened to thine own my amber hair.

Thou art my life — sustainer of my spirit!
Leave me not then in darkness here to pine;
Other hearts love thee, yet do they inherit
A passionate devotedness like mine?

But lo! thou lift'st thy shield o'er yonder tide:
The dun clouds fly before the conquering Sun;
Thou like a monarch up the heavens dost ride, —
And, joy! thou beam'st on me, celestial one!

On me, thy worshipper, thy poor Parsee,
Whose brow adoring types thy face divine;
God of my burning heart's idolatry,
Take root like me, or give me life like thine!

HAROLD THE VALIANT[1]

I mid the hills was born,
Where the skilled bowmen
Send with unerring shaft
Death to the foemen.
But I love to steer my bark —
To fear a stranger —
Over the Maelstrom's edge,
Daring the danger;
And where the mariner
Paleth affrighted,
Over the sunken rocks
I dash on delighted.
The far waters know my keel,
No tide restrains me;
But ah! a Russian maid
Coldly disdains me.

Once round Sicilia's isle
Sailed I, unfearing:
Conflict was on my prow,
Glory was steering.
Where fled the stranger ship
Wildly before me,
Down, like the hungry hawk,
My vessel bore me;
We carved on the craven's deck
The red runes of slaughter:
When my bird whets her beak
I give no quarter.
The far waters know my keel,
No tide restrains me;
But ah! a Russian maid
Coldly disdains me.

Countless as spears of grain
Stood the warriors of Drontheim,
When like the hurricane
I swept down upon them!
Like chaff beneath the flail
They fell in their numbers: —
Their king with the golden hair
I sent to his slumbers.
I love the combat fierce,
No fear restrains me;
But ah! a Russian maid
Coldly disdains me.

Once o'er the Baltic Sea
Swift we were dashing;

[1] See Biographical Note, p. 822.

Bright on our twenty spears
  Sunlight was flashing;
When through the Skager Rack
  The storm-wind was driven,
And from our bending mast
  The broad sail was riven:
Then, while the angry brine
  Foamed like a flagon,
Brimful the yesty rime
  Filled our brown dragon;
But I, with sinewy hand
  Strengthened in slaughter,
Forth from the straining ship
  Bailed the dun water.
The wild waters know my keel,
  No storm restrains me;
But ah! a Russian maid
  Coldly disdains me.

Firmly I curb my steed,
  As e'er Thracian horseman;
My hand throws the javelin true,
  Pride of the Norseman;
And the bold skater marks,
  While his lips quiver,
Where o'er the bending ice
  I skim the river:
Forth to my rapid oar
  The boat swiftly springeth —
Springs like the mettled steed
  When the spur stingeth.
Valiant I am in fight,
  No fear restrains me;
But ah! a Russian maid
  Coldly disdains me.

Saith she, the maiden fair,
  The Norsemen are cravens?
I in the Southland gave
  A feast to the ravens!
Green lay the sward outspread,
  The bright sun was o'er us
When the strong fighting men
  Rushed down before us.
Midway to meet the shock
  My courser bore me,
And like Thor's hammer crashed
  My strong hand before me;
Left we their maids in tears,
  Their city in embers:
The sound of the Viking's spears
  The Southland remembers!
I love the combat fierce,
  No fear restrains me;
But ah! a Russian maid
  Coldly disdains me.

Additional Selections

(VARIOUS POEMS BELONGING TO THIS DIVISION)

I

REQUIEM

FOR ONE SLAIN IN BATTLE

BREATHE, trumpets, breathe
  Slow notes of saddest wailing, —
Sadly responsive peal, ye muffled drums;
Comrades, with downcast eyes
    And banners trailing,
    Attend him home, —
The youthful warrior comes.

Upon his shield,
  Upon his shield returning,
Borne from the field of honor
  Where he fell;
Glory and grief, together clasped
  In mourning,
His fame, his fate
  With sobs exulting tell.

Wrap round his breast
  The flag his breast defended, —
His country's flag,
  In battle's front unrolled:
For it he died;
  On earth forever ended
His brave young life
  Lives in each sacred fold.

With proud fond tears,
By tinge of shame untainted,
Bear him, and lay him
Gently in his grave:
Above the hero write, —
The young, half-sainted, —
His country asked his life,
His life he gave!

GEORGE LUNT

NEW ENGLAND'S DEAD

NEW ENGLAND'S dead! New England's dead!
On every hill they lie;
On every field of strife, made red
By bloody victory.
Each valley, where the battle poured
Its red and awful tide,
Beheld the brave New England sword
With slaughter deeply dyed.
Their bones are on the northern hill,
And on the southern plain,
By brook and river, lake and rill,
And by the roaring main.

The land is holy where they fought,
And holy where they fell;
For by their blood that land was bought,
The land they loved so well.
Then glory to that valiant band,
The honored saviours of the land!

O, few and weak their numbers were, —
A handful of brave men;
But to their God they gave their prayer,
And rushed to battle then.
The God of battles heard their cry,
And sent to them the victory.

They left the ploughshare in the mould,
Their flocks and herds without a fold,
The sickle in the unshorn grain,
The corn, half-garnered, on the plain,
And mustered, in their simple dress,
For wrongs to seek a stern redress,
To right those wrongs, come weal, come woe,
To perish, or o'ercome their foe.

And where are ye, O fearless men?
And where are ye to-day?
I call: — the hills reply again
That ye have passed away;
That on old Bunker's lonely height,
In Trenton, and in Monmouth ground,
The grass grows green, the harvest bright
Above each soldier's mound.
The bugle's wild and warlike blast
Shall muster them no more;
An army now might thunder past,
And they heed not its roar.
The starry flag, 'neath which they fought
In many a bloody day,
From their old graves shall rouse them not,
For they have passed away.

ISAAC McLELLAN

WASHINGTON'S STATUE

THE quarry whence thy form majestic sprung
Has peopled earth with grace,
Heroes and gods that elder bards have sung,
A bright and peerless race;
But from its sleeping veins ne'er rose before
A shape of loftier name
Than his, who Glory's wreath with meekness wore,
The noblest son of Fame.
Sheathed is the sword that Passion never stained;
His gaze around is cast,
As if the joys of Freedom, newly gained,
Before his vision passed;
As if a nation's shout of love and pride
With music filled the air,
And his calm soul was lifted on the tide
Of deep and grateful prayer;
As if the crystal mirror of his life
To fancy sweetly came,
With scenes of patient toil and noble strife,
Undimmed by doubt or shame;
As if the lofty purpose of his soul
Expression would betray, —
The high resolve Ambition to control,
And thrust her crown away!
O, it was well in marble firm and white
To carve our hero's form,
Whose angel guidance was our strength in fight,
Our star amid the storm!
Whose matchless truth has made his name divine,
And human freedom sure,

His country great, his tomb earth's dearest shrine,
While man and time endure!
And it is well to place his image there
Upon the soil he blest:
Let meaner spirits, who its councils share,
Revere that silent guest!

Let us go up with high and sacred love
To look on his pure brow,
And as, with solemn grace, he points above,
Renew the patriot's vow!

HENRY THEODORE TUCKERMAN

II

THE STAR OF CALVARY

It is the same infrequent star, —
The all-mysterious light,
That like a watcher, gazing on
The changes of the night,
Toward the hill of Bethlehem took
Its solitary flight.

It is the same infrequent star;
Its sameness startleth me,
Although the disk is red as blood,
And downward silently
It looketh on another hill, —
The hill of Calvary!

Nor noon, nor night; for to the west
The heavy sun doth glow;
And, like a ship, the lazy mist
Is sailing on below, —
Between the broad sun and the earth
It tacketh to and fro.

There is no living wind astir;
The bat's unholy wing
Threads through the noiseless olive trees,
Like some unquiet thing
Which playeth in the darkness, when
The leaves are whispering.

Mount Calvary! Mount Calvary!
All sorrowfully still,
That mournful tread, it rends the heart
With an unwelcome thrill, —
The mournful tread of them that crowd
Thy melancholy hill!

There is a cross, — not one alone:
'T is even three I count,
Like columns on the mossy marge
Of some old Grecian fount,—
So pale they stand, so drearily,
On that mysterious Mount.

Behold, O Israel! behold,
It is no human One
That ye have dared to crucify.
What evil hath he done?
It is your King, O Israel!
The God-begotten Son!

A wreath of thorns, a wreath of thorns!
Why have ye crowned him so?
That brow is bathed in agony, —
'T is veiled in every woe:
Ye saw not the immortal trace
Of Deity below.

It is the foremost of the Three!
Resignedly they fall,
Those deathlike drooping features,
Unbending, blighted all:
The Man of Sorrows, — how he bears
The agonizing thrall!

'T is fixed on thee, O Israel!
His gaze! — how strange to brook;
But that there 's mercy blended deep
In each reproachful look,
'T would search thee, till the very heart
Its withered home forsook.

To God! to God! how eloquent
The cry, as if it grew,
By those cold lips unuttered, yet
All heartfelt rising through, —
"Father in heaven! forgive them, for
They know not what they do!"

NATHANIEL HAWTHORNE[1]

[1] See BIOGRAPHICAL NOTE, p. 797.

THE CLOUDS

I CANNOT look above and see
  Yon high-piled, pillowy mass
Of evening clouds, so swimmingly
  In gold and purple pass,
And think not, Lord, how thou wast seen
  On Israel's desert way,
Before them, in thy shadowy screen,
  Pavilioned all the day!

Or, of those robes of gorgeous hue
  Which the Redeemer wore,
When, ravished from his followers' view,
  Aloft his flight he bore;
When lifted, as on mighty wing,
  He curtained his ascent,
And, wrapt in clouds, went triumphing
  Above the firmament.

Is it a trail of that same pall
  Of many-colored dyes,
That high above, o'ermantling all,
  Hangs midway down the skies, —
Or borders of those sweeping folds
  Which shall be all unfurled
About the Saviour, when he holds
  His judgment on the world?

For in like manner as he went, —
  My soul, hast thou forgot? —
Shall be his terrible descent,
  When man expecteth not!
Strength, Son of man, against that hour,
  Be to our spirits given,
When thou shalt come again with power,
  Upon the clouds of heaven!

WILLIAM CROSWELL

A WORLD BEYOND

SCIENCE long watched the realms of space,
A planet's devious path to trace:
Convinced of heaven's harmonious law,
"A world beyond" Leverrier saw.

Thus when he views earth's sins and woes,
With a like faith the Christian knows
There is a world beyond, to prove
God's perfect wisdom, power, and love.

NATHANIEL INGERSOLL BOWDITCH

IT IS NOT DEATH TO DIE

IT is not death to die,
  To leave this weary road,
And, midst the brotherhood on high,
  To be at home with God.

It is not death to close
  The eye long dimmed by tears,
And wake in glorious repose,
  To spend eternal years.

It is not death to bear
  The wrench that sets us free
From dungeon-chain, to breathe the air
  Of boundless liberty.

It is not death to fling
  Aside this sinful dust,
And rise on strong, exulting wing,
  To live among the just.

Jesus, thou Prince of Life,
  Thy chosen cannot die!
Like Thee, they conquer in the strife,
  To reign with Thee on high.

GEORGE WASHINGTON BETHUNE

PARAPHRASE OF LUTHER'S HYMN

A MIGHTY fortress is our God,
  A bulwark never failing;
Our helper he amid the flood
  Of mortal ills prevailing.
    For still our ancient foe
    Doth seek to work us woe;
    His craft and power are great,
    And, armed with cruel hate,
  On earth is not his equal.

Did we in our own strength confide,
  Our striving would be losing, —
Were not the right man on our side,
  The man of God's own choosing.
    Dost ask who that may be?
    Christ Jesus, it is he,
    Lord Sabaoth his name,
    From age to age the same,
  And he must win the battle.

And though this world, with devils filled,
  Should threaten to undo us,

We will not fear, for God hath willed
His truth to triumph through us.
The Prince of Darkness grim, —
We tremble not for him;
His rage we can endure,
For lo! his doom is sure:
One little word shall fell him.

That word above all earthly powers,
No thanks to them, abideth;
The spirit and the gifts are ours
Through Him who with us sideth.
Let goods and kindred go,
This mortal life also;
The body they may kill,
God's truth abideth still,
His Kingdom is forever.

Frederic Henry Hedge

DIES IRÆ

Day of wrath, that day of burning,
Seer and Sibyl speak concerning,
All the world to ashes turning.

Oh, what fear shall it engender,
When the Judge shall come in splendor,
Strict to mark and just to render!

Trumpet, scattering sounds of wonder,
Rending sepulchres asunder,
Shall resistless summons thunder.

All aghast then Death shall shiver,
And great Nature's frame shall quiver,
When the graves their dead deliver.

Volume, from which nothing 's blotted,
Evil done nor evil plotted,
Shall be brought and dooms allotted.

When shall sit the Judge unerring,
He 'll unfold all here occurring,
Vengeance then no more deferring.

What shall *I* say, that time pending?
Ask what advocate 's befriending,
When the just man needs defending?

Dreadful King, all power possessing,
Saving freely those confessing,
Save thou me, O Fount of Blessing!

Think, O Jesus, for what reason
Thou didst bear earth's spite and treason,
Nor me lose in that dread season!

Seeking me Thy worn feet hasted,
On the cross Thy soul death tasted:
Let such travail not be wasted!

Righteous Judge of retribution!
Make me gift of absolution
Ere that day of execution!

Culprit-like, I plead, heart-broken,
On my cheek shame's crimson token:
Let the pardoning word be spoken!

Thou, who Mary gav'st remission,
Heard'st the dying Thief's petition,
Cheer'st with hope my lost condition.

Though my prayers be void of merit,
What is needful, Thou confer it,
Lest I endless fire inherit.

Be there, Lord, my place decided
With Thy sheep, from goats divided,
Kindly to Thy right hand guided!

When the accursed away are driven,
To eternal burnings given,
Call me with the blessed to heaven!

I beseech Thee, prostrate lying,
Heart as ashes, contrite, sighing,
Care for me when I am dying!

Day of tears and late repentance,
Man shall rise to hear his sentence:
Him, the child of guilt and error,
Spare, Lord, in that hour of terror!

Abraham Coles

MILTON'S PRAYER OF PATIENCE

I am old and blind!
Men point at me as smitten by God's frown;
Afflicted and deserted of my kind,
Yet am I not cast down.

I am weak, yet strong;
I murmur not that I no longer see;
Poor, old, and helpless, I the more belong,
Father Supreme! to Thee.

All-merciful One!
When men are furthest, then art Thou most near;
When friends pass by, my weaknesses to shun,
Thy chariot I hear.

Thy glorious face
Is leaning toward me, and its holy light
Shines in upon my lonely dwelling-place, —
And there is no more night.

On my bended knee
I recognize Thy purpose clearly shown;
My vision Thou hast dimmed, that I may see
Thyself — Thyself alone.

I have naught to fear:
This darkness is the shadow of Thy wing;
Beneath it I am almost sacred — here
Can come no evil thing.

Oh, I seem to stand
Trembling, where foot of mortal ne'er hath been,
Wrapped in that radiance from the sinless land,
Which eye hath never seen!

Visions come and go:
Shapes of resplendent beauty round me throng;
From angel lips I seem to hear the flow
Of soft and holy song.

It is nothing now,
When heaven is opening on my sightless eyes,
When airs from Paradise refresh my brow,
That earth in darkness lies.

In a purer clime
My being fills with rapture, — waves of thought
Roll in upon my spirit, — strains sublime
Break over me unsought.

Give me now my lyre!
I feel the stirrings of a gift divine:
Within my bosom glows unearthly fire
Lit by no skill of mine.

ELIZABETH LLOYD HOWELL

THE ANGELS' SONG

It came upon the midnight clear,
That glorious song of old,
From angels bending near the earth
To touch their harps of gold:
"Peace to the earth, good-will to men
From heaven's all-gracious King!"
The world in solemn stillness lay
To hear the angels sing.

Still through the cloven skies they come,
With peaceful wings unfurled;
And still their heavenly music floats
O'er all the weary world:
Above its sad and lowly plains
They bend on heavenly wing,
And ever o'er its Babel sounds
The blessed angels sing.

Yet with the woes of sin and strife
The world has suffered long;
Beneath the angel-strain have rolled
Two thousand years of wrong;
And man, at war with man, hears not
The love-song which they bring:
O, hush the noise, ye men of strife,
And hear the angels sing!

And ye, beneath life's crushing load
Whose forms are bending low;
Who toil along the climbing way
With painful steps and slow, —
Look now! for glad and golden hours
Come swiftly on the wing;
O, rest beside the weary road,
And hear the angels sing.

For lo! the days are hastening on,
By prophet-bards foretold,
When with the ever-circling years
Comes round the age of gold;
When Peace shall over all the earth
Its ancient splendors fling,
And the whole world send back the song
Which now the angels sing.

EDMUND HAMILTON SEARS

THE OTHER WORLD

It lies around us like a cloud,
The world we do not see;
Yet the sweet closing of an eye
May bring us there to be.

Its gentle breezes fan our cheeks
  Amid our worldly cares;
Its gentle voices whisper love,
  And mingle with our prayers.

Sweet hearts around us throb and beat,
  Sweet helping hands are stirred,
And palpitates the veil between,
  With breathings almost heard.

The silence, awful, sweet, and calm,
  They have no power to break;
For mortal words are not for them
  To utter or partake.

So thin, so soft, so sweet they glide,
  So near to press they seem,
They lull us gently to our rest,
  They melt into our dream.

And, in the hush of rest they bring,
  'T is easy now to see
How lovely and how sweet a pass
  The hour of death may be; —

To close the eye and close the ear,
  Wrapped in a trance of bliss,
And, gently drawn in loving arms,
  To swoon from that to this: —

Scarce knowing if we wake or sleep,
  Scarce asking where we are,
To feel all evil sink away,
  All sorrow and all care!

Sweet souls around us! watch us still,
  Press nearer to our side;
Into our thoughts, into our prayers,
  With gentle helping glide.

Let death between us be as naught,
  A dried and vanished stream;
Your joy be the reality,
  Our suffering life the dream.

HARRIET ELIZABETH BEECHER STOWE

III

LOVE UNCHANGEABLE

YES, still I love thee! Time, who sets
  His signet on my brow,
And dims my sunken eye, forgets
  The heart he could not bow,
Where love, that cannot perish, grows
For one, alas! that little knows
  How love may sometimes last,
Like sunshine wasting in the skies,
  When clouds are overcast.

The dew-drop hanging o'er the rose,
  Within its robe of light,
Can never touch a leaf that blows,
  Though seeming to the sight;
And yet it still will linger there,
Like hopeless love without despair, —
  A snow-drop in the sun:
A moment finely exquisite,
  Alas! but only one.

I would not have thy married heart
  Think momently of me;
Nor would I tear the cords apart,
  That bind me so to thee;
No! while my thoughts seem pure and
    mild,
Like dew upon the roses wild,
  I would not have thee know
The stream, that seems to thee so still,
  Has such a tide below.

Enough that in delicious dreams
  I see thee and forget,—
Enough, that when the morning beams
  I feel my eyelids wet!
Yet, could I hope, when Time lets fall
The darkness for creation's pall,
  To meet thee, — and to love, —
I would not shrink from aught below,
  Nor ask for more above.

RUFUS DAWES

LOVE UNSOUGHT

THEY tell me that I must not love,
  That thou wilt spurn the free
And unbought tenderness that gives
  Its hidden wealth to thee.

It may be so: I heed it not,
Nor would I change my blissful lot,
When thus I am allowed to make
My heart a bankrupt for thy sake.

They tell me when the fleeting charm
  Of novelty is o'er,
Thou 'lt turn away with careless brow
  And think of me no more.
It may be so! enough for me
If sunny skies still smile o'er thee,
Or I can trace, when thou art far,
Thy pathway like a distant star.

EMMA CATHARINE EMBURY

COME BACK

COME back and bring my life again
  That went with thee beyond my will!
Restore me that which makes me man
  Or leaves me wretched, dead and chill!
Thy presence was of life a part;
  Thine absence leaves the blank of death.
They wait thy presence — eye and heart,
  With straining gaze and bated breath.

The light is darkness, if thine eyes
  Make not the medium of its ray;
I see no star in evening skies,
  Save thou look up and point the way.
Nor bursting buds in May's young bloom,
  Nor sunshine rippling o'er the sea,
Bears up to heaven my heart's perfume
  Save thou my monitor can be.

There are two paths for human feet, —
  One bordered by a duty plain,
And one by phantoms cursed, yet sweet,
  Bewildering heart and maddening brain;
The one will right and reason urge,
  But thou must walk beside me there,
Or else I tread the dizzy verge,
  And thou some guilt of loss must bear.

Come back, there is no cause on earth, —
  No word of shame, no deed of wrong —
Can bury all of truth and worth,
  And sunder bonds once firm and strong.
There is no duty, heaven-imposed,
  That, velvet-gloved — an iron band
Upon my heart-strings crushed and closed—
  Thy hate should all my love withstand.

Days seem like ages — and, ere long,
  On senseless ears the cry may fall;
Or, stilled by bitter shame and wrong,
  The pleading voice may cease to call.
Come back! before the eyes grow dim
  That keep but sight to see thee come,
Ere fail and falter hand and limb,
  Whose strength but waits to fold thee home.

HENRY WILLIAM HERBERT

SONG

'T IS said that absence conquers love!
  But, oh! believe it not;
I 've tried, alas! its power to prove,
  But thou art not forgot.
Lady, though fate has bid us part,
  Yet still thou art as dear,
As fixed in this devoted heart,
  As when I clasped thee here.

I plunge into the busy crowd,
  And smile to hear thy name;
And yet, as if I thought aloud,
  They know me still the same;
And when the wine-cup passes round,
  I toast some other fair, —
But when I ask my heart the sound,
  Thy name is echoed there.

And when some other name I learn,
  And try to whisper love,
Still will my heart to thee return
  Like the returning dove.
In vain! I never can forget,
  And would not be forgot;
For I must bear the same regret,
  Whate'er may be my lot.

E'en as the wounded bird will seek
  Its favorite bower to die,
So, lady! I would hear thee speak,
  And yield my parting sigh.
'T is said that absence conquers love!
  But, oh! believe it not;
I 've tried, alas! its power to prove,
  But thou art not forgot.

FREDERICK WILLIAM THOMAS

IV

A REMEMBRANCE

I SEE thee still! thou art not dead,
  Though dust is mingled with thy form;
The broken sunbeam hath not shed
  The final rainbow on the storm:
In visions of the midnight deep,
  Thine accents through my bosom thrill
Till joy's fond impulse bids me weep, —
  For, wrapt in thought, I see thee still!

I see thee still, — that cheek of rose, —
  Those lips with dewy fragrance wet, —
That forehead in serene repose, —
  Those soul-lit eyes — I see them yet!
Sweet seraph! Sure thou art not dead,
  Thou gracest still this earthly sphere;
An influence still is round me shed,
  Like thine, — and yet thou art not here!

Farewell, beloved! To mortal sight
  Thy vermeil cheek no more may bloom;
No more thy smiles inspire delight,
  For thou art garnered in the tomb, —
Rich harvest for that ruthless power
  Which hath me bound to bear his will:
Yet, as in hope's unclouded hour,
  Throned in my heart I see thee still.

WILLIS GAYLORD CLARKE

A DEATH-BED

HER suffering ended with the day,
  Yet lived she at its close,
And breathed the long, long night away
  In statue-like repose.

But when the sun in all his state
  Illumed the eastern skies,
She passed through Glory's morning gate
  And walked in Paradise!

JAMES ALDRICH

DIRGE

SOFTLY!
  She is lying
    With her lips apart;
Softly!
  She is dying
    Of a broken heart.

Whisper!
  Life is growing
    Dim within her breast;
Whisper!
  She is going
    To her final rest.

Gently!
  She is sleeping,
    She has breathed her last!
Gently!
  While you 're weeping
    She to heaven has passed.

CHARLES GAMAGE EASTMAN

FLORENCE VANE

I LOVED thee long and dearly,
    Florence Vane;
My life's bright dream and early
    Hath come again;
I renew in my fond vision
    My heart's dear pain,
My hope, and thy derision,
    Florence Vane.

The ruin lone and hoary,
    The ruin old,
Where thou didst mark my story,
    At even told, —
That spot — the hues Elysian
    Of sky and plain —
I treasure in my vision,
    Florence Vane.

Thou wast lovelier than the roses
    In their prime;
Thy voice excelled the closes
    Of sweetest rhyme;
Thy heart was as a river
    Without a main.
Would I had loved thee never,
    Florence Vane!

But, fairest, coldest wonder!
    Thy glorious clay

Lieth the green sod under, —
Alas the day!
And it boots not to remember
Thy disdain, —
To quicken love's pale ember,
Florence Vane.

The lilies of the valley
By young graves weep,
The pansies love to dally
Where maidens sleep;
May their bloom, in beauty vying,
Never wane
Where thine earthly part is lying,
Florence Vane!

PHILIP PENDLETON COOKE

THE WIFE

I COULD have stemmed misfortune's tide,
And borne the rich one's sneer, —
Have braved the haughty glance of pride,
Nor shed a single tear;
I could have smiled on every blow
From life's full quiver thrown,
While I might gaze on thee, and know
I should not be alone.

I could — I think I could — have brooked,
E'en for a time, that thou
Upon my fading face hadst looked
With less of love than now;
For then I should at least have felt
The sweet hope still my own
To win thee back, and whilst I dwelt
On earth, not been alone.

But thus to see from day to day
Thy brightening eye and cheek,
And watch thy life-sands waste away,
Unnumbered, slow, and meek;
To meet thy smiles of tenderness,
And catch the feeble tone
Of kindness, ever breathed to bless,
And feel I'll be alone;

To mark thy strength each hour decay,
And yet thy hopes grow stronger,
As, filled with heavenward trust, they say
Earth may not claim thee longer;
Nay, dearest, 't is too much — this heart
Must break when thou art gone:
It must not be; we must not part;
I could not live alone.

ANNA PEYRE DINNIES

BLIND LOUISE

SHE knew that she was growing blind, —
Foresaw the dreary night
That soon would fall, without a star,
Upon her fading sight;

Yet never did she make complaint,
But prayed each day might bring
A beauty to her waning eyes, —
The loveliness of spring!

She dreaded that eclipse which might
Perpetually enclose
Sad memories of a leafless world,
A spectral realm of snows.

She 'd rather that the verdure left
An evergreen to shine
Within her heart, as summer leaves
Its memory on the pine.

She had her wish; for when the sun
O'erhung his eastern towers,
And shed his benediction on
A world of May-time flowers,

We found her seated, as of old,
In her accustomed place,
A midnight in her sightless eyes,
And morn upon her face!

GEORGE WASHINGTON DEWEY

UNDER THE VIOLETS

UNDER the violets, blue and sweet,
Where low the willow droops and weeps,
Where children tread with timid feet,
When twilight o'er the forest creeps,
She sleeps, — my little darling sleeps.

Breathe low and soft, O wind! breathe low
Where so much loveliness is laid!
Pour out thy heart in strains of woe,
O bird! that in the willows' shade
Sing'st till the stars do pale and fade.

It may be that to other eyes,
As in the happy days of old,
The sun doth every morning rise
O'er mountain summits tipped with gold,
And set where sapphire seas are rolled;

But I am so hedged round with woe,
This glory I no more can see.

O weary heart, that throbbest so,
Thou hast but this one wish, — to be
A little dust beneath the tree.

I would thou hadst thy wish to-day,
And we were lying side by side
With her who took our life away
That heavy day whereon she died.
O grave! I would thy gates were wide.

EDWARD YOUNG

THE VOICE OF THE GRASS

HERE I come creeping, creeping everywhere;
By the dusty roadside,
On the sunny hill-side,
Close by the noisy brook,
In every shady nook,
I come creeping, creeping everywhere.

Here I come creeping, smiling everywhere;
All around the open door,
Where sit the aged poor;
Here where the children play,
In the bright and merry May,
I come creeping, creeping everywhere.

Here I come creeping, creeping everywhere;
In the noisy city street
My pleasant face you 'll meet,
Cheering the sick at heart
Toiling his busy part, —
Silently creeping, creeping everywhere.

Here I come creeping, creeping everywhere;
You cannot see me coming,
Nor hear my low sweet humming;
For in the starry night,
And the glad morning light,
I come quietly creeping everywhere.

Here I come creeping, creeping everywhere;
More welcome than the flowers
In summer's pleasant hours:
The gentle cow is glad,
And the merry bird not sad,
To see me creeping, creeping everywhere.

Here I come creeping, creeping everywhere:
When you 're numbered with the dead
In your still and narrow bed,
In the happy spring I 'll come
And deck your silent home —
Creeping, silently creeping everywhere.

Here I come creeping, creeping everywhere;
My humble song of praise
Most joyfully I raise
To Him at whose command
I beautify the land,
Creeping, silently creeping everywhere.

SARAH ROBERTS BOYLE

V

A WINTER WISH

OLD wine to drink!
Ay, give the slippery juice
That drippeth from the grape thrown loose
Within the tun;
Plucked from beneath the cliff
Of sunny-sided Teneriffe,
And ripened 'neath the blink
Of India's sun!
Peat whiskey hot,
Tempered with well-boiled water!
These make the long night shorter, —
Forgetting not
Good stout old English porter.

Old wood to burn!
Ay, bring the hill-side beech
From where the owlets meet and screech,
And ravens croak;
The crackling pine, and cedar sweet;
Bring too a clump of fragrant peat,
Dug 'neath the fern;
The knotted oak,
A fagot too, perhap,
Whose bright flame, dancing, winking,

Shall light us at our drinking;
While the oozing sap
Shall make sweet music to our thinking.

Old books to read!
Ay, bring those nodes of wit,
The brazen-clasped, the vellum writ,
Time-honored tomes!
The same my sire scanned before,
The same my grandsire thumbëd o'er,
The same his sire from college bore,
The well-earned meed
Of Oxford's domes:
Old Homer blind,
Old Horace, rake Anacreon, by
Old Tully, Plautus, Terence lie;
Mort Arthur's olden minstrelsie,
Quaint Burton, quainter Spenser, ay!
And Gervase Markham's venerie —
Nor leave behind
The holye Book by which we live and die.

Old friends to talk!
Ay, bring those chosen few,
The wise, the courtly, and the true,
So rarely found;
Him for my wine, him for my stud,
Him for my easel, distich, bud
In mountain walk!
Bring Walter good,
With soulful Fred, and learned Will,
And thee, my alter ego (dearer still
For every mood).
These add a bouquet to my wine!
These add a sparkle to my pine!
If these I tine,
Can books, or fire, or wine be good?

ROBERT HINCKLEY MESSINGER

A PROEM

WHEN in my walks I meet some ruddy lad —
Or swarthy man — with tray-beladen head,
Whose smile entreats me, or his visage sad,
To buy the images he moulds for bread,

I think that, — though his poor Greek Slave in chains,
His Venus and her Boy with plaster dart,
Be, like the Organ-Grinder's quavering strains,
But farthings in the currency of art, —

Such coins a kingly effigy still wear,
Let metals base or precious in them mix:
The painted vellum hallows not the Prayer,
Nor ivory nor gold the Crucifix.

SAMUEL WARD

HORACE

HE who would echo Horace' lays
Aspires to an Icarian fame;
And borne on waxen wings essays
A flight — may give some sea a name.

My fate perchance! But as I write
I see through Time's reverted glass,
In fleckered mists of shade and light,
The phantoms of the ages pass.

I see an infant, tired with play,
Sleep sweetly in Apulia's wild,
And doves bring myrtle leaves and bay
To cover the courageous child.

A stripling walks the streets of Rome,
With slate and satchel on his arm;
His life abroad, his ways at home,
A loving father's care and charm.

Fulfilment of his boyhood's dream,
Greece welcomes now the freedman's son;
He haunts the groves of Academe,
And quaffs the springs of Helicon.

Light of the World! the central seat
Of wit and wisdom, art and lore, —
In Athens patriot exiles meet
Where bards and sages met before.

No athlete, and no warrior he,
With Brutus on Philippi's field,
The darling of Melpomene,
Not bravely, throws away his shield.

Her fleets dispersed and tempest-tost,
Her armies crushed, their leaders slain, —
Now is the great Republic lost,
Lost never to revive again.

The Julian star ascends the sky,
It shines on groups of learned men,

Law clips the wings of Liberty,
  And Horace wields the Empire's pen.

Names, only names! — the brilliant throng
  That crowd the poet's pictured page:
Still lives in his imperial song
  The soul of the Augustan age.

No longer through the Sacred Way
  The pontiffs lead the vestal train;
Thrones crumble, dynasties decay,
  Of Alaric born, or Charlemagne: —

Saints, Soldiers, Presbyters, and Popes,
  In legions rise and disappear,
And Bards with glowing horoscopes
  Oblivion garners year by year;

But on strong wing, through upper air, —
  Two worlds beneath, the Old and New, —
The Roman Swan is wafted where
  The Roman eagles never flew.

JOHN OSBORNE SARGENT

CHEZ BRÉBANT[1]

THE vicomte is wearing a brow of gloom
As he mounts the stair to his favorite room.
"Breakfast for two!" the *garçons* say,
"Then the pretty young lady is coming to-day!"
But the *patron* mutters, *A Dieu ne plaise!*
I want no clients from Père la Chaise.
Silver and crystal — a splendid show!
And a damask cloth white as driven snow.
The vicomte sits down with a ghastly air, —
His *vis-à-vis* is an empty chair.
But he calls to the *garçon*, "Antoine! *Vite!*
Place a stool for the lady's feet."
"The lady, monsieur?" (in a wavering tone).
"Yes — when have you known me to breakfast alone?
Fill up her glass! *Versez! Versez!*
You see how white are her cheeks to-day:
Sip it, my darling, 't was ordered for thee."
He raises his glass, "*A toi*, Mimi!"
The *garçon* shudders, for nothing is there
In the lady's place but an empty chair.
But still, with an air of fierce unrest,
The vicomte addresses an unseen guest.
"Leave us, Antoine: we have much to say,
And time is precious to me to-day."
When the *garçon* was gone he sprang up with a start:
"Mimi is dead of a broken heart.
Could I think, when she gave it with generous joy,
A woman's heart such a fragile toy?
Her trim little figure no longer I see!
Would I were lying with thee, Mimi!
For what is life but a hell to me?
What splendor and wealth but misery?"
A jet of flame and a whirl of smoke!
A detonation the silence broke.
The landlord enters, and lying there
Is the dead vicomte, with a stony glare
Rigidly fixed on an empty chair.
"*Il faut avertir le commissaire!*
Ma foi! Chez Brébant ces choses sont rares!"

FRANCIS ALEXANDER DURIVAGE

THE POET

GATHER all kindreds of this boundless realm
  To speak a common tongue in thee! Be thou —
Heart, pulse, and voice, whether pent hate o'erwhelm
  The stormy speech or young love whisper low.
Cheer them, immitigable battle-drum!
  Forth, truth-mailed, to the old unconquered field,
And lure them gently to a laurelled home,
  In notes more soft than lutes or viols yield.
Fill all the stops of life with tuneful breath;
Closing their lids, bestow a dirge-like death!

CORNELIUS MATHEWS

[1] See BIOGRAPHICAL NOTE, p. 790.

DIVISION III

(LOWELL, STORY, MRS. HOWE, WHITMAN, PARSONS, BROWNELL, READ, BOKER, THE STODDARDS, TAYLOR, MRS. DORR, MRS. PRESTON, MRS. COOKE, AND OTHERS)

James Russell Lowell

FROM "RHŒCUS"

HEAR now this fairy legend of old Greece,
As full of gracious youth and beauty still
As the immortal freshness of that grace
Carved for all ages on some Attic frieze.

A youth named Rhœcus, wandering in the wood,
Saw an old oak just trembling to its fall,
And, feeling pity of so fair a tree,
He propped its gray trunk with admiring care,
And with a thoughtless footstep loitered on.
But, as he turned, he heard a voice behind
That murmured "Rhœcus!" 'T was as if the leaves,
Stirred by a passing breath, had murmured it,
And, while he paused bewildered, yet again
It murmured "Rhœcus!" softer than a breeze.
He started and beheld with dizzy eyes
What seemed the substance of a happy dream
Stand there before him, spreading a warm glow
Within the green glooms of the shadowy oak.
It seemed a woman's shape, yet far too fair
To be a woman, and with eyes too meek
For any that were wont to mate with gods.
All naked like a goddess stood she there,
And like a goddess all too beautiful
To feel the guilt-born earthliness of shame.
"Rhœcus, I am the Dryad of this tree,"
Thus she began, dropping her low-toned words
Serene, and full, and clear, as drops of dew,
"And with it I am doomed to live and die;
The rain and sunshine are my caterers,
Nor have I other bliss than simple life;
Now ask me what thou wilt, that I can give,
And with a thankful joy it shall be thine."

Then Rhœcus, with a flutter at the heart,
Yet by the prompting of such beauty bold,
Answered: "What is there that can satisfy
The endless craving of the soul but love?
Give me thy love, or but the hope of that
Which must be evermore my nature's goal."
After a little pause she said again,
But with a glimpse of sadness in her tone,
"I give it, Rhœcus, though a perilous gift;
An hour before the sunset meet me here."
And straightway there was nothing he could see
But the green glooms beneath the shadowy oak,
And not a sound came to his straining ears
But the low trickling rustle of the leaves,
And far away upon an emerald slope
The falter of an idle shepherd's pipe.

Now, in those days of simpleness and faith,
Men did not think that happy things were dreams
Because they overstepped the narrow bourn
Of likelihood, but reverently deemed
Nothing too wondrous or too beautiful
To be the guerdon of a daring heart.
So Rhœcus made no doubt that he was blest,
And all along unto the city's gate
Earth seemed to spring beneath him as he walked,
The clear, broad sky looked bluer than its wont,
And he could scarce believe he had not wings,
Such sunshine seemed to glitter through his veins
Instead of blood, so light he felt and strange.

Young Rhœcus had a faithful heart enough,
But one that in the present dwelt too much,
And, taking with blithe welcome whatsoe'er
Chance gave of joy, was wholly bound in that,
Like the contented peasant of a vale,
Deemed it the world, and never looked beyond.
So, haply meeting in the afternoon
Some comrades who were playing at the dice,
He joined them, and forgot all else beside.

The dice were rattling at the merriest,
And Rhœcus, who had met but sorry luck,
Just laughed in triumph at a happy throw,
When through the room there hummed a yellow bee
That buzzed about his ear with down-dropped legs
As if to light. And Rhœcus laughed and said,
Feeling how red and flushed he was with loss,
"By Venus! does he take me for a rose?"
And brushed him off with rough, impatient hand.
But still the bee came back, and thrice again
Rhœcus did beat him off with growing wrath.
Then through the window flew the wounded bee,
And Rhœcus, tracking him with angry eyes,
Saw a sharp mountain-peak of Thessaly
Against the red disk of the setting sun, —
And instantly the blood sank from his heart,
As if its very walls had caved away.
Without a word he turned, and, rushing forth,
Ran madly through the city and the gate,
And o'er the plain, which now the wood's long shade,
By the low sun thrown forward broad and dim,
Darkened wellnigh unto the city's wall.

Quite spent and out of breath he reached the tree,
And, listening fearfully, he heard once more
The low voice murmur "Rhœcus!" close at hand:
Whereat he looked around him, but could see
Naught but the deepening glooms beneath the oak.
Then sighed the voice, "O Rhœcus! never-more
Shalt thou behold me or by day or night,
Me, who would fain have blessed thee with a love
More ripe and bounteous than ever yet
Filled up with nectar any mortal heart:
But thou didst scorn my humble messenger,
And sent'st him back to me with bruisëd wings.
We spirits only show to gentle eyes,
We ever ask an undivided love,
And he who scorns the least of Nature's works
Is thenceforth exiled and shut out from all.
Farewell! for thou canst never see me more."

Then Rhœcus beat his breast and groaned aloud,
And cried "Be pitiful! forgive me yet
This once, and I shall never need it more!"
"Alas!" the voice returned, "'t is thou art blind,
Not I unmerciful; I can forgive,
But have no skill to heal thy spirit's eyes;
Only the soul hath power o'er itself."
With that again there murmured "Never-more!"
And Rhœcus after heard no other sound,
Except the rattling of the oak's crisp leaves,
Like the long surf upon a distant shore
Raking the sea-worn pebbles up and down.
The night had gathered round him: o'er the plain
The city sparkled with its thousand lights,
And sounds of revel fell upon his ear
Harshly and like a curse; above, the sky,
With all its bright sublimity of stars,
Deepened, and on his forehead smote the breeze:
Beauty was all around him and delight,
But from that eve he was alone on earth.

A STANZA ON FREEDOM

THEY are slaves who fear to speak
For the fallen and the weak;
They are slaves who will not choose
Hatred, scoffing, and abuse,

Rather than in silence shrink
From the truth they needs must think;
They are slaves who dare not be
In the right with two or three.

HEBE

I SAW the twinkle of white feet,
I saw the flash of robes descending;
Before her ran an influence fleet,
That bowed my heart like barley bending.

As, in bare fields, the searching bees
Pilot to blooms beyond our finding,
It led me on, by sweet degrees
Joy's simple honey-cells unbinding.

Those Graces were that seemed grim Fates;
With nearer love the sky leaned o'er me;
The long-sought Secret's golden gates
On musical hinges swung before me.

I saw the brimmed bowl in her grasp
Thrilling with godhood; like a lover
I sprang the proffered life to clasp;—
The beaker fell; the luck was over.

The earth has drunk the vintage up;
What boots it patch the goblet's splinters?
Can Summer fill the icy cup,
Whose treacherous crystal is but winter's?

O spendthrift haste! await the Gods;
The nectar crowns the lips of Patience;
Haste scatters on unthankful sods
The immortal gift in vain libations.

Coy Hebe flies from those that woo,
And shuns the hands would seize upon her;
Follow thy life, and she will sue
To pour for thee the cup of honor.

SHE CAME AND WENT

As a twig trembles, which a bird
Lights on to sing, then leaves unbent,
So is my memory thrilled and stirred;—
I only know she came and went.

As clasps some lake, by gusts unriven,
The blue dome's measureless content,
So my soul held that moment's heaven;—
I only know she came and went.

As, at one bound, our swift spring heaps
The orchards full of bloom and scent,
So clove her May my wintry sleeps;—
I only know she came and went.

An angel stood and met my gaze,
Through the low doorway of my tent;
The tent is struck, the vision stays;—
I only know she came and went.

Oh, when the room grows slowly dim,
And life's last oil is nearly spent,
One gush of light these eyes will brim,
Only to think she came and went.

FROM "THE VISION OF SIR LAUNFAL"

FOR a cap and bells our lives we pay,
Bubbles we buy with a whole soul's tasking:
'T is heaven alone that is given away,
'T is only God may be had for the asking;
No price is set on the lavish summer;
June may be had by the poorest comer.

And what is so rare as a day in June?
Then, if ever, come perfect days;
Then Heaven tries earth if it be in tune,
And over it softly her warm ear lays;
Whether we look or whether we listen,
We hear life murmur or see it glisten;
Every clod feels a stir of might,
An instinct within it that reaches and towers,
And, groping blindly above it for light,
Climbs to a soul in grass and flowers;
The flush of life may well be seen
Thrilling back over hills and valleys;
The cowslip startles in meadows green,
The buttercup catches the sun in its chalice,
And there's never a leaf nor a blade too mean
To be some happy creature's palace;
The little bird sits at his door in the sun,
Atilt like a blossom among the leaves,
And lets his illumined being o'errun
With the deluge of summer it receives;
His mate feels the eggs beneath her wings,
And the heart in her dumb breast flutters and sings;
He sings to the wide world and she to her nest,—
In the nice ear of Nature which song is the best?

Now is the high-tide of the year,
And whatever of life hath ebbed away
Comes flooding back with a ripply cheer,
Into every bare inlet and creek and bay;
Now the heart is so full that a drop overfills it,
We are happy now because God wills it;
No matter how barren the past may have been,
'T is enough for us now that the leaves are green;
We sit in the warm shade and feel right well
How the sap creeps up and the blossoms swell;
We may shut our eyes, but we cannot help knowing
That skies are clear and grass is growing;
The breeze comes whispering in our ear,
That dandelions are blossoming near,
That maize has sprouted, that streams are flowing,
That the river is bluer than the sky,
That the robin is plastering his house hard by;
And if the breeze kept the good news back,
For other couriers we should not lack;
We could guess it all by yon heifer's lowing, —
And hark! how clear bold chanticleer,
Warmed with the new wine of the year,
Tells all in his lusty crowing!

FROM "A FABLE FOR CRITICS"

TO HIS COUNTRYMEN

THERE are one or two things I should just like to hint,
For you don't often get the truth told you in print;
The most of you (this is what strikes all beholders)
Have a mental and physical stoop in the shoulders;
Though you ought to be free as the winds and the waves,
You 've the gait and the manners of runaway slaves;
Though you brag of your New World, you don't half believe in it;
And as much of the Old as is possible weave in it;
Your goddess of freedom, a tight, buxom girl,
With lips like a cherry and teeth like a pearl,
With eyes bold as Herë's, and hair floating free,
And full of the sun as the spray of the sea,
Who can sing at a husking or romp at a shearing,
Who can trip through the forests alone without fearing,
Who can drive home the cows with a song through the grass,
Keeps glancing aside into Europe's cracked glass,
Hides her red hands in gloves, pinches up her lithe waist,
And makes herself wretched with transmarine taste;
She loses her fresh country charm when she takes
Any mirror except her own rivers and lakes.

ON HIMSELF

There is Lowell, who 's striving Parnassus to climb
With a whole bale of *isms* tied together with rhyme,
He might get on alone, spite of brambles and boulders,
But he can't with that bundle he has on his shoulders,
The top of the hill he will ne'er come nigh reaching
Till he learns the distinction 'twixt singing and preaching;
His lyre has some chords that would ring pretty well,
But he 'd rather by half make a drum of the shell,
And rattle away till he 's old as Methusalem,
At the head of a march to the last new Jerusalem.

FROM "THE BIGLOW PAPERS"

WHAT MR. ROBINSON THINKS

GUVENER B. is a sensible man;
He stays to his home an' looks arter his folks;
He draws his furrer ez straight ez he can,
An' into nobody's tater-patch pokes;
But John P.
Robinson he
Sez he wunt vote fer Guvener B.

My! aint it terrible? Wut shall we du?
We can't never choose him o' course, — thet 's flat;
Guess we shall hev to come round, (don't you?)
An' go in fer thunder an' guns, an' all that;
Fer John P.
Robinson he
Sez he wunt vote fer Guvener B.

Gineral C. is a dreffle smart man:
He 's ben on all sides thet give places or pelf;
But consistency still wuz a part of his plan, —
He 's ben true to *one* party, — an' thet is himself; —
So John P.
Robinson he
Sez he shall vote fer Gineral C.

Gineral C. he goes in fer the war;
He don't vally princerple morn 'n an old cud;
Wut did God make us raytional creeturs fer,
But glory an' gunpowder, plunder an' blood?
So John P.
Robinson he
Sez he shall vote fer Gineral C.

We were gittin' on nicely up here to our village,
With good old idees o' wut 's right an' wut aint,
We kind o' thought Christ went agin war an' pillage,
An' thet eppyletts worn't the best mark of a saint;
But John P.
Robinson he
Sez this kind o' thing 's an exploded idee.

The side of our country must ollers be took,
An' Presidunt Polk, you know, *he* is our country.
An' the angel thet writes all our sins in a book
Puts the *debit* to him, an' to us the *per contry;*
An' John P.
Robinson he
Sez this is his view o' the thing to a T.

Parson Wilbur he calls all these argimunts lies;
Sez they 're nothin' on airth but jest *fee, faw, fum;*
An' thet all this big talk of our destinies
Is half on it ign'ance, an' t'other half rum;
But John P.
Robinson he
Sez it aint no sech thing; an', of course, so must we.

Parson Wilbur sez *he* never heerd in his life
Thet th' Apostles rigged out in their swaller-tail coats,
An' marched round in front of a drum an' a fife,
To git some on 'em office, an' some on 'em votes;
But John P.
Robinson he
Sez they didn't know everythin' down in Judee.

Wal, it 's a marcy we 've gut folks to tell us
The rights an' the wrongs o' these matters, I vow, —
God sends country lawyers, an' other wise fellers,
To start the world's team wen it gits in a slough;
Fer John P.
Robinson he
Sez the world 'll go right, ef he hollers out Gee!

THE CANDIDATE'S LETTER

Dear Sir, — You wish to know my notions
On sartin pints thet rile the land;
There 's nothin' thet my natur so shuns
Ez bein' mum or underhand;
I 'm a straight-spoken kind o' creetur
Thet blurts right out wut 's in his head,
An' ef I 've one pecooler feetur,
It is a nose thet wunt be led.

So, to begin at the beginnin'
An' come direcly to the pint,

I think the country's underpinnin'
  Is some consid'ble out o' jint;
I aint agoin' to try your patience
  By tellin' who done this or thet,
I don't make no insinooations,
  I jest let on I smell a rat.

Thet is, I mean, it seems to me so,
  But, ef the public think I'm wrong,
I wunt deny but wut I be so, —
  An', fact, it don't smell very strong;
My mind 's tu fair to lose its balance
  An' say wich party hez most sense;
There may be folks o' greater talence
  Thet can't set stiddier on the fence.

I 'm an eclectic; ez to choosin'
  'Twixt this an' thet, I 'm plaguy lawth;
I leave a side thet looks like losin',
  But (wile there 's doubt) I stick to both;
I stan' upon the Constitution,
  Ez preudunt statesmun say, who 've planned
A way to git the most profusion
  O' chances ez to *ware* they 'll stand.

Ez fer the war, I go agin it, —
  I mean to say I kind o' du, —
Thet is, I mean thet, bein' in it,
  The best way wuz to fight it thru;
Not but wut abstract war is horrid,
  I sign to thet with all my heart, —
But civlyzation *doos* git forrid
  Sometimes upon a powder-cart.

About thet darned Proviso matter
  I never hed a grain o' doubt,
Nor I aint one my sense to scatter
  So 'st no one could n't pick it out;
My love fer North an' South is equil,
  So I 'll jest answer plump an' frank,
No matter wut may be the sequil, —
  Yes, Sir, I *am* agin a Bank.

Ez to the answerin' o' questions,
  I 'm an off ox at bein' druv,
Though I aint one thet ary test shuns
  I 'll give our folks a helpin' shove;
Kind o' permiscoous I go it
  Fer the holl country, an' the ground
I take, ez nigh ez I can show it,
  Is pooty gen'ally all round.

I don't appruve o' givin' pledges;
  You 'd ough' to leave a feller free,
An' not go knockin' out the wedges
  To ketch his fingers in the tree;
Pledges air awfle breachy cattle
  Thet preudunt farmers don't turn out, —
Ez long 'z the people git their rattle,
  Wut is there fer 'm to grout about ?

Ez to the slaves, there 's no confusion
  In *my* idees consarnin' them, —
I think they air an Institution,
  A sort of — yes, jest so, — ahem:
Do *I* own any ? Of my merit
  On thet pint you yourself may jedge;
All is, I never drink no sperit,
  Nor I haint never signed no pledge.

Ez to my princerples, I glory
  In hevin' nothin' o' the sort;
I aint a Wig, I aint a Tory,
  I 'm jest a canderdate, in short;
Thet 's fair an' square an' parpendicler
  But, ef the Public cares a fig
To hev me an'thin' in particler,
  Wy, I 'm a kind o' peri-Wig.

P. S.

Ez we 're a sort o' privateerin',
  O' course, you know, it 's sheer an' sheer,
An' there is suthin' wuth your hearin'
  I 'll mention in *your* privit ear;
Ef you git *me* inside the White House,
  Your head with ile I 'll kin' o' 'nint
By gittin' *you* inside the Light-house
  Down to the eend o' Jaalam Pint.

An' ez the North hez took to brustlin'
  At bein' scrouged frum off the roost,
I 'll tell ye wut 'll save all tusslin'
  An' give our side a harnsome boost, —
Tell 'em thet on the Slavery question
  I 'm RIGHT, although to speak I 'm lawth;
This gives you a safe pint to rest on,
  An' leaves me frontin' South by North.

THE COURTIN'

GOD makes sech nights, all white an' still
  Fur 'z you can look or listen,
Moonshine an' snow on field an' hill,
  All silence an' all glisten.

Zekle crep' up quite unbeknown
  An' peeked in thru the winder,
An' there sot Huldy all alone,
  'ith no one nigh to hender.

A fireplace filled the room's one side
  With half a cord o' wood in —
There warn't no stoves (tell comfort died)
  To bake ye to a puddin'.

The wa'nut logs shot sparkles out
  Towards the pootiest, bless her,
An' leetle flames danced all about
  The chiny on the dresser.

Agin the chimbley crook-necks hung,
  An' in amongst 'em rusted
The ole queen's-arm thet gran'ther Young
  Fetched back f'om Concord busted.

The very room, coz she was in,
  Seemed warm f'om floor to ceilin',
An' she looked full ez rosy agin
  Ez the apples she was peelin'.

'T was kin' o' kingdom-come to look
  On sech a blessed cretur;
A dogrose blushin' to a brook
  Ain't modester nor sweeter.

He was six foot o' man, A 1,
  Clear grit an' human natur';
None could n't quicker pitch a ton
  Nor dror a furrer straighter.

He 'd sparked it with full twenty gals,
  He 'd squired 'em, danced 'em, druv 'em,
Fust this one, an' then thet, by spells —
  All is, he could n't love 'em.

But long o' her his veins 'ould run
  All crinkly like curled maple;
The side she breshed felt full o' sun
  Ez a south slope in Ap'il.

She thought no v'ice hed sech a swing
  Ez hisn in the choir;
My! when he made Ole Hunderd ring,
  She *knowed* the Lord was nigher.

An' she 'd blush scarlit, right in prayer,
  When her new meetin'-bunnet
Felt somehow thru its crown a pair
  O' blue eyes sot upun it.

Thet night, I tell ye, she looked *some!*
  She seemed to 've gut a new soul,
For she felt sartin-sure he 'd come,
  Down to her very shoe-sole.

She heered a foot, an' knowed it tu,
  A-raspin' on the scraper, —
All ways to once her feelins flew
  Like sparks in burnt-up paper.

He kin' o' l'itered on the mat,
  Some doubtfle o' the sekle;
His heart kep' goin' pity-pat,
  But hern went pity Zekle.

An' yit she gin her cheer a jerk
  Ez though she wished him furder,
An' on her apples kep' to work,
  Parin' away like murder.

" You want to see my Pa, I s'pose ?"
  " Wal . . . no . . . I come dasignin' " —
" To see my Ma ? She 's sprinklin' clo'es
  Agin to-morrer's i'nin'."

To say why gals acts so or so,
  Or don't, 'ould be presumin';
Mebby to mean *yes* an' say *no*
  Comes nateral to women.

He stood a spell on one foot fust,
  Then stood a spell on t 'other,
An' on which one he felt the wust
  He could n't ha' told ye nuther.

Says he, " I 'd better call agin ";
  Says she, " Think likely, Mister ";
Thet last word pricked him like a pin,
  An' . . . Wal, he up an' kist her.

When Ma bimeby upon 'em slips,
  Huldy sot pale ez ashes,
All kin' o' smily roun' the lips
  An' teary roun' the lashes.

For she was jes' the quiet kind
  Whose naturs never vary,
Like streams that keep a summer mind
  Snowhid in Jenooary.

The blood clost roun' her heart felt glued
  Too tight for all expressin',
Tell mother see how metters stood,
  An' gin 'em both her blessin'.

Then her red come back like the tide
  Down to the Bay o' Fundy,
An' all I know is they was cried
  In meetin' come nex' Sunday.

MR. HOSEA BIGLOW TO THE EDITOR OF "THE ATLANTIC MONTHLY"

WHERE 's Peace? I start, some clear-blown night,
When gaunt stone walls grow numb an' number,
An' creakin' 'cross the snow-crus' white,
Walk the col' starlight into summer;
Up grows the moon, an' swell by swell
Thru the pale pasturs silvers dimmer
Than the last smile thet strives to tell
O' love gone heavenward in its shimmer.

I hev ben gladder o' sech things
Than cocks o' spring or bees o' clover,
They filled my heart with livin' springs,
But now they seem to freeze 'em over;
Sights innercent ez babes on knee,
Peaceful ez eyes o' pastur'd cattle,
Jes' coz they be so, seem to me
To rile me more with thoughts o' battle.

Indoors an' out by spells I try;
Ma'am Natur' keeps her spin-wheel goin',
But leaves my natur' stiff and dry
Ez fiel's o' clover arter mowin';
An' her jes' keepin' on the same,
Calmer 'n a clock, an' never carin',
An' findin' nary thing to blame,
Is wus than ef she took to swearin'.

. . . .

Rat-tat-tat-tattle thru the street
I hear the drummers makin' riot,
An' I set thinkin' o' the feet
Thet follered once an' now are quiet, —
White feet ez snowdrops innercent,
Thet never knowed the paths o' Satan,
Whose comin' step ther 's ears thet won't,
No, not lifelong, leave off awaitin'.

Why, hain't I held 'em on my knee?
Didn't I love to see 'em growin',
Three likely lads ez wal could be,
Hahnsome an' brave an' not tu knowin'?
I set an' look into the blaze
Whose natur', jes' like theirn, keeps climbin',
Ez long 'z it lives, in shinin' ways,
An' half despise myself for rhymin'.

Wut 's words to them whose faith an' truth
On War's red techstone rang true metal,
Who ventered life an' love an' youth
For the gret prize o' death in battle?
To him who, deadly hurt, agen
Flashed on afore the charge's thunder,
Tippin' with fire the bolt of men
Thet rived the Rebel line asunder?

'Tain't right to hev the young go fust,
All throbbin' full o' gifts an' graces,
Leavin' life's paupers dry ez dust
To try an' make b'lieve fill their places:
Nothin' but tells us wut we miss,
Ther 's gaps our lives can't never fay in,
An' *thet* world seems so fur from this
Lef' for us loafers to grow gray in!

My eyes cloud up for rain; my mouth
Will take to twitchin' roun' the corners;
I pity mothers, tu, down South,
For all they sot among the scorners:
I 'd sooner take my chance to stan'
At Jedgment where your meanest slave is,
Than at God's bar hol' up a han'
Ez drippin' red ez yourn, Jeff Davis!

Come, Peace! not like a mourner bowed
For honor lost an' dear ones wasted,
But proud, to meet a people proud,
With eyes thet tell o' triumph tasted!
Come, with han' grippin' on the hilt,
An' step thet proves ye Victory's daughter!
Longin' for you, our sperits wilt
Like shipwrecked men's on raf's for water.

Come, while our country feels the lift
Of a gret instinct shoutin' "Forwards!"
An' knows thet freedom ain't a gift
Thet tarries long in han's o' cowards!
Come, sech ez mothers prayed for, when
They kissed their cross with lips thet quivered,
An' bring fair wages for brave men,
A nation saved, a race delivered!

ODE RECITED AT THE HARVARD COMMEMORATION

JULY 21, 1865

I

WEAK-WINGED is song,
Nor aims at that clear-ethered height
Whither the brave deed climbs for light:
We seem to do them wrong,

Bringing our robin's-leaf to deck their hearse
Who in warm life-blood wrote their nobler verse,
Our trivial song to honor those who come
With ears attuned to strenuous trump and drum,
And shaped in squadron-strophes their desire,
Live battle-odes whose lines were steel and fire:
Yet sometimes feathered words are strong,
A gracious memory to buoy up and save
From Lethe's dreamless ooze, the common grave
Of the unventurous throng.

II

To-day our Reverend Mother welcomes back
Her wisest Scholars, those who understood
The deeper teaching of her mystic tome,
And offered their fresh lives to make it good:
No lore of Greece or Rome,
No science peddling with the names of things,
Or reading stars to find inglorious fates,
Can lift our life with wings
Far from Death's idle gulf that for the many waits
And lengthen out our dates
With that clear fame whose memory sings
In manly hearts to come, and nerves them and dilates:
Nor such thy teaching, Mother of us all!
Not such the trumpet-call
Of thy diviner mood,
That could thy sons entice
From happy homes and toils, the fruitful nest
Of those half-virtues which the world calls best,
Into War's tumult rude;
But rather far that stern device
The sponsors chose that round thy cradle stood
In the dim, unventured wood,
The VERITAS that lurks beneath
The letter's unprolific sheath,
Life of whate'er makes life worth living,
Seed-grain of high emprise, immortal food,
One heavenly thing whereof earth hath the giving.

III

Many loved Truth, and lavished life's best oil
Amid the dust of books to find her,
Content at last, for guerdon of their toil,
With the cast mantle she hath left behind her.
Many in sad faith sought for her,
Many with crossed hands sighed for her;
But these, our brothers, fought for her,
At life's dear peril wrought for her,
So loved her that they died for her,
Tasting the raptured fleetness
Of her divine completeness:
Their higher instinct knew
Those love her best who to themselves are true,
And what they dare to dream of, dare to do;
They followed her and found her
Where all may hope to find,
Not in the ashes of the burnt-out mind,
But beautiful, with danger's sweetness round her.
Where faith made whole with deed
Breathes its awakening breath
Into the lifeless creed,
They saw her plumed and mailed,
With sweet, stern face unveiled,
And all-repaying eyes, look proud on them in death.

IV

Our slender life runs rippling by, and glides
Into the silent hollow of the past;
What is there that abides
To make the next age better for the last?
Is earth too poor to give us
Something to live for here that shall outlive us?
Some more substantial boon
Than such as flows and ebbs with Fortune's fickle moon?
The little that we see
From doubt is never free;
The little that we do

Is but half-nobly true;
With our laborious hiving
What men call treasure, and the gods call dross,
Life seems a jest of Fate's contriving,
Only secure in every one's conniving,
A long account of nothings paid with loss,
Where we poor puppets, jerked by unseen wires,
After our little hour of strut and rave,
With all our pasteboard passions and desires,
Loves, hates, ambitions, and immortal fires,
Are tossed pell-mell together in the grave.
But stay! no age was e'er degenerate,
Unless men held it at too cheap a rate,
For in our likeness still we shape our fate.
Ah, there is something here
Unfathomed by the cynic's sneer,
Something that gives our feeble light
A high immunity from Night,
Something that leaps life's narrow bars
To claim its birthright with the hosts of heaven;
A seed of sunshine that can leaven
Our earthly dullness with the beams of stars,
And glorify our clay
With light from fountains elder than the Day;
A conscience more divine than we,
A gladness fed with secret tears,
A vexing, forward-reaching sense
Of some more noble permanence;
A light across the sea,
Which haunts the soul and will not let it be,
Still beaconing from the heights of undegenerate years.

V

Whither leads the path
To ampler fates that leads?
Not down through flowery meads,
To reap an aftermath
Of youth's vainglorious weeds,
But up the steep, amid the wrath
And shock of deadly-hostile creeds,
Where the world's best hope and stay
By battle's flashes gropes a desperate way,
And every turf the fierce foot clings to bleeds.
Peace hath her not ignoble wreath,
Ere yet the sharp, decisive word
Light the black lips of cannon, and the sword
Dreams in its easeful sheath;
But some day the live coal behind the thought,
Whether from Baäl's stone obscene,
Or from the shrine serene
Of God's pure altar brought,
Bursts up in flame; the war of tongue and pen
Learns with what deadly purpose it was fraught,
And, helpless in the fiery passion caught,
Shakes all the pillared state with shock of men:
Some day the soft Ideal that we wooed
Confronts us fiercely, foe-beset, pursued,
And cries reproachful: "Was it, then, my praise,
And not myself was loved? Prove now thy truth;
I claim of thee the promise of thy youth;
Give me thy life, or cower in empty phrase,
The victim of thy genius, not its mate!"
Life may be given in many ways,
And loyalty to Truth be sealed
As bravely in the closet as the field,
So bountiful is Fate;
But then to stand beside her,
When craven churls deride her,
To front a lie in arms and not to yield,
This shows, methinks, God's plan
And measure of a stalwart man,
Limbed like the old heroic breeds,
Who stand self-poised on manhood's solid earth,
Not forced to frame excuses for his birth,
Fed from within with all the strength he needs.

VI

Such was he, our Martyr-Chief,
Whom late the Nation he had led,
With ashes on her head,
Wept with the passion of an angry grief:
Forgive me, if from present things I turn
To speak what in my heart will beat and burn,
And hang my wreath on his world-honored urn.
Nature, they say, doth dote,
And cannot make a man
Save on some worn-out plan,
Repeating us by rote:

For him her Old-World moulds aside she threw,
And, choosing sweet clay from the breast
Of the unexhausted West,
With stuff untainted shaped a hero new,
Wise, steadfast in the strength of God, and true.
How beautiful to see
Once more a shepherd of mankind indeed,
Who loved his charge, but never loved to lead;
One whose meek flock the people joyed to be,
Not lured by any cheat of birth,
But by his clear-grained human worth,
And brave old wisdom of sincerity!
They knew that outward grace is dust;
They could not choose but trust
In that sure-footed mind's unfaltering skill,
And supple-tempered will
That bent like perfect steel to spring again and thrust.
His was no lonely mountain-peak of mind,
Thrusting to thin air o'er our cloudy bars,
A sea-mark now, now lost in vapor's blind;
Broad prairie rather, genial, level-lined,
Fruitful and friendly for all human kind,
Yet also nigh to heaven and loved of loftiest stars.
Nothing of Europe here,
Or, then, of Europe fronting mornward still,
Ere any names of Serf and Peer
Could Nature's equal scheme deface
And thwart her genial will;
Here was a type of the true elder race,
And one of Plutarch's men talked with us face to face.
I praise him not; it were too late;
And some innative weakness there must be
In him who condescends to victory
Such as the Present gives, and cannot wait,
Safe in himself as in a fate.
So always firmly he:
He knew to bide his time,
And can his fame abide,
Still patient in his simple faith sublime,
Till the wise years decide.
Great captains, with their guns and drums,
Disturb our judgment for the hour,
But at last silence comes;
These all are gone, and, standing like a tower,
Our children shall behold his fame,
The kindly-earnest, brave, foreseeing man,
Sagacious, patient, dreading praise, not blame,
New birth of our new soil, the first American.

VII

Long as man's hope insatiate can discern
Or only guess some more inspiring goal
Outside of Self, enduring as the pole,
Along whose course the flying axles burn
Of spirits bravely-pitched, earth's manlier brood;
Long as below we cannot find
The meed that stills the inexorable mind;
So long this faith to some ideal Good,
Under whatever mortal names it masks,
Freedom, Law, Country, this ethereal mood
That thanks the Fates for their severer tasks,
Feeling its challenged pulses leap,
While others skulk in subterfuges cheap,
And, set in Danger's van, has all the boon it asks,
Shall win man's praise and woman's love,
Shall be a wisdom that we set above
All other skills and gifts to culture dear,
A virtue round whose forehead we inwreathe
Laurels that with a living passion breathe
When other crowns grow, while we twine them, sear.
What brings us thronging these high rites to pay,
And seal these hours the noblest of our year,
Save that our brothers found this better way?

VIII

We sit here in the Promised Land
That flows with Freedom's honey and milk;
But 't was they won it, sword in hand,
Making the nettle danger soft for us as silk.
We welcome back our bravest and our best; —
Ah me! not all! some come not with the rest,
Who went forth brave and bright as any here!

I strive to mix some gladness with my strain,
But the sad strings complain,
And will not please the ear:
I sweep them for a pæan, but they wane
Again and yet again
Into a dirge, and die away, in pain.
In these brave ranks I only see the gaps,
Thinking of dear ones whom the dumb turf wraps,
Dark to the triumph which they died to gain:
Fitlier may others greet the living,
For me the past is unforgiving;
I with uncovered head
Salute the sacred dead,
Who went, and who return not. — Say not so!
'T is not the grapes of Canaan that repay,
But the high faith that failed not by the way;
Virtue treads paths that end not in the grave;
No bar of endless night exiles the brave;
And to the saner mind
We rather seem the dead that stayed behind.
Blow, trumpets, all your exultations blow!
For never shall their aureoled presence lack:
I see them muster in a gleaming row,
With ever-youthful brows that nobler show;
We find in our dull road their shining track;
In every nobler mood
We feel the orient of their spirit glow,
Part of our life's unalterable good,
Of all our saintlier aspiration;
They come transfigured back,
Secure from change in their high-hearted ways,
Beautiful evermore, and with the rays
Of morn on their white Shields of Expectation!

IX

But is there hope to save
Even this ethereal essence from the grave?
What ever 'scaped Oblivion's subtle wrong
Save a few clarion names, or golden threads of song?
Before my musing eye
The mighty ones of old sweep by,
Disvoicëd now and insubstantial things,
As noisy once as we; poor ghosts of kings,
Shadows of empire wholly gone to dust,
And many races, nameless long ago,
To darkness driven by that imperious gust
Of ever-rushing Time that here doth blow:
O visionary world, condition strange,
Where naught abiding is but only Change,
Where the deep-bolted stars themselves still shift and range!
Shall we to more continuance make pretence?
Renown builds tombs; a life-estate is Wit;
And, bit by bit,
The cunning years steal all from us but woe;
Leaves are we, whose decays no harvest sow.
But, when we vanish hence,
Shall they lie forceless in the dark below,
Save to make green their little length of sods,
Or deepen pansies for a year or two,
Who now to us are shining-sweet as gods?
Was dying all they had the skill to do?
That were not fruitless: but the Soul resents
Such short-lived service, as if blind events
Ruled without her, or earth could so endure;
She claims a more divine investiture
Of longer tenure than Fame's airy rents;
Whate'er she touches doth her nature share;
Her inspiration haunts the ennobled air,
Gives eyes to mountains blind,
Ears to the deaf earth, voices to the wind,
And her clear trump sings succor everywhere
By lonely bivouacs to the wakeful mind;
For soul inherits all that soul could dare:
Yea, Manhood hath a wider span
And larger privilege of life than man.
The single deed, the private sacrifice,
So radiant now through proudly-hidden tears,
Is covered up erelong from mortal eyes
With thoughtless drift of the deciduous years;
But that high privilege that makes all men peers,
That leap of heart whereby a people rise
Up to a noble anger's height,
And, flamed on by the Fates, not shrink, but grow more bright,
That swift validity in noble veins,

Of choosing danger and disdaining shame,
Of being set on flame
By the pure fire that flies all contact base
But wraps its chosen with angelic might,
These are imperishable gains,
Sure as the sun, medicinal as light,
These hold great futures in their lusty reins
And certify to earth a new imperial race.

X

Who now shall sneer?
Who dare again to say we trace
Our lines to a plebeian race?
Roundhead and Cavalier!
Dumb are those names erewhile in battle loud;
Dream-footed as the shadow of a cloud,
They flit across the ear:
That is best blood that hath most iron in 't
To edge resolve with, pouring without stint
For what makes manhood dear.
Tell us not of Plantagenets,
Hapsburgs, and Guelfs, whose thin bloods crawl
Down from some victor in a border-brawl!
How poor their outworn coronets,
Matched with one leaf of that plain civic wreath
Our brave for honor's blazon shall bequeath,
Through whose desert a rescued Nation sets
Her heel on treason, and the trumpet hears
Shout victory, tingling Europe's sullen ears
With vain resentments and more vain regrets!

XI

Not in anger, not in pride,
Pure from passion's mixture rude
Ever to base earth allied,
But with far-heard gratitude,
Still with heart and voice renewed,
To heroes living and dear martyrs dead,
The strain should close that consecrates our brave.
Lift the heart and lift the head!
Lofty be its mood and grave,
Not without a martial ring,
Not without a prouder tread
And a peal of exultation:
Little right has he to sing
Through whose heart in such an hour
Beats no march of conscious power,
Sweeps no tumult of elation!
T' is no Man we celebrate,
By his country's victories great,
A hero half, and half the whim of Fate,
But the pith and marrow of a Nation
Drawing force from all her men,
Highest, humblest, weakest, all,
For her time of need, and then
Pulsing it again through them,
Till the basest can no longer cower,
Feeling his soul spring up divinely tall,
Touched but in passing by her mantle-hem.
Come back, then, noble pride, for 't is her dower!
How could poet ever tower,
If his passions, hopes, and fears,
If his triumphs and his tears,
Kept not measure with his people?
Boom, cannon, boom to all the winds and waves!
Clash out, glad bells, from every rocking steeple!
Banners, a-dance with triumph, bend your staves!
And from every mountain-peak
Let beacon-fire to answering beacon speak,
Katahdin tell Monadnock, Whiteface he,
And so leap on in light from sea to sea,
Till the glad news be sent
Across a kindling continent,
Making earth feel more firm and air breathe braver:
"Be proud! for she is saved, and all have helped to save her!
She that lifts up the manhood of the poor,
She of the open soul and open door,
With room about her hearth for all mankind!
The fire is dreadful in her eyes no more;
From her bold front the helm she doth unbind,
Sends all her handmaid armies back to spin,
And bids her navies, that so lately hurled
Their crashing battle, hold their thunders in,
Swimming like birds of calm along the unharmful shore.
No challenge sends she to the elder world,
That looked askance and hated; a light scorn
Plays o'er her mouth, as round her mighty knees
She calls her children back, and waits the morn
Of nobler day, enthroned between her subject seas."

XII

Bow down, dear Land, for thou hast found release!
Thy God, in these distempered days,
Hath taught thee the sure wisdom of His ways,
And through thine enemies hath wrought thy peace!
Bow down in prayer and praise!
No poorest in thy borders but may now
Lift to the juster skies a man's enfranchised brow.
O Beautiful! my Country! ours once more!
Smoothing thy gold of war-dishevelled hair
O'er such sweet brows as never other wore,
And letting thy set lips,
Freed from wrath's pale eclipse,
The rosy edges of their smile lay bare,
What words divine of lover or of poet
Could tell our love and make thee know it,
Among the Nations bright beyond compare?
What were our lives without thee?
What all our lives to save thee?
We reck not what we gave thee;
We will not dare to doubt thee,
But ask whatever else, and we will dare!

THE FIRST SNOW-FALL

The snow had begun in the gloaming,
And busily all the night
Had been heaping field and highway
With a silence deep and white.

Every pine and fir and hemlock
Wore ermine too dear for an earl,
And the poorest twig on the elm-tree
Was ridged inch deep with pearl.

From sheds new-roofed with Carrara
Came Chanticleer's muffled crow,
The stiff rails softened to swan's-down,
And still fluttered down the snow.

I stood and watched by the window
The noiseless work of the sky,
And the sudden flurries of snow-birds,
Like brown leaves whirling by.

I thought of a mound in sweet Auburn
Where a little headstone stood;
How the flakes were folding it gently,
As did robins the babes in the wood.

Up spoke our own little Mabel,
Saying, "Father, who makes it snow?"
And I told of the good All-father
Who cares for us here below.

Again I looked at the snow-fall,
And thought of the leaden sky
That arched o'er our first great sorrow,
When that mound was heaped so high.

I remembered the gradual patience
That fell from that cloud like snow,
Flake by flake, healing and hiding
The scar that renewed our woe.

And again to the child I whispered,
"The snow that husheth all,
Darling, the merciful Father
Alone can make it fall!"

Then, with eyes that saw not, I kissed her;
And she, kissing back, could not know
That *my* kiss was given to her sister,
Folded close under deepening snow.

INTERNATIONAL COPYRIGHT

In vain we call old notions fudge,
And bend our conscience to our dealing;
The Ten Commandments will not budge,
And stealing will continue stealing.

IN A COPY OF OMAR KHAYYÁM

These pearls of thought in Persian gulfs were bred,
Each softly lucent as a rounded moon;
The diver Omar plucked them from their bed,
Fitzgerald strung them on an English thread.

Fit rosary for a queen, in shape and hue,
When Contemplation tells her pensive beads

Of mortal thoughts, forever old and new.
Fit for a queen? Why, surely then for you!

The moral? Where Doubt's eddies toss and twirl
Faith's slender shallop till her footing reel,
Plunge: if you find not peace beneath the whirl,
Groping, you may like Omar grasp a pearl.

AUF WIEDERSEHEN

SUMMER

The little gate was reached at last,
Half hid in lilacs down the lane;
She pushed it wide, and, as she past,
A wistful look she backward cast,
And said, — "*Auf wiedersehen!*"

With hand on latch, a vision white
Lingered reluctant, and again
Half doubting if she did aright,
Soft as the dews that fell that night,
She said, — "*Auf wiedersehen!*"

The lamp's clear gleam flits up the stair;
I linger in delicious pain;
Ah, in that chamber, whose rich air
To breathe in thought I scarcely dare,
Thinks she, — "*Auf wiedersehen!*"

'T is thirteen years; once more I press
The turf that silences the lane;
I hear the rustle of her dress,
I smell the lilacs, and — ah, yes,
I hear, — "*Auf wiedersehen!*"

Sweet piece of bashful maiden art!
The English words had seemed too fain,
But these — they drew us heart to heart,
Yet held us tenderly apart;
She said, — "*Auf wiedersehen!*"

PALINODE

AUTUMN

Still thirteen years: 't is autumn now
On field and hill, in heart and brain;
The naked trees at evening sough;
The leaf to the forsaken bough
Sighs not, — "*Auf wiedersehen!*"

Two watched yon oriole's pendent dome,
That now is void, and dank with rain,
And one, — oh, hope more frail than foam!
The bird to his deserted home
Sings not, — "*Auf wiedersehen!*"

The loath gate swings with rusty creak;
Once, parting there, we played at pain;
There came a parting, when the weak
And fading lips essayed to speak
Vainly, — "*Auf wiedersehen!*"

Somewhere is comfort, somewhere faith,
Though thou in outer dark remain;
One sweet sad voice ennobles death,
And still, for eighteen centuries saith
Softly, — "*Auf wiedersehen!*"

If earth another grave must bear,
Yet heaven hath won a sweeter strain,
And something whispers my despair,
That, from an orient chamber there,
Floats down, — "*Auf wiedersehen!*"

AFTER THE BURIAL

Yes, faith is a goodly anchor;
When skies are sweet as a psalm,
At the bows it lolls so stalwart,
In its bluff, broad-shouldered calm.

And when over breakers to leeward
The tattered surges are hurled,
It may keep our head to the tempest,
With its grip on the base of the world.

But, after the shipwreck, tell me
What help in its iron thews,
Still true to the broken hawser,
Deep down among sea-weed and ooze?

In the breaking gulfs of sorrow,
When the helpless feet stretch out
And find in the deeps of darkness
No footing so solid as doubt,

Then better one spar of Memory,
One broken plank of the Past,
That our human heart may cling to,
Though hopeless of shore at last!

To the spirit its splendid conjectures,
To the flesh its sweet despair,

Its tears o'er the thin-worn locket
With its anguish of deathless hair!

Immortal? I feel it and know it,
Who doubts it of such as she?
But that is the pang's very secret, —
Immortal away from me.

There's a narrow ridge in the graveyard
Would scarce stay a child in his race,
But to me and my thought it is wider
Than the star-sown vague of Space.

Your logic, my friend, is perfect,
Your moral most drearily true;
But, since the earth clashed on *her* coffin,
I keep hearing that, and not you.

Console if you will, I can bear it;
'T is a well-meant alms of breath;
But not all the preaching since Adam
Has made Death other than Death.

It is pagan; but wait till you feel it, —
That jar of our earth, that dull shock
When the ploughshare of deeper passion
Tears down to our primitive rock.

Communion in spirit! Forgive me,
But I, who am earthly and weak,
Would give all my incomes from dreamland
For a touch of her hand on my cheek.

That little shoe in the corner,
So worn and wrinkled and brown,
With its emptiness confutes you,
And argues your wisdom down.

IN THE TWILIGHT

Men say the sullen instrument,
That, from the Master's bow,
With pangs of joy or woe,
Feels music's soul through every fibre sent,
Whispers the ravished strings
More than he knew or meant;
Old summers in its memory glow;
The secrets of the wind it sings;
It hears the April-loosened springs;
And mixes with its mood
All it dreamed when it stood
In the murmurous pine-wood
Long ago!

The magical moonlight then
Steeped every bough and cone;
The roar of the brook in the glen
Came dim from the distance blown;
The wind through its glooms sang low,
And it swayed to and fro
With delight as it stood
In the wonderful wood,
Long ago!

O my life, have we not had seasons
That only said, Live and rejoice?
That asked not for causes and reasons,
But made us all feeling and voice?
When we went with the winds in thei blowing,
When Nature and we were peers,
And we seemed to share in the flowing
Of the inexhaustible years?
Have we not from the earth drawn juices
Too fine for earth's sordid uses?
Have I heard, have I seen
All I feel, all I know?
Doth my heart overween?
Or could it have been
Long ago?

Sometimes a breath floats by me,
An odor from Dreamland sent,
That makes the ghost seem nigh me
Of a splendor that came and went,
Of a life lived somewhere, I know not
In what diviner sphere,
Of memories that stay not and go not,
Like music heard once by an ear
That cannot forget or reclaim it,
A something so shy, it would shame it
To make it a show,
A something too vague, could I name it,
For others to know,
As if I had lived it or dreamed it,
As if I had acted or schemed it,
Long ago!

And yet, could I live it over,
This life that stirs in my brain,
Could I be both maiden and lover,
Moon and tide, bee and clover,
As I seem to have been, once again,
Could I but speak it and show it,
This pleasure more sharp than pain,
That baffles and lures me so,
The world should once more have a poet,
Such as it had
In the ages glad,
Long ago!

AN AUTOGRAPH

O'ER the wet sands an insect crept
Ages ere man on earth was known —
And patient Time, while Nature slept,
The slender tracing turned to stone.

'T was the first autograph: and ours?
Prithee, how much of prose or song,
In league with the creative powers,
Shall 'scape Oblivion's broom so long.

24th June, 1886.

William Wetmore Story

CLEOPATRA

HERE, Charmian, take my bracelets:
They bar with a purple stain
My arms; turn over my pillows —
They are hot where I have lain:
Open the lattice wider,
A gauze o'er my bosom throw,
And let me inhale the odors
That over the garden blow.

I dreamed I was with my Antony,
And in his arms I lay;
Ah, me! the vision has vanished —
The music has died away.
The flame and the perfume have perished —
As this spiced aromatic pastille
That wound the blue smoke of its odor
Is now but an ashy hill.

Scatter upon me rose leaves,
They cool me after my sleep,
And with sandal odors fan me
Till into my veins they creep;
Reach down the lute, and play me
A melancholy tune,
To rhyme with the dream that has vanished
And the slumbering afternoon.

There, drowsing in golden sunlight,
Loiters the slow smooth Nile,
Through slender papyri, that cover
The wary crocodile.
The lotus lolls on the water,
And opens its heart of gold,
And over its broad leaf pavement
Never a ripple is rolled.
The twilight breeze is too lazy
Those feathery palms to wave,
And yon little cloud is as motionless
As a stone above a grave.

Ah, me! this lifeless nature
Oppresses my heart and brain!
Oh! for a storm and thunder —
For lightning and wild fierce rain!
Fling down that lute — I hate it!
Take rather his buckler and sword,
And crash them and clash them together
Till this sleeping world is stirred.

Hark! to my Indian beauty —
My cockatoo, creamy white,
With roses under his feathers —
That flashes across the light.
Look! listen! as backward and forward
To his hoop of gold he clings,
How he trembles, with crest uplifted,
And shrieks as he madly swings!
Oh, cockatoo, shriek for Antony!
Cry, "Come, my love, come home!"
Shriek, "Antony! Antony! Antony!"
Till he hears you even in Rome.

There — leave me, and take from my chamber
That stupid little gazelle,
With its bright black eyes so meaningless,
And its silly tinkling bell!
Take him, — my nerves he vexes —
The thing without blood or brain,
Or, by the body of Isis,
I 'll snap his thin neck in twain!

Leave me to gaze at the landscape
Mistily stretching away,
Where the afternoon's opaline tremors
O'er the mountains quivering play;
Till the fiercer splendor of sunset
Pours from the west its fire,
And melted, as in a crucible,
Their earthy forms expire;
And the bald blear skull of the desert
With glowing mountains is crowned,
That burning like molten jewels
Circle its temples round.

I will lie and dream of the past time,
  Æons of thought away,
And through the jungle of memory
  Loosen my fancy to play;
When, a smooth and velvety tiger,
  Ribbed with yellow and black,
Supple and cushion-footed
  I wandered, where never the track
Of a human creature had rustled
  The silence of mighty woods,
And, fierce in a tyrannous freedom,
  I knew but the law of my moods.
The elephant, trumpeting, started,
  When he heard my footstep near,
And the spotted giraffes fled wildly
  In a yellow cloud of fear.
I sucked in the noontide splendor,
  Quivering along the glade,
Or yawning, panting, and dreaming,
  Basked in the tamarisk shade,
Till I heard my wild mate roaring,
  As the shadows of night came on
To brood in the trees' thick branches,
  And the shadow of sleep was gone;
Then I roused, and roared in answer,
  And unsheathed from my cushioned feet
My curving claws, and stretched me,
  And wandered my mate to greet.
We toyed in the amber moonlight,
  Upon the warm flat sand,
And struck at each other our massive arms —
  How powerful he was and grand!
His yellow eyes flashed fiercely
  As he crouched and gazed at me,
And his quivering tail, like a serpent,
  Twitched curving nervously.
Then like a storm he seized me,
  With a wild triumphant cry,
And we met, as two clouds in heaven
  When the thunders before them fly.
We grappled and struggled together,
  For his love like his rage was rude;
And his teeth in the swelling folds of my neck
  At times, in our play, drew blood.

Often another suitor —
  For I was flexile and fair —
Fought for me in the moonlight,
  While I lay couching there,
Till his blood was drained by the desert;
  And, ruffled with triumph and power,
He licked me and lay beside me
  To breathe him a vast half-hour.
Then down to the fountain we loitered,
  Where the antelopes came to drink;
Like a bolt we sprang upon them,
  Ere they had time to shrink.
We drank their blood and crushed them,
  And tore them limb from limb,
And the hungriest lion doubted
  Ere he disputed with him.

That was a life to live for!
  Not this weak human life,
With its frivolous bloodless passions,
  Its poor and petty strife!

Come to my arms, my hero!
  The shadows of twilight grow,
And the tiger's ancient fierceness
  In my veins begins to flow.
Come not cringing to sue me!
  Take me with triumph and power,
As a warrior storms a fortress!
  I will not shrink or cower.
Come, as you came in the desert,
  Ere we were women and men,
When the tiger passions were in us,
  And love as you loved me then!

IO VICTIS

I SING the hymn of the conquered, who fell in the Battle of Life, —
The hymn of the wounded, the beaten, who died overwhelmed in the strife;
Not the jubilant song of the victors, for whom the resounding acclaim
Of nations was lifted in chorus, whose brows wore the chaplet of fame,
But the hymn of the low and the humble, the weary, the broken in heart,
Who strove and who failed, acting bravely a silent and desperate part;
Whose youth bore no flower on its branches, whose hopes burned in ashes away,
From whose hands slipped the prize they had grasped at, who stood at the dying of day
With the wreck of their life all around them, unpitied, unheeded, alone,
With Death swooping down o'er their failure, and all but their faith overthrown,

While the voice of the world shouts its chorus, — its pæan for those who have won;

While the trumpet is sounding triumphant,
and high to the breeze and the sun
Glad banners are waving, hands clapping,
and hurrying feet
Thronging after the laurel-crowned victors, I stand on the field of defeat,
In the shadow, with those who have fallen,
and wounded, and dying, and there
Chant a requiem low, place my hand on
their pain-knotted brows, breathe a
prayer,
Hold the hand that is helpless, and whisper,
"They only the victory win,
Who have fought the good fight, and have
vanquished the demon that tempts
us within;
Who have held to their faith unseduced
by the prize that the world holds on
high;
Who have dared for a high cause to suffer,
resist, fight, — if need be, to die."

Speak, History! who are Life's victors?
Unroll thy long annals, and say,
Are they those whom the world called the
victors — who won the success of a
day?
The martyrs, or Nero? The Spartans,
who fell at Thermopylæ's tryst,
Or the Persians and Xerxes? His judges
or Socrates? Pilate or Christ?

PRAXITELES AND PHRYNE

A THOUSAND silent years ago,
The twilight faint and pale
Was drawing o'er the sunset glow
Its soft and shadowy veil;

When from his work the Sculptor stayed
His hand, and, turned to one
Who stood beside him, half in shade,
Said, with a sigh, "'T is done.

"Thus much is saved from chance and
change,
That waits for me and thee;
Thus much — how little! — from the range
Of Death and Destiny.

"Phryne, thy human lips shall pale,
Thy rounded limbs decay, —
Nor love nor prayers can aught avail
To bid thy beauty stay;

"But there thy smile for centuries
On marble lips shall live, —
For Art can grant what Love denies,
And fix the fugitive.

"Sad thought! nor age nor death shall fade
The youth of this cold bust;
When this quick brain and hand that made,
And thou and I are dust!

"When all our hopes and fears are dead,
And both our hearts are cold,
And love is like a tune that 's played,
And life a tale that 's told,

"This senseless stone, so coldly fair,
That love nor life can warm,
The same enchanting look shall wear,
The same enchanting form.

"Its peace no sorrow shall destroy;
Its beauty age shall spare
The bitterness of vanished joy,
The wearing waste of care.

"And there upon that silent face
Shall unborn ages see
Perennial youth, perennial grace,
And sealed serenity.

"And strangers, when we sleep in peace,
Shall say, not quite unmoved,
'So smiled upon Praxiteles
The Phryne whom he loved!'"

Julia Ward Howe

BATTLE-HYMN OF THE REPUBLIC

MINE eyes have seen the glory of the coming of the Lord:
He is trampling out the vintage where the
grapes of wrath are stored;
He hath loosed the fateful lightning of his
terrible swift sword:
His truth is marching on.

I have seen Him in the watch-fires of a hundred circling camps;
They have builded Him an altar in the evening dews and damps;
I can read His righteous sentence by the dim and flaring lamps.
His day is marching on.

I have read a fiery gospel, writ in burnished rows of steel:
"As ye deal with my contemners, so with you my grace shall deal;
Let the Hero, born of woman, crush the serpent with his heel,
Since God is marching on."

He has sounded forth the trumpet that shall never call retreat;
He is sifting out the hearts of men before his judgment-seat:
Oh! be swift, my soul, to answer Him! be jubilant, my feet!
Our God is marching on.

In the beauty of the lilies Christ was born across the sea,
With a glory in his bosom that transfigures you and me:
As he died to make men holy, let us die to make men free,
While God is marching on.

OUR ORDERS

WEAVE no more silks, ye Lyons looms,
To deck our girls for gay delights!
The crimson flower of battle blooms,
And solemn marches fill the night.

Weave but the flag whose bars to-day
Drooped heavy o'er our early dead,
And homely garments, coarse and gray,
For orphans that must earn their bread!

Keep back your tunes, ye viols sweet,
That poured delight from other lands!
Rouse there the dancer's restless feet:
The trumpet leads our warrior bands.

And ye that wage the war of words
With mystic fame and subtle power,
Go, chatter to the idle birds,
Or teach the lesson of the hour!

Ye Sibyl Arts, in one stern knot
Be all your offices combined!
Stand close, while Courage draws the lot,
The destiny of human kind.

And if that destiny could fail,
The sun should darken in the sky,
The eternal bloom of Nature pale,
And God, and Truth, and Freedom die!

Walt Whitman

BEGINNERS

How they are provided for upon the earth (appearing at intervals),
How dear and dreadful they are to the earth,
How they inure to themselves as much as to any, what a paradox appears their age,
How people respond to them, yet know them not,
How there is something relentless in their fate all times,
How all times mischoose the objects of their adulation and reward,
And how the same inexorable price must still be paid for the same great purchase.

STILL THOUGH THE ONE I SING

STILL though the one I sing,
(One, yet of contradictions made) I dedicate to Nationality,
I leave in him revolt, (O latent right of insurrection! O quenchless, indispensable fire!)

FROM "THE SONG OF MYSELF"

MYSELF

I CELEBRATE myself, and sing myself,
And what I assume you shall assume,
For every atom belonging to me as good belongs to you.

I loaf and invite my soul,
I lean and loaf at my ease observing a spear of summer grass.

My tongue, every atom of my blood, formed from this soil, this air,
Born here of parents born here from parents the same, and their parents the same,
I, now thirty-seven years old in perfect health begin,
Hoping to cease not till death.

Creeds and schools in abeyance,
Retiring back awhile sufficed at what they are, but never forgotten,
I harbor for good or bad, I permit to speak at every hazard,
Nature without check with original energy.

LEAVES OF GRASS

A child said *What is the grass?* fetching it to me with full hands;
How could I answer the child? I do not know what it is any more than he.

I guess it must be the flag of my disposition, out of hopeful green stuff woven.

Or I guess it is the handkerchief of the Lord,
A scented gift and remembrancer designedly dropped,
Bearing the owner's name someway in the corners, that we may see and remark, and say *Whose?*

Or I guess the grass is itself a child, the produced babe of the vegetation.

Or I guess it is a uniform hieroglyphic,
And it means, Sprouting alike in broad zones and narrow zones,
Growing among black folks as among white,
Kanuck, Tuckahoe, Congressman, Cuff, I give them the same, I receive them the same.

And now it seems to me the beautiful uncut hair of graves.

Tenderly will I use you curling grass,
It may be you transpire from the breasts of young men,
It may be if I had known them I would have loved them,
It may be you are from old people, or from offspring taken soon out of their mothers' laps,
And here you are the mothers' laps.

This grass is very dark to be from the white heads of old mothers,
Darker than the colorless beards of old men,
Dark to come from under the faint red roofs of mouths.

O I perceive after all so many uttering tongues,
And I perceive they do not come from the roofs of mouths for nothing.

I wish I could translate the hints about the dead young men and women,
And the hints about old men and mothers, and the offspring taken soon out of their laps.

What do you think has become of the young and old men?
And what do you think has become of the women and children?

They are alive and well somewhere,
The smallest sprout shows there is really no death,
And if ever there was it led forward life, and does not wait at the end to arrest it,
And ceased the moment life appeared.

All goes onward and outward, nothing collapses,
And to die is different from what any one supposed, and luckier.

. . . .

I know I am deathless,
I know this orbit of mine cannot be swept by a carpenter's compass,
I know I shall not pass like a child's carlacue cut with a burnt stick at night.

. . . .

One world is away and by far the largest to me, and that is myself,
And whether I come to my own to-day or in ten thousand or ten million years,
I can cheerfully take it now, or with equal cheerfulness I can wait.

My foothold is tenoned and mortised in granite,
I laugh at what you call dissolution,
And I know the amplitude of time.

HEROES

I UNDERSTAND the large hearts of heroes,
The courage of present times and all times,
How the skipper saw the crowded and rudderless wreck of the steamship, and Death chasing it up and down the storm,
How he knuckled tight and gave not back an inch, and was faithful of days and faithful of nights,
And chalked in large letters on a board, *Be of good cheer, we will not desert you;*
How he followed with them and tacked with them three days and would not give it up,
How he saved the drifting company at last,
How the lank loose-gowned women looked when boated from the side of their prepared graves,
How the silent old-faced infants, and the lifted sick, and the sharp-lipped unshaved men;
All this I swallow, it tastes good, I like it well, it becomes mine,
I am the man, I suffered, I was there.

. . . .

Agonies are one of my changes of garments,
I do not ask the wounded person how he feels, I myself become the wounded person,
My hurts turn livid upon me as I lean on a cane and observe.

I am the mashed fireman with breast-bone broken,
Tumbling walls buried me in their debris,
Heat and smoke I inspired, I heard the yelling shouts of my comrades,
I heard the distant click of their picks and shovels;
They have cleared the beams away, they tenderly lift me forth.

I lie in the night air in my red shirt, the pervading hush is for my sake,
Painless after all I lie exhausted but not so unhappy,
White and beautiful are the faces around me, the heads are bared of their fire-caps,
The kneeling crowd fades with the light of the torches.

Distant and dead resuscitate,
They show as the dial or move as the hands of me, I am the clock myself.

I am an old artillerist, I tell of my fort's bombardment,
I am there again.

Again the long roll of the drummers,
Again the attacking cannon, mortars,
Again to my listening ears the cannon responsive.

I take part, I see and hear the whole,
The cries, curses, roar, the plaudits for well-aimed shots,
The ambulanza slowly passing trailing its red drip,
Workmen searching after damages, making indispensable repairs,
The fall of grenades through the rent roof, the fan-shaped explosion,
The whizz of limbs, heads, stone, wood, iron, high in the air.

Again gurgles the mouth of my dying general, he furiously waves with his hand,
He gasps through the clot *Mind not me — mind — the entrenchments.*

. . . .

Would you hear of an old-time sea-fight?
Would you learn who won by the light of the moon and stars?
List to the yarn, as my grandmother's father the sailor told it to me.

Our foe was no skulk in his ship I tell you, (said he)
His was the surly English pluck, and there is no tougher or truer, and never was, and never will be;
Along the lowered eve he came horribly raking us.

We closed with him, the yards entangled, the cannon touched,
My captain lashed fast with his own hands.

We had received some eighteen pound shots under the water,
On our lower gun-deck two large pieces had burst at the first fire, killing all around and blowing up overhead.

Fighting at sun-down, fighting at dark,
Ten o'clock at night, the full moon well up, our leaks on the gain, and five feet of water reported,
The master-at-arms loosing the prisoners confined in the after-hold to give them a chance for themselves.

The transit to and from the magazine is now stopped by the sentinels,
They see so many strange faces they do not know whom to trust.

Our frigate takes fire,
The other asks if we demand quarter?
If our colors are struck and the fighting done?

Now I laugh content for I hear the voice of my little captain,
We have not struck, he composedly cries, *we have just begun our part of the fighting.*

Only three guns are in use,
One is directed by the captain himself against the enemy's mainmast,
Two well served with grape and canister silence his musketry and clear his decks.

The tops alone second the fire of this little battery, especially the main-top,
They hold out bravely during the whole of the action.

Not a moment's cease,
The leaks gain fast on the pumps, the fire eats toward the powder-magazine.

One of the pumps has been shot away, it is generally thought we are sinking.

Serene stands the little captain,
He is not hurried, his voice is neither high nor low,
His eyes give more light to us than our battle-lanterns.

Toward twelve there in the beams of the moon they surrender to us.

INFINITY

My feet strike an apex of the apices of the stairs,
On every step bunches of ages, and larger bunches between the steps,
All below duly travelled, and still I mount and mount.

Rise after rise bow the phantoms behind me,
Afar down I see the huge first Nothing, I know I was even there,
I waited unseen and always, and slept through the lethargic mist,
And took my time, and took no hurt from the fetid carbon.

Long I was hugged close — long and long.

Immense have been the preparations for me,
Faithful and friendly the arms that have helped me.
Cycles ferried my cradle, rowing and rowing like cheerful boatmen,
For room to me stars kept aside in their own rings,
They sent influences to look after what was to hold me.

Before I was born out of my mother generations guided me,
My embryo has never been torpid, nothing could overlay it.

For it the nebula cohered to an orb,
The long slow strata piled to rest it on,
Vast vegetables gave it sustenance,
Monstrous sauroids transported it in their mouths and deposited it with care.

All forces have been steadily employed to complete and delight me,
Now on this spot I stand with my robust soul.

. . . .

Old age superbly rising! O welcome, ineffable grace of dying days!

Every condition promulges not only itself, it promulges what grows after and out of itself,
And the dark hush promulges as much as any.

I open my scuttle at night and see the far-sprinkled systems,
And all I see multiplied as high as I can cipher edge but the rim of the farther systems.

Wider and wider they spread, expanding, always expanding,
Outward and outward and forever outward.
My sun has his sun and round him obediently wheels,
He joins with his partners a group of superior circuit,
And greater sets follow, making specks of the greatest inside them.

There is no stoppage and never can be stoppage,
If I, you, and the worlds, and all beneath or upon their surfaces, were this moment reduced back to a pallid float, it would not avail in the long run,
We should surely bring up again where we now stand,
And surely go as much farther, and then farther and farther.

A few quadrillions of eras, a few octillions of cubic leagues, do not hazard the span or make it impatient,
They are but parts, anything is but a part.

See ever so far, there is limitless space outside of that,
Count ever so much, there is limitless time around that.

My rendezvous is appointed, it is certain,
The Lord will be there and wait till I come on perfect terms,
The great Camerado, the lover true for whom I pine will be there.

GIVE ME THE SPLENDID SILENT SUN

GIVE me the splendid silent sun with all his beams full-dazzling,
Give me juicy autumnal fruit ripe and red from the orchard,
Give me a field where the unmowed grass grows,
Give me an arbor, give me the trellised grape,
Give me fresh corn and wheat, give me serene-moving animals teaching content,
Give me nights perfectly quiet as on high plateaus west of the Mississippi, and I looking up at the stars,
Give me odorous at sunrise a garden of beautiful flowers where I can walk undisturbed,
Give me for marriage a sweet-breathed woman of whom I should never tire,
Give me a perfect child, give me, away aside from the noise of the world, a rural domestic life,
Give me to warble spontaneous songs recluse by myself, for my own ears only,
Give me solitude, give me Nature, give me again O Nature your primal sanities!

These demanding to have them, (tired with ceaseless excitement, and racked by the war-strife)
These to procure incessantly asking, rising in cries from my heart,
While yet incessantly asking still I adhere to my city,
Day upon day and year upon year, O city, walking your streets,
Where you hold me enchained a certain time refusing to give me up,
Yet giving to make me glutted, enriched of soul, you give me forever faces;
(O I see what I sought to escape, confronting, reversing my cries,
I see my own soul trampling down what it asked for.)

Keep your splendid silent sun,
Keep your woods, O Nature, and the quiet places by the woods,
Keep your fields of clover and timothy, and your corn-fields and orchards,
Keep the blossoming buckwheat fields where the Ninth-month bees hum;
Give me faces and streets — give me these phantoms incessant and endless along the trottoirs!
Give me interminable eyes — give me women — give me comrades and lovers by the thousand!

Let me see new ones every day — let me hold new ones by the hand every day!
Give me such shows — give me the streets of Manhattan!
Give me Broadway, with the soldiers marching — give me the sound of the trumpets and drums!
(The soldiers in companies or regiments — some starting away flushed and reckless,
Some, their time up, returning with thinned ranks, young, yet very old, worn, marching, noticing nothing;)
Give me the shores and wharves heavy-fringed with black ships!
O such for me! O an intense life, full to repletion and varied!
The life of the theatre, bar-room, huge hotel, for me!
The saloon of the steamer! The crowded excursion for me! The torchlight procession!
The dense brigade bound for the war, with high-piled military wagons following;
People, endless, streaming, with strong voices, passions, pageants,
Manhattan streets with their powerful throbs, with beating drums as now,
The endless and noisy chorus, the rustle and clank of muskets (even the sight of the wounded),
Manhattan crowds, with their turbulent musical chorus!
Manhattan faces and eyes forever for me.

MANNAHATTA

I WAS asking for something specific and perfect for my city,
Whereupon lo! upsprang the aboriginal name.

Now I see what there is in a name, a word, liquid, sane, unruly, musical, self-sufficient,
I see that the word of my city is that word from of old,
Because I see that word nested in nests of water-bays, superb,
Rich, hemmed thick all around with sail ships and steam ships, an island sixteen miles long, solid-founded,
Numberless crowded streets, high growths of iron, slender, strong, light, splendidly uprising toward clear skies,
Tides swift and ample, well-loved by me, towards sundown,
The flowing sea-currents, the little islands, larger adjoining islands, the heights, the villas,
The countless masts, the white shore-steamers, the lighters, the ferry-boats, the black sea-steamers well-modelled,
The down-town streets, the jobbers' houses of business, the houses of business of the ship-merchants and money-brokers, the river-streets,
Immigrants arriving, fifteen or twenty thousand in a week,
The carts hauling goods, the manly race of drivers of horses, the brown-faced sailors,
The summer air, the bright sun shining, and the sailing clouds aloft,
The winter snows, the sleigh-bells, the broken ice in the river, passing along up or down with the flood-tide or ebb-tide,
The mechanics of the city, the masters, well-formed, beautiful-faced, looking you straight in the eyes,
Trottoirs thronged, vehicles, Broadway, the women, the shops and shows,
A million people — manners free and superb — open voices — hospitality — the most courageous and friendly young men,
City of hurried and sparkling waters! city of spires and masts!
City nested in bays! my city!

FROM "CROSSING BROOKLYN FERRY"

AH, what can ever be more stately and admirable to me than mast-hemmed Manhattan?
River and sunset and scallop-edged waves of flood-tide?
The sea-gulls oscillating their bodies, the hay-boat in the twilight, and the belated lighter?
. . . .
Flow on, river! flow with the flood-tide, and ebb with the ebb-tide!
Frolic on, crested and scallop-edged waves!

Gorgeous clouds of the sunset! drench with your splendor me, or the men and women generations after me!
Cross from shore to shore, countless crowds of passengers!
Stand up, tall masts of Mannahatta! Stand up, beautiful hills of Brooklyn!
Throb, baffled and curious brain! throw out questions and answers!
Suspend here and everywhere, eternal float of solution!
Gaze, loving and thirsting eyes, in the house or street or public assembly!
Sound out, voices of young men! loudly and musically call me by my nighest name!
Live, old life! play the part that looks back on the actor or actress!
Play the old role, the role that is great or small according as one makes it!
Consider, you who peruse me, whether I may not in unknown ways be looking upon you;
Be firm, rail over the river, to support those who lean idly, yet haste with the hasting current;
Fly on, sea-birds! fly sideways, or wheel in large circles high in the air;
Receive the summer sky, you water, and faithfully hold it till all downcast eyes have time to take it from you!
Diverge, fine spokes of light, from the shape of my head, or any one's head, in the sunlit water!
Come on, ships from the lower bay! pass up or down, white-sailed schooners, sloops, lighters!
Flaunt away, flags of all nations! be duly lowered at sunset!
Burn high your fires, foundry chimneys! cast black shadows at nightfall! cast red and yellow light over the tops of the houses!
Appearances, now or henceforth, indicate what you are,
You necessary film, continue to envelop the soul,
About my body for me, and your body for you, be hung our divinest aromas,
Thrive, cities — bring your freight, bring your shows, ample and sufficient rivers,
Expand, being than which none else is perhaps more spiritual,
Keep your places, objects than which none else is more lasting.

OUT OF THE CRADLE ENDLESSLY ROCKING

Out of the cradle endlessly rocking,
Out of the mocking-bird's throat, the musical shuttle,
Out of the Ninth-month midnight,
Over the sterile sands and the fields beyond, where the child leaving his bed wandered alone, bareheaded, barefoot,
Down from the showered halo,
Up from the mystic play of shadows twining and twisting as if they were alive,
Out from the patches of briers and blackberries,
From the memories of the bird that chanted to me,
From your memories, sad brother, from the fitful risings and fallings I heard,
From under that yellow half-moon laterisen and swollen as if with tears,
From those beginning notes of yearning and love there in the mist,
From the thousand responses of my heart never to cease,
From the myriad thence-aroused words,
From the word stronger and more delicious than any,
From such as now they start the scene revisiting,
As a flock, twittering, rising, or overhead passing,
Borne hither, ere all eludes me, hurriedly,
A man, yet by these tears a little boy again,
Throwing myself on the sand, confronting the waves,
I, chanter of pains and joys, uniter of here and hereafter,
Taking all hints to use them, but swiftly leaping beyond them,
A reminiscence sing.

Once Paumanok,
When the lilac-scent was in the air and Fifth-month grass was growing,
Up this seashore in some briers,
Two feathered guests from Alabama, two together,
And their nest, and four light-green eggs spotted with brown,
And every day the he-bird to and fro near at hand,
And every day the she-bird crouched on her nest, silent, with bright eyes,

And every day I, a curious boy, never too close, never disturbing them,
Cautiously peering, absorbing, translating.

Shine! shine! shine!
Pour down your warmth, great sun!
While we bask, we two together.

Two together!
Winds blow south, or winds blow north,
Day come white, or night come black,
Home, or rivers and mountains from home,
Singing all time, minding no time,
While we two keep together.

Till of a sudden,
Maybe killed, unknown to her mate,
One forenoon the she-bird crouched not on the nest,
Nor returned that afternoon, nor the next,
Nor ever appeared again.

And thenceforward all summer in the sound of the sea,
And at night under the full of the moon in calmer weather,
Over the hoarse surging of the sea,
Or flitting from brier to brier by day,
I saw, I heard at intervals the remaining one, the he-bird,
The solitary guest from Alabama.

Blow! blow! blow!
Blow up sea-winds along Paumanok's shore;
I wait and I wait till you blow my mate to me.

Yes, when the stars glistened,
All night long on the prong of a moss-scalloped stake,
Down almost amid the slapping waves,
Sat the lone singer wonderful causing tears.

He called on his mate,
He poured forth the meanings which I of all men know.

Yes, my brother, I know, —
The rest might not, but I have treasured every note,
For more than once dimly down to the beach gliding,
Silent, avoiding the moonbeams, blending myself with the shadows,
Recalling now the obscure shapes, the echoes, the sounds and sights after their sorts,
The white arms out in the breakers tirelessly tossing,
I, with bare feet, a child, the wind wafting my hair,
Listened long and long.

Listened to keep, to sing, now translating the notes,
Following you, my brother.

Soothe! soothe! soothe!
Close on its wave soothes the wave behind,
And again another behind embracing and lapping, every one close,
But my love soothes not me, not me.

Low hangs the moon, it rose late,
It is lagging — O I think it is heavy with love, with love.

O madly the sea pushes upon the land,
With love, with love.

O night! do I not see my love fluttering out among the breakers?
What is that little black thing I see there in the white?

Loud! loud! loud!
Loud I call to you, my love!

High and clear I shoot my voice over the waves,
Surely you must know who is here, is here,
You must know who I am, my love.

Low-hanging moon!
What is that dusky spot in your brown yellow?
O it is the shape, the shape of my mate!
O moon, do not keep her from me any longer.

Land! land! O land!
Whichever way I turn, O, I think you could give me my mate back again if you only would,
For I am almost sure I see her dimly whichever way I look.

O rising stars!
Perhaps the one I want so much will rise, will rise with some of you.

O throat! O trembling throat!
Sound clearer through the atmosphere!
Pierce the woods, the earth,
Somewhere listening to catch you must be the one I want.

Shake out carols!
Solitary here, the night's carols!
Carols of lonesome love! death's carols!
Carols under that lagging, yellow, waning moon!
O under that moon where she droops almost down into the sea!
O reckless despairing carols!

But soft! sink low!
Soft! let me just murmur,
And do you wait a moment, you husky-noised sea,
For somewhere I believe I heard my mate responding to me,
So faint, I must be still, be still to listen,
But not altogether still, for then she might not come immediately to me.

Hither, my love!
Here I am! here!
With this just-sustained note I announce myself to you,
This gentle call is for you my love, for you.

Do not be decoyed elsewhere:
That is the whistle of the wind, it is not my voice,
That is the fluttering, the fluttering of the spray,
Those are the shadows of leaves.

O darkness! O in vain!
O I am very sick and sorrowful.

O brown halo in the sky near the moon, drooping upon the sea!
O troubled reflection in the sea!
O throat! O throbbing heart!
And I singing uselessly, uselessly all the night.

O past! O happy life! O songs of joy!
In the air, in the woods, over fields,
Loved! loved! loved! loved! loved!
But my mate no more, no more with me!
We two together no more.

The aria sinking,
All else continuing, the stars shining,
The winds blowing, the notes of the bird continuous echoing,
With angry moans the fierce old mother incessantly moaning,
On the sands of Paumanok's shore gray and rustling,
The yellow half-moon enlarged, sagging down, drooping, the face of the sea almost touching,
The boy ecstatic, with his bare feet the waves, with his hair the atmosphere dallying,
The love in the heart long pent, now loose, now at last tumultuously bursting,
The aria's meaning, the ears, the soul, swiftly depositing,
The strange tears down the cheeks coursing,
The colloquy there, the trio, each uttering,
The undertone, the savage old mother incessantly crying,
To the boy's soul's questions sullenly timing, some drown'd secret hissing,
To the outsetting bard.

Demon or bird! (said the boy's soul)
Is it indeed toward your mate you sing? or is it really to me?
For I, that was a child, my tongue's use sleeping, now I have heard you,
Now in a moment I know what I am for, I awake,
And already a thousand singers, a thousand songs, clearer, louder and more sorrowful than yours,
A thousand warbling echoes have started to life within me, never to die.

O you singers solitary, singing by yourself, projecting me,
O solitary me listening, never more shall I cease perpetuating you,
Never more shall I escape, never more the reverberations,
Never more the cries of unsatisfied love be absent from me,
Never again leave me to be the peaceful child I was before what there in the night,
By the sea under the yellow and sagging moon,
The messenger there aroused, the fire, the sweet hell within,
The unknown want, the destiny of me.

O give me the clew! (it lurks in the night here somewhere)
O if I am to have so much, let me have more!

A word then, (for I will conquer it)
The word final, superior to all,
Subtle, sent up — what is it? — I listen;
Are you whispering it, and have been all the time, you sea-waves?
Is that it from your liquid rims and wet sands?

Whereto answering, the sea,
Delaying not, hurrying not,
Whispered me through the night, and very plainly before daybreak,
Lisped to me the low and delicious word death,
And again death, death, death, death,
Hissing melodious, neither like the bird nor like my aroused child's heart,
But edging near as privately for me, rustling at my feet,
Creeping thence steadily up to my ears and laving me softly all over,
Death, death, death, death, death.

Which I do not forget,
But fuse the song of my dusky demon and brother,
That he sang to me in the moonlight on Paumanok's gray beach,
With the thousand responsive songs at random,
My own songs awaked from that hour,
And with them the key, the word up from the waves,
The word of the sweetest song and all songs,
That strong and delicious word which, creeping to my feet,
(Or like some old crone rocking the cradle, swathed in sweet garments, bending aside)
The sea whispered me.

TO THE MAN-OF-WAR-BIRD

THOU who hast slept all night upon the storm,
Waking renewed on thy prodigious pinions,
(Burst the wild storm? above it thou ascendedst,
And rested on the sky, thy slave that cradled thee)
Now a blue point, far, far in heaven floating,
As to the light emerging here on deck I watch thee,
(Myself a speck, a point on the world's floating vast.)

Far, far at sea,
After the night's fierce drifts have strewn the shore with wrecks,
With re-appearing day as now so happy and serene,
The rosy and elastic dawn, the flashing sun,
The limpid spread of air cerulean,
Thou also re-appearest.

Thou born to match the gale, (thou art all wings)
To cope with heaven and earth and sea and hurricane,
Thou ship of air that never furl'st thy sails,
Days, even weeks untired and onward, through spaces, realms gyrating,
At dusk that look'st on Senegal, at morn America,
That sport'st amid the lightning-flash and thunder-cloud,
In them, in thy experiences, hadst thou my soul,
What joys! what joys were thine!

THE DALLIANCE OF THE EAGLES

SKIRTING the river road (my forenoon walk, my rest),
Skyward in air a sudden muffled sound, the dalliance of the eagles,
The rushing amorous contact high in space together,
The clinching interlocking claws, a living, fierce, gyrating wheel,
Four beating wings, two beaks, a swirling mass tight grappling,
In tumbling turning clustering loops, straight downward falling,
Till o'er the river poised, the twain yet one, a moment's lull,
A motionless still balance in the air, then parting, talons loosing,
Upward again on slow-firm pinions slanting, their separate diverse flight,
She hers, he his, pursuing.

CAVALRY CROSSING A FORD

A LINE in long array where they wind betwixt green islands,
They take a serpentine course, their arms flash in the sun, — hark to the musical clank,
Behold the silvery river, in it the splashing horses loitering stop to drink,
Behold the brown-faced men, each group, each person, a picture, the negligent rest on the saddles,
Some emerge on the opposite bank, others are just entering the ford — while,
Scarlet and blue and snowy white,
The guidon flags flutter gayly in the wind.

BIVOUAC ON A MOUNTAIN SIDE

I SEE before me now a travelling army halting,
Below a fertile valley spread, with barns and the orchards of summer,
Behind, the terraced sides of a mountain, abrupt, in places rising high,
Broken, with rocks, with clinging cedars, with tall shapes dingily seen,
The numerous camp-fires scattered near and far, some away up on the mountain,
The shadowy forms of men and horses, looming, large-sized, flickering,
And over all the sky — the sky! far, far out of reach, studded, breaking out, the eternal stars.

A SIGHT IN CAMP IN THE DAYBREAK GRAY AND DIM

A SIGHT in camp in the daybreak gray and dim,
As from my tent I emerge so early sleepless,
As slow I walk in the cool fresh air the path near by the hospital tent,
Three forms I see on stretchers lying, brought out there untended lying,
Over each the blanket spread, ample brownish woolen blanket,
Gray and heavy blanket, folding, covering all.

Curious I halt and silent stand,
Then with light fingers I from the face of the nearest, the first, just lift the blanket;
Who are you, elderly man so gaunt and grim, with well-grayed hair, and flesh all sunken about the eyes?
Who are you, my dear comrade?

Then to the second I stepped — and who are you, my child and darling?
Who are you, sweet boy with cheeks yet blooming?

Then to the third — a face nor child nor old, very calm, as of beautiful yellow-white ivory;
Young man, I think I know you — I think this face is the face of the Christ himself,
Dead and divine and brother of all, and here again he lies.

O CAPTAIN! MY CAPTAIN!

O CAPTAIN! my Captain! our fearful trip is done,
The ship has weathered every rack, the prize we sought is won,
The port is near, the bells I hear, the people all exulting,
While follow eyes the steady keel, the vessel grim and daring;
But O heart! heart! heart!
O the bleeding drops of red,
Where on the deck my Captain lies,
Fallen cold and dead.

O Captain! my Captain! rise up and hear the bells;
Rise up — for you the flag is flung — for you the bugle trills,
For you bouquets and ribboned wreaths — for you the shores acrowding,
For you they call, the swaying mass, their eager faces turning;
Here Captain! dear father!
This arm beneath your head!
It is some dream that on the deck
You 've fallen cold and dead.

My Captain does not answer, his lips are pale and still,
My father does not feel my arm, he has no pulse nor will,
The ship is anchored safe and sound, its voyage closed and done,
From fearful trip the victor ship comes in with object won;
Exult O shores, and ring O bells!
But I, with mournful tread,
Walk the deck my Captain lies,
Fallen cold and dead.

AFTER AN INTERVAL

(NOVEMBER 22, 1875, MIDNIGHT—SATURN AND MARS IN CONJUNCTION)

AFTER an interval, reading, here in the midnight,
With the great stars looking on—all the stars of Orion looking,
And the silent Pleiades—and the duo looking of Saturn and ruddy Mars;
Pondering, reading my own songs, after a long interval, (sorrow and death familiar now)
Ere closing the book, what pride! what joy! to find them
Standing so well the test of death and night,
And the duo of Saturn and Mars!

DAREST THOU NOW O SOUL

DAREST thou now, O soul,
Walk out with me toward the unknown region,
Where neither ground is for the feet nor any path to follow?

No map there, nor guide,
Nor voice sounding, nor touch of human hand,
Nor face with blooming flesh, nor lips, nor eyes, are in that land.

I know it not, O soul!
Nor dost thou, all is a blank before us,—
All waits undreamed of in that region, that inaccessible land.

Till when the tie is loosened,
All but the ties eternal, Time and Space,
Nor darkness, gravitation, sense, nor any bounds bounding us.

Then we burst forth, we float,
In Time and Space, O soul! prepared for them,
Equal, equipped at last, (O joy! O fruit of all!) them to fulfil, O soul!

Thomas Dunn English

SONGS

THE OLD MILL

HERE from the brow of the hill I look,
Through a lattice of boughs and leaves,
On the old gray mill with its gambrel roof,
And the moss on its rotting eaves.
I hear the clatter that jars its walls,
And the rushing water's sound,
And I see the black floats rise and fall
As the wheel goes slowly round.

I rode there often when I was young,
With my grist on the horse before,
And talked with Nelly, the miller's girl,
As I waited my turn at the door;
And while she tossed her ringlets brown,
And flirted and chatted so free,
The wheel might stop or the wheel might go,
It was all the same to me.

'T is twenty years since last I stood
On the spot where I stand to-day,
And Nelly is wed, and the miller is dead,
And the mill and I are gray.
But both, till we fall into ruin and wreck,
To our fortune of toil are bound;
And the man goes, and the stream flows,
And the wheel moves slowly round.

BEN BOLT

Don't you remember sweet Alice, Ben Bolt, —
Sweet Alice whose hair was so brown,
Who wept with delight when you gave her a smile,
And trembled with fear at your frown?
In the old church-yard in the valley, Ben Bolt,
In a corner obscure and alone,
They have fitted a slab of the granite so gray,
And Alice lies under the stone.

Under the hickory tree, Ben Bolt,
Which stood at the foot of the hill,
Together we've lain in the noonday shade,
And listened to Appleton's mill.
The mill-wheel has fallen to pieces, Ben Bolt,
The rafters have tumbled in,
And a quiet which crawls round the walls as you gaze
Has followed the olden din.

Do you mind of the cabin of logs, Ben Bolt,
At the edge of the pathless wood,
And the button-ball tree with its motley limbs,
Which nigh by the doorstep stood?

The cabin to ruin has gone, Ben Bolt,
The tree you would seek for in vain;
And where once the lords of the forest waved
Are grass and the golden grain.

And don't you remember the school, Ben Bolt,
With the master so cruel and grim,
And the shaded nook in the running brook
Where the children went to swim?
Grass grows on the master's grave, Ben Bolt,
The spring of the brook is dry,
And of all the boys who were schoolmates then
There are only you and I.

There is change in the things I loved, Ben Bolt,
They have changed from the old to the new;
But I feel in the deeps of my spirit the truth,
There never was change in you.
Twelvemonths twenty have past, Ben Bolt,
Since first we were friends — yet I hail
Your presence a blessing, your friendship a truth,
Ben Bolt of the salt-sea gale.

Josiah Gilbert Holland[1]

DANIEL GRAY

If I shall ever win the home in heaven
For whose sweet rest I humbly hope and pray,
In the great company of the forgiven
I shall be sure to find old Daniel Gray.

I knew him well; in truth, few knew him better;
For my young eyes oft read for him the Word,
And saw how meekly from the crystal letter
He drank the life of his beloved Lord.

Old Daniel Gray was not a man who lifted
On ready words his freight of gratitude,
Nor was he called as one among the gifted,
In the prayer-meetings of his neighborhood.

He had a few old-fashioned words and phrases,
Linked in with sacred texts and Sunday rhymes;
And I suppose that in his prayers and graces
I've heard them all at least a thousand times.

I see him now — his form, his face, his motions,
His homespun habit, and his silver hair, —
And hear the language of his trite devotions,
Rising behind the straight-backed kitchen chair.

[1] See, also, p. 588.

I can remember how the sentence sounded —
"Help us, O Lord, to pray and not to faint!"
And how the "conquering and to conquer" rounded
The loftier aspirations of the saint.

He had some notions that did not improve him:
He never kissed his children — so they say;
And finest scenes and fairest flowers would move him
Less than a horse-shoe picked up in the way.

He had a hearty hatred of oppression,
And righteous words for sin of every kind;
Alas, that the transgressor and transgression
Were linked so closely in his honest mind!

He could see naught but vanity in beauty,
And naught but weakness in a fond caress,
And pitied men whose views of Christian duty
Allowed indulgence in such foolishness.

Yet there were love and tenderness within him;
And I am told that when his Charley died,
Nor nature's need nor gentle words could win him
From his fond vigils at the sleeper's side.

And when they came to bury little Charley
They found fresh dew-drops sprinkled in his hair,
And on his breast a rose-bud gathered early,
And guessed, but did not know, who placed it there.

Honest and faithful, constant in his calling,
Strictly attendant on the means of grace,
Instant in prayer, and fearful most of falling,
Old Daniel Gray was always in his place.

A practical old man, and yet a dreamer,
He thought that in some strange, unlooked-for way
His mighty Friend in Heaven, the great Redeemer,
Would honor him with wealth some golden day.

This dream he carried in a hopeful spirit
Until in death his patient eye grew dim,
And his Redeemer called him to inherit
The heaven of wealth long garnered up for him.

So, if I ever win the home in heaven
For whose sweet rest I humbly hope and pray,
In the great company of the forgiven
I shall be sure to find old Daniel Gray.

BABYHOOD

What is the little one thinking about?
Very wonderful things, no doubt!
Unwritten history!
Unfathomed mystery!
Yet he laughs and cries, and eats and drinks,
And chuckles and crows, and nods and winks,
As if his head were as full of kinks
And curious riddles as any sphinx!
Warped by colic, and wet by tears,
Punctured by pins, and tortured by fears,
Our little nephew will lose two years;
And he 'll never know
Where the summers go; —
He need not laugh, for he 'll find it so!

Who can tell what a baby thinks?
Who can follow the gossamer links
By which the manikin feels his way
Out from the shore of the great unknown,
Blind, and wailing, and alone,
Into the light of day? —
Out from the shore of the unknown sea,
Tossing in pitiful agony, —
Of the unknown sea that reels and rolls,
Specked with the barks of little souls —
Barks that were launched on the other side,
And slipped from Heaven on an ebbing tide!
What does he think of his mother's eyes?
What does he think of his mother's hair?
What of the cradle-roof that flies
Forward and backward through the air?
What does he think of his mother's breast —
Bare and beautiful, smooth and white,
Seeking it ever with fresh delight —
Cup of his life and couch of his rest?

What does he think when her quick embrace
Presses his hand and buries his face
Deep where the heart-throbs sink and swell
With a tenderness she can never tell,
Though she murmur the words
Of all the birds —
Words she has learned to murmur well?
Now he thinks he 'll go to sleep!
I can see the shadow creep
Over his eyes, in soft eclipse,
Over his brow, and over his lips,
Out to his little finger-tips!
Softly sinking, down he goes!
Down he goes! Down he goes!
See! He is hushed in sweet repose!

A CHRISTMAS CAROL

There 's a song in the air!
There 's a star in the sky!
There 's a mother's deep prayer
And a baby's low cry!
And the star rains its fire while the Beautiful sing,
For the manger of Bethlehem cradles a king.

There 's a tumult of joy
O'er the wonderful birth,
For the virgin's sweet boy
Is the Lord of the earth.
Ay! the star rains its fire and the Beautiful sing,
For the manger of Bethlehem cradles a king.

In the light of that star
Lie the ages impearled;
And that song from afar
Has swept over the world.
Every hearth is aflame, and the Beautiful sing
In the homes of the nations that Jesus is King.

We rejoice in the light,
And we echo the song
That comes down through the night
From the heavenly throng.
Ay! we shout to the lovely evangel they bring,
And we greet in his cradle our Saviour and King.

Herman Melville

THE COLLEGE COLONEL[1]

He rides at their head;
A crutch by his saddle just slants in view,
One slung arm is in splints you see,
Yet he guides his strong steed — how coldly too.

He brings his regiment home,
Not as they filed two years before;
But a remnant half-tattered, and battered, and worn,
Like castaway sailors, who, stunned
By the surf's loud roar,
Their mates dragged back and seen no more, —
Again and again breast the surge,
And at last crawl, spent, to shore.

A still rigidity and pale,
An Indian aloofness, lones his brow;
He has lived a thousand years
Compressed in battle's pains and prayers,
Marches and watches slow.

There are welcoming shouts and flags;
Old men off hat to the Boy,
Wreaths from gay balconies fall at his feet,
But to him — there comes alloy.

It is not that a leg is lost,
It is not that an arm is maimed,
It is not that the fever has racked, —
Self he has long disclaimed.

But all through the Seven Days' Fight,
And deep in the Wilderness grim,
And in the field-hospital tent,
And Petersburg crater, and dim
Lean brooding in Libby, there came —
Ah heaven! — what *truth* to him!

[1] Copyright, 1866, by Harper & Brothers.

THE EAGLE OF THE BLUE[1]

ALOFT he guards the starry folds
Who is the brother of the star;
The bird whose joy is in the wind
Exulteth in the war.

No painted plume — a sober hue,
His beauty is his power;
That eager calm of gaze intent
Foresees the Sibyl's hour.

Austere, he crowns the swaying perch,
Flapped by the angry flag;
The hurricane from the battery sings,
But his claw has known the crag.

Amid the scream of shells, his scream
Runs shrilling; and the glare
Of eyes that brave the blinding sun
The volleyed flame can bear.

The pride of quenchless strength is his —
Strength which, though chained, avails;
The very rebel looks and thrills —
The anchored Emblem hails.

Though scarred in many a furious fray,
No deadly hurt he knew;
Well may we think his years are charmed —
The Eagle of the Blue.

MEMORIALS

ON THE SLAIN AT CHICKAMAUGA[1]

HAPPY are they and charmed in life
Who through long wars arrive unscarred
At peace. To such the wreath be given,
If they unfalteringly have striven —
In honor, as in limb, unmarred.
Let cheerful praise be rife,
And let them live their years at ease,
Musing on brothers who victorious died —
Loved mates whose memory shall ever please.

And yet mischance is honorable too —
Seeming defeat in conflict justified,
Whose end to closing eyes is hid from view.
The will, that never can relent —
The aim, survivor of the bafflement,
Make this memorial due.

AN UNINSCRIBED MONUMENT ON ONE OF THE BATTLE-FIELDS OF THE WILDERNESS[1]

SILENCE and Solitude may hint
(Whose home is in yon piny wood)
What I, though tableted, could never tell —
The din which here befell,
And striving of the multitude.
The iron cones and spheres of death
Set round me in their rust, —
These, too, if just,
Shall speak with more than animated breath.
Thou who beholdest, if thy thought,
Not narrowed down to personal cheer,
Take in the import of the quiet here —
The after-quiet — the calm full fraught;
Thou too wilt silent stand, —
Silent as I, and lonesome as the land.

CROSSING THE TROPICS

WHILE now the Pole Star sinks from sight
The Southern Cross it climbs the sky;
But losing thee, my love, my light,
O bride but for one bridal night,
The loss no rising joys supply.

Love, love, the Trade Winds urge abaft,
And thee, from thee, they steadfast waft.

By day the blue and silver sea
And chime of waters blandly fanned, —
Nor these, nor Gama's stars to me
May yield delight, since still for thee
I long as Gama longed for land.

I yearn, I yearn, reverting turn,
My heart it streams in wake astern.

When, cut by slanting sleet, we swoop
Where raves the world's inverted year,
If roses all your porch shall loop,
Not less your heart for me will droop,
Doubling the world's last outpost drear.

O love, O love, these oceans vast:
Love, love, it is as death were past!

[1] Copyright, 1866, by HARPER & BROTHERS.

THE ENVIABLE ISLES

Through storms you reach them and from storms are free.
  Afar descried, the foremost drear in hue,
But, nearer, green; and, on the marge, the sea
  Makes thunder low and mist of rain-bowed dew.

But, inland, — where the sleep that folds the hills
A dreamier sleep, the trance of God, instils, —
  On uplands hazed, in wandering airs aswoon,
Slow-swaying palms salute love's cypress tree
  Adown in vale where pebbly runlets croon
A song to lull all sorrow and all glee.

Sweet-fern and moss in many a glade are here,
  Where, strown in flocks, what cheek-flushed myriads lie
Dimpling in dream, unconscious slumberers mere,
  While billows endless round the beaches die.

Thomas William Parsons

ON A BUST OF DANTE

See, from this counterfeit of him
Whom Arno shall remember long,
  How stern of lineament, how grim,
The father was of Tuscan song:
There but the burning sense of wrong,
  Perpetual care and scorn, abide;
Small friendship for the lordly throng;
  Distrust of all the world beside.

  Faithful if this wan image be,
No dream his life was, — but a fight !
  Could any Beatrice see
A lover in that anchorite ?
To that cold Ghibelline's gloomy sight
  Who could have guessed the visions came
Of Beauty, veiled with heavenly light,
  In circles of eternal flame ?

  The lips as Cumæ's cavern close,
The cheeks with fast and sorrow thin,
  The rigid front, almost morose,
But for the patient hope within,
Declare a life whose course hath been
  Unsullied still, though still severe,
Which, through the wavering days of sin,
  Kept itself icy-chaste and clear.

  Not wholly such his haggard look
When wandering once, forlorn, he strayed,
  With no companion save his book,
To Corvo's hushed monastic shade;
Where, as the Benedictine laid
  His palm upon the convent's guest,
The single boon for which he prayed
  Was peace, that pilgrim's one request.

  Peace dwells not here, — this rugged face
Betrays no spirit of repose;
  The sullen warrior sole we trace,
The marble man of many woes.
Such was his mien when first arose
  The thought of that strange tale divine,
When hell he peopled with his foes,
  Dread scourge of many a guilty line.

  War to the last he waged with all
The tyrant canker-worms of earth;
  Baron and duke, in hold and hall,
Cursed the dark hour that gave him birth;
He used Rome's harlot for his mirth;
  Plucked bare hypocrisy and crime;
But valiant souls of knightly worth
  Transmitted to the rolls of Time.

  O Time ! whose verdicts mock our own,
The only righteous judge art thou;
  That poor old exile, sad and lone,
Is Latium's other Virgil now:
Before his name the nations bow;
  His words are parcel of mankind,
Deep in whose hearts, as on his brow,
  The marks have sunk of Dante's mind.

DIRGE

FOR ONE WHO FELL IN BATTLE

Room for a soldier! lay him in the clover;
He loved the fields, and they shall be his cover;
Make his mound with hers who called him once her lover:
Where the rain may rain upon it,
Where the sun may shine upon it,
Where the lamb hath lain upon it,
And the bee will dine upon it.

Bear him to no dismal tomb under city churches;
Take him to the fragrant fields, by the silver birches,
Where the whip-poor-will shall mourn, where the oriole perches:
Make his mound with sunshine on it.
Where the bee will dine upon it,
Where the lamb hath lain upon it,
And the rain will rain upon it.

Busy as the bee was he, and his rest should be the clover;
Gentle as the lamb was he, and the fern should be his cover;
Fern and rosemary shall grow my soldier's pillow over:
Where the rain may rain upon it,
Where the sun may shine upon it,
Where the lamb hath lain upon it,
And the bee will dine upon it.

Sunshine in his heart, the rain would come full often
Out of those tender eyes which evermore did soften:
He never could look cold till we saw him in his coffin.
Make his mound with sunshine on it,
Plant the lordly pine upon it,
Where the moon may stream upon it,
And memory shall dream upon it.

"Captain or Colonel," — whatever invocation
Suit our hymn the best, no matter for thy station, —
On thy grave the rain shall fall from the eyes of a mighty nation!
Long as the sun doth shine upon it
Shall glow the goodly pine upon it,
Long as the stars do gleam upon it
Shall memory come to dream upon it.

MARY BOOTH

What shall we do now, Mary being dead,
Or say or write that shall express the half?
What can we do but pillow that fair head,
And let the Spring-time write her epitaph! —

As it will soon, in snowdrop, violet,
Wind-flower and columbine and maiden's tear;
Each letter of that pretty alphabet,
That spells in flowers the pageant of the year.

She was a maiden for a man to love;
She was a woman for a husband's life;
One that has learned to value, far above
The name of love, the sacred name of wife.

Her little life-dream, rounded so with sleep,
Had all there is of life, except gray hairs, —
Hope, love, trust, passion, and devotion deep;
And that mysterious tie a mother bears.

She hath fulfilled her promise and hath passed;
Set her down gently at the iron door!
Eyes look on that loved image for the last:
Now cover it in earth, — her earth no more.

HER EPITAPH

The handful here, that once was Mary's earth,
Held, while it breathed, so beautiful a soul,
That, when she died, all recognized her birth,
And had their sorrow in serene control.

"Not here! not here!" to every mourner's heart
The wintry wind seemed whispering round her bier:

And when the tomb-door opened, with a start
We heard it echoed from within, —
"Not here!"

Shouldst thou, sad pilgrim, who mayst hither pass,
Note in these flowers a delicater hue,
Should spring come earlier to this hallowed grass,
Or the bee later linger on the dew, —

Know that her spirit to her body lent
Such sweetness, grace, as only goodness can;
That even her dust, and this her monument,
Have yet a spell to stay one lonely man, —

Lonely through life, but looking for the day
When what is mortal of himself shall sleep,
When human passion shall have passed away,
And Love no longer be a thing to weep.

TO A YOUNG GIRL DYING

WITH A GIFT OF FRESH PALM-LEAVES

This is Palm Sunday: mindful of the day,
I bring palm branches, found upon my way:
But these will wither; thine shall never die, —
The sacred palms thou bearest to the sky!
Dear little saint, though but a child in years,
Older in wisdom than my gray compeers!
We doubt and tremble, — *we*, with bated breath,
Talk of this mystery of life and death:
Thou, strong in faith, art gifted to conceive
Beyond thy years, and teach us to believe!

Then take my palms, triumphal, to thy home,
Gentle white palmer, never more to roam!
Only, sweet sister, give me, ere thou go'st,
Thy benediction, — for my love thou know'st!
We, too, are pilgrims, travelling towards the shrine:
Pray that our pilgrimage may end like thine!

INTO THE NOISELESS COUNTRY

Into the noiseless country Annie went,
Among the silent people where no sound
Of wheel or voice or implement — no roar
Of wind or billow moves the tranquil air:

And oft at midnight when my strength is spent
And day's delirium in the lull is drowned
Of deepening darkness, as I kneel before
Her palm and cross, comes to my soul this prayer,
That partly brings me back to my content,
"Oh, that hushed forest! — soon may I be there!"

ANDREW

Ermine or blazonry, he knew them not,
Nor cloth of gold, for Duty was his Queen;
But this he knew, — a soul without a spot,
Judgment untarnished, and a conscience clean.

In peace, in war, a worker day and night,
Laborious chieftain! toiling at his lamp;
The children had the splendor of the fight, —
Home was his battle-field, his room the camp.

Without a wound, without a stain he fell,
But with life rounded, all his acts complete;
And seldom History will have to tell
Of one whom Cato could more gladly greet.

Among the just his welcome should be warm,
Nor will New England let his memory cease;
He was our peacemaker, who mid the storm
Of the great conflict, served the Prince of Peace.

OBITUARY

FINDING Francesca full of tears, I said,
"Tell me thy trouble." "Oh, my dog is dead!
Murdered by poison! — no one knows for what —
Was ever dog born capable of that?"
"Child," — I began to say, but checked my thought, —
"A better dog can easily be bought."
For no — what animal could him replace?
Those loving eyes! That fond, confiding face!
Those dear, dumb touches! Therefore I was dumb.
From word of mine could any comfort come?
A bitter sorrow 't is to lose a brute
Friend, dog or horse, for grief must then be mute, —
So many smile to see the rivers shed
Of tears for one poor, speechless creature dead.
When parents die there 's many a word to say, —
Kind words, consoling — one can always pray;
When children die 't is natural to tell
Their mother, "Certainly, with them 't is well!"
But for a dog, 't was all the life he had,
Since death is end of dogs, or good or bad.
This was his world; he was contented here;
Imagined nothing better, naught more dear,
Than his young mistress; sought no brighter sphere;
Having no sin, asked not to be forgiven;
Ne'er guessed at God nor ever dreamed of heaven.
Now he has passed away, so much of love
Goes from our life, without one hope above!
When a dog dies there 's nothing to be said
But — kiss me, darling! — dear old Smiler 's dead.

TO A LADY

WITH A HEAD OF DIANA

MY Christmas gifts were few: to one
A fan, to keep love's flame alive,
Since even to the constant sun
Twilight and setting must arrive;

And to another — she who sent
That splendid toy, an empty purse —
I gave, though not for satire meant,
An emptier thing — a scrap of verse;

For thee I chose Diana's head,
Graved by a cunning hand in Rome,
To whose dim shop my feet were led
By sweet remembrances of home.

'T was with a kind of pagan feeling
That I my little treasure bought, —
My mood I care not for concealing, —
"Great is Diana!" was my thought.

Methought, howe'er we change our creeds,
Whether to Jove or God we bend,
By various paths religion leads
All spirits to a single end.

The goddess of the woods and fields,
The healthful huntress, undefiled,
Now with her fabled brother yields
To sinless Mary and her Child.

But chastity and truth remain
Still the same virtues as of yore,
Whether we kneel in Christian fane
Or old mythologies adore.

What though the symbol were a lie, —
Since the ripe world hath wiser grown, —
If any goodness grew thereby,
I will not scorn it for mine own.

So I selected Dian's head
From out the artist's glittering show;
And this shall be my gift, I said,
To one that bears the silver bow;

To her whose quiet life has been
The mirror of as calm a heart,
Above temptation from the din
Of cities, and the pomp of art;

Who still hath spent her active days
Cloistered amid her happy hills,
Not ignorant of worldly ways,
But loving more the woods and rills.

And thou art she to whom I give
This image of the virgin queen,
Praying that thou, like her, mayst live
Thrice blest! in being seldom seen.

"LIKE AS THE LARK"

Quale allodetta che in aere si spazia
Prima cantando, e poi tace, contenta,
Dell' ultima dolcezza che la sazia.
DANTE: *Paradiso, XX.*

LIKE as the lark that, soaring higher and higher,
Singeth awhile, then stops as 't were content
With his last sweetness, having filled desire,
So paused our bard; not for his force was spent,
Nor that a string was loosened in his lyre,
But, having said his best and done his best,
He could not better what was given before,
And threescore years and ten, demanding rest,
Whispered, *They want thee on the other shore!*
And now he walks amid the learned throng,
Haply with him who was the sixth of those
Who towered above the multitude in song,
Or by the side of Geoffrey Chaucer goes,
Who shall remember with his wonted smile
How James found music in his antique style.
But we 'll not mingle fancies with our sorrow
Nor from his own imagination borrow;
Holmes, who is left us, best could speak his praise
Who knew his heart so well and loved his lays,
And whom Heaven crowns with greater length of days.

O YE SWEET HEAVENS!

O YE sweet heavens! your silence is to me
More than all music. With what full delight
I come down to my dwelling by the sea
And look from out the lattice on the night!
There the same glories burn serene and bright
As in my boyhood; and if I am old
Are they not also? Thus my spirit is bold
To think perhaps we are coeval. Who
Can tell when first my faculty began
Of thought? Who knows but I was there with you
When first your Maker's mind, celestial spheres,
Contrived your motion ere I was a man?
Else, wherefore do mine eyes thus fill with tears
As I, O Pleiades! your beauty scan?

PARADISI GLORIA

"O frate mio! ciascuna e cittadina
D' una vera città" . . .

THERE is a city, builded by no hand,
And unapproachable by sea or shore,
And unassailable by any band
Of storming soldiery for evermore.

There we no longer shall divide our time
By acts or pleasures, — doing petty things
Of work or warfare, merchandise or rhyme;
But we shall sit beside the silver springs

That flow from God's own footstool, and behold
Sages and martyrs, and those blessed few
Who loved us once and were beloved of old,
To dwell with them and walk with them anew,

In alternations of sublime repose,
Musical motion, the perpetual play
Of every faculty that Heaven bestows
Through the bright, busy, and eternal day.

William Wilberforce Lord

FROM "WORSHIP"

For them, O God, who only worship Thee
In fanes whose fretted roofs shut out the heavens,
Let organs breathe, and chorded psalteries sound:
But let my voice rise with the mingled noise
Of winds and waters; — winds that in the sedge,
And grass, and ripening grain, while nature sleeps,
Practise, in whispered music, soft and low,
Their sweet inventions, and then sing them loud
In caves, and on the hills, and in the woods,
— A moving anthem, that along the air
Dying, then swelling forth in fitful gusts,
Like a full choir of bodiless voices, sweeps, —
Yea, of the great earth that make an instrument,
Awakening with their touch, itself not mute,
Each different thing to difference of tone,
Long, harp-like shrillings, or soft gush of sounds; —
Waters, — to earth, as to the air the winds,
Motion and utterance, and that begin
Even at their source the gently murmured hymn,
Rise with the river, with the torrent swell,
And at the cataract's dizzy, headlong leap,
Break forth in solemn and deep bursts of song.
Yet what is all this deep, perpetual sound, —
These voices of the earth, and sea, and air,
That make it seem to us, as if our Earth,
Into the silent and unruffled deep
Led forth, with thunder-step, the choir of worlds?
All these, — what are they? — in the boundless void,
An insect's whisper in the ear of night,
A voice in that of death, — in thine, O God,
A faint symphony to Heaven ascending
Amid ten thousand, thousand songs of praise.

. . . .

Break forth, ye Winds!
That in the impalpable deep caves of air,
Moving your silent plumes, in dreams of flight,
Tumultuous lie, and from your half-stretched wings
Beat the faint zephyrs that disturb the air; —
Break forth, ye fiercer harmonies, ye Storms
That in the cavernous and unquiet sea
Lie pent, and like imprisoned thunders beat
Your azure confines, making endless moan; —
All sounds, all harmonies, break forth! and be
To these my thoughts and aspirations, voice; —
Rise, rise, not bearing, but upborne by them, —
Rise through the golden gates uplift and wide!
In, through the everlasting doors! and join
The multitude of multitudes whose praise
With mighty burst of full accordant sound
Moves Heaven's whole fabric vast, as move the clouds
That from their swinging censers upward pour,
By wings of hovering seraphim disturbed, —
A sound so deep and loud, that at its might
The pillared heavens would fail, and all their frame
Of ancient strength and grandeur sink at once,
But for its soul of sweetness that supports,
And mightier harmony that builds them still: —
Ye Winds! ye Storms! all sounds and harmonies,
O thither rise! be heard amidst the throng;
Let them that dwell within the gates of light,
And them that sit on thrones — let seraphs hear, —
Let laurelled saints, and let all angels hear, —
A human soul knows and adores its God!

FROM AN "ODE TO ENGLAND"

KEATS

O GOLD Hyperion, love-lorn Porphyro,
Ill-fated! from thine orbëd fire struck back
Just as the parting clouds began to glow,
And stars, like sparks, to bicker in thy track!
Alas! throw down, throw down, ye mighty dead,
The leaves of oak and asphodel
That ye were weaving for that honored head,—
In vain, in vain, your lips would seek a spell
In the few charmëd words the poet sung,
To lure him upward in your seats to dwell,—
As vain your grief! Oh! why should one so young
Sit crowned midst hoary heads with wreaths divine?
Though to his lips Hymettus' bees had clung,
His lips shall never taste the immortal wine,
Who sought to drain the glowing cup too soon,
For he hath perished, and the moon
Hath lost Endymion — but too well
The shaft that pierced him in her arms was sped:
Into that gulf of dark and nameless dread,
Star-like he fell, but a wide splendor shed
Through its deep night, that kindled as he fell.

WORDSWORTH

And Thou! whom earth still holds, and will not yield
To join the mighty brotherhood of ghosts,—
Who, when their lips upon the earth are sealed,
Sing in the presence of the Lord of Hosts:—
Thou that, when first my quickened ear
Thy deeper harmonies might hear,
I imaged to myself as old and blind,
For so were Milton and Mæonides!
And worthy art thou — whether like the wind
Rousing its might among the forest trees,
Thou sing of mountain and of flood,
The voiceful thunder of the seas,
With all their inland symphonies,
Their thousand brooks and rills;
The vale's deep voice, the roaring wood,
The ancient silence of the hills,
Sublimer still than these;
Or in devotion's loftier mood,
Like a solemn organ tone
In some vast minster heard alone,
Feelings that are thoughts inspire;
Or, with thy hand upon the lyre
High victories to celebrate,
Summon from its strings the throng
Of stately numbers intricate
That swell the impetuous tide of song.
O Bard, of soul assured and high,
And god-like calm! we look on thee
With like serene and awful eye,
As when,— of such divinity
Still credulous,— the multitude
One in the concourse might behold,
Whose statue in his life-time stood
Among the gods. O Poet, old
In all the years of future time!
But young in the perpetual youth
And bloom of love, and might of truth,—
To these thy least ambitious rhyme
Is faithful, and partakes their worth;
Yea, true as is the starry chime
To the great strains the sun gives forth.
Bard of our Time! thy name we see,
By golden-haired Mnemosyne,
First graved upon its full-writ page,—
Thee — last relinquished, whom the Age
Doth yield to Immortality.

THE BROOK

A LITTLE blind girl wandering,
While daylight pales beneath the moon,
And with a brook meandering,
To hear its gentle tune.

The little blind girl by the brook,
It told her something — you might guess,
To see her smile, to see her look
Of listening eagerness.

Though blind, a never silent guide
  Flowed with her timid feet along;
And down she wandered by its side
  To hear the running song.

And sometimes it was soft and low,
  A creeping music in the ground;
And then, if something checked its flow,
  A gurgling swell of sound.

And now, upon the other side,
  She seeks her mother's cot;
And still the noise shall be her guide,
  And lead her to the spot.

For to the blind, so little free
  To move about beneath the sun,
Small things like this seem liberty, —
  Something from darkness won.

But soon she heard a meeting stream,
  And on the bank she followed still,
It murmured on, nor could she tell
  It was another rill.

"Ah! whither, whither, my little maid?
  And wherefore dost thou wander here?"
"I seek my mother's cot," she said,
  "And surely it is near."

"There is no cot upon this brook,
  In yonder mountains dark and drear,
Where sinks the sun, its source it took,
  Ah, wherefore art thou here?"

"O sir, thou art not true nor kind!
  It is the brook, I know its sound.
Ah! why would you deceive the blind?
  I hear it in the ground."

And on she stepped, but grew more sad,
  And weary were her tender feet,
The brook's small voice seemed not so glad,
  Its song was not so sweet.

"Ah! whither, whither, my little maid?
  And wherefore dost thou wander here?"
"I seek my mother's cot," she said,
  "And surely it is near."

"There is no cot upon this brook."
  "I hear its sound," the maid replied,
With dreamlike and bewildered look,
  "I have not left its side."

"O go with me, the darkness nears,
  The first pale stars begin to gleam."
The maid replied with bursting tears,
  "It is the stream! it is the stream!"

ON THE DEFEAT OF A GREAT MAN

Fallen? How fallen? States and empires fall;
  O'er towers and rock-built walls,
And perished nations, floods to tempests call
With hollow sound along the sea of time:
  The great man never falls.
He lives, he towers aloft, he stands sublime:
  They fall who give him not
The honor here that suits his future name, —
  They die and are forgot.

O Giant loud and blind! the great man's fame
  Is his own shadow, and not cast by thee, —
  A shadow that shall grow
As down the heaven of time the sun descends,
  And on the world shall throw
His god-like image, till it sinks where blends
  Time's dim horizon with Eternity.

TO ROSINA PICO

Regent of song! who bringest to our shore
  Strains from the passionate land, where shapes of art
Make music of the wind that passes o'er,
  Thou even here hast found the human heart;
And in a thousand hearts thy songs repeat
Their echoes, like remembered poesy sweet,
Witching the soul to warble evermore.

First seen, it seemed as if thy sweetest strain
  Had taken shape, and stood before our sight;
Thy aspect filled the silence with sweet pain
  That made it long for death. O creature bright!

Or ere the trembling silence had ta'en flight
We listened to thy looks, in hushed delight,
And from thy motions sought a sound to gain.

Then on all hearts at once did pour a flood
Of golden sound, in many an eddying tone,
As pours the wind into a breathless wood,
Awakening in it music not its own;
Thy voice controlled all spirits to one mood,
Before all eyes one breathing image stood
Beheld, as if to thee all eyes had grown.

Yet did I seem to be with thee alone,
With thee to stand upon enchanted ground,
And gazed on thee, as if the sculptured stone
Should live before me, (so thy magic bound
My soul, bewildered) while a cloud of sound,
Rising in wreaths, upon the air around
Lingered like incense from a censer thrown.

Henry Howard Brownell

FROM "THE RIVER-FIGHT"

Would you hear of the River-Fight?
It was two of a soft spring night; —
God's stars looked down on all,
And all was clear and bright
But the low fog's chilling breath —
Up the River of Death
Sailed the Great Admiral.

On our high poop-deck he stood,
And round him ranged the men
Who have made their birthright good
Of manhood, once and again, —
Lords of helm and of sail,
Tried in tempest and gale,
Bronzed in battle and wreck:
Bell and Bailey grandly led
Each his Line of the Blue and Red,
Wainwright stood by our starboard rail,
Thornton fought the deck.

And I mind me of more than they,
Of the youthful, steadfast ones,
That have shown them worthy sons
Of the Seamen passed away —
Tyson conned our helm that day,
Watson stood by his guns.

What thought our Admiral then,
Looking down on his men?
Since the terrible day,
(Day of renown and tears!)
When at anchor the Essex lay,
Holding her foes at bay,
When, a boy, by Porter's side he stood
Till deck and plank-sheer were dyed with blood,
'T is half a hundred years —
Half a hundred years to-day!

Who could fail with him?
Who reckon of life or limb?
Not a pulse but beat the higher!
There had you seen, by the starlight dim,
Five hundred faces strong and grim —
The Flag is going under fire!
Right up by the fort, with her helm hard-a-port,
The Hartford is going under fire!

The way to our work was plain,
Caldwell had broken the chain
(Two hulks swung down amain,
Soon as 't was sundered).
Under the night's dark blue,
Steering steady and true,
Ship after ship went through,
Till, as we hove in view,
Jackson out-thundered.

Back echoed Philip! ah, then
Could you have seen our men,
How they sprung, in the dim night haze,
To their work of toil and of clamor!
How the loaders, with sponge and rammer,
And their captains, with cord and hammer,
Kept every muscle ablaze!

How the guns, as with cheer and shout
Our tackle-men hurled them out,
Brought up on the water-ways!

First, as we fired at their flash,
'T was lightning and black eclipse,
With a bellowing roll and crash;
But soon, upon either bow,
What with forts, and fire-rafts, and ships,
(The whole fleet was hard at it now,
All pounding away!) and Porter
Still thundering with shell and mortar,
'T was the mighty sound and form
Of an equatorial storm!

(Such you see in the Far South,
After long heat and drouth,
As day draws nigh to even:
Arching from North to South,
Blinding the tropic sun,
The great black bow comes on,
Till the thunder-veil is riven,
When all is crash and levin,
And the cannonade of heaven
Rolls down the Amazon!)

But, as we worked along higher,
Just where the river enlarges,
Down came a pyramid of fire —
It was one of your long coal barges
(We had often had the like before).
'T was coming down on us to larboard,
Well in with the eastern shore,
And our pilot, to let it pass round,
(You may guess we never stopped to sound)
Giving us a rank sheer to starboard,
Ran the Flag hard and fast aground!

'T was nigh abreast of the Upper Fort,
And straightway a rascal Ram
(She was shaped like the devil's dam)
Puffed away for us with a snort,
And shoved it with spiteful strength
Right alongside of us, to port.
(It was all of our ship's length,
A huge crackling Cradle of the Pit,
Pitch-pine knots to the brim,
Belching flame red and grim)
What a roar came up from it!

Well, for a little it looked bad;
But these things are, somehow, shorter
In the acting than the telling.
There was no singing-out nor yelling,
Nor any fussing and fretting,
No stampede, in short;
But there we were, my lad,
All afire on our port quarter,
Hammocks ablaze in the netting,
Flames spouting in at every port,
Our Fourth Cutter burning at the davit,
No chance to lower away and save it.

In a twinkling the flames had risen
Halfway to maintop and mizzen,
Darting up the shrouds like snakes.
Ah, how we clanked at the brakes!
And the deep steam-pumps throbbed under,
Sending a ceaseless flow.
Our topmen, a dauntless crowd,
Swarmed in rigging and shroud —
There, ('t was a wonder!)
The burning ratlines and strands
They quenched with their bare hard hands;
But the great guns below
Never silenced their thunder!

At last, by backing and sounding,
When we were clear of grounding,
And under headway once more,
The whole rebel fleet came rounding
The point. If we had it hot before,
'T was now, from shore to shore,
One long, loud thundering roar —
Such crashing, splintering, and pounding,
And smashing as you never heard before!

But that we fought foul wrong to wreck,
And to save the Land we loved so well,
You might have deemed our long gun deck
Two hundred feet of hell!

For all above was battle,
Broadside, and blaze, and rattle,
Smoke and thunder alone;
But, down in the sick-bay,
Where our wounded and dying lay,
There was scarce a sob or a moan.

And at last, when the dim day broke,
And the sullen sun awoke,
Drearily blinking

O'er the haze and the cannon-smoke,
That ever such morning dulls,
There were thirteen traitor hulls
On fire and sinking!

THE BURIAL OF THE DANE

Blue gulf all around us,
Blue sky overhead —
Muster all on the quarter,
We must bury the dead!

It is but a Danish sailor,
Rugged of front and form;
A common son of the forecastle,
Grizzled with sun and storm.

His name, and the strand he hailed from
We know, and there 's nothing more!
But perhaps his mother is waiting
In the lonely Island of Fohr.

Still, as he lay there dying,
Reason drifting awreck,
"'T is my watch," he would mutter,
"I must go upon deck!"

Aye, on deck, by the foremast!
But watch and lookout are done;
The Union Jack laid o'er him,
How quiet he lies in the sun!

Slow the ponderous engine,
Stay the hurrying shaft;
Let the roll of the ocean
Cradle our giant craft;
Gather around the grating,
Carry your messmate aft!

Stand in order, and listen
To the holiest page of prayer!
Let every foot be quiet,
Every head be bare —
The soft trade-wind is lifting
A hundred locks of hair.

Our captain reads the service,
(A little spray on his cheeks)
The grand old words of burial,
And the trust a true heart seeks: —
"We therefore commit his body
To the deep" — and, as he speaks,

Launched from the weather railing,
Swift as the eye can mark,
The ghastly, shotted hammock
Plunges, away from the shark,
Down, a thousand fathoms,
Down into the dark!

A thousand summers and winters
The stormy Gulf shall roll
High o'er his canvas coffin;
But, silence to doubt and dole: —
There 's a quiet harbor somewhere
For the poor aweary soul.

Free the fettered engine,
Speed the tireless shaft,
Loose to'gallant and topsail,
The breeze is fair abaft!

Blue sea all around us,
Blue sky bright o'erhead —
Every man to his duty,
We have buried our dead!

THE SPHINX

They glare — those stony eyes!
That in the fierce sun-rays
Showered from these burning skies,
Through untold centuries
Have kept their sleepless and unwinking gaze.

Since what unnumbered year
Hast thou kept watch and ward,
And o'er the buried Land of Fear
So grimly held thy guard?
No faithless slumber snatching,
Still couched in silence brave,
Like some fierce hound long watching
Above her master's grave.

No fabled Shape art thou!
On that thought-freighted brow
And in those smooth weird lineaments we find,
Though traced all darkly, even now,
The relics of a Mind:
And gather dimly thence
A vague, half-human sense —
The strange and sad Intelligence
That sorrow leaves behind.

Dost thou in anguish thus
Still brood o'er Œdipus?
And weave enigmas to mislead anew,
And stultify the blind
Dull heads of human kind,
And inly make thy moan
That mid the hated crew,
Whom thou so long couldst vex,
Bewilder, and perplex,
Thou yet couldst find a subtler than thine own?

Even now, methinks that those
Dark, heavy lips, which close
In such a stern repose,
Seem burdened with some Thought unsaid,
And hoard within their portals dread
Some fearful Secret there, —
Which to the listening earth
She may not whisper forth,
Not even to the air, —

Of awful wonders hid
In yon dread pyramid,
The home of magic Fears,
Of chambers vast and lonely,
Watched by the Genii only,
Who tend their Masters' long-forgotten biers;
And treasures that have shone
On cavern walls alone
Four thousand, thousand years.

Those sullen orbs wouldst thou eclipse,
And ope those massy, tomb-like lips,
Many a riddle thou couldst solve
Which all blindly men revolve.

Would She but tell! She knows
Of the old Pharaohs,
Could count the Ptolemies' long line;
Each mighty Myth's original hath seen,
Apis, Anubis — Ghosts that haunt between
The Bestial and Divine —
(Such, He that sleeps in Philœ — He that stands
In gloom, unworshipped, 'neath his rock-hewn fane —
And They who, sitting on Memnonian sands,
Cast their long shadows o'er the desert plain:)
Hath marked Nitocris pass,
And Ozymandias
Deep-versed in many a dark Egyptian wile;
The Hebrew Boy hath eyed
Cold to the master's bride:
And that Medusan stare hath frozen the smile
Of Her all love and guile,
For whom the Cæsar sighed,
And the World-Loser died —
The Darling of the Nile.

Theodore O'Hara

THE BIVOUAC OF THE DEAD

The muffled drum's sad roll has beat
The soldier's last tattoo;
No more on Life's parade shall meet
That brave and fallen few.
On Fame's eternal camping-ground
Their silent tents are spread,
And Glory guards, with solemn round,
The bivouac of the dead.

No rumor of the foe's advance
Now swells upon the wind;
No troubled thought at midnight haunts
Of loved ones left behind;
No vision of the morrow's strife
The warrior's dream alarms;
No braying horn nor screaming fife
At dawn shall call to arms.

Their shivered swords are red with rust,
Their plumëd heads are bowed;
Their haughty banner, trailed in dust,
Is now their martial shroud.
And plenteous funeral tears have washed
The red stains from each brow,
And the proud forms, by battle gashed,
Are free from anguish now.

The neighing troop, the flashing blade,
The bugle's stirring blast,
The charge, the dreadful cannonade,
The din and shout, are past;

Nor war's wild note nor glory's peal
  Shall thrill with fierce delight
Those breasts that nevermore may feel
  The rapture of the fight.

Like the fierce northern hurricane
  That sweeps his great plateau,
Flushed with the triumph yet to gain,
  Came down the serried foe.
Who heard the thunder of the fray
  Break o'er the field beneath,
Knew well the watchword of that day
  Was "Victory or Death."

Long had the doubtful conflict raged
  O'er all that stricken plain,
For never fiercer fight had waged
  The vengeful blood of Spain;
And still the storm of battle blew,
  Still swelled the gory tide;
Not long, our stout old chieftain knew,
  Such odds his strength could bide.

'T was in that hour his stern command
  Called to a martyr's grave
The flower of his beloved land,
  The nation's flag to save.
By rivers of their fathers' gore
  His first-born laurels grew,
And well he deemed the sons would pour
  Their lives for glory too.

Full many a norther's breath has swept
  O'er Angostura's plain,
And long the pitying sky has wept
  Above its mouldered slain.
The raven's scream, or eagle's flight,
  Or shepherd's pensive lay,
Alone awakes each sullen height
  That frowned o'er that dread fray.

Sons of the Dark and Bloody Ground,
  Ye must not slumber there,
Where stranger steps and tongues resound
  Along the heedless air.
Your own proud land's heroic soil
  Shall be your fitter grave:
She claims from war his richest spoil —
  The ashes of her brave.

Thus 'neath their parent turf they rest,
  Far from the gory field,
Borne to a Spartan mother's breast
  On many a bloody shield;
The sunshine of their native sky
  Smiles sadly on them here,
And kindred eyes and hearts watch by
  The heroes' sepulchre.

Rest on, embalmed and sainted dead!
  Dear as the blood ye gave;
No impious footstep here shall tread
  The herbage of your grave;
Nor shall your glory be forgot
  While Fame her record keeps,
Or Honor points the hallowed spot
  Where Valor proudly sleeps.

Yon marble minstrel's voiceless stone
  In deathless song shall tell,
When many a vanished age hath flown,
  The story how ye fell;
Nor wreck, nor change, nor winter's blight,
  Nor Time's remorseless doom,
Shall dim one ray of glory's light
  That gilds your deathless tomb.

Maria White Lowell

SONG

O BIRD, thou dartest to the sun,
When morning beams first spring,
And I, like thee, would swiftly run;
As sweetly would I sing.
Thy burning heart doth draw thee up
Unto the source of fire;
Thou drinkest from its glowing cup
And quenchest thy desire.

O dew, thou droppest soft below,
And pearlest all the ground,
Yet, when the morning comes, I know
Thou never canst be found.
I would like thine had been my birth;
Then I, without a sigh,
Might sleep the night through on the earth
To waken in the sky.

O clouds, ye little tender sheep,
Pastured in fields of blue,
While moon and stars your fold can keep
And gently shepherd you,
Let me, too, follow in the train
That flocks across the night,
Or lingers on the open plain
With new-shorn fleeces white.

O singing winds, that wander far,
Yet always seem at home,
And freely play 'twixt star and star
Along the bending dome,
I often listen to your song,
Yet never hear you say
One word of all the happy worlds
That sing so far away.

For they are free, ye all are free,
And bird, and dew, and light,
Can dart upon the azure sea
And leave me to my night;
Oh, would like theirs had been my birth,
Then I, without a sigh,
Might sleep this night through on the earth
To waken in the sky.

THE MORNING-GLORY

We wreathed about our darling's head
The morning-glory bright;
Her little face looked out beneath,
So full of life and light,
So lit as with a sunrise,
That we could only say,
"She is the morning-glory true,
And her poor types are they."

So always from that happy time
We called her by their name,
And very fitting did it seem —
For, sure as morning came,
Behind her cradle bars she smiled
To catch the first faint ray,
As from the trellis smiles the flower
And opens to the day.

But not so beautiful they rear
Their airy cups of blue,
As turned her sweet eyes to the light,
Brimmed with sleep's tender dew;
And not so close their tendrils fine
Round their supports are thrown,
As those dear arms whose outstretched plea
Clasped all hearts to her own.

We used to think how she had come,
Even as comes the flower,
The last and perfect added gift
To crown Love's morning hour;
And how in her was imaged forth
The love we could not say,
As on the little dewdrops round
Shines back the heart of day.

We never could have thought, O God,
That she must wither up,
Almost before a day was flown,
Like the morning-glory's cup;
We never thought to see her droop
Her fair and noble head,
Till she lay stretched before our eyes,
Wilted, and cold, and dead!

The morning-glory's blossoming
Will soon be coming round —
We see the rows of heart-shaped leaves
Upspringing from the ground;
The tender things the winter killed
Renew again their birth,
But the glory of our morning
Has passed away from earth.

O Earth! in vain our aching eyes
Stretch over thy green plain!
Too harsh thy dews, too gross thine air
Her spirit to sustain;
But up in groves of Paradise
Full surely we shall see
Our morning-glory beautiful
Twine round our dear Lord's knee.

Thomas Buchanan Read

THE CLOSING SCENE

Within his sober realm of leafless trees
The russet year inhaled the dreamy air;
Like some tanned reaper in his hour of ease,
When all the fields are lying brown and bare.

The gray barns looking from their lazy
hills
O'er the dim waters widening in the
vales,
Sent down the air a greeting to the mills,
On the dull thunder of alternate flails.

All sights were mellowed and all sounds
subdued,
The hills seemed farther and the streams
sang low;
As in a dream the distant woodman
hewed
His winter log with many a muffled
blow.

The embattled forests, erewhile armed in
gold,
Their banners bright with every martial
hue,
Now stood, like some sad beaten host of
old,
Withdrawn afar in Time's remotest
blue.

On slumbrous wings the vulture held his
flight;
The dove scarce heard his sighing mate's
complaint;
And, like a star slow drowning in the
light,
The village church-vane seemed to pale
and faint.

The sentinel-cock upon the hill-side
crew, —
Crew thrice, and all was stiller than before,
Silent till some replying warder blew
His alien horn, and then was heard no
more.

Where erst the jay, within the elm's tall
crest,
Made garrulous trouble round her unfledged young,
And where the oriole hung her swaying
nest,
By every light wind like a censer swung;

Where sang the noisy masons of the
eaves,
The busy swallows, circling ever near,
Foreboding, as the rustic mind believes,
An early harvest and a plenteous year;

Where every bird which charmed the vernal
feast
Shook the sweet slumber from its wings
at morn,
To warn the reaper of the rosy east, —
All now was songless, empty, and forlorn.

Alone from out the stubble piped the
quail,
And croaked the crow through all the
dreamy gloom;
Alone the pheasant, drumming in the
vale,
Made echo to the distant cottage loom.

There was no bud, no bloom upon the
bowers;
The spiders wove their thin shrouds night
by night;
The thistle-down, the only ghost of flowers,
Sailed slowly by, passed noiseless out of
sight.

Amid all this, in this most cheerless air,
And where the woodbine shed upon the
porch
Its crimson leaves, as if the Year stood
there
Firing the floor with his inverted torch;

Amid all this, the centre of the scene,
The white-haired matron, with monotonous tread,
Plied the swift wheel, and with her joyless
mien,
Sat, like a Fate, and watched the flying
thread.

She had known Sorrow, — he had walked
with her,
Oft supped and broke the bitter ashen
crust;
And in the dead leaves still she heard the
stir
Of his black mantle trailing in the dust.

While yet her cheek was bright with summer bloom,
Her country summoned and she gave her
all;
And twice War bowed to her his sable
plume, —
Regave the swords to rust upon her
wall.

Regave the swords, — but not the hand that drew
And struck for Liberty its dying blow,
Nor him who, to his sire and country true,
Fell mid the ranks of the invading foe.

Long, but not loud, the droning wheel went on,
Like the low murmur of a hive at noon;
Long, but not loud, the memory of the gone
Breathed through her lips a sad and tremulous tune.

At last the thread was snapped — her head was bowed;
Life dropped the distaff through his hands serene, —
And loving neighbors smoothed her careful shroud,
While Death and Winter closed the autumn scene.

LINES TO A BLIND GIRL

BLIND as the song of birds,
Feeling its way into the heart,
Or as a thought ere it hath words, —
As blind thou art:

Or as a little stream
A dainty hand might guide apart,
Or Love — young Love's delicious dream —
As blind thou art:

Or as a slender bark,
Where summer's varying breezes start,
Or blossoms blowing in the dark, —
As blind thou art:

Or as the Hope, Desire
Leads from the bosom's crowded mart,
Deluded Hope, that soon must tire, —
As blind thou art:

The chrysalis, that folds
The wings that shall in light depart,
Is not more blind than that which holds
The wings within thy heart.

For when thy soul was given
Unto the earth, a beauteous trust,
To guard its matchless glory, Heaven
Endungeoned it in dust.

DRIFTING

MY soul to-day
Is far away,
Sailing the Vesuvian Bay;
My wingëd boat,
A bird afloat,
Swings round the purple peaks remote: —

Round purple peaks
It sails, and seeks
Blue inlets and their crystal creeks,
Where high rocks throw,
Through deeps below,
A duplicated golden glow.

Far, vague, and dim,
The mountains swim;
While on Vesuvius' misty brim,
With outstretched hands,
The gray smoke stands
O'erlooking the volcanic lands.

Here Ischia smiles
O'er liquid miles;
And yonder, bluest of the isles,
Calm Capri waits,
Her sapphire gates
Beguiling to her bright estates.

I heed not, if
My rippling skiff
Float swift or slow from cliff to cliff;
With dreamful eyes
My spirit lies
Under the walls of Paradise.

Under the walls
Where swells and falls
The Bay's deep breast at intervals
At peace I lie,
Blown softly by,
A cloud upon this liquid sky.

The day, so mild,
Is Heaven's own child,
With Earth and Ocean reconciled;
The airs I feel
Around me steal
Are murmuring to the murmuring keel.

Over the rail
My hand I trail
Within the shadow of the sail,
A joy intense,
The cooling sense
Glides down my drowsy indolence.

With dreamful eyes
My spirit lies
Where Summer sings and never dies, —
O'erveiled with vines
She glows and shines
Among her future oil and wines.

Her children, hid
The cliffs amid,
Are gambolling with the gambolling kid;
Or down the walls,
With tipsy calls,
Laugh on the rocks like waterfalls.

The fisher's child,
With tresses wild,
Unto the smooth, bright sand beguiled,
With glowing lips
Sings as she skips,
Or gazes at the far-off ships.

Yon deep bark goes
Where traffic blows,
From lands of sun to lands of snows;
This happier one, —
Its course is run
From lands of snow to lands of sun.

O happy ship,
To rise and dip,
With the blue crystal at your lip!
O happy crew,
My heart with you
Sails, and sails, and sings anew!

No more, no more
The worldly shore
Upbraids me with its loud uproar:
With dreamful eyes
My spirit lies
Under the walls of Paradise!

Francis Orrery Ticknor

A SONG FOR THE ASKING

A SONG! What songs have died
Upon the earth,
Voices of love and pride —
Of tears and mirth?
Fading as hearts forget,
As shadows flee!
Vain is the voice of song,
And yet —
I sing to thee!

A song! What ocean shell
Were silent long,
If in thy touch might dwell
Its all of song?
A song? Then near my heart
Thy cheek must be,
For, like the shell, it sings —
Sweet Heart —
To thee, of thee!

THE VIRGINIANS OF THE VALLEY

THE knightliest of the knightly race
That, since the days of old,
Have kept the lamp of chivalry
Alight in hearts of gold;
The kindliest of the kindly band
That, rarely hating ease,
Yet rode with Spotswood round the land,
And Raleigh round the seas;

Who climbed the blue Virginian hills
Against embattled foes,
And planted there, in valleys fair,
The lily and the rose;
Whose fragrance lives in many lands,
Whose beauty stars the earth,
And lights the hearths of happy homes
With loveliness and worth.

We thought they slept! — the sons who kept
The names of noble sires,
And slumbered while the darkness crept
Around their vigil fires;
But aye the "Golden Horseshoe" knights
Their old Dominion keep,
Whose foes have found enchanted ground,
But not a knight asleep.

LITTLE GIFFEN

Out of the focal and foremost fire,
Out of the hospital walls as dire;
Smitten of grape-shot and gangrene,
(Eighteenth battle, and *he* sixteen!)
Spectre! such as you seldom see,
Little Giffen, of Tennessee!

"Take him and welcome!" the surgeons said;
Little the doctor can help the dead!
So we took him; and brought him where
The balm was sweet in the summer air;
And we laid him down on a wholesome bed, —
Utter Lazarus, heel to head!

And we watched the war with abated breath, —
Skeleton Boy against skeleton Death.
Months of torture, how many such?
Weary weeks of the stick and crutch;
And still a glint of the steel-blue eye
Told of a spirit that would n't die,

And did n't. Nay, more! in death's despite
The crippled skeleton "learned to write."
"Dear mother," at first, of course; and then
"Dear captain," inquiring about the men.
Captain's answer: "Of eighty-and-five,
Giffen and I are left alive."

Word of gloom from the war, one day;
Johnson pressed at the front, they say.
Little Giffen was up and away;
A tear — his first — as he bade good-by,
Dimmed the glint of his steel-blue eye.
"I 'll write, if spared!" There was news of the fight;
But none of Giffen. — He did not write.

I sometimes fancy that, were I king
Of the princely Knights of the Golden Ring,
With the song of the minstrel in mine ear,
And the tender legend that trembles here,
I 'd give the best on his bended knee,
The whitest soul of my chivalry,
For "Little Giffen," of Tennessee.

Samuel Johnson

THE CITY OF GOD

City of God, how broad and far
Outspread thy walls sublime!
The true thy chartered freemen are,
Of every age and clime.

One holy Church, one army strong,
One steadfast high intent,
One working band, one harvest-song,
One King Omnipotent.

How purely hath thy speech come down
From man's primeval youth;
How grandly hath thine empire grown
Of Freedom, Love, and Truth!

How gleam thy watchfires through the night,
With never fainting ray;
How rise thy towers, serene and bright,
To meet the dawning day!

In vain the surge's angry shock,
In vain the drifting sands;
Unharmed, upon the Eternal Rock,
The Eternal City stands.

INSPIRATION

Life of Ages, richly poured,
Love of God, unspent and free,
Flowing in the Prophet's word
And the People's liberty!

Never was to chosen race
That unstinted tide confined;
Thine is every time and place,
Fountain sweet of heart and mind!

Secret of the morning stars,
Motion of the oldest hours,
Pledge through elemental wars
Of the coming spirit's powers!

Rolling planet, flaming sun,
Stand in nobler man complete;
Prescient laws Thine errands run,
Frame the shrine for Godhead meet.

Homeward led, the wondering eye
Upward yearned in joy or awe,
Found the love that waited nigh,
Guidance of Thy guardian Law.

In the touch of earth it thrilled;
Down from mystic skies it burned:
Right obeyed and passion stilled
Its eternal gladness earned.

Breathing in the thinker's creed,
Pulsing in the hero's blood,
Nerving simplest thought and deed,
Freshening time with truth and good,

Consecrating art and song,
Holy book and pilgrim track,
Hurling floods of tyrant wrong
From the sacred limits back, —

Life of Ages, richly poured,
Love of God, unspent and free,
Flow still in the Prophet's word
And the People's liberty!

Erastus Wolcott Ellsworth

FROM "WHAT IS THE USE?"

I SAW a man, by some accounted wise,
For some things said and done before their eyes,
Quite overcast, and, in a restless muse,
Pacing a path about,
And often giving out:
"What is the use?"

Then I, with true respect: "What meanest thou
By those strange words, and that unsettled brow;
Health, wealth, the fair esteem of ample views?
To these things thou art born."
But he, as one forlorn,
"What is the use?

"I have surveyed the sages and their books,
Man, and the natural world of woods and brooks,
Seeking that perfect good that I would choose;
But find no perfect good,
Settled, and understood.
What is the use?

"Life, in a poise, hangs trembling on the beam,
Even in a breath bounding to each extreme
Of joy and sorrow; therefore I refuse
All beaten ways of bliss,
And only answer this:
'What is the use?'

. . . .

"Who'll care for me when I am dead and gone?
Not many now — and, surely, soon, not one;
And should I sing like an immortal Muse,
Men, if they read the line,
Read for their good, not mine;
What is the use?

"And song, if passable, is doomed to pass —
Common, though sweet as the new-scythëd grass.
Of human deeds and thoughts, Time bears no news,
That, flying, he can lack,
Else they would break his back.
What is the use?

"Spirit of Beauty, breath of golden lyres,
Perpetual tremble of immortal wires,
Divinely torturing rapture of the Muse,
Conspicuous wretchedness —
Thou starry, sole success —
What is the use?

"Doth not all struggle tell, upon its brow,
That he who makes it is not easy now,
But hopes to be? Vain Hope, that dost abuse,
Coquetting with thine eyes,
And fooling him who sighs!
What is the use?

"Go, pry the lintels of the pyramids,
Lift the old kings' mysterious coffin lids:
This dust was theirs, whose names these stones confuse, —

These mighty monuments
Of mighty discontents.
What is the use?

"Did not he sum it all, whose gate of pearls
Blazed royal Ophir, Tyre, and Syrian girls, —
The great, wise, famous monarch of the Jews?
Though rolled in grandeur vast,
He said of all, at last,
'What is the use?'

"Oh, but to take of life the natural good,
Even as a hermit caverned in a wood,
More sweetly fills my sober-suited views,
Than sweating to attain
Any luxurious pain.
What is the use?

"Give me a hermit's life, without his beads,
His lantern-jawed and moral-mouthing creeds;
Systems and creeds the natural heart abuse.
What need of any Book,
Or spiritual crook?
What is the use?

"I love, and God is love. And I behold
Man, nature, God, one triple chain of gold,
Nature in all, sole Oracle and Muse.
What should I seek at all,
More than is natural?
What is the use?"

Seeing this man so heathenly inclined,
So wilted in the mood of a good mind,
I felt a kind of heat of earnest thought,
And studying in reply,
Answered him, eye to eye: —

"Thou dost amaze me that thou dost mistake
The wandering rivers for the fountain lake:
What is the end of living? — happiness? —
An end that none attain
Argues a purpose vain.

"Plainly, this world is not a scope for bliss,
But duty. Yet we see not all that is,
Nor may be, some day, if we love the light:
What man is, in desires,
Whispers where man aspires.

"But what and where are we? — what now — to-day?
Souls on a globe that spins our lives away,
A multitudinous world, where heaven and hell,
Strangely in battle met,
Their gonfalons have set.

"Dust though we are, and shall return to dust,
Yet, being born to battles, fight we must;
Under which ensign is our only choice.
We know to wage our best;
God only knows the rest.

"Then, since we see about us sin and dole,
And some things good, why not, with hand and soul,
Wrestle and succor out of wrong and sorrow;
Grasping the swords of strife;
Making the most of life?

"Yea, all that we can wield is worth the end,
If sought as God's and man's most loyal friend;
Naked we come into the world, and take
Weapons of various skill —
Let us not use them ill."

THE MAYFLOWER

Down in the bleak December bay
The ghostly vessel stands away;
Her spars and halyards white with ice,
Under the dark December skies.
A hundred souls, in company,
Have left the vessel pensively, —
Have touched the frosty desert there,
And touched it with the knees of prayer.
And now the day begins to dip,
The night begins to lower
Over the bay, and over the ship
Mayflower.

Neither the desert nor the sea
Imposes rites: their prayers are free;
Danger and toil the wild imposes,
And thorns must grow before the roses.
And who are these? — and what distress
The savage-acred wilderness
On mother, maid, and child, may bring,
Beseems them for a fearful thing;

For now the day begins to dip,
The night begins to lower
Over the bay, and over the ship
Mayflower.

But Carver leads (in heart and health
A hero of the commonwealth)
The axes that the camp requires,
To build the lodge and heap the fires.
And Standish from his warlike store
Arrays his men along the shore,
Distributes weapons resonant,
And dons his harness militant;
For now the day begins to dip,
The night begins to lower
Over the bay, and over the ship
Mayflower;

And Rose, his wife, unlocks a chest —
She sees a Book, in vellum drest,
She drops a tear and kisses the tome,
Thinking of England and of home:

Might they — the Pilgrims, there and
then
Ordained to do the work of men —
Have seen, in visions of the air,
While pillowed on the breast of prayer
(When now the day began to dip,
The night began to lower
Over the bay, and over the ship
Mayflower),

The Canaan of their wilderness
A boundless empire of success;
And seen the years of future nights
Jewelled with myriad household lights;
And seen the honey fill the hive;
And seen a thousand ships arrive;
And heard the wheels of travel go;
It would have cheered a thought of woe,
When now the day began to dip,
The night began to lower
Over the bay, and over the ship
Mayflower.

Elizabeth Stoddard

THE POET'S SECRET

The poet's secret I must know,
If that will calm my restless mind.
I hail the seasons as they go,
I woo the sunshine, brave the wind.

I scan the lily and the rose,
I nod to every nodding tree,
I follow every stream that flows,
And wait beside the steadfast sea.

I question melancholy eyes,
I touch the lips of women fair:
Their lips and eyes may make me wise,
But what I seek for is not there.

In vain I watch the day and night,
In vain the world through space may
roll;
I never see the mystic light
Which fills the poet's happy soul.

Through life I hear the rhythmic flow
Whose meaning into song must turn;
Revealing all he longs to know,
The secret each alone must learn.

NOVEMBER

Much have I spoken of the faded leaf;
Long have I listened to the wailing wind,
And watched it ploughing through the
heavy clouds,
For autumn charms my melancholy mind.

When autumn comes, the poets sing a
dirge:
The year must perish; all the flowers
are dead;
The sheaves are gathered; and the mottled
quail
Runs in the stubble, but the lark has fled!

Still, autumn ushers in the Christmas cheer,
The holly-berries and the ivy-tree:
They weave a chaplet for the Old Year's
bier,
These waiting mourners do not sing for
me!

I find sweet peace in depths of autumn
woods,
Where grow the ragged ferns and
roughened moss;

The naked, silent trees have taught me this, —
The loss of beauty is not always loss!

UNRETURNING

Now all the flowers that ornament the grass,
Wherever meadows are and placid brooks,
Must fall — the "glory of the grass" must fall.
Year after year I see them sprout and spread, —
The golden, glossy, tossing buttercups,
The tall, straight daisies and red clover globes,
The swinging bellwort and the blue-eyed bent,
With nameless plants as perfect in their hues, —
Perfect in root and branch, their plan of life,
As if the intention of a soul were there:
I see them flourish as I see them fall!
But he, who once was growing with the grass,
And blooming with the flowers, my little son,
Fell, withered — dead, nor has revived again!
Perfect and lovely, needful to my sight,
Why comes he not to ornament my days?
The barren fields forget their barrenness,
The soulless earth mates with these soulless things,
Why should I not obtain *my* recompense?
The budding spring should bring, or summer's prime,
At least a vision of the vanished child,
And let his heart commune with mine again,
Though in a dream — his life was but a dream;
Then might I wait with patient cheerfulness,
That cheerfulness which keeps one's tears unshed,
And blinds the eyes with pain — the passage slow
Of other seasons, and be still and cold
As the earth is when shrouded in the snow,
Or passive, like it, when the boughs are stripped
In autumn, and the leaves roll everywhere.
And he should go again; for winter's snows,
And autumn's melancholy voice, in winds,
In waters, and in woods, belong to me, —
To me, a faded soul; for, as I said,
The sense of all his beauty, sweetness, comes
When blossoms are the sweetest; when the sea,
Sparkling and blue, cries to the sun in joy,
Or, silent, pale, and misty waits the night,
Till the moon, pushing through the veiling cloud,
Hangs naked in its heaving solitude:
When feathery pines wave up and down the shore,
And the vast deep above holds gentle stars,
And the vast world beneath hides him from me!

IN THE STILL, STAR-LIT NIGHT

In the still, star-lit night,
By the full fountain and the willow-tree,
I walked, and not alone —
A spirit walked with me!

A shade fell on the grass;
Upon the water fell a deeper shade:
Something the willow stirred,
For to and fro it swayed.

The grass was in a quiver,
The water trembled, and the willow-tree
Sighed softly; I sighed loud —
The spirit taunted me.

All the night long I walked
By the full fountain, dropping icy tears;
I tore the willow leaves,
I tore the long, green spears!

I clutched the quaking grass,
And beat the rough bark of the willow-tree;
I shook the wreathëd boughs,
To make the spirit flee.

It haunted me till dawn,
By the full fountain and the willow-tree;
For with myself I walked —
How could the spirit flee?

MERCEDES

Under a sultry, yellow sky,
On the yellow sand I lie;
The crinkled vapors smite my brain,
I smoulder in a fiery pain.

Above the crags the condor flies;
He knows where the red gold lies,
He knows where the diamonds shine;—
If I knew, would she be mine?

Mercedes in her hammock swings;
In her court a palm-tree flings
Its slender shadow on the ground,
The fountain falls with silver sound.

Her lips are like this cactus cup;
With my hand I crush it up;
I tear its flaming leaves apart;—
Would that I could tear her heart!

Last night a man was at her gate;
In the hedge I lay in wait;
I saw Mercedes meet him there,
By the fireflies in her hair.

I waited till the break of day,
Then I rose and stole away;
But left my dagger in the gate;—
Now she knows her lover's fate!

ON THE CAMPAGNA

Stop on the Appian Way,
In the Roman Campagna;
Stop at my tomb,
The tomb of Cecilia Metella.
To-day as you see it
Alaric saw it, ages ago,
When he, with his pale-visaged Goths,
Sat at the gates of Rome,
Reading his Runic shield.
Odin, thy curse remains!

Beneath these battlements
My bones were stirred with Roman pride,
Though centuries before my Romans died:
Now my bones are dust; the Goths are dust.
The river-bed is dry where sleeps the king,
My tomb remains!

When Rome commanded the earth
Great were the Metelli:
I was Metellus' wife;
I loved him — and I died.
Then with slow patience built he this memorial:
Each century marks his love.

Pass by on the Appian Way
The tomb of Cecilia Metella;
Wild shepherds alone seek its shelter,
Wild buffaloes tramp at its base.
Deep is its desolation,
Deep as the shadow of Rome!

A SUMMER NIGHT

I feel the breath of the summer night,
Aromatic fire:
The trees, the vines, the flowers are astir
With tender desire.

The white moths flutter about the lamp,
Enamoured with light;
And a thousand creatures softly sing
A song to the night!

But I am alone, and how can I sing
Praises to thee?
Come, Night! unveil the beautiful soul
That waiteth for me.

LAST DAYS

As one who follows a departing friend,
Destined to cross the great, dividing sea,
I watch and follow these departing days,
That go so grandly, lifting up their crowns
Still regal, though their victor Autumn comes.
Gifts they bestow, which I accept, return,
As gifts exchanged between a loving pair,
Who may possess them as memorials
Of pleasures ended by the shadow—Death.
What matter which shall vanish hence, if both
Are transitory — me, and these bright hours —
And of the future ignorant alike?
From all our social thralls I would be free.
Let care go down the wind—as hounds afar,
Within their kennels baying unseen foes,

Give to calm sleepers only calmer dreams.
Here will I rest alone: the morning mist
Conceals no form but mine; the evening dew
Freshens but faded flowers and my worn face.
When the noon basks among the wooded hills
I too will bask, as silent as the air
So thick with sun-motes, dyed like yellow gold,
Or colored purple like an unplucked plum.
The thrush, now lonesome, for her young have flown,
May flutter her brown wings across my path;
And creatures of the sod with brilliant eyes
May leap beside me, and familiar grow.
The moon shall rise among her floating clouds,
Black, vaporous fans, and crinkled globes of pearl,
And her sweet silver light be given to me.
To watch and follow these departing days
Must be my choice; and let me mated be
With Solitude; may memory and hope
Unite to give me faith that nothing dies;
To show me always, what I pray to know,
That man alone may speak the word — *Farewell.*

Thomas Lake Harris

CALIFORNIA

THE Grecian Muse, to earth who bore
  Her goblet filled with wine of gold,
Dispersed the frown that Ages wore
  Upon their foreheads grim and cold,
  What time the lyric thunders rolled.

O'er this new Eden of the West
  The mightier Muse enkindles now:
Her joy-lyre fashions in my breast,
  And wreathes the song-crown for my brow,
  Ere yet her loftier powers avow.

Though like Tithonus old and gray,
  I serve her mid the swords and shields;
Her being opens for my way,
  And there I find Elysian fields;
  And there I dwell while Nature yields.

My Dian of the sparkling West,
  My lady of the silver bow!
Here, where the savage man made quest
  For golden spoils in earth that grow,
  She leads the Golden Age below.

Beneath her feet the maiden May
  Sits crowned with roses where I sing.
My brows with frosted age are gray,
  But all my being glows for spring:
  A golden youth 't is hers to bring.

So in her, for her, I abide,
  And taste the goblets of her bliss;
Upon the hills with morning dyed,
  All as a new acropolis,
  Her shrine shall yet arise, I wis.

And here shall greater Hellas burn,
  Irradiant for the Solar Powers;
And men the love of strife unlearn,
  Tasting from lips that breathe of flowers,
  Made young by joys that live from ours.

FLEDGLINGS

WHY should we waste and weep?
  The Summers weave
A nest of blossoms deep.
  Sad hearts, why grieve?
We downy birdlings are
  Unfledged for flight:
God's love-wind woos afar;
  Its name, Delight.

From arcades vast and dim
  What songs disthrall?
Through Nature's endless hymn,
  Our kindred call.
Mysterious murmurings,
  When night is lone,
Glide, as to lift our wings
  For flights unknown.

In melody we form,
By sweetness fill:
For gladness, pure and warm,
Our bosoms thrill.
Soon shall our choiring bands,
Upborne for glee,
Find in God's garden lands
Their bridal tree.

Eternity prepares
Her gift in Time,
And flows by fragrant airs
That lead the prime.
Chill shadows touch the eyes;
Their orbs are wet;
But God shall for us rise,
When stars have set.

SEA-SLEEP

SLEEP, sleep, sleep
In thy folded waves, O Sea!
Till the quiet breathings creep,
With a low-voiced melody,
Out of the glimmering deep.
For sleep is the close of life;
'T is the end of love, and its birth;
'T is the quieting of strife,
And the silencing of mirth.
Hush and sleep!

Close thou thy lids, O Sea,
On palaces and towers;
Dream on deliciously
Deep in thy dreamland bowers.
Waken us not again,
Beating upon our shore,
Rousing the strife in men
With full and thunderous roar.

Drop from thy crested heights,
To still repose and rest;
Fold us in hushed delights,
With dream-flowers from thy breast:
Not as the poppies are
But lilies cool, that weep
Tears that as kisses scar
To soothe for slumbers deep.

Hush thou the little waves,
Hush with a low-voiced song,
Till the Under-Deep that laves
Thy lucid floor lifts strong;
Till the Under-Word is borne
To this weary world of ours,
And lives, for love that mourn,
Fold as the dew-dipped flowers.

Rest thou in time's unrest,
In the bloom-bell and the brain;
Then loose, all silver-tressed,
The streamings of thy mane:
Gliding, dissolving so,
That we at peace may be,
Sleep in thy silver glow,
Thy azure calm, O Sea;
Make lullaby!

George Henry Boker[1]

A BALLAD OF SIR JOHN FRANKLIN

O, WHITHER sail you, Sir John Franklin?
Cried a whaler in Baffin's Bay.
To know if between the land and the pole
I may find a broad sea-way.

I charge you back, Sir John Franklin,
As you would live and thrive;
For between the land and the frozen pole
No man may sail alive.

But lightly laughed the stout Sir John,
And spoke unto his men:
Half England is wrong, if he be right;
Bear off to westward then.

O, whither sail you, brave Englishman?
Cried the little Esquimau.
Between your land and the polar star
My goodly vessels go.

Come down, if you would journey there,
The little Indian said;
And change your cloth for fur clothing,
Your vessel for a sled.

But lightly laughed the stout Sir John,
And the crew laughed with him too:—

[1] See BIOGRAPHICAL NOTE, p. 780.

A sailor to change from ship to sled,
  I ween, were something new.

All through the long, long polar day,
  The vessels westward sped;
And wherever the sail of Sir John was blown,
  The ice gave way and fled: —

Gave way with many a hollow groan,
  And with many a surly roar,
But it murmured and threatened on every side,
  And closed where he sailed before.

Ho! see ye not, my merry men,
  The broad and open sea?
Bethink ye what the whaler said,
Think of the little Indian's sled!
  The crew laughed out in glee.

Sir John, Sir John, 't is bitter cold,
  The scud drives on the breeze,
The ice comes looming from the north,
  The very sunbeams freeze.

Bright summer goes, dark winter comes, —
  We cannot rule the year;
But long ere summer's sun goes down,
  On yonder sea we 'll steer.

The dripping icebergs dipped and rose,
  And floundered down the gale;
The ships were stayed, the yards were manned,
  And furled the useless sail.

The summer 's gone, the winter 's come, —
  We sail not on yonder sea:
Why sail we not, Sir John Franklin? —
  A silent man was he.

The summer goes, the winter comes, —
  We cannot rule the year:
I ween we cannot rule the ways,
  Sir John, wherein we 'd steer.

The cruel ice came floating on,
  And closed beneath the lee,
Till the thickening waters dashed no more:
'T was ice around, behind, before —
  My God! there is no sea!

What think you of the whaler now?
  What of the Esquimau?
A sled were better than a ship,
  To cruise through ice and snow.

Down sank the baleful crimson sun,
  The northern light came out,
And glared upon the ice-bound ships,
  And shook its spears about.

The snow came down, storm breeding storm,
  And on the decks was laid,
Till the weary sailor, sick at heart,
  Sank down beside his spade.

Sir John, the night is black and long,
  The hissing wind is bleak,
The hard, green ice as strong as death: —
  I prithee, Captain, speak!

The night is neither bright nor short,
  The singing breeze is cold, —
The ice is not so strong as hope,
  The heart of man is bold!

What hope can scale this icy wall,
  High over the main flag-staff?
Above the ridges the wolf and bear
Look down, with a patient, settled stare,
  Look down on us and laugh.

The summer went, the winter came, —
  We could not rule the year;
But summer will melt the ice again,
And open a path to the sunny main,
  Whereon our ships shall steer.

The winter went, the summer went,
  The winter came around;
But the hard, green ice was strong as death,
And the voice of hope sank to a breath,
  Yet caught at every sound.

Hark! heard you not the noise of guns? —
  And there, and there, again?
'T is some uneasy iceberg's roar,
  As he turns in the frozen main.

Hurra! Hurra! the Esquimaux
  Across the ice-fields steal:
God give them grace for their charity! —
  Ye pray for the silly seal.

Sir John, where are the English fields,
  And where are the English trees,

And where are the little English flowers
  That open in the breeze?

Be still, be still, my brave sailors!
  You shall see the fields again,
And smell the scent of the opening flowers,
  The grass, and the waving grain.

Oh! when shall I see my orphan child?
  My Mary waits for me.
Oh! when shall I see my old mother,
  And pray at her trembling knee?

Be still, be still, my brave sailors!
  Think not such thoughts again.
But a tear froze slowly on his cheek:
  He thought of Lady Jane.

Ah! bitter, bitter grows the cold,
  The ice grows more and more;
More settled stare the wolf and bear,
  More patient than before.

O, think you, good Sir John Franklin,
  We 'll ever see the land?
'T was cruel to send us here to starve,
  Without a helping hand.

'T was cruel, Sir John, to send us here,
  So far from help or home,
To starve and freeze on this lonely sea:
I ween the lords of the Admiralty
  Would rather send than come.

Oh! whether we starve to death alone,
  Or sail to our own country,
We have done what man has never done —
The truth is founded, the secret won —
  We passed the Northern Sea!

THE FERRY

THERE was a gay maiden lived down by the mill, —
  Ferry me over the ferry, —
Her hair was as bright as the waves of a rill,
When the sun on the brink of his setting stands still,
  Her lips were as full as a cherry.

A stranger came galloping over the hill, —
  Ferry me over the ferry, —
He gave her broad silver and gold for his will:
She glanced at the stranger, she glanced o'er the sill;
  The maiden was gentle and merry.

"O! what would you give for your virtue again?" —
  Ferry me over the ferry, —
"O! silver and gold on your lordship I 'd rain,
I 'd double your pleasure, I 'd double my pain,
  This moment forever to bury."

TO ENGLAND

LEAR and Cordelia! 't was an ancient tale
Before thy Shakespeare gave it deathless fame:
The times have changed, the moral is the same.
So like an outcast, dowerless, and pale,
Thy daughter went; and in a foreign gale
Spread her young banner, till its sway became
A wonder to the nations. Days of shame
Are close upon thee: prophets raise their wail.
When the rude Cossack with an outstretched hand
Points his long spear across the narrow sea, —
"Lo! there is England!" when thy destiny
Storms on thy straw-crowned head, and thou dost stand
Weak, helpless, mad, a by-word in the land, —
God grant thy daughter a Cordelia be!

TO MY LADY

I

I 'LL call thy frown a headsman, passing grim,
Walking before some wretch foredoomed to death,
Who counts the pantings of his own hard breath,
Wondering how heart can beat, or steadfast limb

Bear its sad burden to life's awful brim.
I'll call thy smile a priest, who slowly sayeth
Soft words of comfort, as the sinner strayeth
Away in thought; or sings a holy hymn,
Full of rich promise, as he walks behind
The fatal axe with face of goodly cheer,
And kind inclinings of his saintly ear.
So, love, thou seest in smiles, or looks unkind,
Some taste of sweet philosophy I find,
That seasons all things in our little sphere.

II

Why shall I chide the hand of wilful Time
When he assaults thy wondrous store of charms?
Why charge the gray-beard with a wanton crime?
Or strive to daunt him with my shrill alarms?
Or seek to lull him with a silly rhyme:
So he, forgetful, pause upon his arms,
And leave thy beauties in their noble prime,
The sole survivors of his grievous harms?
Alas! my love, though I'll indeed bemoan
The fatal ruin of thy majesty;
Yet I'll remember that to Time alone
I owed thy birth, thy charms' maturity,
Thy crowning love with which he vested me,
Nor can reclaim, though all the rest be flown.

DIRGE FOR A SOLDIER

Close his eyes; his work is done!
What to him is friend or foeman,
Rise of moon, or set of sun,
Hand of man, or kiss of woman?
Lay him low, lay him low,
In the clover or the snow!
What cares he? he cannot know:
Lay him low!

As man may, he fought his fight,
Proved his truth by his endeavor;
Let him sleep in solemn night,
Sleep forever and forever.
Lay him low, lay him low,
In the clover or the snow!
What cares he? he cannot know:
Lay him low!

Fold him in his country's stars,
Roll the drum and fire the volley!
What to him are all our wars,
What but death bemocking folly?
Lay him low, lay him low,
In the clover or the snow!
What cares he? he cannot know:
Lay him low!

Leave him to God's watching eye,
Trust him to the hand that made him.
Mortal love weeps idly by:
God alone has power to aid him.
Lay him low, lay him low,
In the clover or the snow!
What cares he? he cannot know:
Lay him low!

John Randolph Thompson

MUSIC IN CAMP

Two armies covered hill and plain,
Where Rappahannock's waters
Ran deeply crimsoned with the stain
Of battle's recent slaughters.

The summer clouds lay pitched like tents
In meads of heavenly azure;
And each dread gun of the elements
Slept in its hid embrasure.

The breeze so softly blew it made
No forest leaf to quiver,
And the smoke of the random cannonade
Rolled slowly from the river.

And now, where circling hills looked down
With cannon grimly planted,
O'er listless camp and silent town
The golden sunset slanted.

When on the fervid air there came
  A strain — now rich, now tender;
The music seemed itself aflame
  With day's departing splendor.

A Federal band, which, eve and morn,
  Played measures brave and nimble,
Had just struck up, with flute and horn
  And lively clash of cymbal.

Down flocked the soldiers to the banks,
  Till, margined by its pebbles,
One wooded shore was blue with "Yanks,"
  And one was gray with "Rebels."

Then all was still, and then the band,
  With movement light and tricksy,
Made stream and forest, hill and strand,
  Reverberate with "Dixie."

The conscious stream with burnished glow
  Went proudly o'er its pebbles,
But thrilled throughout its deepest flow
  With yelling of the Rebels.

Again a pause, and then again
  The trumpets pealed sonorous,
And "Yankee Doodle" was the strain
  To which the shore gave chorus.

The laughing ripple shoreward flew,
  To kiss the shining pebbles;
Loud shrieked the swarming Boys in Blue
  Defiance to the Rebels.

And yet once more the bugles sang
  Above the stormy riot;
No shout upon the evening rang —
  There reigned a holy quiet.

The sad, slow stream its noiseless flood
  Poured o'er the glistening pebbles;
All silent now the Yankees stood,
  And silent stood the Rebels.

No unresponsive soul had heard
  That plaintive note's appealing,
So deeply "Home, Sweet Home" had stirred
  The hidden founts of feeling.

Or Blue or Gray, the soldier sees,
  As by the wand of fairy,
The cottage 'neath the live-oak trees,
  The cabin by the prairie.

Or cold or warm, his native skies
  Bend in their beauty o'er him;
Seen through the tear-mist in his eyes,
  His loved ones stand before him.

As fades the iris after rain
  In April's tearful weather,
The vision vanished, as the strain
  And daylight died together.

But memory, waked by music's art,
  Expressed in simplest numbers,
Subdued the sternest Yankee's heart,
  Made light the Rebel's slumbers.

And fair the form of music shines,
  That bright, celestial creature,
Who still, mid war's embattled lines,
  Gave this one touch of Nature.

ASHBY

To the brave all homage render;
  Weep, ye skies of June!
With a radiance pure and tender,
  Shine, O saddened moon;
"Dead upon the field of glory,"
Hero fit for song and story,
  Lies our bold dragoon.

Well they learned, whose hands have slain him,
  Braver, knightlier foe
Never fought 'gainst Moor or Paynim —
  Rode at Templestowe:
With a mien how high and joyous,
'Gainst the hordes that would destroy us
  Went he forth, we know.

Nevermore, alas! shall sabre
  Gleam around his crest;
Fought his fight, fulfilled his labor,
  Stilled his manly breast;
All unheard sweet nature's cadence,
Trump of fame and voice of maidens;
  Now he takes his rest.

Earth, that all too soon hath bound him,
  Gently wrap his clay!
Linger lovingly around him,
  Light of dying day!
Softly fall, ye summer showers;
Birds and bees among the flowers
  Make the gloom seem gay.

Then, throughout the coming ages, —
When his sword is rust,
And his deeds in classic pages —
Mindful of her trust
Shall Virginia, bending lowly,
Still a ceaseless vigil holy
Keep above his dust.

James Matthew Legaré

AMY

This is the pathway where she walked,
The tender grass pressed by her feet.
The laurel boughs laced overhead,
Shut out the noonday heat.

The sunshine gladly stole between
The softly undulating limbs.
From every blade and leaf arose
The myriad insect hymns.

A brook ran murmuring beneath
The grateful twilight of the trees,
Where from the dripping pebbles swelled
A beech's mossy knees.

And there her robe of spotless white,
(Pure white such purity beseemed !)
Her angel face, and tresses bright
Within the basin gleamed.

The coy sweetbriers half detained
Her light hem as we moved along !
To hear the music of her voice
The mockbird hushed his song.

But now her little feet are still,
Her lips the Everlasting seal;
The hideous secrets of the grave
The weeping eyes reveal.

The path still winds, the brook descends,
The skies are bright as then they were.
My Amy is the only leaf
In all that forest sear.

AHAB MOHAMMED

A peasant stood before a king and said,
"My children starve, I come to thee for bread."
On cushions soft and silken sat enthroned
The king, and looked on him that prayed and moaned,
Who cried again, — "For bread I come to thee."
For grief, like wine, the tongue will render free.
Then said the prince with simple truth, "Behold
I sit on cushions silken-soft, of gold
And wrought with skill the vessels which they bring
To fitly grace the banquet of a king.
But at my gate the Mede triumphant beats,
And die for food my people in the streets.
Yet no good father hears his child complain
And gives him stones for bread, for alms disdain.
Come, thou and I will sup together — come."
The wondering courtiers saw — saw and were dumb:
Then followed with their eyes where Ahab led
With grace the humble guest, amazed, to share his bread.

Him half abashed the royal host withdrew
Into a room, the curtained doorway through.
Silent behind the folds of purple closed,
In marble life the statues stood disposed;
From the high ceiling, perfume breathing, hung
Lamps rich, pomegranate-shaped, and golden-swung.
Gorgeous the board with massive metal shone,
Gorgeous with gems arose in front a throne:
These through the Orient lattice saw the sun.
If gold there was, of meat and bread was none

Save one small loaf; this stretched his hand
and took
Ahab Mohammed, prayed to God, and
broke:
One half his yearning nature bid him crave,
The other gladly to his guest he gave.
"I have no more to give," he cheerily
said:
"With thee I share my only loaf of bread."
Humbly the stranger took the offered
crumb
Yet ate not of it, standing meek and
dumb;
Then lifts his eyes, — the wondering Ahab
saw
His rags fall from him as the snow in
thaw.
Resplendent, blue, those orbs upon him
turned;
All Ahab's soul within him throbbed and
burned.

"Ahab Mohammed," spoke the vision then,
"From this thou shalt be blessëd among
men.
Go forth — thy gates the Mede bewildered
flees,
And Allah thank thy people on their knees.
He who gives somewhat does a worthy
deed,
Of him the recording angel shall take heed.
But he that halves all that his house doth
hold,
His deeds are more to God, yea more than
finest gold."

TO A LILY

Go bow thy head in gentle spite,
Thou lily white,
For she who spies thee waving here,
With thee in beauty can compare
As day with night.

Soft are thy leaves and white: her arms
Boast whiter charms.
Thy stem prone bent with loveliness
Of maiden grace possesseth less:
Therein she charms.

Thou in thy lake dost see
Thyself: so she
Beholds her image in her eyes
Reflected. Thus did Venus rise
From out the sea.

Inconsolate, bloom not again.
Thou rival vain
Of her whose charms have thine outdone,
Whose purity might spot the sun,
And make thy leaf a stain.

Thomas Wentworth Higginson

ODE TO A BUTTERFLY

Thou spark of life that wavest wings of
gold,
Thou songless wanderer mid the songful
birds,
With Nature's secrets in thy tints unrolled
Through gorgeous cipher, past the reach of
words,
Yet dear to every child
In glad pursuit beguiled,
Living his unspoiled days mid flowers and
flocks and herds!

Thou wingëd blossom, liberated thing,
What secret tie binds thee to other flowers,
Still held within the garden's fostering?
Will they too soar with the completed
hours,
Take flight, and be like thee
Irrevocably free,
Hovering at will o'er their parental bowers?

Or is thy lustre drawn from heavenly
hues, —
A sumptuous drifting fragment of the sky,
Caught when the sunset its last glance im-
bues
With sudden splendor, and the tree-tops
high
Grasp that swift blazonry,
Then lend those tints to thee,
On thee to float a few short hours, and
die?

Birds have their nests; they rear their eager young,
And flit on errands all the livelong day;
Each fieldmouse keeps the homestead whence it sprung;
But thou art Nature's freeman, — free to stray
  Unfettered through the wood,
  Seeking thine airy food,
The sweetness spiced on every blossomed spray.

The garden one wide banquet spreads for thee,
O daintiest reveller of the joyous earth!
One drop of honey gives satiety;
A second draught would drug thee past all mirth.
  Thy feast no orgy shows;
  Thy calm eyes never close,
Thou soberest sprite to which the sun gives birth.

And yet the soul of man upon thy wings
Forever soars in aspiration; thou
His emblem of the new career that springs
When death's arrest bids all his spirit bow.
  He seeks his hope in thee
  Of immortality.
Symbol of life, me with such faith endow!

TO DUTY

Light of dim mornings; shield from heat and cold;
Balm for all ailments; substitute for praise;
Comrade of those who plod in lonely ways
(Ways that grow lonelier as the years wax old);
Tonic for fears; check to the over-bold;
Nurse, whose calm hand its strong restriction lays,
Kind but resistless, on our wayward days;
Mart, where high wisdom at vast price is sold;
Gardener, whose touch bids the rose-petals fall,
The thorns endure; surgeon, who human hearts
Searchest with probes, though the death-touch be given;
Spell that knits friends, but yearning lovers parts;
Tyrant relentless o'er our blisses all; —
Oh, can it be, thine other name is Heaven?

"THE SNOWING OF THE PINES"

Softer than silence, stiller than still air
Float down from high pine-boughs the slender leaves.
The forest floor its annual boon receives
That comes like snowfall, tireless, tranquil, fair.
Gently they glide, gently they clothe the bare
Old rocks with grace. Their fall a mantle weaves
Of paler yellow than autumnal sheaves
Or those strange blossoms the witch-hazels wear.
Athwart long aisles the sunbeams pierce their way;
High up, the crows are gathering for the night;
The delicate needles fill the air; the jay
Takes through their golden mist his radiant flight;
They fall and fall, till at November's close
The snow-flakes drop as lightly — snows on snows.

DECORATION

"MANIBUS O DATE LILIA PLENIS"

Mid the flower-wreathed tombs I stand
Bearing lilies in my hand.
Comrades! in what soldier-grave
Sleeps the bravest of the brave?

Is it he who sank to rest
With his colors round his breast?
Friendship makes his tomb a shrine;
Garlands veil it: ask not mine.

One low grave, yon trees beneath,
Bears no roses, wears no wreath;
Yet no heart more high and warm
Ever dared the battle-storm,

Never gleamed a prouder eye
In the front of victory,
Never foot had firmer tread
On the field where hope lay dead,

Than are hid within this tomb,
Where the untended grasses bloom,
And no stone, with feigned distress,
Mocks the sacred loneliness.

Youth and beauty, dauntless will,
Dreams that life could ne'er fulfil,
Here lie buried; here in peace
Wrongs and woes have found release.

Turning from my comrades' eyes,
Kneeling where a woman lies,
I strew lilies on the grave
Of the bravest of the brave.

"SINCE CLEOPATRA DIED"

"SINCE Cleopatra died!" Long years are past,
In Antony's fancy, since the deed was done.
Love counts its epochs, not from sun to sun,
But by the heart-throb. Mercilessly fast
Time has swept onward since she looked her last
On life, a queen. For him the sands have run
Whole ages through their glass, and kings have won
And lost their empires o'er earth's surface vast
Since Cleopatra died. Ah! Love and Pain
Make their own measure of all things that be.
No clock's slow ticking marks their deathless strain;
The life they own is not the life we see;
Love's single moment is eternity:
Eternity, a thought in Shakespeare's brain.

"SUCH STUFF AS DREAMS ARE MADE OF"

Now all the cloudy shapes that float and lie
Within this magic globe we call the brain
Fold quite away, condense, withdraw, refrain,
And show it tenantless — an empty sky.
Return, O parting visions, pass not by;
Nor leave me vacant still, with strivings vain,
Longing to grasp at your dim garment's train,
And be drawn on to sleep's immunity.
I lie and pray for fancies hovering near;
Oblivion's kindly troop, illusions blest;
Dim, trailing phantoms in a world too clear;
Soft, downy, shadowy forms, my spirit's nest;
The warp and woof of sleep; till, freed from fear,
I drift in sweet enchantment back to rest.

Charles Godfrey Leland

EL CAPITAN-GENERAL

THERE was a captain-general who ruled in Vera Cruz,
And what we used to hear of him was always evil news:
He was a pirate on the sea — a robber on the shore,
The Señor Don Alonzo Estabán San Salvador.

There was a Yankee skipper who round about did roam;
His name was Stephen Folger, and Nantucket was his home:
And having gone to Vera Cruz, he had been skinned full sore
By the Señor Don Alonzo Estabán San Salvador.

But having got away alive, though all his cash was gone,
He said, "If there is vengeance, I will surely try it on!
And I do wish I may be damned if I don't clear the score
With Señor Don Alonzo Estabán San Salvador!"

He shipped a crew of seventy men — well-armëd men were they,
And sixty of them in the hold he darkly stowed away;
And, sailing back to Vera Cruz, was sighted from the shore
By the Señor Don Alonzo Estabán San Salvador.

With twenty-five soldados he came on board so pleased,
And said, "*Maldito* Yankee — again your ship is seized.
How many sailors have you got?" Said Folger, "Ten — no more,"
To the Captain Don Alonzo Estabán San Salvador.

"But come into my cabin and take a glass of wine.
I do suppose, as usual, I'll have to pay a fine:
I have got some old Madeira, and we'll talk the matter o'er —
My Captain Don Alonzo Estabán San Salvador."

And as over that Madeira the captain-general boozed,
It seemed to him as if his head was getting quite confused;
For it happened that some morphine had travelled from "the store"
To the glass of Don Alonzo Estabán San Salvador.

"What is it makes the vessel roll? What sounds are these I hear?
It seems as if the rising waves were beating on my ear!" —
"Oh, it is the breaking of the surf — just that and nothing more,
My Captain Don Alonzo Estabán San Salvador!"

The governor was in a sleep which muddled all his brains;
The seventy men had got his gang and put them all in chains;
And when he woke the following day he could not see the shore,
For he was out on the blue water — the Don San Salvador.

"Now do you see that yard-arm — and understand the thing?"
Said Captain Folger. "For all from that yard-arm you shall swing,
Or forty thousand dollars you shall pay me from your store,
My Captain Don Alonzo Estabán San Salvador."

The Capitano took a pen — the order he did sign —
"O Señor Yankee! but you charge amazing high for wine!"
But 't was not till the draft was paid they let him go ashore,
El Señor Don Alonzo Estabán San Salvador.

The greatest sharp some day will find another sharper wit;
It always makes the Devil laugh to see a biter bit;
It takes two Spaniards any day to come a Yankee o'er —
Even two like Don Alonzo Estabán San Salvador.

THE TWO FRIENDS

I HAVE two friends — two glorious friends — two better could not be,
And every night when midnight tolls they meet to laugh with me.

The first was shot by Carlist thieves — ten years ago in Spain.
The second drowned near Alicante — while I alive remain.

I love to see their dim white forms come floating through the night,
And grieve to see them fade away in early morning light.

The first with gnomes in the Under Land is leading a lordly life,
The second has married a mermaiden, a beautiful water-wife.

And since I have friends in the Earth and Sea — with a few, I trust, on high,
'T is a matter of small account to me — the way that I may die.

For whether I sink in the foaming flood, or swing on the triple tree,
Or die in my bed, as a Christian should, is all the same to me.

Bayard Taylor

ARIEL IN THE CLOVEN PINE

Now the frosty stars are gone:
I have watched them one by one,
Fading on the shores of Dawn.
Round and full the glorious sun
Walks with level step the spray,
Through this vestibule of Day,
While the wolves that late did howl
Slink to dens and coverts foul,
Guarded by the demon owl,
Who, last night, with mocking croon,
Wheeled athwart the chilly moon,
And with eyes that blankly glared
On my direful torment stared.

The lark is flickering in the light;
Still the nightingale doth sing; —
All the isle, alive with Spring,
Lies, a jewel of delight,
On the blue sea's heaving breast:
Not a breath from out the west,
But some balmy smell doth bring
From the sprouting myrtle buds,
Or from meadowy vales that lie
Like a green inverted sky,
Which the yellow cowslip stars,
And the bloomy almond woods,
Cloud-like, cross with roseate bars.
All is life that I can spy,
To the farthest sea and sky,
And my own the only pain
Within this ring of Tyrrhene main.

In the gnarled and cloven Pine
Where that hell-born hag did chain me,
All this orb of cloudless shine,
All this youth in Nature's veins
Tingling with the season's wine,
With a sharper torment pain me.
Pansies in soft April rains
Fill their stalks with honeyed sap
Drawn from Earth's prolific lap;
But the sluggish blood she brings
To the tough Pine's hundred rings,
Closer locks their cruel hold,
Closer draws the scaly bark
Round the crevice, damp and cold,
Where my useless wings I fold, —
Sealing me in iron dark.
By this coarse and alien state
Is my dainty essence wronged;
Finer senses, that belonged
To my freedom, chafe at Fate,
Till the happier elves I hate,
Who in moonlight dances turn
Underneath the palmy fern,
Or in light and twinkling bands
Follow on with linkëd hands
To the ocean's yellow sands.

Primrose-eyes each morning ope
In their cool, deep beds of grass;
Violets make the airs that pass
Telltales of their fragrant slope.
I can see them where they spring
Never brushed by fairy wing.
All those corners I can spy
In the island's solitude,
Where the dew is never dry,
Nor the miser bees intrude.
Cups of rarest hue are there,
Full of perfumed wine undrained, —
Mushroom banquets, ne'er profaned,
Canopied by maiden-hair.
Pearls I see upon the sands,
Never touched by other hands,
And the rainbow bubbles shine
On the ridged and frothy brine,
Tenantless of voyager
Till they burst in vacant air.
Oh, the songs that sung might be,
And the mazy dances woven,
Had that witch ne'er crossed the sea
And the Pine been never cloven!

Many years my direst pain
Has made the wave-rocked isle complain
Winds that from the Cyclades
Came to blow in wanton riot
Round its shore's enchanted quiet,
Bore my wailings on the seas:
Sorrowing birds in autumn went
Through the world with my lament.
Still the bitter fate is mine,
All delight unshared to see,
Smarting in the cloven Pine,
While I wait the tardy axe
Which, perchance, shall set me free
From the damned witch Sycorax.

SONG

DAUGHTER of Egypt, veil thine eyes!
  I cannot bear their fire;
Nor will I touch with sacrifice
  Those altars of desire.
For they are flames that shun the day,
  And their unholy light
Is fed from natures gone astray
  In passion and in night.

The stars of Beauty and of Sin,
  They burn amid the dark,
Like beacons that to ruin win
  The fascinated bark.
Then veil their glow, lest I forswear
  The hopes thou canst not crown,
And in the black waves of thy hair
  My struggling manhood drown!

BEDOUIN SONG

FROM the Desert I come to thee
  On a stallion shod with fire;
And the winds are left behind
  In the speed of my desire.
Under thy window I stand,
  And the midnight hears my cry:
I love thee, I love but thee,
  With a love that shall not die
    Till the sun grows cold,
    And the stars are old,
    And the leaves of the Judgment
      Book unfold!

Look from thy window and see
  My passion and my pain;
I lie on the sands below,
  And I faint in thy disdain.
Let the night-winds touch thy brow
  With the heat of my burning sigh,
And melt thee to hear the vow
  Of a love that shall not die
    Till the sun grows cold,
    And the stars are old,
    And the leaves of the Judgment
      Book unfold!

My steps are nightly driven,
  By the fever in my breast,
To hear from thy lattice breathed
  The word that shall give me rest.
Open the door of thy heart,
  And open thy chamber door,
And my kisses shall teach thy lips
  The love that shall fade no more
    Till the sun grows cold,
    And the stars are old,
    And the leaves of the Judgment
      Book unfold!

AMERICA

FROM THE NATIONAL ODE, JULY 4, 1876

FORESEEN in the vision of sages,
  Foretold when martyrs bled,
She was born of the longing of ages,
  By the truth of the noble dead
  And the faith of the living fed!
No blood in her lightest veins
Frets at remembered chains,
Nor shame of bondage has bowed her head.
In her form and features still
The unblenching Puritan will,
Cavalier honor, Huguenot grace,
The Quaker truth and sweetness,
And the strength of the danger-girdled race
Of Holland, blend in a proud completeness.
From the homes of all, where her being began,
She took what she gave to Man;
Justice, that knew no station,
  Belief, as soul decreed,
Free air for aspiration,
Free force for independent deed!
She takes, but to give again,
As the sea returns the rivers in rain;
And gathers the chosen of her seed
From the hunted of every crown and creed.
Her Germany dwells by a gentler Rhine;
Her Ireland sees the old sunburst shine;
Her France pursues some dream divine;
Her Norway keeps his mountain pine;
Her Italy waits by the western brine;
  And, broad-based under all,
Is planted England's oaken-hearted mood,
  As rich in fortitude
As e'er went worldward from the island-wall!
  Fused in her candid light,
To one strong race all races here unite;
Tongues melt in hers, hereditary foemen
Forget their sword and slogan, kith and clan.
  'T was glory, once, to be a Roman:
She makes it glory, now, to be a man!

THE QUAKER WIDOW

THEE finds me in the garden, Hannah, — come in! 'T is kind of thee
To wait until the Friends were gone, who came to comfort me.
The still and quiet company a peace may give, indeed,
But blessed is the single heart that comes to us at need.

Come, sit thee down! Here is the bench where Benjamin would sit
On First-day afternoons in spring, and watch the swallows flit:
He loved to smell the sprouting box, and hear the pleasant bees
Go humming round the lilacs and through the apple-trees.

I think he loved the spring: not that he cared for flowers: most men
Think such things foolishness, — but we were first acquainted then,
One spring: the next he spoke his mind; the third I was his wife,
And in the spring (it happened so) our children entered life.

He was but seventy-five; I did not think to lay him yet
In Kennett graveyard, where at Monthly Meeting first we met.
The Father's mercy shows in this: 't is better I should be
Picked out to bear the heavy cross — alone in age — than he.

We 've lived together fifty years: it seems but one long day,
One quiet Sabbath of the heart, till he was called away;
And as we bring from Meeting-time a sweet contentment home,
So, Hannah, I have store of peace for all the days to come.

I mind (for I can tell thee now) how hard it was to know
If I had heard the spirit right, that told me I should go;
For father had a deep concern upon his mind that day,
But mother spoke for Benjamin, — she knew what best to say.

Then she was still: they sat awhile: at last she spoke again,
"The Lord incline thee to the right!" and "Thou shalt have him, Jane!"
My father said. I cried. Indeed, 't was not the least of shocks,
For Benjamin was Hicksite, and father Orthodox.

I thought of this ten years ago, when daughter Ruth we lost:
Her husband 's of the world, and yet I could not see her crossed.
She wears, thee knows, the gayest gowns, she hears a hireling priest —
Ah, dear! the cross was ours: her life 's a happy one, at least.

Perhaps she 'll wear a plainer dress when she 's as old as I, —
Would thee believe it, Hannah? once *I* felt temptation nigh!
My wedding-gown was ashen silk, too simple for my taste;
I wanted lace around the neck, and a ribbon at the waist.

How strange it seemed to sit with him upon the women's side!
I did not dare to lift my eyes: I felt more fear than pride,
Till, "in the presence of the Lord," he said, and then there came
A holy strength upon my heart, and I could say the same.

I used to blush when he came near, but then I showed no sign;
With all the meeting looking on, I held his hand in mine.
It seemed my bashfulness was gone, now I was his for life:
Thee knows the feeling, Hannah, — thee, too, hast been a wife.

As home we rode, I saw no fields look half so green as ours;
The woods were coming into leaf, the meadows full of flowers;
The neighbors met us in the lane, and every face was kind, —
'T is strange how lively everything comes back upon my mind.

I see, as plain as thee sits there, the wedding-dinner spread:
At our own table we were guests, with father at the head;
And Dinah Passmore helped us both, — 't was she stood up with me,
And Abner Jones with Benjamin, — and now they 're gone, all three!

It is not right to wish for death; the Lord disposes best.
His Spirit comes to quiet hearts, and fits them for His rest;
And that He halved our little flock was merciful, I see:
For Benjamin has two in heaven, and two are left with me.

Eusebius never cared to farm, — 't was not his call, in truth,
And I must rent the dear old place, and go to daughter Ruth.
Thee 'll say her ways are not like mine, — young people now-a-days
Have fallen sadly off, I think, from all the good old ways.

But Ruth is still a Friend at heart; she keeps the simple tongue,
The cheerful, kindly nature we loved when she was young;
And it was brought upon my mind, remembering her, of late,
That we on dress and outward things perhaps lay too much weight.

I once heard Jesse Kersey say, a spirit clothed with grace,
And pure almost as angels are, may have a homely face.
And dress may be of less account: the Lord will look within:
The soul it is that testifies of righteousness or sin.

Thee must n't be too hard on Ruth: she 's anxious I should go,
And she will do her duty as a daughter should, I know.
'T is hard to change so late in life, but we must be resigned:
The Lord looks down contentedly upon a willing mind.

THE SONG OF THE CAMP

"Give us a song!" the soldiers cried,
The outer trenches guarding,
When the heated guns of the camps allied
Grew weary of bombarding.

The dark Redan, in silent scoff,
Lay, grim and threatening, under;
And the tawny mound of the Malakoff
No longer belched its thunder.

There was a pause. A guardsman said,
"We storm the forts to-morrow;
Sing while we may, another day
Will bring enough of sorrow."

They lay along the battery's side,
Below the smoking cannon:
Brave hearts, from Severn and from Clyde,
And from the banks of Shannon.

They sang of love, and not of fame;
Forgot was Britain's glory:
Each heart recalled a different name,
But all sang "Annie Laurie."

Voice after voice caught up the song,
Until its tender passion
Rose like an anthem, rich and strong, —
Their battle-eve confession.

Dear girl, her name he dared not speak,
But, as the song grew louder,
Something upon the soldier's cheek
Washed off the stains of powder.

Beyond the darkening ocean burned
The bloody sunset's embers,
While the Crimean valleys learned
How English love remembers.

And once again a fire of hell
Rained on the Russian quarters,
With scream of shot, and burst of shell,
And bellowing of the mortars!

And Irish Nora's eyes are dim
For a singer, dumb and gory;
And English Mary mourns for him
Who sang of "Annie Laurie."

Sleep, soldiers! still in honored rest
Your truth and valor wearing:
The bravest are the tenderest, —
The loving are the daring.

FROM "THE SUNSHINE OF THE GODS"

AH, moment not to be purchased,
Not to be won by prayer,
Not by toil to be conquered,
But given, lest one despair,
By the Gods in wayward kindness,
Stay — thou art all too fair!
Hour of the dancing measures,
Sylph of the dew and rainbow,
Let us clutch thy shining hair!

For the mist is blown from the mind,
For the impotent yearning is over,
And the wings of the thoughts have power:
In the warmth and the glow creative
Existence mellows and ripens,
And a crowd of swift surprises
Sweetens the fortunate hour;
Till a shudder of rapture loosens
The tears that hang on the eyelids
Like a breeze-suspended shower,
With a sense of heavenly freshness
Blown from beyond the sunshine,
And the blood, like the sap of the roses,
Breaks into bud and flower.

'T is the Sunshine of the Gods,
The sudden light that quickens,
Unites the nimble forces,
And yokes the shy expression
To the thoughts that waited long, —
Waiting and wooing vainly:
But now they meet like lovers
In the time of willing increase,
Each warming each, and giving
The kiss that maketh strong:
And the mind feels fairest May-time
In the marriage of its passions,
For Thought is one with Speech,
In the Sunshine of the Gods,
And Speech is one with Song!
Then a rhythmic pulse makes order
In the troops of wandering fancies:
Held in soft subordination,
Lo! they follow, lead, or fly.
The fields of their feet are endless,
And the heights and the deeps are open
To the glance of the equal sky;
And the Masters sit no longer
In inaccessible distance,
But give to the haughtiest question,
Smiling, a sweet reply.

TO M. T.

THOUGH thy constant love I share,
  Yet its gift is rarer;
In my youth I thought thee fair:
  Thou art older and fairer!

Full of more than young delight
  Now day and night are;
For the presence, then so bright,
  Is closer, brighter.

In the haste of youth we miss
  Its best of blisses:
Sweeter than the stolen kiss
  Are the granted kisses.

Dearer than the words that hide
  The love abiding,
Are the words that fondly chide,
  When love needs chiding.

Higher than the perfect song
  For which love longeth,
Is the tender fear of wrong,
  That never wrongeth.

She whom youth alone makes dear
  May awhile seem nearer:
Thou art mine so many a year,
  The older, the dearer!

Julia Caroline Ripley Dorr

THE FALLOW FIELD

THE sun comes up and the sun goes down;
The night mist shroudeth the sleeping town;
But if it be dark or if it be day,
If the tempests beat or the breezes play,
Still here on this upland slope I lie,
Looking up to the changeful sky.

Naught am I but a fallow field;
Never a crop my acres yield.
Over the wall at my right hand
Stately and green the corn-blades stand,

And I hear at my left the flying feet
Of the winds that rustle the bending wheat.

Often while yet the morn is red
I list for our master's eager tread.
He smiles at the young corn's towering height,
He knows the wheat is a goodly sight,
But he glances not at the fallow field
Whose idle acres no wealth may yield.

Sometimes the shout of the harvesters
The sleeping pulse of my being stirs,
And as one in a dream I seem to feel
The sweep and the rush of the swinging steel,
Or I catch the sound of the gay refrain
As they heap their wains with the golden grain.

Yet, O my neighbors, be not too proud,
Though on every tongue your praise is loud.
Our mother Nature is kind to me,
And I am beloved by bird and bee,
And never a child that passes by
But turns upon me a grateful eye.

Over my head the skies are blue;
I have my share of the rain and dew;
I bask like you in the summer sun
When the long bright days pass, one by one,
And calm as yours is my sweet repose
Wrapped in the warmth of the winter snows.

For little our loving mother cares
Which the corn or the daisy bears,
Which is rich with the ripening wheat,
Which with the violet's breath is sweet,
Which is red with the clover bloom,
Or which for the wild sweet-fern makes room.

Useless under the summer sky
Year after year men say I lie.
Little they know what strength of mine
I give to the trailing blackberry vine;
Little they know how the wild grape grows,
Or how my life-blood flushes the rose.

Little they think of the cups I fill
For the mosses creeping under the hill;
Little they think of the feast I spread
For the wild wee creatures that must be fed:
Squirrel and butterfly, bird and bee,
And the creeping things that no eye may see.

Lord of the harvest, thou dost know
How the summers and winters go.
Never a ship sails east or west
Laden with treasures at my behest,
Yet my being thrills to the voice of God
When I give my gold to the golden-rod.

O EARTH! ART THOU NOT WEARY?

O Earth! art thou not weary of thy graves?
Dear, patient mother Earth, upon thy breast
How are they heaped from farthest east to west!
From the dim north, where the wild storm-wind raves
O'er the cold surge that chills the shore it laves,
To sunlit isles by softest seas caressed,
Where roses bloom alway and song-birds nest,
How thick they lie — like flecks upon the waves!
There is no mountain-top so far and high,
No desert so remote, no vale so deep,
No spot by man so long untenanted,
But the pale moon, slow marching up the sky,
Sees over some lone grave the shadows creep!
O Earth! art thou not weary of thy dead?

WITH A ROSE FROM CONWAY CASTLE

On hoary Conway's battlemented height,
O poet-heart, I pluck for thee a rose!
Through arch and court the sweet wind wandering goes;
Round each high tower the rooks in airy flight
Circle and wheel, all bathed in amber light;
Low at my feet the winding river flows;
Valley and town, entranced in deep repose,
War doth no more appall, nor foes affright.
Thou knowest how softly on the castle walls,
Where mosses creep, and ivies far and free

Fling forth their pennants to the freshening breeze,
Like God's own benison this sunshine falls.
Therefore, O friend, across the sundering seas,
Fair Conway sends this sweet wild rose to thee !

TWO PATHS

A PATH across a meadow fair and sweet,
Where clover-blooms the lithesome grasses greet,
A path worn smooth by his impetuous feet.

A straight, swift path — and at its end, a star
Gleaming behind the lilac's fragrant bar,
And her soft eyes, more luminous by far !

A path across the meadow fair and sweet,
Still sweet and fair where blooms and grasses meet —
A path worn smooth by his reluctant feet.

A long, straight path — and, at its end, a gate
Behind whose bars she doth in silence wait
To keep the tryst, if he come soon or late !

John Williamson Palmer

STONEWALL JACKSON'S WAY

COME, stack arms, men; pile on the rails;
Stir up the camp-fire bright !
No growling if the canteen fails:
We 'll make a roaring night.
Here Shenandoah brawls along,
There burly Blue Ridge echoes strong,
To swell the Brigade's rousing song,
Of Stonewall Jackson's Way.

We see him now — the queer slouched hat,
Cocked o'er his eye askew;
The shrewd, dry smile; the speech so pat,
So calm, so blunt, so true.
The "Blue-light Elder" knows 'em well:
Says he, "That 's Banks; he 's fond of shell.
Lord save his soul ! we 'll give him — ;" Well,
That 's Stonewall Jackson's Way.

Silence ! Ground arms ! Kneel all ! Caps off !
Old Massa 's going to pray.
Strangle the fool that dares to scoff:
Attention ! — it 's his way.
Appealing from his native sod,
In forma pauperis to God,
"Lay bare Thine arm ! Stretch forth Thy rod:
Amen !" — That 's Stonewall's Way.

He 's in the saddle now. Fall in !
Steady ! the whole brigade.
Hill 's at the ford, cut off; we 'll win
His way out, ball and blade.
What matter if our shoes are worn ?
What matter if our feet are torn ?
Quick step ! we 're with him before morn:
That 's Stonewall Jackson's Way.

The sun's bright lances rout the mists
Of morning; and — By George !
Here 's Longstreet, struggling in the lists,
Hemmed in an ugly gorge.
Pope and his Dutchmen ! — whipped before.
"Bay'nets and grape !" hear Stonewall roar.
Charge, Stuart ! Pay off Ashby's score,
In Stonewall Jackson's Way.

Ah, Maiden ! wait and watch and yearn
For news of Stonewall's band.
Ah, Widow ! read, with eyes that burn,
That ring upon thy hand.
Ah, Wife ! sew on, pray on, hope on !
Thy life shall not be all forlorn.
The foe had better ne'er been born,
That gets in Stonewall's Way.

THE FIGHT AT THE SAN JACINTO

"Now for a brisk and cheerful fight !"
Said Harman, big and droll,
As he coaxed his flint and steel for a light,
And puffed at his cold clay bowl;

"For we are a skulking lot," says he,
"Of land-thieves hereabout,
And these bold señores, two to one,
Have come to smoke us out."

Santa Anna and Castillòn,
Almonte brave and gay,
Portilla red from Goliad,
And Cos with his smart array.
Dulces and cigaritos,
And the light guitar, ting-tum!
Sant' Anna courts siesta,
And Sam Houston taps his drum.

The buck stands still in the timber —
"Is it patter of nuts that fall?"
The foal of the wild mare whinnies —
Did he hear the Comanche call?
In the brake by the crawling bayou
The slinking she-wolves howl;
And the mustang's snort in the river sedge
Has startled the paddling fowl.

A soft, low tap, and a muffled tap,
And a roll not loud nor long —
We would not break Sant' Anna's nap,
Nor spoil Almonte's song.
Saddles and knives and rifles!
Lord! but the men were glad
When Deaf Smith muttered "Alamo!"
And Karnes hissed "Goliad!"

The drummer tucked his sticks in his belt,
And the fifer gripped his gun.
Oh, for one free, wild, Texan yell,
As we took the slope in a run!
But never a shout nor a shot we spent,
Nor an oath nor a prayer, that day,
Till we faced the bravos, eye to eye,
And then we blazed away.

Then we knew the rapture of Ben Milam,
And the glory that Travis made,
With Bowie's lunge, and Crockett's shot,
And Fannin's dancing blade;
And the heart of the fighter, bounding free
In his joy so hot and mad —
When Millard charged for Alamo,
Lamar for Goliad.

Deaf Smith rode straight, with reeking spur,
Into the shock and rout:
"I 've hacked and burned the bayou bridge;
There 's no sneak's back-way out!"
Muzzle or butt for Goliad,
Pistol and blade and fist!
Oh, for the knife that never glanced,
And the gun that never missed!

Dulces and cigaritos,
Song and the mandolin!
That gory swamp is a gruesome grove
To dance fandangoes in.
We bridged the bog with the sprawling herd
That fell in that frantic rout;
We slew and slew till the sun set red,
And the Texan star flashed out.

THE MARYLAND BATTALION

SPRUCE Macaronis, and pretty to see,
Tidy and dapper and gallant were we;
Blooded, fine gentlemen, proper and tall,
Bold in a fox-hunt and gay at a ball;
Prancing soldados so martial and bluff,
Billets for bullets, in scarlet and buff —
But our cockades were clasped with a mother's low prayer,
And the sweethearts that braided the sword-knots were fair.

There was grummer of drums humming hoarse in the hills,
And the bugle sang fanfaron down by the mills;
By Flatbush the bagpipes were droning amain,
And keen cracked the rifles in Martense 's lane;
For the Hessians were flecking the hedges with red,
And the grenadiers' tramp marked the roll of the dead.

Three to one, flank and rear, flashed the files of St. George,
The fierce gleam of their steel as the glow of a forge.
The brutal boom-boom of their swart cannoneers

Was sweet music compared with the taunt of their cheers —
For the brunt of their onset, our crippled array,
And the light of God's leading gone out in the fray!

Oh, the rout on the left and the tug on the right!
The mad plunge of the charge and the wreck of the flight!
When the cohorts of Grant held stout Stirling at strain,
And the mongrels of Hesse went tearing the slain;
When at Freeke's Mill the flumes and the sluices ran red,
And the dead choked the dyke and the marsh choked the dead!

"O Stirling, good Stirling! how long must we wait?
Shall the shout of your trumpet unleash us too late?
Have you never a dash for brave Mordecai Gist,
With his heart in his throat, and his blade in his fist?
Are we good for no more than to prance in a ball,
When the drums beat the charge and the clarions call?"

Tralara! Tralara! Now praise we the Lord
For the clang of His call and the flash of His sword!
Tralara! Tralara! Now forward to die;
For the banner, hurrah! and for sweethearts, good-bye!
"Four hundred wild lads!" Maybe so. I 'll be bound
'T will be easy to count us, face up, on the ground.
If we hold the road open, tho' Death take the toll,
We 'll be missed on parade when the States call the roll —
When the flags meet in peace and the guns are at rest,
And fair Freedom is singing Sweet Home in the West.

Richard Henry Stoddard

THE WITCH'S WHELP[1]

ALONG the shore the slimy brine-pits yawn,
Covered with thick green scum; the billows rise,
And fill them to the brim with clouded foam,
And then subside, and leave the scum again.
The ribbëd sand is full of hollow gulfs,
Where monsters from the waters come and lie.
Great serpents bask at noon along the rocks,
To me no terror; coil on coil they roll
Back to their holes before my flying feet.
The Dragon of the Sea, my mother's god,
Enormous Setebos, comes here to sleep;
Him I molest not; when he flaps his wing
A whirlwind rises, when he swims the deep
It threatens to engulf the trembling isle.
Sometimes when winds do blow, and clouds are dark,
I seek the blasted wood whose barkless trunks
Are bleached with summer suns; the creaking trees
Stoop down to me, and swing me right and left
Through crashing limbs, but not a jot care I.
The thunder breaks above, and in their lairs
The panthers roar; from out the stormy clouds
Whose hearts are fire, sharp lightnings rain around
And split the oaks; not faster lizards run
Before the snake up the slant trunks than I,
Not faster down, sliding with hands and feet.
I stamp upon the ground, and adders rouse,
Sharp-eyed, with poisonous fangs; beneath the leaves
They couch, or under rocks, and roots of trees
Felled by the winds; through briery undergrowth

[1] See BIOGRAPHICAL NOTE, p. 824.

They slide with hissing tongues, beneath my feet
To writhe, or in my fingers squeezed to death.
There is a wild and solitary pine,
Deep in the meadows; all the island birds
From far and near fly there, and learn new songs.
Something imprisoned in its wrinkled bark
Wails for its freedom; when the bigger light
Burns in mid-heaven, and dew elsewhere is dried,
There it still falls; the quivering leaves are tongues,
And load the air with syllables of woe.
One day I thrust my spear within a cleft
No wider than its point, and something shrieked,
And falling cones did pelt me sharp as hail:
I picked the seeds that grew between their plates,
And strung them round my neck with sea-mew eggs.
Hard by are swamps and marshes, reedy fens
Knee-deep in water; monsters wade therein
Thick-set with plated scales; sometimes in troops
They crawl on slippery banks; sometimes they lash
The sluggish waves among themselves at war.
Often I heave great rocks from off the crags,
And crush their bones; often I push my spear
Deep in their drowsy eyes, at which they howl
And chase me inland; then I mount their humps
And prick them back again, unwieldy, slow.
At night the wolves are howling round the place,
And bats sail there athwart the silver light,
Flapping their wings; by day in hollow trees
They hide, and slink into the gloom of dens.
We live, my mother Sycorax and I,
In caves with bloated toads and crested snakes.
She can make charms, and philters, and brew storms,
And call the great Sea Dragon from his deeps.
Nothing of this know I, nor care to know.
Give me the milk of goats in gourds or shells,
The flesh of birds and fish, berries and fruit,
Nor want I more, save all day long to lie,
And hear, as now, the voices of the sea.

MELODIES AND CATCHES

SONGS

How are songs begot and bred?
How do golden measures flow?
From the heart, or from the head?
Happy Poet, let me know.

Tell me first how folded flowers
Bud and bloom in vernal bowers;
How the south wind shapes its tune,
The harper, he, of June.

None may answer, none may know,
Winds and flowers come and go,
And the selfsame canons bind
Nature and the Poet's mind.

THE SEA

THROUGH the night, through the night,
In the saddest unrest,
Wrapt in white, all in white,
With her babe on her breast,
Walks the mother so pale,
Staring out on the gale,
Through the night.

Through the night, through the night,
Where the sea lifts the wreck,
Land in sight, close in sight,
On the surf-flooded deck,
Stands the father so brave,
Driving on to his grave,
Through the night.

BIRDS

BIRDS are singing round my window,
Tunes the sweetest ever heard,
And I hang my cage there daily,
But I never catch a bird.

So with thoughts my brain is peopled,
And they sing there all day long:
But they will not fold their pinions
In the little cage of Song!

THE SKY

THE sky is a drinking-cup,
That was overturned of old,
And it pours in the eyes of men
Its wine of airy gold.

We drink that wine all day,
Till the last drop is drained up,
And are lighted off to bed
By the jewels in the cup!

THE SHADOW

THERE is but one great sorrow,
All over the wide, wide world;
But that in turn must come to all —
The Shadow that moves behind the pall,
A flag that never is furled.

Till he in his marching crosses
The threshold of the door,
Usurps a place in the inner room,
Where he broods in the awful hush and gloom,
Till he goes, and comes no more —

Save this there is no sorrow,
Whatever we think we feel;
But when Death comes all 's over:
'T is a blow that we never recover,
A wound that never will heal.

A CATCH

ONCE the head is gray,
And the heart is dead,
There 's no more to do:
Make the man a bed
Six foot under ground,
There he 'll slumber sound.

Golden was my hair,
And my heart did beat
To the viol's voice
Like the dancers' feet.
Not colder now his blood
Who died before the flood.

Fair, and fond, and false,
Mother, wife, and maid,
Never lived a man
They have not betrayed.
None shall 'scape my mirth
But old Mother Earth.

Safely housed with her,
With no company
But my brother Worm,
Who will feed on me,
I shall slumber sound,
Deep down under ground.

THE FLIGHT OF YOUTH

THERE are gains for all our losses,
There are balms for all our pain:
But when youth, the dream, departs,
It takes something from our hearts,
And it never comes again.

We are stronger, and are better,
Under manhood's sterner reign:
Still we feel that something sweet
Followed youth, with flying feet,
And will never come again.

Something beautiful is vanished,
And we sigh for it in vain:
We behold it everywhere,
On the earth, and in the air,
But it never comes again.

ORIENTAL SONGS

THE DIVAN

A LITTLE maid of Astrakan,
An idol on a silk divan;
She sits so still, and never speaks,
She holds a cup of mine;
'T is full of wine, and on her cheeks
Are stains and smears of wine.

Thou little girl of Astrakan,
I join thee on the silk divan:
There is no need to seek the land,
The rich bazaars where rubies shine;
For mines are in that little hand,
And on those little cheeks of thine.

WINE AND DEW

YOU may drink to your leman in gold,
In a great golden goblet of wine;

She 's as ripe as the wine, and as bold
As the glare of the gold:
But this little lady of mine,
I will not profane her in wine.
I go where the garden so still is
(The moon raining through),
To pluck the white bowls of the lilies,
And drink her in dew!

THE JAR

Day and night my thoughts incline
To the blandishments of wine:
Jars were made to drain, I think,
Wine, I know, was made to drink.

When I die, (the day be far!)
Should the potters make a jar
Out of this poor clay of mine,
Let the jar be filled with wine!

THE FALCON

I am a white falcon, hurrah!
My home is the mountains so high;
But away o'er the lands and the waters,
Wherever I please, I can fly.

I wander from city to city,
I dart from the wave to the cloud,
And when I am dead I shall slumber
With my own white wings for a shroud.

ARAB SONG

Break thou my heart, ah, break it,
If such thy pleasure be;
Thy will is mine, what say I?
'T is more than mine to me.

And if my life offend thee,
My passion and my pain,
Take thou my life, ah, take it,
But spare me thy disdain!

THE LOVER

(JAPAN)

It is dark and lonesome here,
Beneath the windy eaves: —
The cold, cold ground my bed,
My coverlet dead leaves,
My only bedfellow
The rain that wets my sleeves!

If it be day, or night,
I know not, cannot say,
For I am like a child
Who has lost his troubled way,
Till I see the white of the hoar-frost —
Then I know it is day!

I touch the silent strings,
The broken lute complains;
The sweets of love are gone,
The bitterness remains,
Like the memory of summer
In the time of the long rains!

A few more days and nights,
My tears will cease to flow;
For I hear a voice within,
Which tells me I shall go,
Before the morning hoar-frost
Becomes the night of snow!

ABRAHAM LINCOLN

Not as when some great Captain falls
In battle, where his Country calls,
Beyond the struggling lines
That push his dread designs

To doom, by some stray ball struck dead:
Or, in the last charge, at the head
Of his determined men,
Who *must* be victors then.

Nor as when sink the civic great,
The safer pillars of the State,
Whose calm, mature, wise words
Suppress the need of swords.

With no such tears as e'er were shed
Above the noblest of our dead
Do we to-day deplore
The Man that is no more.

Our sorrow hath a wider scope,
Too strange for fear, too vast for hope,
A wonder, blind and dumb,
That waits — what is to come!

Not more astounded had we been
If Madness, that dark night, unseen,
Had in our chambers crept,
And murdered while we slept!

We woke to find a mourning earth,
Our Lares shivered on the hearth,
The roof-tree fallen, all
That could affright, appall!

Such thunderbolts, in other lands,
Have smitten the rod from royal hands,
But spared, with us, till now,
Each laurelled Cæsar's brow.

No Cæsar he whom we lament,
A Man without a precedent,
Sent, it would seem, to do
His work, and perish, too.

Not by the weary cares of State,
The endless tasks, which will not wait,
Which, often done in vain,
Must yet be done again:

Not in the dark, wild tide of war,
Which rose so high, and rolled so far,
Sweeping from sea to sea
In awful anarchy:

Four fateful years of mortal strife,
Which slowly drained the nation's life,
(Yet for each drop that ran
There sprang an armëd man!)

Not then; but when, by measures meet,
By victory, and by defeat,
By courage, patience, skill,
The people's fixed "*We will!*"

Had pierced, had crushed Rebellion dead,
Without a hand, without a head,
At last, when all was well,
He fell, O how he fell!

The time, the place, the stealing shape,
The coward shot, the swift escape,
The wife — the widow's scream, —
It is a hideous Dream!

A dream? What means this pageant, then?
These multitudes of solemn men,
Who speak not when they meet,
But throng the silent street?

The flags half-mast that late so high
Flaunted at each new victory?
(The stars no brightness shed,
But bloody looks the red!)

The black festoons that stretch for miles,
And turn the streets to funeral aisles?
(No house too poor to show
The nation's badge of woe.)

The cannon's sudden, sullen boom,
The bells that toll of death and doom,
The rolling of the drums,
The dreadful car that comes?

Cursed be the hand that fired the shot,
The frenzied brain that hatched the plot,
Thy country's Father slain
By thee, thou worse than Cain!

Tyrants have fallen by such as thou,
And good hath followed — may it now!
(God lets bad instruments
Produce the best events.)

But he, the man we mourn to-day,
No tyrant was: so mild a sway
In one such weight who bore
Was never known before.

Cool should he be, of balanced powers,
The ruler of a race like ours,
Impatient, headstrong, wild,
The Man to guide the Child.

And this *he* was, who most unfit
(So hard the sense of God to hit,)
Did seem to fill his place;
With such a homely face,

Such rustic manners, speech uncouth,
(That somehow blundered out the truth,)
Untried, untrained to bear
The more than kingly care.

Ah! And his genius put to scorn
The proudest in the purple born,
Whose wisdom never grew
To what, untaught, he knew,

The People, of whom he was one:
No gentleman, like Washington,
(Whose bones, methinks, make room,
To have him in their tomb!)

A laboring man, with horny hands,
Who swung the axe, who tilled his lands,
Who shrank from nothing new,
But did as poor men do.

One of the People! Born to be
Their curious epitome;
To share yet rise above
Their shifting hate and love.

Common his mind, (it seemed so then,)
His thoughts the thoughts of other men:
Plain were his words, and poor,
But now they will endure!

No hasty fool, of stubborn will,
But prudent, cautious, pliant still;
Who since his work was good
Would do it as he could.

Doubting, was not ashamed to doubt,
And, lacking prescience, went without:
Often appeared to halt,
And was, of course, at fault;

Heard all opinions, nothing loath,
And, loving both sides, angered both:
Was — *not* like Justice, blind,
But watchful, clement, kind.

No hero this of Roman mould,
Nor like our stately sires of old:
Perhaps he was not great,
But he preserved the State!

O honest face, which all men knew!
O tender heart, but known to few!
O wonder of the age,
Cut off by tragic rage!

Peace! Let the long procession come,
For hark, the mournful, muffled drum,
The trumpet's wail afar,
And see, the awful car!

Peace! Let the sad procession go,
While cannon boom and bells toll slow.
And go, thou sacred car,
Bearing our woe afar!

Go, darkly borne, from State to State,
Whose loyal, sorrowing cities wait
To honor all they can
The dust of that good man.

Go, grandly borne, with such a train
As greatest kings might die to gain.
The just, the wise, the brave,
Attend thee to the grave.

And you, the soldiers of our wars,
Bronzed veterans, grim with noble scars,
Salute him once again,
Your late commander — slain!

Yes, let your tears indignant fall,
But leave your muskets on the wall;
Your country needs you now
Beside the forge — the plough.

(When Justice shall unsheathe her brand, —
If Mercy may not stay her hand,
Nor would we have it so, —
She must direct the blow.)

And you, amid the master-race,
Who seem so strangely out of place,
Know ye who cometh? He
Who hath declared ye free.

Bow while the body passes — nay,
Fall on your knees, and weep, and pray!
Weep, weep — I would ye might —
Your poor black faces white!

And, children, you must come in bands,
With garlands in your little hands,
Of blue and white and red,
To strew before the dead.

So sweetly, sadly, sternly goes
The Fallen to his last repose.
Beneath no mighty dome,
But in his modest home;

The churchyard where his children rest,
The quiet spot that suits him best,
There shall his grave be made,
And there his bones be laid.

And there his countrymen shall come,
With memory proud, with pity dumb,
And strangers far and near,
For many and many a year.

For many a year and many an age,
While History on her ample page
The virtues shall enroll
Of that Paternal Soul.

ADSUM

DECEMBER 23–24, 1863

THE Angel came by night
(Such angels still come down),
And like a winter cloud
Passed over London town;
Along its lonesome streets,
Where Want had ceased to weep,
Until it reached a house
Where a great man lay asleep;
The man of all his time
Who knew the most of men,
The soundest head and heart,
The sharpest, kindest pen.
It paused beside his bed,
And whispered in his ear;
He never turned his head,
But answered, "I am here."

Into the night they went.
At morning, side by side,
They gained the sacred Place
Where the greatest Dead abide.
Where grand old Homer sits
In godlike state benign;
Where broods in endless thought
The awful Florentine;
Where sweet Cervantes walks,
A smile on his grave face;
Where gossips quaint Montaigne,
The wisest of his race;
Where Goethe looks through all
With that calm eye of his;
Where — little seen but Light —
The only Shakespeare is!
When the new Spirit came,
They asked him, drawing near,
"Art thou become like us?"
He answered, "I am here."

AN OLD SONG REVERSED

"THERE are gains for all our losses."
So I said when I was young.
If I sang that song again,
'T would not be with that refrain,
Which but suits an idle tongue.

Youth has gone, and hope gone with it,
Gone the strong desire for fame.
Laurels are not for the old.
Take them, lads. Give Senex gold.
What 's an everlasting name?

When my life was in its summer
One fair woman liked my looks:
Now that Time has driven his plough
In deep furrows on my brow,
I 'm no more in her good books.

"There are gains for all our losses?"
Grave beside the wintry sea,
Where my child is, and my heart,
For they would not live apart,
What has been your gain to me?

No, the words I sang were idle,
And will ever so remain:
Death, and Age, and vanished Youth
All declare this bitter truth,
There 's a loss for every gain!

MORS ET VITA

"UNDER the roots of the roses,
Down in the dark, rich mould,
The dust of my dear one reposes
Like a spark which night incloses
When the ashes of day are cold."

"Under the awful wings
Which brood over land and sea,
And whose shadows nor lift nor flee, —
This is the order of things,
And hath been from of old:
First production,
And last destruction;
So the pendulum swings,
While cradles are rocked and bells are tolled."

"*Not* under the roots of the roses,
But under the luminous wings
Of the King of kings
The soul of my love reposes,
With the light of morn in her eyes,
Where the Vision of Life discloses
Life that sleeps not nor dies."

"Under or over the skies
What is it that never dies?
Spirit — if such there be —
Whom no one hath seen nor heard,
We do not acknowledge thee;
For, spoken or written word,
Thou art but a dream, a breath;
Certain is nothing but Death!"

A GAZELLE

LAST night, when my tired eyes were shut with sleep,
I saw the one I love, and heard her speak, —
Heard, in the listening watches of the night,
The sweet words melting from her sweeter lips:
But what she said, or seemed to say, to me
I have forgotten, though, till morning broke,
I kept repeating her melodious words.
Long, long may Jami's eyes be blest with sleep,
Like that which last night stole him from himself, —
That perfect rest which, closing his tired lids,
Disclosed the hidden beauty of his love,
And, filling his soul with music all the while,
Imposed forgetfulness, instructing him
That silence is more significant of love
Than all the burning words in lovers' songs!

THE FLIGHT OF THE ARROW

THE life of man
Is an arrow's flight,
Out of darkness
Into light,
And out of light
Into darkness again;
Perhaps to pleasure,
Perhaps to pain!

There must be Something,
Above, or below;
Somewhere unseen
A mighty Bow,
A Hand that tires not,
A sleepless Eye
That sees the arrows
Fly, and fly;
One who knows
Why we live — and die.

Margaret Junkin Preston

THE VISION OF THE SNOW

"SHE has gone to be with the angels;"
So they had always said
To the little questioner asking
Of his fair, young mother, dead.

They had never told of the darkness
Of the sorrowful, silent tomb,
Nor scared the sensitive spirit
By linking a thought of gloom

With the girl-like, beautiful being,
Who patiently from her breast,
Had laid him in baby-sweetness,
To pass to her early rest.

And when he would lisp — "Where is she?"
Missing the mother-kiss,
They answered — "Away in a country
That is lovelier far than this: —

"A land all a-shine with beauty
Too pure for our mortal sight,
Where the darling ones who have left us
Are walking in robes of white."

And with eagerest face he would listen,
His tremulous lips apart,
Till the thought of the Beautiful Country
Haunted his yearning heart.

One morn, as he gazed from the window,
A miracle of surprise,
A marvellous, mystic vision
Dazzled his wondering eyes.

Born where the winter's harshness
Is tempered with spring-tide glow,
The delicate Southern nursling
Never had seen the snow.

And clasping his childish fingers,
He turned with a flashing brow,
And cried — "We have got to heaven —
Show me my mother now!"

THE HERO OF THE COMMUNE

"GARÇON! You — *you*
Snared along with this cursëd crew?
(Only a child, and yet so bold,
Scarcely as much as ten years old!)

Do you hear? do you know
Why the gendarmes put you there, in the row,
You, with those Commune wretches tall,
With your face to the wall?"

"*Know?* To be sure I know! why not?
We 're here to be shot;
And there, by the pillar 's the very spot,
Fighting for France, my father fell:
Ah, well!
That 's just the way *I* would choose to fall,
With my back to the wall!"

("Sacré! Fair, open fight, I say,
Is something right gallant in its way,
And fine for warming the blood; but who
Wants wolfish work like this to do?
Bah! 't is a butcher's business!) *How?*
(The boy is beckoning to me now:
I knew that his poor child's heart would fail,
. . . Yet his cheek 's not pale:)
Quick! say your say, for don't you see,
When the church-clock yonder tolls out *Three*,
You 're all to be shot?
. . . *What?*
'*Excuse you one moment?*' O, ho, ho!
Do you think to fool a gendarme so?"

"But, sir, here 's a watch that a friend, one day
(My father's friend), just over the way,
Lent me; and if you 'll let me free,
— It still lacks seven minutes of *Three*, —
I 'll come, on the word of a soldier's son,
Straight back into line, when my errand 's done."

"Ha, ha! No doubt of it! Off! Begone!
(Now, good Saint Denis, speed him on!
The work will be easier since *he* 's saved;
For I hardly see how I could have braved
The ardor of that innocent eye,
As he stood and heard,
While I gave the word,
Dooming him like a dog to die.")

"In time! Well, thanks, that my desire
Was granted; and now, I am ready: —
Fire!
One word! — that 's all!
— You 'll let me turn my *back* to the wall?"

"Parbleu! Come out of the line, I say,
Come out! (who said that his name was *Ney?*)
Ha! France will hear of him yet one day!"

A GRAVE IN HOLLYWOOD CEMETERY, RICHMOND

(J. R. T.)

I READ the marble-lettered name,
And half in bitterness I said:
"As Dante from Ravenna came,
Our poet came from exile — dead."
And yet, had it been asked of him
Where he would rather lay his head,
This spot he would have chosen. Dim
The city's hum drifts o'er his grave,
And green above the hollies wave
Their jagged leaves, as when a boy,
On blissful summer afternoons,
He came to sing the birds his runes,
And tell the river of his joy.

Who dreams that in his wanderings wide,
By stern misfortunes tossed and driven,
His soul's electric strands were riven
From home and country? Let betide
What might, what would, his boast, his pride,
Was in his stricken mother-land,
That could but bless and bid him go,
Because no crust was in her hand
To stay her children's need. We know
The mystic cable sank too deep
For surface storm or stress to strain,
Or from his answering heart to keep
The spark from flashing back again!

Think of the thousand mellow rhymes,
The pure idyllic passion-flowers,
Wherewith, in far gone, happier times,
He garlanded this South of ours.
Provençal-like, he wandered long,
And sang at many a stranger's board,
Yet 't was Virginia's name that poured
The tenderest pathos through his song.
We owe the Poet praise and tears,
Whose ringing ballad sends the brave,
Bold Stuart riding down the years —
What have we given him? Just a grave!

Stephen Collins Foster

MY OLD KENTUCKY HOME, GOOD-NIGHT

THE sun shines bright in the old Kentucky home;
'T is summer, the darkeys are gay;
The corn-top 's ripe, and the meadow 's in the bloom,
While the birds make music all the day.
The young folks roll on the little cabin floor,
All merry, all happy and bright;
By-'n'-by hard times comes a-knocking at the door: —
Then my old Kentucky home, good-night!

Weep no more, my lady,
O, weep no more to-day!
We will sing one song for the old Kentucky home,
For the old Kentucky home, far away.

They hunt no more for the possum and the coon,
On the meadow, the hill, and the shore;
They sing no more by the glimmer of the moon,
On the bench by the old cabin door.
The day goes by like a shadow o'er the heart,
With sorrow, where all was delight;
The time has come when the darkeys have to part: —
Then my old Kentucky home, good-night!

The head must bow, and the back will have to bend,
Wherever the darkey may go;
A few more days, and the trouble all will end,
In the field where the sugar-canes grow.
A few more days for to tote the weary load, —
No matter, 't will never be light;
A few more days till we totter on the road: —
Then my old Kentucky home, good-night!

Weep no more, my lady,
O, weep no more to-day!
We will sing one song for the old Kentucky home,
For the old Kentucky home, far away.

OLD FOLKS AT HOME

WAY down upon de Swanee Ribber,
Far, far away,
Dere 's wha my heart is turning ebber,
Dere 's wha de old folks stay.
All up and down de whole creation
Sadly I roam,
Still longing for de old plantation,
And for de old folks at home.

All de world am sad and dreary,
Ebery where I roam;
Oh, darkeys, how my heart grows weary,
Far from de old folks at home!

All round de little farm I wandered
When I was young,
Den many happy days I squandered,
Many de songs I sung.
When I was playing wid my brudder
Happy was I;
Oh, take me to my kind old mudder!
Dere let me live and die.

One little hut among de bushes,
One dat I love,
Still sadly to my memory rushes,
No matter where I rove.
When will I see de bees a-humming
All round de comb?
When will I hear de banjo tumming,
Down in my good old home?

All de world am sad and dreary,
Eberywhere I roam,
Oh, darkeys, how my heart grows weary,
Far from de old folks at home!

MASSA 'S IN DE COLD GROUND

Round de meadows am a-ringing
De darkeys' mournful song,
While de mocking-bird am singing,
Happy as de day am long.
Where de ivy am a-creeping,
O'er de grassy mound,
Dere old massa am a-sleeping,
Sleeping in de cold, cold ground.

Down in de corn-field
Hear dat mournful sound:
All de darkeys am a-weeping, —
Massa 's in de cold, cold ground.

When de autumn leaves were falling,
When de days were cold,
'T was hard to hear old massa calling,
Cayse he was so weak and old.
Now de orange tree am blooming
On de sandy shore,
Now de summer days am coming, —
Massa nebber calls no more.

Massa make de darkeys love him,
Cayse he was so kind;
Now dey sadly weep above him,
Mourning cayse he leave dem behind.
I cannot work before to-morrow,
Cayse de tear-drop flow;
I try to drive away my sorrow,
Pickin' on de old banjo.

Down in de corn-field
Hear dat mournful sound:
All de darkeys am a-weeping, —
Massa 's in de cold, cold ground.

Rose Terry Cooke

SEGOVIA AND MADRID

It sings to me in sunshine,
It whispers all day long,
My heartache like an echo
Repeats the wistful song:
Only a quaint old love-lilt,
Wherein my life is hid, —
"My body is in Segovia,
But my soul is in Madrid!"

I dream, and wake, and wonder,
For dream and day are one,
Alight with vanished faces,
And days forever done.
They smile and shine around me
As long ago they did;
For my body is in Segovia,
But my soul is in Madrid!

Through inland hills and forests
I hear the ocean breeze,
The creak of straining cordage,
The rush of mighty seas,
The lift of angry billows
Through which a swift keel slid;
For my body is in Segovia,
But my soul is in Madrid.

O fair-haired little darlings
Who bore my heart away!
A wide and woful ocean
Between us roars to-day;
Yet am I close beside you
Though time and space forbid;
My body is in Segovia,
But my soul is in Madrid.

If I were once in heaven,
There would be no more sea;
My heart would cease to wander,
My sorrows cease to be;
My sad eyes sleep forever,
In dust and daisies hid,
And my body leave Segovia.
— Would my soul forget Madrid?

ARACHNE

I watch her in the corner there,
As, restless, bold, and unafraid,
She slips and floats along the air
Till all her subtile house is made.

Her home, her bed, her daily food,
All from that hidden store she draws;

She fashions it and knows it good,
By instinct's strong and sacred laws.

No tenuous threads to weave her nest,
She seeks and gathers there or here;
But spins it from her faithful breast,
Renewing still, till leaves are sere.

Then, worn with toil, and tired of life,
In vain her shining traps are set.
Her frost hath hushed the insect strife
And gilded flies her charm forget.

But swinging in the snares she spun,
She sways to every wintry wind:
Her joy, her toil, her errand done,
Her corse the sport of storms unkind.

Poor sister of the spinster clan!
I too from out my store within
My daily life and living plan,
My home, my rest, my pleasure spin.

I know thy heart when heartless hands
Sweep all that hard-earned web away:
Destroy its pearled and glittering bands,
And leave thee homeless by the way.

I know thy peace when all is done.
Each anchored thread, each tiny knot,
Soft shining in the autumn sun;
A sheltered, silent, tranquil lot.

I know what thou hast never known,—
Sad presage to a soul allowed,—
That not for life I spin, alone,
But day by day I spin my shroud.

BLUEBEARD'S CLOSET

Fasten the chamber!
Hide the red key;
Cover the portal,
That eyes may not see.
Get thee to market,
To wedding and prayer;
Labor or revel,
The chamber is there!

In comes a stranger—
"Thy pictures how fine,
Titian or Guido,
Whose is the sign?"
Looks he behind them?
Ah! have a care!
"Here is a finer."
The chamber is there!

Fair spreads the banquet,
Rich the array;
See the bright torches
Mimicking day;
When harp and viol
Thrill the soft air,
Comes a light whisper:
The chamber is there!

Marble and painting,
Jasper and gold,
Purple from Tyrus,
Fold upon fold,
Blossoms and jewels,
Thy palace prepare:
Pale grows the monarch;
The chamber is there!

Once it was open
As shore to the sea;
White were the turrets,
Goodly to see;
All through the casements
Flowed the sweet air;
Now it is darkness;
The chamber is there!

Silence and horror
Brood on the walls;
Through every crevice
A little voice calls:
"Quicken, mad footsteps,
On pavement and stair;
Look not behind thee,
The chamber is there!"

Out of the gateway,
Through the wide world,
Into the tempest
Beaten and hurled,
Vain is thy wandering,
Sure thy despair,
Flying or staying,
The chamber is there!

LISE

If I were a cloud in heaven,
I would hang over thee;

If I were a star of even,
  I 'd rise and set for thee;
For love, life, light, were given
  Thy ministers to be.

If I were a wind's low laughter,
  I 'd kiss thy hair;
Or a sunbeam coming after,
  Lie on thy forehead fair;
For the world and its wide hereafter
  Have nought with thee to compare.

If I were a fountain leaping,
  Thy name should be
The burden of my sweet weeping;
  If I were a bee,
My honeyed treasures keeping,
  'T were all for thee!

There's never a tided ocean
  Without a shore;
Nor a leaf whose downward motion
  No dews deplore;
And I dream that my devotion
  May move thee to sigh once more.

DONE FOR

A WEEK ago to-day, when red-haired Sally
  Down to the sugar-camp came to see me,
I saw her checked frock coming down the valley,
  Far as anybody's eyes could see.
Now I sit before the camp-fire,
  And I can't see the pine-knots blaze,
Nor Sally's pretty face a-shining,
  Though I hear the good words she says.

A week ago to-night I was tired and lonely,
  Sally was gone back to Mason's fort,
And the boys by the sugar-kettles left me only;
  They were hunting coons for sport.
By there snaked a painted Pawnee,
  I was asleep before the fire;
He creased my two eyes with his hatchet,
  And scalped me to his heart's desire.

There they found me on the dry tussocks lying,
  Bloody and cold as a live man could be;
A hoot-owl on the branches overhead was crying,
  Crying murder to the red Pawnee.

They brought me to the camp-fire,
  They washed me in the sweet white spring;
But my eyes were full of flashes,
  And all night my ears would sing.

I thought I was a hunter on the prairie,
  But they saved me for an old blind dog;
When the hunting-grounds are cool and airy,
  I shall lie here like a helpless log.
I can't ride the little wiry pony,
  That scrambles over hills high and low;
I can't set my traps for the cony,
  Or bring down the black buffalo.

I 'm no better than a rusty, bursted rifle,
  And I don't see signs of any other trail;
Here by the camp-fire blaze I lie and stifle,
  And hear Jim fill the kettles with his pail.
It 's no use groaning. I like Sally,
  But a Digger squaw would n't have me!
I wish they had n't found me in the valley, —
  It 's twice dead not to see!

IN VAIN

PUT every tiny robe away!
The stitches all were set with tears,
Slow, tender drops of joys; to-day
Their rain would wither hopes or fears:
Bitter enough to daunt the moth
That longs to fret this dainty cloth.

The filmy lace, the ribbons blue,
The tracery deft of flower and leaf,
The fairy shapes that bloomed and grew
Through happy moments all too brief.
The warm, soft wraps. O God! how cold
It must be in that wintry mould!

Fold carefully the broidered wool:
Its silken wreaths will ne'er grow old,
And lay the linen soft and cool
Above it gently, fold on fold.
So lie the snows on that soft breast,
Where mortal garb will never rest.

How many days in dreamed delight,
With listless fingers, working slow,
I fashioned them from morn till night
And smiled to see them slowly grow.
I thought the task too late begun;
Alas! how soon it all was done!

Go lock them in a cedar chest,
And never bring me back the key!
Will hiding lay this ghost to rest,
Or the turned lock give peace to me?
No matter! — only that I dread
Lest other eyes behold my dead.

I would have laid them in that grave
To perish too, like any weed;
But legends tell that they who save
Such garments, ne'er the like will need:
But give or burn them, — need will be;
I want but one such memory!

Francis Miles Finch

THE BLUE AND THE GRAY

By the flow of the inland river,
Whence the fleets of iron have fled,
Where the blades of the grave-grass quiver,
Asleep are the ranks of the dead:
Under the sod and the dew,
Waiting the judgment-day;
Under the one, the Blue,
Under the other, the Gray.

These in the robings of glory,
Those in the gloom of defeat,
All with the battle-blood gory,
In the dusk of eternity meet:
Under the sod and the dew,
Waiting the judgment-day;
Under the laurel, the Blue,
Under the willow, the Gray.

From the silence of sorrowful hours
The desolate mourners go,
Lovingly laden with flowers
Alike for the friend and the foe:
Under the sod and the dew,
Waiting the judgment-day;
Under the roses, the Blue,
Under the lilies, the Gray.

So with an equal splendor,
The morning sun-rays fall,
With a touch impartially tender,
On the blossoms blooming for all:
Under the sod and the dew,
Waiting the judgment-day;
Broidered with gold, the Blue,
Mellowed with gold, the Gray.

So, when the summer calleth,
On forest and field of grain,
With an equal murmur falleth
The cooling drip of the rain:
Under the sod and the dew,
Waiting the judgment-day;
Wet with the rain, the Blue,
Wet with the rain, the Gray.

Sadly, but not with upbraiding,
The generous deed was done,
In the storm of the years that are fading
No braver battle was won:
Under the sod and the dew,
Waiting the judgment-day;
Under the blossoms, the Blue,
Under the garlands, the Gray.

No more shall the war cry sever,
Or the winding rivers be red;
They banish our anger forever
When they laurel the graves of our dead!
Under the sod and the dew,
Waiting the judgment-day;
Love and tears for the Blue,
Tears and love for the Gray.

John Townsend Trowbridge

THE VAGABONDS

We are two travellers, Roger and I.
Roger's my dog. — Come here, you scamp!
Jump for the gentleman, — mind your eye!
Over the table, — look out for the lamp!
The rogue is growing a little old;
Five years we've tramped through wind and weather,

And slept out-doors when nights were cold,
And ate and drank — and starved — together.

We 've learned what comfort is, I tell you!
A bed on the floor, a bit of rosin,
A fire to thaw our thumbs (poor fellow!
The paw he holds up there 's been frozen),
Plenty of catgut for my fiddle
(This out-door business is bad for strings),
Then a few nice buckwheats hot from the griddle,
And Roger and I set up for kings!

No, thank ye, Sir, — I never drink;
Roger and I are exceedingly moral, —
Are n't we, Roger? — See him wink! —
Well, something hot, then, — we won't quarrel.
He 's thirsty, too, — see him nod his head?
What a pity, Sir, that dogs can't talk!
He understands every word that 's said, —
And he knows good milk from water-and-chalk.

The truth is, Sir, now I reflect,
I 've been so sadly given to grog,
I wonder I 've not lost the respect
(Here 's to you, Sir!) even of my dog.
But he sticks by, through thick and thin;
And this old coat, with its empty pockets,
And rags that smell of tobacco and gin,
He 'll follow while he has eyes in his sockets.

There is n't another creature living
Would do it, and prove, through every disaster,
So fond, so faithful, and so forgiving,
To such a miserable, thankless master!
No, Sir! — see him wag his tail and grin!
By George! it makes my old eyes water!
That is, there 's something in this gin
That chokes a fellow. But no matter!

We 'll have some music, if you 're willing,
And Roger (hem! what a plague a cough is, Sir!)
Shall march a little — Start, you villain!
Paws up! Eyes front! Salute your officer!
'Bout face! Attention! Take your rifle!
(Some dogs have arms, you see!) Now hold your
Cap while the gentlemen give a trifle,
To aid a poor old patriot soldier!

March! Halt! Now show how the rebel shakes
When he stands up to hear his sentence.
Now tell us how many drams it takes
To honor a jolly new acquaintance.
Five yelps, — that 's five; he 's mighty knowing!
The night 's before us, fill the glasses! —
Quick, Sir! I 'm ill, — my brain is going! —
Some brandy, — thank you, — there! — it passes!

Why not reform? That 's easily said;
But I 've gone through such wretched treatment,
Sometimes forgetting the taste of bread,
And scarce remembering what meat meant,
That my poor stomach 's past reform;
And there are times when, mad with thinking,
I 'd sell out heaven for something warm
To prop a horrible inward sinking.

Is there a way to forget to think?
At your age, Sir, home, fortune, friends,
A dear girl's love, — but I took to drink, —
The same old story; you know how it ends.
If you could have seen these classic features, —
You need n't laugh, Sir; they were not then
Such a burning libel on God's creatures:
I was one of your handsome men!

If you had seen *her*, so fair and young,
Whose head was happy on this breast!
If you could have heard the songs I sung
When the wine went round, you would n't have guessed
That ever I, Sir, should be straying
From door to door, with fiddle and dog,
Ragged and penniless, and playing
To you to-night for a glass of grog!

She 's married since, — a parson's wife:
'T was better for her that we should part, —
Better the soberest, prosiest life
Than a blasted home and a broken heart.

I have seen her? Once: I was weak and spent
On the dusty road: a carriage stopped:
But little she dreamed, as on she went,
Who kissed the coin that her fingers dropped!

You 've set me talking, Sir; I'm sorry;
It makes me wild to think of the change!
What do you care for a beggar's story?
Is it amusing? you find it strange?
I had a mother so proud of me!
'T was well she died before. — Do you know
If the happy spirits in heaven can see
The ruin and wretchedness here below?

Another glass, and strong, to deaden
This pain; then Roger and I will start.
I wonder, has he such a lumpish, leaden,
Aching thing in place of a heart?
He is sad sometimes, and would weep, if he could,
No doubt remembering things that were, —
A virtuous kennel, with plenty of food,
And himself a sober, respectable cur.

I 'm better now; that glass was warming. —
You rascal! limber your lazy feet!
We must be fiddling and performing
For supper and bed, or starve in the street. —
Not a very gay life to lead, you think?
But soon we shall go where lodgings are free,
And the sleepers need neither victuals nor drink: —
The sooner, the better for Roger and me!

MIDWINTER

THE speckled sky is dim with snow,
The light flakes falter and fall slow;
Athwart the hill-top, rapt and pale,
Silently drops a silvery veil;
And all the valley is shut in
By flickering curtains gray and thin.

But cheerily the chickadee
Singeth to me on fence and tree;
The snow sails round him as he sings,
White as the down of angels' wings.

I watch the slow flakes as they fall
On bank and brier and broken wall;
Over the orchard, waste and brown,
All noiselessly they settle down,
Tipping the apple-boughs, and each
Light quivering twig of plum and peach.

On turf and curb and bower-roof
The snow-storm spreads its ivory woof;
It paves with pearl the garden-walk;
And lovingly round tattered stalk
And shivering stem its magic weaves
A mantle fair as lily-leaves.

The hooded beehive, small and low,
Stands like a maiden in the snow;
And the old door-slab is half hid
Under an alabaster lid.

All day it snows: the sheeted post
Gleams in the dimness like a ghost;
All day the blasted oak has stood
A muffled wizard of the wood;
Garland and airy cap adorn
The sumach and the wayside thorn,
And clustering spangles lodge and shine
In the dark tresses of the pine.

The ragged bramble, dwarfed and old,
Shrinks like a beggar in the cold;
In surplice white the cedar stands,
And blesses him with priestly hands.

Still cheerily the chickadee
Singeth to me on fence and tree:
But in my inmost ear is heard
The music of a holier bird;
And heavenly thoughts as soft and white
As snow-flakes, on my soul alight,
Clothing with love my lonely heart,
Healing with peace each bruisëd part,
Till all my being seems to be
Transfigured by their purity.

MIDSUMMER

AROUND this lovely valley rise
The purple hills of Paradise.

O, softly on yon banks of haze,
Her rosy face the Summer lays!

Becalmed along the azure sky,
The argosies of cloudland lie,
Whose shores, with many a shining rift,
Far off their pearl-white peaks uplift.

Through all the long midsummer-day
The meadow-sides are sweet with hay.
I seek the coolest sheltered seat,
Just where the field and forest meet, —
Where grow the pine-trees tall and bland,
The ancient oaks austere and grand,
And fringy roots and pebbles fret
The ripples of the rivulet.

I watch the mowers, as they go
Through the tall grass, a white-sleeved row.
With even stroke their scythes they swing,
In tune their merry whetstones ring.
Behind the nimble youngsters run,
And toss the thick swaths in the sun.
The cattle graze, while, warm and still,
Slopes the broad pasture, basks the hill,
And bright, where summer breezes break,
The green wheat crinkles like a lake.

The butterfly and humblebee
Come to the pleasant woods with me;
Quickly before me runs the quail,
Her chickens skulk behind the rail;
High up the lone wood-pigeon sits,
And the woodpecker pecks and flits.
Sweet woodland music sinks and swells,
The brooklet rings its tinkling bells,
The swarming insects drone and hum,
The partridge beats its throbbing drum.
The squirrel leaps among the boughs,
And chatters in his leafy house.
The oriole flashes by; and, look!
Into the mirror of the brook,
Where the vain bluebird trims his coat,
Two tiny feathers fall and float.

As silently, as tenderly,
The down of peace descends on me.
O, this is peace! I have no need
Of friend to talk, of book to read:
A dear Companion here abides;
Close to my thrilling heart He hides;
The holy silence is His Voice:
I lie and listen, and rejoice.

Jeremiah Eames Rankin

THE WORD OF GOD TO LEYDEN CAME

The word of God to Leyden came,
  Dutch town by Zuyder-Zee;
Rise up, my children of no name,
  My kings and priests to be.
There is an empire in the West,
  Which I will soon unfold;
A thousand harvests in her breast,
  Rocks ribbed with iron and gold.

Rise up, my children, time is ripe!
  Old things are passed away.
Bishops and kings from earth I wipe:
  Too long they 've had their day.
A little ship have I prepared
  To bear you o'er the seas;
And in your souls, my will declared,
  Shall grow by slow degrees.

Beneath my throne the martyrs cry:
  I hear their voice, How long?
It mingles with their praises high,
  And with their victor song.
The thing they longed and waited for,
  But died without the sight;
So, this shall be! I wrong abhor,
  The world I 'll now set right.

Leave, then, the hammer and the loom,
  You 've other work to do;
For Freedom's commonwealth there 's room,
  And you shall build it too.
I 'm tired of bishops and their pride,
  I 'm tired of kings as well;
Henceforth I take the people's side,
  And with the people dwell.

Tear off the mitre from the priest,
  And from the king, his crown;
Let all my captives be released;
  Lift up, whom men cast down.
Their pastors let the people choose,
  And choose their rulers too;
Whom they select, I 'll not refuse,
  But bless the work they do.

The Pilgrims rose, at this God's word,
  And sailed the wintry seas:
With their own flesh nor blood conferred,
  Nor thought of wealth or ease.
They left the towers of Leyden town,
  They left the Zuyder-Zee;

And where they cast their anchor down,
  Rose Freedom's realm to be.

THE BABIE[1]

NAE shoon to hide her tiny taes,
  Nae stockin' on her feet;
Her supple ankles white as snaw,
  Or early blossoms sweet.

Her simple dress o' sprinkled pink,
  Her double, dimplit chin,
Her puckered lips, and baumy mou',
  With na ane tooth within.

Her een sae like her mither's een,
  Twa gentle, liquid things;
Her face is like an angel's face:
  We 're glad she has nae wings.

She is the buddin' of our luve,
  A giftie God gied us:
We maun na luve the gift owre weel;
  'T wad be nae blessin' thus.

We still maun lo'e the Giver mair,
  An' see Him in the given;
An' sae she 'll lead us up to Him,
  Our babie straight frae Heaven.

Additional Selections

(VARIOUS POEMS BELONGING TO THIS DIVISION)

I

TWILIGHT AT SEA

THE twilight hours like birds flew by,
  As lightly and as free;
Ten thousand stars were in the sky,
  Ten thousand on the sea;
For every wave with dimpled face,
  That leaped upon the air,
Had caught a star in its embrace,
  And held it trembling there.

AMELIA COPPUCK WELBY

WHY THUS LONGING?

WHY thus longing, thus for ever sighing,
  For the far-off, unattained, and dim,
While the beautiful, all round thee lying,
  Offers up its low, perpetual hymn?

Wouldst thou listen to its gentle teaching,
  All thy restless yearnings it would still;
Leaf and flower and laden bee are preaching
  Thine own sphere, though humble, first to fill.

Poor indeed thou must be, if around thee
  Thou no ray of light and joy canst throw —
If no silken cord of love hath bound thee
  To some little world through weal and woe;

If no dear eyes thy fond love can brighten —
  No fond voices answer to thine own;
If no brother's sorrow thou canst lighten,
  By daily sympathy and gentle tone.

Not by deeds that win the crowd's applauses,
  Not by works that give thee world-renown,
Not by martyrdom or vaunted crosses,
  Canst thou win and wear the immortal crown!

Daily struggling, though unloved and lonely,
  Every day a rich reward will give;
Thou wilt find, by hearty striving only,
  And truly loving, thou canst truly live.

Dost thou revel in the rosy morning,
  When all nature hails the lord of light,
And his smile, the mountain-tops adorning,
  Robes yon fragrant fields in radiance bright?

[1] See BIOGRAPHICAL NOTE, p. 817.

Other hands may grasp the field and forest,
Proud proprietors in pomp may shine;
But with fervent love if thou adorest,
Thou art wealthier — all the world is thine.

Yet if through earth's wide domains thou rovest,
Sighing that they are not thine alone,
Not those fair fields, but thyself, thou lovest,
And their beauty and thy wealth are gone.

Nature wears the color of the spirit;
Sweetly to her worshipper she sings;
All the glow, the grace she doth inherit,
Round her trusting child she fondly flings.

HARRIET WINSLOW SEWALL

BALDER'S WIFE

HER casement like a watchful eye
From the face of the wall looks down,
Lashed round with ivy vines so dry,
And with ivy leaves so brown.
Her golden head in her lily hand
Like a star in the spray o' the sea,
And wearily rocking to and fro,
She sings so sweet and she sings so low
To the little babe on her knee.
But let her sing what tune she may,
Never so light and never so gay,
It slips and slides and dies away
To the moan of the willow water.

Like some bright honey-hearted rose
That the wild wind rudely mocks,
She blooms from the dawn to the day's sweet close
Hemmed in with a world of rocks.
The livelong night she doth not stir,
But keeps at her casement lorn,
And the skirts of the darkness shine with her
As they shine with the light o' the morn,
And all who pass may hear her lay,
But let it be what tune it may,
It slips and slides and dies away
To the moan of the willow water.

And there, within that one-eyed tower,
Lashed round with the ivy brown,
She droops like some unpitied flower
That the rain-fall washes down:
The damp o' the dew in her golden hair,
Her cheek like the spray o' the sea,
And wearily rocking to and fro,
She sings so sweet and she sings so low
To the little babe on her knee.
But let her sing what tune she may,
Never so glad and never so gay,
It slips and slides and dies away
To the moan of the willow water.

ALICE CARY

NEARER HOME

ONE sweetly solemn thought
Comes to me o'er and o'er;
I am nearer home to-day
Than I ever have been before;

Nearer my Father's house,
Where the many mansions be;
Nearer the great white throne,
Nearer the crystal sea;

Nearer the bound of life,
Where we lay our burdens down;
Nearer leaving the cross,
Nearer gaining the crown!

But lying darkly between,
Winding down through the night,
Is the silent, unknown stream,
That leads at last to the light.

Closer and closer my steps
Come to the dread abysm:
Closer Death to my lips
Presses the awful chrism.

Oh, if my mortal feet
Have almost gained the brink;
If it be I am nearer home
Even to-day than I think;

Father, perfect my trust;
Let my spirit feel in death,
That her feet are firmly set
On the rock of a living faith!

PHŒBE CARY

THE MASTER'S INVITATION

DEAR Lord, thy table is outspread;
What other could such feast afford?

And thou art waiting at the head,
But I am all unworthy, Lord;
Yet do I hear thee say, —
(Was ever love so free?)
Come hither, son, to-day
And sit and sup with me.

O master! I am full of doubt,
My heart with sin and fear defiled;
Come thou, and cast the tempter out,
And make me as a little child;
Methinks I hear thee say, —
Come thou, at once, and see
What love can take away,
And what confer on thee.

My Lord! to thee I fain would go,
Yet tarry now I know not why;
Speak, if to tell what well I know,
That none are half so vile as I.
What do I hear thee say? —
Look, trembling one, and see
These tokens, which to-day
Tell what I did for thee.

Nay, Lord! I could not here forget
What thou didst for my ransom give;
The garden prayer, the bloody sweat,
All this and more, that I might live.
I hear thee sadly say, —
If this remembered be,
Why linger thus to-day?
Why doubt and question me?

Oh, love to angels all unknown!
I turn from sin and self aside;
Thou hast the idol self o'erthrown,
I only see the Crucified;
I only hear thee say, —
A feast is spread for thee
On this and every day,
If thou but follow me!

Anson Davies Fitz Randolph

TO A YOUNG CHILD

As doth his heart who travels far from home
Leap up whenever he by chance doth see
One from his mother-country lately come,
Friend from my home — thus do I welcome thee.
Thou art so late arrived that I the tale
Of thy high lineage on thy brow can trace,
And almost feel the breath of that soft gale
That wafted thee unto this desert place,
And half can hear those ravishing sounds that flowed
From out Heaven's gate when it was oped for thee,
That thou awhile mightst leave thy bright abode
Amid these lone and desolate tracks to be
A homesick, weary wanderer, and then
Return unto thy native land again.

Eliza Scudder

THE PILGRIM

A pilgrim am I, on my way
To seek and find the Holy Land;
Scarce had I started, when there lay
And marched round me a fourfold band:
A smiling Joy, a weeping Woe,
A Hope, a Fear, did with me go;
And one may come, or one be gone;
But I am never more alone.

My little Hope, she pines and droops,
And finds it hard to live on earth;
But then some pitying angel stoops
To lift her out of frost and dearth,
And bears her on before, and up,
To taste, out of our Saviour's cup,
Such cheer as here she cannot find,
While patiently I plod behind.

Thus oft I send her from below —
Poor little Hope — for change of air.
I miss her sorely; but I know
That God of her is taking care.
And when my earthly course is done,
To heaven's gate I 'll see her run
To meet me mid the shining bands,
With full fruition in her hands.

My Fear I give to Faith to still
With lullabies upon her breast.
She sings to him, "Our Father's will,
Not ours, be done, for His is best,"
And lays him down to sleep in bowers —
Beneath the cross — of passion-flowers.
But ever yet he wakes in pain,
And finds his way to me again.

But Woe, — she scarce will lose her hold.
  She sits and walks and runs with me,
And watches. Ere the sun with gold
  Pays to the East his entrance fee
    She stirs, and stares me in the face,
    And drives me from each stopping-place.
    A guardian angel in disguise
    Seems looking through her tearful eyes.

Perhaps she hath a charge from God
  To see that ne'er, through Satan's camp,
I slumber on my dangerous way
  Too sound or long. A safety lamp
    Meantime by Joy is carried nigh,
    Somewhat aloof; for he is shy,
    Too shy within my grasp to stay,
    Though seldom is he far away.

Thus, fellow-pilgrims, fare we on;
  But, in what mortals call my death,
My Fear is doomed to die anon;
  When Woe shall leave me safe, — so saith
    My sweet-voiced Hope, — and turn to bring
    Some other soul; while Joy shall spring
    With me through heaven's strait door, to be
    Forever of my company!

SARAH HAMMOND PALFREY

A STRIP OF BLUE

I DO not own an inch of land,
  But all I see is mine, —
The orchard and the mowing-fields,
  The lawns and gardens fine.
The winds my tax-collectors are,
  They bring me tithes divine, —
Wild scents and subtle essences,
  A tribute rare and free;
And, more magnificent than all,
  My window keeps for me
A glimpse of blue immensity, —
  A little strip of sea.

Richer am I than he who owns
  Great fleets and argosies;
I have a share in every ship
  Won by the inland breeze,
To loiter on yon airy road
  Above the apple-trees.
I freight them with my untold dreams;
  Each bears my own picked crew;
And nobler cargoes wait for them
  Than ever India knew, —
My ships that sail into the East
  Across that outlet blue.

Sometimes they seem like living shapes, —
  The people of the sky, —
Guests in white raiment coming down
  From heaven, which is close by;
I call them by familiar names,
  As one by one draws nigh.
So white, so light, so spirit-like,
  From violet mists they bloom!
The aching wastes of the unknown
  Are half reclaimed from gloom,
Since on life's hospitable sea
  All souls find sailing-room.

The ocean grows a weariness
  With nothing else in sight;
Its east and west, its north and south,
  Spread out from morn till night;
We miss the warm, caressing shore,
  Its brooding shade and light.
A part is greater than the whole;
  By hints are mysteries told.
The fringes of eternity, —
  God's sweeping garment-fold,
In that bright shred of glittering sea,
  I reach out for and hold.

The sails, like flakes of roseate pearl,
  Float in upon the mist;
The waves are broken precious stones, —
  Sapphire and amethyst
Washed from celestial basement walls,
  By suns unsetting kist.
Out through the utmost gates of space,
  Past where the gray stars drift,
To the widening Infinite, my soul
  Glides on, a vessel swift,
Yet loses not her anchorage
  In yonder azure rift.

Here sit I, as a little child;
The threshold of God's door
Is that clear band of chrysoprase;
  Now the vast temple floor,
The blinding glory of the dome
  I bow my head before.
Thy universe, O God, is home,
  In height or depth, to me;

Yet here upon thy footstool green
  Content am I to be;
Glad when is oped unto my need
  Some sea-like glimpse of Thee.

LUCY LARCOM

'TIS BUT A LITTLE FADED FLOWER

'T IS but a little faded flower,
  But oh, how fondly dear!
'T will bring me back one golden hour,
  Through many a weary year.
I may not to the world impart
  The secret of its power,
But treasured in my inmost heart,
  I keep my faded flower.

Where is the heart that doth not keep,
  Within its inmost core,
Some fond remembrance, hidden deep,
  Of days that are no more?
Who hath not saved some trifling thing
  More prized than jewels rare —
A faded flower, a broken ring,
  A tress of golden hair?

ELLEN CLEMENTINE HOWARTH

II

OLIVIA

WHAT are the long waves singing so mournfully evermore?
What are they singing so mournfully as they weep on the sandy shore?
"Olivia, oh, Olivia!" — what else can it seem to be?
"Olivia, lost Olivia, will never return to thee!"
"Olivia, lost Olivia!" — what else can the sad song be? —
"Weep and mourn, she will not return, — she cannot return, to thee!"

And strange it is when the low winds sigh, and strange when the loud winds blow,
In the rustle of trees, in the roar of the storm, in the sleepiest streamlet's flow,
Forever, from ocean or river, ariseth the same sad moan, —
"She sleeps; let her sleep; wake her not. It were best she should rest, and alone."
Forever the same sad requiem comes up from the sorrowful sea,
For the lovely, the lost Olivia, who cannot return to me.

Alas! I fear 't is not in the air, or the sea, or the trees, — that strain:
I fear 't is a wrung heart aching, and the throb of a tortured brain;
And the shivering whisper of startled leaves, and the sob of the waves as they roll, —
I fear they are only the echo of the song of a suffering soul, —
Are only the passionless echo of the voice that is ever with me:
"The lovely, the lost Olivia will never return to thee!"

I stand in the dim gray morning, where once I stood, to mark,
Gliding away along the bay, like a bird, her white-winged bark;
And when through the Golden Gate the sunset radiance rolled,
And the tall masts melted to thinnest threads in the glowing haze of gold,
I said, "To thine arms I give her, O kind and shining sea,
And in one long moon from this June eve you shall let her return to me."

But the wind from the far spice islands came back, and it sang with a sigh, —
"The ocean is rich with the treasure it has hidden from you and the sky."
And where, amid rocks and green sea-weed, the storm and the tide were at war,
The nightly-sought waste was still vacant when I looked to the cloud and the star;

And soon the sad wind and dark ocean
unceasingly sang unto me,
"The lovely, the lost Olivia will never return to thee!"

Dim and still the landscape lies, but
shadowless as heaven,
For the growing morn and the low west
moon on everything shine even;
The ghosts of the lost have departed, that
nothing can ever redeem,
And Nature, in light, sweet slumber, is
dreaming her morning dream.
'T is morn and our Lord has awakened, and
the souls of the blessed are free.
O, come from the caves of the ocean!
Olivia, return unto me!

What thrills me? What comes near me?
Do I stand on the sward alone?
Was that a light wind, or a whisper? a
touch, or the pulse of a tone?
Olivia! whose spells from my slumber my
broken heart sway and control,
At length bring'st thou death to me, dear-
est, or rest to my suffering soul?
No sound but the psalm of the ocean:
"Bow down to the solemn decree, —
The lovely, the lost Olivia will never re-
turn to thee!"

And still are the long waves singing so
mournfully evermore;
Still are they singing so mournfully as they
weep on the sandy shore, —
"Olivia, lost Olivia!" so ever 't is doomed
to be, —
"Olivia, lost Olivia will never return to
thee!"
"Olivia, lost Olivia!" — what else could
the sad song be? —
"Weep and mourn, she will not return, —
she cannot return to thee!"

EDWARD POLLOCK

UNDER THE SNOW

It was Christmas Eve in the year fourteen,
And, as ancient dalesmen used to tell,
The wildest winter they ever had seen,
With the snow lying deep on moor and fell,

When Wagoner John got out his team,
Smiler and Whitefoot, Duke and Gray,
With the light in his eyes of a young man's
dream,
As he thought of his wedding on New
Year's Day

To Ruth, the maid with the bonnie brown
hair,
And eyes of the deepest, sunniest blue,
Modest and winsome, and wondrous fair,
And true to her troth, for her heart was
true.

"Thou 's surely not going!" shouted mine
host,
"Thou 'll be lost in the drift, as sure as
thou 's born;
Thy lass winnot want to wed wi' a ghost,
And that 's what thou 'll be on Christmas
morn.

"It 's eleven long miles from Skipton toon
To Blueberg hooses 'e Washburn dale:
Thou had better turn back and sit thee
doon,
And comfort thy heart wi' a drop o' good
ale."

Turn the swallows flying south,
Turn the vines against the sun,
Herds from rivers in the drouth,
Men must dare or nothing 's done.

So what cares the lover for storm or drift,
Or peril of death on the haggard way?
He sings to himself like a lark in the lift,
And the joy in his heart turns December
to May.

But the wind from the north brings a
deadly chill
Creeping into his heart, and the drifts are
deep,
Where the thick of the storm strikes Blueberg hill.
He is weary and falls in a pleasant sleep,

And dreams he is walking by Washburn
side,
Walking with Ruth on a summer's day,
Singing that song to his bonnie bride,
His own wife now forever and aye.

Now read me this riddle, how Ruth should
hear
That song of a heart in the clutch of doom

Steal on her ear, distinct and clear
As if her lover was in the room.

And read me this riddle, how Ruth should know,
As she bounds to throw open the heavy door,
That her lover was lost in the drifting snow,
Dying or dead, on the great wild moor.

"Help! help!" "Lost! lost!"
Rings through the night as she rushes away,
Stumbling, blinded and tempest-tossed,
Straight to the drift where her lover lay.

And swift they leap after her into the night,
Into the drifts by Blueberg hill,
Ridsdale and Robinson, each with a light,
To find her there holding him white and still.

"He was dead in the drift, then,"
I hear them say,
As I listen in wonder,
Forgetting to play,
Fifty years syne come Christmas Day.

"Nay, nay, they were wed!" the dalesman cried,
"By Parson Carmalt o' New Year's Day;
Bless ye! Ruth were me great-great grandsire's bride,
And Maister Frankland gave her away."

"But how did she find him under the snow?"
They cried with a laughter touched with tears.
"Nay, lads," he said softly, "we never can know —
"No, not if we live a hundred years.

"There's a sight o' things gan
To the making o' man."
Then I rushed to my play
With a whoop and away,
Fifty years syne come Christmas Day.

ROBERT COLLYER

TACKING SHIP OFF SHORE

THE weather-leech of the topsail shivers,
The bowlines strain, and the lee-shrouds slacken,
The braces are taut, the lithe boom quivers,
And the waves with the coming squall-cloud blacken.

Open one point on the weather-bow,
Is the light-house tall on Fire Island Head.
There's a shade of doubt on the captain's brow,
And the pilot watches the heaving lead.

I stand at the wheel, and with eager eye
To sea and to sky and to shore I gaze,
Till the muttered order of "Full and by!"
Is suddenly changed for "Full for stays!"

The ship bends lower before the breeze,
As her broadside fair to the blast she lays;
And she swifter springs to the rising seas,
As the pilot calls, "Stand by for stays!"

It is silence all, as each in his place,
With the gathered coil in his hardened hands,
By tack and bowline, by sheet and brace,
Waiting the watchword impatient stands.

And the light on Fire Island Head draws near,
As, trumpet-winged, the pilot's shout
From his post on the bowsprit's heel I hear,
With the welcome call of "Ready! About!"

No time to spare! It is touch and go;
And the captain growls, "Down helm! hard down!"
As my weight on the whirling spokes I throw,
While heaven grows black with the storm-cloud's frown.

High o'er the knight-heads flies the spray,
As we meet the shock of the plunging sea;
And my shoulder stiff to the wheel I lay,
As I answer, "Ay, ay, sir! Ha-a-rd a-lee!"

With the swerving leap of a startled steed
The ship flies fast in the eye of the wind,
The dangerous shoals on the lee recede,
And the headland white we have left behind.

The topsails flutter, the jibs collapse,
  And belly and tug at the groaning cleats;
The spanker slats, and the mainsail flaps;
  And thunders the order, "Tacks and sheets!"

Mid the rattle of blocks and the tramp of the crew,
  Hisses the rain of the rushing squall:
The sails are aback from clew to clew,
  And now is the moment for "Mainsail, haul!"

And the heavy yards, like a baby's toy,
  By fifty strong arms are swiftly swung:
She holds her way, and I look with joy
  For the first white spray o'er the bulwarks flung.

"Let go, and haul!" 'T is the last command,
  And the head-sails fill to the blast once more:
Astern and to leeward lies the land,
  With its breakers white on the shingly shore.

What matters the reef, or the rain, or the squall?
  I steady the helm for the open sea;
The first mate clamors, "Belay, there, all!"
  And the captain's breath once more comes free.

And so off shore let the good ship fly;
  Little care I how the gusts may blow,
In my fo'castle bunk, in a jacket dry.
  Eight bells have struck, and my watch is below.

WALTER MITCHELL

ANTONY TO CLEOPATRA

I AM dying, Egypt, dying!
  Ebbs the crimson life-tide fast,
And the dark Plutonian shadows
  Gather on the evening blast;
Let thine arm, O Queen, enfold me,
  Hush thy sobs and bow thine ear,
Listen to the great heart secrets
  Thou, and thou alone, must hear.

Though my scarred and veteran legions
  Bear their eagles high no more,
And my wrecked and scattered galleys
  Strew dark Actium's fatal shore;
Though no glittering guards surround me,
  Prompt to do their master's will,
I must perish like a Roman,
  Die the great Triumvir still.

Let not Cæsar's servile minions
  Mock the lion thus laid low;
'T was no foeman's arm that felled him,
  'T was his own that struck the blow:
His who, pillowed on thy bosom,
  Turned aside from glory's ray —
His who, drunk with thy caresses,
  Madly threw a world away.

Should the base plebeian rabble
  Dare assail my name at Rome,
Where the noble spouse Octavia
  Weeps within her widowed home,
Seek her; say the gods bear witness, —
  Altars, augurs, circling wings, —
That her blood, with mine commingled,
  Yet shall mount the thrones of kings.

And for thee, star-eyed Egyptian —
  Glorious sorceress of the Nile!
Light the path to Stygian horrors,
  With the splendor of thy smile;
Give the Cæsar crowns and arches,
  Let his brow the laurel twine:
I can scorn the senate's triumphs,
  Triumphing in love like thine.

I am dying, Egypt, dying!
  Hark! the insulting foeman's cry;
They are coming — quick, my falchion!
  Let me front them ere I die.
Ah, no more amid the battle
  Shall my heart exulting swell;
Isis and Osiris guard thee —
  Cleopatra — Rome — farewell!

WILLIAM HAINES LYTLE

THE SECOND MATE

"Ho, there! Fisherman, hold your hand!
  Tell me, what is that far away, —
There, where over the isle of sand
  Hangs the mist-cloud sullen and gray?
See! it rocks with a ghastly life,
  Rising and rolling through clouds of spray,
Right in the midst of the breakers' strife, —
  Tell me what is it, Fisherman, pray?"

"That, good sir, was a steamer stout
As ever paddled around Cape Race;
And many 's the wild and stormy bout
She had with the winds, in that self-same place;
But her time was come; and at ten o'clock
Last night she struck on that lonesome shore;
And her sides were gnawed by the hidden rock,
And at dawn this morning she was no more."

"Come, as you seem to know, good man,
The terrible fate of this gallant ship,
Tell me about her all that you can;
And here 's my flask to moisten your lip.
Tell me how many she had aboard, —
Wives, and husbands, and lovers true, —
How did it fare with her human hoard?
Lost she many, or lost she few?"

"Master, I may not drink of your flask,
Already too moist I feel my lip;
But I 'm ready to do what else you ask,
And spin you my yarn about the ship.
'T was ten o'clock, as I said, last night,
When she struck the breakers and went ashore;
And scarce had broken the morning's light
Than she sank in twelve feet of water or more.

"But long ere this they knew her doom,
And the captain called all hands to prayer;
And solemnly over the ocean's boom
Their orisons wailed on the troublous air.
And round about the vessel there rose
Tall plumes of spray as white as snow,
Like angels in their ascension clothes,
Waiting for those who prayed below.

"So these three hundred people clung
As well as they could, to spar and rope;
With a word of prayer upon every tongue,
Nor on any face a glimmer of hope.
But there was no blubbering weak and wild, —
Of tearful faces I saw but one,
A rough old salt, who cried like a child,
And not for himself, but the captain's son.

"The captain stood on the quarter-deck,
Firm but pale, with trumpet in hand;
Sometimes he looked at the breaking wreck,
Sometimes he sadly looked to land;
And often he smiled to cheer the crew —
But, Lord! the smile was terrible grim —
Till over the quarter a huge sea flew;
And that was the last they saw of him.

"I saw one young fellow with his bride,
Standing amidships upon the wreck;
His face was white as the boiling tide,
And she was clinging about his neck.
And I saw them try to say good-by,
But neither could hear the other speak;
So they floated away through the sea to die —
Shoulder to shoulder, and cheek to cheek.

"And there was a child, but eight at best,
Who went his way in a sea she shipped,
All the while holding upon his breast
A little pet parrot whose wings were clipped.
And, as the boy and the bird went by,
Swinging away on a tall wave's crest,
They were gripped by a man, with a drowning cry,
And together the three went down to rest.

"And so the crew went one by one,
Some with gladness, and few with fear, —
Cold and hardship such work had done
That few seemed frightened when death was near.
Thus every soul on board went down, —
Sailor and passenger, little and great;
The last that sank was a man of my town,
A capital swimmer, — the second mate."

"Now, lonely fisherman, who are you
That say you saw this terrible wreck?
How do I know what you say is true,
When every mortal was swept from the deck?
Where were you in that hour of death?
How did you learn what you relate?"
His answer came in an under-breath:
"Master, I was the second mate!"

FITZ-JAMES O'BRIEN[1]

[1] See BIOGRAPHICAL NOTE, p. 812.

III

TO AN AUTUMN LEAF

The scarlet tide of summer's life
Is ebbing toward a shoreless sea;
Late fell before the reaper's knife
The ripened grain — a type of thee.

How fresh and young the earth looked, when
The sun first kissed thy silken head!
Now blazing grass and smouldering fen
Burn incense for an empress dead.

With gorgeous robes she lies in state,
Her trailing banners cloud the sky:
When Atropos no more will wait,
'T is joy so gloriously to die.

Whose loss is it, if thou and I
Are dropped into the fecund earth?
A privilege it is to die
When life is of no further worth.

Some newer lives will fill the place
Of which we feel ourselves bereft;
Mayhap, though shadows for a space,
Our vital essence will be left.

The spirit of each form that grows
Survives the mould in which 't is cast:
The universe will not repose,
Though death and life each follow fast.

Whence comes, where goes the spark we see?
Till time's last ensign is unfurled,
This miracle of life will be,
For aye, the problem of the world.

Who reads a page of Nature's book,
How clear soe'er the text may be,
Needs something of a wizard's look,
If he would probe her mystery.

Oh, for an art like palmistry,
That I might scan thy mazy veins!
I long to know thy history, —
Why blood thy transient record stains.

The symmetry of thy outline,
The curious function of each part,
Betray the work of love divine: —
Does it conceal a throbbing heart?

Dost know the mortal life of man,
Its wants and wrongs and pangs and fears?
Does sorrow trouble thy brief span,
Although denied relief of tears?

Hast thou a soul as well as I,
To breathe and blush and live the same?
What matters if I make outcry,
And call myself a prouder name?

One made us both by His high will,
He gave alike and takes away:
We grind as small in His great mill,
"Dust unto dust," our roundelay.

Albert Mathews

EBB AND FLOW

I walked beside the evening sea,
And dreamed a dream that could not be;
The waves that plunged along the shore
Said only — "Dreamer, dream no more!"

But still the legions charged the beach;
Loud rang their battle-cry, like speech;
But changed was the imperial strain:
It murmured — "Dreamer, dream again!"

I homeward turned from out the gloom, —
That sound I heard not in my room;
But suddenly a sound, that stirred
Within my very breast, I heard.

It was my heart, that like a sea
Within my breast beat ceaselessly:
But like the waves along the shore,
It said — "Dream on!" and "Dream no more!"

George William Curtis

THALATTA! THALATTA!

CRY OF THE TEN THOUSAND

I stand upon the summit of my life:
Behind, the camp, the court, the field, the grove,
The battle and the burden; vast, afar,
Beyond these weary ways, Behold! the Sea!
The sea o'erswept by clouds and winds and wings,

By thoughts and wishes manifold, whose breath
Is freshness and whose mighty pulse is peace.
Palter no question of the horizon dim, —
Cut loose the bark; such voyage itself is rest,
Majestic motion, unimpeded scope,
A widening heaven, a current without care,
Eternity! — deliverance, promise, course!
Time-tired souls salute thee from the shore.

JOSEPH BROWNLEE BROWN

INCOGNITA OF RAPHAEL

LONG has the summer sunlight shone
On the fair form, the quaint costume;
Yet, nameless still, she sits, unknown,
A lady in her youthful bloom.

Fairer for this! no shadows cast
Their blight upon her perfect lot,
Whate'er her future or her past
In this bright moment matters not.

No record of her high descent
There needs, nor memory of her name;
Enough that Raphael's colors blent
To give her features deathless fame!

'T was his anointing hand that set
The crown of beauty on her brow;
Still lives its early radiance yet,
As at the earliest, even now.

'T is not the ecstasy that glows
In all the rapt Cecilia's grace;
Nor yet the holy, calm repose
He painted on the Virgin's face.

Less of the heavens, and more of earth,
There lurk within these earnest eyes,
The passions that have had their birth
And grown beneath Italian skies.

What mortal thoughts, and cares, and dreams,
What hopes, and fears, and longings rest
Where falls the folded veil, or gleams
The golden necklace on her breast!

What mockery of the painted glow
May shade the secret soul within;
What griefs from passion's overflow,
What shame that follows after sin!

Yet calm as heaven's serenest deeps
Are those pure eyes, those glances pure;
And queenly is the state she keeps,
In beauty's lofty trust secure.

And who has strayed, by happy chance,
Through all those grand and pictured halls,
Nor felt the magic of her glance,
As when a voice of music calls?

Not soon shall I forget the day, —
Sweet day, in spring's unclouded time,
While on the glowing canvas lay
The light of that delicious clime, —

I marked the matchless colors wreathed
On the fair brow, the peerless cheek;
The lips, I fancied, almost breathed
The blessings that they could not speak.

Fair were the eyes with mine that bent
Upon the picture their mild gaze,
And dear the voice that gave consent
To all the utterance of my praise.

O fit companionship of thought;
O happy memories, shrined apart;
The rapture that the painter wrought,
The kindred rapture of the heart!

WILLIAM ALLEN BUTLER

ON ONE WHO DIED IN MAY

WHY, Death, what dost thou here,
This time o' year?
Peach-blow and apple-blossom;
Clouds, white as my love's bosom;
Warm wind o' the west
Cradling the robin's nest;
Young meadows hasting their green laps to fill
With golden dandelion and daffodil:
These are fit sights for spring;
But, oh, thou hateful thing,
What dost thou here?

Why, Death, what dost thou here,
This time o' year?
Fair, at the old oak's knee,
The young anemone;

Fair, the plash places set
With dog-tooth violet;
    The first sloop-sail,
    The shad-flower pale;
Sweet are all sights,
Sweet are all sounds of spring;
But thou, thou ugly thing,
    What dost thou here?

Dark Death let fall a tear.
    Why am I here?
Oh, heart ungrateful! Will man never know
I am his friend, nor ever was his foe?
Whose the sweet season, if it be not mine?
Mine, not the bobolinks, that song divine,
Chasing the shadows o'er the flying wheat!
'T is a dead voice, not his, that sounds so sweet.
Whose passionate heart burns in this flaming rose
But his, whose passionate heart long since lay still?
Whose wan hope pales this snowlike lily tall,
    Beside the garden wall,
But his whose radiant eyes and lily grace
Sleep in the grave that crowns yon tufted hill?

    All hope, all memory,
Have their deep springs in me;
  And love, that else might fade,
  By me immortal made,
Spurns at the grave, leaps to the welcoming skies,
And burns a steadfast star to steadfast eyes.

CLARENCE CHATHAM COOK

BUT ONCE

TELL me, wide wandering soul, in all thy quest
Sipping or draining deep from crystal rim
Where pleasure sparkled, when did overbrim
That draught its goblet with the fullest zest?
Of all thy better bliss what deemst thou best?
Then thus my soul made answer. Ecstasy
Comes once, like birth, like death, and once have I
Been, oh! so madly happy, that the rest
Is tame as surgeless seas. It was a night
Sweet, beautiful as she, my love, my light;
Fair as the memory of that keen delight.
Through trees the moon rose steady, and it blessed
Her forehead chastely. Her uplifted look,
Calm with deep passion, I for answer took,
Then sudden heart to heart was wildly pressed.

THEODORE WINTHROP

IV

ALMA MATER'S ROLL

I SAW her scan her sacred scroll,
I saw her read her record roll
Of men who wrought to win the right,
Of men who fought and died in fight; —
When now, a hundred years by-gone
The day she welcomed Washington,
She showed to him her boys and men,
And told him of their duty then.

"Here are the beardless boys I sent,
And whispered to them my intent
To free a struggling continent.
"The marks upon this scroll will show
Their words a hundred years ago.

"Otis!" "No lesser death was given
To him than by a bolt from heaven!"
"Quincy!" "He died before he heard
The echo of his thunder word."
"And these were stripling lads whom I
Sent out to speak a nation's cry,
In 'glittering generality'
Of living words that cannot die:

"John Hancock!" "Here." "John Adams!" "Here."

"Paine, Gerry, Hooper, Williams!"
"Here."
"My Narragansett Ellery!" "Here."
"Sam Adams, first of freemen!" "Here."
"My beardless boys, my graybeard men,
Summoned to take the fatal pen
Which gave eternal rights to men, —
All present, or accounted for."

I saw her scan again the scroll, —
I heard her read again the roll;
I heard her name her soldier son,
Ward, called from home by Lexington.
He smiled and laid his baton down,
Proud to be next to Washington!
He called her list of boys and men
Who served her for her battles then.
From North to South, from East to West,
He named her bravest and her best,
From distant fort, from bivouac near:
"Brooks, Eustis, Cobb, and Thacher!"
"Here."
Name after name, with quick reply,
As twitched his lip and flashed his eye;
But then he choked and bowed his head, —
"Warren at Bunker Hill lies dead."

The roll was closed; he only said,
"All present, or accounted for."

That scroll is stained with time and dust;
They were not faithless to their trust.

"If those days come again, — if I
Call on the grandsons, — what reply?
What deed of courage new display
These fresher parchments of to-day?"

I saw her take the newest scroll, —
I heard her read the whiter roll;
And as the answers came, the while
Our mother nodded with a smile:
"Charles Adams!" "Here." "George
Bancroft!" "Here."
"The Hoars!" "Both here." "Dick
Dana!" "Here."
"Wadsworth!" "He died at duty's call."
"Webster!" "He fell as brave men
fall."
"Everett!" "Struck down in Faneuil
Hall."
"Sumner!" "A nation bears his pall."
"Shaw, Abbott, Lowell, Savage!" "All
Died there, — to live on yonder wall!"
"Come East, come West, come far, come
near, —
Lee, Bartlett, Davis, Devens!" "Here."
"All present, or accounted for."

Boys, heed the omen! Let the scroll
Fill as it may as years unroll;
But when again she calls her youth
To serve her in the ranks of Truth,
May she find all one heart, one soul, —
At home or on some distant shore,
"All present, or accounted for!"

EDWARD EVERETT HALE

Φ Β Κ DINNER, *Harvard*, 1875

BOOKRA[1]

As I lay asleep in Italy. — SHELLEY.

ONE night I lay asleep in Africa,
In a closed garden by the city gate;
A desert horseman, furious and late,
Came wildly thundering at the massive bar,
"Open in Allah's name! Wake, Mustapha!
Slain is the Sultan, — treason, war, and
hate
Rage from Fez to Tetuan! Open straight."
The watchman heard as thunder from
afar:
"Go to! In peace this city lies asleep;
To all-knowing Allah 't is no news you
bring;"
Then turned in slumber still his watch to
keep.
At once a nightingale began to sing,
In oriental calm the garden lay, —
Panic and war postponed another day.

CHARLES DUDLEY WARNER

[1] *Bookra* = To-morrow.

III

SECOND LYRICAL PERIOD

(IN THREE DIVISIONS)

FROM THE BEGINNING OF THE CIVIL WAR TO THE HUNDREDTH PRESIDENTIAL YEAR

1861–1889

1

Mitchell (S. Weir's) first book of verse, "The Hill of Stones, and Other Poems" (Boston) did not appear until 1882
Hayne (Paul H.'s) "Poems": Boston, 1854
Winter's "Poems": Boston, 1854; "The Queen's Domain": Boston, 1858
Mrs. Moulton's "This, That, and the Other": Boston, 1854; "Poems": Boston, 1877
Aldrich's "The Bells": New York, 1854; "The Ballad of Babie Bell": N. Y. Journal of Commerce, 1855; "The Ballad of Babie Bell, and Other Poems": New York, 1858
Stedman's "Poems Lyrical and Idyllic": New York, 1860
Piatt's and Howells's "Poems of Two Friends": Columbus, 1859
Mr. and Mrs. Piatt's "The Nests at Washington": New York, 1863
Mrs. Spofford's "Amber Gods," prose: Boston, 1863; "Poems": Boston, 1881
Howells's "No Love Lost": New York, 1869; "Poems": Boston, 1873
Harte's "Luck of Roaring Camp": Overland Monthly, 1868; "Poems": Boston, 1870
Miller's "Songs of the Sierras": Boston, 1871
Hay's "Pike County Ballads": Boston, 1871
Mrs. Jackson's "Verses by H. H.": Boston, 1873
Lanier's "Corn": Lippincott's, 1874; "Centennial Cantata," 1876

2

Miss Lazarus's "Poems and Translations": New York, 1866; "Admetus and Other Poems": New York, 1871
Sill's "The Hermitage": New York, 1867
O'Reilly's "Songs from the Southern Seas": Boston, 1873
Gilder's "The New Day": New York, 1875
Miss Coolbrith's "A Perfect Day, and Other Poems": San Francisco, 1881
Mrs. E. M. (Hutchinson) Cortissoz's "Songs and Lyrics": Boston, 1881
Riley's "The Old Swimmin'-Hole, and 'Leven More Poems": Indianapolis, 1883
Thompson's "Songs of Fair Weather": Boston, 1883
Miss Thomas's "A New Year's Masque": Boston, 1884
Bates's "Berries of the Brier": Boston, 1886
Field's "Culture's Garland": Boston, 1887; "A Little Book of Western Verse": Chicago, 1889
Tabb's "Poems": Baltimore, 1882; "Poems": Boston, 1894
Markham's "The Man with the Hoe, and Other Poems": New York, 1899

3

Woodberry's "The North Shore Watch, a Threnody" (privately printed): Cambridge, 1883; "The North Shore Watch, and Other Poems": Boston, 1890
Bunner's "Airs from Arcady": New York, 1884
Miss Guiney's "Songs at the Start": Boston, 1884
Miss Cone's "Oberon and Puck": New York, 1885
Sherman's "Madrigals and Catches": New York, 1887
Miss Reese's "A Branch of May": Baltimore, 1887; "A Handful of Lavender": Boston, 1891
Miss Monroe's "Valeria, and Other Poems": Chicago, 1891; "Commemoration Ode": delivered, Chicago, 1892, published, Chicago, 1893
Garland's "Prairie Songs": Cambridge and Chicago, 1893
Burton's "Dumb in June": Boston, 1895

The dates given are those of copyright entry

SECOND LYRICAL PERIOD

(IN THREE DIVISIONS)

DIVISION I

(MITCHELL, TIMROD, HAYNE, MRS. JACKSON, MISS DICKINSON, STEDMAN, THE PIATTS, MRS. SPOFFORD, MRS. MOULTON, WINTER, ALDRICH, HOWELLS, HAY, HARTE, SILL, MILLER, LANIER, AND OTHERS)

Silas Weir Mitchell[1]

ON A BOY'S FIRST READING OF "KING HENRY V"

WHEN youth was lord of my unchallenged
fate,
And time seemed but the vassal of my will,
I entertainëd certain guests of state —
The great of older days, who, faithful still,
Have kept with me the pact my youth had
made.

And I remember how one galleon rare
From the far distance of a time long dead
Came on the wings of a fair-fortuned air,
With sound of martial music heralded,
In blazonry of storied shields arrayed.

So the *Great Harry* with high trumpetings,
The wind of victory in her burly sails!
And all her deck with clang of armor
rings:
And under-flown the Lily standard trails,
And over-flown the royal Lions ramp.

The waves she rode are strewn with silent
wrecks,
Her proud sea-comrades once; but ever yet
Comes time - defying laughter from her
decks,
Where stands the lion-lord Plantagenet,
Large-hearted, merry, king of court and
camp.

Sail on! sail on! The fatal blasts of time
That spared so few, shall thee with joy
escort;
And with the stormy thunder of thy rhyme
Shalt thou salute full many a centuried port
With "Ho! for Harry and red Agin-
court!"

TO A MAGNOLIA FLOWER IN THE GARDEN OF THE ARMENIAN CONVENT AT VENICE

I SAW thy beauty in its high estate
Of perfect empire, where at set of sun
In the cool twilight of thy lucent leaves
The dewy freshness told that day was
done.

Hast thou no gift beyond thine ivory cone's
Surpassing loveliness? Art thou not
near —
More near than we — to nature's silent-
ness;
Is it not voiceful to thy finer ear?

Thy folded secrecy doth like a charm
Compel to thought. What spring-born
yearning lies
Within the quiet of thy stainless breast
That doth with languorous passion seem
to rise?

The soul doth truant angels entertain
Who with reluctant joy their thoughts
confess:
Low-breathing, to these sister spirits give
The virgin mysteries of thy heart to
guess.

[1] See BIOGRAPHICAL NOTE, p. 810.

What whispers hast thou from yon child-like sea
That sobs all night beside these garden walls ?
Canst thou interpret what the lark hath sung
When from the choir of heaven her music falls ?

If for companionship of purity
The equal pallor of the risen moon
Disturb thy dreams, dost know to read aright
Her silver tracery on the dark lagoon ?

The mischief-making fruitfulness of May
Stirs all the garden folk with vague desires :
Doth there not reach thine apprehensive ear
The faded longing of these dark-robed friars,

When, in the evening hour to memories given,
Some gray-haired man amid the gathering gloom
For one delirious moment sees again
The gleam of eyes and white-walled Erzeroum ?

Hast thou not loved him for this human dream ?
Or sighed with him who yester-evening sat
Upon the low sea-wall, and saw through tears
His ruined home, and snow-clad Ararat ?

If thou art dowered with some refinëd sense
That shares the counsels of the nesting bird,
Canst hear the mighty laughter of the earth,
And all that ear of man hath never heard,

If the abysmal stillness of the night
Be eloquent for thee, if thou canst read
The glowing rubric of the morning song,
Doth each new day no gentle warning breed ?

Shall not the gossip of the maudlin bee,
The fragrant history of the fallen rose,
Unto the prescience of instinctive love
Some humbler prophecy of joy disclose ?

Cold vestal of the leafy convent cell,
The traitor days have thy calm trust betrayed;
The sea-wind boldly parts thy shining leaves
To let the angel in. Be not afraid !

The gold-winged sun, divinely penetrant,
The pure annunciation of the morn
Breathes o'er thy chastity, and to thy soul
The tender thrill of motherhood is borne.

Set wide the glory of thy perfect bloom !
Call every wind to share thy scented breaths !
No life is brief that doth perfection win.
To-day is thine — to-morrow thou art death's !

OF ONE WHO SEEMED TO HAVE FAILED

Death 's but one more to-morrow. Thou art gray
With many a death of many a yesterday.
O yearning heart that lacked the athlete's force
And, stumbling, fell upon the beaten course,
And looked, and saw with ever glazing eyes
Some lower soul that seemed to win the prize !
Lo, Death, the just, who comes to all alike,
Life's sorry scales of right anew shall strike.
Forth, through the night, on unknown shores to win
The peace of God unstirred by sense of sin !
There love without desire shall, like a mist
At evening precious to the drooping flower,
Possess thy soul in ownership, and kissed
By viewless lips, whose touch shall be a dower
Of genius and of winged serenity,
Thou shalt abide in realms of poesy.
There soul hath touch of soul, and there the great
Cast wide to welcome thee joy's golden gate.
Freeborn to untold thoughts that age on age
Caressed sweet singers in their sacred sleep,

Thy soul shall enter on its heritage
Of God's unuttered wisdom. Thou shalt sweep
With hand assured the ringing lyre of life,
Till the fierce anguish of its bitter strife,
Its pain, death, discord, sorrow, and despair,
Break into rhythmic music. Thou shalt share
The prophet-joy that kept forever glad
God's poet-souls when all a world was sad.
Enter and live! Thou hast not lived before;
We were but soul-cast shadows. Ah, no more
The heart shall bear the burdens of the brain;
Now shall the strong heart think, nor think in vain.
In the dear company of peace, and those
Who bore for man life's utmost agony,
Thy soul shall climb to cliffs of still repose,
And see before thee lie Time's mystery,
And that which is God's time, Eternity;
Whence sweeping over thee dim myriad things,
The awful centuries yet to be, in hosts
That stir the vast of heaven with formless wings,
Shall cast for thee their shrouds, and, like to ghosts,
Unriddle all the past, till, awed and still,
Thy soul the secret hath of good and ill.

THE QUAKER GRAVEYARD

Four straight brick walls, severely plain,
  A quiet city square surround;
A level space of nameless graves, —
  The Quakers' burial-ground.

In gown of gray, or coat of drab,
  They trod the common ways of life,
With passions held in sternest leash,
  And hearts that knew not strife.

To yon grim meeting-house they fared,
  With thoughts as sober as their speech,
To voiceless prayer, to songless praise,
  To hear the elders preach.

Through quiet lengths of days they came,
  With scarce a change to this repose;
Of all life's loveliness they took
  The thorn without the rose.

But in the porch and o'er the graves,
  Glad rings the southward robin's glee,
And sparrows fill the autumn air
  With merry mutiny;

While on the graves of drab and gray
  The red and gold of autumn lie,
And wilful Nature decks the sod
  In gentlest mockery.

IDLENESS

There is no dearer lover of lost hours
            Than I.
I can be idler than the idlest flowers;
            More idly lie
Than noonday lilies languidly afloat,
And water pillowed in a windless moat.
  And I can be
Stiller than some gray stone
That hath no motion known.
  It seems to me
That my still idleness doth make my own
  All magic gifts of joy's simplicity.

A DECANTER OF MADEIRA, AGED 86, TO GEORGE BANCROFT, AGED 86, GREETING

Good Master, you and I were born
In "Teacup days" of hoop and hood,
And when the silver cue hung down,
And toasts were drunk, and wine was good;

When kin of mine (a jolly brood)
From sideboards looked, and knew full well
What courage they had given the beau,
How generous made the blushing belle.

Ah me! what gossip could I prate
Of days when doors were locked at dinners!
Believe me, I have kissed the lips
Of many pretty saints — or sinners.

Lip service have I done, alack!
I don't repent, but come what may,
What ready lips, sir, I have kissed,
Be sure at least I shall not say.

Two honest gentlemen are we, —
I Demi John, whole George are you;

When Nature grew us one in years
She meant to make a generous brew.

She bade me store for festal hours
The sun our south-side vineyard knew;
To sterner tasks she set your life,
As statesman, writer, scholar, grew.

Years eighty-six have come and gone;
At last we meet. Your health to-night.
Take from this board of friendly hearts
The memory of a proud delight.

The days that went have made you wise,
There 's wisdom in my rare bouquet.
I 'm rather paler than I was;
And, on my soul, you 're growing gray.

I like to think, when Toper Time
Has drained the last of me and you,
Some here shall say, They both were
good, —
The wine we drank, the man we knew.

1886

Henry Timrod

THE COTTON BOLL

WHILE I recline
At ease beneath
This immemorial pine,
Small sphere!
(By dusky fingers brought this morning
here
And shown with boastful smiles),
I turn thy cloven sheath,
Through which the soft white fibres peer,
That, with their gossamer bands,
Unite, like love, the sea-divided lands,
And slowly, thread by thread,
Draw forth the folded strands,
Than which the trembling line,
By whose frail help yon startled spider
fled
Down the tall spear-grass from his swinging
bed,
Is scarce more fine;
And as the tangled skein
Unravels in my hands,
Betwixt me and the noonday light
A veil seems lifted, and for miles and
miles
The landscape broadens on my sight,
As, in the little boll, there lurked a spell
Like that which, in the ocean shell,
With mystic sound
Breaks down the narrow walls that hem us
round,
And turns some city lane
Into the restless main,
With all his capes and isles!

Yonder bird,
Which floats, as if at rest,
In those blue tracts above the thunder,
where
No vapors cloud the stainless air,
And never sound is heard,
Unless at such rare time
When, from the City of the Blest,
Rings down some golden chime,
Sees not from his high place
So vast a cirque of summer space
As widens round me in one mighty field,
Which, rimmed by seas and sands,
Doth hail its earliest daylight in the beams
Of gray Atlantic dawns;
And, broad as realms made up of many
lands,
Is lost afar
Behind the crimson hills and purple lawns
Of sunset, among plains which roll their
streams
Against the Evening Star!
And lo!
To the remotest point of sight,
Although I gaze upon no waste of snow,
The endless field is white;
And the whole landscape glows,
For many a shining league away,
With such accumulated light
As Polar lands would flash beneath a tropic
day!

Nor lack there (for the vision grows,
And the small charm within my hands —
More potent even than the fabled one,
Which oped whatever golden mystery
Lay hid in fairy wood or magic vale,
The curious ointment of the Arabian tale —
Beyond all mortal sense
Doth stretch my sight's horizon, and I see,
Beneath its simple influence,

As if, with Uriel's crown,
I stood in some great temple of the Sun,
And looked, as Uriel, down!)
Nor lack there pastures rich and fields all green
With all the common gifts of God.
For temperate airs and torrid sheen
Weave Edens of the sod;
Through lands which look one sea of billowy gold
Broad rivers wind their devious ways;
A hundred isles in their embraces fold
A hundred luminous bays;
And through yon purple haze
Vast mountains lift their plumëd peaks cloud-crowned;
And, save where up their sides the ploughman creeps,
An unhewn forest girds them grandly round,
In whose dark shades a future navy sleeps!
Ye Stars, which, though unseen, yet with me gaze
Upon this loveliest fragment of the earth!
Thou Sun, that kindlest all thy gentlest rays
Above it, as to light a favorite hearth!
Ye Clouds, that in your temples in the West
See nothing brighter than its humblest flowers!
And you, ye Winds, that on the ocean's breast
Are kissed to coolness ere ye reach its bowers!
Bear witness with me in my song of praise,
And tell the world that, since the world began,
No fairer land hath fired a poet's lays,
Or given a home to man.

But these are charms already widely blown!
His be the meed whose pencil's trace
Hath touched our very swamps with grace,
And round whose tuneful way
All Southern laurels bloom;
The Poet of "The Woodlands," unto whom
Alike are known
The flute's low breathing and the trumpet's tone,
And the soft west wind's sighs;
But who shall utter all the debt,
O Land wherein all powers are met
That bind a people's heart,
The world doth owe thee at this day,
And which it never can repay,
Yet scarcely deigns to own!
Where sleeps the poet who shall fitly sing
The source wherefrom doth spring
That mighty commerce which, confined
To the mean channels of no selfish mart,
Goes out to every shore
Of this broad earth, and throngs the sea with ships
That bear no thunders; hushes hungry lips
In alien lands;
Joins with a delicate web remotest strands;
And gladdening rich and poor,
Doth gild Parisian domes,
Or feed the cottage-smoke of English homes,
And only bounds its blessings by mankind!
In offices like these, thy mission lies,
My Country! and it shall not end
As long as rain shall fall and Heaven bend
In blue above thee; though thy foes be hard
And cruel as their weapons, it shall guard
Thy hearth-stones as a bulwark; make thee great
In white and bloodless state;
And haply, as the years increase —
Still working through its humbler reach
With that large wisdom which the ages teach —
Revive the half-dead dream of universal peace!
As men who labor in that mine
Of Cornwall, hollowed out beneath the bed
Of ocean, when a storm rolls overhead,
Hear the dull booming of the world of brine
Above them, and a mighty muffled roar
Of winds and waters, yet toil calmly on,
And split the rock, and pile the massive ore,
Or carve a niche, or shape the archëd roof;
So I, as calmly, weave my woof
Of song, chanting the days to come,
Unsilenced, though the quiet summer air
Stirs with the bruit of battles, and each dawn
Wakes from its starry silence to the hum
Of many gathering armies. Still,
In that we sometimes hear,
Upon the Northern winds, the voice of woe
Not wholly drowned in triumph, though I know
The end must crown us, and a few brief years
Dry all our tears,

I may not sing too gladly. To Thy will
Resigned, O Lord! we cannot all forget
That there is much even Victory must regret.
And, therefore, not too long
From the great burthen of our country's wrong
Delay our just release!
And, if it may be, save
These sacred fields of peace
From stain of patriot or of hostile blood!
Oh, help us, Lord! to roll the crimson flood
Back on its course, and, while our banners wing
Northward, strike with us! till the Goth shall cling
To his own blasted altar-stones, and crave
Mercy; and we shall grant it, and dictate
The lenient future of his fate
There, where some rotting ships and crumbling quays
Shall one day mark the Port which ruled the Western seas.

QUATORZAIN

Most men know love but as a part of life;
They hide it in some corner of the breast,
Even from themselves; and only when they rest
In the brief pauses of that daily strife,
Wherewith the world might else be not so rife,
They draw it forth (as one draws forth a toy
To soothe some ardent, kiss-exacting boy)
And hold it up to sister, child, or wife.
Ah me! why may not love and life be one?
Why walk we thus alone, when by our side,
Love, like a visible god, might be our guide?
How would the marts grow noble! and the street,
Worn like a dungeon-floor by weary feet,
Seem then a golden court-way of the Sun!

CHARLESTON

Calm as that second summer which precedes
The first fall of the snow,
In the broad sunlight of heroic deeds,
The city bides the foe.

As yet, behind their ramparts, stern and proud,
Her bolted thunders sleep, —
Dark Sumter, like a battlemented cloud,
Looms o'er the solemn deep.

No Calpe frowns from lofty cliff or scaur
To guard the holy strand;
But Moultrie holds in leash her dogs of war
Above the level sand.

And down the dunes a thousand guns lie couched,
Unseen, beside the flood, —
Like tigers in some Orient jungle crouched,
That wait and watch for blood.

Meanwhile, through streets still echoing with trade,
Walk grave and thoughtful men,
Whose hands may one day wield the patriot's blade
As lightly as the pen.

And maidens, with such eyes as would grow dim
Over a bleeding hound,
Seem each one to have caught the strength of him
Whose sword she sadly bound.

Thus girt without and garrisoned at home,
Day patient following day,
Old Charleston looks from roof and spire and dome,
Across her tranquil bay.

Ships, through a hundred foes, from Saxon lands
And spicy Indian ports,
Bring Saxon steel and iron to her hands,
And summer to her courts.

But still, along yon dim Atlantic line,
The only hostile smoke
Creeps like a harmless mist above the brine,
From some frail floating oak.

Shall the spring dawn, and she, still clad in smiles,
And with an unscathed brow,
Rest in the strong arms of her palm-crowned isles,
As fair and free as now?

We know not; in the temple of the Fates
God has inscribed her doom:
And, all untroubled in her faith, she waits
The triumph or the tomb.
April, 1863.

AT MAGNOLIA CEMETERY

SLEEP sweetly in your humble graves,
Sleep, martyrs of a fallen cause;
Though yet no marble column craves
The pilgrim here to pause.

In seeds of laurel in the earth
The blossom of your fame is blown,
And somewhere, waiting for its birth,
The shaft is in the stone!

Meanwhile, behalf the tardy years
Which keep in trust your storied tombs,
Behold! your sisters bring their tears,
And these memorial blooms.

Small tributes! but your shades will smile
More proudly on these wreaths to-day,
Than when some cannon-moulded pile
Shall overlook this bay.

Stoop, angels, hither from the skies!
There is no holier spot of ground
Than where defeated valor lies,
By mourning beauty crowned.
Charleston, 1867.

Paul Hamilton Hayne

ASPECTS OF THE PINES

TALL, sombre, grim, against the morning sky
They rise, scarce touched by melancholy airs,
Which stir the fadeless foliage dreamfully,
As if from realms of mystical despairs.

Tall, sombre, grim, they stand with dusky gleams
Brightening to gold within the woodland's core,
Beneath the gracious noontide's tranquil beams, —
But the weird winds of morning sigh no more.

A stillness, strange, divine, ineffable,
Broods round and o'er them in the wind's surcease,
And on each tinted copse and shimmering dell
Rests the mute rapture of deep hearted peace.

Last, sunset comes — the solemn joy and might
Borne from the west when cloudless day declines —
Low, flute-like breezes sweep the waves of light,
And, lifting dark green tresses of the pines,

Till every lock is luminous, gently float,
Fraught with hale odors up the heavens afar,
To faint when twilight on her virginal throat
Wears for a gem the tremulous vesper star.

VICKSBURG

FOR sixty days and upwards,
A storm of shell and shot
Rained round us in a flaming shower,
But still we faltered not.
"If the noble city perish,"
Our grand young leader said,
"Let the only walls the foe shall scale
Be ramparts of the dead!"

For sixty days and upwards,
The eye of heaven waxed dim;
And even throughout God's holy morn,
O'er Christian prayer and hymn,
Arose a hissing tumult,
As if the fiends in air

Strove to engulf the voice of faith
  In the shrieks of their despair.

There was wailing in the houses,
  There was trembling on the marts,
While the tempest raged and thundered,
  Mid the silent thrill of hearts;
But the Lord, our shield, was with us,
  And ere a month had sped,
Our very women walked the streets
  With scarce one throb of dread.

And the little children gambolled,
  Their faces purely raised,
Just for a wondering moment,
  As the huge bombs whirled and blazed;
Then turned with silvery laughter
  To the sports which children love,
Thrice-mailed in the sweet, instinctive thought
  That the good God watched above.

Yet the hailing bolts fell faster,
  From scores of flame-clad ships,
And about us, denser, darker,
  Grew the conflict's wild eclipse,
Till a solid cloud closed o'er us,
  Like a type of doom and ire,
Whence shot a thousand quivering tongues
  Of forked and vengeful fire.

But the unseen hands of angels
  Those death-shafts warned aside,
And the dove of heavenly mercy
  Ruled o'er the battle tide;
In the houses ceased the wailing,
  And through the war-scarred marts
The people strode, with step of hope,
  To the music in their hearts.

BETWEEN THE SUNKEN SUN AND THE NEW MOON

BETWEEN the sunken sun and the new moon,
I stood in fields through which a rivulet ran
With scarce perceptible motion, not a span
Of its smooth surface trembling to the tune
Of sunset breezes: "O delicious boon,"
I cried, "of quiet! wise is Nature's plan,
Who, in her realm, as in the soul of man,
Alternates storm with calm, and the loud noon
With dewy evening's soft and sacred lull:
Happy the heart that keeps *its* twilight hour,
And, in the depths of heavenly peace reclined,
Loves to commune with thoughts of tender power;
Thoughts that ascend, like angels beautiful,
A shining Jacob's ladder of the mind."

A STORM IN THE DISTANCE

I SEE the cloud-born squadrons of the gale,
  Their lines of rain like glittering spears depress,
While all the affrighted land grows darkly pale
  In flashing charge on earth's half-shielded breast.

Sounds like the rush of trampling columns float
  From that fierce conflict; volleyed thunders peal,
Blent with the maddened wind's wild bugle-note;
  The lightnings flash, the solid woodlands reel!

Ha! many a foliaged guardian of the height,
  Majestic pine or chestnut, riven and bare,
Falls in the rage of that aerial fight,
  Led by the Prince of all the Powers of air!

Vast boughs like shattered banners hurtling fly
  Down the thick tumult: while, like emerald snow,
Millions of orphaned leaves make wild the sky,
  Or drift in shuddering helplessness below.

Still, still, the levelled lances of the rain
  At earth's half-shielded breast take glittering aim;
All space is rife with fury, racked with pain,
  Earth bathed in vapor, and heaven rent by flame!

At last the cloud-battalions through long rifts
Of luminous mists retire: — the strife is done,
And earth once more her wounded beauty lifts,
To meet the healing kisses of the sun.

THE ROSE AND THORN

SHE 's loveliest of the festal throng
In delicate form and Grecian face, —
A beautiful, incarnate song,
A marvel of harmonious grace,
And yet I know the truth I speak:
From those gay groups she stands apart,
A rose upon her tender cheek,
A thorn within her heart.

Though bright her eyes' bewildering gleams,
Fair tremulous lips and shining hair,
A something born of mournful dreams
Breathes round her sad enchanted air;
No blithesome thoughts at hide and seek
From out her dimples smiling start;
If still the rose be on her cheek,
A thorn is in her heart.

Young lover, tossed 'twixt hope and fear,
Your whispered vow and yearning eyes
Yon marble Clytie pillared near
Could move as soon to soft replies;
Or, if she thrill at words you speak,
Love's memory prompts the sudden start;
The rose has paled upon her cheek,
The thorn has pierced her heart.

A LITTLE WHILE I FAIN WOULD LINGER YET

A LITTLE while (my life is almost set!)
I fain would pause along the downward way,
Musing an hour in this sad sunset-ray,
While, Sweet! our eyes with tender tears are wet:
A little hour I fain would linger yet.

A little while I fain would linger yet,
All for love's sake, for love that cannot tire;
Though fervid youth be dead, with youth's desire,
And hope has faded to a vague regret,
A little while I fain would linger yet.

A little while I fain would linger here:
Behold! who knows what strange, mysterious bars
'Twixt souls that love may rise in other stars?
Nor can love deem the face of death is fair:
A little while I still would linger here.

A little while I yearn to hold thee fast,
Hand locked in hand, and loyal heart to heart;
(O pitying Christ! those woeful words, "We part!")
So ere the darkness fall, the light be past,
A little while I fain would hold thee fast.

A little while, when light and twilight meet, —
Behind, our broken years; before, the deep
Weird wonder of the last unfathomed sleep, —
A little while I still would clasp thee, Sweet,
A little while, when night and twilight meet.

A little while I fain would linger here;
Behold! who knows what soul-dividing bars
Earth's faithful loves may part in other stars?
Nor can love deem the face of death is fair:
A little while I still would linger here.

IN HARBOR

I THINK it is over, over,
I think it is over at last:
Voices of foemen and lover,
The sweet and the bitter have passed:
Life, like a tempest of ocean
Hath outblown its ultimate blast:
There 's but a faint sobbing seaward
While the calm of the tide deepens leeward,
And behold! like the welcoming quiver
Of heart-pulses throbbed through the river,

Those lights in the harbor at last,
The heavenly harbor at last!

I feel it is over! over!
For the winds and the waters surcease;
Ah, few were the days of the rover
That smiled in the beauty of peace,
And distant and dim was the omen
That hinted redress or release!
From the ravage of life, and its riot,
What marvel I yearn for the quiet
Which bides in the harbor at last, —
For the lights, with their welcoming quiver
That throbs through the sanctified river,
Which girdle the harbor at last,
This heavenly harbor at last?

I know it is over, over,
I know it is over at last!
Down sail! the sheathed anchor uncover,
For the stress of the voyage has passed:
Life, like a tempest of ocean,
Hath outbreathed its ultimate blast:
There's but a faint sobbing seaward,
While the calm of the tide deepens leeward;
And behold! like the welcoming quiver
Of heart-pulses throbbed through the river,
Those lights in the harbor at last,
The heavenly harbor at last!

Emily Dickinson[1]

LIFE

LIFE

Our share of night to bear,
Our share of morning,
Our blank in bliss to fill,
Our blank in scorning.

Here a star, and there a star,
Some lose their way.
Here a mist, and there a mist,
Afterwards — day!

A BOOK

He ate and drank the precious words,
His spirit grew robust;
He knew no more that he was poor,
Nor that his frame was dust.
He danced along the dingy days,
And this bequest of wings
Was but a book. What liberty
A loosened spirit brings!

UTTERANCE

I found the phrase to every thought
I ever had, but one;
And that defies me, — as a hand
Did try to chalk the sun

To races nurtured in the dark: —
How would your own begin?
Can blaze be done in cochineal,
Or noon in mazarin?

WITH FLOWERS

If recollecting were forgetting,
Then I remember not;
And if forgetting, recollecting,
How near I had forgot!
And if to miss were merry,
And if to mourn were gay,
How very blithe the fingers
That gathered these to-day!

PARTING

My life closed twice before its close;
It yet remains to see
If Immortality unveil
A third event to me,

So huge, so hopeless to conceive,
As these that twice befell:
Parting is all we know of heaven,
And all we need of hell.

CALLED BACK

Just lost when I was saved!
Just felt the world go by!
Just girt me for the onset with eternity,
When breath blew back,
And on the other side
I heard recede the disappointed tide!

Therefore, as one returned, I feel,
Odd secrets of the line to tell!
Some sailor, skirting foreign shores,

[1] See, also, p. 587.

Some pale reporter from the awful doors
Before the seal!

Next time, to stay!
Next time, the things to see
By ear unheard,
Unscrutinized by eye.

Next time, to tarry,
While the ages steal, —
Slow tramp the centuries,
And the cycles wheel.

LOVE

CHOICE

Of all the souls that stand create
I have elected one.
When sense from spirit files away,
And subterfuge is done;

When that which is and that which was
Apart, intrinsic, stand,
And this brief tragedy of flesh
Is shifted like a sand;

When figures show their royal front
And mists are carved away, —
Behold the atom I preferred
To all the lists of clay!

CONSTANT

Alter? When the hills do.
Falter? When the sun
Question if his glory
Be the perfect one.

Surfeit? When the daffodil
Doth of the dew:
Even as herself, O friend!
I will of you!

HEART, WE WILL FORGET HIM

Heart, we will forget him!
You and I, to-night!
You may forget the warmth he gave,
I will forget the light.

When you have done, pray tell me,
That I my thoughts may dim;
Haste! lest while you 're lagging,
I may remember him!

NATURE

THE WAKING YEAR

A lady red upon the hill
Her annual secret keeps;
A lady white within the field
In placid lily sleeps!

The tidy breezes with their brooms
Sweep vail, and hill, and tree!
Prithee, my pretty housewives!
Who may expected be?

The neighbors do not yet suspect!
The woods exchange a smile, —
Orchard, and buttercup, and bird,
In such a little while!

And yet how still the landscape stands,
How nonchalant the wood,
As if the resurrection
Were nothing very odd!

AUTUMN

The morns are meeker than they were,
The nuts are getting brown;
The berry's cheek is plumper,
The rose is out of town.
The maple wears a gayer scarf,
The field a scarlet gown.
Lest I should be old-fashioned,
I 'll put a trinket on.

BECLOUDED

The sky is low, the clouds are mean,
A travelling flake of snow
Across a barn or through a rut
Debates if it will go.

A narrow wind complains all day
How someone treated him:
Nature, like us, is sometimes caught
Without her diadem.

FRINGED GENTIAN

God made a little gentian;
It tried to be a rose
And failed, and all the summer laughed:
But just before the snows
There came a purple creature
That ravished all the hill;

And summer hid her forehead,
And mockery was still.
The frosts were her condition;
The Tyrian would not come
Until the North evoked it: —
"Creator! shall I bloom?"

TIME AND ETERNITY

TOO LATE

DELAYED till she had ceased to know,
Delayed till in its vest of snow
Her loving bosom lay:
An hour behind the fleeting breath,
Later by just an hour than death, —
Oh, lagging yesterday!

Could she have guessed that it would be;
Could but a crier of the glee
Have climbed the distant hill;
Had not the bliss so slow a pace, —
Who knows but this surrendered face
Were undefeated still?

Oh, if there may departing be
Any forgot by victory
In her imperial round,
Show them this meek apparelled thing,
That could not stop to be a king,
Doubtful if it be crowned!

CHARTLESS

I NEVER saw a moor,
I never saw the sea;
Yet know I how the heather looks,
And what a wave must be.

I never spoke with God,
Nor visited in heaven;
Yet certain am I of the spot
As if the chart were given.

THE BATTLE-FIELD

THEY dropped like flakes, they dropped like stars,
Like petals from a rose,
When suddenly across the June
A wind with finger goes.

They perished in the seamless grass, —
No eye could find the place;
But God on his repealless list
Can summon every face.

VANISHED

SHE died, — this was the way she died;
And when her breath was done,
Took up her simple wardrobe
And started for the sun.

Her little figure at the gate
The angels must have spied,
Since I could never find her
Upon the mortal side.

THAT SUCH HAVE DIED

THAT such have died enables us
The tranquiller to die;
That such have lived, certificate
For immortality.

THE SECRET

I HAVE not told my garden yet,
Lest that should conquer me;
I have not quite the strength now
To break it to the bee.

I will not name it in the street,
For shops would stare, that I,
So shy, so very ignorant,
Should have the face to die.

The hillsides must not know it,
Where I have rambled so,
Nor tell the loving forests
The day that I shall go,

Nor lisp it at the table,
Nor heedless by the way
Hint that within the riddle
One will walk to-day!

ETERNITY

ON this wondrous sea,
Sailing silently,
Ho! pilot, ho!
Knowest thou the shore
Where no breakers roar,
Where the storm is o'er?

In the silent west
Many sails at rest,
Their anchors fast;
Thither I pilot thee, —
Land, ho! Eternity!
Ashore at last!

Will Wallace Harney

ADONAIS

SHALL we meet no more, my love, at the binding of the sheaves,
In the happy harvest-fields, as the sun sinks low,
When the orchard paths are dim with the drift of fallen leaves,
And the reapers sing together, in the mellow, misty eves:
O, happy are the apples when the south winds blow!

Love met us in the orchard, ere the corn had gathered plume, —
O, happy are the apples when the south winds blow!
Sweet as summer days that die when the months are in the bloom,
And the peaks are ripe with sunset, like the tassels of the broom,
In the happy harvest-fields as the sun sinks low.

Sweet as summer days that die, leafing sweeter each to each, —
O, happy are the apples when the south winds blow!
All the heart was full of feeling: love had ripened into speech,
Like the sap that turns to nectar in the velvet of the peach,
In the happy harvest-fields as the sun sinks low.

Sweet as summer days that die at the ripening of the corn, —
O, happy are the apples when the south winds blow!
Sweet as lovers' fickle oaths, sworn to faithless maids forsworn,
When the musty orchard breathes like a mellow drinking-horn,
Over happy harvest-fields as the sun sinks low.

Love left us at the dying of the mellow autumn eves, —
O, happy are the apples when the south winds blow!
When the skies are ripe and fading, like the colors of the leaves,
And the reapers kiss and part, at the binding of the sheaves,
In the happy harvest-fields as the sun sinks low.

Then the reapers gather home, from the gray and misty meres; —
O, happy are the apples when the south winds blow!
Then the reapers gather home, and they bear upon their spears,
One whose face is like the moon, fallen gray among the spheres,
With the daylight's curse upon it, as the sun sinks low.

Faint as far-off bugles blowing, soft and low the reapers sung; —
O, happy are the apples when the south winds blow!
Sweet as summer in the blood, when the heart is ripe and young,
Love is sweetest in the dying, like the sheaves he lies among,
In the happy harvest-fields as the sun sinks low.

THE STAB

ON the road, the lonely road,
Under the cold white moon,
Under the ragged trees he strode;
He whistled and shifted his weary load —
Whistled a foolish tune.

There was a step timed with his own,
A figure that stooped and bowed —
A cold, white blade that gleamed and shone,
Like a splinter of daylight downward thrown —
And the moon went behind a cloud.

But the moon came out so broad and good,
The barn-fowl woke and crowed;
Then roughed his feathers in drowsy mood,
And the brown owl called to his mate in the wood,
That a dead man lay on the road.

Helen Fiske Jackson

("H. H.")

CORONATION

AT the king's gate the subtle noon
Wove filmy yellow nets of sun;
Into the drowsy snare too soon
The guards fell one by one.

Through the king's gate, unquestioned then,
A beggar went, and laughed, "This brings
Me chance at last, to see if men
Fare better, being kings."

The king sat bowed beneath his crown,
Propping his face with listless hand,
Watching the hour-glass sifting down
Too slow its shining sand.

"Poor man, what wouldst thou have of me?"
The beggar turned, and, pitying,
Replied like one in dream, "Of thee,
Nothing. I want the king."

Uprose the king, and from his head
Shook off the crown and threw it by.
"O man, thou must have known," he said,
"A greater king than I."

Through all the gates, unquestioned then,
Went king and beggar hand in hand.
Whispered the king, "Shall I know when
Before His throne I stand?"

The beggar laughed. Free winds in haste
Were wiping from the king's hot brow
The crimson lines the crown had traced.
"This is his presence now."

At the king's gate, the crafty noon
Unwove its yellow nets of sun;
Out of their sleep in terror soon
The guards waked one by one.

"Ho here! Ho there! Has no man seen
The king?" The cry ran to and fro;
Beggar and king, they laughed, I ween,
The laugh that free men know.

On the king's gate the moss grew gray;
The king came not. They called him dead;
And made his eldest son one day
Slave in his father's stead.

MORN

IN what a strange bewilderment do we
Awake each morn from out the brief night's sleep.
Our struggling consciousness doth grope and creep
Its slow way back, as if it could not free
Itself from bonds unseen. Then Memory,
Like sudden light, outflashes from its deep
The joy or grief which it had last to keep
For us; and by the joy or grief we see
The new day dawneth like the yesterday;
We are unchanged; our life the same we knew
Before. I wonder if this is the way
We wake from death's short sleep, to struggle through
A brief bewilderment, and in dismay
Behold our life unto our old life true.

EMIGRAVIT

WITH sails full set, the ship her anchor weighs.
Strange names shine out beneath her figure head.
What glad farewells with eager eyes are said!
What cheer for him who goes, and him who stays!
Fair skies, rich lands, new homes, and untried days
Some go to seek: the rest but wait instead,
Watching the way wherein their comrades led,
Until the next stanch ship her flag doth raise.
Who knows what myriad colonies there are
Of fairest fields, and rich, undreamed-of gains
Thick planted in the distant shining plains
Which we call sky because they lie so far?
Oh, write of me, not "Died in bitter pains,"
But "Emigrated to another star!"

POPPIES IN THE WHEAT

ALONG Ancona's hills the shimmering heat,
A tropic tide of air, with ebb and flow
Bathes all the fields of wheat until they glow
Like flashing seas of green, which toss and beat
Around the vines. The poppies lithe and fleet
Seem running, fiery torchmen, to and fro
To mark the shore. The farmer does not know
That they are there. He walks with heavy feet,
Counting the bread and wine by autumn's gain,
But I, — I smile to think that days remain
Perhaps to me in which, though bread be sweet
No more, and red wine warm my blood in vain,
I shall be glad remembering how the fleet,
Lithe poppies ran like torchmen with the wheat.

A LAST PRAYER

FATHER, I scarcely dare to pray,
So clear I see, now it is done,
That I have wasted half my day,
And left my work but just begun;

So clear I see that things I thought
Were right or harmless were a sin;
So clear I see that I have sought,
Unconscious, selfish aims to win;

So clear I see that I have hurt
The souls I might have helped to save;
That I have slothful been, inert,
Deaf to the calls thy leaders gave.

In outskirts of thy kingdoms vast,
Father, the humblest spot give me;
Set me the lowliest task thou hast;
Let me repentant work for thee!

HABEAS CORPUS

MY body, eh? Friend Death, how now?
Why all this tedious pomp of writ?
Thou hast reclaimed it sure and slow
For half a century, bit by bit.

In faith thou knowest more to-day
Than I do, where it can be found!
This shriveled lump of suffering clay,
To which I now am chained and bound,

Has not of kith or kin a trace
To the good body once I bore;
Look at this shrunken, ghastly face:
Didst ever see that face before?

Ah, well, friend Death, good friend thou art;
Thy only fault thy lagging gait,
Mistaken pity in thy heart
For timorous ones that bid thee wait.

Do quickly all thou hast to do,
Nor I nor mine will hindrance make;
I shall be free when thou art through;
I grudge thee naught that thou must take!

Stay! I have lied: I grudge thee one,
Yes, two I grudge thee at this last, —
Two members which have faithful done
My will and bidding in the past.

I grudge thee this right hand of mine;
I grudge thee this quick-beating heart;
They never gave me coward sign,
Nor played me once a traitor's part.

I see now why in olden days
Men in barbaric love or hate
Nailed enemies' hands at wild crossways,
Shrined leaders' hearts in costly state:

The symbol, sign, and instrument
Of each soul's purpose, passion, strife,
Of fires in which are poured and spent
Their all of love, their all of life.

O feeble, mighty human hand!
O fragile, dauntless human heart!
The universe holds nothing planned
With such sublime, transcendent art!

Yes, Death, I own I grudge thee mine
Poor little hand, so feeble now;
Its wrinkled palm, its altered line,
Its veins so pallid and so slow —

(*Unfinished here.*)

Ah, well, friend Death, good friend thou art:
I shall be free when thou art through.
Take all there is — take hand and heart:
There must be somewhere work to do.

Her last poem: 7 *August*, 1885.

Franklin Benjamin Sanborn

SAMUEL HOAR

A YEAR ago how often did I meet
Under these elms, once more in sober bloom,
Thy tall, sad figure pacing down the street, —
But now the robin sings above thy tomb.
Thy name on other shores may ne'er be known,
Though austere Rome no graver Consul knew;
But Massachusetts her true son doth own:
Out of her soil thy hardy virtues grew.
She loves the man who chose the conquered cause,
The upright soul that bowed to God alone,
The clean hand that upheld her equal laws,
The old religion, never yet outgrown,
The cold demeanor and warm heart beneath,
The simple grandeur of thy life and death.

ARIANA[1]

SWEET saint! whose rising dawned upon the sight
Like fair Aurora chasing mists away,
Our ocean billows, and thy western height
Gave back reflections of the tender ray,
Sparkling and smiling as night turned to day: —
Ah! whither vanished that celestial light?
Suns rise and set, Monadnoc's amethyst
Year-long above the sullen cloud appears,
Daily the waves our summer strand have kissed,
But thou returnest not with days and years:
Or is it thine, yon clear and beckoning star,
Seen o'er the hills that guarded once thy home?
Dost guide thy friend's free steps that widely roam
Toward that far country where his wishes are?

Joel Benton

AT CHAPPAQUA

HIS cherished woods are mute. The stream glides down
The hill as when I knew it years ago;
The dark, pine arbor with its priestly gown
Stands hushed, as if our grief it still would show;
The silver springs are cupless, and the flow
Of friendly feet no more bereaves the grass,
For he is absent who was wont to pass
Along this wooded path. His axe's blow
No more disturbs the impertinent bole or bough;
Nor moves his pen our heedless nation now,
Which, sworn to justice, stirred the people so.
In some far world his much-loved face must glow
With rapture still. This breeze once fanned his brow.
This is the peaceful Mecca all men know!

THE SCARLET TANAGER

A BALL of fire shoots through the tamarack
In scarlet splendor, on voluptuous wings;
Delirious joy the pyrotechnist brings,
Who marks for us high summer's almanac.
How instantly the red-coat hurtles back!
No fiercer flame has flashed beneath the sky.
Note now the rapture in his cautious eye,
The conflagration lit along his track.
Winged soul of beauty, tropic in desire,
Thy love seems alien in our northern zone;
Thou giv'st to our green lands a burst of fire
And callest back the fables we disown.
The hot equator thou mightst well inspire,
Or stand above some Eastern monarch's throne.

[1] See BIOGRAPHICAL NOTE, p. 819.

Elizabeth Akers Allen

("FLORENCE PERCY")

SEA-BIRDS

O LONESOME sea-gull, floating far
Over the ocean's icy waste,
Aimless and wide thy wanderings are,
Forever vainly seeking rest: —
Where is thy mate, and where thy nest?

'Twixt wintry sea and wintry sky,
Cleaving the keen air with thy breast,
Thou sailest slowly, solemnly;
No fetter on thy wing is pressed: —
Where is thy mate, and where thy nest?

O restless, homeless human soul,
Following for aye thy nameless quest,
The gulls float, and the billows roll;
Thou watchest still, and questionest: —
Where is *thy* mate, and where thy nest?

"MY DEARLING"

My Dearling! — thus, in days long fled,
In spite of creed and court and queen,
King Henry wrote to Anne Boleyn, —
The dearest pet name ever said,
And dearly purchased, too, I ween!

Poor child! she played a losing game:
She won a heart, — so Henry said, —
But ah, the price she gave instead!
Men's hearts, at best, are but a name:
She paid for Henry's with her head!

You count men's hearts as something worth?
Not I: were I a maid unwed,
I 'd rather have my own fair head
Than all the lovers on the earth,
Than all the hearts that ever bled!

"My Dearling!" with a love most true,
Having no fear of creed or queen,
I breathe that name my prayers between;
But it shall never bring to you
The hapless fate of Anne Boleyn!

THE LAST LANDLORD

You who dread the cares and labors
Of the tenant's annual quest,
You who long for peace and rest,
And the quietest of neighbors,
You may find them, if you will,
In the city on the hill.

One indulgent landlord leases
All the pleasant dwellings there;
He has tenants everywhere, —
Every day the throng increases;
None may tell their number, yet
He has mansions still to let.

Never presses he for payment;
Gentlest of all landlords he;
And his numerous tenantry
Never lack for food or raiment.
Sculptured portal, grassy roof,
All alike are trouble-proof.

Of the quiet town's frequenters,
Never one is ill at ease;
There are neither locks nor keys,
Yet no robber breaks or enters;
Not a dweller bolts his door,
Fearing for his treasure-store.

Never sound of strife or clamor
Troubles those who dwell therein;
Never toil's distracting din,
Stroke of axe, nor blow of hammer;
Crimson clover sheds its sweets
Even in the widest streets.

Never tenant old or younger
Suffers illness or decline;
There no suffering children pine;
There comes never want nor hunger;
Woe and need no longer reign;
Poverty forgets its pain.

Turmoil and unrest and hurry
Stay forevermore outside;
By the hearts which there abide
Wrong, privation, doubt, and worry
Are forgotten quite, or seem
Only like a long-past dream.

Never slander nor detraction
  Enters there, and never heard
  Is a sharp or cruel word;
No unworthy thought or action,
  Purpose or intent of ill
  Knows the city on the hill.

There your mansion never waxes
  Out of date, nor needs repairs;
  There intrude no sordid cares;
There are neither rent nor taxes;
  And no vexed and burdened brain
  Reckons either loss or gain.

Wanderers, tired with long endeavor,
  You whom, since your being's dawn,
  With the stern command "Move on!"
Ruthless Fate has tracked forever,
  Here at last your footsteps stay
  With no dread of moving-day!

IN A GARRET

THIS realm is sacred to the silent past;
  Within its drowsy shades are treasures rare
Of dust and dreams; the years are long since last
  A stranger's footfall pressed the creaking stair.

This room no housewife's tidy hand disturbs;
  And here, like some strange presence, ever clings
A homesick smell of dry forgotten herbs, —
  A musty odor as of mouldering things.

Here stores of withered roots and leaves repose,
  For fancied virtues prized in days of yore,
Gathered with thoughtful care, mayhap by those
  Whose earthly ills are healed forever more.

Here shy Arachne winds her endless thread,
  And weaves her silken tapestry unseen,
Veiling the rough-hewn timbers overhead,
  And looping gossamer festoons between.

Along the low joists of the sloping roof,
  Moth-eaten garments hang, a gloomy row,
Like tall fantastic ghosts, which stand aloof,
  Holding grim converse with the long ago.

Here lie remembrancers of childish joys, —
  Old fairy-volumes, conned and conned again,
A cradle, and a heap of battered toys,
  Once loved by babes who now are bearded men.

Here, in the summer, at a broken pane,
  The yellow wasps come in, and buzz and build
Among the rafters; wind and snow and rain
  All enter, as the seasons are fulfilled.

This mildewed chest, behind the chimney, holds
  Old letters, stained and nibbled; faintly show
The faded phrases on the tattered folds
  Once kissed, perhaps, or tear-wet — who may know?

I turn a page like one who plans a crime,
  And lo! love's prophecies and sweet regrets,
A tress of chestnut hair, a love-lorn rhyme,
  And fragrant dust that once was violets.

I wonder if the small sleek mouse, that shaped
  His winter nest between these time-stained beams,
Was happier that his bed was lined and draped
  With the bright warp and woof of youthful dreams?

Here where the gray incessant spiders spin,
  Shrouding from view the sunny world outside,
A golden bumblebee has blundered in
  And lost the way to liberty, and died.

So the lost present drops into the past;
  So the warm living heart, that loves the light,
Faints in the unresponsive darkness vast
  Which hides time's buried mysteries from sight.

Why rob these shadows of their sacred trust?
Let the thick cobwebs hide the day once more;
Leave the dead years to silence and to dust,
And close again the long unopened door.

ROCK ME TO SLEEP

BACKWARD, turn backward, O Time, in your flight,
Make me a child again just for to-night!
Mother, come back from the echoless shore,
Take me again to your heart as of yore;
Kiss from my forehead the furrows of care,
Smooth the few silver threads out of my hair;
Over my slumbers your loving watch keep; —
Rock me to sleep, mother, — rock me to sleep!

Backward, flow backward, O tide of the years!
I am so weary of toil and of tears, —
Toil without recompense, tears all in vain, —
Take them, and give me my childhood again!
I have grown weary of dust and decay, —
Weary of flinging my soul-wealth away;
Weary of sowing for others to reap; —
Rock me to sleep, mother, — rock me to sleep!

Tired of the hollow, the base, the untrue,
Mother, O mother, my heart calls for you!
Many a summer the grass has grown green,
Blossomed and faded, our faces between:
Yet, with strong yearning and passionate pain,
Long I to-night for your presence again.
Come from the silence so long and so deep; —
Rock me to sleep, mother, — rock me to sleep!

Over my heart, in the days that are flown,
No love like mother-love ever has shone;
No other worship abides and endures, —
Faithful, unselfish, and patient like yours:
None like a mother can charm away pain
From the sick soul and the world-weary brain.
Slumber's soft calms o'er my heavy lids creep; —
Rock me to sleep, mother, — rock me to sleep!

Come, let your brown hair, just lighted with gold,
Fall on your shoulders again as of old;
Let it drop over my forehead to-night,
Shading my faint eyes away from the light;
For with its sunny-edged shadows once more
Haply will throng the sweet visions of yore;
Lovingly, softly, its bright billows sweep; —
Rock me to sleep, mother, — rock me to sleep!

Mother, dear mother, the years have been long
Since I last listened your lullaby song:
Sing, then, and unto my soul it shall seem
Womanhood's years have been only a dream.
Clasped to your heart in a loving embrace,
With your light lashes just sweeping my face,
Never hereafter to wake or to weep; —
Rock me to sleep, mother, — rock me to sleep!

Mary Ashley Townsend

SONNETS

THE DEAD SINGER

A POET'S soul has sung its way to God;
Has loosed its luminous wings from earthly thongs,
And soared to join the imperishable throngs
Whose feet the immaculate valleys long have trod.
For him, the recompense; for us, the rod;
And we to whom regretfulness belongs
Crown our dead singer with his own sweet songs,
And roof his grave with love's remembering sod.

But yesterday, a beacon on the height;
To-day, a splendor that has passed us by, —
So, one by one into the morning light,
Whilst yet late watchers gaze upon the sky
And wonder what the heavens prophesy,
The shining stars pass silently from sight!

VIRTUOSA

As by the instrument she took her place,
The expectant people, breathing sigh nor word,
Sat hushed, while o'er the waiting ivory stirred
Her supple hands with their suggestive grace.
With sweet notes they began to interlace,
And then with lofty strains their skill to gird,
Then loftier still, till all the echoes heard
Entrancing harmonies float into space.
She paused, and gaily trifled with the keys
Until they laughed in wild delirium,
Then, with rebuking fingers, from their glees
She led them one by one till all grew dumb,
And music seemed to sink upon its knees,
A slave her touch could quicken or benumb.

AT SET OF SUN

A scent of guava-blossoms and the smell
Of bruisëd grass beneath the tamarind-trees;
The hurried humming of belated bees
With pollen-laden thighs; far birds that tell
With faint, last notes of night's approaching spell,
While smoke of supper-fires the low sun sees
Creep through the roofs of palm, and on the breeze
Floats forth the message of the evening bell.
Our footsteps pause, we look toward the west,
And from my heart throbs out one fervent prayer:
O love! O silence! ever to be thus, —
A silence full of love and love its best,
Till in our evening years we two shall share
Together, side by side, life's Angelus!

DOWN THE BAYOU

The cypress swamp around me wraps its spell,
With hushing sounds in moss-hung branches there,
Like congregations rustling down to prayer,
While Solitude, like some unsounded bell,
Hangs full of secrets that it cannot tell,
And leafy litanies on the humid air
Intone themselves, and on the tree-trunks bare
The scarlet lichen writes her rubrics well.
The cypress-knees take on them marvellous shapes
Of pygmy nuns, gnomes, goblins, witches, fays,
The vigorous vine the withered gum-tree drapes,
Across the oozy ground the rabbit plays,
The moccasin to jungle depths escapes,
And through the gloom the wild deer shyly gaze.

RESERVE

The sea tells something, but it tells not all
That rests within its bosom broad and deep;
The psalming winds that o'er the ocean sweep
From compass point to compass point may call,
Nor half their music unto earth let fall;
In far, ethereal spheres night knows to keep
Fair stars whose rays to mortals never creep,
And day uncounted secrets holds in thrall.
He that is strong is stronger if he wear
Something of self beyond all human clasp, —
An inner self, behind unlifted folds
Of life, which men can touch not nor lay bare:
Thus great in what he gives the world to grasp,
Is greater still in that which he withholds.

HER HOROSCOPE

'Tis true, one half of woman's life is hope
And one half resignation. Between there lies
Anguish of broken dreams, — doubt, dire surprise,
And then is born the strength with all to cope.
Unconsciously sublime, life's shadowed slope

She braves; the knowledge in her patient eyes
Of all that love bestows and love denies,
As writ in every woman's horoscope!
She lives, her heart-beats given to others' needs,
Her hands, to lift for others on the way
The burdens which their weariness forsook.
She dies, an uncrowned doer of great deeds.
Remembered? Yes, as is for one brief day
The rose one leaves in some forgotten book.

EMBRYO

I FEEL a poem in my heart to-night,
A still thing growing, —
As if the darkness to the outer light
A song were owing:
A something strangely vague, and sweet, and sad,
Fair, fragile, slender;
Not tearful, yet not daring to be glad,
And oh, so tender!

It may not reach the outer world at all,
Despite its growing;
Upon a poem-bud such cold winds fall
To blight its blowing.
But, oh, whatever may the thing betide,
Free life or fetter,
My heart, just to have held it till it died,
Will be the better!

A GEORGIA VOLUNTEER

FAR up the lonely mountain-side
My wandering footsteps led;
The moss lay thick beneath my feet,
The pine sighed overhead.
The trace of a dismantled fort
Lay in the forest nave,
And in the shadow near my path
I saw a soldier's grave.

The bramble wrestled with the weed
Upon the lowly mound; —
The simple head-board, rudely writ,
Had rotted to the ground;
I raised it with a reverent hand,
From dust its words to clear,
But time had blotted all but these —
"A Georgia Volunteer!"

I saw the toad and scaly snake
From tangled covert start,
And hide themselves among the weeds
Above the dead man's heart;
But undisturbed, in sleep profound,
Unheeding, there he lay;
His coffin but the mountain soil,
His shroud Confederate gray.

I heard the Shenandoah roll
Along the vale below,
I saw the Alleghanies rise
Towards the realms of snow.
The "Valley Campaign" rose to mind —
Its leader's name — and then
I knew the sleeper had been one
Of Stonewall Jackson's men.

Yet whence he came, what lip shall say —
Whose tongue will ever tell
What desolated hearths and hearts
Have been because he fell?
What sad-eyed maiden braids her hair,
Her hair which he held dear?
One lock of which perchance lies with
The Georgia Volunteer!

What mother, with long watching eyes,
And white lips cold and dumb,
Waits with appalling patience for
Her darling boy to come?
Her boy! whose mountain grave swells up
But one of many a scar,
Cut on the face of our fair land,
By gory-handed war.

What fights he fought, what wounds he wore,
Are all unknown to fame;
Remember, on his lonely grave
There is not e'en a name!
That he fought well and bravely too,
And held his country dear,
We know, else he had never been
A Georgia Volunteer.

He sleeps — what need to question now
If he were wrong or right?
He knows, ere this, whose cause was just
In God the Father's sight.
He wields no warlike weapons now,
Returns no foeman's thrust —
Who but a coward would revile
An honest soldier's dust?

Roll, Shenandoah, proudly roll,
Adown thy rocky glen,
Above thee lies the grave of one
Of Stonewall Jackson's men.

Beneath the cedar and the pine,
In solitude austere,
Unknown, unnamed, forgotten, lies
A Georgia Volunteer.

John Albee

MUSIC AND MEMORY

Enchantress, touch no more that strain !
I know not what it may contain,
But in my breast such mood it wakes
My very spirit almost breaks.
Thoughts come from out some hidden realm
Whose dim memorials overwhelm,
Still bring not back the things I lost,—
Still bringing all the pain they cost.

A SOLDIER'S GRAVE

Break not his sweet repose —
Thou whom chance brings to this sequestered ground,
The sacred yard his ashes close,
But go thy way in silence; here no sound
Is ever heard but from the murmuring pines,
Answering the sea's near murmur;
Nor ever here comes rumor
Of anxious world or war's foregathering signs.
The bleaching flag, the faded wreath,
Mark the dead soldier's dust beneath,
And show the death he chose;
Forgotten save by her who weeps alone,
And wrote his fameless name on this low stone:
Break not his sweet repose.

LANDOR

Come, Walter Savage Landor, come this way;
Step through the lintel low, with prose or verse,
Tallest of latter men; the early star
And latest setting sun of great compeers;
Through youth, through manhood, and extremest age,
Strong at the root, and at the top, blossoms
Perennial. When culled the fields around
Still calling up the great for wisest talk,
Or singing clear some fresh, melodious stave,
Not sickly-sweet, but like ripe autumn fruit,
Of which not one but all the senses taste,
And leave uncloyed the dainty appetite.
Great English master of poetic art,
In these late times that dandle every muse,
Here mayst thou air all day thine eloquence,
And I a never weary listener,
If thou at eve wilt sing one witty song,
Or chant some line of cadenced, classic hymn.

BOS'N HILL

The wind blows wild on Bos'n Hill,
Far off is heard the ocean's rote;
Low overhead the gulls scream shrill,
And homeward scuds each little boat.

Then the dead Bos'n wakes in glee
To hear the storm-king's song;
And from the top of mast-pine tree
He blows his whistle loud and long.

The village sailors hear the call,
Lips pale and eyes grow dim;
Well know they, though he pipes them all,
He means but one shall answer him.

He pipes the dead up from their graves,
Whose bones the tansy hides;
He pipes the dead beneath the waves,
They hear and cleave the rising tides.

But sailors know when next they sail
Beyond the Hilltop's view,
There 's one amongst them shall not fail
To join the Bos'n's Crew.

DANDELIONS

Now dandelions in the short, new grass,
Through all their rapid stages daily pass;
No bee yet visits them; each has its place,
Still near enough to see the other's face.
Unkenn'd the bud, so like the grass and ground
In our old country yards where thickest found;
Some morn it opes a little golden sun,
And sets in its own west when day is done.
In few days more 't is old and silvery gray,
And though so close to earth it made its stay,
Lo! now it findeth wings and lightly flies,
A spirit form, till on the sight it dies.

Edmund Clarence Stedman

SONG FROM A DRAMA

Thou art mine, thou hast given thy word;
Close, close in my arms thou art clinging;
Alone for my ear thou art singing
A song which no stranger hath heard:
But afar from me yet, like a bird,
Thy soul, in some region unstirred,
On its mystical circuit is winging.

Thou art mine, I have made thee mine own;
Henceforth we are mingled forever:
But in vain, all in vain, I endeavor —
Though round thee my garlands are thrown,
And thou yieldest thy lips and thy zone —
To master the spell that alone
My hold on thy being can sever.

Thou art mine, thou hast come unto me!
But thy soul, when I strive to be near it —
The innermost fold of thy spirit —
Is as far from my grasp, is as free,
As the stars from the mountain-tops be,
As the pearl, in the depths of the sea,
From the portionless king that would wear it.

THE DISCOVERER

I have a little kinsman
Whose earthly summers are but three,
And yet a voyager is he
Greater than Drake or Frobisher,
Than all their peers together!
He is a brave discoverer,
And, far beyond the tether
Of them who seek the frozen Pole,
Has sailed where the noiseless surges roll.
Ay, he has travelled whither
A winged pilot steered his bark
Through the portals of the dark,
Past hoary Mimir's well and tree,
Across the unknown sea.

Suddenly, in his fair young hour,
Came one who bore a flower,
And laid it in his dimpled hand
With this command:
"Henceforth thou art a rover!
Thou must make a voyage far,
Sail beneath the evening star,
And a wondrous land discover."
— With his sweet smile innocent
Our little kinsman went.

Since that time no word
From the absent has been heard.
Who can tell
How he fares, or answer well
What the little one has found
Since he left us, outward bound?
Would that he might return!
Then should we learn
From the pricking of his chart
How the skyey roadways part.
Hush! does not the baby this way bring,
To lay beside this severed curl,
Some starry offering
Of chrysolite or pearl?

Ah, no! not so!
We may follow on his track,
But he comes not back.
And yet I dare aver
He is a brave discoverer
Of climes his elders do not know.
He has more learning than appears
On the scroll of twice three thousand years,

More than in the groves is taught,
Or from furthest Indies brought;
He knows, perchance, how spirits fare, —
What shapes the angels wear,
What is their guise and speech
In those lands beyond our reach, —
And his eyes behold
Things that shall never, never be to mortal hearers told.

PAN IN WALL STREET

Just where the Treasury's marble front
Looks over Wall Street's mingled nations;
Where Jews and Gentiles most are wont
To throng for trade and last quotations;
Where, hour by hour, the rates of gold
Outrival, in the ears of people,
The quarter-chimes, serenely tolled
From Trinity's undaunted steeple, —

Even there I heard a strange, wild strain
Sound high above the modern clamor,
Above the cries of greed and gain,
The curbstone war, the auction's hammer;
And swift, on Music's misty ways,
It led, from all this strife for millions,
To ancient, sweet-do-nothing days
Among the kirtle-robed Sicilians.

And as it stilled the multitude,
And yet more joyous rose, and shriller,
I saw the minstrel, where he stood
At ease against a Doric pillar:
One hand a droning organ played,
The other held a Pan's-pipe (fashioned
Like those of old) to lips that made
The reeds give out that strain impassioned.

'T was Pan himself had wandered here
A-strolling through this sordid city,
And piping to the civic ear
The prelude of some pastoral ditty!
The demigod had crossed the seas, —
From haunts of shepherd, nymph, and satyr,
And Syracusan times, — to these
Far shores and twenty centuries later.

A ragged cap was on his head;
But — hidden thus — there was no doubting
That, all with crispy locks o'erspread,
His gnarlëd horns were somewhere sprouting;
His club-feet, cased in rusty shoes,
Were crossed, as on some frieze you see them,
And trousers, patched of divers hues,
Concealed his crooked shanks beneath them.

He filled the quivering reeds with sound,
And o'er his mouth their changes shifted,
And with his goat's-eyes looked around
Where'er the passing current drifted;
And soon, as on Trinacrian hills
The nymphs and herdsmen ran to hear him,
Even now the tradesmen from their tills,
With clerks and porters, crowded near him.

The bulls and bears together drew
From Jauncey Court and New Street Alley,
As erst, if pastorals be true,
Came beasts from every wooded valley;
The random passers stayed to list, —
A boxer Ægon, rough and merry,
A Broadway Daphnis, on his tryst
With Nais at the Brooklyn Ferry.

A one-eyed Cyclops halted long
In tattered cloak of army pattern,
And Galatea joined the throng, —
A blowsy, apple-vending slattern;
While old Silenus staggered out
From some new-fangled lunch-house handy,
And bade the piper, with a shout,
To strike up Yankee Doodle Dandy!

A newsboy and a peanut-girl
Like little Fauns began to caper:
His hair was all in tangled curl,
Her tawny legs were bare and taper;
And still the gathering larger grew,
And gave its pence and crowded nigher,
While aye the shepherd-minstrel blew
His pipe, and struck the gamut higher.

O heart of Nature, beating still
With throbs her vernal passion taught her, —
Even here, as on the vine-clad hill,
Or by the Arethusan water!
New forms may fold the speech, new lands
Arise within these ocean-portals,
But Music waves eternal wands, —
Enchantress of the souls of mortals!

So thought I, — but among us trod
A man in blue, with legal baton,
And scoffed the vagrant demigod,
And pushed him from the step I sat on.
Doubting I mused upon the cry,
"Great Pan is dead!" — and all the people
Went on their ways: — and clear and high
The quarter sounded from the steeple.

KEARNY AT SEVEN PINES

So that soldierly legend is still on its journey, —
That story of Kearny who knew not to yield!
'T was the day when with Jameson, fierce Berry, and Birney,
Against twenty thousand he rallied the field.
Where the red volleys poured, where the clamor rose highest,
Where the dead lay in clumps through the dwarf oak and pine,
Where the aim from the thicket was surest and nighest, —
No charge like Phil Kearny's along the whole line.

When the battle went ill, and the bravest were solemn,
Near the dark Seven Pines, where we still held our ground,
He rode down the length of the withering column,
And his heart at our war-cry leapt up with a bound;
He snuffed, like his charger, the wind of the powder, —
His sword waved us on and we answered the sign:
Loud our cheer as we rushed, but his laugh rang the louder,
"There 's the devil's own fun, boys, along the whole line!"

How he strode his brown steed! How we saw his blade brighten
In the one hand still left, — and the reins in his teeth!
He laughed like a boy when the holidays heighten,
But a soldier's glance shot from his visor beneath.
Up came the reserves to the mellay infernal,
Asking where to go in, — through the clearing or pine?
"O, anywhere! Forward! 'T is all the same, Colonel:
You 'll find lovely fighting along the whole line!"

O, evil the black shroud of night at Chantilly,
That hid him from sight of his brave men and tried!
Foul, foul sped the bullet that clipped the white lily,
The flower of our knighthood, the whole army's pride!
Yet we dream that he still, — in that shadowy region
Where the dead form their ranks at the wan drummer's sign, —
Rides on, as of old, down the length of his legion,
And the word still is Forward! along the whole line.

THE HAND OF LINCOLN

Look on this cast, and know the hand
That bore a nation in its hold:
From this mute witness understand
What Lincoln was, — how large of mould

The man who sped the woodman's team,
And deepest sunk the ploughman's share,
And pushed the laden raft astream,
Of fate before him unaware.

This was the hand that knew to swing
The axe — since thus would Freedom train
Her son — and made the forest ring,
And drove the wedge, and toiled amain.

Firm hand, that loftier office took,
A conscious leader's will obeyed,

And, when men sought his word and look,
 With steadfast might the gathering swayed.

No courtier's, toying with a sword,
 Nor minstrel's, laid across a lute;
A chief's, uplifted to the Lord
 When all the kings of earth were mute!

The hand of Anak, sinewed strong,
 The fingers that on greatness clutch;
Yet, lo! the marks their lines along
 Of one who strove and suffered much.

For here in knotted cord and vein
 I trace the varying chart of years;
I know the troubled heart, the strain,
 The weight of Atlas — and the tears.

Again I see the patient brow
 That palm erewhile was wont to press;
And now 't is furrowed deep, and now
 Made smooth with hope and tenderness.

For something of a formless grace
 This moulded outline plays about;
A pitying flame, beyond our trace,
 Breathes like a spirit, in and out, —

The love that cast an aureole
 Round one who, longer to endure,
Called mirth to ease his ceaseless dole,
 Yet kept his nobler purpose sure.

Lo, as I gaze, the statured man,
 Built up from yon large hand, appears:
A type that Nature wills to plan
 But once in all a people's years.

What better than this voiceless cast
 To tell of such a one as he,
Since through its living semblance passed
 The thought that bade a race be free!

SALEM

A. D. 1692

Soe, Mistress Anne, faire neighbour myne,
 How rides a witche when nighte-winds blowe?
Folk saye that you are none too goode
To joyne the crewe in Salem woode,
When one you wot of gives the signe:
 Righte well, methinks, the pathe you knowe.

In Meetinge-time I watched you well,
 Whiles godly Master Parris prayed:
Your folded hands laye on your booke;
But Richard answered to a looke
That fain would tempt him unto hell,
 Where, Mistress Anne, your place is made.

You looke into my Richard's eyes
 With evill glances shamelesse growne;
I found about his wriste a hair,
And guesse what fingers tyed it there:
He shall not lightly be your prize —
 Your Master firste shall take his owne.

'T is not in nature he should be
 (Who loved me soe when Springe was greene)
A childe, to hange upon your gowne!
He loved me well in Salem Towne
Until this wanton witcherie
 His hearte and myne crept dark betweene.

Last Sabbath nighte, the gossips saye,
 Your goodman missed you from his side.
He had no strength to move, untill
Agen, as if in slumber still,
Beside him at the dawne you laye.
 Tell, nowe, what meanwhile did betide.

Dame Anne, mye hate goe with you fleete
 As driftes the Bay fogg overhead —
Or over yonder hill-topp, where
There is a tree ripe fruite shall bear
When, neighbour myne, your wicked feet
 The stones of Gallowes Hill shall tread.

FALSTAFF'S SONG

Where 's he that died o' Wednesday?
 What place on earth hath he?
A tailor's yard beneath, I wot,
 Where worms approaching be;
For the wight that died o' Wednesday,
 Just laid the light below,
Is dead as the varlet turned to clay
 A score of years ago.

Where 's he that died o' Sabba' day?
 Good Lord, I'd not be he!

The best of days is foul enough
  From this world's fare to flee;
And the saint that died o' Sabba' day,
  With his grave turf yet to grow,
Is dead as the sinner brought to pray
  A hundred years ago.

Where 's he that died o' yesterday?
  What better chance hath he
To clink the can and toss the pot
  When this night's junkets be?
For the lad that died o' yesterday
  Is just as dead — ho! ho! —
As the whoreson knave men laid away
  A thousand years ago.

THE WORLD WELL LOST

THAT year? Yes, doubtless I remember still, —
  Though why take count of every wind that blows!
'T was plain, men said, that Fortune used me ill
  That year, — the self-same year I met with Rose.

Crops failed; wealth took a flight; house, treasure, land,
  Slipped from my hold — thus plenty comes and goes.
One friend I had, but he too loosed his hand
  (Or was it I?) the year I met with Rose.

There was a war, I think; some rumor, too,
  Of famine, pestilence, fire, deluge, snows;
Things went awry. My rivals, straight in view,
  Throve, spite of all; but I, — I met with Rose.

That year my white-faced Alma pined and died:
  Some trouble vexed her quiet heart, — who knows?
Not I, who scarcely missed her from my side,
  Or aught else gone, the year I met with Rose.

Was there no more? Yes, that year life began:
  All life before a dream, false joys, light woes, —
All after-life compressed within the span
  Of that one year, — the year I met with Rose!

HELEN KELLER

MUTE, sightless visitant,
  From what uncharted world
Hast voyaged into Life's rude sea,
    With guidance scant;
As if some bark mysteriously
Should hither glide, with spars aslant
    And sails all furled!

  In what perpetual dawn,
  Child of the spotless brow,
Hast kept thy spirit far withdrawn —
  Thy birthright undefiled?
What views to thy sealed eyes appear?
  What voices mayst thou hear
  Speak as we know not how?
  Of grief and sin hast thou,
    O radiant child,
Even thou, a share? Can mortal taint
  Have power on thee unfearing
  The woes our sight, our hearing,
Learn from Earth's crime and plaint?

    Not as we see
Earth, sky, insensate forms, ourselves,
  Thou seest, — but vision-free
  Thy fancy soars and delves,
Albeit no sounds to us relate
    The wondrous things
  Thy brave imaginings
Within their starry night create.

  Pity thy unconfined
Clear spirit, whose enfranchised eyes
  Use not their grosser sense?
Ah, no! thy bright intelligence
  Hath its own Paradise,
A realm wherein to hear and see
  Things hidden from our kind.
  Not thou, not thou — 't is we
  Are deaf, are dumb, are blind!

1888.

MORGAN

Oh, what a set of Vagabundos,
Sons of Neptune, sons of Mars,
Raked from todos otros mundos,
Lascars, Gascons, Portsmouth tars,
Prison mate and dock-yard fellow,
Blades to Meg and Molly dear,
Off to capture Porto Bello
Sailed with Morgan the Buccaneer!

Out they voyaged from Port Royal
(Fathoms deep its ruins be,
Pier and convent, fortress loya ,
Sunk beneath the gaping sea ;
On the Spaniard's beach they landed,
Dead to pity, void of fear, —
Round their blood-red flag embanded,
Led by Morgan the Buccaneer.

Dawn till dusk they stormed the castle,
Beat the gates and gratings down;
Then, with ruthless rout and wassail,
Night and day they sacked the town,
Staved the bins its cellars boasted,
Port and Lisbon, tier on tier,
Quaffed to heart's content, and toasted
Harry Morgan the Buccaneer:

Stripped the church and monastery,
Racked the prior for his gold,
With the traders' wives made merry,
Lipped the young and mocked the old,
Diced for hapless señoritas
(Sire and brother bound anear), —
Juanas, Lolas, Manuelitas,
Cursing Morgan the Buccaneer.

Lust and rapine, flame and slaughter;
Forayed with the Welshman grim:
"Take my pesos, spare my daughter!"
"Ha! ha!" roared that devil's limb,
"These shall jingle in our pouches,
She with us shall find good cheer."
"Lash the graybeard till he crouches!"
Shouted Morgan the Buccaneer.

Out again through reef and breaker,
While the Spaniard moaned his fate,
Back they voyaged to Jamaica,
Flush with doubloons, coins of eight,
Crosses wrung from Popish varlets,
Jewels torn from arm and ear, —
Jesu! how the Jews and harlots
Welcomed Morgan the Buccaneer!

ON A GREAT MAN WHOSE MIND IS CLOUDING

That sovereign thought obscured? That vision clear
Dimmed in the shadow of the sable wing,
And fainter grown the fine interpreting
Which as an oracle was ours to hear!
Nay, but the Gods reclaim not from the seer
Their gift, — although he ceases here to sing,
And, like the antique sage, a covering
Draws round his head, knowing what change is near.

SI JEUNESSE SAVAIT!

When the veil from the eyes is lifted
The seer's head is gray;
When the sailor to shore has drifted
The sirens are far away.
Why must the clearer vision,
The wisdom of Life's late hour,
Come, as in Fate's derision,
When the hand has lost its power?
Is there a rarer being,
Is there a fairer sphere
Where the strong are not unseeing,
And the harvests are not sere;
Where, ere the seasons dwindle,
They yield their due return;
Where the lamps of knowledge kindle
While the flames of youth still burn?
O, for the young man's chances!
O, for the old man's will!
Those flee while this advances,
And the strong years cheat us still.

MORS BENEFICA

Give me to die unwitting of the day,
And stricken in Life's brave heat, with senses clear:
Not swathed and couched until the lines appear
Of Death's wan mask upon this withering clay,
But as that old man eloquent made way
From Earth, a nation's conclave hushed anear;
Or as the chief whose fates, that he may hear
The victory, one glorious moment stay.
Or, if not thus, then with no cry in vain,

No ministrant beside to ward and weep,
Hand upon helm I would my quittance gain
In some wild turmoil of the waters deep,
And sink content into a dreamless sleep
(Spared grave and shroud) below the ancient main.

QUEST

FROM "CORDA CONCORDIA"

WHERE broods the Absolute,
Or shuns our long pursuit
By fiery utmost pathways out of ken?
Fleeter than sunbeams, lo,
Our passionate spirits go,
And traverse immemorial space, and then
Look off, and look in vain, to find
The master-clew to all they left behind.

White orbs like angels pass
Before the triple glass,
That men may scan the record of each flame, —
Of spectral line and line
The legendry divine, —
Finding their mould the same, and aye the same,
The atoms that we knew before
Of which ourselves are made, — dust, and no more.

So let our defter art
Probe the warm brain, and part
Each convolution of the trembling shell:
But whither now has fled
The sense to matter wed
That murmured here? All silence, such as fell
When to the shrine beyond the Ark
The soldiers reached, and found it void and dark.

Seek elsewhere, and in vain
The wings of morning chain;
Their speed transmute to fire, and bring the Light,
The co-eternal beam
Of the blind minstrel's dream;
But think not that bright heat to know aright,
Nor how the trodden seed takes root,
Waked by its glow, and climbs to flower and fruit.

Behind each captured law
Weird shadows give us awe;
Press with your swords, the phantoms still evade;
Through our alertest host
Wanders at ease some ghost,
Now here, now there, by no enchantment laid,
And works upon our souls its will,
Leading us on to subtler mazes still.

We think, we feel, we are;
And light, as of a star,
Gropes through the mist, — a little light is given;
And aye from life and death
We strive, with indrawn breath,
To somehow wrest the truth, and long have striven,
Nor pause, though book and star and clod
Reply, *Canst thou by searching find out God?*

As from the hollow deep
The soul's strong tide must keep
Its purpose still. We rest not, though we hear
No voice from heaven let fall,
No chant antiphonal
Sounding through sunlit clefts that open near;
We look not outward, but within,
And think not quite to end as we begin.

INVOCATION

THOU, — whose endearing hand once laid in sooth
Upon thy follower, no want thenceforth,
Nor toil, nor joy and pain, nor waste of years
Filled with all cares that deaden and subdue,
Can make thee less to him — can make thee less
Than sovereign queen, his first liege, and his last
Remembered to the unconscious dying hour, —
Return and be thou kind, bright Spirit of song,
Thou whom I yet loved most, loved most of all
Even when I left thee — I, now so long strayed
From thy beholding! And renew, renew
Thy gift to me fain clinging to thy robe!
Still be thou kind, for still thou wast most dear.

Tracy Robinson

SONG OF THE PALM

I

Wild is its nature, as it were a token,
Born of the sunshine, and the stars, and sea;
Grand as a passion felt but never spoken,
Lonely and proud and free.

For when the Maker set its crown of beauty,
And for its home ordained the torrid ring,
Assigning unto each its place and duty,
He made the Palm a King.

So when in reverie I look and listen,
Half dream-like floats, within my passive mind,
Why in the sun its branches gleam and glisten,
And harp-wise beat the wind;

Why, when the sea-waves, heralding their tidings,
Come roaring on the shore with crests of down,
In grave acceptance of their sad confidings,
It bows its stately crown;

Why, in the death-like calms of night and morning,
Its quivering spears of green are never still,
But ever tremble, as at solemn warning
A human heart may thrill;

And also why it stands in lonely places,
By the red desert or the sad sea shore,
Or haunts the jungle, or the mountain graces
Where eagles proudly soar!

It is a sense of kingly isolation,
Of royal beauty and enchanting grace,
Proclaiming from the earliest creation
The power and pride of race,

That has almost imbued it with a spirit,
And made it sentient, although still a tree,
With dim perception that it might inherit
An immortality.

The lines of kinship thus so near converging,
It is not strange, O heart of mine, that I,
While stars were shining and old ocean surging,
Should intercept a sigh.

It fell a-sighing when the faint wind, dying,
Had kissed the tropic night a fond adieu —
The starry cross on her warm bosom lying,
Within the southern view.

And when the crescent moon, the west descending,
Drew o'er her face the curtain of the sea,
In the rapt silence, eager senses lending,
Low came the sigh to me.

God of my life! how can I ever render
The full sweet meaning sadly thus conveyed —
The full sad meaning, heart-breakingly tender,
That through the cadence strayed.

II

When the wild North-wind by the sun enchanted,
Seeks the fair South, as lover beauty's shrine,
It bears the moaning of the sorrow-haunted,
Gloomy, storm-beaten Pine.

The waves of ocean catch the miserere,
Far wafted seaward from the wintry main,
They roll it on o'er reaches vast and dreary
With infinite refrain,

Until on coral shores, where endless Summer
Waves golden banners round her queenly throne,
The Palm enfolds the weary spirit roamer
With low responsive moan.

The sea-grape hears it, and the lush banana,
In the sweet indolence of their repose;

The frangipanni, like a crowned Sultana,
The passion flower, and rose;

And the fierce tiger in his darksome lair,
Deep hid away beneath the bamboo-tree;
All the wild habitants of earth and air,
And of the sleeping sea.

It throws a spell of silence so enthralling,
So breathless and intense and mystical,
Not the deep hush of skies when stars are falling
Can fill the soul so full.

A death in life! A calm so deep and brooding
It floods the heart with an ecstatic pain,
Brimming with joy, yet fearfully fore-boding
The dreadful hurricane.

Fail love, fly happiness, yield all things mortal!
Fate, with the living, hath my small lot cast
To dwell beside thee, Palm! Beyond death's portal,
Guard well my sleep at last.

For I do love thee with a lover's passion.
Morn, noon, and night thou art forever grand, —
Type of a glory God alone may fashion
Within the Summer Land.

Sigh not, O Palm! Dread not the final hour;
For oft I 've seen within thy gracious shade,
Amid rose-garlands fair, from Love's own bower,
Lithe, dusky forms displayed,

Clad with the magic of their beauty only;
And it were strange if Paradise should be
Despoiled and made forever sad and lonely,
Bereft of these and thee!

Charles Henry Webb

WITH A NANTUCKET SHELL

I SEND thee a shell from the ocean beach;
But listen thou well, for my shell hath speech.
Hold to thine ear,
And plain thou'lt hear
Tales of ships
That were lost in the rips,
Or that sunk on shoals
Where the bell-buoy tolls,
And ever and ever its iron tongue rolls
In a ceaseless lament for the poor lost souls.

And a song of the sea
Has my shell for thee;
The melody in it
Was hummed at Wauwinet,
And caught at Coatue
By the gull that flew
Outside to the ship with its perishing crew.
But the white wings wave
Where none may save,
And there 's never a stone to mark a grave.

See, its sad heart bleeds
For the sailors' needs;
But it bleeds again
For more mortal pain,
More sorrow and woe,
Than is theirs who go
With shuddering eyes and whitening lips
Down in the sea on their shattered ships.

Thou fearest the sea?
And a tyrant is he, —
A tyrant as cruel as tyrant may be;
But though winds fierce blow,
And the rocks lie low,
And the coast be lee,
This I say to thee:
Of Christian souls more have been wrecked on shore
Than ever were lost at sea!

MARCH

The earth seems a desolate mother, —
  Betrayed like the princess of old,
The ermine stripped from her shoulders,
  And her bosom all naked and cold.

But a joy looks out from her sadness,
  For she feels with a glad unrest
The throb of the unborn summer
  Under her bare, brown breast.

GIL, THE TOREADOR

The Queen sat in her balcony,
  The Loveliest of Spain;
Beneath rode all the chivalry,
  And roses fell like rain
To crown the gallant gentlemen
  The gonfalon who bore:
A woman's favor fell for one, —
  Gil, the Toreador.

Beneath the royal canopy,
  To see the red bull slain,
They sat, like loyal lovers,
  The King and Queen of Spain.
Came marshal, noble, knight and squire,
  Chulo and picador:
Of all a woman saw but one, —
  Gil, the Toreador.

The trumpets clanged, the sport was on,
  The royal sport of Spain;
Maddened by shouts and thrust of lance
  The bull now charged amain:
Down to their death went chulos then,
  And many a matador: —
A woman only knew there fell
  Gil, the Toreador.

When through the streets of proud Madrid
  Swept next the courtly train,
Sat not upon her balcony
  The Loveliest of Spain.
Long live the King and his fair Queen,
  Still loyal thousands roar: —
None know what woman died when fell
  Gil, the Toreador.

DUM VIVIMUS VIGILEMUS

Turn out more ale, turn up the light;
I will not go to bed to-night.
Of all the foes that man should dread
The first and worst one is a bed.
Friends I have had both old and young,
And ale we drank and songs we sung:
Enough you know when this is said,
That, one and all, — they died in bed.
  In bed they died and I'll not go
  Where all my friends have perished so.
  Go you who glad would buried be,
  But not to-night a bed for me.

For me to-night no bed prepare,
But set me out my oaken chair.
And bid no other guests beside
The ghosts that shall around me glide;
In curling smoke-wreaths I shall see
A fair and gentle company.
Though silent all, rare revellers they,
Who leave you not till break of day.
  Go you who would not daylight see,
  But not to-night a bed for me:
  For I've been born and I've been wed —
  All of man's peril comes of bed.

And I'll not seek — whate'er befall —
Him who unbidden comes to all.
A grewsome guest, a lean-jawed wight —
God send he do not come to-night!
But if he do, to claim his own,
He shall not find me lying prone;
But blithely, bravely, sitting up,
And raising high the stirrup-cup.
  Then if you find a pipe unfilled,
  An empty chair, the brown ale spilled;
  Well may you know, though naught be said,
  That I've been borne away to bed.

Richard Realf

INDIRECTION

Fair are the flowers and the children, but their subtle suggestion is fairer;
Rare is the roseburst of dawn, but the secret that clasps it is rarer;
Sweet the exultance of song, but the strain that precedes it is sweeter;
And never was poem yet writ, but the meaning outmastered the metre.

Never a daisy that grows, but a mystery guideth the growing;
Never a river that flows, but a majesty sceptres the flowing;
Never a Shakespeare that soared, but a stronger than he did enfold him,
Nor ever a prophet foretells, but a mightier seer hath foretold him.

Back of the canvas that throbs the painter is hinted and hidden;
Into the statue that breathes the soul of the sculptor is bidden;
Under the joy that is felt lie the infinite issues of feeling;
Crowning the glory revealed is the glory that crowns the revealing.

Great are the symbols of being, but that which is symboled is greater;
Vast the create and beheld, but vaster the inward creator;
Back of the sound broods the silence, back of the gift stands the giving;
Back of the hand that receives thrill the sensitive nerves of receiving.

Space is as nothing to spirit, the deed is outdone by the doing;
The heart of the wooer is warm, but warmer the heart of the wooing;
And up from the pits where these shiver, and up from the heights where those shine,
Twin voices and shadows swim starward, and the essence of life is divine.

THE WORD

O Earth! thou hast not any wind that blows
Which is not music; every weed of thine
Pressed rightly flows in aromatic wine;
And every humble hedgerow flower that grows,
And every little brown bird that doth sing,
Hath something greater than itself, and bears
A living Word to every living thing,
Albeit it hold the Message unawares.
All shapes and sounds have something which is not
Of them: a Spirit broods amid the grass;
Vague outlines of the Everlasting Thought
Lie in the melting shadows as they pass;
The touch of an Eternal Presence thrills
The fringes of the sunsets and the hills.

AN OLD MAN'S IDYL

By the waters of Life we sat together,
Hand in hand in the golden days
Of the beautiful early summer weather,
When skies were purple and breath was praise,
When the heart kept tune to the carol of birds,
And the birds kept tune to the songs which ran
Through shimmer of flowers on grassy swards,
And trees with voices æolian.

By the rivers of Life we walked together,
I and my darling, unafraid;
And lighter than any linnet's feather
The burdens of being on us weighed.
And Love's sweet miracles o'er us threw
Mantles of joy outlasting Time,
And up from the rosy morrows grew
A sound that seemed like a marriage chime.

In the gardens of Life we strayed together;
And the luscious apples were ripe and red,
And the languid lilac and honeyed heather
Swooned with the fragrance which they shed.
And under the trees the angels walked,
And up in the air a sense of wings
Awed us tenderly while we talked
Softly in sacred communings.

In the meadows of Life we strayed together,
Watching the waving harvests grow;
And under the benison of the Father
Our hearts, like the lambs, skipped to and fro.
And the cowslip, hearing our low replies,
Broidered fairer the emerald banks,
And glad tears shone in the daisy's eyes,
And the timid violet glistened thanks.

Who was with us, and what was round us,
Neither myself nor my darling guessed;
Only we knew that something crowned us
Out from the heavens with crowns of rest;
Only we knew that something bright
Lingered lovingly where we stood,
Clothed with the incandescent light
Of something higher than humanhood.

O the riches Love doth inherit!
Ah, the alchemy which doth change
Dross of body and dregs of spirit
Into sanctities rare and strange!

My flesh is feeble and dry and old,
My darling's beautiful hair is gray;
But our elixir and precious gold
Laugh at the footsteps of decay.

Harms of the world have come unto us,
Cups of sorrow we yet shall drain;
But we have a secret which doth show us
Wonderful rainbows in the rain.
And we hear the tread of the years move by,
And the sun is setting behind the hills;
But my darling does not fear to die,
And I am happy in what God wills.

So we sit by our household fires together,
Dreaming the dreams of long ago:
Then it was balmy summer weather,
And now the valleys are laid in snow.
Icicles hang from the slippery eaves;
The wind blows cold, — 't is growing late;
Well, well! we have garnered all our sheaves,
I and my darling, and we wait.

George Arnold

FAREWELL TO SUMMER

SUMMER is fading; the broad leaves that grew
So freshly green, when June was young, are falling;
And, all the whisper-haunted forest through,
The restless birds in saddened tones are calling,
From rustling hazel copse and tangled dell,
"Farewell, sweet Summer,
Fragrant, fruity Summer,
Sweet, farewell!"

Upon the windy hills, in many a field,
The honey-bees hum slow, above the clover,
Gleaning the latest sweets its blooms may yield,
And, knowing that their harvest-time is over,
Sing, half a lullaby and half a knell,
"Farewell, sweet Summer,
Honey-laden Summer,
Sweet, farewell!"

The little brook that babbles mid the ferns,
O'er twisted roots and sandy shallows playing,
Seems fain to linger in its eddied turns,
And with a plaintive, purling voice is saying
(Sadder and sweeter than my song can tell),
"Farewell, sweet Summer,
Warm and dreamy Summer,
Sweet, farewell!"

The fitful breeze sweeps down the winding lane
With gold and crimson leaves before it flying;
Its gusty laughter has no sound of pain,
But in the lulls it sinks to gentle sighing,
And mourns the Summer's early broken spell, —
"Farewell, sweet Summer,
Rosy, blooming Summer,
Sweet, farewell!"

So bird and bee and brook and breeze make moan,
With melancholy song their loss complaining.
I too must join them, as I walk alone
Among the sights and sounds of Summer's waning. . . .
I too have loved the season passing well. . . .
So, farewell, Summer,
Fair but faded Summer,
Sweet, farewell!

BEER

HERE,
With my beer
I sit,
While golden moments flit:
Alas!
They pass
Unheeded by:
And, as they fly,
I,
Being dry,
Sit, idly sipping here
My beer.

O, finer far
Than fame, or riches, are
The graceful smoke-wreaths of this free cigar!
Why
Should I
Weep, wail, or sigh?
What if luck has passed me by?
What if my hopes are dead, —
My pleasures fled?
Have I not still
My fill
Of right good cheer, —
Cigars and beer?

Go, whining youth,
Forsooth!
Go, weep and wail,
Sigh and grow pale,
Weave melancholy rhymes
On the old times,
Whose joys like shadowy ghosts appear,
But leave to me my beer!
Gold is dross, —
Love is loss, —
So, if I gulp my sorrows down,
Or see them drown
In foamy draughts of old nut-brown,
Then do I wear the crown,
Without the cross!

Frances Louisa Bushnell

WORLD MUSIC

JUBILANT the music through the fields a-ringing, —
Carol, warble, whistle, pipe, — endless ways of singing,
Oriole, bobolink, melody of thrushes,
Rustling trees, hum of bees, sudden little hushes,
Broken suddenly again —
Carol, whistle, rustle, humming,
In reiterate refrain,
Thither, hither, going, coming,
While the streamlets' softer voices mingle murmurously together;
Gurgle, whisper, lapses, plashes, — praise of love and summer weather.

Hark! A music finer on the air is blowing, —
Throbs of infinite content, sounds of things a-growing,
Secret sounds, flit of bird under leafy cover,
Odors shy floating by, clouds blown swiftly over,
Kisses of the crimson roses,
Crosses of the lily-lances,
Stirrings when a bud uncloses,
Tripping sun and shadow dances,
Murmur of aërial tides, stealthy zephyrs gliding,
And a thousand nameless things sweeter for their hiding.

Ah! a music more than these floweth on forever,
In and out, yet all beyond our tracing or endeavor,

Far yet clear, strange yet near, sweet
with a profounder sweetness,
Mystical, rhythmical, weaving all into
completeness;
For its wide, harmonious measures
Not one earthly note let fall;
Sorrows, raptures, pains and pleasures,
All in it, and it in all.
Of earth's music the ennobler, of its discord
the refiner,
Pipe of Pan was once its naming, now it
hath a name diviner.

UNFULFILMENT

Ah, June is here, but where is May? —
That lovely, shadowy thing,
Fair promiser of fairer day,
That made my fancy stretch her wing,
In hope-begetting spring.

The spaces vague, the luminous veil,
The drift of bloom and scent,
Those dreamy longings setting sail,
That knew not, asked not, where they
went, —
Ah! was this all they meant, —

This day that lets me dream no more,
This bright, unshadowed round?
On some illimitable shore,
The harbor whither those were bound
Lieth, nor yet is found.

IN THE DARK

Restless, to-night, and ill at ease,
And finding every place too strait,
I leave the porch shut in with trees,
And wander through the garden-gate.

So dark at first, I have to feel
My way before me with my hands;
But soul-like fragrances reveal
My virgin Daphne, where she stands.

Her stars of blossom breathe aloft
Her worship to the stars above;
In wavering pulsations soft,
Climbs the sweet incense of her love;

Those far, celestial eyes can dart
Their glances down through leafy
bars;
The spark that burns within her heart
Was dropped, in answer, from the
stars.

She does not find the space too small,
The night too dark, for sweetest
bloom;
Content within the garden wall,
Since upward there is always room.

Her spotless heart, through all the night,
Holds safe its little vestal spark.
O blessed, if the soul be white,
To breathe and blossom in the dark!

Annie Fields

ON WAKING FROM A DREAMLESS SLEEP

I waked; the sun was in the sky,
The face of heaven was fair;
The silence all about me lay,
Of morning in the air.

I said, Where hast thou been, my soul,
Since the moon set in the west?
I know not where thy feet have trod,
Nor what has been thy quest.

Where wast thou when Orion past
Below the dark-blue sea?
His glittering, silent stars are gone, —
Didst follow them for me?

Where wast thou in that awful hour
When first the night-wind heard
The faint breath of the coming dawn,
And fled before the word?

Where hast thou been, my spirit,
Since the long wave on the shore
Tenderly rocked my sense asleep,
And I heard thee no more?

My limbs like breathing marble
Have lain in the warm down;

No heavenly chant, no earthly care,
  Have stirred a smile or frown.

I wake; thy kiss is on my lips;
  Thou art my day, my sun!
But where, O spirit, where wast thou
  While the sands of night have run?

THEOCRITUS

Ay! Unto thee belong
The pipe and song,
Theocritus, —
Loved by the satyr and the faun!
To thee the olive and the vine,
To thee the Mediterranean pine,
And the soft lapping sea!
Thine, Bacchus,
Thine, the blood-red revels,
Thine, the bearded goat!
Soft valleys unto thee,
And Aphrodite's shrine,
And maidens veiled in falling robes of lawn!
But unto us, to us,
The stalwart glories of the North;
Ours is the sounding main,
And ours the voices uttering forth
By midnight round these cliffs a mighty strain;
A tale of viewless islands in the deep
Washed by the waves' white fire;
Of mariners rocked asleep,
In the great cradle, far from Grecian ire
Of Neptune and his train;
To us, to us,
The dark-leaved shadow and the shining birch,
The flight of gold through hollow woodlands driven,
Soft dying of the year with many a sigh,
These, all, to us are given!
And eyes that eager evermore shall search
The hidden seed, and searching find again
Unfading blossoms of a fadeless spring;
These, these, to us!
The sacred youth and maid,
Coy and half afraid;
The sorrowful earthly pall,
Winter and wintry rain,
And autumn's gathered grain,
With whispering music in their fall;
These unto us!
And unto thee, Theocritus,
To thee,
The immortal childhood of the world,
The laughing waters of an inland sea,
And beckoning signal of a sail unfurled!

LITTLE GUINEVER

"When Queen Guinever of Britain was a little wench."
LOVE'S LABOUR 'S LOST.

Swift across the palace floor
  Flashed her tiny wilful feet;
"Playfellow, I will no more,
  Now I must my task complete."

Arthur kissed her childish hand,
  Sighed to think her task severe,
Walked forth in the garden land,
  Lonely till she reappear.

She has sought her latticed room,
  Overlooking faery seas,
Called Launcelot from a bowery gloom
  To feast of milk and honey of bees.

"Had we bid Prince Arthur too,
  He had shaken his grave head,
Saying, 'My holidays are few!' —
  May queens not have their will?" she said.

Thus she passed the merry day,
  Thus her women spake and smiled:
"All we see we need not say,
  For Guinever is but a child."

THE RETURN

The bright sea washed beneath her feet,
  As it had done of yore,
The well-remembered odor sweet
  Came through her opening door.

Again the grass his ripened head
  Bowed where her raiment swept;
Again the fog-bell told of dread,
  And all the landscape wept.

Again beside the woodland bars
  She found the wilding rose,
With petals fine and heart of stars, —
  The flower our childhood knows.

And there, before that blossom small,
  By its young face beguiled,

The woman saw her burden fall,
And stood a little child.

She knew no more the weight of love,
No more the weight of grief;
So could the simple wild-rose move
And bring her heart relief.

She asked not where her love was gone,
Nor where her grief was fled,
But stood as at the great white throne,
Unmindful of things dead.

"SONG, TO THE GODS, IS SWEETEST SACRIFICE"

"Behold another singer!" Criton said,
And sneered, and in his sneering turned the leaf:
"Who reads the poets now? They are past and dead:
Give me for their vain work unrhymed relief."
A laugh went round. Meanwhile the last ripe sheaf
Of corn was garnered, and the summer birds
Stilled their dear notes, while autumn's voice of grief
Rang through the fields, and wept the gathered herds.
Then in despair men murmured: "Is this all, —
To fade and die within this narrow ring?
Where are the singers, with their hearts aflame,
To tell again what those of old let fall, —
How to decaying worlds fresh promise came,
And how our angels in the night-time sing?"

Harriet McEwen Kimball

THE GUEST

Speechless Sorrow sat with me;
I was sighing wearily;
Lamp and fire were out; the rain
Wildly beat the window-pane.
In the dark I heard a knock,
And a hand was on the lock;
One in waiting spake to me,
Saying sweetly,
"I am come to sup with thee."

All my room was dark and damp:
"Sorrow," said I, "trim the lamp,
Light the fire, and cheer thy face,
Set the guest-chair in its place."
And again I heard the knock;
In the dark I found the lock: —
"Enter, I have turned the key;
Enter, Stranger,
Who art come to sup with me."

Opening wide the door he came,
But I could not speak his name;
In the guest-chair took his place,
But I could not see his face.
When my cheerful fire was beaming,
When my little lamp was gleaming,
And the feast was spread for three,
Lo, my Master
Was the Guest that supped with me!

ALL 'S WELL

The day is ended. Ere I sink to sleep,
My weary spirit seeks repose in Thine.
Father! forgive my trespasses, and keep
This little life of mine.

With loving-kindness curtain Thou my bed,
And cool in rest my burning pilgrim-feet;
Thy pardon be the pillow for my head;
So shall my sleep be sweet.

At peace with all the world, dear Lord, and Thee,
No fears my soul's unwavering faith can shake;
All 's well, whichever side the grave for me
The morning light may break.

WHITE AZALEAS

AZALEAS — whitest of white!
White as the drifted snow
Fresh-fallen out of the night,
Before the coming glow
Tinges the morning light;
When the light is like the snow,
White,
And the silence is like the light:
Light, and silence, and snow, —
All — white!

White! not a hint
Of the creamy tint
A rose will hold,
The whitest rose, in its inmost fold;
Not a possible blush;
White as an embodied hush;
A very rapture of white;
A wedlock of silence and light:
White, white as the wonder undefiled
Of Eve just wakened in Paradise;
Nay, white as the angel of a child
That looks into God's own eyes!

John James Piatt

THE MOWER IN OHIO

THE bees in the clover are making honey, and I am making my hay:
The air is fresh, I seem to draw a young man's breath to-day.

The bees and I are alone in the grass: the air is so very still
I hear the dam, so loud, that shines beyond the sullen mill.

Yes, the air is so still that I hear almost the sounds I cannot hear —
That, when no other sound is plain, ring in my empty ear:

The chime of striking scythes, the fall of the heavy swaths they sweep —
They ring about me, resting, when I waver half asleep;

So still, I am not sure if a cloud, low down, unseen there be,
Or if something brings a rumor home of the cannon so far from me:

Far away in Virginia, where Joseph and Grant, I know,
Will tell them what I meant when first I had my mowers go!

Joseph, he is my eldest one, the only boy of my three
Whose shadow can darken my door again, and lighten my heart for me.

Joseph, he is my eldest — how his scythe was striking ahead!
William was better at shorter heats, but Jo in the long run led.

William, he was my youngest; John, between them I somehow see,
When my eyes are shut, with a little board at his head in Tennessee.

But William came home one morning early, from Gettysburg, last July,
(The mowing was over already, although the only mower was I):

William, my captain, came home for good to his mother; and I 'll be bound
We were proud and cried to see the flag that wrapt his coffin around;

For a company from the town came up ten miles with music and gun:
It seemed his country claimed him then — as well as his mother — her son.

But Joseph is yonder with Grant to-day, a thousand miles or near,
And only the bees are broad at work with me in the clover here.

Was it a murmur of thunder I heard that hummed again in the air?
Yet, may be, the cannon are sounding now their Onward to Richmond there.

But under the beech by the orchard, at noon, I sat an hour it would seem —
It may be I slept a minute, too, or wavered into a dream.

For I saw my boys, across the field, by the flashes as they went,
Tramping a steady tramp as of old, with the strength in their arms unspent;

Tramping a steady tramp, they moved like soldiers that march to the beat
Of music that seems, a part of themselves, to rise and fall with their feet;

Tramping a steady tramp, they came with flashes of silver that shone,
Every step, from their scythes that rang as if they needed the stone —

(The field is wide, and heavy with grass) — and, coming toward me, they beamed
With a shine of light in their faces at once, and — surely I must have dreamed!

For I sat alone in the clover-field, the bees were working ahead.
There were three in my vision — remember, old man: and what if Joseph were dead!

But I hope that he and Grant (the flag above them both, to boot)
Will go into Richmond together, no matter which is ahead or afoot!

Meantime, alone at the mowing here — an old man somewhat gray —
I must stay at home as long as I can, making, myself, the hay.

And so another round — the quail in the orchard whistles blithe; —
But first I 'll drink at the spring below, and whet again my scythe.

ROSE AND ROOT

A FABLE OF TWO LIVES

The Rose aloft in sunny air,
Beloved alike by bird and bee,
Takes for the dark Root little care
That toils below it ceaselessly.

I put my question to the flower:
"Pride of the Summer, garden queen,
Why livest thou thy little hour?"
And the Rose answered, "I am seen."

I put my question to the Root.
"I mine the earth content," it said,
"A hidden miner underfoot:
I know a Rose is overhead."

TO ABRAHAM LINCOLN

Stern be the pilot in the dreadful hour
When a great nation, like a ship at sea
With the wroth breakers whitening at her lee,
Feels her last shudder if her helmsman cower;
A godlike manhood be his mighty dower!
Such and so gifted, Lincoln, mayst thou be,
With thy high wisdom's low simplicity
And awful tenderness of voted power.
From our hot records then thy name shall stand
On Time's calm ledger out of passionate days —
With the pure debt of gratitude begun,
And only paid in never-ending praise —
One of the many of a mighty Land,
Made by God's providence the Anointed One.

1862.

FARTHER

(THE SUGGESTED DEVICE OF A NEW WESTERN STATE)

Far-off a young State rises, full of might:
I paint its brave escutcheon. Near at hand
See the log-cabin in the rough clearing stand;
A woman by its door, with steadfast sight,
Trustful, looks Westward, where, uplifted bright,
Some city's Apparition, weird and grand,
In dazzling quiet fronts the lonely land,
With vast and marvellous structures wrought of light,
Motionless on the burning cloud afar:
The haunting vision of a time to be,
After the heroic age is ended here,
Built on the boundless, still horizon's bar
By the low sun, his gorgeous prophecy
Lighting the doorway of the pioneer!

THE CHILD IN THE STREET

FOR A VOLUME OF DOUBLE AUTHORSHIP

EVEN as tender parents lovingly
Send a dear child in some true servant's care
Forth in the street, for larger light and air,
Feeling the sun her guardian will be,
And dreaming with a blushful pride that she
Will earn sweet smiles and glances everywhere,
From loving faces; and that passers fair
Will bend, and bless, and kiss her, when they see,
And ask her name, and if her home is near,
And think, "O gentle child, how blessed are they
Whose twofold love bears up a single flower!"
And so with softer musing move away, —
We send thee forth, O Book, thy little hour—
The world may pardon us to hold thee dear.

TO A LADY

ON HER ART OF GROWING OLD GRACEFULLY

YOU ask a verse, to sing (ah, laughing face!)
Your happy art of growing old with grace?
O Muse, begin, and let the truth—but hold!
First let me see that you are growing old.

THE GUERDON

To the quick brow Fame grudges her best wreath
While the quick heart to enjoy it throbs beneath:
On the dead forehead's sculptured marble shown,
Lo, her choice crown — its flowers are also stone.

TORCH-LIGHT IN AUTUMN

I LIFT this sumach-bough with crimson flare,
And, touched with subtle pangs of dreamy pain,
Through the dark wood a torch I seem to bear
In Autumn's funeral train.

IRELAND

A SEASIDE PORTRAIT

A GREAT, still Shape, alone,
She sits (her harp has fallen) on the sand,
And sees her children, one by one, depart: —
Her cloak (that hides what sins beside her own!)
Wrapped fold on fold about her. Lo,
She comforts her fierce heart,
As wailing some, and some gay-singing go,
With the far vision of that Greater Land
Deep in the Atlantic skies,
St. Brandan's Paradise!
Another Woman there,
Mighty and wondrous fair,
Stands on her shore-rock: — one uplifted hand
Holds a quick-piercing light
That keeps long sea-ways bright;
She beckons with the other, saying "Come,
O landless, shelterless,
Sharp-faced with hunger, worn with long distress: —
Come hither, finding home!
Lo, my new fields of harvest, open, free,
By winds of blessing blown,
Whose golden corn-blades shake from sea to sea —
Fields without walls that all the people own!"

LEAVES AT MY WINDOW

I WATCH the leaves that flutter in the wind,
Bathing my eyes with coolness and my heart
Filling with springs of grateful sense anew,
Before my window — in wind and rain and sun.
And now the wind is gone and now the rain,
And all a motionless moment breathe; and now
Playful the wind comes back — again the shower,
Again the sunshine! Like a golden swarm
Of butterflies the leaves are fluttering,
The leaves are dancing, singing — all alive
(For Fancy gives her breath to every leaf)
For the blithe moment. Beautiful to me,
Of all inanimate things most beautiful,
And dear as flowers their kindred, are the leaves
In their glad summer life; and, when a child,

I loved to lie through sunny afternoons
With half-shut eyes (familiar then with things
Long unfamiliar, knowing Fairyland
And all the unhidden mysteries of the Earth)
Using my kinship in those earlier days
With Nature and the humbler people, dear
To her green life, in every shade and sun.
The leaves had myriad voices, and their joy
One with the birds' that sang among them seemed;
And, oftentimes, I lay in breezy shade
Till, creeping with the loving stealth he takes
In healthy temperaments, the blessëd Sleep
(Thrice blessëd and thrice blessing now, because
Of sleepless things that will not give us rest!)
Came with his weird processions — dreams that wore
All happy masks — blithe fairies numberless,
Forever passing, never more to pass,
The Spirits of the Leaves. Awaking then,
Behold the sun was swimming in my face
Through mists of his creation, swarming gold,
And all the leaves in sultry languor lay
Above me, for I wakened when they dropped
Asleep, unmoving. Now, when Time has ceased
His holiday, and I am prisoned close
In his harsh service, mastered by his Hours,
The leaves have not forgotten me: behold,
They play with me like children who, awake,
Find one most dear asleep and waken him
To their own gladness from his sultry dream;
But nothing sweeter do they give to me
Than thoughts of one who, far away, perchance
Watches like me the leaves and thinks of me, —
While o'er her window sunnily the shower
Touches all boughs to music, and the rose
Beneath swings lovingly toward the dripping pane,
And she, whom Nature gave the freshest sense
Of all her delicate life, rejoices in
The joy of birds that use the hour to sing
With breasts o'erfull of music. "Little Birds,"
She sings, "sing to my little Bird below!"
And with her child-like fancy, half-belief,
She hears them sing and makes believe they obey,
And the child, wakening, listens motionless.

THE LOST GENIUS

A Giant came to me when I was young,
My instant will to ask —
My earthly Servant, from the earth he sprung
Eager for any task!

"What wilt thou, O my Master?" he began,
"Whatever can be," I.
"Say thy first wish — whate'er thou wilt I can,"
The Strong Slave made reply.

"Enter the earth and bring its riches forth,
For pearls explore the sea."
He brought, from East and West and South and North,
All treasures back to me!

"Build me a palace wherein I may dwell."
"Awake and see it done,"
Spake his great voice at dawn. Oh, miracle
That glittered in the sun!

"Find me the princess fit for my embrace,
The vision of my breast;
For her search every clime and every race."
My yearning arms were blessed!

"Get me all knowledge." Sages with their lore,
And poets with their songs,
Crowded my palace halls at every door,
In still, obedient throngs!

"Now bring me wisdom." Long ago he went;
(The cold task harder seems:)
He did not hasten with the last content —
The rest, meanwhile, were dreams!

Houseless and poor, on many a trackless road,
Without a guide, I found
A white-haired phantom with the world his load,
Bending him to the ground!

"I bring thee wisdom, Master." Is it he,
I marvelled then, in sooth?
"Thy palace-builder, beauty-seeker, see!"
I saw the Ghost of Youth!

PURPOSE

STRONG in thy steadfast purpose, be
Like some brave master of the sea,
Whose keel, by Titan pulses quickened, knows
His will where'er he goes.
Some isle, palm-roofed, in spiced Pacific air
He seeks — though solitary zones apart,
Its place long fixed on his deep-studied chart.
Fierce winds, your wild confusion make!
Waves, wroth with tide and tempest, shake
His iron-wrought hull aside!
However driven, to that far island fair
(His compass not more faithful than his heart)
He makes his path the ocean wide —
His prow is always there!

Harriet Prescott Spofford

PHANTOMS ALL

COME, all you sailors of the southern waters,
You apparitions of the Spanish main,
Who dyed the jewelled depths blood-red with slaughters,
You things of crime and gain!

Come, caravel and pinnace, on whose daring
Rose the low purple of a new world's shore;
Come from your dreams of desperate sea-faring
And sun your sails once more.

Build up again your stately height, storm-harried
Santa Maria, crusted with salt stains;
Come quick, you black and treacherous craft that carried
Columbus home in chains!

And out of all your angry flames and flashes,
Proud with a pride that only homeward yearned,
Swim darkly up and gather from your ashes,
You ships that Cortes burned!

Come, prows, whence climbing into light deific
Undazzled Balboa planted o'er the plain,
The lonely plain of the unguessed Pacific,
The standard of great Spain.

In Caribbean coves, dark vanished vessels,
Lurking and hiding thrice a hundred years,
Figure again your mad and merry wrestles,
Beaks of the buccaneers!

Come, you that bore through boughs of dripping blossom,
Ogeron with his headsman and his priest,
Where Limousin with treasure in his bosom
Dreamed, and in dreaming ceased.

Barks at whose name to-day the nursling shivers,
Come, with the bubble-rafts where men swept down
Along the foam and fall of mighty rivers
To sack the isthmian town!

Through dusky bayous known in old romances
In one great furtive squadron move, you host
That took to death and drowning those free-lances,
The Brethren of the Coast!

Come, Drake, come, Hawkins, to your sad employer,
Come, L'Olonnois and Davila, again,
Come, you great ships of Montbar the Destroyer,
Of Morgan and his men!

Dipping and slipping under shadowy highlands,
Dashing in haste the swifter fate to meet,
Come from your wrecks on haunted keys and islands,
Cervera's valiant fleet!

Galleons, and merchantmen, and sloops of story,
O silent escort, follow in full train
This passing phantom of an ancient glory,
The Navy of Old Spain!

EVANESCENCE

What 's the brightness of a brow?
What 's a mouth of pearls and corals?
Beauty vanishes like a vapor,
Preach the men of musty morals!

Should the crowd then, ages since,
Have shut their ears to singing Homer,
Because the music fled as soon
As fleets the violets' aroma?

Ah, for me, I thrill to see
The bloom a velvet cheek discloses,
Made of dust — I well believe it!
So are lilies, so are roses!

MUSIC IN THE NIGHT

When stars pursue their solemn flight,
Oft in the middle of the night,
A strain of music visits me,
Hushed in a moment silverly, —
Such rich and rapturous strains as make
The very soul of silence ache
With longing for the melody;

Or lovers in the distant dusk
Of summer gardens, sweet as musk,
Pouring the blissful burden out,
The breaking joy, the dying doubt;
Or revellers, all flown with wine,
And in a madness half divine,
Beating the broken tune about;

Or else the rude and rolling notes
That leave some strolling sailors' throats,
Hoarse with the salt sprays, it may be,
Of many a mile of rushing sea;
Or some high-minded dreamer strays
Late through the solitary ways,
Nor heeds the listening night, nor me.

Or how or whence those tones be heard,
Hearing, the slumbering soul is stirred,
As when a swiftly passing light
Startles the shadows into flight;
While one remembrance suddenly
Thrills through the melting melody, —
A strain of music in the night.

Out of the darkness burst the song,
Into the darkness moves along:
Only a chord of memory jars,
Only an old wound burns its scars,
As the wild sweetness of the strain
Smites the heart with passionate pain,
And vanishes among the stars.

A SIGH

It was nothing but a rose I gave her, —
Nothing but a rose
Any wind might rob of half its savor,
Any wind that blows.

When she took it from my trembling fingers
With a hand as chill, —
Ah, the flying touch upon them lingers,
Stays, and thrills them still!

Withered, faded, pressed between the pages,
Crumpled fold on fold, —
Once it lay upon her breast, and ages
Cannot make it old!

THE PINES

Couldst thou, Great Fairy, give to me
The instant's wish, that I might see
Of all the earth's that one dear sight
Known only in a dream's delight,
I would, beneath some island steep,
In some remote and sun-bright deep,
See high in heaven above me now
A palm-tree wave its rhythmic bough!

And yet this old pine's haughty crown,
Shaking its clouds of silver down,
Whispers me snatches of strange tunes
And murmur of those awful runes
Which tell by subtle spell, and power
Of secret sympathies, the hour
When far in the dark North the snow
Among great bergs begins to blow.

Nay, thou sweet South of heats and balms,
Keep all thy proud and plumy palms,

Keep all thy fragrant flowery ease,
Thy purple skies, thy purple seas!
These boughs of blessing shall not fail,
These voices singing in the gale,
The vigor of these mighty lines:
I will content me with my pines!

VOICE

SAID the archangels, moving in their glory,
Seeing the suns bend out along their courses,
Seeing the earth swim up in vernal light,
Seeing the year renew her ancient story, —
Ask we here the Lord of all the finer forces
To make us now a poet whose song shall reach our height!

Fain would we know the impulse ever fleeing,
Fleeing in light o'er the battlements of even,
Fleeing in love that lifts the universe like wings;
Fain would we know the secret of our being,
Blush for a moment with the inmost joy of heaven —
Make us then a poet whose song shall tell these things!

From his rosy cloud, a Voice, — O wonder!
All my harp-strings tremble to sweet singing!
Life, O lovely life, is at the flood!
Hear the torrents' far melodious thunder,
Hear the winds' long sweep, the joyous thickets ringing,
Forests bow and murmur, and blossoms burst their bud!

Israfel, the Voice, was warbling, — Follow
Where the wild swift music winds and doubles!
Follow! When the sap whirls longing for the light,
When the first thrush thrills the dusky hollow,
Every heart on earth with jocund spirit bubbles,
And every soul 's a poet whose song surmounts our height!

THE HUNT

WILD stream the clouds, and the fresh wind is singing,
Red is the dawn, and the world white with rime, —
Music, O music! The hunter's horn ringing!
Over the hilltop the mounted men climb.

Flashing of scarlet, and glitter, and jingle,
The deep bay, the rhythm of hoof and of cry, —
Echo, O echo! The winds rush and mingle!
Halloo, view halloo! And the Hunt has swept by.

Stay! All the morning is hushed and is sober,
Bare is the hilltop and sad as its wont, —
Out of the ghost of a long-dead October
Blows as the dust blows the ghost of the Hunt!

Louise Chandler Moulton[1]

TO-NIGHT

BEND low, O dusky Night,
And give my spirit rest.
Hold me to your deep breast,
And put old cares to flight.
Give back the lost delight
That once my soul possest,
When Love was loveliest.
Bend low, O dusky Night!

Enfold me in your arms —
The sole embrace I crave
Until the embracing grave
Shield me from life's alarms.
I dare your subtlest charms;
Your deepest spell I brave, —
O, strong to slay or save,
Enfold me in your arms!

[1] See, also, the Sonnet on p. 811.

A PAINTED FAN

Roses and butterflies snared on a fan,
All that is left of a summer gone by;
Of swift, bright wings that flashed in the sun,
And loveliest blossoms that bloomed to die!

By what subtle spell did you lure them here,
Fixing a beauty that will not change, —
Roses whose petals never will fall,
Bright, swift wings that never will range?

Had you owned but the skill to snare as well
The swift-winged hours that came and went,
To prison the words that in music died,
And fix with a spell the heart's content,

Then had you been of magicians the chief;
And loved and lovers should bless your art,
If you could but have painted the soul of the thing, —
Not the rose alone, but the rose's heart!

Flown are those days with their winged delights,
As the odor is gone from the summer rose;
Yet still, whenever I wave my fan,
The soft, south wind of memory blows.

THE SHADOW DANCE

She sees her image in the glass, —
How fair a thing to gaze upon!
She lingers while the moments run,
With happy thoughts that come and pass,

Like winds across the meadow grass
When the young June is just begun:
She sees her image in the glass, —
How fair a thing to gaze upon!

What wealth of gold the skies amass!
How glad are all things 'neath the sun!
How true the love her love has won!
She recks not that this hour will pass, —
She sees her image in the glass.

LAUS VENERIS

A PICTURE BY BURNE JONES

Pallid with too much longing,
White with passion and prayer,
Goddess of love and beauty,
She sits in the picture there, —

Sits with her dark eyes seeking
Something more subtle still
Than the old delights of loving
Her measureless days to fill.

She has loved and been loved so often
In her long, immortal years,
That she tires of the worn-out rapture,
Sickens of hopes and fears.

No joys or sorrows move her,
Done with her ancient pride;
For her head she found too heavy
The crown she has cast aside.

Clothed in her scarlet splendor,
Bright with her glory of hair,
Sad that she is not mortal, —
Eternally sad and fair,

Longing for joys she knows not,
Athirst with a vain desire,
There she sits in the picture,
Daughter of foam and fire.

LAURA SLEEPING

Come hither and behold this lady's face,
Who lies asleep, as if strong Death had kissed
Upon her eyes the kiss none can resist,
And held her fast in his prolonged embrace!
See the still lips, which grant no answering grace
To Love's fond prayers, and the sweet, carven smile,
Sign of some dream-born joy which did beguile
The dreaming soul from its fair resting-place!
So will she look when Death indeed has sway
O'er her dear loveliness, and holds her fast
In that last sleep which knows nor night nor day,
Which hopes no future, contemplates no past;

So *will* she look; but now, behold! she wakes —
Thus, from the Night, Dawn's sunlit beauty breaks.

HIC JACET

So Love is dead that has been quick so long!
Close, then, his eyes, and bear him to his rest,
With eglantine and myrtle on his breast,
And leave him there, their pleasant scents among;
And chant a sweet and melancholy song
About the charms whereof he was possessed,
And how of all things he was loveliest,
And to compare with aught were him to wrong.
Leave him beneath the still and solemn stars,
That gather and look down from their far place
With their long calm our brief woes to deride,
Until the Sun the Morning's gate unbars
And mocks, in turn, our sorrows with his face; —
And yet, had Love been Love, he had not died.

THE LAST GOOD-BY

How shall we know it is the last good-by?
The skies will not be darkened in that hour,
No sudden blight will fall on leaf or flower,
No single bird will hush its careless cry,
And you will hold my hands, and smile or sigh
Just as before. Perchance the sudden tears
In your dear eyes will answer to my fears;
But there will come no voice of prophecy, —
No voice to whisper, "Now, and not again,
Space for last words, last kisses, and last prayer,
For all the wild, unmitigated pain
Of those who, parting, clasp hands with despair:" —
"Who knows?" we say, but doubt and fear remain,
Would any *choose* to part thus unaware?

WERE BUT MY SPIRIT LOOSED UPON THE AIR

Were but my spirit loosed upon the air, —
By some High Power who could Life's chains unbind,
Set free to seek what most it longs to find, —
To no proud Court of Kings would I repair:
I would but climb, once more, a narrow stair,
When day was wearing late, and dusk was kind;
And one should greet me to my failings blind,
Content so I but shared his twilight there.
Nay! well I know he waits not as of old, —
I could not find him in the old-time place, —
I must pursue him, made by sorrow bold,
Through worlds unknown, in strange Celestial race,
Whose mystic round no traveller has told,
From star to star, until I see his face.

WE LAY US DOWN TO SLEEP

We lay us down to sleep,
And leave to God the rest:
Whether to wake and weep
Or wake no more be best.

Why vex our souls with care?
The grave is cool and low, —
Have we found life so fair
That we should dread to go?

We 've kissed love's sweet, red lips,
And left them sweet and red:
The rose the wild bee sips
Blooms on when he is dead.

Some faithful friends we 've found;
But they who love us best,
When we are under ground,
Will laugh on with the rest.

No task have we begun
But other hands can take;
No work beneath the sun
For which we need to wake.

Then hold us fast, sweet Death,
If so it seemeth best
To Him who gave us breath
That we should go to rest.

We lay us down to sleep;
Our weary eyes we close:
Whether to wake and weep,
Or wake no more, He knows.

LOUISA MAY ALCOTT

IN MEMORIAM

As the wind at play with a spark
Of fire that glows through the night,
As the speed of the soaring lark
That wings to the sky his flight,
So swiftly thy soul has sped
On its upward, wonderful way,
Like the lark, when the dawn is red,
In search of the shining day.

Thou art not with the frozen dead
Whom earth in the earth we lay,
While the bearers softly tread,
And the mourners kneel and pray;

From thy semblance, dumb and stark,
The soul has taken its flight —
Out of the finite dark,
Into the Infinite Light.

LOVE'S RESURRECTION DAY

ROUND among the quiet graves,
When the sun was low,
Love went grieving, — Love who saves:
Did the sleepers know?

At his touch the flowers awoke,
At his tender call
Birds into sweet singing broke,
And it did befall

From the blooming, bursting sod
All Love's dead arose,
And went flying up to God
By a way Love knows.

William Hayes Ward

TO JOHN GREENLEAF WHITTIER

ON THE DEATH OF LOWELL

DEAR singer of our fathers' day,
Who lingerest in the sunset glow,
Our grateful hearts all bid thee stay;
Bend hitherward and do not go.
Gracious thine age, thy youth was strong,
For Freedom touched thy tongue with fire:
To sing the right and fight the wrong
Thine equal hand held bow or lyre.
O linger, linger long,
Singer of song.

We beg thee stay; thy comrade star
Which later rose is earlier set;
What music and what battle-scar
When side by side the fray ye met!
Thy trumpet and his drum and fife
Gave saucy challenge to the foe
In Liberty's heroic strife;
We mourn for him, thou must not go!
Yet linger, linger long,
Singer of song.

We cannot yield thee; only thou
Art left to us, and one beside
Whose silvered wisdom still can show
How smiles and tears together bide.
And we would bring our boys to thee,
And bid them hold in memory crowned
That they our saintliest bard did see,
The Galahad of our table round.
Then linger, linger long,
Singer of song.

The night is dark; three radiant beams
Are gone that crossed the zenith sky;
For one the water-fowl, meseems,
For two the Elmwood herons cry.
Ye twain that early rose and still
Skirt low the level west along,
Sink when ye must, to rise and fill
The morrow's east with light and song.
But linger, linger long,
Singers of song.

THE NEW CASTALIA

OUT of a cavern on Parnassus' side,
Flows Castaly; and with the flood outblown

From its deep heart of ice, the mountain's breath
Tempers the ardor of the Delphian vale.
Beside the stream from the black mould upsprings
Narcissus, robed in snow, with ruby crowned.
Long ranks of crocus, humble servitors,
But clad in purple, mark his downcast face.
The sward, moist from the flood, is pied with flowers,
Lily and vetch, lupine and melilot,
The hyacinth, cowslip, and gay marigold,
While, on the border of the copse, sweet herbs,
Anise and thyme, breathe incense to the bay
And myrtle. Here thy home, fair Muse! How soft
Thy step falls on the grass whose morning drops
Bedew thy feet! The blossoms bend but break
Not, and thy fingers pluck the eglantine,
The privet and the bilberry; or frame
A rustic whistle from a fresh-cut reed.
Here is thy home, dear Muse, fed on these airs;
The hills, the founts, the woods, the sky are thine!

But who are these? A company of youth
Upon a tesseled pavement in a court,
Under a marble statue of a muse,
Strew hot-house flowers before a mimic fount
Drawn from a faucet in a rockery.
With mutual admiration they repeat
Their bric-a-brackery of rococo verse,
Their versicles and icicles of song!
What know ye, verse-wrights, of the Poet's art?
What noble passion or what holy heat
Is stirred to frenzy when your eyes admire
The peacock feathers on a frescoed wall,
Or painted posies on a lady's fan?

Are these thine only bards, young age, whose eyes
Are blind to Heaven and heart of man; whose blood
Is water, and not wine; unskilled in notes
Of liberty, and holy love of land,
And man, and all things beautiful; deep skilled
To burnish wit in measured feet, to wind
A weary labyrinth of labored rhymes,
And cipher verses on an abacus?

Irving Browne

MY NEW WORLD

My prow is tending toward the west,
Old voices growing faint, dear faces dim,
And all that I have loved the best
Far back upon the waste of memory swim.
My old world disappears:
Few hopes and many fears
Accompany me.

But from the distance fair
A sound of birds, a glimpse of pleasant skies,
A scent of fragant air,
All soothingly arise
In cooing voice, sweet breath, and merry eyes
Of grandson on my knee.
And ere my sails be furled,
Kind Lord, I pray
Thou let me live a day
In my new world.

AT SHAKESPEARE'S GRAVE

(IGNATIUS DONNELLY LOQ.)

Dismiss your apprehension, pseudo bard,
For no one wishes to disturb these stones,
Nor cares if here or in the outer yard
They stow your impudent, deceitful bones.

Your foolish-colored bust upon the wall,
With its preposterous expanse of brow,
Shall rival Humpty Dumpty's famous fall,
And cheats no cultured Boston people now.

Steal deer, hold horses, act your third-rate parts,
Hoard money, booze, neglect Anne Hathaway, —
You can't deceive us with your stolen arts;
Like many a worthier dog, you 've had your day.

I have expresst your history in a cyfer,
I 've done your sum for all ensuing time,
I don't know what you longer wish to lie for
Beneath these stones or in your doggerel rhyme.

Get up and flit, or plunge into the river,
Or walk the chancel with a ghostly squeak,
You were an ignorant and evil liver,
Who could not spell, nor write, nor read much Greek.

Tho' you enslaved the ages by your spell,
And Fame has blown no reputation louder,
Your cake is dough, for I by sifting well
Have quite reduced your dust to Bacon-powder.

MAN'S PILLOW

A BABY lying on his mother's breast
Draws life from that sweet fount;
He takes his rest
And heaves deep sighs;
With brooding eyes
Of soft content
She shelters him within that fragrant nest,
And scarce refrains from crushing him
With tender violence,
His rosebud mouth, each rosy limb
Excite such joy intense;
Rocked on that gentle billow,
She sings into his ear
A song that angels stoop to hear.
Blest child and mother doubly blest!
Such his first pillow.

A man outwearied with the world's mad race
His mother seeks again;
His furrowed face,
His tired gray head,
His heart of lead
Resigned he yields;
She covers him in some secluded place,
And kindly heals the earthy scar
Of spade with snow and flowers,
While glow of sun and gleam of star,
And murmuring rush of showers,
And wind-obeying willow
Attend his unbroken sleep;
In this repose secure and deep,
Forgotten save by One, he leaves no trace.
Such his last pillow.

Lucius Harwood Foote

POETRY

SOMETHING more than the lilt of the strain,
Something more than the touch of the lute;
For the voice of the minstrel is vain,
If the heart of the minstrel is mute.

ON THE HEIGHTS

HE crawls along the mountain walls,
From whence the severed river falls;
Its seething waters writhe and twist,
Then leap, and crumble into mist.
Midway between two boundless seas,
Prone on a ragged reef he lies;
Above him bend the shoreless skies,
While helpless, on his bended knees,
Into that awful gulf profound,
Appalled, he peers with bated breath,
Clutches with fear the yielding ground,
And crouches face to face with death.
The fearful splendor of the sight
Begets in his bewildered brain
A downwright torture of delight,
The very ecstasy of pain.
A sudden frenzy fills his mind, —
If he could break the bonds that bind,
And launch upon the waves of wind;
Only to loose his hold and leap,
Then, cradled like a cloud, to sleep
Wind-rocked upon the soundless deep.
With eyes upturned, he breaks the spell,
And creeps from out the jaws of hell.
Pohono's siren wiles beguile, —
He drinks her kisses in the wind,
He leaves the nether world behind.
Up, and still upward, mile on mile,
With muffled tramp, the pilgrim creeps
Across the frozen winding-sheet,
Where white-faced death in silence sleeps.
Up, and still upward, to the light,
Until at last his leaden feet
Have mocked the eagle in its flight.

Grim-browed and bald, Tis-sa-ack broods
Above these white-robed solitudes.
A mute, awe-stricken mortal stands
Upon the fragment of a world,
And, when the rifted clouds are curled,
Sees far below the steadfast lands.

DON JUAN

DON JUAN has ever the grand old air,
As he greets me with courtly grace;
Like a crown of glory the snow-white hair
That halos his swarthy face;
And he says, with a courtesy rare and fine,
As he ushers me in at the door,
"Panchita mia will bring us the wine,
And the casa is yours, señor."
His fourscore years have a tranquil cast,
For Time has tempered his heart and hand;
Though the seething tide of his blood ran fast
When he ruled like a lord in the land.
In the wild rodeo and mad stampede
He rode, I am told,
In the days of old,
With his brown vaqueros at headlong speed.
From the Toro Peaks to the Carmel Pass
His cattle fed on the rich, wild grass;
And far to the west,
Where the sand-dunes rest
On the rim of the heaving sea,
From the Point of Pines to the river's mouth,
From the Gabilan Hills to the bay on the south,
He held the land in fee.
It was never the same
When the Gringos came,
With their lust of gold and their greed of gain;
And his humble cot,
With its garden plot,
Is all that is left of his wide domain.
But he says with a courtesy rare and fine,
As he ushers me in at the door,
"Panchita mia will bring us the wine,
And the casa is yours, señor."

EL VAQUERO

TINGED with the blood of Aztec lands,
Sphinx-like, the tawny herdsman stands,
A coiled reata in his hands.
Devoid of hope, devoid of fear,
Half brigand and half cavalier, —
This helot, with imperial grace,
Wears ever on his tawny face
A sad, defiant look of pain.
Left by the fierce iconoclast
A living fragment of the past,
Greek of the Greeks he must remain.

THE DERELICT

UNMOORED, unmanned, unheeded on the deep —
Tossed by the restless billow and the breeze,
It drifts o'er sultry leagues of tropic seas,
Where long Pacific surges swell and sweep.
When pale-faced stars their silent watches keep,
From their far rhythmic spheres, the Pleiades,
In calm beatitude and tranquil ease,
Smile sweetly down upon its cradled sleep.
Erewhile, with anchor housed and sails unfurled,
We saw the stout ship breast the open main,
To round the Stormy Cape, and span the world,
In search of ventures which betoken gain.
To-day, somewhere, on some far sea, we know
Her battered hulk is heaving to and fro.

Theodore Tilton

GOD SAVE THE NATION

THOU who ordainest, for the land's salvation,
Famine, and fire, and sword, and lamentation,
Now unto Thee we lift our supplication, —
O, save the Nation!

By the great sign foretold of Thy appearing,
Coming in clouds, while mortal men stand fearing,
Show us, amid the smoke of battle clearing,
Thy chariot nearing.

By the brave blood that floweth like a river,
Hurl Thou a thunderbolt from out Thy quiver!
Break Thou the strong gates! every fetter shiver!
Smite and deliver!

Slay Thou our foes, or turn them to derision!
Then, in the blood-red Valley of Decision,
Clothe Thou the fields, as in the prophet's vision,
With peace Elysian!

CŒUR DE LION TO BERENGARIA

O far-off darling in the South,
Where grapes are loading down the vine,
And songs are in the throstle's mouth,
While love's complaints are here in mine,
Turn from the blue Tyrrhenian Sea!
Come back to me! Come back to me!

Here all the Northern skies are cold,
And in their wintriness they say
(With warnings by the winds foretold)
That love may grow as cold as they!
How ill the omen seems to be!
Come back to me! Come back to me!

Come back, and bring thy wandering heart —
Ere yet it be too far estranged!
Come back, and tell me that thou art
But little chilled, but little changed!
O love, my love, I love but thee!
Come back to me! Come back to me!

I long for thee from morn till night;
I long for thee from night till morn:
But love is proud, and any slight
Can sting it like a piercing thorn.
My bleeding heart cries out to thee —
Come back to me! Come back to me!

Come back, and pluck the nettle out;
Come kiss the wound, or love may die!
How can my heart endure the doubt?
Oh, judge its anguish by its cry!
Its cry goes piercingly to thee —
Come back to me! Come back to me!

What is to thee the summer long?
What is to thee the clustered vine?
What is to thee the throstle's song,
Who sings of love, but not of mine?
Oh, turn from the Tyrrhenian Sea!
Come back to me! Come back to me!

THE FLIGHT FROM THE CONVENT

I see the star-lights quiver,
Like jewels in the river;
The bank is hid with sedge;
What if I slip the edge?
I thought I knew the way
By night as well as day:
But how a lover goes astray!

The place is somewhat lonely —
I mean for just one only;
I brought the boat ashore
An hour ago or more.
Well, I will sit and wait;
She fixed the hour at eight:
Good angels! bring her not too late!

To-morrow's tongues that name her
Will hardly dare to blame her:
A lily still is white
Through all the dark of night:
The morning sun shall show
A bride as pure as snow,
Whose wedding all the world shall know.

O God! that I should gain her!
But what can so detain her?
Hist, yelping cur! thy bark
Will fright her in the dark.
What! striking nine? that 's fast!
Is some one walking past?
— Oho! so thou art come at last!

But why thy long delaying?
Alack! thy beads and praying!
If thou, a saint, dost hope
To kneel and kiss the Pope,
Then I, a sinner, know
Where sweeter kisses grow —
Nay, now, just once before we go!

Nay, twice, and by St. Peter
The second was the sweeter!
Quick now, and in the boat!
Good-by, old tower and moat!
May mildew from the sky
Drop blindness on the eye
That lurks to watch our going by!

O saintly maid! I told thee
No convent-walls could hold thee.
Look! yonder comes the moon!
We started none too soon.
See how we pass that mill!
What! is the night too chill?
— Then I must fold thee closer still!

SIR MARMADUKE'S MUSINGS

I won a noble fame;
But, with a sudden frown,
The people snatched my crown,
And, in the mire, trod down
My lofty name.

I bore a bounteous purse;
And beggars by the way
Then blessed me, day by day;
But I, grown poor as they,
Have now their curse.

I gained what men call friends;
But now their love is hate,
And I have learned, too late,
How mated minds unmate,
And friendship ends.

I clasped a woman's breast, —
As if her heart, I knew,
Or fancied, would be true, —
Who proved, alas! she too!
False like the rest.

I now am all bereft, —
As when some tower doth fall,
With battlement, and wall,
And gate, and bridge, and all, —
And nothing left.

But I account it worth
All pangs of fair hopes crossed —
All loves and honors lost, —
To gain the heavens, at cost
Of losing earth.

So, lest I be inclined
To render ill for ill, —
Henceforth in me instil,
O God, a sweet good-will
To all mankind.

Mary Emily Bradley

A CHRYSALIS

My little Mädchen found one day
A curious something in her play,
That was not fruit, nor flower, nor seed;
It was not anything that grew,
Or crept, or climbed, or swam, or flew;
Had neither legs nor wings, indeed;
And yet she was not sure, she said,
Whether it was alive or dead.

She brought it in her tiny hand
To see if I would understand,
And wondered when I made reply,
"You 've found a baby butterfly."
"A butterfly is not like this,"
With doubtful look she answered me.
So then I told her what would be
Some day within the chrysalis;
How, slowly, in the dull brown thing
Now still as death, a spotted wing,
And then another, would unfold,
Till from the empty shell would fly
A pretty creature, by and by,
All radiant in blue and gold.

"And will it, truly?" questioned she —
Her laughing lips and eager eyes
All in a sparkle of surprise —
"And shall your little Mädchen see?"
"She shall!" I said. How could I tell
That ere the worm within its shell
Its gauzy, splendid wings had spread,
My little Mädchen would be dead?

To-day the butterfly has flown, —
She was not here to see it fly, —
And sorrowing I wonder why
The empty shell is mine alone.
Perhaps the secret lies in this:
I too had found a chrysalis,
And Death that robbed me of delight
Was but the radiant creature's flight!

IN DEATH

How still the room is! But a while ago
The sound of sobbing voices vexed my ears,
And on my face there fell a rain of tears —
I scarce knew why or whence, but now I know.

For this sweet speaking silence, this surcease
Of the dumb, desperate struggle after breath,
This painless consciousness of perfect peace,
Which fills the place of anguish — it is Death!
What folly to have feared it! Not the best
Of all we knew of life can equal this,
Blending in one the sense of utter rest,
The vivid certainty of boundless bliss!
O Death, the loveliness that is in thee,
Could the world know, the world would cease to be.

BEYOND RECALL

There was a time when Death and I
Came face to face together:
I was but young indeed to die,
And it was summer weather;
One happy year a wedded wife,
And I was slipping out of life.

You knelt beside me, and I heard,
As from some far-off distance,
A bitter cry that dimly stirred
My soul to make resistance.
You thought me dead; you called my name;
And back from Death itself I came.

But oh! that you had made no sign,
That I had heard no crying!
For now the yearning voice is mine,
And there is no replying:
Death never could so cruel be
As Life — and you — have proved to me!

A SPRAY OF HONEYSUCKLE

I broke one day a slender stem,
Thick-set with little golden horns,
Half bud, half blossom, and a gem —
Such as one finds in autumn morns
When all the grass with dew is strung —
On every fairy bugle hung.

Careless, I dropped it, in a place
Where no light shone, and so forgot
Its delicate, dewy, flowering grace,
Till presently from the dark spot
A charming sense of sweetness came,
That woke an answering sense of shame.

Quickly I thought, O heart of mine,
A lesson for thee plain to read:
Thou needest not that light should shine,
Or fellow-men thy virtues heed:
Enough — if haply this be so —
That thou hast sweetness to bestow!

John Aylmer Dorgan

THE BEAUTIFUL

The Beautiful, which mocked his fond pursuing,
The poet followed long;
With passionate purpose the shy shadow wooing,
And soul-betraying song.

And still the fervor of his fond endeavor
To him seemed poured in vain,
And all in vain, forever and forever,
The sorrow of his strain.

But when at last he perished broken-hearted,
The world, grown dark and dull,
Bewailed the radiance with him departed
Who was the Beautiful.

THE DEAD SOLOMON

King Solomon stood in the house of the Lord,
And the Genii silently wrought around,
Toiling and moiling without a word,
Building the temple without a sound.

Fear and rage were theirs, but naught,
In mien or face, of fear or rage;
For had he guessed their secret thought,
They had pined in hell for many an age.

Closed were the eyes that the demons feared;
Over his breast streamed his silver beard;
Bowed was his head, as if in prayer,

As if, through the busy silence there,
The answering voice of God he heard.

Solemn peace was on his brow,
Leaning upon his staff in prayer;
And a breath of wind would come and go,
And stir his robe, and beard of snow,
And long white hair;
But he heeded not,
Wrapt afar in holy thought.

King Solomon stood in the house of the Lord,
And the Genii silently wrought around,
Toiling and moiling without a word,
Building the temple without a sound.

And now the work was done,
Perfected in every part;
And the demons rejoiced at heart,
And made ready to depart,
But dared not speak to Solomon,
To tell him their task was done,
And fulfilled the desire of his heart.

So around him they stood with eyes of fire,
Each cursing the king in his secret heart, —
Secretly cursing the silent king,
Waiting but till he should say "Depart;"
Cursing the king,
Each evil thing:
But he heeded them not, nor raised his head;
For King Solomon was dead!

Then the body of the king fell down;
For a worm had gnawed his staff in twain.
He had prayed to the Lord that the house he planned
Might not be left for another hand,
Might not unfinished remain;
So praying, he had died,
But had not prayed in vain.

So the body of the king fell down,
And howling fled the fiends amain;
Bitterly grieved, to be so deceived,
Howling afar they fled;
Idly they had borne his chain,
And done his hateful tasks, in dread
Of mystic penal pain, —
And King Solomon was dead!

Frances Laughton Mace[1]

ALCYONE

I

AMONG the thousand, thousand spheres that roll,
Wheel within wheel, through never-ending space,
A mighty and interminable race,
Yet held by some invisible control,
And led as to a sure and shining goal,
One star alone, with still, unchanging face,
Looks out from her perpetual dwelling-place,
Of these swift orbs the centre and the soul.
Beyond the moons that beam, the stars that blaze,
Past fields of ether, crimson, violet, rose,
The vast star-garden of eternity,
Behold! it shines with white immaculate rays,
The home of peace, the haven of repose,
The lotus-flower of heaven, Alcyone.

II

It is the place where life's long dream comes true;
On many another swift and radiant star
Gather the flaming hosts of those who war
With powers of darkness; those stray seraphs, too,
Who hasten forth God's ministries to do:
But here no sounds of eager trumpets mar
The subtler spell which calls the soul from far,
Its wasted springs of gladness to renew.
It is the morning land of the Ideal,
Where smiles, transfigured to the raptured sight,
The joy whose flitting semblance now we see;
Where we shall know, as visible and real,
Our life's deep aspiration, old yet new,
In the sky-splendor of Alcyone.

[1] See, also, p 684.

III

What lies beyond we ask not. In that hour
When first our feet that shore of beauty press,
It is enough of heaven, its sweet success,
To find our own. Not yet we crave the dower
Of grander action and sublimer power;
We are content that life's long loneliness
Finds in love's welcoming its rich redress,
And hopes, deep hidden, burst in perfect flower.
Wait for me there, O loved of many days!
Though with warm beams some beckoning planet glows,
Its dawning triumphs keep, to share with me:
For soon, far winging through the starry maze,
Past fields of ether, crimson, violet, rose,
I follow, follow to Alcyone!

William Henry Venable

THE SCHOOL GIRL

From some sweet home, the morning train
Brings to the city,
Five days a week, in sun or rain,
Returning like a song's refrain,
A school girl pretty.

A wild flower's unaffected grace
Is dainty miss's;
Yet in her shy, expressive face
The touch of urban arts I trace, —
And artifices.

No one but she and Heaven knows
Of what she 's thinking:
It may be either books or beaux,
Fine scholarship or stylish clothes,
Per cents or prinking.

How happy must the household be,
This morn that kissed her;
Not every one can make so free;
Who sees her, inly wishes she
Were his own sister.

How favored is the book she cons,
The slate she uses,
The hat she lightly doffs and dons,
The orient sunshade that she owns,
The desk she chooses!

Is she familiar with the wars
Of Julius Cæsar?
Do crucibles and Leyden jars,
And French, and earth, and sun, and stars,
And Euclid, please her?

She studies music, I opine;
O day of knowledge!
And all the other arts divine,
Of imitation and design,
Taught in the college.

A charm attends her everywhere, —
A sense of beauty;
Care smiles to see her free of care;
The hard heart loves her unaware;
Age pays her duty.

She is protected by the sky;
Good spirits tend her;
Her innocence is panoply;
God's wrath must on the miscreant lie
Who dares offend her!

MY CATBIRD

A CAPRICCIO

Prime cantante!
Scherzo! Andante!
Piano, pianissimo!
Presto, prestissimo!
Hark! are there nine birds or ninety and nine?
And now a miraculous gurgling gushes
Like nectar from Hebe's Olympian bottle,
The laughter of tune from a rapturous throttle!
Such melody must be a hermit-thrush's!
But that other caroler, nearer,
Outrivalling rivalry with clearer
Sweetness incredibly fine!
Is it oriole, red-bird, or blue-bird,
Or some strange, un-Auduboned new bird?

All one, sir, both this bird and that bird;
The whole flight are all the same catbird!
The whole visible and invisible choir you see
On one lithe twig of yon green tree.
Flitting, feathery Blondel!
Listen to his rondel!
To his lay romantical,
To his sacred canticle.
Hear him lilting!
See him tilting
His saucy head and tail, and fluttering
While uttering
All the difficult operas under the sun
Just for fun;
Or in tipsy revelry,
Or at love devilry,
Or, disdaining his divine gift and art,
Like an inimitable poet
Who captivates the world's heart,
And don't know it.
Hear him lilt!
See him tilt!

Then suddenly he stops,
Peers about, flirts, hops,
As if looking where he might gather up
The wasted ecstasy just spilt
From the quivering cup
Of his bliss overrun.
Then, as in mockery of all
The tuneful spells that e'er did fall
From vocal pipe, or evermore shall rise,
He snarls, and mews, and flies.

Anna Callender Brackett

SONNETS

IN HADES [1]

THEN saw I, with gray eyes fulfilled of rest,
And lulling voice, a woman sweet, and she, —
"Bear thou my word: I am of all most blest;
Nor marvel that I am Eurydice.
I stood and watched those slow feet go from me
Farther and farther; in the light afar,
All clear the figure grew — then suddenly
Into my dark his face flashed like a star! —
And that was all. The purple vaporous door
Left me triumphant over time and space;
Sliding across between forevermore,
It could not hide the glory of that face.
For me no room to doubt, no need to learn —
He knew the whole — *and could not choose but turn!*"

BENEDICITE

"ALL Green Things on the earth, bless ye the Lord!"
So sang the choir while ice-cased branches beat
The frosty window-panes, and at our feet
The frozen, tortured sod but mocked the word,
And seemed to cry like some poor soul in pain,
"Lord, suffering and endurance fill my days;
The growing green things will their Maker praise, —
The happy green things, growing in warm rain!
So God lacks praise while all the fields are white!"
I said; then smiled, remembering southward far
How pampas-grass swayed green in summer light.
Nay, God hears always from this swinging star,
Decani and Cantoris, South and North,
Each answering other, praises pouring forth

[1] Copyright, 1899, by HARPER & BROTHERS.

Charles Frederick Johnson

THE MODERN ROMANS

UNDER the slanting light of the yellow sun of October,
A "gang of Dagos" were working close by the side of the car track.
Pausing a moment to catch a note of their liquid Italian,
Faintly I heard an echo of Rome's imperial accents,
Broken-down forms of Latin words from the Senate and Forum,
Now smoothed over by use to the musical *lingua Romana.*
Then came the thought, Why, these are the heirs of the conquering Romans;
These are the sons of the men who founded the Empire of Cæsar;
These are they whose fathers carried the conquering eagles
Over all Gaul and across the sea to Ultima Thule.
The race-type persists unchanged in their eyes and profiles and figures, —
Muscular, short, and thick-set, with prominent noses, recalling
"*Romanos rerum dominos, gentemque togatam.*"
See, Labienus is swinging a pick with rhythmical motion;
Yonder one pushing the shovel might be Julius Cæsar,
Lean, deep-eyed, broad-browed, and bald, a man of a thousand;
Further along there stands the jolly Horatius Flaccus;
Grim and grave, with rings in his ears, see Cato the Censor;
And the next has precisely the bust of Cneius Pompeius.
Blurred and worn the surface, I grant, and the coin is but copper;
Look more closely, you'll catch a hint of the old superscription, —
Perhaps the stem of a letter, perhaps a leaf of the laurel.

On the side of the street, in proud and gloomy seclusion,
"Bossing the job," stood a Celt, the race enslaved by the legions,
Sold in the market of Rome, to meet the expenses of Cæsar.
And as I loitered, the Celt cried, "'Tind to your worruk, ye Dagos, —
Full up yer shovel, Paythro, ye haythen, I'll dock yees a quarther."
This he said to the one who resembled the great Imperator;
Meekly the dignified Roman kept on patiently digging.

Such are the changes and chances the centuries bring to the nations.
Surely, the ups and downs of this world are past calculation.
How the races troop o'er the stage in endless procession!
Persian, and Arab, and Greek, and Hun, and Roman, and Vandal,
Master the world in turn and then disappear in the darkness,
Leaving a remnant as hewers of wood and drawers of water.
"Possibly," — this I thought to myself, — "the yoke of the Irish
May in turn be lifted from us in the tenth generation.
Now the Celt is on top, — but time may bring his revenges,
Turning the Fenian down once more to be 'bossed by a Dago.'"

THEN AND NOW

To me the earth once seemed to be
Most beautiful and fair;
All living creatures were to me,
In wood or air,
But kindred of a freer class;
I thrilled with keenest joy
To find the young quail in the grass: —
I was a boy.

The robin in the apple-tree,
The brown thrush in the wood,
The meadow larks, all called to me;
I understood:
A sense of union with the whole,
Of love for beast and bird,
Deep chords from man's ancestral soul,
Each wild note stirred.

All that is gone, and now I see
A blood-stained earth, where strife,
Unceasing war, and cruelty,
Make room for life;
Each living thing a helpless prey
To sharper tooth or claw,
Ten thousand murders every day
By nature's law.

But still old earth its glamour casts
O'er the clear eyes of youth,
And still the old illusion lasts
In spite of truth;

For now I find my boy can see
The earth I used to know;
He sees it as it seemed to me
So long ago.

Poor little chap! Sometimes I think
I 'll tell him how he 's fooled,
But when I see his eyes, I shrink,
My purpose cooled:
Why should I cloud his soul with doubt,
Or youth's illusions mar?
Too soon, alas, he will find out
That life is war.

Celia Thaxter

SEAWARD

TO ——

How long it seems since that mild April night,
When, leaning from the window, you and I
Heard, clearly ringing from the shadowy bight,
The loon's unearthly cry!

Southwest the wind blew, million little waves
Ran rippling round the point in mellow tune,
But mournful, like the voice of one who raves,
That laughter of the loon!

We called to him, while blindly through the haze
Uprose the meagre moon behind us, slow,
So dim, the fleet of boats we scarce could trace,
Moored lightly just below.

We called, and, lo, he answered! Half in fear
We sent the note back. Echoing rock and bay
Made melancholy music far and near;
Sadly it died away.

That schooner, you remember? Flying ghost!
Her canvas catching every wandering beam,
Aerial, noiseless, past the glimmering coast
She glided like a dream.

Would we were leaning from your window now,
Together calling to the eerie loon,
The fresh wind blowing care from either brow,
This sumptuous night of June!

So many sighs load this sweet inland air,
'T is hard to breathe, nor can we find relief:
However lightly touched, we all must share
This nobleness of grief.

But sighs are spent before they reach your ear;
Vaguely they mingle with the water's rune;
No sadder sound salutes you than the clear,
Wild laughter of the loon.

THE SANDPIPER

Across the narrow beach we flit,
One little sandpiper and I,
And fast I gather, bit by bit,
The scattered driftwood bleached and dry.
The wild waves reach their hands for it,
The wild wind raves, the tide runs high,
As up and down the beach we flit, —
One little sandpiper and I.

Above our heads the sullen clouds
Scud black and swift across the sky;

Like silent ghosts in misty shrouds
Stand out the white lighthouses high.
Almost as far as eye can reach
I see the close-reefed vessels fly,
As fast we flit along the beach, —
One little sandpiper and I.

I watch him as he skims along,
Uttering his sweet and mournful cry.
He starts not at my fitful song,
Or flash of fluttering drapery.
He has no thought of any wrong;
He scans me with a fearless eye:
Staunch friends are we, well tried and strong,
The little sandpiper and I.

Comrade, where wilt thou be to-night
When the loosed storm breaks furiously?
My driftwood fire will burn so bright!
To what warm shelter canst thou fly?
I do not fear for thee, though wroth
The tempest rushes through the sky:
For are we not God's children both,
Thou, little sandpiper, and I?

SONG

We sail toward evening's lonely star
That trembles in the tender blue;
One single cloud, a dusky bar,
Burnt with dull carmine through and through,
Slow smouldering in the summer sky,
Lies low along the fading west.
How sweet to watch its splendors die,
Wave-cradled thus and wind-caressed!

The soft breeze freshens, leaps the spray
To kiss our cheeks, with sudden cheer;
Upon the dark edge of the bay
Lighthouses kindle, far and near,
And through the warm deeps of the sky
Steal faint star-clusters, while we rest
In deep refreshment, thou and I,
Wave-cradled thus and wind-caressed.

How like a dream are earth and heaven,
Star-beam and darkness, sky and sea;
Thy face, pale in the shadowy even,
Thy quiet eyes that gaze on me!
O realize the moment's charm,
Thou dearest! we are at life's best,
Folded in God's encircling arm,
Wave-cradled thus and wind-caressed.

MAY MORNING

Warm, wild, rainy wind, blowing fitfully,
Stirring dreamy breakers on the slumberous May sea,
What shall fail to answer thee? What thing shall withstand
The spell of thine enchantment, flowing over sea and land?

All along the swamp-edge in the rain I go;
All about my head thou the loosened locks dost blow;
Like the German goose-girl in the fairy tale,
I watch across the shining pool my flock of ducks that sail.

Redly gleam the rose-haws, dripping with the wet,
Fruit of sober autumn, glowing crimson yet;
Slender swords of iris leaves cut the water clear,
And light green creeps the tender grass, thick-spreading far and near.

Every last year's stalk is set with brown or golden studs;
All the boughs of bayberry are thick with scented buds;
Islanded in turfy velvet, where the ferns uncurl,
Lo! the large white duck's egg glimmers like a pearl!

Softly sing the billows, rushing, whispering low;
Freshly, oh, deliciously, the warm, wild wind doth blow!
Plaintive bleat of new-washed lambs comes faint from far away;
And clearly cry the little birds, alert and blithe and gay.

O happy, happy morning! O dear, familiar place!
O warm, sweet tears of Heaven, fast falling on my face!
O well-remembered, rainy wind, blow all my care away,
That I may be a child again this blissful morn of May.

William Winter

MY QUEEN[1]

He loves not well whose love is bold!
I would not have thee come too nigh:
The sun's gold would not seem pure gold
Unless the sun were in the sky;
To take him thence and chain him near
Would make his beauty disappear.

He keeps his state, — keep thou in thine,
And shine upon me from afar!
So shall I bask in light divine,
That falls from love's own guiding star;
So shall thy eminence be high,
And so my passion shall not die.

But all my life shall reach its hands
Of lofty longing toward thy face,
And be as one who speechless stands
In rapture at some perfect grace!
My love, my hope, my all shall be
To look to heaven and look to thee!

Thy eyes shall be the heavenly lights;
Thy voice the gentle summer breeze,
What time it sways, on moonlit nights,
The murmuring tops of leafy trees;
And I shall touch thy beauteous form
In June's red roses, rich and warm.

But thou thyself shalt come not down
From that pure region far above;
But keep thy throne and wear thy crown,
Queen of my heart and queen of love!
A monarch in thy realm complete,
And I a monarch — at thy feet!

ASLEEP[1]

He knelt beside her pillow, in the dead watch of the night,
And he heard her gentle breathing, but her face was still and white,
And on her poor, wan cheek a tear told how the heart can weep,
And he said, "My love was weary — God bless her! she 's asleep."

He knelt beside her gravestone in the shuddering autumn night,
And he heard the dry grass rustle, and his face was thin and white,
And through his heart the tremor ran of grief that cannot weep,
And he said, "My love was weary — God bless her! she 's asleep."

THE NIGHT WATCH[1]

Beneath the midnight moon of May,
Through dusk on either hand,
One sheet of silver spreads the bay,
One crescent jet the land;
The black ships mirrored in the stream
Their ghostly tresses shake —
When will the dead world cease to dream?
When will the morning break?

Beneath a night no longer May,
Where only cold stars shine,
One glimmering ocean spreads away
This haunted life of mine;
And, shattered on the frozen shore,
My harp can never wake —
When will this night of death be o'er?
When will the morning break?

ON THE VERGE[2]

Out in the dark it throbs and glows —
The wide, wild sea, that no man knows!
The wind is chill, the surge is white,
And I must sail that sea to-night.

You shall not sail! The breakers roar
On many a mile of iron shore,
The waves are livid in their wrath,
And no man knows the ocean path.

I must not bide for wind or wave;
I must not heed, though tempest rave;
My course is set, my hour is known,
And I must front the dark, alone.

Your eyes are wild, your face is pale, —
This is no night for ships to sail!
The hungry wind is moaning low,
The storm is up — you shall not go!

'T is not the moaning wind you hear —
It is a sound more dread and drear,
A voice that calls across the tide,
A voice that will not be denied.

Your words are faint, your brow is cold,
Your looks grow sudden gray and old,
The lights burn dim, the casements shake, —
Ah, stay a little, for my sake!

Too late! Too late! The vow you said
This many a year is cold and dead,
And through that darkness, grim and black,
I shall but follow on its track.

Remember all fair things and good
That e'er were dreamed or understood,
For they shall all the Past requite,
So you but shun the sea to-night!

No more of dreams! Nor let there be
One tender thought of them or me, —
For on the way that I must wend
I dread no harm and need no friend!

The golden shafts of sunset fall
Athwart the gray cathedral wall,
While o'er its tombs of old renown
The rose-leaves softly flutter down.

No thought of holy things can save
One relic now from Memory's grave,
And, be it sun or moon or star,
The light that falls must follow far!

I mind the ruined turrets bold,
The ivy, flushed with sunset gold,
The dew-drenched roses, in their sleep,
That seemed to smile, and yet to weep.

There 'll be nor smile nor tear again;
There 'll be the end of every pain;
There 'll be no parting to deplore,
Nor love nor sorrow any more.

I see the sacred river's flow,
The barge in twilight drifting slow,
While o'er the daisied meadow swells
The music of the vesper bells.

It is my knell — so far away!
The night wears on — I must not stay!
My canvas strains before the gale —
My cables part, and I must sail!

. . . .

Loud roars the sea! The dark has come:
He does not move — his lips are dumb. —
Ah, God receive, on shores of light,
The shattered ship that sails to-night!

ADELAIDE NEILSON[1]

AND oh, to think the sun can shine,
  The birds can sing, the flowers can bloom,
And she, whose soul was all divine,
  Be darkly mouldering in the tomb:

That o'er her head the night-wind sighs,
  And the sad cypress droops and moans;
That night has veiled her glorious eyes,
  And silence hushed her heavenly tones:

That those sweet lips no more can smile,
  Nor pity's tender shadows chase,
With many a gentle, child-like wile,
  The rippling laughter o'er her face:

That dust is on the burnished gold
  That floated round her royal head;
That her great heart is dead and cold —
  Her form of fire and beauty dead!

Roll on, gray earth and shining star,
  And coldly mock our dreams of bliss;
There is no glory left to mar,
  Nor any grief so black as this!

ARTHUR[1]

(1872–1886)

I

WHITE sail upon the ocean verge,
  Just crimsoned by the setting sun,
Thou hast thy port beyond the surge,
  Thy happy homeward course to run,
And wingëd hope, with heart of fire,
To gain the bliss of thy desire.

I watch thee till the sombre sky
  Has darkly veiled the lucent plain;
My thoughts, like homeless spirits, fly
  Behind thee o'er the glimmering main;
Thy prow will kiss a golden strand,
But they can never come to land.

And if they could, the fanes are black
  Where once I bent the reverent knee;
No shrine would send an answer back,
  No sacred altar blaze for me,
No holy bell, with silver toll,
Declare the ransom of my soul.

'T is equal darkness, here or there;
  For nothing that this world can give

Could now the ravaged past repair,
Or win the precious dead to live!
Life's crumbling ashes quench its flame,
And every place is now the same.

II

Thou idol of my constant heart,
Thou child of perfect love and light,
That sudden from my side didst part,
And vanish in the sea of night,
Through whatsoever tempests blow
My weary soul with thine would go.

Say, if thy spirit yet have speech,
What port lies hid within the pall,
What shore death's gloomy billows reach,
Or if they reach no shore at all!
One word — one little word — to tell
That thou art safe and all is well!

The anchors of my earthly fate,
As they were cast so must they cling;
And naught is now to do but wait
The sweet release that time will bring,
When all these mortal moorings break,
For one last voyage I must make.

Say that across the shuddering dark —
And whisper that the hour is near —
Thy hand will guide my shattered bark
Till mercy's radiant coasts appear,
Where I shall clasp thee to my breast,
And know once more the name of rest.

THE PASSING BELL AT STRATFORD[1]

(IT IS A TRADITION IN STRATFORD-UPON-AVON THAT THE BELL OF THE GUILD CHAPEL WAS TOLLED AT THE DEATH AND FUNERAL OF SHAKESPEARE)

SWEET bell of Stratford, tolling slow,
In summer gloaming's golden glow,
I hear and feel thy voice divine,
And all my soul responds to thine.

As now I hear thee, even so,
My Shakespeare heard thee long ago,
When lone by Avon's pensive stream
He wandered, in his haunted dream:

Heard thee — and far his fancy sped
Through spectral caverns of the dead,
And strove — and strove in vain — to pierce
The secret of the universe.

As now thou mournest didst thou mourn
On that sad day when he was borne
Through the green aisle of honied limes,
To rest beneath the chambered chimes.

He heard thee not, nor cared to hear!
Another voice was in his ear,
And, freed from all the bonds of men,
He knew the awful secret then.

Sweet bell of Stratford, toll, and be
A sacred promise unto me
Of that great hour when I shall know
The path whereon his footsteps go.

Stratford, 14 *Sept.* 1890.

I. H. B.

DIED, AUGUST 11, 1898

THE dirge is sung, the ritual said,
No more the brooding organ weeps,
And, cool and green, the turf is spread
On that lone grave where BROMLEY sleeps.

Gone — in his ripe, meridian hour!
Gone — when the wave was at its crest!
And wayward Humor's perfect flower
Is turned to darkness and to rest.

No more those honest eyes will beam
With torrid light of proud desire;
No more those fluent lips will teem
With Wit's gay quip or Passion's fire.

Forever gone! And with him fade
The dreams that Youth and Friendship know —
The frolic and the glee that made
The golden time of Long Ago.

The golden time! Ah, many a face, —
And his the merriest of them all, —
That made this world so sweet a place,
Is cold and still, beneath the pall.

His was the heart that over-much
In human goodness puts its trust,
And his the keen, satiric touch
That shrivels falsehood into dust.

His love was like the liberal air, —
  Embracing all, to cheer and bless;
And every grief that mortals share
  Found pity in his tenderness.

His subtle vision deeply saw,
  Through piteous webs of human fate,
The motion of the sovereign law,
  On which all tides of being wait.

No sad recluse, no lettered drone,
  His mirthful spirit, blithely poured,
In many a crescent frolic shone, —
  The light of many a festal board.

No pompous pedant, did he feign,
  With dull conceit of learning's store;
But not for him were writ in vain
  The statesman's craft, the scholar's lore.

Fierce for the right, he bore his part
  In strife with many a valiant foe;
But Laughter winged his polished dart,
  And Kindness tempered every blow.

No selfish purpose marked his way;
  Still for the common good he wrought,
And still enriched the passing day
  With sheen of wit and sheaves of thought.

Shrine him, New-England, in thy breast!
  With wild-flowers grace his hallowed bed,
And guard with love his laurelled rest,
  Forever with thy holiest dead!

For not in all the teeming years
  Of thy long glory hast thou known
A being framed of smiles and tears,
  Humor and force, so like thine own!

And never did thy asters gleam,
  Or through thy pines the night-wind roll,
To soothe, in death's transcendent dream,
  A sweeter or a nobler soul!

UNWRITTEN POEMS[1]

Fairy spirits of the breeze —
Frailer nothing is than these.
Fancies born we know not where —
In the heart or in the air;
Wandering echoes blown unsought
From far crystal peaks of thought;
Shadows, fading at the dawn,
Ghosts of feeling dead and gone:
Alas! Are all fair things that live
Still lovely and still fugitive?

Sarah Morgan Bryan Piatt

AFTER WINGS

This was your butterfly, you see, —
  His fine wings made him vain:
The caterpillars crawl, but he
  Passed them in rich disdain. —
My pretty boy says, "Let him be
  Only a worm again!"

O child, when things have learned to wear
  Wings once, they must be fain
To keep them always high and fair:
  Think of the creeping pain
Which even a butterfly must bear
  To be a worm again!

MY BABES IN THE WOOD

I know a story, fairer, dimmer, sadder,
  Than any story painted in your books.
You are so glad? It will not make you gladder;
  Yet listen, with your pretty restless looks.

"Is it a Fairy Story?" Well, half fairy —
  At least it dates far back as fairies do,
And seems to me as beautiful and airy;
  Yet half, perhaps the fairy half, is true.

You had a baby sister and a brother,
  (Two very dainty people, rosily white,
Each sweeter than all things except the other!)
  Older yet younger — gone from human sight!

And I, who loved them, and shall love them ever,
  And think with yearning tears how each light hand

Crept toward bright bloom or berries — I shall never
  Know how I lost them. Do you understand?

Poor slightly golden heads! I think I missed them
  First, in some dreamy, piteous, doubtful way;
But when and where with lingering lips I kisssed them,
  My gradual parting, I can never say.

Sometimes I fancy that they may have perished
  In shadowy quiet of wet rocks and moss,
Near paths whose very pebbles I have cherished,
  For their small sakes, since my most lovely loss.

I fancy, too, that they were softly covered
  By robins, out of apple-flowers they knew,
Whose nursing wings in far home sunshine hovered,
  Before the timid world had dropped the dew.

Their names were — what yours are! At this you wonder.
  Their pictures are — your own, as you have seen;
And my bird-buried darlings, hidden under
  Lost leaves — why, it is your dead selves I mean!

THE WITCH IN THE GLASS

"My mother says I must not pass
Too near that glass;
She is afraid that I will see
A little witch that looks like me,
With a red, red mouth to whisper low
The very thing I should not know!"

"Alack for all your mother's care!
A bird of the air,
A wistful wind, or (I suppose
Sent by some hapless boy) a rose,
With breath too sweet, will whisper low
The very thing you should not know!"

TRADITION OF CONQUEST

His Grace of Marlborough, legends say,
  Though battle-lightnings proved his worth,
Was scathed like others, in his day,
  By fiercer fires at his own hearth.

The patient chief, thus sadly tried, —
  Madam, the Duchess, was so fair, —
In Blenheim's honors felt less pride
  Than in the lady's lovely hair.

Once (shorn, she had coiled it there to wound
  Her lord when he should pass, 't is said),
Shining across his path he found
  The glory of the woman's head.

No sudden word, nor sullen look,
  In all his after days, confessed
He missed the charm whose absence took
  A scar's pale shape within his breast.

I think she longed to have him blame,
  And soothe him with imperious tears: —
As if her beauty were the same,
  He praised her through his courteous years.

But when the soldier's arm was dust,
  Among the dead man's treasures, where
He laid it as from moth and rust,
  They found his wayward wife's sweet hair.

THE WATCH OF A SWAN

I read somewhere that a swan, snow-white,
In the sun all day, in the moon all night,
Alone by a little grave would sit
  Waiting, and watching it.

Up out of the lake her mate would rise,
And call her down with his piteous cries
Into the waters still and dim: —
  With cries she would answer him.

Hardly a shadow would she let pass
Over the baby's cover of grass;
Only the wind might dare to stir
  The lily that watched with her.

Do I think that the swan was an angel? Oh,
I think it was only a swan, you know,

That for some sweet reason, wingëd and wild,
Had the love of a bird for a child.

IN CLONMEL PARISH CHURCHYARD

AT THE GRAVE OF CHARLES WOLFE

Where the graves were many, we looked for one.
Oh, the Irish rose was red,
And the dark stones saddened the setting sun
With the names of the early dead.
Then, a child who, somehow, had heard of him
In the land we love so well,
Kept lifting the grass till the dew was dim
In the churchyard of Clonmel.

But the sexton came. "Can you tell us where
Charles Wolfe is buried?" "I can.
— See, that is his grave in the corner there.
(Ay, he was a clever man,
If God had spared him!) It 's many that come
To be asking for him," said he.
But the boy kept whispering, "Not a drum
Was heard," — in the dusk to me.

(Then the gray man tore a vine from the wall
Of the roofless church where he lay,
And the leaves that the withering year let fall
He swept, with the ivy, away;
And, as we read on the rock the words
That, writ in the moss, we found,
Right over his bosom a shower of birds
In music fell to the ground.)

. . . Young poet, I wonder did you care,
Did it move you in your rest
To hear that child in his golden hair,
From the mighty woods of the West,
Repeating your verse of his own sweet will,
To the sound of the twilight bell,
Years after your beating heart was still
In the churchyard of Clonmel?

A CALL ON SIR WALTER RALEIGH

AT YOUGHAL, COUNTY CORK

"Ay, not at home, then, didst thou say?
— And, prithee, hath he gone to court?"
"Nay; he hath sailed but yesterday,
With Edmund Spenser, from this port.

"This Spenser, folk do say, hath writ
Twelve cantos, called 'The Faërie Queene.'
To seek for one to publish it,
They go — on a long voyage, I ween."

Ah me! I came so far to see
This ruffed and plumëd cavalier, —
He whom romance and history,
Alike, to all the world make dear.

And I had some strange things to tell
Of our New World, where he hath been;
And now they say — I marked them well —
They say the Master is not in!

The knaves speak not the truth; I see
Sir Walter at the window there.
— That is the hat, the sword, which he
In pictures hath been pleased to wear.

There hangs the very cloak whereon
Elizabeth set foot. (But oh,
Young diplomat, as things have gone,
Pity it is she soiled it so!)

And there — but look! he 's lost in smoke:
(That weirdly charmed Virginia weed!)
Make haste, bring anything; his cloak —
They save him with a shower, indeed!

. . . Ay, lost in smoke. I linger where
He walked his garden. Day is dim,
And death-sweet scents rise to the air
From flowers that gave their breath to him.

There, with its thousand years of tombs,
The dark church glimmers where he prayed;
Here, with that high head shorn of plumes,
The tree he planted gave him shade.

That high head shorn of plumes? Even so
It stained the Tower, when gray with grief.
O tree he planted, as I go,
For him I tenderly take a leaf.

I have been dreaming here, they say,
Of one dead knight forgot at court.
— And yet he sailed but yesterday,
With Edmund Spenser, from this port.

AN IRISH WILD-FLOWER

(A BAREFOOT CHILD BY ——— CASTLE)

She felt, I think, but as a wild-flower can,
Through her bright fluttering rags, the dark, the cold.
Some farthest star, remembering what man
Forgets, had warmed her little head with gold.

Above her, hollow-eyed, long blind to tears,
Leaf-cloaked, a skeleton of stone arose. . . .
O castle-shadow of a thousand years,
Where you have fallen — is this the thing that grows?

TRANSFIGURED

Almost afraid they led her in
(A dwarf more piteous none could find):
Withered as some weird leaf, and thin,
The woman was — and wan and blind.

Into his mirror with a smile —
Not vain to be so fair, but glad —
The South-born painter looked the while,
With eyes than Christ's alone less sad.

"Mother of God," in pale surprise
He whispered, "what am I to paint!"
A voice, that sounded from the skies,
Said to him, "Raphael, a saint."

She sat before him in the sun:
He scarce could look at her, and she
Was still and silent. . . . "It is done,"
He said. — "Oh, call the world to see!"

Ah, this was she in veriest truth —
Transcendent face and haloed hair.
The beauty of divinest youth,
Divinely beautiful, was there.

Herself into her picture passed —
Herself and not her poor disguise,
Made up of time and dust. . . . At last
One saw her with the Master's eyes.

THE TERM OF DEATH

Between the falling leaf and rose-bud's breath;
The bird's forsaken nest and her new song
(And this is all the time there is for Death);
The worm and butterfly — it is not long!

ENVOY

Sweet World, if you will hear me now:
I may not own a sounding Lyre
And wear my name upon my brow
Like some great jewel quick with fire.

But let me, singing, sit apart,
In tender quiet with a few,
And keep my fame upon my heart,
A little blush-rose wet with dew.

David Gray

ON LEBANON

Those days we spent on Lebanon,
Held captive by the sieging snow —
What bright things are forgot and gone,
While these have kept their after-glow!

It seemed but monotone, in truth,
That morning gaze o'er mountain mass,
Our council with the hamlet's youth,
The daily sortie up the pass, —
And, last, your father's fire o' nights,
Sweet Maiden of the Maronites!

Sometimes the battling clouds would break,
And from the rifted azure, fair,
We saw an eagle slant, and take,
Broad-winged, the stormy slopes of air.
And once, when winter's stubborn heart
Half broke in sunshine o'er the place,
We held our bridles to depart,
Eager and gleeful; but your face —
It did not mirror our delights,
O Maiden of the Maronites!

Bright face! how Arab-wild would glow,
Through shifting mood of storm or calm,
Its beauty, born of sun and snow,
Between the cedar and the palm.
Nor, as I watched its changing thought,
Could alien speech be long disguise;
For ere one English phrase she caught
I learned the Arabic of her eyes —
The love-lore of their dusks and lights,
My Maiden of the Maronites!

We parted soon, and upward fared,
Snow-fettered, till the pass was ours,
And all beneath us, golden-aired,
Lay Syria, in a dream of flowers.
Then spurred we, for before us burned
White Baalbec's signal in the noon,
And, ere to wayside camp we turned,
'Twixt us and you and far Bhâmdun,
All Lebanon raised his icy heights,
My Maiden of the Maronites!

Yet, still, those days on Lebanon
As steadfast keep their after-glow
As if they owned a summer sun,
And roses blossomed in the snow;
And when, with fire of heart and brain,
And the quick pulse's speed increased,
And wordless longings, come again
Vision and passion of the East,
I dream — ah! wild are Fancy's flights,
O Maiden of the Maronites!

DIVIDED

THE half-world's width divides us; where she sits
Noonday has broadened o'er the prairied West;
For me, beneath an alien sky, unblest,
The day dies and the bird of evening flits.
Nor do I dream that in her happier breast
Stirs thought of me. Untroubled beams the star,
And recks not of the drifting mariner's quest,
Who, for dear life, may seek it on mid-sea.
The half-world's width divides us; yet, from far —
And though I know that nearer may not be
In all the years — yet, O beloved, to thee
Goes out my heart, and, past the crimson bar
Of Sunset, westward yearns away — away —
And dieth towards thee with the dying day!

THE CROSS OF GOLD

THE fifth from the north wall;
Row innermost; and the pall
Plain black — all black — except
The cross on which she wept,
Ere she lay down and slept.

This one is hers, and this —
The marble next it — his.
So lie in brave accord
The lady and her lord,
Her cross and his red sword.

And, now, what seekst thou here;
Having nor care nor fear
To vex with thy hot tread
These halls of the long dead, —
To flash the torch's light
Upon their utter night? —
What word hast thou to thrust
Into her ear of dust?

Spake then the haggard priest:
"In lands of the far East
I dreamed of finding rest —
What time my lips had prest
The cross on this dead breast.

"And if my sin be shriven,
And mercy live in heaven,
Surely this hour, and here,
My long woe's end is near —
Is near — and I am brought
To peace, and painless thought
Of her who lies at rest,
This cross upon her breast;

"Whose passionate heart is cold
Beneath this cross of gold;

Who lieth, still and mute,
In sleep so absolute.
Yea, by this precious sign
Shall sleep most sweet be mine;

And I, at last, am blest,
Knowing she went to rest
This cross upon her breast."

Thomas Bailey Aldrich

APPRECIATION

To the sea-shell's spiral round
'T is your heart that brings the sound:
The soft sea-murmurs that you hear
Within, are captured from your ear.

You do poets and their song
A grievous wrong,
If your own soul does not bring
To their high imagining
As much beauty as they sing.

TO HAFIZ

THOUGH gifts like thine the fates gave not to me,
One thing, O Hafiz, we both hold in fee —
Nay, it holds us; for when the June wind blows
We both are slaves and lovers to the rose.
In vain the pale Circassian lily shows
Her face at her green lattice, and in vain
The violet beckons, with unveilëd face —
The bosom's white, the lip's light purple stain,
These touch our liking, yet no passion stir.
But when the rose comes, Hafiz — in that place
Where she stands smiling, we kneel down to her!

WHEN THE SULTAN GOES TO ISPAHAN

When the Sultan Shah-Zaman
Goes to the city Ispahan,
Even before he gets so far
As the place where the clustered palm-trees are,
At the last of the thirty palace-gates,
The flower of the harem, Rose-in-Bloom,
Orders a feast in his favorite room —
Glittering squares of colored ice,
Sweetened with syrop, tinctured with spice,
Creams, and cordials, and sugared dates,
Syrian apples, Othmanee quinces,
Limes, and citrons, and apricots,
And wines that are known to Eastern princes;
And Nubian slaves, with smoking pots
Of spicëd meats and costliest fish
And all that the curious palate could wish,
Pass in and out of the cedarn doors;
Scattered over mosaic floors
Are anemones, myrtles, and violets,
And a musical fountain throws its jets
Of a hundred colors into the air.
The dusk Sultana loosens her hair,
And stains with the henna-plant the tips
Of her pointed nails, and bites her lips
Till they bloom again; but, alas, *that* rose
Not for the Sultan buds and blows,
Not for the Sultan Shah-Zaman
When he goes to the city Ispahan.

Then at a wave of her sunny hand
The dancing-girls of Samarcand
Glide in like shapes from fairy-land,
Making a sudden mist in air
Of fleecy veils and floating hair
And white arms lifted. Orient blood
Runs in their veins, shines in their eyes.
And there, in this Eastern Paradise,
Filled with the breath of sandal-wood,
And Khoten musk, and aloes and myrrh,
Sits Rose-in-Bloom on a silk divan,
Sipping the wines of Astrakhan;
And her Arab lover sits with her.
That's when the Sultan Shah-Zaman
Goes to the city Ispahan.

Now, when I see an extra light,
Flaming, flickering on the night
From my neighbor's casement opposite,
I know as well as I know to pray,
I know as well as a tongue can say,
That the innocent Sultan Shah-Zaman
Has gone to the city Ispahan.

PALABRAS CARIÑOSAS

GOOD-NIGHT! I have to say good-night
To such a host of peerless things!
Good-night unto the slender hand
All queenly with its weight of rings;
Good-night to fond, uplifted eyes,
Good-night to chestnut braids of hair,
Good-night unto the perfect mouth,
And all the sweetness nestled there —
The snowy hand detains me, then
I'll have to say Good-night again!

But there will come a time, my love,
When, if I read our stars aright,
I shall not linger by this porch
With my farewells. Till then, good-night!
You wish the time were now? And I.
You do not blush to wish it so?
You would have blushed yourself to death
To own so much a year ago —
What, both these snowy hands! ah, then
I'll have to say Good-night again!

HEREDITY

A SOLDIER of the Cromwell stamp,
With sword and psalm-book by his side,
At home alike in church and camp:
Austere he lived, and smileless died.

But she, a creature soft and fine —
From Spain, some say, some say from France;
Within her veins leapt blood like wine —
She led her Roundhead lord a dance!

In Grantham church they lie asleep;
Just where, the verger may not know.
Strange that two hundred years should keep
The old ancestral fires aglow!

In me these two have met again;
To each my nature owes a part:
To one, the cool and reasoning brain;
To one, the quick, unreasoning heart.

IDENTITY

SOMEWHERE — in desolate wind-swept space —
In Twilight-land — in No-man's-land —
Two hurrying Shapes met face to face,
And bade each other stand.

"And who are you?" cried one a-gape,
Shuddering in the gloaming light.
"I know not," said the second Shape,
"I only died last night!"

UNGUARDED GATES

WIDE open and unguarded stand our gates,
Named of the four winds, North, South, East, and West;
Portals that lead to an enchanted land
Of cities, forests, fields of living gold,
Vast prairies, lordly summits touched with snow,
Majestic rivers sweeping proudly past
The Arab's date-palm and the Norseman's pine —
A realm wherein are fruits of every zone,
Airs of all climes, for, lo! throughout the year
The red rose blossoms somewhere — a rich land,
A later Eden planted in the wilds,
With not an inch of earth within its bound
But if a slave's foot press it sets him free.
Here, it is written, Toil shall have its wage,
And Honor honor, and the humblest man
Stand level with the highest in the law.
Of such a land have men in dungeons dreamed,
And with the vision brightening in their eyes
Gone smiling to the fagot and the sword.

Wide open and unguarded stand our gates,
And through them presses a wild motley throng —
Men from the Volga and the Tartar steppes,
Featureless figures of the Hoang-Ho,
Malayan, Scythian, Teuton, Kelt, and Slav,
Flying the Old World's poverty and scorn;
These bringing with them unknown gods and rites, —
Those, tiger passions, here to stretch their claws.
In street and alley what strange tongues are loud,
Accents of menace alien to our air,
Voices that once the Tower of Babel knew!

O Liberty, white Goddess! is it well
To leave the gates unguarded? On thy breast

Fold Sorrow's children, soothe the hurts of fate,
Lift the down-trodden, but with hand of steel
Stay those who to thy sacred portals come
To waste the gifts of freedom. Have a care
Lest from thy brow the clustered stars be torn
And trampled in the dust. For so of old
The thronging Goth and Vandal trampled Rome,
And where the temples of the Cæsars stood
The lean wolf unmolested made her lair.

GUILIELMUS REX

THE folk who lived in Shakespeare's day
And saw that gentle figure pass
By London Bridge, his frequent way —
They little knew what man he was.

The pointed beard, the courteous mien,
The equal port to high and low,
All this they saw or might have seen —
But not the light behind the brow!

The doublet's modest gray or brown,
The slender sword-hilt's plain device,
What sign had these for prince or clown?
Few turned, or none, to scan him twice.

Yet 't was the king of England's kings!
The rest with all their pomps and trains
Are mouldered, half-remembered things —
'T is he alone that lives and reigns!

SARGENT'S PORTRAIT OF EDWIN BOOTH AT "THE PLAYERS"

THAT face which no man ever saw
And from his memory banished quite,
With eyes in which are Hamlet's awe
And Cardinal Richelieu's subtle light
Looks from this frame. A master's hand
Has set the master-player here,
In the fair temple that he planned
Not for himself. To us most dear
This image of him! "It was thus
He looked; such pallor touched his cheek;
With that same grace he greeted us —
Nay, 't is the man, could it but speak!"
Sad words that shall be said some day —
Far fall the day! O cruel Time,
Whose breath sweeps mortal things away,
Spare long this image of his prime,
That others standing in the place
Where, save as ghosts, we come no more,
May know what sweet majestic face
The gentle Prince of Players wore!

TENNYSON

SHAKESPEARE and Milton — what third blazoned name
Shall lips of after-ages link to these?
His who, beside the wild encircling sea,
Was England's voice, her voice with one acclaim,
For threescore years; whose word of praise was fame,
Whose scorn gave pause to man's iniquities.

What strain was his in that Crimean war?
A bugle-call in battle; a low breath,
Plaintive and sweet, above the fields of death!
So year by year the music rolled afar,
From Euxine wastes to flowery Kandahar,
Bearing the laurel or the cypress wreath.

Others shall have their little space of time,
Their proper niche and bust, then fade away
Into the darkness, poets of a day;
But thou, O builder of enduring rhyme,
Thou shalt not pass! Thy fame in every clime
On earth shall live where Saxon speech has sway.

Waft me this verse across the winter sea,
Through light and dark, through mist and blinding sleet,
O winter winds, and lay it at his feet;
Though the poor gift betray my poverty,
At his feet lay it: it may chance that he
Will find no gift, where reverence is, unmeet.

A SHADOW OF THE NIGHT

CLOSE on the edge of a midsummer dawn
In troubled dreams I went from land to land,
Each seven-colored like the rainbow's arc,

Regions where never fancy's foot had trod
Till then; yet all the strangeness seemed not strange,
At which I wondered, reasoning in my dream
With two-fold sense, well knowing that I slept.
At last I came to this our cloud-hung earth,
And somewhere by the seashore was a grave,
A woman's grave, new-made, and heaped with flowers;
And near it stood an ancient holy man
That fain would comfort me, who sorrowed not
For this unknown dead woman at my feet.
But I, because his sacred office held
My reverence, listened; and 't was thus he spake:
"When next thou comest thou shalt find her still
In all the rare perfection that she was.
Thou shalt have gentle greeting of thy love!
Her eyelids will have turned to violets,
Her bosom to white lilies, and her breath
To roses. What is lovely never dies,
But passes into other loveliness,
Star-dust, or sea-foam, flower, or wingëd air.
If this befalls our poor unworthy flesh,
Think thee what destiny awaits the soul!
What glorious vesture it shall wear at last!"
While yet he spoke, seashore and grave and priest
Vanished, and faintly from a neighboring spire
Fell five slow solemn strokes upon my ear.
Then I awoke with a keen pain at heart,
A sense of swift unutterable loss,
And through the darkness reached my hand to touch
Her cheek, soft pillowed on one restful palm —
To be quite sure!

SONNETS

ENAMOURED ARCHITECT OF AIRY RHYME

ENAMOURED architect of airy rhyme,
Build as thou wilt; heed not what each man says:
Good souls, but innocent of dreamers' ways,
Will come, and marvel why thou wastest time;
Others, beholding how thy turrets climb
'Twixt theirs and heaven, will hate thee all thy days;
But most beware of those who come to praise.
O Wondersmith, O worker in sublime
And heaven-sent dreams, let art be all in all;
Build as thou wilt, unspoiled by praise or blame,
Build as thou wilt, and as thy light is given:
Then, if at last the airy structure fall,
Dissolve, and vanish — take thyself no shame.
They fail, and they alone, who have not striven.

REMINISCENCE

THOUGH I am native to this frozen zone
That half the twelvemonth torpid lies, or dead;
Though the cold azure arching overhead
And the Atlantic's never-ending moan
Are mine by heritage, I must have known
Life otherwhere in epochs long since fled;
For in my veins some Orient blood is red,
And through my thought are lotus blossoms blown.
I do remember . . . it was just at dusk,
Near a walled garden at the river's turn
(A thousand summers seem but yesterday!),
A Nubian girl, more sweet than Khoorja musk,
Came to the water-tank to fill her urn,
And, with the urn, she bore my heart away!

OUTWARD BOUND

I LEAVE behind me the elm-shadowed square
And carven portals of the silent street,
And wander on with listless, vagrant feet
Through seaward-leading alleys, till the air
Smells of the sea, and straightway then the care
Slips from my heart, and life once more is sweet.
At the lane's ending lie the white-winged fleet.
O restless Fancy, whither wouldst thou fare?

Here are brave pinions that shall take thee
far —
Gaunt hulks of Norway; ships of red
Ceylon;
Slim-masted lovers of the blue Azores!
'T is but an instant hence to Zanzibar,
Or to the regions of the Midnight Sun;
Ionian isles are thine, and all the fairy
shores!

ANDROMEDA

The smooth-worn coin and threadbare
classic phrase
Of Grecian myths that did beguile my
youth,
Beguile me not as in the olden days:
I think more grief and beauty dwell with
truth.
Andromeda, in fetters by the sea,
Star-pale with anguish till young Perseus
came,
Less moves me with her suffering than she,
The slim girl figure fettered to dark shame,
That nightly haunts the park, there, like a
shade,
Trailing her wretchedness from street to
street.
See where she passes — neither wife nor
maid;
How all mere fiction crumbles at her feet!
Here is woe's self, and not the mask of woe:
A legend's shadow shall not move you so!

THE UNDISCOVERED COUNTRY

Forever am I conscious, moving here,
That should I step a little space aside
I pass the boundary of some glorified
Invisible domain — it lies so near!
Yet nothing know we of that dim frontier
Which each must cross, whatever fate be-
tide,
To reach the heavenly cities where abide
(Thus Sorrow whispers) those that were
most dear,
Now all transfigured in celestial light!
Shall we indeed behold them, thine and
mine,
Whose going hence made black the noon-
day sun? —
Strange is it that across the narrow night
They fling us not some token, or make
sign
That all beyond is not Oblivion.

SLEEP

When to soft sleep we give ourselves
away,
And in a dream as in a fairy bark
Drift on and on through the enchanted
dark
To purple daybreak — little thought we
pay
To that sweet bitter world we know by
day.
We are clean quit of it, as is a lark
So high in heaven no human eye can
mark
The thin swift pinion cleaving through the
gray.
Till we awake ill fate can do no ill,
The resting heart shall not take up again
The heavy load that yet must make it
bleed;
For this brief space the loud world's voice
is still,
No faintest echo of it brings us pain.
How will it be when we shall sleep in-
deed?

PRESCIENCE

The new moon hung in the sky,
The sun was low in the west,
And my betrothed and I
In the churchyard paused to rest —
Happy maiden and lover,
Dreaming the old dream over:
The light winds wandered by,
And robins chirped from the nest.

And, lo! in the meadow-sweet
Was the grave of a little child,
With a crumbling stone at the feet,
And the ivy running wild —
Tangled ivy and clover
Folding it over and over:
Close to my sweetheart's feet
Was the little mound up-piled.

Stricken with nameless fears,
She shrank and clung to me,
And her eyes were filled with tears
For a sorrow I did not see:
Lightly the winds were blowing,
Softly her tears were flowing —
Tears for the unknown years
And a sorrow that was to be!

MEMORY

My mind lets go a thousand things,
Like dates of wars and deaths of kings,
And yet recalls the very hour —
'T was noon by yonder village tower,
And on the last blue noon in May —
The wind came briskly up this way,
Crisping the brook beside the road;
Then, pausing here, set down its load
Of pine-scents, and shook listlessly
Two petals from that wild-rose tree.

THALIA

A MIDDLE-AGED LYRICAL POET IS SUPPOSED TO BE TAKING LEAVE OF THE MUSE OF COMEDY

I say it under the rose —
  Oh, thanks ! — yes, under the laurel,
We part lovers, not foes;
  We are not going to quarrel.

We have too long been friends
  On foot and in gilded coaches,
Now that the whole thing ends,
  To spoil our kiss with reproaches.

I leave you; my soul is wrung;
  I pause, look back from the portal —
Ah, I no more am young,
  And you, child, you are immortal !

Mine is the glacier's way,
  Yours is the blossom's weather —
When were December and May
  Known to be happy together ?

Before my kisses grow tame,
  Before my moodiness grieve you,
While yet my heart is flame,
  And I all lover, I leave you.

So, in the coming time,
  When you count the rich years over,
Think of me in my prime,
  And not as a white-haired lover,

Fretful, pierced with regret,
  The wraith of a dead Desire,
Thrumming a cracked spinet
  By a slowly dying fire.

When, at last, I am cold —
  Years hence, if the gods so will it —
Say, "He was true as gold,"
  And wear a rose in your fillet !

Others, tender as I,
  Will come and sue for caresses,
Woo you, win you, and die —
  Mind you, a rose in your tresses !

Some Melpomene woo,
  Some hold Clio the nearest;
You, sweet Comedy, — you
  Were ever sweetest and dearest !

Nay, it is time to go.
  When writing your tragic sister
Say to that child of woe
  How sorry I was I missed her.

Really, I cannot stay,
  Though "parting is such sweet sorrow" . . .
Perhaps I will, on my way
  Down-town, look in to-morrow !

QUATRAINS

MASKS

Black Tragedy lets slip her grim disguise
And shows you laughing lips and roguish eyes;
But when, unmasked, gay Comedy appears,
How wan her cheeks are, and what heavy tears !

MEMORIES

Two things there are with Memory will abide,
Whatever else befall, while life flows by:
That soft cold hand-touch at the altar side;
The thrill that shook you at your child's first cry.

CIRCUMSTANCE

  Linked to a clod, harassed, and sad
With sordid cares, she knew not life was sweet
Who should have moved in marble halls, and had
  Kings and crown-princes at her feet.

ON READING ——

Great thoughts in crude, unshapely verse set forth
Lose half their preciousness, and ever must.
Unless the diamond with its own rich dust
Be cut and polished, it seems little worth.

QUITS

If my best wines mislike thy taste,
And my best service win thy frown,
Then tarry not, I bid thee haste;
There 's many another Inn in town.

AN ODE

ON THE UNVEILING OF THE SHAW MEMORIAL ON BOSTON COMMON, MAY THIRTY-FIRST, 1897

I

Not with slow, funereal sound
Come we to this sacred ground;
Not with wailing fife and solemn muffled drum,
Bringing a cypress wreath
To lay, with bended knee,
On the cold brows of Death —
Not so, dear God, we come,
But with the trumpets' blare
And shot-torn battle-banners flung to air,
As for a victory!

Hark to the measured tread of martial feet,
The music and the murmurs of the street!
No bugle breathes this day
Disaster and retreat! —
Hark, how the iron lips
Of the great battle-ships
Salute the City from her azure Bay!

II

Time was — time was, ah, unforgotten years! —
We paid our hero tribute of our tears.
But now let go
All sounds and signs and formulas of woe:
'T is Life, not Death, we celebrate;
To Life, not Death, we dedicate
This storied bronze, whereon is wrought
The lithe immortal figure of our thought,
To show forever to men's eyes,
Our children's children's children's eyes,
How once he stood
In that heroic mood,
He and his dusky braves
So fain of glorious graves! —
One instant stood, and then
Drave through that cloud of purple steel and flame,
Which wrapt him, held him, gave him not again,
But in its trampled ashes left to Fame
An everlasting name!

III

That was indeed to live —
At one bold swoop to wrest
From darkling death the best
That death to life can give.
He fell as Roland fell
That day at Roncevaux,
With foot upon the ramparts of the foe!
A pæan, not a knell,
For heroes dying so!
No need for sorrow here,
No room for sigh or tear,
Save such rich tears as happy eyelids know.
See where he rides, our Knight!
Within his eyes the light
Of battle, and youth's gold about his brow;
Our Paladin, our Soldier of the Cross,
Not weighing gain with loss —
World-loser, that won all
Obeying duty's call!
Not his, at peril's frown,
A pulse of quicker beat;
Not his to hesitate
And parley hold with Fate,
But proudly to fling down
His gauntlet at her feet.
O soul of loyal valor and white truth,
Here, by this iron gate,
Thy serried ranks about thee as of yore,
Stand thou for evermore
In thy undying youth!

The tender heart, the eagle eye!
Oh, unto him belong
The homages of Song;
Our praises and the praise
Of coming days
To him belong —
To him, to him, the dead that shall not die!

A PETITION

To spring belongs the violet, and the blown
Spice of the roses let the summer own.
Grant me this favor, Muse — all else withhold —
That I may not write verse when I am old.

And yet I pray you, Muse, delay the time!
Be not too ready to deny me rhyme;
And when the hour strikes, as it must, dear Muse,
I beg you very gently break the news.

William Dean Howells

IN EARLIEST SPRING

TOSSING his mane of snows in wildest eddies and tangles,
Lion-like, March cometh in, hoarse, with tempestuous breath,
Through all the moaning chimneys, and thwart all the hollows and angles
Round the shuddering house, threating of winter and death.

But in my heart I feel the life of the wood and the meadow
Thrilling the pulses that own kindred with fibres that lift
Bud and blade to the sunward, within the inscrutable shadow,
Deep in the oak's chill core, under the gathering drift.

Nay, to earth's life in mine some prescience, or dream, or desire
(How shall I name it aright ?) comes for a moment and goes, —
Rapture of life ineffable, perfect — as if in the brier,
Leafless there by my door, trembled a sense of the rose.

THE TWO WIVES

THE colonel rode by his picket-line
In the pleasant morning sun,
That glanced from him far off to shine
On the crouching rebel picket's gun.

From his command the captain strode
Out with a grave salute,
And talked with the colonel as he rode: —
The picket levelled his piece to shoot.

The colonel rode and the captain walked, —
The arm of the picket tired;
Their faces almost touched as they talked,
And, swerved from his aim, the picket fired.

The captain fell at the horse's feet,
Wounded and hurt to death,
Calling upon a name that was sweet
As God is good, with his dying breath.

And the colonel that leaped from his horse and knelt
To close the eyes so dim,
A high remorse for God's mercy felt,
Knowing the shot was meant for him.

And he whispered, prayer-like, under his breath,
The name of his own young wife:
For Love, that had made his friend's peace with Death,
Alone could make his with life.

FROM GENERATION TO GENERATION[1]

INNOCENT spirits, bright, immaculate ghosts !
Why throng your heavenly hosts,
As eager for their birth
In this sad home of death, this sorrow-haunted earth ?

Beware ! Beware ! Content you where you are,
And shun this evil star,
Where we who are doomed to die
Have our brief being, and pass, we know not where or why.

We have not to consent or to refuse ;
It is not ours to choose :
We come because we must,
We know not by what law, if unjust or if just.

The doom is on us, as it is on you,
That nothing can undo ;
And all in vain you warn :
As your fate is to die, our fate is to be born.

CHANGE[1]

SOMETIMES, when after spirited debate
Of letters or affairs, in thought I go
Smiling unto myself, and all aglow
With some immediate purpose, and elate
As if my little, trivial scheme were great,
And what I would so were already so:
Suddenly I think of her that died, and know,

Whatever friendly or unfriendly fate
Befall me in my hope or in my pride,
It is all nothing but a mockery,
And nothing can be what it used to be,
When I could bid my happy life abide,
And build on earth for perpetuity,
Then, in the deathless days before she died.

IF[1]

Yes, death is at the bottom of the cup,
And every one that lives must drink it up;
And yet between the sparkle at the top
And the black lees where lurks that bitter drop,
There swims enough good liquor, Heaven knows,
To ease our hearts of all their other woes.

The bubbles rise in sunshine at the brim;
That drop below is very far and dim;
The quick fumes spread, and shape us such bright dreams
That in the glad delirium it seems
As though by some deft sleight, if so we willed,
That drop untasted might be somehow spilled.

HOPE[1]

We sailed and sailed upon the desert sea
Where for whole days we alone seemed to be.
At last we saw a dim, vague line arise
Between the empty billows and the skies,
That grew and grew until it wore the shape
Of cove and inlet, promontory and cape;
Then hills and valleys, rivers, fields, and woods,
Steeples and roofs, and village neighborhoods.
And then I thought, "Sometime I shall embark
Upon a sea more desert and more dark
Than ever this was, and between the skies
And empty billows I shall see arise
Another world out of that waste and lapse,
Like yonder land. Perhaps — perhaps — perhaps!"

VISION[1]

Within a poor man's squalid home I stood:
The one bare chamber, where his work-worn wife
Above the stove and wash-tub passed her life,
Next the sty where they slept with all their brood.
But I saw not that sunless, breathless lair,
The chamber's sagging roof and reeking floor;
The smeared walls, broken sash, and battered door;
The foulness and forlornness everywhere.
I saw a great house with the portals wide
Upon a banquet room, and, from without,
The guests descending in a brilliant line
By the stair's statued niches, and beside
The loveliest of the gemmed and silken rout
The poor man's landlord leading down to dine.

JUDGMENT DAY[1]

Before Him weltered like a shoreless sea
The souls of them that had not sought to be,
With all their guilt upon them, and they cried,
They that had sinned from hate and lust and pride,
"Thou that didst make us what we might become,
Judge us!" The Judge of all the earth was dumb;
But high above them, in His sovereign place,
He lifted up the pity of His face.

WHAT SHALL IT PROFIT?[1]

If I lay waste and wither up with doubt
The blessed fields of heaven where once my faith
Possessed itself serenely safe from death;
If I deny the things past finding out;
Or if I orphan my own soul of One
That seemed a Father, and make void the place
Within me where He dwelt in power and grace,
What do I gain by that I have undone?

Forceythe Willson

THE OLD SERGEANT

(1863)

"Come a little nearer, Doctor, — thank you, — let me take the cup:
Draw your chair up, — draw it closer, — just another little sup!
May be you may think I'm better; but I'm pretty well used up: —
Doctor, you've done all you could do, but I'm just a going up!

"Feel my pulse, sir, if you want to, but it ain't much use to try:" —
"Never say that," said the Surgeon as he smothered down a sigh;
"It will never do, old comrade, for a soldier to say die!"
"What you *say* will make no difference, Doctor, when you come to die.

"Doctor, what has been the matter?" "You were very faint, they say;
You must try to get to sleep now." "Doctor, have I been away?"
"Not that anybody knows of!" "Doctor — Doctor, please to stay!
There is something I must tell you, and you won't have long to stay!

"I have got my marching orders, and I'm ready now to go;
Doctor, did you say I fainted? — but it could n't ha' been so, —
For as sure as I'm a sergeant, and was wounded at Shiloh,
I've this very night been back there, on the old field of Shiloh!

"This is all that I remember: the last time the Lighter came,
And the lights had all been lowered, and the noises much the same,
He had not been gone five minutes before something called my name:
'Orderly Sergeant — Robert Burton!' — just that way it called my name.

"And I wondered who could call me so distinctly and so slow,
Knew it could n't be the Lighter, — he could not have spoken so, —
And I tried to answer, 'Here, sir!' but I could n't make it go;
For I could n't move a muscle, and I could n't make it go!

"Then I thought: it's all a nightmare, all a humbug and a bore;
Just another foolish grape-vine,[1] — and it won't come any more;
But it came, sir, notwithstanding, just the same way as before:
'Orderly Sergeant — Robert Burton!' — even plainer than before.

"That is all that I remember, till a sudden burst of light,
And I stood beside the river, where we stood that Sunday night,
Waiting to be ferried over to the dark bluffs opposite,
When the river was perdition and all hell was opposite! —

"And the same old palpitation came again in all its power,
And I heard a Bugle sounding, as from some celestial Tower;
And the same mysterious voice said: 'It is the eleventh hour!
Orderly Sergeant — Robert Burton — it is the eleventh hour!'

"Doctor Austin! — what *day* is this?" "It is Wednesday night, you know."
"Yes, — to-morrow will be New Year's, and a right good time below!
What *time* is it, Doctor Austin?" "Nearly Twelve." "Then don't you go!
Can it be that all this happened — all this — not an hour ago!

"There was where the gunboats opened on the dark rebellious host;
And where Webster semicircled his last guns upon the coast;
There were still the two log-houses, just the same, or else their ghost, —
And the same old transport came and took me over — or its ghost!

[1] Canard.

"And the old field lay before me all deserted far and wide;
There was where they fell on Prentiss, — there McClernand met the tide;
There was where stern Sherman rallied, and where Hurlbut's heroes died, —
Lower down, where Wallace charged them, and kept charging till he died.

"There was where Lew Wallace showed them he was of the canny kin,
There was where old Nelson thundered, and where Rousseau waded in;
There McCook sent 'em to breakfast, and we all began to win —
There was where the grape-shot took me, just as we began to win.

"Now, a shroud of snow and silence over everything was spread;
And but for this old blue mantle and the old hat on my head,
I should not have even doubted, to this moment, I was dead, —
For my footsteps were as silent as the snow upon the dead!

"Death and silence! — Death and silence! all around me as I sped!
And, behold, a mighty TOWER, as if builded to the dead,
To the Heaven of the heavens lifted up its mighty head,
Till the Stars and Stripes of Heaven all seemed waving from its head!

"Round and mighty-based it towered — up into the infinite —
And I knew no mortal mason could have built a shaft so bright;
For it shone like solid sunshine; and a winding stair of light
Wound around it and around it till it wound clear out of sight!

"And, behold, as I approached it, — with a rapt and dazzled stare, —
Thinking that I saw old comrades just ascending the great Stair, —
Suddenly the solemn challenge broke of, 'Halt, and who goes there!'
'I'm a friend,' I said, 'if you are.' 'Then advance, sir, to the Stair!'

"I advanced! — That sentry, Doctor, was Elijah Ballantyne! —
First of all to fall on Monday, after we had formed the line! —
'Welcome, my old Sergeant, welcome! welcome by that countersign!'
And he pointed to the scar there, under this old cloak of mine!

"As he grasped my hand, I shuddered, thinking only of the grave;
But he smiled and pointed upward with a bright and bloodless glaive:
'That's the way, sir, to Headquarters.' 'What Headquarters?' 'Of the Brave.'
'But the great Tower?' 'That,' he answered, 'is the way, sir, of the Brave!'

"Then a sudden shame came o'er me at his uniform of light;
At my own so old and tattered, and at his so new and bright:
'Ah!' said he, 'you have forgotten the New Uniform to-night, —
Hurry back, for you must be here at just twelve o'clock to-night!'

"And the next thing I remember, you were sitting *there*, and I —
Doctor — did you hear a footstep? Hark! — God bless you all! Good by!
Doctor, please to give my musket and my knapsack, when I die,
To my son — my son that's coming, — he won't get here till I die!

"Tell him his old father blessed him as he never did before, —
And to carry that old musket — hark! a knock is at the door! —
Till the Union — See! it opens!" "Father! father! speak once more!"
"*Bless you!*" gasped the old, gray Sergeant, and he lay and said no more!

FROM "IN STATE"

O KEEPER of the Sacred Key,
And the Great Seal of Destiny,
Whose eye is the blue canopy,
Look down upon the warring world, and tell us what the end will be.

"Lo, through the wintry atmosphere,
On the white bosom of the sphere,
A cluster of five lakes appear;
And all the land looks like a couch, or warrior's shield, or sheeted bier.

"And on that vast and hollow field,
With both lips closed and both eyes sealed,
A mighty Figure is revealed, —
Stretched at full length, and stiff and stark, as in the hollow of a shield.

"The winds have tied the drifted snow
Around the face and chin; and, lo!
The sceptred Giants come and go,
And shake their shadowy crowns and say: 'We always feared it would be so!'

"She came of an heroic race:
A giant's strength, a maiden's grace,
Like two in one seem to embrace,
And match, and blend, and thorough-blend, in her colossal form and face.

"Where can her dazzling falchion be?
One hand is fallen in the sea;
The Gulf-Stream drifts it far and free;
And in that hand her shining brand gleams from the depths resplendently.

"And by the other, in its rest,
The starry banner of the West
Is clasped forever to her breast;
And of her silver helmet, lo, a soaring eagle is the crest.

"And on her brow, a softened light,
As of a star concealed from sight
By some thin veil of fleecy white, —
Or of the rising moon behind the rainy vapors of the night.

"The Sisterhood that was so sweet,
The Starry System sphered complete,
Which the mazed Orient used to greet,
The Four and Thirty fallen Stars glimmer and glitter at her feet.

"And over her, — and over all,
For panoply and coronal, —
The mighty Immemorial,
And everlasting Canopy and starry Arch and Shield of All."

William Reed Huntington

TELLUS

Why here, on this third planet from the Sun,
Fret we and smite against our prison-bars?
Why not in Saturn, Mercury, or Mars,
Mourn we our sins, the things undone and done?
Where was the soul's bewildering course begun?
In what sad land among the scattered stars
Wrought she the ill which now forever scars
By bitter consequence each victory won?
I know not, dearest friend, yet this I see,
That thou for holier fellowships wast meant.
Through some strange blunder thou art here; and we
Who on the convict ship were hither sent,
By judgment just, must not be named with thee
Whose tranquil presence shames our discontent.

AUTHORITY

Launched upon ether float the worlds secure.
Naught hath the truthful Maker to conceal.
No trestle-work of adamant or steel
Is that high firmament where these endure.
Patient, majestic, round their cynosure
In secular procession see them wheel;
Self-poised, but not self-centred, for they feel
In each tense fibre one all-conquering lure.
And need I fret me, Father, for that Thou
Dost will the weightiest verities to swing
On viewless orbits? Nay, henceforth I cleave
More firmly to the Credo; and my vow
With readier footstep to thine altar bring,
As one who counts it freedom to believe.

Margaret Elizabeth Sangster

WHITTIER[1]

His fourscore years and five
Are gone, like a tale that is told.
The quick tears start, there 's an ache at the heart,
For we never thought him old.

Straight as a mountain pine,
With the mountain eagle's eye,
With the hand-clasp strong, and the unhushed song,
Was it time for him to die?

Prophet and priest he stood
In the storm of embattled years;
The broken chain was his harp's refrain,
And the peace that is balm for tears.

The hills and the valleys knew
The poet who kept their tryst.
To our common life and our daily strife
He brought the blessing of Christ.

And we never thought him old,
Though his locks were white as snow.
O heart of gold, grown suddenly cold,
It was not time to go!

[1] Copyright, 1893, by Harper & Brothers.

AWAKENING[2]

Never yet was a springtime,
Late though lingered the snow,
That the sap stirred not at the whisper
Of the south wind, sweet and low;
Never yet was a springtime
When the buds forgot to blow.

Ever the wings of the summer
Are folded under the mould;
Life, that has known no dying,
Is Love's, to have and to hold,
Till, sudden, the burgeoning Easter!
The song! the green and the gold!

[2] Copyright, 1897, by Harper & Brothers.

Henry Ames Blood

COMRADES

One steed I have of common clay,
And one no less than regal;
By day I jog on old Saddlebags,
By night I fly upon Eagle:
To store, to market, to field, to mill,
One plods with patient patter,
Nor hears along the far-off heights
The hoofs of his comrade clatter.

To field, to market, to mill he goes,
Nor sees his comrade gleaming
Where he flies along the purple hills,
Nor the flame from his bridle streaming;
Sees not his track, nor the sparks of fire
So terribly flashing from it,
As they flashed from the track of Alborak
When he bravely carried Mahomet.

One steed, in a few short years, will rest
Under the grasses yonder;
The other will come there centuries hence
To linger and dream and ponder;
And yet both steeds are mine to-day,
The immortal and the mortal:
One beats alone the clods of earth,
One stamps at heaven's portal.

SHAKESPEARE

I wish that I could have my wish to-night,
For all the fairies should assist my flight
Back into the abyss of years;
Till I could see the streaming light,
And hear the music of the spheres
That sang together at the joyous birth
Of that immortal mind,
The noblest of his kind,—
The only Shakespeare that has graced our earth.

Oh that I might behold
Those gentle sprites, by others all unseen,
Queen Mab and Puck the bold,
With curtseys manifold
Glide round his cradle every morn and e'en;

That I might see the nimble shapes that ran
And frisked and frolicked by his side,
When school-hours ended or began,
At morn or eventide;
That I might see the very shoes he wore
Upon the dusty street,
His little gown and pinafore,
His satchel and his schoolboy rig complete!

If I could have the wish I rhyme,
Then should this night and all it doth contain
Be set far back upon the rim of Time,
And I would wildered be upon a stormy plain;
The wanton waves of winter wind and storm
Should beat upon my ruddy face,
And on my streaming hair;
And hags and witches multiform,
And beldames past all saintly grace,
Should hover round me in the sleety air.

Then, hungry, cold, and frightened by these imps of sin,
And breathless all with buffeting the storm,
Betimes I would arrive at some old English inn,
Wainscoted, high, and warm.
The fire should blaze in antique chimney-place;
And on the high-backed settles, here and there,
The village gossip and the merry laugh
Should follow brimming cups of half-an'-half;
Before the fire, in hospitable chair,
The landlord fat should bask his shining face,
And slowly twirl his pewter can;
And there in his consummate grace,
The perfect lord of wit,
The immortal man,
The only Shakespeare of this earth should sit.

There, too, that Spanish galleon of a hulk,
Ben Jonson, lying at full length,
Should so dispose his goodly bulk
That he might lie at ease upon his back,
To test the tone and strength
Of Boniface's sherris-sack.

And there should be some compeers of these two,
Rare wits and poets of the land,
Whom all good England knew,
And who are now her dear forget-me-nots;
And they should lounge on Shakespeare's either hand,
And sip their punch from queer old cans and pots.

Oh, then, such drollery should begin,
Such wit flash out, such humor run
Around the fire in this old English inn,
The veriest clod would be convulsed with fun;
And Boniface's merry sides would ache,
And his round belly like a pudding shake.

Never since the world began
Has been such repartee;
And never till the next begins
Will greater things be said by man,
Than this same company
Were wont to say so oft in those old English inns.

Dear artist, if you paint this picture mine,
Do not forget the storm that roars
Above the merry din and laughter within doors;
But let some stroke divine
Make all within appear more rich and warm,
By contrast with the outer storm.

23 *April*, 1864.

Mary Mapes Dodge[1]

THE TWO MYSTERIES

We know not what it is, dear, this sleep so deep and still;
The folded hands, the awful calm, the cheek so pale and chill;
The lids that will not lift again, though we may call and call;
The strange, white solitude of peace that settles over all.

[1] See, also, p. 587.

We know not what it means, dear, this
desolate heart-pain;
This dread to take our daily way, and walk
in it again;
We know not to what other sphere the
loved who leave us go,
Nor why we're left to wonder still, nor
why we do not know.

But this we know: Our loved and dead, if
they should come this day, —
Should come and ask us, "What is life?"
— not one of us could say.
Life is a mystery as deep as ever death can
be;
Yet oh, how dear it is to us, this life we
live and see!

Then might they say, — these vanished
ones, — and blessëd is the thought,
"So death is sweet to us, beloved! though
we may show you naught;
We may not to the quick reveal the mystery of death —
Ye cannot tell us, if ye would, the mystery
of breath."

The child who enters life comes not with
knowledge or intent,
So those who enter death must go as little
children sent.
Nothing is known. But I believe that God
is overhead;
And as life is to the living, so death is to
the dead.

ONCE BEFORE

Once before, this self-same air
Passed me, though I know not where.
Strange! how very like it came!
Touch and fragrance were the same;
Sound of mingled voices, too,
With a light laugh ringing through;
Some one moving, — here or there, —
Some one passing up the stair,
Some one calling from without,
Or a far-off childish shout, —
Simple, home-like, nothing more,
Yet it all hath been before!

No: not to-day, nor yesterday,
Nor any day! But far away —
So long ago, so very far,
It might have been on other star.
How was it spent? and where? and when?
This life that went, yet comes again?
Was sleep its world, or death its shore?
I still the silent Past implore.
Ah! never dream had power to show
Such vexing glimpse of Long Ago.
Never a death could follow death
With love between, and home, and breath.

The spell has passed. What spendthrifts we,
Of simple, household certainty!
What golden grain we trample low
Searching for flowers that never grow!
Why, home is real, and love is real;
Nor false our honest high ideal.
Life, — it is bounding, warm, and strong, —
And all my heart resounds with song.
It must be true, whate'er befall,
This and the world to come are all.
And yet it puzzles me — alack! —
When life that could not be, comes back!

THE STARS

They wait all day unseen by us, unfelt;
Patient they bide behind the day's full glare;
And we, who watched the dawn when they
were there,
Thought we had seen them in the daylight
melt,
While the slow sun upon the earth-line
knelt.
Because the teeming sky seemed void and
bare,
When we explored it through the dazzled
air,
We had no thought that there all day they
dwelt.
Yet were they over us, alive and true,
In the vast shades far up above the blue, —
The brooding shades beyond our daylight
ken, —
Serene and patient in their conscious light,
Ready to sparkle for our joy again, —
The eternal jewels of the short-lived night.

EMERSON

We took it to the woods, we two,
The book well worn and brown,
To read his words where stirring leaves
Rained their soft shadows down.

Yet as we sat and breathed the scene,
We opened not a page;
Enough that he was with us there,
Our silent, friendly sage!

His fresh "Rhodora" bloomed again;
His "Humble-bee" buzzed near;
And oh, the "Wood-notes" beautiful
He taught our souls to hear.

So our unopened book was read;
And so, in restful mood,
We and our poet, arm in arm,
Went sauntering through the wood.

SHADOW-EVIDENCE

SWIFT o'er the sunny grass,
I saw a shadow pass
With subtle charm, —
So quick, so full of life,
With thrilling joy so rife,
I started lest, unknown,
My step — ere it was flown —
Had done it harm.

Why look up to the blue?
The bird was gone, I knew,
Far out of sight.
Steady and keen of wing,
The slight, impassioned thing,
Intent on a goal unknown,
Had held its course alone
In silent flight.

Dear little bird, and fleet,
Flinging down at my feet
Shadow for song:
More sure am I of thee —
Unseen, unheard by me —
Than of some things felt and known,
And guarded as my own,
All my life long.

William Bull Wright

FROM "THE BROOK"

THROUGH his million veins are poured
The splendors of the heaven whence he fell.
Wise above his thought is he:
Deep things he has to tell
To such as with a swift dexterity
Can aptly gloss his tangled word.
To an eternal song he frames his dance,
And urges his advance
Through numbers, motions intricately woven.
No pedant's eye avails to scan
The tumult of his foaming line,
Whose music owns a rule divine
To ears that once have caught the plan.
His notes so delicate and fine
My rudely fingered stop would crumble;
Only some easier tones I twine
To wreathe my homely line.
But, ah, the strength, the scope, the vision,
. . . the cadence sweet!
What bard could in his rhyme imprison,
Or bind with a melodious fetter,
The prance of these fine feet!

"Whence I come or whither I go,
I little question, for well I know
What I am, 't is joy to be;
Laughter is my vesture,
And a god of revelry
Beckons in my gesture.
I love my proper daemon well;
Summons he, I haste to follow
Through balmy grove or grassy dell,
Or mountain's tempest-haunted hollow.

"Only to the sober eye
The gods withdraw the curtains of the sky
Pressed from an immortal vine,
Temperance is eternal wine.
Who drinks my liquors chaste and cool
May slight the Heliconian pool:
He has no need to steal a sip
From Hafiz' bowl, or bathe his lip
In honey pressed from Pindar's comb,
Or taste of Bacchus' philtered foam,
Or filch from Chaucer's bounteous grace
Some liquid, limpid, purling phrase.
He shall take with heavenly sleight
In springe of couchant rhyme
The holy syllables, that in their flight
Skim the meads of Time,
And sometimes tarry for a night.
Lark-like they warble sweet and clear
Up and down the bustling sphere:

Happy he that skills to hear
Their feathery oarage light.

"Wide waves the harvest of sweet song,
Long since the gods have sown the seed:
Thither a thousand reapers throng,
But since the flinty stalks grow strong
Their sickles clip the easier weed.
Strives one with sweat and sober heed,
And limbs that ache and hands that bleed,
To sheave some score of stems:
The dear wise world, that loves the weed,
His heavenly task condemns.

"I know ye, folk of birth and death,
And of what troublous stuff is spun
The feeble tissue of your breath:
I know your fashions every one, —
Your gait and features smooth or grim,
From him that wakes a raw papoose
To him whose tongue his parents loose
With babbling of a Christian hymn.
Well I know the woman's wail,
Who comes, like bird from forage-quest,
With loaded bill unto her nest,
And finds her tender chitlings dead:
What beak hath brought ye death instead?
Sorrowful numbers flock around,
Earth-born ditties full of tears,
The loss, the cross, the myriad fears
That sting and madden and confound.
Ye call the law of your own fate
Rough to the feet, unfriendly, cold;
But if the heart be free and bold,
It turns to beautiful and great.
Come forth and love it, and 't is thine,
Works like a strong man by thy side;
But dodge or weep or fall supine,
Or take a lesser thought for guide,
The pebble of the rill
Has power to kill.

"For my frolic lyre refuses
Fellowship of moping muses:
Touched by a single note of pain,
His simple chords would crack atwain.
He to heaven is strongly sworn
To sound the hymns of utmost joy
And things of joyance born;
Pledged to a large, exulting song,
To which no sombre tones belong,
That, riding high above man's narrow state,
Perfect and full, and beyond sweetness sweet,
Teaches the maiden stars their heavenly gait,
And those soft flashings of their silver feet."

John Hay

LIBERTY

What man is there so bold that he should say,
"Thus, and thus only, would I have the Sea"?
For whether lying calm and beautiful,
Clasping the earth in love, and throwing back
The smile of Heaven from waves of amethyst;
Or whether, freshened by the busy winds,
It bears the trade and navies of the world
To ends of use or stern activity;
Or whether, lashed by tempests, it gives way
To elemental fury, howls and roars
At all its rocky barriers, in wild lust
Of ruin drinks the blood of living things,
And strews its wrecks o'er leagues of desolate shore, —
Always it is the Sea, and men bow down
Before its vast and varied majesty.

So all in vain will timorous ones essay
To set the metes and bounds of Liberty.
For Freedom is its own eternal law:
It makes its own conditions, and in storm
Or calm alike fulfils the unerring Will.
Let us not then despise it when it lies
Still as a sleeping lion, while a swarm
Of gnat-like evils hover round its head;
Nor doubt it when in mad, disjointed times
It shakes the torch of terror, and its cry
Shrills o'er the quaking earth, and in the flame
Of riot and war we see its awful form
Rise by the scaffold, where the crimson axe
Rings down its grooves the knell of shuddering kings.
For ever in thine eyes, O Liberty,

Shines that high light whereby the world is saved,
And though thou slay us, we will trust in thee!

THE SURRENDER OF SPAIN

Land of unconquered Pelayo! land of the Cid Campeador!
Sea-girdled mother of men! Spain, name of glory and power;
Cradle of world-grasping Emperors, grave of the reckless invader,
How art thou fallen, my Spain! how art thou sunk at this hour!

Once thy magnanimous sons trod, victors, the portals of Asia,
Once the Pacific waves rushed, joyful thy banners to see;
For it was Trajan that carried the battle-flushed eagles to Dacia,
Cortés that planted thy flag fast by the uttermost sea.

Hast thou forgotten those days illumined with glory and honor,
When the far isles of the sea thrilled to the tread of Castile?
When every land under heaven was flecked by the shade of thy banner, —
When every beam of the sun flashed on thy conquering steel?

Then through red fields of slaughter, through death and defeat and disaster,
Still flared thy banner aloft, tattered, but free from a stain;
Now to the upstart Savoyard thou bendest to beg for a master.
How the red flush of her shame mars the proud beauty of Spain!

Has the red blood run cold that boiled by the Xenil and Darro?
Are the high deeds of the sires sung to the children no more?
On the dun hills of the North hast thou heard of no plough-boy Pizarro?
Roams no young swineherd Cortés hid by the Tagus' wild shore?

Once again does Hispania bend low to the yoke of the stranger!
Once again will she rise, flinging her gyves in the sea!
Princeling of Piedmont! unwitting thou weddest with doubt and with danger,
King over men who have learned all that it costs to be free.

CHRISTINE

The beauty of the northern dawns,
Their pure, pale light is thine;
Yet all the dreams of tropic nights
Within thy blue eyes shine.
Not statelier in their prisoning seas
The icebergs grandly move,
But in thy smile is youth and joy,
And in thy voice is love.

Thou art like Hecla's crest that stands
So lonely, proud, and high,
No earthly thing may come between
Her summit and the sky.
The sun in vain may strive to melt
Her crown of virgin snow,
But the great heart of the mountain glows
With deathless fire below.

PIKE COUNTY BALLADS

JIM BLUDSO OF THE PRAIRIE BELLE

Wall, no! I can't tell whar he lives,
Becase he don't live, you see;
Leastways, he 's got out of the habit
Of livin' like you and me.
Whar have you been for the last three year
That you haven't heard folks tell
How Jimmy Bludso passed in his checks
The night of the Prairie Belle?

He were n't no saint, — them engineers
Is all pretty much alike, —
One wife in Natchez-under-the-Hill
And another one here, in Pike;
A keerless man in his talk was Jim,
And an awkward hand in a row,
But he never flunked, and he never lied, —
I reckon he never knowed how.

And this was all the religion he had, —
To treat his engine well;
Never be passed on the river;
To mind the pilot's bell;

And if ever the Prairie Belle took fire, —
  A thousand times he swore
He 'd hold her nozzle agin the bank
  Till the last soul got ashore.

All boats has their day on the Mississip,
  And her day come at last, —
The Movastar was a better boat,
  But the Belle she *would n't* be passed.
And so she come tearin' along that night —
  The oldest craft on the line —
With a nigger squat on her safety-valve,
  And her furnace crammed, rosin and pine.

The fire bust out as she clared the bar,
  And burnt a hole in the night,
And quick as a flash she turned, and made
  For that willer-bank on the right.
There was runnin' and cursin', but Jim yelled out,
  Over all the infernal roar,
"I 'll hold her nozzle agin the bank
  Till the last galoot 's ashore."

Through the hot, black breath of the burnin' boat
  Jim Bludso's voice was heard,
And they all had trust in his cussedness,
  And knowed he would keep his word.
And, sure 's you 're born, they all got off
  Afore the smokestacks fell, —
And Bludso's ghost went up alone
  In the smoke of the Prairie Belle.

He were n't no saint, — but at jedgment
  I 'd run my chance with Jim,
'Longside of some pious gentlemen
  That would n't shook hands with him.
He seen his duty, a dead-sure thing, —
  And went for it thar and then;
And Christ ain't a going to be too hard
  On a man that died for men.

LITTLE BREECHES

I DON'T go much on religion,
  I never ain't had no show;
But I 've got a middlin' tight grip, sir,
  On the handful o' things I know.
I don't pan out on the prophets
  And free-will and that sort of thing, —
But I b'lieve in God and the angels,
  Ever sence one night last spring.

I come into town with some turnips,
  And my little Gabe come along, —
No four-year-old in the county
  Could beat him for pretty and strong, —
Peart and chipper and sassy,
  Always ready to swear and fight, —
And I 'd larnt him to chaw terbacker
  Jest to keep his milk-teeth white.

The snow come down like a blanket
  As I passed by Taggart's store;
I went in for a jug of molasses
  And left the team at the door.
They scared at something and started, —
  I heard one little squall,
And hell-to-split over the prairie
  Went team, Little Breeches, and all.

Hell-to-split over the prairie!
  I was almost froze with skeer;
But we rousted up some torches,
  And sarched for 'em far and near.
At last we struck hosses and wagon,
  Snowed under a soft white mound,
Upsot, dead beat, — but of little Gabe
  No hide nor hair was found.

And here all hope soured on me
  Of my fellow-critter's aid; —
I jest flopped down on my marrow-bones,
  Crotch-deep in the snow, and prayed.

. . . .

By this, the torches was played out,
  And me and Isrul Parr
Went off for some wood to a sheepfold
  That he said was somewhar thar.

We found it at last, and a little shed
  Where they shut up the lambs at night.
We looked in and seen them huddled thar,
  So warm and sleepy and white;
And thar sot Little Breeches and chirped,
  As peart as ever you see,
"I want a chaw of terbacker,
  And that 's what 's the matter of me."

How did he git thar? Angels.
  He could never have walked in that storm:
They jest scooped down and toted him
  To whar it was safe and warm.
And I think that saving a little child,
  And fotching him to his own,
Is a derned sight better business
  Than loafing around The Throne.

THE STIRRUP-CUP

My short and happy day is done,
The long and dreary night comes on,
And at my door the pale horse stands
To carry me to unknown lands.

His whinny shrill, his pawing hoof,
Sound dreadful as a gathering storm;
And I must leave this sheltering roof
And joys of life so soft and warm.

Tender and warm the joys of life, —
Good friends, the faithful and the true;
My rosy children and my wife,
So sweet to kiss, so fair to view, —

So sweet to kiss, so fair to view:
The night comes down, the lights burn blue;
And at my door the pale horse stands
To bear me forth to unknown lands.

Edna Dean Proctor

FROM "THE SONG OF THE ANCIENT PEOPLE"

We are the Ancient People;
Our father is the Sun;
Our mother, the Earth, where the mountains tower
And the rivers seaward run;
The stars are the children of the sky,
The red men of the plain;
And ages over us both had rolled
Before you crossed the main; —
For we are the Ancient People,
Born with the wind and rain.

And ours is the ancient wisdom,
The lore of Earth and cloud: —
We know what the awful lightnings mean,
Wí-lo-lo-a-ne with arrows keen,
And the thunder crashing loud;
And why with his glorious, burning shield
His face the Sun-God hides,
As, glad from the east, while night recedes,
Over the Path of Day he speeds
To his home in the ocean tides;
For the Deathless One at eve must die,
To flame anew in the nether sky, —
Must die, to mount when the Morning Star,
First of his warrior-host afar,
Bold at the dawning rides!
And we carry our new-born children forth
His earliest beams to face,
And pray he will make them strong and brave
As he looks from his shining place,
Wise in council and firm in war,
And fleet as the wind in the chase;
And why the Moon, the Mother of Souls,
On summer nights serene,
Fair from the azure vault of heaven
To Earth will fondly lean,
While her sister laughs from the tranquil lake,
Soft-robed in rippling sheen;
For the Moon is the bride of the glowing Sun,
But the Goddess of Love is she
Who beckons and smiles from the placid depths
Of the lake and the shell-strown sea.

. . . .

We know why the down of the Northland drifts
O'er wood and waste and hill;
And how the light-winged butterflies
To the brown fields summer bear,
And the balmy breath of the Corn-maids floats
In June's enchanted air;
And when to pluck the Medicine flowers
On the brow of the mountain peak,
The lilies of Té-na-tsa-li,
That brighten the faded cheek,
And heal the wounds of the warrior
And the hunter worn and weak;
And where in the hills the crystal stones
And the turquoise blue to seek;
And how to plant the earliest maize,
Sprinkling the sacred meal,
And setting our prayer-plumes in the midst
As full to the east we kneel, —
The plumes whose life shall waft our wish
To the heights the skies conceal;
Nay, when the stalks are parched on the plain
And the deepest springs are dry,
And the Water-God, the jewelled toad,
Is lost to every eye,

With song and dance and voice of flutes
That soothe the Regions Seven,
We can call the blessed summer showers
Down from the listening heaven!
For ours is the lore of a dateless past,
And we have power thereby, —
Power which our vanished fathers sought
Through toil and watch and pain,
Till the spirits of wood and wave and air
To grant us help were fain;
For we are the Ancient People,
Born with the wind and rain.

HEAVEN, O LORD, I CANNOT LOSE

Now Summer finds her perfect prime;
Sweet blows the wind from western calms;
On every bower red roses climb;
The meadows sleep in mingled balms.
Nor stream, nor bank the wayside by,
But lilies float and daisies throng;
Nor space of blue and sunny sky
That is not cleft with soaring song.
O flowery morns, O tuneful eves,
Fly swift! my soul ye cannot fill!
Bring the ripe fruit, the garnered sheaves,
The drifting snows on plain and hill.
Alike, to me, fall frosts and dews;
But Heaven, O Lord, I cannot lose!

Warm hands to-day are clasped in mine;
Fond hearts my mirth or mourning share;
And, over hope's horizon line,
The future dawns, serenely fair.
Yet still, though fervent vow denies,
I know the rapture will not stay;
Some wind of grief or doubt will rise
And turn my rosy sky to gray.
I shall awake, in rainy morn,
To find my hearth left lone and drear;
Thus, half in sadness, half in scorn,
I let my life burn on as clear
Though friends grow cold or fond love woos;
But Heaven, O Lord, I cannot lose!

In golden hours the angel Peace
Comes down and broods me with her wings:
I gain from sorrow sweet release;
I mate me with divinest things;
When shapes of guilt and gloom arise
And far the radiant angel flees,
My song is lost in mournful sighs,
My wine of triumph left but lees;
In vain for me her pinions shine,
And pure, celestial days begin;
Earth's passion-flowers I still must twine,
Nor braid one beauteous lily in.
Ah! is it good or ill I choose?
But Heaven, O Lord, I cannot lose!

So wait I. Every day that dies
With flush and fragrance born of June,
I know shall more resplendent rise
Where summer needs nor sun nor moon.
And every bud, on love's low tree,
Whose mocking crimson flames and falls,
In fullest flower I yet shall see
High-blooming by the jasper walls.
Nay, every sin that dims my days,
And wild regrets that veil the sun,
Shall fade before those dazzling rays,
And my long glory be begun!
Let the years come to bless or bruise:
Thy Heaven, O Lord, I shall not lose!

Charlotte Fiske Bates

(MADAME ROGÉ)

A CHARACTER

HIS face is truly of the Roman mould,
He bears within the heart of Cato, too;
Although his look may seem severe and cold,
He never would be false to truth or you.

And deepest feeling hides about the mouth;
His soul-wind blows not always from the north,
But sometimes also from the gentle south,
And then, like flowers, the tender words steal forth.

The light and fickle still have love to spare,
If Death has taken from them even thrice;

But she who has this noble's love to wear
May know it never will be given twice.

Yes, whom he chooses may be always sure
That no one else will ever take her place;
Of his whole heart eternally secure,
Less need she tremble at Death's chilling face.

And should she leave him, he will not wax weak
With noisy woe, till Solace bare her breast;
Not in those soft and soothing arms would seek
To dim the sense of loss in childish rest.

Nay! such as he, not months and years alone,
Will keep the grave's grass green, its marble white;
The cherished rose will blow about the stone
Till hands that plighted troth shall re-unite.

THE CLUE

OH, frame some little word for me
None else shall ever hear or see, —
Something my soul can call her own,
When suddenly she feels alone;
Something that she can take away
When God shall draw the veil of clay;
Something that thou wilt know her by
Among the billions of the sky;
Something no other soul will fit
Save hers for whom thou makest it.

DELAY

I DO affirm that thou hast saved the race
As much as thou hast ever made it lose:
Men of quick action may thy name abuse,
But the world's life and theirs attest thy grace.
An hour of thee doth sometimes turn the face
Of men and kingdoms, bidding them refuse
What, chosen last, it had been death to choose:
Through thee alone, they missed the fatal place.
How often dies the guileful thought or end
When guileless eyes detain us on our way!
What sin and shame that hindrance may forefend,
Which we so hate and storm against to-day!
What mighty evils over all impend,
Averted graciously by kind Delay!

WOODBINES IN OCTOBER

As dyed in blood the streaming vines appear,
While long and low the wind about them grieves:
The heart of Autumn must have broken here,
And poured its treasure out upon the leaves.

THE LIVING BOOK

THIS bears the seal of immortality,
For every soul that reads it feels the search
Of answering thought, and thousands there may be
Saying at once, "How straight that looks at me!"
Nor child nor fool it leaveth in the lurch;
But, like the eyes that mark great Guido's fame,
It follows every one, as if by name.

James Ryder Randall

MY MARYLAND

THE despot's heel is on thy shore,
Maryland!
His torch is at thy temple door,
Maryland!
Avenge the patriotic gore
That flecked the streets of Baltimore,
And be the battle-queen of yore,
Maryland, my Maryland!

Hark to an exiled son's appeal,
Maryland !
My Mother State, to thee I kneel,
Maryland !
For life and death, for woe and weal,
Thy peerless chivalry reveal,
And gird thy beauteous limbs with steel,
Maryland, my Maryland !

Thou wilt not cower in the dust,
Maryland !
Thy beaming sword shall never rust,
Maryland !
Remember Carroll's sacred trust,
Remember Howard's warlike thrust,
And all thy slumberers with the just,
Maryland, my Maryland !

Come ! 't is the red dawn of the day,
Maryland !
Come with thy panoplied array,
Maryland !
With Ringgold's spirit for the fray,
With Watson's blood at Monterey,
With fearless Lowe and dashing May,
Maryland, my Maryland !

Dear Mother, burst the tyrant's chain,
Maryland !
Virginia should not call in vain,
Maryland !
She meets her sisters on the plain, —
"*Sic semper !*" 't is the proud refrain
That baffles minions back amain,
Maryland !
Arise in majesty again,
Maryland, my Maryland !

Come ! for thy shield is bright and strong,
Maryland !
Come ! for thy dalliance does thee wrong,
Maryland !
Come to thine own heroic throng
Stalking with Liberty along,
And chant thy dauntless slogan-song,
Maryland, my Maryland !

I see the blush upon thy cheek,
Maryland !
For thou wast ever bravely meek,
Maryland!
But lo ! there surges forth a shriek,
From hill to hill, from creek to creek,
Potomac calls to Chesapeake,
Maryland, my Maryland !

Thou wilt not yield the Vandal toll,
Maryland !
Thou wilt not crook to his control,
Maryland !
Better the fire upon thee roll,
Better the shot, the blade, the bowl,
Than crucifixion of the soul,
Maryland, My Maryland !

I hear the distant thunder hum,
Maryland !
The Old Line's bugle, fife, and drum,
Maryland !
She is not dead, nor deaf, nor dumb;
Huzza ! she spurns the Northern scum !
She breathes ! She burns ! She 'll come !
She 'll come !
Maryland, My Maryland !

JOHN PELHAM

JUST as the spring came laughing through the strife,
With all its gorgeous cheer,
In the bright April of historic life
Fell the great cannoneer.

The wondrous lulling of a hero's breath
His bleeding country weeps ;
Hushed, in the alabaster arms of Death,
Our young Marcellus sleeps.

Nobler and grander than the child of Rome,
Curbing his chariot steeds,
The knightly scion of a Southern home
Dazzled the land with deeds.

Gentlest and bravest in the battle-brunt —
The Champion of the Truth —
He bore his banner to the very front
Of our immortal youth.

A clang of sabres mid Virginian snow,
The fiery pang of shells, —
And there 's a wail of immemorial woe
In Alabama dells:

The pennon drops, that led the sacred band
Along the crimson field;
The meteor blade sinks from the nerveless hand,
Over the spotless shield.

We gazed and gazed upon that beauteous face,
While, round the lips and eyes,
Couched in their marble slumber, flashed the grace
Of a divine surprise.

O, mother of a blessëd soul on high,
Thy tears may soon be shed!
Think of thy boy, with princes of the sky,
Among the Southern dead!

How must he smile on this dull world beneath,
Fevered with swift renown —
He, with the martyr's amaranthine wreath,
Twining the victor's crown!

WHY THE ROBIN'S BREAST WAS RED

The Saviour, bowed beneath his cross, climbed up the dreary hill,
And from the agonizing wreath ran many a crimson rill;
The cruel Roman thrust him on with unrelenting hand,
Till, staggering slowly mid the crowd, He fell upon the sand.

A little bird that warbled near, that memorable day,
Flitted around and strove to wrench one single thorn away;
The cruel spike impaled his breast, — and thus, 't is sweetly said,
The Robin has his silver vest incarnadined with red.

Ah, Jesu! Jesu! Son of man! My dolor and my sighs
Reveal the lesson taught by this winged Ishmael of the skies.
I, in the palace of delight or cavern of despair,
Have plucked no thorns from thy dear brow, but planted thousands there!

Abram Joseph Ryan

THE CONQUERED BANNER

Furl that Banner, for 't is weary;
Round its staff 't is drooping dreary:
Furl it, fold it, — it is best;
For there 's not a man to wave it,
And there 's not a sword to save it,
And there's not one left to lave it
In the blood which heroes gave it,
And its foes now scorn and brave it:
Furl it, hide it, — let it rest!

Take that Banner down! 't is tattered;
Broken is its staff and shattered;
And the valiant hosts are scattered,
Over whom it floated high.
Oh, 't is hard for us to fold it,
Hard to think there 's none to hold it,
Hard that those who once unrolled it
Now must furl it with a sigh!

Furl that Banner — furl it sadly!
Once ten thousands hailed it gladly,
And ten thousands wildly, madly,
Swore it should forever wave;
Swore that foeman's sword should never
Hearts like theirs entwined dissever,
Till that flag should float forever
O'er their freedom or their grave!

Furl it! for the hands that grasped it,
And the hearts that fondly clasped it,
Cold and dead are lying low;
And that Banner — it is trailing,
While around it sounds the wailing
Of its people in their woe.

For, though conquered, they adore it, —
Love the cold, dead hands that bore it,
Weep for those who fell before it,
Pardon those who trailed and tore it;
And oh, wildly they deplore it,
Now to furl and fold it so!

Furl that Banner! True, 't is gory,
Yet 't is wreathed around with glory,
And 't will live in song and story
Though its folds are in the dust!
For its fame on brightest pages,
Penned by poets and by sages,

Shall go sounding down the ages —
Furl its folds though now we must.

Furl that Banner, softly, slowly!
Treat it gently — it is holy,
For it droops above the dead.
Touch it not — unfold it never;
Let it droop there, furled forever, —
For its people's hopes are fled!

A CHILD'S WISH

BEFORE AN ALTAR

I WISH I were the little key
That locks Love's Captive in,
And lets Him out to go and free
A sinful heart from sin.

I wish I were the little bell
That tinkles for the Host,
When God comes down each day to dwell
With hearts He loves the most.

I wish I were the chalice fair,
That holds the Blood of Love,
When every gleam lights holy prayer
Upon its way above.

I wish I were the little flower
So near the Host's sweet face,
Or like the light that half an hour
Burns on the shrine of grace.

I wish I were the altar where,
As on His mother's breast,
Christ nestles, like a child, fore'er
In Eucharistic rest.

But, oh! my God, I wish the most
That my poor heart may be
A home all holy for each Host
That comes in love to me.

Francis Bret Harte

AT THE HACIENDA

KNOW I not who thou mayst be
Carved upon this olive-tree, —
"Manuela of La Torre," —
For around on broken walls
Summer sun and spring rain falls,
And in vain the low wind calls
"Manuela of La Torre."

Of that song no words remain
But the musical refrain, —
"Manuela of La Torre."
Yet at night, when winds are still,
Tinkles on the distant hill
A guitar, and words that thrill
Tell to me the old, old story, —
Old when first thy charms were sung,
Old when these old walls were young,
"Manuela of La Torre."

CHIQUITA

BEAUTIFUL! Sir, you may say so. Thar is n't her match in the county;
Is thar, old gal, — Chiquita, my darling, my beauty?
Feel of that neck, sir, — thar 's velvet! Whoa! steady, — ah, will you, you vixen!
Whoa! I say. Jack, trot her out; let the gentleman look at her paces.

Morgan! — she ain't nothing else, and I 've got the papers to prove it.
Sired by Chippewa Chief, and twelve hundred dollars won't buy her.
Briggs of Tuolumne owned her. Did you know Briggs of Tuolumne?
Busted hisself in White Pine, and blew out his brains down in 'Frisco?

Hed n't no savey, hed Briggs. Thar, Jack! that 'll do, — quit that foolin'!
Nothin' to what she kin do, when she's got her work cut out before her.
Hosses is hosses, you know, and likewise, too, jockeys is jockeys:
And 't ain't ev'ry man as can ride as knows what a hoss has got in him.

Know the old ford on the Fork, that nearly got Flanigan's leaders?

Nasty in daylight, you bet, and a mighty rough ford in low water!
Well, it ain't six weeks ago that me and the Jedge and his nevey
Struck for that ford in the night, in the rain, and the water all round us;

Up to our flanks in the gulch, and Rattlesnake Creek jest a-bilin',
Not a plank left in the dam, and nary a bridge on the river.
I had the gray, and the Jedge had his roan, and his nevey, Chiquita;
And after us trundled the rocks jest loosed from the top of the cañon.

Lickity, lickity, switch, we came to the ford, and Chiquita
Buckled right down to her work, and, afore I could yell to her rider,
Took water jest at the ford, and there was the Jedge and me standing,
And twelve hundred dollars of hoss-flesh afloat, and a-driftin' to thunder!

Would ye b'lieve it? That night, that hoss, that 'ar filly, Chiquita,
Walked herself into her stall, and stood there, all quiet and dripping:
Clean as a beaver or rat, with nary a buckle of harness,
Jest as she swam the Fork, — that hoss, that ar' filly, Chiquita.

That's what I call a hoss! and — What did you say? — Oh, the nevey?
Drownded, I reckon, — leastways, he never kem back to deny it.
Ye see the derned fool had no seat, ye could n't have made him a rider;
And then, ye know, boys will be boys, and hosses — well, hosses is hosses!

GRIZZLY

Coward, — of heroic size,
In whose lazy muscles lies
Strength we fear and yet despise;
Savage, — whose relentless tusks
Are content with acorn husks;
Robber, — whose exploits ne'er soared
O'er the bee's or squirrel's hoard;
Whiskered chin, and feeble nose,
Claws of steel on baby toes, —
Here, in solitude and shade,
Shambling, shuffling plantigrade,
Be thy courses undismayed!

Here, where Nature makes thy bed,
Let thy rude, half-human tread
Point to hidden Indian springs,
Lost in ferns and fragrant grasses,
Hovered o'er by timid wings,
Where the wood-duck lightly passes,
Where the wild bee holds her sweets,
Epicurean retreats,
Fit for thee, and better than
Fearful spoils of dangerous man.
In thy fat-jowled deviltry
Friar Tuck shall live in thee;
Thou mayest levy tithe and dole;
Thou shalt spread the woodland cheer,
From the pilgrim taking toll;
Match thy cunning with his fear;
Eat, and drink, and have thy fill;
Yet remain an outlaw still!

CROTALUS

No life in earth, or air, or sky;
The sunbeams, broken silently,
On the bared rocks around me lie, —

Cold rocks with half-warmed lichens scarred,
And scales of moss; and scarce a yard
Away, one long strip, yellow-barred.

Lost in a cleft! T is but a stride
To reach it, thrust its roots aside,
And lift it on thy stick astride!

Yet stay! That moment is thy grace!
For round thee, thrilling air and space,
A chattering terror fills the place!

A sound as of dry bones that stir
In the Dead Valley! By yon fir
The locust stops its noonday whir!

The wild bird hears; smote with the sound,
As if by bullet brought to ground,
On broken wing, dips, wheeling round!

The hare, transfixed, with trembling lip,
Halts, breathless, on pulsating hip,
And palsied tread, and heels that slip.

. . . .

Enough, old friend! — 't is thou. Forget
My heedless foot, nor longer fret
The peace with thy grim castanet!

I know thee! Yes! Thou mayst forego
That lifted crest; the measured blow
Beyond which thy pride scorns to go,

Or yet retract! For me no spell
Lights those slit orbs, where, some think, dwell
Machicolated fires of hell!

I only know thee humble, bold,
Haughty, with miseries untold,
And the old Curse that left thee cold,

And drove thee ever to the sun,
On blistering rocks; nor made thee shun
Our cabin's hearth, when day was done,

And the spent ashes warmed thee best;
We knew thee, — silent, joyless guest
Of our rude ingle. E'en thy quest

Of the rare milk-bowl seemed to be
Naught but a brother's poverty
And Spartan taste that kept thee free

From lust and rapine. Thou! whose fame
Searches the grass with tongue of flame,
Making all creatures seem thy game;

When the whole woods before thee run,
Asked but — when all was said and done —
To lie, untrodden, in the sun!

"JIM"

Say there! P'r'aps
Some on you chaps
  Might know Jim Wild?
Well, — no offense:
Thar aint no sense
  In gittin' riled!

Jim was my chum
  Up on the Bar:
That 's why I come
  Down from up yar,
Lookin' for Jim.
Thank ye, sir! *You*
Ain't of that crew, —
  Blest if you are!
Money? Not much:
  That ain't my kind;
I ain't no such.
  Rum? I don't mind,
Seein' it 's you.

Well, this yer Jim, —
Did you know him?
Jes' 'bout your size;
Same kind of eyes; —
Well, that is strange:
  Why, it's two year
  Since he came here,
Sick, for a change.

Well, here 's to us:
  Eh?
The h—— you say!
  Dead?
That little cuss?

What makes you star',
You over thar?
Can't a man drop
'S glass in yer shop
But you must r'ar?
  It would n't take
D——d much to break
You and your bar.

  Dead!
Poor — little — Jim!
Why, thar was me,
Jones, and Bob Lee,
Harry and Ben, —
No-account men:
Then to take *him!*

Well, thar — Good-by —
No more, sir — I —
  Eh?
What 's that you say?
Why, dern it! — sho —
No? Yes! By Joe!
  Sold!
Sold! Why, you limb,
You ornery,
  Derned old
Long-legged Jim.

THE SOCIETY UPON THE STANISLAUS

I reside at Table Mountain, and my name is Truthful James;
I am not up to small deceit, or any sinful games;

And I 'll tell in simple language what I know about the row
That broke up our Society upon the Stanislow.

But first I would remark, that it is not a proper plan
For any scientific gent to whale his fellow-man,
And, if a member don't agree with his peculiar whim,
To lay for that same member for to "put a head" on him.

Now nothing could be finer or more beautiful to see
Than the first six months' proceedings of that same Society,
Till Brown of Calaveras brought a lot of fossil bones
That he found within a tunnel near the tenement of Jones.

Then Brown he read a paper, and he reconstructed there,
From those same bones, an animal that was extremely rare;
And Jones then asked the Chair for a suspension of the rules,
Till he could prove that those same bones was one of his lost mules.

Then Brown he smiled a bitter smile, and said he was at fault, —
It seemed he had been trespassing on Jones's family vault:
He was a most sarcastic man, this quiet Mr. Brown,
And on several occasions he had cleaned out the town.

Now I hold it is not decent for a scientific gent
To say another is an ass, — at least, to all intent;
Nor should the individual who happens to be meant
Reply by heaving rocks at him, to any great extent.

Then Abner Dean of Angel's raised a point of order — when
A chunk of old red sandstone took him in the abdomen,
And he smiled a kind of sickly smile, and curled up on the floor,
And the subsequent proceedings interested him no more.

For, in less time than I write it, every member did engage
In a warfare with the remnants of a palæozoic age;
And the way they heaved those fossils in their anger was a sin,
Till the skull of an old mammoth caved the head of Thompson in.

And this is all I have to say of these improper games,
For I live at Table Mountain, and my name is Truthful James;
And I 've told in simple language what I know about the row
That broke up our Society upon the Stanislow.

THE AGED STRANGER

AN INCIDENT OF THE WAR

"I was with Grant" — the stranger said;
Said the farmer, "Say no more,
But rest thee here at my cottage porch,
For thy feet are weary and sore."

"I was with Grant" — the stranger said;
Said the farmer, "Nay, no more, —
I prithee sit at my frugal board,
And eat of my humble store.

"How fares my boy, — my soldier boy,
Of the old Ninth Army Corps?
I warrant he bore him gallantly
In the smoke and the battle's roar!"

"I know him not," said the aged man,
"And, as I remarked before,
I was with Grant" — "Nay, nay, I know,"
Said the farmer, "say no more:

"He fell in battle, — I see, alas!
Thou 'dst smooth these tidings o'er, —
Nay, speak the truth, whatever it be,
Though it rend my bosom's core.

"How fell he, — with his face to the foe,
Upholding the flag he bore?
Oh, say not that my boy disgraced
The uniform that he wore!"

"I cannot tell," said the aged man,
"And should have remarked before,
That I was with Grant, — in Illinois, —
Some three years before the war."

Then the farmer spake him never a word,
But beat with his fist full sore
That aged man, who had worked for Grant
Some three years before the war.

MADROÑO

CAPTAIN of the Western wood,
Thou that apest Robin Hood!
Green above thy scarlet hose,
How thy velvet mantle shows!
Never tree like thee arrayed,
O thou gallant of the glade!

When the fervid August sun
Scorches all it looks upon,
And the balsam of the pine
Drips from stem to needle fine,
Round thy compact shade arranged,
Not a leaf of thee is changed!

When the yellow autumn sun
Saddens all it looks upon,
Spreads its sackcloth on the hills,
Strews its ashes in the rills,
Thou thy scarlet hose dost doff,
And in limbs of purest buff
Challengest the sombre glade
For a sylvan masquerade.

Where, oh, where, shall he begin
Who would paint thee, Harlequin?
With thy waxen burnished leaf,
With thy branches' red relief,
With thy polytinted fruit, —
In thy spring or autumn suit, —
Where begin, and, oh, where end,
Thou whose charms all art transcend!

WHAT THE BULLET SANG

O JOY of creation
To be!
O rapture to fly
And be free!
Be the battle lost or won,
Though its smoke shall hide the sun,
I shall find my love, — the one
Born for me!

I shall know him where he stands,
All alone,
With the power in his hands
Not o'erthrown;
I shall know him by his face,
By his godlike front and grace;
I shall hold him for a space,
All my own!

It is he — O my love!
So bold!
It is I — all thy love
Foretold!
It is I. O love! what bliss!
Dost thou answer to my kiss?
O sweetheart! what is this
Lieth there so cold?

Stephen Henry Thayer

EUROPA

GREAT Sovereign of the earth and sea,
Whose sceptre shall forever be
The reign supreme of Liberty,
Draw thou the veil that dims our sight, light thou our eyes,
That we may see!

Beyond the waters, east and west,
Six giant legions ominous rest,
Equipped and armed from sole to crest;
The burdened nations groan and reel and listen for
The dread behest.

The Ottoman by the Ægean tide
Is bonded; there the navies ride
And train their armaments to bide
The menace from the eagle's north, or who will dare
The kings allied.

The cringing Sultan can but wait
The will of other crowns; his fate
Is graven in the hearts that hate
And tremble at his wasting power — the curse of men —
So weak, so great.

His doom is written in the skies;
His Orient Empire palsied lies,
And still and still he crucifies
The last bare hope that yet might save, and mocks his knell,
And still defies.

I hear the Empires muttering now, —
The northern Cæsar keeps his vow,
And waits and wills both where and how
His sheathless sword shall smite at last; he waits and knits
His iron brow.

I see the Austrians mustering where
The Adriatic's waters glare,
Or by the Danube; and they swear
Eternal vigilance against the Cossack hordes
So sleepless there.

The crafty Chancellor, outworn,
Who guards the German state, in scorn
Watches the French frontier, — his thorn;
Looks north to the Crimean gates, and eastward to
The Golden Horn.

Europa waits the signal, swells
Imperial armies, still compels,
From Britain to the Dardanelles,
Fresh millions to her warrior camps, and millions more,
For ships and shells.

Till on her mighty, martial field
The greatest products she can yield
Are armëd men and sword and shield:
Whole nations bent and strung for what?
O Lord, thy thought
Is still concealed!

Great Sovereign of the earth and sea,
Whose sceptre shall forever be
The reign supreme of Liberty,
Draw thou the veil that dims our sight, light thou our eyes,
That we may see!

CHARMIAN, *16 Feb., 1888*

POET OF EARTH

OH, be not ether-borne, poet of earth;
Stretch not thy wings to such a cloudless height
As ne'er to know the darkness of the night,
As ne'er to feel the touch of grief or mirth
That lives in human sympathy, whose birth
Is longed for in this world of love and blight;
Thou, too, must drink of sorrow and delight,
Must taste the joy of hope, and feel its dearth;
God's service lies not out of reach, and heaven
Is found alone through lowly ministry;
Some souls there are whose dumb chords wait the breath
Of other souls, divinely gifted, given
To voice the deeper tones, and lead the way
To immortality, through life and death!

THE WAITING CHORDS

HEEDLESS she strayed from note to note,
A maid, scarce knowing that she sang;
The dainty accents from her throat
In undulations lightly rang.

She sang in laughing rhythms sweet;
A bird of spring was in her voice;
Till, on through measures deft and fleet,
She caught the ditty of her choice.

A song of love, in words of fire,
Now made her breast with passion stir;
It breathed across her living lyre,
And thrilled the waiting chords in her.

Uplifted like a quivering dart,
One moment poised the tones on high,
To tell the language of her heart,
And swell the pæan ere it die.

She smote the keys with will and force,
Like storm-winds swept the sounds along;
Her flying fingers in their course
Vied with the tumult of her song.

Her eyes flashed with the burning theme;
A glow of triumph flushed her cheek;
No need of words to tell the dream
Of love her lips would never speak.

When the wild cadence died in air,
And all the chords to silence fell,
I knew the spirit lurking there —
The secret that had wrought the spell.

Rossiter Johnson

EVELYN

If I could know
That here about the place where last you
played, —
Within this room, and yonder in the shade
Of branches low, —
Your spirit lingered, I would never go,
But evermore a hermit pace the round
Of sunny paths across this garden ground,
And o'er the fleckered lawn
Whereon your baby chariot was drawn,
And round these lonely walls,
Where no sound ever falls
So pretty as your prattle or your crow, —
If I could only know!

If I could know
That to some distant clime or planet rare
Sweet souls like thine repair,
Where love's own fountains fail not as they
flow, —
I 'd be a traveller, and would ever go,
Day after day, along the selfsame road,
Leaving behind this desolate abode,
My head upon my pillow only lay
To dream myself still farther on the way,
Until at last I rest,
Clasping my little daughter to my breast,
Though half eternity were wasted so, —
If I could only know!

If I could know
That you a child with childlike ways remain,
I 'd never wish to be a man again,
But only try to grow
As childlike, using all the idle toys
That you and I have played with, till their
noise
Brought back the echoes of your merry
laugh,
When paper windmill whirled upon its staff,
Or painted ball went rolling on the floor,
Or puss peeped out behind the door,
Or watch, held half in fear,
With its mysterious pulses thrilled your ear:
All manly occupation I 'd forego,
If I could only know!

If I could know
That henceforth, in some pure eternal
sphere,
The little life that grew so swiftly here
Would still expand and grow,
How should I strive against my wasting
years,
With toil from sun to sun, and midnight
tears,
To build my soul up to the height of yours,
And catch the light that lures,
The inspiration that impels,
The strength that dwells,
Beyond the bounds of earthly cares and
fears,
Beyond this bitter woe, —
If I could only know!

Alas! what do I know?
I know your world scarce compassed yonder
stone —
As little seems my own!
I know you never knew unhappiness —
Would I could mourn the less!
I know you never saw death's darker side —
The shore where we abide!
I know you never felt the nameless
dread —
Ah, but if mine were fled!
I know you never heard a lover's vow —
And I 'm your lover now!
I know no answer to my wail can come —
Let me be dumb!

A SOLDIER POET

Where swell the songs thou shouldst have
sung
By peaceful rivers yet to flow?
Where bloom the smiles thy ready tongue
Would call to lips that loved thee so?
On what far shore of being tossed,
Dost thou resume the genial stave,
And strike again the lyre we lost
By Rappahannock's troubled wave?

If that new world hath hill and stream,
And breezy bank, and quiet dell,
If forests murmur, waters gleam,
And wayside flowers their story tell,
Thy hand ere this has plucked the reed
That wavered by the wooded shore;
Its prisoned soul thy fingers freed,
To float melodious evermore.

So seems it to my musing mood,
  So runs it in my surer thought,
That much of beauty, more of good,
  For thee the rounded years have wrought;

That life will live, however blown
  Like vapor on the summer air;
That power perpetuates its own;
  That silence here is music there.

Amelia Walstien Carpenter

THE RIDE TO CHEROKEE

IT's only we, Grimalkin, both fond and fancy free,
So do your best, my beauty, for a home for you and me;
For you the oats and leisure, for me the pipe and book,
With sometimes, just at sunset, the long gray eastward look.
For once there was another: ah, Kathrine! who shall say
What wilful fancy seized you that sunny summer day;
You turned and nodded, smiling as you went gayly by,
And the man who strolled beside you had a braver front than I;
It meant a day's undoing, a night's black watch for me,
And this mad ride, Grimalkin, to-day for Cherokee.

The great crowd forges forward, like fire in fury blown,
Each urging to the utmost, and God help him that 's down,
Shoulder to shoulder rising like shapes in horror cast,
And my good mare aflashing a star along the blast;
So — so — my brave Grimalkin, it 's home for you and me
If we ride the distance safely to the line in Cherokee:
We 'll pass our lives together, — you 'll have a stall with me,
And a blanket — if we win it — in the home in Cherokee.

There 's one that 's riding with us, with many a good steed passed,
Look well, little Grimalkin, or you 're left, too, at the last;
He 's singing as he 's riding with his brave and gallant air,
With the fierce light falling hotly on his face and yellow hair.
A rush — a shout; he 's falling; God help the man that 's down
As the wild steeds thunder onward, on the hard earth baked and brown.
On, on; and look, Grimalkin! we 're safe, 't is victory!
We 'll stake the claim and hold the home, here in the Cherokee.

And he that fell! a breath space I saw his glazing eyes
As he lay staring upward into the dust-filled skies:
Eyes one star-flash of memory told me I 'd met before,
Eyes that a woman's loving would brighten nevermore.
And fancy flung me backward, from that madding rush and whirl,
To an old Long Island garden and a violet-laden girl;
Ah well, he stole my treasure, my sweetheart's heart, from me, —
God rest him! I 'm the victor, to-day in Cherokee!

RECOLLECTION

A SILVER birch-tree like a sacred maid
Set with a guard of stalwart hemlocks round,
Whose low-toned airs stole by with sighing sound,
Stirred, shivering slightly, as if half afraid
Where the black shadow crept along the ground.
Breathless she stood, — as one whose work is stayed,
But threads her shuttle while her thought has strayed
To times when wild fauns haunted all the rills,
And piped among the deep noon-checkered hills

Till all the land with song was over-
laid.
O Pan, dear Pan! come forth from out the
dark
Of those dream days; outsing our thrush
and lark
Till laughter-loving youths from window-
sills
Shall whisper, "Hark! who sang that love-
song? Hark!"

OLD FLEMISH LACE

A LONG, rich breadth of Holland lace,
A window by a Flemish sea;
Huge men go by with mighty pace, —
Great Anne was Queen these days, may
be,
And strange ships prowled for spoil the
sea —
For you — old lace!

Stitch after stitch enwrought with grace,
The mist falls cold on Zuyder-Zee;
The silver tankards hang in place
Along the wall; across her knee
Dame Snuyder spreads her square of lace,
A veil — for me?

The Holland dames put by their lace,
The bells of Bruges ring out in glee;
The mill-wheels move in sluggish race: —
Farewell, sweet bells! Then down the
sea
The slow ship brings the bridal grace —
The veil — for me!

Manhattan shores — a New World place,
The Pinxter-blows their sweetest be:
And now — come close, O love-bright
face —
Bend low — . . .
Nay, not old Trinity,
To Olde Sainte Marke's i' the Bowerie,
Dear Hal, — with thee!

John Lancaster Spalding

BELIEVE AND TAKE HEART

WHAT can console for a dead world?
We tread on dust which once was life;
To nothingness all things are hurled:
What meaning in a hopeless strife?
Time's awful storm
Breaks but the form.

Whatever comes, whatever goes,
Still throbs the heart whereby we live;
The primal joys still lighten woes,
And time which steals doth also give.
Fear not, be brave:
God can thee save.

The essential truth of life remains,
Its goodness and its beauty too,
Pure love's unutterable gains,
And hope which thrills us through and
through:
God has not fled,
Souls are not dead.

Not in most ancient Palestine,
Nor in the lightsome air of Greece,
Were human struggles more divine,
More blessed with guerdon of increase:
Take thou thy stand
In the workers' band.

Hast then no faith? Thine is the fault: —
What prophets, heroes, sages, saints,
Have loved, on thee still makes assault,
Thee with immortal things acquaints.
On life then seize:
Doubt is disease.

THE STARRY HOST

THE countless stars, which to our human
eye
Are fixed and steadfast, each in proper
place,
Forever bound to changeless points in
space,
Rush with our sun and planets through the
sky,
And like a flock of birds still onward
fly;
Returning never whence began their race,

They speed their ceaseless way with gleaming face
As though God bade them win Infinity.
Ah whither, whither is their forward flight
Through endless time and limitless expanse?
What power with unimaginable might
First hurled them forth to spin in tireless dance?
What beauty lures them on through primal night,
So that for them to be is to advance?

SILENCE

INAUDIBLE move day and night,
And noiseless grows the flower;
Silent are pulsing wings of light,
And voiceless fleets the hour.

The moon utters no word when she
Walks through the heavens bare;
The stars forever silent flee,
And songless gleam through air.

The deepest love is voiceless too;
Heart sorrow makes no moan:
How still the zephyrs when they woo!
How calm the rose full blown!

The bird winging the evening sky
Flies onward without song;
The crowding years as they pass by
Flow on in mutest throng.

The fishes glide through liquid deep
And never speak a word;
The angels round about us sweep,
And yet no voice is heard.

The highest thoughts no utterance find,
The holiest hope is dumb,
In silence grows the immortal mind,
And speechless deep joys come.

Rapt adoration has no tongue,
No words has holiest prayer;
The loftiest mountain peaks among
Is stillness everywhere.

With sweetest music silence blends,
And silent praise is best;
In silence life begins and ends:
God cannot be expressed.

FOREPLEDGED

O WOMAN, let thy heart not cleave
To any poet's soul;
For he the muse will never leave,
But follow to life's goal.

Then trust him not, he is not thine,
Whate'er he seems to be;
Strong unseen tendrils round him twine,
And keep him still from thee.

His words with passion are athrill,
And bear contagious fire;
He knows the charmer's perfect skill
To wake the heart's desire.

But love him not, his love is woe;
The genius at his side
Would prove for thee a fatal foe
Wert thou his wedded bride.

FROM "GOD AND THE SOUL"

NATURE AND THE CHILD

FOR many bessings I to God upraise
A thankful heart; the life He gives is fair
And sweet and good, since He is everywhere,
Still with me even in the darkest ways.
But most I thank Him for my earliest days,
Passed in the fields and in the open air,
With flocks and birds and flowers, free from all care,
And glad as brook that through a meadow strays.
O balmy air, O orchards white with bloom,
O waving fields of ever-varying green,
O deep, mysterious woods, whose leafy gloom
Invites to pensive dreams of worlds unseen,
To thoughts as solemn as the silent tomb,
No power from you my heart can ever wean!

ET MORI LUCRUM

THE star must cease to burn with its own light
Before it can become the dwelling-place
Of hearts that love, — beings of godlike race,
Through its own death attaining to the height
Of excellence, and sinking into night,

That it may glow with a more perfect grace,
And bear a nobler life through boundless space,
Till time shall bring eternity in sight.
So man, if he would truly live, must die,
Descending through the grave that he may rise
To higher worlds and dwell in purer sky;
Making of seeming life the sacrifice
To share the perfect life with God on high,
Where love divine is the infinite prize.

THE VOID BETWEEN

When from the gloom of earth we see the sky,
The happy stars seem each to other near,
And their low-whispered words we almost hear,
As in sweet company they smile or sigh.
Alas ! infinite worlds between them lie,
And solitary each within its sphere
Rolls lonely ever onward without cheer,
Is born, and lives and dies with no one near.
And so men's souls seem close together bound,
But worlds immeasurable lie between,
And each is centre in a void profound,
Wherein he lonely lives sad or serene,
And, planet-like, moves higher centre round,
Whence light he draws as from the sun night's Queen.

AT THE NINTH HOUR

Eli, Eli, lama sabacthani ?
O sadder than the ocean's wailing moan,
Sadder than homes whence life and joy have flown,
Than graves where those we love in darkness lie;
More full of anguish than all agony
Of broken hearts, forsaken of their own
And left in hopeless misery alone,
Is this, O sweet and loving Christ, Thy cry !
For this, this only is infinite pain:
To feel that God Himself has turned away.
If He abide, all loss may still be gain,
And darkest night be beautiful as day.
But lacking Him the universe is vain,
And man's immortal soul is turned to clay.

Henry Bernard Carpenter

THE REED

"ET ARUNDINEM IN DEXTERA EJUS"

Beneath the Memnonian shadows of Memphis, it rose from the slime,
A reed of the river, self-hid, as though shunning the curse of its crime,
And it shook as it measured in whispers the lapses of tide and of time.

It shuddered, it stooped, and was dumb, when the kings of the earth passed along.
For what could this reed of the river in the race of the swift and the strong, —
Where the wolf met the bear and the panther, blood-bathed, at the banquets of wrong ?

These loved the bright brass, the hard steel, and the gods that kill and condemn;
Yea, theirs was the robe silver-tissued, and theirs was the sun-colored gem;
If they touched thee, O reed, 't was to wing with swift death thy sharp arrowy stem.

Then the strong took the corn and the wine, and the poor, who had scattered the seed,
Went forth to the wilderness weeping, and sought out a sign in their need,
And the gods laughed in rapturous thunder, and showed them the wind-shaken reed.

O dower of the poor and the helpless ! O key to Thought's palace unpriced !
When the strong mocked with cruel crimson and spat in the face of their Christ,
When the thorns were his crown — in his faint palm this reed for a sceptre sufficed;

This reed in whose fire-pith Prometheus
brought life, and the arts began,
When Man, the god of time's twilight, grew
godlike by dying for Man,
Ere Redemption fell bound and bleeding,
priest-carved to the priests' poor
plan.

Come hither, ye kings of the earth, and ye
priests without pity, draw near:
Ye girded your loins for a curse, and ye
builded dark temples to Fear;
Ye gathered from rune-scroll and symbol
great syllables deathful and drear.

Then ye summoned mankind to your Idol,
the many bowed down to the few,
As ye told in loud anthems how all things
were framed for the saints and for
you, —
"Lord, not on these sun-blistered rocks,
but on Gideon's fleece falls thy
dew."

Man was taken from prison to judgment;
a bulrush he bent at your nod;
Ye stripped him of rights, his last garment,
and bared his broad back for the rod,
And ye lisped, as he writhed down in anguish, "This woe is the sweet will
of God."

But lo! whilst ye braided the thorn-crown
for Man and the children of men,
Whilst ye reft him of worship and wealth,
and he stood mute and dazed in your
den,
A reed-stalk remained for a sceptre; ye left
in his hand the pen.

Sweet wooer, strong winner of kingship,
above crown, crosier and sword,
By thee shall the mighty be broken, and the
spoil which their might hath stored
Shall be stamped small as dust, and be wafted
away by the breath of the Lord.

His decree is gone forth, it is planted, and
these are the words which he
spake, —
No smouldering flax of first fancy, no full
flame of thought, will he slake,
No bruisëd reed of the writer shall the
strength of eternities break.

Behold your sign and your sceptre. Arise,
imperial reed,
Go forth to discrown king and captain and
disinherit the creed;
O strike through the iron war-tower and
cast out the murderer's seed;

Go forth — like the swell of the spring-tide,
sweep on in measureless sway,
Till raised over each throned falsehood, in
bright omnipresence like day,
Thou shalt bruise them with rod of iron,
and break them like vessels of clay.

Robert Kelley Weeks

MEDUSA

One calm and cloudless winter night,
Under a moonless sky,
Whence I had seen the gracious light
Of sunset fade and die,

I stood alone a little space,
Where tree nor building bars
Its outlook, in a desert place,
The best to see the stars.

No sound was in the frosty air,
No light below the skies;
I looked above, and unaware
Looked in Medusa's eyes: —

The eyes that neither laugh nor weep,
That neither hope nor fear,
That neither watch nor dream nor sleep,
Nor sympathize nor sneer;

The eyes that neither spurn nor choose,
Nor question nor reply,
That neither pardon nor accuse,
That yield not nor defy;

The eyes that hide not nor reveal,
That trust not nor betray,
That acquiesce not nor appeal, —
The eyes that never pray.

O love that will not be forgot!
  O love that leaves alone!
O love that blinds and blesses not!
  O love that turns to stone!

A SONG FOR LEXINGTON

The spring came earlier on
Than usual that year;
The shadiest snow was gone,
The slowest brook was clear,
And warming in the sun
Shy flowers began to peer.

'T was more like middle May,
The earth so seemed to thrive,
That Nineteenth April day
Of Seventeen Seventy-Five;
Winter was well away,
New England was alive!

Alive and sternly glad!
Her doubts were with the snow;
Her courage, long forbade,
Ran full to overflow;
And every hope she had
Began to bud and grow.

She rose betimes that morn,
For there was work to do;
A planting, not of corn,
Of what she hardly knew, —
Blessings for men unborn;
And well she did it too!

With open hand she stood,
And sowed for all the years,
And watered it with blood,
And watered it with tears,
The seed of quickening food
For both the hemispheres.

This was the planting done
That April morn of fame;
Honor to every one
To that seed-field that came!
Honor to Lexington,
Our first immortal name!

MAN AND NATURE

O steadfast trees that know
Rain, hail, and sleet, and snow,
And all the winds that blow;
  But when spring comes, can then
  So freshly bud again
Forgetful of the wrong!

Waters that deep below
The stubborn ice can go
With quiet underflow,
  Contented to be dumb
  Till spring herself shall come
To listen to your song!

Stars that the clouds pass o'er
And stain not, but make more
Alluring than before: —
  How good it is for us
  That your lives are not thus
Prevented, but made strong!

John White Chadwick

THE MAKING OF MAN

As the insect from the rock
  Takes the color of its wing;
As the boulder from the shock
  Of the ocean's rhythmic swing
Makes itself a perfect form,
  Learns a calmer front to raise;
As the shell, enamelled warm
  With the prism's mystic rays,
Praises wind and wave that make
  All its chambers fair and strong;
As the mighty poets take
  Grief and pain to build their song:
Even so for every soul,
  Whatsoe'er its lot may be, —
Building, as the heavens roll,
  Something large and strong and free, —
Things that hurt and things that mar
  Shape the man for perfect praise;
Shock and strain and ruin are
  Friendlier than the smiling days.

THE GOLDEN-ROBIN'S NEST

THE golden-robin came to build his nest
High in the elm-tree's ever-nodding crest;
All the long day, upon his task intent,
Backward and forward busily he went,

Gathering from far and near the tiny shreds
That birdies weave for little birdies' beds;
Now bits of grass, now bits of vagrant string,
And now some queerer, dearer sort of thing.

For on the lawn, where he was wont to come
In search of stuff to build his pretty home,
We dropped one day a lock of golden hair
Which our wee darling easily could spare;

And close beside it tenderly we placed
A lock that had the stooping shoulders graced
Of her old grandsire; it was white as snow,
Or cherry-trees when they are all ablow.

Then throve the golden-robin's work apace;
Hundreds of times he sought the lucky place
Where sure, he thought, in his bird-fashion dim,
Wondrous provision had been made for him.

Both locks, the white and golden, disappeared;
The nest was finished, and the brood was reared;
And then there came a pleasant summer's day
When the last golden-robin flew away.

Ere long, in triumph, from its leafy height,
We bore the nest so wonderfully dight,
And saw how prettily the white and gold
Made warp and woof of many a gleaming fold.

But when again the golden-robins came,
Cleaving the orchards with their breasts aflame,
Grandsire's white locks and baby's golden head
Were lying low, both in one grassy bed.

And so more dear than ever is the nest
Ta'en from the elm-tree's ever nodding crest.
Little the golden-robin thought how rare
A thing he wrought of white and golden hair!

RECOGNITION

WHEN souls that have put off their mortal gear
Stand in the pure, sweet light of heaven's day,
And wondering deeply what to do or say,
And trembling more with rapture than with fear,
Desire some token of their friends most dear,
Who there some time have made their happy stay,
And much have longed for them to come that way,
What shall it be, this sign of hope and cheer?
Shall it be tone of voice or glance of eye?
Shall it be touch of hand or gleam of hair
Blown back from spirit-brows by heaven's air,—
Things which of old we knew our dearest by?
Oh, naught of this; but, if our love is true,
Some secret sense shall cry, 'T is you and—you!

STARLIGHT

"LOOK up," she said; and all the heavens blazed
With countless myriads of quiet stars,
Whereon a moment silently he gazed,
And drank that peace no trouble ever mars.
Then looking down into her face upturned,
Two other stars that did outshine the rest
Upward to him with such soft splendor yearned
That all her secret was at once confessed.
Then he with kisses did put out their light,
And said, "O strange, but more, dear love, to me
Are thy pure eyes than all the stars of night
That shine in heaven everlastingly!

Night still is night, with every star aglow;
But light were night didst thou not love me so."

THE RISE OF MAN

Thou for whose birth the whole creation yearned
Through countless ages of the morning world,
Who, first in fiery vapors dimly hurled,
Next to the senseless crystal slowly turned,
Then to the plant which grew to something more,—
Humblest of creatures that draw breath of life,—
Wherefrom through infinites of patient pain
Came conscious man to reason and adore:
Shall we be shamed because such things have been,
Or bate one jot of our ancestral pride?
Nay, in thyself art thou not deified
That from such depths thou couldst such summits win?
While the long way behind is prophecy
Of those perfections which are yet to be.

HIS MOTHER'S JOY

Little, I ween, did Mary guess,
As on her arm her baby lay,
What tides of joy would swell and beat,
Through ages long, on Christmas day.

And what if she had known it all,—
The awful splendor of his fame?
The inmost heart of all her joy
Would still, methinks, have been the same:
The joy that every mother knows
Who feels her babe against her breast:
The voyage long is overpast,
And now is calm and peace and rest.

"Art thou the Christ?" The wonder came
As easy as her infant's breath:
But answer none. Enough for her,
That love had triumphed over death.

A WEDDING-SONG

I said: "My heart, now let us sing a song
For a fair lady on her wedding-day;
Some solemn hymn or pretty roundelay,
That shall be with her as she goes along
To meet her joy, and for her happy feet
Shall make a pleasant music, low and sweet."

Then said my heart: "It is right bold of thee
To think that any song that we could sing
Would for this lady be an offering
Meet for such gladness as hers needs must be,
What time she goes to don her bridal ring,
And her own heart makes sweetest caroling."

And so it is that with my lute unstrung,
Lady, I come to greet thy wedding-day;
But once, methinks, I heard a poet say,
The sweetest songs remain for aye unsung.
So mine, unsung, at thy dear feet I lay,
And with a "Peace be with you!" go my way.

George Alfred Townsend

ARMY CORRESPONDENT'S LAST RIDE

FIVE FORKS, APRIL 1ST, 1865.

Ho! pony. Down the lonely road
Strike now your cheeriest pace!
The woods on fire do not burn higher
Than burns my anxious face;
Far have you sped, but all this night
Must feel my nervous spur;
If we be late, the world must wait
The tidings we aver:—
To home and hamlet, town and hearth,
To thrill child, mother, man,
I carry to the waiting North
Great news from Sheridan!

The birds are dead among the pines,
Slain by the battle fright,
Prone in the road the steed reclines
That never reached the fight;

Yet on we go, — the wreck below
  Of many a tumbled wain, —
By ghastly pools where stranded mules
  Die, drinking of the rain;
With but my list of killed and missed
  I spur my stumbling nag,
To tell of death at many a tryst,
  But victory to the flag!

"Halt! who comes there? The counter-sign!" —
  "A friend." — "Advance! The fight, —
How goes it, say?" — "We won the day!" —
  "Huzza! Pass on!" — "Good-night!"—
And parts the darkness on before,
  And down the mire we tramp,
And the black sky is painted o'er
  With many a pulsing camp;
O'er stumps and ruts, by ruined huts,
  Where ghosts look through the gloam, —
Behind my tread I hear the dead
  Follow the news toward home!

The hunted souls I see behind,
  In swamp and in ravine,
Whose cry for mercy thrills the wind
  Till cracks the sure carbine;
The moving lights, which scare the dark,
  And show the trampled place
Where, in his blood, some mother's bud
  Turns up his young, dead face;
The captives spent, whose standards rent
  The conqueror parades,
As at the Five Forks roads arrive
  The General's dashing aides.

O wondrous Youth! through this grand ruth
  Runs my boy's life its thread;
The General's fame, the battle's name,
  The rolls of maimed and dead
I bear, with my thrilled soul astir,
  And lonely thoughts and fears,
And am but History's courier
  To bind the conquering years;
A battle-ray, through ages gray
  To light to deeds sublime,
And flash the lustre of this day
  Down all the aisles of Time!

Ho! pony, — 't is the signal gun
  The night-assault decreed;
On Petersburg the thunderbolts
  Crash from the lines of Meade;
Fade the pale, frightened stars o'erhead,
  And shrieks the bursting air;
The forest foliage, tinted red,
  Grows ghastlier in the glare;
Though in her towers, reached her last hours,
  Rocks proud Rebellion's crest —
The world may sag, if but my nag
  Get in before the rest!

With bloody flank, and fetlocks dank,
  And goad, and lash, and shout —
Great God! as every hoof-beat falls
  A hundred lives beat out!
As weary as this broken steed
  Reels down the corduroys,
So, weary, fight for morning light
  Our hot and grimy boys;
Through ditches wet, o'er parapet
  And guns barbette, they catch
The last, lost breach; and I, — I reach
  The mail with my despatch!

Sure it shall speed, the land to read,
  As sped the happiest shell!
The shot I send strike the world's end;
  This tells my pony's knell;
His long race run, the long war done,
  My occupation gone, —
Above his bier, prone on the pier,
  The vultures fleck the dawn.
Still, rest his bones where soldiers dwell,
  Till the Long Roll they catch.
He fell the day that Richmond fell,
  And took the first despatch!

IN RAMA

A LITTLE face there was,
  When all her pains were done,
Beside that face I loved:
  They said it was a son.
A son to me — how strange! —
  Who never was a man,
But lived from change to change
  A boy, as I began.

More boyish still the hope
  That leaped within me then,
That I, matured in him,
  Should found a house of men;
And all my wasted sheaves,
  Bound up in his ripe shock,
Give seed to sterner times
  And name to sterner stock.

He grew to that ideal,
And blossomed in my sight;
Strange questions filled his day,
Sweet visions in the night,
Till he could walk with me,
Companion, hand in hand;
But nothing seemed to be
Like him, in Wonder-land.

For he was leading me
Beyond the bounds of mind,
Far down Eternity,
And I so far behind.

One day an angel stepped
Out of the idle sphere;
The man had entered in,
The boy is weeping here.

My house is founded there
In heaven that he has won.
Shall I be outlawed, then,
O Lord who hast my son?
This grief that makes me old,
These tears that make me pure,
They tell me time is time,
And only heaven mature.

Edward Rowland Sill

THE FOOL'S PRAYER

THE royal feast was done; the King
Sought some new sport to banish care,
And to his jester cried: "Sir Fool,
Kneel now, and make for us a prayer!"

The jester doffed his cap and bells,
And stood the mocking court before;
They could not see the bitter smile
Behind the painted grin he wore.

He bowed his head, and bent his knee
Upon the monarch's silken stool;
His pleading voice arose: "O Lord,
Be merciful to me, a fool!

"No pity, Lord, could change the heart
From red with wrong to white as wool:
The rod must heal the sin; but, Lord,
Be merciful to me, a fool!

"'T is not by guilt the onward sweep
Of truth and right, O Lord, we stay;
'T is by our follies that so long
We hold the earth from heaven away.

"These clumsy feet, still in the mire,
Go crushing blossoms without end;
These hard, well-meaning hands we thrust
Among the heart-strings of a friend.

"The ill-timed truth we might have kept —
Who knows how sharp it pierced and stung!
The word we had not sense to say —
Who knows how grandly it had rung!

"Our faults no tenderness should ask,
The chastening stripes must cleanse them all;
But for our blunders — oh, in shame
Before the eyes of heaven we fall.

"Earth bears no balsam for mistakes;
Men crown the knave, and scourge the tool
That did his will; but Thou, O Lord,
Be merciful to me, a fool!"

The room was hushed; in silence rose
The King, and sought his gardens cool,
And walked apart, and murmured low,
"Be merciful to me, a fool!"

BEFORE SUNRISE IN WINTER

A PURPLE cloud hangs half-way down;
Sky, yellow gold below;
The naked trees, beyond the town,
Like masts against it show, —

Bare masts and spars of our earth-ship,
With shining snow-sails furled;
And through the sea of space we slip,
That flows all round the world.

THE LOVER'S SONG

LEND me thy fillet, Love!
 I would no longer see:
Cover mine eyelids close awhile,
 And make me blind like thee.

Then might I pass her sunny face,
 And know not it was fair;
Then might I hear her voice, nor guess
 Her starry eyes were there.

Ah! Banished so from stars and sun —
 Why need it be my fate?
If only she might dream me good
 And wise, and be my mate!

Lend her thy fillet, Love!
 Let her no longer see:
If there is hope for me at all,
 She must be blind like thee.

THE COUP DE GRACE

 IF I were very sure
That all was over betwixt you and me, —
 That, while this endless absence I endure
With but one mood, one dream, one misery
Of waiting, you were happier to be free, —

 Then I might find again
In cloud and stream and all the winds that blow,
 Yea, even in the faces of my fellow-men,
The old companionship; and I might know
Once more the pulse of action, ere I go.

 But now I cannot rest,
While this one pleading, querulous tone without
 Breaks in and mars the music in my breast.
I open the closed door — lo! all about,
What seem your lingering footprints; then I doubt.

 Waken me from this sleep!
Strike fearless, let the naked truth-edge gleam!
 For while the beautiful old past I keep,
I am a phantom, and all mortals seem
But phantoms, and my life fades as a dream.

TEMPTED

YES, I know what you say:
 Since it cannot be soul to soul,
Be it flesh to flesh, as it may;
 But is Earth the whole?

Shall a man betray the Past
 For all Earth gives?
"But the Past is dead?" At last,
 It is all that lives.

Which were the nobler goal, —
 To snatch at the moment's bliss,
Or to swear I will keep my soul
 Clean for her kiss?

FORCE

THE stars know a secret
 They do not tell;
And morn brings a message
 Hidden well.

There 's a blush on the apple,
 A tint on the wing,
And the bright wind whistles,
 And the pulses sting.

Perish dark memories!
 There 's light ahead;
This world 's for the living,
 Not for the dead.

In the shining city,
 On the loud pave,
The life-tide is running
 Like a leaping wave.

How the stream quickens,
 As noon draws near!
No room for loiterers,
 No time for fear.

Out on the farm lands
 Earth smiles as well;
Gold-crusted grain-fields,
 With sweet, warm smell;

Whir of the reaper,
 Like a giant bee;
Like a Titan cricket,
 Thrilling with glee.

On mart and meadow,
Pavement or plain;
On azure mountain,
Or azure main, —

Heaven bends in blessing;
Lost is but won;
Goes the good rain-cloud,
Comes the good sun:

Only babes whimper,
And sick men wail,
And faint hearts and feeble hearts,
And weaklings fail.

Down the great currents
Let the boat swing;
There was never winter
But brought the spring.

A PRAYER

O God, our Father, if we had but truth!
Lost truth — which thou perchance
Didst let man lose, lest all his wayward youth
He waste in song and dance;
That he might gain, in searching, mightier powers
For manlier use in those foreshadowed hours.

If, blindly groping, he shall oft mistake,
And follow twinkling motes
Thinking them stars, and the one voice forsake
Of Wisdom for the notes
Which mocking Beauty utters here and there,
Thou surely wilt forgive him, and forbear!

Oh love us, for we love thee, Maker — God!
And would creep near thy hand,
And call thee "Father, Father," from the sod
Where by our graves we stand,
And pray to touch, fearless of scorn or blame,
Thy garment's hem, which Truth and Good we name.

William Gordon McCabe

CHRISTMAS NIGHT OF '62

The wintry blast goes wailing by,
The snow is falling overhead;
I hear the lonely sentry's tread,
And distant watch-fires light the sky.

Dim forms go flitting through the gloom;
The soldiers cluster round the blaze
To talk of other Christmas days,
And softly speak of home and home.

My sabre swinging overhead
Gleams in the watch-fire's fitful glow,
While fiercely drives the blinding snow,
And memory leads me to the dead.

My thoughts go wandering to and fro,
Vibrating 'twixt the Now and Then;
I see the low-browed home again,
The old hall wreathed with mistletoe.

And sweetly from the far-off years
Comes borne the laughter faint and low,
The voices of the Long Ago!
My eyes are wet with tender tears.

I feel again the mother-kiss,
I see again the glad surprise
That lightened up the tranquil eyes
And brimmed them o'er with tears of bliss,

As, rushing from the old hall-door,
She fondly clasped her wayward boy —
Her face all radiant with the joy
She felt to see him home once more.

My sabre swinging on the bough
Gleams in the watch-fire's fitful glow,
While fiercely drives the blinding snow
Aslant upon my saddened brow.

Those cherished faces all are gone!
Asleep within the quiet graves
Where lies the snow in drifting waves, —
And I am sitting here alone.

There 's not a comrade here to-night
But knows that loved ones far away
On bended knees this night will pray:
"God bring our darling from the fight."

But there are none to wish me back,
For me no yearning prayers arise.
The lips are mute and closed the eyes —
My home is in the bivouac.

In the Army of Northern Virginia.

DREAMING IN THE TRENCHES

I PICTURE her there in the quaint old room,
Where the fading fire-light starts and falls,
Alone in the twilight's tender gloom
With the shadows that dance on the dim-lit walls.

Alone, while those faces look silently down
From their antique frames in a grim repose —
Slight scholarly Ralph in his Oxford gown,
And stanch Sir Alan, who died for Montrose.

There are gallants gay in crimson and gold,
There are smiling beauties with powdered hair,
But she sits there, fairer a thousand-fold,
Leaning dreamily back in her low arm-chair.

And the roseate shadows of fading light
Softly clear steal over the sweet young face,
Where a woman's tenderness blends to-night
With the guileless pride of a knightly race.

Her hands lie clasped in a listless way
On the old *Romance* — which she holds on her knee —
Of Tristram the bravest of knights in the fray,
And Iseult, who waits by the sounding sea.

And her proud, dark eyes wear a softened look
As she watches the dying embers fall:
Perhaps she dreams of the knight in the book,
Perhaps of the pictures that smile on the wall.

What fancies I wonder are thronging her brain,
For her cheeks flush warm with a crimson glow!
Perhaps — ah! me, how foolish and vain!
But I 'd give my life to believe it so!

Well, whether I ever march home again
To offer my love and a stainless name,
Or whether I die at the head of my men, —
I 'll be true to the end all the same.

Petersburg Trenches, 1864.

Titus Munson Coan

A DREAM OF FLOWERS

EVEN at their fairest still I love the less
The blossoms of the garden than the blooms
Won by the mountain climber: theirs the tints
And forms that most delight me, — theirs the charm
That lends an aureole to the azure heights
Whereon they flourish, children of the dews
And mountain streamlets.
But in sleep sometimes
Mountain and meadow blend their gifts in one.
This morn I trod the secret path of dreams,
And, lo! my wilding flowers sprang thick around me,
Alpine and lowland too; and with them sprang
Blossoms that never had I known before
Except in poets' pages — fancied forms
And hues that shone in more than Alpine light.
Poppies incarnadine and rosemary,
And violets with gentle eyes were there,
And their sweet cousinry, the periwinkles;
Night-blooming cereus, agrimony, rue,
And stately damask roses, Eastern queens,
The noblest-born of flowers; and by their side

The panthers of the meadow, tiger-lilies;
Came with her trembling banner of perfumed bells
The lily of the valley, and the jessamine,
Princesses twain with maiden fragrance pure;
The azure of the Alpine gentian shone
Intense beneath the rival blue of heaven;
Along the heights blossomed the Alpine rose,
And higher yet the starry edelweiss, —
And sweet the wind came o'er the visioned Alp.

. . . .

But now I seemed to wonder at the view,
To my dimmed sense a riddle; then was 'ware
Of daytime colors blending with my dream,
And cleared my eyes, and saw my roguish girl,
A witch of seven, with flowers in both her hands,
Fresh-gathered in my garden, stealing in
Upon my morning vision, and waving me
Their fragrance. "Wake!" she cried, and I awoke
To her, a sweeter flower than all the rest!

THE CRYSTAL

Olympian sunlight is the Poet's sphere;
Yet of his rapt unconscious thought at play
The wintry stream gave image but to-day,
When first the frost his magic made appear;
The darkling water dreamed, and mirrored clear,
A thousand miles adown, the clouds' array,
Nor any gleam or stirring did betray
The secret of the transformation near —
When, lo! what beauty flashing from the night
Of formless atoms! Nature stirs amain,
Building her crystal arches firm and well,
And framing fairy cantilevers bright.
So broods the vision in the Poet's brain,
And leaps to life beneath a kindred spell.

NIHIL HUMANI ALIENUM

In the loud waking world I come and go,
And yet the twofold gates of dreams are mine;
I have seen the battle-lightnings round me shine,
And won the stillness of Hawaiian snow;
The votary's sad surrender do I know;
Joy have I had of passion and of wine;
Nor shines the light of poesy less divine
Though science's white cressets round me glow.
Yet never in me are these things at feud;
They make one sum of rapture; in my heart
Their memories rise and glow, a living good;
Dreams, banquets, battles, prayers, carousals, art,
All form for me a vital brotherhood;
From nothing human let me hold apart!

Nora Perry

CRESSID

Has any one seen my Fair,
Has any one seen my Dear?
Could any one tell me where
And whither she went from here?

The road is winding and long,
With many a turn and twist,
And one could easy go wrong,
Or ever one thought or list.

How should one know my Fair,
And how should one know my Dear?
By the dazzle of sunlight hair
That smites like a golden spear.
By the eyes that say "Beware,"
By the smile that beckons you near, —
This is to know my Fair,
This is to know my Dear.

Rough and bitter as gall
The voice that suddenly comes
Over the windy wall
Where the fishermen have their homes: —

"Ay, ay, we know full well
The way your fair one went:
She led by the ways of Hell,
And into its torments sent

"The boldest and bravest here,
Who knew nor guilt nor guile,
Who knew not shadow of fear
Till he followed that beckoning smile.

"Now would you find your Fair,
Now would you find your Dear?
Go, turn and follow her where
And whither she went from here,

"Along by the winding path
That leads by the old sea-wall:
The wind blows wild with wrath,
And one could easily fall

"From over the rampart there,
If one should lean too near,
To look for the sunlight hair
That smites like a golden spear!"

THE LOVE-KNOT

TYING her bonnet under her chin,
She tied her raven ringlets in;
But not alone in the silken snare
Did she catch her lovely floating hair,
For, tying her bonnet under her chin,
She tied a young man's heart within.

They were strolling together up the hill,
Where the wind comes blowing merry and chill;
And it blew the curls, a frolicsome race,
All over the happy peach-colored face,
Till, scolding and laughing, she tied them in,
Under her beautiful dimpled chin.

And it blew a color, bright as the bloom
Of the pinkest fuchsia's tossing plume,
All over the cheeks of the prettiest girl
That ever imprisoned a romping curl,
Or, tying her bonnet under her chin,
Tied a young man's heart within.

Steeper and steeper grew the hill;
Madder, merrier, chillier still
The western wind blew down, and played
The wildest tricks with the little maid,
As, tying her bonnet under her chin,
She tied a young man's heart within.

O western wind, do you think it was fair
To play such tricks with her floating hair?
To gladly, gleefully do your best
To blow her against the young man's breast,
Where he as gladly folded her in,
And kissed her mouth and her dimpled chin?

Ah! Ellery Vane, you little thought,
An hour ago, when you besought
This country lass to walk with you,
After the sun had dried the dew,
What perilous danger you'd be in,
As she tied her bonnet under her chin!

RIDING DOWN

OH, did you see him riding down,
And riding down, while all the town
Came out to see, came out to see,
And all the bells rang mad with glee?

Oh, did you hear those bells ring out,
The bells ring out, the people shout,
And did you hear that cheer on cheer
That over all the bells rang clear?

And did you see the waving flags,
The fluttering flags, the tattered flags,
Red, white, and blue, shot through and through,
Baptized with battle's deadly dew?

And did you hear the drums' gay beat,
The drums' gay beat, the bugles sweet,
The cymbals' clash, the cannons' crash,
That rent the sky with sound and flash?

And did you see me waiting there,
Just waiting there and watching there,
One little lass, amid the mass
That pressed to see the hero pass?

And did you see him smiling down,
And smiling down, as riding down
With slowest pace, with stately grace,
He caught the vision of a face, —

My face uplifted red and white,
Turned red and white with sheer delight.
To meet the eyes, the smiling eyes,
Outflashing in their swift surprise?

Oh, did you see how swift it came,
How swift it came, like sudden flame,
That smile to me, to only me,
The little lass who blushed to see?

And at the windows all along,
Oh, all along, a lovely throng
Of faces fair, beyond compare,
Beamed out upon him riding there!

Each face was like a radiant gem,
A sparkling gem, and yet for them
No swift smile came, like sudden flame,
No arrowy glance took certain aim.

He turned away from all their grace,
From all that grace of perfect face,
He turned to me, to only me,
The little lass who blushed to see!

WHO KNOWS?

WHO knows the thoughts of a child,
The angel unreconciled
To the new strange world that lies
Outstretched to its wondering eyes?

Who knows if a piteous fear,
Too deep for a sob or a tear,
Is beneath that breathless gaze
Of sudden and swift amaze, —

Some fear from the dim unknown,
Some shadow like black mist blown
Across the heavenly ray
Of this new-come dawning day?

But the smile which as sudden and swift
Breaks through the shadowy rift, —
From what far heaven or near,
What unseen blissful sphere,

Comes the smile of a little child,
This angel unreconciled
To the new, strange world that lies
Outstretched to its wondering eyes?

James Herbert Morse

SILENCE

COME, Silence, thou sweet reasoner,
Lay thy soft hand on all that stir —
On grass and shrub and tree and flower,
And let this be thine own dear hour.

No more across the neighbor rill
To that lone cottage on the hill
Shall wonder with her questions go,
Seeking if joy be there or no.

No longer shall the listening ear
Go seeking grief afar, or near;
Or eye be turned to find a stain
In the dear God's well-ruled domain.

The cricket tunes his slender throat
And lifts an early evening note.
The late bird ventures one last flight
Of song, and nestles for the night.

High up beyond the cloud-rift dun
One spot of blue yet shows the sun;
On that I fix a silent eye:
All earth, all life, all else pass by.

BROOK SONG

BROOK, would thou couldst flow
With a music all thine own —
Thy babble of music alone —
Not a word of the Long Ago
In thy brawling down below,
Not a sigh of the wind by thee,
The wind in the willow tree!

Or, Brook, if thou couldst go,
As once, in the prime of May,
For a whole long holiday,
When the cowslips down below,
And the violets watched thy flow,
With the babble of two by thee,
And the wind in the willow tree!

O Brook, if thou couldst so
Make a living music, and sing
Of a faded, bygone spring,
And down by the violets flow
With that babble of Long Ago, --
I would listen forever to thee
And the wind in the willow tree.

THE WILD GEESE

THE wild geese, flying in the night, behold
Our sunken towns lie underneath a sea,
Which buoys them on its billows. Liberty
They have, but such as those frail barques of old
That crossed unsounded mains to search our wold.
To them the night unspeakable is free;
They have the moon and stars for company;
To them no foe but the remorseless cold,
And froth of polar currents darting past,
That have been nigh the world's-end lair of storms.
Enormous billows float their fragile forms.
Yes, those frail beings, tossing on the Vast
Of wild revolving winds, feel no dismay!
'T is we who dread the thunder, and not they.

HIS STATEMENT OF THE CASE

"Now half a hundred years had I been born —
So many and so brief — when made aware,
By Time's blunt looks, of hoar-frost in my hair.
I turned to one of twenty, in the corn,
At husking time, that blissful autumn morn,
And said, 'What if the red ear fall to me?'
I would not for the world have any see
The look, half doubtful, mazeful, half in scorn,
That grew through all degrees, then broke in laughter,
As she ran down among the beardless men.
I left the husking, nor returned thereafter,
That autumn morn, nor any morn since then.
But you shall see gray beards in a long row,
Upon the rustic roads where I now go."

THE WAYSIDE

THERE are some quiet ways —
Ay, not a few —
Where the affections grow,
And noble days
Distil a gentle praise
That, as cool dew,
Or aromatic gums
Within a bower,
In after-times becomes
A calm, perennial dower.

There wayside bush and briar!
These lend a grace,
Flashing a glad assent
To sweet desire.
All their interior choir
The woodlands place
At service to command;
Man need not know,
In such a favored land,
The ways that proud folk go.

Perhaps the day may be,
Dear heart of mine,
When riches press too near
Outside, and we,
To live unfettered, flee
The great and fine,
And hide our little home
In some deep grove,
Where they alone may come
Who only come for love.

Joaquin Miller

COLUMBUS

BEHIND him lay the gray Azores,
Behind the Gates of Hercules;
Before him not the ghost of shores,
Before him only shoreless seas.
The good mate said: "Now must we pray,
For lo! the very stars are gone.
Brave Admiral, speak, what shall I say?"
"Why, say, 'Sail on! sail on! and on!'"

"My men grow mutinous day by day;
My men grow ghastly wan and weak."
The stout mate thought of home; a spray
Of salt wave washed his swarthy cheek.
"What shall I say, brave Admiral, say,
If we sight naught but seas at dawn?"
"Why, you shall say at break of day,
'Sail on! sail on! sail on! and on!'"

They sailed and sailed, as winds might blow,
 Until at last the blanched mate said:
"Why, now not even God would know
 Should I and all my men fall dead.
These very winds forget their way,
 For God from these dread seas is gone.
Now speak, brave Admiral, speak and say"—
 He said: "Sail on! sail on! and on!"

They sailed. They sailed. Then spake the mate:
 "This mad sea shows his teeth to-night.
He curls his lip, he lies in wait,
 With lifted teeth, as if to bite!
Brave Admiral, say but one good word:
 What shall we do when hope is gone?"
The words leapt like a leaping sword:
 "Sail on! sail on! sail on! and on!"

Then, pale and worn, he kept his deck,
 And peered through darkness. Ah, that night
Of all dark nights! And then a speck—
 A light! A light! A light! A light!
It grew, a starlit flag unfurled!
 It grew to be Time's burst of dawn.
He gained a world; he gave that world
 Its grandest lesson: "On! sail on!"

AT THE GRAVE OF WALKER

He lies low in the levelled sand,
Unsheltered from the tropic sun,
And now of all he knew not one
Will speak him fair in that far land.
Perhaps 'twas this that made me seek,
Disguised, his grave one winter-tide;
A weakness for the weaker side,
A siding with the helpless weak.

A palm not far held out a hand,
Hard by a long green bamboo swung,
And bent like some great bow unstrung,
And quivered like a willow wand;
Perched on its fruits that crooked hang,
Beneath a broad banana's leaf,
A bird in rainbow splendor sang
A low, sad song, of tempered grief.

No sod, no sign, no cross nor stone,
But at his side a cactus green
Upheld its lances long and keen;
It stood in sacred sands alone,
Flat-palmed and fierce with lifted spears;
One bloom of crimson crowned its head,
A drop of blood, so bright, so red,
Yet redolent as roses' tears.

In my left hand I held a shell,
All rosy lipped and pearly red;
I laid it by his lowly bed,
For he did love so passing well
The grand songs of the solemn sea.
O shell! sing well, wild, with a will,
When storms blow loud and birds be still,
The wildest sea-song known to thee!

I said some things with folded hands,
Soft whispered in the dim sea-sound,
And eyes held humbly to the ground,
And frail knees sunken in the sands.
He had done more than this for me,
And yet I could not well do more:
I turned me down the olive shore,
And set a sad face to the sea.

WESTWARD HO!

What strength! what strife! what rude unrest!
What shocks! what half-shaped armies met!
A mighty nation moving west,
With all its steely sinews set
Against the living forests. Hear
The shouts, the shots of pioneer,
The rended forests, rolling wheels,
As if some half-checked army reels,
Recoils, redoubles, comes again,
Loud-sounding like a hurricane.

O bearded, stalwart, westmost men,
So tower-like, so Gothic built!
A kingdom won without the guilt
Of studied battle, that hath been
Your blood's inheritance. . . . Your heirs
Know not your tombs: the great ploughshares
Cleave softly through the mellow loam
Where you have made eternal home,
And set no sign. Your epitaphs
Are writ in furrows. Beauty laughs
While through the green ways wandering
Beside her love, slow gathering
White, starry-hearted May-time blooms
Above your lowly levelled tombs;
And then below the spotted sky

She stops, she leans, she wonders why
The ground is heaved and broken so,
And why the grasses darker grow
And droop and trail like wounded wing.

Yea, Time, the grand old harvester,
Has gathered you from wood and plain.
We call to you again, again;
The rush and rumble of the car
Comes back in answer. Deep and wide
The wheels of progress have passed on;
The silent pioneer is gone.
His ghost is moving down the trees,
And now we push the memories
Of bluff, bold men who dared and died
In foremost battle, quite aside.

CROSSING THE PLAINS

WHAT great yoked brutes with briskets low,
With wrinkled necks like buffalo,
With round, brown, liquid, pleading eyes,
That turned so slow and sad to you,
That shone like love's eyes soft with tears,
That seemed to plead, and make replies,
The while they bowed their necks and drew
The creaking load; and looked at you.
Their sable briskets swept the ground,
Their cloven feet kept solemn sound.

Two sullen bullocks led the line,
Their great eyes shining bright like wine;
Two sullen captive kings were they,
That had in time held herds at bay,
And even now they crushed the sod
With stolid sense of majesty,
And stately stepped and stately trod,
As if 't were something still to be
Kings even in captivity.

VAQUERO

HIS broad-brimmed hat pushed back with careless air,
The proud vaquero sits his steed as free
As winds that toss his black abundant hair.
No rover ever swept a lawless sea
With such a haught and heedless air as he
Who scorns the path, and bounds with swift disdain
Away, a peon born, yet born to be
A splendid king; behold him ride and reign.

How brave he takes his herds in branding days,
On timbered hills that belt about the plain;
He climbs, he wheels, he shouts through winding ways
Of hiding ferns and hanging fir; the rein
Is loose, the rattling spur drives swift; the mane
Blows free; the bullocks rush in storms before;
They turn with lifted heads, they rush again,
Then sudden plunge from out the wood, and pour
A cloud upon the plain with one terrific roar.

Now sweeps the tawny man on stormy steed,
His gaudy trappings tossed about and blown
About the limbs as lithe as any reed;
The swift long lasso twirled above is thrown
From flying hand; the fall, the fearful groan
Of bullock toiled and tumbled in the dust —
The black herds onward sweep, and all disown
The fallen, struggling monarch that has thrust
His tongue in rage and rolled his red eyes in disgust.

BY THE PACIFIC OCEAN

HERE room and kingly silence keep
Companionship in state austere;
The dignity of death is here,
The large, lone vastness of the deep;
Here toil has pitched his camp to rest:
The west is banked against the west.

Above yon gleaming skies of gold
One lone imperial peak is seen;
While gathered at his feet in green
Ten thousand foresters are told:
And all so still! so still the air
That duty drops the web of care.

Beneath the sunset's golden sheaves
The awful deep walks with the deep,
Where silent sea doves slip and sweep,
And commerce keeps her loom and weaves
The dead red men refuse to rest;
Their ghosts illume my lurid West.

TWILIGHT AT THE HEIGHTS

THE brave young city by the Balboa seas
Lies compassed about by the hosts of night —
Lies humming, low, like a hive of bees;
And the day lies dead. And its spirit's flight
Is far to the west; while the golden bars
That bound it are broken to a dust of stars.

Come under my oaks, oh, drowsy dusk!
The wolf and the dog; dear incense hour
When Mother Earth hath a smell of musk,
And things of the spirit assert their power —
When candles are set to burn in the west —
Set head and foot to the day at rest.

DEAD IN THE SIERRAS

HIS footprints have failed us,
Where berries are red,
And madroños are rankest, —
The hunter is dead!

The grizzly may pass
By his half-open door;
May pass and repass
On his path, as of yore;

The panther may crouch
In the leaves on his limb;
May scream and may scream, —
It is nothing to him.

Prone, bearded, and breasted
Like columns of stone;
And tall as a pine —
As a pine overthrown!

His camp-fires gone,
What else can be done
Than let him sleep on
Till the light of the sun?

Ay, tombless! what of it?
Marble is dust,
Cold and repellent;
And iron is rust.

PETER COOPER

GIVE honor and love for evermore
To this great man gone to rest;
Peace on the dim Plutonian shore,
Rest in the land of the blest.

I reckon him greater than any man
That ever drew sword in war;
I reckon him nobler than king or khan,
Braver and better by far.

And wisest he in this whole wide land
Of hoarding till bent and gray;
For all you can hold in your cold dead hand
Is what you have given away.

So whether to wander the stars or to rest
Forever hushed and dumb,
He gave with a zest and he gave his best —
Give him the best to come.

1883.

TO RUSSIA

WHO tamed your lawless Tartar blood?
What David bearded in her den
The Russian bear in ages when
You strode your black, unbridled stud,
A skin-clad savage of your steppes?
Why, one who now sits low and weeps,
Why, one who now wails out to you, —
The Jew, the Jew, the homeless Jew.

Who girt the thews of your young prime
And bound your fierce divided force?
Why, who but Moses shaped your course
United down the grooves of time?
Your mighty millions all to-day
The hated, homeless Jew obey.
Who taught all poetry to you?
The Jew, the Jew, the hated Jew.

Who taught you tender Bible tales
Of honey-lands, of milk and wine?
Of happy, peaceful Palestine?
Of Jordan's holy harvest vales?
Who gave the patient Christ? I say,
Who gave your Christian creed? Yea, yea,
Who gave your very God to you?
Your Jew! Your Jew! Your hated Jew!

THE VOICE OF THE DOVE

COME listen, O Love, to the voice of the dove,
Come, hearken and hear him say,

There are many To-morrows, my Love,
my Love, —
There is only one To-day.

And all day long you can hear him say
This day in purple is rolled,
And the baby stars of the milky-way —
They are cradled in cradles of gold.

Now what is thy secret, serene gray dove,
Of singing so sweetly alway ?
"There are many To-morrows, my Love,
my Love, —
There is only one To-day."

JUANITA

You will come, my bird, Bonita ?
Come ! For I by steep and stone
Have built such nest for you, Juanita,
As not eagle bird hath known.

Rugged ! Rugged as Parnassus !
Rude, as all roads I have trod —
Yet are steeps and stone-strewn passes
Smooth o'erhead, and nearest God.

Here black thunders of my cañon
Shake its walls in Titan wars !
Here white sea-born clouds companion
With such peaks as know the stars !

Here madrona, manzanita —
Here the snarling chaparral
House and hang o'er steeps, Juanita,
Where the gaunt wolf loved to dwell !

Dear, I took these trackless masses
Fresh from Him who fashioned them;
Wrought in rock, and hewed fair passes,
Flower set, as sets a gem.

Aye, I built in woe. God willed it;
Woe that passeth ghosts of guilt;
Yet I built as His birds builded —
Builded, singing as I built.

All is finished ! Roads of flowers
Wait your loyal little feet.
All completed ? Nay, the hours
Till you come are incomplete.

Steep below me lies the valley,
Deep below me lies the town,
Where great sea-ships ride and rally,
And the world walks up and down.

O, the sea of lights far streaming
When the thousand flags are furled —
When the gleaming bay lies dreaming
As it duplicates the world !

You will come, my dearest, truest ?
Come, my sovereign queen of ten;
My blue skies will then be bluest;
My white rose be whitest then:

Then the song ! Ah, then the sabre
Flashing up the walls of night !
Hate of wrong and love of neighbor —
Rhymes of battle for the Right !

Joseph O'Connor

WHAT WAS MY DREAM?

"AND MY SPIRIT WAS TROUBLED TO KNOW THE DREAM"

What was my dream ? Though consciousness be clear,
I hold no memory of the potent thing,
Yet feel the force of it — a creeping fear,
A hope, a horror, and a sense austere
Of revelation, stayed at thought's extreme:
As when the wind is passed, the pines still swing;
Or when the storm has blown, the waves yet fling
To shore the battered corpse and shattered beam;
So sways my troubled mind. What was my dream ?

What was my dream ? A heath, starlit and wide,
With marching giants marshalled to and fro
As if for strife ? A moonlit river's tide,
Where every form I love may be descried
Afloat and past all effort to redeem ?

A garden rare, with Nature all aglow
Among her fruits and flowers, that, as they grow,
Breathe perfumed melody, full glad to teem
With every germ of life? What was my dream?

What was my dream? A distant, unknown world
That elemental ether doth immerse,
With matter in a wild disorder hurled,
And primal forces in contention whirled,
A senseless demon over all supreme,
Who seeks with apish malice to reverse
Creative influences, and coerce
A universe to death, and bring its scheme
To chaos whence it came? What was my dream?

What was my dream? Some Indian sage's scroll
May keep for me, perchance, a glimpse or glint;
Some Hebrew prophet's vision may unroll
Its veils and show this secret of the soul;
At times, among the murmurs of a stream,
I catch the far, faint echo of a hint, —
Or seem to feel in some suggestive tint,
Where golden glories of the sunset gleam,
A presence unrevealed. What was my dream?

What was my dream? A silver trumpet blown
Thrills with a touch of the strong mystery;
The buds of spring, the leaves of autumn strown,
The tempest's flashing blade and braggart tone
Remind me of the unremembered theme.
Where billows curve along the shining sea,
It breaks through lucent green in foamy glee,
And hides uncaught; not seldom do I deem
Love's sigh its harbinger? What was my dream?

THE GENERAL'S DEATH

THE general dashed along the road
Amid the pelting rain;
How joyously his bold face glowed
To hear our cheers' refrain!

His blue blouse flapped in wind and wet,
His boots were splashed with mire,
But round his lips a smile was set,
And in his eyes a fire.

A laughing word, a gesture kind, —
We did not ask for more,
With thirty weary miles behind,
A weary fight before.

The gun grew light to every man,
The crossed belts ceased their stress,
As onward to the column's van
We watched our leader press.

Within an hour we saw him lie,
A bullet in his brain,
His manly face turned to the sky,
And beaten by the rain.

Charles Goodrich Whiting

BLUE HILLS BENEATH THE HAZE

BLUE hills beneath the haze
That broods o'er distant ways,
Whether ye may not hold
Secrets more dear than gold, —
This is the ever new
Puzzle within your blue.

Is 't not a softer sun
Whose smiles yon hills have won?
Is 't not a sweeter air
That folds the fields so fair?
Is 't not a finer rest
That I so fain would test?

The far thing beckons most,
The near becomes the lost.

Not what we have is worth,
But that which has no birth
Or breath within the ken
Of transitory men.

THE EAGLE'S FALL

THE eagle, did ye see him fall? —
Aflight beyond mid-air
Erewhile his mighty pinions bore him,
His eyry left, the sun before him;
And not a bird could dare
To match with that tremendous motion,
Through fire and flood, 'twixt sky and ocean, —
But did ye see the eagle fall?

And so ye saw the eagle fall!
Struck in his flight of pride
He hung in air one lightning moment,
As wondering what the deadly blow meant,
And what his blood's ebb tide.
Whirling off sailed a loosened feather;
Then headlong, pride and flight together, —
'T was thus ye saw the eagle fall!

Thus did ye see the eagle fall!
But on the sedgy plain,
Where closed the monarch's eye in dying,
Marked ye the screaming and the vying
Wherewith the feathered train,
Sparrow and jackdaw, hawk and vulture,
Gathered exulting to insult your
Great eagle in his fall?

THE WAY TO HEAVEN

HEAVEN is open every day;
In night also
He that would wend his upward way
May surely go.
There is no wall to that demesne
Where God resides; nor any screen
To hide the glories of that scene, —
If man will know.

The ladder which the Hebrew saw
Whenas he slept,
From earth God never doth updraw,
But still hath kept;
And angels ever to and fro
On errands swiftly glide and glow, —
For love above, for love below,
Its rounds have stept.

Thereon the saint doth daily mount
Above the stars,
Caring nowhit to take account
Of earthly bars;
Since well 't is known to such as he
There are no guards but pass him free;
He hath the watchword and the key,
In peace, or wars.

Charles Edward Carryl

THE SONG IN THE DELL

I KNOW a way
Of hearing what the larks and linnets say:
The larks tell of the sunshine and the sky;
The linnets from the hedges make reply,
And boast of hidden nests with mocking lay.

I know a way
Of keeping near the rabbits at their play:
They tell me of the cool and shady nooks
Where waterfalls disturb the placid brooks
That I may go and frolic in the spray.

I know a way
Of catching dewdrops on a night in May,
And threading them upon a spear of green,
That through their sides translucent may be seen
The sparkling hue that emeralds display.

I know a way
Of trapping sunbeams as they nimbly play
At hide-and-seek with meadow-grass and flowers,
And holding them in store for dreary hours
When winds are chill and all the sky is gray.

I know a way
Of stealing fragrance from the new-mown hay
And storing it in flasks of petals made,
To scent the air when all the flowers fade
And leave the woodland world to sad decay.

I know a way
Of coaxing snowflakes in their flight to stay
So still awhile, that, as they hang in air,
I weave them into frosty lace, to wear
About my head upon a sultry day.

ROBINSON CRUSOE

The night was thick and hazy
When the Piccadilly Daisy
Carried down the crew and captain in the sea;
And I think the water drowned 'em,
For they never, never found 'em,
And I know they did n't come ashore with me.

Oh! 'twas very sad and lonely
When I found myself the only
Population on this cultivated shore;
But I 've made a little tavern
In a rocky little cavern,
And I sit and watch for people at the door.

I spent no time in looking
For a girl to do my cooking,
As I 'm quite a clever hand at making stews;
But I had that fellow Friday
Just to keep the tavern tidy,
And to put a Sunday polish on my shoes.

I have a little garden
That I 'm cultivating lard in,
As the things I eat are rather tough and dry;
For I live on toasted lizards,
Prickly pears, and parrot gizzards,
And I 'm really very fond of beetle-pie.

The clothes I had were furry,
And it made me fret and worry
When I found the moths were eating off the hair;
And I had to scrape and sand 'em,
And I boiled 'em and I tanned 'em,
Till I got the fine morocco suit I wear.

I sometimes seek diversion
In a family excursion
With the few domestic animals you see;
And we take along a carrot
As refreshments for the parrot,
And a little can of jungleberry tea.

Then we gather as we travel
Bits of moss and dirty gravel,
And we chip off little specimens of stone;
And we carry home as prizes
Funny bugs of handy sizes,
Just to give the day a scientific tone.

If the roads are wet and muddy
We remain at home and study, —
For the Goat is very clever at a sum, —
And the Dog, instead of fighting,
Studies ornamental writing,
While the Cat is taking lessons on the drum.

We retire at eleven,
And we rise again at seven;
And I wish to call attention, as I close,
To the fact that all the scholars
Are correct about their collars,
And particular in turning out their toes.

Sidney Lanier

SONG FOR "THE JAQUERIE"

BETRAYAL

The sun has kissed the violet sea,
And burned the violet to a rose.
O Sea! wouldst thou not better be
Mere violet still? Who knows? Who knows?
Well hides the violet in the wood:
The dead leaf wrinkles her a hood,
And winter's ill is violet's good;

But the bold glory of the rose,
It quickly comes and quickly goes, —
Red petals whirling in white snows,
Ah me!

The sun has burnt the rose-red sea:
The rose is turned to ashes gray.
O Sea, O Sea, mightst thou but be
The violet thou hast been to-day!
The sun is brave, the sun is bright,
The sun is lord of love and light,
But after him it cometh night.
Dim anguish of the lonesome dark! —
Once a girl's body, stiff and stark,
Was laid in a tomb without a mark,
Ah me!

THE HOUND

THE hound was cuffed, the hound was kicked,
O' the ears was cropped, o' the tail was nicked,
(*All.*) Oo-hoo-o, howled the hound.
The hound into his kennel crept;
He rarely wept, he never slept.
His mouth he always open kept,
Licking his bitter wound,
The hound,
(*All.*) *U-lu-lo*, howled the hound.

A star upon his kennel shone
That showed the hound a meat-bare bone.
(*All.*) O hungry was the hound!
The hound had but a churlish wit:
He seized the bone, he crunched, he bit.
"An thou wert Master, I had slit
Thy throat with a huge wound,"
Quo' hound.
(*All.*) O, angry was the hound.

The star in castle-windows shone,
The Master lay abed, alone.
(*All.*) Oh ho, why not? quo' hound.
He leapt, he seized the throat, he tore
The Master, head from neck, to floor,
And rolled the head i' the kennel door,
And fled and salved his wound,
Good hound!
(*All.*) *U-lu-lo*, howled the hound.

NIGHT AND DAY

THE innocent, sweet Day is dead.
Dark Night hath slain her in her bed.
O, Moors are as fierce to kill as to wed!
— Put out the light, said he.

A sweeter light than ever rayed
From star of heaven or eye of maid
Has vanished in the unknown Shade.
— She 's dead, she 's dead, said he.

Now, in a wild, sad after-mood
The tawny Night sits still to brood
Upon the dawn-time when he wooed.
— I would she lived, said he.

Star-memories of happier times,
Of loving deeds and lovers' rhymes,
Throng forth in silvery pantomimes.
— Come back, O Day! said he.

THE STIRRUP-CUP

DEATH, thou 'rt a cordial old and rare:
Look how compounded, with what care
Time got his wrinkles reaping thee
Sweet herbs from all antiquity.

David to thy distillage went,
Keats, and Gotama excellent,
Omar Khayyám, and Chaucer bright,
And Shakespeare for a king-delight.

Then, Time, let not a drop be spilt:
Hand me the cup whene'er thou wilt;
'T is thy rich stirrup-cup to me;
I 'll drink it down right smilingly.

SONG OF THE CHATTAHOOCHEE

OUT of the hills of Habersham,
Down the valleys of Hall,
I hurry amain to reach the plain,
Run the rapid and leap the fall,
Split at the rock and together again,
Accept my bed, or narrow or wide,
And flee from folly on every side
With a lover's pain to attain the plain
Far from the hills of Habersham,
Far from the valleys of Hall.

All down the hills of Habersham,
All through the valleys of Hall,
The rushes cried *Abide, abide*,
The wilful waterweeds held me thrall,
The laving laurel turned my tide,

The ferns and the fondling grass said *Stay*,
The dewberry dipped for to work delay,
And the little reeds sighed *Abide, abide,*
Here in the hills of Habersham,
Here in the valleys of Hall.

High o'er the hills of Habersham,
Veiling the valleys of Hall,
The hickory told me manifold
Fair tales of shade, the poplar tall
Wrought me her shadowy self to hold,
The chestnut, the oak, the walnut, the pine,
Overleaning, with flickering meaning and sign,
Said, *Pass not, so cold, these manifold*
Deep shades of the hills of Habersham,
These glades in the valleys of Hall.

And oft in the hills of Habersham,
And oft in the valleys of Hall,
The white quartz shone, and the smooth brook-stone
Did bar me of passage with friendly brawl,
And many a luminous jewel lone
— Crystals clear or a-cloud with mist,
Ruby, garnet, and amethyst —
Made lures with the lights of streaming stone
In the clefts of the hills of Habersham,
In the beds of the valleys of Hall.

But oh, not the hills of Habersham,
And oh, not the valleys of Hall
Avail: I am fain for to water the plain.
Downward the voices of Duty call —
Downward, to toil and be mixed with the main,
The dry fields burn, and the mills are to turn,
And a myriad flowers mortally yearn,
And the lordly main from beyond the plain
Calls o'er the hills of Habersham,
Calls through the valleys of Hall.

THE MARSHES OF GLYNN

Glooms of the live-oaks, beautiful-braided and woven
With intricate shades of the vines that myriad-cloven
Clamber the forks of the multiform boughs, —
Emerald twilights, —
Virginal shy lights,
Wrought of the leaves to allure to the whisper of vows,
When lovers pace timidly down through the green colonnades
Of the dim sweet woods, of the dear dark woods,
Of the heavenly woods and glades,
That run to the radiant marginal sand-beach within
The wide sea-marshes of Glynn; —

Beautiful glooms, soft dusks in the noon-day fire, —
Wildwood privacies, closets of lone desire,
Chamber from chamber parted with wavering arras of leaves, —
Cells for the passionate pleasure of prayer to the soul that grieves,
Pure with a sense of the passing of saints through the wood,
Cool for the dutiful weighing of ill with good; —

O braided dusks of the oak and woven shades of the vine,
While the riotous noonday sun of the June-day long did shine
Ye held me fast in your heart and I held you fast in mine;
But now when the noon is no more, and riot is rest,
And the sun is a-wait at the ponderous gate of the West,
And the slant yellow beam down the wood-aisle doth seem
Like a lane into heaven that leads from a dream, —
Ay, now, when my soul all day hath drunken the soul of the oak,
And my heart is at ease from men, and the wearisome sound of the stroke
Of the scythe of time and the trowel of trade is low,
And belief overmasters doubt, and I know that I know,
And my spirit is grown to a lordly great compass within,
That the length and the breadth and the sweep of the marshes of Glynn
Will work me no fear like the fear they have wrought me of yore
When length was fatigue, and when breadth was but bitterness sore,

And when terror and shrinking and dreary unnamable pain
Drew over me out of the merciless miles of the plain, —

Oh, now, unafraid, I am fain to face
The vast sweet visage of space.
To the edge of the wood I am drawn, I am drawn,
Where the gray beach glimmering runs, as a belt of the dawn,
For a mete and a mark
To the forest-dark: —
So:
Affable live-oak, leaning low, —
Thus — with your favor — soft, with a reverent hand,
(Not lightly touching your person, Lord of the land!)
Bending your beauty aside, with a step I stand
On the firm-packed sand,
Free
By a world of marsh that borders a world of sea.
Sinuous southward and sinuous northward the shimmering band
Of the sand-beach fastens the fringe of the marsh to the folds of the land.
Inward and outward to northward and southward the beach-lines linger and curl
As a silver-wrought garment that clings to and follows the firm sweet limbs of a girl.
Vanishing, swerving, evermore curving again into sight,
Softly the sand-beach wavers away to a dim gray looping of light.
And what if behind me to westward the wall of the woods stands high?
The world lies east: how ample, the marsh and the sea and the sky!
A league and a league of marsh-grass, waist-high, broad in the blade,
Green, and all of a height, and unflecked with a light or a shade,
Stretch leisurely off, in a pleasant plain,
To the terminal blue of the main.

Oh, what is abroad in the marsh and the terminal sea?
Somehow my soul seems suddenly free
From the weighing of fate and the sad discussion of sin,
By the length and the breadth and the sweep of the marshes of Glynn.

Ye marshes, how candid and simple and nothing-withholding and free
Ye publish yourselves to the sky and offer yourselves to the sea!
Tolerant plains, that suffer the sea and the rains and the sun,
Ye spread and span like the catholic man who hath mightily won
God out of knowledge and good out of infinite pain
And sight out of blindness and purity out of a stain.

As the marsh-hen secretly builds on the watery sod,
Behold I will build me a nest on the greatness of God:
I will fly in the greatness of God as the marsh-hen flies
In the freedom that fills all the space 'twixt the marsh and the skies:
By so many roots as the marsh-grass sends in the sod
I will heartily lay me a-hold on the greatness of God:
Oh, like to the greatness of God is the greatness within
The range of the marshes, the liberal marshes of Glynn.

And the sea lends large, as the marsh: lo, out of his plenty the sea
Pours fast: full soon the time of the flood-tide must be:
Look how the grace of the sea doth go
About and about through the intricate channels that flow
Here and there,
Everywhere,
Till his waters have flooded the uttermost creeks and the low-lying lanes,
And the marsh is meshed with a million veins,
That like as with rosy and silvery essences flow
In the rose-and-silver evening glow.
Farewell, my lord Sun!
The creeks overflow: a thousand rivulets run

'Twixt the roots of the sod; the blades of the marsh-grass stir;
Passeth a hurrying sound of wings that westward whirr;
Passeth, and all is still; and the currents cease to run;
And the sea and the marsh are one.

How still the plains of the waters be!
The tide is in his ecstasy;
The tide is at his highest height;
And it is night.

And now from the Vast of the Lord will the waters of sleep
Roll in on the souls of men,
But who will reveal to our waking ken
The forms that swim and the shapes that creep
Under the waters of sleep?
And I would I could know what swimmeth below when the tide comes in
On the length and the breadth of the marvellous marshes of Glynn.

THE MOCKING BIRD

SUPERB and sole, upon a plumëd spray
That o'er the general leafage boldly grew,
He summ'd the woods in song; or typic drew
The watch of hungry hawks, the lone dismay
Of languid doves when long their lovers stray,
And all birds' passion-plays that sprinkle dew
At morn in brake or bosky avenue.
Whate'er birds did or dreamed, this bird could say.
Then down he shot, bounced airily along
The sward, twitched in a grasshopper, made song
Midflight, perched, prinked, and to his art again.
Sweet Science, this large riddle read me plain:
How may the death of that dull insect be
The life of yon trim Shakespeare on the tree?

THE HARLEQUIN OF DREAMS

SWIFT, through some trap mine eyes have never found,
Dim-panelled in the painted scene of Sleep,
Thou, giant Harlequin of Dreams, dost leap
Upon my spirit's stage. Then Sight and Sound,
Then Space and Time, then Language, Mete and Bound,
And all familiar Forms that firmly keep
Man's reason in the road, change faces, peep
Betwixt the legs and mock the daily round.
Yet thou canst more than mock: sometimes my tears
At midnight break through bounden lids — a sign
Thou hast a heart; and oft thy little leaven
Of dream-taught wisdom works me bettered years.
In one night witch, saint, trickster, fool divine,
I think thou 'rt Jester at the Court of Heaven!

A BALLAD OF TREES AND THE MASTER

INTO the woods my Master went,
Clean forspent, forspent.
Into the woods my Master came,
Forspent with love and shame.
But the olives they were not blind to Him;
The little gray leaves were kind to Him;
The thorn-tree had a mind to Him
When into the woods He came.

Out of the woods my Master went,
And He was well content.
Out of the woods my Master came,
Content with death and shame.
When Death and Shame would woo Him last,
From under the trees they drew Him last:
'Twas on a tree they slew Him — last,
When out of the woods He came.

SUNRISE

IN my sleep I was fain of their fellowship, fain
Of the live-oak, the marsh, and the main.
The little green leaves would not let me alone in my sleep;
Up-breathed from the marshes, a message of range and of sweep,

Interwoven with waftures of wild sea-liberties, drifting,
Came through the lapped leaves sifting, sifting,
Came to the gates of sleep.
Then my thoughts, in the dark of the dungeon-keep
Of the Castle of Captives hid in the City of Sleep,
Upstarted, by twos and by threes assembling;
The gates of sleep fell a-trembling
Like as the lips of a lady that forth falter *yes*,
Shaken with happiness:
The gates of sleep stood wide.

I have waked, I have come, my beloved!
I might not abide:
I have come ere the dawn, O beloved, my live-oaks, to hide
In your gospelling glooms, — to be
As a lover in heaven, the marsh my marsh and the sea my sea.

Tell me, sweet burly-barked, man-embodied Tree
That mine arms in the dark are embracing, dost know
From what fount are these tears at thy feet which flow?
They rise not from reason, but deeper inconsequent deeps.
Reason 's not one that weeps.
What logic of greeting lies
Betwixt dear over-beautiful trees and the rain of the eyes?

O cunning green leaves, little masters! like as ye gloss
All the dull-tissued dark with your luminous darks that emboss
The vague blackness of night into pattern and plan,
So,
(But would I could know, but would I could know,)
With your question embroidering the dark of the question of man, —
So, with your silences purfling this silence of man
While his cry to the dead for some knowledge is under the ban,
Under the ban, —
So, ye have wrought me
Designs on the night of our knowledge, — yea, ye have taught me,
So,
That haply we know somewhat more than we know.

Ye lispers, whisperers, singers in storms,
Ye consciences murmuring faiths under forms,
Ye ministers meet for each passion that grieves,
Friendly, sisterly, sweetheart leaves,
Oh, rain me down from your darks that contain me
Wisdoms ye winnow from winds that pain me, —
Sift down tremors of sweet-within-sweet
That advise me of more than they bring, — repeat
Me the woods-smell that swiftly but now brought breath
From the heaven-side bank of the river of death, —
Teach me the terms of silence, — preach me
The passion of patience, — sift me, — impeach me, —
And there, oh there
As ye hang with your myriad palms upturned in the air,
Pray me a myriad prayer.

My gossip, the owl, — is it thou
That out of the leaves of the low-hanging bough,
As I pass to the beach, art stirred?
Dumb woods, have ye uttered a bird?

. . . .

Reverend Marsh, low-couched along the sea,
Old chemist, rapt in alchemy,
Distilling silence, — lo,
That which our father-age had died to know —
The menstruum that dissolves all matter — thou
Hast found it; for this silence, filling now
The globëd charity of receiving space,
This solves us all: man, matter, doubt, disgrace,
Death, love, sin, sanity,
Must in yon silence, clear solution lie, —
Too clear! That crystal nothing who 'll peruse?

The blackest night could bring us brighter
news.
Yet precious qualities of silence haunt
Round these vast margins, ministrant.
Oh, if thy soul 's at latter gasp for space,
With trying to breathe no bigger than thy
race
Just to be fellowed, when that thou hast
found
No man with room, or grace enough of
bound,
To entertain that New thou tellst, thou
art, —
'T is here, 't is here, thou canst unhand
thy heart
And breathe it free, and breathe it free,
By rangy marsh, in lone sea-liberty.

The tide 's at full; the marsh with flooded
streams
Glimmers, a limpid labyrinth of dreams.
Each winding creek in grave entrancement
lies
A rhapsody of morning-stars. The skies
Shine scant with one forked galaxy, —
The marsh brags ten: looped on his breast
they lie.

Oh, what if a sound should be made!
Oh, what if a bound should be laid
To this bow-and-string tension of beauty
and silence a-spring, —
To the bend of beauty the bow, or the hold
of silence the string!
I fear me, I fear me yon dome of diapha-
nous gleam
Will break as a bubble o'er-blown in a
dream, —
Yon dome of too-tenuous tissues of space
and of night,
Over-weighted with stars, over-freighted
with light,
Over-sated with beauty and silence, will
seem
But a bubble that broke in a dream,
If a bound of degree to this grace be laid,
Or a sound or a motion made.

But no: it is made: list! somewhere, —
mystery, where?
In the leaves? in the air?
In my heart? is a motion made:
'T is a motion of dawn, like a flicker of
shade on shade.
In the leaves 't is palpable: low multitudi-
nous stirring
Upwinds through the woods; the little ones,
softly conferring,
Have settled my lord's to be looked for;
so, they are still;
But the air and my heart and the earth are
a-thrill, —
And look where the wild duck sails round
the bend of the river, —
And look where a passionate shiver
Expectant is bending the blades
Of the marsh-grass in serial shimmers and
shades, —
And invisible wings, fast fleeting, fast
fleeting,
Are beating
The dark overhead as my heart beats, —
and steady and free
Is the ebb-tide flowing from marsh to sea —
(Run home, little streams,
With your lapfuls of stars and
dreams), —
And a sailor unseen is hoisting a-peak,
For list, down the inshore curve of the
creek
How merrily flutters the sail, —
And lo, in the East! Will the East un-
veil?
The East is unveiled, the East hath con-
fessed
A flush: 't is dead; 't is alive: 't is dead, ere
the West
Was aware of it: nay, 't is abiding, 't is un-
withdrawn:
Have a care, sweet Heaven! 'T is
Dawn.

Now a dream of a flame through that
dream of a flush is uprolled:
To the zenith ascending, a dome of
undazzling gold
Is builded, in shape as a bee-hive, from
out of the sea:
The hive is of gold undazzling, but oh, the
Bee,
The star-fed Bee, the build-fire Bee,
Of dazzling gold is the great Sun-Bee
That shall flash from the hive-hole over
the sea.

Yet now the dewdrop, now the morning gray,
Shall live their little lucid sober day

Ere with the sun their souls exhale
away.
Now in each pettiest personal sphere of dew
The summed moon shines complete as in
the blue
Big dewdrop of all heaven: with these lit
shrines
O'ersilvered to the farthest sea-confines,
The sacramental marsh one pious plain
Of worship lies. Peace to the ante-reign
Of Mary Morning, blissful mother mild,
Minded of nought but peace, and of a child,

Not slower than Majesty moves, for a mean
and a measure
Of motion, — not faster than dateless
Olympian leisure
Might pace with unblown ample garments
from pleasure to pleasure, —
The wave-serrate sea-rim sinks unjarring,
unreeling,
Forever revealing, revealing, revealing,
Edgewise, bladewise, halfwise, wholewise,
— 't is done!
Good-morrow, Lord Sun!
With several voice, with ascription one,
The woods and the marsh and the sea and
my soul
Unto thee, whence the glittering stream of
all morrows doth roll,
Cry good and past good and most heav-
enly morrow, Lord Sun.

O Artisan born in the purple, — Workman
Heat, —
Parter of passionate atoms that travail to
meet
And be mixed in the death-cold oneness, —
innermost Guest
At the marriage of elements, — fellow of
publicans, — blest
King in the blouse of flame, that loiterest
o'er
The idle skies yet laborest past evermore, —
Thou, in the fine forge-thunder, thou,
in the beat
Of the heart of a man, thou Motive, —
Laborer Heat:
Yea, Artist, thou, of whose art yon sea 's
all news,
With his inshore greens and manifold mid-
sea blues,
Pearl-glint, shell-tint, ancientest, perfectest
hues
Ever shaming the maidens, — lily and rose
Confess thee, and each mild flame that
glows
In the clarified virginal bosoms of stones
that shine,
It is thine, it is thine:

Thou chemist of storms, whether driving
the winds a-swirl
Or a-flicker the subtiler essences polar that
whirl
In the magnet earth, — yea, thou with a
storm for a heart,
Rent with debate, many-spotted with question, part
From part oft sundered, yet ever a globèd
light,
Yet ever the artist, ever more large and
bright
Than the eye of a man may avail of: —
manifold One,
I must pass from the face, I must pass
from the face of the Sun:
Old Want is awake and agog, every wrinkle
a-frown;
The worker must pass to his work in the
terrible town:
But I fear not, nay, and I fear not the
thing to be done;
I am strong with the strength of my
lord the Sun:
How dark, how dark soever the race that
must needs be run,
I am lit with the Sun.

Oh, never the mast-high run of the seas
Of traffic shall hide thee,
Never the hell-colored smoke of the facto-
ries
Hide thee,
Never the reek of the time's fen-politics
Hide thee,
And ever my heart through the night shall
with knowledge abide thee,
And ever by day shall my spirit, as one
that hath tried thee,
Labor, at leisure, in art, — till yonder be-
side thee
My soul shall float, friend Sun,
The day being done.

May Riley Smith

MY UNINVITED GUEST

One day there entered at my chamber door
A presence whose light footfall on the floor
No token gave; and, ere I could withstand,
Within her clasp she drew my trembling hand.

"Intrusive guest," I cried, "my palm I lend
But to the gracious pressure of a friend!
Why comest thou, unbidden and in gloom,
Trailing thy cold gray garments in my room?

"I know thee, Pain! Thou art the sullen foe
Of every sweet enjoyment here below;
Thou art the comrade and ally of Death,
And timid mortals shrink from thy cold breath.

"No fragrant balms grow in thy garden beds,
Nor slumbrous poppies droop their crimson heads;
And well I know thou comest to me now
To bind thy burning chains upon my brow!"

And though my puny will stood straightly up,
From that day forth I drank her pungent cup,
And ate her bitter bread, — with leaves of rue,
Which in her sunless gardens rankly grew.

And now, so long it is, I scarce can tell
When Pain within my chamber came to dwell;
And though she is not fair of mien or face,
She hath attracted to my humble place

A company most gracious and refined,
Whose touches are like balm, whose voices kind:
Sweet Sympathy, with box of ointment rare;
Courage, who sings while she sits weaving there;

Brave Patience, whom my heart esteemeth much,
And who hath wondrous virtue in her touch.
Such is the chaste and sweet society
Which Pain, my faithful foe, hath brought to me.

And now upon my threshold there she stands,
Reaching to me her rough yet kindly hands
In silent truce. Thus for a time we part,
And a great gladness overflows my heart;

For she is so ungentle in her way
That no host welcomes her or bids her stay;
Yet, though men bolt and bar their house from thee,
To every door, O Pain, thou hast a key!

DEPARTURE

Adieu, kind Life, though thou hast often been
Lavish of quip, and scant of courtesy,
Beneath thy roughness I have found in thee
A host who doth my parting favor win.
Friend, teacher, sage, and sometimes harlequin,
Thine every mood hath held some good for me, —
Nor ever friendlier seemed thy company
Than on this night when I must quit thine inn.
I love thee, Life, in spite of thy rude ways!
Dear is thy pleasant house, so long my home.
I thank thee for the hospitable days,
The friends, the rugged cheer. Then, landlord, come!
Pour me a stirrup cup, — our parting nears;
I ever liked thy wine, though salt with tears.

Henry Abbey

DONALD

O WHITE, white, light moon, that sailest in the sky,
Look down upon the whirling world, for thou art up so high,
And tell me where my Donald is who sailed across the sea,
And make a path of silver light to lead him back to me.

O white, white, bright moon, thy cheek is coldly fair;
A little cloud beside thee seems thy wildly floating hair;
And if thou wouldst not have me wan, and pale, and cold like thee,
Go, make a mighty tide to draw my Donald back to me.

O light, white, bright moon, that dost so fondly shine,
There is not a lily in the world but hides its face from thine:
I too shall go and hide my face close in the dust from thee,
Unless with light and tide thou bring my Donald back to me.

WINTER DAYS

Now comes the graybeard of the north:
The forests bare their rugged breasts
To every wind that wanders forth,
And, in their arms, the lonely nests
That housed the birdlings months ago
Are egged with flakes of drifted snow.

No more the robin pipes his lay
To greet the flushed advance of morn;
He sings in valleys far away;
His heart is with the south to-day;
He cannot shrill among the corn:
For all the hay and corn are down
And garnered; and the withered leaf,
Against the branches bare and brown,
Rattles; and all the days are brief.

An icy hand is on the land;
The cloudy sky is sad and gray;
But through the misty sorrow streams,
Outspreading wide, a golden ray.
And on the brook that cuts the plain
A diamond wonder is aglow,
Fairer than that which, long ago,
De Rohan staked a name to gain.

IN MEMORY OF GENERAL GRANT

WHITE wings of commerce sailing far,
Hot steam that drives the weltering wheel,
Tamed lightning speeding on the wire,
Iron postman on the way of steel, —
These, circling all the world, have told
The loss that makes us desolate;
For we give back to dust this day
The God-sent man who saved the state.

When black the sky and dire with war,
When every heart was wrung with fear,
He rose serene, and took his place,
The great occasion's mighty peer.
He smote armed opposition down,
He bade the storm and darkness cease,
And o'er the long-distracted land
Shone out the smiling sun of peace.

The famous captains of the past
March in review before the mind:
Some fought for glory, some for gold,
But most to yoke and rule mankind.
Not so the captain dead to-day,
For whom our half-mast banners wave:
He fought to keep the Union whole,
And break the shackles of the slave.

A silent man, in friendship true,
He made point-blank his certain aim,
And, born a stranger to defeat,
To steadfast purpose linked his name:
For while the angry flood of war
Surged down between its gloomy banks,
He followed duty, with the mien
Of but a soldier in the ranks.

How well he wore white honor's flower,
The gratitude and praise of men,
As General, as President,
And then as simple citizen!
He was a hero to the end:
The dark rebellion raised by Death

Against the Powers of Life and Light,
He battled hard, with failing breath.

O hero of Fort Donelson,
And wooded Shiloh's frightful strife!
Sleep on! for honor loves the tomb
More than the garish ways of life.
Sleep on! sleep on! Thy wondrous life
Is freedom's most illustrious page;
And fame shall loudly sound thy praise
In every clime, to every age.

FAITH'S VISTA

WHEN from the vaulted wonder of the sky
The curtain of the light is drawn aside,
And I behold the stars in all their wide
Significance and glorious mystery,
Assured that those more distant orbs are suns
Round which innumerable worlds revolve, —
My faith grows strong, my day-born doubts dissolve,
And death, that dread annulment which life shuns,
Or fain would shun, becomes to life the way,
The thoroughfare to greater worlds on high,
The bridge from star to star. Seek how we may,
There is no other road across the sky;
And, looking up, I hear star-voices say:
"You could not reach us if you did not die."

Ambrose Bierce

THE DEATH OF GRANT

FATHER! whose hard and cruel law
Is part of thy compassion's plan,
Thy works presumptuously we scan
For what the prophets say they saw.

Unbidden still, the awful slope
Walling us in, we climb to gain
Assurance of the shining plain
That faith has certified to hope.

In vain: beyond the circling hill
The shadow and the cloud abide;
Subdue the doubt, our spirits guide
To trust the Record and be still;

To trust it loyally as he
Who, heedful of his high design,
Ne'er raised a seeking eye to thine,
But wrought thy will unconsciously,

Disputing not of chance or fate,
Nor questioning of cause or creed:
For anything but duty's deed
Too simply wise, too humbly great.

The cannon syllabled his name;
His shadow shifted o'er the land,
Portentous, as at his command
Successive cities sprang to flame!

He fringed the continent with fire,
The rivers ran in lines of light!
Thy will be done on earth — if right
Or wrong he cared not to inquire.

His was the heavy hand, and his
The service of the despot blade;
His the soft answer that allayed
War's giant animosities.

Let us have peace: our clouded eyes
Fill, Father, with another light,
That we may see with clearer sight
Thy servant's soul in Paradise.

THE BRIDE

"YOU know, my friends, with what a brave carouse
I made a second marriage in my house, —
Divorced old barren Reason from my bed
And took the Daughter of the Vine to spouse."

So sang the Lord of Poets. In a gleam
Of light that made her like an angel seem,
The Daughter of the Vine said: "I myself
Am Reason, and the Other was a Dream."

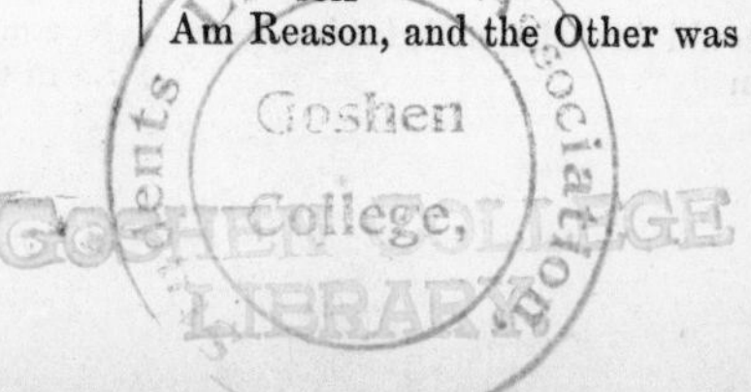

ANOTHER WAY

I LAY in silence, dead. A woman came
And laid a rose upon my breast, and said,
"May God be merciful." She spoke my name,
And added, "It is strange to think him dead.

"He loved me well enough, but 't was his way
To speak it lightly." Then, beneath her breath:
"Besides" — I knew what further she would say,
But then a footfall broke my dream of death.

To-day the words are mine. I lay the rose
Upon her breast, and speak her name, and deem
It strange indeed that she is dead. God knows
I had more pleasure in the other dream.

MONTEFIORE

I SAW — 't was in a dream, the other night —
A man whose hair with age was thin and white;
One hundred years had bettered by his birth,
And still his step was firm, his eye was bright.

Before him and about him pressed a crowd.
Each head in reverence was bared and bowed,
And Jews and Gentiles in a hundred tongues
Extolled his deeds and spake his fame aloud.

I joined the throng and, pushing forward, cried,
"Montefiore!" with the rest, and vied
In efforts to caress the hand that ne'er
To want and worth had charity denied.

So closely round him swarmed our shouting clan
He scarce could breathe, and, taking from a pan
A gleaming coin, he tossed it o'er ou heads,
And in a moment was a lonely man!

PRESENTIMENT

WITH saintly grace and reverent tread
She walked among the graves with me;
Her every footfall seemed to be
A benediction on the dead.

The guardian spirit of the place
She seemed, and I some ghost forlorn,
Surprised by the untimely morn
She made with her resplendent face.

Moved by some waywardness of will,
Three paces from the path apart
She stepped and stood — my prescient heart
Was stricken with a passing chill.

My child-lore of the years agone
Remembering, I smiled and thought,
"Who shudders suddenly at naught,
His grave is being trod upon."

But now I know that it was more
Than idle fancy. O, my sweet,
I did not know such little feet
Could make a buried heart so sore!

CREATION

GOD dreamed — the suns sprang flaming into place,
And sailing worlds with many a venturous race.
He woke — His smile alone illumined space.

T. A. H.

YES, he was that, or that, as you prefer, —
Did so and so, though, faith, it was n't all;
Lived like a fool, or a philosopher,
And had whatever 's needful to a fall.
As rough inflections on a planet merge
In the true bend of the gigantic sphere,
Nor mar the perfect circle of its verge,
So in the survey of his worth the small

Asperities of spirit disappear,
Lost in the grander curves of character.
He lately was hit hard; none knew but I
The strength and terror of that ghastly stroke, —
Not even herself. He uttered not a cry,
But set his teeth and made a revelry;
Drank like a devil, — staining sometimes red
The goblet's edge; diced with his conscience; spread,
Like Sisyphus, a feast for Death, and spoke
His welcome in a tongue so long forgot
That even his ancient guest remembered not
What race had cursed him in it. Thus my friend,
Still conjugating with each failing sense
The verb "to die" in every mood and tense,
Pursued his awful humor to the end.
When, like a stormy dawn, the crim broke
From his white lips, he smiled and mutely bled,
And, having meanly lived, is grandly dead.

Charles Warren Stoddard

THE ROYAL MUMMY TO BOHEMIA[1]

Wherefore these revels that my dull eyes greet?
These dancers, dancing at my fleshless feet;
The harpers, harping vainly at my ears
Deaf to the world, lo, thrice a thousand years!

Time was when even I was blithe: I knew
The murmur of the flowing wave, where grew
The lean, lithe rushes; I have heard the moan
Of Nilus in prophetic undertone.

My sire was monarch of a mighty race:
Daughter of Pharaoh, I! before my face
Myriads of groveling creatures crawled, to thrust
Their fearful foreheads in the desert dust.

Above me gleamed and glowed my palace walls:
There bloomed my bowers; and there, my waterfalls
Lulled me in languors; slaves with feather flails
Fretted the tranquil air to gentle gales.

O, my proud palms! my royal palms that stood
In stately groups, a queenly sisterhood!
And O, my sphinxes, gazing eye in eye,
Down the dim vistas of eternity!

Where be ye now? And where am I at last?
With gay Bohemia is my portion cast:
Born of the oldest East, I seek my rest
In the fair city of the youngest West.

Farewell, O Egypt! Naught can thee avail:
What tarries now to tell thy sorry tale?
A sunken temple that the sands have hid
The tapering shadow of a pyramid!

And now, my children, harbor me not ill:
I was a princess, am a woman still.
Gibe me no gibes, but greet me at your best,
As I was wont to greet the stranger guest.

Feast well, drink well, make merry while ye may,
For e'en the best of you must pass my way.
The elder as the youngster, fair to see,
Must gird his marble loins and follow me.

Bohemian Club, San Francisco.

WIND AND WAVE

O, when I hear at sea
The water on our lee,
I fancy that I hear the wind
That combs my hemlock tree:

But when beneath that tree
I listen eagerly,

[1] See Biographical Note, p. 823.

I seem to hear the rushing wave
I heard far out at sea.

ALBATROSS

TIME cannot age thy sinews, nor the gale
Batter the network of thy feathered mail,
Lone sentry of the deep!
Among the crashing caverns of the storm,
With wing unfettered, lo! thy frigid form
Is whirled in dreamless sleep!

Where shall thy wing find rest for all its might?
Where shall thy lidless eye, that scours the night,
Grow blank in utter death?
When shall thy thousand years have stripped thee bare,
Invulnerable spirit of the air,
And sealed thy giant-breath?

Not till thy bosom hugs the icy wave, —
Not till thy palsied limbs sink in that grave,
Caught by the shrieking blast,
And hurled upon the sea with broad wings locked,
On an eternity of waters rocked,
Defiant to the last!

THE COCOA-TREE

CAST on the water by a careless hand,
Day after day the winds persuaded me:
Onward I drifted till a coral tree
Stayed me among its branches, where the sand
Gathered about me, and I slowly grew,
Fed by the constant sun and the inconstant dew.

The sea-birds build their nests against my root,
And eye my slender body's horny case.
Widowed within this solitary place
Into the thankless sea I cast my fruit;
Joyless I thrive, for no man may partake
Of all the store I bear and harvest for his sake.

No more I heed the kisses of the morn;
The harsh winds rob me of the life they gave;
I watch my tattered shadow in the wave,
And hourly droop and nod my crest forlorn,
While all my fibres stiffen and grow numb
Beckoning the tardy ships, the ships that never come!

Francis Fisher Browne

VANQUISHED

I

NOT by the ball or brand
Sped by a mortal hand,
Not by the lightning stroke
When fiery tempests broke, —
Not mid the ranks of War
Fell the great Conqueror.

II

Unmovëd, undismayed,
In the crash and carnage of the cannonade, —
Eye that dimmed not, hand that failed not,
Brain that swerved not, heart that quailed not,
Steel nerve, iron form, —
The dauntless spirit that o'erruled the storm.

III

While the Hero peaceful slept
A foeman to his chamber crept,
Lightly to the slumberer came,
Touched his brow and breathed his name:
O'er the stricken form there passed
Suddenly an icy blast.

IV

The Hero woke, rose undismayed,
Saluted Death, and sheathed his blade.

V

The Conqueror of a hundred fields
To a mightier Conqueror yields;

No mortal foeman's blow
Laid the great Soldier low:
Victor in his latest breath —
Vanquished but by Death.

UNDER THE BLUE

THE skies are low, the winds are slow,
The woods are filled with autumn glory;
The mists are still on field and hill,
The brooklet sings its dreamy story.

I careless rove through glen and grove;
I dream by hill and copse and river;
Or in the shade by aspen made
I watch the restless shadows quiver.

I lift my eyes to azure skies
That shed their tinted glory o'er me;
While memories sweet around me fleet,
As radiant as the scene before me.

For while I muse upon the hues
Of autumn skies in splendor given,
Sweet thoughts arise of rare deep eyes
Whose blue is like the blue of heaven.

Bend low, fair skies! Smile sweet, fair eyes!
From radiant skies rich hues are streaming;
But in the blue of pure eyes true
The radiance of my life is beaming.

O skies of blue! ye fade from view;
Faint grow the hues that o'er me quiver;
But the sure light of sweet eyes bright
Shines on forever and forever.

SANTA BARBARA

BETWEEN the mountains and the sea,
Walled by the rock, fringed by the foam,
A valley stretches fair and free
Beneath the blue of heaven's dome.

At rest in that fair valley lies
Saint Barbara, the beauteous maid;
Above her head the cloudless skies
Smile down upon her charms displayed.

The sunlit mountains o'er her shed
The splendor of their purple tinge;
While round her like a mantle spread
The blue seas with their silver fringe.

Enfolded in that soothing calm,
The earth seems sweet, and heaven near;
The flowers bloom free, the air is balm,
And summer rules the radiant year.

Mary Ainge De Vere

("MADELINE BRIDGES")

THE WIND-SWEPT WHEAT

FAINT, faint and clear,
Faint as the music that in dreams we hear
Shaking the curtain-fold of sleep,
That shuts away
The world's hoarse voice, the sights and sounds of day,
Her sorry joys, her phantoms false and fleet, —
So softly, softly stirs
The wind's low murmur in the rippled wheat.

From west to east
The warm breath blows, the slender heads droop low
As if in prayer;
Again, more lightly tossed in merry play,
They bend and bow and sway
With measured beat,
But never rest, — through shadow and through sun
Goes on the tender rustle of the wheat.

Dreams more than sleep
Fall on the listening heart and lull its care;
Dead years send back
Some treasured, unforgotten tune.
Ah, long ago,
When sun and sky were sweet,
In happy noon,

We stood breast-high, mid waves of ripened grain,
And heard the wind make music in the wheat.

Not for to-day —
Not for this hour alone — the melody
So soft and ceaseless thrills the dreamer's ear:
Of all that was and is, of all that yet shall be,
It holds a part.
Love, sorrow, longing, pain,
The restlessness that yearns,
The thirst that burns,
The bliss that like a fountain overflows,
The deep repose,
Good that we might have known, but shall not know,
The hope God took, the joy He made complete, —
Life's chords all answer from the wind-swept wheat!

A FAREWELL

I PUT thy hand aside, and turn away:
Why should I blame the slight and fickle heart
That cannot bravely go, nor boldly stay,
Too weak to cling, and yet too fond to part?
Dead Passion chains thee where her ashes lie.
Cold is the shrine, ah, cold for evermore!
Why linger, then, while golden moments fly
And sunshine waits beyond the open door?
Nay — fare thee well, for memory and I
Must tarry here and wait. . . . We have no choice
Nor other better joy, until we die,
Only to wait, and hear nor step nor voice,
Nor any happy advent come to break
The watch we keep alone — for Love's dear sake!

FAITH TREMBLING

WERE I a happy bird,
Building my little nest each early spring,
It might be easy then to keep God's word,
His praise to sing;
Easy to live content,
Tending my little ones, — of love secure,
Knowing no agony for time misspent,
Or thought impure!

Were I a butterfly,
A bright-winged creature of the sunshine born,
Idle and lovely I could live and die
Without self-scorn;
I need not fear
To take my utmost will of summer sweet;
Nor dread, when the swift end came near,
My Judge to meet!

If I were only made
Patient, and calm, and pure, as angels are,
I had not been so doubtful, — sore afraid
Of sin and care;
It would seem sweet and good
To bear the heavy cross that martyrs take,
The passion and the pain of womanhood
For my Lord's sake.

But strong, and fair, and young,
I dread my glowing limbs, — my heart of fire,
My soul that trembles like a harp full strung
To keen desire!
O, wild and idle words!
Will God's large charity and patience be
Given unto butterflies and singing birds,
And not to me?

THE SPINNER

THE spinner twisted her slender thread
As she sat and spun:
"The earth and the heavens are mine," she said,
"And the moon and sun;
Into my web the sunlight goes,
And the breath of May,
And the crimson life of the new-blown rose
That was born to-day."

The spinner sang in the hush of noon
And her song was low:
" Ah, morning, you pass away too soon,
You are swift to go.
My heart o'erflows like a brimming cup
With its hopes and fears.
Love, come and drink the sweetness up
Ere it turn to tears."

The spinner looked at the falling sun:
" Is it time to rest ?
My hands are weary, — my work is done,
I have wrought my best;
I have spun and woven with patient eyes
And with fingers fleet.
Lo ! where the toil of a lifetime lies
In a winding-sheet ! "

WHEN THE MOST IS SAID

What 's love, when the most is said ?
The flash of the lightning fleet,
Then, darkness that shrouds the soul, — but the earth is firm to my feet;
The rocks and the tides endure, the grasses and herbs return,
The path to my foot is sure, and the sods to my bosom yearn.

What 's fame, when the truth is told ? A shout to a distant hill,
The craigs may echo a while, but fainter, and fainter still;
Yet forever the wind blows wide the sweetness of all the skies,
The rain cries and the snow flies, and the storm in its bosom lies.

What 's life, what 's life, little heart ? A dream when the nights are long,
Toil in the waking days, — tears, and a kiss, a song.
What 's life, what 's life, little heart ? To beat and be glad of breath
While death waits on either side, — before and behind us, Death !

POET AND LARK

When leaves turn outward to the light,
And all the roads are fringed with green,
When larks are pouring, high, unseen,
The joy they find in song and flight,
Then I, too, with the lark would wing
My little flight, and, soaring, sing.

When larks drop downward to the nest,
And day drops downward to the sea,
And song and wing are fain to rest,
The lark's dear wisdom guideth me,
And I too turn within my door,
Content to dream, and sing no more.

A BREATH

A breath can fan love's flame to burning, —
Make firm resolve of trembling doubt.
But, strange ! at fickle fancy's turning,
The selfsame breath can blow it out.

FRIEND AND LOVER

When Psyche's friend becomes her lover,
How sweetly these conditions blend !
But, oh, what anguish to discover
Her lover has become — her friend !

GOD KEEP YOU

God keep you, dearest, all this lonely night:
The winds are still,
The moon drops down behind the western hill;
God keep you safely, dearest, till the light.

God keep you then when slumber melts away,
And care and strife
Take up new arms to fret our waking life,
God keep you through the battle of the day.

God keep you. Nay, beloved soul, how vain,
How poor is prayer !
I can but say again, and yet again,
God keep you every time and everywhere.

Additional Selections

(VARIOUS POEMS BELONGING TO THIS DIVISION)

I

THE THANKSGIVING IN BOSTON HARBOR

"PRAISE ye the Lord!" The psalm to-day
Still rises on our ears,
Borne from the hills of Boston Bay
Through five times fifty years,
When Winthrop's fleet from Yarmouth crept
Out to the open main,
And through the widening waters swept,
In April sun and rain.
"Pray to the Lord with fervent lips,"
The leader shouted, "pray;"
And prayer arose from all the ships
As faded Yarmouth Bay.

They passed the Scilly Isles that day,
And May-days came, and June,
And thrice upon the ocean lay
The full orb of the moon.
And as that day, on Yarmouth Bay,
Ere England sunk from view,
While yet the rippling Solent lay
In April skies of blue,
"Pray to the Lord with fervent lips,"
Each morn was shouted, "pray;"
And prayer arose from all the ships,
As first in Yarmouth Bay;

Blew warm the breeze o'er Western seas,
Through Maytime morns, and June,
Till hailed these souls the Isles of Shoals,
Low 'neath the summer moon;
And as Cape Ann arose to view,
And Norman's Woe they passed,
The wood-doves came the white mists through,
And circled round each mast.
"Pray to the Lord with fervent lips,"
Then called the leader, "pray;"
And prayer arose from all the ships,
As first in Yarmouth Bay.

Above the sea the hill-tops fair —
God's towers — began to rise,
And odors rare breathe through the air,
Like balms of Paradise.

Through burning skies the ospreys flew,
And near the pine-cooled shores
Danced airy boat and thin canoe,
To flash of sunlit oars.
"Pray to the Lord with fervent lips,"
The leader shouted, "pray!"
Then prayer arose, and all the ships
Sailed into Boston Bay.

The white wings folded, anchors down,
The sea-worn fleet in line,
Fair rose the hills where Boston town
Should rise from clouds of pine;
Fair was the harbor, summit-walled,
And placid lay the sea.
"Praise ye the Lord," the leader called;
"Praise ye the Lord," spake he.
"Give thanks to God with fervent lips,
Give thanks to God to-day,"
The anthem rose from all the ships,
Safe moored in Boston Bay.

"Praise ye the Lord!" Primeval woods
First heard the ancient song,
And summer hills and solitudes
The echoes rolled along.
The Red Cross flag of England blew
Above the fleet that day,
While Shawmut's triple peaks in view
In amber hazes lay.
"Praise ye the Lord with fervent lips.
Praise ye the Lord to-day,"
The anthem rose from all the ships
Safe moored in Boston Bay.

The Arabella leads the song —
The Mayflower sings below,
That erst the Pilgrims bore along
The Plymouth reefs of snow.
Oh! never be that psalm forgot
That rose o'er Boston Bay,
When Winthrop sang, and Endicott,
And Saltonstall, that day:
"Praise ye the Lord with fervent lips,
Praise ye the Lord to-day;"
And praise arose from all the ships,
Like prayers in Yarmouth Bay.

That psalm our fathers sang we sing,
That psalm of peace and wars,
While o'er our heads unfolds its wing
The flag of forty stars.
And while the nation finds a tongue
For nobler gifts to pray,
'T will ever sing the song they sung
That first Thanksgiving Day:
"Praise ye the Lord with fervent lips,
Praise ye the Lord to-day;"
So rose the song from all the ships,
Safe moored in Boston Bay.

Our fathers' prayers have changed to psalms,
As David's treasures old
Turned, on the Temple's giant arms,
To lily-work of gold.
Ho! vanished ships from Yarmouth's tide,
Ho! ships of Boston Bay,
Your prayers have crossed the centuries wide
To this Thanksgiving Day!
We pray to God with fervent lips,
We praise the Lord to-day,
As prayers arose from Yarmouth ships,
But psalms from Boston Bay.

HEZEKIAH BUTTERWORTH

CARMEN BELLICOSUM

IN their ragged regimentals,
Stood the old Continentals,
Yielding not,
While the grenadiers were lunging,
And like hail fell the plunging
Cannon-shot;
When the files
Of the isles,
From the smoky night-encampment, bore the banner of the rampant
Unicorn;
And grummer, grummer, grummer, rolled the roll of the drummer
Through the morn!

Then with eyes to the front all,
And with guns horizontal,
Stood our sires;
While the balls whistled deadly,
And in streams flashing redly
Blazed the fires:
As the roar
On the shore
Swept the strong battle-breakers o'er the green-sodded acres
Of the plain;
And louder, louder, louder, cracked the black gunpowder,
Cracking amain!

Now like smiths at their forges
Worked the red St. George's
Cannoneers,
And the villainous saltpetre
Rang a fierce, discordant metre
Round our ears:
As the swift
Storm-drift,
With hot sweeping anger, came the horse-guards' clangor
On our flanks.
Then higher, higher, higher, burned the old-fashioned fire
Through the ranks!

Then the bare-headed Colonel
Galloped through the white infernal
Powder-cloud;
And his broadsword was swinging,
And his brazen throat was ringing
Trumpet-loud;
Then the blue
Bullets flew,
And the trooper-jackets redden at the touch of the leaden
Rifle-breath;
And rounder, rounder, rounder, roared the iron six-pounder,
Hurling death!

GUY HUMPHREYS MCMASTER[1]

AT MARSHFIELD

FROM "WEBSTER: AN ODE"

HIS way in farming all men knew;
Way wide, forecasting, free,
A liberal tilth that made the tiller poor.
That huge Websterian plough what furrows drew
Through fallows fattened from the barren sea!
Yoked to that plough and matched for mighty size,
What oxen moved! — in progress equal, sure,
Unconscious of resistance, as of force

[1] See BIOGRAPHICAL NOTE, p. 809.

Not finite, elemental, like his own,
Taking its way with unimpeded course.
He loved to look into their meek brown eyes,
That with a light of love half human shone
Calmly on him from out the ample front,
While, with a kind of mutual, wise,
Mute recognition of some kin,
Superior to surprise,
And schooled by immemorial wont,
They seemed to say, We let him in,
He is of us, he is, by natural dower,
One in our brotherhood of great and peaceful power.

So, when he came to die
At Marshfield by the sea,
And now the end is nigh,
Up from the pleasant lea
Move his dumb friends in solemn, slow,
Funereal procession, and before
Their master's door
In melancholy file compassionately go;
He will be glad to see his trusty friends once more.
Now let him look a look that shall suffice,
Lo, let the dying man
Take all the peace he can
From those large tranquil brows and deep soft eyes.
Rest it will be to him,
Before his eyes grow dim,
To bathe his aged eyes in one deep gaze
Commingled with old days,
On faces of such friends sincere,
With fondness brought from boyhood, dear.

Farewell, a long look and the last,
And these have turned and passed.
Henceforth he will no more,
As was his wont before,
Step forth from yonder door
To taste the freshness of the early dawn,
The whiteness of the sky,
The whitening stars on high,
The dews yet white that lie
Far spread in pearl upon the glimmering lawn;
Never at evening go,
Sole pacing to and fro,
With musing step and slow,
Beneath the cope of heaven set thick with stars,
Considering by whose hand
Those works, in wisdom planned,
Were fashioned, and still stand
Serenely fast and fair above these earthly jars.
Never again. Forth he will soon be brought
By neighbors that have loved him, having known,
Plain farmers, with the farmer's natural thought
And feeling, sympathetic to his own.
All in a temperate air, a golden light,
Rich with October, sad with afternoon,
Fitly let him be laid, with rustic rite,
To rest amid the ripened harvest boon.
He loved the ocean's mighty murmur deep,
And this shall lull him through his dreamless sleep.
But those plain men will speak above his head,
This is a lonesome world, and WEBSTER dead!

WILLIAM CLEAVER WILKINSON

THE COWBOY

"WHAT care I, what cares he,
What cares the world of the life we know?
Little they reck of the shadowless plains,
The shelterless mesa, the sun and the rains,
The wild, free life, as the winds that blow."
With his broad sombrero,
His worn chapparejos,
And clinking spurs,
Like a Centaur he speeds,
Where the wild bull feeds;
And he laughs, ha, ha! — who cares, who cares!

Ruddy and brown — careless and free —
A king in the saddle — he rides at will
O'er the measureless range where rarely change
The swart gray plains so weird and strange,
Treeless, and streamless, and wondrous still!
With his slouch sombrero,
His torn chapparejos,
And clinking spurs,
Like a Centaur he speeds
Where the wild bull feeds;
And he laughs, ha, ha! — who cares, who cares!

He of the towns, he of the East,
Has only a vague, dull thought of him;
In his far-off dreams the cowboy seems
A mythical thing, a thing he deems
A Hun or a Goth as swart and grim!
With his stained sombrero,
His rough chapparejos,
And clinking spurs,
Like a Centaur he speeds,
Where the wild bull feeds;
And he laughs, ha, ha! — who cares, who cares!

Often alone, his saddle a throne,
He scans like a sheik the numberless herd;
Where the buffalo-grass and the sage-grass dry
In the hot white glare of a cloudless sky,
And the music of streams is never heard.
With his gay sombrero,
His brown chapparejos,
And clinking spurs,
Like a Centaur he speeds,
Where the wild bull feeds;
And he laughs, ha, ha! — who cares, who cares!

Swift and strong, and ever alert,
Yet sometimes he rests on the dreary vast;
And his thoughts, like the thoughts of other men,
Go back to his childhood days again,
And to many a loved one in the past.
With his gay sombrero,
His rude chapparejos,
And clinking spurs,
He rests awhile,
With a tear and a smile,
Then he laughs, ha, ha! — who cares, who cares!

Sometimes his mood from solitude
Hurries him, heedless, off to the town!
Where mirth and wine through the goblet shine,
And treacherous sirens twist and twine
The lasso that often brings him down;
With his soaked sombrero,
His rent chapparejos,
And clinking spurs,
He staggers back
On the homeward track,
And shouts to the plains — who cares, who cares!

On his broncho's back he sways and swings,
Yet mad and wild with the city's fume;
His pace is the pace of the song he sings,
And the ribald oath that maudlin clings
Like the wicked stench of the harlot's room.
With his ragged sombrero,
His torn chapparejos,
His rowel-less spurs,
He dashes amain
Through the trackless rain;
Reeling and reckless — who cares, who cares!

'T is over late at the ranchman's gate —
He and his fellows, perhaps a score,
Halt in a quarrel o'er night begun,
With a ready blow and a random gun —
There 's a dead, dead comrade! nothing more.
With his slouched sombrero,
His dark chapparejos,
And clinking spurs,
He dashes past,
With face o'ercast,
And growls in his throat — who cares, who cares!

Away on the range there is little change;
He blinks in the sun, he herds the steers;
But a trail on the wind keeps close behind,
And whispers that stagger and blanch the mind
Through the hum of the solemn noon he hears.
With his dark sombrero,
His stained chapparejos,
His clinking spurs,
He sidles down
Where the grasses brown
May hide his face, while he sobs — who cares!

But what care I, and what cares he —
This is the strain, common at least;
He is free and vain of his bridle-rein,
Of his spurs, of his gun, of the dull, gray plain;
He is ever vain of his broncho beast!
With his gray sombrero,
His brown chapparejos,
And clinking spurs,
Like a Centaur he speeds,
Where the wild bull feeds;
And he laughs, ha, ha! — who cares! who cares!

JOHN ANTROBUS

II

ALL QUIET ALONG THE POTOMAC

"All quiet along the Potomac," they say,
"Except now and then a stray picket
Is shot, as he walks on his beat to and fro,
By a rifleman hid in the thicket.
'T is nothing — a private or two now and then
Will not count in the news of the battle;
Not an officer lost — only one of the men,
Moaning out, all alone, the death-rattle."

All quiet along the Potomac to-night,
Where the soldiers lie peacefully dreaming;
Their tents in the rays of the clear autumn moon,
Or the light of the watch-fire, are gleaming.
A tremulous sigh of the gentle night-wind
Through the forest leaves softly is creeping;
While stars up above, with their glittering eyes,
Keep guard, for the army is sleeping.

There 's only the sound of the lone sentry's tread,
As he tramps from the rock to the fountain,
And thinks of the two in the low trundle-bed
Far away in the cot on the mountain.
His musket falls slack; his face, dark and grim,
Grows gentle with memories tender,
As he mutters a prayer for the children asleep,
For their mother; may Heaven defend her!

The moon seems to shine just as brightly as then,
That night, when the love yet unspoken
Leaped up to his lips — when low-murmured vows
Were pledged to be ever unbroken.
Then drawing his sleeve roughly over his eyes,
He dashes off tears that are welling,
And gathers his gun closer up to its place,
As if to keep down the heart-swelling.

He passes the fountain, the blasted pine-tree,
The footstep is lagging and weary;
Yet onward he goes, through the broad belt of light,
Toward the shade of the forest so dreary.
Hark! was it the night-wind that rustled the leaves?
Was it moonlight so wondrously flashing?
It looked like a rifle . . . "Ha! Mary, good-bye!"
The red life-blood is ebbing and plashing.

All quiet along the Potomac to-night;
No sound save the rush of the river;
While soft falls the dew on the face of the dead —
The picket 's off duty forever!

Ethel Lynn Beers

SAMBO'S RIGHT TO BE KILT

Some tell us 't is a burnin' shame
To make the naygers fight;
An' that the thrade of bein' kilt
Belongs but to the white:
But as for me, upon my sowl!
So liberal are we here,
I'll let Sambo be murthered instead of myself,
On every day in the year.
On every day in the year, boys,
And in every hour of the day;
The right to be kilt I'll divide wid him,
An' divil a word I'll say.

In battle's wild commotion
I should n't at all object
If Sambo's body should stop a ball
That was comin' for me direct;
And the prod of a Southern bagnet,
So ginerous are we here,
I'll resign, and let Sambo take it
On every day in the year.
On every day in the year, boys,
And wid none o' your nasty pride,
All my right in a Southern bagnet prod
Wid Sambo I'll divide!

The men who object to Sambo
Should take his place and fight;
And it 's betther to have a nayger's hue
Than a liver that 's wake an' white.
Though Sambo 's black as the ace of spades,
His finger a thrigger can pull,
And his eye runs sthraight on the barrel-sights
From undher its thatch of wool.
So hear me all, boys darlin',
Don't think I 'm tippin' you chaff,
The right to be kilt we 'll divide wid him,
And give him the largest half!

CHARLES GRAHAM HALPINE

THE BAND IN THE PINES

(AFTER PELHAM DIED)

Oh, band in the pine-wood, cease!
Cease with your splendid call;
The living are brave and noble,
But the dead are bravest of all!

They throng to the martial summons,
To the loud triumphant strain,
And the dear bright eyes of long-dead friends
Come to the heart again!

They come with the ringing bugle,
And the deep drums' mellow roar;
Till the soul is faint with longing
For the hands we clasp no more!

Oh, band in the pine-wood, cease!
Or the heart will melt with tears,
For the gallant eyes and the smiling lips,
And the voices of old years.

JOHN ESTEN COOKE

THE VOLUNTEER

"At dawn," he said, "I bid them all farewell,
To go where bugles call and rifles gleam."
And with the restless thought asleep he fell,
And glided into dream.

A great hot plain from sea to mountain spread, —
Through it a level river slowly drawn:
He moved with a vast crowd, and at its head
Streamed banners like the dawn.

There came a blinding flash, a deafening roar,
And dissonant cries of triumph and dismay;
Blood trickled down the river's reedy shore,
And with the dead he lay.

The morn broke in upon his solemn dream,
And still, with steady pulse and deepening eye,
"Where bugles call," he said, "and rifles gleam,
I follow, though I die!"

ELBRIDGE JEFFERSON CUTLER

STONEWALL JACKSON

Not midst the lightning of the stormy fight,
Nor in the rush upon the vandal foe,
Did kingly Death, with his resistless might,
Lay the great leader low.

His warrior soul its earthly shackles broke
In the full sunshine of a peaceful town;
When all the storm was hushed, the trusty oak
That propped our cause went down.

Though his alone the blood that flecks the ground,
Recalling all his grand heroic deeds,
Freedom herself is writhing in the wound,
And all the country bleeds.

He entered not the nation's Promised Land
At the red belching of the cannon's mouth,
But broke the House of Bondage with his hand —
The Moses of the South!

O gracious God! not gainless is the loss:
A glorious sunbeam gilds thy sternest frown;
And while his country staggers 'neath the Cross,
He rises with the Crown!

HENRY LYNDEN FLASH

ROLL-CALL

"Corporal Green!" the Orderly cried;
"Here!" was the answer loud and clear,
From the lips of a soldier who stood near, —
And "Here!" was the word the next replied.

"Cyrus Drew!" — then a silence fell;
This time no answer followed the call;
Only his rear-man had seen him fall:
Killed or wounded — he could not tell.

There they stood in the failing light,
These men of battle, with grave, dark looks,
As plain to be read as open books,
While slowly gathered the shades of night.

The fern on the hillsides was splashed with blood,
And down in the corn, where the poppies grew,
Were redder stains than the poppies knew,
And crimson-dyed was the river's flood.

For the foe had crossed from the other side,
That day, in the face of a murderous fire
That swept them down in its terrible ire;
And their life-blood went to color the tide.

"Herbert Cline!" — At the call there came
Two stalwart soldiers into the line,
Bearing between them this Herbert Cline,
Wounded and bleeding, to answer his name.

"Ezra Kerr!" — and a voice answered "Here!"
"Hiram Kerr!" — but no man replied.
They were brothers, these two; the sad wind sighed,
And a shudder crept through the cornfield near.

"Ephraim Deane!" — then a soldier spoke:
"Deane carried our regiment's colors," he said,
"When our ensign was shot; I left him dead
Just after the enemy wavered and broke.

"Close to the roadside his body lies;
I paused a moment and gave him to drink;
He murmured his mother's name, I think,
And Death came with it and closed his eyes."

'T was a victory, — yes; but it cost us dear:
For that company's roll, when called at night,
Of a hundred men who went into the fight,
Numbered but twenty that answered "*Here!*"

Nathaniel Graham Shepherd

"PICCIOLA"

It was a Sergeant old and gray,
Well singed and bronzed from siege and pillage,
Went tramping in an army's wake
Along the turnpike of the village.

For days and nights the winding host
Had through the little place been marching,
And ever loud the rustics cheered,
Till every throat was hoarse and parching.

The Squire and Farmer, maid and dame,
All took the sight's electric stirring,
And hats were waved and staves were sung,
And kerchiefs white were countless whirring.

They only saw a gallant show
Of heroes stalwart under banners,
And, in the fierce heroic glow,
'T was theirs to yield but wild hosannas.

The Sergeant heard the shrill hurrahs,
Where he behind in step was keeping;
But glancing down beside the road
He saw a little maid sit weeping.

"And how is this?" he gruffly said,
A moment pausing to regard her; —
"Why weepest thou, my little chit?"
And then she only cried the harder.

"And how is this, my little chit?"
The sturdy trooper straight repeated,

"When all the village cheers us on,
That you, in tears, apart are seated?

"We march two hundred thousand strong,
And that 's a sight, my baby beauty,
To quicken silence into song
And glorify the soldier's duty."

"It 's very, very grand, I know,"
The little maid gave soft replying;
"And Father, Mother, Brother too,
All say 'Hurrah' while I am crying;

"But think — O Mr. Soldier, think, —
How many little sisters' brothers
Are going all away to fight
And may be *killed*, as well as others!"

"Why, bless thee, child," the Sergeant said,
His brawny hand her curls caressing,
"'T is left for little ones like thee
To find that War 's not all a blessing."

And "Bless thee!" once again he cried;
Then cleared his throat and looked indignant,
And marched away with wrinkled brow
To stop the struggling tear benignant.

And still the ringing shouts went up
From doorway, thatch, and fields of tillage;
The pall behind the standard seen
By one alone of all the village.

The oak and cedar bend and writhe
When roars the wind through gap and braken;
But 't is the tenderest reed of all
That trembles first when Earth is shaken.

ROBERT HENRY NEWELL

REVEILLE

THE morning is cheery, my boys, arouse!
The dew shines bright on the chestnut boughs,
And the sleepy mist on the river lies,
Though the east is flushing with crimson dyes.
Awake! awake! awake!
O'er field and wood and brake,
With glories newly born,
Comes on the blushing morn.
Awake! awake!

You have dreamed of your homes and friends all night;
You have basked in your sweethearts' smiles so bright;
Come, part with them all for a while again, —
Be lovers in dreams; when awake, be men.
Turn out! turn out! turn out!
You have dreamed full long, I know.
Turn out! turn out! turn out!
The east is all aglow.
Turn out! turn out!

From every valley and hill there come
The clamoring voices of fife and drum;
And out in the fresh, cool morning air
The soldiers are swarming everywhere.
Fall in! fall in! fall in!
Every man in his place,
Fall in! fall in! fall in!
Each with a cheerful face,
Fall in! fall in!

MICHAEL O'CONNOR

FARRAGUT

MOBILE BAY, 5 AUGUST, 1864

FARRAGUT, Farragut,
Old Heart of Oak,
Daring Dave Farragut,
Thunderbolt stroke,
Watches the hoary mist
Lift from the bay,
Till his flag, glory-kissed,
Greets the young day.

Far, by gray Morgan's walls,
Looms the black fleet.
Hark, deck to rampart calls
With the drums' beat!
Buoy your chains overboard,
While the steam hums;
Men! to the battlement,
Farragut comes.

See, as the hurricane
Hurtles in wrath
Squadrons of clouds amain
Back from its path!
Back to the parapet,
To the guns' lips,
Thunderbolt Farragut
Hurls the black ships.

Now through the battle's roar
Clear the boy sings,
"By the mark fathoms four,"
While his lead swings.
Steady the wheelmen five
"Nor' by East keep her,"
"Steady," but two alive:
How the shells sweep her!

Lashed to the mast that sways
Over red decks,
Over the flame that plays
Round the torn wrecks,
Over the dying lips
Framed for a cheer,
Farragut leads his ships,
Guides the line clear.

On by heights cannon-browed,
While the spars quiver;
Onward still flames the cloud
Where the hulks shiver.
See, yon fort's star is set,
Storm and fire past.
Cheer him, lads — Farragut,
Lashed to the mast!

Oh! while Atlantic's breast
Bears a white sail,
While the Gulf's towering crest
Tops a green vale,
Men thy bold deeds shall tell,
Old Heart of Oak,
Daring Dave Farragut,
Thunderbolt stroke!

William Tuckey Meredith

DRIVING HOME THE COWS

Out of the clover and blue-eyed grass
He turned them into the river-lane;
One after another he let them pass,
Then fastened the meadow-bars again.

Under the willows, and over the hill,
He patiently followed their sober pace;
The merry whistle for once was still,
And something shadowed the sunny face.

Only a boy! and his father had said
He never could let his youngest go:
Two already were lying dead
Under the feet of the trampling foe.

But after the evening work was done,
And the frogs were loud in the meadow-swamp,
Over his shoulder he slung his gun
And stealthily followed the foot-path damp.

Across the clover, and through the wheat,
With resolute heart and purpose grim,
Though cold was the dew on his hurrying feet
And the blind bat's flitting startled him.

Thrice since then had the lanes been white,
And the orchards sweet with apple-bloom;
And now, when the cows came back at night,
The feeble father drove them home.

For news had come to the lonely farm
That three were lying where two had lain;
And the old man's tremulous, palsied arm
Could never lean on a son's again.

The summer day grew cool and late.
He went for the cows when the work was done;
But down the lane, as he opened the gate,
He saw them coming one by one:

Brindle, Ebony, Speckle, and Bess,
Shaking their horns in the evening wind;
Cropping the buttercups out of the grass —
But who was it following close behind?

Loosely swung in the idle air
The empty sleeve of army blue;
And worn and pale, from the crisping hair,
Looked out a face that the father knew.

For Southern prisons will sometimes yawn,
And yield their dead unto life again;
And the day that comes with a cloudy dawn
In golden glory at last may wane.

The great tears sprang to their meeting eyes;
For the heart must speak when the lips are dumb:
And under the silent evening skies
Together they followed the cattle home.

Kate Putnam Osgood

III

NEGRO SPIRITUALS[1]

IN DAT GREAT GITTIN'-UP MORNIN'

I 'M a gwine to tell you bout de comin' ob
de Saviour, —
Fare you well, Fare you well,
Dere 's a better day a-comin',
When my Lord speaks to his Fader,
Says, Fader, I 'm tired o' bearin',
Tired o' bearin' for poor sinners:
O preachers, fold your Bibles;
Prayer-makers, pray no more,
For de last soul 's converted.
In dat great gittin'-up Mornin',
Fare you well, Fare you well.

De Lord spoke to Gabriel:
Say, go look behind de altar,
Take down de silver trumpet,
Go down to de sea-side,
Place one foot on de dry land,
Place de oder on de sea,
Raise your hand to heaven,
Declare by your Maker,
Dat time shall be no longer,
In dat great gittin'-up Mornin', etc.

Blow your trumpet, Gabriel.
Lord, how loud shall I blow it ?
Blow it right calm and easy,
Do not alarm my people,
Tell dem to come to judgment,
In dat great gittin'-up Mornin', etc.

. . . .

Gabriel, blow your trumpet.
Lord, how loud shall I blow it ?
Loud as seven peals of thunder,
Wake de sleepin' nations.
Den you see poor sinner risin',
See de dry bones a creepin',
In dat great gittin'-up Mornin', etc.

Den you see de world on fire,
You see de moon a bleedin',
See de stars a fallin',
See de elements meltin',
See de forked lightnin',
Hear de rumblin' thunder.
Earth shall reel and totter,
Hell shall be uncapped,
De dragon shall be loosened.
Fare you well, poor sinner.
In dat great gittin'-up Mornin',
Fare you well, Fare you well.

STARS BEGIN TO FALL

I TINK I hear my brudder say,
Call de nation great and small;
I lookee on de God's right hand
When de stars begin to fall.
Oh, what a mournin', sister, —
Oh, what a mournin', brudder, —
Oh, what a mournin',
When de stars begin to fall !

ROLL, JORDAN, ROLL

My brudder sittin' on de tree of life
An' he yearde when Jordan roll.
Roll, Jordan,
Roll, Jordan,
Roll, Jordan, roll !
O march de angel march;
O my soul arise in Heaven, Lord,
For to yearde when Jordan roll.

Little chil'en, learn to fear de Lord,
And let your days be long.
Roll, Jordan, etc.

O let no false nor spiteful word
Be found upon your tongue.
Roll, Jordan, etc.

SWING LOW, SWEET CHARIOT

OH, de good ole chariot swing so low, —
I don't want to leave me behind.
O swing low, sweet chariot,
Swing low, sweet chariot,
I don't want to leave me behind.

Oh, de good ole chariot will take us all
home, —
I don't want to leave me behind.
Swing low, sweet chariot, etc.

[1] See NOTE, p. 812.

BRIGHT SPARKLES IN DE CHURCHYARD

MAY de Lord — He will be glad of me —
In de heaven He 'll rejoice.
In de heaven, once,
In de heaven, twice,
In de heaven He 'll rejoice.

Bright sparkles in de churchyard
Give light unto de tomb;
Bright summer, spring 's over,
Sweet flowers in der bloom.

My mother, once,
My mother, twice,
My mother she 'll rejoice.
In de heaven once, etc.

Mother, rock me in de cradle all de day; —
All de day, etc.
Oh, mother, don't yer love yer darlin' child ?
Oh, rock me in de cradle all de day.
Rock me, etc.
You may lay me down to sleep, my mother dear,
Oh, rock me in de cradle all de day.

IV

THE PYXIDANTHERA

SWEET child of April, I have found thy place
Of deep retirement. Where the low swamp ferns
Curl upward from their sheaths, and lichens creep
Upon the fallen branch, and mosses dark
Deepen and brighten, where the ardent sun
Doth enter with restrained and chastened beam,
And the light cadence of the blue-bird's song
Doth falter in the cedar, — there the Spring
In gratitude hath wrought the sweet surprise
And marvel of thy unobtrusive bloom.

Most perfect symbol of my purest thought, —
A thought so close and warm within my heart
No words can shape its secret, and no prayer
Can breathe its sacredness — be thou my type,
And breathe to one, who wanders here at dawn,
The deep devotion, which, transcending speech,
Lights all the folded silence of my heart
As thy sweet beauty doth the shadow here.

So let thy clusters brighten, star on star
Of pink and white about his lingering feet,
Till, dreaming and enchanted, there shall pass
Into his life the story that my soul
Hath given thee. So shall his will be stirred
To purest purpose and divinest deed,
And every hour be touched with grace and light.

AUGUSTA COOPER BRISTOL

YELLOW JESSAMINE

IN tangled wreaths, in clustered gleaming stars,
In floating, curling sprays,
The golden flower comes shining through the woods
These February days;
Forth go all hearts, all hands, from out the town,
To bring her gayly in,
This wild, sweet Princess of far Florida —
The yellow jessamine.

The live-oaks smile to see her lovely face
Peep from the thickets; shy,
She hides behind the leaves her golden buds
Till, bolder grown, on high
She curls a tendril, throws a spray, then flings
Herself aloft in glee,
And, bursting into thousand blossoms swings
In wreaths from tree to tree.

The dwarf-palmetto on his knees adores
This Princess of the air;
The lone pine-barren broods afar and sighs,
"Ah! come, lest I despair;"
The myrtle-thickets and ill-tempered thorns
Quiver and thrill within,
As through their leaves they feel the dainty touch
Of yellow jessamine.

The garden-roses wonder as they see
The wreaths of golden bloom,
Brought in from the far woods with eager haste
To deck the poorest room,
The rich man's house, alike; the loaded hands
Give sprays to all they meet,
Till, gay with flowers, the people come and go,
And all the air is sweet.

The Southern land, well weary of its green
Which may not fall nor fade,
Bestirs itself to greet the lovely flower
With leaves of fresher shade;
The pine has tassels, and the orange-trees
Their fragrant work begin:
The spring has come — has come to Florida,
With yellow jessamine.

CONSTANCE FENIMORE WOOLSON

THE PETRIFIED FERN

IN a valley, centuries ago,
Grew a little fern-leaf, green and slender,
Veining delicate and fibres tender;
Waving when the wind crept down so low;
Rushes tall, and moss, and grass grew round it,
Playful sunbeams darted in and found it,
Drops of dew stole in by night, and crowned it,
But no foot of man e'er trod that way;
Earth was young and keeping holiday.

Monster fishes swam the silent main,
Stately forests waved their giant branches,
Mountains hurled their snowy avalanches,
Mammoth creatures stalked across the plain;
Nature revelled in grand mysteries;
But the little fern was not of these,
Did not number with the hills and trees,
Only grew and waved its wild sweet way, —
No one came to note it day by day.

Earth, one time, put on a frolic mood,
Heaved the rocks and changed the mighty motion
Of the deep, strong currents of the ocean;
Moved the plain and shook the haughty wood,
Crushed the little fern in soft moist clay,
Covered it, and hid it safe away.
Oh the long, long centuries since that day!
Oh the agony, oh life's bitter cost,
Since that useless little fern was lost!

Useless! Lost! There came a thoughtful man
Searching Nature's secrets, far and deep;
From a fissure in a rocky steep
He withdrew a stone, o'er which there ran
Fairy pencillings, a quaint design,
Veinings, leafage, fibres clear and fine,
And the fern's life lay in every line!
So, I think, God hides some souls away,
Sweetly to surprise us the last day.

MARY BOLLES BRANCH

THE DAWNING O' THE YEAR

ALL ye who love the springtime — and who but loves it well
When the little birds do sing, and the buds begin to swell! —
Think not ye ken its beauty, or know its face so dear,
Till ye look upon old Ireland, in the dawning o' the year!

For where in all the earth is there any joy like this,
When the skylark sings and soars like a spirit into bliss,
While the thrushes in the bush strain their small brown mottled throats,
Making all the air rejoice with their clear and mellow notes;

And the blackbird on the hedge in the golden sunset glow
Trills with saucy, side-tipped head to the bonny nest below;
And the dancing wind slips down through the leaves of the boreen,
And all the world rejoices in the wearing o' the green!

For 't is green, green, green, where the ruined towers are gray,
And it 's green, green, green, all the happy night and day;
Green of leaf and green of sod, green of ivy on the wall,
And the blessed Irish shamrock with the fairest green of all.

There the primrose breath is sweet, and the yellow gorse is set
A crown of shining gold on the headlands brown and wet;
Not a nook of all the land but the daisies make to glow,
And the happy violets pray in their hidden cells below.

And it 's there the earth is merry, like a young thing newly made
Running wild amid the blossoms in the field and in the glade,
Babbling ever into music under skies with soft clouds piled,
Like the laughter and the tears in the blue eyes of a child.

But the green, green, green, O 't is that is blithe and fair!
In the fells and on the hills, gay and gladsome as the air,
Lying warm above the bog, floating brave on crag and glen,
Thrusting forty banners high where another land has ten.

Sure Mother Nature knows of her sore and heavy grief,
And thus with soft caress would give solace and relief;
Would fold her close in loveliness to keep her from the cold,
And clasp the mantle o'er her heart with emeralds and gold.

So ye who love the springtime, — and who but loves it well
When the little birds do sing, and the buds begin to swell! —
Think not ye ken its beauty or know its face so dear
Till ye meet it in old Ireland in the dawning o' the year!

MARY ELIZABETH BLAKE

THE WILLIS

THE Willis are out to-night,
In the ghostly pale moonlight,
With robes and faces white.

Swiftly they circle round,
And make not any sound,
Nor footprint on the ground.

The forest is asleep;
All things that fly or creep
A death-like silence keep.

A fear is over all;
From spectral trees and tall
The gathering night-dews fall.

Moveless are leaf and limb,
While through the forest dim
Slow glides a figure slim.

A figure slim and fair,
With loosened, streaming hair,
Watching the Willis there!

"These are the ghosts," she said,
"Of hapless ones unwed,
Who loved and now are dead."

Her hair was drenched with dew;
The moonlight shimmered through,
And showed its raven hue.

"Each one of these," she cried,
"Or ever she was a bride,
For love's sake sinned and died."

"I come," she said, "I too;
Ye are by one too few,"
And joined the phantom crew.

Swiftly they circled round,
Nor was there any sound,
Nor footprint on the ground.

DAVID LAW PROUDFIT

TWO OF A TRADE

THE dragon-fly and I together
Sail up the stream in the summer weather;
He at the stern all green and gold,
And I at the oars, our course to hold.

Above the floor of the level river
The bent blades dip and spring and quiver;
And the dragon-fly is here and there,
Along the water and in the air.

And thus we go as the sunshine mellows;
A pair of Nature's merriest fellows;
For the Spanish cedar is light and true,
And instead of one, it has carried two.

And thus we sail without care or sorrow,
With trust for to-day and hope for to-morrow;
He at the stern, all green and gold,
And I at the oars, our course to hold.

SAMUEL WILLOUGHBY DUFFIELD

V

SONNETS

AN OPEN SECRET

WOULD the lark sing the sweeter if he knew
A thousand hearts hung breathless on his lay?
And if "How fair!" the rose could hear us say,
Would she, her primal fairness to outdo,
Take on a richer scent, a lovelier hue?
Who knows or cares to answer yea or nay?
O tuneful lark! sail, singing, on your way,
Brimmed with excess of ecstasy; and you,
Sweet rose! renew with every perfect June
Your perfect blossoming! Still Nature-wise,
Sing, bloom, because ye must, and not for praise.
If only we, who covet the fair boon
Of well-earned fame, and wonder where it lies,
Would read the secret in your simple ways!

RECONCILIATION

IF thou wert lying cold and still and white
In death's embraces, O mine enemy!
I think that if I came and looked on thee,
I should forgive; that something in the sight
Of thy still face would conquer me, by right
Of death's sad impotence, and I should see
How pitiful a thing it is to be
At feud with aught that 's mortal. So to-night,
My soul, unfurling her white flag of peace,
Forestalling that dread hour when we may meet, —
The dead face and the living, — fain would cry,
Across the years, "Oh, let our warfare cease!
Life is so short, and hatred is not sweet;
Let there be peace between us ere we die!"

CAROLINE ATHERTON MASON

NOW

UPON my bier no garlands lay,
To shrivel at death's icy touch;
Pansies for thought bequeathed to-day,
Were worth a thousand such!
Rare flowers too often serve the pride
Which grants them — naught beside.

No lavish tears that laggard be,
Pour vainly on my pulseless clay;
A single drop of sympathy
Were richer boon to-day;
To-day I need it — but, thank God,
No need is in the sod.

Yield now the sign, or let me go
Unlaurelled into waiting space;
Not taunted by a hollow show
Of friendship's tardy grace;
Not mocked by fruits that would not fall
Save as an idle pall.

Fair blossoms with love's dewdrops wet,
And fondly laid in folded hands,
Must hold the grateful spirit yet
While wandering in strange lands;
But wounded souls the meed must spurn
That only Death can earn!

MARY BARKER DODGE

A LIVING MEMORY

My absent daughter — gentle, gentle maid,
Your life doth never fade!
O, everywhere I see your blue eyes shine,
And on my heart, in healing or command,
I feel the pressure of your small, warm hand
That slipped at dawn, almost without a sign,
So softly out of mine!

The birds all sing of you, my darling one;
Your day was just begun,
But you had learned to love all things that grew;
And when I linger by the streamlet's side
Where weed and bush to you were glorified,
The violet looks up as if it knew,
And talks to me of you.

The lily dreams of you. The pensive rose
Reveals you where it glows
In purple trance above the waterfall;
The fragrant fern rejoices by the pond,
And sets your dear face in its feathery frond;
The winds blow chill, but, sounding over all,
I hear your sweet voice call!

My gentle daughter! With us you have stayed.
Your life doth never fade!
O, evermore I see your blue eyes shine.
In subtle moods I cannot understand,
I feel the flutter of your tender hand
That slipped at dawn, almost without a sign,
So softly out of mine!

WILLIAM AUGUSTUS CROFFUT

WAITING

Serene, I fold my hands and wait,
Nor care for wind, or tide, or sea;
I rave no more 'gainst time or fate,
For, lo! my own shall come to me.

I stay my haste, I make delays,
For what avails this eager pace?
I stand amid the eternal ways,
And what is mine shall know my face.

Asleep, awake, by night or day,
The friends I seek are seeking me;
No wind can drive my bark astray,
Nor change the tide of destiny.

What matter if I stand alone?
I wait with joy the coming years;
My heart shall reap where it has sown,
And garner up its fruit of tears.

The waters know their own and draw
The brook that springs in yonder height;
So flows the good with equal law
Unto the soul of pure delight.

The stars come nightly to the sky;
The tidal wave unto the sea;
Nor time, nor space, nor deep, nor high,
Can keep my own away from me.

JOHN BURROUGHS

DEAD LOVE

Two loves had I. Now both are dead,
And both are marked by tombstones white.
The one stands in the churchyard near,
The other hid from mortal sight.

The name on one all men may read,
And learn who lies beneath the stone;
The other name is written where
No eyes can read it but my own.

On one I plant a living flower,
And cherish it with loving hands;
I shun the single withered leaf
That tells me where the other stands.

To that white tombstone on the hill
In summer days I often go;
From this white stone that nearer lies
I turn me with unuttered woe.

O God, I pray, if love must die,
And make no more of life a part,

Let witness be where all can see,
And not within a living heart.

MARY MATHEWS ADAMS

DISARMED

O LOVE, so sweet at first,
So bitter in the end!
Thou canst be fiercest foe,
As well as fairest friend.
Are these poor withered leaves
The fruitage of thy May?
Thou that wert strong to save,
How art thou swift to slay!

Ay, thou art swift to slay,
Despite thy kiss and clasp,
Thy long, caressing look,
Thy subtle, thrilling grasp!
Ay, swifter far to slay
Than thou art strong to save,
And selfish in thy need,
And cruel as the grave.

Yes, cruel as the grave, —
Go, go, and come no more!
But canst thou set my heart
Just where it was before?
Go, go, — and come no more!
Go, leave me with my tears,
The only gift of thine
That shall outlive the years.

Yet shall outlive the years
One other, cherished thing,
Slight as a vagrant plume
Shed from some passing wing: —
The memory of thy first
Divine, half-timid kiss.
Go! I forgive thee all
In weeping over this!

LAURA REDDEN SEARING
("Howard Glyndon")

POST-MERIDIAN[1]

AFTERNOON

WHEN in thy glass thou studiest thy face,
Not long, nor yet not seldom, half repelled
And half attracted; when thou hast beheld
Of Time's slow ravages the crumbling trace,
(Deciphered now with many an interspace
The characters erewhile that Beauty spelled),
And in thy throat a choking fear hath swelled
Of Love, grown cold, eluding thy embrace:
Couldst thou but read my gaze of tenderness —
Affection fused with pity — precious tears
Would bring relief to thy unjust distress;
Thy visage, even as it to me appears,
Would seem to thee transfigured; thou wouldst bless
Me, who am also, Dearest! scarred with years.

EVENING

AGE cannot wither her whom not gray hairs
Nor furrowed cheeks have made the thrall of Time;
For Spring lies hidden under Winter's rime,
And violets know the victory is theirs.
Even so the corn of Egypt, unawares,
Proud Nilus shelters with engulfing slime;
So Etna's hardening crust a more sublime
Volley of pent-up fires at last prepares.
O face yet fair, if paler, and serene
With sense of duty done without complaint!
O venerable crown! — a living green,
Strength to the weak, and courage to the faint —
Thy bleaching locks, thy wrinkles, have but been
Fresh beads upon the rosary of a saint!

WENDELL PHILLIPS GARRISON

VI

THOREAU'S FLUTE

WE, sighing, said, "Our Pan is dead;
His pipe hangs mute beside the river;
Around it wistful sunbeams quiver,
But Music's airy voice is fled.
Spring mourns as for untimely frost;
The bluebird chants a requiem;
The willow-blossom waits for him; —
The Genius of the wood is lost."

[1] See, also, the Sonnet on p. 794.

Then from the flute, untouched by hands,
There came a low, harmonious breath:
"For such as he there is no death;
His life the eternal life commands;
Above man's aims his nature rose:
The wisdom of a just content
Made one small spot a continent,
And turned to poetry Life's prose.

"Haunting the hills, the stream, the wild,
Swallow and aster, lake and pine,
To him grew human or divine, —
Fit mates for this large-hearted child.
Such homage Nature ne'er forgets,
And yearly on the coverlid
'Neath which her darling lieth hid
Will write his name in violets.

"To him no vain regrets belong,
Whose soul, that finer instrument,
Gave to the world no poor lament,
But wood-notes ever sweet and strong.
O lonely friend! he still will be
A potent presence, though unseen, —
Steadfast, sagacious, and serene:
Seek not for him, — he is with thee."

Louisa May Alcott

OPPORTUNITY

"Master of human destinies am I!
Fame, love, and fortune on my footsteps wait.
Cities and fields I walk; I penetrate
Deserts and seas remote, and passing by
Hovel and mart and palace — soon or late
I knock unbidden once at every gate!

"If sleeping, wake — if feasting, rise before
I turn away. It is the hour of fate,
And they who follow me reach every state
Mortals desire, and conquer every foe
Save death; but those who doubt or hesitate,
Condemned to failure, penury, and woe,
Seek me in vain and uselessly implore.
I answer not, and I return no more!"

John James Ingalls

THE CONDEMNED

Read me no moral, priest, upon my life, —
Reserve that for your flock.
A few short hours will end my mortal strife,
Upon the gallows block.

Before the gaping crowd, who come to see
A fellow mortal die,
Preach if you choose, and take your text from me, —
To them I cannot lie.

And still the less can I, a finite man,
Pretend to cheat my God:
By him the workings of his mighty plan
Are clearly understood.

Conceived in lust, brought up in sordid sin,
How could I hope to be
Aught but the outcast I have ever been,
Fruit for the gallows tree?

Go teach the children swarming through the town,
To-day exposed to all
The poverty and vice that drew me down, —
Save them before they fall.

But as for me, I die as I have lived,
As all men must,
Believing as I always have believed
That God is just.

Edward Howland

MY BIRTH

I had my birth where stars were born,
In the dim æons of the past:
My cradle cosmic forces rocked,
And to my first was linked my last.

Through boundless space the shuttle flew,
To weave the warp and woof of fate:
In my begetting were conjoined
The infinitely small and great.

The outmost star on being's rim,
The tiniest sand-grain of the earth,
The farthest thrill and nearest stir
Were not indifferent to my birth.

And when at last the earth swung free,
A little planet by the moon,
For me the continent arose,
For me the ocean roared its tune;

For me the forests grew; for me
The electric force ran to and fro;
For me tribes wandered o'er the earth,
Kingdoms arose, and cities grew;

For me religions waxed and waned;
For me the ages garnered store;
For me ships traversed every sea;
For me the wise ones learned their lore;

For me, through fire and blood and tears,
Man struggled onward up the height,
On which, at last, from heaven falls
An ever clearer, broader light.

The child of all the ages, I,
Nursed on the exhaustless breasts of time;
By heroes thrilled, by sages taught,
Sung to by bards of every clime.

Quintessence of the universe,
Distilled at last from God's own heart,
In me concentred now abides
Of all that is the subtlest part.

The product of the ages past,
Heir of the future, then, am I:
So much am I divine that God
Cannot afford to let me die.

If I should ever cease to be,
The farthest star its mate would miss,
And, looking after me, would fall
Down headlong darkening to the abyss.

For, if aught real that is could cease,
If the All-Father ever nods,
That day across the heavens would fall
Ragnarok, twilight of the gods.

MINOT JUDSON SAVAGE

THE INEVITABLE

I LIKE the man who faces what he must
With step triumphant and a heart of cheer;
Who fights the daily battle without fear;
Sees his hopes fail, yet keeps unfaltering trust
That God is God, — that somehow, true and just
His plans work out for mortals; not a tear
Is shed when fortune, which the world holds dear,
Falls from his grasp — better, with love, a crust
Than living in dishonor; envies not,
Nor loses faith in man; but does his best,
Nor ever murmurs at his humbler lot;
But, with a smile and words of hope, gives zest
To every toiler. He alone is great
Who by a life heroic conquers fate.

SARAH KNOWLES BOLTON

QUATRAINS

TIME

TIME has no flight — 'tis we who speed along;
The days and nights are but the same as when
The earth awoke with the first rush of song,
And felt the swiftly passing feet of men.

INFALLIBILITY

"BELIEVE in me," the Prophet cried, —
"I hold the key of life and light:"
And, lo, one touched him, and he died
Within the passing of a night.

POWER

HAROUN, the Caliph, through the sunlit street
Walked slowly with bent head and weary breath,
And cried, "Alas, I cannot stay my feet,
That move unceasing toward the gate of Death."

DISAPPOINTMENT

FROM the drear wastes of unfulfilled desire,
We harvest dreams that never come to pass,
Then pour our wine amid the dying fire,
And on the cold hearth break the empty glass.

COMPENSATION

No ceaseless vigil with hard toil we keep,
And to grim want give but a passing breath;
For after labor comes the rest of sleep,
And hunger cannot make its home with death.

THOMAS STEPHENS COLLIER

VII

ANCIENT OF DAYS

Ancient of days, Who sittest, throned in glory;
To Thee all knees are bent, all voices pray;
Thy love has blest the wide world's wondrous story,
With light and life since Eden's dawning day.

O Holy Father, Who hast led Thy children
In all the ages, with the Fire and Cloud,
Through seas dry-shod; through weary wastes bewildering;
To Thee, in reverent love, our hearts are bowed.

O Holy Jesus, Prince of Peace and Saviour,
To Thee we owe the peace that still prevails,
Stilling the rude wills of men's wild behavior,
And calming passion's fierce and stormy gales.

O Holy Ghost, the Lord and the Life-giver,
Thine is the quickening power that gives increase;
From Thee have flowed, as from a pleasant river,
Our plenty, wealth, prosperity, and peace.

O Triune God, with heart and voice adoring,
Praise we the goodness that doth crown our days;
Pray we, that Thou wilt hear us, still imploring
Thy love and favor, kept to us always.

William Croswell Doane

O LITTLE TOWN OF BETHLEHEM

O little town of Bethlehem,
How still we see thee lie!
Above thy deep and dreamless sleep
The silent stars go by;
Yet in thy dark streets shineth
The everlasting Light;
The hopes and fears of all the years
Are met in thee to-night.

For Christ is born of Mary,
And, gathered all above,
While mortals sleep, the angels keep
Their watch of wondering love.
O morning stars, together
Proclaim the holy birth!
And praises sing to God the King,
And peace to men on earth.

How silently, how silently,
The wondrous gift is given!
So God imparts to human hearts
The blessings of His heaven.
No ear may hear His coming,
But in this world of sin,
Where meek souls will receive Him still,
The dear Christ enters in.

O holy Child of Bethlehem!
Descend to us, we pray;
Cast out our sin, and enter in,
Be born in us to-day.
We hear the Christmas angels
The great glad tidings tell;
Oh come to us, abide with us,
Our Lord Emmanuel!

Phillips Brooks

IN GALILEE

Roman and Jew upon one level lie;
Great Herod's palaces are ground to dust;
Upon the synagogues are mould and rust;
Night winds among the tottering columns sigh;
Yet sparrows through the massive ruins fly,
And o'er the sacred earth's embroidered crust
Still goes the sower forth to sow, still must
The shepherd with his sheep sit listlessly.
There towers the mountain where the Teacher spake
In those old times the sweet Beatitudes,
Surviving kings and codes, fair words and feuds.
There creeps the Jordan to its destined lake,
The fisher casts his net into the sea,
And still the lilies bloom in Galilee.

Mary Frances Butts[1]

[1] See also p. 588.

REINCARNATION

It cannot be that He who made
This wondrous world for our delight,
Designed that all its charms should fade
And pass forever from our sight;
That all shall wither and decay,
And know on earth no life but this,
With only one finite survey
Of all its beauty and its bliss.

It cannot be that all the years
Of toil and care and grief we live
Shall find no recompense but tears,
No sweet return that earth can give;
That all that leads us to aspire,
And struggle onward to achieve,
And every unattained desire
Were given only to deceive.

It cannot be that, after all
The mighty conquests of the mind,
Our thoughts shall pass beyond recall
And leave no record here behind;
That all our dreams of love and fame,
And hopes that time has swept away, —
All that enthralled this mortal frame, —
Shall not return some other day.

It cannot be that all the ties
Of kindred souls and loving hearts
Are broken when this body dies,
And the immortal mind departs;
That no serener light shall break
At last upon our mortal eyes,
To guide us as our footsteps make
The pilgrimage to Paradise.

David Banks Sickels

ROLL OUT, O SONG

Roll out, O song to God!
Move on, ye throngs of men!
Chances and changes come and go:
God changeth not! Amen.
And on the throngs of men,
On worrying care and strife,
Sinks down, as if from angel tongues,
The word of hope and life.

Down in the darksome ways
And worrying whirl of life
Sinks, like a strain of vesper-song,
The thought of his great strife
Who, of the Virgin born,
Made all our chains His own,
And broke them with His own right arm,
Nor left us more alone.

Amid the weak, one strong,
Amid the false, one true,
Amid all change, one changing not, —
One hope we ne'er shall rue.
In whose sight all is now,
In whose love all is best:
The things of this world pass away, —
Come, let us in Him rest.
Amen.

Frank Sewall

NOT KNOWING[1]

Not knowing the things that shall befall me there. Acts xx. 22.

I know not what will befall me: God hangs a mist o'er my eyes;
And thus, each step of my onward path, He makes new scenes arise,
And every joy He sends to me comes like a sweet surprise.

I see not a step before me as I tread on another year;
But I 've left the past in God's keeping, — the future His mercy shall clear,
And what looks dark in the distance may brighten as I draw near.

For perhaps the dreaded future is less bitter than I think;
The Lord may sweeten the waters before I stoop to drink;
Or, if Marah must be Marah, He will stand beside its brink.

It may be He keeps waiting, for the coming of my feet,
Some gift of such rare blessedness, some joy so strangely sweet,
That my lips shall only tremble with the thanks they cannot speak.

O restful, blissful ignorance! 't is blessëd not to know;
It keeps me still in those mighty arms which will not let me go,
And lulls my weariness to rest on the bosom that loves me so.

[1] See Biographical Note, p. 781.

So I go on not knowing, — I would not if I might;
I would rather walk in the dark with God than go alone in the light;
I would rather walk with Him by faith than walk alone by sight.

My heart shrinks back from trials which the future may disclose,
Yet I never had sorrow but what the dear Lord chose;
So I send the coming tears back with the whispered word, "He knows."

MARY GARDINER BRAINARD

TO ST. MARY MAGDALEN

MID the white spouses of the Sacred Heart,
After its queen, the nearest, dearest thou:
Yet the aureola around thy brow
Is not the virgins' — thine a throne apart.
Nor yet, my Saint, does faith-illumined art
Thy hand with palm of martyrdom endow:
And when thy hair is all it will allow
Of glory to thy head, we do not start.
O more than virgin in thy penitent love!
And more than martyr in thy passionate woe!
Who knelt not with thee on the gory sod,
How should they now sit throned with thee above?
Or where the crown our worship could bestow
Like that long gold which wiped the feet of God?

BENJAMIN DIONYSIUS HILL
(Father Edmund, of the Heart of Mary, C. P.)

VIII

NOW I LAY ME DOWN TO SLEEP[1]

"Now I lay me down to sleep:
I pray the Lord my soul to keep,"
Was my childhood's early prayer
Taught by my mother's love and care.
Many years since then have fled;
Mother slumbers with the dead;
Yet methinks I see her now,
With love-lit eye and holy brow,
As, kneeling by her side to pray,
She gently taught me how to say,
"Now I lay me down to sleep:
I pray the Lord my soul to keep."

Oh! could the faith of childhood's days,
Oh! could its little hymns of praise,
Oh! could its simple, joyous trust
Be recreated from the dust
That lies around a wasted life,
The fruit of many a bitter strife!
Oh! then at night in prayer I 'd bend,
And call my God, my Father, Friend,
And pray with childlike faith once more
The prayer my mother taught of yore, —
"Now I lay me down to sleep:
I pray the Lord my soul to keep."

EUGENE HENRY PULLEN

ONE SATURDAY

I NEVER had a happier time,
And I am forty-three,
Than one midsummer afternoon,
When it was May with me:
Life's fragrant May,
And Saturday,
And you came out with me to play;
And up and down the garden walks,
Among the flowering beans,
We proudly walked and tossed our heads
And played that we were queens.

Thrice prudent sovereigns, we made
The diadems we wore,
And fashioned for our royal hands
The sceptres which they bore;
But good Queen Bess
Had surely less
Than we, of proud self-consciousness,
While wreaths of honeysuckle hung
Around your rosy neck,
And tufts of marigold looped up
My gown, a "gingham check."

Our chosen land was parted out,
Like Israel's, by lot;
My kingdom, from the garden wall
Reached to the strawberry plot;

[1] See BIOGRAPHICAL NOTE, p. 817.

The onion-bed,
The beet-tops red,
The corn which waved above my head,
The gooseberry bushes, hung with fruit,
The wandering melon-vine,
The carrots and the cabbages,
All, all of them, were mine!

Beneath the cherry-tree was placed
Your throne, a broken chair;
Your realm was narrower than mine,
But it was twice as fair:
Tall hollyhocks,
And purple phlox,
And time-observing four-o'clocks,
Blue lavender, and candytuft,
And pink and white sweet peas,
Your loyal subjects, waved their heads
In every passing breeze.

Oh! gay and prosperous was our reign
Till we were called to tea; —
But years, since then, have come and gone,
And I am forty-three!
Yet, journeying
On rapid wing,
Time has not brought, and cannot bring,
For you or me, a happier day
Than when, among the beans,
We proudly walked and tossed our heads,
And fancied we were queens.

Annie Douglas Robinson
("Marian Douglas")

MY LADDIE'S HOUNDS

(VIRGINIA MOUNTAINS)

They are my laddie's hounds
That rin the wood at brak o' day.
Wha is it taks them hence? Can ony say
Wha is it taks my laddie's hounds
At brak o' day?

They cleek aff thegither,
An' then fa' back, wi' room atween
For ane to walk; sae aften, I hae seen
The baith cleek aff thegither
Wi' ane atween!

And when toward the pines
Up yonder lane they loup alang,
I see ae bonnie laddie brent and strang,
I see ae laddie loup alang
Toward the pines.

I follow them, in mind,
Ilk time; right weel I ken the way, —
They thrid the wood, an' speel the staney brae,
An' skir the field; I follow them,
I ken the way.

They daddle at the creek,
Whaur down fra aff the reaching-logs
I stoup, wi' my dear laddie, an' the dogs,
An' drink o' springs that spait the creek
Maist to the logs.

He 's but a bairn, atho'
He hunts the mountain's lonely bree,
His doggies' ears abune their brows wi' glee
He ties; he 's but a bairn, atho'
He hunts the bree.

Fu' length they a' stretch out
Upon ae bink that green trees hap
In shade. He whusslits saft; the beagles nap
Wi' een half shut, a' stretchin' out
Whaur green trees hap.

And noo he fades awa'
Frae 'tween the twa — into the blue.
My sight gats blind; gude Lord, it isna true
That he has gane for aye, awa' —
Into the blue!

They are my laddie's hounds
That mak the hill at fa' o' day
Wi' dowie heads hung laigh; can ony say
Wha is it hunts my laddie's hounds
Till fa' o' day?

Marguerite Elizabeth Easter

THE CHILDREN

When the lessons and tasks are all ended,
And the school for the day is dismissed,
The little ones gather around me,
To bid me good night and be kissed:
Oh, the little white arms that encircle
My neck in their tender embrace!
Oh, the smiles that are halos of heaven,
Shedding sunshine of love on my face!

And when they are gone, I sit dreaming
Of my childhood too lovely to last, —
Of joy that my heart will remember,
While it wakes to the pulse of the past,
Ere the world and its wickedness made me
A partner of sorrow and sin,
When the glory of God was about me,
And the glory of gladness within.

All my heart grows as weak as a woman's,
And the fountain of feeling will flow,
When I think of the paths steep and stony,
Where the feet of the dear ones must go, —
Of the mountains of sin hanging o'er them,
Of the tempest of fate blowing wild:
Oh, there 's nothing on earth half so holy
As the innocent heart of a child!

They are idols of hearts and of households;
They are angels of God in disguise:
His sunlight still sleeps in their tresses,
His glory still shines in their eyes;
Those truants from home and from heaven, —
They have made me more manly and mild;
And I know now how Jesus could liken
The kingdom of God to a child.

I ask not a life for the dear ones,
All radiant, as others have done,
But that life may have just enough shadow
To temper the glare of the sun;
I would pray God to guard them from evil,
But my prayer would bound back to myself:
Ah! a seraph may pray for a sinner,
But a sinner must pray for himself.

The twig is so easily bended,
I have banished the rule and the rod;
I have taught them the goodness of knowledge,
They have taught me the goodness of God:
My heart is the dungeon of darkness
Where I shut them for breaking a rule;
My frown is sufficient correction;
My love is the law of the school.

I shall leave the old house in the autumn,
To traverse its threshold no more:
Ah, how I shall sigh for the dear ones
That meet me each morn at the door!
I shall miss the "good nights" and the kisses,
And the gush of their innocent glee,
The group on the green, and the flowers
That are brought every morning for me.

I shall miss them at morn and at even,
Their song in the school and the street;
I shall miss the low hum of their voices,
And the tread of their delicate feet.
When the lessons of life are all ended,
And Death says "The school is dismissed!"
May the little ones gather around me,
To bid me good night and be kissed!

CHARLES MONROE DICKINSON

IX

"THE DOVES OF VENICE"

As the Transatlantic tourists
Have been rowed on the Lagoon,
They have mourned its ancient glories,
They have watched the Germans spoon.

As they 've sailed these famous highways,
As they 've floated on these tides,
The arts that most impressed them
Were the artless German brides.

As they 've listened to the music
Of the poor Italian bands,
Heard the same old tunes repeated,
Seen the Germans holding hands, —

They have wondered why all Venice,
From San Marco to Lagoon,
Is now illumined only
By a German honeymoon;

Why the steeds on the Duomo
Have not laughed horse-laughs, and shied
At the too transparent fondness
Of the modern German bride!

Why the very stones of Venice,
Which the great John Ruskin loves,
Are nothing but a roosting-place
For German turtle-doves!

LAURENCE HUTTON

MOTHER GOOSE SONNETS

JACK AND JILL

AH, Jack it was, and with him little Jill,
Of the same age and size, a neighbor's daughter,
Who on a breezy morning climbed the hill
To fetch down to the house a pail of water.
Jack put his best foot foremost on that day, —
Vaulting ambition we have seen before, —
He stepped too far, of course, and soon he lay
In the vile path, his little crown so sore!
The next act in the tragedy was played
By Jill, whose eager foothold, too, was brief.
Epitome of life, that boy and maid
Together hoped, together came to grief.
And in their simple story lies concealed
The germ of half that 's plucked in fiction's field.

SIMPLE SIMON

A BOY named Simon sojourned in a dale;
Some said that he was simple, but I 'm sure
That he was nothing less than simon pure;
They thought him so because, forsooth, a whale
He tried to catch in Mother's water-pail.
Ah! little boy, timid, composed, demure, —
He had imagination. Yet endure
Defeat he could, for he of course did fail.
But there are Simons of a larger growth,
Who, too, in shallow waters fish for whales,
And when they fail they are "unfortunate."
If the small boy is simple, then are both,
And the big Simon more, who often rails
At what he calls ill luck or unkind fate.

HARRIET S. MORGRIDGE

A THRENODY

The Ahkoond of Swat is dead. — *London Papers.*

WHAT, what, what,
What 's the news from Swat?
Sad news,
Bad news,
Comes by the cable led
Through the Indian Ocean's bed,
Through the Persian Gulf, the Red
Sea and the Med-
Iterranean — he 's dead;
The Ahkoond is dead!

For the Ahkoond I mourn,
Who would n't?
He strove to disregard the message stern,
But he Ahkoodn't.
Dead, dead, dead;
(Sorrow Swats!)
Swats wha hae wi' Ahkoond bled,
Swats whom he hath often led
Onward to a gory bed,
Or to victory,
As the case might be,
Sorrow Swats!
Tears shed,
Shed tears like water,
Your great Ahkoond is dead!
That Swats the matter!

Mourn, city of Swat!
Your great Ahkoond is not,
But lain 'mid worms to rot.
His mortal part alone, his soul was caught
(Because he was a good Ahkoond)
Up to the bosom of Mahound.
Though earthy walls his frame surround
(Forever hallowed be the ground!)
And sceptics mock the lowly mound
And say "He 's now of no Ahkoond!"
His soul is in the skies, —
The azure skies that bend above his loved
Metropolis of Swat.
He sees with larger, other eyes,
Athwart all earthly mysteries —
He knows what 's Swat.

Let Swat bury the great Ahkoond
With a noise of mourning and
of lamentation!
Let Swat bury the great Ahkoond
With the noise of the mourning
of the Swattish nation!

Fallen is at length
Its tower of strength,
Its sun is dimmed ere it had nooned;
Dead lies the great Ahkoond,
The great Ahkoond of Swat
Is not!

GEORGE THOMAS LANIGAN

DIVISION II

(GILDER, O'REILLY, MAURICE THOMPSON, FATHER TABB, EMMA LAZARUS, MRS. CORTISSOZ, EDITH THOMAS, EUGENE FIELD, BATES, MARKHAM, WHITCOMB RILEY, INA COOLBRITH, R. U. JOHNSON, AND OTHERS)

Richard Watson Gilder

ODE

I

I AM the spirit of the morning sea;
I am the awakening and the glad surprise;
I fill the skies
With laughter and with light.
Not tears, but jollity
At birth of day brim the strong man-child's eyes.
Behold the white
Wide three-fold beams that from the hidden sun
Rise swift and far, —
One where Orion keeps
His armëd watch, and one
That to the midmost starry heaven upleaps;
The third blots out the firm-fixed Northern Star.
I am the wind that shakes the glittering wave,
Hurries the snowy spume along the shore
And dies at last in some far-murmuring cave.
My voice thou hearest in the breaker's roar —
That sound which never failed since time began,
And first around the world the shining tumult ran.

II

I light the sea and wake the sleeping land.
My footsteps on the hills make music, and my hand
Plays like a harper's on the wind-swept pines.

With the wind and the day
I follow round the world — away ! away !
Wide over lake and plain my sunlight shines
And every wave and every blade of grass
Doth know me as I pass;
And me the western sloping mountains know, and me
The far-off, golden sea.

O sea, whereon the passing sun doth lie !
O man, who watchest by that golden sea !
Grieve not, — O grieve not thou, but lift thine eye
And see me glorious in the sunset sky !

III

I love not the night
Save when the stars are bright,
Or when the moon
Fills the white air with silence like a tune.
Yea, even the night is mine
When the Northern Lights outshine,
And all the wild heavens throb in ecstasy divine; —
Yea, mine deep midnight, though the black sky lowers,
When the sea burns white and breaks on the shore in starry showers.

IV

I am the laughter of the new-born child
On whose soft-breathing sleep an angel smiled.
And I all sweet first things that are:
First songs of birds, not perfect as at last, —
Broken and incomplete, —
But sweet, oh, sweet !
And I the first faint glimmer of a star
To the wrecked ship that tells the storm is past;
The first keen smells and stirrings of the Spring;
First snow-flakes, and first May-flowers after snow;
The silver glow
Of the new moon's ethereal ring;
The song the morning stars together made,
And the first kiss of lovers under the first June shade.

V

My sword is quick, my arm is strong to smite
In the dread joy and fury of the fight.
I am with those who win, not those who fly;
With those who live I am, not those who die.
Who die? Nay, nay, that word
Where I am is unheard;
For I am the spirit of youth that cannot change,
Nor cease, nor suffer woe;
And I am the spirit of beauty that doth range
Through natural forms and motions, and each show
Of outward loveliness. With me have birth
All gentleness and joy in all the earth.
Raphael knew me, and showed the world my face;
Me Homer knew, and all the singing race, —
For I am the spirit of light, and life, and mirth.

THE CELESTIAL PASSION

O WHITE and midnight sky! O starry bath!
Wash me in thy pure, heavenly, crystal flood;
Cleanse me, ye stars, from earthly soil and scath;
Let not one taint remain in spirit or blood!
Receive my soul, ye burning, awful deeps;
Touch and baptize me with the mighty power
That in ye thrills, while the dark planet sleeps;
Make me all yours for one blest, secret hour!
O glittering host! O high angelic choir!
Silence each tone that with thy music jars;
Fill me even as an urn with thy white fire
Till all I am is kindred to the stars!
Make me thy child, thou infinite, holy night —
So shall my days be full of heavenly light!

I COUNT MY TIME BY TIMES THAT I MEET THEE

I COUNT my time by times that I meet thee;
These are my yesterdays, my morrows, noons,
And nights; these my old moons and my new moons.
Slow fly the hours, or fast the hours do flee,
If thou art far from or art near to me:
If thou art far, the bird tunes are no tunes;
If thou art near, the wintry days are Junes, —
Darkness is light, and sorrow cannot be.
Thou art my dream come true, and thou my dream;
The air I breathe, the world wherein I dwell;
My journey's end thou art, and thou the way;
Thou art what I would be, yet only seem;
Thou art my heaven and thou art my hell;
Thou art my ever-living judgment-day.

SONGS

I

NOT from the whole wide world I chose thee,
Sweetheart, light of the land and the sea!
The wide, wide world could not inclose thee,
For thou art the whole wide world to me.

II

Years have flown since I knew thee first,
And I know thee as water is known of thirst;
Yet I knew thee of old at the first sweet sight,
And thou art strange to me, Love, to-night.

ON THE LIFE-MASK OF ABRAHAM LINCOLN

THIS bronze doth keep the very form and mould
Of our great martyr's face. Yes, this is he:
That brow all wisdom, all benignity;
That human, humorous mouth; those cheeks that hold
Like some harsh landscape all the summer's gold;
That spirit fit for sorrow, as the sea
For storms to beat on; the lone agony
Those silent, patient lips too well foretold.

Yes, this is he who ruled a world of men
As might some prophet of the elder day —
Brooding above the tempest and the fray
With deep-eyed thought and more than mortal ken.
A power was his beyond the touch of art
Or armëd strength — his pure and mighty heart.

THE SONNET

What is a sonnet? 'T is the pearly shell
That murmurs of the far-off murmuring sea;
A precious jewel carved most curiously;
It is a little picture painted well.
What is a sonnet? 'T is the tear that fell
From a great poet's hidden ecstasy;
A two-edged sword, a star, a song, — ah me!
Sometimes a heavy-tolling funeral bell.
This was the flame that shook with Dante's breath,
The solemn organ whereon Milton played,
And the clear glass where Shakespeare's shadow falls:
A sea this is, — beware who ventureth!
For like a fiord the narrow floor is laid
Mid-ocean deep to the sheer mountain walls.

EVENING IN TYRINGHAM VALLEY

What domes and pinnacles of mist and fire
Are builded in yon spacious realms of light
All silently, as did the walls aspire
Templing the ark of God by day and night!
Noiseless and swift, from darkening ridge to ridge,
Through purple air that deepens down the day,
Over the valley springs a shadowy bridge.
The evening star's keen, solitary ray
Makes more intense the silence, and the glad,
Unmelancholy, restful, twilight gloom —
So full of tenderness, that even the sad
Remembrances that haunt the soul take bloom
Like that on yonder mountain. Now the bars
Of sunset all burn black; the day doth fail,
And the skies whiten with the eternal stars.
Oh, let thy spirit stay with me, sweet vale!

SHERMAN

Glory and honor and fame and everlasting laudation
For our captains who loved not war, but fought for the life of the nation;
Who knew that, in all the land, one slave meant strife, not peace;
Who fought for freedom, not glory; made war that war might cease.

Glory and honor and fame; the beating of muffled drums;
The wailing funeral dirge, as the flag-wrapped coffin comes;
Fame and honor and glory; and joy for a noble soul,
For a full and splendid life, and laurelled rest at the goal.

Glory and honor and fame; the pomp that a soldier prizes;
The league-long waving line as the marching falls and rises;
Rumbling of caissons and guns; the clatter of horses' feet,
And a million awe-struck faces far down the waiting street.

But better than martial woe, and the pageant of civic sorrow;
Better than praise of to-day, or the statue we build to-morrow;
Better than honor and glory, and history's iron pen,
Was the thought of duty done and the love of his fellow-men.

HAST THOU HEARD THE NIGHTINGALE?

Yes, I have heard the nightingale.
As in dark woods I wandered,
And dreamed and pondered,
A voice passed by all fire
And passion and desire;

I rather felt than heard
The song of that lone bird:
Yes, I have heard the nightingale.

Yes, I have heard the nightingale.
I heard it, and I followed;
The warm night swallowed
This soul and body of mine,
As burning thirst takes wine,
While on and on I pressed
Close to that singing breast:
Yes, I have heard the nightingale.

Yes, I have heard the nightingale.
Well doth each throbbing ember
The flame remember;
And I, how quick that sound
Turned drops from a deep wound!
How this heart was the thorn
Which pierced that breast forlorn!
Yes, I have heard the nightingale.

THE CELLO

When late I heard the trembling cello play,
In every face I read sad memories
That from dark, secret chambers where they lay
Rose, and looked forth from melancholy eyes.
So every mournful thought found there a tone
To match despondence: sorrow knew its mate;
Ill fortune sighed, and mute despair made moan;
And one deep chord gave answer, "Late, — too late."
Then ceased the quivering strain, and swift returned
Into its depths the secret of each heart;
Each face took on its mask, where lately burned
A spirit charmed to sight by music's art;
But unto one who caught that inner flame
No face of all can ever seem the same.

A CHILD

Her voice was like the song of birds;
Her eyes were like the stars;
Her little waving hands were like
Birds' wings that beat the bars.

And when those waving hands were still, —
Her soul had fled away, —
The music faded from the air,
The color from the day.

AH, BE NOT FALSE

Ah, be not false, sweet Splendor!
Be true, be good;
Be wise as thou art tender;
Be all that Beauty should.

Not lightly be thy citadel subdued;
Not ignobly, not untimely.
Take praise in solemn mood;
Take love sublimely.

OF ONE WHO NEITHER SEES NOR HEARS[1]

She lives in light, not shadow;
Not silence, but the sound
Which thrills the stars of heaven
And trembles from the ground.

She breathes a finer ether,
Beholds a keener sun;
In her supernal being
Music and light are one.

Unknown the subtle senses
That lead her through the day;
Love, light, and song and color
Come by another way.

Sight brings she to the seeing,
New song to those that hear;
Her braver spirit sounding
Where mortals fail and fear.

She at the heart of being
Serene and glad doth dwell;
Spirit with scarce a veil of flesh;
A soul made visible.

Or is it only a lovely girl,
With flowers at her maiden breast?
— Helen, here is a book of song
From the poet who loves you best.

[1] Helen Keller.

THE BIRDS OF BETHLEHEM

I HEARD the bells of Bethlehem ring —
Their voice was sweeter than the priests';
I heard the birds of Bethlehem sing
Unbidden in the churchly feasts.

They clung and sung on the swinging chain
High in the dim and incensed air;
The priests, with repetitions vain,
Chanted a never-ending prayer.

So bell and bird and priest I heard,
But voice of bird was most to me;
It had no ritual, no word,
And yet it sounded true and free.

I thought Child Jesus, were he there,
Would like the singing birds the best,
And clutch his little hands in air
And smile upon his mother's breast.

BETHLEHEM, *Holy Week*, 1896.

NOËL

STAR-DUST and vaporous light, —
The mist of worlds unborn, —
A shuddering in the awful night
Of winds that bring the morn.

Now comes the dawn: the circling earth;
Creatures that fly and crawl;
And Man, that last, imperial birth;
And Christ, the flower of all.

THE SONG OF A HEATHEN

(SOJOURNING IN GALILEE, A. D. 32)

IF Jesus Christ is a man, —
And only a man, — I say
That of all mankind I cleave to him,
And to him will I cleave alway.

If Jesus Christ is a God, —
And the only God, — I swear
I will follow Him through heaven and hell,
The earth, the sea, and the air!

THE HEROIC AGE

HE speaks not well who doth his time deplore,
Naming it new and little and obscure,
Ignoble and unfit for lofty deeds.
All times were modern in the time of them,
And this no more than others. Do thy part
Here in the living day, as did the great
Who made old days immortal! So shall men,
Gazing long back to this far-looming hour,
Say: "Then the time when men were truly men;
Though wars grew less, their spirits met the test
Of new conditions; conquering civic wrong;
Saving the state anew by virtuous lives;
Guarding the country's honor as their own,
And their own as their country's and their sons';
Defying leaguëd fraud with single truth;
Not fearing loss, and daring to be pure.
When error through the land raged like a pest,
They calmed the madness caught from mind to mind
By wisdom drawn from eld, and counsel sane;
And as the martyrs of the ancient world
Gave Death for man, so nobly gave they Life:
Those the great days, and that the heroic age."

ATHENS, 1896.

AFTER-SONG

THROUGH love to light! Oh wonderful the way
That leads from darkness to the perfect day!
From darkness and from sorrow of the night
To morning that comes singing o'er the sea.
Through love to light! Through light, O God, to thee,
Who art the love of love, the eternal light of light!

Edward Willard Watson

ABSOLUTION

I

PRIEST of God, unto thee I come;
Day doth dawn, though the mist lies deep.
Trembling with dread from my home I fled;
I have slain a man in the land of sleep.

Him I met in a region dim,
Where ever the sun shines faint and low,
Where the moon is far as a tiny star,
And rivers speed with a noiseless flow.

In the tangled wood he was lying hid;
But I saw him lurking, and then I knew
'T was the soul of the one since time begun
That had made me false when I would be
true.

My heart was hot and my anger fierce;
I knew in my dreaming his life I sought.
But with all my power, as I saw him cower,
I willed the deed that my hands have
wrought.

Ask me not if his name I know,
For all the rest of my dream is hid;
I only remember the river's flow,
And the dim gray light and the deed I did.

But demons of death and hate that wait
For the soul that sins, my soul pursue,
And my hands are red with the blood of
the dead,
And ever they cry the long hours through:

"Murderer, though in dreams and sleep,
Done is the deed with thy soul's consent,
And there is no hope for Heaven's gate to
ope,
Nor will men have pity nor God relent."

II

Son, no sin on thy soul doth rest;
Blood shows not on thy trembling hands.
Unto thee can cling no awful thing;
Thy soul was roaming in unreal lands.

'T was but a dream when all things seem
Mingled with fantasy strange and wild,
And the soul of man, do the worst it can,
Is sinless in slumber and undefiled.

For life is the life of the waking day;
Time enough in it for crime and sin.
But we sleep in the hours, like the sinless
flowers
That heed not the world and its madden-
ing din.

III

Out from the living, O God, I creep,
Naked and chill, to thy silent land;
Friend have I none, I stand alone,
To wait my doom at thy mighty hand.

Naked and chill, though wrapped in sin,
In the dark and cold with only thee,
Nor glint of a star that 's faint and far,
To light the night of thy world for me.

Whither, O God, wilt thou send the soul
Thou hast planted on earth and plucked
away?
For it grew, with the weeds of its evil
deeds,
In the wood and fen, in the mire and clay.

IV

Child of the earth, thou fragile flower
Bending down to the wind that blew,
Life shall seem but an evil dream;
Wake to the life that is real and true.

Cease thy dreaming, the world forget;
Lulled be the pain I made thee bear.
Sin and shame are only the name
Of the lesson I taught thee in sorrow
there.

Thou hast learned how the soul of man
Lifts, through error, its heart on high,
Up from the sin I placed it in,
To the bright, clear light in the starry
sky.

Ages hence, when thy world and stars
Fade away in the mist they are,
Thou shalt weep, and in pity creep
Back to the life of some lonely star.

Love shall well in thy heart, and tears
Fall for the sorrows thou couldst not know
But for the years of sins and fears
Spent in the dream of thy life below.

John Boyle O'Reilly

FROM "WENDELL PHILLIPS"

What shall we mourn? For the prostrate tree that sheltered the young green wood?
For the fallen cliff that fronted the sea, and guarded the fields from the flood?
For the eagle that died in the tempest, afar from its eyrie's brood?

Nay, not for these shall we weep; for the silver cord must be worn,
And the golden fillet shrink back at last, and the dust to its earth return;
And tears are never for those who die with their face to the duty done;
But we mourn for the fledglings left on the waste, and the fields where the wild waves run.

From the midst of the flock he defended, the brave one has gone to his rest;
And the tears of the poor he befriended their wealth of affliction attest.
From the midst of the people is stricken a symbol they daily saw,
Set over against the law books, of a Higher than human Law;
For his life was a ceaseless protest, and his voice was a prophet's cry
To be true to the Truth and faithful, though the world were arrayed for the Lie.

From the hearing of those who hated, a threatening voice has past;
But the lives of those who believe and die are not blown like a leaf on the blast.
A sower of infinite seed was he, a woodman that hewed toward the light,
Who dared to be traitor to Union when Union was traitor to Right!

AT BEST

The faithful helm commands the keel,
From port to port fair breezes blow;
But the ship must sail the convex sea,
Nor may she straighter go.

So, man to man; in fair accord,
On thought and will the winds may wait;
But the world will bend the passing word,
Though its shortest course be straight.

From soul to soul the shortest line
At best will bended be:
The ship that holds the straightest course
Still sails the convex sea.

AN ART MASTER

He gathered cherry-stones, and carved them quaintly
Into fine semblances of flies and flowers;
With subtle skill, he even imaged faintly
The forms of tiny maids and ivied towers.

His little blocks he loved to file and polish;
And ampler means he asked not, but despised.
All art but cherry-stones he would abolish,
For then his genius would be rightly prized.

For such rude hands as dealt with wrongs and passions,
And throbbing hearts, he had a pitying smile;
Serene his way through surging years and fashions,
While Heaven gave him his cherry-stones and file!

A SAVAGE

Dixon, a Choctaw, twenty years of age,
Had killed a miner in a Leadville brawl;
Tried and condemned, the rough-beards curb their rage,
And watch him stride in freedom from the hall.

"*Return on Friday, to be shot to death!*"
So ran the sentence, — it was Monday night.
The dead man's comrades drew a well-pleased breath;
Then all night long the gambling-dens were bright.

The days sped slowly; but the Friday came,
And flocked the miners to the shooting-ground;
They chose six riflemen of deadly aim,
And with low voices sat and lounged around.

"He will not come." "He 's not a fool." "The men
Who set the savage free must face the blame."
A Choctaw brave smiled bitterly, and then
Smiled proudly, with raised head, as Dixon came.

Silent and stern, a woman at his heels,
He motions to the brave, who stays her tread.
Next minute flame the guns, — the woman reels
And drops without a moan: Dixon is dead.

A WHITE ROSE

THE red rose whispers of passion,
And the white rose breathes of love;
Oh, the red rose is a falcon,
And the white rose is a dove.

But I send you a cream-white rosebud
With a flush on its petal tips;
For the love that is purest and sweetest
Has a kiss of desire on the lips.

MAYFLOWER

THUNDER our thanks to her — guns, hearts, and lips!
Cheer from the ranks to her,
Shout from the banks to her —
Mayflower! Foremost and best of our ships.

Mayflower! Twice in the national story
Thy dear name in letters of gold —
Woven in texture that never grows old —
Winning a home and winning glory!
Sailing the years to us, welcomed for aye;
Cherished for centuries, dearest to-day.
Every heart throbs for her, every flag dips —
Mayflower! First and last, best of our ships.

White as a seagull, she swept the long passage.
True as the homing-bird flies with its message.
Love her? O, richer than silk every sail of her.
Trust her? More precious than gold every nail of her.
Write we down faithfully every man's part in her;
Greet we all gratefully every true heart in her.
More than a name to us, sailing the fleetest,
Symbol of that which is purest and sweetest:
More than a keel to us, steering the straightest,
Emblem of that which is freest and greatest:
More than a dove-bosomed sail to the windward,
Flame passing on while the night-clouds fly hindward.
Kiss every plank of her! None shall take rank of her;
Frontward or weatherward, none can eclipse.
Thunder our thanks to her! Cheer from the banks to her!
Mayflower! Foremost and best of our ships!

Elizabeth Stuart Phelps Ward

THE LOST COLORS

FROWNING, the mountain stronghold stood,
Whose front no mortal could assail;
For more than twice three hundred years
The terror of the Indian vale.
By blood and fire the robber band
Answered the helpless village wail.

Hot was his heart and cool his thought,
When Napier from his Englishmen
Up to the bandits' rampart glanced,

And down upon his ranks again.
Summoned to dare a deed like that,
Which of them all would answer then?

What sullen regiment is this
That lifts its eyes to dread Cutchee?
Abased, its standard bears no flag.
For thus the punishment shall be
That England metes to Englishmen
Who shame her once by mutiny.

From out the disgraced Sixty-Fourth
There stepped a hundred men of might.
Cried Napier: "Now prove to me
I read my soldiers' hearts aright!
Form! Forward! Charge, my volunteers!
Your colors are on yonder height!"

So sad is shame, so wise is trust!
The challenge echoed bugle-clear.
Like fire along the Sixty-Fourth
From rank to file rang cheer on cheer.
In death and glory up the pass
They fought for all to brave men dear.

Old is the tale, but read anew
In every warring human heart.
What rebel hours, what coward shame,
Upon the aching memory start!
To find the ideal forfeited,
— What tears can teach the holy art?

Thou great Commander! leading on
Through weakest darkness to strong light;
By any anguish, give us back
Our life's young standard, pure and bright.
O fair, lost Colors of the soul!
For your sake storm we any height.

THE ROOM'S WIDTH

I THINK if I should cross the room,
Far as fear;
Should stand beside you like a thought —
Touch you, dear,

Like a fancy, — to your sad heart
It would seem
That my vision passed and prayed you,
Or my dream.

Then you would look with lonely eyes —
Lift your head —
And you would stir, and sigh, and say,
"She is dead."

Baffled by death and love, I lean
Through the gloom.
O Lord of life! am I forbid
To cross the room?

GLOUCESTER HARBOR

ONE shadow glides from the dumb shore,
And one from every silent sail.
One cloud the averted heavens wear,
A soft mask, thin and frail.

Oh, silver is the lessening rain,
And yellow was the weary drouth.
The reef her warning finger puts
Upon the harbor's mouth.

Her thin, wan finger, stiff and stark,
She holds by night, she holds by day.
Ask, if you will: no answer makes
The sombre, guarded bay.

The fleet, with idle canvas hung,
Like a brute life, sleeps patiently.
The headlights nod across the cliff,
The fog blows out to sea.

There is no color on the tide,
No color on the helpless sky;
Across the beach — a safe, small sound —
The grass-hid crickets cry.

And through the dusk I hear the keels
Of home-bound boats grate low and sweet.
O happy lights! O watching eyes!
Leap out the sound to greet.

O tender arms that meet and clasp!
Gather and cherish while ye may.
The morrow knoweth God. Ye know
Your own are yours to-day.

Forever from the Gloucester winds
The cries of hungry children start.
There breaks in every Gloucester wave
A widowed woman's heart.

Francis Howard Williams

ELECTRA

My Love too stately is to be but fair,
Too fair she is for naught but stateliness;
She bids me Nay, and yet a silent Yes
Dwells in the dusk her shadowy eyelids wear.
My Love's step makes a music in the air,
Touching the sense with a divine caress,
And all the rapture of the dawn doth bless
The light that leaps to life across her hair.
Her mouth is just the love-couch for a song,
And mid the fragrance of its riven flowers
Low laughter breaks and trembles close to tears
Mingled of mirth and melody, as a throng
Of bird notes wakes to joy the drowsy hours
And weaves delight through all the grieving years.

WALT WHITMAN

Darkness and death? Nay, Pioneer, for thee
The day of deeper vision has begun;
There is no darkness for the central sun
Nor any death for immortality.
At last the song of all fair songs that be,
At last the guerdon of a race well run,
The upswelling joy to know the victory won,
The river's rapture when it finds the sea.
Ah, thou art wrought in an heroic mould,
The modern man upon whose brow yet stays
A gleam of glory from the age of gold, —
A diadem which all the gods have kissed.
Hail and farewell! flower of the antique days, —
Democracy's divine protagonist.

March 26, 1892.

SONG

A bird in my bower
Sat calling, a-calling;
A bird answered low from the garden afar.
His note came with power,
While falling, a-falling,
Her note quivered faint as the light of a star.
"I am Life! I am Life!"
From the bower a-ringing,
Trilled forth a mad melody, soaring above;
"I am Love! I am Love!"
From the garden a-singing,
Came soft as a dream, and the echoes sang "Love."

They joined, and together
Fast flying, a-flying,
Were lost to my gaze in the arch of the sky.
The wind through the heather
Is sighing, a-sighing;
Ah! how should it ever do other than sigh?
Where art thou, where art thou,
Life, flying, a-flying?
Where art thou, O Love, sweetest child of the dawn?
The song in the meadow
Is dying, a-dying;
My heart groweth heavy, and whispereth — "Gone."

Maurice Thompson

THE LION'S CUB

The whelp that nipped its mother's dug in turning from her breast,
And smacked its lusty lips and built its own lair in the West,
Has stretched its limbs and looked about and roared across the sea:
"Oh, mother, I did bite thee hard, but still thou lovest me!"

She lifts her head and listens, as waking from a dream,
Her great jaw set, her claws outspread, her lion eyes agleam;
The voice is deep as thunder on the far horizon rim,
And up the mother spoke and said: "It can be none but him!"

Cried England to America: "My ancient love abides,
And the old Trafalgar courage still upon the ocean rides."
America to England spake: "The God of Liberty
Goes with us marching up the land and sailing down the sea."

And the twain are joined for hunting, — let all the packs beware,
The tiger's kith, the panther's kin, the race-hordes of the bear.
They two step forth together, God's hand has struck the hour,
All pathways lead to freedom, each foot-step broadens power.

The world is still in dull amaze, agape and dazed to hear;
There is a rustling of the thrones, uneasy far and near,
King leaning unto king, and on Oppression's hateful lips
A pallor as the wind brings in the booming of the ships.

And who shall cower, who recoil, or choose the craven's tack,
And strain the law (by heroes made) to hold his country back?
Ah, who? Let children lisp his shame and women cry him down
What time our glorious banner waves o'er stormëd tower and town.

The star is up, the star of splendor, never to set or wane;
The flag leads on, the flag of glory, never to turn again;
And where it goes we cheer and follow, no man of us will fail;
We all are where our armies camp and where our navies sail.

World-conquering mother, hard we bit in parting from thy breast;
Yet still we smack our lusty lips and love thy milk the best;
For the blood our mother gave us is the true imperial strain;
She bore one cub, one only, but it wears the lion's mane!

AN EARLY BLUEBIRD

LEAP to the highest height of spring,
And trill thy sweetest note,
Bird of the heavenly plumes and twinkling wing
And silver-tonëd throat!

Sing, while the maple's deepest root
Thrills with a pulse of fire
That lights its buds. Blow, blow thy tender flute,
Thy reed of rich desire!

Breathe in thy syrinx Freedom's breath,
Quaver the fresh and true,
Dispel this lingering wintry mist of death
And charm the world anew!

Thou first sky-dipped spring-bud of song,
Whose heavenly ecstasy
Foretells the May while yet March winds are strong,
Fresh faith appears with thee!

How sweet, how magically rich,
Through filmy splendor blown,
Thy hopeful voice set to the promise-pitch
Of melody yet unknown!

O land of mine (where hope can grow
And send a deeper root
With every spring), hear, heed the free bird blow
Hope's charmëd flute!

Ah! who will hear, and who will care,
And who will heed thy song,
As prophecy, as hope, as promise rare,
Budding to bloom ere long?

From swelling bulbs and sprouting seed,
Sweet sap and fragrant dew,
And human hearts, grown doubly warm at need,
Leaps answer strong and true:

We see, we hear (thou liberty-loving thing,
That down spring winds doth float),
The promise of thine empyrean wing,
The hope that floods thy throat!

WRITTEN ON A FLY-LEAF OF THEOCRITUS

THOSE were good times, in olden days,
Of which the poet has his dreams,
When gods beset the woodland ways,
And lay in wait by all the streams.

One could be sure of something then
Severely simple, simply grand,
Or keenly, subtly sweet, as when
Venus and Love went hand in hand.

Now I would give (such is my need)
All the world's store of rhythm and rhyme
To see Pan fluting on a reed
And with his goat-hoof keeping time!

A FLIGHT SHOT

WE were twin brothers, tall and hale,
Glad wanderers over hill and dale.

We stood within the twilight shade
Of pines that rimmed a Southern glade.

He said: "Let 's settle, if we can,
Which of us is the stronger man.

"We 'll try a flight shot, high and good,
Across the green glade toward the wood."

And so we bent in sheer delight
Our old yew bows with all our might.

Our long keen shafts, drawn to the head,
Were poised a moment ere they sped.

As we leaned back a breath of air
Mingled the brown locks of our hair.

We loosed. As one our bow-cords rang,
As one away our arrows sprang.

Away they sprang; the wind of June
Thrilled to their softly whistled tune.

We watched their flight, and saw them strike
Deep in the ground slantwise alike,

So far away that they might pass
For two thin straws of broom-sedge grass!

Then arm in arm we doubting went
To find whose shaft was farthest sent,

Each fearing in his loving heart
That brother's shaft had fallen short.

But who could tell by such a plan
Which of us was the stronger man?

There at the margin of the wood,
Side by side our arrows stood,

Their red cock-feathers wing and wing,
Their amber nocks still quivering,

Their points deep-planted where they fell
An inch apart and parallel!

We clasped each other's hands; said he,
"Twin champions of the world are we!"

A CREOLE SLAVE-SONG

(*Ah, lo zo-zo chan' dan' branche*)

WHAT bird is that, with voice so sweet,
Sings to the sun from yonder tree?
What girl is that so slim and fleet,
Comes through the cane her love to meet?
Foli zo-zo, sing merrily.
The pretty girl she comes to me!

What wind is that upon the cane?
What perfume from a far-off rose
Fills me with dreams? What strange, vague pain
Stirs in my heart? What longing vain
Is this that through my bosom goes?
O south wind, perfume and desire,
You kiss, you soothe, you burn like fire!

Ah, no! Ah, no! It is a cheat.
There is no bird; my love comes not;
The wind chills me from head to feet,
And oh, it brings no perfume sweet.
My slender girl the white man bought,
And took her far across the bay —
I cannot cut the cane to-day!

I cannot cut the cane to-day —
  O zo-zo, moquer, come and sing!
O warm wind, through the cane-field stray,
Wave the long moss so soft and gray!
  I have no heart for anything;
But life was heaven and work was play
When my love loved me every day!

White man, how I worked for you
  When I was young and blithe and strong!
The earth was green, the sky was blue,
My love's eyes were as bright as dew;
  And life was like the *zo-zo's* song!
But you — you sold my love away —
I cannot cut the cane to-day!

I did not dream a slave could be
  A man, and right a grievous wrong.
I writhed and bore your cruelty;
I felt the soul go out of me;
  And yet, I was so lion-strong
I could have torn your heart away —
I cannot cut the cane to-day!

Freedom! I feel it when too late,
  Like spring wind on a blasted tree,
A waft of mockery and hate!
Bring back my chains, O cruel Fate!
  Bring youth and slavery back to me;
Bring back the lash, the hound, the pain,
So that my own love come again!

But hark! A gentle voice afar
  Calls me to go, I know not where —
Yes, past the sun and past the star,
Into God's land. A golden car
  And milk-white horses — *she* is there!
So sweet — I dream — I float away —
I cannot cut the cane to-day!

A PROPHECY

(FROM "LINCOLN'S GRAVE")

OLD soldiers true, ah, them all men can trust,
Who fought, with conscience clear, on either side;
Who bearded Death and thought their cause was just;
Their stainless honor cannot be denied;
All patriots they beyond the farthest doubt;
Ring it and sing it up and down the land,
And let no voice dare answer it with sneers,
  Or shut its meaning out;
Ring it and sing it, we go hand in hand,
Old infantry, old cavalry, old cannoneers.

And if Virginia's vales shall ring again
To battle-yell of Moseby or Mahone,
If Wilder's wild brigade or Morgan's men
Once more wheel into line; or all alone
A Sheridan shall ride, a Cleburne fall, —
There will not be two flags above them flying,
But both in one, welded in that pure flame
  Upflaring in us all,
When kindred unto kindred, loudly crying,
Rally and cheer in freedom's holy name!

Mary Thacher Higginson

CHANGELINGS

  THE ghosts of flowers went sailing
  Through the dreamy autumn air, —
The gossamer wings of the milkweed brown,
And the sheeny silk of the thistle-down;
  But there was no bewailing,
  And never a hint of despair.

  From the mountain-ash was swinging
  A gray, deserted nest;
Scarlet berries where eggs had been;
Softly the flower-wraiths floated in:
  And the brook and breeze were singing
  When the sun sank down in the west.

IN THE DARK

THE fields were silent, and the woodland drear,
  The moon had set, and clouds hid all the stars;
And blindly, when a footfall met my ear,
  I reached across the bars.

And swift as thought this hand was clasped in thine,
  Though darkness hung around us and above;
Not guided by uncertain fate to mine,
  But by the law of love.

I know not which of us may first go hence
  And leave the other to be brave alone,
Unable to dispel the shadows dense
  That veil the life unknown;

But if I linger last, and stretch once more
  A longing hand when fades this earthly day,
Again it will be grasped by thine, before
  My steps can lose the way.

GHOST-FLOWERS

(MONOTROPA UNIFLORA)

In shining groups, each stem a pearly ray,
Weird flecks of light within the shadowed wood,
They dwell aloof, a spotless sisterhood.
No Angelus, except the wild bird's lay,
Awakes these forest nuns; yet night and day
Their heads are bent, as if in prayerful mood.
A touch will mar their snow, and tempests rude
Defile; but in the mist fresh blossoms stray
From spirit-gardens just beyond our ken.
Each year we seek their virgin haunts, to look
Upon new loveliness, and watch again
Their shy devotions near the singing brook;
Then, mingling in the dizzy stir of men,
Forget the vows made in that cloistered nook.

INHERITANCE

We wondered why he always turned aside
When mirth and gladness filled the brimming days:
Who else so fit as he for pleasure's ways?
Men thought him frozen by a selfish pride;
But that his voice was music none denied,
Or that his smile was like the sun's warm rays.
One day upon the sands he spoke in praise
Of swimmers who were buffeting the tide:
"The swelling waves of life they dare to meet.
I may not plunge where others safely go, —
Unbidden longings in my pulses beat."
O blind and thoughtless world! you little know
That ever round this hero's steadfast feet
Surges and tugs the dreaded undertow.

John Henry Boner

POE'S COTTAGE AT FORDHAM

Here lived the soul enchanted
  By melody of song;
Here dwelt the spirit haunted
  By a demoniac throng;
Here sang the lips elated;
Here grief and death were sated;
Here loved and here unmated
  Was he, so frail, so strong.

Here wintry winds and cheerless
  The dying firelight blew,
While he whose song was peerless
  Dreamed the drear midnight through,
And from dull embers chilling
Crept shadows darkly filling
The silent place, and thrilling
  His fancy as they grew.

Here, with brow bared to heaven,
  In starry night he stood,
With the lost star of seven
  Feeling sad brotherhood.
Here in the sobbing showers
Of dark autumnal hours
He heard suspected powers
  Shriek through the stormy wood.

From visions of Apollo
  And of Astarte's bliss,
He gazed into the hollow
  And hopeless vale of Dis,
And though earth were surrounded
By heaven, it still was mounded
With graves. His soul had sounded
  The dolorous abyss.

Proud, mad, but not defiant,
  He touched at heaven and hell.

Fate found a rare soul pliant
And rung her changes well.
Alternately his lyre,
Stranded with strings of fire,
Led earth's most happy choir,
Or flashed with Israfel.

No singer of old story
Luting accustomed lays,
No harper for new glory,
No mendicant for praise,
He struck high chords and splendid,
Wherein were fiercely blended
Tones that unfinished ended
With his unfinished days.

Here through this lowly portal,
Made sacred by his name,
Unheralded immortal
The mortal went and came.
And fate that then denied him,
And envy that decried him,
And malice that belied him,
Have cenotaphed his fame.

REMEMBRANCE

I THINK that we retain of our dead friends
And absent ones no general portraiture;
That perfect memory does not long endure,
But fades and fades until our own life ends.
Unconsciously, forgetfulness attends
That grief for which there is no other cure,
But leaves of each lost one some record sure, —
A look, an act, a tone, — something that lends
Relief and consolation, not regret.
Even that poor mother mourning her dead child,
Whose agonizing eyes with tears are wet,
Whose bleeding heart cannot be reconciled
Unto the grave's embrace, — even she shall yet
Remember only when her babe first smiled.

WE WALKED AMONG THE WHISPERING PINES

IT was a still autumnal day —
So sadly still and strangely bright —
The hectic glow of quick decay
Tinged everything with lovely light.
It warmly touched the fragrant air
And fields of corn and crumbling vines
Along the golden Yadkin, where
We walked among the whispering pines

Alas, that tender hectic glow
Shone in her gentle, pallid face,
And none save God in heaven could know
My agony to see its trace —
To watch those fatal roses bloom
Upon her cheeks — red, cruel signs —
But all of love, not of the tomb,
We spoke among the whispering pines.

Ah, fatal roses — never yet
Have they deceived. She drooped and died.
We parted and we never met
Again; but often at my side
An angel walks, — her step I know, —
A viewless arm my neck entwines.
O angel love, so years ago
We walked among the whispering pines.

THE LIGHT'OOD FIRE

WHEN wintry days are dark and drear
And all the forest ways grow still,
When gray snow-laden clouds appear
Along the bleak horizon hill,
When cattle all are snugly penned
And sheep go huddling close together,
When steady streams of smoke ascend
From farm-house chimneys, — in such weather
Give me old Carolina's own,
A great log house, a great hearth-stone,
A cheering pipe of cob or briar,
And a red, leaping light'ood fire.

When dreary day draws to a close
And all the silent land is dark,
When Boreas down the chimney blows
And sparks fly from the crackling bark,
When limbs are bent with snow or sleet
And owls hoot from the hollow tree,
With hounds asleep about your feet,
Then is the time for reverie.
Give me old Carolina's own,
A hospitable wide hearthstone,
A cheering pipe of cob or briar,
And a red, rousing light'ood fire.

John Banister Tabb

EVOLUTION

Out of the dusk a shadow,
Then, a spark;
Out of the cloud a silence,
Then, a lark;
Out of the heart a rapture,
Then, a pain;
Out of the dead, cold ashes,
Life again.

THE WATER-LILY

Whence, O fragrant form of light,
Hast thou drifted through the night,
Swanlike, to a leafy nest,
On the restless waves, at rest?

Art thou from the snowy zone
Of a mountain-summit blown,
Or the blossom of a dream,
Fashioned in the foamy stream?

Nay, — methinks the maiden moon,
When the daylight came too soon,
Fleeting from her bath to hide,
Left her garment in the tide.

TO SHELLEY

At Shelley's birth,
The Lark, dawn-spirit, with an anthem loud
Rose from the dusky earth
To tell it to the Cloud,
That, like a flower night-folded in the gloom,
Burst into morning bloom.

At Shelley's death,
The Sea, that deemed him an immortal, saw
A god's extinguished breath,
And landward, as in awe,
Upbore him to the altar whence he came,
And the rekindling flame.

THE SISTERS

The waves forever move;
The hills forever rest:
Yet each the heavens approve,
And Love alike hath blessed
A Martha's household care,
A Mary's cloistered prayer.

ANONYMOUS

Anonymous — nor needs a name
To tell the secret whence the flame,
With light, and warmth, and incense, came
A new creation to proclaim.

So was it when, His labor done,
God saw His work, and smiled thereon:
His glory in the picture shone,
But name upon the canvas, none.

CLOVER

Little masters, hat in hand
Let me in your presence stand,
Till your silence solve for me
This your threefold mystery.

Tell me — for I long to know —
How, in darkness there below,
Was your fairy fabric spun,
Spread and fashioned, three in one

Did your gossips gold and blue,
Sky and Sunshine, choose for you,
Ere your triple forms were seen,
Suited liveries of green?

Can ye, — if ye dwelt indeed
Captives of a prison seed, —
Like the Genie, once again
Get you back into the grain?

Little masters, may I stand
In your presence, hat in hand,
Waiting till you solve for me
This your threefold mystery?

THE DEPARTED

They cannot wholly pass away,
How far soe'er above;

Nor we, the lingerers, wholly stay
Apart from those we love:
For spirits in eternity,
As shadows in the sun,
Reach backward into Time, as we,
Like lifted clouds, reach on.

INDIAN SUMMER

No more the battle or the chase
The phantom tribes pursue,
But each in its accustomed place
The Autumn hails anew:
And still from solemn councils set
On every hill and plain,
The smoke of many a calumet
Ascends to heaven again.

THE DRUID

Godlike beneath his grave divinities,
The last of all their worshippers, he stood.
The shadows of a vanished multitude
Enwound him, and their voices in the breeze
Made murmur, while the meditative trees
Reared of their strong fraternal branches rude
A temple meet for prayer. What blossoms strewed
The path between Life's morning hours and these?
What lay beyond the darkness? He alone
The sunshine and the shadow and the dew
Had shared alike with leaf, and flower, and stem:
Their life had been his lesson; and from them
A dream of immortality he drew,
As in their fate foreshadowing his own.

THE CHILD

AT BETHLEHEM

I

Long, long before the Babe could speak,
When he would kiss his mother's cheek
And to her bosom press,
The brightest angels standing near
Would turn away to hide a tear —
For they are motherless.

II

Where were ye, Birds, that bless His name,
When wingless to the world He came,
And wordless, though Himself the Word
That made the blossom and the bird?

III

TO HIS MOTHER

He brought a Lily white,
That bowed its fragrant head
And blushed a rosy red
Before her fairer light.

He brought a Rose; and, lo,
The crimson blossom saw
Her beauty, and in awe
Became as white as snow.

QUATRAINS

THE BUBBLE

Why should I stay? Nor seed nor fruit have I.
But, sprung at once to beauty's perfect round,
Nor loss, nor gain, nor change in me is found, —
A life — complete in death — complete to die.

BECALMED

The bar is crossed; but Death — the pilot — stands
In seeming doubt before the tranquil deep;
The fathom-line still trembling in his hands,
As when upon the treacherous shoals of sleep.

FAME

Their noonday never knows
What names immortal are:
'T is night alone that shows
How star surpasseth star.

Sarah Chauncey Woolsey

("SUSAN COOLIDGE")

HELEN

THE autumn seems to cry for thee,
  Best lover of the autumn days!
Each scarlet-tipped and wine-red tree,
  Each russet branch and branch of gold,
Gleams through its veil of shimmering haze,
  And seeks thee as they sought of old:
For all the glory of their dress,
They wear a look of wistfulness.

In every wood I see thee stand,
  The ruddy boughs above thy head,
And heaped in either slender hand
  The frosted white and amber ferns,
The sumach's deep, resplendent red,
  Which like a fiery feather burns,
And, over all, thy happy eyes,
Shining as clear as autumn skies.

I hear thy call upon the breeze,
  Gay as the dancing wind, and sweet,
And, underneath the radiant trees,
  O'er lichens gray and darkling moss,
Follow the trace of those light feet
  Which never were at fault or loss,
But, by some forest instinct led,
Knew where to turn and how to tread.

Where art thou, comrade true and tried?
  The woodlands call for thee in vain,
And sadly burns the autumn-tide
  Before my eyes, made dim and blind
By blurring, puzzling mists of pain.
  I look before, I look behind;
Beauty and loss seem everywhere,
And grief and glory fill the air.

Already, in these few short weeks,
  A hundred things I leave unsaid,
Because there is no voice that speaks
  In answer, and no listening ear,
No one to care now thou art dead!
  And month by month, and year by year,
I shall but miss thee more, and go
With half my thought untold, I know.

I do not think thou hast forgot,
I know that I shall not forget,
  And some day, glad, but wondering not,
We two shall meet, and, face to face,
In still, fair fields unseen as yet,
  Shall talk of each old time and place,
And smile at pain interpreted
By wisdom learned since we were dead.

GULF STREAM

LONELY and cold and fierce I keep my way,
  Scourge of the lands, companioned by the storm,
Tossing to heaven my frontlet, wild and gray,
  Mateless, yet conscious ever of a warm
And brooding presence close to mine all day.

What is this alien thing, so near, so far,
  Close to my life always, but blending never, —
Hemmed in by walls whose crystal gates unbar
  Not at the instance of my strong endeavor
To pierce the stronghold where their secrets are?

Buoyant, impalpable, relentless, thin,
  Rise the clear, mocking walls. I strive in vain
To reach the pulsing heart that beats within,
  Or, with persistence of a cold disdain,
To quell the gladness which I may not win.

Forever sundered and forever one,
  Linked by a bond whose spell I may not guess,
Our hostile yet embracing currents run;
  Such wedlock lonelier is than loneliness.
Baffled, withheld, I clasp the bride I shun.

Yet even in my wrath a wild regret
  Mingles; a bitterness of jealous strife
Tinges my fury as I foam and fret
  Against the borders of that calmer life,
Beside whose course my wrathful course is set.

But all my anger, all my pain and woe,
Are vain to daunt her gladness; all the while
She goes rejoicing, and I do not know,
Catching the soft irradiance of her smile,
If I am most her lover or her foe.

Gertrude Bloede

("STUART STERNE")

NIGHT AFTER NIGHT

NIGHT after night we dauntlessly embark
On slumber's stream, in whose deep waves are drowned
Sorrow and care, and with all senses bound
Drift for a while beneath the sombre arc
Of that full circle made of light and dark
Called life, yet have no fear, and know refound
Lost consciousness shall be, even at the sound
Of the first warble of some early lark
Or touch of sunbeam. Oh, and why not then
Lie down to our last sleep, still trusting Him
Who guided us so oft through shadows dim,
Believing somewhere on our sense again
Some lark's sweet note, some golden beam, shall break,
And with glad voices cry, "Awake! awake!"

MY FATHER'S CHILD

ABOUT her head or floating feet
No halo's starry gleam,
Still dark and swift uprising, like
A bubble in a stream, —

A soul, from whose rejoicing heart
The bonds of earth were riven,
Sped upward through the silent night
To the closed Gates of Heaven.

And waiting heard a voice, — "Who comes
To claim Eternity?
Hero or saint that bled and died
Mankind to save and free?"

She bent her head. The voice once more, —
"Didst thou then toil and live
For home and children — to thy Love
Last breath and heart's blood give?"

Her head sank lower still, she clasped
Her hands upon her breast:
"Oh, no!" she whispered, "my dim life
Has never been so blest!

"I trod a lonely, barren path,
And neither great nor good,
Gained not a hero's palm, nor won
The crown of motherhood!

"Oh, I was naught!" Yet suddenly
The white lips faintly smiled —
"Save, oh, methinks I was mayhap
My Heavenly Father's Child!"

A flash of light, a cry of joy,
And with uplifted eyes
The soul, through gates rolled open wide,
Passed into Paradise.

SOUL, WHEREFORE FRET THEE?

SOUL, wherefore fret thee? Striving still to throw
Some light upon the primal mystery
Through rolling ages pondered ceaselessly,
Whence thou hast come, and whither thou shalt go!
Some deepest, secret voice gives thee to know
How, older than created earth and sea,
Thou hast been ever, shalt forever be, —
Unborn — undying! Thy own life doth show,
Yester, to-day, to-morrow, but a chain
Of dusky pearls, whereof we seek in vain
End or beginning, though perchance the one
We call To-day gleams whitest in the sun.
Ay, Soul, thy very Self is unto thee
Immortal pledge of Immortality!

Will Carleton

OUT OF THE OLD HOUSE, NANCY[1]

Out of the old house, Nancy — moved up
into the new;
All the hurry and worry is just as good as
through.
Only a bounden duty remains for you
and I —
And that 's to stand on the doorstep
here, and bid the old house good-
by.

What a shell we 've lived in, these nineteen
or twenty years!
Wonder it had n't smashed in, and tumbled
about our ears;
Wonder it 's stuck together, and answered
till to-day;
But every individual log was put up here
to stay.

Things looked rather new, though, when
this old house was built;
And things that blossomed you would 've
made some women wilt;
And every other day, then, as sure as day
would break,
My neighbor Ager come this way, invitin'
me to "shake."

And you, for want of neighbors, was sometimes blue and sad,
For wolves and bears and wildcats was the
nearest ones you had;
But, lookin' ahead to the clearin', we
worked with all our might,
Until we was fairly out of the woods, and
things was goin' right.

Look up there at our new house! — ain't it
a thing to see?
Tall and big and handsome, and new as new
can be;
All in apple-pie order, especially the
shelves,
And never a debt to say but what we own
it all ourselves.

Look at our old log-house — how little it
now appears!
But it 's never gone back on us for nineteen
or twenty years;
An' I won't go back on it now, or go to
pokin' fun —
There 's such a thing as praisin' a thing for
the good that it has done.

Probably you remember how rich we was
that night,
When we was fairly settled, an' had things
snug and tight:
We feel as proud as you please, Nancy,
over our house that 's new,
But we felt as proud under this old roof,
and a good deal prouder, too.

Never a handsomer house was seen beneath
the sun:
Kitchen and parlor and bedroom — we
had 'em all in one;
And the fat old wooden clock, that we
bought when we come West,
Was tickin' away in the corner there, and
doin' its level best.

Trees was all around us, a-whisperin' cheering words;
Loud was the squirrel's chatter, and sweet
the songs of birds;
And home grew sweeter and brighter — our
courage began to mount —
And things looked hearty and happy then,
and work appeared to count.

And here one night it happened, when
things was goin' bad,
We fell in a deep old quarrel — the first
we ever had;
And when you give out and cried, then I,
like a fool, give in,
And then we agreed to rub all out, and start
the thing ag'in.

Here it was, you remember, we sat when
the day was done,
And you was a-makin' clothing *that was n't
for either one*;
And often a soft word of love I was soft
enough to say,
And the wolves was howlin' in the woods
not twenty rods away.

[1] Copyright, 1873, by Harper & Brothers.

Then our first-born baby — a regular little joy,
Though I fretted a little because it was n't a boy:
Wa' n't she a little flirt, though, with all her pouts and smiles?
Why, settlers come to see that show a half a dozen miles.

Yonder sat the cradle — a homely, home-made thing, —
And many a night I rocked it, providin' you would sing;
And many a little squatter brought up with us to stay, —
And so that cradle, for many a year, was never put away.

How they kept a-comin', so cunnin' and fat and small!
How they growed! 't was a wonder how we found room for 'em all;
But though the house was crowded, it empty seemed that day
When Jennie lay by the fireplace there, and moaned her life away.

An' right in there the preacher, with Bible and hymn-book, stood,
"'Twixt the dead and the living," and "hoped 't would do us good;"
And the little whitewood coffin on the table there was set,
And now as I rub my eyes it seems as if I could see it yet.

Then that fit of sickness it brought on you, you know;
Just by a thread you hung, and you e'en-a'-most let go;
And here is the spot I tumbled, an' give the Lord his due,
When the doctor said the fever 'd turned, an' he could fetch you through.

Yes, a deal has happened to make this old house dear:
Christenin's, funerals, weddin's — what have n't we had here?
Not a log in this buildin' but its memories has got,
And not a nail in this old floor but touches a tender spot.

Out of the old house, Nancy, — moved up into the new;
All the hurry and worry is just as good as through;
But I tell you a thing right here, that I ain't ashamed to say,
There 's precious things in this old house we never can take away.

Here the old house will stand, but not as it stood before:
Winds will whistle through it, and rains will flood the floor;
And over the hearth, once blazing, the snow-drifts oft will pile,
And the old thing will seem to be a-mournin' all the while.

Fare you well, old house! you 're naught that can feel or see,
But you seem like a human being — a dear old friend to me;
And we never will have a better home, if *my* opinion stands,
Until we commence a-keepin' house in the house not made with hands.

Ina Coolbrith

WHEN THE GRASS SHALL COVER ME

WHEN the grass shall cover me,
Head to foot where I am lying;
When not any wind that blows,
Summer blooms nor winter snows,
Shall awake me to your sighing:
Close above me as you pass,
You will say, "How kind she was,"
You will say, "How true she was,"
When the grass grows over me.

When the grass shall cover me,
Holden close to earth's warm bosom, —
While I laugh, or weep, or sing
Nevermore, for anything,
You will find in blade and blossom,
Sweet small voices, odorous,
Tender pleaders in my cause,
That shall speak me as I was —
When the grass grows over me.

When the grass shall cover me!
Ah, belovëd, in my sorrow

Very patient, I can wait,
Knowing that, or soon or late,
There will dawn a clearer morrow:
When your heart will moan "Alas!
Now I know how true she was;
Now I know how dear she was" —
When the grass grows over me!

THE MARIPOSA LILY

INSECT or blossom? Fragile, fairy thing,
Poised upon slender tip, and quivering
To flight! a flower of the fields of air;
A jewelled moth; a butterfly, with rare
And tender tints upon his downy wing,
A moment resting in our happy sight;
A flower held captive by a thread so slight
Its petal-wings of broidered gossamer
Are, light as the wind, with every wind astir, —
Wafting sweet odor, faint and exquisite.
O dainty nursling of the field and sky,
What fairer thing looks up to heaven's blue
And drinks the noontide sun, the dawning's dew?
Thou wingëd bloom! thou blossom-butterfly!

FRUITIONLESS

AH! little flower, upspringing, azure-eyed,
The meadow-brook beside,
Dropping delicious balms
Into the tender palms
Of lover-winds, that woo with light caress,
In still contentedness,
Living and blooming thy brief summer-day: —
So, wiser far than I,
That only dream and sigh,
And, sighing, dream my listless life away.

Ah! sweetheart birds, a-building your wee house
In the broad-leavëd boughs,
Pausing with merry trill
To praise each other's skill,
And nod your pretty heads with pretty pride;
Serenely satisfied
To trill and twitter love's sweet roundelay: —
So, happier than I,
That, lonely, dream and sigh,
And, sighing, dream my lonely life away.

Brown-bodied bees, that scent with nostrils fine
The odorous blossom-wine,
Sipping, with heads half thrust
Into the pollen dust
Of rose and hyacinth and daffodil,
To hive, in amber cell,
A honey feasting for the winter-day: —
So, better far than I,
Self-wrapt, that dream and sigh,
And, sighing, dream my useless life away.

HELEN HUNT JACKSON

WHAT songs found voice upon those lips,
What magic dwelt within the pen,
Whose music into silence slips,
Whose spell lives not again!

For her the clamorous to-day
The dreamful yesterday became;
The brands upon dead hearths that lay
Leaped into living flame.

Clear ring the silvery Mission bells
Their calls to vesper and to mass;
O'er vineyard slopes, through fruited dells,
The long processions pass;

The pale Franciscan lifts in air
The Cross above the kneeling throng;
Their simple world how sweet with prayer,
With chant and matin-song!

There, with her dimpled, lifted hands,
Parting the mustard's golden plumes,
The dusky maid, Ramona, stands
Amid the sea of blooms.

And Alessandro, type of all
His broken tribe, for evermore
An exile, hears the stranger call
Within his father's door.

The visions vanish and are not,
Still are the sounds of peace and strife, —
Passed with the earnest heart and thought
Which lured them back to life.

O sunset land! O land of vine,
And rose, and bay! in silence here
Let fall one little leaf of thine,
With love, upon her bier.

Lloyd Mifflin

SONNETS

I

THE SOVEREIGNS

THEY who create rob death of half its stings;
They, from the dim inane and vague opaque
Of nothingness, build with their thought, and make
Enduring entities and beauteous things;
They are the Poets — they give airy wings
To shapes marmorean; or they overtake
The Ideal with the brush, or, soaring, wake
Far in the rolling clouds their glorious strings.
The Poet is the only potentate;
His sceptre reaches o'er remotest zones;
His thought remembered and his golden tones
Shall, in the ears of nations uncreate,
Roll on for ages and reverberate
When Kings are dust beside forgotten thrones.

MILTON

HIS feet were shod with music and had wings
Like Hermes: far upon the peaks of song
His sandals sounded silverly along;
The dull world blossomed into beauteous things
Where'er he trod; and Heliconian springs
Gushed from the rocks he touched; round him a throng
Of fair invisibles, seraphic, strong,
Struck Orphean murmurs out of golden strings;
But he, spreading keen pinions for a white
Immensity of radiance and of peace,
Up-looming to the Empyrean infinite,
Far through ethereal fields, and zenith seas,
High, with strong wing-beats and with eagle ease,
Soared in a solitude of glorious light!

II

THE SHIP

I LAY on Delos of the Cyclades
At evening, on a cape of golden land;
The blind Bard's book was open in my hand,
There where the Cyclops makes the Odyssey's
Calm pages tremble as Odysseus flees.
Then, stately, like a mirage o'er the sand,
A phantom ship across the sunset strand
Rose out of dreams and clave the purple seas;
Straight on that city's bastions did she run —
Whose toppling turrets on their donjons hold
Bells that to mortal ears have never tolled —
Then drifted down the gateways of the sun
With fading pennon and with gonfalon,
And cast her anchors in the pools of gold.

TO AN OLD VENETIAN WINE-GLASS

DAUGHTER of Venice, fairer than the moon!
From thy dark casement leaning, half divine,
And to the lutes of love that low repine
Across the midnight of the hushed lagoon
Listening with languor in a dreamful swoon —
On such a night as this thou didst entwine
Thy lily fingers round this glass of wine,
And clasped thy climbing lover — none too soon!
Thy lover left, but ere he left thy room
From this he drank, his warm lips at the brim;
Thou kissed it as he vanished in the gloom;
That kiss, because of thy true love for him —
Long, long ago, when thou wast in thy bloom, —
Hath left it ever rosy round the rim!

III

THESEUS AND ARIADNE

Thes. Nay, I have loved thee!
Ari. Thou hast loved, didst say?
Thes. I loved thee well at Crete.
Ari. Lov'st me no more?
Thes. Ah! who can hold the wave upon the shore?
Ari. Thou, if thou wouldst; and, oh! is that the way

Thou speak'st to me, who gave thee, on that day,
My flower of life ?
Thes. My ship is ready — sail and oar ! . . .
Ari. Did I not save thee from the Minotaur, —
And wilt thou leave me ?
Thes. Who can make love stay ? . . .
Wax is my heart and takes full easily
The last print on 't. Past love is past recall.
Adieu ! . . . Love has the helm — he guides, not we . . .
Ari. Beloved Traitor ! May thy black sail pall
Deep in the brine, thee, and thy maidens all ! . . .
Ye gods ! he leaves me and my babe to be !

IV

TO THE MILKWEED

None call thee flower ! . . . I will not so malign
The satin softness of thy plumëd seed,
Nor so profane thee as to call thee weed,
Thou tuft of ermine down, fit to entwine
About a queen; or, fitter still, to line
The nest of birds of strange exotic breed.
The orient cunning, and the somnolent speed
Of looms of dusky Ind weave not so fine
A gossamer . . . Ah me ! could he who sings,
On such adventurous and aërial wings
Far over lands and undiscovered seas
Waft the dark seeds of his imaginings,
That, flowering, men might say, Lo ! look on these
Wild Weeds of Song — not all ungracious things !

TO A MAPLE SEED

Art thou some wingëd Sprite, that, fluttering round,
Exhausted on the grass at last doth lie,
Or wayward Fay ? Ah, weakling, by and by
Thyself shalt grow a giant, strong and sound,
When, like Antaeus, thou dost touch the ground.
O happy Seed ! it is not thine to die;
Thy wings bestow thine immortality,
And thou canst bridge the deep and dark profound.
I hear the ecstatic song the wild bird flings,
In future summers, from thy leafy head !
What hopes ! what fears ! what rapturous sufferings !
What burning words of love will there be said !
What sobs — what tears ! what passionate whisperings !
Under thy boughs, when I, alas ! am dead.

V

SESOSTRIS

Sole Lord of Lords and very King of Kings,
He sits within the desert, carved in stone;
Inscrutable, colossal, and alone,
And ancienter than memory of things.
Graved on his front the sacred beetle clings;
Disdain sits on his lips; and in a frown
Scorn lives upon his forehead for a crown.
The affrighted ostrich dare not dust her wings
Anear this Presence. The long caravan's
Dazed camels stop, and mute the Bedouins stare.
This symbol of past power more than man's
Presages doom. Kings look — and Kings despair:
Their sceptres tremble in their jewelled hands,
And dark thrones totter in the baleful air !

THE DOORS

As through the Void we went I heard his plumes
Strike on the darkness. It was passing sweet
To hold his hand and feel that thin air beat
Against our pinions as we winged those glooms
Of Ebon, through which Atropos still dooms
Each soul to pass. Then presently our feet
Found footing on a ledge of dark retreat,
And opposite appeared two doors of tombs
Seen by the star upon the angel's head
That made dim twilight; there I caught my breath:
"Why pause we here ?" The angel answering said,
"The journey ends. These are the Doors of Death;

Lo, now they open, inward, for the dead."
And then a Voice, — "Who next that entereth?"

THE FLIGHT

UPON a cloud among the stars we stood.
The angel raised his hand and looked and said,
"Which world, of all yon starry myriad,
Shall we make wing to?" The still solitude
Became a harp whereon his voice and mood
Made spheral music round his haloed head.
I spake — for then I had not long been dead —
"Let me look round upon the vasts, and brood
A moment on these orbs ere I decide . . .
What is yon lower star that beauteous shines
And with soft splendor now incarnadines
Our wings? — *There* would I go and there abide."
He smiled as one who some child's thought divines:
"That is the world where yesternight you died."

FIAT LUX

THEN that dread angel near the awful throne,
Leaving the seraphs ranged in flaming tiers,
Winged his dark way through those unpinioned spheres,
And on the void's black beetling edge, alone,
Stood with raised wings, and listened for the tone
Of God's command to reach his eager ears,
While Chaos wavered, for she felt her years
Unsceptred now in that convulsive zone.
Night trembled. And, as one hath oft beheld
A lamp lit in a vase light up its gloom,
So God's voice lighted him, from heel to plume:
Let there be Light, It said, and Darkness, quelled,
Shrunk noiseless backward in her monstrous womb
Through vasts unwinnowed by the wings of eld!

James Jeffrey Roche

THE KEARSARGE

IN the gloomy ocean bed
Dwelt a formless thing, and said,
In the dim and countless eons long ago,
"I will build a stronghold high,
Ocean's power to defy,
And the pride of haughty man to lay low."

Crept the minutes for the sad,
Sped the cycles for the glad,
But the march of time was neither less nor more;
While the formless atom died,
Myriad millions by its side,
And above them slowly lifted Roncador.

Roncador of Caribee,
Coral dragon of the sea,
Ever sleeping with his teeth below the wave;
Woe to him who breaks the sleep!
Woe to them who sail the deep!
Woe to ship and man that fear a shipman's grave!

Hither many a galleon old,
Heavy-keeled with guilty gold,
Fled before the hardy rover smiting sore;
But the sleeper silent lay
Till the preyer and his prey
Brought their plunder and their bones to Roncador.

Be content, O conqueror!
Now our bravest ship of war,
War and tempest who had often braved before,
All her storied prowess past,
Strikes her glorious flag at last
To the formless thing that builded Roncador.

ANDROMEDA

THEY chained her fair young body to the cold and cruel stone;
The beast begot of sea and slime had marked her for his own;

The callous world beheld the wrong, and left her there alone.
Base caitiffs who belied her, false kinsmen who denied her,
Ye left her there alone!

My Beautiful, they left thee in thy peril and thy pain;
The night that hath no morrow was brooding on the main:
But, lo! a light is breaking of hope for thee again;
'T is Perseus' sword a-flaming, thy dawn of day proclaiming
Across the western main.
O Ireland! O my country! he comes to break thy chain!

MY COMRADE

The love of man and woman is as fire,
To warm, to light, but surely to consume
And self-consuming die. There is no room
For constancy and passionate desire.
We stand at last beside a wasted pyre,
Touch its dead embers, groping in the gloom;
And where an altar stood, erect a tomb,
And sing a requiem to a broken lyre.
But comrade-love is as a welding blast
Of candid flame and ardent temperature:
Glowing most fervent, it doth bind more fast;
And melting both, but makes the union sure.
The dross alone is burnt — till at the last
The steel, if cold, is one, and strong and pure.

THE SKELETON AT THE FEAST

We summoned not the Silent Guest,
And no man spake his name;
By lips unseen our Cup was pressed,
And mid the merry song and jest,
The Uninvited came.

Wise were they in the days of old,
Who gave the Stranger place;
And when the joyous catch was trolled,
And toasts were quaffed and tales were told,
They looked him in the face.

God save us from the skeleton
Who sitteth at the feast!
God rest the manly spirit gone,
Who sat beside the Silent One,
And dreaded him the least!

Alice Wellington Rollins

THE DEATH OF AZRON

He caught his chisel, hastened to his bench,
And, kneeling on one knee before one more
Pale page of uncarved marble, murmured fast,
"Here will I ask it! here in marble! here
Will I carve well the restless, patient sphinx,
With eyes that burn, though prisoned all the while
In dull, cold stone: what is Life for? what for?"
And he wrought well; but suddenly there came
A tremor and a chill through his right arm.
Turning his face, he saw beside him there
A woman like an angel, or perchance
An angel like a woman; so supreme
The look she bent upon him where she stood,
Silent, superb, and beautiful, that he,
Still holding fast his chisel, stammered forth,
"What art thou? art thou Love? — at last, for me?"
"Not Love," she answered; "Azron, I am Death!"
"Nay," and he grasped his chisel firmer still,
"I cannot die! See, I am young! not yet
Have I fulfilled all that is in my soul.
I ask not for dull life of plodding clods

That know not the divine; I ask not life
For a wild round of pleasure or mad deeds;
I ask not love, if it be not for me.
I ask but work! I would but finish this!
If all the thoughts burning within my brain—
Not foolish thoughts, but thoughts for which men wait—
Are to die now unuttered, if my strength
Of will and purpose, of proud energy,
Of eagerness to see but the divine,
And then reveal it to blind, waiting men,
Must perish unexpressed, what is it for?"
"Azron," the angel answered him, "thy sphinx
Asks, but it answers also; what hast thou
Answered to those who ask of thine own work,
'What is it for?' Didst thou not say to them,
'It matters not, so it be beautiful'?
Thy sphinx, with restless eyes that ask, would fain
Question, 'What is Life for?' but the proud mouth,
The patient sweetness of the even brows,
The perfect poise of changeless attitude,
The finely modelled cheek, the unparted lips,
Answer, 'It matters not! it matters not!
If only it be beautiful!' Nay, this,
Thy greater work, this glorious tomb of thine,
Not for a living woman, but for her,
The sphinx that asks and answers, is it not
A living answer to the living cry?
'What is it for?' they ask; and thou hast said,
'It matters not, for it is beautiful.'
It may be I have secrets to reveal
When thou hast crossed the portal of the dead;
It may be, I have none: it matters not.
Lay each straight marble firm in its white place;
Choose well each burnished gem; let all be fair
And orderly; and then it matters not
What it is for, or when the chisel falls.
Despair not, Azron, thou hast builded well;
But now—ask me no more!—it matters not!"
And Azron's head sank slowly on his breast,
The chisel fell.

MANY THINGS THOU HAST GIVEN ME, DEAR HEART

MANY things thou hast given me, dear heart;
But one thing thou hast taken: that high dream
Of heaven as of a country that should seem
Beyond all glory that divinest art
Has pictured:—with this I have had to part
Since knowing thee;—how long, love, will the gleam
Of each day's sunlight on my pathway stream,
Richer than what seemed richest at the start?
Make my days happy, love; yet I entreat
Make not each happier than the last for me;
Lest heaven itself should dawn to me, complete
In joy, not the surprise I dreamed 't would be,
But simply as the natural and sweet
Continuance of days spent here with thee.

VITA BENEFICA

ON softest pillows my dim eyes unclose;
No pain,—delicious weariness instead;
Sweet silence broods around the quiet bed,
And round me breathes the fragrance of the rose.
The moonlight leans against the pane, and shows
The little leaves outside in watchful dread
Keeping their guard; while with swift, noiseless tread
Love in its lovelier service comes and goes.
A hand I love brings nectar; near me bends
A face I love; ah! it is over!—this
Indeed is heaven. Could I only tell
Dear ones whose hearts the sorrow for me rends
How easily one meets Death's gentle kiss,—
And then I woke—to find that I was well!

Alice Williams Brotherton

THE BLAZING HEART

WHO are ye, spirits, that stand
In the outer gloom,
Each with a blazing heart in hand,
Which lighteth the dark beyond the tomb?

"Oh, we be souls that loved
Too well, too well!
Yet, for that love, though sore reproved,
(Oh, sore reproved!) have we 'scaped hell.

"'Scaped hell, but gained not heaven.
Woe, woe and alas!
Only — to us this grace is given,
To light the dark where the dead must pass.

"Behind us the shadows throng,
And the mists are gray;
But our blazing hearts light the soul along
From grave to yon gate that hides the day."

Who may this lady be
At my right hand?
"This is the heart which for Anthony
Changed from soft flesh to a burning brand."

"This for Æneas glowed,
Is glowing still."
"This kindled for Phaon; the flame it showed
No waters of ocean could quench or kill."

This shape, with the flowing hair?
"She loved so much
That even the Sinless heard her prayer,
Pitied her pangs, and suffered her touch."

Bid the sounds of crackling cease!
"They blaze, they burn!"
Let me flee back to my coffined peace!
"Pass on (they beckon); there's no return."

Spirits, why press ye close?
I am faint with fear!
"Already *thy* heart like an ember glows;
Pluck it forth from thy bosom, thy place is here."

Happy Francesca! thine
Is the fairer lot.
Better with him in hell to pine
Than stand in cool shadows by him forgot!

MY ENEMY

I

MY foe was dark, and stern, and grim,
I lived my life in fear of him.
I passed no secret, darkened nook
Without a shuddering, furtive look,
Lest he should take me unawares
In some one of his subtle snares.
Even in broad noon the thought of him
Turned all the blessed sunlight dim,
Stole the rich color from the rose,
The perfume from the elder-blows.

I saw him not, I heard no sound;
But traces everywhere I found
Of his fell plotting. Now, the flower
Most prized lay blasted by his power;
From the locked casket, rent apart,
The jewel dearest to my heart
Was stolen; or, from out the dark,
Some swift blow made my heart its mark.

Sweet eyes I loved grew glazed and dim
That had but caught a glimpse of him;
And ears, were wont to hear each sigh
Of mine, were deafened utterly,
Even to my shrieks; and lips I pressed
Struck a cold horror to my breast.
This hath he done, my enemy.
From him, O God, deliver me!

II

I reached but now this place of gloom
Through yon small gateway, where is room
For only one to pass. This calm
Is healing as a Sabbath psalm.
A sound, as if the hard earth slid
Down-rattling on a coffin-lid,
Was in mine ears. Now all is still,
And I am free to fare at will —
Whither? I seem but tarrying
For one who doth a message bring.

Who meets me in the way, whose face
Is radiant with an angel's grace ?
Smiling, he saith in underbreath :
" I am thy foe long dreaded, — Death."
" O Death, sweet Death, and is it *thou*
I called mine enemy but now ? "
I place my trusting palms in his,
And lift my chill lips for his kiss.
" Press close, be near me to the end,
When all are fled, my one true friend ! "

" Yea, *friend*," he answereth. " All, and more
Than all I took, do I restore —
Blossom and jewel, youth and hope ;
And see, this little key doth ope
The shining portal that we see,
Beyond which — *love* awaiteth thee."
" O blinded eyes ! Ah, foolish heart !
Adieu, dear Death — one kiss ! We part."

Walter Learned

WITH A SPRAY OF APPLE BLOSSOMS

The promise of these fragrant flowers,
The fruit that 'neath these blossoms lies
Once hung, they say, in Eden's bowers,
And tempted Eve in Paradise.

O fairest daughter of Eve's blood,
Lest her misprision thine should be,
I 've nipped temptation in the bud
And send this snowy spray to thee.

THE LAST RESERVATION

Sullen and dull, in the September day,
On the bank of the river,
They waited the boat that should bear them away
From their poor homes forever.

For progress strides on, and the order had gone
To these wards of the nation:
" Give us land and more room," was the cry, " and move on
To the next reservation."

With her babe, she looked back at her home 'neath the trees
From which they were driven,
Where the last camp-fire's smoke, borne out on the breeze,
Rose slowly toward heaven.

Behind her, fair fields, and the forest and glade,
The home of her nation;
Around her, the gleam of the bayonet and blade
Of civilization.

Clasping close to her bosom the small dusky form
With tender caressing,
She bent down, on the cheek of her babe soft and warm
A mother's kiss pressing.

A splash in the river — the column moves on
Close-guarded and narrow,
Noting as little the two that are gone
As the fall of a sparrow.

Only an Indian ! Wretched, obscure,
To refinement a stranger,
And a babe, that was born in a wigwam as poor
And rude as a manger.

Moved on — to make room for the growth in the West
Of a brave Christian nation,
Moved on — thank God, forever at rest
In the last reservation.

ON THE FLY-LEAF OF MANON LESCAUT

To you, whose temperate pulses flow
With measured beat, serene and slow,
The even tenor of whose way
Is undisturbed by passion's sway,
This tale of wayward love may seem
The record of a fevered dream.
And yet, we two have that within

To make us what our kind have been.
A lure more strong, a wish more faint,
Makes one a monster, one a saint;
And even love, by difference nice,
Becomes a virtue or a vice.
The briar, that o'er the garden wall
Trails its sweet blossoms till they fall
Across the dusty road, and then
Are trodden under foot of men,
Is sister to the decorous rose
Within the garden's well-kept close,
Whose pinioned branches may not roam
Out and beyond their latticed home.
There 's many a life of sweet content
Whose virtue is environment.
They erred, they fell; and yet, 'tis true,
They hold the mirror up to you.

IN EXPLANATION

Her lips were so near
That — what else could I do?
You 'll be angry, I fear,
But her lips were so near —
Well, I can't make it clear,
Or explain it to you,
But — her lips were so near
That — what else could I do?

TO CRITICS

When I was seventeen I heard
From each censorious tongue,
"I 'd not do that if I were you;
You see you 're rather young."

Now that I number forty years,
I 'm quite as often told
Of this or that I should n't do
Because I 'm quite too old.

O carping world! If there 's an age
Where youth and manhood keep
An equal poise, alas! I must
Have passed it in my sleep.

Henry Augustin Beers

POSTHUMOUS

Put them in print?
Make one more dint
In the ages' furrowed rock? No, no!
Let his name and his verses go.
These idle scraps, they would but wrong
His memory, whom we honored long,
And men would ask: "Is this the best —
Is this the whole his life expressed?"
Haply he had no care to tell
To all the thoughts which flung their spell
Around us when the night grew deep,
Making it seem a loss to sleep,
Exalting the low, dingy room
To some high auditorium.
And when we parted homeward, still
They followed us beyond the hill.
The heaven had brought new stars to sight,
Opening the map of later night;
And the wide silence of the snow,
And the dark whispers of the pines,
And those keen fires that glittered slow
Along the zodiac's wintry signs,
Seemed witnesses and near of kin
To the high dreams we held within.

Yet what is left
To us bereft,
Save these remains,
Which now the moth
Will fret, or swifter fire consume?
These inky stains
On his table-cloth;
These prints that decked his room;
His throne, this ragged easy-chair;
This battered pipe, his councillor.
This is the sum and inventory.
No son he left to tell his story,
No gold, no lands, no fame, no book.
Yet one of us, his heirs, who took
The impress of his brain and heart,
May gain from Heaven the lucky art
His untold meanings to impart
In words that will not soon decay.
Then gratefully will such one say:
"This phrase, dear friend, perhaps, is mine;
The breath that gave it life was thine."

ON A MINIATURE

THINE old-world eyes — each one a violet
Big as the baby rose that is thy mouth —
Set me a-dreaming. Have our eyes not met
In childhood — in a garden of the South ?

Thy lips are trembling with a song of France,
My cousin, and thine eyes are dimly sweet;
'Wildered with reading in an old romance
All afternoon upon the garden seat.

The summer wind read with thee, and the bees
That on the sunny pages loved to crawl;
A skipping reader was the impatient breeze,
And turned the leaves, but the slow bees read all.

And now thy foot descends the terrace stair;
I hear the rustle of thy silk attire;
I breathe the musky odors of thy hair,
And airs that from thy painted fan respire.

Idly thou pausest in the shady walk,
Thine ear attentive to the fountain's fall;
Thou mark'st the flower-de-luce sway on her stalk,
The speckled vergalieus ripening on the wall.

Thou hast the feature of my mother's race,
The gilded comb she wore, her smile, her eye;
The blood that flushes softly in thy face
Crawls through my veins beneath this northern sky.

As one disherited, though next of kin,
Who lingers at the barred ancestral gate,
And sadly sees the happy heir within
Stroll careless through his forfeited estate, —

Even so I watch thy southern eyes, Lisette,
Lady of my lost paradise, and heir
Of summer days that were my birthright. Yet
Beauty like thine makes usurpation fair.

BIFTEK AUX CHAMPIGNONS

MIMI, do you remember —
Don't get behind your fan —
That morning in September
On the cliffs of Grand Manan,
Where to the shock of Fundy
The topmost harebells sway
(*Campanula rotundifolia: cf.* Gray) ?

On the pastures high and level,
That overlook the sea,
Where I wondered what the devil
Those little things could be
That Mimi stooped to gather,
As she strolled across the down,
And held her dress skirt rather —
Oh, now, you need n't frown.

For you know the dew was heavy,
And your boots, *I* know, were thin;
So a little extra brevi-
ty in skirts was, sure, no sin.
Besides, who minds a cousin ?
First, second, even third, —
I 've kissed 'em by the dozen,
And they never once demurred.

" If one 's allowed to ask it,"
Quoth I, " *Ma belle cousine,*
What have you in your basket ? "
(Those baskets white and green
The brave Passamaquoddies
Weave out of scented grass,
And sell to tourist bodies
Who through Mt. Desert pass.)

You answered, slightly frowning,
" Put down your stupid book —
That everlasting Browning ! —
And come and help me look.
Mushroom you spik him English,
I call him *champignon :*
I 'll teach you to distinguish
The right kind from the wrong."

There was no fog on Fundy
That blue September day;
The west wind, for that one day,
Had swept it all away.
The lighthouse glasses twinkled,
The white gulls screamed and flew,
The merry sheep-bells tinkled,
The merry breezes blew.

The bayberry aromatic,
The papery immortelles
(That give our grandma's attic
That sentimental smell,
Tied up in little brush-brooms)
Were sweet as new-mown hay,
While we went hunting mushrooms
That blue September day.

ECCE IN DESERTO

The wilderness a secret keeps
Upon whose guess I go:
Eye hath not seen, ear hath not heard;
And yet I know, I know,

Some day the viewless latch will lift,
The door of air swing wide
To one lost chamber of the wood
Where those shy mysteries hide, —

One yet unfound, receding depth,
From which the wood-thrush sings,
Still luring in to darker shades,
In — in to colder springs.

There is no wind abroad to-day.
But hark ! — the pine-tops' roar,
That sleep and in their dreams repeat
The music of the shore.

What wisdom in their needles stirs ?
What song is that they sing ?
Those airs that search the forest's heart,
What rumor do they bring ?

A hushed excitement fills the gloom,
And, in the stillness, clear
The vireo's tell-tale warning rings:
"'T is near — 't is near — 't is near !"

As, in the fairy-tale, more loud
The ghostly music plays
When, toward the enchanted bower, the prince
Draws closer through the maze.

Nay — nay. I track a fleeter game,
A wilder than ye know,
To lairs beyond the inmost haunt
Of thrush or vireo.

This way it passed : the scent lies fresh;
The ferns still lightly shake.
Ever I follow hard upon,
But never overtake.

To other woods the trail leads on,
To other worlds and new,
Where they who keep the secret here
Will keep the promise too.

THE SINGER OF ONE SONG[1]

He sang one song and died — no more but that:
A single song and carelessly complete.
He would not bind and thresh his chance-grown wheat,
Nor bring his wild fruit to the common vat,
To store the acid rinsings, thin and flat,
Squeezed from the press or trodden under feet.
A few slow beads, blood-red and honey-sweet,
Oozed from the grape, which burst and spilled its fat.
But Time, who soonest drops the heaviest things
That weight his pack, will carry diamonds long.
So through the poets' orchestra, which weaves
One music from a thousand stops and strings,
Pierces the note of that immortal song:
"High over all the lonely bugle grieves."

Arthur Sherburne Hardy

DUALITY

Within me are two souls that pity each
The other for the ends they seek, yet smile
Forgiveness, as two friends that love the while
The folly against which each feigns to preach.

[1] See page 89.

And while one barters in the market-place,
Or drains the cup before the tavern fire,
The other, winged with a divine desire,
Searches the solitary wastes of space.

And if o'ercome with pleasure this one sleeps,
The other steals away to lay its ear
Upon some lip just cold, perchance to hear
Those wondrous secrets which it knows — and keeps.

IMMORTALITY

My window is the open sky,
The flower in farthest wood is mine;
I am the heir to all gone by,
The eldest son of all the line.
And when the robbers Time and Death
Athwart my path conspiring stand,
I cheat them with a clod, a breath,
And pass the sword from hand to hand!

ITER SUPREMUM

Oh, what a night for a soul to go!
The wind a hawk, and the fields in snow;
No screening cover of leaves in the wood,
Nor a star abroad the way to show.

Do they part in peace, — soul with its clay?
Tenant and landlord, what do they say?
Was it sigh of sorrow or of release
I heard just now as the face turned gray?

What if, aghast on the shoreless main
Of Eternity, it sought again
The shelter and rest of the isle of Time,
And knocked at the door of its house of pain!

On the tavern hearth the embers glow,
The laugh is deep, and the flagons low;
But without, the wind and the trackless sky,
And night at the gates where a soul would go.

William Young

FROM "WISHMAKERS' TOWN"

THE BELLS

I

Awake! Awake!
All living things that be,
In nest or fold! —
All lives that solace take,
And dreamful ease, in tent, or wind-blown tree,
Or curtained couch, your wanderings forsake
In the dim realms of unreality!
Awake, for shame
Of languor's soft delight!
Lo, once again earth's heaving disk is rolled
In rosy flame,
And through the camps of night,
The flying Moon, beneath her splintered targe,
Sore-stricken by the feathered shafts of Dawn,
And harried by her hounds, like Actaeon,
Kneels,
Stoops, and wheels
Adown the western marge!

II

Awake to toil!
In wood, and rock-ribbed hill,
And loamy mead,
What golden largess lies!
Awake to strife, and far-resounding deed,
In love's sweet quest, or honor's high emprise,
With trumpets blown, and clash of steed with steed!
Awake to care,
And triumph's frequent foil!
But still pursue! O hand with strength to take —
O dauntless heart, to suffer, and to dare —
O swerveless will,
To bend, or else to break —
To life, to love, to conquest, and to spoil,
Awake! Awake!

THE FLOWER-SELLER

Myrtle, and eglantine,
For the old love and the new!
And the columbine,
With its cap and bells, for folly!

And the daffodil, for the hopes of youth!
And the rue,
For melancholy!
But of all the blossoms that blow,
Fair gallants all, I charge you to win, if ye may,
This gentle guest,
Who dreams apart, in her wimple of purple and gray,
Like the blessed Virgin, with meek head bending low
Upon her breast.

For the orange flower
Ye may buy as ye will; but the violet of the wood
Is the love of maidenhood;
And he that hath worn it but once, though but for an hour, —
He shall never again, though he wander by many a stream,
No, never again shall he meet with a flower that shall seem
So sweet and pure; and forever, in after years,
At the thought of its bloom, or the fragrance of its breath,
The past shall arise,
And his eyes shall be dim with tears,
And his soul shall be far in the gardens of Paradise,
Though he stand in the shambles of death.

THE CONSCIENCE-KEEPER

REPENT, O ye, predestinate to woe!
'T is mine to cry — albeit, well I wis,
Ye may not heed. And ye, elect to bliss,
Must e'en be saved, whether I cry or no.

And yet, repent! Repent ye, and atone,
In either case. Forswear your wisdom's pride,
And pray for faith — though some must be denied!
Nor yet by prayer, nor yet by faith alone,

But by your works, attest your penitence.
Give to the poor! — of whom ye see in me
God's almoner — and in your charity
Deign to forget not Peter and his pence.

THE PAWNS

PRINCE, and Bishop, and Knight, and Dame,
Plot, and plunder, and disagree!
O but the game is a royal game!
O but your tourneys are fair to see!

None too hopeful we found our lives;
Sore was labor from day to day;
Still we strove for our babes and wives —
Now, to the trumpet, we march away!

"Why?" — For some one hath willed it so!
Nothing we know of the why or the where —
To swamp, or jungle, or wastes of snow —
Nothing we know, and little we care.

Give us to kill! — since this is the end
Of love and labor in Nature's plan;
Give us to kill and ravish and rend,
Yea, since this is the end of man.

States shall perish, and states be born:
Leaders, out of the throng, shall press, —
Some to honor, and some to scorn:
We, that are little, shall yet be less.

Over our lines shall the vulture soar;
Hard on our flanks shall the jackals cry;
And the dead shall be as the sands of the shore;
And daily the living shall pray to die.

Nay, what matter! — When all is said,
Prince and Bishop will plunder still:
Lord and Lady must dance and wed.
Pity us, pray for us, ye that will!

THE BRIDAL PAIR

He

THOUGH the roving bee, as lightly,
Sip the sweets of thyme and clover,
Though the moon of May, as whitely,
Silver all the greensward over,
Yet, beneath the trysting tree,
That hath been which shall not be!

She

Drip the viols, ne'er so sweetly,
  With the honey-dew of pleasure —
Trip the dancers, ne'er so featly,
  Through the old remembered measure,
    Yet, the lighted lanthorn round,
  What is lost shall not be found!

False the logic that breeds the fear.
  Buds will blossom, and pipes will play.
So it was in that early year;
  So shall it be till the world is gray.
But the petted darling, if need shall be,
  As swift to the saddle will vault again;
And those that follow will ride as free
  As ever of old rode Marion's men.

JUDITH

FLOWER of youth, in the ancient frame —
  Maid of the mettlesome lip and eye,
Lightly wearing the fateful name,
  And the rakish beaver of days gone by!
Pink of fashion! Yet this is she
  That once, through midnight forest and fen,
Guided the horsemen of "Old Santee,"
  And rode to the death with Marion's men.

Rare the picture that decks the wall;
  Rare and dainty, in life, below,
My century-later belle of the ball,
  Mocking the beauty of long ago.
If now the summons should come to ride,
  Through such a darkness as brooded then,
How would it please you to serve as guide?
  And where, ah, where were Marion's men?

PHILOMEL TO CORYDON

SHEPHERD, wilt thou take counsel of the bird
That oft hath hearkened, from this leafy lair,
To love's entreaty, and the parting word? —
Sue not so humbly to the haughty fair.
Pipe in her praise upon thine oaten straw,
And pipe the louder when she says thee nay;
Swear that her lightest wish to thee is law,
But break the law twice twenty times a day.
Trust not to argument, or thou 'rt undone;
But calmly, gently, when she doth protest
Her course is East, impel her to the West;
Approve her way, but lead her in thine own.
For learn, fond youth, wouldst thou escape disaster,
That woman likes a slave — but loves a master.

Will Henry Thompson

THE HIGH TIDE AT GETTYSBURG

A CLOUD possessed the hollow field,
The gathering battle's smoky shield.
Athwart the gloom the lightning flashed,
And through the cloud some horsemen dashed,
And from the heights the thunder pealed.

Then at the brief command of Lee
Moved out that matchless infantry,
With Pickett leading grandly down,
To rush against the roaring crown
Of those dread heights of destiny.

Far heard above the angry guns
A cry across the tumult runs, —
The voice that rang through Shiloh's woods
And Chickamauga's solitudes,
The fierce South cheering on her sons!

Ah, how the withering tempest blew
Against the front of Pettigrew!
A Khamsin wind that scorched and singed
Like that infernal flame that fringed
The British squares at Waterloo!

A thousand fell where Kemper led;
A thousand died where Garnett bled:
In blinding flame and strangling smoke

The remnant through the batteries broke
And crossed the works with Armistead.

"Once more in Glory's van with me!"
Virginia cried to Tennessee;
"We two together, come what may,
Shall stand upon these works to-day!"
(The reddest day in history.)

Brave Tennessee! In reckless way
Virginia heard her comrade say:
"Close round this rent and riddled rag!"
What time she set her battle-flag
Amid the guns of Doubleday.

But who shall break the guards that wait
Before the awful face of Fate?
The tattered standards of the South
Were shriveled at the cannon's mouth,
And all her hopes were desolate.

In vain the Tennesseean set
His breast against the bayonet!
In vain Virginia charged and raged,
A tigress in her wrath uncaged,
Till all the hill was red and wet!

Above the bayonets, mixed and crossed,
Men saw a gray, gigantic ghost
Receding through the battle-cloud,
And heard across the tempest loud
The death-cry of a nation lost!

The brave went down! Without disgrace
They leaped to Ruin's red embrace.
They only heard Fame's thunders wake,
And saw the dazzling sun-burst break
In smiles on Glory's bloody face!

They fell, who lifted up a hand
And bade the sun in heaven to stand!
They smote and fell, who set the bars
Against the progress of the stars,
And stayed the march of Motherland!

They stood, who saw the future come
On through the fight's delirium!
They smote and stood, who held the hope
Of nations on that slippery slope
Amid the cheers of Christendom.

God lives! He forged the iron will
That clutched and held that trembling hill.
God lives and reigns! He built and lent
The heights for Freedom's battlement
Where floats her flag in triumph still!

Fold up the banners! Smelt the guns!
Love rules. Her gentler purpose runs.
A mighty mother turns in tears
The pages of her battle years,
Lamenting all her fallen sons!

COME LOVE OR DEATH

O LIFTED face of mute appeal!
  Poor tongueless pantomime of prayer!
O sullen sea, whose deeps conceal
  The children of despair!
O heart that will not look above!
  Poor staggering feet that seek the wave!
I would come quick, if I were Love,
  And I had power to save.

O sinking sunset loneliness
  Aflame in hot, unmoving eyes!
Poor wan lips, creeping in distress
  To cover up your cries!
O broken speech, and sobbing breath!
  Poor restless and uncertain will!
I would come quick, if I were Death,
  And I had power to kill!

Charles de Kay

ARCANA SYLVARUM

HARK! . . .
What booming
Faints on the high-strung ear?
Through the damp woods (so dark
No flowers are blooming)
I hear, I hear
The twang of harps, the leap
Of hairy feet, and know the revel 's ripe,
While, like a coral stripe,
The lizard cool doth creep,
Monster, but monarch there, up the pale
    Indian Pipe.

Hush! . . .
Your panting
Will scare them from their game.

Let not a footfall crush
Their rites enchanting!
The deadwood's flame,
Bellies of murdered fire-flies,
And glimmering moonstones thick with treasured rays
Shall help our round-eyed gaze
Antics unholy to surprise,
Which the ungodly crew round the red lizard plays.

Now! . . .
No breathing
To spoil the heathenish dance!
Lest from each pendent bough
Poison be seething, —
A hair-fine lance
Pierce to our brain, and slowly slay.
But look your breathless fill, and mark them swing,
Man and maid a-capering,
Ugly, fair, morosely gay,
Round the red lizard smooth, crowned for their wicked king.

Back! . . .
Inhuman
Are gestures, laughs, and jeers.
Off, ere we lose the track!
Nor man nor woman
May stand your leers,
Shameless and loose, uncovered creatures!
Quick, lest we join their orgies in the dark!
Back! For the madness stark
Is crawling through our natures
To touch the red lizard vile, spread on the damp white bark.

ULF IN IRELAND

(A. D. 790)

WHAT then, what if my lips do burn,
Husband, husband;
What though thou see'st my red lips burn,
Why look'st thou with a look so stern,
Husband?

It was the keen wind through the reed,
Husband, husband:
'T was wind made sharp with sword-edge reed
That made my tender lips to bleed,
Husband.

And hath the wind a human tooth,
Woman, woman?
Can light wind mark like human tooth
A shameful scar of love uncouth,
Woman?

What horror lurks within your eyes,
Husband, husband?
What lurking horror strains your eyes,
What black thoughts from your heart arise,
Husband?

Who stood beside you at the gate,
Woman, woman?
Who stood so near you by the gate
No moon your shapes could separate,
Woman?

So God me save, 't was I alone,
Husband, husband!
So Christ me save, 't was I alone
Stood listening to the ocean moan,
Husband!

Then hast thou four feet at the least,
Woman, woman!
Thy Christ hath lent thee four at least,
Oh, viler than four-footed beast,
Woman!

A heathen witch hath thee unmanned,
Husband, husband!
A foul witchcraft, alas, unmanned:
Thou saw'st some old tracks down the sand,
Husband!

Yet were they tracks that went not far,
Woman, woman;
Those ancient foot-marks went not far,
Or else you search the harbor bar,
Woman.

It is not yours alone that bleed,
Woman, woman;
Smooth lips not yours may also bleed,
Your wound has been avenged with speed,
Woman!

What talk you so of bar and wound,
Husband, husband?
What ghastly sign of sudden wound
And kinsman smitten to the ground,
Husband?

I saw your blood upon his cheek,
Woman, woman;
The moon had marked his treacherous cheek,
I marked his heart beside the creek,
Woman!

What, have you crushed the only flower,
Husband, husband!
Among our weeds the only flower?
Henceforward get you from my bower,
Husband!

I love you not; I loved but him,
Husband, husband!
In all the world I loved but him;
Not hell my love for Brenn shall dim,
Husband!

He 's caught her by her jet-black hair;
Sorrow, sorrow!
He 's bent her head back by the hair
Till all her throbbing throat lies bare —
Sorrow!

You knew me fiercer than the wolf,
Woman, woman;
You knew I well am named the wolf;
I shall both you and him engulf,
Woman.

Yet I to you was always kind,
Woman, woman;
To serpents only fools are kind;
Yet still with love of you I'm blind,
Woman.

I'll look no more upon your face,
Woman, woman;
These eyes shall never read your face,
For you shall die in this small space,
Woman!

He 's laid his mouth below her chin,
Horror!
That throat he kissed below the chin
No breath thereafter entered in:
Horror, horror!

Edward King

THE TSIGANE'S CANZONET

I

No! No!
Bird in the darkness singing,
I will not forget!
Trill me thy tender lay again, —
Thy song of passion and of pain;
Set all the sweet vale ringing
With thy canzonet.
Cling to thy branch, O bird, and cry,
"Love me, my love, or let me die!"
With ecstasy I hear thee,
And trembling linger near thee;
So let thine exquisite pure melody o'erflow this narrow space, and inundate the sky!
The winds that wander by
Will bear it to my love;
But I need not to prove
My loyalty with song,
For I have loved her long!
No! No!
Bird in the darkness singing,
I will not forget!

II

No! No!
Great river nobly flowing,
I will not forget!
Tell every flower that bends to kiss
Thy wave, how truest lover's bliss
Within my heart is glowing,
In my soul stays yet!
With murmur sweet, fair stream, proclaim
The magic of my lady's name
To every graceful willow
That sways above each billow;
To every reed beside thy banks so broad and low tell of her beauty and her spotless fame.
But seek not me to blame,
For I am loyal still;
My heart knows but her will;
The thought of her caress
Is ever here to bless:
No! No!
Great river nobly flowing,
I will not forget.

A WOMAN'S EXECUTION

(PARIS, 1871)

SWEET-BREATHED and young,
The people's daughter,
No nerves unstrung,
Going to slaughter!

"Good morning, friends,
You 'll love us better, —
Make us amends:
We 've burst your fetter!

"How the sun gleams!
(Women are snarling):
Give me your beams,
Liberty's darling!

"Marie 's my name;
Christ's mother bore it.
That badge? No shame:
Glad that I wore it!"

(Hair to her waist,
Limbs like a Venus):
Robes are displaced:
"Soldiers, please screen us!

"He at the front?
That is my lover:
Stood all the brunt; —
Now — the fight 's over.

"Powder and bread
Gave out together:
Droll! to be dead
In this bright weather!

"Jean, boy, we might
Have married in June!
This the wall? Right!
Vive la Commune!"

Hjalmar Hjorth Boyesen

THORALF AND SYNNÖV

O, HAVE you been in Gudbrand's dale, where Laagen's mighty flood
Chants evermore its wild refrain unto the listening wood?
And have you seen the evening sun on those bright glaciers glow,
When valleyward it shoots and darts like shafts from elfin bow?

Have you beheld the maidens when the saeter path they tread
With ribbons in their sunny hair and milk-pails on the head?
And have you heard the fiddles when they strike the lusty dance?
Then you have heard of Synnöv Houg, and of myself perchance.

For Synnöv Houg is lissome as the limber willow spray;
And when you think you hold her fast, and she is yours for aye,
Then, like the airy blowball that dances o'er the lea,
She gently through your fingers slips and lightly floateth free.

Then it was last St. John's Eve, — I remember it so well, —
We lads had lit a bonfire in a grass-grown little dell;
And all the pretty maidens were seated in a ring,
And some were telling stories, while the rest were listening;

Till up sprang little Synnöv, and she sang a stave as clear
As the skylark's earliest greeting in the morning of the year;
And I — I hardly knew myself, but up they saw me dart,
For every note of Synnöv's stave went straight unto my heart.

And like the rushing currents that from the glaciers flow,
And down into the sunny bays their icy waters throw,
So streamed my heavy bass-notes through the forests far and wide,
And Synnöv's treble rocked like a feather on the tide.

"My little Synnöv," sang I, "thou art good and very fair."
"And little Thoralf," sang she, "of what you say, beware!"
"My fairest Synnöv," quoth I, "my heart was ever thine,
My homestead and my goodly farm, my herds of lowing kine."

"O Thoralf, dearest Thoralf, if that your meaning be, —
If your big heart can hold such a little thing as me, —
Then I shall truly tell you if e'er I want a man,
And you are free to catch me, handsome Thoralf — if you can!"

And down the hillside ran she, where the tangled thicket weaves
A closely latticed bower with its intertwining leaves,
And through the copse she bounded, light-footed as a hare,
And with her merry laughter rang the forest far and near.

Whenever I beheld little Synnöv, all that year,
She fled from my sight as from hunter's shaft the deer;
I lay awake full half the nights and knew not what to do,
For I loved the little Synnöv so tenderly and true.

Then 'twas a summer even up in the birchen glen,
I sat listening to the cuckoo and the twitter of the wren,
When suddenly above me rang out a silver voice;
It rose above the twittering birds and o'er the river's noise.

There sat my little maid, where the rocks had made a seat;
And tiny crimson flowers grew all around her feet,
And on her yellow locks clung a tiny roguish hood;
Its edge was made of swan's-down, but the cloth was red as blood.

And noiselessly behind her I had stolen through the copse.
I cursed the restless birch-trees for rustling in their tops;
How merrily my heart beat! And forth I leapt in haste,
And flung a slender birch-bough around the maiden's waist.

She blushed and she fluttered, — then turned away to run,
But straight into my sturdy arms I caught the little one.
I put her gently down on the heather at my side,
Where tiny crimson flowers the rocky ledges hide.

And as the prisoned birdling, when he knows his cage full well,
Pours forth his notes full blithely, and naught his mirth can quell,
So little Synnöv, striving in vain my hold to flee,
Turned quick on me her roguish eyes and laughed full heartily.

"My little Synnöv," said I, "if I remember right,
'Twas something that you promised me a year ago to-night."
Then straight she stayed her laughter and serious she grew,
And whispered, "Dearest Thoralf, you promised something too."

Joel Chandler Harris

THE PLOUGH-HANDS' SONG

NIGGER mighty happy w'en he layin' by co'n —
Dat sun 's a-slantin';
Nigger mighty happy w'en he year de dinner ho'n —
Dat sun 's a-slantin';
En he mo' happy still w'en de night draws on —
Dat sun 's a-slantin';
Dat sun 's a-slantin' des ez sho 's you bo'n!
En it's rise up, Primus! fetch anudder yell:

Dat ole dun cow des a-shakin' up 'er bell,
En de frogs chunin' up 'fo de jew done fell:
Good-night, Mr. Killdee! I wish you mighty well! —
Mr. Kildee! I wish you mighty well! —
I wish you mighty well!

De c'on 'll be ready 'g'inst dumplin' day,
Dat sun 's a-slantin';
But nigger gotter watch, en stick, en stay,
Dat sun 's a-slantin';
Same ez de bee-martin watchin' un de jay,
Dat sun 's a slantin';
Dat sun 's a-slantin' en a-slippin' away!
Den it 's rise up, Primus! en gin it t' um strong:
De cow 's gwine home wid der ding-dang-dong;
Sling in anudder tech er de ole time song:
Good-night, Mr. Whipperwill! don't stay long! —
Mr. Whipperwill! don't stay long! —
Don't stay long!

De shadders, dey er creepin' todes de top er de hill,
Dat sun 's a-slantin';
But night don't 'stroy w'at de day done buil',
Dat sun 's a-slantin';
'Less de noddin' er de nigger give de ash-cake a chill —
Dat sun 's a-slantin';
Dat sun's a-slantin' en slippin' down still!
Den sing it out, Primus! des holler en bawl,
En w'ilst we er strippin' deze mules fer de stall,
Let de gals ketch de soun' er de plantashun call:
Oh, it 's good-night, ladies! my love unter you all! —
Ladies! my love unter you all! —
My love unter you all!

MY HONEY, MY LOVE

Hit 's a mighty fur ways up de Far'well Lane,
My honey, my love!
You may ax Mister Crow, you may ax Mister Crane,
My honey, my love!
Dey 'll make you a bow, en dey 'll tell you de same,
My honey, my love!
Hit 's a mighty fur ways fer ter go in de night,
My honey, my love!
My honey, my love, my heart's delight —
My honey, my love!

Mister Mink, he creeps twel he wake up de snipe,
My honey, my love!
Mister Bull-Frog holler, Come alight my pipe!
My honey, my love!
En de Pa'tridge ax, Ain't yo' peas ripe?
My honey, my love!
Better not walk erlong dar much atter night,
My honey, my love!
My honey, my love, my heart's delight —
My honey, my love!

De Bully-Bat fly mighty close ter de groun',
My honey, my love!
Mister Fox, he coax 'er, Do come down!
My honey, my love!
Mister Coon, he rack all 'roun 'en 'roun',
My honey, my love!
In de darkes' night, oh, de nigger, he 's a sight!
My honey, my love!
My honey, my love, my heart's delight —
My honey, my love!

Oh, flee, Miss Nancy, flee ter my knee,
My honey, my love!
'Lev'n big, fat coons liv' in one tree,
My honey, my love.
Oh, ladies all, won't you marry me?
My honey, my love!
Tu'n lef,' tu'n right, we 'll dance all night,
My honey, my love!
My honey, my love, my heart's delight —
My honey, my love!

De big Owl holler en cry fer his mate,
My honey, my love!
Oh, don't stay long! Oh, don't stay late!
My honey, my love.
Hit ain't so mighty fur ter de Good-by Gate,
My honey, my love!
Whar we all got ter go w'en we sing out de night,
My honey, my love!
My honey, my love, my heart's delight —
My honey, my love!

John Vance Cheney[1]

THE HAPPIEST HEART

WHO drives the horses of the sun
Shall lord it but a day;
Better the lowly deed were done,
And kept the humble way.

The rust will find the sword of fame,
The dust will hide the crown;
Ay, none shall nail so high his name
Time will not tear it down.

The happiest heart that ever beat
Was in some quiet breast
That found the common daylight sweet,
And left to Heaven the rest.

THE STRONG

DOST deem him weak that owns his strength is tried?
Nay, we may safely lean on him that grieves:
The pine has immemorially sighed,
The enduring poplar's are the trembling leaves.

To feel, and bow the head, is not to fear;
To cheat with jest — that is the coward's art:
Beware the laugh that battles back the tear;
He 's false to all that 's traitor to his heart.

He of great deeds does grope amid the throng
Like him whose steps toward Dagon's temple bore;
There 's ever something sad about the strong —
A look, a moan, like that on ocean's shore.

EVERY ONE TO HIS OWN WAY

OAK leaves are big as the mouse's ear,
So, farmer, go plant. But the frost —
Beware! the witch o' the year,
See that her palm be crossed.
The bee is abroad, and the ant;
Spider is busy; ho, farmer, go plant.

The winds blow soft from the glazy sea,
So, merchant, rig ship. But the wave —
Beware! salt water can be
A highway, can be a grave.
Bring silks for milady; a trip
For wines and spices; ho, merchant, rig ship.

I heard round oath at the churchyard door,
So, preacher, go preach. But the Book —
Say yea and nay, and no more;
Look to the wording, look.
A heaven and a hell within reach,
'T is one or the other; good preacher, go preach.

Farmer, go till; ride, merchant, the sea;
Good preacher, have at the mewed folk:
From frost and storm be you free,
And spared That Old Serpent's joke.
I'll sit in my doorway, God please,
Quietly looking between the green trees.

EVENING SONGS

I

THE birds have hid, the winds are low,
The brake is awake, the grass aglow:
The bat is the rover,
No bee on the clover,
The day is over,
And evening come.

The heavy beetle spreads her wings,
The toad has the road, the cricket sings:
The bat is the rover,
No bee on the clover,
The day is over,
And evening come.

II

It is that pale, delaying hour
When nature closes like a flower,
And on the spirit lies
The silence of the earth and skies.

The world has thoughts she will not own
When shade and dream with night have flown;
Bright overhead, a star
Makes golden guesses what they are.

[1] See also p. 586.

III

Now is Light, sweet mother, down the west,
With little Song against her breast;
She took him up, all tired with play,
And fondly bore him far away.

While he sleeps, one wanders in his stead,
A fainter glory round her head;
She follows happy waters after,
Leaving behind low, rippling laughter.

IV

Behind the hilltop drops the sun,
The curled heat falters on the sand,
While evening's ushers, one by one,
Lead in the guests of Twilight Land.

The bird is silent overhead,
Below the beast has laid him down;
Afar, the marbles watch the dead,
The lonely steeple guards the town.

The south wind feels its amorous course
To cloistered sweet in thickets found;
The leaves obey its tender force,
And stir 'twixt silence and a sound.

THE SKILFUL LISTENER

THE skilful listener, he, methinks, may hear
The grass blades clash in sunny field together,
The roses kissing, and the lily, whether
It joy or sorrow in the summer's ear,
The jewel dew-bells of the mead ring clear
When morning lightly moves them in June weather,
The flocked hours flitting by on stealthy feather,
The last leaves' wail at waning of the year.
Haply, from these we catch a passing sound,
(The best of verities, perchance, but seem)
We overhear close Nature, on her round,
When least she thinks it; bird and bough and stream
Not only, but her silences profound,
Surprised by softer footfall of our dream.

WHITHER

WHITHER leads this pathway, little one? —
It runs just on and on, is never done.

Whither leads this pathway, mistress fair? —
That path to town, sir; to the village square.

Whither leads this pathway, father old? —
To the white quiet of the churchyard fold.

O. C. Auringer

THE FLIGHT OF THE WAR-EAGLE

THE eagle of the armies of the West,
Dying upon his alp, near to the sky,
Through the slow days that paled the imperial eye,
But could not tame the proud fire of his breast, —
Gone with the mighty pathos! Only rest
Remains where passed that struggle stern and high;
Rest, silence, broken sometimes by the cry
Of mother and eaglets round the ravaged nest.
'T was when the death-cloud touched the mountain crest,
A singer among the awed flocks cowering nigh,
Looked up and saw against the sunrise sky
An eagle, in ethereal plumage dressed,
Break from the veil, and flame his buoyant flight
Far toward the hills of heaven unveiled and bright.

July 23, 1885.

THE BALLAD OF ORISKANY

She leaned her cheek upon her hand,
And looked across the glooming land;
She saw the wood from farm to farm
Touched by the twilight's ghostly charm;
And heard the owl's cry sound forlorn
Across the fields of waving corn,
And sighed with sad voice dreamily:
Oriskany! Oriskany!

The moonlight through the open door
Laid its broad square upon the floor;
A beetle plunging through the gloom
Hummed fitfully within the room;
Across the casement's opening
Night creatures sped on purring wing,
And still she murmured musically
The fatal name, Oriskany.

She raised her face to the dim night skies,
A dream of peace was in her eyes;
Like memory speaking from the dead
Her voice seemed, as she spoke and said:
"'T is two years past this very morn
That he came riding through the corn,
With his gay comrades gallantly,
To wed me in Oriskany.

"At eve the rooms were all alight,
The bride and bridesmaids clad in white,
As we stood side by side apart,
I trembling, but how blest at heart!
The lights, the flowers, the sparkling eyes,
Were sweet to me as paradise;
The vows like music were to me,
That bound us in Oriskany.

"The feast that flowed mid converse fleet,
The music and the dancing feet,
The games that flew from room to room,
The cries, the laughter, and the bloom,
And in the midst, so fair and tall,
My bridegroom, prince among them all, —
'T was all one glad, sweet dream to me,
That night in gay Oriskany.

"And then the parting groups, the flight,
The voices fading through the night;
The homestead lying dim and lone,
The rooms deserted, lights outblown;
The holy hush wherein befell
The things too wondrous dear to tell —
O sacred fire of love! Ah me —
Oriskany! Oriskany!

"The year went round, there came a guest —
A lovely babe lay on my breast, —
Ah, we were blest! Then came the sound
Of drum and trump the valley round:
'T was just one year ago this morn
That he went armed across the corn,
In strength of heart and patriot glee,
To meet the foe on Oriskany.

"Below the hill the battle broke;
I heard the din, I saw the smoke;
Road-weary bands paused at the door,
And drank, and onward rode once more;
Poor wounded souls came crawling by
To find some quiet place to die;
My heart beat proud but fearfully
That day in wild Oriskany.

"At eve, amid the drip of rain,
They brought me home my soldier slain!
With calm great looks and quiet tread
They came and laid him on my bed —
As fair as life. A bloodless blow
They said had slain him; but his foe
He stabbed ere dying, through and through —
My brave! His country's enemy
He smote on red Oriskany!

"My babe died with the dying year;
Two mounds have I in the churchyard near,
But not a loving voice or form
To keep the earth-flame in me warm;
My dead life to the live world clings,
I feel no joy in natural things,—
Strangely has death mistaken me,
Who died on dark Oriskany.

"All day within the homestead dim
I think of him, I dream of him;
My tasks of hands and feet and soul
Lead true to him as to their goal;
In woman's heart God wrote it thus:
That men should be as gods to us.
I feel the pangs, the weakness see,
Yet worship — in Oriskany.

"I cannot think of him as dead
Upon our one-year's bridal bed,
Oriskany, Oriskany!
Nor dream of him within the tomb,
Amid the willowed churchyard's gloom,
Oriskany, Oriskany!

I see him as he passed that morn,
Warm with all life, across the corn:
'T is thus he shall return to me
At last, far from Oriskany."

APRIL

Weary at heart with winter yesterday,
I sought the fields for something green to see,
Some budded turf or mossbank quietly
Uncovered in the sweet familiar way.
Crossing a pasture slope that sunward lay,
I suddenly surprised beneath a tree
A girlish creature who at sight of me
Sprang up all wild with daintiest dismay.
"Stay, pretty one!" I cried, — "who art thou, pray?"
Mid tears and freaks of pettish misery,
And sighing, "I am April," answered she;
"I rear the field flowers for my sister May."
Then with an arch laugh sidewise, clear and strong,
Turned blithely up the valley with a song.

Emma Lazarus

ON THE PROPOSAL TO ERECT A MONUMENT IN ENGLAND TO LORD BYRON

The grass of fifty Aprils hath waved green
Above the spent heart, the Olympian head,
The hands crost idly, the shut eyes unseen,
Unseeing, the locked lips whose song hath fled;
Yet mystic-lived, like some rich, tropic flower,
His fame puts forth fresh blossoms hour by hour;
Wide spread the laden branches dropping dew
On the low, laurelled brow misunderstood,
That bent not, neither bowed, until subdued
By the last foe who crowned while he o'erthrew.

Fair was the Easter Sabbath morn when first
Men heard he had not wakened to its light:
The end had come, and time had done its worst,
For the black cloud had fallen of endless night.
Then in the town, as Greek accosted Greek,
'Twas not the wonted festal words to speak,
"Christ is arisen," but "Our chief is gone,"
With such wan aspect and grief-smitten head
As when the awful cry of "Pan is dead!"
Filled echoing hill and valley with its moan.

"I am more fit for death than the world deems,"
So spake he as life's light was growing dim,
And turned to sleep as unto soothing dreams.
What terrors could its darkness hold for him,
Familiar with all anguish, but with fear
Still unacquainted? On his martial bier
They laid a sword, a helmet, and a crown —
Meed of the warrior, but not these among
His voiceless lyre, whose silent chords unstrung
Shall wait — how long? — for touches like his own.

An alien country mourned him as her son,
And hailed him hero: his sole, fitting tomb
Were Theseus' temple or the Parthenon,
Fondly she deemed. His brethren bare him home,
Their exiled glory, past the guarded gate
Where England's Abbey shelters England's great.
Afar he rests whose very name hath shed
New lustre on her with the song he sings.
So Shakespeare rests who scorned to lie with kings,
Sleeping at peace midst the unhonored dead.

And fifty years suffice to overgrow
With gentle memories the foul weeds of hate
That shamed his grave. The world begins to know
Her loss, and view with other eyes his fate.
Even as the cunning workman brings to pass
The sculptor's thought from out the unwieldy mass
Of shapeless marble, so Time lops away
The stony crust of falsehood that concealed
His just proportions, and, at last revealed,
The statue issues to the light of day,

Most beautiful, most human. Let them fling
The first stone who are tempted even as he,
And have not swerved. When did that rare soul sing
The victim's shame, the tyrant's eulogy,
The great belittle, or exalt the small,
Or grudge his gift, his blood, to disenthrall
The slaves of tyranny or ignorance?
Stung by fierce tongues himself, whose rightful fame
Hath he reviled? Upon what noble name
Did the winged arrows of that barbed wit glance?

The years' thick, clinging curtains backward pull,
And show him as he is, crowned with bright beams,
"*Beauteous, and yet not all as beautiful*
As he hath been or might be; Sorrow seems
Half of his immortality." He needs
No monument whose name and song and deeds
Are graven in all foreign hearts; but she,
His mother, England, slow and last to wake,
Needs raise the votive shaft for her fame's sake:
Hers is the shame if such forgotten be!

VENUS OF THE LOUVRE

Down the long hall she glistens like a star,
The foam-born mother of Love, transfixed to stone,
Yet none the less immortal, breathing on.
Time's brutal hand hath maimed but could not mar.
When first the enthralled enchantress from afar
Dazzled mine eyes, I saw not her alone,
Serenely poised on her world-worshipped throne,
As when she guided once her dove-drawn car, —
But at her feet a pale, death-stricken Jew,
Her life adorer, sobbed farewell to love.
Here *Heine* wept! Here still he weeps anew,
Nor ever shall his shadow lift or move,
While mourns one ardent heart, one poet-brain,
For vanished Hellas and Hebraic pain.

THE CRANES OF IBYCUS

There was a man who watched the river flow
Past the huge town, one gray November day.
Round him in narrow high-piled streets at play
The boys made merry as they saw him go,
Murmuring half-loud, with eyes upon the stream,
The immortal screed he held within his hand.
For he was walking in an April land
With Faust and Helen. Shadowy as a dream
Was the prose-world, the river and the town.
Wild joy possessed him; through enchanted skies
He saw the cranes of Ibycus swoop down.
He closed the page, he lifted up his eyes,
Lo — a black line of birds in wavering thread
Bore him the greetings of the deathless dead!

THE BANNER OF THE JEW

Wake, Israel, wake! Recall to-day
The glorious Maccabean rage,
The sire heroic, hoary-gray,
His five-fold lion-lineage:

The Wise, the Elect, the Help-of-God,
The Burst-of-Spring, the Avenging Rod.[1]

From Mizpeh's mountain-ridge they saw
Jerusalem's empty streets, her shrine
Laid waste where Greeks profaned the Law
With idol and with pagan sign.
Mourners in tattered black were there,
With ashes sprinkled on their hair.

Then from the stony peak there rang
A blast to ope the graves: down poured
The Maccabean clan, who sang
Their battle-anthem to the Lord.
Five heroes lead, and, following, see
Ten thousand rush to victory!

Oh for Jerusalem's trumpet now,
To blow a blast of shattering power,
To wake the sleepers high and low,
And rouse them to the urgent hour!
No hand for vengeance — but to save,
A million naked swords should wave.

Oh deem not dead that martial fire,
Say not the mystic flame is spent!
With Moses' law and David's lyre,
Your ancient strength remains unbent.
Let but an Ezra rise anew,
To lift the *Banner of the Jew!*

A rag, a mock at first — erelong,
When men have bled and women wept,
To guard its precious folds from wrong,
Even they who shrunk, even they who slept,
Shall leap to bless it, and to save.
Strike! for the brave revere the brave!

THE CROWING OF THE RED COCK

Across the Eastern sky has glowed
The flicker of a blood-red dawn;
Once more the clarion cock has crowed,
Once more the sword of Christ is drawn.
A million burning roof-trees light
The world-wide path of Israel's flight.

Where is the Hebrew's fatherland?
The folk of Christ is sore bestead;
The Son of Man is bruised and banned,
Nor finds whereon to lay his head.
His cup is gall, his meat is tears,
His passion lasts a thousand years.

Each crime that wakes in man the beast,
Is visited upon his kind.
The lust of mobs, the greed of priest,
The tyranny of kings, combined
To root his seed from earth again,
His record is one cry of pain.

When the long roll of Christian guilt
Against his sires and kin is known,
The flood of tears, the life-blood spilt,
The agony of ages shown,
What oceans can the stain remove
From Christian law and Christian love?

Nay, close the book; not now, not here,
The hideous tale of sin narrate;
Reëchoing in the martyr's ear,
Even he might nurse revengeful hate,
Even he might turn in wrath sublime,
With blood for blood and crime for crime.

Coward? Not he, who faces death,
Who singly against worlds has fought,
For what? A name he may not breathe,
For liberty of prayer and thought.
The angry sword he will not whet,
His nobler task is — to forget.

THE NEW EZEKIEL

What, can these dead bones live, whose sap is dried
By twenty scorching centuries of wrong?
Is this the House of Israel, whose pride
Is as a tale that 's told, an ancient song?
Are these ignoble relics all that live
Of psalmist, priest, and prophet? Can the breath
Of very heaven bid these bones revive,
Open the graves and clothe the ribs of death?

Yea, Prophesy, the Lord hath said. Again
Say to the wind, Come forth and breathe afresh,
Even that they may live upon these slain,
And bone to bone shall leap, and flesh to flesh.
The Spirit is not dead, proclaim the word,
Where lay dead bones, a host of armed men stand!
I ope your graves, my people, saith the Lord,
And I shall place you living in your land.

[1] The sons of Matthias — Jonathan, John, Eleazar, Simon (also called the Jewel), and Judas, the Prince.

Grace Denio Litchfield

MY LETTER

From far away, from far away,
It journeyed swiftly night and day,
It rested not. With cruel haste
It crossed the ocean's trackless waste.
It swerved no moment in its flight
Through mist and storm and deepest night.
No mercy prompted it to stay,
No pity moved it to delay.
O'er seas that rose up to detain,
Silent as Death it sped amain.
Through cities crowding close and strong,
Undazed, untired, it fled along.
No voice cried out through all the land,
Great Heaven saw, yet stirred no hand.
No angel, kinder than the rest,
Held his white shield before my breast.
Across the land, across the sea,
Straight, swift, and sure, it came to me!
Unlet, unhindered, undeterred,
Straight, swift, and sure, it brought me word!

TO A HURT CHILD

What, are you hurt, Sweet? So am I;
Cut to the heart;
Though I may neither moan nor cry,
To ease the smart.

Where was it, Love? Just here! So wide
Upon your cheek!
Oh happy pain that needs no pride,
And may dare speak.

Lay here your pretty head. One touch
Will heal its worst,
While I, whose wound bleeds overmuch,
Go all unnursed.

There, Sweet. Run back now to your play,
Forget your woes.
I too was sorely hurt this day, —
But no one knows.

MY OTHER ME

Children, do you ever,
In walks by land or sea,
Meet a little maiden
Long time lost to me!

She is gay and gladsome,
Has a laughing face,
And a heart as sunny;
And her name is Grace.

Naught she knows of sorrow,
Naught of doubt or blight;
Heaven is just above her —
All her thoughts are white.

Long time since I lost her,
That other Me of mine;
She crossed into Time's shadow
Out of Youth's sunshine.

Now the darkness keeps her;
And, call her as I will,
The years that lie between us
Hide her from me still.

I am dull and pain-worn,
And lonely as can be —
Oh, children, if you meet her,
Send back my other Me!

Francis Saltus Saltus

THE ANDALUSIAN SERENO

With oaken staff and swinging lantern bright,
He strolls at midnight when the world is still
Through dismal lanes and plazas plumed with light,
Guarding the drowsy thousands in Seville.

Gazing upon his ever star-thronged sky,
With careless step he wanders to and fro;

The gloomy streets reëcho with his cry,
His slow, low, sad, and dreary "*Se-re-no!*"

He sees the blond moon fleck the rosy towers
Of old giralda with its opal sheen,
And in broad alamedas, warm with flowers,
He sees the Moorish cypress bend and lean.

Then, vaguely dreaming, he recalls the nights
His father passed beneath those very stars,
The tales of escaladed walls, the fights,
The mirth, the songs, the Babel of guitars!

And all his sire had told him years ago,
How, often, in the gardens dim and dark,
He met full many a mantled Romeo,
And stumbled over corpses cold and stark.

But he, alas! had heard no serenade;
No ladder hangs from Donna Linda's bars,
And the wan glint of an assassin's blade
He ne'er has seen beneath these quiet stars.

So, weary, in the dead calm of the town,
His soul regrets the Past's romantic glow,
While mute, despondent, pacing up and down,
He sadly moans his dreary "*Se-re-no!*"

But sometimes in the grayish light of dawn
He stops and trembles in his clinging cape,
For he can see a lady's curtain drawn,
And, in the street below, a phantom shape,

Draped in quaint, antique garb, with sword and glove,
Sombrero vast, and mandolin on arm,
Which seems to play a weird, wild lay of love,
And at his coming shows no quick alarm;

But turns, and there a skeleton, all lean
And haggard, leers within the lightless lane!
And the Sereno knows that he has seen
The spectre of the Past, the ghost of Spain.

THE SPHINX SPEAKS

Carved by a mighty race whose vanished hands
Formed empires more destructible than I,
In sultry silence I forever lie,
Wrapped in the shifting garment of the sands.
Below me, Pharaoh's scintillating bands
With clashings of loud cymbals have passed by,
And the eternal reverence of the sky
Falls royally on me and all my lands.
The record of the future broods in me;
I have with worlds of blazing stars been crowned,
But none my subtle mystery hath known
Save one, who made his way through blood and sea,
The Corsican, prophetic and renowned,
To whom I spake, one awful night alone!

THE BAYADERE

Near strange, weird temples, where the Ganges' tide
Bathes domed Lahore, I watched, by spice-trees fanned,
Her agile form in some quaint saraband,
A marvel of passionate chastity and pride.
Nude to the loins, superb and leopard-eyed,
With fragrant roses in her jewelled hand,
Before some Kaât-drunk Rajah, mute and grand,
Her flexile body bends, her white feet glide.
The dull Kinoors throb one monotonous tune,
And wail with zeal as in a hasheesh trance;
Her scintillant eyes in vague, ecstatic charm
Burn like black stars below the Orient moon,
While the suave, dreamy languor of the dance
Lulls the grim, drowsy cobra on her arm.

PASTEL

Among the priceless gems and treasures rare
Old Versailles shelters in its halls sublime,
I can recall one faded image fair,
A girl's sad face, praised once in every clime.
Poets have sung, in rich and happy rhyme,
Her violet eyes, the wonder of her hair.
An art-bijou it was, but dimmed by time,
A dreamy pastel of La Valliere!
I, too, remember in my heart a face
Whose charm I deemed would ever with me dwell;
But as the days went by, its peerless grace
Fled like those dreams that blooming dawn dispel,
Till of its beauty there was left no trace,
Time having blurred it like that pale pastel!

THE IDEAL

Toil on, poor muser, to attain that goal
Where Art conceals its grandest, noblest prize;
Count every tear that dims your aching eyes,
Count all the years that seem as days, and roll
The death-tides slowly on; count all your sighs;
Search the wide, wondrous earth from pole to pole,
Tear unbelief from out your martyred soul;
Succumb not, chase despondency, be wise;
Work, toil, and struggle with the brush or pen,
Revel in rhyme, strain intellect and ken;
Live on and hope despite man's sceptic leers;
Praise the Ideal with your every breath,
Give it life, youth and glory, blood and tears,
And to possess it pay its tribute — Death.

Lucy White Jennison

("OWEN INNSLEY")

A DREAM OF DEATH

HELENA

"Du hast mich beschworen aus dem Grab"

I died; they wrapped me in a shroud,
With hollow mourning, far too loud,
And sighs that were but empty sound,
And laid me low within the ground.
I felt *her* tears through all the rest;
Past sheet and shroud they reached my breast;
They warmed to life the frozen clay,
And I began to smile and say:
At last thou lov'st me, Helena!

I rose up in the dead of night;
I sought her window; — 't was alight.
A pebble clattered 'gainst the pane, —
"Who 's there? the wind and falling rain?"
"Ah! no; but one thy tears have led
To leave his chill and narrow bed
To warm himself before thy breath;
Who for thy sake has conquered death.
Arise, and love me, Helena!"

She oped the door, she drew me in.
Her mouth was pale, her cheek was thin;
Her eyes were dim; its length unrolled,
Fell loosely down her hair of gold.
My presence wrought her grief's eclipse;
She pressed her lips upon my lips,
She held me fast in her embrace,
Her hands went wandering o'er my face:
At last thou lov'st me, Helena!

The days are dark, the days are cold,
And heavy lies the churchyard mould.
But ever, at the deep of night,
Their faith the dead and living plight.
Who would not die if certain bliss
Could be foreknown? and such as this
No life — away! the hour is nigh,
With heart on fire she waits my cry:
Arise, and love me, Helena!

BONDAGE

"AND this is freedom!" cried the serf;
"At last
I tread free soil, the free air blows on me;"
And, wild to learn the sweets of liberty,
With eager hope his bosom bounded fast.
But not for naught had the long years amassed
Habit of slavery; among the free
He still was servile, and, disheartened, he
Crept back to the old bondage of the past.
Long did I bear a hard and heavy chain
Wreathëd with amaranth and asphodel,
But through the flower-breaths stole the weary pain.
I cast it off and fled, but 't was in vain;
For when once more I passed by where it fell,
I took it up and bound it on again.

THE BURDEN OF LOVE

I BEAR an unseen burden constantly;
Waking or sleeping I can never thrust
The load aside; through summer's heat and dust
And winter's snows it still abides with me.
I cannot let it fall, though I should be
Never so weary; carry it I must.
Nor can the bands that bind it on me rust
Or break, nor ever shall I be set free.
Sometimes 't is heavy as the weight that bore
Atlas on giant shoulders; sometimes light
As the frail message of the carrier dove;
But, light or heavy, shifting nevermore.
What is it thus oppressing, day and night?
The burden, dearest, of a mighty love.

Laura Elizabeth Richards

A SONG OF TWO ANGELS

Two angels came through the gate of Heaven.
(White and soft is a mother's breast!)
Stayed them both by the gate of Heaven;
Rested a little on folded wings,
Spake a little of holy things.
(In Heaven alone is perfect rest!)

Over them rose the golden steeps,
Heaven's castled and golden steeps;
Under them, depth on depth of space
Fell away from the holy place.

"Brother, and now I must take my way,
Glad and joyful must take my way,
Down to the realm of day and night;
Down to yon earth that rolls so bright."

"Brother, I too am thither sent;
Sad and silent, am thither sent.
Let us together softly wing
Our flight to yon world of sorrowing."

Down they swept through the shining air,
Swiftly sped through the shining air, —
This one bright as the sunset's glow,
That one white as the falling snow.

"Brother, and tell me your errand now!
Tell me your joyful errand now!"
"A little new soul must wake on earth,
And I carry the blessing for its birth."

"And tell me, brother, what task is yours?
Dear white angel, what task is yours?"
"To bear a soul back to Heaven's height, —
A mother, whose child is born to-night."

"Ah! will the mother be sad to go?
Loath to leave her baby and go?"
"Hush, dear angel! she will not know.
God in His mercy wills it so."

"Ah! will the baby wake forlorn?
Seek its mother, and weep forlorn?"
"Hush, dear angel! we may not know.
God, knowing all things, wills it so."

Down they swept through the dusky air,
Swiftly sped through the dusky air;
Trod the dim earth with noiseless feet;
Softly stole through a village street.

Now they came to a cottage door,
Stayed them both at a cottage door, —
This one bright as the sunset's glow,
That one white as the falling snow.

"Brother, I trow we here must part!
Dear white angel, we here must part!
For this low door I must enter by."
"Alas! and alas! so too must I!"

Sad they gazed in each other's face;
(White and soft is a mother's breast;)
Lingered and looked in each other's face;
Then folded their hands in silent prayer,
And so together they entered there.
(In Heaven alone is perfect rest.)

WHERE HELEN SITS[1]

WHERE Helen sits, the darkness is so deep,
No golden sunbeam strikes athwart the gloom;
No mother's smile, no glance of loving eyes,
Lightens the shadow of that lonely room.

Yet the clear whiteness of her radiant soul
Decks the dim walls, like angel vestments shed.
The lovely light of holy innocence
Shines like a halo round her bended head,
Where Helen sits.

Where Helen sits, the stillness is so deep,
No children's laughter comes, no song of bird.
The great world storms along its noisy way,
But in this place no sound is ever heard.

Yet do her gentle thoughts make melody
Sweeter than aught from harp or viol flung;
And Love and Beauty, quiring each to each,
Sing as the stars of Eden's morning sung,
Where Helen sits.

A VALENTINE

OH! little loveliest lady mine,
What shall I send for your valentine?
Summer and flowers are far away;
Gloomy old Winter is king to-day;
Buds will not blow, and sun will not shine:
What shall I do for a valentine?

I 've searched the gardens all through and through
For a bud to tell of my love so true;
But buds are asleep, and blossoms are dead,
And the snow beats down on my poor little head:
So, little loveliest lady mine,
Here is my heart for your valentine!

George Houghton

SANDY HOOK

WHITE sand and cedars; cedars, sand;
Light-houses here and there; a strand
Strewn o'er with driftwood; tangled weeds;
A squad of fish-hawks poised above
The nets, too anxious-eyed to move;
Flame-flowering cactus; wingëd seeds,
That on a sea of sunshine lie
Unfanned, save by some butterfly;
A sun now reddening toward the west; —
And under and through all one hears
That mellow voice, old as the years,
The waves' low monotone of unrest.
So wanes the summer afternoon
In drowsy stillness, and the moon
Appears; when, sudden, round about
The wind-cocks wheel, — hoarse fog-horns shout
A warning, and in gathering gloom
Against the sea's white anger loom
Tall shapes of wreckers, torch in hand,
Rattling their life-boats down the sand!

THE HANDSEL RING

"HERE, O lily-white lady mine,
Here by thy warrior sire's own shrine,
Handsel I thee by this golden sign,
This sunshiny thing."
Weeping she reached her hand so slim,
Smiled, though her eyes were wet and dim,

[1] Helen Keller.

Saying: "I swear, by Heaven, by him,
And by this handsel ring!"

But as she bended her eyes abashed,
Out of his fingers the jewel flashed,
On the gray flags of the kirk it clashed,
That treacherous thing;
Clashed, and bounded, and circled, and sped,
Till through a crevice it flamed and fled,—
Down in the tomb of the knightly dead
Darted the handsel ring.

"Matters not, darling! Ere day be o'er,
Goldsmiths shall forge for thy hands a score;
Let not thy heart be harried and sore
For a little thing!"
"Nay! but behold what broodeth there!
See the cold sheen of his silvery hair!
Look how his eyeballs roll and stare,
Seeking thy handsel ring!"

"I see nothing, my precious, my own!
'Tis a black vision that sorrow hath sown;
Haste, let us hence, for dark it hath grown,
And moths are on wing."
"Nay, but his shrunken fist, behold,
Looses his lance-hilt and scatters the mould!
What is that his long fingers hold?
Christ! 't is our handsel ring!"

And when the bridegroom bends over her,
Neither the lips nor the eyelids stir;
Naught to her, now, but music and myrrh,—
Needless his handsel ring.

THE MANOR LORD

BESIDE the landsman knelt a dame,
And slowly pushed the pages o'er;
Still by the hearth-fire's spending flame
She waited, while a hollow roar
Came from the chimney, and the breath
Of twice seven hounds upon the floor;
And, save the old man's labored moan,
The night had no sound more.

The fire flickered; with a start
The master hound upflung his head;
Sudden he whined, when with one spring
Each hunter bounded from his bed,—
And through rent blind and bolted door
All voiceless every creature fled;
The blinking watcher closed her book:
"Amen, our lord is dead!"

Eugene Field

WYNKEN, BLYNKEN, AND NOD

WYNKEN, Blynken, and Nod one night
Sailed off in a wooden shoe,—
Sailed on a river of crystal light
Into a sea of dew.
"Where are you going, and what do you wish?"
The old moon asked the three.
"We have come to fish for the herring-fish
That live in this beautiful sea;
Nets of silver and gold have we,"
Said Wynken,
Blynken,
And Nod.

The old moon laughed and sang a song,
As they rocked in the wooden shoe;
And the wind that sped them all night long
Ruffled the waves of dew;
The little stars were the herring-fish
That lived in the beautiful sea.
"Now cast your nets wherever you wish,—
Never afeard are we!"
So cried the stars to the fishermen three,
Wynken,
Blynken,
And Nod.

All night long their nets they threw
To the stars in the twinkling foam,—
Then down from the skies came the wooden shoe,
Bringing the fishermen home:
'T was all so pretty a sail, it seemed
As if it could not be;
And some folk thought 'twas a dream they 'd dreamed
Of sailing that beautiful sea;
But I shall name you the fishermen three:
Wynken,
Blynken,
And Nod.

Wynken and Blynken are two little eyes,
  And Nod is a little head,
And the wooden shoe that sailed the skies
  Is a wee one's trundle-bed;
So shut your eyes while Mother sings
  Of wonderful sights that be,
And you shall see the beautiful things
  As you rock on the misty sea
  Where the old shoe rocked the fishermen three, —
      Wynken,
      Blynken,
      And Nod.

GARDEN AND CRADLE

When our babe he goeth walking in his garden,
  Around his tinkling feet the sunbeams play;
    The posies they are good to him,
    And bow them as they should to him,
  As fareth he upon his kingly way;
    And birdlings of the wood to him
  Make music, gentle music, all the day,
When our babe he goeth walking in his garden.

When our babe he goeth swinging in his cradle,
  Then the night it looketh ever sweetly down;
    The little stars are kind to him,
    The moon she hath a mind to him,
  And layeth on his head a golden crown;
    And singeth then the wind to him
  A song, the gentle song of Bethle'm town,
When our babe he goeth swinging in his cradle.

IN THE FIRELIGHT

The fire upon the hearth is low,
  And there is stillness everywhere,
  And, like winged spirits, here and there
The firelight shadows fluttering go.
And as the shadows round me creep,
  A childish treble breaks the gloom,
  And softly from a further room
Comes: "Now I lay me down to sleep."

And, somehow, with that little prayer
  And that sweet treble in my ears,
  My thought goes back to distant years,
And lingers with a dear one there;
And as I hear my child's amen,
  My mother's faith comes back to me, —
  Crouched at her side I seem to be,
And mother holds my hands again.

Oh for an hour in that dear place,
  Oh for the peace of that dear time,
  Oh for that childish trust sublime,
Oh for a glimpse of mother's face!
Yet, as the shadows round me creep,
  I do not seem to be alone —
  Sweet magic of that treble tone
And "Now I lay me down to sleep!"

NIGHTFALL IN DORDRECHT

The mill goes toiling slowly around
  With steady and solemn creak,
And my little one hears in the kindly sound
  The voice of the old mill speak.
While round and round those big white wings
  Grimly and ghostlike creep,
My little one hears that the old mill sings
  "Sleep, little tulip, sleep!"

The sails are reefed and the nets are drawn,
  And, over his pot of beer,
The fisher, against the morrow's dawn,
  Lustily maketh cheer.
He mocks at the winds that caper along
  From the far-off clamorous deep, —
But we — we love their lullaby song
  Of "Sleep, little tulip, sleep!"

Old dog Fritz in slumber sound
  Groans of the stony mart:
To-morrow how proudly he'll trot you round,
  Hitched to our new milk-cart!
And you shall help me blanket the kine
  And fold the gentle sheep,
And set the herring a-soak in brine, —
  But now, little tulip, sleep!

A Dream-One comes to button the eyes
  That wearily droop and blink,
While the old mill buffets the frowning skies
  And scolds at the stars that wink;
Over your face the misty wings
  Of that beautiful Dream-One sweep,
And rocking your cradle she softly sings
  "Sleep, little tulip, sleep!"

THE DINKEY-BIRD

In an ocean, 'way out yonder
 (As all sapient people know,)
Is the land of Wonder-wander,
 Whither children love to go:
It 's their playing, romping, swinging,
 That give great joy to me
While the Dinkey-Bird goes singing
 In the amfalula tree!

There the gum-drops grow like cherries,
 And taffy 's thick as peas, —
Caramels you pick like berries
 When, and where, and how you please;
Big red sugar-plums are clinging
 To the cliffs beside that sea
Where the Dinkey-Bird is singing
 In the amfalula tree.

So when children shout and scamper
 And make merry all the day,
When there 's naught to put a damper
 To the ardor of their play;
When I hear their laughter ringing,
 Then I 'm sure as sure can be
That the Dinkey-Bird is singing
 In the amfalula tree.

For the Dinkey-Bird's bravuras
 And staccatos are so sweet, —
His roulades, appoggiaturas,
 And robustos so complete,
That the youth of every nation —
 Be they near or far away —
Have especial delectation
 In that gladsome roundelay.

Their eyes grow bright and brighter,
 Their lungs begin to crow,
Their hearts get light and lighter,
 And their cheeks are all aglow;
For an echo cometh bringing
 The news to all and me,
That the Dinkey-Bird is singing
 In the amfalula tree.

I 'm sure you like to go there
 To see your feathered friend, —
And so many goodies grow there
 You would like to comprehend!
Speed, little dreams, your winging
 To that land across the sea
Where the Dinkey-Bird is singing
 In the amfalula tree!

LITTLE BOY BLUE

The little toy dog is covered with dust,
 But sturdy and stanch he stands;
And the little toy soldier is red with rust,
 And his musket moulds in his hands.
Time was when the little toy dog was new,
 And the soldier was passing fair;
And that was the time when our Little Boy Blue
 Kissed them and put them there.

"Now, don't you go till I come," he said,
 "And don't you make any noise!"
So, toddling off to his trundle-bed,
 He dreamt of the pretty toys;
And, as he was dreaming, an angel song
 Awakened our Little Boy Blue —
Oh! the years are many, the years are long,
 But the little toy friends are true!

Ay, faithful to Little Boy Blue they stand,
 Each in the same old place,
Awaiting the touch of a little hand,
 The smile of a little face;
And they wonder, as waiting the long years through
 In the dust of that little chair,
What has become of our Little Boy Blue,
 Since he kissed them and put them there.

THE LYTTEL BOY

Some time there ben a lyttel boy
 That wolde not renne and play,
And helpless like that little tyke
 Ben allwais in the way.
"Goe, make you merrie with the rest,"
 His weary moder cried;
But with a frown he catcht her gown
 And hong untill her side.

That boy did love his moder well,
 Which spake him faire, I ween;
He loved to stand and hold her hand
 And ken her with his een;
His cosset bleated in the croft,
 His toys unheeded lay, —
He wolde not goe, but, tarrying soe,
 Ben allwais in the way.

Godde loveth children and doth gird
His throne with soche as these,
And he doth smile in plaisaunce while
They cluster at his knees;
And some time, when he looked on earth
And watched the bairns at play,
He kenned with joy a lyttel boy
Ben allwais in the way.

And then a moder felt her heart
How that it ben to-torne,
She kissed eche day till she ben gray
The shoon he use to worn;
No bairn let hold untill her gown
Nor played upon the floore, —
Godde's was the joy; a lyttel boy
Ben in the way no more!

OUR TWO OPINIONS

Us two wuz boys when we fell out, —
Nigh to the age uv my youngest now;
Don't rec'lect what 't wuz about,
Some small deeff'rence, I 'll allow.
Lived next neighbors twenty years,
A-hatin' each other, me 'nd Jim, —
He havin' *his* opinyin uv *me*,
'Nd *I* havin' *my* opinyin uv *him*.

Grew up together 'nd would n't speak,
Courted sisters, 'nd marr'd 'em, too;
'Tended same meetin'-house oncet a week,
A-hatin' each other through 'nd through!
But when Abe Linkern asked the West
F'r soldiers, we answered, — me 'nd Jim, —
He havin' *his* opinyin uv *me*,
'Nd *I* havin' *my* opinyin uv *him*.

But down in Tennessee one night
Ther' wuz sound uv firin' fur away,
'Nd the sergeant allowed ther' 'd be a fight
With the Johnnie Rebs some time nex' day;
'Nd as I wuz thinkin' uv Lizzie 'nd home
Jim stood afore me, long 'nd slim, —
He havin' *his* opinyin uv *me*,
'Nd *I* havin' *my* opinyin uv *him*.

Seemed like we knew there wuz goin' to be
Serious trouble f'r me 'nd him;
Us two shuck hands, did Jim 'nd me,
But never a word from me or Jim!
He went *his* way 'nd *I* went *mine*,
'Nd into the battle's roar went we, —
I havin' *my* opinyin uv Jim,
'Nd *he* havin' *his* opinyin uv *me*.

Jim never come back from the war again,
But I hain't forgot that last, last night
When, waitin' f'r orders, us two men
Made up 'nd shuck hands, afore the fight.
'Nd, after it all, it 's soothin' to know
That here *I* be 'nd yonder 's Jim, —
He havin' *his* opinyin uv *me*,
'Nd *I* havin' *my* opinyin uv *him*.

THE BIBLIOMANIAC'S PRAYER

Keep me, I pray, in wisdom's way,
That I may truths eternal seek;
I need protecting care to-day, —
My purse is light, my flesh is weak.
So banish from my erring heart
All baleful appetites and hints
Of Satan's fascinating art,
Of first editions, and of prints.
Direct me in some godly walk
Which leads away from bookish strife,
That I with pious deed and talk
May extra-illustrate my life.

But if, O Lord, it pleaseth Thee
To keep me in temptation's way,
I humbly ask that I may be
Most notably beset to-day;
Let my temptation be a book,
Which I shall purchase, hold, and keep,
Whereon, when other men shall look,
They 'll wail to know I got it cheap.
Oh, let it such a volume be
As in rare copperplates abounds,
Large paper, clean, and fair to see,
Uncut, unique, unknown to Lowndes.

DIBDIN'S GHOST

Dear wife, last midnight, whilst I read
The tomes you so despise,
A spectre rose beside the bed,
And spake in this true wise:
"From Canaan's beatific coast
I 've come to visit thee,
For I am Frognall Dibdin's ghost,"
Says Dibdin's ghost to me.

I bade him welcome, and we twain
  Discussed with buoyant hearts
The various things that appertain
  To bibliomaniac arts.
"Since you are fresh from t'other side,
  Pray tell me of that host
That treasured books before they died,"
  Says I to Dibdin's ghost.

"They 've entered into perfect rest;
  For in the life they 've won
There are no auctions to molest,
  No creditors to dun.
Their heavenly rapture has no bounds
  Beside that jasper sea;
It is a joy unknown to Lowndes,"
  Says Dibdin's ghost to me.

Much I rejoiced to hear him speak
  Of biblio-bliss above,
For I am one of those who seek
  What bibliomaniacs love.
"But tell me, for I long to hear.
  What doth concern me most,
Are wives admitted to that sphere?"
  Says I to Dibdin's ghost.

"The women folk are few up there;
  For 't were not fair, you know,
That they our heavenly joy should share
  Who vex us here below.
The few are those who have been kind
  To husbands such as we;
They knew our fads, and did n't mind,"
  Says Dibdin's ghost to me.

"But what of those who scold at us
  When we would read in bed?
Or, wanting victuals, make a fuss
  If we buy books instead?
And what of those who 've dusted not
  Our motley pride and boast, —
Shall they profane that sacred spot?"
  Says I to Dibdin's ghost.

"Oh, no! they tread that other path,
  Which leads where torments roll,
And worms, yes, bookworms, vent their wrath
  Upon the guilty soul.
Untouched of bibliomaniac grace,
  That saveth such as we,
They wallow in that dreadful place,"
  Says Dibdin's ghost to me.

"To my dear wife will I recite
  What things I 've heard you say;
She 'll let me read the books by night
  She 's let me buy by day.
For we together by and by
  Would join that heavenly host;
She 's earned a rest as well as I,"
  Says I to Dibdin's ghost.

ECHOES FROM THE SABINE FARM

TO THE FOUNTAIN OF BANDUSIA

O FOUNTAIN of Bandusia!
  Whence crystal waters flow,
With garlands gay and wine I 'll pay
  The sacrifice I owe;
A sportive kid with budding horns
  I have, whose crimson blood
Anon shall dye and sanctify
  Thy cool and babbling flood.

O fountain of Bandusia!
  The Dog-star's hateful spell
No evil brings into the springs
  That from thy bosom well;
Here oxen, wearied by the plow,
  The roving cattle here
Hasten in quest of certain rest,
  And quaff thy gracious cheer.

O fountain of Bandusia!
  Ennobled shalt thou be,
For I shall sing the joys that spring
  Beneath yon ilex-tree.
Yes, fountain of Bandusia,
  Posterity shall know
The cooling brooks that from thy nooks
  Singing and dancing go.

TO LEUCONÖE

I

WHAT end the gods may have ordained for me,
And what for thee,
  Seek not to learn, Leuconöe, — we may not know.
Chaldean tables cannot bring us rest.
'T is for the best
  To bear in patience what may come, or weal or woe.

If for more winters our poor lot is cast,
Or this the last,
  Which on the crumbling rocks has dashed Etruscan seas,

Strain clear the wine; this life is short, at best.
Take hope with zest,
And, trusting not To-morrow, snatch To-day for ease!

TO LEUCONÖE

II

Seek not, Leuconöe, to know how long you 're going to live yet,
What boons the gods will yet withhold, or what they 're going to give yet;
For Jupiter will have his way, despite how much we worry: —
Some will hang on for many a day, and some die in a hurry.

The wisest thing for you to do is to embark this diem
Upon a merry escapade with some such bard as I am.
And while we sport I 'll reel you off such odes as shall surprise ye;
To-morrow, when the headache comes, — well, then I 'll satirize ye!

Robert Burns Wilson

IT IS IN WINTER THAT WE DREAM OF SPRING

It is in Winter that we dream of Spring;
For all the barren bleakness and the cold,
The longing fancy sees the frozen mould
Decked with sweet blossoming.

Though all the birds be silent, — though
The fettered stream's soft voice be still,
And on the leafless bough the snow
Be rested, marble-like and chill, —
Yet will the fancy build, from these,
The transient but well-pleasing dream
Of leaf and bloom among the trees,
And sunlight glancing on the stream.

Though, to the eye, the joyless landscape yields
No faintest sign to which the hope might cling, —
Amidst the pallid desert of the fields, —
It is in Winter that we dream of Spring.

THE DEAD PLAYER

Sure and exact, — the master's quiet touch,
Thus perfect, was his art;
Ambitious, generous, sad, and loving much,
Was his pain-haunted heart.

To him, the blissful burthen of her love
Did stern-browed Fortune give;
In hell, in heaven, beneath life and above,
Such souls as his must live.

Who wears Fame's Tyrian garb, as well must wear
The heavy robe of Grief;
Who bears aloft the palm, must also bear
Hid woundings past belief.

Both he did wear and bear, as well as most
Of Earth's soon-counted few
That stand distinguished from the unknown host
By having work to do.

Souls seek their doom. A costly-freighted bark
That sails a perilous sea,
Rounds every bar, and goes down, in the dark
At port, — e'en such was he.

A classic shade, — he walks the unknown lands
Death-silent and death-dim;
But, like a noble Phidian marble, stands
The memory of him.

TO A CROW

Bold, amiable, ebon outlaw, grave and wise!
For many a good green year hast thou withstood —
By dangerous, planted field and haunted wood —
All the devices of thine enemies,
Gleaning thy grudgëd bread with watchful eyes

And self-relying soul. Come ill or good,
Blithe days thou see'st, thou feathered Robin Hood!
Thou mak'st a jest of farm-land boundaries.
Take all thou may'st, and never count it crime
To rob the greatest robber of the earth,
Weak-visioned, dull, self-lauding man, whose worth
Is in his own esteem. Bide thou thy time;
Thou know'st far more of Nature's lore than he,
And her wide lap shall still provide for thee.

THE SUNRISE OF THE POOR

A DARKENED hut outlined against the sky,
A forward-looking slope, — some cedar trees,
Gaunt grasses stirred by the awaking breeze,
And nearer, where the grayer shadows lie,
Within a small paled square, one may descry
The beds wherein the Poor first taste of ease,
Where dewy rose-vines drop their spicy lees
Above the dreamless ashes, silently.
A lonely woman leans there, — bent and gray:
Outlined in part against the shadowed hill,
In part against the sky, in which the day
Begins to blaze. O earth, so sweet, — so still! —
The woman sighs, and draws a long, deep breath:
It is the call to labor, — not to death.

SUCH IS THE DEATH THE SOLDIER DIES

SUCH is the death the soldier dies:
He falls, — the column speeds away;
Upon the dabbled grass he lies,
His brave heart following, still, the fray.

The smoke-wraiths drift among the trees,
The battle storms along the hill;
The glint of distant arms he sees;
He hears his comrades shouting still.

A glimpse of far-borne flags, that fade
And vanish in the rolling din:
He knows the sweeping charge is made,
The cheering lines are closing in.

Unmindful of his mortal wound,
He faintly calls and seeks to rise;
But weakness drags him to the ground: —
Such is the death the soldier dies.

BALLAD OF THE FADED FIELD

BROAD bars of sunset-slanted gold
Are laid along the field, and here
The silence sings, as if some old
Refrain, that once rang long and clear,
Came softly, stealing to the ear
Without the aid of sound. The rill
Is voiceless, and the grass is sere,
But beauty's soul abideth still.

Trance-like, the mellow air doth hold
The sorrow of the passing year;
The heart of Nature groweth cold,
The time of falling snow is near;
On phantom feet, which none may hear,
Creeps — with the shadow of the hill —
The semblance of departed cheer,
But beauty's soul abideth still.

The dead, gray-clustered weeds enfold
The well-known summer path, and drear
The dusking hills, like billows rolled
Against the distant sky, appear.
From lonely haunts, where Night and Fear
Keep ghostly tryst, when mists are chill,
The dark pine lifts a jaggëd spear,
But beauty's soul abideth still.

ENVOY

Dear love, the days that once were dear
May come no more; life may fulfill
Her fleeting dreams with many a tear,
But beauty's soul abideth still.

Arlo Bates

AMERICA

(FROM "THE TORCH-BEARERS")

FOR, O America, our country! — land
Hid in the west through centuries, till men
Through countless tyrannies could understand
The priceless worth of freedom, — once again
The world was new-created when thy shore
First knew the Pilgrim keels, that one last test
The race might make of manhood, nor give o'er
The strife with evil till it proved its best.
Thy true sons stand as torch-bearers, to hold
A guiding light. Here the last stand is made.
If we fail here, what new Columbus bold,
Steering brave prow through black seas unafraid,
Finds out a fresh land where man may abide
And freedom yet be saved? The whole round earth
Has seen the battle fought. Where shall men hide
From tyranny and wrong, where life have worth,
If here the cause succumb? If greed of gold
Or lust of power or falsehood triumph here,
The race is lost! A globe dispeopled, cold,
Rolled down the void a voiceless, lifeless sphere,
Were not so stamped by all which hope debars
As were this earth, plunging along through space
Conquered by evil, shamed among the stars,
Bearing a base, enslaved, dishonored race!
Here has the battle its last vantage ground;
Here all is won, or here must all be lost,
Here freedom's trumpets one last rally sound;
Here to the breeze its blood-stained flag is tossed.
America, last hope of man and truth,
Thy name must through all coming ages be
The badge unspeakable of shame and ruth,
Or glorious pledge that man through truth is free.
This is thy destiny; the choice is thine
To lead all nations and outshine them all:
But if thou failest, deeper shame is thine,
And none shall spare to mock thee in thy fall.

IN PARADISE

"O PITYING angel, pause, and say
To me, new come to Paradise,
How I may drive one pain away
By penitence or sacrifice.
From deeps below of nether Hell
I hear a lost soul's bitter cry:
Alas! It was through me she fell, —
What price forgetfulness may buy?"

The passing angel paused in flight,
Poised like fair stars which first arise,
And looked on that pale suppliant white,
With piercing pity in his eyes.
"Ah, woe!" he said. "Thy joy and peace
Cannot be bought with prayer or price.
For thee that wail will never cease,
Though thou hast won to Paradise!"

THE CYCLAMEN

OVER the plains where Persian hosts
Laid down their lives for glory
Flutter the cyclamens, like ghosts
That witness to their story.
Oh, fair! Oh, white! Oh, pure as snow!
On countless graves how sweet they grow!

Or crimson, like the cruel wounds
From which the life-blood, flowing,
Poured out where now on grassy mounds
The low, soft winds are blowing:

Oh, fair! Oh, red! Like blood of slain;
Not even time can cleanse that stain.

But when my dear these blossoms holds,
All loveliness her dower,
All woe and joy the past enfolds
In her find fullest flower.
Oh, fair! Oh, pure! Oh, white and red!
If she but live, what are the dead!

CONCEITS

I

KITTY'S LAUGH

THY laugh 's a song an oriole trilled,
Romping in glee the sky, —
Sunshine in lucent drops distilled,
And showered from on high.

So perfect in his song thou art,
That when thy laughter rings
I long to clasp thee to my heart,
Lest, too, thou have his wings!

II

KITTY'S "NO"

Kit, the recording angel wrote
That cruel "no" you said,
And smiled to think how in your throat
You choked a "yes" instead;

Then sighed in envy of the look
That promised me your grace;
And on the margin of his book
Limned in excuse your face.

LIKE TO A COIN

LIKE to a coin, passing from hand to hand,
Are common memories, and day by day
The sharpness of their impress wears away.
But love's remembrances unspoiled withstand
The touch of time, as in an antique land
Where some proud town old centuries did slay,
Intaglios buried lie, still in decay
Perfect and precious spite of grinding sand.
What fame or joy or sorrow has been ours,
What we have hoped or feared, we may forget.
The clearness of all memory time deflours,
Save that of love alone, persistent yet
Though sure oblivion all things else devours,
Its tracings firm as when they first were set.

THE WATCHERS

WE must be nobler for our dead, be sure,
Than for the quick. We might their living eyes
Deceive with gloss of seeming; but all lies
Were vain to cheat a prescience spirit-pure.
Our soul's true worth and aim, however poor,
They see who watch us from some deathless skies
With glance death-quickened. That no sad surprise
Sting them in seeing, be ours to secure.
Living, our loved ones make us what they dream;
Dead, if they see, they know us as we are.
Henceforward we must be, not merely seem.
Bitterer woe than death it were by far
To fail their hopes who love us to redeem;
Loss were thrice loss that thus their faith should mar.

ON THE ROAD TO CHORRERA

THREE horsemen galloped the dusty way
While sun and moon were both in the sky;
An old crone crouched in the cactus' shade,
And craved an alms as they rode by.
A friendless hag she seemed to be,
But the queen of a bandit crew was she.

One horseman tossed her a scanty dole,
A scoffing couplet the second trolled;
But the third, from his blue eyes frank and free,
No glance vouchsafed the beldam old;
As toward the sunset and the sea,
No evil fearing, rode the three.

A curse she gave for the pittance small,
A gibe for the couplet's ribald word;
But that which once had been her heart

At sight of the silent horseman stirred:
And safe through the ambushed band they speed
For the sake of the rider who would not heed!

A WINTER TWILIGHT

PALE beryl sky, with clouds
Hued like dove's wing,
O'ershadowing
The dying day,
And whose edge half enshrouds
The first fair evening star,
Most crystalline by far
Of all the stars that night enring,
Half human in its ray, —
What blessed, soothing sense of calm
Comes with this twilight, — sovereign balm
That takes at last the bitter sting
Of day's keen pain away.

Florence Earle Coates

PERDITA

(ON SEEING MISS ANDERSON IN THE RÔLE)

SHE dances,
And I seem to be
In primrose vales of Sicily,
Beside the streams once looked upon
By Thyrsis and by Corydon:
The sunlight laughs as she advances,
Shyly the zephyrs kiss her hair,
And she seems to me as the wood-fawn, free,
And as the wild rose, fair.

Dance, Perdita! and, shepherds, blow!
Your reeds restrain no longer!
Till weald and welkin gleeful ring,
Blow, shepherds, blow! and, lasses, sing
Yet sweeter strains and stronger!
Let far Helorus softer flow
'Twixt rushy banks, that he may hear;
Let Pan, great Pan himself, draw near!

Stately
She moves, half smiling,
With girlish look beguiling, —
A dawn-like grace in all her face;
Stately she moves, sedately,
Through the crowd circling round her;
But — swift as light —
See! she takes flight!
Empty, alas! is her place.

Follow her, follow her, let her not go!
Mirth ended so —
Why, 't is but woe!
Follow her, follow her! Perdita! — lo,
Love hath with wreaths enwound her!

She dances,
And I seem to see
The nymph divine, Terpsichore,
As when her beauty dazzling shone
On eerie heights of Helicon.
With bursts of song her voice entrances
The dreamy, blossom-scented air,
And she seems to me as the wood-fawn, free,
And as the wild rose, fair.

SURVIVAL

THE knell that dooms the voiceless and obscure
Stills Memnon's music with its ghostly chime;
Strength is as weakness in the clasp of Time,
And for the things that were there is no cure.
The vineyard with its fair investiture,
The mountain summit with its hoary rime,
The throne of Cæsar, Cheops' tomb sublime,
Alike decay, and only dreams endure.
Dreams for Assyria her worship won,
And India is hallowed by her dreams;
The Sphinx with deathless visage views the race
That like the lotus of a summer seems;
And, rudderless, immortally sails on
The wingëd Victory of Samothrace.

INDIA

SILENT amidst unbroken silence deep
Of dateless years, in loneliness supreme,
She pondered patiently one mighty theme,
And let the hours, uncounted, by her creep.

The motionless Himalayas, the broad sweep
Of glacial cataracts, great Ganges' stream, —
All these to her were but as things that seem,
Doomed all to pass, like phantoms viewed in sleep.
Her history? She has none, — scarce a name.
The life she lived is lost in the profound
Of time, which she despised; but nothing mars
The memory that, single, gives her fame:
She dreamed eternal dreams, and from the ground
Still raised her yearning vision to the stars.

TENNYSON

How beautiful to live as thou didst live!
How beautiful to die as thou didst die, —
In moonlight of the night, without a sigh,
At rest in all the best that love could give!

How excellent to bear into old age
The poet's ardor and the heart of youth, —
To keep to the last sleep the vow of truth,
And leave to lands that grieve a glowing page!

How glorious to feel the spirit's power
Unbroken by the near approach of death,
To breathe blest prophecies with failing breath,
Soul-bound to beauty in that latest hour!

How sweet to greet, in final kinship owned,
The master-spirit to thy dreams so dear, —
At last from his immortal lips to hear
The dirge for Imogen, and thee, intoned!

How beautiful to live as thou didst live!
How beautiful to die as thou didst die, —
In moonlight of the night, without a sigh,
At rest in all the best that love could give!

SONGS

THE WORLD IS MINE

For me the jasmine buds unfold
And silver daisies star the lea,
The crocus hoards the sunset gold,
And the wild rose breathes for me.
I feel the sap through the bough returning,
I share the skylark's transport fine,
I know the fountain's wayward yearning;
I love, and the world is mine!

I love, and thoughts that sometime grieved,
Still well remembered, grieve not me;
From all that darkened and deceived
Upsoars my spirit free.
For soft the hours repeat one story,
Sings the sea one strain divine,
My clouds arise all flushed with glory;
I love, and the world is mine!

TO-MORROW

The robin chants when the thrush is dumb,
Snow smooths a bed for the clover,
Life flames anew, and days to come
Are sweet as the days that are over.

The tide that ebbs by the moon flows back,
Faith builds on the ruins of sorrow,
The halcyon flutters in winter's track,
And night makes way for the morrow.

And ever a strain, of joys the sum,
Sings on in the heart of the lover —
In death sings on — that days to come
Are sweet as the days that are over!

George Parsons Lathrop

THE FLOWN SOUL

Come not again! I dwell with you
Above the realm of frost and dew,
Of pain and fire, and growth to death.
I dwell with you where never breath
Is drawn, but fragrance vital flows
From life to life, even as a rose
Unseen pours sweetness through each vein,
And from the air distils again.
You are my rose unseen: we live
Where each to other joy may give
In ways untold, by means unknown
And secret as the magnet-stone.

For which of us, indeed, is dead?
No more I lean to kiss your head, —
The gold-red hair so thick upon it:
Joy feels no more the touch that won it,
When o'er my brow your pearl-cool palm
In tenderness so childish, calm,
Crept softly, once. Yet, see, my arm
Is strong, and still my blood runs warm:

I still can work and think and weep.
But all this show of life I keep
Is but the shadow of your shine,
Flicker of your fire, husk of your vine;
Therefore you are not dead, nor I,
Who hear your laughter's minstrelsy.
Among the stars your feet are set;
Your little feet are dancing yet
Their rhythmic beat, as when on earth.
So swift, so slight, are death and birth!

Come not again, dear child. If thou
By any chance couldst break that vow
Of silence, at thy last hour made;
If to this grim life unafraid
Thou couldst return, and melt the frost
Wherein thy bright limbs' power was lost;
Still would I whisper — since so fair
The silent comradeship we share —
Yes, whisper mid the unbidden rain
Of tears: "Come not! Come not again!"

SOUTH-WIND

SOFT-THROATED South, breathing of summer's ease
(Sweet breath, whereof the violet's life is made!)
Through lips moist-warm, as thou hadst lately stayed
'Mong rosebuds, wooing to the cheeks of these
Loth blushes faint and maidenly, — rich breeze,
Still doth thy honeyed blowing bring a shade
Of sad foreboding. In thy hand is laid
The power to build or blight the fruit of trees,
The deep, cool grass, and field of thick-combed grain.
Even so my Love may bring me joy or woe,
Both measureless, but either counted gain
Since given by her. For pain and pleasure flow
Like tides upon us of the selfsame sea:
Tears are the gems of joy and misery.

THE SUNSHINE OF THINE EYES

THE sunshine of thine eyes,
(O still, celestial beam!)
Whatever it touches it fills
With the life of its lambent gleam.

The sunshine of thine eyes,
Oh, let it fall on me!
Though I be but a mote of the air,
I could turn to gold for thee.

REMEMBRANCE

UNDER the apple bough
Love, in a dream of leaves,
Dreamed we of love, as now, —
All that gives beauty or grieves.

Over the sad world then
Curved like the sky that bough;
I was in heaven then, —
You are in heaven now.

THE VOICE OF THE VOID

I WARN, like the one drop of rain
On your face, ere the storm;
Or tremble in whispered refrain
With your blood, beating warm.
I am the presence that ever
Baffles your touch's endeavor, —
Gone like the glimmer of dust
Dispersed by a gust.
I am the absence that taunts you,
The fancy that haunts you;
The ever unsatisfied guess
That, questioning emptiness,
Wins a sigh for reply.
Nay, nothing am I,
But the flight of a breath —
For I am Death!

THE CHILD'S WISH GRANTED

Do you remember, my sweet, absent son,
How in the soft June days forever done
You loved the heavens so warm and clear and high;
And, when I lifted you, soft came your cry, —
"Put me 'way up, — 'way, 'way up in blue sky"?

I laughed and said I could not, — set you down,
Your gray eyes wonder-filled beneath that crown
Of bright hair gladdening me as you raced by.
Another Father now, more strong than I,
Has borne you voiceless to your dear blue sky.

KEENAN'S CHARGE

I

THE sun had set;
The leaves with dew were wet:
Down fell a bloody dusk
On the woods, that second of May,
Where Stonewall's corps, like a beast of prey,
Tore through, with angry tusk.

"They 've trapped us, boys!"
Rose from our flank a voice.
With a rush of steel and smoke
On came the rebels straight,
Eager as love and wild as hate;
And our line reeled and broke:

Broke and fled.
No one stayed — but the dead!
With curses, shrieks, and cries,
Horses and wagons and men
Tumbled back through the shuddering glen,
And above us the fading skies.

There 's one hope still, —
Those batteries parked on the hill!
"Battery, wheel!" (mid the roar)
"Pass pieces; fix prolonge to fire
Retiring. Trot!" In the panic dire
A bugle rings "Trot!" — and no more.

The horses plunged,
The cannon lurched and lunged,
To join the hopeless rout.
But suddenly rode a form
Calmly in front of the human storm,
With a stern, commanding shout:

"Align those guns!"
(We knew it was Pleasonton's.)
The cannoneers bent to obey,
And worked with a will at his word:
And the black guns moved as if *they* had heard.
But ah the dread delay!

"To wait is crime;
O God, for ten minutes' time!"
The General looked around.
There Keenan sat, like a stone,
With his three hundred horse alone,
Less shaken than the ground.

"Major, your men?"
"Are soldiers, General." "Then
Charge, Major! Do your best:
Hold the enemy back, at all cost,
Till my guns are placed, — else the army is lost.
You die to save the rest!"

II

BY the shrouded gleam of the western skies,
Brave Keenan looked into Pleasonton's eyes
For an instant, — clear, and cool, and still;
Then, with a smile, he said: "I will."

"Cavalry, charge!" Not a man of them shrank.
Their sharp, full cheer, from rank on rank,
Rose joyously, with a willing breath, —
Rose like a greeting hail to death.
Then forward they sprang, and spurred and clashed;
Shouted the officers, crimson-sashed;
Rode well the men, each brave as his fellow,
In their faded coats of the blue and yellow;
And above in the air, with an instinct true,
Like a bird of war their pennon flew.

With clank of scabbards and thunder of steeds,
And blades that shine like sunlit reeds,
And strong brown faces bravely pale
For fear their proud attempt shall fail,
Three hundred Pennsylvanians close
On twice ten thousand gallant foes.

Line after line the troopers came
To the edge of the wood that was ringed with flame;
Rode in and sabred and shot — and fell;
Nor came one back his wounds to tell.
And full in the midst rose Keenan, tall
In the gloom, like a martyr awaiting his fall,

While the circle-stroke of his sabre, swung
'Round his head, like a halo there, luminous hung.
Line after line — ay, whole platoons,
Struck dead in their saddles — of brave dragoons
By the maddened horses were onward borne
And into the vortex flung, trampled and torn;
As Keenan fought with his men, side by side.

So they rode, till there were no more to ride.

But over them, lying there, shattered and mute,
What deep echo rolls? — 'Tis a death-salute
From the cannon in place; for, heroes, you braved
Your fate not in vain: the army was saved!

Over them now — year following year —
Over their graves the pine-cones fall,
And the whippoorwill chants his spectre-call;
But they stir not again; they raise no cheer:
They have ceased. But their glory shall never cease,
Nor their light be quenched in the light of peace.
The rush of their charge is resounding still
That saved the army at Chancellorsville.

Rose Hawthorne Lathrop

GIVE ME NOT TEARS

DESPAIR

Dear, when you see my grave,
Oh, shall you weep?
Ah, no! That were to have
Mistaken care;
But when you see my grave,
I pray you keep
Sunshine of heart that time doth lay me there,
Where veiling mists of dream guard endless sleep.
Though the young life we mourn
That, blooming, dies, —
Ere grief hath made forlorn
This other face, —
Still sadder are the eyes,
The cheeks more worn
Than show the dead, of those who seek love's grace:
Death is the gentlest of the world's replies.

JOY

Dear, when the sun is set
From my life's air,
And your eyes, newly wet
With tears for me,
Make my sky darker yet, —
Remember where
Your eyes in light laved all my destiny:
Weep not, weep not, since so much love was there!

Remember that through you
My rapture came:
I gained from faith so true
More than I asked, —
For not the half I knew
My need might name,
Until I saw the soul your love unmasked:
Then crave not of the night my vanished flame.

DOROTHY

Dear little Dorothy, she is no more!
I have wandered world-wide from shore to shore,
I have seen as great beauties as ever were wed;
But none can console me for Dorothy dead.

Dear little Dorothy! How strange it seems
That her face is less real than the faces of dreams;
That the love which kept true, and the lips which so spoke,
Are more lost than my heart, which died not when it broke!

A SONG BEFORE GRIEF

SORROW, my friend,
When shall you come again?
The wind is slow, and the bent willows send
Their silvery motions wearily down the plain.
The bird is dead
That sang this morning through the summer rain!

Sorrow, my friend,
I owe my soul to you.
And if my life with any glory end
Of tenderness for others, and the words are true,
Said, honoring, when I 'm dead, —
Sorrow, to you, the mellow praise, the funeral wreath, are due.

And yet, my friend,
When love and joy are strong,
Your terrible visage from my sight I rend
With glances to blue heaven. Hovering along,
By mine your shadow led,
"Away!" I shriek, "nor dare to work my new-sprung mercies wrong!"

Still, you are near:
Who can your care withstand?
When deep eternity shall look most clear,
Sending bright waves to kiss the trembling land,
My joy shall disappear, —
A flaming torch thrown to the golden sea by your pale hand.

THE CLOCK'S SONG

EILEEN of four,
Eileen of smiles;
Eileen of five,
Eileen of tears;
Eileen of ten, of fifteen years,
Eileen of youth
And woman's wiles;
Eileen of twenty,
In love's land,
Eileen all tender
In her bliss,
Untouched by sorrow's treacherous kiss,
And the sly weapon in life's hand, —
Eileen aroused to share all fate,
Eileen a wife,
Pale, beautiful,
Eileen most grave and dutiful,
Mourning her dreams in queenly state.
Eileen! Eileen! . . .

Charles Francis Richardson

PRAYER

If, when I kneel to pray,
With eager lips I say:
"Lord, give me all the things that I desire, —
Health, wealth, fame, friends, brave heart, religious fire,
The power to sway my fellow-men at will,
And strength for mighty works to banish ill," —
In such a prayer as this
The blessing I must miss.

Or if I only dare
To raise this fainting prayer:
"Thou seest, Lord, that I am poor and weak,
And cannot tell what things I ought to seek;
I therefore do not ask at all, but still
I trust thy bounty all my wants to fill," —
My lips shall thus grow dumb,
The blessing shall not come.

But if I lowly fall,
And thus in faith I call:
"Through Christ, O Lord, I pray thee give to me
Not what I would, but what seems best to thee
Of life, of health, of service, and of strength,
Until to thy full joy I come at length," —
My prayer shall then avail,
The blessing shall not fail.

AFTER DEATH

When I forth fare beyond this narrow earth,
With all its metes and bounds of now and here,
And brooding clouds of ignorance and fear
That overhung me on my day of birth,
Wherethrough the jocund sun's perennial mirth
Has shone more inly bright each coming year
With some new glory of that outer sphere
Where length and breadth and height are little worth,
Then shall I find that even here below
We guessed the secret of eternity,
And learned in years the yearless mystery;
For in our earliest world we came to know
The master-lesson and the riddle's key:
Unending love unending growth shall be.

A CONJECTURE

I wonder, dear, if you had been
The maiden queen's pet maid of honor,
A flower of that fair time wherein
A court of roses smiled upon her,

And I, erewhile, by Trojan wall
Had fiercely fought for Grecian glory,
Beheld the pride of Priam fall,
And home in Athens told the story,

Whether we, wandering in the glow
Of the Hereafter's radiant spaces,
Would there have mutely met, and so
Seen love make bright our yearning faces

Edwin Markham

THE MAN WITH THE HOE

WRITTEN AFTER SEEING THE PAINTING BY MILLET

God made man in His own image, in the image of God made He him. — Genesis.

Bowed by the weight of centuries he leans
Upon his hoe and gazes on the ground,
The emptiness of ages in his face,
And on his back the burden of the world.
Who made him dead to rapture and despair,
A thing that grieves not and that never hopes,
Stolid and stunned, a brother to the ox?
Who loosened and let down this brutal jaw?
Whose was the hand that slanted back this brow?
Whose breath blew out the light within this brain?

Is this the Thing the Lord God made and gave
To have dominion over sea and land;
To trace the stars and search the heavens for power;
To feel the passion of Eternity?
Is this the Dream He dreamed who shaped the suns
And pillared the blue firmament with light?
Down all the stretch of Hell to its last gulf
There is no shape more terrible than this —
More tongued with censure of the world's blind greed —
More filled with signs and portents for the soul —
More fraught with menace to the universe.

What gulfs between him and the seraphim!
Slave of the wheel of labor, what to him
Are Plato and the swing of Pleiades?
What the long reaches of the peaks of song,
The rift of dawn, the reddening of the rose?
Through this dread shape the suffering ages look;
Time's tragedy is in that aching stoop;
Through this dread shape humanity betrayed,
Plundered, profaned, and disinherited,
Cries protest to the Judges of the World,
A protest that is also prophecy.

O masters, lords, and rulers in all lands,
Is this the handiwork you give to God,
This monstrous thing distorted and soul-quenched?
How will you ever straighten up this shape;
Touch it again with immortality;
Give back the upward looking and the light;
Rebuild in it the music and the dream;
Make right the immemorial infamies,
Perfidious wrongs, immedicable woes?

O masters, lords, and rulers in all lands,
How will the Future reckon with this Man?
How answer his brute question in that hour
When whirlwinds of rebellion shake the world?
How will it be with kingdoms and with kings —
With those who shaped him to the thing he is —
When this dumb Terror shall reply to God,
After the silence of the centuries?

MY COMRADE

I NEVER build a song by night or day,
Of breaking ocean or of blowing whin,
But in some wondrous unexpected way,
Like light upon a road, my Love comes in.

And when I go at night upon the hill,
My heart is lifted on mysterious wings:
My Love is there to strengthen and to still,
For she can take away the dread of things.

POETRY

SHE comes like the hush and beauty of the night,
And sees too deep for laughter;
Her touch is a vibration and a light
From worlds before and after.

A LOOK INTO THE GULF

I LOOKED one night, and there Semiramis,
With all her mourning doves about her head,
Sat rocking on an ancient road of Hell,
Withered and eyeless, chanting to the moon
Snatches of song they sang to her of old
Upon the lighted roofs of Nineveh.
And then her voice rang out with rattling laugh:
"The bugles! they are crying back again —
Bugles that broke the nights of Babylon,
And then went crying on through Nineveh.
. . . .
Stand back, ye trembling messengers of ill!
Women, let go my hair: I am the Queen,
A whirlwind and a blaze of swords to quell
Insurgent cities. Let the iron tread
Of armies shake the earth. Look, lofty towers:
Assyria goes by upon the wind!"
And so she babbles by the ancient road,
While cities turned to dust upon the Earth
Rise through her whirling brain to live again —
Babbles all night, and when her voice is dead
Her weary lips beat on without a sound

THE LAST FURROW

THE Spirit of Earth with still, restoring hands,
Mid ruin moves, in glimmering chasm gropes,
And mosses mantle and the bright flower opes;
But Death the Ploughman wanders in all lands,
And to the last of Earth his furrow stands.
The grave is never hidden: fearful hopes
Follow the dead upon the fading slopes,
And there wild memories meet upon the sands.
When willows fling their banners to the plain,
When rumor of winds and sound of sudden showers
Disturb the dream of winter, all in vain
The grasses hurry to the graves, the flowers
Toss their wild torches on their windy towers;
Yet are the bleak graves lonely in the rain.

THE WHIRLWIND ROAD

THE Muses wrapped in mysteries of light
Came in a rush of music on the night;
And I was lifted wildly on quick wings,
And borne away into the deep of things.
The dead doors of my being broke apart;
A wind of rapture blew across the heart;
The inward song of worlds rang still and clear;
I felt the Mystery the Muses fear;

Yet they went swiftening on the ways untrod,
And hurled me breathless at the feet of God.

I felt faint touches of the Final Truth, —
Moments of trembling love, moments of youth.
A vision swept away the human wall;
Slowly I saw the meaning of it all —
Meaning of life and time and death and birth, —
But cannot tell it to the men of Earth.
I only point the way, and they must go
The whirlwind road of song if they would know.

JOY OF THE MORNING

I HEAR you, little bird,
Shouting a-swing above the broken wall.
Shout louder yet: no song can tell it all.
Sing to my soul in the deep, still wood:
'T is wonderful beyond the wildest word:
I 'd tell it, too, if I could.

Oft when the white still dawn
Lifted the skies and pushed the hills apart,
I 've felt it like a glory in my heart,
(The world's mysterious stir)
But had no throat like yours, my bird,
Nor such a listener.

Richard Edwin Day

ENGLAND

THOU art as a lone watcher on a rock,
With Saxon hair back floating in the wind,
Gazing where stranger ships, to doom consigned,
Upon the sullen ledges grind and knock.
Fair were the barks round which the breakers flock,
Rich freights had they of treasure for mankind,
And gallant were the hearts that left behind
The sea's broad buffet for the channel's shock.
Slow, slow the ship that brings thy liberties
Cuts the white tempest or the bright, blue brine,
And wanders oft before the whelming storm,
And ever the swift straits and shallows flees.
But near, more near, the haven's sheltering line,
Up the long sea-curve rides its stately form.

TO SHAKESPEARE

THOU, who didst lay all other bosoms bare,
Impenetrable shade didst round thee throw;
And of the ready tears thou makest flow,
Monarch of tears, thou hast not any share.
Sad Petrarch, sadder Byron their despair
Unlocked, their dismal theatres of woe
Unclosed: thou showest Hamlet, Romeo,
And maddened Lear, with tempest on his hair.
Hadst thou no suffering men's tears could suage?
No comedy of thine own life, shut in?
No lurid tragedy — perhaps of sin —
That walked with muffled steps its curtained stage?
Confession troubles ne'er thy godlike look;
Thou art, thyself, thy one unopened book.

Maurice Francis Egan

MAURICE DE GUÉRIN

THE old wine filled him, and he saw, with eyes
Anoint of Nature, fauns and dryads fair
Unseen by others; to him maidenhair
And waxen lilacs, and those birds that rise
A-sudden from tall reeds at slight surprise,
Brought charmëd thoughts; and in earth everywhere
He, like sad Jaques, found a music rare
As that of Syrinx to old Grecians wise.

A pagan heart, a Christian soul had he,
He followed Christ, yet for dead Pan he sighed,
Till earth and heaven met within his breast;
As if Theocritus in Sicily
Had come upon the Figure crucified
And lost his gods in deep, Christ-given rest.

HE MADE US FREE

As flame streams upward, so my longing thought
Flies up with Thee,
Thou God and Saviour, who hast truly wrought
Life out of death, and to us, loving, brought
A fresh, new world; and in Thy sweet chains caught,
And made us free!

As hyacinths make way from out the dark,
My soul awakes,
At thought of Thee, like sap beneath the bark;
As little violets in field and park
Rise to the trilling thrush and meadow-lark,
New hope it takes.

As thou goest upward through the nameless space
We call the sky,
Like jonquil perfume softly falls Thy grace;
It seems to touch and brighten every place;
Fresh flowers crown our wan and weary race,
O Thou on high!

Hadst Thou not risen, there would be no joy
Upon earth's sod;
Life would be still with us a wound or toy,
A cloud without the sun, — O Babe, O Boy,
O Man of Mother pure, with no alloy,
O risen God!

Thou, God and King, didst "mingle in the game,"
(Cease, all fears; cease!)
For love of us, — not to give Virgil's fame
Or Croesus' wealth, not to make well the lame,
Or save the sinner from deservëd shame,
But for sweet Peace!

For peace, for joy, — not that the slave might lie
In luxury,
Not that all woe from us should always fly,
Or golden crops with Syrian roses vie
In every field; but in Thy peace to die
And rise, — be free!

THE OLD VIOLIN

THOUGH tuneless, stringless, it lies there in dust,
Like some great thought on a forgotten page;
The soul of music cannot fade or rust, —
The voice within it stronger grows with age;
Its strings and bow are only trifling things —
A master-touch! — its sweet soul wakes and sings.

THE SHAMROCK

WHEN April rains make flowers bloom
And Johnny-jump-ups come to light,
And clouds of color and perfume
Float from the orchards pink and white,
I see my shamrock in the rain,
An emerald spray with raindrops set,
Like jewels on Spring's coronet,
So fair, and yet it breathes of pain.

The shamrock on an older shore
Sprang from a rich and sacred soil
Where saint and hero lived of yore,
And where their sons in sorrow toil;
And here, transplanted, it to me
Seems weeping for the soil it left:
The diamonds that all others see
Are tears drawn from its heart bereft.

When April rain makes flowers grow,
And sparkles on their tiny buds
That in June nights will over-blow
And fill the world with scented floods,
The lonely shamrock in our land —
So fine among the clover leaves —
For the old springtimes often grieves, —
I feel its tears upon my hand.

Nathan Haskell Dole

RUSSIA

SATURNIAN mother! why dost thou devour
Thy offspring, who by loving thee are curst?
Why must they fear thee who would fain be first
To add new glories to thy matchless dower?
Why must they flee before thy cruel power,
That punishes their best as treason's worst, —
The treason that despotic chains would burst, —
That makes men heroes who in slavery cower?
Upon thy brow the stars of empire burn;
Thy bearing has a majesty sublime.
Thy exiled children ever toward thee yearn;
Nor should their ardent love be deemed a crime.
O, mighty mother of men, to mildness turn,
And haste the advent of a happier time!

TO AN IMPERILLED TRAVELLER

UNFLINCHING Dante of a later day,
Thou who hast wandered through the realms of pain
And seen with aching breast and whirling brain
Woes which thou wert unable to allay,
What frightful visions hast thou brought away:
Of torments, passions, agonies, struggles vain
To break the prison walls, to rend the chain, —
Of hopeless hearts too desperate to pray!
Men are the devils of that pitiless hell!
Men guard the labyrinth of that ninefold curse!
Marvel of marvels! Thou hast lived to tell,
In prose more sorrowful than Dante's verse,
Of pangs more grievous, sufferings more fell,
Than Dante or his master dared rehearse!

A RUSSIAN FANTASY

O'ER the yellow crocus on the lawn
Floats a light white butterfly.
Breezes waft it! See, 'tis gone!
Dushka, little soul, when didst thou die?

Henry Van Dyke

AN ANGLER'S WISH

I

WHEN tulips bloom in Union Square,
And timid breaths of vernal air
Go wandering down the dusty town,
Like children lost in Vanity Fair;

When every long, unlovely row
Of westward houses stands aglow,
And leads the eyes towards sunset skies
Beyond the hills where green trees grow, —

Then weary seems the street parade,
And weary books, and weary trade:
I 'm only wishing to go a-fishing;
For this the month of May was made.

II

I guess the pussy-willows now
Are creeping out on every bough
Along the brook; and robins look
For early worms behind the plough.

The thistle-birds have changed their dun
For yellow coats, to match the sun;
And in the same array of flame
The dandelion show 's begun.

The flocks of young anemones
Are dancing round the budding trees:
Who can help wishing to go a-fishing
In days as full of joy as these?

III

I think the meadow-lark's clear sound
Leaks upward slowly from the ground,
While on the wing the blue-birds ring
Their wedding-bells to woods around.

The flirting chewink calls his dear
Behind the bush; and very near,
Where water flows, where green grass grows,
Song-sparrows gently sing, "Good cheer."

And, best of all, through twilight's calm
The hermit-thrush repeats his psalm.
How much I 'm wishing to go a-fishing
In days so sweet with music's balm!

IV

'T is not a proud desire of mine;
I ask for nothing superfine;
No heavy weight, no salmon great,
To break the record — or my line:

Only an idle little stream,
Whose amber waters softly gleam,
Where I may wade, through woodland shade,
And cast the fly, and loaf, and dream:

Only a trout or two, to dart
From foaming pools, and try my art:
No more I 'm wishing — old-fashioned fishing,
And just a day on Nature's heart.

THE VEERY

The moonbeams over Arno's vale in silver flood were pouring,
When first I heard the nightingale a long-lost love deploring.
So passionate, so full of pain, it sounded strange and eerie;
I longed to hear a simpler strain, — the wood-notes of the veery.

The laverock sings a bonny lay above the Scottish heather;
It sprinkles down from far away like light and love together;
He drops the golden notes to greet his brooding mate, his dearie;
I only know one song more sweet, — the vespers of the veery.

In English gardens, green and bright and full of fruity treasure,
I heard the blackbird with delight repeat his merry measure:
The ballad was a pleasant one, the tune was loud and cheery,
And yet, with every setting sun, I listened for the veery.

But far away, and far away, the tawny thrush is singing;
New England woods, at close of day, with that clear chant are ringing:
And when my light of life is low, and heart and flesh are weary,
I fain would hear, before I go, the wood-notes of the veery.

ROSLIN AND HAWTHORNDEN

Fair Roslin Chapel, how divine
The art that reared thy costly shrine!
Thy carven columns must have grown
By magic, like a dream in stone.

Yet not within thy storied wall
Would I in adoration fall,
So gladly as within the glen
That leads to lovely Hawthornden:

A long-drawn aisle, with roof of green
And vine-clad pillars, while between
The Esk runs murmuring on its way,
In living music, night and day.

Within the temple of this wood
The martyrs of the covenant stood,
And rolled the psalm, and poured the prayer,
From Nature's solemn altar-stair.

THE LILY OF YORROW

Deep in the heart of the forest the lily of Yorrow is growing;
Blue is its cup as the sky, and with mystical odor o'erflowing;
Faintly it falls through the shadowy glades when the south wind is blowing;

Sweet are the primroses pale, and the violets after a shower;
Sweet are the borders of pinks, and the blossoming grapes on the bower:

Sweeter by far is the breath of that far-away woodland flower.

Searching and strange in its sweetness, it steals like a perfume enchanted
Under the arch of the forest, and all who perceive it are haunted,
Seeking and seeking forever, till sight of the lily is granted.

Who can describe how it grows, with its chalice of lazuli leaning
Over a crystalline spring, where the ferns and the mosses are greening?
Who can imagine its beauty, or utter the depth of its meaning?

Calm of the journeying stars, and repose of the mountains olden,
Joy of the swift-running rivers, and glory of sunsets golden,
Secrets that cannot be told in the heart of the flower are holden.

Surely to see it is peace and the crown of a life-long endeavor;
Surely to pluck it is gladness, — but they who have found it can never
Tell of the gladness and peace: they are hid from our vision forever.

'T was but a moment ago that a comrade was wandering near me:
Turning aside from the pathway, he murmured a greeting to cheer me, —
Then he was lost in the shade, and I called, but he did not hear me.

Why should I dream he is dead, and bewail him with passionate sorrow?
Surely I know there is gladness in finding the lily of Yorrow:
He has discovered it first, and perhaps I shall find it to-morrow.

TENNYSON

IN LUCEM TRANSITUS, OCTOBER, 1892

FROM the misty shores of midnight, touched with splendors of the moon,
To the singing tides of heaven, and the light more clear than noon,
Passed a soul that grew to music till it was with God in tune.

Brother of the greatest poets, true to nature, true to art;
Lover of Immortal Love, uplifter of the human heart, —
Who shall cheer us with high music, who shall sing, if thou depart?

Silence here — for love is silent, gazing on the lessening sail;
Silence here — for grief is voiceless when the mighty minstrels fail;
Silence here — but, far beyond us, many voices crying, Hail!

FOUR THINGS

FOUR things a man must learn to do
If he would make his record true:
To think without confusion clearly;
To love his fellow-men sincerely;
To act from honest motives purely;
To trust in God and Heaven securely.

Joseph I. C. Clarke

THE FIGHTING RACE

"READ out the names!" and Burke sat back,
And Kelly drooped his head.
While Shea — they call him Scholar Jack —
Went down the list of the dead.
Officers, seamen, gunners, marines,
The crews of the gig and yawl,
The bearded man and the lad in his teens,
Carpenters, coal passers — all.
Then, knocking the ashes from out his pipe,
Said Burke in an offhand way:
"We 're all in that dead man's list, by Cripe!
Kelly and Burke and Shea."
"Well, here 's to the Maine, and I 'm sorry for Spain,"
Said Kelly and Burke and Shea.

"Wherever there 's Kellys there 's trouble," said Burke.
"Wherever fighting 's the game,
Or a spice of danger in grown man's work,"
Said Kelly, "you 'll find my name."
"And do we fall short," said Burke, getting mad,
"When it 's touch and go for life ?"
Said Shea, "It 's thirty-odd years, bedad,
Since I charged to drum and fife
Up Marye's Heights, and my old canteen
Stopped a rebel ball on its way.
There were blossoms of blood on our sprigs of green —
Kelly and Burke and Shea —
And the dead did n't brag." "Well, here 's to the flag!"
Said Kelly and Burke and Shea.

"I wish 't was in Ireland, for there 's the place,"
Said Burke, "that we 'd die by right,
In the cradle of our soldier race,
After one good stand-up fight.
My grandfather fell on Vinegar Hill,
And fighting was not his trade;
But his rusty pike 's in the cabin still,
With Hessian blood on the blade."
"Aye, aye," said Kelly, "the pikes were great
When the word was 'clear the way!'
We were thick on the roll in ninety-eight —
Kelly and Burke and Shea."
"Well, here 's to the pike and the sword and the like!"
Said Kelly and Burke and Shea.

And Shea, the scholar, with rising joy,
Said, "We were at Ramillies;
We left our bones at Fontenoy
And up in the Pyrenees;
Before Dunkirk, on Landen's plain,
Cremona, Lille, and Ghent,
We 're all over Austria, France, and Spain,
Wherever they pitched a tent.
We 've died for England from Waterloo
To Egypt and Dargai;
And still there 's enough for a corps or crew,
Kelly and Burke and Shea."
"Well, here is to good honest fighting blood!"
Said Kelly and Burke and Shea.

"Oh, the fighting races don't die out,
If they seldom die in bed,
For love is first in their hearts, no doubt,"
Said Burke; then Kelly said:
"When Michael, the Irish Archangel, stands,
The angel with the sword,
And the battle-dead from a hundred lands
Are ranged in one big horde,
Our line, that for Gabriel's trumpet waits,
Will stretch three deep that day,
From Jehoshaphat to the Golden Gates —
Kelly and Burke and Shea."
"Well, here 's thank God for the race and the sod!"
Said Kelly and Burke and Shea.

1898

Charles Henry Phelps

HENRY WARD BEECHER

His tongue was touched with sacred fire,
He could not rest, he must speak out,
When Liberty lay stabbed, and doubt
Stalked through the night in vestments dire, —

When slaves uplifted manacled hands,
Praying in agony and despair,
And answer came not anywhere,
But gloom through all the stricken lands, —

His voice for freedom instant rang.
"For shame!" he cried; "spare thou the rod;
All men are free before their God!"
The dragon answered with its fang.

'T is brave to face embrasured death
Hot belching from the cannon's mouth,
Yet brave it is, for North or South,
And Truth, to face the mob's mad breath.

So spake he then, — he and the few
Who prized their manhood more than praise;

Their faith failed not of better days
After the nights of bloody dew.

England's great heart misunderstood:
She looked upon her child askance;
But heard his words and lowered her lance,
Remembering her motherhood.

Majestic Liberty, serene
Thou frontest on the chaste white sea!
Quench thou awhile thy torch, for he
Lies dead on whom thou once did lean.

Thy cause was ever his, — the slave
In any fetters was his friend;
His warfare never knew an end;
Wherever men lay bound he clave.

RARE MOMENTS

Each of us is like Balboa: once in all our lives do we,
Gazing from some tropic summit, look upon an unknown sea;

But upon the dreary morrow, every way our footsteps seek,
Rank and tangled vine and jungle block our pathway to the peak.

YUMA

Weary, weary, desolate,
Sand-swept, parched, and cursed of fate;
Burning, but how passionless!
Barren, bald, and pitiless!

Through all ages baleful moons
Glared upon thy whited dunes;

And malignant, wrathful suns
Fiercely drank thy streamless runs;

So that Nature's only tune
Is the blare of the simoon,
Piercing burnt unweeping skies
With its awful monodies.

Not a flower lifts its head
Where the emigrant lies dead;

Not a living creature calls
Where the Gila Monster crawls,
Hot and hideous as the sun,
To the dead man's skeleton;

But the desert and the dead,
And the hot hell overhead,
And the blazing, seething air,
And the dread mirage are there.

Robert Underwood Johnson

FROM "THE VOICE OF WEBSTER"

Silence was envious of the only voice
That mightier seemed than she. So, cloaked as Death,
With potion borrowed from Oblivion,
Yet with slow step and tear-averted look,
She sealed his lips, closed his extinguished eyes,
And, veiling him with darkness, deemed him dead.
But no! — There 's something vital in the great
That blunts the edge of Death, and sages say
You should stab deep if you would kill a king.

In vain! The conqueror's conqueror he remains,
Surviving his survivors. And as when,
The prophet gone, his least disciple stands
Newly invested with a twilight awe,
So linger men beside his listeners
While they recount that miracle of speech
And the hushed wonder over which it fell.

What do they tell us of that storied voice,
Breathing an upper air, wherein he dwelt
Mid shifting clouds a mountain of resolve,
And falling like Sierra's April flood
That pours in ponderous cadence from the cliff,
Waking Yosemite from its sleep of snow,
And less by warmth than by its massive power

Thawing a thousand torrents into one?
Such was his speech, and, were his fame to die,
Such for its requiem alone were fit:
Some kindred voice of Nature, as the Sea
When autumn tides redouble their lament
On Marshfield shore; some elemental force
Kindred to Nature in the mind of man —
A far-felt, rhythmic, and resounding wave
Of Homer, or a freedom-breathing wind
Sweeping the height of Milton's loftiest mood.
Most fit of all, could his own words pronounce
His eulogy, eclipsing old with new,
As though a dying star should burst in light.

And yet he spoke not only with his voice.
His full brow, buttressing a dome of thought,
Moved the imagination like the rise
Of some vast temple covering nothing mean.
His eyes were sibyls' caves, wherein the wise
Read sibyls' secrets; and the iron clasp
Of those broad lips, serene or saturnine,
Made proclamation of majestic will.
His glance could silence like a frowning Fate.
His mighty frame was refuge, while his mien
Did make dispute of stature with the gods.

AS A BELL IN A CHIME

As a bell in a chime
Sets its twin-note a-ringing,
As one poet's rhyme
Wakes another to singing,
So, once she has smiled,
All your thoughts are beguiled,
And flowers and song from your childhood are bringing.

Though moving through sorrow
As the star through the night,
She needs not to borrow,
She lavishes, light.
The path of yon star
Seemeth dark but afar:
Like hers it is sure, and like hers it is bright.

Each grace is a jewel
Would ransom the town;
Her speech has no cruel,
Her praise is renown;
'T is in her as though Beauty,
Resigning to Duty
The sceptre, had still kept the purple and crown.

THE WISTFUL DAYS

What is there wanting in the Spring?
The air is soft as yesteryear;
The happy-nested green is here,
And half the world is on the wing.
The morning beckons, and like balm
Are westward waters blue and calm.
Yet something 's wanting in the Spring.

What is it wanting in the Spring?
O April, lover to us all,
What is so poignant in thy thrall
When children's merry voices ring?
What haunts us in the cooing dove
More subtle than the speech of Love,
What nameless lack or loss of Spring?

Let Youth go dally with the Spring,
Call her the dear, the fair, the young;
And all her graces ever sung
Let him, once more rehearsing, sing.
They know, who keep a broken tryst,
Till something from the Spring be missed
We have not truly known the Spring.

IN TESLA'S LABORATORY

Here in the dark what ghostly figures press! —
No phantom of the Past, or grim or sad;
No wailing spirit of woe; no spectre, clad
In white and wandering cloud, whose dumb distress
Is that its crime it never may confess;
No shape from the strewn sea; nor they that add
The link of Life and Death, — the tearless mad,
That live nor die in dreary nothingness:
But blessed spirits waiting to be born —
Thoughts to unlock the fettering chains of Things;

The Better Time; the Universal Good.
Their smile is like the joyous break of morn;
How fair, how near, how wistfully they
brood!
Listen! that murmur is of angels' wings.

BROWNING AT ASOLO

THIS is the loggia Browning loved,
High on the flank of the friendly town;
These are the hills that his keen eye roved,
The green like a cataract leaping down
To the plain that his pen gave new
renown.

There to the West what a range of blue! —
The very background Titian drew
To his peerless Loves! O tranquil
scene!
Who than thy poet fondlier knew
The peaks and the shore and the lore
between?

See! yonder's his Venice — the valiant
Spire,
Highest one of the perfect three,
Guarding the others: the Palace choir,
The Temple flashing with opal fire —
Bubble and foam of the sunlit sea.

Yesterday he was part of it all —
Sat here, discerning cloud from snow
In the flush of the Alpine afterglow,
Or mused on the vineyard whose wine-
stirred row
Meets in a leafy bacchanal.

Listen a moment — how oft did he! —
To the bells from Fontalto's distant
tower
Leading the evening in . . . ah, me!
Here breathes the whole soul of Italy
As one rose breathes with the breath of
the bower.

Sighs were meant for an hour like this
When joy is keen as a thrust of pain.
Do you wonder the poet's heart should miss
This touch of rapture in Nature's kiss
And dream of Asolo ever again?

"Part of it yesterday," we moan?
Nay, he is part of it now, no fear.
What most we love we are that alone.
His body lies under the Minster stone,
But the love of the warm heart lingers
here.

THE BLOSSOM OF THE SOUL

THOU half-unfolded flower
With fragrance-laden heart,
What is the secret power
That doth thy petals part?
What gave thee most thy hue —
The sunshine or the dew?

Thou wonder-wakened soul!
As Dawn doth steal on Night,
On thee soft Love hath stole.
Thine eye, that blooms with light,
What makes its charm so new —
Its sunshine, or its dew?

Richard Kendall Munkittrick

AT THE SHRINE

A PALE Italian peasant,
Beside the dusty way,
Upon this morning pleasant
Kneels in the sun to pray.

Silent in her devotion,
With fervent glance she pleads;
Her fingers' only motion,
Telling her amber beads.

Dreaming of ilex bowers
Beyond the purple brine,
Once more she sees the flowers
Bloom at the wayside shrine.

And, while the mad crowd jostles,
She, with a visage sweet,
Prays where the bisque apostles
Are sold on Barclay Street.

GHOSTS

OUT in the misty moonlight
The first snowflakes I see,

As they frolic among the leafless
 Limbs of the apple-tree.

Faintly they seem to whisper,
 As round the boughs they wing:
"We are the ghosts of the blossoms
 That died in the early spring."

A BULB

MISSHAPEN, black, unlovely to the sight,
 O mute companion of the murky mole,
You must feel overjoyed to have a white,
 Imperious, dainty lily for a soul.

TO MIGUEL DE CERVANTES SAAVADRA

A BLUEBIRD lives in yonder tree,
Likewise a little chickadee,
In two woodpeckers' nests — rent free!

There, where the weeping willow weeps,
A dainty housewren sweetly cheeps —
From an old oriole's nest she peeps.
I see the English sparrow tilt
Upon the limb with sun begilt, —
His nest an ancient swallow built.

So it was one of your old jests,
Eh, Mig. Cervantes, that attests
"There are no birds in last year's nests"?

Craven Langstroth Betts

THE HOLLYHOCKS

SOME space beyond the garden close
 I sauntered down the shadowed lawn;
It was the hour when sluggards doze,
 The cheerful, zephyr-breathing dawn.
The sun had not yet bathed his face,
 Dark reddened from the night's carouse,
When, lo! in festive gypsy grace
 The hollyhocks stood nodding brows.

They shone full bold and debonair —
 That fine, trim band of frolic blades;
Their ruffles, pinked and purfled fair,
 Flamed with their riotous rainbow shades.
They whispered light each comrade's ears,
 They flirted with the wooing breeze;
The grassy army's stanchest spears
 Rose merely to their stalwart knees!

My heart flushed warm with welcome cheer,
 They were so royal tall to see;
No high-placed rivals need they fear,
 All flowers paid them fealty.
The haughtiest wild rose standing near
 Their girdles hardly might attain;
They glowed, the courtiers of a year,
 Blithe pages in the Summer's train!

Their radiance mocked the ruddy morn,
 So jocund and so saucy free;
Gay vagrants, Flora's bravest born,
 They brightened all the emerald lea.

I said: "Glad hearts, the crabbed frost
 Will soon your sun-dyed glories blight;
No evil eye your pride has crossed,
 You know not the designs of night.

"You have not thought that beauty fades;
 It is in vain you bloom so free;
While you are flaunting in the glades
 The gale may wreck your wanton glee."
They shook their silken frills in scorn,
 And to my warning seemed to say,
"Dull rhymester, look! 'tis summer morn,
 And round us is the court of Day!"

DON QUIXOTE

GAUNT, rueful knight, on raw-boned, shambling hack,
Thy battered morion, shield and rusty spear,
Jog ever down the road in strange career,
Both tears and laughter following on thy track,
Stout Sancho hard behind, whose leathern back
Is curved in clownish sufferance, mutual cheer
The quest beguiling as devoid of fear,
Thou spurrest to rid the world of rogues, alack!
Despite fantastic creed and addled pate,
Of awkward arms and weight of creaking steel,

Nobility is thine — the high estate
That arms knights errant for all human weal;
How rare, La Mancha, grow such souls of late, —
Dear, foiled enthusiast, teach our hearts to feel!

TO THE MOONFLOWER

PALE, climbing disk, who dost lone vigil keep
When all the flower-heads droop in drowsy swoon;
When lily bells fold to the zephyr's tune,
And wearied bees are lapped in sugared sleep;
What secret hope is thine? What purpose deep?
Art thou enamored of the siren moon
That thus thy white face from the god of noon
Thou coverest, while his chariot rounds the steep?
Poor, frail Endymion! know her lustre's line
Is but the cold, reflected majesty
That clothes the great sun's regent-borrowed shine
Of him who yields restricted ministry,
Thy bright creator; he did ne'er design
The proud, false queen should fealty take of thee!

Ellen Mackay Hutchinson Cortissoz

MOTH-SONG

WHAT dost thou here,
Thou dusky courtier,
Within the pinky palace of the rose?
Here is no bed for thee,
No honeyed spicery, —
But for the golden bee,
And the gay wind, and me,
Its sweetness grows.
Rover, thou dost forget; —
Seek thou the passion-flower
Bloom of one twilight hour.
Haste, thou art late!
Its hidden savors wait.
For thee is spread
Its soft, purple coverlet;
Moth, art thou sped?
— Dim as a ghost he flies
Thorough the night mysteries.

HER PICTURE

AUTUMN was cold in Plymouth town;
The wind ran round the shore,
Now softly passing up and down,
Now wild and fierce and fleet,
Wavering overhead,
Moaning in the narrow street
As one beside the dead.

The leaves of wrinkled gold and brown
Fluttered here and there,
But not quite heedless where;
For as in hood and sad-hued gown
The Rose of Plymouth took the air,
They whirled, and whirled, and fell to rest
Upon her gentle breast,
Then on the happy earth her foot had pressed.

Autumn is wild in Plymouth town,
Barren and bleak and cold,
And still the dead leaves flutter down
As the years grow old.
And still — forever gravely fair —
Beneath their fitful whirl,
New England's sweetest girl,
Rose Standish, takes the air.

ON KINGSTON BRIDGE

On All Souls' Night the dead walk on Kingston Bridge. — OLD LEGEND.

ON Kingston Bridge the starlight shone
Through hurrying mists in shrouded glow;
The boding night-wind made its moan,
The mighty river crept below.
'T was All Souls' night, and to and fro
The quick and dead together walked,
The quick and dead together talked,
On Kingston Bridge.

Two met who had not met for years;
Once was their hate too deep for fears:
One drew his rapier as he came,
Upleapt his anger like a flame.
With clash of mail he faced his foe,
And bade him stand and meet him so.
He felt a graveyard wind go by
Cold, cold as was his enemy.
A stony horror held him fast.
The Dead looked with a ghastly stare,
And sighed "I know thee not," and passed
Like to the mist, and left him there
On Kingston Bridge.

'T was All Souls' night, and to and fro
The quick and dead together walked,
The quick and dead together talked,
On Kingston Bridge.

Two met who had not met for years:
With grief that was too deep for tears
They parted last.
He clasped her hand, and in her eyes
He sought Love's rapturous surprise.
"Oh Sweet!" he cried, "hast thou come back
To say thou lov'st thy lover still?"
— Into the starlight, pale and cold,
She gazed afar, — her hand was chill:
"Dost thou remember how we kept
Our ardent vigils? — how we kissed? —
Take thou these kisses as of old!"
An icy wind about him swept;
"I know thee not," she sighed, and passed
Into the dim and shrouding mist
On Kingston Bridge.

'T was All Souls' night, and to and fro
The quick and dead together walked,
The quick and dead together talked,
On Kingston Bridge.

SO WAGS THE WORLD

MEMORY cannot linger long,
Joy must die the death.
Hope 's like a little silver song
Fading in a breath.
So wags the weary world away
Forever and a day.

But love, that sweetest madness,
Leaps and grows in toil and sadness,
Makes unseeing eyes to see,
And heapeth wealth in penury.
So wags the good old world away
Forever and a day.

PRAISE-GOD BAREBONES

I AND my cousin Wildair met
And tossed a pot together; —
Burnt sack it was that Molly brewed,
For it was nipping weather.
'Fore George! To see Dick buss the wench
Set all the inn folk laughing!
They dubbed him pearl of cavaliers
At kissing and at quaffing.

"Oddsfish!" says Dick, "the sack is rare,
And rarely burnt, fair Molly;
'T would cure the sourest Crop-ear yet
Of Pious Melancholy."
"Egad!" says I, "here cometh one
Hath been at 's prayers but lately."
— Sooth, Master Praise-God Barebones stepped
Along the street sedately.

Dick Wildair, with a swashing bow,
And touch of his Toledo,
Gave Merry Xmas to the rogue
And bade him say his Credo;
Next crush a cup to the King's health,
And eke to pretty Molly;
"'T will cure your Saintliness," says Dick,
"Of Pious Melancholy."

Then Master Barebones stopped and frowned;
My heart stood still a minute:
Thinks I, both Dick and I will hang,
Or else the devil 's in it!
For me, I care not for old Noll,
Nor all the Rump together.
Yet, faith! 't is best to be alive
In pleasant Xmas weather.

His worship, Barebones, grimly smiled; —
"I love not blows nor brawling;
Yet will I give thee, fool, a pledge!"
And, zooks! he sent Dick sprawling!
When Moll and I helped Wildair up,
No longer trim and jolly, —
"Feel'st not, Sir Dick," says saucy Moll,
"A Pious Melancholy?"

PAMELA IN TOWN

THE fair Pamela came to town,
To London town, in early summer;
And up and down and round about
The beaux discussed the bright new-comer,
With "Gadzooks, sir," and "Ma'am, my duty,"
And "Odds my life, but 't is a Beauty!"

To Ranelagh went Mistress Pam,
Sweet Mistress Pam so fair and merry,
With cheeks of cream and roses blent,
With voice of lark and lip of cherry.
Then all the beaux vow'd 't was their duty
To win and wear this country Beauty.

And first Frank Lovelace tried his wit,
With whispers bold and eyes still bolder;
The warmer grew his saucy flame,
Cold grew the charming fair and colder.
'T was "icy bosom" — "cruel beauty" —
"To love, sweet Mistress, 't is a duty."

Then Jack Carew his arts essayed,
With honeyed sighs and feignëd weeping.
Good lack! his billets bound the curls
That pretty Pam she wore a-sleeping.
Next day these curls had richer beauty,
So well Jack's fervor did its duty.

Then Cousin Will came up to view
The way Pamela ruled the fashion;
He watched the gallants crowd about,
And flew into a rustic passion, —
Left "Squire, his mark," on divers faces,
And pinked Carew beneath his laces.

Alack! one night at Ranelagh
The pretty Sly-boots fell a-blushing;
And all the mettled bloods look'd round
To see what caused that telltale flushing.
Up stepp'd a grizzled Poet Fellow
To dance with Pam a saltarello.

Then Jack and Frank and Will resolved,
With hand on sword and cutting glances,
That they would lead that Graybeard forth
To livelier tunes and other dances.
But who that saw Pam's eyes a-shining
With love and joy would see her pining!

And — oons! Their wrath cool'd as they looked —
That Poet stared as fierce as any!
He was a mighty proper man,
With blade on hip and inches many;
The beaux all vow'd it was their duty
To toast some newer, softer Beauty.

Sweet Pam she bridled, blush'd, and smiled —
The wild thing loved and could but show it!
Mayhap some day you'll see in town
Pamela and her grizzled Poet.
Forsooth he taught the rogue her duty,
And won her faith, her love, her beauty.

APRIL FANTASIE

THE fresh, bright bloom of the daffodils
Makes gold in the garden bed,
Gold that is like the sunbeams
Loitering overhead.
Bloom, bloom
In the sun and the wind, —
April hath a fickle mind.

The budding twigs of the sweetbrier
Stir as with hope and bliss
Under the sun's soft glances,
Under the wind's sly kiss.
Swing, swing
In the sun and the wind, —
April hath a fickle mind.

May, she calls to her little ones,
Her flowers hiding away,
"Never put off till to-morrow
What you may do to-day.
Come, come
Through the sun and the wind, —
April hath a fickle mind."

QUAKER LADIES

MORE shy than the shy violet,
Hiding when the wind doth pass,
Nestled in the nodding grass,
With morning mist all wet,
In open woodland ways
The Quaker Lady[1] strays.

[1] Houstonia Cærulea.

Pale as noonday cloudlets are,
  Floating in the blue,
This little wildwood star
  Blooms in light and dew.

Sun and shadow on her hair,
  Flowers about her feet,
  Pale and still and sweet;
As a nun all pure and fair,
Through the soft spring air,
  In the light of God
  Deborah walks abroad.

Her little cap it hath a grace
  Most demure and grave,
And her kerchief's modest lace
  Veils the lovely wave
Above her maiden heart,
Where only gentle thoughts have part.
  Even the tying of her shoe
  Hath beauty in it, too,
A delicate, sweet art.

Hiding when the wind goes by,
  Not afraid, yet shy,
The tiny flower takes from the sky
  Life's own light and dew,
  And its exquisite hue.
And the little Quaker maid,
Timidly, yet not afraid,
Unfolds the sweetness of her soul
  To Heavenly control,
And wears upon her quiet face
The Spirit's tender grace.

THE BRIDE'S TOILETTE

(THE CONCIERGERIE, 1793)

"DAME, how the moments go —
  And the bride is not ready!
Call all her tiring maids,
  Paul, Jean, and Thedie.
Is this your robe, my dear?
  Faith, but she 's steady!
The bridegroom is blest who gets
  Such a brave lady."

"Pardi! That throat is fair —
  How he will kiss it!
Here is your kerchief, girl;
  Did you not miss it?
Quick, don these little shoes,
  White as your foot is.
Ho, Jean, Saint Guillotine
  Loves these fine beauties!"

"Now those long locks must go, —
  The bridegroom is waiting;
Short is the hour he gives
  To wooing and mating.
Thedie, you fool, the shears! —
  Time this was ended." —
Down falls the golden hair,
  Once lovingly tended.

So from her prison doors
  Forth went the lady;
Silent the Bridegroom stood,
  Not a sound made he.
Oh, but he clasped her close!
  'T was a brave lover. —
"Dance, dance La Carmagnole!
  The bridal is over!"

A CRY FROM THE SHORE

COME down, ye graybeard mariners,
  Unto the wasting shore!
The morning winds are up, — the gods
  Bid me to dream no more.
Come, tell me whither I must sail,
  What peril there may be,
Before I take my life in hand
  And venture out to sea!

"We may not tell thee where to sail,
  Nor what the dangers are;
Each sailor soundeth for himself,
  Each hath a separate star:
Each sailor soundeth for himself,
  And on the awful sea
What we have learned is ours alone;
  We may not tell it thee."

Come back, O ghostly mariners,
  Ye who have gone before!
I dread the dark, impetuous tides;
  I dread the farther shore.
Tell me the secret of the waves;
  Say what my fate shall be, —
Quick! for the mighty winds are up,
  And will not wait for me.

"Hail and farewell, O voyager!
  Thyself must read the waves;
What we have learned of sun and storm
  Lies with us in our graves:

What we have learned of sun and storm
Is ours alone to know.
The winds are blowing out to sea,
Take up thy life and go!"

SEA-WAY

The tide slips up the silver sand,
Dark night and rosy day;
It brings sea-treasures to the land,
Then bears them all away.
On mighty shores from east to west
It wails, and gropes, and cannot rest.

O Tide, that still doth ebb and flow
Through night to golden day: —
Wit, learning, beauty, come and go,
Thou giv'st — thou tak'st away.
But some time, on some gracious shore,
Thou shalt lie still and ebb no more.

HARVEST

Sweet, sweet, sweet,
Is the wind's song,
Astir in the rippled wheat
All day long.
It hath the brook's wild gayety,
The sorrowful cry of the sea.
Oh hush and hear!
Sweet, sweet and clear,
Above the locust's whirr
And hum of bee
Rises that soft, pathetic harmony.

In the meadow-grass
The innocent white daisies blow,
The dandelion plume doth pass
Vaguely to and fro, —
The unquiet spirit of a flower
That hath too brief an hour.

Now doth a little cloud all white,
Or golden bright,
Drift down the warm, blue sky;
And now on the horizon line,
Where dusky woodlands lie,
A sunny mist doth shine,
Like to a veil before a holy shrine,
Concealing, half-revealing
Things Divine.

Sweet, sweet, sweet,
Is the wind's song,
Astir in the rippled wheat
All day long.
That exquisite music calls
The reaper everywhere —
Life and death must share,
The golden harvest falls.

So doth all end, —
Honored Philosophy,
Science and Art,
The bloom of the heart; —
Master, Consoler, Friend,
Make Thou the harvest of our days
To fall within Thy ways.

Thomas Nelson Page

UNCLE GABE'S WHITE FOLKS

Sarvent, Marster! Yes, sah, dat 's me —
Ole Unc' Gabe 's my name;
I thankee, Marster, I 'm 'bout, yo' see.
"An' de ole 'ooman?" She 's much de same,
Po'ly an' 'plainin', thank de Lord!
But de Marster 's gwine ter come back from 'broad.

"Fine ole place?" Yes, sah, 't is so;
An' mighty fine people my white folks war —
But you ought ter 'a' seen it years ago,
When de Marster an' de Mistis lived up dyah;
When de niggers 'd stan' all roun' de do',
Like grains o' corn on de cornhouse flo'.

"Live mons'ous high?" Yes, Marster, yes;
Cut 'n' onroyal 'n' gordly dash;
Eat an' drink till you could n' res'.
My folks war 'n' none o' yo' po'-white-trash;
No, sah, dey was ob high degree —
Dis heah nigger am quality!

"Tell you 'bout 'em?" You mus' 'a' hearn
'Bout my ole white folks, sho'!
I tell you, suh, dey was gre't an' stern;
D' did n' have nuttin' at all to learn;
D' knowed all dar was to know;
Gol' ober de' head an' onder dey feet;
An' silber! dey sowed 't like folks sows wheat.

"Use ter be rich?" Dat war n' de wud!
Jes' wallowed an' roll' in wealf.
Why, none o' my white folks ever stir'd
Ter lif' a han' for d'self;
De niggers use ter be stan'in' roun'
Jes' d' same ez leaves when dey fus' fall down;
De stable-stalls up heah at home
Looked like teef in a fine-toof comb;
De cattle was p'digious — mus' tell de fac'!
An' de hogs mecked de hillsides look like black;
An' de flocks ob sheep was so gre't an' white
Dey 'peared like clouds on a moonshine night.
An' when my ole Mistis use' ter walk —
Jes' ter her kerridge (dat was fur
Ez ever she walked) — I tell you, sir,
You could almos' heah her silk dress talk;
Hit use' ter soun' like de mornin' breeze,
When it wakes an' rustles de Gre't House trees.
An' de Marster's face! — de Marster's face,
Whenever de Marster got right pleased —
Well, I 'clar' ter Gord, 't would shine wid grace
De same ez his countenance had been greased.
De cellar, too, had de bes' ob wine,
An' brandy, an' sperrits dat yo' could fine;
An' ev'ything in dyah was stored,
'Skusin' de glory of de Lord!

"Warn' dyah a son?" Yes, sah, you knows
He's de young Marster now;
But we heah dat dey tooken he very clo'es
Ter pay what ole Marster owe;
He's done been gone ten year, I s'pose.
But he's comin' back some day, of co'se;
An' my ole 'ooman is aluz pyard,
An' meckin' de Blue-Room baid,
An' ev'y day dem sheets is ayard,
An' will be till *she's* daid;
An' de styars she 'll scour,
An' dat room she 'll ten',
Ev'y blessed day dat de Lord do sen'!

What say, Marster? Yo' say, you knows? —
He's young an' slender-like an' fyah;
Better-lookin' 'n you, of co'se!
Hi! you's he? 'Fo Gord, 't is him!
'T is de very voice an' eyes an' hyah,
An' mouf an' smile, on'y yo' ain' so slim —
I wonder whah — whah 's de ole 'ooman?
Now let my soul
Depart in peace,
For I behol'
Dy glory, Lord! — I knowed you, chile —
I knowed you soon 's I see'd your face!
Whar has you been dis blessed while?
Done come back an' buy de place?
Oh, bless de Lord for all his grace!
De ravins shell hunger, an' shell not lack,
De Marster, de young Marster 's done come back!

ASHCAKE

Well, yes, sir, dat am a comical name —
It are so, for a fac' —
But I knowed one, down in Ferginyer,
Could 'a' toted dat on its back.

"What was it?" I 'm gwine to tell you —
'T was mons'us long ago:
'T was "Ashcake," sah; an' all on us
Use' ter call 'im jes' "Ashcake," so.

You see, sir, my ole Marster, he
Was a pow'ful wealfy man,
Wid mo' plantations dan hyahs on you haid —
Gre't acres o' low-groun' lan'.

Jeems River bottoms, dat used ter stall
A fo'-hoss plough, no time;
An' he 'd knock you down ef you jes' had dyared
Ter study 'bout guano 'n' lime.

De corn used ter stan' in de row dat thick
You jes' could follow de balk;
An' rank! well, I 'clar 'ter de king, I 'se seed
Five 'coons up a single stalk!

He owned mo' niggers 'n arr' a man
  About dyar, black an' bright;
He owned so many, b'fo' de Lord,
  He didn' know all by sight!

Well, sir, one evelin', long to'ds dusk,
  I seen de Marster stan'
An' watch a yaller boy pass de gate
  Wid a ashcake in his han'.

He never had no mammy at all —
  Leastways, she was dead by dat —
An' de cook an' de hands about on de place
  Used ter see dat de boy kep' fat.

Well, he trotted along down de parf dat night,
  An' de Marster he seen him go,
An' hollered, "Say, boy — say, what 's yer name?"
  "A—ashcake, sir," says Joe.

It 'peared ter tickle de Marster much,
  An' he called him up to de do'.
"Well, dat is a curisome name," says he;
  "But I guess it suits you, sho'."

"Whose son are you?" de Marster axed.
  "Young Jane's," says Joe; "she 's daid."
A sperrit cudden 'a' growed mo' pale,
  An' "By Gord!" I heerd him said.

He tuk de child 'long in de house,
  Jes' 'count o' dat ar whim;
An', dat-time-out, you never see
  Sich sto' as he sot by him.

An' Ashcake swung his cradle, too,
  As clean as ever you see;
An' stuck as close ter ole Marster's heel
  As de shader sticks to de tree.

'Twel one dark night, when de river was out,
  De Marster an' Ashcake Joe
Was comin' home an' de skiff upsot,
  An' Marster 'd 'a' drownded, sho',

Excusin' dat Ashcake cotch'd him hard
  An' gin him holt o' de boat,
An' saved him so; but 't was mo'n a week
  B'fo' *his* body comed afloat.

An' de Marster he grieved so 'bouten dat thing,
  It warn' long, sah, befo' he died;
An' he 's sleep, way down in Ferginyer,
  Not fur from young Ashcake's side.

James Whitcomb Riley

WHEN SHE COMES HOME

When she comes home again! A thousand ways
I fashion, to myself, the tenderness
Of my glad welcome: I shall tremble — yes;
And touch her, as when first in the old days
I touched her girlish hand, nor dared upraise
Mine eyes, such was my faint heart's sweet distress.
Then silence: and the perfume of her dress:
The room will sway a little, and a haze
Cloy eyesight — soulsight, even — for a space;
And tears — yes; and the ache here in the throat,
To know that I so ill deserve the place
Her arms make for me; and the sobbing note
I stay with kisses, ere the tearful face
Again is hidden in the old embrace.

THE OLD MAN AND JIM

Old man never had much to say —
  'Ceptin' to Jim, —
And Jim was the wildest boy he had,
  And the old man jes' wrapped up in him!
Never heerd him speak but once
Er twice in my life, — and first time was
When the army broke out, and Jim he went,
The old man backin' him, fer three months;
And all 'at I heerd the old man say
Was, jes' as we turned to start away, —
  "Well, good-by, Jim:
  Take keer of yourse'f!"

'Peared like he was more satisfied
  Jes' *lookin'* at Jim

And likin' him all to hisse'f-like, see? —
'Cause he was jes' wrapped up in him!
And over and over I mind the day
The old man come and stood round in the way
While we was drillin', a-watchin' Jim;
And down at the deepot a-heerin' him say, —
"Well, good-by, Jim:
Take keer of yourse'f!"

Never was nothin' about the farm
Disting'ished Jim;
Neighbors all ust to wonder why
The old man 'peared wrapped up in him:
But when Cap. Biggler, he writ back
'At Jim was the bravest boy we had
In the whole dern rigiment, white er black,
And his fightin' good as his farmin' bad, —
'At he had led, with a bullet clean
Bored through his thigh, and carried the flag
Through the bloodiest battle you ever seen, —
The old man wound up a letter to him
'At Cap. read to us, 'at said, — "Tell Jim
Good-by;
And take keer of hisse'f!"

Jim come home jes' long enough
To take the whim
'At he 'd like to go back in the calvery —
And the old man jes' wrapped up in him!
Jim 'lowed 'at he 'd had sich luck afore,
Guessed he 'd tackle her three years more.
And the old man give him a colt he 'd raised,
And follered him over to Camp Ben Wade,
And laid around fer a week er so,
Watchin' Jim on dress-parade;
'Tel finally he rid away,
And last he heerd was the old man say, —
"Well, good-by, Jim:
Take keer of yourse'f!"

Tuk the papers, the old man did,
A-watchin' fer Jim,
Fully believin' he 'd make his mark
Some way — jes' wrapped up in him!
And many a time the word 'ud come
'At stirred him up like the tap of a drum:
At Petersburg, fer instunce, where
Jim rid right into their cannons there,
And tuk 'em, and p'inted 'em t' other way,
And socked it home to the boys in gray,
As they skooted fer timber, and on and on —
Jim a lieutenant, — and one arm gone, —
And the old man's words in his mind all day, —
"Well, good-by, Jim:
Take keer of yourse'f!"

Think of a private, now, perhaps,
We 'll say like Jim,
'At 's clumb clean up to the shoulder-straps —
And the old man jes' wrapped up in him!
Think of him — with the war plum' through,
And the glorious old Red-White-and-Blue
A-laughin' the news down over Jim,
And the old man, bendin' over him —
The surgeon turnin' away with tears
'At had n't leaked fer years and years,
As the hand of the dyin' boy clung to
His Father's, the old voice in his ears, —
"Well, good-by, Jim:
Take keer of yourse'f!"

A LIFE-LESSON

THERE! little girl, don't cry!
They have broken your doll, I know;
And your tea-set blue,
And your play-house, too,
Are things of the long ago;
But childish troubles will soon pass by. —
There! little girl, don't cry!

There! little girl, don't cry!
They have broken your slate, I know;
And the glad, wild ways
Of your school-girl days
Are things of the long ago;
But life and love will soon come by. —
There! little girl, don't cry!

There! little girl, don't cry!
They have broken your heart, I know;
And the rainbow gleams
Of your youthful dreams
Are things of the long ago;
But Heaven holds all for which you sigh. —
There! little girl, don't cry!

THE WAY THE BABY WOKE

AND this is the way the baby woke:
As when in deepest drops of dew
The shine and shadows sink and soak,

The sweet eyes glimmered through and through;
And eddyings and dimples broke
About the lips, and no one knew
Or could divine the words they spoke, —
And this is the way the baby woke.

THE WAY THE BABY SLEPT

This is the way the baby slept:
A mist of tresses backward thrown
By quavering sighs where kisses crept
With yearnings she had never known:
The little hands were closely kept
About a lily newly blown —
And God was with her. And we wept. —
And this is the way the baby slept.

BEREAVED

Let me come in where you sit weeping, — ay,
Let me, who have not any child to die,
Weep with you for the little one whose love
I have known nothing of.

The little arms that slowly, slowly loosed
Their pressure round your neck; the hands you used
To kiss. — Such arms — such hands I never knew.
May I not weep with you?

Fain would I be of service — say some thing,
Between the tears, that would be comforting, —
But ah! so sadder than yourselves am I,
Who have no child to die.

IKE WALTON'S PRAYER

I crave, dear Lord,
No boundless hoard
Of gold and gear,
Nor jewels fine,
Nor lands, nor kine,
Nor treasure-heaps of anything. —
Let but a little hut be mine
Where at the hearthstone I may hear
The cricket sing,
And have the shine
Of one glad woman's eyes to make,
For my poor sake,
Our simple home a place divine: —
Just the wee cot — the cricket's chirr —
Love, and the smiling face of her.

I pray not for
Great riches, nor
For vast estates and castle-halls: —
Give me to hear the bare footfalls
Of children o'er
An oaken floor
New-rinsed with sunshine, or bespread
With but the tiny coverlet
And pillow for the baby's head;
And, pray Thou, may
The door stand open and the day
Send ever in a gentle breeze,
With fragrance from the locust-trees,
And drowsy moan of doves, and blur
Of robin-chirps, and drone of bees,
With after-hushes of the stir
Of intermingling sounds, and then
The goodwife and the smile of her
Filling the silences again —
The cricket's call
And the wee cot,
Dear Lord of all,
Deny me not!

I pray not that
Men tremble at
My power of place
And lordly sway, —
I only pray for simple grace
To look my neighbor in the face
Full honestly from day to day —
Yield me his horny palm to hold,
And I'll not pray
For gold: —
The tanned face, garlanded with mirth,
It hath the kingliest smile on earth;
The swart brow, diamonded with sweat,
Hath never need of coronet.
And so I reach,
Dear Lord, to Thee,
And do beseech
Thou givest me
The wee cot, and the cricket's chirr,
Love, and the glad sweet face of her.

ON THE DEATH OF LITTLE MAHALA ASHCRAFT

"Little Haly! Little Haly!" cheeps the robin in the tree;
"Little Haly!" sighs the clover, "Little Haly!" moans the bee;

"Little Haly! Little Haly!" calls the kill-deer at twilight;
And the katydids and crickets hollers "Haly!" all the night.

The sunflowers and the hollyhawks droops over the garden fence;
The old path down the garden-walks still holds her footprints' dents;
And the well-sweep's swingin' bucket seems to wait fer her to come
And start it on its wortery errant down the old bee-gum.

The bee-hives all is quiet; and the little Jersey steer,
When any one comes nigh it, acts so lonesome-like and queer;
And the little Banty chickens kindo' cutters faint and low,
Like the hand that now was feedin' 'em was one they did n't know.

They's sorrow in the wavin' leaves of all the apple-trees;
And sorrow in the harvest-sheaves, and sorrow in the breeze;
And sorrow in the twitter of the swallers 'round the shed;
And all the song her red-bird sings is "Little Haly's dead!"

The medder 'pears to miss her, and the pathway through the grass,
Whare the dewdrops ust to kiss her little bare feet as she passed;
And the old pin in the gate-post seems to kindo'-sorto' doubt
That Haly's little sunburnt hands 'll ever pull it out.

Did her father er her mother ever love her more 'n me,
Er her sisters er her brother prize her love more tendurly?
I question — and what answer? — only tears, and tears alone,
And ev'ry neghbor's eyes is full o' teardrops as my own.

"Little Haly! Little Haly!" cheeps the robin in the tree;
"Little Haly!" sighs the clover; "Little Haly!" moans the bee;
"Little Haly! Little Haly!" calls the kill-deer at twilight,
And the katydids and crickets hollers "Haly!" all the night.

LITTLE ORPHANT ANNIE

LITTLE Orphant Annie 's come to our house to stay,
An' wash the cups and saucers up, an' brush the crumbs away,
An' shoo the chickens off the porch, an' dust the hearth, an' sweep,
An' make the fire, an' bake the bread, an' earn her board-an'-keep;
An' all us other children, when the supper things is done,
We set around the kitchen fire an' has the mostest fun
A-list'nin' to the witch-tales 'at Annie tells about,
An' the Gobble-uns 'at gits you
Ef you
Don't
Watch
Out!

Onc't they was a little boy would n't say his pray'rs —
An' when he went to bed at night, away up stairs,
His mammy heerd him holler, an' his daddy heerd him bawl,
An' when they turn't the kivvers down, he was n't there at all!
An' they seeked him in the rafter-room, an' cubby-hole, an' press,
An' seeked him up the chimbly-flue, an' ever'wheres, I guess;
But all they ever found was thist his pants an' roundabout!
An' the Gobble-uns 'll git you
Ef you
Don't
Watch
Out!

An' one time a little girl 'ud allus laugh an' grin,
An' make fun of ever' one, an' all her blood-an'-kin;
An' onc't when they was "company," an' ole folks was there,

She mocked 'em an' shocked 'em, an' said she did n't care !
An' thist as she kicked her heels, an' turn't to run an' hide,
They was two great big Black Things a-standin' by her side,
An' they snatched her through the ceilin' 'fore she knowed what she 's about !
An' the Gobble-uns 'll git you
Ef you
Don't
Watch
Out !

An' little Orphant Annie says, when the blaze is blue,
An' the lampwick sputters, an' the wind goes woo-oo !
An' you hear the crickets quit, an' the moon is gray,
An' the lightnin'-bugs in dew is all squenched away, —
You better mind yer parents, and yer teachers fond and dear,
An' churish them 'at loves you, an' dry the orphant's tear,
An' he'p the pore an' needy ones 'at clusters all about,
Er the Gobble-uns 'll git you
Ef you
Don't
Watch
Out !

DWAINIE

FROM "THE FLYING ISLANDS OF THE NIGHT"

Ay, Dwainie ! — My Dwainie !
The lurloo ever sings,
A tremor in his flossy crest
And in his glossy wings.
And Dwainie ! — My Dwainie !
The winno-welvers call; —
But Dwainie hides in Spirkland
And answers not at all.

The teeper twitters Dwainie ! —
The tcheucker on his spray
Teeters up and down the wind,
And will not fly away:
And Dwainie ! — My Dwainie !
The drowsy oovers drawl; —
But Dwainie hides in Spirkland
And answers not at all.

O Dwainie ! — My Dwainie !
The breezes hold their breath, —
The stars are pale as blossoms,
And the night as still as death;
And Dwainie ! — My Dwainie !
The fainting echoes fall; —
But Dwainie hides in Spirkland
And answers not at all.

HONEY DRIPPING FROM THE COMB

How slight a thing may set one's fancy drifting
Upon the dead sea of the Past ! — A view —
Sometimes an odor — or a rooster lifting
A far-off "*Ooh ! ooh-ooh !*"

And suddenly we find ourselves astray
In some wood's-pasture of the Long Ago, —
Or idly dream again upon a day
Of rest we used to know.

I bit an apple but a moment since, —
A wilted apple that the worm had spurned, —
Yet hidden in the taste were happy hints
Of good old days returned.

And so my heart, like some enraptured lute,
Tinkles a tune so tender and complete,
God's blessing must be resting on the fruit —
So bitter, yet so sweet !

A MAN BY THE NAME OF BOLUS

A MAN by the name of Bolus — (all 'at we 'll ever know
Of the stranger's name, I reckon — and I'm kindo' glad it 's so !) —
Got off here, Christmas morning, looked 'round the town, and then
Kindo' sized up the folks, I guess, and — went away again !

The fac's is, this man Bolus got "run in," Christmas-day;
The town turned out to see it, and cheered, and blocked the way;
And they dragged him 'fore the Mayor — fer he could n't er would n't walk —
And socked him down fer trial — though he could n't er would n't talk !

Drunk? They was no doubt of it! —
W'y, the marshal of the town
Laughed and testified 'at he fell *up*-stairs
'stid o' *down!*
This man by the name of Bolus? — W'y,
he even drapped his jaw
And snored on through his "hearin'" —
drunk as you ever saw!

One feller spit in his boot-leg, and another
'n' drapped a small
Little chunk o' ice down his collar, — but
he did n't wake at all!
And they all nearly split when his Honor
said, in one of his witty ways,
To "chalk it down fer him, 'Called away
— be back in thirty days!'"

That's where this man named Bolus slid,
kindo' like in a fit,
Flat on the floor; and — drat my ears! —
I hear 'em a-laughin' yit!
Somebody fetched Doc Sifers from jest
acrost the hall, —
And all Doc said was, "Morphine! We're
too late!" and that's all!

That's how they found his name out —
piece of a letter 'at read:
"Your wife has lost her reason, and little
Nathan's dead —
Come ef you kin, — fergive *her* — but
Bolus, as fer *me*,
This hour I send a bullet through where
my heart *ort* to be!"

Man by the name of Bolus! — As his re-
vilers broke
Fer the open air, 'peared like, to me, I
heard a voice 'at spoke —
*Man by the name of Bolus! git up from
where you lay —
Git up and smile white at 'em with your hands
crossed thataway!*

LONGFELLOW

The winds have talked with him confid-
ingly;
The trees have whispered to him; and the
night
Hath held him gently as a mother might,
And taught him all sad tones of melody;
The mountains have bowed to him; and
the sea,
In clamorous waves, and murmurs exquisite,
Hath told him all her sorrow and delight, —
Her legends fair, — her darkest mystery.
His verse blooms like a flower, night and
day;
Bees cluster round his rhymes; and twit-
terings
Of lark and swallow, in an endless May,
Are mingling with the tender songs he
sings.
Nor shall he cease to sing — in every lay
Of Nature's voice he sings — and will
alway.

LOVE'S PRAYER

Dear Lord! kind Lord!
Gracious Lord! I pray
Thou wilt look on all I love,
Tenderly to-day!
Weed their hearts of weariness;
Scatter every care,
Down a wake of angel wings
Winnowing the air.

Bring unto the sorrowing
All release from pain;
Let the lips of laughter
Overflow again;
And with all the needy
O divide, I pray,
This vast treasure of content
That is mine to-day!

Louis James Block

THE GARDEN WHERE THERE IS NO WINTER

"Se Dio ti lasci, lettor, prender frutto
Di tua lezione."

Behold the portal: open wide it stands,
And the long reaches shine and still allure
To seek their nobler depths serene, secure,
And watch the waters kiss the yellow
sands
That gentle winds stir with their sweet
commands;
These stately growths from age to age
endure,

These splendid blooms glow in the sunlight pure,
These wondrous works of human hearts and hands.
Over the charmëd space no storm may rest,
The gloomy hours avoid the magic bound,
Homer dwells here, Vergil, and all the blest
Whose perfumed color lights Time's mighty round;
Pluck the fruit freely, reader, and partake,
God wills it — for the enchanted Soul's fair sake.

TUBEROSE

Flower, that I hold in my hand,
Waxen and white and unwoful,
Perfect with your race's lovely perfection,
Pure as the dream of a child just descended from the heavens,
Chaste as the thought of the maid on whose sight first shines the glow of love's planet,
Trustful as a boy who holds the world in hands of power unrelaxing,
Flower, graceful, lovely,
Lo! I give you to the waves that roll across the ocean's expanses.

I watch you like a star on the waters,
I watch you floating away in the distance;
The ocean gives you reception and dwelling,
The ocean with the sweep of its world-encircling currents,
With its storms and winds, —
Mutable home where all is each and each is other.

You show no signs of terror,
You float to the mid-most whirlpool,
You are made one with the unending streams,
The moon and stars are reflected in your changed bosom,
The measureless winds enfold you with love as a garment.
Night and day and time are contained in your embraces,
Clouds emerge from your heart and return,
Life and death are as slender ripples across your central calmness,
Hope and wishing and longing and tumult are over,
Unto the all, your cradle and grave, your father-mother,
You have returned,
O flower transfigured!
O flower having reached your fruition!

FATE

Three steps and I reach the door,
But a whole month rolls between
Since last I stood before
My shut room's simple scene.

I pause at the door and shrink,
My hand is at point to turn,
But I stand and dimly think
Of all I long for and yearn.

My life leaps up to me there,
The past with its every deed,
And I tremble and hardly dare
The open mystery to read.

A year and a day and awhile,
Ay me! there is none escape;
Each thought, each dream, each smile
Will front me in questioning shape.

I open and see what no eyes
Save mine have the power to see:
Dead scenes and dead griefs arise,
Dead follies make mouths at me.

Yea, so: through the dark I peer,
And shudder away from the door;
Voices once heard I hear,
Know faces seen long before.

WORK

Ah, blessedness of work! the aimless mind,
Left to pursue at will its fancies wild,
Returns at length, like some play-wearied child,
Unto its labor's knee, and leaves behind
Its little games, and learns to soothe its blind
Wide longings in the sweet tranquillity

Of limited tasks, whose mild successions wind
In pauseless waves unto the distant sea;
For blank infinity is cold as ice,
And drear the void of space unsown with stars,
And dolorous the barren line of shore;
Therefore it was with lover-like device
This lower world was built, through whose cleft bars
The limitless sun of Truth shines more and more.

Maybury Fleming

TO DEMETER

Thou ever young! Persephone but gazes
Upon thy face, and shows thee back thine own;
And every flock that on thy hillsides grazes,
And every breeze from thy fair rivers blown,
And all the nestlings from thy branches flown,
Are eloquent in thy praises,
Demeter, mother of truth.

Thy seasons of grief, thy winters white with snowing,
More lovely make thy face, adorn thy head,
Add beauty to thy sweet eyes, ever glowing
With love and strength and godhead; and thy tread
Sweetens the earth; and all the gods are dead
But thee, — thee only, strowing
Ever the land with youth.

And all the dead gods are in thee united,
Woman and girl and lover and friend and queen;
And this tame, time-worn world is full requited
For that the Christ has cost us, and the teen
Bred of swift time. And thy kissed palms between —
Thy dear kissed hands — are righted
The heart-knot and the ruth.

WHAT THOUGH THE GREEN LEAF GROW?

What though the green leaf grow?
'T will last a month and day;
In all sweet flowers that blow
Lurks Death, his slave Decay.

But if my lady smile
There is no Death at all;
The world is fair the while, —
What though the red leaf fall?

TO SLEEP

Sweet wooded way in life, forgetful Sleep!
Dim, drowsy realm where restful shadows fall,
And where the world's glare enters not at all,
Or in soft glimmer making rest more deep;
Where sound comes not, or else like brooks that keep
The world's noise out, as by a slumberous wall
Of gentlest murmur; where still whispers call
To smileless gladness those that waking weep;
Beneath the dense veil of thy stirless leaves,
Where no air is except the calm of space,
Vexed souls of men have grateful widowhood
Of tedious sense; there thoughts are bound in sheaves
By viewless hands as silent as the place;
And man, unsinning, finds all nature good.

William Cranston Lawton

SONG, YOUTH, AND SORROW

LOFTY against our Western dawn uprises Achilles:
He among heroes alone singeth or toucheth the lyre.
Few, and dimmed by grief, are the days that to him are appointed!
Love he shall know but to lose, life but to cast it away.
Dreaming of peace and a bride, he sees not the foes at the portal:
Paris, a traitor to love; Phœbus, accorder of song!

Freely he chose, do ye deem, and clave to the anguish and glory?
Rather the Fates at his birth chose, yet he gladly assents.
Is it a warning that death untimely and bitterest sorrow,
Sorrow in love, and death, follow the children of song?
Yet will the young man's heart still cling to the choice of Achilles —
Grief, an untimely doom, fame that eternal abides.

MY FATHERLAND

THE imperial boy had fallen in his pride
Before the gates of golden Babylon.
The host, who deemed that priceless treasure won,
For many a day since then had wandered wide,
By famine thinned, by savage hordes defied.
In a deep vale, beneath the setting sun,
They saw at last a swift black river run,
While shouting spearmen thronged the farther side.

Then eagerly, with startled, joyous eyes,
Toward the desponding chief a soldier flew:
"I was a slave in Athens, never knew
My native country; but I understand
The meaning of yon wild barbarian cries,
And I believe this is my fatherland!"

This glimpse have we, no more. Did parents fond,
Brothers, or kinsmen, hail his late return?
Or did he, doubly exiled, only yearn
To greet the Euxine's waves at Trebizond,
The blue Ægean, and Pallas' towers beyond?
Mute is the record. We shall never learn.
But as once more the well-worn page I turn,
Forever by reluctant schoolboys conned,

A parable to me the tale appears,
Of blacker waters in a drearier vale.
Ah me! When on that brink we exiles stand,
As earthly lights and mortal accents fail,
Shall voices long forgotten reach our ears,
To tell us we have found our fatherland?

Katherine Eleanor Conway

THE HEAVIEST CROSS OF ALL

I'VE borne full many a sorrow, I've suffered many a loss —
But now, with a strange, new anguish, I carry this last dread cross;
For of this be sure, my dearest, whatever thy life befall,
The cross that our own hands fashion is the heaviest cross of all.

Heavy and hard I made it in the days of my fair strong youth,
Veiling mine eyes from the blessed light, and closing my heart to truth.
Pity me, Lord, whose mercy passeth my wildest thought,
For I never dreamed of the bitter end of the work my hands had wrought!

In the sweet morn's flush and fragrance I wandered o'er dewy meadows,

And I hid from the fervid noontide glow in the cool green woodland shadows;
And I never recked, as I sang aloud in my wilful, selfish glee,
Of the mighty woe that was drawing nigh to darken the world for me.

But it came at last, my dearest, — what need to tell thee how?
Mayst never know of the wild, wild woe that my heart is bearing now!
Over my summer's glory crept a damp and chilling shade,
And I staggered under the heavy cross that my sinful hands had made.

I go where the shadows deepen, and the end seems far off yet —
God keep thee safe from the sharing of this woeful late regret!
For of this be sure, my dearest, whatever thy life befall,
The crosses we make for ourselves, alas! are the heaviest ones of all.

SATURNINUS

He might have won the highest guerdon that heaven to earth can give,
For whoso falleth for justice — dying, he yet shall live.

He might have left us his memory to flame as a beacon light,
When clouds of the false world's raising shut the stars of heaven from sight.

He might have left us his name to ring in our triumph song
When we stand, as we 'll stand at to-morrow's dawn, by the grave of a world-old wrong.

For he gave thee, O mother of valiant sons, thou fair, and sore oppressed,
The love of his youth and his manhood's choice — first-fruits of his life, and best.

Thine were throb of his heart and thought of his brain and toil of his strong right hand;
For thee he braved scorn and reviling, and loss of gold and land,

Threat and lure and false-hearted friend, and blight of a broken word —
Terrors of night and delay of light — prison and rack and sword.

For thee he bade death defiance — till the heavens opened wide,
And his face grew bright with reflex of light from the face of the Crucified.

And his crown was in sight and his palm in reach and his glory all but won,
And then — he failed — God help us! with the worst of dying done.

Only to die on the treacherous down by the hands of the tempters spread —
Nay, nay — make way for the strangers! we have no right in the dead.

But oh, for the beacon quenched, that we dreamed would kindle and flame!
And oh, for the standard smirched and shamed, and the name we dare not name!

Over the lonesome grave the shadows gather fast;
Only the mother, like God, forgives, and comforts her heart with the past.

Irwin Russell

DE FUST BANJO

Go 'way, fiddle! folks is tired o' hearin' you a-squawkin'.
Keep silence fur yo' betters! — don't you heah de banjo talkin'?
About de 'possum's tail she 's gwine to lecter — ladies, listen! —
About de ha'r whut is n't dar, an' why de ha'r is missin':

"Dar's gwine to be a' oberflow," said Noah, lookin' solemn —
Fur Noah tuk the "Herald," an' he read de ribber column —

An' so he sot his hands to wuk a-cl'arin' timber-patches,
An' 'lowed he 's gwine to build a boat to beat the steamah *Natchez.*

Ol' Noah kep' a-nailin' an' a-chippin' an' a-sawin';
An' all de wicked neighbors kep' a-laughin' an' a-pshawin';
But Noah did n't min' 'em, knowin' whut wuz gwine to happen:
An' forty days an' forty nights de rain it kep' a-drappin'.

Now, Noah had done cotched a lot ob ebry sort o' beas'es —
Ob all de shows a-trabbelin', it beat 'em all to pieces!
He had a Morgan colt an' sebral head o' Jarsey cattle —
An' druv 'em 'board de Ark as soon 's he heered de thunder rattle.

Den sech anoder fall ob rain! — it come so awful hebby,
De ribber riz immejitly, an' busted troo de lebbee;
De people all wuz drownded out — 'cep' Noah an' de critters,
An' men he 'd hired to work de boat — an' one to mix de bitters.

De Ark she kep' a-sailin' an' a-sailin' *an'* a-sailin';
De lion got his dander up, an' like to bruk de palin';
De sarpints hissed; de painters yelled; tell, whut wid all de fussin',
You c'u'd n't hardly heah de mate a-bossin' 'roun' an' cussin'.

Now Ham, de only nigger whut wuz runnin' on de packet,
Got lonesome in de barber-shop, an' c'u'd n't stan' de racket;
An' so, fur to amuse he-se'f, he steamed some wood an' bent it,
An' soon he had a banjo made — de fust dat wuz invented.

He wet de ledder, stretched it on; made bridge an' screws an' aprin;
An' fitted in a proper neck — 't wuz berry long an' tap'rin';
He tuk some tin, an' twisted him a thimble fur to ring it;
An' den de mighty question riz: how wuz he gwine to string it?

De 'possum had as fine a tail as dis dat I 's a-singin';
De ha'r 's so long an' thick an' strong, — des fit fur banjo-stringin';
Dat nigger shaved 'em off as short as wash-day-dinner graces;
An' sorted ob 'em by de size, f'om little E's to basses.

He strung her, tuned her, struck a jig, — 't wuz "Nebber min' de wedder," —
She soun' like forty-lebben bands a-playin' all togedder;
Some went to pattin'; some to dancin': Noah called de figgers;
An' Ham he sot an' knocked de tune, de happiest ob niggers!

Now, sence dat time — it 's mighty strange — dere 's not de slightes' showin'
Ob any ha'r at all upon de 'possum's tail a-growin';
An' curi's, too, dat nigger's ways: his people nebber los' 'em —
Fur whar you finds de nigger — dar 's de banjo an' de 'possum!

Charles Leonard Moore

TO ENGLAND

Now England lessens on my sight;
The bastioned front of Wales,
Discolored and indefinite,
There like a cloud-wreath sails:
A league, and all those thronging hills
Must sink beneath the sea;
But while one touch of Memory thrills,
They yet shall stay with me.

I claim no birthright in yon sod,
Though thence my blood and name;
My sires another region trod,
Fought for another fame;

Yet a son's tear this moment wrongs
  My eager watching eyes,
Land of the lordliest deeds and songs
  Since Greece was great and wise!

Thou hedgerow thing that queenest the
    Earth,
  What magic hast? — what art?
A thousand years of work and worth
  Are clustered at thy heart:
The ghosts of those that made thee free
  To throng thy hearth are wont;
And as thy richest reliquary
  Thou wearest thy Abbey's front!

Aye, ere my distance is complete
  I see thy heroes come
And crowd yon shadowy mountain seat,
  Still guardians of their home;
Thy Drake, thy Nelson, and thy Bruce
  Glow out o'er dusky tides;
The rival Roses blend in truce,
  And King with Roundhead rides.

And with these phantoms born to last,
  A storm of music breaks;
And bards, pavilioned in the past, —
  Each from his tomb awakes!
The ring and glitter of thy swords,
  Thy lovers' bloom and breath,
By them transmuted into words,
  Redeem the world from death.

My path is West! My heart before
  Bounds o'er the dancing wave;
Yet something 's left I must deplore —
  A magic wild and grave:
Though Honor live and Romance dwell
  By mine own streams and woods,
Yet not in spire and keep so well
  Are built such lofty moods.

England, perchance our love were more
  If we were matched and met
In battle squadron on the shore,
  Or here on ocean set:
How were all other banners furled
  If that great duel rose!
For we alone in all the world
  Are worthy to be foes.

If we should fail or you should fly,
  'T were but a twinned disgrace,
For both are bound to bear on high
  The laurels of one race: —

No fear! new blooms shall bud above
  Upon the ancient wreath,
For both can gentle be to Love,
  And insolent to Death.

Land of the lion-hearted brood,
  I breathe a last adieu;
To Her who reigns across the flood
  My loyalty is true:
But with my service to her o'er,
  Thou, England, ownest the rest,
For I must worship and adore
  Whate'er is brave and best.

FROM THE "BOOK OF DAY-DREAMS"

SOUL UNTO SOUL GLOOMS DARKLING

DISGUISE upon disguise, and then disguise,
Equivocations at the rose's heart,
Life's surest pay a poet's forgeries,
The gossamer gold coinage of our art.
Why hope for truth? Thy very being
    slips,
Lost from thee, in thy crowd of masking
    moods.
Why hope for love? Between quick-kiss-
    ing lips
Is room and stage for all hate's interludes.
One with thy love thou art! — her eyes,
    her hair
Known to thy soul, a pure estate of bliss;
But some least motion, look, or changëd air,
And nadir unto zenith nearer is:
Thou mayst control her limbs, but not begin
To know what planet rules the tides within.

DISENCHANTMENT

THE mighty soul that is ambition's mate,
Tied to the shiftings of a certain star,
Forgets the circle of its mortal state
And what its planetary aspects are,
Till, in conjunctive course and wandering,
Out of its trance and treasure-dream of
    hope
It wakens, poor illusionary thing,
Wingless, without desire, or deed, or scope.
So have I with imaginations played
Till I have lost life's sure and single good,
Forgotten friendships, broken vows, and
    made
My heart a highway for ingratitude,

And, driven to the desert of the sky,
Fear now no thing but immortality.

OR EVER THE EARTH WAS

THAT which shall last for aye can have no birth.
Thou art immortal! therefore thou hast been
A voyage to which the journey of the earth
Is but the shifting of some tawdry scene.
Thou wert not absent when the camp began
Of the great captains of the middle air, —
Sirius and Vega and Aldebaran, —
Myriads, and but the marshals numbered there;
Ay, earlier yet in the God-purposed void,
The dream and desert of oblivion,
Thou livedst, — a thought of one to be employed
Ere yet Time's garments thou didst take and don:
Guest that no footprint on my threshold leaves, —
Speak, O dim traveller, speak: thy host believes!

THOU LIVEST, O SOUL!

THOU livest, O soul! be sure, though earth be flames,
Though lost be all the paths the planets trod,
Thou hast not aught to do with signs and names,
With Life's false art or Time's brief period.
Thy being wast ere yet the heavens were not,
Gently thy breath the waves of ether stirred,
And often hast thou feared and oft forgot,
Yet knew thyself when rang the parent Word.
Long hast thou played at change through chain on chain
Of beings, drooping now in strange descent,
Now adding bloom to bloom and beauty's gain,
Through subtle growths of glory evident.
O earnest play, thyself apart oft smilest,
One still at heart, that so thyself beguilest.

THEN SHALL WE SEE

THEN shall we see and know the group divine,
The sure immortals of the world's vague throng,
Ceaseless continuers of the purple line,
The equal-sceptred kings of Deed and Song:
From sire to sire to Orpheus and beyond,
Thrilled with the blood of Hector do they come,
Blazoned on eyes believing, eyes too fond
To fail to follow them unto their home.
Hark! their thin tread outechoes the vast hosts
That shake the valleys of the globe beneath;
Their smile is fire; their eyes (O, subtle ghosts!)
Have waked in me the passion of the Wreath
Without whose round not heaven itself is bliss,
Nor immortality immortal is.

Edith Matilda Thomas[1]

THE BETRAYAL OF THE ROSE

A WHITE rose had a sorrow —
And a strange sorrow!
For her sisters they had none,
As they all sat around her
Each on her feudal throne.
A strange sorrow
For one with no to-morrow,
No yesterday, to call her own,
But only to-day.

A white rose had a sorrow —
And a sweet sorrow!
She had locked it in her breast
Save that one outer petal,
Less guarded than the rest
(Oh, fond sorrow!),

[1] See, also, p. 588.

From the red rose did borrow
Blushes, and the truth confessed
In the red rose's way!

THE TEARS OF THE POPLARS

HATH not the dark stream closed above thy head,
With envy of thy light, thou shining one?
Hast thou not, murmuring, made thy dreamless bed
Where blooms the asphodel, far from all sun?
But thou — thou dost obtain oblivious ease,
While here we rock and moan — thy funeral trees.

Have we not flung our tresses on the stream?
Hath not thy friend, the snowy cygnet, grieved,
And ofttimes watched for thy returning beam,
With archëd neck — and ofttimes been deceived?
A thousand years, and yet a thousand more,
Hast thou been mourned upon this reedy shore.

How long, how long since, all the summer day,
Earth heard the heavens sound from pole to pole,
While legion clouds stood forth in bright array;
Yet no rain followed on the thunder's roll!
Beneath that glittering legion shrank the seas,
And fire unseen was borne upon the breeze.

The ground was smouldering fire beneath our tread,
The forest dropped the leaf, and failed all grass.
The souls of stricken men their bodies fled,
And, sighing, flocked the wind. — We heard them pass!
The priest, that scanned the portent of the skies,
Fell reeling back, with pierced and shrivelled eyes.

But ah, he saw not what our sight discerned —
The flying chariot-wheel, with fervid tire —
The steeds that unaccustomed guidance spurned
With fateful hoof and breath that scattered fire —
He saw not thee and thine unmeasured fall,
And Jove, unheeding, in his cloudy hall!

Dragged headlong by those swift immortal horse,
Up to our sire went thy vain cry for aid;
Neither he cast a bound, to check their course,
Nor on the golden rein a hand he laid.
Brother beloved, what foe could so deceive,
Bidding thee dare what scarcely gods achieve?

Alas! that we remember — and forget!
For, if we sometimes gain a brief repose,
Soon are we roused, by sudden fear beset;
Then, through our silver boughs a shudder goes,
Our heads we lift, we search the azure gloom,
As though thou still wert falling to thy doom!

Upon the earth no loves were ever ours;
Man greets us from afar, but comes not near,
Nor even round our dark unwindowed towers
Throng the light birds — so much our grief they fear!
We sigh — we tremble — 't is not to the breeze —
Brother beloved, we are thy funeral trees!

THE QUIET PILGRIM

ISAIAH XXXVIII. 15

WHEN on my soul in nakedness
His swift, avertless hand did press,
Then I stood still, nor cried aloud,
Nor murmured low in ashes bowed;
And, since my woe is utterless,
To supreme quiet I am vowed;
Afar from me be moan and tears, —
I shall go softly all my years.

Whenso my quick, light-sandaled feet
Bring me where Joys and Pleasures meet,
I mingle with their throng at will;
They know me not an alien still,
Since neither words nor ways unsweet
Of storëd bitterness I spill;
Youth shuns me not, nor gladness fears, —
For I go softly all my years.

Whenso I come where Griefs convene,
And in my ear their voice is keen,
They know me not, as on I glide,
That with Arch Sorrow I abide.
They haggard are, and drooped of mien,
And round their brows have cypress tied:
Such shows I leave to light Grief's peers, —
I shall go softly all my years.

Yea, softly! heart of hearts unknown.
Silence hath speech that passeth moan,
More piercing-keen than breathëd cries
To such as heed, made sorrow-wise.
But save this voice without a tone,
That runs before me to the skies,
And rings above thy ringing spheres,
Lord, I go softly all my years!

MOTHER ENGLAND

I

There was a rover from a western shore,
England! whose eyes the sudden tears did drown,
Beholding the white cliff and sunny down
Of thy good realm, beyond the sea's uproar.
I, for a moment, dreamed that, long before,
I had beheld them thus, when, with the frown
Of sovereignty, the victor's palm and crown
Thou from the tilting-field of nations bore.
Thy prowess and thy glory dazzled first;
But when in fields I saw the tender flame
Of primroses, and full-fleeced lambs at play,
Meseemed I at thy breast, like these, was nursed;
Then mother — Mother England! — home I came,
Like one who hath been all too long away!

II

As nestling at thy feet in peace I lay,
A thought awoke and restless stirred in me:
"My land and congeners are beyond the sea,
Theirs is the morning and the evening day.
Wilt thou give ear while this of them I say:
'Haughty art thou, and they are bold and free,
As well befits who have descent from thee,
And who have trodden brave the forlorn way.
Children of thine, but grown to strong estate;
Nor scorn from thee would they be slow to pay,
Nor check from thee submissly would they bear;
Yet, Mother England! yet their hearts are great,
And if for thee should dawn some darkest day,
At cry of thine, how proudly would they dare!'"

BREATH OF HAMPSTEAD HEATH

The wind of Hampstead Heath still burns my cheek
As, home returned, I muse, and see arise
Those rounded hills beneath the low, gray skies,
With gleams of haze-lapped cities far to seek.
These can I picture, but how fitly speak
Of what might not be seen with searching eyes,
And all beyond the listening ear that lies,
Best known to bards and seers in times antique?
The winds that of the spirit rise and blow
Kindle my thought, and shall for many a day,
Recalling what blithe presence filled the place
Of one who oftentimes passed up that way,
By garden close and lane where boughs bend low,
Until the breath of Hampstead touched his face.

THEFTS OF THE MORNING

BIND us the Morning, mother of the stars
And of the winds that usher in the day!
Ere her light fingers slide the eastern bars,
A netted snare before her footsteps lay;
Ere the pale roses of the mist be strown,
Bind us the Morning, and restore our own!

With her have passed all things we held most dear,
Most subtly guarded from her amorous stealth;
We nothing gathered, toiling year by year,
But she hath claimed it for increase of wealth;
Our gems make bright her crown, incrust her throne:
Bind us the Morning, and restore our own!

Where are they gone, who round our myrtles played,
Or bent the vines' rich fruitage to our hands,
Or breathed deep song from out the laurels' shade?
She drew them to her, — who can slack the bands?
What lure she used, what toils, was never known:
Bind us the Morning, and restore our own!

Enough that for her sake Orion died,
Slain by the silver Archer of the sky, —
That Ilion's prince amid her splendors wide
Lies chained by age, nor wins his prayer to die;
Enough! but hark! Our captive loves make moan:
Bind us the Morning, and restore our own!

We have beheld them whom we lost of old,
Among her choiring Hours, in sorrow bowed.
A moment gleam their faces, faint and cold,
Through some high oriel window wreathed with cloud,
Or on the wind before her they are blown:
Bind us the Morning, and restore our own!

They do her service at the noiseless looms
That weave the misty vesture of the hills;
Their tears are drink to thirsting grass and blooms,
Their breath the darkling wood-bird wakes and thrills;
Us too they seek, but far adrift are thrown:
Bind us the Morning, and restore our own!

Yea, cry her *Thief!* from where the light doth break
To where it merges in the western deep!
If aught of ours she, startled, should forsake,
Such waifs the waiting Night for us will keep.
But stay not; still pursue her, falsely flown:
Bind us the Morning, and restore our own!

FROST

How small a tooth hath mined the season's heart!
How cold a touch hath set the wood on fire,
Until it blazes like a costly pyre
Built for some Ganges emperor, old and swart,
Soul-sped on clouds of incense! Whose the art
That webs the streams, each morn, with silver wire,
Delicate as the tension of a lyre, —
Whose falchion pries the chestnut-burr apart?
It is the Frost, a rude and Gothic sprite,
Who doth unbuild the Summer's palaced wealth,
And puts her dear loves all to sword or flight;
Yet in the hushed, unmindful winter's night
The spoiler builds again with jealous stealth,
And sets a mimic garden, cold and bright.

QUATRAINS

THE SOUL IN THE BODY

WHAT if the Soul her real life elsewhere holds,
Her faint reflex Time's darkling stream enfolds,
And thou and I, though seeming dwellers here,
Live somewhere yonder in the starlit sphere?

INSOMNIA

A HOUSE of sleepers — I, alone unblest,
Am yet awake and empty vigil keep.
When these, who spend life's day with me, find rest,
Oh, let me not be last to fall asleep!

TO IMAGINATION

ONE day thou didst desert me — then I learned
How looks the world to men that lack thy grace,
And toward the shadowy night sick-hearted turned, —
When, lo! the first star brought me back thy face!

A FAR CRY TO HEAVEN

WHAT! dost thou pray that the outgone tide be rolled back on the strand,
The flame be rekindled that mounted away from the smouldering brand,
The past-summer harvest flow golden through stubble-lands naked and sere,
The winter-gray woods upgather and quicken the leaves of last year? —
Thy prayers are as clouds in a drouth; regardless, unfruitful, they roll;
For this, that thou prayest vain things, 't is a far cry to Heaven, my soul, —
Oh, a far cry to Heaven!

Thou dreamest the word shall return, shot arrow-like into the air,
The wound in the breast where it lodged be balmed and closed for thy prayer,
The ear of the dead be unsealed, till thou whisper a boon once denied,
The white hour of life be restored, that passed thee unprized, undescribed! —
Thy prayers are as runners that faint, that fail, within sight of the goal,
For this, that thou prayest fond things, 't is a far cry to Heaven, my soul, —
Oh, a far cry to Heaven!

And cravest thou fondly the quivering sands shall be firm to thy feet,
The brackish pool of the waste to thy lips be made wholesome and sweet?
And cravest thou subtly the bane thou desirest be wrought to thy good,
As forth from a poisonous flower a bee conveyeth safe food?
For this, that thou prayest ill things, thy prayers are an anger-rent scroll;
The chamber of audit is closed, — 't is a far cry to Heaven, my soul, —
Oh, a far cry to Heaven!

THE MOTHER WHO DIED TOO

SHE was so little — little in her grave,
The wide earth all around so hard and cold —
She was so little! therefore did I crave
My arms might still her tender form enfold.
She was so little, and her cry so weak
When she among the heavenly children came —
She was so little — I alone might speak
For her who knew no word nor her own name.

WINTER SLEEP

I KNOW it must be winter (though I sleep) —
I know it must be winter, for I dream
I dip my bare feet in the running stream,
And flowers are many, and the grass grows deep.

I know I must be old (how age deceives!) —
I know I must be old, for, all unseen,
My heart grows young, as autumn fields grow green,
When late rains patter on the falling sheaves.

I know I must be tired (and tired souls err) —
I know I must be tired, for all my soul
To deeds of daring beats a glad, faint roll,
As storms the riven pine to music stir.

I know I must be dying (Death draws near) —
I know I must be dying, for I crave
Life — life, strong life, and think not of the grave,
And turf-bound silence, in the frosty year.

FROM "THE INVERTED TORCH"

WHEN IN THE FIRST GREAT HOUR

When in the first great hour of sleep supreme
I saw my Dearest fair and tranquil lie,
Swift ran through all my soul this wonder-cry:
"How hast thou met and vanquished hate extreme!"
For by thy faint white smiling thou didst seem,
Sweet Magnanimity! to half defy,
Half pity, those ill things thou hadst put by,
That are the haunters of our life's dim dream.
Pain, error, grief, and fear — poor shadows all —
I, to thy triumph caught, saw fail and fade.

. . . .

Yet as some muser, when the embers fall,
The low lamp flickers out, starts up dismayed,
So I awoke, to find me still Time's thrall,
Time's sport, — nor by thy warm, safe presence stayed.

TELL ME

Tell me, is there sovereign cure
For heart-ache, heart-ache, —
Cordial quick and potion sure,
For heart-ache, heart-ache?

Fret thou not. If all else fail
For heart-ache, heart-ache,
One thing surely will avail, —
That 's heart-break, heart-break!

IF STILL THEY LIVE

If still they live, whom touch nor sight
Nor any subtlest sense can prove,
Though dwelling past our day and night,
At farthest star's remove, —

Oh, not because these skies they change
For upper deeps of sky unknown,
Shall that which made them ours grow strange,
For spirit holds its own;

Whether it pace this earth around,
Or cross, with printless, buoyant feet,
The unreverberant Profound
That hath no name nor mete!

WILL IT BE SO?

Oft have I wakened ere the spring of day,
And, from my window looking forth, have found
All dim and strange the long-familiar ground.
But soon I saw the mist glide slow away,
And leave the hills in wonted green array,
While from the stream-sides and the fields around
Rose many a pensive day-entreating sound,
And the deep-breasted woodlands seemed to pray.
Will it be even so when first we wake
Beyond the Night in which are merged all nights, —
The soul sleep-heavy and forlorn will ache,
Deeming herself midst alien sounds and sights?
Then will the gradual Day with comfort break
Along the old deeps of being, the old heights?

Samuel Minturn Peck

SASSAFRAS

Fringing cypress forests dim
Where the owl makes weird abode,
Bending down with spicy limb
O'er the old plantation road,

Through the swamp and up the hill,
Where the dappled byways run,
Round the gin-house, by the mill,
Floats its incense to the sun.

Swift to catch the voice of spring,
Soon its tasselled blooms appear;
Modest is their blossoming,
Breathing balm and waving cheer;
Rare the greeting that they send
To the fragrant wildwood blooms,
Bidding every blossom blend
In a chorus of perfumes.

On it leans the blackberry vine,
With white sprays caressingly;
Round its knees the wild peas twine,
Beckoning to the yellow bee;
Through its boughs the red-bird flits
Like a living flake of fire,
And with love-enlightened wits
Weaves his nest and tunes his lyre.

Oh, where skies are summer-kissed,
And the drowsy days are long,
'Neath the sassafras to list
To the field-hand's mellow song!
Or, more sweet than chimes that hang
In some old cathedral dome,
Catch the distant klingle-klang
Of the cow-bells tinkling home!

A SOUTHERN GIRL

HER dimpled cheeks are pale;
She 's a lily of the vale,
Not a rose.
In a muslin or a lawn
She is fairer than the dawn
To her beaux.

Her boots are slim and neat,—
She is vain about her feet,
It is said.
She amputates her r's,
But her eyes are like the stars
Overhead.

On a balcony at night,
With a fleecy cloud of white
Round her hair—
Her grace, ah, who could paint?
She would fascinate a saint,
I declare.

'T is a matter of regret,
She 's a bit of a coquette,
Whom I sing:
On her cruel path she goes
With a half a dozen beaux
To her string.

But let all that pass by,
As her maiden moments fly,
Dew-empearled;
When she marries, on my life,
She will make the dearest wife
In the world.

THE CAPTAIN'S FEATHER

THE dew is on the heather,
The moon is in the sky,
And the captain's waving feather
Proclaims the hour is nigh
When some upon their horses
Shall through the battle ride,
And some with bleeding corses
Must on the heather bide.

The dust is on the heather,
The moon is in the sky,
And about the captain's feather
The bolts of battle fly;
But hark, what sudden wonder
Breaks forth upon the gloom?
It is the cannon's thunder—
It is the voice of doom!

The blood is on the heather,
The night is in the sky,
And the gallant captain's feather
Shall wave no more on high;
The grave and holy brother
To God is saying Mass,
But who shall tell his mother,
And who shall tell his lass?

MY LITTLE GIRL

MY little girl is nested
Within her tiny bed,
With amber ringlets crested
Around her dainty head;
She lies so calm and stilly,
She breathes so soft and low,
She calls to mind a lily
Half-hidden in the snow.

A weary little mortal
Has gone to slumberland;
The Pixies at the portal
Have caught her by the hand.
She dreams her broken dolly
Will soon be mended there,
That looks so melancholy
Upon the rocking-chair.

I kiss your wayward tresses,
My drowsy little queen;
I know you have caresses
From floating forms unseen.

O, Angels, let me keep her
To kiss away my cares,
This darling little sleeper,
Who has my love and prayers!

Arthur Wentworth Hamilton Eaton

PRAY FOR THE DEAD

PRAY for the dead — who bids thee not?
Do all our human loves grow pale,
Or are the old needs all forgot
When men have passed within the veil?

Shall prayer's strong pleadings pierce the skies
For those we still keep with us here,
And not a single wish arise
For loved ones in a happier sphere?

Have they no conquests yet to win,
No rugged heights of truth to climb;
Does no strange syllable of sin
Mar the soft cadence of their rhyme;

Or has God snapped the strong, sweet ties
He took such loving pains to weld,
And said, "Henceforth their memories
In prayerless silence must be held"?

Pray for the dead: the links that bound
Thy soul to theirs were forged on high;
Borne upward, they have surely found
The chain still fastened in the sky.

And who of us so wise to say
That they have lost the need of prayer!
Heaven's gates are not so far away
That earth goes unremembered there.

Pray for the dead, nor dare repress
Thy longings at the throne of grace;
Our dead ones are more dear, not less,
In the pure presence of God's face.

And strength and faith are needed, there
As here, inspired life to win —
Nor see alone the gateways fair
Of Heaven's great life, but enter in.

Love well and pray for all thy dead:
God gives thee such sweet liberty,
He means where'er their souls are sped,
That they shall be in touch with thee.

THE EGYPTIAN LOTUS

(IN AN ARTIFICIAL POND)

PROUD, languid lily of the sacred Nile,
'T is strange to see thee on our Western wave,
Far from those sandy shores, that mile on mile,
Papyrus-plumed, stretch silent as the grave.

O'er dark, mysterious pool and sheltered bay,
And round deep dreaming isles thy leaves expand,
Where Alexandrian barges plough their way,
Full-freighted, to the ancient Theban land.

On Karnak's lofty columns thou wert seen,
And spacious Luxor's temple-palace walls,
Each royal Pharaoh's emeralded queen
Chose thee to deck her glittering banquet halls;

Yet thou art blossoming on this fairy lake
As regally, amidst these common things,
As on the shores where Nile's soft ripples break,
As in the halls of old Egyptian kings.

Thy grace charms, day by day, men's curious eyes,
But he whose outer senses thought has probed,
Looking at thee, sees stately temples rise
About him, and long lines of priests, white-robed,

That chant strange music as they slowly pace
Dim columned aisles; hears, trembling overhead,
Echoes that lose themselves in that vast space,
Of Egypt's solemn ritual for the dead.

Ay, deeper thoughts than these, though undefined,
Wake in the quickened soul at sight of thee,
For this majestic orient faith enshrined
Man's yearning hope of immortality.

And thou wert Egypt's symbol of the power
That under all decaying form lies hid;
The old world worshipped thee, O Lotus flower,
Then carved its sphinx and reared its pyramid.

Additional Selections

(VARIOUS POEMS BELONGING TO THIS DIVISION)

I

LITTLE WILD BABY[1]

THROUGH the fierce fever I nursed him, and then he said
I was the woman — I !— that he would wed;
He sent a boat with men for his own white priest,
And he gave my father horses, and made a feast.
I am his wife: if he has forgotten me,
I will not live for scorning eyes to see.
(*Little wild baby, that knowest not where thou art going,*
Lie still! lie still! Thy mother will do the rowing.)

Three moons ago — it was but three moons ago —
He took his gun, and started across the snow;
For the river was frozen, the river that still goes down
Every day, as I watch it, to find the town;
The town whose name I caught from his sleeping lips,
A place of many people and many ships.
(*Little wild baby, that knowest not where thou art going,*
Lie still! lie still! Thy mother will do the rowing.)

I to that town am going, to search the place,
With his little white son in my arms, till I see his face.
Only once shall I need to look in his eyes,
To see if his soul, as I knew it, lives or dies.
If it lives, we live, and if it is dead, we die,
And the soul of my baby will never ask me why.
(*Little wild baby, that knowest not where thou art going,*
Lie still! lie still! Thy mother will do the rowing.)

I have asked about the river: one answered me,
That after the town it goes to find the sea;
That great waves, able to break the stoutest bark,
Are there, and the sea is very deep and dark.
If he is happy without me, so best, so best;
I will take his baby, and go away to my rest.
(*Little wild baby, that knowest not where thou art going,*
Lie still! lie still! Thy mother will do the rowing.
The river flows swiftly, the sea is dark and deep;
Little wild baby, lie still! Lie still and sleep.)

MARGARET THOMSON JANVIER
("Margaret Vandegrift")

VIVÉROLS

BEYOND the sea, I know not where,
There is a town called Vivérols;
I know not if 'tis near or far,
I know not what its features are,
I only know 'tis Vivérols.

[1] See BIOGRAPHICAL NOTE, p. 803.

I know not if its ancient walls
By vine and moss be overgrown;
I know not if the night-owl calls
From feudal battlements of stone,
Inhabited by him alone.

I know not if mid meadow-lands
Knee-deep in corn stands Vivérols;
I know not if prosperity
Has robbed its life of poesy;
That could not be in Vivérols,
They would not call it Vivérols.

Perchance upon its terraced heights
The grapes grow purple in the sun;
Or down its wild untrodden crags,
Its broken cliffs and frost-bit jags,
The mountain brooks unfettered run.

I cannot fancy Vivérols
A place of gaudy pomp and show,
A "Grand Établissement des Eaux,"
Where to restore their withered lives
The roués of the city go.

Nor yet a place where Poverty
No ray of happiness lets in;
Where wanders hopeless beggary
Mid scenes of sorrow, want, and sin.
That could not be in Vivérols;
There 's life and cheer in Vivérols!

Perchance among the clouds it lies,
Mid vapors out from Dreamland blown;
Built up from vague remembrances,
That never yet had form in stone, —
Its castles built of cloud alone.

I only know, should thou and I
Through its old walls of crumbling stone
Together wander all alone,
No spot on earth could be more fair
Than ivy-covered Vivérols!
No grass be greener anywhere,
No bluer sky nor softer air
Than we should find in Vivérols.

Love, we may wander far or near,
The sun shines bright o'er Vivérols;
Green is the grass, the skies are clear;
No clouds obscure our pathway, dear;
Where love is, there is Vivérols, —
There is no other Vivérols.

David Starr Jordan

HE 'D NOTHING BUT HIS VIOLIN

He 'd nothing but his violin,
I 'd nothing but my song,
But we were wed when skies were blue
And summer days were long;
And when we rested by the hedge,
The robins came and told
How they had dared to woo and win,
When early Spring was cold.

We sometimes supped on dew-berries,
Or slept among the hay,
But oft the farmers' wives at eve
Came out to hear us play;
The rare old songs, the dear old tunes, —
We could not starve for long
While my man had his violin,
And I my sweet love-song.

Mary Kyle Dallas

WHAT MY LOVER SAID

By the merest chance, in the twilight gloom,
In the orchard path he met me;
In the tall, wet grass, with its faint perfume,
And I tried to pass, but he made no room,
Oh, I tried, but he would not let me.
So I stood and blushed till the grass grew red,
With my face bent down above it,
While he took my hand as he whispering said —
(*How the clover lifted each pink, sweet head*
To listen to all that my lover said, —
Oh, the clover in bloom, I love it!)

In the high, wet grass went the path to hide,
And the low, wet leaves hung over;
But I could not pass upon either side,
For I found myself, when I vainly tried,
In the arms of my steadfast lover.
And he held me there and he raised my head,
While he closed the path before me,
And he looked down into my eyes and said —
(*How the leaves bent down from the boughs o'erhead,*
To listen to all that my lover said, —
Oh, the leaves hanging lowly o'er me!)

Had he moved aside but a little way,
I could surely then have passed him;

And he knew I never could wish to stay,
And would not have heard what he had to say,
Could I only aside have cast him.
It was almost dark, and the moments sped,
And the searching night wind found us,
But he drew me nearer and softly said —
(*How the pure sweet wind grew still, instead,*
To listen to all that my lover said, —
Oh, the whispering wind around us!)

I am sure he knew, when he held me fast,
That I must be all unwilling;
For I tried to go, and I would have passed,
As the night was come with its dew, at last,
And the sky with its stars was filling.
But he clasped me close when I would have fled,
And he made me hear his story,
And his soul came out from his lips and said —
(*How the stars crept out where the white moon led,*
To listen to all that my lover said, —
Oh, the moon and the stars in glory!)

I know that the grass and the leaves will not tell,
And I'm sure that the wind, precious rover,
Will carry my secret so safely and well
That no being shall ever discover
One word of the many that rapidly fell
From the soul-speaking lips of my lover;
And the moon and the stars that looked over
Shall never reveal what a fairy-like spell
They wove round about us that night in the dell,
In the path through the dew-laden clover,
Nor echo the whispers that made my heart swell
As they fell from the lips of my lover.

HOMER GREENE

UNLESS

O TOUCH me not, unless thy soul
Can claim my soul as thine;
Give me no earthly flowers that fade,
No love, but love divine:
For I gave thee immortal flowers,
That bloomed serene in heavenly bowers.

Look not with favor on my face,
Nor answer my caress,
Unless my soul have first found grace
Within thy sight; express
Only the truth, though it should be
Cold as the ice on northern sea.

O never speak of love to me,
Unless thy heart can feel
That in the face of Deity
Thou wouldst that love reveal:
For God is love, and His bright law
Should find our hearts without one flaw.

ELLA DIETZ GLYNES

WINTER TWILIGHT

SOFT-SANDALLED twilight, handmaid of the night,
Before her noble lady's radiant face
Doth slowly come, with gentle, quiet pace,
And draweth rose and azure curtains light
Around the snowy couch, so pure, so white,
Whereon her mistress soon will rest. With grace
Celestial she doth cover every trace
Of toil, and daily soil doth hide from sight.
So would I that before thy face my love
Might gently move, and ever from above
Such tender beauty draw about thy way
That when thou liest down to nightly rest
Earth-thoughts should fade, and there should only stay
The peace of heaven within thy tranquil breast.

GEORGE TRACY ELLIOT

II

UNDER THE RED CROSS

SHE came and went as comes and goes
A fragrance in the morning air,
Where lay the shadowy shapes of those
Who died in her sweet care.

Some doubted, when her face had flown,
Whether it was or only seemed, —
Whether one saw what he had known
Or something he had dreamed.

And near a trampled field at night
  Wan eyes, still following her afar,
Saw round that head a saintlier light
    Than came from moon or star.

The wreck, the roar, the murk, the glare
  Were nought to her; she simply knew
God's broken images were there
    Where healing hands were few.

CHAUNCEY HICKOX

A CHILD'S QUESTION

"WHAT is it to be dead?" O Life,
  Close-held within my own,
What foul breath in the air is rife?
  What voice malign, unknown,
Hath dared this whisper faint and dread,
"What is — what is it to be dead?"

Who told you that the song-bird died?
  They had no right to say
This to my child — I know we cried
  When Robin "went away;"
But this strange thing we never said,
That what we loved so could be dead.

Give me your hands, my only boy!
  Health throbs in every vein;
Thou hast not dreamed of earth's alloy,
  Nor stepped where guilt has lain;
O sweet young life! O baby breath!
What hast thou now to do with death?

I even framed for thy dear sake
  Anew the childish prayer,
Lest, "If I die before I wake,"
  Should rouse a thought or care.
Mother of Christ, was this a sin —
To watch where death might enter in?

Too late! The Angel of the Flame
  Relentless cries: "Go hence!"
I think of Eden's sin and shame;
  I gaze — on innocence!
And still the curse? Must I arise
And lead my own from Paradise!

I see the wide, the awful world
  Loom up beyond the gate;
I see his pure soul tossed and whirled —
  My child! I pray thee wait!
Ask me not what the Angel saith;
My soul this day hath tasted death!

EMMA HUNTINGTON NASON

THE MYSTERY

YOU gave me roses, love, last night,
When the sea was blue and the skies were bright;
And the earth was aglow with a golden light
When you gave me roses, love, last night.

Lilies I lay by your side to-day,
And your face — it is colder and whiter than they;
And I linger and listen and wonder and pray,
As I bring you lilies to-day.

LILIAN WHITING

THOMAS À KEMPIS

(DE IMITATIONE CHRISTI)

TURN with me from the city's clamorous street,
Where throng and push passions and lusts and hate,
And enter, through this age-browned, ivied gate,
For many summers' birds a sure retreat,
The place of perfect peace. And here, most meet
For meditation, where no idle prate
Of the world's ways may come, rest thee and wait.
'T is very quiet. Thus doth still Heaven entreat.
With reverent feet, his face so worn, so fair,
Walks one who bears the cross, who waits the crown.
Tumult is past. In those calm eyes I see
The image of the Master, Christ, alone,
And from those patient lips I hear one prayer:
"Dear Lord, dear Lord, that I may be like thee!"

RICHARD ROGERS BOWKER

KELPIUS'S HYMN

O GOD, thy moon is on the hills,
  Thy stars are in the sky,
Thy Spirit this mortal vessel fills,
  I feel the end is nigh;

Swift meteors flame across the north,
The golden planets wheel and sink,
Soon steps thy trumpet-angel forth
From Heaven's eternal brink;
Then peace illumes these warlike ways,
Christ's joyful chiliad has its birth,
A round of Eden's perfect days,
Thy kingdom comes upon the earth!

My eyes are dim, my hands are weak,
My soul is scarred with sin,
But day and night thy Word I seek,
That I a crown may win.
Cleanse thou and make my spirit pure
As are the spirits of thy saints;
Like them in bliss would I endure
When earthly body faints.
Far up on Heaven's resplendent height
I hear the circling cherubs sing,
As downward to this world of night
The New Jerusalem they bring!

ARTHUR PETERSON

III

TWO ARGOSIES[1]

(ANTONIO'S AND SHAKESPEARE'S)

"THE ducats take! I'll sign the bond to-day:
No storm can wreck Antonio's white-winged fleet;
My stately ships secure ride every bay
From Tripolis to Indies' golden seat.
The ducats take, Bassanio, go thy way;
Thy Portia win, and bid me to the feast;
Ten thousand men Antonio's nod obey,
And of ten thousand Shylock is the least.
I'll sign the bond, thy words cannot avail,
No chance can reach the wealth I share with thee:
I stand secure, let cruel fortune rail
Till Venice sleeps beneath bright Adria's sea."
Fate heard the boast — a thousand vessels lay
'Mid rocks and sands to waves an idle prey.

The dramas take! That bond at least is sure;
Twelve thousand words more dear than ducats are
Outride the storms of ages and endure,
Safe anchored here within the shifting bar
Of changing speech. Eternal now his tongue,
By right divine, sways all the world with grace:
Great bond of all — the words sweet Shakespeare sung;
His commerce brings the nations face to face.
His dramas take! Their wealth shall still survive;
His argosies care not for time or fate;
All else may pass, and crowding centuries strive,
That bond alone is not determinate.
In him proud Albion lives entire and hale,
Her titled language crowned in high entail.

WALLACE BRUCE

[1] Copyright, 1894, by HARPER & BROTHERS.

IN THE OLD CHURCHYARD AT FREDERICKSBURG[2]

IN the old churchyard at Fredericksburg
A gravestone stands to-day,
Marking the place where a grave has been,
Though many and many a year has it seen
Since its tenant mouldered away.
And that quaintly carved old stone
Tells its simple tale to all: —
"Here lies a bearer of the pall
At the funeral of Shakespeare."

There in the churchyard at Fredericksburg
I wandered all alone,
Thinking sadly on empty fame,
How the great dead are but a name, —
To few are they really known.
Then upon this battered stone
My listless eye did fall,
Where lay the bearer of the pall
At the funeral of Shakespeare.

[2] See BIOGRAPHICAL NOTE, p. 807.

Then in the churchyard at Fredericksburg
It seemed as though the air
Were peopled with phantoms that swept by,
Flitting along before my eye,
So sad, so sweet, so fair;
Hovering about this stone,
By some strange spirit's call,
Where lay a bearer of the pall
At the funeral of Shakespeare.

For in the churchyard at Fredericksburg
Juliet seemed to love,
Hamlet mused, and the old Lear fell,
Beatrice laughed, and Ariel
Gleamed through the skies above,
As here, beneath this stone,
Lay in his narrow hall
He who before had borne the pall
At the funeral of Shakespeare.

And I left the old churchyard at Fredericksburg;
Still did the tall grass wave,
With a strange and beautiful grace,
Over the sad and lonely place,
Where hidden lay the grave;
And still did the quaint old stone
Tell its wonderful tale to all: —
"Here lies a bearer of the pall
At the funeral of Shakespeare."

FREDERICK WADSWORTH LORING

IV

THE AZTEC CITY

THERE is a clouded city, gone to rest
Beyond the crest
Where cordilleras mar the mystic west.

There suns unheeded rise and re-arise;
And in the skies
The harvest moon unnoticed lives and dies.

And yet this clouded city has no night —
Volcanic light
Compels eternal noontide, redly bright.

A thousand wells, whence cooling waters came,
No more the same,
Now send aloft a thousand jets of flame.

This clouded city is enchanting fair,
For rich and rare
From sculptured frieze the gilded griffins stare.

With level look — with loving, hopeful face,
Fixed upon space,
Stand caryatides of unknown race,

And colonnades of dark green serpentine,
Of strange design,
Carved on whose shafts queer alphabets combine.

And there are lofty temples, rich and great,
And at the gate,
Carved in obsidian, the lions wait.

And from triumphant arches, looking down
Upon the town,
In porphyry, sad, unknown statesmen frown.

And there are palace homes, and stately walls,
And open halls
Where fountains are, with voiceless waterfalls.

The ruddy fire incessantly illumes
Temples and tombs,
And in its blaze the stone-wrought cactus blooms.

From clouds congealed the mercury distils,
And, forming rills,
Adown the streets in double streamlet trills.

As rains from clouds, that summer skies eclipse,
From turret-tips
And spire and porch the mobile metal drips.

No one that visited this fiery hive
Ever alive
Came out but me — I, I alone, survive.

EUGENE FITCH WARE
("Ironquill")

WERE-WOLF

RUNS the wind along the waste,
Run the clouds across the moon,
Ghastly shadows run in haste
From snowy dune to dune —
Blue shadows o'er the ghastly white
Spectral gleaming in the night.
But ghastlier, more spectral still,
What fearful thing speeds hither,
Running, running, running
Swifter than cloud or wind?
What omen of nameless ill,
Whence coming, speeding whither,
Running, running, running,
Leaves all save fear behind?

Leaning, leaning in the race,
Breath keen-drawn through nostrils tense,
Fell eyes in ruthless face,
What goblin of malevolence
Runs through the frozen night
In superhuman flight?
See it run, run, run,
Outstripping the shadows that fly!
Hear the fiend's heart beat, beat,
Beat, beat, beat in its breast!
Running, running, running on
Under the frozen sky,
Fleet, so fearfully fleet,
Pausing never to rest.

Clutched — what is clutched so tight
In its lean, cold hands as it speeds?
Something soft, something white,
Something human, that bleeds?
Is it an infant's curly head,
And innocent limbs, gnawed and red?
Fleeter and yet more fleet
It leans, leans and runs;
Dabbled with blood are its awful lips,
Grinning in horrible glee.
The wolves that follow with scurrying feet,
Sniffing that goblin scent, at once
Scatter in terror, while it slips
Away, to the shore of the frozen sea.

Away! is it man? is it woman,
On such dread meat to feed?
Away! is it beast? is it human?
Or is it a fiend indeed?
Fiend from human loins begotten,
Hell-inspired, God-forgotten!
Now the midnight hour draws on:
Human form no fiend may keep
Or ever that mystic hour is told.
Lower, lower, lower it bends.
Midnight is come — is come and gone!
Down on all fours see it plunge and leap!
A human yell in a wolf's howl ends! . . .
What gaunt, gray thing gallops on o'er the world?

JULIAN HAWTHORNE

V

THE GOLDEN AGE

THIS world was not
As it now is seen:
It once was clothed
With a deeper green;
And rarer gems
Than the ice-caves hold
The sea brought up
On the sands of gold.

But rust of ages,
The breath of Time,
The meadows covered
With early rime;
And the wild grass faded,
The gems were gone,
And the wave fell cold
As it thundered on.

In bygone ages
The world was fair,
And the moon-god played
With her golden hair;
And the paling stars
With love-white arms
Bent down to welcome
A sister's charms.

The air lay sweet
With the breath of pines;
The hill-tops glowed
With their wealth of mines;
And sweet, and low,
And rich, and free,
The wild, dark music
Stole over the sea.

And the sea-waves laughed
At the saffron moon;
And the musk-rose smiled
With her soul of June;
And the golden age
Of Nature's years
No warning heard
Of her coming tears.

But the hand of man
Was the sword of death:
A poison lurked
In his savage breath,
And the wealth of years
And the glow of years
Were drowned in a flood
Of swelling tears.

The world was fair
In the days of yore;
But that golden age
Shall come no more.
The sun may shine,
And wild flowers bloom;
But the goal of all
Is the open tomb, —

The end of all
Is the silent grave;
And beauty lies
In the cold still wave.
And the world shall harden
The hearts of men
Till it hear the voice
Of its Christ again.

ERNEST FRANCISCO FENOLLOSA

THE MAN WITH THE HOE

A REPLY

Let us a little permit Nature to take her own way: she better understands her own affairs than we. — MONTAIGNE.

NATURE reads not our labels, "great" and "small";
Accepts she one and all

Who, striving, win and hold the vacant place;
All are of royal race.

Him, there, rough-cast, with rigid arm and limb,
The Mother moulded him,

Of his rude realm ruler and demigod,
Lord of the rock and clod.

With Nature is no "better" and no "worse,"
On this bared head no curse.

Humbled it is and bowed; so is he crowned
Whose kingdom is the ground.

Diverse the burdens on the one stern road
Where bears each back its load;

Varied the toil, but neither high nor low.
With pen or sword or hoe,

He that has put out strength, lo, he is strong;
Of him with spade or song

Nature but questions, — "This one, shall he stay?"
She answers "Yea," or "Nay,"

"Well, ill, he digs, he sings;" and he bides on,
Or shudders, and is gone.

Strength shall he have, the toiler, strength and grace,
So fitted to his place

As he leaned, there, an oak where sea winds blow,
Our brother with the hoe.

No blot, no monster, no unsightly thing,
The soil's long-lineaged king;

His changeless realm, he knows it and commands;
Erect enough he stands,

Tall as his toil. Nor does he bow unblest:
Labor he has, and rest.

Need was, need is, and need will ever be
For him and such as he;

Cast for the gap, with gnarlëd arm and limb,
The Mother moulded him, —

Long wrought, and moulded him with mother's care,
Before she set him there.

And aye she gives him, mindful of her own,
Peace of the plant, the stone;

Yea, since above his work he may not rise,
She makes the field his skies.

See! she that bore him, and metes out the lot,
He serves her. Vex him not

To scorn the rock whence he was hewn, the pit
And what was digged from it;

Lest he no more in native virtue stand,
The earth-sword in his hand,

But follow sorry phantoms to and fro,
And let a kingdom go.

JOHN VANCE CHENEY[1]

VI

"GOSSAMER WEFT"

WHENEVER A LITTLE CHILD IS BORN

WHENEVER a little child is born,
All night a soft wind rocks the corn;
One more buttercup wakes to the morn,
Somewhere, somewhere.

One more rosebud shy will unfold,
One more grass-blade push through the mold,
One more bird-song the air will hold,
Somewhere, somewhere.

AGNES CARTER MASON

MORNING

WILL there really be a morning?
Is there such a thing as day?
Could I see it from the mountains
If I were as tall as they?
Has it feet like water lilies?
Has it feathers like a bird?
Is it brought from famous countries
Of which I've never heard?
Oh some scholar, oh some sailor,
Oh some wise man from the skies,
Please to tell a little pilgrim
Where the place called morning lies.

EMILY DICKINSON[2]

SNOWFLAKES

WHENEVER a snowflake leaves the sky,
It turns and turns to say "Good-by!
Good-by, dear clouds, so cool and gray!"
Then lightly travels on its way.

And when a snowflake finds a tree,
"Good-day!" it says — "Good-day to thee!
Thou art so bare and lonely, dear,
I'll rest and call my comrades here."

But when a snowflake, brave and meek,
Lights on a rosy maiden's cheek,
It starts — "How warm and soft the day!
'T is summer!" — and it melts away.

MARY MAPES DODGE[3]

WHY IT WAS COLD IN MAY

THE Year had all the Days in charge,
And promised them that they
Should each one see the World in turn,
But ten Days ran away!
Ten Days that should have gone abroad
Sometime in early May —
So, when May came, and all was fair,
These Days were sent to bed,
And ten *good* Winter Days were sent,
To see the World instead!

HENRIETTA ROBINS ELIOT

THISTLE-DOWN

NEVER a beak has my white bird,
Nor throat for song;
But wings of silk by soft wind stirred
Bear it along.

With wings of silk and a heart of seed,
Over field and town
It sails,— ah! quaint little bird indeed
Is the thistle-down.

CLARA DOTY BATES

1 See p. 515; also, BIOGRAPHICAL NOTE, p. 785.

2 See, also, p. 320.

3 See, also, p. 392.

A LITTLE BOY'S VAIN REGRET

He was six years old, just six that day,
And I saw he had something important to say
As he held in his hand a broken toy.
He looked in my face for an instant, and then
He said, with a sigh, and a downcast eye,
"If I could live my life over again,
I think I could be a better boy!"

Edith Matilda Thomas[1]

A MORTIFYING MISTAKE

I studied my tables over and over, and backward and forward, too;
But I could n't remember six times nine, and I did n't know what to do,
Till sister told me to play with my doll, and not to bother my head.
"If you call her 'Fifty-four' for a while, you 'll learn it by heart," she said.

So I took my favorite, Mary Ann (though I thought 't was a dreadful shame
To give such a perfectly lovely child such a perfectly horrid name),
And I called her my dear little "Fifty-four" a hundred times, till I knew
The answer of six times nine as well as the answer of two times two.

Next day Elizabeth Wigglesworth, who always acts so proud,
Said, "Six times nine is fifty-two," and I nearly laughed aloud!
But I wished I had n't when teacher said, "Now, Dorothy, tell if you can."
For I thought of my doll and — sakes alive! — I answered, "*Mary Ann!*"

Anna M. Pratt

EARLY NEWS

The sparrow told it to the robin,
The robin told it to the wren,
Who passed it on, with sweet remark,
To thrush, and bobolink, and lark,
The news that dawn had come again.

Anna M. Pratt

A MILLION LITTLE DIAMONDS

A million little diamonds
Twinkled on the trees;
And all the little maidens said:
"A jewel, if you please!"
But while they held their hands outstretched,
To catch the diamonds gay,
A million little sunbeams came,
And stole them all away.

Mary Frances Butts[2]

ONLY ONE

Hundreds of stars in the pretty sky;
Hundreds of shells on the shore together;
Hundreds of birds that go singing by;
Hundreds of bees in the sunny weather.

Hundreds of dewdrops to greet the dawn;
Hundreds of lambs in the purple clover;
Hundreds of butterflies on the lawn;
But only one mother the wide world over.

George Cooper

LULLABY

Rockaby, lullaby, bees in the clover!
Crooning so drowsily, crying so low,
Rockaby, lullaby, dear little rover!
Down into wonderland,
Down to the under-land,
Go, now go!
Down into wonderland go.

Rockaby, lullaby, rain on the clover,
(Tears on the eyelids that waver and weep!)
Rockaby, lullaby — bending it over!
Down on the mother-world,
Down on the other world,
Sleep, oh sleep!
Down on the mother-world sleep.

Rockaby, lullaby, dew on the clover,
Dew on the eyes that will sparkle at dawn!
Rockaby, lullaby, dear little rover!
Into the stilly world,
Into the lily world,
Gone! now gone!
Into the lily world gone.

Josiah Gilbert Holland[3]

[1] See, also, p. 571.
[2] See, also, p. 468.
[3] See, also, p. 233.

VII

IMPROMPTUS

WRITTEN IN THE VISITORS' BOOK AT THE BIRTHPLACE OF ROBERT BURNS

Of heavenly stature, but most human smile,
Gyved with our faults he stands,
Truth's white and Love's red roses tendering us,
Whose thorns are in his hands.

THE NEW ARRIVAL

There came to port last Sunday night
The queerest little craft,
Without an inch of rigging on;
I looked and looked — and laughed!
It seemed so curious that she
Should cross the Unknown water,
And moor herself within my room —
My daughter! O, my daughter!

Yet by these presents witness all
She 's welcome fifty times,
And comes consigned in hope and love —
And common-metre rhymes.
She has no manifest but this;
No flag floats o'er the water;
She 's too new for the British Lloyds —
My daughter! O, my daughter!

Ring out, wild bells — and tame ones too;
Ring out the lover's moon.
Ring in the little worsted socks,
Ring in the bib and spoon.
Ring out the muse, ring in the nurse,
Ring in the milk and water.
Away with paper, pen, and ink —
My daughter! O, my daughter!

George Washington Cable

THOUGHTS ON THE COMMANDMENTS

"Love your neighbor as yourself," —
So the parson preaches:
That 's one half the Decalogue, —
So the prayer-book teaches.
Half my duty I can do
With but little labor,
For with all my heart and soul
I do love my neighbor.

Mighty little credit, that,
To my self-denial;
Not to love her, though, might be
Something of a trial.
Why, the rosy light, that peeps
Through the glass above her,
Lingers round her lips, — you see
E'en the sunbeams love her.

So to make my merit more,
I 'll go beyond the letter: —
Love my neighbor as myself?
Yes, and ten times better.
For she 's sweeter than the breath
Of the Spring, that passes
Through the fragrant, budding woods,
O'er the meadow-grasses.

And I 've preached the word I know,
For it was my duty
To convert the stubborn heart
Of the little beauty.
Once again success has crowned
Missionary labor,
For her sweet eyes own that she
Also loves her neighbor.

George Augustus Baker

AN AMERICAN GIRL

She 's had a Vassar education,
And points with pride to her degrees;
She 's studied household decoration;
She knows a dado from a frieze,
And tells Corots from Boldonis;
A Jacquemart etching, or a Haden,
A Whistler, too, perchance might please
A free and frank young Yankee maiden.

She does not care for meditation;
Within her bonnet are no bees;
She has a gentle animation,
She joins in singing simple glees.
She tries no trills, no rivalries
With Lucca (now Baronin Räden),
With Nilsson or with Gerster; she 's
A frank and free young Yankee maiden.

I'm blessed above the whole creation,
Far, far above all other he's;
I ask you for congratulation
On this the best of jubilees:

I go with her across the seas
Unto what Poe would call an Aiden, —
I hope no serpent 's there to tease
A frank and free young Yankee maiden.

ENVOY

Princes, to you the western breeze
Bears many a ship and heavy laden.
What is the best we send in these?
A free and frank young Yankee maiden.

BRANDER MATTHEWS

TO JESSIE'S DANCING FEET

How, as a spider's web is spun
With subtle grace and art,
Do thy light footsteps, every one,
Cross and recross my heart!
Now here, now there, and to and fro,
Their winding mazes turn;
Thy fairy feet so lightly go
They seem the earth to spurn.
Yet every step leaves there behind
A something, in thy dance,
That serves to tangle up my mind
And all my soul entrance.

How, as the web the spiders spin
And wanton breezes blow,
Thy soft and filmy laces in
A swirl around thee flow!
The cobweb 'neath thy chin that 's crossed
Remains demurely put,
While those are ever whirled and tossed
That show thy saucy foot;
That show the silver grayness of
Thy stockings' silken sheen,
And mesh of snowy skirts above
The silver that is seen.

How, as the spider, from his web,
Dangles in light suspense,
Do thy sweet measures' flow and ebb
Sway my enraptured sense!
Thy fluttering lace, thy dainty airs,
Thy every charming pose —
There are not more alluring snares
To bind me with than those.
Swing on! Sway on! With easy grace
Thy witching steps repeat!
The love I dare not — to thy face —
I offer at thy feet.

WILLIAM DE LANCEY ELLWANGER

DIVISION III

(WOODBERRY, BUNNER, MRS. PULLEN, MISS REESE, H. S. MORRIS, MISS CONE, BURTON, SHERMAN, GARLAND, MISS MONROE, MISS GUINEY, AND OTHERS)

George Edward Woodberry

FROM "WILD EDEN"[1]

WHEN FIRST I SAW HER

WHEN first I saw her, at the stroke
The heart of nature in me spoke;
The very landscape smiled more sweet,
Lit by her eyes, pressed by her feet;
She made the stars of heaven more bright
By sleeping under them at night;
And fairer made the flowers of May
By being lovelier than they.

Softly down where the sunshine spread,
Dark in the grass I laid my head;
And let the lights of earth depart
To find her image in my heart;
While through my being came and went
Tones of some heavenly instrument,
As if where its blind motions roll
This world should wake and be a soul.

THE SECRET

NIGHTINGALES warble about it
All night under blossom and star;
The wild swan is dying without it,
And the eagle crieth afar;
The sun, he doth mount but to find it,
Searching the green earth o'er;
But more doth a man's heart mind it —
O more, more, more!

[1] Copyright, 1899, by THE MACMILLAN COMPANY.

Over the gray leagues of ocean
  The infinite yearneth alone;
The forests with wandering emotion
  The thing they know not intone;
Creation arose but to see it,
  A million lamps in the blue;
But a lover, he shall be it,
  If one sweet maid is true.

O, INEXPRESSIBLE AS SWEET

O, INEXPRESSIBLE as sweet,
  Love takes my voice away;
I cannot tell thee when we meet
  What most I long to say.

But hadst thou hearing in thy heart
  To know what beats in mine,
Then shouldst thou walk, where'er thou art,
  In melodies divine.

So warbling birds lift higher notes
  Than to our ears belong;
The music fills their throbbing throats,
  But silence steals the song.

THE ROSE OF STARS

WHEN Love, our great Immortal,
  Put on mortality,
And down from Eden's portal
  Brought this sweet life to be,
At the sublime archangel
  He laughed with veilëd eyes,
For he bore within his bosom
  The seed of Paradise.

He hid it in his bosom,
  And there such warmth it found,
It brake in bud and blossom,
  And the rose fell on the ground;
As the green light on the prairie,
  As the red light on the sea,
Through fragrant belts of summer
  Came this sweet life to be.

And the grave archangel seeing
  Spread his mighty wings for flight,
But the glow hung round him fleeing
  Like the rose of an Arctic night;
And sadly moving heavenward
  By Venus and by Mars,
He heard the joyful planets
  Hail Earth, the Rose of Stars.

DIVINE AWE

To tremble, when I touch her hands,
With awe that no man understands;
To feel soft reverence arise
When, lover-sweet, I meet her eyes;
To see her beauty grow and shine
When most I feel this awe divine, —
Whate'er befall me, this is mine;
And where about the room she moves,
My spirit follows her, and loves.

HOMEWARD BOUND

I

INTO the west of the waters on the living ocean's foam,
Into the west of the sunset where the young adventurers roam,
Into the west of the shining star, I am sailing, sailing home;
Home from the lonely cities, time's wreck, and the naked woe,
Home through the clean great waters where freemen's pennants blow,
Home to the land men dream of, where all the nations go;
'T is home but to be on the waters, 't is home already here,
Through the weird red-billowing sunset into the west to steer,
To fall asleep in the rocking dark with home a day more near.

II

By morning light the ship holds on, alive with happy freight,
A thousand hearts with one still joy, and with one hope elate,
To reach the land that mothered them and sweetly guides their fate;
Whether the purple furrow heaps the bows with dazzling spray,
Or buried in green-based masses they dip the storm-swept day,
Or the white fog ribbons o'er them, the strong ship holds her way;
And when another day is done, by the star of love we steer
To the land of all that we love best and all that we hold dear;
We are sailing westward, homeward; our western home is near.

THE CHILD

It was only the clinging touch
Of a child's hand in the street,
But it made the whole day sweet;
Caught, as he ran full-speed,
In my own stretched out to his need,
Caught, and saved from the fall,
As I held, for the moment's poise,
In my circling arms the whole boy's
Delicate slightness, warmëd mould;
Mine, for an instant mine,
The sweetest thing the heart can divine,
More precious than fame or gold,
The crown of many joys,
Lay in my breast, all mine.

I was nothing to him;
He neither looked up nor spoke;
I never saw his eyes;
He was gone ere my mind awoke
From the action's quick surprise
With vision blurred and dim.

You say I ask too much:
It was only the clinging touch
Of a child in a city street;
It hath made the whole day sweet.

O, STRUCK BENEATH THE LAUREL

O, struck beneath the laurel, where the singing fountains are,
I saw from heaven falling the star of love afar;
O, slain in Eden's bower nigh the bourn where lovers rest,
I fell upon the arrow that was buried in my breast;
Farewell the noble labor, farewell the silent pain,
Farewell the perfect honor of the long years lived in vain;
I lie upon the moorland where the wood and pasture meet,
And the cords that no man breaketh are bound about my feet.

SO SLOW TO DIE

The rainbow on the ocean
A moment bright,
The nightingale's devotion
That dies on night,
Eve's rosy star a-tremble
Its hour of light, —
All things that love resemble
Too soon take flight.

The violets we cherish
Died in the spring;
Roses and lilies perish
In what they bring;
And joy and beauty wholly
With life depart;
But love leaves slow, how slowly!
Life's empty heart.

O, strange to me, and wondrous,
The storm passed by,
With sound of voices thund'rous
Swept from the sky;
But stranger, love, thy fashion, —
O, tell me why
Art thou, dark storm of passion,
So slow to die?

As roll the billowy ridges
When the great gale has blown o'er;
As the long winter-dirges
From frozen branches pour;
As the whole sea's harsh December
Pounds on the pine-hung shore;
So will love's deep remember,
So will deep love deplore.

SEAWARD

I will rise, I will go from the places that are dark with passion and pain,
From the sorrow-changëd woodlands and a thousand memories slain.
O light gone out in darkness on the cliff I seek no more
Where she I worshipped met me in her girlhood at the door!
O, bright though years how many! farewell, sweet guiding star —
The wild wind blows me seaward over the harbor-bar!
Better thy waste, gray Ocean, the homeless, heaving plain,
Than to choke the fount of life and the flower of honor stain!
I will seek thy blessed shelter, deep bosom of sun and storm,
From the fever and fret of the earth and the things that debase and deform;
For I am thine; from of old thou didst lay me, a child, at rest

In thy cradle of many waters, and gav'st to my hunger thy breast;
Remember the dreamful boy whom thy beauty preserved from wrong, —
Thou taughtest me music, O Singer of the never-silent song!
Man-grown, I will seek thy healing; though from worse than death I fly,
Not mine the heart of the craven, not here I mean to die!
Let me taste on my lips thy salt, let me live with the sun and the rain,
Let me lean to the rolling wave and feel me man again!
O, make thee a sheaf of arrows as when thy winters rage forth, —
Whiten me as thy deep-sea waves with the blanching breath of the North!
O, take thee a bundle of spears from thine azure of burning drouth,
Smite into my pulses the tremors, the fervors, the blaze of the South!
So might my breath be snow-cold, and my blood be pure like fire,
The heavenly souls that have left me will come back to sustain and inspire.
Take me — I come — O, save me in the paths my fathers trod!
Then fling me back to the battle where men labor the peace of God!

FROM "MY COUNTRY"

O DESTINED Land, unto thy citadel,
What founding fates even now doth peace compel,
That through the world thy name is sweet to tell!
O thronëd Freedom, unto thee is brought
  Empire; nor falsehood nor blood-payment asked;
Who never through deceit thy ends hast sought,
  Nor toiling millions for ambition tasked;
  Unlike the fools who build the throne
    On fraud, and wrong, and woe;
  For man at last will take his own,
    Nor count the overthrow;
But far from these is set thy continent,
  Nor fears the Revolution in man's rise;
On laws that with the weal of all consent,
  And saving truths that make the people wise:
For thou art founded in the eternal fact
That every man doth greaten with the act
Of freedom; and doth strengthen with the weight
Of duty; and diviner moulds his fate,
By sharp experience taught the thing he lacked,
God's pupil; thy large maxim framed, though late,
Who masters best himself best serves the State.
This wisdom is thy Corner: next the stone
Of Bounty; thou hast given all; thy store,
Free as the air, and broadcast as the light,
Thou flingest; and the fair and gracious sight,
More rich, doth teach thy sons this happy lore:
That no man lives who takes not priceless gifts
Both of thy substance and thy laws, whereto
He may not plead desert, but holds of thee
A childhood title, shared with all who grew,
His brethren of the hearth; whence no man lifts
Above the common right his claim; nor dares
To fence his pastures of the common good:
For common are thy fields; common the toil;
Common the charter of prosperity,
That gives to each that all may blessed be.
This is the very counsel of thy soil.
Therefore, if any thrive, mean-souled he spares
The alms he took; let him not think subdued
The State's first law, that civic rights are strong
But while the fruits of all to all belong;
Although he heir the fortune of the earth,
Let him not hoard, nor spend it for his mirth,
But match his private means with public worth.
That man in whom the people's riches lie
Is the great citizen, in his country's eye.
Justice, the third great base, that shall secure
To each his earnings, howsoever poor,
From each his duties, howsoever great.
She bids the future for the past atone.
Behold her symbols on the hoary stone —

The awful scales and that war-hammered beam
Which whoso thinks to break doth fondly dream,
Or Czars who tyrannize or mobs that rage;
These are her charge, and heaven's eternal law.
She from old fountains doth new judgment draw.
Till, word by word, the ancient order swerves
To the true course more nigh; in every age
A little she creates, but more preserves.
Hope stands the last, a mighty prop of fate.
These thy foundations are, O firm-set State!

ON A PORTRAIT OF COLUMBUS

WAS this his face, and these the finding eyes
That plucked a new world from the rolling seas?
Who, serving Christ, whom most he sought to please,
Willed his one thought until he saw arise
Man's other home and earthly paradise —
His early vision, when with stalwart knees
He pushed the boat from his young olive-trees,
And sailed to wrest the secret of the skies?
He on the waters dared to set his feet,
And through believing planted earth's last race.
What faith in man must in our new world beat,
Thinking how once he saw before his face
The west and all the host of stars retreat
Into the silent infinite of space!

1892

AMERICA TO ENGLAND

MOTHER of nations, of them eldest we,
Well is it found, and happy for the state,
When that which makes men proud first makest them great,
And such our fortune is who sprang from thee,
And brought to this new land from over sea
The faith that can with every household mate,
And freedom whereof law is magistrate,
And thoughts that make men brave, and leave them free.
O Mother of our faith, our law, our lore,
What shall we answer thee if thou shouldst ask
How this fair birthright doth in us increase?
There is no home but Christ is at the door;
Freely our toiling millions choose life's task;
Justice we love, and next to justice peace.

AT GIBRALTAR

I

ENGLAND, I stand on thy imperial ground,
Not all a stranger; as thy bugles blow,
I feel within my blood old battles flow, —
The blood whose ancient founts in thee are found.
Still surging dark against the Christian bound
Wide Islam presses; well its peoples know
Thy heights that watch them wandering below;
I think how Lucknow heard their gathering sound.
I turn, and meet the cruel, turbaned face.
England, 'tis sweet to be so much thy son!
I feel the conqueror in my blood and race;
Last night Trafalgar awed me, and to-day
Gibraltar wakened; hark, thy evening gun
Startles the desert over Africa!

II

Thou art the rock of empire, set mid-seas
Between the East and West, that God has built;
Advance thy Roman borders where thou wilt,
While run thy armies true with his decrees;
Law, justice, liberty, — great gifts are these:
Watch that they spread where English blood is spilt,
Lest, mixed and sullied with his country's guilt,
The soldier's life-stream flow, and Heaven displease!
Two swords there are: one naked, apt to smite,
Thy blade of war; and, battle-storied, one
Rejoices in the sheath, and hides from light.
American I am; would wars were done!

Now westward, look, my country bids good-night, —
Peace to the world from ports without a gun!
Then, where the cluster of my hearth-stone shone,
"Bid me not live," I sigh, "till all be gone."

LOVE'S ROSARY

SWEET names, the rosary of my evening prayer,
Told on my lips like kisses of good-night
To friends who go a little from my sight,
And some through distant years shine clear and fair! —
So this dear burden that I daily bear
Mighty God taketh, and doth loose me quite;
And soft I sink in slumbers pure and light
With thoughts of human love and heavenly care;
But when I mark how into shadow slips
My manhood's prime, and weep fast-passing friends,
And heaven's riches making poor my lips,
And think how in the dust love's labor ends,

SONG OF EROS, IN "AGATHON"

WHEN love in the faint heart trembles,
And the eyes with tears are wet,
Oh, tell me what resembles
Thee, young Regret?
Violets with dewdrops drooping;
Lilies o'erfull of gold,
Roses in June rains stooping,
That weep for the cold,
Are like thee, young Regret.

Bloom, violets, lilies, and roses!
But what, young Desire,
Like thee, when love discloses
Thy heart of fire?
The wild swan unreturning,
The eagle alone with the sun,
The long-winged storm-gulls burning
Seaward when day is done,
Are like thee, young Desire.

Francis Barton Gummere

JOHN BRIGHT

I

FEW men of hero-mould
The Quaker counts amid his ranks to-day;
But, in the troublous times of old,
Before commodity's loud gold
Drowned with its clank the clash of steel,
The Quaker held no devious way;
For him to see was but to feel,
To feel was but to say.

II

All hail those men of yore!
Amid innumerable disasters true
To that brave standard which they bore;
Whether amid the maddened roar
Of priest-led mobs, or scourged and flung
To die in gaols, or where the few
Sat waiting for the cloven tongue,
But one straight path they knew.

III

Yet peace breeds doubtful virtues. When the flame
Of persecution flickered, fell, expired,
So dimmed the old lustre; no hot shame
The wavering conscience fired.
So, when wild storms are past, and winds grow tame,
And the foiled tempest holds his hand,
The vessels cast safe anchor near the strand;
And sweet it seems a gentle sea to ride,
While lapping waters lave
The weary, battered side: —
"Ah, linger thus," the shipmen cry, "near land,
Nor tempt again the buffets of the wave!"
They will not heed the voice
That calls from far and chides their choice:
He must not dally with the shore
Who thinks on noble gain,
But bend him stoutly to the oar,
And seek the midmost main,
And wrest their treasure from the clasp of wave and hurricane.

IV

Ho! pilot of the roaring seas!
No summer sailor thou;

It was no idle breeze
That set those manly lines upon thy brow;
For thou hast done what all to do are fain,
Yet few, ah, few attain, —
Hast never struck thy sail
And fled before the gale
Till it had spent its force, —
But sawest clear upon the chart of life
Thy straight-drawn track; and though the storm blew loud,
And elemental strife
In one mad whirl joined sea and cloud,
Thou hast but lashed thy helm and held thy course.
And for the manly heart and manly deed
Thy country loves thee, — gives
Honor unstinted as thy meed;
And they that still can hold
The Quaker name rejoice that one man lives
Who fills the measure of their hero-mould.

V

At glimpse of wrong, thy voice that knows not fear,
As sword from scabbard still hath leapt, and fills
With noblest echoes these wide halls of time.
We too, when tempests shook our western clime,
And all the air was rife with bodings grave,
Have felt new hope to hear
That voice of manly cheer,
And mark the signal of a friendly hand
From yon far strand
Where thy bluff England dashes back the wave.

VI

Brief be our word, yet strong.
So we this greeting send,
Stout English heart, across the severing sea,
Whose chainless waters blend
The breezes of two nations that are free;
Free, free for evermore!
And shore shall call to shore
In sister freedom till the end of time;
And still the thunder chime
Of that vast sea shall chorus the same song.
Ay, he who bends his ear
To those great tones, shall hear
Exultant voices, swelling high, proclaim
That thou, undaunted heart,
Hast played a hero's part,
Joining with freedom's deathless song thy deathless name.

Henry Cuyler Bunner

THE WAY TO ARCADY

Oh, what 's the way to Arcady,
To Arcady, to Arcady;
Oh, what 's the way to Arcady,
Where all the leaves are merry?

Oh, what 's the way to Arcady?
The spring is rustling in the tree, —
The tree the wind is blowing through, —
It sets the blossoms flickering white.
I knew not skies could burn so blue
Nor any breezes blow so light.
They blow an old-time way for me,
Across the world to Arcady.

Oh, what 's the way to Arcady?
Sir Poet, with the rusty coat,
Quit mocking of the song-bird's note.
How have you heart for any tune,
You with the wayworn russet shoon?
Your scrip, a-swinging by your side,
Gapes with a gaunt mouth hungry-wide.
I 'll brim it well with pieces red,
If you will tell the way to tread.

Oh, I am bound for Arcady,
And if you but keep pace with me
You tread the way to Arcady.

And where away lies Arcady,
And how long yet may the journey be?

Ah, that (quoth he) *I do not know:*
Across the clover and the snow —
Across the frost, across the flowers —
Through summer seconds and winter hours,
I 've trod the way my whole life long,
And know not now where it may be;
My guide is but the stir to song,
That tells me I cannot go wrong,
Or clear or dark the pathway be
Upon the road to Arcady.

But how shall I do who cannot sing?
  I was wont to sing, once on a time, —
There is never an echo now to ring
  Remembrance back to the trick of rhyme.

'T is strange you cannot sing (quoth he), —
The folk all sing in Arcady.

But how may he find Arcady
Who hath nor youth nor melody?

What, know you not, old man (quoth he), —
  Your hair is white, your face is wise, —
  That Love must kiss that Mortal's eyes
Who hopes to see fair Arcady?
No gold can buy you entrance there;
But beggared Love may go all bare —
No wisdom won with weariness;
But Love goes in with Folly's dress —
No fame that wit could ever win;
But only Love may lead Love in
  To Arcady, to Arcady.

Ah, woe is me, through all my days
  Wisdom and wealth I both have got,
And fame and name, and great men's praise;
  But Love, ah Love! I have it not.
There was a time, when life was new —
  But far away, and half forgot —
I only know her eyes were blue;
  But Love — I fear I knew it not.
We did not wed, for lack of gold,
And she is dead, and I am old.
All things have come since then to me,
Save Love, ah Love! and Arcady.

Ah, then I fear we part (quoth he), —
My way 's for Love and Arcady.

But you, you fare alone, like me;
  The gray is likewise in your hair.
  What love have you to lead you there,
To Arcady, to Arcady?

Ah, no, not lonely do I fare;
  My true companion 's Memory.
With Love he fills the Spring-time air;
  With Love he clothes the Winter tree.
Oh, past this poor horizon's bound
  My song goes straight to one who stands, —
Her face all gladdening at the sound, —
  To lead me to the Spring-green lands,
To wander with enlacing hands.
The songs within my breast that stir
Are all of her, are all of her.
My maid is dead long years (quoth he), —
She waits for me in Arcady.

Oh, yon 's the way to Arcady,
  To Arcady, to Arcady;
Oh, yon 's the way to Arcady,
  Where all the leaves are merry.

SHE WAS A BEAUTY

SHE was a beauty in the days
  When Madison was President,
And quite coquettish in her ways, —
  On conquests of the heart intent.

  Grandpapa, on his right knee bent,
Wooed her in stiff, old-fashioned phrase, —
She was a beauty in the days
  When Madison was President.

  And when your roses where hers went
Shall go, my Rose, who date from Hayes,
  I hope you 'll wear her sweet content
Of whom tradition lightly says:
She was a beauty in the days
  When Madison was President.

A PITCHER OF MIGNONETTE

A PITCHER of mignonette
  In a tenement's highest casement, —
Queer sort of flower-pot — yet
That pitcher of mignonette
Is a garden in heaven set,
  To the little sick child in the basement —
The pitcher of mignonette,
  In the tenement's highest casement.

DEAF

As to a bird's song she were listening,
Her beautiful head is ever sidewise bent;
Her questioning eyes lift up their depths intent —
She, who will never hear the wild-birds sing.
My words within her ears' cold chambers ring
Faint, with the city's murmurous sub-tones blent;

Though with such sounds as suppliants may have sent
To high-throned goddesses, my speech takes wing.
Not for the side-poised head's appealing grace
I gaze, nor hair where fire in shadow lies —
For her this world's unhallowed noises base
Melt into silence; not our groans, our cries,
Our curses, reach that high-removëd place
Where dwells her spirit, innocently wise.

LES MORTS VONT VITE

Les morts vont vite! Ay, for a little space
We miss and mourn them fallen from their place;
To take our portion in their rest are fain;
But by-and-by, having wept, press on again,
Perchance to win their laurels in the race.

What man would find the old in the new love's face?
Seek on the fresher lips the old kisses' trace?
For withered roses newer blooms disdain?
Les morts vont vite!

But when disease brings thee in piteous case,
Thou shalt thy dead recall, and thy ill grace
To them for whom remembrance plead in vain.
Then, shuddering, think, while thy bed-fellow Pain
Clasps thee with arms that cling like Death's embrace:
Les morts vont vite!

THE APPEAL TO HAROLD

Haro! Haro!
Judge now betwixt this woman and me,
Haro!
She leaves me bond, who found me free.
Of love and hope she hath drained me dry —
Yea, barren as a drought-struck sky;
She hath not left me tears for weeping,
Nor will my eyelids close in sleeping.
I have gathered all my life's-blood up —
Haro!
She hath drunk and thrown aside the cup.

Shall she not give me back my days?
Haro!
I made them perfect for her praise.
There was no flower in all the brake
I found not fairer for her sake;
There was no sweet thought I did not fashion
For aid and servant to my passion.
Labor and learning worthless were,
Haro!
Save that I made them gifts for her.

Shall she not give me back my nights?
Haro!
Give me sweet sleep for brief delights?
Lo, in the night's wan mid I lie,
And ghosts of hours that are dead go by, —
Hours of a love that died unshriven;
Of a love in change for my manhood given.
She caressed and slew my soul's white truth,
Haro!
Shall she not give me back my youth?

Haro! Haro!
Tell thou me not of a greater judge,
Haro!
It is He who hath my sin in grudge.
Yea, from God I appeal to thee;
God hath not part or place for me.
Thou who hast sinned, judge thou my sinning:
I have staked my life for a woman's winning;
She hath stripped me of all save remembering —
Haro!
Right thou me, right thou me, Harold the King!

ON READING A POET'S FIRST BOOK

This is a breath of summer wind
That comes — we know not how — that goes
As softly, — leaving us behind,
Pleased with a smell of vine and rose.

Poet, shall this be all thy word?
  Blow on us with a bolder breeze,
Until we rise, as having heard
  The sob, the song of far-off seas.

Blow in thy shell until thou draw,
  From inner whorls where still they sleep,
The notes unguessed of love and awe,
  And all thy song grow full and deep.

Feeble may be the scanty phrase, —
  Thy dream a dream tongue never spake,—
Yet shall thy note, through doubtful days,
  Swell stronger for Endeavor's sake.

As Jacob, wrestling through the night,
  Felt all his muscles strengthen fast
With wakening strength, and met the light
  Blessed and strong, though overcast.

FEMININE

SHE might have known it in the earlier Spring, —
  That all my heart with vague desire was stirred;
And, ere the Summer winds had taken wing,
  I told her; but she smiled and said no word.

The Autumn's eager hand his red gold grasped,
  And she was silent; till from skies grown drear
Fell soft one fine, first snow-flake, and she clasped
  My neck and cried, "Love, we have lost a year!"

J. B.

JUNE 7, 1880

THE Actor 's dead, and memory alone
Recalls the genial magic of his tone;
Marble nor canvas nor the printed page
Shall tell his genius to another age:
A memory, doomed to dwindle less and less,
His world-wide fame shrinks to this little-ness.
Yet if, a half a century from to-day,
A tender smile about our old lips play,
And if our grandchild query whence it came,
We 'll say: "A thought of Brougham." —
                    And that is Fame!

TO A JUNE BREEZE

BEING A LOVER'S MESSAGE TO HIS MISTRESS A-SUMMERING

WIND of the City Streets,
    Impatient to be free,
In this dull time of heats
    My love takes wings to flee:
Leave thou this idle Town
And hunt Her down.

  Wherever She may stay,
    By Sea or Mountain-side,
  Make thou thy airy Way,
    If there She bide;
  If sea-spray kiss Her face;
  Or hills find grace.

And, having found Her out,
    On Sands or under Trees,
Say that I wait in doubt,
    To melt with love, or freeze:
Nor yet hath Summer stirred,
But waits Her word.

  Say that, if She so please,
    These ways so dusty-dry,
  With their poor song-shunned Trees,
    Shall ring with Melody;
  And turn Love's Wilderness,
  If She say Yes.

But if my Fate fall so
    That She will naught of me,
Tell Her the Winter's snow
    Shall strip the greenest tree:
One only Frost I fear —
She makes my year.

  Go, then, sweet Wind, and pray
    That She remember
  She makes my March or May,
    June or December —

If Town grow green with trees,
If the new Blossoms freeze,
    Hers it is but to say, —
Pray Her that so She please —
    Pray Her remember!

THE CHAPERON

I TAKE my chaperon to the play —
She thinks she 's taking me.
And the gilded youth who owns the box,
A proud young man is he;
But how would his young heart be hurt
If he could only know
That not for his sweet sake I go
Nor yet to see the trifling show;
But to see my chaperon flirt.

Her eyes beneath her snowy hair
They sparkle young as mine;
There 's scarce a wrinkle in her hand
So delicate and fine.
And when my chaperon is seen,
They come from everywhere —
The dear old boys with silvery hair,
With old-time grace and old-time air,
To greet their old-time queen.

They bow as my young Midas here
Will never learn to bow
(The dancing-masters do not teach
That gracious reverence now);
With voices quavering just a bit,
They play their old parts through,
They talk of folk who used to woo,
Of hearts that broke in 'fifty-two —
Now none the worse for it.

And as those aged crickets chirp
I watch my chaperon's face,
And see the dear old features take
A new and tender grace;
And in her happy eyes I see
Her youth awakening bright,
With all its hope, desire, delight —
Ah, me! I wish that I were quite
As young — as young as she!

Wilbur Larremore

MADAM HICKORY

FIT theme for song, the sylvan maid
Who, if she knew not fauns or satyrs,
Had conjured oft in mossy shade
Visions of savage pale-face haters;
I trow she dined on pork and maize
In cabin, single-roomed and sooted,
Quite innocent of frills and stays,
Warm-hearted and bare-footed.

Her beauty surely brought her note, —
Its praises fed her soul like manna;
Gossip o'er furtive tales did gloat,
Sacred to Venus not Diana;
But when the valiant lover came
He crushed the scandal pests like vermin;
A terror hedged the hero's name
And she was white as ermine.

Thenceforth, a matron fair and fat,
She shared the doting warrior's station.
Thais with Alexander sat
And heard the plaudits of a nation;
Though envious souls with poisoned leer
Offset her new life by the other,
The hero held her yet more dear,
Stainless as Mary Mother.

Weary of fortune's smile and frown
She died without the White House portal,
But never wife wore richer crown,
A sacred troth and love immortal:
That love had made a queen of her
Whom haughty dames turned prudish backs on,
And History smiles but has no slur
For Mistress Andrew Jackson.

BLOSSOM TIME

SPRING came with tiny lances thrusting,
And earth was clad in peeping green;
In russet bark, the twigs incrusting,
Tenderest blossom-points were seen;
A robin courier proclaimed good cheer:
Summer will soon arrive, for I am here.

And now from cherry boughs in flower
The languid breeze arousing shakes,
With every honeyed breath, a shower
Of feather snow in drifting flakes;
And apple trees in bloom, like ricks of white,
Are veiled with smoky, amethystine light.

Ah, little soul, on thy first spring
  Unclosing merry, puzzled eyes,
Would that a father's thought could bring
  Prophetic counsel more than wise
To guide thee as a father's love would yearn, —
Thou hast so much to suffer and to learn!

I cannot live thy life for thee,
  My precepts would be dull and trite,
Barren as last year's leaves to me
  Beneath the apple blossoms white;
But in thy new horizon's vaster range
Our hearts close knit shall feel no chilling change.

Elisabeth (Cavazza) Pullen

HER SHADOW

STILL as I move thou movest,
Sister of mine, silent and left of the light.
  Why dost thou follow my way
  All through the hours of the day?
Where dost thou wait all the night
For the coming of light?

Is it then that thou lovest
Me, that forever must stand between thee and the sun?
  For whose sake thy life is made
  The dim, cold life of a shade —
A life that, until it be done,
Is unkissed of the sun.

Hearken, I whisper a word —
Thy lips too part, yet breathless are they, without fire;
  My hands stretch forth, and they clasp
  Roses and lilies —
Gray ghosts of bloom, and desire
Ashes for fire!

Look how my veil is stirred
By the beating beneath it — thine too moves, ah, poor shade!
  What of warm life canst thou know?
  When I die where wilt thou go —
Wilt thou be lonely, afraid?
I, too, a shade!

ALICIA'S BONNET

LAST night Alicia wore a Tuscan bonnet,
And many humming-birds were fastened on it.

I sat beside Alicia at the play;
  Her violet eyes with tender tears were wet
(The diamonds in her ears less bright than they)
  For pity of the woes of Juliet:
  Alicia's sighs a poet might have set
To delicate music in a dainty sonnet.

Last night Alicia wore a Tuscan bonnet,
And many humming-birds were fastened on it.

And yet to me her graceful ready words
  Sounded like tinkling silver bells that jangled,
For on her golden hair the humming-birds
  Were fixed as if within a sunbeam tangled,
  Their quick life quenched, their tiny bodies mangled,
Poor pretty birds upon Alicia's bonnet.

Last night Alicia wore a Tuscan bonnet,
And many humming-birds were fastened on it.

Caught in a net of delicate creamy crêpe,
  The dainty captives lay there dead together;
No dart of slender bill, no fragile shape
  Fluttering, no stir of any radiant feather:
  Alicia looked so calm, I wondered whether
She cared if birds were killed to trim her bonnet.

Last night Alicia wore a Tuscan bonnet,
And many humming-birds were fastened on it.

If rubies and if sapphires have a spirit,
  Though deep they lie below the weight of earth,

If emeralds can a conscious life inherit
  And beryls rise again to wingëd birth —
  Being changed to birds but not to lesser worth —
Alicia's golden head had such upon it.

Last night Alicia wore a Tuscan bonnet,
And many humming-birds were fastened on it.

Perhaps I dreamed — the house was very still —
  But on a sudden the Academy
Of Music seemed a forest of Brazil,
  Each pillar that supports the balcony
  Took form and stature of a tropic tree
With scarlet odorous flowers blooming on it.

Last night Alicia wore a Tuscan bonnet,
And many humming-birds were fastened on it.

A fragrance of delicious drowsy death
  Was in the air; the lithe lianas clung
About the mighty tree, and birds beneath
  More swift than arrows flashed and flew among
  The perfumed poisonous blossoms as they swung,
The heavy-honeyed flowers that hung upon it.

Last night Alicia wore a Tuscan bonnet,
And many humming-birds were fastened on it.

Like rain-drops when the sun breaks up the shower,
  Or weavers' shuttles carrying golden thread,
Or flying petals of a wind-blown flower,
  Myriads of humming-birds flew over-head —
  Purple and gold and green and blue and red —
Above each scarlet cup, or poised upon it.

Last night Alicia wore a Tuscan bonnet,
And many humming-birds were fastened on it.

What rapid flight! Each one a wingëd flame,
  Burning with brilliant joy of life and all
Delight of motion; to and fro they came,
  An endless dance, a fairy festival;
  Then suddenly I saw them pause and fall,
Slain only to adorn Alicia's bonnet.

Last night Alicia wore a Tuscan bonnet,
And many humming-birds were fastened on it.

My mind came back from the Brazilian land;
  For, as a snowflake falls to earth beneath,
Alicia's hand fell lightly on my hand;
  And yet I fancied that a stain of death,
  Like that which doomed the lady of Macbeth,
Was on her hand: could I perhaps have won it?

Last night Alicia wore a Tuscan bonnet,
And many humming-birds were fastened on it.

LOVE AND POVERTY

One sat within a hung and lighted room —
A little shape, with face between his wings,
And in the light made of all golden things
He seemed a warm and living rose abloom;
And one without sobbed in the night and gloom,
And all about him was a pilgrim's weed,
His little hands and cold he held for meed
Of his long waiting, sad as by a tomb:
He entered at the door, the other flew
Out at the casement — and with sudden day
The lamps burned faint, and he who came most new
Was fair, and he who went was wan and gray.
"For I am Love who came," and "Be content,"
Sang this one, "It was Poverty who went!"

DERELICT

She wanders up and down the main
  Without a master, nowhere bound;
  The currents turn her round and round,
Her track is like a tangled skein;

And never helmsman by his chart
So strange a way as hers may steer
To enter port or to depart
For any harbor far or near.

The waters clamor at her sides,
The winds cry through her cordage torn,
The last sail hangs, to tatters worn;
Upon the waves the vessel rides
This way or that, as winds may shift,
In ghastly dance when airs blow balm,
Or held in a lethargic calm,
Or fury-hunted, wild, adrift.

When south winds blow, does she recall
Spices and golden fruits in store?
Or north winds — nets off Labrador
And icebergs' iridescent wall?
Or east — the isles of Indian seas?
Or west — new ports and sails unfurled?
Her voyages all around the world
To mock her with old memories?

For her no light-house sheds a ray
Of crimson warning from its tower;
No watchers wait in hope the hour
To greet her coming up the bay;
No trumpet speaks her, hearty, hoarse —
Or if a captain hail at first,
He sees her for a thing accursed,
And turns his own ship from her course.

Alone, in desperate liberty
She forges on; and how she fares
No man alive inquires, or cares
Though she were sunk beneath the sea.
Her helm obeys no firm control,
She drifts — a prey for storms to take,
For sands to clutch, for rocks to break —
A ship condemned, like a lost soul.

THE SEA-WEED

The flying sea-bird mocked the floating dulse:
"Poor wandering water-weed, where dost thou go,
Astray upon the ocean's restless pulse?"
It said: "I do not know.

"At a cliff's foot I clung and was content,
Swayed to and fro by warm and shallow waves;
Along the coast the storm-wind raging went,
And tore me from my caves.

"I am the bitter herbage of that plain
Where no flocks pasture, and no man shall have
Homestead, nor any tenure there may gain
But only for a grave.

"A worthless weed, a drifting, broken weed,
What can I do in all this boundless sea?
No creature of the universe has need
Or any thought of me."

Hither and yonder, as the winds might blow,
The sea-weed floated. Then a refluent tide
Swept it along to meet a galleon's prow —
"Land ho!" Columbus cried.

Daniel Lewis Dawson

THE SEEKER IN THE MARSHES

Thanksgiving to the gods!
Shaken and shivering in the autumn rains,
With clay feet clinging to the weary sods,
I wait below the clouds, amid the plains,
As though I stood in some remote, strange clime,
Waiting to kneel upon the tomb of time.
The harvest swaths are gathered in the garth,
The aftermath is floating in the fields,
The house-carl bides beside the roaring hearth,
And clustered cattle batten in the shields.
Thank ye the gods, O dwellers in the land,
For home and hearth and ever-giving hand.
Stretch hands to pray and feed and sleep and die,

And then be gathered to your kindred gods,
Low in dank barrows ever more to lie,
So long as autumn over wood-ways plods,
Forgetting the green earth as ye forgot
Its glory in the day when it was born
To you, on some fair tide in grove and grot,
As though new-made upon a glimmering morn.

And it shall so be meted unto you
As ye did mete when all things were to do.
The wild rains cling around me in the night
Closer than woman in the sunny days,
And through these shaken veins a weird delight
Of loneliness and storm and sodden ways
And desolation, made most populous,
Builds up the roof-trees of the gloomy house
Of grief to hide and help my lonely path,
A sateless seeker for the aftermath.

Thanksgiving to the gods!
No hidden grapes are leaning to the sods,
No purple apple glances through green leaves,
Nor any fruit or flower is in the rains,
Nor any corn to garner in long sheaves,
And hard the toil is on these scanty plains.
Howbeit I thank the ever-giving ones,
Who dwell in high Olympus near the stars,
They have not walked in ever-burning suns,
Nor has the hard earth hurt their feet with scars.
Never the soft rains beat them, nor the snow,
Nor the sharp winds that we marsh-stalkers know.
In the sad halls of heaven they sleep the sleep,
Yea, and no morn breaks through their slumber deep.

These things they cast me forth at even-tide to bear
With curving sickle over sod and sand;
And no wild tempest drowns me to despair,
No terrors fear me in a barren land.
Perchance somewhere, across the hollow hill,
Or in the thickets in these dreary meads,
Great grapes, uncut, are on the limp vine still,
And waving corn still wears its summer weeds,
Unseen, ungathered in the earlier tide,
When larger summer o'er the earth did glide.
Who knows? Belike from this same sterile path
My harvest hand, heaped with an aftermath,
Shall cast the garner forth before their feet,
Shapely and shaven clean and very sweet.

Thanksgiving to the gods!
Wet with the falling rain,
My face and sides are beaten as with rods,
And soft and sodden is the endless plain —
How long — how long do I endure in vain?

Lewis Frank Tooker

THE LAST FIGHT

That night I think that no one slept;
No bells were struck, no whistle blew,
And when the watch was changed I crept
From man to man of all the crew
With whispered orders. Though we swept
Through roaring seas, we hushed the clock,
And muffled every clanking block.

So when one fool, unheeding, cried
Some petty order, straight I ran,
And threw him sprawling o'er the side.
All life is but a narrow span:
It little matters that one bide
A moment longer here, for all
Fare the same road, whate'er befall.

But vain my care; for when the day
Broke gray and wet, we saw the foe
But half a stormy league away.
By noon we saw his black bows throw
Five fathoms high a wall of spray:
A little more, we heard the drum,
And knew that our last hour had come.

All day our crew had lined the side
With grim, set faces, muttering;
And once a boy (the first that died)
One of our wild songs tried to sing:
But when their first shot missed us wide,
A dozen sprang above our rail,
Shook fists, and roared a cursing hail.

Thereon, all hot for war, they bound
Their heads with cool, wet bands, and drew
Their belts close, and their keen blades ground;
Then, at the next gun's puff of blue,
We set the grog-cup on its round,
And pledged for life or pledged for death
Our last sigh of expiring breath.

Laughing, our brown young singer fell
As their next shot crashed through our rail;
Then 'twixt us flashed the fire of hell,
That shattered spar and riddled sail.
What ill we wrought we could not tell;
But blood-red all their scuppers dripped
When their black hull to starboard dipped.

Nine times I saw our helmsman fall,
And nine times sent new men, who took
The whirling wheel as at death's call;
But when I saw the last one look
From sky to deck, then, reeling, crawl
Under the shattered rail to die,
I knew where I should surely lie.

I could not send more men to stand
And turn in idleness the wheel
Until they took death's beckoning hand,
While others, meeting steel with steel,
Flamed out their lives — an eager band,
Cheers on their lips, and in their eyes
The goal-rapt look of high emprise.

So to the wheel I went. Like bees
I heard the shot go darting by;
There came a trembling in my knees,
And black spots whirled about the sky.
I thought of things beyond the seas —
The little town where I was born,
And swallows twittering in the morn.

A wounded creature drew him where
I grasped the wheel, and begged to steer.
It mattered not how he might fare
The little time he had for fear;
So if I left this to his care
He too might serve us yet, he said.
He died there while I shook my head.

I would not fall so like a dog,
My helpless back turned to the foe;
So when his great hulk, like a log,
Came surging past our quarter, lo!
With helm hard down, straight through the fog
Of battle smoke, and luffing wide,
I sent our sharp bow through his side.

The willing waves came rushing in
The ragged entrance that we gave;
Like snakes I heard their green coils spin
Up, up, around our floating grave;
But dauntless still, amid a din
Of clashing steel and battle-shout,
We rushed to drive their boarders out.

Around me in a closing ring
My grim-faced foemen darkly drew;
Then, sweeter than the lark in spring,
Loud rang our blades; the red sparks flew.
Twice, thrice, I felt the sudden sting
Of some keen stroke; then, swinging fair,
My own clave more than empty air.

The fight went raging past me when
My good blade cleared a silent place;
Then in a ring of fallen men
I paused to breathe a little space.
Elsewhere the deck roared like a glen
When mountain torrents meet; the fray
A moment then seemed far away.

The barren sea swept to the sky;
The empty sky dipped to the sea;
Such utter waste could scarcely lie
Beyond death's starved periphery.
Only one living thing went by:
Far overhead an ominous bird
Rode down the gale with wings unstirred.

Windward I saw the billows swing
Dark crests to beckon others on
To see our end; then, hurrying
To reach us ere we should be gone,
They came, like tigers mad to fling
Their jostling bodies on our ships,
And snarl at us with foaming lips.

There was no time to spare: a wave
 E'en then broke growling at my feet;
One last look to the sky I gave,
 Then sprang my eager foes to meet.
Loud rang the fray above our grave —
 I felt the vessel downward reel
 As my last thrust met thrusting steel.

I heard a roaring in my ears;
 A green wall pressed against my eyes;
Down, down I passed; the vanished years
 I saw in mimicry arise.
Yet even then I felt no fears,
 And with my last expiring breath
 My past rose up and mocked at death.

SLEEP

In a tangled, scented hollow,
On a bed of crimson roses,
Stilly now the wind reposes;
Hardly can the breezes borrow
Breath to stir the night-swept river.
Motionless the water-sedges,
And within the dusky hedges
Sounds no leaf's impatient shiver.
Sleep has come, that rare rest-giver.

Light and song have flown away
With the sun and twilight swallow;
Scarcely will the unknown morrow
Bring again so sweet a day.
Song was born of Joy and Thought;
Light, of Love and her caress.
Nothing 's left me but a tress;
Death and Sleep the rest have wrought —
Death and Sleep, who came unsought.

HIS QUEST

What seek'st thou at this madman's pace?
"I seek my love's new dwelling place:
Her house is dark, her doors are wide,
There bat and owl and beetle bide,
And there, breast-high, the rank weeds grow,
And drowsy poppies nod and blow.
So mount I swift to ride me through
The world to find my love anew.
I have no token of the way;
I haste by night, I press by day.
Through busy cities I am borne,
On lonely heights I watch the morn
Climb up the east, and see the light
Of waning moon gleam thwart my flight.
Sometimes a light before me flees;
I follow it, till stormy seas
Break wide before, then all is dark.
Sometimes on plains, wide, still, and stark,
I hear a voice; I seek the sound,
And ride into a hush profound.
To find her dwelling I will ride
Worlds through and through, whate'er betide."

To find her dwelling rode he forth,
In vain rode south, in vain rode north;
In vain in mountain, plain, and mart
He searched, but never searched his heart.

Armistead Churchill Gordon

KREE

 My boy Kree?
He played wid you when you was a chile?
 You an' he
Growed up tergether? Wait! Lemme see!
Closer! so I can look in yer face! —
 Mars' George's smile!
 Lord love you, Marster!
Dar 'neaf dat cypress is whar Kree lays.

 Sunburnt an' grown!
Mars' George, I shudden ha' knowed you, son,
'Count o' de beard dat yer face has on,
But for dat ole-time smile o' your'n —
 "An' Kree?" you say.
 Had n't you heerd, Marster,
He 'ceasded de year dat you went away?

 Kree an' you!
How de ole times comes back onst mo' —
Moonlight fishin's, an' hyars in de sno';
Squirrels an' jaybirds up overhead,
In de oak-trees dat de sun shined through! —
 Look at me, Marster!
Here is me livin'; an' Kree, he 's dead.

'Pears ter me strange
Now, when I thinks on 'em, dose ole years:
Mars' George, sometimes de b'ilin' tears
Fills up my eyes,
'Count o' de mizery now, an' de change —
De sun dims, Marster,
Ter an ole man, when his one boy dies.

Did you say "How?"
Out in de dug-out, one moonshine night,
Fishin' wid your baby brother — he
Wid de curls o' yaller, like streaks o' light,
An' de dancin' big blue eyes. Dead, now —
Kree died for him;
An' yearnin' for Kree,
De Lord tuk him, Marster:
De green grass kivers 'em bofe f'om sight.

Heerd o' de tale?
Did n' know Kree was de one dat drowned
Sav'n' Mars' Charley? Well, 't were he.
De boy waxed weaker, his face mo' pale,
Arter de corpse o' poor Kree were found.
Two months later he went, you see:
God bless you, Marster!
Nine years has rolled over bofe onder ground.

Worn out an' gray,
Here I sets waitin', Mars' George, alone.
All on 'em's gone —
Marster an' Mistis, an' Charley an' he.
You an' me only is lef'. Some day,
When you 's gone back ter yer ship on de sea,
I 'll hear him say,
Jes' as he used ter, a-fishin', ter me:
"Daddy, come over!" An' passin' away,
Dat side de river, again I 'll be
Wid my boy Kree.

ROSES OF MEMORY

A ROSE's crimson stain,
A rose's stainless white,
Fitly become the immortal slain
Who fell in the great fight.
When Armistead died amid his foes,
Girt by the rebel cheer,
God plucked a soul like a white rose
In June time o' the year.

The blood in Pickett's heart
Was of a ruddier hue
Than the reddest bloom whose petals part
To welcome heaven's dew.
I think the fairest flowers that blow
Should greet the life-stream shed
In that historic long ago
By this historic dead.

The immemorial years
Such valor never knew
As poured a flood of crimson blood
At Gettysburg with you.
Living and dead, in faith the same,
I see you on that height,
Crowned with the rosy wreath of fame
Won in the fatal fight.

Not these had made afraid
King Arthur's mystic sword —
Not Bayard's most chivalric blade,
Nor Gideon's, for the Lord.
Yours was the strain of high emprise,
Yours the unfaltering faith, —
The honor lofty as the skies,
The duty strong as death.

When Douglas flung the heart
Of Bruce amid his foes,
And said: "He leads. We do not part:
I follow where he goes,"
No mightier impulse stirred his soul
Than that which up yon height
Moved you with Pickett toward the goal
Of freedom in that fight.

The fair goal was not won,
The famous fight was lost;
But never shone the all-seeing sun
On more heroic host.
Your deeds of mighty prowess shame
All deeds of derring-do
With which Time's bloody pages flame.
— Hail and farewell to you!

Unto the dead farewell!
They are hid in the dark and cold;
And the broken shaft and the roses tell
What is left of the tale untold.
They are deaf to the martial music's call
Till a judgment dawn shall break,
When the trumpet of Truth shall proclaim to all:
"They perished for my sake!"

Let them be quiet here
  Where birds and blossoms be; —
And hail to you, who bring the tear
  And the rose of memory
    To water and deck each lowly grave
      Of those who in God's sight
    With loyal hearts their hearts' blood gave
      For the eternal right!

Alike for low and high
  The roses white and red:
For valor and honor cannot die,
  And they were of these dead.
    The private in his jacket of gray
      And the general with his star
    The Lord God knighted alike that day,
      In the red front of War.

Edward Sanford Martin

A GIRL OF POMPEII

A PUBLIC haunt they found her in:
  She lay asleep, a lovely child;
  The only thing left undefiled
Where all things else bore taint of sin.

Her charming contours fixed in clay
  The universal law suspend,
  And turn Time's chariot back, and blend
A thousand years with yesterday.

A sinless touch, austere yet warm,
  Around her girlish figure pressed,
  Caught the sweet imprint of her breast,
And held her, surely clasped, from harm.

Truer than work of sculptor's art
  Comes this dear maid of long ago,
  Sheltered from woeful chance, to show
A spirit's lovely counterpart,

And bid mistrustful men be sure
  That form shall fate of flesh escape,
  And, quit of earth's corruptions, shape
Itself, imperishably pure.

A LITTLE BROTHER OF THE RICH

To put new shingles on old roofs;
  To give old women wadded skirts;
To treat premonitory coughs
  With seasonable flannel shirts;
To soothe the stings of poverty
  And keep the jackal from the door, —
These are the works that occupy
  The Little Sister of the Poor.

She carries, everywhere she goes,
  Kind words and chickens, jams and coals;
Poultices for corporeal woes,
  And sympathy for downcast souls:
Her currant jelly, her quinine,
  The lips of fever move to bless;
She makes the humble sick-room shine
  With unaccustomed tidiness.

A heart of hers the instant twin
  And vivid counterpart is mine;
I also serve my fellow-men,
  Though in a somewhat different line.
The Poor, and their concerns, she has
  Monopolized, because of which
It falls to me to labor as
  A Little Brother of the Rich.

For their sake at no sacrifice
  Does my devoted spirit quail;
I give their horses exercise;
  As ballast on their yachts I sail.
Upon their tallyhos I ride
  And brave the chances of a storm;
I even use my own inside
  To keep their wines and victuals warm.

Those whom we strive to benefit
  Dear to our hearts soon grow to be;
I love my Rich, and I admit
  That they are very good to me.
Succor the Poor, my sisters, — I,
  While heaven shall still vouchsafe me health,
Will strive to share and mollify
  The trials of abounding wealth.

EGOTISM

WITHOUT him still this whirling earth
  Might spin its course around the sun,
And death still dog the heels of birth,
  And life be lived, and duty done.

Without him let the rapt earth dree
  What doom its twin rotations earn;
Whither or whence, are naught to me,
  Save as his being they concern.

Comets may crash, or inner fire
  Burn out and leave an arid crust,
Or earth may lose Cohesion's tire,
  And melt to planetary dust.

It 's naught to me if he 's not here,
  I 'll not lament, nor even sigh;
I shall not feel the jar, nor fear,
  For I am he, and he is I.

Lizette Woodworth Reese

LYDIA

Break forth, break forth, O Sudbury town,
  And bid your yards be gay
Up all your gusty streets and down,
  For Lydia comes to-day!

I hear it on the wharves below;
  And if I buy or sell,
The good folk as they churchward go
  Have only this to tell.

My mother, just for love of her,
  Unlocks her carvëd drawers;
And sprigs of withered lavender
  Drop down upon the floors.

For Lydia's bed must have the sheet
  Spun out of linen sheer,
And Lydia's room be passing sweet
  With odors of last year.

The violet flags are out once more
  In lanes salt with the sea;
The thorn-bush at Saint Martin's door
  Grows white for such as she.

So, Sudbury, bid your gardens blow,
  For Lydia comes to-day;
Of all the words that I do know,
  I have but this to say.

ANNE

SUDBURY MEETING-HOUSE, 1653

Her eyes be like the violets,
  Ablow in Sudbury lane;
When she doth smile, her face is sweet
  As blossoms after rain;
With grief I think of my gray hairs,
  And wish me young again.

In comes she through the dark old door
  Upon this Sabbath day;
And she doth bring the tender wind
  That sings in bush and tree;
And hints of all the apple boughs
  That kissed her by the way.

Our parson stands up straight and tall,
  For our dear souls to pray,
And of the place where sinners go
  Some grewsome things doth say:
Now, she is highest Heaven to me;
  So Hell is far away.

Most stiff and still the good folk sit
  To hear the sermon through;
But if our God be such a God,
  And if these things be true,
Why did He make her then so fair,
  And both her eyes so blue?

A flickering light, the sun creeps in,
  And finds her sitting there;
And touches soft her lilac gown,
  And soft her yellow hair;
I look across to that old pew,
  And have both praise and prayer.

Oh, violets in Sudbury lane,
  Amid the grasses green,
This maid who stirs ye with her feet
  Is far more fair, I ween!
I wonder how my forty years
  Look by her sweet sixteen!

DAFFODILS

Fathered by March, the daffodils are
  here.
First, all the air grew keen with yesterday,

And once a thrush from out some hollow gray
On a field's edge, where whitening stalks made cheer,
Fluted the last unto the budding year;
Now that the wind lets loose from orchard spray
Plum bloom and peach bloom down the dripping way,
Their punctual gold through the wet blades they rear.
Oh, fleet and sweet! A light to all that pass
Below, in the cramped yard, close to the street,
Long-stemmed ones flame behind the palings bare,
The whole of April in a tuft of grass.
Scarce here, soon will it be — oh, sweet and fleet! —
Gone like a snatch of song upon the stair.

TEARS

When I consider Life and its few years —
A wisp of fog betwixt us and the sun;
A call to battle, and the battle done
Ere the last echo dies within our ears;
A rose choked in the grass; an hour of fears;
The gusts that past a darkening shore do beat;
The burst of music down an unlistening street —
I wonder at the idleness of tears.
Ye old, old dead, and ye of yesternight,
Chieftains, and bards, and keepers of the sheep,
By every cup of sorrow that you had,
Loose me from tears, and make me see aright
How each hath back what once he stayed to weep;
Homer his sight, David his little lad!

IMMORTALITY

Battles nor songs can from oblivion save,
But Fame upon a white deed loves to build:
From out that cup of water Sidney gave,
Not one drop has been spilled.

THOMAS À KEMPIS

Brother of mine, good monk with cowlëd head,
Walled from that world which thou hast long since fled,
And pacing thy green close beyond the sea,
I send my heart to thee.

Down gust-sweet walks, bordered by lavender,
While eastward, westward, the mad swallows whir,
All afternoon poring thy missal fair,
Serene thou pacest there.

Mixed with the words and fitting like a tune,
Thou hearest distantly the voice of June, —
The little, gossipping noises in the grass,
The bees that come and pass.

Fades the long day; the pool behind the hedge
Burns like a rose within the windy sedge;
The lilies ghostlier grow in the dim air;
The convent windows flare.

Yet still thou lingerest; from pastures steep,
Past the barred gate the shepherd drives his sheep;
A nightingale breaks forth, and for a space
Makes sweeter the sweet place.

Then the gray monks by hooded twos and threes
Move chapelward beneath the flaming trees;
Closing thy book, back by the alleys fair
Thou followest to prayer.

Born to these brawling days, this work-sick age,
Oft long I for thy simpler heritage;
A thought of thee is like a breath of bloom
Blown through a noisy room.

For thou art quick, not dead. I picture thee
Forever in that close beyond the sea;
And find, despite this weather's headlong stir,
Peace and a comforter.

TELLING THE BEES

Bathsheba came out to the sun,
Out to our wallëd cherry-trees;
The tears adown her cheek did run,
Bathsheba standing in the sun,
Telling the bees.

My mother had that moment died;
Unknowing, sped I to the trees,
And plucked Bathsheba's hand aside;
Then caught the name that there she cried
Telling the bees.

Her look I never can forget,
I that held sobbing to her knees;
The cherry-boughs above us met;
I think I see Bathsheba yet
Telling the bees.

IN TIME OF GRIEF

Dark, thinned, beside the wall of stone,
The box dripped in the air;
Its odor through my house was blown
Into the chamber there.

Remote and yet distinct the scent,
The sole thing of the kind,
As though one spoke a word half meant
That left a sting behind.

I knew not Grief would go from me,
And naught of it be plain,
Except how keen the box can be
After a fall of rain.

TO A TOWN POET

Snatch the departing mood;
Make yours its emptying reed, and pipe us still
Faith in the time, faith in our common blood,
Faith in the least of good:
Song cannot fail if these its spirits fill!

What if your heritage be
The huddled trees along the smoky ways;
At a street's end the stretch of lilac sea;
The vender, swart but free,
Crying his yellow wares across the haze?

Your verse awaits you there;
For Love is Love though Latin swords be rust,
The keen Greek driven from gossipping mall and square;
And Care is still but Care
Though Homer and his seven towns are dust.

Thus Beauty lasts, and, lo!
Now Proserpine is barred from Enna's hills,
The flower she plucked yet makes an April show,
Sets some town still a-glow,
And yours the Vision of the Daffodils.

The Old-World folk knew not
More surge-like sounds than urban winters bring
Up from the wharves at dusk to every spot;
And no Sicilian plot
More fire than heaps our tulips in the spring.

Strait is the road of Song,
And they that be the last are oft the first;
Fret not for fame; the years are kind though long;
You, in the teasing throng,
May take all time with one shrewd lyric burst.

Be reverend and know
Ill shall not last, or waste the ploughëd land;
Or creeds sting timid souls; and naught at all,
Whatever else befall,
Can keep us from the hollow of God's hand.

Let trick of words be past;
Strict with the thought, unfearful of the form,
So shall you find the way and hold it fast,
The world hear, at the last,
The horns of morning sound above the storm.

TRUST

I am Thy grass, O Lord!
I grow up sweet and tall
But for a day, beneath Thy sword
To lie at evenfall.

Yet have I not enough
  In that brief day of mine?
The wind, the bees, the wholesome stuff
  The sun pours out like wine.

Behold, this is my crown, —
  Love will not let me be;
Love holds me here; Love cuts me down;
  And it is well with me.

Lord, Love, keep it but so;
  Thy purpose is full plain:
I die that after I may grow
  As tall, as sweet again.

A HOLIDAY

Along the pastoral ways I go,
To get the healing of the trees,
The ghostly news the hedges know;
To hive me honey like the bees,
Against the time of snow.

The common hawthorn that I see,
Beside the sunken wall astir,
Or any other blossoming tree,
Is each God's fair white gospeller,
His book upon the knee.

A gust-broken bough; a pilfered nest;
Rumors of orchard or of bin;
The thrifty things of east and west, —
The countryside becomes my Inn,
And I its happy guest.

KEATS

An English lad, who, reading in a book,
A ponderous, leathern thing set on his knee,
Saw the broad violet of the Egean Sea
Lap at his feet as it were village brook.
Wide was the east; the gusts of morning shook;
Immortal laughter beat along that shore;
Pan, crouching in the reeds, piped as of yore;
The gods came down and thundered from that book.
He lifted his sad eyes; his London street
Swarmed in the sun, and strove to make him heed;
Boys spun their tops, shouting and fair of cheek:
But, still, that violet lapping at his feet, —
An English lad had he sat down to read;
But he rose up and knew himself a Greek.

RESERVE

Keep back the one word more,
Nor give of your whole store;
For, it may be, in Art's sole hour of need,
Lacking that word, you shall be poor indeed.

William Hamilton Hayne

THE SOUTHERN SNOW-BIRD

I see a tiny fluttering form
Beneath the soft snow's soundless storm,
'Mid a strange noonlight palely shed
Through mocking cloud-rifts overhead.

All other birds are far from sight, —
They think the day has turned to night;
But he is cast in hardier mould,
This chirping courier of the cold.

He does not come from lands forlorn,
Where midnight takes the place of morn;
Nor did his dauntless heart, I know,
Beat first above Siberian snow;
And yet an arctic bird he seems;
Though nurtured near our southern streams,
The tip of his small tail may be
A snow-storm in epitome.

TO A CHEROKEE ROSE

Thy one white leaf is open to the sky,
  And o'er thy heart swift lights and shadows pass, —
The wooing winds seem loath to wander by,
  Jealous of sunshine and the summer grass.

Thy sylvan loveliness is pure and strong,
  For thou art bright and yet not overbold —

Like a young maid apart from fashion's
throng —
A virgin dowered with a heart of gold.

QUATRAINS

MOONLIGHT SONG OF THE MOCKING-BIRD

EACH golden note of music greets
The listening leaves, divinely stirred,
As if the vanished soul of Keats
Had found its new birth in a bird.

NIGHT MISTS

SOMETIMES, when Nature falls asleep,
Around her woods and streams
The mists of night serenely creep —
For they are Nature's dreams.

AN AUTUMN BREEZE

THIS gentle and half melancholy breeze
Is but a wandering Hamlet of the trees,
Who finds a tongue in every lingering leaf
To voice some subtlety of sylvan grief.

EXILES

HOPES grimly banished from the heart
Are the sad exiles that depart
To melancholy's rayless goal, —
A bleak Siberia of the soul.

A CYCLONE AT SEA

A THROAT of thunder, a tameless heart,
And a passion malign and free,
He is no sheik of the desert sand.
But an Arab of the sea!

He sprang from the womb of some wild
cloud,
And was born to smite and slay:
To soar like a million hawks set free,
And swoop on his ocean prey!

He has scourged the Sea till her mighty
breast
Responds to his heart's fierce beat,
And has torn brave souls from their bodies
frail
To fling them at Allah's feet.

Possessed by a demon's lust of life,
He revels o'er wrecks and graves,
And hurtles onward in curbless speed, —
Dark Bedouin of the waves.

"SLEEP AND HIS BROTHER DEATH"

JUST ere the darkness is withdrawn,
In seasons of cold or heat,
Close to the boundary line of Dawn
These mystical brothers meet.

They clasp their weird and shadowy
hands,
As they listen each to each,
But never a mortal understands
Their strange immortal speech.

THE YULE LOG

OUT of the mighty Yule log came
The crooning of the lithe wood-flame, —
A single bar of music fraught
With cheerful yet half pensive thought, —
A thought elusive: out of reach,
Yet trembling on the verge of speech.

George Edgar Montgomery

ENGLAND

I

THE voice of England is a trumpet tone
When that inviolate Mother wills it so:
Nations may rise and fall, and tyrants go
Upon their devious, darkened paths: alone
England preserves her people and her
throne,
Her ancient freedom, her perpetual
flow
Of broad and brightened life; time shall
not show
This mighty Nation pitiful and prone.

II

It is the Saxon soul that speaks in her,
The stanchest soul that earth has ever wrought
To guide humanity in faith and light.
The shivering slave has been her worshipper,
And with defiant courage she has taught
Red Tyranny to cringe before the Right.

TO A CHILD

I LOOK upon thy happy face —
Dear child with those undarkened eyes
Like glimpses of transparent skies —
And dream of things which have no place

In that small, golden head of thine;
Things that no ten-year-old has yet
Dared in his roguish wit to set
To thought, or word, or rhythmic line.

And it is better so, I think,
Better the child should be a child,
That he should grow as glad and wild
As flowers upon a river's brink.

Laugh, then, and romp, and kiss the sun,
And be as if this ancient earth
Were but the resting-place of mirth
Since time was born and joy begun.

Laugh, and I 'll be a child with thee,
Forgetful of the days which fly,
Forgetful of the nights which die,
And sipping sweetness like the bee.

For, oh ! remember, little sir,
Childhood is but a passing spring,
Loath to await the burgeoning
Of summer and its fiery stir. . . .

But no, my dreams will not be stilled;
I cannot turn the long years back,
And life for me has ploughed its track;
The man must be the man, as willed;

Not dreams, I warn thee, such as they,
Our languid-hearted poets make,
Nor such as many love to wake
From fable or the Grecian lay;

But dreams of an aspiring soul,
That yearns with all its human might
To steal the secrets of the night,
To reach some high millennial goal.

Here, at this hour, I view the sweep
Of a vast century to its close,
Sublime in its titanic throes,
And in its plummet ocean-deep —

A century thrilled from start to end
With fearless striving, fearless hope,
Whose larger mind and wider scope
In one eternal progress tend. . . .

Yet thine will be the loftier tread,
And thine will be the swifter pace;
When thou shalt be as I, the race
Will scorn the marvels of the dead.

Ah, thou shalt look so clear, so far,
That all I wonder at will seem
Like the first mistings of a dream
Which dawns into a perfect star.

A DEAD SOLDIER

HE sleeps at last — a hero of his race.
Dead ! — and the night lies softly on his face,
While the faint summer stars, like sentinels,
Hover above his lonely resting-place.

A soldier, yet less soldier than a man,
Who gave to justice what a soldier can, —
The courage of his arm, a patient heart,
And the fire-soul that flamed when wrong began.

Not Caesar, Alexander, Antonine,
No despot born of the old warrior line,
Napoleons of the sword, whose cruel hands
Caught at the throat of love upon its shrine, —

But one who worshipped in the sweeter years
Those rights that men have gained with blood and tears;
Who led his armies like a priest of men,
And fought his battles with anointed spears.

AT NIGHT

THE sun is sinking over hill and sea,
Its red light fires a spectral line of shore;
Night droops upon our half-world mistily
With sombre glory and ghost-haunted lore;
The stars show dim and pallid in the sky,
Vague, wraith-white glimmerings of volcanic spheres,
And a slim crescent of the moon appears
Like some young herald in the hours that die.

Soon we who watch the fading of a day,
Who feel the cool winds of the ocean blow
Upon our dusk fields in sweet, vagrant way,
Freshening earth's arid spaces with their glow,
Stand forth amid the infinite peace of night,
An infinite peace for high and holy souls
That strive to find their far, mysterious goals
Beyond the horizon of their eager sight.

At this sequestered hour when tender sleep
Holds out to listless lives its precious boon,
When men grow weary of the fruits they reap,
Grow weary of recurrent dawn and noon,
Peace dwells upon them for a little while,
Like dew and shade upon the growing grass,
And, mindless of uncounted hours that pass,
They woo a deep oblivion and they smile.

Yet I, whose nights are full of waking dreams,
Sleep not — but watch the furtive moments drift
Like sluggish waves, and watch the fire-bright gleam
Of vibrant planets rolling straight and swift
Along their orbit pathways, even as life
Moves in its earthward orbit to the grave,
Till I, an atom, doomed to weep and slave,
Feel my fast kinship with celestial strife.

For now I see the universe outspread
Within my vision, as with close-shut lids
One may read clear the history of the dead
And stand with Pharaohs by the Pyramids,
Or sit within some rare Athenian home;
Yes, as the words and deeds of men are brought
Into the widening circle of my thought,
The stars grow real to me like deathless Rome.

Ella Wheeler Wilcox

RECRIMINATION

I

SAID Life to Death: "Methinks, if I were you,
I would not carry such an awesome face
To terrify the helpless human race;
And if indeed those wondrous tales be true
Of happiness beyond, and if I knew
About the boasted blessings of that place,
I would not hide so miserly all trace
Of my vast knowledge, Death, if I were you:
But, like a glorious angel, I would lean
Above the pathway of each sorrowing soul,
Hope in my eyes, and comfort in my breath,
And strong conviction in my radiant mien,
The while I whispered of that beauteous goal.
This would I do if I were you, O Death."

II

Said Death to Life: "If I were you, my friend,
I would not lure confiding souls each day
With fair, false smiles to enter on a way
So filled with pain and trouble to the end;
I would not tempt those whom I should defend,
Nor stand unmoved and see them go astray;
Nor would I force unwilling souls to stay
Who longed for freedom, were I you, my friend:
But, like a tender mother, I would take

The weary world upon my sheltering breast,
And wipe away its tears, and soothe its strife;
I would fulfil my promises, and make
My children bless me as they sank to rest
Where now they curse — if I were you, O Life."

III

Life made no answer, and Death spoke again:
"I would not woo from God's sweet nothingness
A soul to being, if I could not bless
And crown it with all joy. If unto men
My face seems awesome, tell me, Life, why then
Do they pursue me, mad for my caress,
Believing in my silence lies redress
For your loud falsehoods?" (so Death spoke again).
"Oh, it is well for you I am not fair —
Well that I hide behind a voiceless tomb
The mighty secrets of that other place:
Else would you stand in impotent despair,
While unfledged souls straight from the mother's womb
Rushed to my arms and spat upon your face!"

Charles Lotin Hildreth

TO AN OBSCURE POET WHO LIVES ON MY HEARTH

Why shouldst thou cease thy plaintive song
When I draw near?
Has mankind done thee any wrong,
That thou shouldst fear?

To see thee scampering to thy den,
So wild and shy,
'T would seem thou know'st the ways of men
As well as I.

'T is true the palmy days are o'er
When all thy kind —
Poor minstrel folk — at every door
Might welcome find;

For song was certain password then
To every breast,
And current coin that bought from men
Food, fire, and rest;

And these are more discerning days,
More coldly just:
I doubt thy rustic virelays
Would earn a crust.

The age is shrill and choral-like;
For many sing,
And he who would be heard must strike
Life's loudest string.

And thou, poor minstrel of the field,
With slender tone,
Art type of many a singer sealed
To die unknown.

And many a heart that would have sung
Songs sweet to hear,
Could passion give itself a tongue
To catch the ear.

But, cricket, thou shouldst trust in me,
For thou and I
Are brothers in adversity, —
Both poor and shy.

And since the height of thy desire
Is but to live,
Thy little share of food and fire
I freely give.

And thou shalt sing of fields and hills
And forest streams,
Till thy rapt invocation stills
My troubled dreams.

IMPLORA PACE

I stood within the cypress gloom
Where old Ferrara's dead are laid,
And mused on many a sculptured tomb,
Moss-grown and mouldering in the shade.

And there was one the eye might pass,
And careless foot might tread upon
A crumbling tablet in the grass,
With weeds and wild vines overrun.

In the dim light I stooped to trace
The lines the time-worn marble bore,
Of reverent praise or prayer for grace —
"*Implora Pace!*" — nothing more.

Name, fame, and rank, if any were,
Had long since vanished from the stone,
Leaving the meek, pathetic prayer,
"Peace I implore!" and this alone.

AT THE MERMAID INN

AFTER THE FIRST PERFORMANCE OF "HAMLET"

At table yonder sits the man we seek,
Beside the ingle, where the crimson flare
Reveals him through the eddying tavern reek,
Reclining easeful in his leathern chair;
In russet doublet, bearded and benign,
He looks a worthy burgher at his wine.

Even so; but when thy veins ran fire to-night,
Thy hand crept knotted to thy sword-hilt there,
And through all moods of madness and delight
Thy soul was hurried headlong, unaware,
It seemed the genius or the scene should be
Some radiant shape, brow-bound with majesty.

And lo! a man unsingled from the crowd
By quick recognizance of reverent eyes,
A dim, inobvious presence, kindly-browed,
That sits apart, observant, thoughtful-wise,
Weaving — who knows? — what wondrous woof of song,
What other Hamlet, from the shifting throng.

A pale, plain-favored face, the smile whereof
Is beautiful; the eyes gray, changeful, bright,
Low-lidded now, and luminous as love;
Anon soul-searching, ominous as night,
Seer-like, inscrutable, revealing deeps
Wherein a mighty spirit wakes or sleeps.

Here, where my outstretched hand might touch his arm,
I gaze upon that mild and lofty mien,
With that deep awe and unexpressive charm
I feel in wide sea-solitudes serene;
Or on some immemorial mountain's crest —
Eternity unveiled and manifest.

For he hath wrought with nature and made known
The marvel and the majesty of life;
Translating from the pages of his own
The mighty heart of man, the stress and strife,
The pain, the passion, and the bitter leaven,
The cares that quell, the dreams that soar to heaven.

So, whatsoever time shall make or mar,
Or fate decree of benison or blame,
This poet-player, like a wondrous star,
Shall shed the solemn splendor of his fame,
Wide as the world, while beauty has a shrine,
While youth has hope, and love is yet divine.

Harrison Smith Morris

DESTINY

A. D. 1899

Our many years are made of clay and cloud,
And quick desire is but as morning dew;
And love and life, that linger and are proud,
Dissolve and are again the arching blue.

For who shall answer what the ages ask?
Or who undo a one-day-earlier bud?
We are but atoms in the larger task
Of law that seeks not to be understood.

Shall we then gather to our meagre mien
The purple of power, and sit above the seed,

While still abroad the acres of the green
  Invisible feet leave imprint of their speed?

We are but part; the whole within the part
  Trembles, as heaven steadied in a stream.
Not ours to question whence the leafage start,
  Or doubt the prescience of a people's dream.

For these are cradled in the dark of time,
  And move in larger order than we know;
The isolate act interpreted a crime,
  In perfect circle, shows the Mind below.

Forth from the hush of equatorial heat
  The wiser mother drove her sable kin —
Was it that through our vitiated wheat
  A lustier grain should swell the life, grown thin?

Was it that upward through a waste of blood
  The brutal tribe should struggle to a soul, —
That white and black, in interchange of good,
  Might grope through ages to a loftier whole?

Who knows, who knows? For while we mock with doubt
  The ceaseless loom thrids through its slow design;
The waning artifice is woven out,
  And simple manhood rears a nobler line.

Then wherefore clamor to your idols thus
  For bands to hold the Nation from its growth,
And wax in terror at the overplus
  Won from dishonor and imperial sloth?

Wherefore implore the Power that lifts our might
  To punish what His providence ordains;
To fix our star forever in its night;
  To hold us fettered in our ancient chains?

The Nation in God's garden swells to fruit,
  And He is glad, and blesses. Shall we then
Shrink inward to the dulness of the root,
  And vanish from the onward march of men?

Give up the lands we won in loyal war;
  Give up the gain and glory, rule, renown,
The orient commerce of the open door,
  The conquest, and the wide imperial crown?

Yea, were these all, 't were well to let them go;
  For idle gold is but an empty gain:
An empire, reared on ashes of its foe,
  Falls, as have fallen the island-walls of Spain.

Treasure is dust. They need it not who build
  On better things. Our gain is in the loss:
In love and tears, self victories fulfilled,
  In manhood bending to the bitter cross.

In burdens that make wise the bearer, wounds
  Taken in hate that sanctify the heart,
In sympathies and sorrows, and in sounds
  That up from all the open waters start;

In brotherhood that binds the broken ties
  And clasps the whole world closer into peace;
In East and West enwoven loverwise,
  Mated for happy arts and home's increase.

What though the sere leaf circle to the ground, —
  Its summer task is done, the bough is clean
For Spring's ascent; the lost is later found
  In some new recess of the risen green.

We are but Nature's menials. 'T is her might
  Sets our strange feet on Australasian sands,
Bids us to pluck the races from their night
  And build a State from out the brawling bands.

Serene, she sweeps aside the more or less,
  The man or people, if her end be sure;
Her brooding eyes, that ever bend to bless,
  Find guerdon for the dead that shall endure.

Truth marches on, though crafty ignorance
  Heed not the footfall of the eternal tread.

The land that shrinks from Nature's armed advance
  Shall lie dishonored with her wasted dead.

Yea, it behooves us that the light be free.
  We are but bearers, — it is Nature's own, —
Runners who speed the way of Destiny,
  Yielding the torch whose flame is forward blown.

We are in His wide grasp who holds the law,
  Who heaves the tidal sea, and rounds the year;
We may return not, though the weak withdraw;
  We must move onward to the last frontier.

THE LONELY-BIRD

IN THE ADIRONDACKS

O DAPPLED throat of white! Shy, hidden bird!
  Perched in green dimness of the dewy wood,
  And murmuring, in that lonely, lover mood,
    Thy heart-ache, softly heard,
Sweetened by distance, over land and lake.

Why, like a kinsman, do I feel thy voice
  Awaken voices in me free and sweet?
  Was there some far ancestral birdhood fleet
    That rose and would rejoice:
A broken cycle rounded in a song?

The lake, like steady wine in a deep cup,
  Lay crystal in the curving mountain deeps;
  And now the air brought that long lyric up
    That sobs, then falls and weeps,
And hushes silence into listening hope.

Is it that we were sprung of one old kin,
  Children of brooding earth, that lets us tell,
  Thou from thy rhythmic throat, I deep within,
    These syllables of her spell,
This hymnëd wisdom of her pondering years?

For thou hast spoken song-wise in a tongue
  I knew not till I heard the buried air
  Burst from the boughs and bring me what thou sung,
    Here where the lake lies bare
To reaching summits and the azure sky.

Thy music is a language of the trees,
  The brown soil, and the never-trodden brake;
  Translatress art thou of dumb mysteries
    That dream through wood and lake;
And I, in thee, have uttered what I am!

A PINE-TREE BUOY

WHERE all the winds were tranquil,
  And all the odors sweet,
And rings of tumbling upland
  Sloped down to kiss your feet:

There, in a nest of verdure,
  You grew from bud to bough;
You heard the song at mid-day, —
  At eve the plighted vow.

But fate that gives a guerdon
  Takes back a double fee:
She hewed you from your homestead
  And set you in the sea.

And every bowling billow
  Bends down your barren head
To hearken if the whisper
  Of what you knew is dead.

MOHAMMED AND SEID

SWEPT by the hot wind, stark, untrackable,
The stony desert stretches to the sky.
Deep-printed shadows at the tent-door lie,
And camels slumber by the burning well.
One weeps within, wrinkled and dusk of face,
White-haired and lordly, o'er the new-brought dead:
Mohammed over Seid, who loved and read
Truth in the master when a fierce disgrace
Burned in his blood and none would heed the word.
"Behold the Prophet how he mourns a slave!"
So the slave's daughter, and Mohammed heard:

"A friend has lost a friend. What Allah gave
His wisdom takes. He never yet has erred!"
Thus said, and made the slain a martial grave.

WALT WHITMAN

He was in love with Truth and knew her near —
Her comrade, not her suppliant on the knee:
She gave him wild melodious words to be
Made music that should haunt the atmosphere.
She drew him to her bosom, day-long dear,
And pointed to the stars and to the sea,
And taught him miracles and mystery,
And made him master of the rounded year.
Yet one gift did she keep. He looked in vain,
Brow-shaded, through the darkness of the mist,
Marking a beauty like a wandering breath
That beckoned, yet denied his soul a tryst:
He sang a passion, yet he saw not plain
Till kind earth held him and he spake with death.

FICKLE HOPE

Hope, is this thy hand
Lies warm as life in mine?
Is this thy sign
Of peace none understand?

What! art thou not steadfast?
From off the blue air's beach
Wilt lean and reach
The price of pity past?

I know not if I may
Believe thee, Hope, or doubt:
With pretty pout
Wilt flee, or wilt thou stay?

Ernest Crosby

CHOIR PRACTICE

As I sit on a log here in the woods among the clean-faced beeches,
The trunks of the trees seem to me like the pipes of a mighty organ,
Thrilling my soul with wave on wave of the harmonies of the universal anthem —
The grand, divine, eonic "I am" chorus.

The red squirrel scolding in yonder hickory tree,
The flock of blackbirds chattering in council overhead,
The monotonous crickets in the unseen meadow,
Even the silent ants travelling their narrow highway with enormous burdens at my feet —
All, like choristers, sing in the green-arched cathedral
The heaven-prompted mystery, "I am, I am."
The rays of sunshine shoot down through the branches and touch the delicate ferns and the blades of coarse grass piercing up through last year's dead leaves,
And all cry out together, "I am."

We used to call upon all these works of the Lord to praise the Lord, and they did praise Him.
But now they praise no longer, for they have been taught a new song, and with one accord they chant the "I am."

I too would learn the new music, and I begin hesitatingly to take part in the world-wide choir practice.
After all these quiet private rehearsals,
At last in my own place you may look for me also in the final, vast, eternal chorus.
And we, all of us, as you see us, are but mouth-pieces.
Who is it that behind and beneath sings ever through us, now whispering, now thundering, "I am"?

THE SEARCH

No one could tell me where my Soul might be.
I searched for God, but God eluded me.
I sought my Brother out, and found all three.

THE SOUL OF THE WORLD

The soul of the world is abroad to-night —
Not in yon silvery amalgam of moonbeam and ocean, nor in the pink heat-lightning tremulous on the horizon;
Not in the embrace of yonder pair of lovers either, heart beating to heart in the shadow of the fishing-smack drawn up on the beach.
All that — shall I call it illusion? Nay, but at best it is a pale reflection of the truth.
I am not to be put off with symbols, for the soul of the world is itself abroad to-night.

I neither see nor hear nor smell nor taste nor touch it, but faintly I feel it powerfully stirring.
I feel it as the blind heaving sea feels the moon bending over it.
I feel it as the needle feels the serpentine magnetic current coiling itself about the earth.
I open my arms to embrace it as the lovers embrace each other, but my embrace is all inclusive.
My heart beats to heart likewise, but it is to the heart universal, for the soul of the world is abroad to-night.

Harry Thurston Peck

HELIOTROPE

Amid the chapel's chequered gloom
She laughed with Dora and with Flora,
And chattered in the lecture-room, —
That saucy little sophomora!
Yet while, as in her other schools,
She was a privileged transgressor,
She never broke the simple rules
Of one particular professor.

But when he spoke of varied lore,
Paroxytones and modes potential,
She listened with a face that wore
A look half fond, half reverential.
To her that earnest voice was sweet,
And though her love had no confessor,
Her girlish heart lay at the feet
Of that particular professor.

And he had learned, among his books
That held the lore of ages olden,
To watch those ever changing looks,
The wistful eyes, the tresses golden,
That stirred his pulse with passion's pain
And thrilled his soul with soft desire,
And bade fond youth return again
Crowned with his coronet of fire.

Her sunny smile, her winsome ways,
Were more to him than all his knowledge,
And she preferred his words of praise
To all the honors of the college.
Yet "What am foolish I to him?"
She whispered to her heart's confessor.
"She thinks me old and gray and grim,"
In silence pondered the professor.

Yet once when Christmas bells were rung
Above ten thousand solemn churches,
And swelling anthems grandly sung
Pealed through the dim cathedral arches, —
Ere home returning, filled with hope,
Softly she stole by gate and gable,
And a sweet spray of heliotrope
Left on his littered study-table.

Nor came she more from day to day
Like sunshine through the shadows rifting:
Above her grave, far, far away,
The ever silent snows were drifting;

And those who mourned her winsome face
Found in its stead a swift successor
And loved another in her place —
All, save the silent old professor.

But, in the tender twilight gray,
Shut from the sight of carping critic,
His lonely thoughts would often stray
From Vedic verse and tongues Semitic,
Bidding the ghost of vanished hope
Mock with its past the sad possessor
Of the dead spray of heliotrope
That once she gave the old professor.

WONDERLAND

SWEET eyes by sorrow still unwet,
To you the world is radiant yet,
A palace-hall of splendid truth
Touched by the golden haze of youth,
Where hopes and joys are ever rife
Amid the mystery of life;
And seeking all to understand,
The world to you is Wonderland.

I turn and watch with unshed tears
The furrowed track of ended years;
I see the eager hopes that wane,
The joys that die in deathless pain,
The coward Faith that falsehoods shake,
The souls that faint, the hearts that break,
The Truth by livid lips bemoaned,
The Right defiled, the Wrong enthroned, —
And, striving still to understand,
The world to me is Wonderland.

A little time, then by and by
The puzzled thought itself shall die.
When, like the throb of distant drums,
The call inevitable comes
To blurring brain and weary limb,
And when the aching eyes grow dim,
And fast the gathering shadows creep
To lull the drowsy sense asleep,
We two shall slumber hand in hand
To wake, perhaps, in Wonderland.

THE OTHER ONE

SWEET little maid with winsome eyes
That laugh all day through the tangled hair;
Gazing with baby looks so wise
Over the arm of the oaken chair,
Dearer than you is none to me,
Dearer than you there can be none;
Since in your laughing face I see
Eyes that tell of another one.

Here where the firelight softly glows,
Sheltered and safe and snug and warm,
What to you is the wind that blows,
Driving the sleet of the winter storm?
Round your head the ruddy light
Glints on the gold from your tresses spun,
But deep is the drifting snow to-night
Over the head of the other one.

Hold me close as you sagely stand,
Watching the dying embers shine;
Then shall I feel another hand
That nestled once in this hand of mine;
Poor little hand, so cold and chill,
Shut from the light of stars and sun,
Clasping the withered roses still
That hide the face of the sleeping one.

Laugh, little maid, while laugh you may,
Sorrow comes to us all, I know;
Better perhaps for her to stay
Under the robe of drifting snow.
Sing while you may your baby songs,
Sing till your baby days are done;
But oh the ache of the heart that longs
Night and day for the other one!

Frank Lebby Stanton

ONE COUNTRY

AFTER all,
One country, brethren! We must rise or fall
With the Supreme Republic. We must be
The makers of her immortality, —
Her freedom, fame,
Her glory or her shame:
Liegemen to God and fathers of the free!

After all —
Hark! from the heights the clear, strong, clarion call
And the command imperious: "Stand forth,
Sons of the South and brothers of the North!
Stand forth and be
As one on soil and sea —
Your country's honor more than empire's worth!"

After all,
'T is Freedom wears the loveliest coronal;
Her brow is to the morning; in the sod
She breathes the breath of patriots; every clod
Answers her call
And rises like a wall
Against the foes of liberty and God!

A PLANTATION DITTY

De gray owl sing fum de chimbly top:
"Who — who — is — you-oo?"
En I say: "Good Lawd, hit 's des po' me,
En I ain't quite ready fer de Jasper Sea;
I 'm po' en sinful, en you 'lowed I 'd be;
Oh, wait, good Lawd, 'twell ter-morror!"

De gray owl sing fum de cypress tree:
"Who — who — is — you-oo?"
En I say: "Good Lawd, ef you look you 'll see
Hit ain't nobody but des po' me,
En I like ter stay 'twell my time is free;
Oh, wait, good Lawd, 'twell ter-morror!"

THE GRAVEYARD RABBIT

In the white moonlight, where the willow waves,
He halfway gallops among the graves —
A tiny ghost in the gloom and gleam,
Content to dwell where the dead men dream,

But wary still!
For they plot him ill;
For the graveyard rabbit hath a charm
(May God defend us!) to shield from harm.

Over the shimmering slabs he goes —
Every grave in the dark he knows;
But his nest is hidden from human eye
Where headstones broken on old graves lie.

Wary still!
For they plot him ill;
For the graveyard rabbit, though sceptics scoff,
Charmeth the witch and the wizard off!

The black man creeps, when the night is dim,
Fearful, still, on the track of him;
Or fleetly follows the way he runs,
For he heals the hurts of the conjured ones.

Wary still!
For they plot him ill;
The soul 's bewitched that would find release, —
To the graveyard rabbit go for peace!

He holds their secret — he brings a boon
Where winds moan wild in the dark o' the moon;
And gold shall glitter and love smile sweet
To whoever shall sever his furry feet!

Wary still!
For they plot him ill;
For the graveyard rabbit hath a charm
(May God defend us!) to shield from harm.

THE MOCKING-BIRD

He did n't know much music
When first he come along;
An' all the birds went wonderin'
Why he did n't sing a song.

They primped their feathers in the sun,
An' sung their sweetest notes;
An' music jest come on the run
From all their purty throats!

But still that bird was silent
In summer time an' fall;
He jest set still an' listened,
An' he would n't sing at all!

But one night when them songsters
Was tired out an' still,

An' the wind sighed down the valley
An' went creepin' up the hill;

When the stars was all a-tremble
In the dreamin' fields o' blue,
An' the daisy in the darkness
Felt the fallin' o' the dew, —

There come a sound o' melody
No mortal ever heard,
An' all the birds seemed singin'
From the throat o' one sweet bird!

Then the other birds went Mayin'
In a land too fur to call;
Fer there warn't no use in stayin'
When one bird could sing fer all!

A LITTLE WAY

A LITTLE way to walk with you, my own —
Only a little way,
Then one of us must weep and walk alone
Until God's day.

A little way! It is so sweet to live
Together, that I know
Life would not have one withered rose to give
If one of us should go.

And if these lips should ever learn to smile,
With thy heart far from mine,
'T would be for joy that in a little while
They would be kissed by thine!

Margaret Deland

LOVE AND DEATH

ALAS! that men must see
Love, before Death!
Else they content might be
With their short breath;
Aye, glad, when the pale sun
Showed restless Day was done,
And endless Rest begun.

Glad, when with strong, cool hand
Death clasped their own,
And with a strange command
Hushed every moan;
Glad to have finished pain,
And labor wrought in vain,
Blurred by Sin's deepening stain.

But Love's insistent voice
Bids Self to flee —
"Live that I may rejoice,
Live on, for me!"
So, for Love's cruel mind,
Men fear this Rest to find,
Nor know great Death is kind!

SENT WITH A ROSE TO A YOUNG LADY

DEEP in a Rose's glowing heart
I dropped a single kiss,
And then I bade it quick depart,
And tell my Lady this:

"The love thy Lover tried to send
O'erflows my fragrant bowl,
But my soft leaves would break and bend,
Should he send half the whole!"

THE CLOVER

O RUDDY Lover —
O brave red Clover!
Didst think to win her
Thou dost adore?
She will not love thee,
She looks above thee,
The Daisy's gold doth move her more.
If gold can win her,
Then Love 's not in her;
So leave the Sinner,
And sigh no more!

LOVE'S WISDOM

How long I 've loved thee, and how well —
I dare not tell!
Because, if thou shouldst once divine
This love of mine,
Or did but once my tongue confess
My heart's distress,
Far, far too plainly thou wouldst see
My slavery,
And, guessing what Love's wit should hide,
Rest satisfied!

So, though I worship at thy feet,
I 'll be discreet —
And all my love shall not be told,
Lest thou be cold,
And, knowing I was always thine,
Scorn to be mine.
So am I dumb, to rescue thee
From tyranny —
And, by my silence, I do prove
Wisdom and Love!

Tudor Jenks

SMALL AND EARLY

WHEN Dorothy and I took tea, we sat upon the floor;
No matter how much tea I drank, she always gave me more;
Our table was the scarlet box in which her tea-set came;
Our guests, an armless one-eyed doll, a wooden horse gone lame.
She poured out nothing, very fast, — the tea-pot tipped on high, —
And in the bowl found sugar lumps unseen by my dull eye.
She added rich (pretended) cream — it seemed a wilful waste,
For though she overflowed the cup, it did not change the taste.
She asked, "Take milk?" or "Sugar?" and though I answered, "No,"
She put them in, and told me that I "*must* take it so!"
She 'd say "Another cup, Papa?" and I, "No, thank you, Ma'am,"
But then I *had* to take it — her courtesy was sham.
Still, being neither green, nor black, nor English-breakfast tea,
It did not give her guests the "nerves" — whatever those may be.
Though often I upset my cup, she only minded when
I would mistake the empty cups for those she 'd filled again.
She tasted my cup gingerly, for fear I 'd burn my tongue;
Indeed, she really hurt my pride — she made me feel so young.
I must have drunk some twoscore cups, and Dorothy sixteen,
Allowing only needful time to pour them, in between.
We stirred with massive pewter spoons, and sipped in courtly ease,
With all the ceremony of the stately Japanese.
At length she put the cups away. "Good-night, Papa," she said;
And I went to a real tea, and Dorothy to bed.

THE SPIRIT OF THE MAINE

IN battle-line of sombre gray
Our ships-of-war advance,
As Red Cross Knights in holy fray
Charged with avenging lance.
And terrible shall be thy plight,
O fleet of cruel Spain!
For ever in our van doth fight
The spirit of the Maine!

As when beside Regillus Lake
The Great Twin Brethren came
A righteous fight for Rome to make
Against the Deed of Shame —
So now a ghostly ship shall doom
The fleet of treacherous Spain:
Before her guilty soul doth loom
The spirit of the Maine!

A wraith arrayed in peaceful white,
As when asleep she lay
Above the traitorous mine that night
Within Havana Bay,
She glides before the avenging fleet,
A sign of woe to Spain.
Brave though her sons, how shall they meet
The spirit of the Maine!

Alice Brown

CANDLEMAS

O HEARKEN, all ye little weeds
That lie beneath the snow,
(So low, dear hearts, in poverty so low!)
The sun hath risen for royal deeds,
A valiant wind the vanguard leads;
Now quicken ye, lest unborn seeds
Before ye rise and blow.

O furry living things, adream
On Winter's drowsy breast,
(How rest ye there, how softly, safely rest!)
Arise and follow where a gleam
Of wizard gold unbinds the stream,
And all the woodland windings seem
With sweet expectance blest.

My birds, come back! the hollow sky
Is weary for your note.
(Sweet-throat, come back! O liquid, mellow throat!)
Ere May's soft minions hereward fly,
Shame on ye, laggards, to deny
The brooding breast, the sun-bright eye,
The tawny, shining coat!

TRILBY

O LIVING image of eternal youth!
Wrought with such large simplicity of truth
That, now the pattern 's made and on the shelf,
Each vows he might have cut it for himself;
Nor marvels that we sang of empty days,
Of rank-grown laurel and unprunëd bays,
While yet, in all this lonely Crusoe land,
The Trilby footprint had not touched the sand.
Here 's a new carelessness of Titan play.
Here 's Ariel's witchery to lead the way
In such sweet artifice of dainty wit
That men shall die with imitating it.
Now every man's old grief turns in its bed,
And bleeds a drop or two, divinely red;
Fair baby joys do rouse them, one by one,
Dancing a lightsome round, though love be done;
And Memory takes off her frontlet dim
To bind a bit of tinsel round the rim.
Dreams come to life, and faint foreshadowings
Flutter anear us on reluctant wings.
But not one pang, nay, though 't were gall of bliss,
And not one such awakening would we miss.
O comrades, here 's true stuff! ours to adore,
And swear we 'll carve our cherry-stones no more.

CLOISTERED

SEAL thou the window! Yea, shut out the light
And bar my door to all the airs of spring.
Yet in my cell, concealed from curious sight,
Here will I sit and sing.

Deaf, blind, and wilt Thou have me dumb, also,
Telling in silence these sad beads of days?
So let it be: though no sweet numbers flow,
My breath shall be Thy praise.

Yea, though Thou slay the life wherein men see
The upward-mounting flame, the failing spark,
My heart of love, that heart Thou gavest me,
Shall beat on in the dark.

LIFE

WHAT, comrade of a night,
No sooner meet than fight?
Before the word, the blow?
Well, be it so.

Yet think not Thou I yield,
Lost on a lonely field.
Lo! to my fainting breath,
My champion, Death!

SLEEP

WITHDRAW thee, soul, from strife.
Enter thine unseen bark,
And sail across the dark,
The silent sea of life.
Leave Care and Grief, feared now no more,
To wave and beckon from the shore.

Thy tenement is bare.
Shut are the burning eyes,
Ears deaf against surprise,
Limbs in a posture fair.
The body sleeps, unheeding thee,
And thou, my sailing soul, art free.

Rouse not to choose thy way;
To make it long or short,
Or seek some golden port
In haste, ere springs the day.
Desire is naught, and effort vain:
Here he who seeks shall ne'er attain.

Dream-winged, thy boat may drift
Where lands lie warm in light;
Or sail, with silent flight,
Oblivion cleaving swift.
Still, dusk or dawning, art thou blest,
O Fortune's darling, dowered with rest!

William Morton Payne

INCIPIT VITA NOVA

WHAT time the earth takes on the garb of Spring,
And new-born joy runs riot in the blood,
When the year's tide turns refluent to its flood,
And blissful birds their songs are caroling, —
When life once more is fair, and everything
In nature smiles, when tender flowrets bud,
And deck the mead as stars the heavens stud, —
What wonder that my heart leaps up to sing!
What wonder that to thee my song of praise
I bring, and burn sweet incense at thy shrine,
And offer all the worship of my lays
To thee, whose loveliness hath lent my days
That life renewed whereof the Florentine
Sang ere he wrote the Comedy Divine!

"EJ BLOT TIL LYST"

("Not for pleasure only," — the motto of the Royal Theatre at Copenhagen.)

NOT merely for our pleasure, but to purge
The soul from baseness, from ignoble fear,
And all the passions that make dim the clear
Calm vision of the world; our feet to urge
On to ideal far-set goals; to merge
Our being with the heart of things; brought near
The springs of life, to make us see and hear
And feel its swelling and pulsating surge: —
Such, Thespian art divine, thy nobler aim;
For this the tale of Œdipus was told,
Of frenzied Lear, Harpagon's greed of gold; —
And, knowing this, how must we view with shame
Thy low estate, and hear the plaudits loud
That mark thee now but pander to the crowd!

TANNHÄUSER

SIN-SATIATE, and haggard with despair,
Freed from the unholy mountain's baleful spell,
Forth coming from the very pit of Hell,
The fallen knight repentant kneels in prayer.
But hark! what solemn strains fill all the air?
What pilgrim chants now on the morning swell,
And pour hope's balm upon his soul, and tell
Of pardon, if he to Christ's seat repair?

With fervent heart he treads the weary way,
Kneels at the throne of God's anointed, hears
The fearful doom repentance may not stay:
And yet, in death's last gasp — if he but heed —
An angel voice soft whispers in his ears
That for him too the Saviour once did bleed.

LOHENGRIN

STRAIN, strain thine eyes, this parting is for aye!
Grief have her will of thee! Thy faith confessed
To his unequal, he must go, the quest
Fulfilled that brought him hither on thy day
Of imminent, direst peril. Now away
To other shores bids him the Grail's behest.
Thou knewest him too late to spare thy breast
This keen remorse, thy soul this dark dismay.
Yet canst thou face not all disconsolate
The coming years. The horn remains, the sword,
The ring he left thee, and the child whom late
Thou mournedst; while beyond the power of fate
To dim the memory of that love outpoured
Upon thee by thy stainless knight and lord.

Milicent Washburn Shinn

SONG AND SCIENCE

"THE TWILIGHT OF THE POETS"

SPIRIT of song, whose shining wings have borne
Our souls of old to many a clear blue height,
Comes there the day that leaves our world forlorn
Of thy clear singing in the haunted night?
For while from out the western radiance low
Like stars the great dead shining upward go,
Behold, thy wings are poised to join their flight:
Yet follow not within the golden door
Those starry souls; but when the time is full,
Let thy fair-shining garments, white as wool,
Glimmer once more across our earth's green floor.

Well was it for thee when the moonlight filled
The Syrian nights, and all the air was stilled
With large and simple faith, until men felt
Somewhat most stern and mighty brooding o'er them,
And grimly as Jehovah's warriors bore them.
Well was it for thee where the glad gods dwelt
In happy Hellas, clasped by silver nights,
When on the clear blue of Olympian heights
Apollo's lyre, and by the reedy stream
Pan's shrill, sweet pipe made life a sunny dream.
Well was it for thee in the English wood,
When red, new leaves were bursting out of bud,
And hearts were fresh as young leaves on the elm.
And well, through all the centuries since, thy realm
Has loyally been kept for thee, and thou,
Departing oft, hast still returned; but now
New powers devour thy kingdom day by day.
How shouldst thou come amidst such waste to stay?

For even now, across that western glow,
A keen light whitens coldly in the east,
And glittering on the slopes of morning, lo,
One comes in silver arms; and aye increased
The sharp light shines, and men beholding turn

From thee, and kneel before this wonder new,
Upon whose crest the conquered stars do burn.
No white wings gleam like thine against the blue,
Yet swift his foot and strong; and in his hand —
Ah, bright and terrible! — he bears the brand
Of truth, and in its gleam the lightning plays.
Exultant, young, full-armed from spur to helm,
Spirit of song, he comes to claim thy realm;
And coldly o'er thy lingering radiance low
The keener splendors that attend him flow.
What place is left for thee in all earth's ways?

Yet that strong warrior that recks not of thee
Shall one day turn his eyes and see thy face
Shine like a star from some far deep of space, —
And all his spirit unto thee shall yearn,
Until he call thee back, and win thy grace.
And on thy brow his captive stars shall burn;
And in wide realms, new-conquered unto thee
By that great sword, thine olden smile shall shine;
Unto deep chords of many an unknown sea,
Thy voice shall join its world-old notes divine.

WHEN ALMONDS BLOOM

When almond buds unclose,
Soft white and tender rose, —
A swarm of white moth things,
With sunset on their wings,
That fluttering settle down
On branches chill and brown;
When all the sky is blue,
And up from grasses new
Blithe springs the meadow lark, —
Sweet, sweet, from dawn to dark; —
When all the young year's way
Grows sweeter day by day; —
When almond buds unclose,
Who doubts of May's red rose?

YOSEMITE

FROM "THE WASHINGTON SEQUOIA"

Soul of a tree ungrown, new life out of God's life proceeding,
Folded close in the seed, waking — O wonder of wonders —
Waking with power as a spirit to clothe thee in leaves and in branches,
What, in thine age-long future, is the word thou art set here to say?

Far in the great Sierra dwell the mighty groups of thy kindred;
Aisles of the sounding pines; and colonnades dusky and fragrant,
Pillared with ridgy shafts of tall and wonderful cedar,
Lead to their presence; and round them forever the mountains stand.

Deep in that inner temple listens the fortunate pilgrim,
Low where the red lilies tremble he lies while the still hours pass by him,
Baring his brows to the silence, the dear and intimate greatness,
The touch of the friendly air, like a quiet and infinite hand.

Far, far up from the earth, in the lower spaces of heaven,
Shadowy green on the blue, rests the moving lace of the branches,
Holding the faint winds captive, dropping but lightest of murmurs,
Spirits of far-away sound, to the windless reaches below.

Deep in that inner temple listens the fortunate pilgrim;
Infinite things they say to him, the mighty groups of thy kindred, —
Life beyond life, and soul within soul, and God around all as an ocean, —
Whispers his heart dimly guesses, secrets he never may know.

James Benjamin Kenyon

TACITA

She roves through shadowy solitudes,
Where scentless herbs and fragile flowers
Pine in the gloom that ever broods
Around her sylvan bowers.

No winds amid the branches sigh,
No footfall wakes the sodden ground;
And the cold streams that hurry by
Flow on without a sound.

Strange, voiceless birds from spray to spray
Flit silently; and all day long
The dancing midges round her play,
But sing no elfin song.

The haunting twilight ebbs and flows;
Chill is the night, wan is the morn;
Through this dim wood no minstrel goes,
No hunter winds his horn.

No panting stag seeks yon dark pool;
No shepherd calls his bleating sheep
From sunburnt meads to shadows cool,
And grasses green and deep.

Across her path, from reed to reed,
The spider weaves his gossamer;
She recks not where her footsteps lead,
The world is dead to her.

Her eyes are sad, her face is pale,
Her head droops sidewise wearily;
Her dusky tresses, like a veil,
Down ripple to her knee.

How many a cycle hath she trod
Each mossy aisle, each leafy dell!
Alas, her feet with silence shod
Ne'er flee the hateful spell!

QUATRAINS

THE BEDOUINS OF THE SKIES

Yon clouds that roam the deserts of the air,
On wind-swift barbs, o'er many an azure plain,
Scarce pause to lift to Allah one small prayer,
Ere Ishmael's spirit drives them forth again.

THE TWO SPIRITS

I dreamed two spirits came — one dusk as night:
"Mortals miscall me Life," he sadly saith;
The other, with a smile like morning light,
Flashed his strong wings and spake,
"Men name me Death."

A CHALLENGE

Arise, O soul, and gird thee up anew,
Though the black camel Death kneel at thy gate;
No beggar thou that thou for alms shouldst sue;
Be the proud captain still of thine own fate!

DEATH AND NIGHT

The bearded grass waves in the summer breeze;
The sunlight sleeps along the distant hills;
Faint is the music of the murmuring rills,
And faint the drowsy piping of the bees.
The languid leaves scarce stir upon the trees,
And scarce is heard the clangor of the mills
In the far distance, and the high, sharp trills
Of the cicada die upon the leas.
O death, what art thou? Hast thou peace like this?
Or, underneath the daisies, out of sight,
Hast thou in keep some higher, calmer bliss?
Ah me! 't is pleasant to behold the light,
And missing this, O death, would we not miss
That weariness which makes us love the night?

BRING THEM NOT BACK

Yet, O my friend — pale conjurer, I call
Thee friend — bring, bring the dead not back again,
Since for the tears, the darkness and the pain
Of unrequited friendship — for the gall
That hatred mingles with fond love — for all
Life's endless turmoil, bitterness and bane,
Thou hast given dreamless rest. Still let the rain,
And sunshine, and the dews from heaven fall
Upon the graves of those whose peaceful eyes
Thy breath hath sealed forever. Let the song
Of summer birds be theirs, and in the skies
Let the pale stars keep vigil all night long.
O death, call not the holy dead to rise,
Again to feel the cold world's ruth and wrong.

COME SLOWLY, PARADISE

O dawn upon me slowly, Paradise!
Come not too suddenly,
Lest my just-opened, unaccustomed eyes
Smitten with blindness be.

To those who from Time's penury and woe
Rise to thy heights afar,
Down which the floods of glory fall and flow,
Too great thy splendors are.

So grow upon me slowly; sweetly break
Across death's silent deep,
Till to thy morning brightness I shall wake
As one from happy sleep.

Charles Henry Crandall

STELLA

Home from the observatory,
Now I take her on my knee,
And I tell her all the glory
That the lenses showed to me.
Pleased, she listens to my story,
Earnest look then turneth she

Where the stars are softly blinking
In the blue of summer skies.
Ah! she sees beyond my thinking,
Even into Paradise!
Very humbly I am drinking
What o'erfloweth from her eyes.

THE HUMAN PLAN

Child, weary of thy baubles of to-day —
Child with the golden or the silver hair —
Say, how wouldst thou have built creation's stair,
Hadst thou been free to have thy puny way?
Could thy intelligence have shot the ray
That lit the universe of upper air?
Wouldst thou have bid the surging stars to dare
Their glorious flight and never stop nor stay?
Yet, casting on this life thy weak disdain,
Thou triest to guess thy lot in loftier places,
To draw the heaven of our human need;
A door of rest, a flash of wings, a strain
Of 'trancing music, and the long-lost faces!
But, after all, what may be Heaven indeed?

WITH LILACS

I beg the pardon of these flowers
For bringing them to one whose hair
Alone doth shame, beyond compare,
The sweetest blooms of richest bowers.

I beg the pardon of this maid
For offering them with hand less pure,
A heart less perfect, needing cure
By Love's own music, softly played.

Charles Henry Luders

THE FOUR WINDS

Wind of the North,
Wind of the Norland snows,
Wind of the winnowed skies, and sharp, clear stars, —
Blow cold and keen across the naked hills,
And crisp the lowland pools with crystal films,
And blur the casement squares with glittering ice,
But go not near my love.

Wind of the West,
Wind of the few, far clouds,
Wind of the gold and crimson sunset lands, —
Blow fresh and pure across the peaks and plains,
And broaden the blue spaces of the heavens,
And sway the grasses and the mountain pines,
But let my dear one rest.

Wind of the East,
Wind of the sunrise seas,
Wind of the clinging mists and gray, harsh rains, —
Blow moist and chill across the wastes of brine,
And shut the sun out, and the moon and stars,
And lash the boughs against the dripping eaves,
Yet keep thou from my love.

But thou, sweet wind!
Wind of the fragrant South,
Wind from the bowers of jasmine and of rose, —
Over magnolia blooms and lilied lakes
And flowering forests come with dewy wings,
And stir the petals at her feet, and kiss
The low mound where she lies.

THE HAUNTS OF THE HALCYON

To stand within a gently gliding boat,
Urged by a noiseless paddle at the stern,
Whipping the crystal mirror of the fern
In fairy bays where water-lilies float;
To hear your reel's whirr echoed by the throat
Of a wild mocking-bird, or round some turn
To chance upon a wood-duck's brood that churn
Swift passage toward their mother's warning note, —
This is to rule a realm that nevermore
May aught but restful weariness invade;
This is to live again the old days o'er,
When nymph and dryad haunted stream and glade;
To dream sweet, idle dreams of having strayed
To Arcady, with all its golden lore.

HEART OF OAK

Lean close and set thine ear against the bark;
Then tell me what faint, murmurous sounds are heard:
Hath not the oak stored up the song of bird,
Whisper of wind and rain-lisp? Ay, and hark!
The shadowy elves that fret the summer dark,
With clash of horny winglets swiftly whirred,
Hear'st thou not them, with myriad noises, blurred,
Yet well defined if one but shrewdly mark?
And thou, — when thy Familiar setteth ear
Unto thy bosom, doth he note the same
Sweet concord of harmonious sounds within?
Or is all hushed in hollow silence drear?
An 't be, pray Heaven to save thee from thy shame
Ere thy whole soul be slain by cankerous sin.

AN OLD THOUGHT

Framed in the cavernous fire-place sits a boy,
Watching the embers from his grandsire's knee:
One sees red castles rise, and laughs with joy;
The other marks them crumble, silently.

THE MOUNTEBANKS

Over our heads the branches made
A canopy of woven shade.

The birds about this beechen tent
Like deft attendants came and went.

A shy wood-robin, fluting low,
Furnished the music for the show.

The cricket and the grasshopper
A portion of the audience were.

Thither did Fancy leap to fling
Light summersaults around the ring.

Wit, the sly jester of the Town,
And rustic Humor played the clown;

Reason was ringmaster, and waved
His whip when these his anger braved;

Wishes were horses that each rode
Unto his heart's desire's abode.

There Laughter and Delight and Glee
Performed their parts that all might see,

Till a sweet wind across the clover
Whispered, "At last, the show is over,"

And the broad shadow of a cloud
Moved from us like a moving crowd.

Mary Augusta Mason

THE SCARLET TANAGER

A flame went flitting through the wood;
The neighboring birds all understood
Here was a marvel of their kind;
And silent was each feathered throat
To catch the brilliant stranger's note,
And folded every songster's wing
To hide its sober coloring.
Against the tender green outlined,
He bore himself with splendid ease,
As though alone among the trees.
The glory passed from bough to bough —
The maple was in blossom now,
And then the oak, remembering
The crimson hint it gave in spring,
And every tree its branches swayed
And offered its inviting shade;
Where'er a bough detained him long,
A slender, silver thread of song
Was lightly, merrily unspun.
From early morn till day was done
The vision flitted to and fro.
At last the wood was all alone;
But, ere the restless flame had flown,
He left a secret with each bough,
And in the Fall, where one is now,
A thousand tanagers will glow.

MY LITTLE NEIGHBOR

My little neighbor's table 's set,
And slyly he comes down the tree,
His feet firm in each tiny fret
The bark has fashioned cunningly.

He pauses on a favorite knot;
Beneath the oak his feast is spread;
He asks no friend to share his lot,
Or dine with him on acorn bread.

He keeps his whiskers trim and neat,
His tail with care he brushes through;
He runs about on all four feet —
When dining he sits up on two.

He has the latest stripe in furs,
And wears them all the year around;
He does not mind the prick of burs
When there are chestnuts to be found.

I watch his home and guard his store,
A cozy hollow in a tree;
He often sits within his door
And chatters wondrous things to me.

Henry Jerome Stockard

OVER THEIR GRAVES

OVER their graves rang once the bugle's call,
The searching shrapnel and the crashing ball;
The shriek, the shock of battle, and the neigh
Of horse; the cries of anguish and dismay;
And the loud cannon's thunders that appall.

Now through the years the brown pine-needles fall,
The vines run riot by the old stone wall,
By hedge, by meadow streamlet, far away,
Over their graves.

We love our dead where'er so held in thrall.
Than they no Greek more bravely died, nor Gaul —
A love that 's deathless ! — but they look to-day
With no reproaches on us when we say,
" Come, let us clasp your hands, we 're brothers all,
Over their graves ! "

AS SOME MYSTERIOUS WANDERER OF THE SKIES

As some mysterious wanderer of the skies,
Emerging from the deeps of outer dark,
Traces for once in human ken the arc
Of its stupendous curve, then swiftly flies
Out through some orbit veiled in space, which lies
Where no imagination may embark, —
Some onward-reaching track that God did mark
For all eternity beneath his eyes, —
So comes the soul forth from Creation's vast;
So clothed with mystery moves through mortal sight;
Then sinks away into the Great Unknown.
What systems it hath seen in all the past,
What worlds shall blaze upon its future flight,
Thou knowest, eternal God, and thou alone !

THE MOCKING-BIRD

THE name thou wearest does thee grievous wrong.
No mimic thou ! That voice is thine alone !
The poets sing but strains of Shakespeare's song;
The birds, but notes of thine imperial own !

Sarah Pratt McLean Greene

THE LAMP

HAST thou a lamp, a little lamp,
Put in that hand of thine ?
And did He say, who gave it thee,
The world hath need this light should be,
Now, therefore, let it shine ?

And dost thou say, with bated breath,
It is a little flame;
I 'll let the lamps of broader wick
Seek out the lost and cheer the sick,
While I seek wealth and fame ?

But on the shore where thy small house
Stands dark, stands dark, this night,
Full many a wanderer, thither tossed,
Is driven on that rock and lost,
Where thou hast hid thy light.

Though but a candle thou didst have,
Its trimmed and glowing ray
Is infinite. With God, no light
Is great or small, but only bright,
As is his perfect day.

The world hath sorrow, nothing more,
To give or keep for thee;
Duty is in that hidden flame,
And soaring joy: then rise for shame
That thou so dark shouldst be.

Rise, trim thy lamp; the feeble past
Behind thee put and spurn.

With God it is not soon or late,
So that thy light, now flaming great,
Doth ever fiercer burn, —

Fierce with its love, and flaming great
In its humility;
Shunning no soul in sinful need,
Fearing no path where He may lead,
Glowing consumingly.

Thou shalt not want for light enough,
When earthly moons grow dim;
The dawn is but begun for thee,
When thou shalt hand, so tremblingly,
Thy empty lamp to Him.

DE SHEEPFOL'

De massa ob de sheepfol',
Dat guards de sheepfol' bin,
Look out in de gloomerin' meadows,
Wha'r de long night rain begin —
So he call to de hirelin' shepa'd,
"Is my sheep, is dey all come in?"

Oh den, says de hirelin' shepa'd:
"Dey 's some, dey 's black and thin,
And some, dey 's po' ol' wedda's;
But de res', dey 's all brung in.
But de res', dey 's all brung in."

Den de massa ob de sheepfol',
Dat guards de sheepfol' bin,
Goes down in de gloomerin' meadows,
Wha'r de long night rain begin —
So he le' down de ba's ob de sheepfol',
Callin' sof', "Come in. Come in."
Callin' sof', "Come in. Come in."

Den up t'ro' de gloomerin' meadows,
T'ro' de col' night rain and win',
And up t'ro' de gloomerin' rain-paf',
Wha'r de sleet fa' pie'cin' thin,
De po' los' sheep ob de sheepfol',
Dey all comes gadderin' in.
De po' los' sheep ob de sheepfol',
Dey all comes gadderin' in.

Clarence Urmy

AS I CAME DOWN MOUNT TAMALPAIS

As I came down Mount Tamalpais,
To north the fair Sonoma Hills
Lay like a trembling thread of blue
Beneath a sky of daffodils;
Through tules green a silver stream
Ran south to meet the tranquil bay,
Whispering a dreamy, tender tale
Of vales and valleys far away.

As I came down Mount Tamalpais,
To south the city brightly shone,
Touched by the sunset's good-night kiss
Across the golden ocean blown;
I saw its hills, its tapering masts,
I almost heard its tramp and tread,
And saw against the sky the cross
Which marks the City of the Dead.

As I came down Mount Tamalpais
To east San Pablo's water lay,
Touched with a holy purple light,
The benediction of the day;
No ripple on its twilight tide,
No parting of its evening veil,
Save dimly in the far-off haze
One dreamy, yellow sunset sail.

As I came down Mount Tamalpais,
To west Heaven's gateway opened wide,
And through it, freighted with day-cares,
The cloud-ships floated with the tide;
Then, silently through stilly air,
Starlight flew down from Paradise,
Folded her silver wings and slept
Upon the slopes of Tamalpais.

BLONDEL

Within my heart I long have kept
A little chamber cleanly swept,
Embroidered with a fleur-de-lis,
And lintel boughs of redwood-tree;
A bed, a book, a crucifix,
Two little copper candlesticks
With tapers ready for the match
The moment I his footfall catch,

That when in thought he comes to me
He straightway at his ease may be.
This guest I love so to allure —
Blondel, King Richard's Troubadour!

He often comes, but sings no more
(He says his singing days are o'er!);
Still, sweet of tongue and filled with tales
Of knights and ladies, bowers and vales,
He caps our frugal meal with talk
Of langue d'oïl and langue d'oc,
Of Picardy and Aquitaine,
Blanche of Castile and Charlemagne,
Of ménestrel, trouvère, conteur,
Mime, histrion, and old harpeur —
Small wonder that I love him well,
King Richard's troubadour, Blondel!

Still, as he comes at candle-light
And goes before the east is bright,
I have no heart to beg him keep
Late hour with me when wooed by sleep;
But one request I ever make,
And ever no for answer take:
He will not make the secret mine,
What song he sang at Dürrenstein!
Sleep, troubadour! Enough that thou
With that sweet lay didst keep thy vow
And link thy name by deathless art
With Richard of the Lion Heart!

Susan Marr Spalding

A SONG'S WORTH

I MADE a song for my dear love's delight;
I wrought with all sweet words my heart could lend
To longing lips, and thrilled with joy to send
The message only love could read aright.
He came; and while I trembled in his sight,
He kissed my hands and said, "To what sweet end,
Unknowing, hast thou wrought, O gentle friend?
Singing thy song, I learned to woo, despite
My loved one's frown; and now she is my own."
Blessing me then, he went his happy way.
The whole world sings my song, and I alone
Am silent; yet through tears I sometimes say,
"To which of us doth greater joy belong?
He hath his love; but I — I have my song."

THE SEA'S SPELL

BENEATH thy spell, O radiant summer sea, —
Lulled by thy voice, rocked on thy shining breast,
Fanned by thy soft breath, by thy touch caressed, —
Let all thy treacheries forgotten be.
Let me still dream the ships I gave to thee
All golden-freighted in fair harbors rest;
Let me believe each sparkling wave's white crest
Bears from thy depths my loved and lost to me.
Let me not heed thy wrecks, nor count thy slain.
As o'er-fond lovers for love's sake forget
Their dearest wrongs, so I, with eyes still wet
With thy salt tears, with heart still wrung with pain,
Back to thy fierce, sweet beauty turn again,
And though thou wreck me, will I love thee yet!

FATE

Two shall be born the whole wide world apart;
And speak in different tongues, and have no thought
Each of the other's being, and no heed;
And these o'er unknown seas to unknown lands
Shall cross, escaping wreck, defying death,
And all unconsciously shape every act
And bend each wandering step to this one end, —
That, one day, out of darkness, they shall meet
And read life's meaning in each other's eyes.

And two shall walk some narrow way of life
So nearly side by side, that should one turn
Ever so little space to left or right
They needs must stand acknowledged face to face.
And yet, with wistful eyes that never meet,
With groping hands that never clasp, and lips
Calling in vain to ears that never hear,
They seek each other all their weary days
And die unsatisfied — and this is Fate!

Robert Bridges

"THE UNILLUMINED VERGE"

THEY tell you that Death 's at the turn of the road,
That under the shade of a cypress you 'll find him,
And, struggling on wearily, lashed by the goad
Of pain, you will enter the black mist behind him.

I can walk with you up to the ridge of the hill,
And we 'll talk of the way we have come through the valley;
Down below there a bird breaks into a trill,
And a groaning slave bends to the oar of his galley.

You are up on the heights now, you pity the slave —
"Poor soul, how fate lashes him on at his rowing!
Yet it 's joyful to live, and it 's hard to be brave
When you watch the sun sink and the daylight is going."

We are almost there — our last walk on this height —
I must bid you good-by at that cross on the mountain.
See the sun glowing red, and the pulsating light
Fill the valley, and rise like the flood in a fountain!

And it shines in your face and illumines your soul;
We are comrades as ever, right here at your going;
You may rest if you will within sight of the goal,
While I must return to my oar and the rowing.

We must part now? Well, here is the hand of a friend;
I will keep you in sight till the road makes its turning
Just over the ridge within reach of the end
Of your arduous toil, — the beginning of learning.

You will call to me once from the mist, on the verge,
"Au revoir!" and "Good night!" while the twilight is creeping
Up luminous peaks, and the pale stars emerge?
Yes, I hear your faint voice: "This is rest, and like sleeping!"

JAMES McCOSH

YOUNG to the end through sympathy with youth,
Gray man of learning, — champion of truth!
Direct in rugged speech, alert in mind,
He felt his kinship with all humankind,
And never feared to trace development
Of high from low, — assured and full content
That man paid homage to the Mind above,
Uplifted by the "Royal Law of Love."

The laws of nature that he loved to trace
Have worked, at last, to veil from us his face;
The dear old elms and ivy-covered walls
Will miss his presence, and the stately halls
His trumpet voice. And in their joys
Sorrow will shadow those he called "my boys"!

William Lindsey

EN GARDE, MESSIEURS

En garde, Messieurs, too long have I endured,
Too long with patience borne the world's rebuff;
Now he who shoulders me shall find me rough;
The weakness of an easy soul is cured.

I 've shouted, leathern-lunged, when fame or gold
Were won by others, turned to aid my friend; —
Dull-pated ever, — but such follies end;
Only a fool 's content, and in the cold.

My doublet is in tatters, and my purse
Waves in the wind, light as my lady's fan;
Only my sword is bright; with it I plan
To win success, or put my sword to nurse.

I wait no longer for the primal blow;
Henceforth my stroke is first, I give offense;
I claim no more an over-dainty sense,
I brook no blocking where I plan to go.

En garde, Messieurs! and if my hand is hard,
Remember I 've been buffeted at will;
I am a whit impatient, and 'tis ill
To cross a hungry dog, Messieurs, en garde.

THE HUNDRED-YARD DASH

Give me a race that is run in a breath,
Straight from the start to the "tape;"
Distance hath charms, but a "Ding Dong" means death,
Death without flowers and crape.

"On your mark," "Set," — for a moment we strain,
Held by a leash all unseen;
"P'ff," we are off, from the pistol we gain
Yards, if the starter 's not keen.

Off like lean greyhounds, the cinders scarce stir
Under the touch of our feet;
Flashes of sunlight, the crowd's muffled purr,
The rush of the wind, warm and sweet.

One last fierce effort; the red worsted breaks,
Struggle and strain are all past;
Only ten ticks of the watch, but it makes
First, second, third, and the last.

Horace L. Traubel

I SERVED IN A GREAT CAUSE

I served in a great cause:
Long had I doubted the call I heard, wantoning the seasons dead;
The opportune days were deserts, the sunlight fell on a waste,
But the dawn brought me face to face with itself, with the opening flowers:
I looked upon my sea casting its wrecks down the shore in the storm,
The wrecks, my useless volitions, disordered, missent, ill-protected, to the deep,
The resurrected programme of self veined red with the blood of my birth,
The futile hours past, the distrusted images recalled,
In tumult of desire, in quietude of achievement, in effacement of unbelief.

I served the great cause, the great cause served me;
There were never any debts between us, the compact was without obligation;
I answered its cry, it answered my cry;
The seed in the ground hungered for light, the light pierced the earth with unerring love —
We met, we ran together, appointed mates.

I served not as one who follows or one who
 leads;
I served not in abasement, on my knees,
 with my head in the dust;
I served proudly, accepted, accepting,
The cloudland phantoms never misting the
 prospect,
The sunshine sirens never dazing the day
 with their splendor,
Ever in my heart crowding ancient and
 unborn dreams,
Cresting the hills and making the valleys
 fertile.

I served in a great cause:
I served without heroism, without virtue,
 with no promises of success, with no
 near destination of treasure;
I was on the march, I contained that which
 persevered me to ends unseen, no
 footsore night relaxed my pace;
There was only the press of invisible hands,
 only gray-brown eyes of invitation,
Only my franchised heart to fuel the fires
 to suns.

IF ALL THE VOICES OF MEN

If all the voices of men called out warning
 you, and you could not join your
 voice with their voices,
If all the faces of men were turned one
 way and you met them face to face,
 you going another, —
You still must not be persuaded to capitu-
 lation; you will remember that the
 road runs east as well as west.

EPICEDIUM

Like to the leaf that falls,
 Like to the rose that fades,
 Thou art — and still art not!
We whom this thought enthralls,
 We whom this mystery shades,
 Are bared before our lot!

Like to the light gone out,
 Like to the sun gone down,
 Thou art — and yet we feel
That something more than doubt,
 And more than Nature's frown,
 The Great Good must reveal.

'T is not with thankless heart,
 Nor yet with covert hand,
 We reach from deeps to thee:
We take our grief apart,
 And with it bravely stand
 Beside the voiceless sea!

O, gentle memory mine —
 I fill the world with thee,
 And with thy blessing sleep!
But for thy love divine
 To warm the day for me,
 Why should I wake or weep?

Danske Dandridge

THE DEAD MOON

We are ghost-ridden:
 Through the deep night
Wanders a spirit,
 Noiseless and white;
Loiters not, lingers not, knoweth not rest,
Ceaselessly haunting the East and the
 West.

She, whose undoing the ages have wrought,
Moves on to the time of God's rhythmical
 thought.
 In the dark, swinging sea,
 As she speedeth through space,
She reads her pale image;
 The wounds are agape on her face.
She sees her grim nakedness
 Pierced by the eyes
Of the Spirits of God
 In their flight through the skies.
(Her wounds, — they are many and hol-
 low.)
The Earth turns and wheels as she flies,
And this Spectre, this Ancient, must follow.

When, in the æons,
 Had she beginning?
What is her story?
 What was her sinning?

Do the ranks of the Holy Ones
  Know of her crime ?
Does it loom in the mists
  Of the birthplace of Time ?
The stars, do they speak of her
  Under their breath,
" Will this Wraith be forever
  Thus restless in death ? "
On, through immensity,
  Sliding and stealing,
On, through infinity,
  Nothing revealing ?

I see the fond lovers:
  They walk in her light;
They charge the " soft maiden "
  To bless their love-plight.
Does she laugh in her place,
  As she glideth through space ?
Does she laugh in her orbit with never a sound ?
  That to her, a dead body,
With nothing but rents in her round —
  Blighted and marred,
  Wrinkled and scarred,
    Barren and cold,
    Wizened and old —
    That to her should be told,
That to her should be sung
The yearning and burning of them that are young ?

  Our Earth that is young,
    That is throbbing with life,
  Has fiery upheavals,
    Has boisterous strife ;
But she that is dead has no stir, breathes no air;
She is calm, she is voiceless, in lonely despair.

We dart through the void;
  We have cries, we have laughter;
The phantom that haunts us
  Comes silently after.
This Ghost-lady follows,
  Though none hear her tread;
On, on, we are flying,
  Still tracked by our Dead —
By this white, awful Mystery,
  Haggard and dead.

THE SPIRIT OF THE FALL

Come, on thy swaying feet,
Wild Spirit of the Fall !
With wind-blown skirts, loose hair of russet-brown,
Crowned with bright berries of the bitter-sweet.

Trip a light measure with the hurrying leaf,
Straining thy few late roses to thy breast,
With laughter over-gay, sweet eyes drooped down,
That none may guess thy grief.
Dare not to pause for rest
Lest the slow tears should gather to their fall.

But when the cold moon rises o'er the hill,
The last numb crickets cease, and all is still,
Face down thou liest on the frosty ground
Strewed with thy fortune's wreck, alas, thine all —

. . . .

There, on a winter dawn, thy corse I found,
Lone Spirit of the Fall.

William Roscoe Thayer

("PAUL HERMES")

THE LAST HUNT

Oh, it 's twenty gallant gentlemen
  Rode out to hunt the deer,
With mirth upon the silver horn
  And gleam upon the spear;
They galloped through the meadow-grass,
  They sought the forest's gloom,
And loudest rang Sir Morven's laugh,
  And lightest tost his plume.
    There 's no delight by day or night
    Like hunting in the morn;
  So busk ye, gallant gentlemen,
    And sound the silver horn !

They rode into the dark greenwood
  By ferny dell and glade,

And now and then upon their cloaks
The yellow sunshine played;
They heard the timid forest-birds
Break off amid their glee,
They saw the startled leveret,
But not a stag did see.
Wind, wind the horn, on summer morn!
Though ne'er a buck appear,
There 's health for horse and gentleman
A-hunting of the deer!

They panted up Ben Lomond's side
Where thick the leafage grew,
And when they bent the branches back
The sunbeams darted through;
Sir Morven in his saddle turned,
And to his comrades spake,
"Now quiet! we shall find a stag
Beside the Brownies' Lake."
Then sound not on the bugle-horn,
Bend bush and do not break,
Lest ye should start the timid hart
A-drinking at the lake.

Now they have reached the Brownies' Lake, —
A blue eye in the wood, —
And on its brink a moment's space
All motionless they stood:
When, suddenly, the silence broke
With fifty bowstrings' twang,
And hurtling through the drowsy air
Full fifty arrows sang.
Ah, better for those gentlemen,
Than horn and slender spear,
Were morion and buckler true,
A-hunting of the deer.

Not one of that brave company
Shall hunt the deer again;
Some fell beside the Brownies' Pool,
Some dropt in dell or glen;
An arrow pierced Sir Morven's breast,
His horse plunged in the lake,
And swimming to the farther bank
He left a bloody wake.
Ah, what avails the silver horn,
And what the slender spear?
There 's other quarry in the wood
Beside the fallow deer!

O'er ridge and hollow sped the horse
Besprent with blood and foam,
Nor slackened pace until at eve
He brought his master home.

How tenderly the Lady Ruth
The cruel dart withdrew!
"False Tirrell shot the bolt," she said,
"That my Sir Morven slew!"
Deep in the forest lurks the foe,
While gayly shines the morn:
Hang up the broken spear, and blow
A dirge upon the horn.

MAN IN NATURE

CLIMBING up the hillside beneath the summer stars
I listen to the murmur of the drowsy ebbing sea;
The newly-risen moon has loosed her silver zone
On the undulating waters where the ships are sailing free.

O moon, and O stars, and O drowsy summer sea
Drawing thy tide from the city up the bay,
I know how you will look and what your bounds must be,
When we and our sons have forever passed away.

You shall not change, but a nobler race of men
Shall walk beneath the stars and wander by the shore;
I cannot guess their glory, but I think the sky and sea
Will bring to them more gladness than they brought to us of yore.

THE VIOLIN'S COMPLAINT

HONEST Stradivari made me:
With the gift of love he blest me;
Once, delight, a master played me,
Love awoke when he caressed me!

Oh the deep, ecstatic burning!
Oh the secrets low and tender!
Oh the passion and the yearning
At our love's complete surrender!

Heartless men, so long to hide me
With the costly toys you cherish;
I'm a soul — again confide me
To a lover, ere I perish!

Helen Gray Cone

THE RIDE TO THE LADY

"Now since mine even is come at last, —
For I have been the sport of steel,
And hot life ebbeth from me fast,
And I in saddle roll and reel, —
Come bind me, bind me on my steed!
Of fingering leech I have no need!"
The chaplain clasped his mailëd knee.
"Nor need I more thy whine and thee!
No time is left my sins to tell;
But look ye bind me, bind me well!"
They bound him strong with leathern thong,
For the ride to the lady should be long.

Day was dying; the poplars fled,
Thin as ghosts, on a sky blood-red;
Out of the sky the fierce hue fell,
And made the streams as the streams of hell.
All his thoughts as a river flowed,
Flowed aflame as fleet he rode,
Onward flowed to her abode,
Ceased at her feet, mirrored her face.
(Viewless Death apace, apace,
Rode behind him in that race.)

"Face, mine own, mine alone,
Trembling lips my lips have known,
Birdlike stir of the dove-soft eyne
Under the kisses that make them mine!
Only of thee, of thee, my need!
Only to thee, to thee, I speed!"
The Cross flashed by at the highway's turn;
In a beam of the moon the Face shone stern.

Far behind had the fight's din died;
The shuddering stars in the welkin wide
Crowded, crowded, to see him ride.
The beating hearts of the stars aloof
Kept time to the beat of the horse's hoof.
"What is the throb that thrills so sweet?
Heart of my lady, I feel it beat!"
But his own strong pulse the fainter fell,
Like the failing tongue of a hushing bell.
The flank of the great-limbed steed was wet
Not alone with the started sweat.

Fast, and fast, and the thick black wood
Arched its cowl like a black friar's hood;
Fast, and fast, and they plunged therein, —
But the viewless rider rode to win.

Out of the wood to the highway's light
Galloped the great-limbed steed in fright;
The mail clashed cold, and the sad owl cried,
And the weight of the dead oppressed his side.

Fast, and fast, by the road he knew;
And slow, and slow, the stars withdrew;
And the waiting heaven turned weirdly blue,
As a garment worn of a wizard grim.
He neighed at the gate in the morning dim.

She heard no sound before her gate,
Though very quiet was her bower.
All was as her hand had left it late:
The needle slept on the broidered vine,
Where the hammer and spikes of the passion-flower
Her fashioning did wait.
On the couch lay something fair,
With steadfast lips and veilëd eyne;
But the lady was not there.
On the wings of shrift and prayer,
Pure as winds that winnow snow,
Her soul had risen twelve hours ago.
The burdened steed at the barred gate stood,
No whit the nearer to his goal.
Now God's great grace assoil the soul
That went out in the wood!

ARRAIGNMENT

"Not ye who have stoned, not ye who have smitten us," cry
The sad, great souls, as they go out hence into dark, —
"Not ye we accuse, though for you was our passion borne;
And ye we reproach not, who silently passed us by.
We forgive blind eyes and the ears that would not hark,
The careless and causeless hate and the shallow scorn.

"But ye, who have seemed to know us, have seen and heard;
Who have set us at feasts and have crowned with the costly rose;
Who have spread us the purple of praises beneath our feet;
Yet guessed not the word that we spake was a living word,
Applauding the sound, — we account you as worse than foes!
We sobbed you our message: ye said, 'It is song, and sweet!'"

THISBE

The garden within was shaded,
And guarded about from sight;
The fragrance flowed to the south wind,
The fountain leaped to the light.

And the street without was narrow,
And dusty, and hot, and mean;
But the bush that bore white roses,
She leaned to the fence between:

And softly she sought a crevice
In that barrier blank and tall,
And shyly she thrust out through it
Her loveliest bud of all.

And tender to touch, and gracious,
And pure as the moon's pure shine,
The full rose paled and was perfect, —
For whose eyes, for whose lips, but mine!

THE CONTRAST

He loved her, having felt his love begin
With that first look, — as lover oft avers.
He made pale flowers his pleading ministers,
Impressed sweet music, drew the spring-time in
To serve his suit; but when he could not win,
Forgot her face and those gray eyes of hers;
And at her name his pulse no longer stirs,
And life goes on as though she had not been.
She never loved him; but she loved Love so,
So reverenced Love, that all her being shook
At his demand whose entrance she denied.
Her thoughts of him such tender color took
As western skies that keep the afterglow.
The words he spoke were with her till she died.

THE LAST CUP OF CANARY

SIR HARRY LOVELOCK, 1645

So, the powder 's low, and the larder 's clean,
And surrender drapes, with its blacks impending,
All the stage for a sorry and sullen scene:
Yet indulge me my whim of a madcap ending!

Let us once more fill, ere the final chill,
Every vein with the glow of the rich canary!
Since the sweet hot liquor of life 's to spill,
Of the last of the cellar what boots be chary?

Then hear the conclusion: I 'll yield my breath,
But my leal old house and my good blade never!
Better one bitter kiss on the lips of Death
Than despoiled Defeat as a wife forever!

Let the faithful fire hold the walls in ward
Till the roof-tree crash! Be the smoke once riven
While we flash from the gate like a single sword,
True steel to the hilt, though in dull earth driven!

Do you frown, Sir Richard, above your ruff,
In the Holbein yonder? My deed ensures you!
For the flame like a fencer shall give rebuff
To your blades that blunder, you Round-head boors, you!

And my ladies, a-row on the gallery wall,
Not a sing-song sergeant or corporal sainted
Shall pierce their breasts with his Puritan ball,
To annul the charms of the flesh, though painted!

I have worn like a jewel the life they gave;
As the ring in mine ear I can lightly lose it.
If my days be done, why, my days were brave!
If the end arrive, I as master choose it!

Then fill to the brim, and a health, I say,
To our liege King Charles, and I pray God bless him!
'T would amend worse vintage to drink dismay
To the clamorous mongrel pack that press him!

And a health to the fair women, past recall,
That like birds astray through the heart's hall flitted;
To the lean devil Failure last of all,
And the lees in his beard for a fiend outwitted!

THE SPRING BEAUTIES

The Puritan Spring Beauties stood freshly clad for church;
A Thrush, white-breasted, o'er them sat singing on his perch.
"Happy be! for fair are ye!" the gentle singer told them,
But presently a buff-coat Bee came booming up to scold them.
"Vanity, oh, vanity!
Young maids, beware of vanity!"
Grumbled out the buff-coat Bee,
Half parson-like, half soldierly.

The sweet-faced maidens trembled, with pretty, pinky blushes,
Convinced that it was wicked to listen to the Thrushes;
And when, that shady afternoon, I chanced that way to pass,
They hung their little bonnets down and looked into the grass.
All because the buff-coat Bee
Lectured them so solemnly: —
"Vanity, oh, vanity!
Young maids, beware of vanity!"

FAIR ENGLAND

White England shouldering from the sea,
Green England in thy rainy veil,
Old island-nest of Liberty
And loveliest Song, all hail!
God guard thee long from scath and grief!
Not any wish of ours would mar
One richly glooming ivy-leaf,
One rosy daisy-star.

What! phantoms are we, spectre-thin,
Unfathered, out of nothing born?
Did Being in this world begin
With blaze of yestermorn?

Nay! sacred Life, a scarlet thread,
Through lost unnumbered lives has run;
No strength can tear us from the dead;
The sire is in the son.

Nay! through the years God's purpose glides,
And links in sequence deed with deed;
Hoar Time along his chaplet slides
Bead after jewel-bead.

O brother, breathing English air!
If both be just, if both be free,
A lordlier heritage we share
Than any earth can be:

If hearts be high, if hands be pure,
A bond unseen shall bind us still, —
The only bond that can endure,
Being welded with God's will!

A bond unseen! and yet God speed
The apparent sign, when He finds good;
When in His sight it types indeed
That inward brotherhood.

For not the rose-and-emerald bow
Can bid the battling storm to cease,
But leaps at last, that all may know
The sign, not source, of peace.

Oh, what shall shameful peace avail,
If east or west, if there or here,
Men sprung of ancient England fail
To hold their birthright dear?

If west or east, if here or there,
Brute Mammon sit in Freedom's place,
And judge a wailing world's despair
With hard, averted face?

O great Co-heir, whose lot is cast
  Beside the hearthstone loved of yore!
Inherit with us that best Past
  That lives for evermore!

Inherit with us! Lo, the days
  Are evil; who may know the end?
Strike hands, and dare the darkening ways,
  Twin strengths, with God to friend!

Richard Burton

THE FIRST SONG

A POET writ a song of May
  That checked his breath awhile;
He kept it for a summer day,
  Then spake with half a smile:

"Oh, little song of purity,
  Of mystic to-and-fro,
You are so much a part of me
  I dare not let you go."

And so he made a sister-song
  With more of cunning art;
But held the first his whole life long
  Deep hidden in his heart.

ON A FERRY BOAT

THE river widens to a pathless sea
  Beneath the rain and mist and sullen skies.
  Look out the window; 't is a gray emprise,
This piloting of massed humanity
  On such a day, from shore to busy shore,
  And breeds the thought that beauty is no more.

But see yon woman in the cabin seat,
  The Southland in her face and foreign dress;
  She bends above a babe, with tenderness
That mothers use; her mouth grows soft and sweet.
  Then, lifting eyes, ye saints in heaven, what pain
  In that strange look of hers into the rain!

There lies a vivid band of scarlet red
  With careless grace across her raven hair;
  Her cheek burns brown; and 't is her way to wear
A gown where colors stand in satin's stead.
  Her eye gleams dark as any you may see
  Along the winding roads of Italy.

What dreamings must be hers of sunny climes,
  This beggar woman midst the draggled throng!
  How must she pine for solaces of song,
For warmth and love to furnish laughing-times!
  Her every glance upon the waters gray
  Is piteous with some lost yesterday.

I 've seen a dove, storm-beaten, far at sea;
  And once a flower growing stark alone
  From out a rock; I 've heard a hound make moan,
Left masterless: but never came to me
  Ere this such sense of creatures torn apart
  From all that fondles life and feeds the heart.

BLACK SHEEP

FROM their folded mates they wander far,
  Their ways seem harsh and wild:
They follow the beck of a baleful star,
  Their paths are dream-beguiled.

Yet haply they sought but a wider range,
  Some loftier mountain slope,
And little recked of the country strange
  Beyond the gates of hope.

And haply a bell, with a luring call
  Summoned their feet to tread
Midst the cruel rocks, where the deep pitfall
  And the lurking snare are spread.

Maybe, in spite of their tameless days
Of outcast liberty,
They 're sick at heart for the homely ways
Where their gathered brothers be.

And oft at night, when the plains fall dark
And the hills loom large and dim,
For the shepherd's voice they mutely hark,
And their souls go out to him.

Meanwhile, "Black sheep! black sheep!" we cry,
Safe in the inner fold;
And maybe they hear, and wonder why,
And marvel, out in the cold.

THE FOREFATHER

HERE at the country inn,
I lie in my quiet bed,
And the ardent onrush of armies
Throbs and throbs in my head.

Why, in this calm, sweet place,
Where only silence is heard,
Am I ware of the crash of conflict, —
Is my blood to battle stirred?

Without, the night is blessed
With the smell of pines, with stars;
Within, is the mood of slumber,
The healing of daytime scars.

'T is strange, — yet I am thrall
To epic agonies;
The tumult of myriads dying
Is borne to me on the breeze.

Mayhap in the long ago
My forefather grim and stark
Stood in some hell of carnage,
Faced forward, fell in the dark;

And I, who have always known
Peace with her dove-like ways,
Am gripped by his martial spirit
Here in the after days.

I cannot rightly tell:
I lie, from all stress apart,
And the ardent onrush of armies
Surges hot through my heart.

"EXTRAS"

THE crocuses in the Square
Lend a winsome touch to the May;
The clouds are vanished away,
The weather is bland and fair;
Now peace seems everywhere.
Hark to the raucous, sullen cries:
"Extra! extra!" — tersely flies
The news, and a great hope mounts, or dies.

About the bulletin-boards
Dark knots of people surge;
Strained faces show, then merge
In the inconspicuous hordes
That yet are the Nation's lords.
"Extra! extra! Big fight at sea!"
Was the luck with us? Is it victory?
Dear God, they died for you and me!

Meanwhile the crocuses down the street
With heaven's own patience are calm and sweet.

LOVE IS STRONG

A VIEWLESS thing is the wind,
But its strength is mightier far
Than a phalanxed host in battle line,
Than the limbs of a Samson are.

And a viewless thing is Love,
And a name that vanisheth;
But her strength is the wind's wild strength above,
For she conquers shame and Death.

AN UNPRAISED PICTURE

I SAW a picture once by Angelo.
"Unfinished," said the critic; "done in youth;"
And that was all, no thought of praise, forsooth!
He was informed, and doubtless it was so.
And yet, I let an hour of dreaming go
The way of all time, touched to tears and ruth,
Passion and joy, the prick of conscience' tooth,
Before that careworn Christ's divine, soft glow.

The painter's yearning with an unsure hand
Had moved me more than might his master days;
He seemed to speak like one whose Mecca-land
Is first beheld, though faint and far the ways;
Who may not then his shaken voice command,
Yet trembles forth a word of prayer and praise.

THE POLAR QUEST

UNCONQUERABLY, men venture on the quest
And seek an ocean amplitude unsailed,
Cold, virgin, awful. Scorning ease and rest,
And heedless of the heroes who have failed,
They face the ice floes with a dauntless zest.

The polar quest! Life's offer to the strong!
To pass beyond the pale, to do and dare,
Leaving a name that stirs us like a song.
And making captive some strange Otherwhere,
Though grim the conquest, and the labor long.

Forever courage kindles, faith moves forth
To find the mystic floodway of the North.

IN SLEEP

NOT drowsihood and dreams and mere idless,
Nor yet the blessedness of strength regained,
Alone are in what men call sleep. The past,
My unsuspected soul, my parents' voice,
The generations of my forbears, yea,
The very will of God himself are there
And potent-working: so that many a doubt
Is wiped away at daylight, many a soil
Washed cleanlier, many a puzzle riddled plain.
Strong, silent forces push my puny self
Towards unguessed issues, and the waking man
Rises a Greatheart where a Slave lay down.

Katharine Lee Bates

ROBIN'S SECRET

'TIS the blithest, bonniest weather for a bird to flirt a feather,
For a bird to trill and warble, all his wee red breast a-swell.
I 've a secret. You may listen till your blue eyes dance and glisten,
Little maiden, but I 'll never, never, never, never tell.

You 'll find no more wary piper, till the strawberries wax riper
In December than in June — aha! all up and down the dell,
Where my nest is set, for certain, with a pink and snowy curtain,
East or west, but which I 'll never, never, never, never tell.

You may prick me with a thistle, if you ever hear me whistle
How my brooding mate, whose weariness my carols sweet dispel,
All between the clouds and clover, apple-blossoms drooping over,
Twitters low that I must never, never, never, never tell.

Oh, I swear no closer fellow stains his bill in cherries mellow.
Tra la la! and tirra lirra! I 'm the jauntiest sentinel,
Perched beside my jewel-casket, where lie hidden — don't you ask it,
For of those three eggs I 'll never, never, never, never tell.

Chirp! chirp! chirp! alack! for pity! Who hath marred my merry ditty?
Who hath stirred the scented petals, peeping in where robins dwell?
Oh, my mate! May Heaven defend her!
Little maidens' hearts are tender,
And I never, never, never, never, never *meant* to tell.

A SONG OF RICHES

WHAT will you give to a barefoot lass,
Morning with breath like wine?
Wade, bare feet! In my wide morass
Starry marigolds shine.

Alms, sweet Noon, for a barefoot lass,
With her laughing looks aglow!
Run, bare feet! In my fragrant grass
Golden buttercups blow.

Gift, a gift for a barefoot lass,
O twilight hour of dreams!
Rest, bare feet, by my lake of glass,
Where the mirrored sunset gleams.

Homeward the weary merchants pass,
With the gold bedimmed by care.
Little they wis that the barefoot lass
Is the only millionaire.

THE LITTLE KNIGHT IN GREEN

WHAT fragrant-footed comer
Is stepping o'er my head?
Behold, my queen! the Summer!
Who deems her warriors dead.
Now rise, ye knights of many fights,
From out your sleep profound!
Make sharp your spears, my gallant peers,
And prick the frozen ground.

Before the White Host harm her,
We'll hurry to her aid;
We 'll don our elfin armor,
And every tiny blade
Shall bear atop a dewy drop,
The life-blood of the frost,
Till from their king the order ring:
"Fall back! the day is lost."

Now shame to knighthood, brothers!
Must Summer plead in vain?
And shall I wait till others
My crown of sunshine gain?
Alone this day I 'll dare the fray,
Alone the victory win;
In me my queen shall find, I ween,
A sturdy paladin.

To battle! Ho! King Winter
Hath rushed on me apace, —
My fragile blade doth splinter
Beneath his icy mace.
I stagger back. I yield — alack!
I fall. My senses pass.
Woe worth the chance for doughtiest lance
Of all the House of Grass!

Last hope my heart gives over.
But hark! a shout of cheer!
Don Daisy and Count Clover,
Sir Buttercup, are here!
Behold! behold! with shield of gold
Prince Dandelion comes.
Lord Bumble-Bee beats valiantly
His rolling battle-drums.

My brothers leave their slumbers
And lead the van of war;
Before our swelling numbers
The foes are driven far.
The day 's our own; but, overthrown,
A little Knight in green,
I kiss her feet and deem it sweet
To perish for my queen.

George Pellew

ON A CAST FROM AN ANTIQUE

HEADLESS, without an arm, a figure leans
By something vaguely Greek, — a fount, an urn;
Dim stairs climb past her where one's thoughts discern
A temple or a palace. Some great queen's
Daughter art thou? or humbly one of those

Who serve a queen? Is this the sacred thing
That holds thy child, thy husband, or thy
king?
Or lightly-laughing water? No one knows.
A woman once, now merely womanhood,
In gentle pose of un-selfconscious dream
That consecrates all ministry of love.
Gone are thy temples and the gods thereof,
But through the ruin of centuries sublime
Heart speaks to heart, and still is understood.

DEATH

Calm Death, God of crossed hands and passionless eyes,
Thou God that never heedest gift nor prayer,
Men blindly call thee cruel, unaware
That everything is dearer since it dies.
Worn by the chain of years, without surprise,
The wise man welcomes thee, and leaves the glare
Of noisy sunshine gladly, and his share
He chose not in mad life and windy skies.
Passions and dreams of love, the fever and fret
Of toil, seem vain and petty when we gaze
On the imperious Lords who have no breath:
Atoms or worlds, — we call them lifeless, yet
In thy unending peaceful day of days
They are divine, all-comprehending Death.

Robert Mowry Bell

THE TUTELAGE[1]

In the coiled shell sounds Ocean's distant roar,
Oft to our listening hearts come heavenly strains; —
Men say, "That was the blood in our own veins,
And this, — but the echo of our hope; no more."
And yet, the murmuring sea exists, which bore
That frail creation o'er its watery plains;
And on Time's sands full many a shell remains
Tossed by Eternity upon its shore.
Its tongue our hope from Nature's self has caught.
Matter nor force is lost as æons roll.
And mind? — Love life conserves and death abates, —
Through the long ages this has nature taught.
Under the stars she plights the wistful soul:
"Life ruled by Love nor dies nor dissipates."

THE SECOND VOLUME

In the groined alcoves of an ancient tower
Amid a wealth of treasured tomes I found
A little book, in choicest vellum bound:
Therein a romance of such magic power
It held me rapt through many a trancëd hour;
And then, the threads of interest all unwound,
Abruptly closed. I searched that palace round,
And for its mate still earth's preserves I scour.
Perchance that was the whole? Then purposeless
The pain of conflict, and the bitter doubt
But half resolved; love in a dire distress,
Deserted, baffled, with its joy left out.
Could life so end, half told; its school so fail?
Soul, soul, there is a sequel to thy tale!

[1] See Biographical Note, p. 779.

Frank Dempster Sherman

ON A GREEK VASE

DIVINELY shapen cup, thy lip
  Unto me seemeth thus to speak:
"Behold in me the workmanship,
  The grace and cunning of a Greek!

"Long ages since he mixed the clay,
  Whose sense of symmetry was such,
The labor of a single day
  Immortal grew beneath his touch.

"For dreaming while his fingers went
  Around this slender neck of mine,
The form of her he loved was blent
  With every matchless curve and line.

"Her loveliness to me he gave
  Who gave unto herself his heart,
That love and beauty from the grave
  Might rise and live again in art."

And hearing from thy lips this tale
  Of love and skill, of art and grace,
Thou seem'st to me no more the frail
  Memento of an older race:

But in thy form divinely wrought
  And figured o'er with fret and scroll,
I dream, by happy chance was caught,
  And dwelleth now, that maiden's soul.

TO A ROSE

GO, Rose, and in her golden hair
  You shall forget the garden soon;
The sunshine is a captive there
  And crowns her with a constant noon.

And when your spicy odor goes,
  And fades the beauty of your bloom,
Think what a lovely hand, O Rose,
  Shall place your body in the tomb!

ON SOME BUTTERCUPS

A LITTLE way below her chin,
  Caught in her bosom's snowy hem,
Some buttercups are fastened in, —
  Ah, how I envy them!

They do not miss their meadow place,
  Nor are they conscious that their skies
Are not the heavens, but her face,
  Her hair, and mild blue eyes.

There, in the downy meshes pinned,
  Such sweet illusions haunt their rest;
They think her breath the fragrant wind,
  And tremble on her breast;

As if, close to her heart, they heard
  A captive secret slip its cell,
And with desire were sudden stirred
  To find a voice and tell!

THE LIBRARY

GIVE me the room whose every nook
Is dedicated to a book:
Two windows will suffice for air
And grant the light admission there, —
One looking to the south, and one
To speed the red, departing sun.
The eastern wall from frieze to plinth
Shall be the Poet's labyrinth,
Where one may find the lords of rhyme
From Homer's down to Dobson's time;
And at the northern side a space
Shall show an open chimney-place,
Set round with ancient tiles that tell
Some legend old, and weave a spell
About the firedog-guarded seat,
Where, musing, one may taste the heat:
Above, the mantel should not lack
For curios and bric-à-brac, —
Not much, but just enough to light
The room up when the fire is bright.
The volumes on this wall should be
All prose and all philosophy,
From Plato down to those who are
The dim reflections of that star;
And these tomes all should serve to show
How much we write — how little know;
For since the problem first was set
No one has ever solved it yet.
Upon the shelves along the west
The scientific books shall rest;
Beside them, History; above, —
Religion, — hope, and faith, and love:
Lastly, the southern wall should hold
The story-tellers, new and old;

Haroun al Raschid, who was truth
And happiness to all my youth,
Shall have the honored place of all
That dwell upon the sunny wall;
And with him there shall stand a throng
Of those who help mankind along
More by their fascinating lies
Than all the learning of the wise.

Such be the library; and take
This motto of a Latin make
To grace the door through which I pass:
Hic habitat Felicitas!

QUATRAINS

A QUATRAIN

HARK at the lips of this pink whorl of shell
And you shall hear the ocean's surge and roar:
So in the quatrain's measure, written well,
A thousand lines shall all be sung in four!

A HOLLYHOCK

SERAGLIO of the Sultan Bee!
I listen at the waxen door,
And hear the zithern's melody
And sound of dancing on the floor.

MOONRISE

WITHIN this silent palace of the Night,
See how the moon, like some huge, phantom moth,
Creeps slowly up across the azure cloth
That hangs between the darkness and the light.

THE ROSE'S CUP

DOWN in a garden olden, —
Just where, I do not know, —
A buttercup all golden
Chanced near a rose to grow;
And every morning early,
Before the birds were up,
A tiny dewdrop pearly
Fell in this little cup.

This was the drink of water
The rose had every day;
But no one yet has caught her
While drinking in this way.
Surely, it is no treason
To say she drinks so yet,
For that may be the reason
Her lips with dew are wet.

THE SHADOWS

ALL up and down in shadow-town
The shadow children go;
In every street you 're sure to meet
Them running to and fro.

They move around without a sound,
They play at hide-and-seek,
But no one yet that I have met
Has ever heard them speak.

Beneath the tree you often see
Them dancing in and out,
And in the sun there 's always one
To follow you about.

Go where you will, he follows still,
Or sometimes runs before,
And, home at last, you 'll find him fast
Beside you at the door.

A faithful friend is he to lend
His presence everywhere;
Blow out the light — to bed at night —
Your shadow-mate is there!

Then he will call the shadows all
Into your room to leap,
And such a pack! they make it black,
And fill your eyes with sleep!

AT MIDNIGHT

SEE, yonder, the belfry tower
That gleams in the moon's pale light;
Or is it a ghostly flower
That dreams in the silent night?

I listen and hear the chime
Go quavering o'er the town,
And out of this flower of Time
Twelve petals are wafted down.

John Hall Ingham

GEORGE WASHINGTON

THIS was the man God gave us when the hour
Proclaimed the dawn of Liberty begun;
Who dared a deed, and died when it was done
Patient in triumph, temperate in power,—
Not striving like the Corsican to tower
To heaven, nor like great Philip's greater son
To win the world and weep for worlds unwon,
Or lose the star to revel in the flower.
The lives that serve the eternal verities
Alone do mould mankind. Pleasure and pride
Sparkle awhile and perish, as the spray
Smoking across the crests of cavernous seas
Is impotent to hasten or delay
The everlasting surges of the tide.

GENESIS

DID Chaos form,—and water, air, and fire,
Rocks, trees, the worm, work toward Humanity,—
That Man at last, beneath the churchyard spire,
Might be once more the worm, the rock, the tree?

A SUMMER SANCTUARY

I FOUND a yellow flower in the grass,
A tiny flower with petals like a bell,
And yet, methought, more than a flower it was,—
More like a miracle.

Above, the sky was clear, save where at times
Soft-tinted fleeces drifted dreamily,
Bearing a benison to sunny climes
From altars of the sea.

In vestments green the pines about me gleamed
Like priests that tend the sacrificial fire;
And the faint-lowing cattle almost seemed
Some far intoning choir.

It was a place and an occasion meet
For some high, solemn wonder to befall;
And, when I saw the flower at my feet,
I understood it all.

Harry Lyman Koopman

SEA AND SHORE

OUR Mother, loved of all thy sons
So dear, they die, not dying for thee;
Yet are thy fondest, tenderest ones
Thy wanderers far at sea.

Life-long the bitter blue they stem,
Till custom makes it almost fair;
Sweet grow the splintering gales to them,
The icy gloom, the scorching glare.

But thy dear eyes, which shine for all,
They see not, save through homesick tears,
Or when thy smile, through battle-pall,
Pays death and all their painful years.

Fair freedom's gospel soundeth now
Through softer lips than those of steel;
Rust gathers on the iron prow,
And shore weeds clog the resting keel;

To-day thou askest life, not death;
Our lives, for life and death, are thine:
Sweet are long years, and peaceful breath,
And sunny age beneath its vine;

But there are those that deem more fair
(O Mother, seen at last again!)
That smile the dying see thee wear,
Choosing thine own among the slain.

Yet, being thine, we shall be brave,
And, being thine, we will be true;

Where'er thou callest, on field or wave,
  We wait, thy will to do.

JOHN BROWN

THE sea-bound landsman, looking back to shore,
Now learns what land is highest: — not the ring
Of hills that erewhile shut out everything
Beyond them from him: these are seen no more;
Nor yet the loftier heights that, from the lower,
He saw far inland, blue, and, worshipping,
Believed they touched the sky; the gull's white wing
Long since flashed o'er them sunk in the sea-floor.
These were but uplands hiding the true height,
Which looms above them as they sink, and rears
Its greatness ever greater on the sight.
So thou, across the widening sea of years,
Aye risest great, as on through gloom and bright
Our tossing bark of Progress sunward steers.

ICARUS

'T IS something from that tangle to have won;
'T is something to have matched the wild-bird's flight;
'T is something to have soared and touched the sun.
What though the lashing billows roar beneath?
Better than death in life is life in death: —
  Good night!

THE SATIRIST

NOT mine to draw the cloth-yard shaft
  From straining palm to thrilling ear;
Then launch it through the monster's hulk,
  One thrust, from front to rear.

Mine is the Bushman's tiny bow,
  Whose wounds the foeman hardly feels;
He laughs, and lifts his hand to smite,
  Then suddenly he reels.

REVEALED

Now, on a sudden, I know it, the secret, the secret of life.
Why, the very green of the grass in the fields with betrayal is rife!
The whirr of the grasshopper by the wayside proclaims it to all;
'T is unrolled as a scroll to all eyes in the curve of the waterfall.
But, for me, I can only wonder at mortals, — the secret out;
For they see, hear, taste, smell, feel not what Heaven reveals all about.

Oscar Fay Adams

AT LINCOLN

WHEN I went up the minster tower,
The minster clock rang out the hour;
  The restless organ far below
  Sent tides of music to and fro,
  That rolled through nave and angel choir,
  Whose builder knew what lines inspire,
  And filled the lantern's space profound
  With climbing waves of glorious sound,
As I went up the minster tower
What time the chimes gave forth the hour.

When I stood on the minster tower
The lark above me sent a shower
  Of happy notes, that filtered through

The clouds that flecked the sky's soft blue,
And mingled with the nearer tones
Of jackdaws' calls and stockdoves' moans,
While every breeze that round me swirled
Brought some sweet murmur from the world,
As I stood on the minster tower
What time the lark forsook her bower.

When I came down the minster tower,
Again the chimes proclaimed the hour,
Again the mighty organ rolled
Its thunders through the arches old,
While blended with its note so strong
Soft rose and fell the evensong,
And all the earth, it seemed to me,
Was still by music held in fee,
As I came down the minster tower
What time the clock slow chimed the hour.

ON A GRAVE IN CHRIST-CHURCH, HANTS

TURNING from Shelley's sculptured face aside,
And pacing thoughtfully the silent aisles
Of the gray church that overlooks the smiles
Of the glad Avon hastening its tide
To join the seaward-winding Stour, I spied
Close at my feet a slab among the tiles
That paved the minster, where the sculptor's files
Had graven only "*Died of Grief*," beside
The name of her who slept below. Sad soul!
A century has fled since kindly death
Cut short that life which nothing knew but grief,
And still your fate stirs pity. Yet the whole
Wide world is full of graves like yours, for breath
Of sorrow kills as oft as frost the leaf.

Hamlin Garland

PIONEERS

THEY rise to mastery of wind and snow;
They go like soldiers grimly into strife
To colonize the plain. They plough and sow,
And fertilize the sod with their own life,
As did the Indian and the buffalo.

IN THE GRASS [1]

O TO lie in long grasses!
O to dream of the plain!
Where the west wind sings as it passes
A weird and unceasing refrain;
Where the rank grass wallows and tosses,
And the plains' ring dazzles the eye;
Where hardly a silver cloud bosses
The flashing steel arch of the sky.

To watch the gay gulls as they flutter
Like snowflakes and fall down the sky,
To swoop in the deeps of the hollows,
Where the crow's-foot tosses awry,
And gnats in the lee of the thickets
Are swirling like waltzers in glee
To the harsh, shrill creak of the crickets,
And the song of the lark and the bee.

O far-off plains of my west land!
O lands of winds and the free,
Swift deer — my mist-clad plain!
From my bed in the heart of the forest,
From the clasp and the girdle of pain
Your light through my darkness passes;
To your meadows in dreaming I fly
To plunge in the deeps of your grasses,
To bask in the light of your sky!

THE MEADOW LARK

A BRAVE little bird that fears not God,
A voice that breaks from the snow-wet clod
With prophecy of sunny sod,
Set thick with wind-waved goldenrod.

From the first bare clod in the raw, cold spring,
From the last bare clod, when fall winds sting,
The farm-boy hears his brave song ring,
And work for the time is a pleasant thing.

THE MASSASAUGA

A COLD coiled line of mottled lead,
He lies where grazing cattle tread,
And lifts a fanged and spiteful head.

His touch is deadly, and his eyes
Are hot with hatred and surprise —
Death waits and watches where he lies!

His hate is turned toward everything!
He is the undisputed king
Of every path and woodland spring.

His naked fang is raised to smite
All passing things; light
Is not swifter than his bite.

His touch is deadly, and his eyes
Are hot with hatred and surprise —
Death waits and watches where he lies!

A TRIBUTE OF GRASSES

TO W. W.

SERENE, vast head, with silver cloud of hair
Lined on the purple dusk of death,
A stern medallion, velvet set —
Old Norseman, throned, not chained upon thy chair,
Thy grasp of hand, thy hearty breath
Of welcome thrills me yet
As when I faced thee there!

Loving my plain as thou thy sea,
Facing the East as thou the West,
I bring a handful of grass to thee, —
The prairie grasses I know the best;
Type of the wealth and width of the plain,
Strong of the strength of the wind and sleet,
Fragrant with sunlight and cool with rain,
I bring it and lay it low at thy feet,
Here by the eastern sea.

A WISH[1]

ALL day and many days I rode,
My horse's head set toward the sea;
And as I rode a longing came to me
That I might keep the sunset road,
Riding my horse right on and on,
O'ertake the day still lagging at the west,
And so reach boyhood from the dawn,
And be with all the days at rest.

For then the odor of the growing wheat,
The flare of sumach on the hills,
The touch of grasses to my feet
Would cure my brain of all its ills, —
Would fill my heart so full of joy
That no stern lines could fret my face.
There would I be forever boy,
Lit by the sky's unfailing grace.

THE GIFT OF WATER[1]

"Is water nigh?"
The plainsmen cry,
As they meet and pass in the desert grass.
With finger tip
Across the lip
I ask the sombre Navajo.
The brown man smiles and answers "Sho!"
With fingers high, he signs the miles
To the desert spring,
And so we pass in the dry dead grass,
Brothers in bond of the water's ring.

THE UTE LOVER[1]

BENEATH the burning brazen sky,
The yellowed tepees stand.
Not far away a singing river
Sets through the sand.
Within the shadow of a lonely elm tree
The tired ponies keep.
The wild land, throbbing with the sun's hot magic,
Is rapt as sleep.

From out a clump of scanty willows
A low wail floats, —
The endless repetition of a lover's
Melancholy notes,
So sad, so sweet, so elemental,
All lovers' pain
Seems borne upon its sobbing cadence, —
The love-song of the plain.
From frenzied cry forever falling,
To the wind's wild moan,
It seems the voice of anguish calling
Alone! alone!

Caught from the winds forever moaning
On the plain,
Wrought from the agonies of woman
In maternal pain,

It holds within its simple measure
All death of joy,
Breathed though it be by smiling maiden
Or lithe brown boy.

It hath this magic, sad though its cadence
And short refrain —
It helps the exiled people of the mountain
Endure the plain;
For when at night the stars a-glitter
Defy the moon,
The maiden listens, leans to seek her lover
Where waters croon.

Flute on, O lithe and tuneful Utah, —
Reply, brown jade;
There are no other joys secure to either
Man or maid.
Soon you are old and heavy-hearted,
Lost to mirth;
While on you lies the white man's gory
Greed of earth.

Strange that to me that burning desert
Seems so dear.
The endless sky and lonely mesa,
Flat and drear,
Calls me, calls me as the flute of Utah
Calls his mate, —
This wild, sad, sunny, brazen country,
Hot as hate.

Again the glittering sky uplifts star-blazing;
Again the stream
From out the far-off snowy mountains
Sings through my dream;
And on the air I hear the flute-voice calling
The lover's croon,
And see the listening, longing maiden
Lit by the moon.

DO YOU FEAR THE WIND?[1]

Do you fear the force of the wind,
The slash of the rain?
Go face them and fight them,
Be savage again.
Go hungry and cold like the wolf,
Go wade like the crane:
The palms of your hands will thicken,
The skin of your cheek will tan,
You 'll grow ragged and weary and swarthy,
But you 'll walk like a man!

THE GOLD-SEEKERS[1]

I SAW these dreamers of dreams go by,
I trod in their footsteps a space;
Each marched with his eyes on the sky,
Each passed with a light on his face.

They came from the hopeless and sad,
They faced the future and gold;
Some the tooth of want's wolf had made mad,
And some at the forge had grown old.

Behind them these serfs of the tool
The rags of their service had flung;
No longer of fortune the fool,
This word from each bearded lip rung:

"Once more I 'm a man, I am free!
No man is my master, I say;
To-morrow I fail, it may be, —
No matter, I 'm freeman to-day."

They go to a toil that is sure,
To despair and hunger and cold;
Their sickness no warning can cure,
They are mad with a longing for gold.

The light will fade from each eye,
The smile from each face;
They will curse the impassable sky,
And the earth when the snow torrents race.

Some will sink by the way and be laid
In the frost of the desolate earth;
And some will return to a maid,
Empty of hand as at birth.

But this out of all will remain,
They have lived and have tossed;
So much in the game will be gain,
Though the gold of the dice has been lost.

THE GREETING OF THE ROSES[1]

WE had been long in mountain snow,
In valleys bleak, and broad, and bare,
Where only moss and willows grow,
And no bird wings the silent air.
And so, when on our downward way
Wild roses met us, we were glad:
They were so girlish fair, so gay,
It seemed the sun had made them mad.

[1] Copyright, 1899, by THE MACMILLAN COMPANY.

Virginia Woodward Cloud

THE MOTHER'S SONG

"Two women shall be grinding at the mill: the one shall be taken and the other left."

ALL day and all day, as I sit at my measureless turning,
They come and they go, —
The little ones down on the rocks, — and the sunlight is burning
On vineyards below;
All day and all day, as I sit at my stone and am ceaselessly grinding,
The almond boughs blow.

When she was here — O my first-born ! — here, grinding and singing,
My hand against hers,
What did I reck of the wind where the aloe is swinging,
And the cypress vine stirs ?
What of a bird to its little ones hastening, flying and crying,
Through the dark of the firs ?

When she was here — O my beautiful — here by me grinding,
I saw not the glow
Of the grape; for the bloom of her face that the sunlight was finding,
And the pomegranate blow
Of her mouth, and the joy of her eyes, and her voice like a dove to me singing,
Made my garden agrow.

Was it I ? Was it I for whom Death came seeking and calling
When he found her so fair ?
At the wheel, at the wheel, from dawn till the dew shall be falling,
I will wait for him there.
Death! (I shall cry) I am old, but yon shadow of plums that are purpling
Was the hue of her hair.

Death! (I shall cry) in the sound of the mill ever turning
Till dark brings release,
Till the sun on the vineyards below me to crimson is burning,
There is measure of peace;
For all day and all day — with the wheel — are her eyes to mine turning:
But, Death ! (I shall call) take me hence ere the daylight its shadow is spurning !
Hence, ere the night-time can wrap me around with my tears and my yearning, —
When the grinding shall cease !

AN OLD STREET

THE Past walks here, noiseless, unasked, alone;
Knockers are silent, and beside each stone
Grass peers, unharmed by lagging steps and slow
That with the dark and dawn pass to and fro.
The Past walks here, unseen forevermore,
Save by some heart who, in her half-closed door,
Looks forth and hears the great pulse beat afar, —
The hum and thrill and all the sounds that are,
And listening remembers, half in fear,
As a forgotten tune reëchoes near,
Or from some lilac bush a breath blows sweet
Through the unanswering dusk, the voiceless street, —
Looks forth and sighs, — with candle held above, —
"*It is too late for laughter, — or for love.*"

CARE

ALL in the leafy darkness, when sleep had passed me by,
I knew the surging of the sea —
Though never wave were nigh.
All in the leafy darkness, unbroken by a star,
There came the clamorous call of day,
While yet the day was far.
All in the leafy darkness, woven with hushes deep,
I heard the vulture wings of Fear
Above me tireless sweep;
The sea of Doubt, the dread of day, upon me surged and swept
All in the leafy darkness,
And while the whole world slept.

YOUTH

OUT of the heart there flew a little singing bird,
Past the dawn and the dew, where leaves of morning stirred,
And the heart, which followed on, said: "Though the bird be flown
Which sang in the dew and the dawn, the song is still my own."

Over the foot-worn track, over the rock and thorn,
The tired heart looked back to the olive leaves of morn,
To the fair, lost fields again, and said: "I hear it! Oh, hark!" —
Though the bird were long since slain, though the song had died in the dark.

Clinton Scollard

SIDNEY GODOLPHIN

THEY rode from the camp at morn
With clash of sword and spur.
The birds were loud in the thorn,
The sky was an azure blur.
A gallant show they made
That warm noontide of the year,
Led on by a dashing blade,
By the poet-cavalier.

They laughed through the leafy lanes,
The long lanes of Dartmoor;
And they sang their soldier strains,
Pledged "death" to the Roundhead boor;
Then they came at the middle day
To a hamlet quaint and brown
Where the hated troopers lay,
And they cheered for the King and crown.

They fought in the fervid heat,
Fought fearlessly and well,
But low at the foeman's feet
Their valorous leader fell.
Full on his fair young face
The blinding sun beat down;
In the morn of his manly grace
He died for the King and crown.

Oh the pitiless blow,
The vengeance-thrust of strife,
That blotted the golden glow
From the sky of his glad, brave life!
The glorious promise gone; —
Night with its grim black frown!
Never again the dawn,
And all for the King and crown.

Hidden his sad fate now
In the sealëd book of the years;
Few are the heads that bow,
Or the eyes that brim with tears,
Reading 'twixt blots and stains
From a musty tome that saith
How he rode through the Dartmoor lanes
To his woful, dauntless death.

But I, in the summer's prime,
From that lovely leafy land
Look back to the olden time
And the leal and loyal band.
I see them dash along, —
I hear them charge and cheer,
And my heart goes out in a song
To the poet-cavalier.

AS I CAME DOWN FROM LEBANON

As I came down from Lebanon,
Came winding, wandering slowly down
Through mountain passes bleak and brown,
The cloudless day was well-nigh done.
The city, like an opal set
In emerald, showed each minaret
Afire with radiant beams of sun,
And glistened orange, fig, and lime,
Where song-birds made melodious chime,
As I came down from Lebanon.

As I came down from Lebanon,
Like lava in the dying glow,
Through olive orchards far below
I saw the murmuring river run;
And 'neath the wall upon the sand
Swart sheiks from distant Samarcand,

With precious spices they had won,
Lay long and languidly in wait
Till they might pass the guarded gate,
As I came down from Lebanon.

As I came down from Lebanon,
I saw strange men from lands afar,
In mosque and square and gay bazar,
The Magi that the Moslem shun,
And Grave Effendi from Stamboul,
Who sherbet sipped in corners cool;
And, from the balconies o'errun
With roses, gleamed the eyes of those
Who dwell in still seraglios,
As I came down from Lebanon.

As I came down from Lebanon
The flaming flower of daytime died,
And Night, arrayed as is a bride
Of some great king, in garments spun
Of purple and the finest gold,
Outbloomed in glories manifold,
Until the moon, above the dun
And darkening desert, void of shade,
Shone like a keen Damascus blade,
As I came down from Lebanon.

KHAMSIN

OH, the wind from the desert blew in! — Khamsin,
The wind from the desert blew in!
It blew from the heart of the fiery south,
From the fervid sand and the hills of drouth,
And it kissed the land with its scorching mouth;
The wind from the desert blew in!

It blasted the buds on the almond bough,
And shrivelled the fruit on the orange-tree;
The wizened dervish breathed no vow,
So weary and parched was he.
The lean muezzin could not cry;
The dogs ran mad, and bayed the sky;
The hot sun shone like a copper disk,
And prone in the shade of an obelisk
The water-carrier sank with a sigh,
For limp and dry was his water-skin;
And the wind from the desert blew in.

The camel crouched by the crumbling wall,
And oh the pitiful moan it made!
The minarets, taper and slim and tall,
Reeled and swam in the brazen light;
And prayers went up by day and night,
But thin and drawn were the lips that prayed.
The river writhed in its slimy bed,
Shrunk to a tortuous, turbid thread;
The burnt earth cracked like a cloven rind;
And still the wind, the ruthless wind,
Khamsin,
The wind from the desert blew in.

Into the cool of the mosque it crept,
Where the poor sought rest at the Prophet's shrine;
Its breath was fire to the jasmine vine;
It fevered the brow of the maid who slept,
And men grew haggard with revel of wine.
The tiny fledgelings died in the nest;
The sick babe gasped at the mother's breast.
Then a rumor rose and swelled and spread
From a tremulous whisper, faint and vague,
Till it burst in a terrible cry of dread,
The plague! the plague! the plague! —
Oh the wind, Khamsin,
The scourge from the desert, blew in!

MEMNON

WHY dost thou hail with songful lips no more
The glorious sunrise? — Why is Memnon mute,
Whose voice was tuned as is the silvery flute
When Thebes sat queenly by the Nile's low shore?
The chained slaves sweat no longer at the oar,
No longer shrines are raised to man and brute,
Yet dawn by dawn the sun thou didst salute
Gives thee the greeting that it gave of yore.
What nameless spell is on thee? Dost thou wait
(Hoping and yearning through the years forlorn)
The old-time splendor and the regal state,
The glory and the power of empire shorn?
Oh, break the silence deep, defying fate,
And cry again melodious to the morn!

BE YE IN LOVE WITH APRIL-TIDE?

Be ye in love with April-tide?
I' faith, in love am I!
For now 't is sun, and now 't is shower,
And now 't is frost, and now 't is flower,
And now 't is Laura laughing-eyed,
And now 't is Laura shy.

Ye doubtful days, O slower glide!
Still smile and frown, O sky!
Some beauty unforeseen I trace
In every change of Laura's face:
Be ye in love with April-tide?
I' faith, in love am I!

A BELL

Had I the power
To cast a bell that should from some grand tower,
At the first Christmas hour,
Outring,
And fling
A jubilant message wide,
The forgëd metals should be thus allied: —
No iron Pride,
But soft Humility, and rich-veined Hope
Cleft from a sunny slope;
And there should be
White Charity,
And silvery Love, that knows not Doubt nor Fear,
To make the peal more clear;
And then to firmly fix the fine alloy,
There should be Joy!

Harriet Monroe

FROM THE "COMMEMORATION ODE"

WORLD'S COLUMBIAN EXPOSITION, CHICAGO, OCTOBER 21, 1892

WASHINGTON

When dreaming kings, at odds with swift-paced time,
Would strike that banner down,
A nobler knight than ever writ or rhyme
With fame's bright wreath did crown
Through armed hosts bore it till it floated high
Beyond the clouds, a light that cannot die!
Ah, hero of our younger race!
Great builder of a temple new!
Ruler, who sought no lordly place!
Warrior, who sheathed the sword he drew!
Lover of men, who saw afar
A world unmarred by want or war,
Who knew the path, and yet forbore
To tread, till all men should implore;
Who saw the light, and led the way
Where the gray world might greet the day;
Father and leader, prophet sure,
Whose will in vast works shall endure,
How shall we praise him on this day of days,
Great son of fame who has no need of praise?

How shall we praise him? Open wide the doors
Of the fair temple whose broad base he laid.
Through its white halls a shadowy cavalcade
Of heroes moves o'er unresounding floors —
Men whose brawned arms upraised these columns high,
And reared the towers that vanish in the sky, —
The strong who, having wrought, can never die.

LINCOLN

And, lo! leading a blessed host comes one
Who held a warring nation in his heart;
Who knew love's agony, but had no part
In love's delight; whose mighty task was done

Through blood and tears that we might walk in joy,
And this day's rapture own no sad alloy.
Around him heirs of bliss, whose bright brows wear
Palm-leaves amid their laurels ever fair.
Gaily they come, as though the drum
Beat out the call their glad hearts knew so well:
Brothers once more, dear as of yore,
Who in a noble conflict nobly fell.
Their blood washed pure yon banner in the sky,
And quenched the brands laid 'neath these arches high —
The brave who, having fought, can never die.

Then surging through the vastness rise once more
The aureoled heirs of light, who onward bore
Through darksome times and trackless realms of ruth
The flag of beauty and the torch of truth.
They tore the mask from the foul face of wrong;
Even to God's mysteries they dared aspire;
High in the choir they built yon altar-fire,
And filled these aisles with color and with song:
The ever-young, the unfallen, wreathing for time
Fresh garlands of the seeming-vanished years;
Faces long luminous, remote, sublime,
And shining brows still dewy with our tears.
Back with the old glad smile comes one we knew —
We bade him rear our house of joy to-day.
But Beauty opened wide her starry way,
And he passed on. Bright champions of the true,
Soldiers of peace, seers, singers ever blest, —
From the wide ether of a loftier quest
Their winged souls throng our rites to glorify, —
The wise who, having known, can never die.

DEMOCRACY

For, lo! the living God doth bare his arm.
No more he makes his house of clouds and gloom.
Lightly the shuttles move within his loom;
Unveiled his thunder leaps to meet the storm.
From God's right hand man takes the powers that sway
A universe of stars.
He bows them down; he bids them go or stay;
He tames them for his wars.
He scans the burning paces of the sun,
And names the invisible orbs whose courses run
Through the dim deeps of space.
He sees in dew upon a rose impearled
The swarming legions of a monad world
Begin life's upward race.
Voices of hope he hears
Long dumb to his despair,
And dreams of golden years
Meet for a world so fair.
For now Democracy doth wake and rise
From the sweet sloth of youth.
By storms made strong, by many dreams made wise,
He clasps the hand of Truth.
Through the armed nations lies his path of peace,
The open book of knowledge in his hand.
Food to the starving, to the oppressed release,
And love to all he bears from land to land.
Before his march the barriers fall,
The laws grow gentle at his call.
His glowing breath blows far away
The fogs that veil the coming day, —
That wondrous day
When earth shall sing as through the blue she rolls
Laden with joy for all her thronging souls.
Then shall want's call to sin resound no more
Across her teeming fields. And pain shall sleep,
Soothed by brave science with her magic lore;
And war no more shall bid the nations weep.
Then the worn chains shall slip from man's desire,
And ever higher and higher
His swift foot shall aspire;
Still deeper and more deep

His soul its watch shall keep,
Till love shall make the world a holy place,
Where knowledge dare unveil God's very face.

Not yet the angels hear life's last sweet song.
Music unutterably pure and strong
From earth shall rise to haunt the peopled skies,
When the long march of time,
Patient in birth and death, in growth and blight,
Shall lead man up through happy realms of light
Unto his goal sublime.

IN THE BEGINNING

When sunshine met the wave,
Then love was born;
Then Venus rose to save
A world forlorn.

For light a thousand wings
Of joy unfurled,
And bound with golden rings
The icy world.

And color flamed the earth
With glad desire,
Till life sprang to the birth,
Fire answering fire.

And so the world awoke,
And all was done,
When first the ocean spoke
Unto the sun.

THE FORTUNATE ONE

Beside her ashen hearth she sate her down,
Whence he she loved had fled, —
His children plucking at her sombre gown
And calling for the dead.

One came to her clad in the robes of May,
And said sweet words of cheer,
Bidding her bear the burden in God's way,
And feel her loved ones near.

And she who spake thus would have given, thrice blest,
Long lives of happy years,
To clasp his children to a mother's breast,
And weep his widow's tears.

THE NIGHT-BLOOMING CEREUS

Flower of the moon!
Still white is her brow whom we worshiped on earth long ago;
Yea, purer than pearls in deep seas, and more virgin than snow.
The dull years veil their eyes from her shining, and vanish afraid,
Nor profane her with age — the immortal, nor dim her with shade.

It is we are unworthy, we worldlings, to dwell in her ways;
We have broken her altars and silenced her voices of praise.
She hath hearkened to singing more silvern, seen raptures more bright;
To some planet more pure she hath fled on the wings of the night, —
Flower of the moon!

Yet she loveth the world that forsook her, for, lo! once a year
She, Diana, translucent, pale, scintillant, down from her sphere
Floateth earthward like star-laden music, to bloom in a flower,
And our hearts feel the spell of the goddess once more for an hour.

See! she sitteth in splendor nor knoweth desire nor decay,
And the night is a glory around her more bright than the day,
And her breath hath the sweetness of worlds where no sorrow is known;
And we long as we worship to follow her back to her own, —
Flower of the moon!

A FAREWELL

Good-by: nay, do not grieve that it is over —
The perfect hour;
That the winged joy, sweet honey-loving rover,
Flits from the flower.

Grieve not, — it is the law. Love will be flying —
Yea, love and all.
Glad was the living; blessed be the dying!
Let the leaves fall.

Charlotte Perkins Stetson

A COMMON INFERENCE

A NIGHT: mysterious, tender, quiet, deep;
Heavy with flowers; full of life asleep;
Thrilling with insect voices; thick with stars;
No cloud between the dewdrops and red Mars;
The small earth whirling softly on her way,
The moonbeams and the waterfalls at play;
A million million worlds that move in peace,
A million mighty laws that never cease;
And one small ant-heap, hidden by small weeds,
Rich with eggs, slaves, and store of millet seeds.
They sleep beneath the sod
And trust in God.

A day: all glorious, royal, blazing bright;
Heavy with flowers; full of life and light;
Great fields of corn and sunshine; courteous trees;
Snow-sainted mountains; earth-embracing seas;
Wide golden deserts; slender silver streams;
Clear rainbows where the tossing fountain gleams;
And everywhere, in happiness and peace,
A million forms of life that never cease;
And one small ant-heap, crushed by passing tread,
Hath scarce enough alive to mourn the dead!
They shriek beneath the sod,
"There is no God!"

THE BEDS OF FLEUR-DE-LYS

HIGH-LYING, sea-blown stretches of green turf,
Wind-bitten close, salt-colored by the sea,
Low curve on curve spread far to the cool sky,
And, curving over them as long they lie,
Beds of wild fleur-de-lys.

Wide-flowing, self-sown, stealing near and far,
Breaking the green like islands in the sea;
Great stretches at your feet, and spots that bend
Dwindling over the horizon's end, —
Wild beds of fleur-de-lys.

The light keen wind streams on across the lifts,
Their wind of western springtime by the sea;
The close turf smiles unmoved, but over her
Is the far-flying rustle and sweet stir
In beds of fleur-de-lys.

And here and there across the smooth, low grass
Tall maidens wander, thinking of the sea;
And bend, and bend, with light robes blown aside,
For the blue lily-flowers that bloom so wide, —
The beds of fleur-de-lys.

A CONSERVATIVE

THE garden beds I wandered by
One bright and cheerful morn,
When I found a new-fledged butterfly,
A-sitting on a thorn,
A black and crimson butterfly,
All doleful and forlorn.

I thought that life could have no sting
To infant butterflies,
So I gazed on this unhappy thing
With wonder and surprise,
While sadly with his waving wing
He wiped his weeping eyes.

Said I, "What can the matter be?
Why weepest thou so sore?
With garden fair and sunlight free
And flowers in goodly store:" —
But he only turned away from me
And burst into a roar.

Cried he, "My legs are thin and few
Where once I had a swarm!
Soft fuzzy fur — a joy to view —
Once kept my body warm,
Before these flapping wing-things grew,
To hamper and deform!"

At that outrageous bug I shot
The fury of mine eye;
Said I, in scorn all burning hot,
In rage and anger high,
"You ignominious idiot!
Those wings are made to fly!"

"I do not want to fly," said he,
"I only want to squirm!"
And he drooped his wings dejectedly,
But still his voice was firm:
"I do not want to be a fly!
I want to be a worm!"

O yesterday of unknown lack!
To-day of unknown bliss!
I left my fool in red and black,
The last I saw was this, —
The creature madly climbing back
Into his chrysalis.

Louise Imogen Guiney

ODE FOR A MASTER MARINER ASHORE

There in his room, whene'er the moon looks in,
And silvers now a shell, and now a fin,
And o'er his chart glides like an argosy,
Quiet and old sits he.
Danger! he hath grown homesick for thy smile.
Where hidest thou the while, heart's boast,
Strange face of beauty sought and lost,
Star-face that lured him out from boyhood's isle?

Blown clear from dull indoors, his dreams behold
Night-water smoke and sparkle as of old,
The taffrail lurch, the sheets triumphant toss
Their phosphor-flowers across.
Towards ocean's either rim the long-exiled
Wears on, till stunted cedars throw
A lace-like shadow over snow,
Or tropic fountains wash their agates wild.

Awhile, play up and down the briny spar
Odors of Surinam and Zanzibar,
Till blithely thence he ploughs, in visions new,
The Labradorian blue;
All homeless hurricanes about him break;
The purples of spent day he sees
From Samos to the Hebrides,
And drowned men dancing darkly in his wake.

Where the small deadly foam-caps, well descried,
Top, tier on tier, the hundred-mountained tide,
Away, and far away, his pride is borne,
Riding the noisy morn,
Plunges, and preens her wings, and laughs to know
The helm and tightening halyards still
Follow the urging of his will,
And scoff at sullen earth a league below.

Mischance hath barred him from his heirdom high,
And shackled him with many an inland tie,
And of his only wisdom made a jibe
Amid an alien tribe:
No wave abroad but moans his fallen state.
The trade-wind ranges now, the trade-wind roars!
Why is it on a yellowing page he pores?
Ah, why this hawser fast to a garden gate?

Thou friend so long withdrawn, so deaf, so dim,
Familiar Danger, O forget not him!
Repeat of thine evangel yet the whole
Unto his subject soul,
Who suffers no such palsy of her drouth,
Nor hath so tamely worn her chain,
But she may know that voice again,
And shake the reefs with answer of her mouth.

O give him back, before his passion fail,
The singing cordage and the hollow sail,
And level with those aged eyes let be
The bright unsteady sea;
And move like any film from off his brain
The pasture wall, the boughs that run
Their evening arches to the sun,
The hamlet spire across the sown champaign;

And on the shut space and the trivial hour,
Turn the great floods! and to thy spousal bower,
With rapt arrest and solemn loitering,
Him whom thou lovedst bring:
That he, thy faithful one, with praising lip,
Not having, at the last, less grace
Of thee than had his roving race,
Sum up his strength to perish with a ship.

IN LEINSTER

I TRY to knead and spin, but my life is low the while.
Oh, I long to be alone, and walk abroad a mile;
Yet if I walk alone, and think of naught at all,
Why from me that 's young should the wild tears fall?

The shower-stricken earth, the earth-colored streams,
They breathe on me awake, and moan to me in dreams;
And yonder ivy fondling the broke castle-wall,
It pulls upon my heart till the wild tears fall.

The cabin-door looks down a furze-lighted hill,
And far as Leighlin Cross the fields are green and still;
But once I hear the blackbird in Leighlin hedges call,
The foolishness is on me, and the wild tears fall!

PAX PAGANICA

GOOD oars, for Arnold's sake,
By Laleham lightly bound,
And near the bank, O soft,
Darling swan!
Let not the o'erweary wake
Anew from natal ground,
But where he slumbered oft,
Slumber on.

Be less than boat or bird,
The pensive stream along;
No murmur make, nor gleam,
At his side.
Where was it he had heard
Of warfare and of wrong?—
Not there, in any dream
Since he died.

ON FIRST ENTERING WESTMINSTER ABBEY

HOLY of England! since my light is short
And faint, O rather by the sun anew
Of timeless passion set my dial true,
That with thy saints and thee I may consort,
And, wafted in the cool, enshadowed port
Of poets, seem a little sail long due,
And be as one the call of memory drew
Unto the saddle void since Agincourt!
Not now, for secular love's unquiet lease,
Receive my soul, who, rapt in thee erewhile,
Hath broken tryst with transitory things;
But seal with her a marriage and a peace
Eternal, on thine Edward's altar-isle,
Above the oval sea of ended kings.

MARTYR'S MEMORIAL

SUCH natural debts of love our Oxford knows,
So many ancient dues undesecrate,
I marvel how the landmark of a hate
For witness unto future time she chose;
How out of her corroborate ranks arose
The three, in great denial only great,
For Art's enshrining! . . . Thus, averted straight,
My soul to seek a holier captain goes:
That sweet adventurer whom Truth befell
When as the synagogues were watching not;
Whose crystal name on royal Oriel
Hangs like a shield; who, to an outland spot
Led hence, beholds his Star, and counts it well
Of all his dear domain to live forgot.

A FOOTNOTE TO A FAMOUS LYRIC

TRUE love's own talisman, which here
Shakespeare and Sidney failed to teach,
A steel-and-velvet Cavalier
Gave to our Saxon speech:

Chief miracle of theme and touch
That upstart enviers adore:
I could not love thee, dear, so much,
Loved I not Honour more.

No critic born since Charles was king
But sighed in smiling, as he read:
"Here 's theft of the supremest thing
A poet might have said!"

Young knight and wit and beau, who won,
Mid war's adventure, ladies' praise,
Was 't well of you, ere you had done,
To blight our modern bays?

O yet to you, whose random hand
Struck from the dark whole gems like these,
Archaic beauty, never planned
Nor reared by wan degrees,

Which leaves an artist poor, and art
An earldom richer all her years;
To you, dead on your shield apart,
Be "Ave!" passed in tears.

How shall this singing era spurn
Her master, and in lauds be loath?
Your worth, your work, bid us discern
Light exquisite in both.

'T was virtue's breath inflamed your lyre,
Heroic from the heart it ran;
Nor for the shedding of such fire
Lives since a manlier man.

And till your strophe sweet and bold
So lovely aye, so lonely long,
Love's self outdo, dear Lovelace! hold
The pinnacles of song.

THE WILD RIDE

I HEAR in my heart, I hear in its ominous pulses,
All day, on the road, the hoofs of invisible horses;
All night, from their stalls, the importunate tramping and neighing.

Let cowards and laggards fall back! but alert to the saddle,
Straight, grim, and abreast, go the weather-worn, galloping legion,
With a stirrup-cup each to the lily of women that loves him.

The trail is through dolor and dread, over crags and morasses;
There are shapes by the way, there are things that appal or entice us:
What odds? We are knights, and our souls are but bent on the riding.

I hear in my heart, I hear in its ominous pulses,
All day, on the road, the hoofs of invisible horses;
All night, from their stalls, the importunate tramping and neighing.

We spur to a land of no name, out-racing the storm-wind;
We leap to the infinite dark, like the sparks from the anvil.
Thou leadest, O God! All 's well with Thy troopers that follow.

VALSE JEUNE

ARE there favoring ladies above thee?
  Are there dowries and lands? Do they say
Seven others are fair? But I love thee:
  Aultre n'auray!

All the sea is a lawn in our county;
  All the morrow, our star of delay.
I am King: let me live on thy bounty!
  Aultre n'auray!

To the fingers so light and so rosy
  That have pinioned my heart, (welladay!)
Be a kiss, be a ring with this posy:
  Aultre n'auray!

OF JOAN'S YOUTH

I WOULD unto my fair restore
A simple thing:
The flushing cheek she had before!
Out-velveting
No more, no more,
By Severn shore,
The carmine grape, the moth's auroral wing.

Ah, say how winds in flooding grass
Unmoor the rose;
Or guileful ways the salmon pass
To sea, disclose;
For so, alas,
With Love, alas,
With fatal, fatal Love, a girlhood goes.

SANCTUARY

High above hate I dwell:
O storms! farewell.
Though at my sill your daggered thunders play,
Lawless and loud to-morrow as to-day,
To me they sound more small
Than a young fay's footfall:
Soft and far-sunken, forty fathoms low
In Long Ago,
And winnowed into silence on that wind
Which takes wars like a dust, and leaves but love behind.

Hither Felicity
Doth climb to me,
And bank me in with turf and marjoram
Such as bees lip, or the new-weanëd lamb;
With golden barberry-wreath,
And bluets thick beneath;
One grosbeak, too, mid apple-buds a guest
With bud-red breast,
Is singing, singing! All the hells that rage
Float less than April fog below our hermitage.

Lilla Cabot Perry

MEETING AFTER LONG ABSENCE

I

AS SHE FEARED IT WOULD BE

Here in this room where first we met,
And where we said farewell with tears,
Here, where you swore "Though you forget,
My love shall deeper grow with years,"

Here, where the pictures on the wall,
The very rugs upon the floor,
The smallest objects you recall, —
I am awaiting you once more.

The books that we together read, —
From off their shelves they beckon me.
All here seems living! What is dead?
What is the ghost I fear to see?

Unchanged am I. Did you despise
My love as "small"? — it fills my heart!
You come — a stranger from your eyes
Looks out — and, meeting, first we part.

II

AS IT WAS

I told myself in singing words
That you were changed and I was true;
I would not trust winds, waves, and birds
That change was not in you.

I sang love's dirge before we met, —
"As murdered corpse in river bed
In eyes my heart cannot forget
I see Love lying dead!"

You came — one look — no word was spoken,
Our hands, once clasped, forgot to part,
And, though our silence is unbroken,
Heart has found rest on heart.

LIFE AND DEATH

O ye who see with other eyes than ours,
And speak with tongues we are too deaf to hear,
Whose touch we cannot feel yet know ye near,
When, with a sense of yet undreamed-of powers,
We sudden pierce the cloud of sense that lowers,
Enwrapping us as 't were our spirit's tomb,
And catch some sudden glory through the gloom,
As Arctic sufferers dream of sun and flowers!

Do ye not sometimes long for power to speak
To our dull ears, and pierce their shroud of clay
With a loud cry, "Why, then, this grief at 'death'?
We are the living, you the dead to-day!
This truth you soon shall see, dear hearts, yet weak,
In God's bright mirror cleared from mortal breath!"

ART

WOULDST know the artist? Then go seek
Him in his labors. Though he strive
That Nature's voice alone should speak
From page or canvas to the heart,
Yet is it passionately alive
With his own soul! Of him 't is part! —
This happy failure, this is Art.

Hannah Parker Kimball

BEYOND

ONCE when the wind was on the roof,
And nature seemed to question fate,
A fiery angel, in a dream,
Called on a soul to contemplate,

"Look well about thy precincts, learn
What is thy gain, thy final stock,
Obtained from living day by day."
(Hark, how the winds the elm-trees rock!)

The man's soul cast a glance about.
The place wherein it dwelt was small, —
No vast horizon; every side
Was bounded by a narrow wall.

But well it knew those precincts, well
The carven furniture; the shelf,
Laden with books; the tinted wall
Adorned with pictures of itself,

And of the Father and the Son,
And myriad saints; and then the earth,
With all the senses' arabesques,
That man had planned since man had birth.

"Are these thy treasures? These are dead,"
The fiery angel, in despite,
Cried out: "What wouldst thou gain for these,
If thou shouldst stand in God's own light? —

"If He should rive these walls away?
What sayest thou? Lo, the drifting sun,
The moon, the stars, the sky, God's sky,
Are sights a soul should look upon.

"Pray Him to break these walls away."
The soul shrank back, with hanging head:
"The moon rides free, the stars dance high,
The sun shines bright: these sights I dread."

The walls seemed riven by a sword;
The moon rode free, the wind blew sweet,
The stars danced high; then sunshine lay
In glory at the soul's free feet.

It seemed to stand in a wide land;
Around it high the heavens soared;
It seemed to wither with the light,
Yet joy through all its being poured.

Then darkened grew the sky on high,
And suddenly the sunshine fled;
The wind howled shrill; the soul, aghast,
Awoke and trembled on its bed.

It saw the carven furniture,
The painted pictures on the wall,
The shelf, bowed under heavy lore,
The costly treasures one and all.

Moonlight lay ghostly over them
(Outside the wind was in the trees,
The wind blew free, the stars shone high),
And all the life seemed gone from these.

The soul arose and paced about.
"It was a vision of the night;
Still must I linger in this place:
But O the wind, the sun, the light!"

SOUL AND SENSE

Myriads of motley molecules through space
Move round triumphant. By their whirlpool pace
  Shall *we* be shaken? All in earth's vast span,
Our very bodies, veer to other shapes;
Mid the mad dance one stubborn power escapes,
  Looks on and marvels, — 't is the soul of man.

ONE WAY OF TRUSTING

Not trust you, dear? Nay, 't is not true.
  As sailors trust the shifting sea
From day to day, so I trust you.
  They know how smooth the sea can be;
And well they know its treachery
  When tempests blow; yet forth they thrust
Their ships, as in security.
  They trust it, dear, because they must.

Albert Bigelow Paine

THE LITTLE CHILD

A simple-hearted child was He,
  And He was nothing more;
In summer days, like you and me,
  He played about the door,
Or gathered, where the father toiled,
  The shavings from the floor.

Sometimes He lay upon the grass,
  The same as you and I,
And saw the hawks above Him pass
  Like specks against the sky;
Or, clinging to the gate, He watched
  The stranger passing by.

A simple child, and yet, I think,
  The bird-folk must have known,
The sparrow and the bobolink,
  And claimed Him for their own, —
They gathered round Him fearlessly
  When He was all alone.

The lark, the linnet, and the dove,
  The chaffinch and the wren,
They must have known His watchful love
  And given their worship then;
They must have known and glorified
  The child who died for men.

And when the sun at break of day
  Crept in upon His hair,
I think it must have left a ray
  Of unseen glory there,
A kiss of love on that little brow
  For the thorns that it must wear.

IN LOUISIANA

The long, gray moss that softly swings
    In solemn grandeur from the trees,
    Like mournful funeral draperies, —
A brown-winged bird that never sings.

A shallow, stagnant, inland sea,
    Where rank swamp grasses wave, and where
    A deadliness lurks in the air, —
A sere leaf falling silently.

The death-like calm on every hand,
    That one might deem it sin to break,
    So pure, so perfect, — these things make
The mournful beauty of this land.

Ernest McGaffey

AS THE DAY BREAKS

I pray you, what 's asleep?
  The lily-pads, and riffles, and the reeds;
No longer inward do the waters creep,
  No longer outwardly their force recedes,
And widowed Night, in blackness wide and deep,
  Resumes her weeds.

I pray you, what 's awake?
  A host of stars, the long, long milky way
That stretches out, a glistening silver flake,
  All glorious beneath the moon's cold ray,
And myriad reflections on the lake
  Where star-gleams lay.

I pray you, what 's astir?
  Why, naught but rustling leaves, dry, sere, and brown:
The East's broad gates are yet a dusky blur,
  And star-gems twinkle in fair Luna's crown,
And minor chords of wailing winds that were
  Die slowly down.

I pray you, what 's o'clock?
  Nay! who shall answer that but gray-stoled dawn?
See, how from out the shadows looms yon rock,
  Like some great figure on a canvas drawn;
And heard you not the crowing of the cock?
  The night is gone.

"MARK"

THE heavy mists have crept away,
  Heavily swims the sun,
And dim in mystic cloudlands gray
  The stars fade one by one;
Out of the dusk enveloping
  Come marsh and sky and tree,
Where erst has rested night's dark ring
  Over the Kankakee.

"Mark right!" Afar and faint outlined
  A flock of mallards fly,
We crouch within the reedy blind
  Instantly at the cry.
"Mark left!" We peer through wild rice-blades,
  And distant shadows see,
A wedge-shaped phalanx from the shades
  Of far-off Kankakee.

"Mark overhead!" A canvas-back!
  "Mark! mark!" A bunch of teal!
And swiftly on each flying track
  Follows the shotgun's peal;
Thus rings that call, till twilight's tide
  Rolls in like some gray sea,
And whippoorwills complain beside
  The lonely Kankakee.

A "RISE"

UNDER the shadows of a cliff
Crowned with a growth of stately pine
An angler moors his rocking skiff
And o'er the ripple casts his line,
And where the darkling current crawls
Like thistle-down the gay lure falls.

Then from the depths a silver gleam
Quick flashes, like a jewel bright,
Up through the waters of the stream
An instant visible to sight —
As lightning cleaves the sombre sky
The black bass rises to the fly.

GERONIMO

BESIDE that tent and under guard
In majesty alone he stands,
As some chained eagle, broken-winged,
With eyes that gleam like smouldering brands, —
A savage face, streaked o'er with paint,
And coal-black hair in unkempt mane.
Thin, cruel lips, set rigidly, —
A red Apache Tamerlane.

As restless as the desert winds,
Yet here he stands like carven stone,
His raven locks by breezes moved
And backward o'er his shoulders blown;
Silent, yet watchful as he waits
Robed in his strange, barbaric guise,
While here and there go searchingly
The cat-like wanderings of his eyes.

The eagle feather on his head
Is dull with many a bloody stain,
While darkly on his lowering brow
Forever rests the mark of Cain.
Have you but seen a tiger caged
And sullen through his barriers glare?
Mark well his human prototype,
The fierce Apache fettered there.

I FEAR NO POWER A WOMAN WIELDS

I FEAR no power a woman wields
While I can have the woods and fields,
With comradeship alone of gun,
Gray marsh-wastes and the burning sun.

For aye the heart's most poignant pain
Will wear away 'neath hail and rain,
And rush of winds through branches bare
With something still to do and dare, —

The lonely watch beside the shore,
The wild-fowl's cry, the sweep of oar,
And paths of virgin sky to scan
Untrod, and so uncursed by man.

Gramercy, for thy haunting face,
Thy charm of voice and lissome grace,
I fear no power a woman wields
While I can have the woods and fields.

Katrina Trask

SORROW

O THORN-CROWNED Sorrow, pitiless and stern,
I sit alone with broken heart, my head
Low bowed, keeping long vigil with my dead.
My soul, unutterably sad, doth yearn
Beyond relief in tears — they only burn
My aching eyelids to fall back unshed
Upon the throbbing brain like molten lead,
Making it frenzied. Shall I ever learn
To face you fearlessly, as by my door
You stand with haunting eyes and death-damp hair,
Through the night-watches, whispering solemnly,
"Behold, I am thy guest forevermore."
It chills my soul to know that you are there.
Great God, have mercy on my misery!

LOVE

O POWER of Love, O wondrous mystery!
How is my dark illumined by thy light,
That maketh morning of my gloomy night,
Setting my soul from Sorrow's bondage free
With swift-sent revelation! yea, I see
Beyond the limitation of my sight
And senses, comprehending now, aright,
To-day's proportion to Eternity.
Through thee, my faith in God is made more sure,
My searching eyes have pierced the misty veil;
The pain and anguish which stern Sorrow brings
Through thee become more easy to endure.
Love-strong I mount, and Heaven's high summit scale;
Through thee, my soul has spread her folded wings.

AT LAST

BEYOND the bourn of mortal death and birth,
Two lovers — parted sorrowing on earth —
Met in the land of dim and ghostly space.
Wondering, he gazed on her illumined face:
"Alone you bear the burden now," he said,
"Of bondage; mine is ended, — I am dead."
With rapturous note of victory, she cried,
"The Lord of Life be praised! I, too, have died."

AIDENN

HEAVEN is mirrored, Love, deep in thine eyes,
Soft falls its shimmering light upon thy face;
Tell me, Beloved, is this Paradise,
Or but Love's bower in some deep-sheltered place?

Is that God's burning bush that now appears,
Or but the sunlight slanting through the trees?
Is that sweet song the music of the spheres,
Or but the deep andante of the breeze?

Are we blest spirits of some glad new birth
Floating at last in God's eternity?
Or art thou, Love, still but a man on earth,
And I a woman clinging close to thee?

Additional Selections

(VARIOUS POEMS BELONGING TO THIS DIVISION)

I

BIRTH

Just when each bud was big with bloom,
And as prophetic of perfume,
When spring, with her bright horoscope,
Was sweet as an unuttered hope;

Just when the last star flickered out,
And twilight, like a soul in doubt,
Hovered between the dark and dawn,
And day lay waiting to be born;

Just when the gray and dewy air
Grew sacred as an unvoiced prayer,
And somewhere through the dusk she heard
The stirring of a nested bird, —

Four angels glorified the place:
Wan Pain unveiled her awful face;
Joy, soaring, sang; Love, brooding, smiled;
Peace laid upon her breast a child.

Annie R. Stillman
("Grace Raymond")

THE FIRST STEP

My little one begins his feet to try,
A tottering, feeble, inconsistent way;
Pleased with the effort, he forgets his play,
And leaves his infant baubles where they lie.
Laughing and proud his mother flutters nigh,
Turning to go, yet joy-compelled to stay,
And, bird-like, singing what her heart would say;
But not so certain of my bliss am I.
For I bethink me of the days in store
Wherein those feet must traverse realms unknown,
And half forget the pathway to our door.
And I recall that in the seasons flown
We were his all — as he was all our own —
But never can be quite so any more.

Andrew Bice Saxton

TO O. S. C.

Spirit of "fire and dew,"
Whither hast fled?
Thy soul they never knew
Who call thee dead.

Deep thoughts of why and how
Shadowed thine eyes:
Thou hast the answers now
Straight from the skies.

Thrilled with a double power,
Nature and Art, —
Dowered with a double dower,
Reason and heart, —

Not souls like thine, in vain
God fashioneth;
Leadeth them forth again,
Gently, by death.

Annie Eliot Trumbull

A PLAIN MAN'S DREAM

Were I transported to some distant star
With fifty little children, girls and boys,
Or to some fabled land unknown, afar,
Where never sound could come of this world's noise;

Our world begun anew, as when of yore
Sad Adam fled from Eden; I alone
The sole custodian of all human lore, —
No books to aid, all rules and records gone, —

What could I teach each tender, untaught child?
How much of this world's wisdom could I give
To raise him from the savage, fierce and wild,
And train each soul a worthy life to live?

Plain human speech, some simple laws of life,
A little tillage, household arts a few;
The law of rectitude o'ercoming strife;
Things clean and sane, the simple and the true.

But of Man's long, slow climb from Error's reach, —
The hard-won, precious wisdom of the ages, —
What (and, alas, how little!) could I teach
Which changes men from savages to sages?

Some things I've known I never would impart.
Somewhat I'd tell of building, writing, preaching;
Some hints I'd give on healing, science, art;
Love they would learn full soon without my teaching!

FREDERICK KEPPEL

A CHILD OF TO-DAY

O CHILD, had I thy lease of time! such unimagined things
Are waiting for that soul of thine to spread its untried wings!

Shalt thou not speak the stars, and go on journeys through the sky?
And read the soul of man as clear as now we read the eye?

Who knows if science may not find some art to make thee new, —
To mend the garments of thy flesh when thou hast worn them through?

'T is fearful, aye, and beautiful, thy future that may be.
How strange! — perhaps death's conqueror sits smiling on my knee!

JAMES BUCKHAM

VINGTAINE

I

SEPARATION

COULD she come back who has been dead so long,
How could I tell her of these years of wrong?
To what wild discords has my life been set
Striving the olden love-song to forget!
How could she know, in the abode of bliss,
The utter loneliness of life in this, —
The weariness that comes of nights unslept,
The hopeless agony of tears unwept?
Could she come back, between would lie those years,
And I could only look at her — through tears.

II

IMMUTABILIS

FOR death must come, and change, and, though the loss
Seems to the lonely soul the heaviest cross,
More bitter is the fate that day by day
Sees with sick heart the slow and sure decay
Of Faith and Love; and all our days we spend
In sorrow that these deathless things can end.
Far kinder then were death, for so should we
Be left with an unchanging memory,
And after-years this comfort would restore, —
That which Death takes is ours forevermore.

ALICE LEARNED BUNNER

WHEN EVEN COMETH ON

THE mother-heart doth yearn at eventide,
And, wheresoe'er the straying ones may roam,
When even cometh on they all fare home.
'Neath feathered sheltering the brood doth hide;
In eager flights the birds wing to their nest,
While happy lambs and children miss the sun,
And to the folds do hurtle one by one,
As night doth gather slowly in the west.
All ye who hurry through life's busy day,
Hark to the greeting that the Ages tell,

"The sun doth rise and set, hail and farewell."
But comfort ye your heart where'er ye stray,
For those who through this little day do roam,
When even cometh on shall all fare home.

LUCY EVANGELINE TILLEY

II

THE STATUE OF LORENZO DE' MEDICI

MARK me how still I am! — The sound of feet
Unnumbered echoing through this vaulted hall,
Or voices harsh, on me unheeded fall,
Placed high in my memorial niche and seat,
In cold and marble meditation meet
Among proud tombs and pomp funereal
Of rich sarcophagi and sculptured wall, —
In death's elaborate elect retreat.
I was a Prince, — this monument was wrought
That I in honor might eternal stand;
In vain, subdued by Buonarroti's hand,
The conscious stone is pregnant with his thought;
He to this brooding rock his fame devised,
And he, not I, is here immortalized.

JAMES ERNEST NESMITH

AHMED

WITH wrath-flushed cheeks, and eyelids red
Where anger's fiercest sign was spread,
And hands whose clenched nails left their print
In the brown palm's deep, sun-warmed tint,
The chieftains sate in circle wide,
And in the centre, on his side,
Thrown like a dog, a thieving brute,
Lay Ahmed, frowning, bound and mute.

"The man who takes an offered bribe
From chieftain of an alien tribe
Shall die." So ran the Arab law,
Read by a scribe; and Ahmed saw
In every eye that scanned his face
Burn the hot fury of his race.
His fate was told. All men must die
Some time: what cared he how or why?

They loosed his tight-swathed arms and feet,
Unwound the cashmere turban, sweet
With spice and attar, stripped the vest
Of gold and crimson from his breast,
And laid his broad, brown bosom bare
To scimeter and desert air.
He stood as moulded statues stand,
With sightless eye and nerveless hand:

As moulded statues stand, but through
The dark skin, at each breath he drew,
The wild heart's wilder beating showed.
Then on the sand he kneeled, and bowed
His head to meet the ready stroke;
The headsman threw aside his cloak,
The curved steel circled in the sun —
Ahmed was dead, and justice done.

JAMES BERRY BENSEL

AVE! NERO IMPERATOR

WHAT! Roses on thy tomb! and was there then
One who could sorrow o'er thy wretched fate?
One heart that echoed not the cry of men, —
Its joy and triumph, its contempt and hate?
One being in all the circle of the lands
Who owed a kindness to thy blood-stained hands?

What though thy wrist, adown the chariot course,
Guided thy bounding chargers to the prize!
What though shamed theatres, with plaudits hoarse,
Extolled thy lyre o'er his that decks the skies!
Is glory won from slaves whose nights are stored
With dreams of poisoned draught and proffered sword?

Nero, poor triumphs these; nor broidered gown,
Nor ivory car upon the Sacred Way,
Nor laureled imperator's golden crown
For unwon battles borne in vain display,
Can win thee worship or adorn a name,
The scourge of nations — Rome's imperial shame.

But here, where all is silent, where no turn
Of fear or greed can prompt the courtier's art,
Thine only glory hangs upon thine urn
To tell that thou hast triumphed o'er a heart;
And souls of flowers, when mortal lips are dumb,
May plead for thy poor shade in days to come.

DUFFIELD OSBORNE

A NIGHT IN LESBOS

Δέδυκε μὲν ἁ σελάννα
καὶ Πληΐαδες, μέσαι δέ
νύκτες, πάρα δ' ἔρχετ' ὥρα,
ἔγω δὲ μόνα κατεύδω. — SAPPHO.

THE moon has left the sky,
The Pleiades are flown,
Midnight is creeping nigh,
And I am still alone.

Ah me! how long, how long
Are all these weary hours!
I hate the night-bird's song
Among the Lesbian flowers.

I hate the soft, sweet breeze
That comes to kiss my hair
From oleander trees
And waters cool and fair.

My heart is fierce and wild;
The winds should rave and moan.
Ah! why is Nature mild
When I am here alone?

While yet the silver moon
Rode o'er the laughing sea,
My heart was glad, for, "Soon,"
I said, "he comes to me."

But when its placid sphere
Slid swiftly 'neath the wave,
I sighed, "He is not here.
Be brave, my heart, be brave!"

Then for an age of woe,
Of doubts and hopings vain,
I watched the white stars snow
On yon Ægean plain.

I named them by their names —
Alcyone, and all
Those far and happy flames
On which we mortals call.

"Ere that one sets," I said,
"My soul shall swim in bliss;"
And then, "Ere that is fled
My lips shall feel his kiss."

The moon has left the Pole,
The Pleiades are flown;
'T is midnight in my soul,
And I am here alone!

GEORGE HORTON

BACCHYLIDES

FAIR star, new-risen to our wondering eyes
With brighter glory from thy long eclipse!
Poet, imprisoned in dead centuries!
Some god unlocks thy music now, and strips
The seal of envious silence from thy lips;
And we are fain to hear thy wakening melodies.

Thou comest from the darkness of the tomb
To sing once more the happy olden time, —
Victor and hero, youth and youth's fair bloom,
The joy of life in manhood's golden prime;
And I, of alien tongue and harsher clime,
Listen, and lose awhile life's endless fret and fume.

Thus in a sunset isle, long years agone,
Some shepherd, telling 'neath the ilex trees
The straying sheep that browsed on upland lawn,

Marked with wide eyes across the purple seas
Odysseus' long-lost bark before the breeze
Glide ghost-like from the glooms of Ocean toward the dawn;

And straight forgot his silly flock aspace
In marvel of the strange return from death,
While to the harbor-mouth he ran apace
To hear their tale with wistful, indrawn breath:
"And aye mine eyes are dimmed with dreams" (he saith)
"Of that far land where bide the dead heroic race."

GEORGE MEASON WHICHER

CARLYLE AND EMERSON

A BALE-FIRE kindled in the night,
By night a blaze, by day a cloud,
With flame and smoke all England woke, —
It climbed so high, it roared so loud:

While over Massachusetts' pines
Uprose a white and steadfast star;
And many a night it hung unwatched, —
It shone so still, it seemed so far.

But Light is Fire, and Fire is Light;
And mariners are glad for these, —
The torch that flares along the coast,
The star that beams above the seas.

MONTGOMERY SCHUYLER

III

THE TOWN OF HAY

THE town of Hay is far away,
The town of Hay is far;
Between its hills of green and gray
Its winding meadows are.
Within the quiet town of Hay
Is many a quiet glen,
And there by many a shaded way
Are homes of quiet men:
And there are many hearts alway
That turn with longing, night and day,
Back to the town of Hay.

Within that good old town of Hay
There was no pride of birth,
And no man there pursued his way
A stranger in the earth;
And none were high and none were low,
Of golden hair or gray,
And each would grieve at other's woe
Down in the town of Hay;
And many a world-scorned soul to-day
Mid crowded thousands far away
Weeps for the town of Hay.

A road leads from the town of Hay
Forth to a world of din,
And winds and wanders far away, —
And many walked therein;
Far in the crowds of toil and stress
Their restless footsteps stray, —
Their souls have lost the quietness
Of that old town of Hay;
But in some respite of the fray,
In transient dreams they float away,
Back to the town of Hay.

Old men are in that town of Hay,
Amid its quiet trees,
Who dream of strong sons far away
Upon the stormy seas;
Old mothers, when the twilight dew
The woodbine leaves have pearled,
Dream of their boys who wander through
The wideness of the world:
And tears fall in the twilight gray,
And prayers go up at close of day
In that old town of Hay.

A hillside in the town of Hay
Is slanting toward the sun,
And gathered 'neath its headstones gray
Are sleepers, one by one;
And there are tears in distant lands,
And grief too deep for tears,
And farewells waved from phantom hands
Across the gulf of years:
And when they place that headstone gray,
It crushes hearts so far away
From that old town of Hay.

SAM WALTER FOSS

A DROP OF INK

THIS drop of ink chance leaves upon my pen,
What might it write in Milton's mighty hand!

What might it speak at Shakespeare's high command !
What words to thrill the throbbing hearts of men !
Or from Beethoven's soul a grand amen,
All life and death in one full compass spanned !
Who could its power in Goethe's touch withstand ?
What words of truth it holds beyond our ken, —
What blessed promise we would fain be told,
And cannot, — what grim sentence dread as death, —
What venomous lie, that never shall unfold, —
What law, undoing science with a breath !
But — mockery of life's quick-wasted lot —
Dropped on a virgin sheet 't is but a blot !

JOSEPH ERNEST WHITNEY

SEA IRONY

ONE day I saw a ship upon the sands
Careened upon beam ends, her tilted deck
Swept clear of rubbish of her long-past wreck;
Her colors struck, but not by human hands;
Her masts the driftwood of what distant strands !
Her frowning ports, where at the Admiral's beck
Grim-visaged cannon held the foe in check,
Gaped for the frolic of the minnow bands.
The seaweed banners in her fo'ks'le waved,
A turtle basked upon her capstan head;
Her cabin's pomp the clownish sculpin braved,
And on her prow, where the lost figure-head
Once scorned the brine, a name forgot was graved.
It was "The Irresistible" I read !

JOHN LANGDON HEATON

BERMUDA, *February, 1896.*

SOLITUDE

IT is the bittern's solemn cry
Far out upon the lonely moors,
Where steel-gray pools reflect the sky,
And mists arise in dim contours.

Save this, no murmur on their verge
Doth stir the stillness of the reeds;
Silent the water-snakes emerge
From writhing depths of water-weeds.

Through sedge or gorse of that morass
There shines no light of moon or star;
Only the fen-fires gleam and pass
Along the low horizon bar.

It is the bittern's solemn cry,
As if it voiced, with mournful stress,
The strange hereditary sigh
Of age on age of loneliness.

FREDERICK PETERSON

AN EPILOGUE AT WALLACK'S

THE play was done;
The mimic lovers of the stage
Were safe united, with their mimic battles won;
But while the prompter closed his well-scored page,
And on his bell a willing finger laid,
An old man, stately, kind, and hale,
In mould of courtly fashion made,
Set forth the moral of the tale.

Much bent with time,
The frost that silvered on his brow
Had left its markings, lined and figured like the rime,
Which on the pane the warming noon-day glow
Has smoothed and softened with its cheery smile.
And while he spoke they lent him willing ears;
For warmest youth of heart the while
Shone through the winter of his years.

'T was not the words,
For they were simple as the tales
Some good old nurse's well-taxed memory hoards
Against the time when fairy folk-lore fails.
He spoke in well-worn terms of good advice:
How fathers should not draw too ready rein,
Nor sons take umbrage in a trice
At fathers' counsels, — these and more again.

But as he spoke
The threadbare words they knew so well,
Came rippling streamlets of applause that broke
In throbbing oceans as the curtain fell.

For youth and age, pride, poverty, e'en sin,
Fair maid and bloodless pedagogue,
All felt the world of nearer kin
The while John Gilbert spoke — The Epilogue.

John Elton Wayland
("Idas")

IV

"THE TUNE OF THE TIME"

I

WHEN LOVE COMES KNOCKING

When Love comes knocking at thy gate,
Bid him at once depart:
He will be patient, and will wait
The bidding of thy heart.

Tell him he knocketh there in vain;
That he may ne'er come in:
He 'll smiling leave, but come again,
Thy loving heart to win.

Then, when at last he knocks in tears,
Oh! open wide Love's gate:
He 'll soon forget his foolish fears,
And vow 't was sweet to wait.

William Henry Gardner

IF I BUT KNEW

If I but knew what the tree-tops say,
Whispering secrets night and day,
I 'd make a song, my love, for you,
If I but knew — if I but knew.

If I but knew how the lilies brew
Nectar rare from a drop of dew,
A crystal glass I 'd fill for you,
If I but knew — if I but knew.

Love, if I knew but one tender word,
Sweet as the note of a wooing bird,
I 'd tell my ardent love to you,
If I but knew — if I but knew.

Amy E. Leigh

SONG FROM "BEN HUR"[1]

Wake not, but hear me, love!
Adrift, adrift on slumber's sea,
Thy spirit call to list to me.
Wake not, but hear me, love!
A gift from Sleep, the restful king,
All happy, happy dreams I bring.

Wake not, but hear me, love!
Of all the world of dreams 't is thine
This once to choose the most divine.
So choose, and sleep, my love!
But ne'er again in choice be free,
Unless, unless — thou dream'st of me.

Lew Wallace

II

AT TWILIGHT

The roses of yesteryear
Were all of them white and red:
It fills my heart with silent fear
To find all their beauty fled.

The roses of white are sere,
All faded the roses of red;
And one who loves me is not here,
And one that I love is dead.

Peyton Van Rensselaer

ART THOU THE SAME

Art thou the same, thou sobbing winter wind?
The same that rocked the cradle of the May,
That whispered through the leaves in summer noon,
And swelled the anthem of the full-crowned year?
Art thou the same, thou piteous, moaning thing,
Beating against the pane with ghostly hands,
Wailing in agony across the waste, —
Art thou the same — the same?

Art thou the same, thou poor heart bruised and faint,
Treading thy way alone through twilight gloom?
Art thou the same that sang to greet the dawn,
Carolling in the sunlight like a bird,
Too glad for speech, too glad for aught but song?
Art thou the same that prayest but for night,
For night to come and ease thee of thy pain, —
Art thou the same — the same?

Thou winter wind that wailest through the night,
Thou broken heart too crushed to moan or cry,
There will be rest even for ye, poor things,
And more than rest, — a joy new-washed in tears;
For through the portals of the fading year
Lie sunny hills and fields fresh-clad in green,
And after night who knows what day may bring? —
And ye unchanged, the same — the same?

FRANCES DORR (SWIFT) TATNALL

III

THE SONG OF THE TURNKEY

I

IN the darkness deep
Of the donjon-keep,
Where the spiders spin their strands;
In the home of bats
And of old gray rats,
Are my lord the turnkey's lands.
O, his task is light,
But from morn till night
On his rounds he needs must go.
It is tramp, tramp, tramp,
With his keys and lamp,
In the corridors down below.

Then it 's ho! ho! ho!
I am king of the donjon deep.
There is music of bolt and chain
In the turnkey's dark domain.
How merrily jingle the chains that cling!
How cheerily tinkle the keys that swing!
I am king — king — king of the donjon-keep!

2

Though the ravens scream
From the gallows beam,
It is little heed he takes;
And a song he roars
Through the corridors,
As his watchful round he makes.
None are false to him
In his kingdom grim,
For their monarch never sleeps.
O, there 's none dare say
To the turnkey nay;
He is king of the donjon deeps.

Then it 's ho! ho! ho! etc.

HARRY BACHE SMITH

THE ARMORER'S SONG

I

LET hammer on anvil ring,
And the forge fire brightly shine;
Let wars rage still,
While I work with a will
At this peaceful trade of mine.
The sword is a weapon to conquer fields;
I honor the man who shakes it:
But naught is the lad who the broad-sword wields
Compared to the lad who makes it.

Clang! Clang! Clang!
Then huzzah for the anvil, the forge, and the sledge!
Huzzah for the sparks that fly!
If I had a cup I would straightway pledge
The armorer — that is I!

2

Let others of glory sing,
As they struggle in glory's quest.
Let them wave their brands
In their mailëd hands,
While the sword smites shield and crest.
Oh, war is a trade I have not essayed,
Though goodliest fame attends it.
I sing of the one who, when fight is done,
Takes every good sword and mends it.

Clang! Clang! Clang!
Then huzzah for the valiant, the squire, or the knight,
Who loveth the battle-cry!
But here 's to the swordsman that maketh them fight,
The armorer — that is I!

HARRY BACHE SMITH[1]

HIS MAJESTY

I 'M king of the road! I gather
My toll on the world's highways.
They pave the street for my royal feet,
And the man in the wagon pays.
With my sturdy heels I laugh at wheels;
I hurry at no man's will,
For the rich who ride my meat provide;
They must feed the king to his fill.

I 'm king of the road! Before me
My way lies over the land,
With a wild rose train from meadow and lane
And the hail of a song-bird band.
They are slaves who team by wagon or steam:
The footman carries the crown.
What cares the tramp whose supper and camp
Are waiting in every town?

I 'm king of the road all summer;
In winter I still go free.
Let the snow-blast come, in a nook I'll chum
With a gipsy crew like me.
I 'll ask no shares with home-proud heirs;
They 're the scorn of my soul while I
Can tread the floors of the great Out-doors,
And nobody ask me why.

THERON BROWN

IV

LITTLE ALABAMA COON

I 's a little Alabama Coon,
And I has n't been born very long;
I 'member seein' a great big round moon;
I 'member hearin' one sweet song.
When dey tote me down to de cotton field,
Dar I roll and I tumble in de sun;
While my daddy pick de cotton, mammy watch me grow,
And dis am de song she sung:

Go to sleep, my little pickaninny, —
Brer' Fox 'll catch you if yo' don't;
Slumber on de bosom of yo' ole Mammy Jinny, —
Mammy 's gwine to swat yo' if you won't.

Sh! sh! sh!
Lu-la, lu-la lu-la lu-la lu!
Underneaf de silver Southern moon;
Rock-a-by! hush-a-by!
Mammy's little baby,
Mammy's little Alabama Coon.

Dis hyar little Alabama Coon
Specks to be a growed-up man some day;
Dey 's gwine to christen me hyar very soon, —
My name 's gwine to be "Henry Clay."
When I 's big, I 's gwine to wed a yellow gal;
Den we 'll hab pickaninnies ob our own;
Den dat yellow gal shall rock 'em on her bosom,
And dis am de song she 'll croon:

Go to sleep, my little pickaninny, —
Brer' Fox 'll catch you if yo' don't;
Slumber on de bosom of yo' ole Mammy Jinny, —
Mammy 's gwine to swat yo' if you won't.

Sh! sh! sh!
Lu-la, lu-la lu-la lu-la lu!
Underneaf de silver Southern moon;
Rock-a-by! hush-a-by!
Mammy's little baby,
Mammy's little Alabama Coon.

HATTIE STARR

GO SLEEP, MA HONEY

WHIPP'WILL 's singin' to de moon, —
Go sleep, ma honey, m—m.
He sing a pow'ful mo'nful tune,
Go sleep, ma honey, m—m.
De day bird 's sleepin' on his nes',
He know it time to take a res',
An' he gwine ter do his lebel bes', —
Go sleep, ma honey, m—m.

Old banjo 's laid away, —
Go sleep, ma honey, m—m.
Its pickin 's froo for to-day, —
Go sleep, ma honey, m—m.
De night time surely come to pass,
De cricket 's chirpin' in de grass,
An' de ole mule 's gone to sleep at las', —
Go sleep, ma honey, m—m.

[1] See, also, p. 760.

I hear de night win' in de corn, —
Go sleep, ma honey, m—m.
Dey 's a ghos' out dah, sure 's yo' born, —
Go sleep, ma honey, m—m.
But he dassent come where we keep a light,
An' de candle 's burnin' all de night,
So sink to res', des be all right, —
Go sleep, ma honey, m—m.

EDWARD D. BARKER

KENTUCKY BABE

'SKEETERS am a hummin' on de honeysuckle vine, —
Sleep, Kentucky Babe!
Sandman am a comin' to dis little coon of mine, —
Sleep, Kentucky Babe!
Silv'ry moon am shinin' in de heabens up above,
Bobolink am pinin' fo' his little lady love:
Yo' is mighty lucky,
Babe of old Kentucky, —
Close yo' eyes in sleep.

Fly away,
Fly away, Kentucky Babe, fly away to rest,
Fly away,
Lay yo' kinky, woolly head on yo' mammy's breast, —
Um—um—,
Close yo' eyes in sleep.

Daddy 's in de cane-brake wid his little dog and gun, —
Sleep, Kentucky Babe!
'Possum fo' yo' breakfast when yo' sleepin' time is done, —
Sleep, Kentucky Babe!
Bogie man 'll catch yo' sure unless yo' close yo' eyes,
Waitin' jes outside de doo' to take yo' by surprise:
Bes' be keepin' shady,
Little colored lady, —
Close yo' eyes in sleep.

RICHARD HENRY BUCK

V

A LITTLE DUTCH GARDEN

I PASSED by a garden, a little Dutch garden,
Where useful and pretty things grew, —
Heart's-ease and tomatoes, and pinks and potatoes,
And lilies and onions and rue.

I saw in that garden, that little Dutch garden,
A chubby Dutch man with a spade,
And a rosy Dutch frau with a shoe like a scow,
And a flaxen haired little Dutch maid.

There grew in that garden, that little Dutch garden,
Blue flag flowers lovely and tall,
And early blush roses, and little pink posies,
But Gretchen was fairer than all.

My heart 's in that garden, that little Dutch garden, —
It tumbled right in as I passed,
Mid wildering mazes of spinach and daisies,
And Gretchen is holding it fast.

HATTIE WHITNEY

V

"A SONG THAT OLD WAS SUNG"

THE OLD SEXTON

NIGH to a grave that was newly made,
Leaned a sexton old on his earth-worn spade;
His work was done, and he paused to wait
The funeral train at the open gate.
A relic of bygone days was he,
And his locks were white as the foamy sea;
And these words came from his lips so thin:
"I gather them in: I gather them in.

"I gather them in! for man and boy,
Year after year of grief and joy,
I've builded the houses that lie around,
In every nook of this burial ground;
Mother and daughter, father and son,
Come to my solitude, one by one:
But come they strangers or come they kin —
I gather them in, I gather them in.

"Many are with me, but still I'm alone,
I'm king of the dead — and I make my throne
On a monument slab of marble cold;
And my sceptre of rule is the spade I hold:
Come they from cottage or come they from hall,
Mankind are my subjects, all, all, all!
Let them loiter in pleasure or toilfully spin —
I gather them in, I gather them in.

"I gather them in, and their final rest
Is here, down here, in the earth's dark breast!"
And the sexton ceased, for the funeral train
Wound mutely o'er that solemn plain!
And I said to my heart, when time is told,
A mightier voice than that sexton's old
Will sound o'er the last trump's dreadful din —
"I gather them in, I gather them in."

PARK BENJAMIN[1]

HE CAME TOO LATE

HE came too late! — Neglect had tried
Her constancy too long;
Her love had yielded to her pride,
And the deep sense of wrong.
She scorned the offering of a heart
Which lingered on its way,
Till it could no delight impart,
Nor spread one cheering ray.

He came too late! — At once he felt
That all his power was o'er:
Indifference in her calm smile dwelt —
She thought of him no more.
Anger and grief had passed away,
Her heart and thoughts were free;
She met him, and her words were gay —
No spell had Memory.

He came too late! — The subtle chords
Of love were all unbound,
Not by offence of spoken words,
But by the slights that wound.
She knew that life held nothing now
That could the past repay;
Yet she disdained his tardy vow,
And coldly turned away.

He came too late! — Her countless dreams
Of hope had long since flown;
No charms dwelt in his chosen themes,
Nor in his whispered tone.
And when, with word and smile, he tried
Affection still to prove,
She nerved her heart with woman's pride,
And spurned his fickle love.

ELIZABETH BOGART[2]

[1] See BIOGRAPHICAL NOTE, p. 779.
[2] See BIOGRAPHICAL NOTE, p. 780.

IV

CLOSE OF THE CENTURY

(TYPICAL POETS AND POETRY OF THE FINAL YEARS)

1890–1900

THE SUCCESSION

As one by one the singers of our land,
  Summoned away by Death's unfailing dart,
  Unto the greater mystery depart,
Sadly we watch them from the desolate strand.
Oh! who shall fill their places in the band
  Of tuneful voices? Who with equal art
  Speak the unwritten language of the heart,
And the mute signs of Nature understand?
Yet poetry from earth has never ceased:
  It is a fire perpetual, which has caught
  Its flame from off the altar-place of Heaven.
Never has failed, in darkest days, a priest
  Who, by no price of gain or glory bought,
For his soul's peace his life to song has given.

FRANCES LAUGHTON MACE

CLOSE OF THE CENTURY

(TYPICAL POETS AND POETRY OF THE FINAL YEARS)

Langdon Elwyn Mitchell

("JOHN PHILIP VARLEY")

FROM "TO A WRITER OF THE DAY"

TECHNIQUE

Could but this be brought
Into your ken, — that the technique is thought!
Escape from "Style," the notion men can use
Words without thoughts, — so wrench and so abuse
The innocent language to their ends that they
Will seem to be respectful, honest, gay,
Grave, or what else, — and all the glorious while
The authors' selves sit with the wise and smile:
"'T is but a trick, 't is words, it is a style!"

Your technique, then, is thought, just as I say.
And if you 'll write a poem, there 's no way
But first to think it clearly; pin your mind
Upon your thought; fasten it there, and bind
The thought into your heart: when your veins burn and flow
With love or hate, the thoughts to music go,
Melt into music, and pour fully out
In a rich flood; — but to take thought about
The "music" of your words, 't is matter quite
Beyond your conscious power! For rhymes, they 're right
Or wrong according as they hear, not look
When printed by a printer in a book!
And their "correctness" may be measured best,
And indeed only, by a certain test:
That, namely, for rebellions, — which are so
Until they have succeeded, when they go
By quite another name. Forget not, too,
That every English poet known to you,
That is to say all of them, rhymed just as
The spirit took them and their pleasure was,
And, masters that they were, rhymed "falsely," so
As now no poetaster dares to do!

PURPOSE

So then, at last, let me awake this sleep
And languor of yourself: it is too deep,
And 't is too long!
Oh, I would have you look
With judgment on your life, and not to brook
The less in art, as not in truth; — forgive
Much in you now I can, never that you less live!
I may put by whatever choice of themes,
But not this air of being by rich dreams
Roofed over, and floored under, and walled in.
As Eastern princes in a palanquin
Luxuriously ride, by eunuchs round
Held and supported, lifted from the ground,
And softly borne, — so you, on the mild shoulders,
Effeminate, of dreams! — Your spirit moulders;
The freshness of your soul withers away
As roses do that cannot find the day.

Oh, free yourself! — take up your life and share
The splendor of this day, the world's great air,
And this new land's delight, — this land that we
Adore, this people, this great liberty
Of nations in new birth, — a happy shower
Of golden States, — a many-blossomed flower! —
Now grown a Commonwealth, whose strength and state
And health are dangerous to all that hate
Freedom, and fatal to all those who'd be
Sunk in the dark of Time's abysmal sea,
Safe anchored in the past — safe dead! — that none
Might longer make them fear a change beneath the sun,
To fright them with new good. — But oh, to those
Whose blood within them leaps and laughs and flows;
To all who proudly hope; to all who fain
With their right hands and with their heart and brain
Would throne the right, and make the good to reign;
To all who'd lift man up, and who, heart-free,
Haste toward the light, — this Land and State should be
Dear as their life! — And to her sons should she
Be born again in love, since with her noblest blood
And her right hand of youth she smote the brood
Of her own loins, nested in servitude,
Shadowing the world's detraction with fair peace.
Dear mother of her sons, whose wealth is these;
Her more than gold, their valor, mercy, truth;
Her mighty age, immortal in their youth: —
Dear light of hope, oh, needs she not to be
Forever saved into new liberty?
The fallen blood of martyrs is in vain
If ours be not as free to fall again!
But her salvation is a rigorous task,
Eternally accomplishing. — I ask
You, therefore, as one owing more than most
To her, who is your happiness and boast,
That you cast from you all that will not wake
Men's hearts from sensual sleep: — for her great sake
Put by the velvet touch, the easy grace,
The fingers dreaming on the lyre, the face
Forgetful, listening to light melodies;
Cease thou thy toying with the hours, and cease
This riot of thy youth, this wantoning
With all the sap and spirit of thy Spring.
Not twice that verdure 's given thee; the Tree
Of Life not twice shall blossom; and to be
Young, 't is to be in heaven, 't is to be
Full of ambition, filled with hot desire,
Pregnant with life, and steeped in such a fire
As sets a world in hope! — Oh, could I say
That which I would, you could not say me nay.
But let your country plead with you; give heed
To her dumb call; sow the eternal seed
Of Truth, and Righteousness, and Love; — though you
Shall be, as poets should, known to but few,
Yet your reward is great: it is to be
Sown in the hearts of men, to make men free;
And in your thoughts to be your land's firm stay,
And her salvation in a falling day,
More than dread cannon, than bright thousands more:
For thoughts, like angels, wage eternal war.

SONGS

FEAR

THERE is a sound I would not hear,
  Although it music's self might be;
Lest in my breast a crystal sphere
  Might burst, might break for melody.

There is a face I would not see
  Tho' like the springtime it were fair;
Lest love that was a barren tree
  Should burst in bloom — should blossoms bear.

SWEETS THAT DIE

How fades that native breath
The rose exhales,
  Whenas her bloom is o'er!

Altho' her petals on the evening gales
Are wafted by, a fleet of fairy sails,
She is, alas! no more.

And love dies like the rose,
And fills the air
With many a deep drawn sigh:
Shall I not both embalm with sacred care,
That they may have, in sweetly-breathëd air,
Their immortality!

TO ONE BEING OLD

HER aged hands are worn with works of love;
Dear aged hands that oft on me are laid;
Her heart's below, but, oh, her love's above,
As flowers do sunward turn though in the shade.

The set of sun is dear that lasts not long,
And she is sweeter far than light that dies:
But if her aged body's weak, she's strong;
Her folly, wisdom in a softer guise.

The very smile of love is hers, and she
Hath him long known where others knew a shade;
Forget thine eyes, and learn herewith to see
Within this time-worn sheath the snowy blade.

Upon her lovely cheek there still doth play
A maiden's blush, for her heart grows not old;
Her silver locks go sweetly all astray;
Though silver are her locks, her heart is gold!

THE WAYSIDE VIRGIN

FRANCE

I AM the Virgin; from this granite ledge
A hundred weary winters have I watched
The lonely road that wanders at my feet;
And many days I've sat here, in my lap
A little heap of snow, and overheard
The dry, dead voices of sere, rustling leaves;
While scarce a beggar creaked across the way.
How very old I am! I have forgot
The day they fixed me here; and whence I came,
With crown of gold, and all my tarnished blue.

How green the grass is now, and all around
Blossoms the May; but it is cold in here,
Sunless and cold. — Now comes a little maid
To kneel among the asters at my feet;
What a sweet noise she makes, like murmurings
Of bees in June! I wonder what they say,
These rosy mortals, when they look at me?
I wonder why
They call me Mary and bow down to me?
Oh, I am weary of my painted box, —
Come, child,
And lay thy warm face on my wooden cheek,
That I may feel it glow as once of yore
It glowed when I, a cedar's happy heart,
Felt the first sunshine of the early spring!

WRITTEN AT THE END OF A BOOK

THIS is the end of the book
Written by God.
I am the earth he took,
I am the sod,
The wood and iron which he struck
With his sounding rod.

I am the reed that he blew:
Once quietly
By the riverside I grew,
Till one day he
Rooted me up and breathed a new
Delirium in me.

Would he had left me there,
Where all is still;

To lean on the heavy air,
 Silent, at will
To be, and joy, yet not to share,
 The avenging thrill.

I am the reed that he blew,
 Which yet he blows,
(For this is his breath too,
 And these, like those,
Are his own words blown unto you,
 — Hearken if you choose !)

This is the end of the book;
 And, if you read
Ought that is evil, why, look,
 I but obeyed,
— When deep his voice in my ear shook,
 I blew as he said !

Wallace Rice

UNDER THE STARS

Tell me what sail the seas
 Under the stars?
Ships, and ships' companies,
 Off to the wars.

Steel are the ship's great sides,
 Steel are her guns,
Backward she thrusts the tides,
 Swiftly she runs;

Steel is the sailor's heart,
 Stalwart his arm,
His the Republic's part
 Through cloud and storm.

Tell me what standard rare
 Streams from the spars?
Red stripes and white they bear,
 Blue, with bright stars:

Red for brave hearts that burn
 With liberty,
White for the peace they earn
 Making men free,

Stars for the Heaven above, —
 Blue for the deep,
Where, in their country's love,
 Heroes shall sleep.

Tell me why on the breeze
 These banners blow?
Ships, and ships' companies,
 Eagerly go

Warring, like all our line,
 Freedom to friend
Under this starry sign,
 True to the end.

Fair is the Flag's renown,
 Sacred her scars,
Sweet the death she shall crown
 Under the stars.

THE END

No freeman, saith the wise, thinks much on
 death:
No man with soul he dareth call his own
Liveth in dread lest there be no atone
In time to come for yesterday's warm
 breath,
No more than he for such end hungereth
As falls to those who speed their souls
 a-groan;
Death may be King, to sit a tottering
 throne
And hale men hence — let cowards cringe
 to Death!
Who giveth, taketh; and the days go by:
No seed sowed we; let him who did come
 reap:
Sweet peace is ours — and everlastingly, —
A little sleep, a little slumber! Ay,
This much is known: there is for thee and
 me
A little folding of the hands to sleep.

IMMORTAL FLOWERS

Of old, a man who died
Had, in his pride,
Woman and steed and slave
Heaped at his grave;
Given this sudden end
Their souls to send,
Still serving, whitherward
Their lord had fared.

Grown wiser, we, to-day,
A happier way
Find for our love and grief
And death's relief:
Flowers their fragrance strew
Where he must go,
Gladden the narrow gate
Whereat we wait.

And there be those of us
Who, amorous
Of life and hope, can see
How gleefully
He, lonely, greets beyond
These flowers so fond,
Even as our common doom
Saddens their bloom.

Robert Cameron Rogers

THE DANCING FAUN

Thou dancer of two thousand years,
Thou dancer of to-day,
What silent music fills thine ears,
What Bacchic lay,
That thou shouldst dance the centuries
Down their forgotten way?

What mystic strain of pagan mirth
Has charmed eternally
Those lithe, strong limbs, that spurn the earth?
What melody,
Unheard of men, has Father Pan
Left lingering with thee?

Ah! where is now the wanton throng
That round thee used to meet?
On dead lips died the drinking-song,
But wild and sweet,
What silent music urged thee on,
To its unuttered beat,

That when at last Time's weary will
Brought thee again to sight,
Thou cam'st forth dancing, dancing still,
Into the light,
Unwearied from the murk and dusk
Of centuries of night?

Alas for thee! — Alas, again,
The early faith is gone!
The Gods are no more seen of men,
All, all are gone, —
The shaggy forests no more shield
The Satyr and the Faun.

On Attic slopes the bee still hums,
On many an Elian hill
The wild-grape swells, but never comes
The distant trill
Of reedy flutes; for Pan is dead,
Broken his pipes and still.

And yet within thy listening ears
The pagan measures ring, —
Those limbs that have outdanced the years
Yet tireless spring:
How canst thou dream Pan dead when still
Thou seem'st to hear him sing!

A SLEEPING PRIESTESS OF APHRODITE

She dreams of Love upon the temple stair, —
About her feet the lithe green lizards play
In all the drowsy, warm, Sicilian air.

The winds have loosed the fillet from her hair,
Sea winds, salt-lipped, that laugh and seem to say,
"She dreams of Love, upon the temple stair.

"Then let us twine soft fingers, here and there,
Amid the gleaming threads that drift and stray
In all the drowsy, warm, Sicilian air,

"And let us weave of them a subtle snare
To cast about and bind her, as to-day
She dreams of Love, upon the temple stair."

Alas, the madcap winds, — how much they dare!
They wove the web, and in their wanton way,
In all the drowsy, warm, Sicilian air,

They bound her sleeping, in her own bright hair.
And as she slept came Love — and passed away, —
She dreams of Love, upon the temple stair,
In all the drowsy, warm, Sicilian air.

VIRGIL'S TOMB

"CECINI PASCUA, RURA, DUCES"

On an olive-crested steep
Hanging o'er the dusty road,
Lieth in his last abode,
Wrapped in everlasting sleep,

He who in the days of yore
Sang of pastures, sang of farms,
Sang of heroes and their arms,
Sang of passion, sang of war.

When the lark at dawning tells,
Herald like, the coming day,
And along the dusty way
Comes the sound of tinkling bells,

Rising to the tomb aloft,
While some modern Corydon
Drives his bleating cattle on
From the stable to the croft:

Then the soul of Virgil seems
To awaken from its dreams,
To sing again the melodies
Of which he often tells, —
The music of the birds,
The lowing of the herds,
The tinkling of the bells.

THE SHADOW ROSE

A noisette on my garden path
An ever-swaying shadow throws;
But if I pluck it strolling by,
I pluck the shadow with the rose.

Just near enough my heart you stood
To shadow it, — but was it fair
In him, who plucked and bore you off,
To leave your shadow lingering there?

DOUBT

Slow, groping giant, whose unsteady limbs
Waver and bend and cannot keep the path,
Thy feet are foul with mire, and thy knees
Torn by the nettles of the wayside fen;
The dust of dogmas dead is in thy mouth,
Yet down the ages thou hast followed him —
Clear-eyed Belief — who journeys with light heart.

The leaves of Hope about his head are green,
Firm falls his foot upon the path he treads,
To every day he suits his pilgrimage,
And rest at dusk is his, — complete and deep.

For thee — the bramble: thorns of vain debate
Harrow the hundred furrows of thy brow:
Sleep is not thine, — the darkness has no balm
For thy torn spirit. Deep into the night
Thy feet that gain no guidance from the stars
Press on, until before the silent tent,
Where deep and dreamlessly he lies asleep,
Thou comest with tired limbs to sink beside
The ashes of his fire and find them cold.

A HEALTH AT THE FORD

Broncho Dan halts midway of the stream,
Sucking up the water that goes tugging at his knees;
High noon and dry noon, — to-day it does n't seem
As if the country ever knew the blessing of a breeze.
A torn felt hat with the brim cockled up,
A dip from the saddle — there you are —
It 's the brew of old Snake River in a cowboy's drinking-cup —
At the ford of Deadman's Bar.

"Now for a toast, a health before we go, —
A health to the life that makes living worth a try;

A long drink, a deep drink, it 's bumpers,
Dan, you know;
No heel-taps now, old pony, you must drink
the river dry!
Here 's to her then, — every sunrise knows
her name,
I've given it away to every star;
Cold water in a hat! Pretty tough, but
what of that? —
It 's the best — at Deadman's Bar.

"Where Summer camps all the year by the
sea,
By the broad Pacific where your widened
waters pour,
Old Snake River, take a message down for
me,
Tell the waves that sing to her along the
Southern Shore;
Say that I 'm a-rustling, though the
trail that leads to wealth
Is mighty hard to find and dim and
far,
But tell her that I love her, and say I drank
her health
To-day at Deadman's Bar."

THE ROSARY

THE hours I spent with thee, dear heart,
Are as a string of pearls to me;
I count them over, every one apart,
My rosary.

Each hour a pearl, each pearl a prayer,
To still a heart in absence wrung;
I tell each bead unto the end and there
A cross is hung.

Oh memories that bless — and burn!
Oh barren gain — and bitter loss!
I kiss each bead, and strive at last to learn
To kiss the cross,
Sweetheart,
To kiss the cross.

Vance Thompson

SYMBOLS

GREEN grew the reeds and pale they were,
And all the sunless grass was gray;
The sluggish coils of marsh-water
Dripped thickly over root and stone;
In the deep woods there was no day,
No day within them, shine or sun, —
Only the night alway.

And evermore the cypresses
Against the cold sky rocked and swung;
The lurching of the high, black trees,
Their sprawling black tops tossed and flung
Against the sky. She made a hut
Of dripping stone and wattled clay,
And the small window-space was shut
With woven reeds, green and gray.

The comely stars paced soberly
In the blue gardens overhead,
And morn and eve the housing sky
Shifted in blue and gold and red;
But She who dwelt in the stone hut
Knew not these things; on gathered
knees
She leaned her face, her thick hair shut
Her from the stars and trees.

LINEN BANDS

I WEEP those dead lips, white and dry,
On which no kisses lie,
Those eyes deserted of desire,
And love's soft fire.

I weep the folded feet and hands,
Held fast in linen bands;
Still heart, cold breasts, — for them my
dole:
God hath the soul.

Ella Higginson

BEGGARS[1]

CHILD with the hungry eyes,
The pallid mouth and brow,
And the lifted, asking hands,
I am more starved than thou.

I beg not on the street;
But where the sinner stands,
In secret place, I beg
Of God, with outstretched hands.

As thou hast asked of me,
Raising thy downcast head,
So have I asked of Him,
So, trembling, have I plead.

Take this and go thy way;
Thy hunger shall soon cease.
Thou prayest but for bread,
And I, alas! for peace.

MOONRISE IN THE ROCKIES[1]

THE trembling train clings to the leaning wall
Of solid stone; a thousand feet below
Sinks a black gulf; the sky hangs like a pall
Upon the peaks of everlasting snow.

Then of a sudden springs a rim of light,
Curved like a silver sickle. High and higher —
Till the full moon burns on the breast of night,
And a million firs stand tipped with lucent fire.

THE LAMP IN THE WEST[1]

VENUS has lit her silver lamp
Low in the purple West,
Casting a soft and mellow light
Upon the sea's full breast;
In one clear path — as if to guide
Some pale, wayfaring guest.

Far out, far out the restless bar
Starts from a troubled sleep,
Where, roaring through the narrow straits,
The meeting waters leap;
But still that shining pathway leads
Across the lonely deep.

When I sail out the narrow straits
Where unknown dangers be,
And cross the troubled, moaning bar
To the mysterious sea,
Dear God, wilt thou not set a lamp
Low in the West for me?

THE GRAND RONDE VALLEY[1]

AH, me! I know how like a golden flower
The Grand Ronde valley lies this August night,
Locked in by dimpled hills where purple light
Lies wavering. There at the sunset hour
Sink downward, like a rainbow-tinted shower,
A thousand colored rays, soft, changeful, bright.
Later the large moon rises, round and white,
And three Blue Mountain pines against it tower,
Lonely and dark. A coyote's mournful cry
Sinks from the cañon, — whence the river leaps
A blade of silver underneath the moon.
Like restful seas the yellow wheat-fields lie,
Dreamless and still. And while the valley sleeps,
O hear! — the lullabies that low winds croon.

FOUR-LEAF CLOVER[1]

I KNOW a place where the sun is like gold,
And the cherry blooms burst with snow,
And down underneath is the loveliest nook,
Where the four-leaf clovers grow.

One leaf is for hope, and one is for faith,
And one is for love, you know,
And God put another in for luck, —
If you search, you will find where they grow.

But you must have hope, and you must have faith,
You must love and be strong — and so,
If you work, if you wait, you will find the place
Where the four-leaf clovers grow.

John Kendrick Bangs

TO A WITHERED ROSE[1]

THY span of life was all too short —
A week or two at best —
From budding-time, through blossoming,
To withering and rest.

Yet compensation hast thou — aye ! —
For all thy little woes;
For was it not thy happy lot
To live and die a rose ?

MAY 30, 1893[1]

IT seemed to be but chance, yet who shall say
That 't was not part of Nature 's own sweet way,

That on the field where once the cannon's breath
Laid many a hero cold and stark in death,
Some little children, in the after-years,
Had come to play among the grassy spears,

And, all unheeding, when their romp was done,
Had left a wreath of wild flowers over one

Who fought to save his country, and whose lot
It was to die unknown and rest forgot ?

THE LITTLE ELF

I MET a little Elf-man, once,
Down where the lilies blow.
I asked him why he was so small
And why he did n't grow.

He slightly frowned, and with his eye
He looked me through and through.
" I 'm quite as big for me," said he,
" As you are big for you."

Sophie Jewett

("ELLEN BURROUGHS")

"IF SPIRITS WALK"[2]

IF spirits walk, love, when the night climbs slow
The slant footpath where we were wont to go,
Be sure that I shall take the selfsame way
To the hill-crest, and shoreward, down the gray,
Sheer, gravelled slope, where vetches straggling grow.

Look for me not when gusts of winter blow,
When at thy pane beat hands of sleet and snow;
I would not come thy dear eyes to affray,
If spirits walk.

But when, in June, the pines are whispering low,
And when their breath plays with thy bright hair so
As some one's fingers once were used to play —
That hour when birds leave song, and children pray,
Keep the old tryst, sweetheart, and thou shalt know
If spirits walk.

ARMISTICE[2]

THE water sings along our keel,
The wind falls to a whispering breath;
I look into your eyes and feel
No fear of life or death;
So near is love, so far away
The losing strife of yesterday.

We watch the swallow skim and dip;
Some magic bids the world be still;
Life stands with finger upon lip;
Love hath his gentle will;

Though hearts have bled, and tears have burned,
The river floweth unconcerned.

We pray the fickle flag of truce
Still float deceitfully and fair;
Our eyes must love its sweet abuse;
This hour we will not care,
Though just beyond to-morrow's gate,
Arrayed and strong, the battle wait.

SONG[1]

THY face I have seen as one seeth
A face in a dream,
Soft drifting before me as drifteth
A leaf on the stream:
A face such as evermore fleeth
From following feet,
A face such as hideth and shifteth
Evasive and sweet.

Thy voice I have heard as one heareth,
Afar and apart,
The wood-thrush that rapturous poureth
The song of his heart;
Who heedeth is blest, but who neareth,
In wary pursuit,
May see where the singer upsoareth,
The forest is mute.

WHEN NATURE HATH BETRAYED THE HEART THAT LOVED HER[1]

THE gray waves rock against the gray sky-line,
And break complaining on the long gray sand,
Here where I sit, who cannot understand
Their voice of pain, nor this dumb pain of mine;

For I, who thought to fare till my days end,
Armed sorrow-proof in sorrow, having known
How hearts bleed slow when brave lips make no moan,
How Life can torture, how Death may befriend

When Love entreats him hasten, — even I,
Who feared no human anguish that may be,
I cannot bear the loud grief of the sea,
I cannot bear the still grief of the sky.

A SMILING DEMON OF NOTRE DAME[1]

QUIET as are the quiet skies
He watches where the city lies
Floating in vision clear or dim
Through sun or rain beneath his eyes;
Her songs, her laughter, and her cries
Hour after hour drift up to him.

Her days of glory or disgrace
He watches with unchanging face;
He knows what midnight crimes are done,
What horrors under summer sun;
And souls that pass in holy death
Sweep by him on the morning's breath.

Alike to holiness and sin
He feels nor alien nor akin;
Five hundred creeping mortal years
He smiles on human joy and tears,
Man-made, immortal, scorning man;
Serene, grotesque Olympian.

Evaleen Stein

BUDDING-TIME TOO BRIEF

O LITTLE buds, break not so fast!
The spring 's but new.
The skies will yet be brighter blue,
And sunny too.
I would you might thus sweetly last
Till this glad season 's overpast,
Nor hasten through.

It is so exquisite to feel
The light warm sun;
To merely know the winter done,
And life begun;

And to my heart no blooms appeal
For tenderness so deep and real,
As any one

Of these first April buds, that hold
The hint of spring's
Rare perfectness that May-time brings.
So take not wings!
Oh, linger, linger, nor unfold
Too swiftly though the mellow mould,
Sweet growing things!

And errant birds, and honey-bees,
Seek not to wile;
And, sun, let not your warmest smile
Quite yet beguile
The young peach-boughs and apple-trees
To trust their beauty to the breeze;
Wait yet awhile!

IN MEXICO

THE cactus towers, straight and tall,
Through fallow fields of chapparal;
And here and there, in paths apart,
A dusky peon guides his cart,
And yokes of oxen journey slow,
In Mexico.

And oft some distant tinkling tells
Of muleteers, with wagon bells
That jangle sweet across the maize,
And green agave stalks that raise
Rich spires of blossoms, row on row,
In Mexico.

Upon the whitened city walls
The golden sunshine softly falls,
On archways set with orange trees,
On paven courts and balconies
Where trailing vines toss to and fro,
In Mexico.

And patient little donkeys fare
With laden saddle-bags, and bear
Through narrow ways quaint water-jars
Wreathed round with waxen lily stars
And scarlet poppy-buds that blow,
In Mexico.

When twilight falls, more near and clear
The tender southern skies appear,
And down green slopes of blooming limes
Come cascades of cathedral chimes;
And prayerful figures worship low,
In Mexico.

A land of lutes and witching tones,
Of silver, onyx, opal stones;
A lazy land, wherein all seems
Enchanted into endless dreams;
And never any need they know,
In Mexico,

Of life's unquiet, swift advance;
But slipped into such gracious trance,
The restless world speeds on, unfelt,
Unheeded, as by those who dwelt
In olden ages, long ago,
In Mexico.

IN YOUTH

NOT lips of mine have ever said:
"Would God that I were dead!"
Nay, cruel griefs! ye cannot break
My love of life; nor can ye make
Oblivion blest in any wise,
Nor death seem sweet for sorrow's sake.
Life! life! my every pulse outcries
For life, and love, and quickened breath,
O God, — not, *not* for death!

FLOOD-TIME ON THE MARSHES

DEAR marshes, by no hand of man
Laboriously sown,
My river clasps you in its arms
And claims you for its own!
It laughs, and laughs, and twinkles on
Across the reedy soil,
That heed of harvest vexes not,
Nor need of any toil.

And in my heart I joy to know
That safe within this spot
Sweet nature reigns; let other fields
Bear bread, it matters not.
— What matters aught of anything
When one may drift away
Into the realms of all-delight,
As I drift on to-day?

Beneath the budded swamp-rose sprays
The blue-eyed grasses stand,
Submerged within a crystal world,
A limpid wonderland;
And where the clustered sedges show
Their silky-tasselled sheaves,
The slender arrow-lily lifts
Its quiver of green leaves.

The tiny waves lap softly past,
So musical and round,
I think they must be moulded out
Of sunshine and sweet sound.
And here and there some little knoll,
More lofty than the rest,
Stands out above the happy tide,
An island of the blest;

Where fringed with lacy fronds of fern
The grass grows rich and high,
And flowering spider-worts have caught
The color of the sky;

Where water-oaks are thickly strung
With green and golden balls,
And from tall tilting iris tips
The wild canary calls.

— O gracious world! I seem to feel
A kinship with the trees;
I am first-cousin to the marsh,
A sister to the breeze!
My heartstrings tremble to its touch,
In throbs supremely sweet,
And through my pulses light and life
And love divinely meet.

Far off, the sunbeams smite the woods,
And pearly fleeces sail
Athwart the light, and leave below
A purple-shadowed trail;
The essence of the perfect June
So subtly is distilled,
Until my very soul of souls
Is filled, and overfilled!

Lucy Robinson

(LUCY CATLIN BULL)

THE FIRE I' THE FLINT

THE sudden thrust of speech is no mean test
Of man or woman. Caesar, with his cry
Of anguish, — Pilate, putting justice by, —
Into three words a human soul compressed;
Three broke from Galileo's brooding breast;
And Desdemona, instant to reply,
"Nobody — I myself," is by that lie
In all her purity made manifest.
But Tito, Tito, standing so secure, —
Tito, the idol of the market-place,
Who muttering to himself, "Some madman, sure!"
Could look his stricken father in the face,
From a yet deeper well his falsehood drew,
And lived more base than that young wife died true.

"HIC ME, PATER OPTIME, FESSAM DESERIS"

ERE yet in Vergil I could scan or spell,
Or through the enchanted portal of that lay
Dear to old Rome had found my faltering way,
How oft with heaving breast I heard thee tell
Of horrors that the Trojan fleet befell:
How for a time they were the tempest's prey,
And how at last into a little bay
Their boats came gliding on the peaceful swell.
There, though thick shade might threaten from above,
Were rest and peace, nor any need to roam.
Alas! I did not dream how soon for thee,
Best father, sweetest friend, the quiet cove
Would stretch its arms, while I, half blind with foam,
Should still be tossing on the open sea.

A BALLADE OF ISLANDS

I WOULD I had been island-born.
I dearly love things insular:
The coral bed, the quaint bazaar,

The palm and breadfruit never shorn,
The smoking cone that cannot char
The azure of a tropic morn,
The dancing girl in soft cymar, —
All these such lures, such wonders are —
Oh, why was I not island-born?

In island crossed of Capricorn —
In Otaheite, wild Happar —
Lurk all the powers that make or mar.
The ogress, wrinkled like a Norn,
The parrot-fish, the nenuphar,
The tides that leave in quiet scorn
The moon out of their calendar,
Miranda's cave, Nausicaa's car, —
All these are for the island-born.

'T was on a far-off isle forlorn
That Haidee wore her golden bar,
Virginia seemed a drifted spar,
Rarahu's loving heart was torn,
Sweet Allan Bane, in peace and war,
Awoke St. Modan's harp outworn,
And Graziella her guitar;
She bore the brimming water-jar
Not grieving to be island-born.

ENVOY

Prince, on three islands, sundered far,
Thine were life's flower, its husk, its thorn.
Ripe grew thy wrath on Elba's scar,
In St. Helena sank thy star.
Napoleon, thou wast island-born!

Oliver Herford

PROEM

If this little world to-night
  Suddenly should fall through space
In a hissing, headlong flight,
  Shrivelling from off its face,
As it falls into the sun,
  In an instant every trace
Of the little crawling things —
  Ants, philosophers, and lice,
Cattle, cockroaches, and kings,
  Beggars, millionaires, and mice,
Men and maggots, — all as one
  As it falls into the sun, —
Who can say but at the same
  Instant from some planet far
A child may watch us and exclaim:
  "See the pretty shooting star!"

A BELATED VIOLET

Very dark the autumn sky,
  Dark the clouds that hurried by;
Very rough the autumn breeze
  Shouting rudely to the trees.

Listening, frightened, pale, and cold,
  Through the withered leaves and mould
Peered a violet all in dread —
  "Where, oh, where is spring?" she said.

Sighed the trees, "Poor little thing!
  She may call in vain for spring."
And the grasses whispered low,
  "We must never let her know."

"What 's this whispering?" roared the breeze;
  "Hush! a violet," sobbed the trees,
"Thinks it 's spring, — poor child, we fear
  She will die if she should hear!"

Softly stole the wind away,
  Tenderly he murmured, "Stay!"
To a late thrush on the wing,
  "Stay with her one day and sing!"

Sang the thrush so sweet and clear
  That the sun came out to hear,
And, in answer to her song,
  Beamed on violet all day long;

And the last leaves here and there
  Fluttered with a spring-like air.
Then the violet raised her head, —
  "Spring has come at last!" she said.

Happy dreams had violet
  All that night — but happier yet,
When the dawn came dark with snow,
  Violet never woke to know.

WHY YE BLOSSOME COMETH BEFORE YE LEAFE

Once hoary Winter chanced — alas!
Alas! hys waye mistaking —
A leafless apple-tree to pass
Where Spring lay dreaming. "Fie, ye lass!

Ye lass had best be waking,"
Quoth he, and shook hys robe, and, lo!
Lo! forth didde flye a cloud of snowe.

Now in ye bough an elfe there dwelte,
An elfe of wondrous powere,
That when ye chillye snowe didde pelte,
With magic charm each flake didde melte,
Didde melte into a flowere;
And Spring didde wake and marvelle how,
How blossomed so ye leafless bough.

THE ELF AND THE DORMOUSE

UNDER a toadstool
Crept a wee Elf,
Out of the rain,
To shelter himself.

Under the toadstool,
Sound asleep,
Sat a big Dormouse
All in a heap.

Trembled the wee Elf,
Frightened, and yet
Fearing to fly away
Lest he get wet.

To the next shelter —
Maybe a mile!
Sudden the wee Elf
Smiled a wee smile,

Tugged till the toadstool
Toppled in two.
Holding it over him,
Gayly he flew.

Soon he was safe home,
Dry as could be.
Soon woke the Dormouse —
"Good gracious me!

"Where is my toadstool?"
Loud he lamented.
— And that 's how umbrellas
First were invented.

THE MON-GOOS

THIS, Children, is the famed Mon-goos.
He has an ap-pe-tite ab-struse:
Strange to re-late, this crea-ture takes
A cu-ri-ous joy in eat-ing snakes —
All kinds — though, it must be con-fessed,
He likes the poi-son-ous ones the best.
From him we learn how ve-ry small
A thing can bring a-bout a Fall.
O Mon-goos, where were you that day
When Mistress Eve was led a-stray?
If you 'd but seen the ser-pent first,
Our parents would not have been cursed,
And so there would be no ex-cuse
For MILTON, but for you — Mon-goos!

Amélie Troubetzkoy

A MOOD[1]

IT is good to strive against wind and rain
In the keen, sweet weather that autumn brings.
The wild horse shakes not the drops from his mane,
The wild bird flicks not the wet from her wings,
In gladder fashion than I toss free
The mist-dulled gold of my bright hair's flag,
What time the winds on their heel-wings lag,
And all the tempest is friends with me.
None can reach me to wound or cheer;
Sound of weeping and sound of song —
Neither may trouble me: I can hear
But the wind's loud laugh, and the sibilant, strong,
Lulled rush of the rain through the sapless weeds.
O rare, dear days, ye are here again!
I will woo ye as maidens are wooed of men, —
With oaths forgotten and broken creeds!

Ye shall not lack for the sun's fierce shining —
With the gold of my hair will I make ye glad;

For your blown, red forests give no repining —
Here are my lips: will ye still be sad?
Comfort ye, comfort ye, days of cloud,
Days of shadow, of wrath, of blast —
I who love ye am come at last.
Laugh to welcome me! cry aloud!

For wild am I as thy winds and rains —
Free to come and to go as they;
Love's moon sways not the tides of my veins;
There is no voice that can bid me stay.
Out and away on the drenched, brown lea!
Out to the great, glad heart of the year!
Nothing to grieve for, nothing to fear, —
Fetterless, lawless, a maiden free!

BEFORE THE RAIN[1]

The blackcaps pipe among the reeds,
And there 'll be rain to follow;
There is a murmur as of wind
In every coign and hollow;
The wrens do chatter of their fears
While swinging on the barley-ears.

Come, hurry, while there yet is time,
Pull up thy scarlet bonnet.
Now, sweetheart, as my love is thine,
There is a drop upon it.

So trip it ere the storm-hag weird
Doth pluck the barley by the beard!

Lo! not a whit too soon we're housed;
The storm-witch yells above us;
The branches rapping on the panes
Seem not in truth to love us.
And look where through the clover bush
The nimble-footed rain doth rush!

A SONNET[2]

Take all of me, — I am thine own, heart, soul,
Brain, body, — all; all that I am or dream
Is thine forever; yea, though space should teem
With thy conditions, I 'd fulfil the whole —
Were to fulfil them to be loved of thee.
Oh, love me! — were to love me but a way
To kill me — love me; so to die would be
To live forever. Let me hear thee say
Once only, "Dear, I love thee," — then all life
Would be one sweet remembrance, thou its king:
Nay, thou art that already, and the strife
Of twenty worlds could not uncrown thee. Bring,
O Time! my monarch to possess his throne
Which is my heart and for himself alone.

Gertrude Hall

MRS. GOLIGHTLY

The time is come to speak, I think:
For on the square I met
My beauteous widow, fresh and pink,
Her black gown touched at every brink
With tender violet;

And at her throat the white *crêpe lisse*
Spoke, in a fluffy bow,
Of woe that should perhaps ne'er cease —
(Peace to thy shade, Golightly, peace!)
Yet mitigated woe.

In her soft eye, that used to scan
The ground, nor seem to see,
The hazel legend sweetly ran,
"I *could* not wholly hate a man
For quite adoring me."

And when she drew her 'kerchief fine,
A hint of heliotrope
Its snow edged with an inky line
Exhaled, — from which scent you divine
Through old regrets new hope.

And then her step, so soft and slow,
She scarcely seemed to lift
From off the sward her widowed toe, —
One year, one little year ago! —
So soft yet, yet so swift;

[1] Copyright, 1887, by Harper & Brothers.

[2] Copyright, 1886, by Harper & Brothers.

Then, too, her blush, her side glance coy,
Tell me in easy Greek
(I wonder could her little boy
Prove source of serious annoy?)
The time has come to speak.

ANGELS

How shall we tell an angel
From another guest?
How, from the common worldly herd,
One of the blest?

Hint of suppressed halo,
Rustle of hidden wings,
Wafture of heavenly frankincense, —
Which of these things?

The old Sphinx smiles so subtly:
"I give no golden rule, —
Yet would I warn thee, World: treat well
Whom thou call'st fool."

THE DUST

It settles softly on your things,
Impalpable, fine, light, dull, gray:
Her dingy dust-clout Betty brings,
And singing brushes it away:

And it's a queen's robe, once so proud,
And it's the moths fed in its fold,
It's leaves, and roses, and the shroud
Wherein an ancient saint was rolled.

And it is Beauty's golden hair,
And it is Genius' crown of bay,
And it is lips once warm and fair
That kissed in some forgotten May. . . .

MY OLD COUNSELOR

The Sun looked from his everlasting skies,
He laughed into my daily-dying eyes;
He said to me, the brutal shining Sun:
"Poor, fretful, hot, rebellious, little one!

"Thou shalt not find it, yet there shall be truth;
Thou shalt grow old, but yet there shall be youth;
Thou shalt not do, yet great deeds shall be done, —
Believe me, child, I am an old, old Sun!

"Thou mayst go blind, yet fair will bloom the spring;
Thou mayst not hear them, but the birds will sing;
Thou mayst despair, no less will hope be rife;
Thou must lie dead, but many will have life.

"Thou mayst declare of love: it is a dream!
Yet long with love, my love, the Earth will teem:
Let not thy foolish heart be borne so low, —
Lift up thy heart! Exult that it is so!"

Elaine Goodale Eastman

A COUNTRYWOMAN OF MINE

Handsome? I hardly know. Her profile's fine —
Delightful, intellectual, aquiline.

Her keen eyes light it; keen, yet often kind;
Her fair hair crowns it to an artist's mind.

Fine figure and fine manners, without doubt,
Determine half her charm, and bear me out.

Learned? Well, rather. See them for yourself —
Mill, Spencer, Darwin, on her favorite shelf.

Well educated, certainly well read;
Well born, of course, and (not of course) well bred.

Provincial? Never! Cockney? Not at all.
Her world is small enough, yet not too small.

To prove she knows it, only watch a while
That humorous, tender, half-sarcastic smile.

Accomplished? She says not; but who can tell?
She does some simple things, and does them well.

She walks well, stands well, sits well — things so rare,
To praise as they deserve I hardly dare!

She rows, rides, dances — admirably done!
Delights in each, and yet depends on none.

What to take up she knows, and what to drop;
How to say clever things, and when to stop.

Few dress so well; she does what few can do,
Forgets what she has on; and so do you?

She 's not too careless, not conventional quite;
Does what she likes; knows what she does is right.

Takes New World freedom and with Old World ease;
She 's but to please herself the world to please.

ASHES OF ROSES

Soft on the sunset sky
Bright daylight closes,
Leaving, when light doth die,
Pale hues that mingling lie, —
Ashes of roses.

When love's warm sun is set,
Love's brightness closes;
Eyes with hot tears are wet,
In hearts there linger yet
Ashes of roses.

BABY

Dimpled and flushed and dewy pink he lies,
Crumpled and tossed and lapt in snowy bands;
Aimlessly reaching with his tiny hands,
Lifting in wondering gaze his great blue eyes.
Sweet pouting lips, parted by breathing sighs;
Soft cheeks, warm-tinted as from tropic lands;
Framed with brown hair in shining silken strands, —
All fair, all pure, a sunbeam from the skies!
O perfect innocence! O soul enshrined
In blissful ignorance of good or ill,
By never gale of idle passion crossed!
Although thou art no alien from thy kind,
Though pain and death may take thee captive, still
Through sin, at least, thine Eden is not lost.

Winifred Howells

FORTHFARING

I tripped along a narrow way,
Plucking the same flowers, day by day;
The sun which round about me lay
Had never seemed to sink.

But now at once the path divides;
I see new flowers bloom on all sides;
I stop, while doubt the sun half hides:
I have begun to think.

THE POET AND THE CHILD

"And you, Sir Poet, shall you make, I pray,
This child a poet with that insight rare
They tell me poets have, that everywhere
He sees new beauties lost to common clay?"

"Nay," said the poet, "rather lend the boy
Your scarf of gauze, to veil his questioning eye,
Lest in his pleasure he should aught descry
But what is fair; so shall he much enjoy."

She lightly laughed as she regained the band
Now strolling on (to her it seemed a jest
Turned for her pleasure); but behind the rest
The poet and the child walked hand in hand.

A WASTED SYMPATHY

Do not waste your pity, friend,
When you see me weep as now;
Keep it to some better end.
When dry-eyed I went about
With a leaden heart locked in
By a silent tongue, ah! then
Had you brought it, it had been
Sweet indeed to me; but now
When the depths of my despair
Are upheaved and through the portals
Of my heart come free as air,
It is useless. If you please,
Give your thanks that to a woman
Tears are given, and be at ease.

PAST

There, as she sewed, came floating through her head
Odd bits of poems, learned in other days
And long forgotten in the noisier ways
Through which the fortunes of her life now led;
And looking up, she saw upon the shelf
In dusty rank her favorite poets stand,
All uncaressed by her fond eye or hand;
And her heart smote her, thinking how herself
Had loved them once and found in them all good
As well as beauty, filling every need;
But now they could not fill the emptiness
Of heart she felt ev'n in her gayest mood.
She wanted once no work her heart to feed,
And to be idle once was no distress.

A MOOD

The wind exultant swept
Through the new leaves overhead,
Till at once my pulses leapt
With a life I thought long dead,
And I woke, as one who has slept,
To my childhood, — that had not fled.
On the wind my spirit flew;
Its freedom was mine as well.
For a moment the world was new;
What came there to break the spell?
The wind still freshly blew;
My spirit it was that fell.

Richard Hovey

THE WANDER-LOVERS

Down the world with Marna!
That 's the life for me!
Wandering with the wandering wind,
Vagabond and unconfined!
Roving with the roving rain
Its unboundaried domain!
Kith and kin of wander-kind,
Children of the sea!

Petrels of the sea-drift!
Swallows of the lea!
Arabs of the whole wide girth
Of the wind-encircled earth!
In all climes we pitch our tents,
Cronies of the elements,
With the secret lords of birth
Intimate and free.

All the seaboard knows us
From Fundy to the Keys;
Every bend and every creek
Of abundant Chesapeake;
Ardise hills and Newport coves
And the far-off orange groves,
Where Floridian oceans break,
Tropic tiger seas.

Down the world with Marna,
Tarrying there and here!
Just as much at home in Spain
As in Tangier or Touraine!
Shakespeare's Avon knows us well,
And the crags of Neufchâtel;
And the ancient Nile is fain
Of our coming near.

Down the world with Marna,
Daughter of the air!
Marna of the subtle grace,
And the vision in her face!
Moving in the measures trod
By the angels before God!
With her sky-blue eyes amaze
And her sea-blue hair!

Marna with the trees' life
In her veins a-stir!
Marna of the aspen heart
Where the sudden quivers start!
Quick-responsive, subtle, wild!
Artless as an artless child,
Spite of all her reach of art!
Oh, to roam with her!

Marna with the wind's will,
Daughter of the sea!
Marna of the quick disdain,
Starting at the dream of stain!
At a smile with love aglow,
At a frown a statued woe,
Standing pinnacled in pain
Till a kiss sets free!

Down the world with Marna,
Daughter of the fire!
Marna of the deathless hope,
Still alert to win new scope
Where the wings of life may spread
For a flight unhazarded!
Dreaming of the speech to cope
With the heart's desire!

Marna of the far quest
After the divine!
Striving ever for some goal
Past the blunder-god's control!
Dreaming of potential years
When no day shall dawn in fears!
That 's the Marna of my soul,
Wander-bride of mine!

ENVOY

TO "MORE SONGS FROM VAGABONDIA"

I

Whose furthest footstep never strayed
Beyond the village of his birth
Is but a lodger for the night
In this old wayside inn of earth.

To-morrow he shall take his pack,
And set out for the ways beyond
On the old trail from star to star,
An alien and a vagabond.

II

If any record of our names
Be blown about the hills of time,
Let no one sunder us in death, —
The man of paint, the men of rhyme.

Of all our good, of all our bad,
This one thing only is of worth, —
We held the league of heart to heart
The only purpose of the earth.

THE CALL OF THE BUGLES

Bugles!
And the Great Nation thrills and leaps to
arms!
Prompt, unconstrained, immediate,
Without misgiving and without debate,
Too calm, too strong for fury or alarms,
The people blossoms armies and puts forth
The splendid summer of its noiseless might;
For the old sap of fight
Mounts up in South and North,
The thrill
That tingled in our veins at Bunker Hill
And brought to bloom July of 'Seventy-
Six!
Pine and palmetto mix
With the sequoia of the giant West
Their ready banners, and the hosts of war,
Near and far,
Sudden as dawn,
Innumerable as forests, hear the call
Of the bugles,
The battle-birds!
For not alone the brave, the fortunate,
Who first of all
Have put their knapsacks on —

They are the valiant vanguard of the rest! —
Not they alone, but all our millions wait,
Hand on sword,
For the word
That bids them bid the nations know us sons of Fate.

Bugles!
And in my heart a cry,
— Like a dim echo far and mournfully
Blown back to answer them from yesterday!
A soldier's burial!
November hillsides and the falling leaves
Where the Potomac broadens to the tide —
The crisp autumnal silence and the gray
(As of a solemn ritual
Whose congregation glories as it grieves,
Widowed but still a bride) —
The long hills sloping to the wave,
And the lone bugler standing by the grave!

Taps!
The lonely call over the lonely woodlands —
Rising like the soaring of wings,
Like the flight of an eagle —
Taps!
They sound forever in my heart.
From farther still,
The echoes — still the echoes!
The bugles of the dead
Blowing from spectral ranks an answering cry!
The ghostly roll of immaterial drums,
Beating reveille in the camps of dream,
As from far meadows comes,
Over the pathless hill,
The irremeable stream.
I hear the tread
Of the great armies of the Past go by;
I hear,
Across the wide sea wash of years between,
Concord and Valley Forge shout back from the unseen,
And Vicksburg give a cheer.

Our cheer goes back to them, the valiant dead!
Laurels and roses on their graves to-day,
Lilies and laurels over them we lay,
And violets o'er each unforgotten head.
Their honor still with the returning May
Puts on its springtime in our memories,
Nor till the last American with them lies
Shall the young year forget to strew their bed.
Peace to their ashes, sleep and honored rest!
But we — awake!
Ours to remember them with deeds like theirs!
From sea to sea the insistent bugle blares,
The drums will not be still for any sake;
And as an eagle rears his crest,
Defiant, from some tall pine of the North,
And spreads his wings to fly,
The banners of America go forth
Against the clarion sky.
Veteran and volunteer,
They who were comrades of that shadow host,
And the young brood whose veins renew the fires
That burned in their great sires,
Alike we hear
The summons sounding clear
From coast to coast, —
The cry of the bugles,
The battle-birds!

. . . .

Bugles!
The imperious bugles!
Still their call
Soars like an exaltation to the sky.
They call on men to fall,
To die, —
Remembered or forgotten, but a part
Of the great beating of the Nation's heart!
A call to sacrifice!
A call to victory!
Hark, in the Empyrean
The battle-birds!
The bugles!

UNMANIFEST DESTINY

To what new fates, my country, far
And unforeseen of foe or friend,
Beneath what unexpected star,
Compelled to what unchosen end,

Across the sea that knows no beach
The Admiral of Nations guides
Thy blind obedient keels to reach
The harbor where thy future rides!

The guns that spoke at Lexington
Knew not that God was planning then
The trumpet word of Jefferson
To bugle forth the rights of men.

To them that wept and cursed Bull Run,
  What was it but despair and shame?
Who saw behind the cloud the sun?
  Who knew that God was in the flame?

Had not defeat upon defeat,
  Disaster on disaster come,
The slave's emancipated feet
  Had never marched behind the drum.

There is a Hand that bends our deeds
  To mightier issues than we planned,
Each son that triumphs, each that bleeds,
  My country, serves Its dark command.

I do not know beneath what sky
  Nor on what seas shall be thy fate;
I only know it shall be high,
  I only know it shall be great.

July, 1898.

LOVE IN THE WINDS

When I am standing on a mountain crest,
Or hold the tiller in the dashing spray,
My love of you leaps foaming in my breast,
Shouts with the winds and sweeps to their foray;
My heart bounds with the horses of the sea,
And plunges in the wild ride of the night,
Flaunts in the teeth of tempest the large glee
That rides out Fate and welcomes gods to fight.
Ho, love, I laugh aloud for love of you,
Glad that our love is fellow to rough weather, —
No fretful orchid hothoused from the dew,
But hale and hardy as the highland heather,
Rejoicing in the wind that stings and thrills,
Comrade of ocean, playmate of the hills.

DARTMOUTH WINTER-SONG

Ho, a song by the fire!
(Pass the pipes, fill the bowl!)
Ho, a song by the fire!
— With a skoal! . . .
For the wolf wind is whining in the doorways,
And the snow drifts deep along the road,
And the ice-gnomes are marching from their Norways,
And the great white cold walks abroad.
(Boo-oo-o! pass the bowl!)
    For here by the fire
    We defy frost and storm.
    Ha, ha! we are warm
    And we have our hearts' desire;
    For here's four good fellows
    And the beechwood and the bellows,
    And the cup is at the lip
    In the pledge of fellowship.
        Skoal!

LAURANA'S SONG

FOR "A LADY OF VENICE"

Who 'll have the crumpled pieces of a heart?
Let him take mine!
Who 'll give his whole of passion for a part,
And call 't divine?
Who 'll have the soiled remainder of desire?
Who 'll warm his fingers at a burnt-out fire?
Who 'll drink the lees of love, and cast i' the mire
The nobler wine?

Let him come here, and kiss me on the mouth,
And have his will!
Love dead and dry as summer in the South
When winds are still,
And all the leafage shrivels in the heat!
Let him come here and linger at my feet
Till he grow weary with the over-sweet,
And die, or kill.

FROM "THE BIRTH OF GALAHAD"

YLEN'S SONG

And if he should come again
In the old glad way,
I should smile and take his hand.
What were there to say?

I should close my eyes and smile,
And my soul would be
Like the peace of summer noons
Beside the sea.

FROM "TALIESIN: A MASQUE"

Voices of Unseen Spirits

HERE falls no light of sun nor stars;
No stir nor striving here intrudes;
No moan nor merry-making mars
The quiet of these solitudes.

Submerged in sleep, the passive soul
Is one with all the things that seem;
Night blurs in one confusëd whole
Alike the dreamer and the dream.

O dwellers in the busy town!
For dreams you smile, for dreams you weep.
Come out, and lay your burdens down!
Come out; there is no God but Sleep.

Sleep, and renounce the vital day;
For evil is the child of life.
Let be the will to live, and pray
To find forgetfulness of strife.

Beneath the thicket of these leaves
No light discriminates each from each.
No Self that wrongs, no Self that grieves,
Hath longer deed nor creed nor speech.

Sleep on the mighty Mother's breast!
Sleep, and no more be separate!
Then, one with Nature's ageless rest,
There shall be no more sin to hate.

Taliesin

Spirits of Sleep,
That swell and sink
In the sea of Being
Like waves on the deep,
Forming, crumbling,
Fumbling, and tumbling
Forever, unseeing,
From brink to brink!

Perishing voices,
That call and call
From the coves of dream
With hollow noises!
I hear the sweep
Of the tides of sleep,
The ocean stream
Where the ages fall.

But not for these
Will I let me die,
Though my heart remembers
The calling seas;
For the cycles fought
Till form was wrought
And Might had members
And I was I.

Yet still to you,
O Dreams, I turn;
Not with a prayer
But a bidding to do!
I surmount and subdue you;
Not without you but through you
I shall forge and fare
To the chosen bourne.

Voices

We are ware of a will
Cries "Peace, be still!"
And our waters cease
To a troubled peace.

Taliesin

Lo, star upon star!
They dwell alone
Sirius, Altair,
Algebar!
Their ways are asunder, —
Aloof, in thunder
They march and flare
From zone to zone.

But the formless ether
Far and far
Enfolds their places.
Therein together
At one they sweep
From deep to deep,
And over its spaces
Star calls to star.

Through its waves they reach
Beyond their spheres
To their fellow fires.
Each yearns to each,
And the straight wills swerve
To a yielding curve,
And a moth's desires
Deflect the years.

And with urge on urge
Of the rippling wave
Light speeds through space;
The domes emerge;
And the halls of Night
Behold each light
Reveal his face
To the vast conclave.

The centred Soul
By these is known.
Its will it wreaks
At its own control;
But dumb, unseeing,
The sea of Being
Washes the peaks
Where it strives alone.

Voices

As the dawn awaits
The recoiling gates
Of the eastern air,
We are calm and hear.

Julie Mathilde Lippmann

LOVE AND LIFE

"GIVE me a fillet, Love," quoth I,
"To bind my Sweeting's heart to me,
So ne'er a chance of earth or sky
Shall part us ruthlessly:
A fillet, Love, but not to chafe
My Sweeting's soul, to cause her pain;
But just to bind her close and safe
Through snow and blossom and sun and rain:
A fillet, boy!"
Love said, "Here 's joy."

"Give me a fetter, Life," quoth I,
"To bind to mine my Sweeting's heart,
So Death himself must fail to pry
With Time the two apart:
A fetter, Life, that each shall wear,
Whose precious bondage each shall know.
I prithee, Life, no more forbear —
Why dost thou wait and falter so?
Haste, Life — be brief!"
Said Life: — "Here 's grief."

STONE WALLS

ALONG the country roadside, stone on stone,
Past waving grain-field, and near broken stile,
The walls stretch onward, an uneven pile,
With rankling vines and lichen overgrown:
So stand they sentinel. Unchanged, alone,
They 're left to watch the seasons' passing slow:
The summer's sunlight or the winter's snow,
The spring-time's birdling, or the autumn's moan.
Who placed the stones now gray with many years?
And did the rough hands tire, the sore hearts ache,
The eyes grow dim with all their weight of tears?
Or did the work seem light for some dear sake?
Those lives are over. All their hopes and fears
Are lost like shadows in the morning-break.

THE PINES

THROUGHOUT the soft and sunlit day
The pennoned pines, in strict array,
Stand grim and silent, gaunt and gray.

But when the blasts of winter keen,
They whisper each to each, and lean
Like comrades with a bond between.

And seeing them deport them so,
One almost thinks they seek to show
How mortal-like mere trees may grow.

For men, in peace time, stand aloof,
One from the other, asking proof
Of lineage and race and roof.

But let the blast of battle call, —
Lo! they 're unquestioning comrades all,
Who side by side will stand or fall.

Mark A. De Wolfe Howe

THE TRAVELLERS

THEY made them ready and we saw them go
Out of our very lives;
Yet this world holds them all,
And soon it must befall
That we shall know
How this one fares, how that one thrives;
And one day — who knows when?
They shall be with us here again.

Another traveller left us late
Whose life was as the soul of ours;
A stranger guest went with him to the gate,
And closed it breathing back a breath of flowers.
And what the eyes we loved now look upon,
What industries the hands employ,
In what new speech the tongue hath joy,
We may not know — until one day,
And then another, as our toil is done,
The same still guest shall visit us,
And one by one
Shall take us by the hand and say,
"Come with me to the country marvellous,
Where he has dwelt so long beyond your sight.
'T were idle waiting for his own return
That ne'er shall be; face the perpetual light,
And with him learn
Whate'er the heavens unfold of knowledge infinite."
Each after each then shall we rise,
And follow through the stranger's secret gate,
And we shall ask and hear, beyond surmise,
What glorious life is his, since desolate
We stood about the bed
Where our blind eyes looked down on him as dead.

DISTINCTION

THE village sleeps, a name unknown, till men
With life-blood stain its soil, and pay the due
That lifts it to eternal fame, — for then
'T is grown a Gettysburg or Waterloo.

"WHOM THE GODS LOVE"

"WHOM the gods love die young;" — if gods ye be,
Then generously might ye have spared to us
One from your vast unnumbered overplus,
One youth we loved as tenderly as ye.

Madison Cawein

PROEM

THERE is no rhyme that is half so sweet
As the song of the wind in the rippling wheat;
There is no metre that 's half so fine
As the lilt of the brook under rock and vine;
And the loveliest lyric I ever heard
Was the wildwood strain of a forest bird. —
If the wind and the brook and the bird would teach
My heart their beautiful parts of speech,
And the natural art that they say these with,
My soul would sing of beauty and myth
In a rhyme and a metre that none before
Have sung in their love, or dreamed in their lore,
And the world would be richer one poet the more.

THE RAIN-CROW

CAN freckled August, — drowsing warm and blonde
Beside a wheat-shock in the white-topped mead,
In her hot hair the oxeyed daisies wound, —
O bird of rain, lend aught but sleepy heed
To thee? when no plumed weed, no feather'd seed

Blows by her; and no ripple breaks the pond,
That gleams like flint between its rim of grasses,
Through which the dragonfly forever passes
Like splintered diamond.

Drouth weights the trees, and from the farmhouse eaves
The locust, pulse-beat of the summer day,
Throbs; and the lane, that shambles under leaves
Limp with the heat — a league of rutty way —
Is lost in dust; and sultry scents of hay
Breathe from the panting meadows heaped with sheaves.
Now, now, O bird, what hint is there of rain,
In thirsty heaven or on burning plain,
That thy keen eye perceives?

But thou art right. Thou prophesiest true.
For hardly hast thou ceased thy forecasting,
When, up the western fierceness of scorched blue,
Great water-carrier winds their buckets bring
Brimming with freshness. How their dippers ring
And flash and rumble! lavishing dark dew
On corn and forestland, that, streaming wet,
Their hilly backs against the downpour set,
Like giants vague in view.

The butterfly, safe under leaf and flower,
Has found a roof, knowing how true thou art;
The bumble-bee, within the last half-hour,
Has ceased to hug the honey to its heart;
While in the barnyard, under shed and cart,
Brood-hens have housed. — But I, who scorned thy power,
Barometer of the birds, — like August there, —
Beneath a beech, dripping from foot to hair,
Like some drenched truant, cower.

TO A WIND-FLOWER

TEACH me the secret of thy loveliness,
That, being made wise, I may aspire to be
As beautiful in thought, and so express
Immortal truths to earth's mortality;
Though to my soul ability be less
Than 't is to thee, O sweet anemone.

Teach me the secret of thy innocence,
That in simplicity I may grow wise,
Asking from Art no other recompense
Than the approval of her own just eyes;
So may I rise to some fair eminence,
Though less than thine, O cousin of the skies.

Teach me these things, through whose high knowledge, I, —
When Death hath poured oblivion through my veins,
And brought me home, as all are brought, to lie
In that vast house, common to serfs and Thanes, —
I shall not die, I shall not utterly die,
For beauty born of beauty — *that* remains.

DEATH

THROUGH some strange sense of sight or touch
I find what all have found before,
The presence I have feared so much,
The unknown's immaterial door.

I seek not and it comes to me;
I do not know the thing I find:
The fillet of fatality
Drops from my brows that made me blind.

Point forward now or backward, light!
The way I take I may not choose:
Out of the night into the night,
And in the night no certain clews.

But on the future, dim and vast,
And dark with dust and sacrifice,
Death's towering ruin from the past
Makes black the land that round me lies.

THE SOUL

An heritage of hopes and fears
And dreams and memory,
And vices of ten thousand years
God gives to thee.

A house of clay, the home of Fate,
Haunted of Love and Sin,
Where Death stands knocking at the gate
To let him in.

THE CREEK-ROAD

Calling, the heron flies athwart the blue
That sleeps above it; reach on rocky reach
Of water sings by sycamore and beech,
In whose warm shade bloom lilies not a few.
It is a page whereon the sun and dew
Scrawl sparkling words in dawn's delicious speech;
A laboratory where the wood-winds teach,
Dissect each scent and analyze each hue.
Not otherwise than beautiful, doth it
Record the happenings of each summer day;
Where we may read, as in a catalogue,
When passed a thresher; when a load of hay;
Or when a rabbit; or a bird that lit;
And now a barefoot truant and his dog.

KU KLUX

We have sent him seeds of the melon's core,
And nailed a warning upon his door;
By the Ku Klux laws we can do no more.

Down in the hollow, mid crib and stack,
The roof of his low-porched house looms black,
Not a line of light at the doorsill's crack.

Yet arm and mount! and mask and ride!
The hounds can sense though the fox may hide!
And for a word too much men oft have died.

The clouds blow heavy towards the moon.
The edge of the storm will reach it soon.
The killdee cries and the lonesome loon.

The clouds shall flush with a wilder glare
Than the lightning makes with its angled flare,
When the Ku Klux verdict is given there.

In the pause of the thunder rolling low,
A rifle's answer — who shall know
From the wind's fierce hurl and the rain's black blow?

Only the signature written grim
At the end of the message brought to him, —
A hempen rope and a twisted limb.

So arm and mount! and mask and ride!
The hounds can sense though the fox may hide!
And for a word too much men oft have died.

QUATRAINS

THE WIND IN THE PINES

When winds go organing through the pines
On hill and headland, darkly gleaming,
Meseems I hear sonorous lines
Of Iliads that the woods are dreaming.

OPPORTUNITY

Behold a hag whom Life denies a kiss
As he rides questward in knight-errant-wise;
Only when he hath passed her is it his
To know, too late, the Fairy in disguise.

COMRADERY

With eyes hand-arched he looks into
The morning's face, then turns away
With schoolboy feet, all wet with dew,
Out for a holiday.

The hill brook sings, incessant stars,
Foam-fashioned, on its restless breast;
And where he wades its water-bars
Its song is happiest.

A comrade of the chinquapin,
He looks into its knotted eyes
And sees its heart; and, deep within,
Its soul that makes him wise.

The wood-thrush knows and follows him,
Who whistles up the birds and bees;
And round him all the perfumes swim
Of woodland loam and trees.

Where'er he pass, the supple springs'
Foam-people sing the flowers awake;
And sappy lips of bark-clad things
Laugh ripe each fruited brake.

His touch is a companionship;
His word, an old authority:
He comes, a lyric at his lip,
Unstudied Poesy.

FLIGHT

THE song-birds? are they flown away?
The song-birds of the summer-time,
That sang their souls into the day,
And set the laughing days to rhyme? —
No catbird scatters through the hush
The sparkling crystals of its song;
Within the woods no hermit-thrush
Trails an enchanted flute along,
A sweet assertion of the hush.

All day the crows fly cawing past;
The acorns drop; the forests scowl:
At night I hear the bitter blast
Hoot with the hooting of the owl.
The wild creeks freeze; the ways are strewn
With leaves that rot: beneath the tree
The bird, that set its toil to tune,
And made a home for melody,
Lies dead beneath the death-white moon.

DIRGE

WHAT shall her silence keep
Under the sun?
Here, where the willows weep
And waters run;
Here, where she lies asleep,
And all is done.

Lights, when the tree-top swings;
Scents that are sown;
Sounds of the wood-bird's wings;
And the bee's drone:
These be her comfortings
Under the stone.

What shall watch o'er her here
When day is fled?
Here, when the night is near
And skies are red;
Here, where she lieth dear
And young and dead.

Shadows, and winds that spill
Dew, and the tune
Of the wild whippoorwill,
And the white moon, —
These be the watchers still
Over her stone.

John Bennett

SONGS FROM "MASTER SKY-LARK"

THE SKY-LARK'S SONG

HEY, laddie, hark, to the merry, merry lark;
How high he singeth clear:
Oh, a morn in spring is the sweetest thing
That cometh in all the year!
Oh, a morn in spring is the sweetest thing
That cometh in all the year!

Ring, ting! it is the merry spring-time;
How full of heart a body feels!
Sing hey, trolly lolly, oh, to live is to be jolly,
When spring-time cometh with the summer at her heels!

God bless us all, my jolly gentlemen!
We 'll merry be to-day;
For the cuckoo sings till the greenwood rings,
And it is the month of May!
For the cuckoo sings till the greenwood rings,
And it is the month of May!

Ring, ting! it is the merry spring-time,
How full of heart a body feels!
Sing hey, trolly lolly, oh, to live is to be jolly,
When spring-time cometh with the summer at her heels!

THE SONG OF THE HUNT

(OLD WARWICKSHIRE)

THE hunt is up, the hunt is up;
Sing merrily we, the hunt is up!
The wild birds sing,
The dun deer fling,
The forest aisles with music ring!
Tantara, tantara, tantara!

Then ride along, ride along,
Stout and strong!
Farewell to grief and care;
With a rollicking cheer
For the high dun deer
And a life in the open air!
Tantara, the hunt is up, lads;
Tantara, the bugles bray!
Tantara, tantara, tantara,
Hio, hark away!

GOD BLESS YOU, DEAR, TO-DAY!

IF there be graveyards in the heart
From which no roses spring,
A place of wrecks and old gray tombs
From which no birds take wing,
Where linger buried hopes and dreams
Like ghosts among the graves,
Why, buried hopes are dismal things,
And lonely ghosts are knaves!

If there come dreary winter days,
When summer roses fall
And lie, forgot, in withered drifts
Along the garden wall;
If all the wreaths a lover weaves
Turn thorns upon the brow, —
Then out upon the silly fool
Who makes not merry now!

For if we cannot keep the past,
Why care for what 's to come?
The instant's prick is all that stings,
And then the place is numb.
If Life 's a lie and Love 's a cheat,
As I have heard men say,
Then here 's a health to fond deceit —
God bless you, dear, to-day!

HER ANSWER

TO-DAY, dear heart, but just to-day,
The sunshine over all,
The roses crimsoning the air
Along the garden wall!
Then let the dream and dreamer die;
Whate'er shall be, shall be —
To-day will still be thine and mine
To all eternity.

And oh, there is no glory, dear,
When all the world is done,
There is no splendor lasteth out
The sinking of the sun;
There is no thing that lasts, not one,
When we have turned to clay,
But this: *you loved me* — all the rest
Fades with the world away.

So little while, so little while
This world doth last for us,
There is no way to keep it, dear,
But just to spend it thus.
There is no hand may stop the sand
From flowing fast away
But his who turns the whole glass down
And dreams 't is all to-day.

Edward Lucas White

THE LAST BOWSTRINGS

THEY had brought in such sheafs of hair,
And flung them all about us there
In the loud noonday's heat and glare:
Gold tresses, far too fine to wind,
And brown, with copper curls entwined,
And black coils, black as all my mind.

In the low, stifling armory,
Whence we could hear, but might not flee,
The roar of that engirdling sea,
Whose waves were helmet-crests of foes,
Winding the cords we sat, in rows,
Beside a mound of stringless bows.

Since the first hill-scouts panted in,
Before siege-fires and battle din
Filled night and day, and filled within
Our hearts and brains with flame and sound,
We had sat, huddled on the ground,
Our tears hot on the cords we wound.

We knew, when the first tidings came,
That not the gods from death or shame
Could save us, fighting clothed in flame.
The mid-sea's marshalled waves are few
Beside the warriors, girt with blue,
The gorged hill-passes then let through.

Their spears shook like ripe, standing corn,
Gold lakes that on the plains are born,
And nod to greet the golden morn;
After these years the earth yet reels,
And after snows and showers feels
The deluge of their chariot wheels.

Against our walls their flood was dammed,
Within which, till each porch was jammed,
Farm-folk and fisher-folk were crammed;
Heaped stones inside the gates were piled,
While all above us, calm and mild,
In bitter scorn the heavens smiled.

Our men dwelt on the walls and towers,
From over which, for endless hours,
The hissing arrows flew in showers;
The sling-stones, too, came crashing down,
As though the gods of far renown
Hurled thunderbolts into the town.

Where the hung temples showed their
lights,
Some women prayed upon the heights;
Some stole about throughout the nights, —
Who bore the warriors food by day, —
Gleaning the arrows as they lay
That they might hurtle back to slay.

And where the rooms were heaped with
stores,
Because the stringless bows were scores,
We were shut in with guarded doors;
All day at hurried toil we kept,
And when the darkness on us crept
We lay, each in her place, and slept.

Quick as we worked, we could not make
Strings fast as bowmen came to take
Fresh bows; and oh, the grinding ache
Of hearts and fingers: maid and slave
And princess, we toiled on to save
Home that already was our grave.

Six days we wound the cords with speed;
Naught else from us had any heed,
For bitter was our rage and need.
At last, upon the seventh day,
Into the fury of the fray
They called our very guard away.

No food was brought us. Faint with thirst,
What wonder was it if, at first,
Some wailed that the town gates were
burst?
If, later, to the last embraces
Of child or mother, from their places
Some slunk away with ashen faces?

I cursed them through the door unbarred;
I vowed I would not move a yard,
Lest some one man of ours, pressed hard,
Might be left weaponless alone.
Until I died or turned to stone,
I would wind, were the hair mine own.

A sudden shiver shook my frame,
I looked up with my face aflame;
But oh, no tongue has any name
For the despair I saw enthroned
In my love's eyes, all purple-zoned!
I smiled to greet him, and I groaned.

He buckled on a fresh cuirass, —
His own was but a tattered mass
Of gory thongs. I saw him pass
Out of the portal; with good-byes
And blessings filled, and yearning sighs,
For the last time I saw his eyes.

Each moment, all my blood areel,
I felt the thrust of deadly steel
I knew his body soon must feel.
My heart was choked with prayerful speech;
The high, deaf gods were out of reach,
My eyes dry as a noonday beach.

More cowards left. Few now remained.
Still at our task we strove and strained

With bleeding hands, and iron-brained;
And still my fingers all were fleet,
Though in my temples burned and beat
The murmur of the stunning heat.

There rushed in for fresh arms just then
Some of our allies, — small, dark men;
It slowly dawned upon my ken
That one, who by a spear-heap kneeled,
Fierce-browed and grimy from the field,
Carried my brother's painted shield.

My heart beat in long, tearing throbs;
Sharp torch-lights stormed my eyes in mobs,
And my breath came in rasping sobs;
The tears from both my cheeks I wrung;
So wet my hands were that they clung
Slipping along the cord I strung.

Mutely we toiled until my maid,
Her lips tense as the strands she laid,
Grew wan; her deft, quick fingers strayed:
Then she pitched forward with a groan,
And lay, white, motionless, and prone.
I wound on hastily, alone.

Harsh and unevenly outside
Shields clanged. Men called, and cursed,
and cried;
And when again the latch was tried
My knife lay somewhere on the floor.
Alas ! I found it not before
Three armored foemen burst the door.

GENIUS

He cried aloud to God: "The men below
Are happy, for I see them come and go,
Parents and mates and friends, paired,
clothed with love;
They heed not, see not, need not me above, —
I am alone here. Grant me love and peace,
Or, if not them, grant me at least release."

God answered him: "I set you here on high
Upon my beacon-tower, you know not why.
Your soul-torch by the cruel gale is blown,
As desperate as your aching heart is lone.
You may not guess but that it shines in
vain,
Yet, till it is burned out, you must remain."

Martha Gilbert Dickinson

REALITY

These are my scales to weigh reality, —
A dream, a chord, a longing, love of Thee.
Real as the violets of April days,
Or those soft-hid in unfrequented ways;
Real as the noiseless tune to which we tread
The measure we by life's old song are led;
Real as man's wonder what his soul may be, —
A guest for time or for eternity.
Real as the ocean, seen, alas ! no more,
Whose tide still beats along my heart's in-
shore.
These are my scales to weigh reality, —
A chord, a dream, a longing, love of Thee !

A PRIEST'S PRAYER

Over the dim confessional cried
Father Amatus, — cloistered young, —
Dropping his rosary by his side,
Careless where his crucifix swung:

"I have been priest since — an endless when !
Sat by the living, consoled the dead,
Fasted and prayed for women and men,
Fed the poor with my daily bread.

"The wind blows cold, — how the snow-
flakes creep !
I will sin one sin, ere past recall,
Lest life should faint in this pallid sleep:
Kiss me, Jessica ! Once for all."

FORGIVENESS LANE

Forgiveness Lane is old as youth,
You cannot miss your way;
'T is hedged with flowering thorn forsooth
Where white doves fearless stray.

You must walk gently with your Love,
Frail blossoms dread your feet —
And bloomy branches close above
Make heaven near and sweet.

Some lovers fear the stile of pride
And turn away in pain —
But more have kissed where white doves hide
And blessed Forgiveness Lane !

SEPARATION

THERE be many kinds of parting — yes, I know
Some with fond, grieving eyes that overflow,
Some with brave hands that strengthen as they go;
Ah yes, I know — I know.

But there be partings harder still to tell,
That fall in silence, like an evil spell,
Without one wistful message of farewell;
Ah yes, too hard to tell.

There is no claiming of one sacred kiss, —
One token for the days when life shall miss
A spirit from the world of vanished bliss;
Ah no — not even this.

There is no rising ere the birds have sung
Their skyward songs, to journey with the sun, —
Nor folded hands to show that life is done;
Ah no, for life is young.

There are no seas, no mountains rising wide,
No centuries of absence to divide, —
Just soul-space, standing daily side by side;
Ah, wiser to have died.

Hands still clasp hands, eyes still reflect their own; —
Yet had one over universes flown,
So far each heart hath from the other grown,
Alone were less alone.

UNANSWERED

I WANTED you when skies were red,
And now the sky is gray;
I thought of you when shadows fled —
Now falls the end of day.

I called you when the hills were flame,
And now the hills are bare;
I sought you when the snowflakes came,
And now the swallows pair!

HER MUSIC

IT trembled off the keys, — a parting kiss
So sweet, — the angel slept upon his sword
As through the gate of Paradise we swept, —
Partakers of creation's primal bliss!
— The air was heavy with the breath
Of violets and love till death. —
Forgetful of eternal banishment —
Deep down the dusk of passion-haunted ways,
Lost in the dreaming alchemies of tone, —
Drenched in the dew no other wings frequent,
— Our thirsting hearts drank in the breath
Of violets and love in death. —
There was no world, no flesh, no boundary line, —
Spirit to spirit, — chord and dissonance,
Beyond the jealousy of space or time
Her life in one low cry broke over mine!
— The waking angel drew a shuddering breath
Of violets and love and death.

HEAVEN

ONLY to find Forever, blest
By thine encircling arm;
Only to lie beyond unrest
In passion's dreamy calm!

Only to meet and never part,
To sleep and never wake, —
Heart unto heart and soul to soul,
Dead for each other's sake.

Walter Malone

OCTOBER IN TENNESSEE

FAR, far away, beyond a hazy height,
The turquoise skies are hung in dreamy sleep;
Below, the fields of cotton, fleecy-white,
Are spreading like a mighty flock of sheep.

Now, like Aladdin of the days of old,
October robes the weeds in purple gowns;

He sprinkles all the sterile fields with gold,
And all the rustic trees wear royal crowns.

The straggling fences all are interlaced
With pink and purple morning-glory blooms;
The starry asters glorify the waste,
While grasses stand on guard with pikes and plumes.

Yet still amid the splendor of decay
The chill winds call for blossoms that are dead,
The cricket chirps for sunshine passed away, —
The lovely summer songsters that have fled.

And lonesome in a haunt of withered vines,
Amid the flutter of her withered leaves,
Pale Summer for her perished kingdom pines,
And all the glories of her golden sheaves.

In vain October wooes her to remain
Within the palace of his scarlet bowers, —
Entreats her to forget her heart-break pain,
And weep no more above her faded flowers.

At last November, like a conqueror, comes
To storm the golden city of his foe;
We hear his rude winds like the roll of drums,
Bringing their desolation and their woe.

The sunset, like a vast vermilion flood,
Splashes its giant glowing waves on high,
The forest flames with blazes red as blood, —
A conflagration sweeping to the sky.

Then all the treasures of that brilliant state
Are gathered in a mighty funeral pyre;
October, like a King resigned to fate,
Dies in his forests with their sunset fire.

HE WHO HATH LOVED

He who hath loved hath borne a vassal's chain,
And worn the royal purple of a king;
Hath shrunk beneath the icy Winter's sting,
Then revelled in the golden Summer's reign;
He hath within the dust and ashes lain,
Then soared o'er mountains on an eagle's wing;
A hut hath slept in, worn with wandering,
And hath been lord of castle-towers in Spain.
He who hath loved hath starved in beggar's cell,
Then in Aladdin's jewelled chariot driven;
He hath with passion roamed a demon fell,
And had an angel's raiment to him given;
His restless soul hath burned with flames of hell,
And winged through ever-blooming fields of heaven.

John Jerome Rooney

JOINED THE BLUES

Says Stonewall Jackson to "Little Phil:"
"Phil, have you heard the news?
Why, our 'Joe' Wheeler — 'Fighting Joe' — has gone and joined the blues.

"Ay, no mistake — I saw him come — I heard the oath he took —
And you 'll find it duly entered up in yon great Record Book.

"Yes, 'Phil,' it is a change since then (we give the Lord due thanks)
When 'Joe' came swooping like a hawk upon your Sherman's flanks!

"Why, 'Phil,' you knew the trick yourself — but 'Joe' had all the points —
And we 've yet to hear his horses died of stiff or rusty joints!

"But what of that? — the deed I saw to-day in yonder town

Leads all we did and all 'Joe' did in troopings up and down;

"For, 'Phil,' that oath shall be the heal of many a bleeding wound,
And many a Southland song shall yet to that same oath be tuned!

"The oath 'Joe' swore has done the work of thrice a score of years —
Ay, more than oath — he swore away mistrust and hate and tears!"

"Yes, yes," says "Phil," "he was, indeed, a right good worthy foe,
And well he knew, in those fierce days, to give us blow for blow.

"When 'Joe' came round to pay a call — the commissaries said —
Full many a swearing, grumbling 'Yank' went supperless to bed:

"He seemed to have a pesky knack — so Sherman used to say —
Of calling, when he should by rights be ninety miles away!

"Come, Stonewall, put your hand in mine, — 'Joe''s sworn old Samuel's oath —
We're never North or South again — he kissed the Book for both!"

THE HOMING

ADMIRAL, Admiral, sailing home —
Sailing home through the far, dim seas,
Know you the sound that over the foam
Rises and sinks in the sunset breeze?

Know you the thrill and know you the start
That pulses and runs through the wind and the spray,
Pulses and runs from a nation's heart
To meet you and greet you over the way?

Not for the might of your guns alone,
Thundering doom by the Eastern gate;
Not for the bugle of victory blown, —
Not for these do we watch and wait!

The glory is sweet — ay, sweet to the soul
Of a people proud in the pride of youth,
But sweeter to know, as the seasons roll,
Our men, as of old, are men in truth!

THE MEN BEHIND THE GUNS

A CHEER and salute for the Admiral, and here's to the Captain bold,
And never forget the Commodore's debt when the deeds of might are told!
They stand to the deck through the battle's wreck when the great shells roar and screech —
And never they fear when the foe is near to practice what they preach:
But off with your hat and three times three for Columbia's true-blue sons,
The men below who batter the foe — the men behind the guns!

Oh, light and merry of heart are they when they swing into port once more,
When, with more than enough of the "green-backed stuff," they start for their leave-o'-shore;
And you'd think, perhaps, that the blue-bloused chaps who loll along the street
Are a tender bit, with salt on it, for some fierce "mustache" to eat —
Some warrior bold, with straps of gold, who dazzles and fairly stuns
The modest worth of the sailor boys — the lads who serve the guns.

But say not a word till the shot is heard that tells the fight is on,
Till the long, deep roar grows more and more from the ships of "Yank" and "Don,"
Till over the deep the tempests sweep of fire and bursting shell,
And the very air is a mad Despair in the throes of a living hell;
Then down, deep down, in the mighty ship, unseen by the midday suns,
You'll find the chaps who are giving the raps — the men behind the guns!

Oh, well they know how the cyclones blow that they loose from their cloud of death,
And they know is heard the thunder-word their fierce ten-incher saith!
The steel decks rock with the lightning shock, and shake with the great recoil,
And the sea grows red with the blood of the dead and reaches for his spoil —
But not till the foe has gone below or turns his prow and runs,
Shall the voice of peace bring sweet release to the men behind the guns!

WHERE HELEN COMES

WHERE Helen comes, as falls the dew,
Where Helen comes Peace cometh too!
From out the golden, western lands,
White lilies blooming in her hands,
A light of beauty in her face,
She passeth on with nameless grace.
Before her fly the shades of life —
The darkling, wheeling bats of strife —
They flee her very garments' stir,
And greater fear the soul of her;
For hath she not the magic touch —
The sesame of loving much?
Where'er her morning footsteps pass
The daisies sing unto the grass;
Soft whispers full of praises sweet
Her evening presence rise to greet,
And if she go through deserts bare
The angels of the heart are there:
They find no spot to weave their spells
So fair as that where Helen dwells!
Where Helen comes, as falls the dew,
Where Helen comes Peace cometh too!

THE RÁHAT

UPON Nirwána's brink the ráhat stood;
Beneath him rolled the Ocean of the All:
Responsive flowed the current of his blood
To meet the tidal call —

Save one red drop within his mortal veins
Wherein the image of Zuleika shone;
He gazed a moment on Nirwána's gains —
And Earthward he was gone!

A BEAM OF LIGHT

A BEAM of light, from the infinite depths of the midnight sky,
Painted with infinite love a star in a convict's eye;
When, lo! the ghosts of his sins were afraid and fled with a curse,
And the soul of the man walked free in the fields of the universe!

Anne Reeve Aldrich

A SONG ABOUT SINGING

O NIGHTINGALE, the poet's bird,
A kinsman dear thou art,
Who never sings so well as when
The rose-thorns bruise his heart.

But since thy agony can make
A listening world so blest,
Be sure it cares but little for
Thy wounded, bleeding breast!

IN NOVEMBER

BROWN earth-line meets gray heaven,
And all the land looks sad;
But Love 's the little leaven
That works the whole world glad.
Sigh, bitter wind; lower, frore clouds of gray:
My Love and I are living now in May!

MUSIC OF HUNGARY

MY body answers you, my blood
Leaps at your maddening, piercing call.
The fierce notes startle, and the veil
Of this dull present seems to fall.
My soul responds to that long cry;
It wants its country, Hungary!

Not mine by birth. Yet have I not
Some strain of that old Magyar race?
Else why the secret stir of sense

At sight of swarthy Tzigane face,
That warns me: "Lo, thy kinsmen nigh."
All 's dear that tastes of Hungary.

Once more, O let me hear once more
The passion and barbaric rage!
Let me forget my exile here
In this mild land, in this mild age;
Once more that unrestrained wild cry
That takes me to my Hungary!

They listen with approving smile,
But I, O God, I want my home!
I want the Tzigane tongue, the dance,
The nights in tents, the days to roam.
O music, O fierce life and free,
God made my soul for Hungary!

A CROWNED POET

In thy coach of state
Pass, O King, along:
He no envy feels
To whom God giveth song.

Starving, still I smile,
Laugh at want and wrong:
He is fed and crowned
To whom God giveth song.

Better than all pomps
That to rank belong, —
One such dream as his
To whom God giveth song.

Let us greet, O King,
As we pass along:
He, too, is a king
To whom God giveth song.

LOVE'S CHANGE

I went to dig a grave for Love,
But the earth was so stiff and cold
That, though I strove through the bitter night,
I could not break the mould.

And I said: "Must he lie in my house in state,
And stay in his wonted place?
Must I have him with me another day,
With that awful change in his face?"

FRATERNITY

I ask not how thy suffering came,
Or if by sin, or if by shame,
Or if by Fate's capricious rulings:
To my large pity all 's the same.

Come close and lean against a heart
Eaten by pain and stung by smart;
It is enough if thou hast suffered, —
Brother or sister then thou art.

We will not speak of what we know,
Rehearse the pang, nor count the throe,
Nor ask what agony admitted
Thee to the Brotherhood of Woe.

But in our anguish-darkened land
Let us draw close, and clasp the hand;
Our whispered password holds assuagement, —
The solemn "Yea, I understand!"

RECOLLECTION

How can it be that I forget
The way he phrased my doom,
When I recall the arabesques
That carpeted the room?

How can it be that I forget
His look and mien that hour,
When I recall I wore a rose,
And still can smell the flower?

How can it be that I forget
Those words that were the last,
When I recall the tune a man
Was whistling as he passed?

These things are what we keep from life's
Supremest joy or pain;
For Memory locks her chaff in bins
And throws away the grain.

APRIL — AND DYING

Green blood fresh pulsing through the trees,
Black buds, that sun and shower distend;
All other things begin anew,
But I must end.

Warm sunlight on faint-colored sward,
  Warm fragrance in the breezes' breath;
For other things are heat and life,
  For me is death.

A LITTLE PARABLE

I MADE the cross myself whose weight
  Was later laid on me.
This thought is torture as I toil
  Up life's steep Calvary.

To think mine own hands drove the nails!
  I sang a merry song,
And chose the heaviest wood I had
  To build it firm and strong.

If I had guessed — if I had dreamed
  Its weight was meant for me,
I should have made a lighter cross
  To bear up Calvary!

DEATH AT DAYBREAK

I SHALL go out when the light comes in —
  There lie my cast-off form and face;
I shall pass Dawn on her way to earth,
  As I seek for a path through space.

I shall go out when the light comes in;
  Would I might take one ray with me!
It is blackest night between the worlds,
  And how is a soul to see?

THE ETERNAL JUSTICE

THANK God that God shall judge my soul, not man!
  I marvel when they say,
  "Think of that awful Day
No pitying fellow-sinner's eyes shall scan
  With tolerance thy soul,
  But His who knows the whole,
The God whom all men own is wholly just."
  Hold thou that last word dear,
  And live untouched by fear.
He knows with what strange fires He mixed this dust.
  The heritage of race,
  The circumstance and place
Which make us what we are — were from His hand,
  That left us, faint of voice,
  Small margin for a choice.
He gave, I took: shall I not fearless stand?
  Hereditary bent
  That hedges in intent
He knows, be sure, the God who shaped thy brain.
  He loves the souls He made;
  He knows His own hand laid
On each the mark of some ancestral stain.
  Not souls severely white,
  But groping for more light,
Are what Eternal Justice here demands.
  Fear not: He made thee dust;
  Cling to that sweet word — "Just;"
All 's well with thee if thou art in just hands.

Herbert Bates

PRAIRIE

ACROSS the sombre prairie sea
The dark swells billow heavily.
Are the looming ridges near or far
That heave to the smooth horizon-bar?

The russet reach of grassy roll
Sickens the heart and numbs the soul;
The thin wind gives no air for breath;
The stillness is the pause of death.

This width was never shaped to be
The home of man's mortality,
A breathless vacuum of peace,
Where life's spent ripples spread and cease.

No end, no source, its spaces know;
Wide as the sea's perpetual flow
Is its dead stand — dull wall on wall
Of sullen waves unspiritual.

God give me but in dream to come
Back to the pine-clad hills of home,
Back to the old eternity
Of placid, all-consoling sea.

THE HEAVENS ARE OUR RIDDLE

THE heavens are our riddle; and the sea,
Forested earth, the grassy rustling plain,
Snows, rains, and thunders. Yea, and even we
Before ourselves stand ominous. In vain!
The stars still march their way, the sea still rolls,
The forests wave, the plain drinks in the sun,
And we stand silent, naked, — with tremulous souls, —
Before our unsolved selves. We pray to one
Whose hand should help us. But we hear no voice;
Skies clear and darken; the days pale and pass,
Nor any bids us weep or bids rejoice.
Only the wind sobs in the shrivelling grass, —
Only the wind, — and we with upward eyes
Expectant of the silence of the skies.

John Russell Hayes

FROM "THE OLD-FASHIONED GARDEN"

FAIR is each budding thing the garden shows,
From spring's frail crocus to the latest bloom
Of fading autumn. Every wind that blows
Across that glowing tract sips rare perfume
From all the tangled blossoms tossing there; —
Soft winds, they fain would linger long, nor any farther fare.

The morning-glories ripple o'er the hedge
And fleck its greenness with their tinted foam;
Sweet wilding things, up to the garden's edge
They love to wander from their meadow home,
To take what little pleasure here they may
Ere all their silken trumpets close before the warm midday.

The larkspur lifts on high its azure spires,
And up the arbor's lattices are rolled
The quaint nasturtium's many-colored fires;
The tall carnation's breast of faded gold
Is striped with many a faintly-flushing streak,
Pale as the tender tints that blush upon a baby's cheek.

The old sweet-rocket sheds its fine perfumes;
With golden stars the coreopsis flames;
And here are scores of sweet old-fashioned blooms
Dear for the very fragrance of their names, —
Poppies and gillyflowers and four-o'clocks,
Cowslips and candytuft and heliotrope and hollyhocks,

Harebells and peonies and dragon-head,
Petunias, scarlet sage, and bergamot,
Verbenas, ragged-robins, soft gold-thread,
The bright primrose and pale forget-me-not,
Wall-flowers and crocuses and columbines,
Narcissus, asters, hyacinths, and honeysuckle vines,

Foxgloves and marigolds and mignonette,
Dahlias and lavender and damask rose.
O dear old flowers, ye are blooming yet, —
Each year afresh your lovely radiance glows:
But where are they who saw your beauty's dawn?
Ah, with the flowers of other years they long ago have gone!

They long have gone, but ye are still as fair
As when the brides of eighty years ago
Plucked your soft roses for their waving hair,
And blossoms o'er their bridal-veils to strow.

Alas, your myrtle on a later day
Marked those low mounds where 'neath the willows' shade at last they lay!

Beside the walk the drowsy poppies sway,
More deep of hue than is the reddest rose,
And dreamy-warm as summer's midmost day:
Proud, languorous queens of slumberous repose —
Within their little chalices they keep
The mystic witchery that brings mild, purple-lidded sleep.

Drowse on, soft flowers of quiet afternoons, —
The breezes sleep beneath your lulling spell;
In dreamy silence all the garden swoons,
Save where the lily's aromatic bell
Is murmurous with one low-humming bee,
As oozy honey-drops are pilfered by that filcher wee.

. . . .

And now is gone the dreamy afternoon, —
The sun has sunk below yon western height;
The pallid silver of the harvest-moon
Floods all the garden with its soft, weird light.
The flowers long since have told their dewy beads,
And naught is heard except the frogs' small choir in distant meads.

Dora Read Goodale

THE FLIGHT OF THE HEART

THE heart soars up like a bird
From a nest of care;
Up, up to a larger sky,
To a softer air.
No eye can measure its flight
And no hand can tame;
It mounts in beauty and light,
In music and flame.
Of all the changes of Time
There is none like this;
The heart soars up like a bird
At the stroke of bliss.

The heart soars up like a bird,
But its wings soon tire;
Enough of rapture and song,
The cloud and the fire!
Its look, the look of a king —
Of a slave, its birth,
The poor, tired, impotent thing
Sinks back to the earth.
And the mother spreads her lap,
And she lulls its pain:
"Oh, thou who sighed for the sun,
Art thou mine again?"

THE SOUL OF MAN

SAY, in a hut of mean estate
A light just glimmers and then is gone,
Nature is seen to hesitate, —
Put forth and then retract her pawn;

Say, in the alembic of an eye
Haughty is mixed with poor and low;
Say, Truth herself is not so high
But Error laughs to see her so;

Say, all that strength failed in its trust;
Say, all that wit crept but a span;
Say, 't is a drop spilled in the dust, —
And then say *brother* — then say *man!*

THE JUDGMENT

THOU hast done evil
And given place to the devil;
Yet so cunningly thou concealest
The thing which thou feelest,
That no eye espieth it,
Satan himself denieth it.
Go where it chooseth thee,
There is none that accuseth thee;
Neither foe nor lover
Will the wrong uncover;
The world's breath raiseth thee,
And thy own past praiseth thee.

Yet know thou this:
At quick of thy being
Is an eye all-seeing,

The snake's wit evadeth not,
The charmed lip persuadeth not;
So thoroughly it despiseth
The thing thy hand prizeth,
Though the sun were thy clothing,
It should count thee for nothing.
Thine own eye divineth thee,
Thine own soul arraigneth thee;
God himself cannot shrive thee
Till that judge forgive thee.

Joseph Russell Taylor

THE FLUTE

PUFFED up with luring to her knees
The rabbits from the blackberries,
Quaint little satyrs, and shy and mute,
That limped reluctant to the flute,
She needs must seek the forest's womb
And pipe up tigers from green gloom.

Grouped round the dreaming oaten quill
Those sumptuous savages were still,
Rich spectral beasts that feared to stir,
And haughty and wistful gazed on her,
And swayed their sleepy masks in time
And growled a drowsy under-rhyme.

Tune done, that agile fancy stopped,
The lingering notes in mid-air dropped;
The flute stole from her parted kiss,
Her cheeks for sorcery burned with bliss.
Then grew a deadly muttering there;
And sudden yellow eyes aglare
Blazed furious over wrinkled lips
And teeth on her. Her finger-tips
Trembled a little as they woke
The second tune beneath the oak,
A lilt that charmed and lulled to mute
The uneasy soul within the brute.

And all that warbling ecstasy
Was winged with terror, and daintily
Ceased on the wild and tragic face
And desperate huddle of her grace:
For with the hush began to gride
Their sullen, soulless, evil-eyed,
Intolerable rage, blown hot
Upon her. The third tune was caught
With trouble from unuttered air:
And still as autumn they sat there.

The breathless seventh tune died out
Like withered laughter: all about
The frantic silence ran a race.
She stirred, she moaned, she crawled a space.
There leaped a vast and thunderous roar;
A huge heart-shaking tumult tore
About the oak. Filing away,
They trod the stained flute where it lay.

THE VEERY-THRUSH

BLOW softly, thrush, upon the hush
That makes the least leaf loud,
Blow, wild of heart, remote, apart
From all the vocal crowd,
Apart, remote, a spirit note
That dances meltingly afloat,
Blow faintly, thrush!
And build the green-hid waterfall
I hated for its beauty, and all
The unloved vernal rapture and flush,
The old forgotten lonely time,
Delicate thrush!
Spring's at the prime, the world's in chime,
And my love is listening nearly;
O lightly blow the ancient woe,
Flute of the wood, blow clearly!
Blow, she is here, and the world all dear,
Melting flute of the hush,
Old sorrow estranged, enriched, sea-changed,
Breathe it, veery-thrush!

Arthur Colton

A SONG WITH A DISCORD

THOUGH Winter come with dripping skies,
And laden winds and strong,
Yet I'll read summer in her eyes
Whose voice is summer's song.

Who grieves because the world is old,
Or cares how long it last,

If no gray threads are in our gold,
The shade our marbles cast,

How, creeping near, we may not see?
Time's heirs are Love and I,
And spend our minted days — Ah, me!
For anything they 'll buy.

TO FAUSTINE

SOMETIME, it may be, you and I
In some deserted yard will lie
Where Memory fades away;
Caring no more for Love his dreams,
Busy with new and alien themes,
The saints and sages say.

But let our graves be side by side,
So idlers may at evening tide
Pause there a moment's space:
"Ah, they were lovers who lie here;
Else why these low graves laid so near,
In this forgotten place?"

Philip Henry Savage

MORNING

NOT least, 't is ever my delight
To drink the early morning light;
To take the air upon my tongue
And taste it while the day is young.
So let my solace be the breath
Of morning, when I move to death.

SILKWEED

LIGHTER than dandelion down,
Or feathers from the white moth's wing,
Out of the gates of bramble-town
The silkweed goes a-gypsying.

Too fair to fly in autumn's rout,
All winter in the sheath it lay;
But now, when spring is pushing out,
The zephyr calls, "Away! away!"

Through mullein, bramble, brake, and fern,
Up from their cradle-spring they fly,
Beyond the boundary wall to turn
And voyage through the friendly sky.

Softly, as if instinct with thought,
They float and drift, delay and turn;
And one avoids and one is caught
Between an oak-leaf and a fern.

And one holds by an airy line
The spider drew from tree to tree;
And if the web is light and fine,
'T is not so light and fine as he!

And one goes questing up the wall
As if to find a door; and then,
As if he did not care at all,
Goes over, and adown the glen.

And all in airiest fashion fare
Adventuring, as if, indeed,
'T were not so grave a thing to bear
The burden of a seed!

SOLITUDE

As one advances up the slow ascent
Along the pathway in the woods, the trees
Change aspect, nor alone in this, but change
In stature and in power till Solitude
Seems cut out of the ancient forest. Here
Was Solitude! where man had lived of old,
Loved, serving God, and built himself a home.
Man smooths an acre on the rolling earth,
Turns up the mould and reaps the gifts of God;
Plucks down the apple from the tree, the tree
From empire in the forest, builds a home;
Turns for a bout among his brothers, wins
A sister to his wife and gets an heir;
And then as here in Solitude departs
And leaves small mark behind. The place is rare
In this high epic of the human life.
Where wildness has been wilderness shall be,

But give God time; and life is but a span,
Nine inches, while before it and behind
Stretches the garden of the cosmic gods;
For after London, England shall be wild,
And none can thaw the iceberg at the pole.
In Solitude one sees the winding trace
Of what has been a road, a block of stone
Footworn, that lies along the dim pathway
Before one old foundation; and the rest
Is freaks of grass among the rising growth
Of birch and maple that another year
Shall see almost a forest.

INFINITY

I DARE not think that thou art by, to stand
And face omnipotence so near at hand!
When I consider thee, how must I shrink;
How must I say, I do not understand,
I dare not think!

I cannot stand before the thought of thee,
Infinite Fulness of Eternity!
So close that all the outlines of the land
Are lost, — in the inflowing of thy sea
I cannot stand.

I think of thee, and as the crystal bowl
Is broken, and the waters of the soul
Go down to death within the crystal sea,
I faint and fail when (thou, the perfect whole)
I think of thee.

Barrett Eastman

RICHARD SOMERS

HIS body lies upon the shore,
Afar from his beloved land,
And over him shine tropic suns;
No more he thrills at sound of guns,
No longer, cutlass in his hand,
Cries, "Follow me!" and goes before.

Above him droop the languid trees,
Athirst and fainting with the noon;
Around him drowsy lizards crawl.
No more he hears the boatswain's call,
Nor sees the waters rock the moon,
Nor smells the keen and salty breeze.

Vain roars old Ocean in his ear,
Calling to him from mighty deeps,
Yearning for him who loved the main.
Never shall he make sail again;
Under the restless sands he sleeps,
He is at rest, he cannot hear.

But when the Trumpet sounds alarms
On that great day when all shall rise,
And earth and sea give up their dead,
Then out from his unquiet bed
Where now heroic SOMERS lies
His soul will leap to Ocean's arms!

JOY ENOUGH

INTO the caverns of the sea
Shall all at last descend,
Who now press forward gallantly
Unrecking of the end.

And no man knoweth what is there,
Nor when his time shall come
To yield his soul and take his share
With all those gone and dumb.

It may be we shall find our kin
Waiting to grasp our hands,
And lead us glorified within,
Over the shining sands;

It may be we with them shall lie,
While heaven and earth abide,
Swaying silent with sightless eye
There in the sluggish tide.

It matters nothing if to-day,
Beneath the splendid sun,
We hold to the appointed way,
Doing what must be done.

Reward? What would you? Have not we
The waves beneath us bent?
The winds about us blowing free?
Above — the firmament?

William Vaughn Moody

FROM "AN ODE IN TIME OF HESITATION"

1900

ROBERT GOULD SHAW

THE wars we wage
Are noble, and our battles still are won
By justice for us, ere we lift the gage.
We have not sold our loftiest heritage.
The proud republic hath not stooped to cheat
And scramble in the market place of war;
Her forehead weareth yet its solemn star.
Here is her witness: this, her perfect son,
This delicate and proud New England soul
Who leads despisëd men, with just-unshackled feet,
Up the large ways where death and glory meet,
To show all peoples that our shame is done,
That once more we are clean and spirit-whole.

Crouched in the sea fog on the moaning sand
All night he lay, speaking some simple word
From hour to hour to the slow minds that heard,
Holding each poor life gently in his hand
And breathing on the base rejected clay
Till each dark face shone mystical and grand
Against the breaking day;
And lo, the shard the potter cast away
Was grown a fiery chalice crystal-fine,
Fulfilled of the divine
Great wine of battle wrath by God's ring-finger stirred.
Then upward, where the shadowy bastion loomed
Huge on the mountain in the wet sea light,
Whence now, and now, infernal flowerage bloomed,
Bloomed, burst, and scattered down its deadly seed, —
They swept, and died like freemen on the height,
Like freemen, and like men of noble breed;
And when the battle fell away at night
By hasty and contemptuous hands were thrust
Obscurely in a common grave with him
The fair-haired keeper of their love and trust.
Now limb doth mingle with dissolvëd limb
In nature's busy old democracy
To flush the mountain laurel when she blows
Sweet by the southern sea,
And heart with crumbled heart climbs in the rose: —
The untaught hearts with the high heart that knew
This mountain fortress for no earthly hold
Of temporal quarrel, but the bastion old
Of spiritual wrong,
Built by an unjust nation sheer and strong,
Expugnable but by a nation's rue
And bowing down before that equal shrine
By all men held divine,
Whereof his band and he were the most holy sign.

"NO HINT OF STAIN"

We are our fathers' sons: let those who lead us know!
'T was only yesterday sick Cuba's cry
Came up the tropic wind, "Now help us, for we die!"
Then Alabama heard,
And rising, pale, to Maine and Idaho
Shouted a burning word;
Proud state with proud impassioned state conferred,
And at the lifting of a hand sprang forth,
East, west, and south, and north,
Beautiful armies. Oh, by the sweet blood and young
Shed on the awful hill slope at San Juan,
By the unforgotten names of eager boys
Who might have tasted girls' love and been stung
With the old mystic joys
And starry griefs, now the spring nights come on,
But that the heart of youth is generous, —
We charge you, ye who lead us,
Breathe on their chivalry no hint of stain!
Turn not their new-world victories to gain!
One least leaf plucked for chaffer from the bays
Of their dear praise,
One jot of their pure conquest put to hire,
The implacable republic will require;

With clamor, in the glare and gaze of
noon,
Or subtly, coming as a thief at night,
But surely, very surely, slow or soon
That insult deep we deeply will requite.
Tempt not our weakness, our cupidity!
For save we let the island men go free,
Those baffled and dislaureled ghosts
Will curse us from the lamentable coasts
Where walk the frustrate dead.
The cup of trembling shall be drainëd quite,
Eaten the sour bread of astonishment,
With ashes of the hearth shall be made
white
Our hair, and wailing shall be in the tent:
Then on your guiltier head
Shall our intolerable self-disdain
Wreak suddenly its anger and its pain;
For manifest in that disastrous light
We shall discern the right
And do it, tardily. — O ye who lead,
Take heed!
Blindness we may forgive, but baseness we
will smite.

Frederic Lawrence Knowles

NATURE: THE ARTIST

SUCH hints as untaught Nature yields! —
The calm disorder of the sea,
The straggling splendor of the fields,
The wind's gay incivility.

O workman with your conscious plan,
Compass and square are little worth;
Copy (nay, only poets can)
The artless masonry of earth.

Go watch the windy spring's carouse,
And mark the winter wonders grow, —
The graceful gracelessness of boughs,
The careless carpentry of snow!

A PASTURE

ROUGH pasture where the blackberries
grow! —
It bears upon its churlish face
No sign of beauty, art, or grace;
Not here the silvery coverts glow
That April and the angler know.

There sleeps no brooklet in this wild,
Smooth-resting on its mosses sleek,
Like loving lips upon a cheek
Soft as the face of maid or child, —
Just boulders, helter-skelter piled.

Ungenerous nature but endows
These acres with the stumps and stocks
Which should be trees, with rude, gray
rocks;
Over these humps and hollows browse,
Daily, the awkward, shambling cows.

Here on the right a straggling wall
Of crazy, granite stones, and there
A rotten pine-trunk, brown and bare,
A mass of huge brakes, rank and tall, —
The burning blue sky over all.

And yet these blackberries shy and chaste!
The noisy markets know no such, —
So ripe they tumble when you touch;
Long, taper — rarer wines they waste
Than ever town-bred topers taste.

And tell me! have you looked o'erhead,
From lawns where lazy hammocks swing,
And seen such orioles on the wing?
Such flames of song that flashed and fled?
Well, maybe — I'm not city-bred.

Edwin Arlington Robinson

LUKE HAVERGAL

Go to the western gate, Luke Havergal, —
There where the vines cling crimson on the
wall, —
And in the twilight wait for what will come.
The wind will moan, the leaves will whisper
some, —
Whisper of her, and strike you as they fall;
But go, and if you trust her she will call.

Go to the western gate, Luke Havergal —
Luke Havergal.

No, there is not a dawn in eastern skies
To rift the fiery night that 's in your eyes;
But there, where western glooms are gathering,
The dark will end the dark, if anything:
God slays Himself with every leaf that flies,
And hell is more than half of paradise.
No, there is not a dawn in eastern skies —
In eastern skies.

Out of a grave I come to tell you this, —
Out of a grave I come to quench the kiss
That flames upon your forehead with a glow
That blinds you to the way that you must go.
Yes, there is yet one way to where she is, —
Bitter, but one that faith can never miss.
Out of a grave I come to tell you this —
To tell you this.

There is the western gate, Luke Havergal,
There are the crimson leaves upon the wall.
Go, — for the winds are tearing them away, —
Nor think to riddle the dead words they say,
Nor any more to feel them as they fall;
But go! and if you trust her she will call.
There is the western gate, Luke Havergal —
Luke Havergal.

BALLADE OF DEAD FRIENDS

As we the withered ferns
By the roadway lying,
Time, the jester, spurns
All our prayers and prying —
All our tears and sighing,
Sorrow, change, and woe —
All our where-and-whying
For friends that come and go.

Life awakes and burns,
Age and death defying,
Till at last it learns
All but Love is dying;
Love 's the trade we 're plying,
God has willed it so;
Shrouds are what we 're buying
For friends that come and go.

Man forever yearns
For the thing that 's flying.
Everywhere he turns,
Men to dust are drying, —
Dust that wanders, eying
(With eyes that hardly glow)
New faces, dimly spying
For friends that come and go.

ENVOY

And thus we all are nighing
The truth we fear to know:
Death will end our crying
For friends that come and go.

THE CLERKS

I DID not think that I should find them there
When I came back again; but there they stood,
As in the days they dreamed of when young blood
Was in their cheeks and women called them fair.
Be sure, they met me with an ancient air, —
And, yes, there was a shop-worn brotherhood
About them; but the men were just as good,
And just as human as they ever were.
And you that ache so much to be sublime,
And you that feed yourselves with your descent,
What comes of all your visions and your fears?
Poets and kings are but the clerks of Time,
Tiering the same dull webs of discontent,
Clipping the same sad alnage of the years.

THE PITY OF THE LEAVES

VENGEFUL across the cold November moors,
Loud with ancestral shame there came the bleak,
Sad wind that shrieked, and answered with a shriek,
Reverberant through lonely corridors.
The old man heard it; and he heard, perforce,
Words out of lips that were no more to speak —
Words of the past that shook the old man's cheek

Like dead, remembered footsteps on old floors.
And then there were the leaves that plagued him so!
The brown, thin leaves that on the stones outside
Skipped with a freezing whisper. Now and then
They stopped, and stayed there — just to let him know
How dead they were; but if the old man cried,
They fluttered off like withered souls of men.

THE HOUSE ON THE HILL

THEY are all gone away,
The House is shut and still,
There is nothing more to say.

Through broken walls and gray
The winds blow bleak and shrill:
They are all gone away.

Nor is there one to-day
To speak them good or ill:
There is nothing more to say.

Why is it then we stray
Around that sunken sill?
They are all gone away,

And our poor fancy-play
For them is wasted skill:
There is nothing more to say.

There is ruin and decay
In the House on the Hill:
They are all gone away,
There is nothing more to say.

Caroline Duer

AN INTERNATIONAL EPISODE

(MARCH 15, 1889)

WE were ordered to Samoa from the coast of Panama,
And for two long months we sailed the unequal sea,
Till we made the horseshoe harbor with its curving coral bar,
Smelt the good green smell of grass and shrub and tree.
We had barely room for swinging with the tide —
There were many of us crowded in the bay:
Three Germans, and the English ship, beside
Our three — and from the Trenton where she lay,
Through the sunset calms and after,
We could hear the shrill, sweet laughter
Of the children's voices on the shore at play.

We all knew a storm was coming, but, dear God! no man could dream
Of the furious hell-horrors of that day:
Through the roar of winds and waters we could hear wild voices scream —
See the rocking masts reel by us through the spray.
In the gale we drove and drifted helplessly,
With our rudder gone, our engine-fires drowned,
And none might hope another hour to see;
For all the air was desperate with the sound
Of the brave ships rent asunder —
Of the shrieking souls sucked under,
'Neath the waves, where many a good man's grave was found.

About noon, upon our quarter, from the deeper gloom afar,
Came the English man-of-war Calliope.
"We have lost our anchors, comrades, and, though small the chances are,
We must steer for safety and the open sea."
Then we climbed aloft to cheer her as she passed
Through the tempest and the blackness and the foam:

"Now, God speed you, though the shout should be our last,
Through the channel where the maddened breakers comb,
Through the wild sea's hill and hollow,
On the path we cannot follow,
To your women and your children and your home."

Oh! remember it, good brothers. We two people speak one tongue,
And your native land was mother to our land;
But the head, perhaps, is hasty when the nation's heart is young,
And we prate of things we do not understand.
But the day when we stood face to face with death,
(Upon whose face few men may look and tell),
As long as you could hear, or we had breath,
Four hundred voices cheered you out of hell!
By the will of that stern chorus,
By the motherland which bore us,
Judge if we do not love each other well.

A PORTRAIT

A MAN more kindly, in his careless way,
Than many who profess a higher creed;
Whose fickle love might change from day to day,
And yet be faithful to a friend in need;
Whose manners covered, through life's outs and ins,
Like charity, a multitude of sins.

A man of honor, too, as such things go;
Discreet and secret — qualities of use —
Selfish, but not self-conscious, generous, slow
To anger, but most ready in excuse.
His wit and cleverness consisted not
So much in what he said as what he got.

His principles one might not quite commend,
And they were much too simple to mistake:
Never to turn his back upon a friend,
Never to lie, but for a woman's sake,
To take the sweets that came within his way,
And pay the price if there were price to pay.

Idle, good-looking, negatively wise,
Lazy in action, plausible in speech;
Favor he found in many women's eyes,
And valued most that which was hard to reach.
Few are both true and tender, and he grew,
In time, a little tenderer than true.

Knowing much evil, half-regretting good,
As we regret a childish impulse — lost,
Wearied with knowledge best not understood,
Bored with the disenchantment that it cost;
But, in conclusion, with no failings hid:
A gentleman, no matter what he did.

A WORD TO THE WISE

IF wisdom's height is only disenchantment,
As say the cynics of a certain school,
And sages grow more sad in their advancement,
Then folly is the wisdom of the fool.

Since fools know happiness through lack of knowledge,
And see things fair because they shut their eyes,
Then any one can tell, who's been to college,
That wisdom is the folly of the wise.

Alice Duer Miller

SONG

THE light of spring
On the emerald earth,
A man, a maid,
And a mood of mirth,
A foolish jest,

That a smile amends —
It took no more
To make us friends.

An evening breeze,
The year in bloom,
Lips quickly met
In the garden's gloom;
The trees about us,
The stars above —
It took no more
To teach us love.

Frost in the air —
The air like wine —
Go you your way,
And I 'll go mine.
Lightly we part
Who lightly met —
What more is needed,
When both forget?

A SONNET

Dear, if you love me, hold me most your friend,
Chosen from out the many who would bear
Your gladness gladly — heavily your care;
Who best can sympathize, best comprehend,
Where others fail; who, breathless to the end,
Follows your tale of joy or of despair.
Hold me your counsellor, because I dare
To lift my hand to guide you, that I lend
My love to help you. And I would you knew
That I am fair enough to win men's hearts,
If so I willed; yet honor me above
All other women, since I am too true
To trap you with my sex's smaller arts.
Deem me all these, but love me as your love.

Edward A. U. Valentine

HELEN

She sits within the white oak hall,
Hung with the trophies of the chase —
Helen, a stately maid and tall,
Dark-haired and pale of face;
With drooping lids and eyes that brood,
Sunk in the depths of some strange mood,
She gazes in the fireplace, where
The oozing pine logs snap and flare,
Wafting the perfume of their native wood.

The wind is whining in the garth,
The leaves are at their dervish rounds,
The flexile flames upon the hearth
Hang out their tongues like panting hounds.
The fire, I deem, she holds in thrall;
Its red light fawns as she lets fall
Escaloped pine-cones, dried and brown,
From loose, white hands, till up and down
The colored shadows dye the dusky wall.

The tawny lamp flame tugs its wick;
Upon the landing of the stair
The ancient clock is heard to tick
In shadows dark as Helen's hair;
And by a gentle accolade
A squire to languid silence made,
I lean upon my palms, with eyes
O'er which a rack of fancy flies,
While dreams like gorgeous sunsets flame and fade.

And as I muse on Helen's face,
Within the firelight's ruddy shine,
Its beauty takes an olden grace
Like hers whose fairness was divine;
The dying embers leap, and, lo!
Troy wavers vaguely all aglow,
And in the north wind leashed without,
I hear the conquering Argives' shout;
And Helen feeds the flames as long ago!

THE SPIRIT OF THE WHEAT

Such times as windy moods do stir
The foamless billows of the wheat,
I glimpse the floating limbs of her
In instant visions melting sweet.

A milky shoulder's dip and gleam,
Or arms that clasp upon the air,
An upturned face's rosy dream,
Half blinded by the sunlit hair.

A haunting mermaid mid the swell
And rapture of that summer sea;
A siren of elusive spell,
Born of the womb of mystery,—

That, airy-limbed, swims fancy free,
Glad in the summer's perfect prime,
Full-veined with life's felicity
And faith that knows no winter-time.

At eve, when firefly lustre burns
On that green flood like mirrored stars,
Against the hush her faint voice yearns,
Breathed to a light harp's happy bars.

Till sinks at last in sunset slow
Midsummer's long, luxurious day,
And amber-red the ripe waves glow,
Ah, then it is she slips away!

For with the blighting dog-star's blaze,
The reapers wade within the wheat,
And as they work in harvest ways,
What amorous sights their vision cheat!

For lo, upon some eddying wash
Or hollow of the wind-swept grain,
Her wafted fingers foam-like flash,
Her laughing body drifts amain.

It is the sylph's divine farewell;
A sighing ebbs along the wheat;
Borne onward by a golden swell,
She fades into the wrinkling heat.

Alice Archer (Sewall) James

SINFONIA EROICA[1]

He comes, the happy warrior,
The wind has blown him on!
He is great and terrible and sweet,
From flaming hair to rapid feet.
His presence strides the earth full-armed, complete.

Oh, underneath his helmet-rim
The crowded lilies lie.
From some Elysian feast he comes,
Struck with the passion of the drums,
And fragrant from the feast, behold, he comes!

He holds all morning in his face,
All fury and all fire.
His panting heart bursts with disdain
Of all that hinders him from pain;
And mine with longing that he might remain.

THE BUTTERFLY[1]

I am not what I was yesterday,
God knows my name.
I am made in a smooth and beautiful way,
And full of flame.

The color of corn are my pretty wings,
My flower is blue.
I kiss its topmost pearl, it swings
And I swing too.

I dance above the tawny grass
In the sunny air,
So tantalized to have to pass
Love everywhere.

O Earth, O Sky, you are mine to roam
In liberty.
I am the soul and I have no home,—
Take care of me.

For double I drift through a double world
Of spirit and sense;
I and my symbol together whirled
From who knows whence?

There 's a tiny weed, God knows what good,—
It sits in the moss.
Its wings are heavy and spotted with blood
Across and across.

I sometimes settle a moment there,
And I am so sweet,
That what it lacks of the glad and fair
I fill complete.

The little white moon was once like me;
But her wings are one.

Or perhaps they closëd together be
As she swings in the sun.

When the clovers close their three green wings
Just as I do,
I creep to the primrose heart of things,
And close mine, too.

And then wide opens the candid night,
Serene and intense;
For she has, instead of love and light,
God's confidence.

And I watch that other butterfly,
The one-winged moon,
Till, drunk with sweets in which I lie,
I dream and swoon.

And then when I to three days grow,
I find out pain.
For swift there comes an ache, — I know
That I am twain.

And nevermore can I be one
In liberty.

O Earth, O Sky, your use is done,
Take care of me.

PROCESSIONAL[1]

My love leads the white bulls to sacrifice.
He is white, and he leans against their folded necks.
Blue is the sky behind them, and the dust from the highway yellows his ivory limbs.
He leans and moves, restraining, yet drawn on by tossing heads.
He feels the festal music; rapid and strong are his arms and breast;
Yet from his waist beneath, loose and slow is his resting pace,
Flowers are in his hair, and he is fair.
He thinks he is but strong; he can overcome,
And his mind sees only the impatient horns;
But my heart sees his slimness, and would care for him like a mother.
My love leads the white bulls to sacrifice.

Stephen Crane

THE PEAKS

In the night
Gray, heavy clouds muffled the valleys,
And the peaks looked toward God alone.
"O Master, that movest the wind with a finger,
Humble, idle, futile peaks are we.
Grant that we may run swiftly across the world
To huddle in worship at Thy feet."

In the morning
A noise of men at work came the clear blue miles,
And the little black cities were apparent.
"O Master, that knowest the meaning of raindrops,
Humble, idle, futile peaks are we.
Give voice to us, we pray, O Lord,
That we may sing Thy goodness to the sun."

In the evening
The far valleys were sprinkled with tiny lights.
"O Master,
Thou that knowest the value of kings and birds,
Thou hast made us humble, idle, futile peaks.
Thou only needest eternal patience;
We bow to Thy wisdom, O Lord —
Humble, idle, futile peaks."

In the night
Gray, heavy clouds muffled the valleys,
And the peaks looked toward God alone.

'SCAPED

Once I knew a fine song,
— It is true, believe me, —
It was all of birds,
And I held them in a basket;
When I opened the wicket,
Heavens! they all flew away.
I cried, "Come back, Little Thoughts!"
But they only laughed.
They flew on
Until they were as sand
Thrown between me and the sky.

[1] Copyright, 1899, by Harper & Brothers.

THE BLACK RIDERS

Black riders came from the sea.
There was clang and clang of spear and shield,
And clash and clash of hoof and heel,
Wild shouts and the wave of hair
In the rush upon the wind:
Thus the ride of sin.

WHY?

Behold, the grave of a wicked man,
And near it, a stern spirit.

There came a drooping maid with violets,
But the spirit grasped her arm.
"No flowers for him," he said.
The maid wept:
"Ah, I loved him."
But the spirit, grim and frowning:
"No flowers for him."

Now, this is it —
If the spirit was just,
Why did the maid weep?

THE WAYFARER

The wayfarer,
Perceiving the pathway to truth,
Was struck with astonishment.
It was thickly grown with weeds.
"Ha," he said,
"I see that none has passed here
In a long time."
Later he saw that each weed
Was a singular knife.
"Well," he mumbled at last,
"Doubtless there are other roads."

CONTENT

A youth in apparel that glittered
Went to walk in a grim forest.
There he met an assassin
Attired all in garb of old days;
He, scowling through the thickets,
And dagger poised quivering,
Rushed upon the youth.
"Sir," said this latter,
"I am enchanted, believe me.
To die thus,
In this mediæval fashion,
According to the best legends;
Ah, what joy!"
Then took he the wound, smiling,
And died, content.

ANCESTRY

Once I saw mountains angry,
And ranged in battle-front.
Against them stood a little man;
Ay, he was no bigger than my finger.
I laughed, and spoke to one near me,
"Will he prevail?"
"Surely," replied this other;
"His grandfathers beat them many times."
Then did I see much virtue in grandfathers, —
At least, for the little man
Who stood against the mountains.

THE VIOLETS

There was a land where lived no violets.
A traveller at once demanded: "Why?"
The people told him:
"Once the violets of this place spoke thus:
'Until some woman freely gives her lover
To another woman
We will fight in bloody scuffle.'"
Sadly the people added:
"There are no violets here."

I EXPLAIN

I explain the silvered passing of a ship at night,
The sweep of each sad lost wave,
The dwindling boom of the steel thing's striving,
The little cry of a man to a man,
A shadow falling across the grayer night,
And the sinking of the small star;

Then the waste, the far waste of waters,
And the soft lashing of black waves
For long and in loneliness.

Remember, thou, O ship of love,
Thou leavest a far waste of waters,
And the soft lashing of black waves
For long and in loneliness.

Herbert Bashford

THE ARID LANDS

THESE lands are clothed in burning weather,
These parched lands pant for God's cool rain;
I look away where strike together
The burnished sky and barren plain.

I look away; no green thing gladdens
My weary eye — no flower, no tree,
Naught save the earth, the sage-brush saddens
The scorched, gray earth that sickens me.

Oh for the pines, where the sweet wind revels!
The ringing laugh of the crystal creek!
Alas, gaunt Hunger haunts these levels,
And Thirst goes wandering wan and weak.

No shadow falls where swiftly passes
The gray coyote's noiseless feet,
No song of bird, no hint of grasses —
The home of Silence and of Heat!

BY THE PACIFIC

FROM this quaint cabin window I can see
The strange, vague line of ghostly driftwood, though
No ray of silver moon or soft star-glow
Steals through the summer night's solemnity.
Pale forms drive landward and wild figures flee
Like spectres up the shore; I hear the slow,
Firm tread of marching billows which I know
Will walk beside the years that are to be.
Sweet, gentle sleep is banished from mine eyes;
I lie and think of wrecks until the sobs
And groans of drowning sailors, lost at sea,
Come mingled with the gray gulls' plaintive cries
And those tumultuous, incessant throbs —
The heavy heart-beats of Eternity.

NIGHT IN CAMP

FIERCE burns our fire of driftwood; overhead
Gaunt maples lift long arms against the night;
The stars are sobbing, — sorrow-shaken, white,
And high they hang, or show sad eyes grown red
With weeping for their queen, — the moon, just dead.
Black shadows backward reel when tall and bright
The broad flames stand and fling a golden light
On mats of soft green moss around us spread.
A sudden breeze comes in from off the sea,
The vast, old forest draws a troubled breath,
A leaf awakens; up the shore of sand
The slow tide, silver-lipped, creeps noiselessly;
The campfire dies; then silence deep as death;
The darkness pushing down upon the land.

MORNING IN CAMP

A BED of ashes and a half-burned brand
Now mark the spot where last night's campfire sprung
And licked the dark with slender, scarlet tongue;
The sea draws back from shores of yellow sand,
Nor speaks lest he awake the sleeping land.
Tall trees grow out of shadows; high among
Their sombre boughs one clear, sweet song is sung,
In deep ravine by drooping cedars spanned,
All drowned in gloom; a flying pheasant's whirr
Rends morning's solemn hush; gray rabbits run
Across the clovered glade, while far away
Upon the hills each huge, expectant fir
Holds open arms in welcome to the sun —
Great, pulsing heart of bold, advancing day!

QUATRAINS

MOUNT RAINIER

Long hours we toiled up through the solemn wood
 Beneath moss-banners stretched from tree to tree;
At last upon a barren hill we stood
 And, lo, above loomed Majesty!

ALONG SHORE

What wondrous sermons these seas preach to men!
What lofty pinnacles they seek to climb!
How old and bent they are, yet strong as when
 They rocked the infant Time!

SUNSET

Like some huge bird that sinks to rest,
 The sun goes down — a weary thing —
And o'er the water's placid breast
 It lays a scarlet, outstretched wing.

Rupert Hughes

FOR DECORATION DAY

I

1861–1865

But do we truly mourn our soldier dead,
Or understand at all their precious fame —
We that were born too late to feel the flame
That leapt from lowly hearths, and grew, dispread,
And, like a pillar of fire, our armies led?
Or you that knew them — do the long years tame
The memory-anguish? Are they more than name?
Oh, let no stinted grief profane their bed!
Let tears bedew each wreath that decks the lawn
Of every grave! and raise a solemn prayer
That their battalioned souls be joined to fare
Dim roads, beyond the trumpets of the dawn,
Yet perfumed, somehow, by our flowers that heap
The peaceful barracks where their bodies sleep.

II

1898–1899

And now the long, long lines of the Nation's graves
Grow longer; and the venerate slopes reveal
The fresh spring turf gashed thick with tombs to seal
Away another army of our braves.
So hang black garlands from the architraves
Of all the capitols. The dying peal
Of bugles wails their final Taps. So kneel
And give the dead the due their virtue craves.
Thank God, the olden sinew still is bred;
The milk of American mothers still is sweet;
The sword of Seventy-six is sharp and bright;
The Flag still floats unblotted with defeat!
But ah the blood that keeps its ripples red,
The starry lives that keep its field alight;
The pangs of women and the tears they've bled

The Lord enlarge our spirits till we feel
The greatness of these spirits upward fled.
A kind of genius it has been that fed
Them strength to be, above all passions, leal.
They put aside the velvet for the steel,
Left love, and hope, and ease at home; and sped
To the wilderness of war and every dread.
Their blood is mortar for our commonweal;
Their deeds its decoration and its boast.
So mix with dirges, triumph; smiles, with tears.
Make sorrow perfect with exultant pride —
Our vanished armies have not truly died;

They march to-day before the heavenly host;
And history's veterans raise a storm of cheers,
As the Yankee troops — with glory armed and shod —
In Grand Review swing past the throne of God.

Paul Laurence Dunbar

A CORN-SONG

On the wide veranda white,
In the purple failing light,
Sits the master while the sun is lowly burning;
And his dreamy thoughts are drowned
In the softly flowing sound
Of the corn-songs of the field-hands slow returning.

Oh, we hoe de co'n
Since de ehly mo'n;
Now de sinkin' sun
Says de day is done.

O'er the fields with heavy tread,
Light of heart and high of head,
Though the halting steps be labored, slow, and weary;
Still the spirits brave and strong
Find a comforter in song,
And their corn-song rises ever loud and cheery.

Oh, we hoe de co'n
Since de ehly mo'n;
Now de sinkin' sun
Says de day is done.

To the master in his seat,
Comes the burden, full and sweet,
Of the mellow minor music growing clearer,
As the toilers raise the hymn,
Thro' the silence dusk and dim,
To the cabin's restful shelter drawing nearer.

Oh, we hoe de co'n
Since de ehly mo'n;
Now de sinkin' sun
Says de day is done.

And a tear is in the eye
Of the master sitting by,
As he listens to the echoes low-replying,
To the music's fading calls,
As it faints away and falls
Into silence, deep within the cabin dying.

Oh, we hoe de co'n
Since de ehly mo'n;
Now de sinkin' sun
Says de day is done.

HARRIET BEECHER STOWE

She told the story, and the whole world wept
At wrongs and cruelties it had not known
But for this fearless woman's voice alone.
She spoke to consciences that long had slept:
Her message, Freedom's clear reveille, swept
From heedless hovel to complacent throne.
Command and prophecy were in the tone,
And from its sheath the sword of justice leapt.
Around two peoples swelled a fiery wave,
But both came forth transfigured from the flame.
Blest be the hand that dared be strong to save,
And blest be she who in our weakness came —
Prophet and priestess! At one stroke she gave
A race to freedom and herself to fame.

RETORT

"Thou art a fool," said my head to my heart,
"Indeed, the greatest of fools thou art,
To be led astray by the trick of a tress,
By a smiling face or a ribbon smart;"
And my heart was in sore distress.

Then Phyllis came by, and her face was fair,
The light gleamed soft on her raven hair;

And her lips were blooming a rosy red.
Then my heart spoke out with a right bold air:
"Thou art worse than a fool, O head!"

ON THE ROAD

I 's boun' to see my gal to-night —
Oh, lone de way, my dearie!
De moon ain't out, de stars ain't bright —
Oh, lone de way, my dearie!
Dis hoss o' mine is pow'ful slow,
But when I does git to yo' do'
Yo' kiss 'll pay me back, an' mo',
Dough lone de way, my dearie.

De night is skeery-lak an' still —
Oh, lone de way, my dearie!
'Cept fu' dat mou'nful whippo'will —
Oh, lone de way, my dearie!
De way so long wif dis slow pace,
'T 'u'd seem to me lak savin' grace
Ef you was on a nearer place,
Fu' lone de way, my dearie.

I hyeah de hootin' of de owl —
Oh, lone de way, my dearie!
I wish dat watch-dog would n't howl —
Oh, lone de way, my dearie!
An' evaht'ing bofe right an' lef',
Seem p'in'tly lak hit put itse'f
In shape to skeer me half to def —
Oh, lone de way, my dearie!

I whistles so 's I won't be feared —
Oh, lone de way, my dearie!
But anyhow I 's kin' o' skeered,
Fu' lone de way, my dearie.
De sky been lookin' mighty glum,
But you kin mek hit lighten some,
Ef you 'll jes' say you 's glad I come,
Dough lone de way, my dearie.

HYMN

O li'l' lamb out in de col',
De Mastah call you to de fol',
O li'l' lamb!
He hyeah you bleatin' on de hill;
Come hyeah an' keep yo' mou'nin' still,
O li'l' lamb!

De Mastah sen' de Shepud fo'f;
He wandah souf, he wandah no'f,
O li'l' lamb!
He wandah eas', he wandah wes';
De win' a-wrenchin' at his breas',
O li'l' lamb!

Oh, tell de Shepud whaih you hide;
He want you walkin' by his side,
O li'l' lamb!
He know you weak, he know you so';
But come, don' stay away no mo',
O li'l' lamb!

An' af' ah while de lamb he hyeah
De Shepud's voice a-callin' cleah —
Sweet li'l' lamb!
He answah f'om de brambles thick,
"O Shepud, I 's a-comin' quick" —
O li'l' lamb!

A DEATH SONG

Lay me down beneaf de willers in de grass,
Whah de branch 'll go a-singin' as it pass.
An' w'en I 's a-layin' low,
I kin hyeah it as it go
Singin', "Sleep, my honey, tek yo' res' at las'."

Lay me nigh to whah hit meks a little pool,
An' de watah stan's so quiet lak an' cool,
Whah de little birds in spring
Ust to come an' drink an' sing,
An' de chillen waded on dey way to school.

Let me settle w'en my shouldahs draps dey load
Nigh enough to hyeah de noises in de road;
Fu' I t'ink de las' long res'
Gwine to soothe my sperrit bes'
Ef I 's layin' 'mong de t'ings I 's allus knowed.

Mary McNeil Fenollosa

SUNRISE IN THE HILLS OF SATSUMA

The day unfolds like a lotus bloom,
Pink at the tip and gold at the core,
Rising up swiftly through waters of gloom
That lave night's shore.

Down bamboo-stalks the sunbeams slide,
Darting like glittering elves at play,
To the thin arched grass where crickets hide
And sing all day.

The old crows caw from the camphor boughs,
They have builded there for a thousand years;
Their nestlings stir in a huddled drowse
To pipe shrill fears.

A white fox creeps to his home in the hill,
A small gray ape peers up at the sun;
Crickets and sunbeams are quarrelling still;
Day has begun.

FLYING FISH

Out where the sky and the sky-blue sea
Merge in a mist of sheen,
There started a vision of silver things,
A leap and a quiver, a flash of wings
The sky and the sea between.

Is it of birds from the blue above,
Or fish from the depths that be?
Or is it the ghosts
In silver hosts
Of birds that were drowned at sea?

MIYOKO SAN

Snare me the soul of a dragon-fly,
The jewelled heart of a dew-tipped spray,
A star's quick eye,
Or the scarlet cry
Of a lonely wing on a dawn-lit bay.
Then add the gleam of a golden fan,
And I will paint you Miyoko San.

Find me the thought of a rose, at sight
Of her own pale face in a fawning stream,
The polished night
Of a crow's slow flight,
And the long, sweet grace of a willow's dream.
Then add the droop of a golden fan,
And I will paint you Miyoko San.

Lure me a lay from a sunbeam's throat,
The chant of bees in a perfumed lair,
Or a single note
Gone mad to float
To its own sweet death in the upper air.
Then add the click of a golden fan,
And I have painted Miyoko San.

A DRIFTING PETAL

If I, athirst by a stream, should kneel
With never a blossom or bud in sight,
Till down on the theme of its liquid night
The moon-white tip of a sudden keel,
A fairy boat,
Should dawn and float
To my hand, as only the Gods deserve,
The cloud-like curve,
The loosened sheaf,
The ineffable pink of a lotus leaf, —
I should know, I should feel, that far away
On the dimpled rim of a brighter day
A thought had blossomed, and shaken free
One sheath of its innermost soul for me.

YUKI

When cherry flowers begin to blow
With Yuki's face beneath them,
The richest petals lose their glow,
And small buds haste to sheath them.

When blue wistaria hangs its head
And Yuki leans above it,

The swallow flits discomforted, —
  With none to see or love it.

When lotus blossoms open wide,
  And beckon men to dreaming,
My Yuki smiles, — and all their pride
  Is but a perfumed seeming.

When snow is white on moat and tree
  And crusts each bamboo feather,
My Yuki lifts her eyes to me, —
  'T is all I know of weather.

MORNING FANCY

O LET me die a-singing!
  O let me drown in light!
Another day is winging
  Out from the nest of night.

The morning-glory's velvet eye
  Brims with a jewelled bead.
To-day my soul 's a dragon-fly,
  The world a swaying reed.

Grace Ellery Channing-Stetson

ENGLAND

WHO comes to England not to learn
  The love for her his fathers bore,
Breathing her air, can still return
  No kindlier than he was before.
  In vain, for him, from shore to shore
Those fathers strewed an alien strand
  With the loved names that evermore
Are native to our ear and land.

Who sees the English elm-trees fling
  Long shadows where his footsteps pass,
Or marks the crocuses that spring
  Sets starlike in the English grass,
  And sees not, as within a glass,
New England's loved reflection rise, —
  Mists darker and more dense, alas!
Than England's fogs are in his eyes.

And who can walk by English streams,
  Through sunny meadows gently led,
Nor feel, as one who lives in dreams,
  The wound with which his fathers bled, —
  The homesick tears which must, unshed,
Have dimmed the brave, unfaltering eyes
  That saw New England's elms outspread
Green branches to her loftier skies?

How dear to exiled hearts the sound
  Of little brooks that run and sing!
How dear, in scanty garden ground,
  The crocus calling back the spring
  To English hearts remembering!
How dear that aching memory
  Of cuckoo cry and lark's light wing!
And for their sake how dear to me!

Who owns not how, so often tried,
  The bond all trial hath withstood;
The leaping pulse, the racial pride
  In more than common brotherhood;
  Nor feels his kinship like a flood
Rise blotting every dissonant trace, —
  He is not of the ancient blood!
He is not of the Island race!

WAR

THE great Republic goes to war,
  But spring still comes as spring has done,
  And all the summer months will run
Their summer sequence as before;
  And every bird will build its nest,
  The sun sink daily in the west,
    And rising eastward bring new day
    In the old way.
But ah, those dawns will have a light,
Those western skies burn golden bright,
  With what a note the birds will sing,
  And winter's self be turned to spring
    Than any springtime sweeter far,
  When once again, calm entering,
    The great Republic comes from war!

JUDGMENT

A DEAD Soul lay in the light of day,
  Desperate, wan, it had passed;

Oft foiled, it had toiled on its upward way,
Till it perished, spent, aghast,
After a thousand defeats the prey
Of its conquering sin at last.

Said a stranger: — "Lo, how in shame and woe
Is Satan's seal ever set!"
Laughed a foe: — "Doth the carrion lie so low?
Death and a coward well met."
Said a friend: — "His strength was great, I know,
But his weakness was stronger yet."

Moaned his love unwed: — "Peace to the dead;
And as God shall forgive — let be!"
But an angel spread o'er the prostrate head
His wings in humility;
As he gazed: — "Be praised, great God," he said,
"For a glorious victory!"

A SONG OF ARNO

It is the hour when Arno turns
Her gold to chrysoprase;
When each low-hanging star outburns
Its faint, mysterious rays,
As from the prison of faery urns
Which faery hands upraise.

It is the hour when life 's constraint
A moment's ease is given;
When Earth is like a holy saint,
Stilled, sanctified, and shriven,
And the deep-breathing heart grows faint
To be so near to Heaven.

Guy Wetmore Carryl

WHEN THE GREAT GRAY SHIPS COME IN[1]

(NEW YORK HARBOR, AUGUST 20, 1898)

To eastward ringing, to westward winging, o'er mapless miles of sea,
On winds and tides the gospel rides that the furthermost isles are free,
And the furthermost isles make answer, harbor, and height, and hill,
Breaker and beach cry each to each, "'T is the Mother who calls! Be still!"
Mother! new-found, beloved, and strong to hold from harm,
Stretching to these across the seas the shield of her sovereign arm,
Who summoned the guns of her sailor sons, who bade her navies roam,
Who calls again to the leagues of main, and who calls them this time home!

And the great gray ships are silent, and the weary watchers rest,
The black cloud dies in the August skies, and deep in the golden west
Invisible hands are limning a glory of crimson bars,
And far above is the wonder of a myriad wakened stars!
Peace! As the tidings silence the strenuous cannonade,
Peace at last! is the bugle blast the length of the long blockade,
And eyes of vigil weary are lit with the glad release,
From ship to ship and from lip to lip it is "Peace! Thank God for peace."

Ah, in the sweet hereafter Columbia still shall show
The sons of these who swept the seas how she bade them rise and go, —
How, when the stirring summons smote on her children's ear,
South and North at the call stood forth, and the whole land answered, "Here!"
For the soul of the soldier's story and the heart of the sailor's song
Are all of those who meet their foes as right should meet with wrong,
Who fight their guns till the foeman runs, and then, on the decks they trod,
Brave faces raise, and give the praise to the grace of their country's God!

Yes, it is good to battle, and good to be strong and free,
To carry the hearts of a people to the uttermost ends of sea,

To see the day steal up the bay where the enemy lies in wait,
To run your ship to the harbor's lip and sink her across the strait: —
But better the golden evening when the ships round heads for home,
And the long gray miles slip swiftly past in a swirl of seething foam,
And the people wait at the haven's gate to greet the men who win!
Thank God for peace! Thank God for peace, when the great gray ships come in!

THE SYCOPHANTIC FOX AND THE GULLIBLE RAVEN[1]

A RAVEN sat upon a tree,
And not a word he spoke, for
His beak contained a piece of Brie,
Or, maybe, it was Roquefort:
We 'll make it any kind you please —
At all events, it was a cheese.

Beneath the tree's umbrageous limb
A hungry fox sat smiling;
He saw the raven watching him,
And spoke in words beguiling:
"*J'admire*," said he, "*ton beau plumage*,"
(The which was simply persiflage).

Two things there are, no doubt you know,
To which a fox is used, —
A rooster that is bound to crow,
A crow that 's bound to roost,
And whichsoever he espies
He tells the most unblushing lies.

"Sweet fowl," he said, "I understand
You 're more than merely natty:
I hear you sing to beat the band
And Adelina Patti.
Pray render with your liquid tongue
A bit from 'Götterdämmerung.'"

This subtle speech was aimed to please
The crow, and it succeeded:
He thought no bird in all the trees
Could sing as well as he did.
In flattery completely doused,
He gave the "Jewel Song" from "Faust."

But gravitation's law, of course,
As Isaac Newton showed it,
Exerted on the cheese its force,
And elsewhere soon bestowed it.
In fact, there is no need to tell
What happened when to earth it fell.

I blush to add that when the bird
Took in the situation
He said one brief, emphatic word,
Unfit for publication.
The fox was greatly startled, but
He only sighed and answered "Tut!"

THE MORAL is: A fox is bound
To be a shameless sinner.
And also: When the cheese comes round
You know it 's after dinner.
But (what is only known to few)
The fox is after dinner, too.

Mildred Howells

ROMANCE

DOWN from a sunken doorstep to the road,
Through a warm garden full of old-time flowers,
Stretches a pathway, where the wrinkled toad
Sits lost in sunlight through long summer hours.

Ah, little dream the passers in the street
That there, a few yards from the old house door,
Just where the apple and the pear trees meet,
The noble deeds of old are lived once more! —

That there, within the gold-lit wavering shade,
To Joan of Arc angelic voices sing,

And once again the brave inspired maid
Gives up her life for France and for her king.

Or, now no more the fields of France are seen,
They change to England's rougher, colder shore,
Where rules Elizabeth, the Virgin Queen,
Or where King Arthur holds his court once more.

The stupid village folk they cannot see;
Their eyes are old, and as they pass their way,
It only seems to them beneath the tree
They see a little dark-eyed girl at play.

A MORAL IN SEVRES

Upon my mantel-piece they stand,
While all its length between them lies;
He throws a kiss with graceful hand,
She glances back with bashful eyes.

The china Shepherdess is fair,
The Shepherd's face denotes a heart
Burning with ardor and despair.
Alas, they stand so far apart!

And yet, perhaps, if they were moved,
And stood together day by day,
Their love had not so constant proved,
Nor would they still have smiled so gay.

His hand the Shepherd might have kissed
The match-box Angel's heart to win;
The Shepherdess, his love have missed,
And flirted with the Mandarin.

But on my mantel-piece they stand,
While all its length between them lies;
He throws a kiss with graceful hand,
She glances back with bashful eyes.

DOWN A WOODLAND WAY

As I was strolling down a woodland way,
I met fair Spring, a garland on her arm;
She stood a moment gazing in dismay,
Then turned and fled away in swift alarm.

And as I strove to follow her swift flight
Along the way that I had seen her pass,
No trace of her remained to meet my sight
Save three wild violets among the grass.

George Cabot Lodge

A SONG OF THE WAVE

This is the song of the wave! The mighty one!
Child of the soul of silence, beating the air to sound.
White as a live terror, as a drawn sword,
This is the wave!

This is the song of the wave, the white-maned steed of the Tempest,
Whose veins are swollen with life,
In whose flanks abide the four winds,
This is the wave!

This is the song of the wave! The dawn leaped out of the sea
And the waters lay smooth as a silver shield,
And the sun-rays smote on the waters like a golden sword.

Then a wind blew out of the morning
And the waters rustled,
And the wave was born!

This is the song of the wave! The wind blew out of the noon,
And the white sea-birds like driven foam
Winged in from the ocean that lay beyond the sky;
And the face of the waters was barred with white,
For the wave had many brothers,
And the wave leaped up in its strength
To the chant of the choral air:
This is the wave!

This is the song of the wave! The wind blew out of the sunset
And the west was lurid as Hell;
The black clouds closed like a tomb, for the sun was dead.

Then the wind smote full as the breath of God,
And the wave called to its brothers,
"This is the crest of life!"

This is the song of the wave, that rises to fall,
Rises a sheer green wall like a barrier of glass
That has caught the soul of the moonlight,
Caught and prisoned the moonbeams.
And its edge is frittered with blossoms of foam —
This is the wave!

This is the song of the wave, of the wave that falls,
Wild as a burst of day-gold blown through the colors of morning;
It shivers in infinite jewels, in eddies of wind-driven foam
Up the rumbling steep of sand.
This is the wave!

This is the song of the wave, that died in the fulness of life.
The prodigal this, that lavished its largess of strength
In the lust of attainment.
Aiming at things for Heaven too high,
Sure in the pride of life, in the richness of strength.
So tried it the impossible height, till the end was found:
When ends the soul that yearns for the fillet of morning stars —
The soul in the toils of the journeying worlds,
Whose eye is filled with the Image of God —
And the end is death!

YOUTH

If I must die,
The earth is inarticulate to sing
The dirge I crave:
The sorrow of the murmur-laden wave,
The sea-born wind complaining 'neath the sky,
And round my head the waters' silver ring.

If I must live,
And feel the ashes of oblivion
About my soul,
Let life be fearful, let me feel the whole,
Despair, and face the sunrise — if I grieve
Let it but be the tarrying of the sun.

Hildegarde Hawthorne

A SONG

Sing me a sweet, low song of night
Before the moon is risen,
A song that tells of the stars' delight
Escaped from day's bright prison,
A song that croons with the cricket's voice,
That sleeps with the shadowed trees,
A song that shall bid my heart rejoice
At its tender mysteries!

And then when the song is ended, love,
Bend down your head unto me,
Whisper the word that was born above
Ere the moon had swayed the sea;
Ere the oldest star began to shine,
Or the farthest sun to burn, —
The oldest of words, O heart of mine,
Yet newest, and sweet to learn.

MY ROSE

On a green slope, most fragrant with the spring,
One sweet, fair day I planted a red rose,
That grew, beneath my tender nourishing,
So tall, so riotous of bloom, that those
Who passed the little valley where it grew
Smiled at its beauty. All the air was sweet
About it! Still I tended it, and knew
That he would come, e'en as it grew complete.

And a day brought him! Up I led him, where
In the warm sun my rose bloomed gloriously —

Smiling and saying, "So, is it not fair?
And all for thee — all thine!" But he passed by
Coldly, and answered, "Rose? I see no rose,"
Leaving me standing in the barren vale
Alone! alone! feeling the darkness close
Deep o'er my heart, and all my being fail.

Then came one, gently, yet with eager tread,
Begging one rosebud — but my rose was dead.

Josephine Preston Peabody

PRELUDE

Words, words,
Ye are like birds.
Would I might fold you,
In my hands hold you
Till ye were warm and your feathers a-flutter;
Till, in your throats,
Tremulous notes
Foretold the songs ye would utter.

Words, words,
Ye are all birds!
Would ye might linger
Here on my finger,
Till I kissed each, and then sent you a-winging
Wild, perfect flight,
Through morn to night,
Singing and singing and singing!

WOOD-SONG

Love must be a fearsome thing
That can bind a maid
Glad of life as leaves in spring,
Swift and unafraid.

I could find a heart to sing
Death and darkness, praise or blame;
But before that name,
Heedfully, oh, heedfully
Do I lock my breast;
I am silent as a tree,
Guardful of the nest.

Ah, my passing Woodlander,
Heard you any note?
Would you find a leaf astir
From a wilding throat?
Surely, all the paths defer
Unto such a gentle quest.
Would you take the nest?
Follow where the sun-motes are!
Truly 't is a sorrow
I must bid you fare so far;
Speed you, and good-morrow!

SONNET IN A GARDEN

Dumb Mother of all music, let me rest
On thy great heart while summer days pass by;
While all the heat up-quivers, let me lie
Close gathered to the fragrance of thy breast.
Let not the pipe of birds from some high nest
Give voice unto a thought of melody,
Nor dreaming clouds afloat along the sky
Meet any wind of promise from the west.
Save for that grassy breath that never mars
The peace, but seems a musing of thine own,
Keep thy dear silence. So, embraced, alone,
Forgetful of relentless prison-bars,
My soul shall hear all songs, unsung, unknown,
Uprising with the breath of all the stars.

A CHANGELING GRATEFUL

Here they give me greeting,
House me warm within,
Break their bread and share it
With the heart of kin.

Here the ruddy hearth-light
Singes not a moth,
Gives a summer welcome
As a red rose doth.

I would leave a gift here
If I might: not I! —
Like a homeless laughter,
Vagrant wind gone by.

But while I am a glow-worm
I will shine and stay:
When I am a shadow . . .
I will creep away.

CARAVANS

WHAT bring ye me, O camels, across the southern desert,
The wan and parching desert, pale beneath the dusk?
Ye great slow-moving ones, faithful as care is faithful,
Uncouth as dreams may be, sluggish as far-off ships, —
What bring ye me, O camels?

"We bring thee gold like sunshine, saving that it warms not;
And rarest purple bring we, as dark as all the garnered
Bloom of many grape-vines; and spices subtly mingled
For a lasting savor: the precious nard and aloes;
The bitter-sweet of myrrh, like a sorrow having wings;
Ghostly breath of lilies bruised — how white they were! —
And the captive life of many a far rose-garden.
Jewels bring we hither, surely stars once fallen,
Torn again from darkness: the sunlit frost of topaz,
Moon-fire pent in opals, pearls that even the sea loves.
Webs of marvel bring we, broideries that have drunken
Deep of all life-color from a thousand lives, —
Each the royal cere-cloth of a century.
We come! What wouldst thou more?"

All this dust, these ashes, have ye brought so far?
All these days, these years, have I waited in the sun?
I would have had the wingëd Mirage of yonder desert.

RUBRIC

I'LL not believe the dullard dark,
Nor all the winds that weep,
But I shall find the farthest dream
That kisses me, asleep.

ISOLATION

O BROTHER Planets, unto whom I cry,
Know ye, in all the worlds, a gladder thing
Than this glad life of ours, this wandering
Among the eternal winds that wander by?
Ever to fly, with white star-faces set
Quenchless against the darkness, and the wet
Pinions of all the storms, — on, on alone,
With radiant locks outblown,
And sun-strong eyes to see
Into the sunless maze of all futurity!

Not ours the little measure of the years,
The bitter-sweet of summer that soon wanes,
The briefer benison of springtime rains;
Nay, but the thirst of all the living spheres,
Full-fed with mighty draughts of dark and light, —
The soul of all the dawns, the love of night,
The strength of deathless winters, and the boon
Of endless summer noon.
Look down, from star to star,
And see the centuries, — a flock of birds, afar.

Afar! But we, each one God's sentinel,
Lifting on high the torches that are His,
Look forth to one another o'er the abyss,
And cry, *Eternity, — and all is well!*
So ever journey we, and only know
The way is His, and unto Him we go.
Through all the voiceless desert of the air
Through all the star-dust there,
Where none has ever gone,
Still singing, seeking still, we wander on and on.

O brother Planets, ye to whom I cry,
Yet hath a strange dream touched me; for a cloud
Flared like a moth, within mine eyes. I bowed
My head, and, looking down through all the sky,
I saw the little Earth, far down below, —
The Earth that all the wandering winds do know.
Like some ground-bird, the small, beloved one
Fluttered about the sun.
Ah, were that little star
Only a signal-light of love for us, afar!

AFTER MUSIC

I SAW not they were strange, the ways I roam,
Until the music called, and called me thence,
And tears stirred in my heart as tears may come
To lonely children straying far from home,
Who know not how they wandered so, nor whence.

If I might follow far and far away
Unto the country where these songs abide,
I think my soul would wake and find it day,
Would tell me who I am, and why I stray, —
Would tell me who I was before I died.

A FAR-OFF ROSE

O FAR-OFF rose of long ago,
An hour of sweet, an hour of red,
To live, to breathe, and then to go
Into the dark ere June was dead!

Why say they: Roses shall return
With every year as years go on?
New springtime and strange bloom, my rose,
And alien June; but thou art gone.

Joseph Leiser

KOL NIDRA

FROM "THE DAY OF ATONEMENT"

Lo! above the mournful chanting,
Rise the fuller-sounded wailings
Of the soul's most solemn anthem.
Hark! the strains of deep Kol Nidra —
Saddest music ever mortal
Taught his lips to hymn or sound!

Not the heart of one lone mortal
Told his anguish in that strain;
All the sorrow, pain, and struggles
Of a people in despair,
Gathered from the vale of weeping,
Through the ages of distress.
'T is a mighty cry of beings
Held in bondage and affliction;
All the wailing and lamenting
Of a homeless people, roaming
O'er the plains and scattered hamlets
Of a world without a refuge,
All the sorrows, trials, bereavements, —
Loss of country, home, and people, —
In one mighty strain uniting,
Chant for every age its wail;
Make the suffering years reëcho
With the wounds and pains of yore;
Give a voice to every martyr
Ever hushed to death by pain,
Every smothered shriek of daughter
Burned upon the fagot's bier;
Bring the wander-years and exile,
Persecution's harsh assailment,
Ghetto misery and hounding,
To the ears of men to-day;
Link the dark and dreary ages
With the brighter future's glow;
Weave the past and hopeful present;
Bind the living with the sleeping,
Dust unto the dust confessing,
Even with the dead uniting,
When the soul would join with God.

. . . .

Slowly creep the muffled murmurs.
As the leaves and flowers, conspiring,
Steal a breeze from summer's chamber,
Hum and mumble as they stroke it,
Smooth, caress, and gently coy it,
So this murmur spreads the voices

Of the praying synagogue,
As each lip repeats the sinning
Of his selfish, godless living,
By each mutter low recounting
Every single sin and crime —
How he falsified his neighbor,
Made a stumbling-block for blindness,
Cursed the deaf, unstaid the cripple,
Played his son and daughter wrong,
Tattled of his wife's behavior,
Made his father's age a load,
Spoke belittling of his mother,
Took advantage of the stupid,
Made the hungry buy their bread,
Turned the needy from his threshold,
Clothed the naked with his bareness,
Shut the stranger from his fold,
Never begged forgiveness, pardon,
For a wrong aimed at a foe,
Never weighed the love or mercy
Of the Father of the world.
Low the lips are now repenting;
Every mutter is a sob
Ebbing from the font of being;
Conscience speaks in lowest accents,
Lest the voice cry out to men.

Who has ever heard Kol Nidra
Gushing from the breast of man,
Rising, falling, as the ocean
Lifts the waves in joy or fear.
From Time's ocean has it risen;
Every age has lent a murmur,
Every cycle built a wail;
Every sorrow ever dwelling
In the tortured heart of man,
Tears and sighs together swelling,
Answer for the pangs of ages.
'T is the voice of countless pilgrims,
Sons of Jacob, with a cry,
Moaning, sighing, grieving, wailing,
Answering in thousand voices
Fate and destiny of man,
Winning soul a consolation
For their sad allotment's creed;
Wander-song of homeless traveller,
Outcast from the ranks of men;
Echoes from the throes of mortals,
Questioning the ways of God;
Song hummed by the lonely desert,
Prompted by the heart of night,
Lisped across the sandy borders
By the desert's trailing wind;
Hymn of midnight and the silence,
Song the friendless stars intone,
Sung whene'er the tempest hurtles,
Bruits destruction to the world;
Song of every song of sorrow,
Wail for every grief and woe,
World affliction, world lamenting;
Sorrow of the lonely desert;
Sadness of a homeless people;
Anguish of a chided mortal,
Hounded, tracked, oppressed, and beaten,
Made the scourge of God on earth;
Outcry of a sinful bosom
Warring with his guilt and wrong.
'T is a saintly aspiration
Of a holy soul in prayer;
'T is the music hummed by mercy,
When the heart is touched by love.
'T is the welding of all mercy,
Love, forgiveness, in a union,
Sweeping o'er the span of ages,
Flooding earth with one majestic,
Universal hymn of woe,
As if God had willed his children
Weep in but one human strain.

Who can hear this strange Kol Nidra
Without dropping in the spell?
Lift the vestige of the present,
Link the momentary fleeting
Of the evening with the past;
Dwell a spirit in the ages,
Living in the heart of time:
Lose the sense of outer worlds,
Soul alone in endless time,
Breathing but the breath of ages.

Howard Weeden

THE BANJO OF THE PAST

You ax about dat music made
  On banjos long ago,
An' wants to know why it ain't played
  By niggers any mo'.

Dem banjos b'longed to by-gone days
  When times an' chunes was rare,
When we was gay as children — 'case
  We did n't have a care.

But when we got our freedom, we
  Found projeckin' was done;
Our livin' was to make — you see,
  An' dat lef' out de fun.

We learned to vote an' read an' spell,
  We learned de taste ob tears —
An' when you gets dat 'sponsible,
  De banjo disappears !

THE BORROWED CHILD

My chile ? Lord, no, she 's none o' mine ;
  She 's des one I have tried
To put in place of Anna Jane —
  My little one what died.

Dat 's long ago; no one but me
  Knows even where she lies:
But in her place I 've always kept
  A borrowed chile, her size.

As soon as it outgrows my chile,
  I lets it go, right straight —
An' takes another in its place
  To match dat Heabenly mate.

It 's took a sight o' chillin, sho',
  To ease dat dull ol' pàin,
An' keep de pretty likeness fresh
  Of my dead Anna Jane.

Der 's more den forty years, you see,
  Since she has been in Heaben,
But wid de angels years don't count —
  So she 's still only seben.

Time treats us all up dere, des lak
  It do white ladies here —
It teches 'em so light — one 's still
  A gal at forty year !

Wilbur Underwood

THE CATTLE OF HIS HAND

All night long through the starlit air and the stillness,
Through the cool wanness of dawn and the burning of noontide,
Onward we strain with a mighty resounding of hoof-beats.

Heaven and earth are ashake with the terrible trampling;
Wild, straying feet of a vast and hastening army;
Wistful eyes that helplessly seek one another.

Hushed is the dark to hear the plaint of our lowing,
Mournful cry of the dumb-tired hearts within us,
Faint to death with thirst and the gnawing of hunger.

Day by day through the dust and heat have we thirsted;
Day by day through stony ways have we hungered;
Naught but a few bitter herbs that grew by the wayside.

What we flee that is far behind in the darkness,
Where the place of abiding for us, we know not;
Only we hark for the voice of the Master Herdsman.

Many a weary day must pass ere we hear it,
Blown on the winds, now close, now far in the distance,
Deep as the void above us and sweet as the dawn-star.

He it is who drives us and urges us always,
Faint with a need that is ever present within us,
Struggling onward and toiling one by the other.

Ever we long and cry for rest, but it comes not;
Broke are our feet and sore and bruised by the climbing;
Sharp is his goad in our quivering flanks when we falter,

And some fall down with a plaintive moaning, and perish;

But upward we strain nor stop, for the Voice comes to us,
Driving us on once more to the press and the struggle.

Then when we know His Presence the hard way lightens;
Turn we our piteous eyes to the far-stretching highway;
Struggle ahead in the dark as trusting as children.

What we flee that is far behind in the darkness,
Where the place of abiding for us, we know not;
Only we hark for the Voice — till hope fades from us.

Heaven and earth are ashake with the terrible trampling,
Wild straying feet of a vast and hastening army,
Wistful hearts that helplessly seek one another.

All night long through the star-lit air and the stillness,
Through the cool wanness of dawn and the burning of noontide,
Onward we strain with a mighty resounding of hoof-beats.

Ednah Proctor (Clarke) Hayes

TO A WILD ROSE FOUND IN OCTOBER

THOU foolish blossom, all untimely blown!
  Poor jest of summer, come when woods are chill!
Thy sister buds, in June's warm redness grown,
  That lit with laughter all the upland hill,

Have traceless passed; save on each thornèd stem
  Red drops tell how their hearts, in dying, bled.
Theirs was the noon's rich languor, and for them
  The maiden moon her haloed beauty spread;

For them the bobolink his music spilled
  In bubbling streams; and well the wild bee knew
Their honeyed hearts. Now bird and bee are stilled;
  Now southward swallows hurry down the blue,

Fleeing the murderous Frost that even now
  Hath smote the marshes with his bitter breath,
Quenching the flames that danced on vine and bough, —
  Think'st thou thy beauty will make truce with Death,

Or hold in summer's leash his loosened wrath?
  See! o'er the shrunk grass trail the blackened vines;
And, hark! the wind, tracking the snow's fell path,
  Snarls like a fretted hound among the pines.

The pallid sunshine fails, — a sudden gloom
  Sweeps up the vale, a-thrill with boding fear.
What place for thee? Too late thy pride and bloom!
  Born out of time, — poor fool, — what dost thou here?

. . . .

What do I here when speeds the threatening blight?
  June stirred my heart, and so June is for me.
Who feels life's impulse bourgeon into light
  Recks not of seasons, knows not bird nor bee.

I can but bloom, — did the June roses more?
  I can but droop, — did they not also die?
The Moment is: the After or Before
  Hides all from sight, — canst thou tell more than I?

What matter if to-night come swirling snow
And Death? The Power that makes, that mars, is One.
I know nor care not: when that Power bids blow,
I ope my curlëd petals to the sun.

A GOOD-BY

THE wakening bugles cut the night:
"To horse! To horse! Away!"
And thine the lips that bid me go,
The eyes that bid me stay.

God make me blind for this one hour!
God make me only hear
That hurrying drum, — that cry, "They come!"
And thy "Good-by!" so near.

O eyes that hold me with your tears!
Think not your prayers I spurn:
Eyes that must for a soldier dim,
Not from a craven turn.

O lips that bid me forth to fight,
I take your challenge — so!
Where red death waits without the gates,
Thy knight, and God's, — I go!

THE DEATHLESS

WHAT charlatans in this later day
Beat at the gates of Art!
Each with his trick of speech or brush, —
Forgetting, that apart

From all the brawling of an age,
Its feverish fantasy,
She waits, who only unto Time
The soul of Art sets free!

God's handmaid Beauty, — whose touch rounds
A dewdrop or a world, —
God-sprung when first through Chaos' night
The morning wings unfurled;

Beauty, — who still the secret gives
Whispered the ages through, —
Recurrent as the flush of dawn,
Essential as the dew.

O babblers of some surer guide! —
Knowledge goes changing by;
Caprice may bloom its little hour,
And creeds are born and die;

Still Melos on her worshippers
Looks with calm-lidded eyes;
Still Helen, though Troy sleeps in dust,
Smiles through the centuries;

Still she who gleaned on Judah's plain
Love in her sheaves doth bind;
Still, down the glades of Arden, dance
The feet of Rosalind.

THE MOCKING-BIRD

LIST to that bird! His song — what poet pens it?
Brigand of birds, he 's stolen every note!
Prince though of thieves — hark! how the rascal spends it!
Pours the whole forest from one tiny throat!

THE DANCER

SKIN creamy as the furled magnolia bud
That stabs the dusky shadows of her hair;
Great startled eyes, and sudden-pulsing blood
Staining her cheek and throat and shoulder bare.

(*Ah Manuelita!*
Lita Pepita!
List the cachucha!
Dance! dance!)

Swaying she stands, the while one rounded arm
Draws her mantilla's folds in shy disguise,
Till in the music's subtle, quickening charm
Her trancëd soul forgets the alien eyes.

Fades the swift flush, save from the rose-soft mouth,
And all the conquering memories of Spain
Fling wide her veil; the vintage of the South
Leaps in her heart, and laughs through every vein!

(Ah Manuelita!
Star of Cordova!
Passion and innocence!
Dance! dance!)

Gone from her gaze the stage, the mimicry:
Yon painted scene? It is Cordova's walls!
The eager trumpets ring to revelry —
The banderillero cries — the toro falls!

The vision thrills to heart, to eyes, to lips;
Her castanets click out in conscious pride;
Curved throat, arched foot, and lissome-swaying hips,
The music sweeps her in its swirling tide.

Love and denial, mockery and desire,
A fountain tossing in its moody play,
Tempest of sunshine, cloud, and dew, and fire,
Dancing in joyance to the jocund day!

(Ah Manuelita!
Till the moon swoons in mist!
Till the stars dim and die!
Dance! dance!)

Soft! through the music steals a yearning strain, —
Now distant viols grieve down the drowsy night, —
Her fluttering feet are poised; then drift again,
Luring in languor, dreamy with delight.

(Ah Manuelita!
Witch of the wingëd feet!
Lead on to dream or death!
Dance! dance!)

Hushed in her heart are raptures and alarms;
Falling, as water falleth, to her knees,
She spreads the drifted foam-wreath of her arms;
The music dies in whispered ecstacies.

Frederic Ridgely Torrence

FROM "THE HOUSE OF A HUNDRED LIGHTS"

THE YOUNG LOVERS

I SAW them kissing in the shade and knew the sum of all my lore:
God gave them Youth, God gave them Love, and even God can give no more.

. . . .

I know not from the fading Rose with parted lips what whisper went.
I only know the Nightingale sang once again his old lament.

YOUTH AND AGE

A NIGHTINGALE once lost his voice from too much love, and he who flees
From Thirst to Wine-of-his-Desire must not forget the last — the lees.

Night is a woman vaguely veiled and made to woo, I see her now:
The newborn moon is suddenly her slender, golden, arched eyebrow.

I know a Thief who longs to steal from the moon's granary on high,
Or snatch the bunch of Pleiades from out the cornfield of the sky.

Desire's gold gates are always barred and open at no call or knock.
Age knows the only key is Pain, but Youth still thinks to force the lock.

You invalids who cannot drink much wine or love, I say to you:
"Content yourselves with laughing at the antics of the fools who do."

COMPENSATION

TELL Youth to play with Wine and Love and never bear away the scars!
I may as well tilt up the sky and yet try not to spill the stars.

Yet even for Youth's fevered blood there is a certain balm herein
This maiden's mouth: O sweet disease! and happy, happy medicine!

And, maiden, should these bitter tears you
shed be burdensome, know this:
There is a cure worth all the pain — to-
night — beneath the moon — a kiss.

Girl, when he gives you kisses twain, use
one, and let the other stay,
And hoard it; for moons die, red fades, and
you may need a kiss — some day.

One says, — "Truth 's false and false is
true." Well, since I 've seen this
maiden's eyes,
I 'll be so false as to be true, and such a
fool as to be wise.

CARPE DIEM

When I 'm in health and asked to choose
between the This and That, alas!
I all too gladly yield my throne up there
beside the Sea of Glass.

. . . .

Why! 'mongst all languages of earth
there 's none so sweet nor yet so fine
As that one spoken daily thrice by two and
thirty teeth of mine.

Yet what have I to do with sweets like
Love, or Wine, or Fame's dear
curse?
For I can do without all things except —
except the universe.

The sieve-like cup of Earthly Joy still
foams for me with many a bead,
But I have found another wine called
Charity-without-a-Creed.

And if I want to sleep, I 'll sleep more
than Religion's laws allow.
We 'll have a long sleep in the grave erelong; and should we not learn how?

Whether my days are cooled with calm or
filled with fever's ardent taint,
I have the same blue sky as God, I have the
same God as the saint.

THE CONCLUSION OF THE WHOLE MATTER

The Great Sword Bearer only knows just
when He 'll wound my heart, —
not I:
But since He is the one who gives the
balm, what does it signify?

If my Control should lose its hold on Fortune's collar through some hurt,
What then? — Why then I 'd simply cling
to old gray Resignation's skirt.

Of all the languages of earth in which the
human kind confer
The Master Speaker is the Tear: it is the
Great Interpreter.

Man's life is like a tide that weaves the
sea within its daily web.
It rises, surges, swells, and grows, — a pause
— then comes the evening ebb.

In this rough field of earthly life I have
reaped cause for tears enough,
Yet, after all, I think I 've gleaned my
modicum of Laughing-Stuff.

Helen Hay

TO DIANE

The ruddy poppies bend and bow,
Diane! do you remember?
The sun you knew shines proudly now,
The lake still lists the breeze's vow,
Your towers are fairer for their stains,
Each stone you smiled upon remains.
Sing low — where is Diane?
Diane! do you remember?

I come to find you through the years,
Diane! do you remember?
For none may rule my love's soft fears.
The ladies now are not your peers,
I seek you through your tarnished halls,
Pale sorrow on my spirit falls,
High, low — where is Diane?
Diane! do you remember?

I crush the poppies where I tread,
Diane! do you remember?
Your flower of life, so bright, so red —
She does not hear — Diane is dead.
I pace the sunny bowers alone
Where naught of her remains but stone.
Sing low — where is Diane?
Diane does not remember.

A WOMAN'S PRIDE

I WILL not look for him, I will not hear
My heart's loud beating, as I strain to see
Across the rain forlorn and hopelessly,
Nor, starting, think 't is he that draws so near.
I will forget how tenderly and dear
He might in coming hold his arms to me,
For I will prove what woman's pride can be
When faint love lingers in the darkness drear.
I will not — ah, but should he come to-night
I think my life might break through very bliss,
This little will should so be torn apart
That all my soul might fail in golden light
And let me die; so do I long for this.
Ah, love, thine eyes! — Nay, love — Thy heart, thy heart!

LOVE'S KISS

KISS me but once, and in that space supreme
My whole dark life shall quiver to an end,
Sweet Death shall see my heart and comprehend
That life is crowned, and in an endless gleam
Will fix the color of the dying stream,
That Life and Death may meet as friend with friend
An endless immortality to blend;
Kiss me but once, and so shall end my dream.
And then Love heard me and bestowed his kiss,
And straight I cried to Death: I will not die!
Earth is so fair when one remembers this;
Life is but just begun! Ah, come not yet!
The very world smiles up to kiss the sky,
And in the grave one may forget — forget.

WAS THERE ANOTHER SPRING

WAS there another Spring than this?
I half remember, through the haze
Of glimmering nights and golden days,
A broken-pinioned birdling's note,
An angry sky, a sea-wrecked boat,
A wandering through rain-beaten ways!
Lean closer, love — I have thy kiss!
Was there another Spring than this?

DOES THE PEARL KNOW?

DOES the pearl know, that in its shade and sheen,
The dreamy rose and tender wavering green,
Are hid the hearts of all the ranging seas,
That Beauty weeps for gifts as fair as these?
Does it desire aught else when its rare blush
Reflects Aurora in the morning's hush,
Encircling all perfection can bestow,
Does the pearl know?

Does the bird know, when, through the waking dawn,
He soaring sees below the silvered lawn,
And weary men who wait to watch the day
Steal o'er the heights where he may wheel and stray?
Can he conceive his fee divine to share,
As a free, joyous peer with sun and air,
And pity the sad things that creep below,
Does the bird know?

Does the heart know, when, filled to utter brim,
The least quick throb, a sacrificial hymn
To a great god who scorns the frown of Jove,
That here it finds the awful power of love?
Think you the new-born babe in first wise sleep
Fathoms the gift the heavens have bade him keep?
Yet if this be — if all these things are so —
Does the heart know?

SIGH NOT FOR LOVE

SIGH not for love, — the ways of love are dark!
Sweet Child, hold up the hollow of your hand

And catch the sparks that flutter from the stars!
See how the late sky spreads in flushing bars!
They are dead roses from your own dear land,
Tossed high by kindly breezes; lean, and hark,
And you shall know how Morning glads her lark!

The timid Dawn, herself a little child,
Casts up shy eyes in loving worship, dear,
Is it not yet enough? The Spring is here,
And would you weep for winter's tempest wild?
Sigh not for love, — the ways of love are dark!

George Sidney Hellman[1]

COLERIDGE

THINE is the mystic melody,
The far-off murmur of some dreamland sea
Lifting throughout the night,
Up to the moon's mild light,
Waves silver-lustrous, silvery-white,
That beat in rhythm on the shadowy shore,
And burst in music, and are seen no more.

THE HUDSON

WHERE in its old historic splendor stands
The home of England's far-famed Parliament,
And waters of the Thames in calm content
At England's fame flow slowly o'er their sands;
And where the Rhine past vine-entwinèd lands
Courses in castled beauty, there I went;
And far to Southern rivers, flower-besprent;
And to the icy streams of Northern strands.
Then mine own native shores I trod once more,
And, gazing on thy waters' majesty,
The memory, O Hudson, came to me
Of one who went to seek the wide world o'er
For Love, but found it not. Then home turned he
And saw his mother waiting at the door.

Beatrix Demarest Lloyd

LOVE AND TIME

ACROSS the gardens of Life they go,
A strange, ill-mated pair;
By paths where naught but blossoms blow,
By paths neglected where gaunt weeds grow,
But hand in hand, through joy, through care,
Across the gardens of Life they go.

The one is old, and grim, and gray:
His eyes stare off, like one in dreams;
Across his breast his white locks stray;
The sands in his glass fall day by day;
Over his shoulder his scythe-blade gleams, —
And he is old, and grim, and gray.

And one is young, and bright, and fair:
The golden curls about his head
Shine as a halo; his red lips dare
The birds in song; he knows no care,
Joy in his heart is never dead, —
He lives to love and he is fair.

Hoar-headed Time was never young,
And Love on earth cannot grow old;
And yet, since first to that hand he clung —
Since first his tender song he sung,
Since first his love-tale had he told,
And to a dart his bow had strung —

Together, through ways of joy, of woe,
Though one is old and one is fair,
By paths where naught but blossoms blow,
By paths neglected where gaunt weeds grow,
Together, a strange, ill-mated pair,
Across the gardens of Life they go.

[1] See, also, p. 768.

WITH ROSES

In each green leaf a memory let lie:
The pain that follows on the heels of bliss
In every thorn; each waft of incense be a sigh
For love: each petal of each rose a kiss!

NIGHT-WIND

Like some great pearl from out the Orient,
Upheld by unseen hands, — in its rich weight
An offering to adorn a queen's proud state
That some dependent princeling did present, —
The moon slow rises into night's dark tent.
The pulseless air, with longings vague befreight,
Now quickens 'neath her gaze, now doth inflate
The still-poised midnight clouds in heaven pent.
With jealous haste he draws them o'er her face,
And by his right forbids all other eyes
To note her beauty and to praise her grace;
Then up on lover's wings to her he flies
Impatient for the joy of her embrace;
And to the earth are wafted down his sighs.

Additional Selections

(FROM THE BALLADRY, LYRICS, SONNETS, AND LIGHTER VERSE OF THE FINAL DECADE)

I

THE FLAG GOES BY

Hats off!
Along the street there comes
A blare of bugles, a ruffle of drums,
A flash of color beneath the sky:
Hats off!
The flag is passing by!

Blue and crimson and white it shines,
Over the steel-tipped, ordered lines.
Hats off!
The colors before us fly;
But more than the flag is passing by.

Sea-fights and land-fights, grim and great,
Fought to make and to save the State:
Weary marches and sinking ships;
Cheers of victory on dying lips;

Days of plenty and years of peace;
March of a strong land's swift increase;
Equal justice, right and law,
Stately honor and reverend awe;

Sign of a nation, great and strong
To ward her people from foreign wrong:
Pride and glory and honor, — all
Live in the colors to stand or fall.

Hats off!
Along the street there comes
A blare of bugles, a ruffle of drums;
And loyal hearts are beating high:
Hats off!
The flag is passing by!

Henry Holcomb Bennett

THE COASTERS

Overloaded, undermanned,
Trusting to a lee,
Playing I-spy with the land,
Jockeying the sea —
That 's the way the Coaster goes,
Through calm and hurricane:
Everywhere the tide flows,
Everywhere the wind blows,
From Mexico to Maine.

O East and West! O North and South!
We ply along the shore,
From famous Fundy's foggy mouth,
From voes of Labrador;
Through pass and strait, on sound and sea,
From port to port we stand —
The rocks of Race fade on our lee,
We hail the Rio Grande.

Our sails are never lost to sight;
  On every gulf and bay
They gleam, in winter wind-cloud white,
  In summer rain-cloud gray.

We hold the coast with slippery grip;
  We dare from cape to cape:
Our leaden fingers feel the dip
  And trace the channel's shape.
We sail or bide as serves the tide;
  Inshore we cheat its flow,
And side by side at anchor ride
  When stormy head-winds blow.
We are the offspring of the shoal,
  The hucksters of the sea;
From customs theft and pilot toll
  Thank God that we are free.

Legging on and off the beach,
  Drifting up the strait,
Fluking down the river reach,
  Towing through the gate —
That 's the way the Coaster goes,
  Flirting with the gale:
Everywhere the tide flows,
Everywhere the wind blows,
  From York to Beavertail.

Here and there to get a load,
  Freighting anything ;
Running off with spanker stowed,
  Loafing wing-a-wing —
That 's the way the Coaster goes,
  Chumming with the land :
Everywhere the tide flows,
Everywhere the wind blows,
  From Ray to Rio Grande.

We split the swell where rings the bell
  On many a shallow's edge,
We take our flight past many a light
  That guards the deadly ledge;
We greet Montauk across the foam,
  We work the Vineyard Sound,
The Diamond sees us running home,
  The Georges outward bound;
Absecom hears our canvas beat
  When tacked off Brigantine;
We raise the Gulls with lifted sheet,
  Pass wing-and-wing between.

Off Monomoy we fight the gale,
  We drift off Sandy Key;
The watch of Fenwick sees our sail
  Scud for Henlopen's lee.
With decks awash and canvas torn
  We wallow up the Stream;
We drag dismasted, cargo borne,
  And fright the ships of steam.
Death grips us with his frosty hands
  In calm and hurricane;
We spill our bones on fifty sands
  From Mexico to Maine.

Cargo reef in main and fore,
  Manned by half a crew,
Romping up the weather shore,
  Edging down the Blue —
That 's the way the Coaster goes,
  Scouting with the lead :
Everywhere the tide flows,
Everywhere the wind blows,
  From Cruz to Quoddy Head.

THOMAS FLEMING DAY

OF THE LOST SHIP

WHAT has become of the good ship Kite?
  Where is her hull of chosen oak?
Who were the Victors, what the Fight?
  The old Wives — whom did they invoke,
That should tell them so uncannily:

"*Fell through a crack in the Floor of the Sea*"?

"Trafficked with death in a cruise foredone,"
  The Preachers drone to the Salem Folk,
When the Sea has swallowed up the Sun
  And the white gulls glint — was it they who spoke?
Wes'-Sou'-West from the Devil's Quay:

"*Fell through a crack in the Floor of the Sea*"?

Of the old-time Band there 's not a man
  Who has ever told how the ship went down.
Were they marked by God with the fearsome ban?
  Butchered they priests in a sun-white town?
Do they harry Hell where they may be:

"*Fell through a crack in the Floor of the Sea*"?

Though ye searched the West to the guttering sun,
  Or the East till the baffled lights burn black,
Or North to the bergs till the South be won,
  The changeling shadows answer back,
And their trembling lips pale piteously:

"*Fell through a crack in the Floor of the Sea*"?

And when the great grim Finger becks
  The whining Seas from their ancient bed,
Shall some tongue speak from the world-old wrecks
  To read the log of the Thwarted Dead?
Is there never an end on the mystery:

"*Fell through a crack in the Floor of the Sea*"?

EUGENE RICHARD WHITE

CAMILLA

Now Camilla's fair fingers are plucking in rapture the pulsating strings,
And her far-away eyes are intent on the scene and the story she sings —
Singing her song of Felipe, her hero intrepid and true;
Singing his praise, and recounting what deeds for her love he would do.

See the wild race after cattle, the broncho's wide nostrils blood red;
Hear the hello of the herder, Felipe, who dashes ahead!
Hist, how the lariat sings as it flies o'er the horns of a steer!
See the wild plunge, and the horse standing firm — hear the bellow of fear!

Then on the trail of Apaches, who leads the long marches by night?
Who but Felipe would dare to press on o'er the mesa to fight?
Who but Felipe sits firm in his saddle when rifles ring out in the dark?
Coolly he levels his weapon, the bullet flies true to its mark.

Such is the song sweet Camilla is singing with gaze far-away —
Such is the song, for she knows not how long her Felipe will stay —
Knows not that lone in the waste of the sage-brush her master lies, slain —
Ah, sweet Camilla, thy songs for Felipe, the fearless, are vain!

CHARLES AUGUSTUS KEELER

THE SONG OF THE SONS OF ESAU

YE smooth-faced sons of Jacob, hug close your ingleside;
Guard well the market in its wealth, the palace in its pride!
  Oh, blithe it is to wander, and the world is wide!

Hard straining at their cables, the captive vessels ride:
Haul up the prisoning anchor, swing out upon the tide!
  Oh, grandly fills the canvas, and the sea is wide!

Mysterious spreads the forest, where strange, shy creatures bide:
Within its dim remoteness, who knows what wonders hide?
  Oh, softly step the wild things, and the jungle's wide!

Across the stretching desert the tireless camels stride,
The scorching sun above them, the scorching sands beside.
  Oh, steady swing the camels, and the plain is wide!

Through leagues on leagues of ice-fields, the time-old glaciers slide
Across the drifted valley, from drifted mountain-side.
  Oh, keenly stings the Northwind, and the snow is wide!

It is our weird to wander, whatever fate betide;
We seek the vast far places, nor trail nor chart to guide.
  The restlessness is on us, and the world is wide!

O canny sons of Jacob, to fret and toiling tied,
We grudge you not the birthright for which your father lied!

We own the right of roaming, and the world is wide!

For you the pomp and power, prosperity and pride:
For us the happy wilderness, and not a care to chide.
To give us room to wander was the world made wide!

BERTHA BROOKS RUNKLE

II

THE UNBORN

THOU art my very own,
A part of me,
Bone of my bone
And flesh of my flesh.
And thou shalt be
Heart of my heart
And brain of brain —
In years that are to come to me and thee.

Before thou wast a being, made
Of spirit, as of flesh,
Thou didst sleep beneath the beats
Of my tumultuous heart, and drink,
With little aimless lips
And blind, unseeing eyes,
From every bursting vein
Replete with life's abundant flood.
Ay! even of my very breath,
And from my blood
Thou didst imbibe the fresh
And glorious air, that holds the sweets
Of nature's sure and slow eclipse;
That ceaseless round of life and death
Which are the close entwinëd braid
Of all the seasons' subtle mesh
And endless chain.

In a soft and silken chamber set apart —
Here, just beneath my happy heart, —
Thou didst lie at dreamy ease
While all my being paid
Its tribute unto thee.
What happy hours for thee and me!
As when a bird
Broods on its downy nest —
So would I sit
And watch the flit
Of idle shadows to and fro,
And brood upon my treasure hid
Within my willing flesh.
And when there stirred
A little limb — a tiny hand! —
What rapturous thrills of ecstasy
Shook all my being to its inmost citadel!
Ah! none but she who has borne
A child beneath her breast may know
What wondrous thrill and subtle spell
Comes from this wondrous woven band
That binds a mother to her unborn child
Within her womb.
As in the earth —
That fragrant tomb
Of all that lives, or man or beast —
Soft blossoms bud and bloom and swell,
So didst thou from my body gain
Sweet sustenance and royal feast.

Then through the gates of priceless pain
Thou camest to me — fair, so fair,
And so complete
From rose-tipped feet
To silken hair!
And there beneath each pearly lid,
There glowed a jewel — passing rare!
It moves and breathes! It slakes its thirst
At my all-abundant breast!
Oh, moment born of life — of love!
Oh, rapture of all earth's high, high above!
Three lives in one —
By loving won!
My own — and thine —
Oh, bond divine!
Our little child! Our little child!

JULIA NEELY FINCH

III

DEEP WATERS

DEATH could not come between us two:
What fear of death could be,
If thou, its shadow passing through,
But turned and looked at me?
Nor yet could pain the vision dim
With misty blur of tears;

The cup now clouded to the brim,
For him who drinketh, clears.

Deep waters could not quench the light,
The tender light that lies,
Like splendor of the Northern night,
In thy unquestioning eyes.
Though wide the wild, unfurrowed sea,
Though high the skylark sings,
My love should build a bridge to thee,
My heart should find its wings.

I could not miss thee in the throng,
Nor pass thy dwelling-place,
No noise of war could drown thy song,
Nor darkness veil thy face.
With thee to mount from earth to sky,
With thee in dust to sleep,
What height for love could be too high,
Or depth for love too deep?

VAN TASSEL SUTPHEN

MORITURA

I AM the mown grass, dying at your feet,
The pale grass, gasping faintly in the sun.
I shall be dead, long, long ere day is done,
That you may say: "The air, to-day, was sweet."
I am the mown grass, dying at your feet.

I am the white syringa, falling now,
When some one shakes the bough.
What matter if I lose my life's brief noon?
You laugh, "A snow in June!"
I am the white syringa, falling now.

I am the waning lamp that flickers on, —
Trying to give my old, unclouded light
Among the rest that make your garden bright.
Let me still burn till all my oil is gone.
I am the waning lamp that flickers on.

I am your singer, singing my last note.
Death's fingers clutch my throat.
New grass will grow, new flowers bloom and fall;
New lamps blaze out against your garden wall:
I am your singer, singing my last note.

MARGARET GILMAN (GEORGE) DAVIDSON

THE LONG NIGHT

WHO will watch thee, little mound,
When a few more years are done,
And I go with them to rest
In the silence that is best?
Grave of my belovëd one,
When that I mine own have found,
Who will watch thee, little mound?

Who will love thee, little grave?
Thou must be as others are.
Hearts low in the dust lie here,
Unloved, alone, unwept, and drear,
Forgotten as a fallen star.
Only from some dark sobbing wave
The clouds shall bring their tears to lave
Thy withered lilies, little grave.

Airs that hover over thee,
Little mound, are strangely sweet;
Strangely sweet the odors shed
By the blossoms round thy bed, —
Blossoms for a maiden meet;
But, alas! how will it be
When I lie at rest by thee?

After years that are a day
In the swiftness of their flight,
None among us will there be
Who will live remembering thee
And thy beauty. Into night
We who mourn must take our way
When the twilight cometh gray,
After years that are a day.

Silent cities of the dead
Grow as old as hearts of men;
Flowers sanctified, that bloom
In the sunshine on a tomb,
Have their little day, and then,
All their grace and glory fled,
They are dead amid the dead.

Ah, God! how miserably lost
The loveliest must be; for naught
After a little space there lives
(Save the poor words the grave-stone gives
To heedless eyes and careless thought)
Of pure and blest or passion-tost:
A few brief hours of bloom and frost,
And where are those who loved the lost?

Even our sorrows, seeming long,
Must pass, as grains of sand must fall
Beneath the infinite calm sea
Of ages and eternity.
We are faint shadows on a wall;
We look our last on love and wrong,
Then fade as doth a silenced song.

Harry Bache Smith[1]

WHITE ROSES[2]

There was a rose-tree grew so high
And white with all its seven roses,
It seemed a cloud 'twixt earth and sky.

There was one rose among the seven
That grew alone on topmost bough,
Like a white star caught down from heaven.

I plucked it that it should not be
Deflowered by rainy, wild west winds
In all its white virginity.

There was a little maiden dead
In a dark room in a lone place —
Two candles at her feet and head.

Her two hands crossed upon her breast,
Like frail rose petals, but more still —
Glad to be folded thus at rest.

Her pale lips smiling all the while,
In such a solemn, perfect peace,
Alas, as our lips never smile.

I gave my white rose to the dead —
It seemed less white than her young brow:
The others wept — "Alas!" they said.

I gave my white rose to the child,
Both plucked in their young purity,
And while the others wept I smiled.

Cora Fabbri

IV

STEVENSON'S BIRTHDAY

"How I should like a birthday!" said the child,
"I have so few, and they so far apart."
She spoke to Stevenson — the Master smiled —
"Mine is to-day; I would with all my heart
That it were yours; too many years have I!
Too swift they come, and all too swiftly fly."

So by a formal deed he there conveyed
All right and title in his natal day,
To have and hold, to sell or give away, —
Then signed, and gave it to the little maid.

Joyful, yet fearing to believe too much,
She took the deed, but scarcely dared unfold.
Ah, liberal Genius! at whose potent touch
All common things shine with transmuted gold!
A day of Stevenson's will prove to be
Not part of Time, but Immortality.

Katherine Miller

SONNETS

ON THE DEATH OF A METAPHYSICIAN

Unhappy dreamer, who outwinged in flight
The pleasant region of the things I love,
And soared beyond the sunshine, and above
The golden cornfields and the dear and bright
Warmth of the hearth, — blasphemer of delight,
Was your proud bosom not at peace with Jove,
That you sought, thankless for his guarded grove,
The empty horror of abysmal night?
Ah, the thin air is cold above the moon!
I stood and saw you fall, befooled in death,
As, in your numbëd spirit's fatal swoon,
You cried you were a god, or were to be;
I heard with feeble moan your boastful breath
Bubble from depths of the Icarian sea.

ON A PIECE OF TAPESTRY

Hold high the woof, dear friends, that we may see
The cunning mixture of its colors rare.

[1] See also, p. 679.

Nothing in nature purposely is fair, —
Her mingled beauties never quite agree;
But here all vivid dyes that garish be,
To that tint mellowed which the sense will bear,
Glow, and not wound the eye that, resting there,
Lingers to feed its gentle ecstasy.
Crimson and purple and all hues of wine,
Saffron and russet, brown and sober green
Are rich the shadowy depths of blue between;
While silver threads with golden intertwine,
To catch the glimmer of a fickle sheen, —
All the long labor of some captive queen.

GEORGE SANTAYANA

THE ARTIST

HE wrought with patience long and weary years
Upon his masterpiece, entitled "Fate,"
And dreamed sweet dreams, the while his crust he ate,
And gave his work his soul, his strength, and tears.
His task complete at last, he had no fears
The world would not pronounce his genius great,
But poor, unknown — pray, what could *he* create?
The mad world laughed, and gave not praise, but jeers.
Impelled to ask wherein his work was wrong,
He sought, despairing, one whose art was dead,
But on whose brow were wreathed the bays of Fame:
The master gazed upon the picture long;
"It lacks one thing to make it great," he said,
And signed the canvas with his own great name!

ARTHUR GRISSOM

THE MOUNTAIN TO THE PINE

THOU tall, majestic monarch of the wood,
That standeth where no wild vines dare to creep,
Men call thee old, and say that thou hast stood
A century upon my rugged steep;
Yet unto me thy life is but a day,
When I recall the things that I have seen, —
The forest monarchs that have passed away
Upon the spot where first I saw thy green;
For I am older than the age of man,
Or all the living things that crawl or creep,
Or birds of air, or creatures of the deep;
I was the first dim outline of God's plan:
Only the waters of the restless sea
And the infinite stars in heaven are old to me.

CLARENCE HAWKES

EXPERIENCE

I

LIKE Crusoe with the bootless gold we stand
Upon the desert verge of death, and say:
"What shall avail the woes of yesterday
To buy to-morrow's wisdom, in the land
Whose currency is strange unto our hand?
In life's small market they had served to pay
Some late-found rapture, could we but delay
Till Time hath matched our means to our demand."
But otherwise Fate wills it, for, behold,
Our gathered strength of individual pain,
When Time's long alchemy hath made it gold,
Dies with us — hoarded all these years in vain,
Since those that might be heir to it the mould
Renew, and coin themselves new griefs again.

II

O Death, we come full-handed to thy gate,
Rich with strange burden of the mingled years,
Gains and renunciations, mirth and tears,
And love's oblivion, and remembering hate,
Nor know we what compulsion laid such freight
Upon our souls — and shall our hopes and fears
Buy nothing of thee, Death? Behold our wares,

And sell us the one joy for which we wait.
Had we lived longer, life had such for sale,
With the last coin of sorrow purchased cheap,
But now we stand before thy shadowy pale,
And all our longings lie within thy keep —
Death, can it be the years shall naught avail?

"Not so," Death answered, "they shall purchase sleep."
EDITH WHARTON

V

INTAGLIOS

TENNESSEE

In Tennessee, the dogwood tree
Blossoms to-night: towards the sea
The Cumberland makes melody,
In Tennessee.

And Morgan mounts his steed once more;
In phantom file his troopers pour
Along; the stars hear once again
The song of Morgan and his men.

In Tennessee, the slave is free
To-night; but waking he can see
The raiders — hears them — tremblingly,
In Tennessee.

ON THE PLAINS

Circling on high, in cloudless sky,
The shadowed hawk with passioned eye
In widening orbits floats, a spy,
Circling on high.

He marks the gopher's clean-picked bones,
Whitening upon the hot dry stones
Of the dust-choked gulch, and strikes straightway,
In fancy strikes, the hastening prey.

But all is still — noon hath her will;
Not e'en a snake crawls on the hill;
Only the hawk moves, fain to kill,
Circling on high.

FRANCIS BROOKS

QUATRAINS

A DIAMOND

Look how it sparkles, see it greet
With laughing light the ambient air;
One little drop of sunshine sweet
Held in eternal bondage there.

SPRING

A whisper on the heath I hear,
And blossoms deck the waking wood;
Ah! surely now the virgin year
Is in her blushing maidenhood.

MARCH

Whither doth now this fellow flee
With outstretched arms at such mad pace?
Can the young rascal thinking be
To catch a glimpse of April's face?

APRIL

Maiden, thy cheeks with tears are wet,
And ruefully thine eyebrows arch;
Is 't as they say, thou thinkest yet
Of that inconstant madcap March?

A SUNSET

The Sun, departing, kissed the summer Sky,
Then bent an instant o'er her beating breast;
She lifts to him a timid, tear-stained eye,
And, lo! her blushes crimson all the west.

ROBERT LOVEMAN

VI

THE RECRUIT

Sez Corporal Madden to Private McFadden:
"Bedad, yer a bad 'un!
Now turn out yer toes!
Yer belt is unhookit,
Yer cap is on crookit,
Ye may not be dhrunk,
But, be jabers, ye look it!
Wan — two!
Wan — two!
Ye monkey-faced divil, I'll jolly ye through!
Wan — two! —
Time! Mark!
Ye march like the aigle in Cintheral Parrk!"

Sez Corporal Madden to Private McFadden:
"A saint it ud sadden
To dhrill such a mug!
Eyes front! — ye baboon, ye! —
Chin up! — ye gossoon, ye!
Ye 've jaws like a goat —
Halt! ye leather-lipped loon, ye!
Wan — two!
Wan — two!
Ye whiskered orang-outang, I'll fix you!
Wan — two! —
Time! Mark!
Ye 've eyes like a bat! — can ye see in the dark?"

Sez Corporal Madden to Private McFadden:
"Yer figger wants padd'n' —
Sure, man, ye 've no shape!
Behind ye yer shoulders
Stick out like two bowlders;
Yer shins is as thin
As a pair of pen-holders!
Wan — two!
Wan — two!
Yer belly belongs on yer back, ye Jew!
Wan — two! —
Time! Mark!
I'm dhry as a dog — I can't shpake but I bark!"

Sez Corporal Madden to Private McFadden:
"Me heart it ud gladden
To blacken yer eye.
Ye 're gettin' too bold, ye
Compel me to scold ye, —
'T is halt! that I say, —
Will ye heed what I told ye?
Wan — two!
Wan — two!
Be jabers, I 'm dhryer than Brian Boru!
Wan — two! —
Time! Mark!
What 's wur-ruk for chickens is sport for the lark!"

Sez Corporal Madden to Private McFadden:
"I 'll not stay a gadd'n
Wid dagoes like you!
I 'll travel no farther,
I 'm dyin' for — wather; —
Come on, if ye like, —
Can ye loan me a quather?
Ya-as, you,
What, — two?
And ye 'll pay the potheen? Ye 're a daisy! Whurroo!
You 'll do!
Whist! Mark!
The Rigiment 's flatthered to own ye, me spark!"

Robert William Chambers

THE LITTLE NIPPER AN' 'IS MA

"Yer know me little nipper,"
Said 'Enery 'Awkins, M. P.
"Well, 'e 's a little champion,
An' tikes on arfter me.
Larst Sunday me an' the missus
Went out fer a little walk —
I should say the nipper took us,
Yer should o' 'eard 'im tork!

"We went along through Tyburn,
An' then by 'Endon way,
W'ere I ust ter do me courtin'
In those sweet nights o' May.
We 'd been walkin' out an 'our,
W'en Sal she sez ter me,
''Ere, 'Arry, is yer gime, dear,
Fer shrimps an' a cup o' tea.'

"'Garn,' sez I ter Sally,
'I 'm in fer 'arf an 'arf.'
Lor lumme, yer should jist o' 'eard
My little Sally larf!
'O' course,' she sez, 'I likes me nip
O' gin an' glarss o' beer,
But did not like ter say it out
Before the nipper 'ere.'

"The nipper 'e war n't lookin'
As we neared the Brokers' Arms;
An' in we 'ops ter get a wet,
Not dreamin' any 'arm.
But the nipper 'e were cagy,
An' followed in the rear,
An' 'ears me give me order:
''Ere, miss, two pots o' beer.'

"An' w'en I gives me order,
I turns ter speak ter Sal,
Ter arsk if she remembered
The day she was me gal.
I felt some one a-tuggin'
An' pullin' at me back;
I looks around surprised-like,
An' sees that rascal Jack.

"Sez I, 'See 'ere, me nipper,
I wont 'ave yer 'angin' 'ere.'
Sez 'e, 'D' yer think I 'm goin'?
Not me. No bally fear.
Now, then, wot 'ave yer ordered?
Sez I, 'Two 'arf an' 'arf.'
Sez 'e, 'Ain't mother in it?'
An' yer should o' 'eard 'im larf."

GEORGE FAUVEL GOURAUD

VII

SOME RECENT COLLEGE VERSE

I

D'ARTAGNAN'S RIDE

FIFTY leagues, fifty leagues — and I ride, and I ride —
Fifty leagues as the black crow flies.
None of the three are by my side . . .
The bay horse reels, and the bay horse dies —
But I ride, and I ride
To Callice.

We were four, we were four — and I ride, and I ride —
We were four, but Porthos lies
God knows where by the highway side . . .
The roan horse reels, and the roan horse dies —
But I ride, and I ride
To Callice.

We were three, we were three — and I ride, and I ride —
We were three, but Aramis lies
Bludgeoned and bound and thrown aside . . .
The dun horse reels, and the dun horse dies —
But I ride, and I ride
To Callice.

We were two, we were two — and I ride, and I ride —
We were two, but Athos lies
With a lead-crushed rib and a steel-torn side . . .
The black horse reels, and the black horse dies —
But I ride, and I ride
To Callice.

All alone, all alone — and I ride, and I ride —
All alone, and an ambush lies
God knows where by the highway side . . .
The gray horse reels, and the gray horse dies —
But I ride, and I ride
To Callice,
Yes — I ride and I ride and I ride and I ride
And I ride and I ride
To Callice.

GOUVERNEUR MORRIS

II

TO A MOTH

CRUSHED WITHIN THE LEAVES OF AN ILIAD

POOR Creature! nay, I 'll not say poor,
Why, surely, thou art wondrous blest;
Right royal is this sepulchre
Fate gave thee for thy last long rest.

See here — 't is but two lines above
The spot that marks thy early tomb —
Here Paris breathes his burning love
To her who compassed Ilia's doom.

And here, upon a neighboring page,
The great Achilles moans his friend,
All careless, in his kingly rage,
Of bane or curse the gods may send.

Above, below thee, everywhere,
Fierce Trojan strives with wily Greek;
And mighty lords, with tawny hair,
Deep words of war and wisdom speak.

The high gods gaze upon thee here,
Great warriors guard thy resting-place —
Perchance thou see'st a burning tear
Steal down Briseis' home-turned face.

Ay! rest content, for thou hast won
A tomb that kings might wish in vain;
About thee shines the all-seeing sun,
And roars the many-sounding main.

CHARLES EDWARD THOMAS

METHINKS THE MEASURE

METHINKS the measure of a man is not
To save a state in midst of fierce alarms,
Do noble deeds and mighty feats of arms,
And feel the breath of battle waxing hot.
There have been Cæsars whose more humble lot
Forbade that they should bear the victor's palms;
Cromwells who never left their peaceful farms;
Napoleons without ambition's blot.
Not in the deed that 's done before the eyes
Of wonder-stricken lands upturned to view,
But in the will, though no occasion rise,
And sleeping still, that dares such deeds to do,
Is drawn the line which parts him from the clods
And gives a man a kinship with the gods.

PERCY ADAMS HUTCHISON

HELIOS

OH, I am weary of a heart that brings
Star-worship even to the shining sun:
Rather a savage whose whole heart hath won
Radiance and joy from sunlight than whose wings
Flutter and fade before the twilight rings:
Why should we falter when the night is done, —
Dream-weavers, trembling in dim mists that stun
All things divorced from thought, and thought from things?
I am thy child, O Sun, as Julian was:
I crouch not in the shadows of my soul,
And grapple with dark terrors; nor, rewon,
Drink I of darkness when the shadows pass:
Even at death, when nearest is the goal,
I shall cry out to heaven, "The sun! the sun!"

JOEL ELIAS SPINGARN

DARKNESS

OFT have I stood upon the foaming strand
Watching the moonlight tremble on the sea;
Oft have I seen the stars fade silently
When gleaming dawn drove night across the land;
Oft have I watched the storm lift o'er the sand
The ocean in his might and majesty;
Now are these joys a mockery to me
Since on mine eyes, God, Thou hast laid Thine Hand.
Have I too much exulted in the light,
Forgetting Thee from whom these glories rise,
That Thou hast struck me with this darkling blight,
Robbed me of day and of the sunny skies,
Transforming them into continuous night, —
Is it for this that Thou hast shut mine eyes?

JAMES NAUMBERG ROSENBERG

WHITHER

AGNES, thou child of harmony, now fled
From scenes once bright-illumined with thy smile,
So innocent and kind, free from the guile
Of Orient charm, mysterious and dread, —
Where shall I seek thee, maid? Thou art not dead.
No, Nature's heart would break, count all else vile,
Bereft of thee e'en for a little while.

Where art thou, then? Hast to the violet sped
That with its gentle blue bespeaks thine eye?
To rippling stream, the echo of thy voice?
To wooing wind that, kissing, says 'Rejoice!'
Or to the rosebush with its fainting sigh,
'Ah! too lovely for a season long!' —
Or, art thou on fair angel lips a song?

PHILIP BECKER GOETZ

ATTAINMENT

THROUGH my open window comes the sweet perfuming
Of roses reddening under skies of June;
No sight more fair than roses in red bloom,
No air more sweet than doth the rose perfume;
And yet was never there a rose but died in blooming.

ALGERNON TASSIN

GOD'S WILL

I KNOW, I know where violets blow
Upon a sweet hillside,
And very bashfully they grow
And in the grasses hide —
It is the fairest field, I trow,
In the whole world wide.

One spring I saw two lassies go,
Brown cheek and laughing eye;
They swung their aprons to and fro,
They filled them very high
With violets — then whispered low
So strange, I wondered why.

I know where violet tendrils creep
And crumbled tombstones lie,
The green churchyard is silence-deep;
The village folk go by,
And lassies laugh and women weep,
And God knows why.

ROBERT LOUIS MUNGER

III

CAMEOS

I

A VALENTINE

THE wise forget, dear heart;
They leave the past
And play the hero's part,
Brave to the last.

They weep not nor regret,
Calm are their eyes.
Dear heart, the wise forget. —
I am not wise!

2

FORGIVEN?

I SAW Love stand,
Not as he was ere we in conflict met,
But pale and wan. I knelt — I caught his hand —
"O Love," I cried, "I did not understand!
Forgive — forget!"

Love raised his head
And smiled at me, with weary eyes and worn.
"I have forgot — what was it all?" he said;
"Only — my hands are scarred where they have bled;
My wings are torn."

JEANNETTE BLISS GILLESPY

THE SONG

A SONG lay silent in my pen
Where yesterday I found it,
Right cozy in its gloomy den,
With a melody wrapped round it.
Through all the years 't was waiting so,
To hear the summons of that minute;
I thought I loved the pen; but no!
It was the song within it!

To-day my lady sang to me
My song in sweetest fashion:
Unwrapped it from the melody
In the radiance of its passion.
As one might see a blossom grow,
Yet never see the sun above it,
I thought I loved the song; but no!
It was her singing of it!

JOHN ERSKINE

IV

ALPHEUS AND ARETHUSA

(NEW DORIC)

A NYMPH there was in Arcadie
Who owned a crystal spring;

And there she 'd wash, sans mackintosh,
B'gosh, or anything.

A youth there was in Arcadie
Who hunted o'er the brooks;
He would not tote an overcoat,
But travelled on his looks.

Though ancient Greece had no police,
The gods did as they 'd oughter;
To put them quite from mortal sight
They turned them into water!

EUGENE HOWELL DALY

ON A MAGAZINE SONNET

"SCORN not the sonnet," though its strength be sapped,
Nor say malignant its inventor blundered;
The corpse that here in fourteen lines is wrapped
Had otherwise been covered with a hundred.

RUSSELL HILLARD LOINES

A CREW POEM

So happy were Columbia's eight,
As near the goal they drew,
Each struggling hero all elate,
The cock-swain almost crew.

EDWARD AUGUSTUS BLOUNT, JR.

IN A CHINA SHOP

A DRESDEN shepherdess was one day
Milking a small Delft cow,
When a Sevres Marquis came along —
I saw him smile and bow:
"O lovely shepherdess, hear my song,"
I think I heard him say,
"For thou hast captured my porcelain heart,
And by my sword I swear thou art
A star in the Milky Way."

GEORGE SIDNEY HELLMAN[1]

CLASSICAL CRITICISM

21 B. C.

OLD Horace on a summer afternoon,
Well primed with sweet Falernian, let us say,
Lulled by the far-off brooklet's drowsy croon
To a half-doze in a haphazard way,
Scratched off a half a dozen careless rhymes,
As was his habit. When next day he came
Awake to work, he read them several times,
In vain attempt to catch their sense and aim.
"What was I thinking of? Blest if I know,
Jupiter! What's the difference? Let them go!"

1886 A. D.

"LINES twelve to twenty are in great dispute,"
(Most learnedly the lecturer doth speak,)
"I think I shall be able to refute
Orelli's claim they 're taken from the Greek.
I think, with Bentley, Horace's purpose here
Is irony, and yet I do not know
But Dillenberger's reading is more clear,
For which he gives eight arguments, although
Wilkins gives twelve objections to the same" —
So on (*ad infinitum*). Such is fame!

GEORGE LYNDE RICHARDSON

FOR SALE, A HORSE

IN good condition,
Cheap, on account of competition,
Well-broken, easy on his bridle,
With curb or snaffle never idle.
A very little child can ride him,
And carry three or four beside him.
Why plod when you can ride so cheaply?
There is no need to ponder deeply.
I'll warrant he 'll not bite nor kick you;
I 've not the slightest wish to stick you!
However short you are, you 're suited,
For low-stand men can mount when booted.
Come, buy my steed with manner gracious.
He 'll aid your reading of Horatius.

CHARLES EDWARD TAYLOR

[1] See, also, p. 755.

PERSICOS ODI

Boy, I detest these modern innovations,
The *Voice* crusade may alter some men's habit,
But, as for me, I 'll stick to my old rations,
Ale and a rarebit.

In vino vis. The pious dames of Ipswich,
Knowing its worth and fearing lest men waste it,
Condemn its use in christening battle-ships which
Can't even taste it.

Old Cato Major (and, no doubt, his wife, too)
Found in Falernian, mixed with milder Massic,
Courage which led him, at his time of life, to
Read the Greek classic.

Yes, Cato drank, nor should we lightly damn a
Man who, at eighty and without coercion,
Mastered Liddell and Scott, and Hadley's grammar,
My pet aversion.

Elihu's ways, they say, are growing sinful;
Crimes that are nameless are committed daily.
Oscar! my toby, and I 'll sin a skinful,
So to bed gayly.

Charles Edmund Merrill, Jr

VIII

MISS NANCY'S GOWN

In days when George the Third was King
And ruled the Old Dominion,
And Law and Fashion owned the sway
Of Parliament's opinion,
A good ship brought across the sea
A treasure fair and fine, —
Miss Nancy's gown from London town,
The latest Court design!

The plaited waist from neck to belt
Scarce measured half a span;
The sleeves, balloon-like, at the top
Could hold her feather fan;
The narrow skirt with bias gore
Revealed an ankle neat,
Whene'er she put her dainty foot
From carriage step to street!

By skilful hands this wondrous gown
Of costliest stuff was made,
Cocoons of France on Antwerp looms
Wrought to embossed brocade,
Where roses red and violets
In blooming beauty grew,
As if young May were there alway,
And June and April too!

And from this bower of delight
Miss Nancy reigned a Queen,
Nor one disloyal heart rebelled
In all her wide demesne:
The noble House of Burgesses
Forgot its fierce debate
O'er rights of Crown, when Nancy's gown
Appeared in Halls of State!

Through jocund reel, or measured tread
Of stately minuet,
Like fairy vision shone the bloom
Of rose and violet,
As, hand in hand with Washington,
The hero of the day,
The smiling face and nymph-like grace
Of Nancy led the way!

A century, since that gay time
The merry dance was trod,
Has passed, and Nancy long has slept
Beneath the churchyard sod;
Yet on the brocade velvet gown
The rose and violet
Are blooming bright as on the night
She danced the minuet!

Zitella Cocke

THE JOURNEY

Reluctantly I laid aside my smiles,
Those little, pleasing knickknacks of the face,
And dropped the words accustomed to my tongue,
And took just half a breath in breathing's space;

And then I drew the curtains of my eyes
And ceased to move, and rallied all my thought,
Selecting all the verity that lies
Through daily life, with false pretences fraught;
I sorted and arranged and packed my hope
And my despair together, in my heart;
I tied the strings and sealed the envelope
In which ambition, stifled, used to smart;
Took out my conscience — long since laid away —
And shook it, folded it, with thoughts like tears;
Revised my errors, sorted out the years
When doubt and egotism held their sway;
All this I did the night I heard them say
Beside the pillow, "She will die at dawn" —
And then they wept and called me by my name:
I would have liked to soothe them, but in vain —
I had so very little time to stay,
And so much packing to be done before
I put my fires out and closed my door
To catch the stage-coach which would pass that way
At dawn, and bear me down eternity.
I hurried — and grew weary and turned weak —
The time drew near, — oh, how I longed to speak
And tell them I was sorry to have been
So great a trouble; then a distant din,
A muffled rumble, and the coach drew near;
One weary moment, it will soon be here!
I sighed, and sank and dreamed myself away,
And then "Thank God, thank God!" I heard them say,
While with a pang, half wonderment, half pain,
I woke — and found the coach had missed the train!

MARY BERRI (CHAPMAN) HANSBROUGH

IX

LITTLE THEOCRITUS

YE white Sicilian goats, who wander all
About the slopes of this wild mountain pass,
Take heed your horny footsteps do not fall
Upon the baby dreamer in the grass.

Let him lie there, half waking, and rejoice
In the safe shelter of his resting-place,
In hearing of his shepherd father's voice,
In reach of fruity clusters o'er his face.

Look up, sweet baby eyes, look up on high,
To where Olympus merges in the blue.
There dwell the deathless gods in majesty,
The gods who hold a mighty gift for you.

Those little, clinging hands shall write one day,
Rare, golden words, to lift the hearts of men;
Those curling, downy locks shall wear the bay,
A crown that they shall never lose again.

Little Theocritus! Look up and smile,
Immortal child, for there are coming years,
When the great, busy world shall pause awhile
To listen to your singing through its tears.

CAROLINE WILDER (FELLOWES) PARADISE

NOW IS THE CHERRY IN BLOSSOM [1]

Now is the cherry in blossom, Love,
Love of my heart, with the apple to follow;
Over the village at nightfall now
Merrily veers and darts the swallow.

At nightfall now in the dark marsh grass
Awakes the chorus that sings old sorrow;
The evening star is dim for the dew,
And the apple and lilac will bloom to-morrow.

The honeysuckle is red on the rock;
The willow floats over the brook like a feather;
In every shadow some love lies hid,
And you and I in the world together.

MARY ELEANOR WILKINS

[1] Copyright, 1890, by HARPER & BROTHERS.

HEY NONNY NO

There is a race from eld descent,
Of heaven by earth in joyous mood,
Before the world grew wise and bent
In sad, decadent attitude.
To these each waking is a birth
That makes them heir to all the earth,
Singing, for pure abandoned mirth,
Non nonny non, hey nonny no.

Perchance ye meet them in the mart,
In fashion's toil or folly's throe,
And yet their souls are far apart
Where primrose winds from uplands blow.
At heart on oaten pipes they play
Thro' meadows green and gold with May,
Affined to bird and brook and brae.
Sing nonny non, hey nonny no.

Their gage they win in fame's despite,
While lyric alms to life they fling, —
Children of laughter, sons of light,
With equal heart to starve or sing.
Counting no human creature vile,
They find the good old world worth while;
Care cannot rob them of a smile.
Sing nonny non, hey nonny no.

For creed, the up-reach of a spire,
An arching elm-tree's leafy spread,
A song that lifts the spirit higher
To star or sunshine overhead.
Misfortune they but deem God's jest
To prove His children at their best,
Who, dauntless, rise to His attest.
Sing nonny non, hey nonny no.

Successful ones will brush these by,
Calling them failure as they pass.
What reck they this who claim the sky
For roof, for bed the cosmic grass!
When, failures all, we come to lie,
The grass betwixt us and the sky,
The gift of gladness will not die!
Sing nonny non, hey nonny no.

Marguerite Merington

GOLD-OF-OPHIR ROSES

CALIFORNIA

1

O flower of passion, rocked by balmy gales,
Flushed with life's ecstasy,
Before whose golden glow the poppy pales
And yields her sovereignty!

Child of the ardent south, thy burning heart
Has felt the sun's hot kiss.
Thy creamy petals falling half apart
Quiver with recent bliss.

For joy at thy unequalled loveliness,
He woos with fierce delight;
And thy glad soul, half faint with his caress,
Yet glories in his might.

Thy sighs go out in perfume on the air,
Rich incense of thy love,
And mystic lights, an opalescence rare,
Play round thee from above.

2

So thou dost riot through the glad spring days,
Sun-wooed and revelling in eager life,
Till all the shadowed fragrance of the ways
With thy rich bloom and glowing tints is rife.

A joyous smile that hides a secret tear,
A note of music with a minor strain,
A heart of gold where crimson wounds appear,
Thou breathest all love's sweetness and its pain.

Yet suddenly, even at thy loveliest,
Thou palest with thine own intensity.
Ah, Passion's child, thou art most truly blest,
To bloom one perfect day, and then to die.

Grace Atherton Dennen

I KNOW NOT WHY

I LIFT mine eyes against the sky,
The clouds are weeping, so am I;
I lift mine eyes again on high,
The sun is smiling, so am I.
Why do I smile? Why do I weep?
I do not know; it lies too deep.

I hear the winds of autumn sigh,
They break my heart, they make me cry;
I hear the birds of lovely spring,
My hopes revive, I help them sing.
Why do I sing? Why do I cry?
It lies so deep, I know not why.

MORRIS ROSENFELD

GENTIAN

So all day long I followed through the fields
The voice of Autumn, calling from afar;
And now I thought: "Yon hazel thicket yields
A glimpse of her," and now: "These asters are
Sure sign that she of late has passed this way;
Lo! here the traces of her yellow car."

And once I looked and seemed to see her stand
Beneath a golden maple's black-drawn boughs;
But when I reached the place, naught but a band
Of crickets did perform their tuneful vows
To the soon fading grass, and through the leaves
The quiet sunlight, falling, blessed my brows.

Till, as the long rays lengthened from the west,
I came upon an altar of gray stone,
O'er which a creeper flung with pious zest
Her flickering flames. About that altar lone,
The crowding sumac burned with steady fire;
Before it, stately, stood a priestess; one

Who turned to me her melancholy eyes.
I saw her beauty, ripe with color's breath,
Yet veiled, as when on wood and hill there lies
A mist, a shadow, as of coming death.
And while I gazed she faded; swift I clutched
Her fringed cloak, which rent, my grasp beneath.

And she was gone. As fluttered to the ground
Its many fragments, I, with sudden fears,
Stooped, vainly seeking them, when all around
The blue fringed gentian smiled up through my tears,
As one who knows his welcome will be warm,
Although sad news to his beloved he bears.

ELIZABETH GREEN CRANE

DRYAD SONG

I AM immortal! I know it! I feel it!
Hope floods my heart with delight!
Running on air, mad with life, dizzy, reeling,
Upward I mount, — faith is sight, life is feeling,
Hope is the day-star of might!

It was thy kiss, Love, that made me immortal, —
"'Kiss,' Love? Our lips have not met!"
Ah, but I felt thy soul through night's portal
Swoon on my lips at night's sweet, silent portal,
Wild and as sweet as regret.

Come, let us mount on the wings of the morning,
Flying for joy of the flight,
Wild with all longing, now soaring, now staying,
Mingling like day and dawn, swinging and swaying,
Hung like a cloud in the light:
I am immortal! I feel it! I feel it!
Love bears me up, love is might!

Chance cannot touch me! Time cannot hush me!
Fear, Hope, and Longing, at strife,
Sink as I rise, on, on, upward forever,

Gathering strength, gaining breath, — naught can sever
Me from the Spirit of Life!

MARGARET FULLER

SING AGAIN

YOU sang me a song:
'T was the close of the year —
Sing again!
I cannot remember the name
Or the words:
'T is the same
We listen to hear
When the windows are open in spring,
And the air 's full of birds;
One calls from the branch some sweet thing,
And one sings on the wing
The refrain.

You sang me a song
My heart thrilled to hear.
The refrain
Has run like a fillet of gold
Through the woof
Of the cold
Dark days of a year.
To-night there 's a year at its start,
All the birds are aloof,
Your eyes hold the sun for my part,
And the Spring 's in your heart —
Sing again!

MARIE VAN VORST

THE PARTING OF THE WAYS[1]

UNTRAMMELLED Giant of the West,
With all of Nature's gifts endowed,
With all of Heaven's mercies blessed,
Nor of thy power unduly proud —
Peerless in courage, force, and skill,
And godlike in thy strength of will, —

Before thy feet the ways divide:
One path leads up to heights sublime;
Downward the other slopes, where bide
The refuse and the wrecks of Time.
Choose then, nor falter at the start,
O choose the nobler path and part!

Be thou the guardian of the weak,
Of the unfriended, thou the friend;
No guerdon for thy valor seek,
No end beyond the avowëd end.
Wouldst thou thy godlike power preserve,
Be godlike in the will to serve!

JOSEPH B. GILDER

BIOGRAPHICAL NOTES

BIOGRAPHICAL NOTES

These Notes are restricted, usually, to succinct biographical data concerning the poets quoted in this volume, with mention of their leading works. In some cases, chiefly those of the most recent poets, brief comments are added. The reader will find in "Poets of America" — the book, by the present editor, to which "An American Anthology" is adapted — a critical review of those among the following authors who became known earlier than the last decade of the Nineteenth Century.

Where records of birth, death, etc., differ from those previously accepted, the editor now has good authority for the statements made. He also has endeavored to present correctly the names and dates of publications, as far as given.[1]

ABBEY, Henry, b. Rondout, N. Y., 1842. For some years a journalist in New York City, but after 1864 a merchant in his native town, and now residing at Kingston, N. Y. He has issued "May Dreams," 1862; "Ballads of Good Deeds," 1872; "The City of Success," 1883; complete "Poems," 1886, 2d edition, 1895.

ADAMS, John Quincy, b. Braintree, Mass., 1767; d. Washington, D. C., 1848. Sixth President of the United States. A volume of his quaint, old-fashioned verse, "Poems," appeared in 1848.

ADAMS, Mary (Mathews) (Barnes), b. Brooklyn, N. Y., 18—. Educated at Packer Institute, and became the wife of Alfred S. Barnes, the publisher. Some years after his death married to Charles Kendall Adams, president of the University of Wisconsin. Her volume of poems, "The Choir Visible," was published in 1897. (D. Redlands, Cal., 1902.)

ADAMS, Oscar Fay, b. Worcester, Mass., 18—. A lecturer to classes upon English literature and history and Gothic architecture. His standard "Dictionary of American Authors" was first published in 1884. It has been revised and much enlarged in recent editions. Among his other works are "Post-Laureate Idyls," 1886, and "The Archbishop's Unguarded Moment, and Other Stories," 1899.

ALBEE, John, b. Bellingham, Mass., 1833. Studied divinity at Harvard, but has been devoted to philosophy, nature study, literary and linguistic research. While pursuing these, he has otherwise divided his life between foreign travel and tillage of his ocean farm at New Castle, N. H., and his mountain farm near Chocorua in the same state. A lecturer before the Concord School of Philosophy and elsewhere. Author of "Literary Art," 1881; "Poems," 1883; "New Castle, Historic and Picturesque," 1884; "Prose Idyls," 1892.

ALCOTT, Amos Bronson, philosopher, b. Wolcott, Conn., 1799; d. Boston, Mass., 1888. His early life was spent in teaching young children in his native State, and afterwards in Boston, where he went to reside in 1828. His ideas being denounced as too advanced, he gave up his school and interested himself in the study of philosophy, at Concord, Mass., and in the upbuilding of various reforms. In 1848, after visiting England, he, with some English friends, made an unsuccessful attempt to establish a new community on a farm called "Fruitlands," near Harvard. He then began to instruct by means of more or less formal "conversations," held wherever there might be a demand for them. The friend and colleague of Emerson, and dean of the Concord School of Philosophy, and for many years the hierarch of our transcendental group of poets and illuminati. Contributed to "The Dial," 1839–42, and other periodicals. Published "Conversations with Children on the Gospels," 1836; "Tablets," 1868; "Concord Days," 1872; "Table Talk," 1877; "New Connecticut," 1881; "Sonnets and Canzonets," 1882. The last two volumes were edited by F. B. Sanborn.

ALCOTT, Louisa May, daughter of A. B. Alcott, b. Germantown, Penn., 1832; d. Boston, Mass., 1888. In 1840 her family removed to Concord, Mass., where she grew up under the influence of such men as Thoreau and her father. To assist her kindred, she tried one occupation after another, as her story "Work" and her "Life, Letters, and Journals," edited by Ednah D. Cheney, show, but finally came into wide favor as a writer for the young. Her famous "Little Women," 1867–68, was followed by numerous stories of its class. The poem given in this volume appeared in "The Atlantic Monthly," 1863.

ALDRICH, Anne Reeve, b. New York, N. Y., 1866; d. there, 1892. Grand-niece of the poet James Aldrich. Her first book, "The Rose of Flame," 1889, was adversely criticized for its naïve and unrestrained expression, but its verse showed that she possessed the gifts of a poet. It was followed in 1890 by a novel, "The Feet of Love." She died before her last volume, "Songs about Love, Life, and Death," was published, and many of its short lyrics, in

[1] Where an author has died since the preparation of these biographies the date of decease is appended.

the revelation of a suffering but maturer and truer womanhood, are very touching.

ALDRICH, James, editor and writer, b. Mattituck, L. I., 1810; d. New York, N. Y., 1856. Founder of the "Literary Gazette," N. Y., 1840, in which paper many of his poems appeared. His daughter, Mrs. Ely, issued a collection of his poems for private circulation, 1884.

ALDRICH, Thomas Bailey, b. Portsmouth, N. H., 11 Nov., 1836. Part of his childhood was spent in Louisiana. At the age of seventeen he went to New York, gained the friendship of N. P. Willis, and soon became a regular contributor to the "Mirror" and "Home Journal." His "Ballad of Babie Bell," printed in the N. Y. "Journal of Commerce," 1855, touched the popular heart. After some years of literary journalism in New York, — where he was intimately associated with Bayard Taylor and the Stoddards, O'Brien, Winter, and the present annalist, and added the zest and wit of his brilliant companionship to the gatherings of the bright young writers cheerily struggling for subsistence and reputation in that unfriendly time, — he removed to Boston, where he edited "Every Saturday," 1865–74, and "The Atlantic Monthly," 1881–90. His first volume of verse was "The Bells," 1854. It was followed by "The Ballad of Babie Bell, and Other Poems," 1858; "Pampinea, and Other Poems," 1861; "Cloth of Gold, and Other Poems," 1874; "Flower and Thorn," 1876; "Friar Jerome's Beautiful Book," 1881; "Mercedes, and Later Lyrics," 1884; "Wyndham Towers," 1889; "The Sisters' Tragedy, and other Poems," 1891. In "Complete Poems," 1882, and his "Household Edition," 1895, he brought together his metrical writings, but in 1898 gave a final revision to all of his poems which he wished to preserve, re-arranging them with great care and taste for publication in two volumes. In prose he has written: "Out of His Head, A Romance," 1862; "The Story of a Bad Boy," 1870; "Marjorie Daw, and Other People," 1873; "Prudence Palfrey," 1874; "The Queen of Sheba," 1877; "The Stillwater Tragedy," 1880; etc. The play of "Mercedes" was staged at Palmer's Theatre, 1893. "Judith of Bethulîa," a heroic drama, was played in Boston and New York, with Miss O'Neil in the title-role, 1904. Cp. "Poets of America," pp. 440, 462. (D. Boston, Mass., 19 Mar., 1907.)

ALLEN, Elizabeth Ann (Chase) (Akers), "Florence Percy," b. Strong, Me., 1832. Her first husband was the sculptor, Paul Akers, who died in 1861. In 1865 she was married to E. M. Allen of New York, and lives near that city. Among her writings are "Forest Buds," 1855; "The Silver Bridge, and Other Poems," 1866; "Poems," 1866; "The High-Top Sweeting, and Other Poems," 1891; "The Proud Lady of Stavoren," 1898. Her authorship of the ballad "Rock me to Sleep, Mother" is no longer questioned.

ALLSTON, Washington, artist, b. Waccamaw, near Georgetown, S. C., 1779; d. Cambridge, Mass., 1843. Scion of a distinguished South Carolina family, and closely associated with the beginnings of literature and art in America. Graduated at Harvard, 1800. Spent three years in London, a student at the Royal Academy, and studied afterward in Paris and Rome. Returned to America in 1809, and married a sister of the Rev. Dr. Channing. Went again, in 1811, to London, where his wife died; afterward, in 1830, married a sister of Richard H. Dana. From 1818 until his death was a resident of Boston and of Cambridge, Mass. Is best known as a painter, but made also important contributions to the literature of his period. His writings are "The Sylphs of the Seasons, and Other Poems," 1813; "Monaldi, a Tale," 1841; "Lectures on Art, and Poems," published after his death, in 1850.

ANTROBUS, John, artist, b. Walsall, Staffordshire, England, 1831. Since 1849 he has lived in America; and, though for some time an art student in London and Paris, has usually made his home in Detroit, Mich. His own painting, "The Cowboy," suggested his poem of the same name.

ARNOLD, George, journalist, b. New York City, 1834; d. Strawberry Farms, N. J., 1865. Studied painting, but adopted literature as his profession. Was a versatile writer for the magazines. His "McArone Papers" commenced in "Vanity Fair" in 1860 and continued in that and other journals until his death. Two volumes of poems entitled "Drift: a Sea-Shore Idyl, and Other Poems," and "Poems Grave and Gay," were edited by William Winter and first published in 1866.

AURINGER, Obadiah Cyrus, clergyman, b. Glens Falls, N. Y., 1849. Studied under private tuition. Joined the U. S. Marine Corps, 1871, serving until 1875. He was occupied with agricultural pursuits, 1875–89. In 1890 he was ordained a Presbyterian minister, and became pastor of the Third Presbyterian Church of Troy, N. Y., at which town he still resides. His volumes of poems are "Scythe and Sword," 1887; "The Heart of the Golden Roan," 1891; "Episode of Jane McCrae," 1893; and, with J. Oliver Smith, "The Christ," 1899.

AUTHOR UNFOUND. What is usually the fifth stanza of the old-time ballad "The Yankee Man-of-War" (still familiar to the officers and tars of the U. S. Navy) was omitted from the text on pp. 8, 9, because it was manifestly faulty and inaccurate in the only nautical ballad-book, at the present editor's command, which then contained it. A probably correct version has been found in Walsh's "Patriotic and Naval Songster," 1898, as follows: —

The nightly robes our good ship wore were her whole topsails three,
Her spanker and her standing jib — the courses being free,

"Now, lay aloft! my heroes bold, not a moment must
be passed!"
And royals and top-gallant sails were quickly on each
mast.

The editor inserts the stanza here, regretting that it was not earlier available, but thinks that the ballad, as given in this Anthology, goes along quite as well without it.

BAKER, George Augustus, lawyer, b. New York, N. Y., 1849. Graduated at the City College of New York and from the Columbia University Law School. Author of several prose works, and of "Point-Lace and Diamonds," verse, 1875.

BANGS, John Kendrick, b. Yonkers, N.Y., 1862. Graduated at Columbia. He was associate editor of "Life," 1884-88. He edited Harper's "Drawer," 1888-98, and "Literature," 1899; at the close of which year he became editor of "Harper's Weekly." Some of his many books are "Coffee and Repartee," 1886; "A House Boat on the Styx," 1896; "Cobwebs from a Library Corner," verse, 1899.

BARKER, Edward D. His song, "Go Sleep, Ma Honey," first appeared in the Chicago "Record," and was afterwards successfully set to music by Eugene Cowles.

BASHFORD, Herbert, librarian, b. Sioux City, Iowa, 1871. In 189- he became state librarian of Washington. Author of "Nature Stories of the Northwest," 189-, and "Songs from Puget Sea," 1898.

BATES, Arlo, educator and novelist, b. East Machias, Me., 1850. Graduated from Bowdoin, and in 1880 became editor of the Boston "Sunday Courier." Was afterwards appointed professor of English literature in the Mass. Inst. of Technology. Among his poetical works are "Berries of the Brier," 1886; "Sonnets in Shadow," 1887; "A Poet and His Self," 1891; "Told in the Gate," 1892; "The Torch-Bearers," 1894. His novels include: "The Pagans," 1884; "A Wheel of Fire," 1885; "A Lad's Love," 1887; "The Philistines," 1888; "The Puritans," 1898. His Lowell Institute lectures have been published as "Talks on Writing English," 1896, and "Talks on the Study of Literature," 1897.

BATES, Charlotte Fiske (Madame Rogé), b. New York, N. Y., 1838. Her life has been passed mostly in New York and in Cambridge, Mass. In 1891 she was married to M. Adolphe Rogé, who died in 1896. She was Longfellow's assistant in the compilation of "Poems of Places," and editor of "The Cambridge Book of Poetry," 1882. Invented the "Longfellow Birthday Book," the pioneer of others of the kind. Author of "Risk, and Other Poems," 1879. (Her decease has been falsely reported in a biographical encyclopædia.)

BATES, Clara (Doty), b. Ann Arbor, Mich., 1838; d. Chicago, Ill., 1895. Was married, in 1869, to Morgan Bates, a publisher. Mrs. Bates has been chiefly known as a writer of juvenile verse and stories. Some of her publications are "Blind Jakey," 1868; "Child Lore: its Classics, Traditions, and Jingles," 1880; "On the Way to Wonderland," 1884; "From Heart's Content," verse, 1892.

BATES, Herbert, educator, b. Hyde Park, Mass., 1868. Graduated from Harvard University, class of 1890. Since 1897 Mr. Bates has held the position of head teacher of English in the Manual Training High School of Brooklyn, N. Y. Author of "Songs of Exile," 1896, and the editor of several classics for school use.

BATES, Katharine Lee, educator, b. Falmouth, Mass., 1859. Graduated at Wellesley College, where she became associate professor, and is now professor of English literature. Besides editing editions of various English classics, she has published, "The College Beautiful, and Other Poems," 1887; "Sunshine, and Other Verses for Children," 1890.

BEERS, Ethelinda (Eliot), "Ethel Lynn Beers," b. Goshen, N. Y., 1827; d. Orange, N. J., 1879. A descendant of John Eliot, the Indian missionary, to the spelling of whose surname "Eliot" she and her family reverted, the spelling "Elliott" having been adopted by her immediate ancestors. The title-poem of her volume "All Quiet Along the Potomac, and Other Poems," 1879, first appeared in "Harper's Weekly," Sept. 30, 1861, under the title "The Picket Guard."

"BEERS, Ethel Lynn." — See *Ethelinda Eliot Beers.*

BEERS, Henry Augustin, b. Buffalo, N. Y., 1847. Graduated at Yale, 1869, where he has been tutor, assistant professor, and, since 1880, professor of English literature. Author of "Odds and Ends," 1878; "Life of N. P. Willis," 1885; "The Thankless Muse," verse, 1885; "Outline Sketches of English and American Literature," 1886-87; "From Chaucer to Tennyson," 1890; "A Suburban Pastoral, and Other Tales," 1894; "The Ways of Yale," 1895; "A History of English Romanticism in the Eighteenth Century," 1899; and editor of "A Century of American Literature," 1878; "Selections from Willis's Prose Writings," 1885.

BELL, Robert Mowry, physician, b. Chicago, Ill., 1860. Graduated at the University of Minnesota and the Harvard Medical School, and spent several years of study in Europe. Resided chiefly in Minneapolis, until in 1893 ill-health obliged him to give up practising and to remove to California. Is now studying in Germany with a view to work as an instructor. His verse, contributed to periodicals, is of an elevated order. "The Tutelage," it may be noted, is a fresh variant upon the shell-theme of Landor and Wordsworth, and an optimistic summing up of the questions involved. Cp. "The Nature and Elements of Poetry," pp. 205-208.

BENJAMIN, Park, journalist and lecturer, b. Demerara, British Guiana, 1809; d. New

York, N. Y., 1864. Editor of the "New England Magazine," 1835-37, when he transferred it to New York City as the "American Monthly Magazine." He also assisted Greeley upon the "Tribune." In 1840 Mr. Benjamin established "Our New World." Of his many poems, which never have been collected, "The Old Sexton" is a familiar example. It was recalled by the present editor too late for insertion with poems of its date.

BENNETT, Henry Holcomb, journalist, b. Chillicothe, O., 1863. A writer of stories of army and frontier life. Much of his time is devoted to the science of ornithology.

BENNETT, John, b. Chillicothe, O., 1865. A writer of romantic historical fiction and children's stories. The prose of his "Master Skylark," in which we have Warwickshire, and London, and Shakespeare's time, and glimpses of gentle Will himself, is in choice keeping with the songs detached from it for this Anthology.

BENSEL, James Berry, b. New York, N. Y., 1856; d. there, 1886. The greater portion of his life was passed at Lynn, Mass. Ill-health and inability to complete his literary work, which at one time showed great promise, saddened his last years. Author of "King Kophetua's Wife," novel, 1883; "In the King's Garden, and other Poems," 1885.

BENTON, Joel, b. Amenia, N. Y., 1832. Editor for a while of the Amenia "Times," and a frequent literary contributor to newspapers and magazines. Has published "Emerson as a Poet," 1883; "In the Poe Circle," 1899.

BETHUNE, George Washington, b. New York, N. Y., 1805; d. Florence, Italy, 1862. Minister of note in the Dutch Reformed Church, Brooklyn, N. Y., and author of "Lays of Love and Faith," 1848; "Orations and Discourses," 1850. His edition of Walton's "The Compleat Angler" appeared in 1846.

BETTS, Craven Langstroth, b. St. John, New Brunswick, 1853. Of Loyalist descent. Was educated in his native city. Resided in New York after 1879, engaged in literary work. "Songs from Béranger," translations, 1888; "The Perfume Holder: a Persian Love Poem," 1892; "Tales of a Garrison Town," with A. W. Eaton, 1892; "A Garland of Sonnets," 1899.

BIERCE, Ambrose, critic and journalist, b. Ohio, 1842, of New England parentage. He served as private and then as officer, through the Civil War. The remainder of his life, except a few years in England, has been passed chiefly in California, where he has written his pungent criticisms for the "Examiner" and other periodicals. Author of "Soldiers and Civilians;" "Can Such Things Be?" short stories; "Black Beetles in Amber," satires in verse, 1892; and "Fantastic Fables."

BLAKE, Mary Elizabeth (McGrath), b. Dungarven, Ireland, 1840. Her family removed to Quincy, Mass., when she was six years old. Since her marriage to Dr. J. G. Blake she has lived in Boston. Author of "Poems," 1881; "Youth in Twelve Centuries," 1886; "Verses Along the Way," 1890; and several books of travel. (D. Boston, 1907.)

BLOCK, Louis James, educator, b. 1851. His childhood was passed in St. Louis. A graduate of Washington University. For some years Mr. Block has resided in Chicago, and is principal of one of its high schools. Author of "Exile, a Dramatic Episode," 1880; "Dramatic Sketches and Poems," 1891; "The New World, with Other Verse," 1895; "Capriccios," 1898.

BLOEDE, Gertrude, "Stuart Sterne," b. Dresden, Germany, 1845. Came to America in 1850; a resident of Brooklyn, N. Y., since 1861. She was an associate and protégé of Mr. and Mrs. Bayard Taylor, and the devoted friend of the poet Dorgan for some years preceding his death. Author of "Poems," 1874; "Giorgio, and Other Poems," 1881; "Beyond the Shadow," 1888; "Piero da Castiglione," 1890; "The Story of Two Lives," novel, 1891. (D. 1905.)

BLOOD, Henry Ames, b. Temple, N. H., 1838. Graduating at Dartmouth College, he afterwards taught for a number of years. At the beginning of President Lincoln's administration he became connected with the State Department at Washington, where he has permanently remained. Mr. Blood's quaint and original lyrics have not been collected. He is the author of several unpublished dramas.

BLOUNT, Edward Augustus, Jr., Columbia University, Class of 1895.

BOGART, Elizabeth, b. New York, N. Y., 180–. Daughter of the late Rev. D. S. Bogart. About 1825, Miss Bogart began to write, under the pseudonym "Estelle," for the "Mirror." Her prose and verse have never been collected, though there is material sufficient for several volumes. Her poem "He Came too Late," a favorite and typical example of old-time lyrical sentiment, was remembered "too late" for insertion with verse of its day.

BOKER, George Henry, dramatist and diplomat, b. Philadelphia, Penn., 6 Oct., 1823; d. there, 2 Jan., 1890. Graduated at Princeton, and, after a period of travel in Europe, made his permanent home in Philadelphia. His first volume of verse, "The Lesson of Life, and Other Poems," was issued in 1847. It was succeeded the following year by "Calaynos," a blank-verse tragedy, which was successfully produced in 1849 at a London theatre. "Francesca da Rimini" is now the best known of the metrical dramas which, with his miscellaneous poems, were published in two volumes, "Plays and Poems," 1856. Mr. Boker was secretary of the Union League of Philadelphia from 1861 to 1871, and was actively patriotic during the Civil War. "Poems of the War," containing some lyrics widely familiar, appeared in 1864. Later volumes are "Königsmark, and Other Poems," 1869; "The Book of the Dead," 1882; and

"Sonnets," 1886. He was U. S. minister to Turkey from 1871 to 1875, and to Russia from 1875 to 1879. Throughout his literary career he was closely associated with Bayard Taylor and R. H. Stoddard. To represent Boker with fairness, extracts should be given from the dramatic work to which he devoted his best powers, and for which the repeated success of "Calaynos" and "Francesca da Rimini" showed that he possessed both literary and practical equipments. The ballads, sonnets, etc., to which this Anthology is restricted, exhibit his lyrical strength and quality. Cp. "Poets of America," pp. 56, 404.

BOLTON, Sarah Knowles, b. Farmington, Conn., 1841. She was married to Charles E. Bolton, and removed with him to Cleveland, O. A fertile and excellent writer of books for the young. Author of "Girls Who Became Famous," 1886; "Famous American Authors," 1887; "Famous Types of Womanhood," 1892; "The Inevitable," poems, 1895.

BONER, John Henry, b. Salem, N. C., 1845. Edited papers in Salem and Asheville, N. C. Chief clerk of the N. C. House of Representatives, 1869–70. Entered the civil service at Washington, 1871; removed to New York in 1887, and was on the staffs of "The Century Dictionary," "The New York World," "Literary Digest," and "A Library of American Literature." Published "Whispering Pines," poems, 1883. He afterwards returned to bureau work in Washington. D. 1903.

BOWDITCH, Nathaniel Ingersoll, lawyer, b. Salem, Mass., 1805; d. Boston, Mass., 1861. He entered Harvard at thirteen, graduated in 1822, and lived in Boston. His memoir of his father, the mathematician and astronomer, was published in 1839, in the same volume with a translation of Laplace's "Mécanique Céleste."

BOWKER, Richard Rogers, b. Salem, Mass., 1848. A graduate of the College of New York. He was literary editor of the N. Y. "Evening Mail," and became editor and owner of "The Publishers' Weekly," an editor of the "Library Journal," and compiler of the "American Catalogue," 2 vols. 1885. He has published: "Of Work and Wealth," 1883; "Copyright: its Law and its Literature," 1886, and various economic and political treatises. Secretary of the American Publishers' Copyright League and active in the movement for International Copyright, 1884–91.

BOYESEN, Hjalmar Hjorth, b. Fredericksvaern, Norway, 1848; d. New York City, 1895. He was graduated at the University of Christiana, and removed to Chicago, Ill., where he was associate editor of the Scandinavian paper "Fremad." In 1872–74 he studied philology at Leipsic, Germany. In 1874 he became professor of German at Cornell, and in 1880 professor of Germanic languages at Columbia College. He published: "Gunnar, a Norse Romance," 1874; "Goethe and Schiller, Their Lives and Works," 1878; "Ilka on the Hill-Top, and other Stories," 1881, of which the title-story, dramatized as "Alpine Roses," was produced in 1884; "Essays on Scandinavian Literature;" "Essays on German Literature;" "Idyls of Norway, and Other Poems," 1883; "Vagabond Tales," 1889; the "Norseland" series of books for boys, etc.

BOYLE, Sarah (Roberts), b. Portsmouth, N. H., 1812; d. New York, N. Y., 1869. Daughter of E. Q. Roberts of the diplomatic service. After her marriage to Dr. James Boyle she lived in New York City. Author of several favorite poems.

BRACKETT, Anna Callender, distinguished instructor, b. Boston, Mass., 18—. Educated in the schools of that city, and graduated from the State Normal School, Framingham, Mass., 1856, to which she returned as a teacher, remaining three years. For two years Miss Brackett was vice-principal of the Normal School in Charleston, S. C., resigning that position in 1861. One year's teaching in the High School, Cambridge, Mass., preceded her appointment as principal of the Normal School, St. Louis, Mo. She was the first woman to hold such a position. After teaching there nine years, she founded her well-known school for girls in New York City, which she conducted for twenty years. Miss Brackett is the author of many educational essays, sketches, stories, and poems, and was a scholarly writer for Professor W. T. Harris's "Journal of Speculative Philosophy." Her books are: "Education of American Girls," 1874; "Poetry for Home and School," edited collection, 1876; "Philosophy of Education, Translation from Rosenkranz," 1886; "Technique of Rest," 1892.

BRADLEY, Mrs. Mary Emily (Neeley), b. Easton, Md., 1835; d. Washington, D. C., 1898. She was married in New York City to George T. Bradley, and formed a friendship with R. H. Stoddard, who as editor of the "Aldine" encouraged her in verse-writing. She published "Hidden Sweetness," poems, 1886, and more than twenty stories for girls.

BRAINARD, John Gardiner Calkens, b. New London, Conn., 1796; d. 1828. Graduated at Yale; studied and practised law, but soon devoted himself to journalism. Wrote for the "Microscope," a New Haven paper; became editor of the "Connecticut Mirror," Hartford, Conn., 1822, which post he held until his health failed in 1827. Published his first volume of poems in 1825. A new edition called "Literary Remains," with a sketch of the author by Whittier, was issued in 1832.

BRAINARD, Mary Gardiner, b. 18—. Daughter of a prominent lawyer of New London, Conn., and niece of the poet J. G. C. Brainard. "Not Knowing" appeared first in the "Congregationalist" in 1869. The editor of this Anthology was unable for years to discover the authorship of this womanly and touching expression of a faith that is its own beatitude.

BRANCH, Mary Lydia (Bolles), b. New London, Conn., 1840. Married, in 1870, John L. Branch, a lawyer. Author of "The Kanter Girls" and other stories for young people.

"**BRIDGES**, Madeline." — See *Mary Ainge De Vere.*

BRIDGES, Robert, "Droch," b. Shippensburg, Penn., 1858. Graduated at Princeton. He was assistant news-editor of the N. Y. "Evening Post" from 1881 until his appointment as assistant editor of "Scribner's Magazine" in 1887. Has been literary editor of "Life" since 1883. Author of "Overheard in Arcady," 1894; "Suppressed Chapters and Other Bookishness," 1895; and of various poems.

BRISTOL, Augusta (Cooper), b. Croydon, N. H., 1835. Has chiefly been occupied as an educator and lecturer. Was married in 1866 to Louis Bristol of New Haven, Conn., removing to Vineland, N. J., in 1872. She is the author of several books on social topics and of a volume of poems, "The Web of Life," 1895.

BROOKS, Francis, lawyer and physician, b. Memphis, Tenn., 1867; drowned, Lake Geneva, Wis., 1898. Entered the class of 1889 at Harvard, but left before graduating; and subsequently obtained a degree from the Chicago College of Law; and later studied at the University of Virginia. For a few months a lawyer; then a doctor of no mean distinction; and always devoted to literature, Francis Brooks died at what seemed to be the beginning of his true career. His initial volume, "Margins," appeared in 1897, and a posthumous edition of his complete poems, edited, with a prefatory memoir, by Wallace Rice, was issued in 1898.

BROOKS, Maria (Gowen), "Maria del Occidente," b. Medford, Mass., about 1795; d. Matanzas, Cuba, 1845. Of Welsh descent. Her father, a man of refinement, died when she was young, and she was educated by Mr. Brooks, a merchant of Boston, to whom she became engaged at the age of fourteen. Her "Judith, Esther, and Other Poems," appeared in 1820. Became a widow in 1823; went to live with an uncle in Cuba; and at his death inherited his property. Returned to the United States and lived at Hanover, N. H. Visited Europe in 1830; met Southey; finished writing "Zophiël, or the Bride of Seven," while at his home in Keswick, the first part having been completed in Cuba, and published in 1825. Southey edited the complete poem published in London, 1833, where it excited much attention. In 1843 she issued for private circulation a semi-autobiographical prose romance, "Idomen, or the Vale of Yamuri." The "Ode to the Departed" was written in Cuba, 1844.

BROOKS, Phillips, Protestant Episcopal bishop, b. Boston, Mass., 1835; d. there, 1893. A graduate of Harvard, he was ordained in the Episcopal ministry, 1859. He became rector of Trinity Church in Boston, 1869, and bishop of Massachusetts, 1891, and was honored for his gifts and beloved for the beauty and sincerity of his nature. He published many volumes of sermons, and was the author of several favorite hymns.

BROTHERTON, Alice (Williams), b. Cambridge, Ind., 18—. Since her marriage, 1876, to William E. Brotherton, she has lived in Covington, Ky., and near Cincinnati, O. She has published: "Beyond the Veil," poems, 1886; "The Sailing of King Olaf, and Other Poems," 1888; and has delivered lectures on literature.

BROWN, Alice, b. Hampton Falls, N. H., 1857. Removed to Boston, where she expected to teach, but soon devoted her attention to literature. She is on the staff of the "Youth's Companion," and is the author of several volumes of prose, and of "The Road to Castaly," verse, 1896.

BROWN, Joseph Brownlee, b. Charleston, S. C., 1824; d. Brooklyn, N. Y., 1888. Graduated at Dartmouth. One of the younger transcendentalists who wrote for "The Atlantic Monthly." He was prevented by ill-health from fulfilling the promise of his youth.

BROWN, Phœbe (Hinsdale), b. Canaan, N. Y., 1783; d. Henry, Ill., 1861. Daughter of George Hinsdale, the composer. She resided in Connecticut and Massachusetts until her removal in 1849 to Illinois. Her famous hymn, beginning "I love to steal awhile away," was written in 1818.

BROWN, Theron, clergyman and author, b. Willimantic, Conn., 1832. Graduated at Yale, 1856. Entered the Baptist ministry, 1859. Editorially connected with "Youth's Companion" since 1870. Besides much work in prose, Mr. Brown has published "Life Songs," a volume of poems, 1894.

BROWNE, Francis Fisher, b. South Halifax, Vt., 1843. Before enlisting as a volunteer in the U. S. army, he worked in his father's newspaper office at Chicopee, Mass. At the end of the war he went to Chicago, where, in 1880, he founded his critical semi-monthly, "The Dial," which he has invariably maintained at a high standard. Author of "The Every-Day Life of Abraham Lincoln," 1886; "Volunteer Grain," poems, 1895, and editor of several excellent collections of verse.

BROWNE, Irving, b. Marshall, N. Y., 1835; d. Buffalo, N. Y., 1899. He practised law in Troy, N. Y., edited the Albany "Law Journal," and finally made his home in Buffalo. Wrote and edited numerous legal treatises, and was a collector of rare books. Among his works are: "Law and Lawyers in Literature," 1883; "Iconoclasm and Whitewash," essays, 1885; "Our Best Society," comedy; "The House of the Heart," poems, 1897; and "The Track of the Book-Worm," an essay, with ballads on books.

BROWNELL, Henry Howard, b. Providence, R. I., 6 Feb., 1820; d. Hartford, Conn.

1872. Graduated at Trinity College. Was admitted to the bar in 1844, but practised only five years. Early in the civil war, a poem of his on Farragut attracted that commander's attention, and led to Brownell's appointment as acting ensign on board the Hartford. He witnessed the battle of Mobile Bay, and at the close of the war accompanied Farragut on his cruise to the European ports, resigning in 1868. His poetical works are "Poems," 1847; "Lyrics of a Day," 1864; "War Lyrics, and Other Poems," with an appreciative preface by T. B. Aldrich, 1866.

BRUCE, Wallace, lecturer, b. Hillsdale, N. Y., 1844. Graduated at Yale. After extensive travels in Europe, began work as a lecturer in 1870. Was U. S. consul at Edinburgh, 1889–93. Author of many poems on occasions, and of "The Land of Burns," 1879; "Old Homestead Poems," 1887; "Wayside Poems," 1895; etc.

BRYANT, William Cullen, journalist and poet, b. Cummington, Mass., 3 Nov., 1794; d. New York City, 12 June, 1878. His first published poem, on the Progress of Knowledge, appeared in the "Hampshire Gazette," 1807. In 1808 his philippic "The Embargo," a political satire, was published in Boston and attracted much attention. He seems, however, to have received little commendation from his father for his efforts in versification, and often oversevere criticism, but was apparently undiscouraged. In an autobiography of his early life, it appears that his education was rather elementary, until his fourteenth year, when he began his preparations for college. He entered Williams College, October, 1810, as a sophomore, and left, May, 1811, intending to go to Yale. In this he was disappointed, and forced to give up all hope of a thorough college education. From 1814–15 he studied law. During this period his work assumes a morbid tone, which, following considerable amatory verse, suggests an unhappy attachment. In 1815 he was admitted to the bar. It is interesting to observe that it was in this year, when he attained his majority, he struck the poetic note which became most characteristic with him, for he began here to interpret nature, and his verse shows a marked improvement in sincerity of tone. It was not until 1817 that "Thanatopsis" was published in the "North American Review," though written in his eighteenth year. Shorter poems followed, and in response to a request from the Phi Beta Kappa Society, he delivered a poem, "The Ages," at Harvard, 1821, published in the same year with other poems. It was in this year that he married Miss Frances Fairchild, at Great Barrington. In 1825 he went to New York, and, abandoning the law, devoted himself to literature. After a rather depressing service on the staff of a literary review, he became assistant editor of the "Evening Post." Later, in 1828, he became editor in chief, a position he held for fifty years, until his death. During his connection with the "Post," he took many trips abroad and into the East, described in letters to the paper, and afterward published in book-form: "Letters of a Traveller," 1852; "Letters from Spain and Other Countries," 1859; "Letters from the East," 1869. "The Fountain and Other Poems" appeared in 1842; "The White-Footed Deer, and Other Poems," in 1844. Editions of his "Poems" were published in 1832, 1846, 1855, and 1876. "Orations and Addresses" appeared in 1873; "Thirty Poems" in 1864; blank verse translations of the "Iliad" and "Odyssey" in 1870–72. A comprehensive edition of "The Poetical Works and Prose Works of William Cullen Bryant," edited by Parke Godwin, was published in 1884. Mr. Bryant was often called "the first citizen of the republic," and his death, from sunstroke and a fall, was regarded by all classes as a national calamity. Cp. "Poets of America," chap. iii., and "Nature and Elements of Poetry," p. 252. [B. D. L.]

BUCK, Richard Henry, song-writer, b. Philadelphia, Penn., 1869. Educated in the public schools of that city. In 1896 he became associated with Professor Geibel, the composer, who wrote the music to "Kentucky Babe," a good example of the modern "coon song." Mr. Buck's verse will soon be collected in book-form.

BUCKHAM, James, b. Burlington, Vt., 1858. Author of "The Heart of Life," 1897.

BULL, Lucy Catlin. — See *L. C. B. Robinson.*

BUNNER, Alice (Learned), b. New London, Conn., 186–. A sister of Walter Learned, and wife of the late Henry Cuyler Bunner, whom she married in 1880. Mrs. Bunner contributes poems and sketches to the periodicals.

BUNNER, Henry Cuyler, journalist, b. Oswego, N. Y., 3 Aug., 1855; d. Nutley, N. J., 11 May, 1896. Entered a business firm in New York, and was afterwards a reporter. He became assistant-editor of "Puck" in 1887, and some years later its editorial chief. Well known as a writer of fiction and verse, whose early death was deplored. Author of "A Woman of Honor," 1883; "Airs from Arcady and Elsewhere," poems, 1884; "The Midge," 1886; "The Story of a New York House," 1887; "Zadoc Pine, and Other Stories," 1891; "Rowen," verse, 1892; Jersey Street and Jersey Lane," 1896. A collection of his poems was edited by Brander Matthews and published in 1896.

"BURROUGHS, ELLEN." — See *Sophie Jewett.*

BURROUGHS, John, essayist, b. Roxbury, N. Y., 3 April, 1837. A close student of nature, notably of bird-life in the northern seaboard States. He grew up on his father's farm, and received a common-school education. Was in the Treasury Department at Washington, 1863–72. In 1874 he removed to the fruit-farm still his home, at West Park, N. Y. In some respects a pupil of Emerson, and for years the most effective and high-minded eulogist of his friend Walt Whitman, his habit of thought is original, and he is recognized as a naturalist-philosopher, whose writings have wholesome sentiment and poetic charm. He has published "Notes on Walt Whitman as Poet and Person," 1867; "Wake Robin," 1871; "Winter Sunshine," 1875; "Birds and Poets," 1877; "Locusts and Wild Honey," 1879; "Pepacton," 1881; "Fresh Fields," 1884; "Signs and Seasons," 1886; "Indoor Studies," 1889; "Riverby," 1894; "Walt Whitman, A Study," 1897; "The Light of Day," 1900; "Literary Values," 1902; "Far and Near," 1904; "Ways of Nature," 1905; "Bird and Bough" (his only book of poems), 1906; "Camping and Tramping with Roosevelt," 1907; "Leaf and Tendril," 1908.

BURTON, Richard, educator, b. Hartford, Conn., 1859. Graduated at Trinity, 1883, and Johns Hopkins, 1887. He was literary editor of the Hartford "Courant," 1890-97, and in 1898 was made professor of English literature at the University of Minnesota. His books of verse are "Dumb in June, and Other Poems," 1895; "Memorial Day, and Other Poems," 1897; "Lyrics of Brotherhood," 1900.

BUSHNELL, Frances Louisa, b. Hartford, Conn., 1834; d. 1899. A daughter of Horace Bushnell, the eminent divine. She has contributed thoughtful and refined verse to "The Atlantic Monthly" and other magazines.

BUTLER, William Allen, son of Benjamin F. Butler, b. Albany, N. Y., 1825. Graduated at the University of New York, 1843. For many years a distinguished member of the New York bar. His society poem, "Nothing to Wear," published anonymously in "Harper's Weekly," 1857, and afterwards in book form, took the town, and gave him a wide reputation. He has written other successful satires; "Domesticus," a story; besides legal and biographical works. His poems were collected in 1871, and again in 1899. (D. Yonkers, N. Y., 1902.)

BUTTERWORTH, Hezekiah, editor and balladist, b. Warren, R. I., 1839. Connected with the "Youth's Companion," Boston, since 1871. Author of the series "Zig-zag Journeys," for children, 1876-90; "Poems for Christmas, Easter, and New Year's," 1883; "Poems and Ballads upon Important Episodes in American History," 1887; "The Wampum Belt, or the Fairest Page of History," 1896. (D. Warren, 1905.)

BUTTS, Mary Frances (Barber), b. Hopkinton, R. I., 183-. Married in 1865. Has done much journalistic work, and has written many books for children. — "A Fence of Trust," verse, 1898.

CABLE, George Washington, novelist and humanitarian, b. New Orleans, La., 1844. This distinguished romancer, whose exquisite and most poetic stories of life in the French quarter of his native city, and of plantation life in Louisiana, gave him his first fame, has printed little, as yet, in verse-form.

CARLETON, Will, b. Hudson, Mich., 1845. He was educated at Hillsdale College, Mich., and engaged in journalism in Chicago, but finally removed to Brooklyn, N. Y. A successful lecturer, and reader of his own ballads. He has issued "Poems," 1871; "Farm Ballads," 1873; "Farm Legends," 1875; "Farm Festivals," 1881; "City Ballads," 1885; "City Legends," 1889; "City Festivals," 1892; "Rhymes of our Planet;" "The Old Infant, and Similar Stories," 1896.

CARPENTER, Amelia Walstien (Jolls), b. Stephentown, N. Y., 1840. She was married, when eighteen, to Mr. Cromwell Carpenter, with whom she removed to Kalamazoo and St. Louis, returning, after his death, to her native town. She has contributed her poems and stories to "The Springfield Republican," "The Christian Union," "Lippincott's Magazine," and other periodicals.

CARPENTER, Henry Bernard, b. Dublin, Ireland, 1840; d. Sorrento, Me., 1890. Having graduated at Oxford, he took orders in the Church, and was chaplain to the Earl of Belmore. He came to America in 1874, and was pastor of the Hollis Street Unitarian Church, in Boston, Mass., from 1878 to 1887. Author of "Liber Amoris," 1886; and of a posthumous collection, "A Poet's Last Songs," with a memoir by J. J. Roche.

CARRYL, Charles Edward, b. New York, N. Y., 1841. Mr. Carryl has long been a successful member of the N. Y. Stock Exchange, while closely associated with the literary and artistic life of the metropolis, and devoting much time to bookish pursuits. Author of the delicately fanciful dream-stories "Davy and the Goblin," 1885, and "The Admiral's Caravan," 1892; and of "The River Syndicate, and Other Stories," 1899.

CARRYL, Guy Wetmore, b. New York, N. Y., 1873. Son of Charles E. Carryl. He was educated at Columbia, and has taken literature as a profession. Engaged in various editorial duties until he became the Paris representative of Harper and Brothers. Author of many poems and other contributions to the periodicals, and of the unique "Fables for the Frivolous," 1898. (D. New York, N. Y., 1904.)

CARY, Alice, b. Miami Valley, near Cincinnati, O., 1820; d. New York, N. Y., 1871. She came to New York with her sister in 1852, where their weekly receptions were soon a feature of artistic and literary life. "Poems by Alice and Phœbe Cary" appeared in 1850, and was followed by Alice's "Clovernook," two series of prose sketches — 1851-53; "Lyra, and Other Poems," 1853; "Pictures of Country Life," 1859; "Ballads, Lyrics, and Hymns," 1866, and "The Lover's Diary," 1867.

CARY, Phœbe, sister of Alice, b. 1824; d. 1871. Author of "Poems and Parodies;" "Poems of Faith, Hope, and Love."

CAVAZZA, Elisabeth. — See *E. J. Pullen.*

CAWEIN, Madison Julius, b. Louisville, Ky., 1865. Since the appearance of his first book, "Blooms of the Berry," 1887, Mr. Cawein has devoted himself to poetic composition more assiduously than any other American writer of standing. His maturer volumes are his best, and have been received with favor. They comprise "Red Leaves and Roses," 1893; "Poems of Nature and Love," 1893; "Intimations of the Beautiful," 1894; "The Garden of Dreams," 1896; "Idyllic Monologues," 1898; "Myth and Romance," 1899.

CHADWICK, John White, b. Marblehead, Mass., 1840. A graduate of the Harvard Divinity School. He is pastor of the Liberal Second Unitarian Society of Brooklyn, N. Y., and a justly noted preacher. Some of the best critical and biographical papers in "The Nation" have been from his pen. His sermons, appearing in successive series for many years, constitute a noble body of ethical literature. Author of "A Book of Poems," 1876; "Thomas Paine, the Method and Value of His Religious Teaching," 1877; "In Nazareth Town, a Christmas Fantasy, and Other Poems," 1883; "A Legend of Good Poets," 1885; "A Few Verses," 1900; and other scholarly works in prose. (D. Brooklyn, N. Y., 1904.)

CHAMBERS, Robert William, artist and novelist, b. Brooklyn, N. Y., 1865. Studied at the Ecole des Beaux Arts, Paris. Returned to New York in 1893. His first novel, "In the Quarter," 1894, was followed by "The King in Yellow," 1895; "The Red Republic," 1895; "Ashes of Empire," 1899. "With the Band," 1896, is a collection of military poems.

CHANLER, Amélie (Rives). — See *Princess Troubetskoy.*

CHANNING, Grace Ellery. — See *Mrs. Channing-Stetson.*

CHANNING-STETSON, Grace Ellery, b. Providence, R. I., 186–. Daughter of Dr. William Francis Channing, the distinguished savant; and granddaughter of Channing, the divine. Since 1884 a resident of Southern California and at times of Italy. In 1894 she was married to the artist, Charles Walter Stetson, of Providence. Mrs. Stetson's published works are "Dr. Channing's Note Book," 1887; "The Sister of a Saint," 1895; "Sea Drift," verse, 1899; "The Fortune of a Day," 1900.

CHANNING, William Ellery, 2d, poet and essayist, b. Boston, Mass., 1818. Nephew of the great Unitarian divine. Studied at Harvard, but did not take a degree. Married a sister of Margaret Fuller Ossoli. Engaged in editorial work at New York City and New Bedford, Mass. Went to reside at Concord, Mass., in 1842. Author of "Poems," 1843 and 1847; "The Woodman," 1849; "Near Home," 1858; "The Wanderer," 1872; "Conversations in Rome," 1847; and "Thoreau: the Poet-Naturalist" (prose), 1873. A true poet, though criticised by Poe as an exemplar of the transcendental school. (D. Concord, Mass., 1901.)

CHAPMAN, Mary Berri. — See *M. B. (C.) Hansbrough.*

CHENEY, John Vance, librarian, b. Groveland, N. Y., 1848. Son of the musician and author Simeon P. Cheney. He was admitted to the Massachusetts bar, and practised law in New York City. In 1887 he took charge of the Free Public Library, San Francisco, Cal., and is now librarian of the Newberry Library, Chicago, Ill. He has written "The Old Doctor," prose, 1881; "Thistle-Drift," poems, 1887; "Wood-Blooms," poems, 1888; "The Golden Guess," essays, 1892; "Ninette, a Redwoods Idyl," 1894; "Queen Helen, and Other Poems," 1895, and "That Dome in Air," essays, 1895; "Out of the Silence," poems, 1897. Editor of "Wood Notes Wild," by Simeon Pease Cheney, 1892. Mr. Cheney's poem on p. 586 won the first prize in the competition for a rejoinder to Edwin Markham's "The Man with the Hoe," 1900.

CHILD, Lydia Maria (Francis), b. Medford, Mass., 1802; d. Wayland, Mass., 1880. Her first novel, "Hobomok," appeared in 1821. "An Appeal for that Class of Americans called Africans," 1833, was the first Abolitionist volume published in the United States. With her husband, David L. Child, she edited the "National Anti-Slavery Standard" from 1840 to 1844. She published many works of fiction and general literature.

CLARK, Willis Gaylord, journalist, b. Otisco, N. Y., 1810; d. Philadelphia, Penn., 1841. When about twenty years old engaged in newspaper work, and became owner and editor of "The Philadelphia Gazette." Was a contributor to his twin brother's "Knickerbocker Magazine," New York. After his death the brother, Lewis Gaylord Clark, edited his "Literary Remains," 1844, and his complete poems, 1847.

CLARKE, Ednah Proctor. — See *E. P. (C.) Hayes.*

CLARKE, Joseph Ignatius Constantine, editor and playwright, b. Kingstown, Ireland, 1846. In 1868 he came to America, where he has since resided. Two years later he joined the editorial staff of the N. Y. "Herald," and continued in its service until 1883, when he became managing editor of the N. Y. "Journal." Since 1898 Mr. Clarke has been the editor of the "Criterion." Author of "Robert Emmet," a tragedy, 1888; "Malmorda, a Metrical Romance," 1893, and of various plays.

CLOUD, Virginia Woodward, b. Baltimore, Md., 186–. A favorite contributor to select periodicals.

CLYMER, Ella Maria (Dietz). — See *E. M. D. Glynes.*

COAN, Titus Munson, physician, b. Hilo, Hawaiian Islands, 1836; educated in Honolulu at the Royal and Punahou schools. He graduated at Williams College, 1859, and in medicine in New York City, at the College of Physicians and Surgeons. Served as assistant surgeon in the U. S. army, and under Admiral Farragut in the West Gulf squadron, 1863-65. Subsequently took up literature as a profession. Established the New York Bureau of Revision in 1880. Author of many articles and poems in the magazines, and of "Ounces of Prevention," 1885.

COATES, Florence (Earle), b. Philadelphia, Penn., 185–. A granddaughter of Thomas Earle, the philanthropist. She received her education at the Convent of the Sacred Heart in Paris, and at Brussels. She was married, in 1879, to Edward H. Coates, president of the Pennsylvania Academy of Fine Arts. Mrs. Coates was elected president of the Browning Society of Philadelphia in 189–. Her "Poems" were collected in 1898.

COCKE, Zitella, b. Perry Co., Ala., 186–. She is of English and Huguenot descent, and grew up on a plantation. Of late a resident of Boston, Mass. Her first literary ventures were translations from the French and German. Author of "A Doric Reed," 1895.

COLES, Abraham, LL. D., physician, b. Scotch Plains, N. J., 1813; d. Monterey, Cal., 1891. Graduated at Jefferson Med. Coll., Phila., 1835. He published "Dies Iræ, in Thirteen Original Versions," 1859; "Old Gems in New Settings," 1866; "The Microcosm," 1866; "Latin Hymns," 1868; "The Evangel of Verse," 1874; "The Light of the World," 1884. — Cp. "Poets of America," p. 300.

COLLYER, Robert, clergyman, b. Keighley, Yorkshire, England, 1823. He learned the blacksmith's trade, and in 1850 came to America. For some years, without abandoning his trade, he had followed the calling of a Methodist minister, but in 1859 he founded a Unitarian church in Chicago. In 1879 he became pastor of the Church of the Messiah in New York, and finally pastor emeritus. The beautiful ballad "Under the Snow" is perhaps his best-known poem.

COLLYER, Thomas Stephens, b. New York, N. Y., 1842; d. New London, Conn., 1893. He served in the U. S. navy during the Civil War; became boatswain, 1866, and was placed on the retired list in 1883; after which he made his home in New London, Conn. He wrote "Song Spray," poems, 1889.

COLTON, Arthur Willis, b. Washington, Conn., 1868. Graduated at Yale, where he received the degree of Ph. D. in 1893, and taught English in the academic department for two years. A resident of his native town, and a contributor to the magazines.

CONE, Helen Gray, educator, b. New York, N. Y., 1859. Graduated at the Normal College of New York, where she was appointed instructor in English literature. Two volumes of her poems have appeared: "Oberon and Puck: Verses Grave and Gay," 1885; "The Ride to the Lady, and Other Poems," 1891. Miss Cone assisted Miss Jeannette L. Gilder in editing "Pen Portraits of Literary Women." From the first she has displayed the traits of a true poet, and of an artist too genuine to seek attention by devices. Her verse, always womanly, is often notable for strength, and for a certain elevation of thought and feeling.

CONWAY, Katherine Eleanor, b. Rochester, N. Y., 1853. A member of the editorial staff of the Boston "Pilot" since 1883. Miss Conway is the editor of "Watchwords from John Boyle O'Reilly," 1891, and is the author of "Songs of the Sunrise Slope," 1881; "A Dream of Lilies," verse, 1893; "A Lady and Her Letters," 1895; "Making Friends and Keeping Them," 1895.

COOK, Clarence Chatham, art-critic, b. Dorchester, Mass., 1828; d. 1900. He edited "The Studio" of New York, and has published "The Central Park," 1868; "The House Beautiful: Essays on Beds and Tables, Stools and Candlesticks," 1877.

COOKE, John Esten, b. Winchester, Va., 1830; d. near Boyce, Va., 1886. Brother of Philip Pendleton Cooke. He gave up the practice of law for literary work. His best-known tale, "The Virginian Comedians," 1854, was followed by other Virginian romances of colonial life, or relating to the Civil War, in which he served as a Confederate soldier. He wrote a life of Stonewall Jackson, 1863, and of Robert E. Lee, 1871; "Virginia, a History of the People," 1883, and numerous poems.

COOKE, Philip Pendleton, lawyer, b. Martinsburg, Va., 1816; d. near Boyce, Va., 1850. Entered Princeton at the age of fifteen, where he was specially distinguished for his love of outdoor sports. Wrote for the "Knickerbocker Magazine," when seventeen years old. Was admitted to the bar at Winchester, Va. His best-known lyric is "Florence Vane." Author of "Froissart Ballads, and Other Poems," 1847.

COOKE, Rose (Terry), b. West Hartford, Conn., 17 Feb., 1827; d. Pittsfield, Mass., 18 July, 1892. She lived at Hartford during the first half of her life, where she attended the Hartford Female Seminary. After her marriage to Rollin H. Cooke, in 1873, her home was at Winsted, in the same State. Her last years were spent in Pittsfield, Mass. "Poems by Rose Terry," 1860, attracted general attention to her literary talent, and she also gained reputation as a writer of notable short stories of New England life. The latter were published in four volumes. "Poems," a collective edition, appeared in 1888.

COOLBRITH, Ina Donna, b. near Springfield, Ill., 184–. After a long residence in Los Angeles she removed to San Francisco, and in 1874 became librarian of the Oakland free library. She is a frequent contributor to magazines, and has published "A Perfect Day, and Other Poems," 1881, and "Songs of the Golden Gate," 1895. The last-named collection has met with just praise at home and abroad.

"COOLIDGE, Susan." — See *Sarah Chauncey Woolsey*.

COOPER, George, song-writer, b. New York, N. Y., 1840. A contributor of songs to juvenile and other magazines. A resident of West Hoboken, N. J.

COOPER, James Fenimore, b. Burlington, N. J., 15 Sept., 1789; d. Cooperstown, N. Y., 14 Sept., 1851. Studied at Yale and served as midshipman in U. S. navy, 1808–11. The first book of perhaps the most American of our novelists appeared in 1820. The few songs scattered through his works are usually put in the mouths of his characters. "My Brigantine" is given in "The Water-Witch," 1830.

CORTISSOZ, Ellen Mackay Hutchinson, b. Caledonia, N. Y., 18—. She obtained a position, at an early age, in the office of the N. Y. "Tribune," soon becoming a member of its editorial staff. To her care and taste the literary department of that journal's Sunday supplement has owed its repute. Her husband is Royal Cortissoz, the author and art-critic, also of the "Tribune" staff. In 1881 Mrs. Cortissoz, then Miss Hutchinson, collected some of her verse in a little volume, "Songs and Lyrics," remarkable for the exquisite beauty, in feeling and lyrical charm, of almost every poem which it contained. In her lyrics and ballads, tinged with old colonial and eighteenth-century effects, she has had more than one follower but no equal. She edited, with E. C. Stedman, "A Library of American Literature," in 11 vols., 1888–89.

COXE, Arthur Cleveland, Episcopal bishop of Western New York, b. Mendham, N. J., 1818; d. Clifton Springs, N. Y., 1896. He was graduated at the University of New York; was rector of St. John's Church, Hartford, Calvary Church, New York City, and Grace Church, Baltimore. He became assistant bishop in 1863, and bishop two years later. Among his many works in verse and prose are: "Christian Ballads," perhaps his best-known volume, 1840; "Athanasion, and Other Poems," 1842; "Saul, a Mystery, and Other Poems," 1845; "Hallowe'en, a Romaunt, with Lays Meditative and Devotional," 1869; "The Ladye Chace," 1878; "Institutes of Christian History," 1887.

CRANCH, Christopher Pearse, artist, b. Alexandria, Va., 1813; d. Cambridge, Mass., 1892. Was an ordained Unitarian minister, but soon abandoned the clerical profession and devoted himself to painting. Connected with the New England "Transcendentalists" as a writer for "The Dial," 1840–43. Resided in Europe, 1846–63. Spent the later years of his life at Cambridge, Mass. Author of "Poems," 1844; "The Æneid in English Blank Verse," 1872; "The Bird and the Bell," 1875; "Ariel and Caliban, with Other Poems," 1887.

CRANDALL, Charles Henry, journalist, b. Greenwich, N. Y., 1858. A resident of Springdale, Conn., where he devotes his time to literature. Author of two volumes of verse, "Wayside Music," 1893, and "The Chords of Life," 1898, and editor of "Representative Sonnets," 1890.

CRANE, Elizabeth Green, b. New York, N. Y., 18—. With the exception of occasional trips abroad, Miss Crane has lived in the country since her childhood. Her first book was an historic drama, "Berquin," 1897. It has been followed by a volume of poems, "Sylva," 1900.

CRANE, Stephen, b. Newark, N. J., 1871; d. Baden Weiler, Germany, 1900. Studied at Lafayette College, was occupied for some years with newspaper work, and was correspondent for a New York paper in the Græco-Turkish war of 1897, and in Cuba, 1898. Removed to a suburb of London, England, 1898. Author of "The Black Riders, and Other Lines," verse, 1895; "War is Kind," verse, 1899; and of several volumes of fiction, including "The Red Badge of Courage," 1896; "The Little Regiment," 1897; "The Third Violet," 1899, etc.

CROFFUT, William Augustus, journalist, b. Redding, Conn., 1836. Entered journalism in 1858. He has published several prose volumes as well as "Bourbon Ballads," 1880, and "The Prophecy, and Other Poems," 1896.

CROSBY, Ernest Howard, humanitarian, b. New York, N. Y., 1856. Graduated from the University of New York and the Columbia College Law School. He was appointed judge of the international court of Alexandria, Egypt, in 1889; resigned in 1894. On his way back to America he visited Count Tolstoi, and since has given up the law to devote his attention to social reform. He was first president of the New York Social Reform Club. Author of two volumes of verse: "War Echoes," 1898; "Plain Talk in Psalm and Parable," 1899. (D. 1907.)

CROSWELL, William, b. Hudson, N. Y., 1804; d. Boston, Mass., 1851. He graduated at Yale, and was the first rector of the Church of the Advent, Boston. His first poem appeared in "The Episcopal Watchman," which he edited at Hartford, with Mr. Doane, afterwards bishop of New Jersey. Much of his verse is found in Arthur Cleveland Coxe's compilation, "Poems Sacred and Secular," 1859.

CURTIS, George William, man of letters, orator, and a leader in social and political reform, b. Providence, R. I., 24 Feb., 1824; d. Staten Island, N. Y., 31 Aug., 1892. From his youth, when at eighteen he became a member of the Community at Brook Farm, until his death after years of service in every good and perfect work, he was a practical idealist, and the typical American exemplar of "sweetness and light." His earlier prose writings were "Nile Notes of a Howadji," 1851; "The Potiphar Papers," 1853; "Prue and I," 1856. Their pages were charged with poetic sentiment. One of his very infrequent pieces in verse-form is given in this Anthology. A condensed but admirable biography of Curtis, by Edward Cary, constitutes a volume of the "American Men of Letters" series.

CUTLER, Elbridge Jefferson, b. Holliston,

Mass., 1831; d. Cambridge, Mass., 1870. Professor of modern languages at Harvard, 1865–70. Author of "War Poems," 1867; "Stella," 1868.

DALLAS, **Mary (Kyle)**, b. Philadelphia, Penn., 18—; d. New York, N. Y., 1897. A contributor, for many years, of fiction and verse to family story papers. Some of her novels were published in book-form. Her poem, "Brave Love," has been set to music by Harry Pepper.

DALY, **Eugene Howell**, Columbia University, Class of 1894.

DANA, **Richard Henry**, poet, critic, and essayist, b. Cambridge, Mass., 15 Aug., 1787; d. Boston, Mass., 2 Feb., 1879. After leaving Harvard College, without graduation, on account of being involved in the students' rebellion of 1807, he entered upon the study of law, and was admitted to the bar of Boston in 1811. He was active in politics as a Federalist, and was elected to the Massachusetts legislature. As a journalist he is conspicuous for his connection with the "North American Review," of which he was associate editor with Edward Tyrrel Channing (1818–1820). He began the publication at New York of the "Idle Man," a literary periodical, to which Bryant, Allston, and others contributed, but which reached only six numbers. Dana's first volume of "Poems," containing "The Buccaneer," appeared in 1833. His lectures on Shakespeare, delivered in several Eastern cities, are representative, and he was the first eminent American to appreciate the beauties of Wordsworth. A collective edition of his "Poems and Prose Writings" was brought out in Boston in 1833 (enlarged edition 1850).

DANDRIDGE, **Danske (Bedinger)**, b. Copenhagen, Denmark, 186–. Greatgranddaughter of Eliza Southgate Bowne. In 1877 she married Stephen Dandridge. Her published works are "Joy, and Other Poems," 1888, and "Rose Brake," 1890. She has in preparation a book to be entitled "The Heroes of La Vendée," and a collective edition of her poems.

DAVIDSON, **Margaret Gilman (George)**, b. Columbia, Mo., 1869; d. Lewistown, Ill., 1897. She was married, in 1895, to W. T. Davidson, a journalist, who has in view a memorial collection of her poems.

DAWES, **Rufus**, lawyer, b. Boston, Mass., 1803; d. Washington, D. C., 1859. Author of "The Valley of the Nashaway, and Other Poems," 1830; "Geraldine," 1839; "Miscellaneous Poems," 1839; "Nixie's Mate," "Story," 1840.

DAWSON, **Daniel Lewis**, b. Lewistown, Penn., 1855; d. Philadelphia, Penn., 1893. He attended La Salle College, but completed the college course under private tuition. At one time he went through professional training in athletics and figured as a pugilist. Was an iron-founder at the time of his death. A posthumous collection of his poems, "The Seeker of the Marshes, and Other Poems," appeared in 1893.

DAY, **Richard Edwin**, b. Granby, N. Y., 1852. Graduated at Syracuse University, and taught at various schools. Was associate editor of the Syracuse "Standard," 1880–98.—"Lines in the Sand," 1878; "Thor: a Drama," 1880; "Lyrics and Satires," 1883; "Poems," 1888.

DAY, **Thomas Fleming**, b. Weston-Super-Mare, Somersetshire, England, 1861. Came to the United States in 1868. Son of Edward H. Day, professor of natural science at Normal College, New York City. Editor of a yachting monthly at New York, "The Rudder," since 1895. Author of "Songs of Sea and Sail," 1899.

DE KAY, **Charles**, art-critic, b. Washington, D. C., 1848. Grandson of Joseph Rodman Drake. He was graduated at Yale, and in 1877 joined the staff of the New York "Times." His works include "The Bohemian," 1878; "Hesperus, and Other Poems," 1880; "The Vision of Nimrod," 1881; "The Love Poems of Louis Barnaval," 1883; "Barye, Life and Works," 1889; "The Family Life of Heinrich Heine," translation, 1892; "Bird Gods of Ancient Europe," 1898. Mr. De Kay was the projector of "The Authors Club," New York, and U. S. Consul General, Berlin, 1894–97.

DELAND, **Margaret**.—See *M. W. C. Deland*.

DELAND, **Margaretta Wade (Campbell) (Margaret Deland)**, b. Allegheny, Penn., 1857. She was married, in 1880, to Lorin F. Deland, of Boston, Mass., which city became her residence. Among her writings are: "The Old Garden, and Other Verses," 1886, and "John Ward, Preacher," 1888. The latter is a novel which deals with theological questions, and which brought wide reputation to its author.

DENNEN, **Grace Atherton**, educator, b. Woburn, Mass., 18—. Graduated at Smith College. Removed to California, 1894, and engaged in teaching and literary work. Is a tutor in the English department of Leland Stanford, Jr., University. Edited "The Ebell," 1898.

DE VERE, **Mary Ainge**, **"Madeline Bridges,"** b. Brooklyn, N. Y., 184–. She has always lived in Brooklyn, devoting herself to literature, and making frequent contributions to the "Galaxy," "Century," "Independent," "Life," and many other periodicals. Author of "Love Songs, and Other Poems," 1870; "Poems," 1890.

DEWEY, **George Washington**, b. Baltimore, Md., 1818; d. Philadelphia, Penn., 1860. His father was a painter from Westfield, Mass. The son lived in Philadelphia, where he followed the occupation of an accountant, and afterwards that of a merchant. His poems, essays, and reviews were never collected in book-form. Mr. Dewey held an official position in The Art Union of Philadelphia.

DICKINSON, Charles Monroe, b. Lowville, N. Y., 1842. He was admitted to the New York bar, 1865, and practised law in Binghamton and New York City. In 1878 he became editor and owner of the Binghamton "Republican." Published "The Children, and Other Verses," 1889.

DICKINSON, Emily, b. Amherst, Mass., 1830; d. there, 1886. Her father, Hon. Edward Dickinson, was treasurer of Amherst College. Her life for the most part was spent in close seclusion, and it was only under protest that a few of her poems were printed during her lifetime. In 1862 she was moved to write to Col. Thomas W. Higginson, enclosing four pieces, and seeking his criticism and advice. This led to a correspondence of many years, and to the posthumous volume, "Poems by Emily Dickinson, Edited by Two of Her Friends, Mabel Loomis Todd and T. W. Higginson," 1890. In later volumes more of her pieces were given to the world. Her letters, 1847-1886, have been edited by Mrs. M. L. Todd.

DICKINSON, Martha Gilbert, niece of Emily Dickinson, b. at Amherst, Mass., 18— of Puritan stock. Since 1892 her poems have appeared in various periodicals. Author of "Within the Hedge," 1899; "The Cathedral," 1901. (In 1903 m. Capt. A. Bianchi.)

DINNIES, Anna Peyre (Shackelford), b. Pineville, S. C., 1805; d. New Orleans, La., 1886. Was a resident of St. Louis and New Orleans. In 1847 she published one hundred poems under the title, "The Floral Year."

DOANE, George Washington, Episcopal bishop, b. Trenton, N. J., 1799; d. Burlington, N. J., 1859. Graduated at Union College. He became bishop of New Jersey in 1832. Some of his hymns are standard favorites. His "Life and Writings," edited by his son, appeared in 1860.

DOANE, William Croswell, Episcopal bishop, b. Boston, Mass., 1832. Son of the preceding. He graduated at Burlington (N. J.) College, and entered the Episcopal ministry in 1853. In 1869 he was made bishop of Albany, N. Y. He is the author of several theological works and of much devotional verse.

DODGE, Mary Barker (Carter), b. Bridgewater, Penn., 184–. She was educated in Philadelphia, and married, 1850, to Charles F. Dodge, after which she lived in Williamsport, Mass., and elsewhere. She has published: "Belfry Voices," 1870; "The Gray Masque, and Other Poems," 1885.

DODGE, Mary Elizabeth (Mapes), b. New York, N. Y., 1838. Daughter of Professor James J. Mapes. After the death of her husband, William Dodge, she wrote for the N. Y. "Hearth and Home," of which she and Donald G. Mitchell were the editors. "St. Nicholas," the successful juvenile magazine, has been under her editorial management since it was founded, in 1873. Her works include "Irvington Stories," for children, 1864; "Hans Brinker, or the Silver Skates," 1865, crowned by the French Academy and translated into the principal languages of Europe; "A Few Friends, and How They Amused Themselves," 1869; "Rhymes and Jingles," 1874; "Theophilus and Others," 1876; "Along the Way," poems, 1879; "Donald and Dorothy," 1883; "When Life is Young," poems for young people, 1894. (D. Onteora Park, N. Y., 1905.)

DOLE, Nathan Haskell, man of letters, b. Chelsea, Mass., 1852. Graduating at Harvard, 1874, he was preceptor of Derby Academy, Hingham, Mass., 1876–78, and since has been engaged in scholarly work. At one time a critic on the Philadelphia "Press," and afterwards editor of the N. Y. "Epoch." Has been active as a translator, and is now editing a twenty-volume edition of Tolstoi's works. In 1896 he edited a multivariorum edition of the "Rubáiyát of Omar Khayyám." Author of several novels and a volume of verse, "The Hawthorne Tree, and Other Poems," 1895.

DORGAN, John Aylmer, lawyer, b. Philadelphia, 1836; d. there, 1867. He published a volume of verse, "Studies," 1862, twice reissued. His premature death, by consumption, was much lamented.

DORR, Julia Caroline (Ripley), b. Charleston, S. C., 1825. Her family removed to New York, where she was married, in 1847, to the Hon. Seneca R. Dorr of Rutland, Vt., which city became her residence. She is the author of "Poems," 1871 (complete edition, 1892); "Friar Anselmo, and Other Poems," 1879; "Daybreak, an Easter Poem," 1882; and "Afternoon Songs," 1885; "The Flower of England's Face," prose, 1895; "A Cathedral Pilgrimage," prose, 1896; "In Kings' Houses," novel, 1898. Mrs. Dorr holds a distinguished and enviable position among American women.

"DOUGLAS, Marion." — See *A. D. (G.) Robinson.*

DRAKE, Joseph Rodman, b. New York, N. Y., 17 Aug., 1795; d. there, 21 Sept., 1820. Left an orphan at an early age, Drake had a hard struggle with poverty, but obtained a good education, graduating in medicine in 1816. His marriage in the same year to the daughter of Henry Eckford, the marine architect, placed him in comfortable circumstances. He travelled with his wife in Europe in 1818. In 1819 he went to New Orleans, hoping to benefit his health, but returned to die of consumption in New York in 1820. His first recorded poem, "The Mocking Bird," was written at the age of fourteen. "The Croakers," a series of witty poems appearing in the "Evening Post," — the first in 1819, — dealt with local celebrities and current events, and created much amusement and curiosity as to their authorship. It was finally proved that Drake wrote the first three. Others were written separately by Halleck and Drake, or by the two poets in collaboration. These poems were collected and published in 1860 by the Bradford Club, of New York. "The Culprit Fay," Drake's longest production, grew out of an assertion by some friends that American rivers were not adapted by romantic associations for poetic use. Gen. James Grant Wilson says that Drake composed this poem, a charming example of pure fancy, and read it to his friends as a refutation of their theory. A collection of Drake's poems, containing that national classic "The American Flag" (of which Halleck is said to have written the closing quatrain) was published under the title, "The Culprit Fay, and Other Poems," by his daughter in 1836 (later editions, 1847, 1865).

"DROCH." — See *Robert Bridges*.

DUER, Alice. — See *A. D. Miller*.

DUER, Caroline, b. New York, N. Y., 18—, where she now resides. Daughter of James G. King Miller. Miss Duer's lyrics comprise the larger portion of "Poems by Caroline and Alice Duer," 1896, a volume that won friends by the grace and frequent vigor of its verse, and by a certain air of distinction.

DUFFIELD, Samuel Augustus Willoughby, clergyman, b. Brooklyn, N. Y., 1843; d. Bloomfield, N. J., 1887. A graduate of Yale. Entered the Presbyterian ministry, and held a pastorate at Bloomfield for the greater part of his life. Author of a volume of poems, "Warp and Woof," 1870, and of "English Hymns, their Authors and History," 1886.

DUNBAR, Paul Laurence, b. Dayton, Ohio, 1872. Of African blood. Graduated at the Dayton High School, and engaged in newspaper work. His verse soon attracted attention, and he has given successful readings from his poems. In 1899 he accepted a position in the Library of Congress at Washington. His maturer poems are to be found in "Lyrics of Lowly Life," 1896; "Lyrics of the Hearthside," 1899. "Folks from Dixie," stories, 1897, and "The Uncalled," novel, 1898, are among his books of fiction. (D. 1906.)

DURIVAGE, Francis Alexander, b. Boston, Mass., 1814; d. New York, N. Y., 1881. Nephew of Edward Everett. A journalist and writer of verse and fiction. Among his books are "Life Scenes from the World around Us," 1853; "The Fatal Casket," 1866; and A Cyclopedia of History. The poem "Chez Brébant" is an interesting example of a poem that, although composed by one of the early American school, is quite in the manner of the latter-day verse of which Dobson's "Proverbs in Porcelain" is a typical example.

DWIGHT, Timothy, educator and theologian, b. Northampton, Mass., 14 May, 1752; d. New Haven, 11 Jan., 1817. Was a precocious child and entered Yale when but thirteen years old; became a tutor there when he was nineteen. Licensed to preach in 1777. While serving as chaplain in the American army against Burgoyne, he wrote his famous poem, "Columbia." In 1794 he was elected president of Yale College, and by his dignity, learning, and character proved himself a great educator, whose memory will always be revered. He belonged, with Trumbull, Barlow, etc., to the group known as "The Hartford Wits," contributing anonymous satirical prose and verse to the papers during the decade following the Revolutionary war. A posthumous edition of his divinity sermons was published in five volumes, "Theology, Explained and Defended," 1818. This work has passed through many editions in America and Europe. His metrical works are: "The Conquest of Canaan," 1785; "The Triumph of Infidelity," 1788; "Greenfield Hill," 1794. Under the presidency of Dr. Dwight's grandson Timothy Dwight, in whom the traditions and character of the elder of the name have been nobly revived, Yale College became a university.

EASTER, Marguerite Elizabeth (Miller), b. Leesburg, Va., 1839; d. Baltimore, Md., 1894. She was of German ancestry, and was married, in 1859, to James Washington Easter, a prominent Baltimore merchant. Author of "Clytie, and Other Poems," 1891.

EASTMAN, Barrett, journalist, b. Chicago, Ill., 1869. Educated at Racine College, and became an editorial writer and dramatic critic on various Chicago and New York papers. Since 1898 he has been conducting a newspaper syndicate in New York City. His writings include many contributions in prose and verse to the journals and magazines, and (with Wallace Rice) "Under the Star and other Songs of the Sea," 1898.

EASTMAN, Charles Gamage, journalist, b. Fryeburg, Me., 1816; d. Montpelier, Vt., 1861. A graduate of the University of Vermont. He founded the "Lamoille River Express" at Johnson, Vt., 1838, and "The Spirit of the Age" at Woodstock, Vt., 1840; and became editor of "The Vermont Patriot," Montpelier, 1846. Member of the State Senate, 1851–52. Author of "Poems," 1848, of which a revised edition was issued in 1880.

EASTMAN, Elaine (Goodale), b. Mount Washington, Mass., 1863. She and her younger sister, Dora Read Goodale, attracted attention when children by the publication of several volumes of poems, some of the verse appearing as early as 1877. She became interested in the Indian schools; was first a government teacher in Dakota, and afterwards, in 1890, was appointed superintendent of all Indian schools in South Dakota. In 1891 she married Dr. Charles A. Eastman, a Sioux Indian. She has published separately "Journal of a Farmer's Daughter," 1881.

EATON, Arthur Wentworth Hamilton, clergyman, b. Kentville, Nova Scotia, 1854.

Graduated at Harvard. A minister of the Episcopal Church, and a resident of New York City. He has published several prose works, and a volume of poems, "Acadian Legends and Lyrics," 1889.

EGAN, Maurice Francis, educator, b. Philadelphia, Penn., 1852. Graduated at La Salle College. Was for some years professor of English literature at Notre Dame University, Ind., and now holds the same position at the Catholic University, Washington. From 1880–1888 he was editor of the N. Y. "Freeman's Journal." In verse he has written: "Preludes," 1881; "Songs and Sonnets," 1885, enlarged edition, 1892. His prose volumes include, beside various novels, "Lectures on English Literature," 1889; "The Leopard of Lancianus, and Other Tales," 1899.

ELIOT, Henrietta Robins (Mack), b. Amherst, Mass., 18—. Now resident in Portland, Ore. Mrs. Eliot is a writer of verse and short stories, and has published "Laura's Holidays," 1898.

ELLIOT, George Tracy, b. Mason, N. H., 1853. Educated at the Massachusetts Institute of Technology. Since 1884 he has been a corrector at the Riverside Press, Cambridge, Mass.

ELLSWORTH, Erastus Wolcott, inventor, b. East Windsor, Conn., 1822. Graduated at Amherst. Studied law, but did not follow the profession. Has resided chiefly at East Windsor Hill, where he has been occupied as an inventor of mechanical appliances and with farming. Of late years he has led a secluded life. He was a brilliant contributor to "Putnam's Monthly" and other magazines. A volume of his poems was published in 1855.

ELLWANGER, William De Lancey, lawyer, b. Rochester, N. Y., 1854. Brother of the well-known bookman and essayist, George Herman Ellwanger, and like him interested in books and letters. His poems have appeared in prominent magazines.

EMBURY, Emma Catherine (Manly), b. New York, N. Y., 1806; d. Brooklyn, N. Y., 1863. She was married to Mr. Daniel Embury, of Brooklyn, in 1828. She published "Guido, and Other Poems," 1828; "Love's Token Flowers," verse, 1846; a number of stories; and "Poems," issued posthumously, 1869. A favorite writer in the time of Griswold and Poe.

EMERSON, Ralph Waldo, b. Boston, Mass., 25 May, 1803; d. Concord, Mass., 27 April, 1882. He seems to have made little noteworthy impression upon his schoolmates save for diligent and intelligent work. After leaving Harvard, in 1821, he taught school and studied for the ministry, being ordained 11 March, 1829, the same year in which he was married to Miss Ellen Louisa Tucker. He took an active interest in public affairs, was on the School Board, chosen chaplain of the State Senate, etc. In 1832 he resigned his clerical position in the "Second Church." This step marks a great change in his life. Though he continued to preach, and in many different churches, he would never accept a call, owing to his scruples relating to the communion service. In 1834, after a trip abroad, he became a resident of Concord, Mass. In September, 1835, he married Miss Lydia Jackson, his first wife having died in 1832. In 1835 he began his courses of lectures in Boston. He continued to preach until the autumn of 1838 in the church at East Lexington. In 1836 his first book appeared, a very small volume entitled "Nature." It made no immediate sensation, undoubtedly because incomprehensible to the greater fraction. Carlyle and men of his stamp gave it unstinted praise. His next publication was "The American Scholar," which he delivered before the Phi Beta Kappa Society, at Cambridge, 1837. Holmes has dubbed this oration our "intellectual declaration of independence." His lectures and orations were continued all through his life, and were published as noted below. In 1841 "Brook Farm" was organized. Emerson had only tangential relations with the experiment, and wrote of it in a humorous though kindly manner. His first volume of "Essays" was published in 1841. In 1842 he lost his little son, whose death was the inspiration of the "Threnody." In 1846 his first volume of poems was published. In 1867 his later poems were published under the title "May Day and Other Pieces." Collective editions of his verse appeared in 1876 and subsequently. His prose works, composed principally of his lectures, are "Essays," 1841; "Essays, Second Series," 1844; "Miscellanies," 1849; "Representative Men," 1850; "English Traits," 1856; "The Conduct of Life," 1860; "Society and Solitude," 1870; "Letters and Social Aims," 1875; and a posthumous volume, "Lectures and Biographical Sketches." He also contributed to the "Memoirs of Margaret Fuller Ossoli," 1852; and edited "Parnassus," 1874, a collection of his poetical favorites. It is impossible to overestimate the influence of Emerson on the American people. His lectures were a stimulus as well as a guide for the thought of the day. The latter years of his life were peaceful and happy, though his memory failed him, and his mind lost its alert poise. He died of pneumonia after a short illness, and was buried in ground which he himself had consecrated twenty-seven years before. He was mourned not only by his country but by all the world, though his refined and luminous soul lives forever in his immortal work. For a critical analysis of Emerson's life, philosophy, and writings, cp. "Poets of America," chap. v. [B. D. L.]

ENGLISH, Thomas Dunn, physician and legislator, b. Philadelphia, Penn., 29 June, 1819. He graduated at the medical school of the University of Pennsylvania, 1839, and afterwards studied law, entering the Philadelphia bar in 1842. After 1844 he was occupied in New York as a journalist, establishing "The Aristidean," 1845. From 1859 he practised medicine in Newark, N. J., and he represented his district in the U. S. House of Representatives, 1891–95. The controversy of this literary veteran with Edgar Allan Poe is well remembered, but more recently Dr. English did generously by Poe's memory in contributions to the press. His popular ballad, "Ben Bolt," appeared in the "New Mirror," 1843. Among his books are "American Ballads," 1882; "The Boy's Book of Battle Lyrics," 1885; "Jacob Schuyler's Millions," novel, 1886; "Fairy Stories and Wonder Tales," 1897. His "Select Poems," edited by his daughter, were published, 1894. D. Newark, N. J., 1 April, 1902.

ERSKINE, John, Columbia University, Class of 1900.

FABBRI, Cora Randall, b. New York, N. Y., 1871; d. San Remo, Italy, 1892. Daughter of Ernesto G. Fabbri, Florence, and of Sara Randall, New York. The tender verses of this young girl, upon whom many fair hopes centred, are in a volume of "Lyrics," 1892, published just before her death.

FATHER EDMUND of the Heart of Mary, C. P. — See *Benjamin Dionysius Hill.*

FENOLLOSA, Ernest Francisco, educator and art connoisseur, b. Salem, Mass., 1853. Graduated at Harvard. In 1878 was appointed professor of political economy at the Imperial University in Tokio, Japan, and also began his studies of Japanese art. He was made imperial commissioner of fine arts, 1886, and has held similar positions in the United States. Is now professor of English and English literature in the Higher Normal School of Tokio, and is making a special study of Chinese and Japanese poetry. — "East and West," poems, 1893.

FENOLLOSA, Mary (McNeil), (Mary McNeil Scott), b. Mobile, Ala., 18—. Wife of E. F. Fenollosa. Author of "Out of the Nest: A Flight of Verses," 1899. Her charming stories and poems, since her brief sojourn, 1890, in the province of Satsuma, have related mostly to Japanese themes.

FIELD, Eugene, journalist, b. St. Louis, Mo., 3 Sept., 1850; d. Buena Park, Chicago, Ill., 4 Nov., 1895. He received his schooling at Amherst, Mass., and later at Williams and Knox Colleges and the University of Missouri. In 1873 he began newspaper work at St. Louis, which he continued in St. Joseph, Kansas City, and Denver until 1883, when he was called by Melville E. Stone to the Chicago "Daily News," with which paper he was connected until his death. His "Denver Tribune Primer" appeared in 1882. Soon after his arrival in Chicago, he began the composition of more serious work in prose and verse than the light contributions which had secured him recognition. Material of both kinds is found in "Culture's Garland," published in 1887. It was followed by "A Little Book of Western Verse," 1889; "A Little Book of Profitable Tales," 1889; "With Trumpet and Drum," poems about children, 1892; "Second Book of Verse," 1893; "Echoes from the Sabine Farm," with Roswell M. Field, 1893; "The Holy Cross and Other Tales," 1893; and "Love Songs of Childhood," 1894. "The Love Affairs of a Bibliomaniac," "The House," "Songs and Other Verse," and "Second Book of Tales" (posthumous volumes) were included in the complete edition of "Works of Eugene Field," published in 1896. This rare and original minstrel of the West was the Yorick of American poetry, childhood's born laureate, and no less a scholar by nature than a man of infinite humor, and of inimitable, if sometimes too eccentric, jest.

FIELDS, Annie (Adams), b. Boston, Mass., 1834. She attended George B. Emerson's school in Boston. She was married to Mr. James T. Fields, 1854, and has published: "Under the Olive," poems, 1880; "How to Help the Poor," 1883; "The Singing Shepherd, and Other Poems," 1895; "Authors and Friends," 1896; "A Shelf of Old Books," 1896. She has also written biographies of Whittier, Harriet Beecher Stowe, and James T. Fields.

FIELDS, James Thomas, publisher, b. Portsmouth, N. H., 31 Dec., 1816; d. Boston, Mass., 24 April, 1881. His father was a shipmaster, and died when James was four years old. The latter graduated at the Portsmouth High School at thirteen, and the next year obtained a clerkship in the bookstore of Carter & Hendee at Boston. In 1832, William D. Ticknor bought the business, and Fields remained with him, becoming a partner in 1845, when the firm was reorganized. In 1854 the house assumed the afterward famous name of Ticknor & Fields, associated with the publication of the works of Emerson, Hawthorne, Longfellow, Whittier, Lowell, Holmes, and the remainder of the great Boston group of authors. Of all of these, Mr. Fields, himself an author of repute, and a still better editor, was the personal associate and adviser. He took the editorship of "The Atlantic Monthly," on Mr. Lowell's retirement in 1861, and held it until his own retirement from the publishing house, then Fields, Osgood, & Co., on Jan. 1, 1871. After his retirement from business, Mr. Fields became a favorite lecturer upon literary subjects. He married Miss Annie Adams, 1854. (See *Annie Fields.*) He published: "Poems," 1849; "A Few Verses for a Few Friends," 1858; "Yesterdays with Authors," 1871 (20th edition, 1881); "Hawthorne," 1876; "In and Out of Doors with Charles Dickens," 1876; "Underbrush," 1877; "Ballads and Other Verses," 1880.

FINCH, Francis Miles, jurist, b. Ithaca, N. Y., 1827. Graduated at Yale, 1849. Was the Class Poet and delivered a memorable Class Poem. He practised law at Ithaca until 1881, when he was elected a justice of the N. Y. Court of Appeals. From 1892 he was dean of the law school of Cornell University. "The Blue and the Gray," which appeared in "The Atlantic Monthly" for 1867, has become a national classic. (D. 1907.)

FINCH, Julia (Neely), b. Mobile, Ala., 18—. A musician and composer of Birmingham, Ala. Her pure and womanly lyric of motherhood, "The Unborn," first appeared in an Atlanta periodical.

FLASH, Henry Lynden, b. Cincinnati, O., 1835. Graduated at the Western Military Institute of Kentucky. He was an officer in the Confederate army, and after the war made his home in New Orleans until 1886, when he removed to Los Angeles, Cal. Besides his "Poems," 1860, he wrote several pieces popular in war-time.

FLEMING, Maybury, journalist, b. Boston, Mass., 1853. Was educated at the University of New York, and afterwards joined the editorial staff of the N. Y. "Mail and Express." A contributor to the magazines.

FOOTE, General Lucius Harwood, b. Winfield, N. Y., 1826. His father, a Congregational clergyman, made his home in Ohio and later in Rockford, Ill. The son was educated at Adelbert College, Cleveland, O. In 1861 President Lincoln appointed him collector of the port of Sacramento. He has also been adjutant-general of California; U. S. consul at Valparaiso, Chile; and U. S. minister to Corea. Author of "A Red Letter Day, and Other Poems," 1882; "On the Heights," 1897.

"**FORESTER**, Fanny." — See *Emily Chubbuck Judson*.

"**FORESTER**, Frank." — See *Henry William Herbert*.

FOSS, Sam Walter, librarian, b. Candia, N. H., 1858. Graduated at Brown University. Became librarian of the Somerville Public Library in 1898. His published works are: "Back Country Poems," 1892; "Whiffs from Wild Meadows," 1896; "Dreams in Homespun," 1898; "Songs of War and Peace," 1899.

FOSTER, Stephen Collins, composer, b. Pittsburg, Penn., 1826; d. New York, N. Y., 1864. He was the earliest and chief member of the school of composers of that idealized negro melody which characterizes a fourth of the 125 or more songs, for which he wrote both music and words. His "Old Folks at Home" was written before he was twenty and was published in 1850. Other well-known pieces are "The Suwanee River," "My Old Kentucky Home," "Nellie Bly," etc.

"**FOXTON**, E." — See *Sarah Hammond Palfrey*.

FRENEAU, Philip, mariner, journalist, and patriot, b. New York, N. Y., 1752; d. near Monmouth, N. J., 1832. The true pioneer of our national poets, and the first to display a notable though irregular lyrical gift. Freneau and Hugh Brackenridge, while students at Princeton, wrote, and delivered at their graduation, in 1771, a metrical dialogue, "The Rising Glory of America." During the Revolutionary War, Freneau's pen was most active and satirical. Between 1770 and 1790 he made many sea-voyages to the West Indies and other ports, often in command of mercantile vessels. "The British Prison-Ship," in four cantos, records the capture, in 1780, of a vessel in which he and all on board were taken prisoners. Many of his poems were published in "The Freeman's Journal," with which he was connected in Philadelphia. He edited the "Daily Advertiser," New York, 1790; and the "National Gazette," Philadelphia, 1791. After an interval of sea-life, he made, in 1812, his permanent home in New Jersey. Author of "Poems of Philip Freneau, Written chiefly during the Late War," 1786; "Poems Written between the Years 1788 and 1794," 1795; "Poems Written and Published during the American Revolutionary War," 1809; and "A Collection of Poems on American Affairs," 1815. The edition of 1795 came from the author's own press at Monmouth, N. J. — Cp. "Poets of America," pp. 35, 36.

FROTHINGHAM, Nathaniel Langdon, clergyman, b. Boston, Mass., 1793; d. there, 1870. A graduate of Harvard. He was pastor of a Unitarian church at Boston from 1815 to 1850. Besides various theological writings, he was the author of "Metrical Pieces," 1855 and 1870. His poem, "The Crossed Swords," was written "on seeing the swords of Col. Prescott and Capt. Linzee, now crossed through a carved wreath of olive leaves, in the hall of the Massachusetts Historical Society."

FULLER, Margaret Witter, b. Brooklyn, N. Y., 187-. Daughter of James Ebenezer Fuller, of Norwich, Conn., in which city she has resided since her childhood.

FURNESS, William Henry, clergyman, b. Boston, Mass., 1802; d. Philadelphia, Penn., 1896. He was a graduate of Harvard and of the Harvard Theological school, and in 1825 became pastor of the Unitarian church in Philadelphia. He wrote many theological works. His "Verses: Translations and Hymns," was issued in 1886. His son, Horace Howard Furness, is the most eminent Shakespearean scholar living, and editor of the Variorum Edition of Shakespeare's plays.

GALLAGHER, William Davis, b. Philadelphia, Penn., 1808; d. Louisville, Ky., 1894. Associate editor Cincinnati "Gazette" and Louisville "Courier." Delegate to the convention of 1860 that nominated Lincoln. Private secretary to Thomas Corwin and to S. P. Chase. President Ohio Historical Society. He strove to diffuse a taste for letters, and compiled the earliest anthology of Western poetry: "Selections from the Poetical Literature of the West," Cincinnati, 1840. His "Erato," poems, appeared in 1835-37; his "Miami Woods, A Golden Wedding, and Other Poems," in 1881.

GARDNER, William Henry, song-writer, b. Boston, Mass., 1865. Has devoted himself chiefly to verse-writing for music. His lyrics have been interpreted by both American and English composers. Author of "Work and Play Songs," 1899.

GARLAND, Hamlin, novelist, b. West Salem, Wis., 1860. Graduated at Cedar Valley Seminary, Osage, Ia. Taught school in Illinois, 1882–83, and preëmpted a claim in Dakota, 1883, but in the following year removed to Boston, Mass., where he devoted himself to study and literary work, at the same time teaching in the School of Oratory. Has resided in Chicago and West Salem since 1891, with the exception of trips northwest, and to the East and Europe, in connection with his literary and historical researches. He has published "Prairie Songs," 1893; "Crumbling Idols," essays, 1894; "Ulysses Grant: an Interpretation," 1898; "The Trail of the Gold-Seekers," 1899. Mr. Garland's books of fiction include "Main-Travelled Roads," 1890; "A Little Norsk," 1891; "A Spoil of Office," 1892; "Rose of Dutcher's Coolly," 1895.

GARRISON, Wendell Phillips, b. Cambridgeport, Mass., 1840; d. Orange, N. J., 1907. Graduated at Harvard. A son of William Lloyd Garrison, and literary editor of the New York "Nation" from its foundation in 1865 till 1906. Among other works, he published, in collaboration with his brother, Francis J. Garrison, "William Lloyd Garrison: The Story of His Life, Told by His Children," four volumes, 1885–89. An exquisite private edition of his "Sonnets and Lyrics of the Ever-Womanly," printed in 1898, contains "The Post-Meridian" sonnets. The book itself was examined by the editor of this anthology too late for the insertion, heretofore, of the following beautiful sonnet: —

AT GREENWOOD CEMETERY

Here was the ancient strand, the utmost reach,
Of the great Northern ice-wave; hitherto
With its last pulse it mounted, then withdrew,
Leaving its fringe of wreckage on the beach:
Boulder and pebble and sand-matrix — each
From crag or valley ravished; scanty clue
To its old site affording in its new,
Yet real, as the men of science teach.
Life hath not less its terminal moraine:
Look how on that discharged from melting snows
Another rears itself, the spoil of plain
And mountain also, marked by stones in rows,
With legend meet for such promiscuous pain:
Here rests — Hier ruhet, or *Ici repose.*

GARRISON, William Lloyd, abolitionist, b. Newburyport, Mass., 1805; d. New York, N. Y., 1879. Established "The Liberator," Boston, 1831, and conducted it until 1865. Was founder of the American Anti-Slavery Society, and its president from 1843 to 1865. Suffered imprisonment in Boston and Maryland. In Georgia a reward was set upon his head. After his death his statue was erected in Boston, where he had been mobbed for his principles. His "Sonnets and Poems," chiefly devoted to freedom, appeared in 1843.

GEORGE, Margaret Gilman. — See *M. G. Davidson.*

GILDER, Joseph B., journalist, b. Flushing, N. Y., 1858. Brother of Richard Watson Gilder. Entered the United States Naval Academy at Annapolis, Md., 1872, but resigned two years later. Engaged in journalism until 1881, when, with his sister, Miss Jeannette L. Gilder, he organized "The Critic," and with her has edited it ever since. Mr. Gilder is also the editor of the life and speeches of Hon. Chauncey M. Depew, and of an edition of Lowell's "Impressions of Spain."

GILDER, Richard Watson, editor and reformer, b. Bordentown, N. J., 8 Feb., 1844. He studied at Bellevue Seminary, the college founded in Bordentown by his father, Rev. William H. Gilder. During the Confederate invasion of Pennsylvania he served in Landis's Philadelphia Battery. His father's death put an end to his law studies, and he joined the staff of the Newark, N. J., "Daily Advertiser," 1864. In 1868 he established and edited with Newton Crane the Newark "Morning Register," and afterwards was editor of the New York "Hours at Home." Was associate editor of "Scribner's Monthly" (afterwards "The Century") from its foundation in 1870; and on the death of Dr. J. G. Holland, 1881, became editor-in-chief. His volume of poems, "The New Day," 1875, was followed by several others afterwards included in "Lyrics, and Other Poems," 1885; "Two Worlds, and Other Poems," 1891; "The Great Remembrance, and Other Poems," 1893; "Five Books of Song," complete to date, 1894; "For the Country," poems, 1897; "In Palestine, and Other Poems," 1898. For some years past, Mr. Gilder, always a sincere humanitarian, has been prominent in social and political reform, and especially successful as chairman of the Commission for the Inspection and Betterment of the Tenement House System in New York City. He gave effective aid to the cause of International Copyright. The Authors Club was founded at his home. He is married to the artist, Helena De Kay, sister of Charles De Kay, and granddaughter of Joseph Rodman Drake. His influence has been propitious in many directions taken by our literary and artistic movements of recent years. From the first, the growth and excellence of the "Century Magazine" have been largely due to Mr. Gilder's editorial sense, tact, and unenvious appreciation. His poetry is of a pure cast, finished in the extreme, and often notably lyrical. Cp. "Poets of America," p. 442. His complete Poems appeared in 1908.

GILLESPY, Jeannette Bliss, Barnard College, Class of 1900.

GLYNDON, Howard. — See *L. R. Searing.*

GLYNES, Ella Maria (Dietz), b. New York, N. Y., 185–. She made her débût as an actress in New York, 1872, but played chiefly in England for some years. In 1881 ill-health compelled her to leave the stage. Her first husband was Edward Clymer, a merchant. In 1899 she was married in London to Webster Glynes, barrister. Mrs. Glynes was a founder of the Sorosis Society and its fifth president. She also helped to form the Church and Stage Guild, 1880. Author of "The Triumph of Love," 1878; "The Triumph of Time," 1884; "The Triumph of Life," 1885.

GOETZ, Philip Becker, Harvard University, Class of 1893.

GOODALE, Dora Reed, b. Mount Washington, Mass., 1866. Sister of Mrs. Charles A. Eastman, and author with her, in childhood, of "Apple Blossoms," 1878; "In Berkshire with Wild Flowers," 1879, and "All Round the Year," 1880. Has since contributed to many magazines. Her separate volume, "Heralds of Easter," appeared in 1887.

GOODALE, Elaine. — See *Elaine Eastman.*

GOODRICH, Samuel Griswold, b. Ridgefield, Conn., 1793; d. New York, N. Y., 1860. During his career as publisher and author in Hartford and Boston he edited and wrote one hundred and seventy volumes, chiefly over the pseudonym "Peter Parley." Many of these books achieved a wide popularity. He edited "The Token," an annual, from 1828 to 1832. "The Outcast, and Other Poems," appeared in 1836.

GORDON, Armistead Churchill, b. Albemarle Co., Va., 1855. A graduate of the Virginia University, founded by his grandfather, General W. F. Gordon. While in college he contributed to the New York magazines, and in 1880 published, with Thomas Nelson Page, "Befo' de War," poems. This was followed by "Echoes in Negro Dialect," 1888, and "For Truth and Freedom," 1898. Mr. Gordon is a lawyer and ex-mayor of Staunton, Va.

GOULD, Hannah Flagg, b. Lancaster, Mass., 1789; d. Newburyport, Mass., 1865. She was a sister of Benjamin Apthorp Gould, the classical scholar, and resided at Newburyport for the greater part of her life. Her three volumes of "Poems" appeared in 1832, 1836, and 1841.

GOURAUD, George Fauvel, lawyer, b. New York, N. Y., 1872. Studied at Harrow, England, and the Polytechnicum, Hanover, Germany. Graduated at the Yale Law School, and was admitted to the New York bar, 1896. — "Ballads of Coster-Land," 1897.

GRAY, David, b. Edinburgh, Scotland, 1836; d. Binghamton, 1888. In 1856 he joined the staff of the Buffalo, N. Y., "Courier," of which he afterward became editor, resigning on account of ill-health. His Letters, Prose Writings, Poems, etc., were edited by J. N. Larned in 1888.

GREENE, Albert Gorton, lawyer, b. Providence, R. I., 1802; d. Cleveland, O., 1868. Graduated at Brown University. Was for twenty-five years clerk of the Municipal Court at Providence, and its judge 1858–67. The original school bill of Rhode Island was drafted by his hand. He was conspicuous in the founding of the Providence Athenæum. For fourteen years president of the Rhode Island Historical Society. His poems have never been published in a collected form. Judge Greene was the founder of the "Harris Collection of American Poetry," bequeathed to Brown University by the late Senator Anthony. The editor of the present Anthology has frequently profited by the resources of this collection.

GREENE, Homer, lawyer, b. Ariel, Penn., 1853. A graduate of Union College, and now a resident of Honesdale, Penn., where he has practised law since 1879. Author of several books of fiction and of occasional poems. His winsome and melodious ballad, "What my Lover Said," fairly deserves its popularity.

GREENE, Sarah Pratt (McLean), b. Simsbury, Conn., 1858. Educated at Mt. Holyoke, Mass. Taught school near Plymouth, Mass., where she obtained the material for her "Cape Cod-Folks," 1881. She was married to F. L. Greene, and removed to the West. Since his death she has resided in New England. Among her books are "Towhead," 1884, containing her best-known poem, "De Sheepfol';" "Lastchance Junction," 1889.

GRISSOM, Arthur, b. Payson, Ill., 1869. Well-known as editor of "Spirit," and a member of Mr. Munsey's staff. He was interested in the "Kansas City Independent," and he was editor of "The Smart Set." He published a volume of society verse entitled "Beaux and Belles," 1896. D. New York, N. Y., 1901.

"GROOT, Cecil de." — See *Wallace Rice.*

GUINEY, Louise Imogen, b. Boston, Mass., 1861. Daughter of the late Gen. Patrick Robert Guiney. She graduated from Elmhurst Academy, Providence, R. I., and since has resided chiefly in and near Boston, engaged in literary pursuits. Her works include "Songs at the Start," 1884; "Goose Quill Papers," 1885; "The White Sail," 1887; "Brownies and Bogies," 1888; "Monsieur Henri: a Footnote to French History," 1892; "A Roadside Harp," 1893; "Three Heroines of New England Romance," with Mrs. Spofford and Alice Brown, 1894; "A Little English Gallery," 1894; "Patrins," essays, 1897; "The Martyr's Idyl, and Shorter Poems," 1899.

GUMMERE, Francis Barton, educator, b. Burlington, N. J., 1855. Studied at Haverford College, Harvard, and Freiburg University. In 1887 he became professor of English at Haverford College, Penn. Author of "The Anglo-Saxon Metaphor," 1881; "Handbook of Poetics," 1885; "Germanic Origins: a Study in Primitive Culture," 1892.

HALE, Edward Everett, clergyman and author, b. Boston, Mass., 3 April, 1822. Dr. Hale has been identified with humanitarian projects for over half a century, and his influence as pastor, writer, and philanthropist will long be felt. His patriotic tale, "The Man Without a Country," the best short story of its time, is enough for one author's fame. The poem which represents him in this collection is a vivid expression of his striking personality, and of university traditions in which his record and bearing are an essential part. In addition to his prose works, Dr. Hale has published a volume of poems under the title of "For Fifty Years."

HALE, Sarah Josepha (Buell), b. Newport, N. H., 1788; d. Philadelphia, Penn., 1879. Editor of the "Ladies' Magazine" at Boston, 1828-37, and of "Godey's Ladies' Book" until 1877. An early advocate of the higher education of women. It is said that the celebration of Thanksgiving as a national festival was largely due to her influence. Her first publication was "Genius of Oblivion, and Other Original Poems," 1828. Her literary reputation rests upon the collection "Three Hours, or the Vigil of Love, and Other Poems."

HALL, Gertrude, b. Boston, Mass., 186-. She was educated in Italy. Her first volume, "Verses," appeared in 1890, and was followed by "Allegretto," 1894, and "The Age of Fairy Gold," 1899. She has also written several books of short stories, and has made translations from Paul Verlaine, and one of Rostand's "Cyrano de Bergerac."

HALLECK, Fitz-Greene, b. Guilford, Conn., 8 July, 1790; d. there, 19 Nov., 1867. He was of Puritan and Pilgrim descent, and counted John Eliot, the apostle to the Indians, among his ancestors. Educated at the schools of his native town, he took a position as a clerk in the store of his relative, Andrew Eliot, of Guilford, when fifteen years old. Six years later, in 1811, he came to New York, and obtained a place in the banking house of Jacob Barker, with whom he remained until 1832. From 1832 to 1849 he was employed as an accountant by John Jacob Astor, receiving a pension on the latter's death, and retiring to Guilford, where the remainder of his life was passed. His friendship with Joseph Rodman Drake resulted in their series of satirical "Croaker" papers, published anonymously in the New York "Evening Post" in 1819 (see *Drake, J. R.*). The reputation gained by this work was further enhanced by the appearance of Halleck's poem "Fanny" in the same year, a travesty of the manners of the time. His best-known poem, "Marco Bozzaris," was printed by Bryant in the "New York Review," in 1825. "Alnwick Castle, with Other Poems," his first volume, came out in 1827. The collective edition of his "Poetical Writings," 1869, and "The Life and Letters of Fitz-Greene Halleck," 1869, were prepared by General James Grant Wilson.

HALPINE, Charles Graham, "Miles O'Reilly," b. Oldcastle, County Meath, Ireland, 1829; d. New York, N. Y., 1868. He was graduated at the University of Dublin, and came to America about 1851. He joined the staff of the Boston "Post," and in 1857 became editor of the New York "Leader." Enlisting early in the Union army, he rose to the rank of brigadier-general of volunteers. After the war, in 1864, he returned to newspaper life and politics in New York. His "Life and Adventures, Songs, etc., of Private Miles O'Reilly," 1864, and "Baked Meats of the Funeral," 1866, first appeared as papers in the New York "Herald." "The Poetical Works of Charles G. Halpine," 1869, was a posthumous volume.

HANSBROUGH, Mary Berri (Chapman), b. Washington, D. C., 187-. A writer of prose and verse. She was married in 1897 to Henry Clay Hansbrough, senator from North Dakota. Her volume "Lyrics of Love and Nature" appeared in 1895.

HARDY, Arthur Sherburne, novelist and mathematician, b. Andover, Mass., 13 Aug., 1847. Graduated at West Point, and was made 2d lieutenant in the 3d artillery regiment, U. S. A., 1869. He resigned from the army the following year, and after a period of travel and study abroad was appointed professor of civil engineering at Iowa College. From 1878 to 1893 he was professor of mathematics at Dartmouth. After a brief connection with the "Cosmopolitan" magazine, Mr. Hardy was made minister to Persia in 1897, and two years later was transferred to the ministry at Athens. Author of "Francesca of Rimini," poem, 1878; "But yet a Woman," 1883; "The Wind of Destiny," 1886; "Passe Rose," 1889; "Life and Letters of Joseph Hardy Neesima," 1891.

HARNEY, Will Wallace, b. Bloomington, Ind., 1831. He studied at Louisville College and taught in the Kentucky State Normal School. He succeeded his father as editor of the Louisville "Democrat" in 1869, but soon removed to an orange grove in Florida. His contributions to different periodicals have not been collected.

HARRIS, Joel Chandler, b. Eatonton, Ga., 9 Dec., 1848. He learned the printer's trade in the office of the Georgia "Countryman," and his early compositions appeared in that paper. In 1890 he became editor of the Atlanta "Constitution," in which journal he had first published his "Uncle Remus, His Songs and His Sayings," 1880, now a veritable classic. His works include "Nights with Uncle Remus," 1882; "Mingo, and Other Sketches," 1884; "Daddy Jake the Runaway," 1889; a biography of Henry W. Grady, 1890; "Balaam and his Master," 1891; "Little Mr. Thimblefinger and his Queer Country," 1894; "Aaron in the Wildwoods," 1897; "Tales of the Home Folks in Peace and War," 1898; "Georgia from the Invasion of De Soto to Recent Times," 1899.

HARRIS, Thomas Lake, b. Fenny Stratford, England, 1823. He founded the Brotherhood of the New Life, a mystical organization at Salem-on-Erie, near Brocton, N. Y., and afterwards became a resident of California. "The Great Republic, a Poem of the Sun," 1867; "Star Flowers," verse, 1886; and "God's Breath in Man," 1891, are among his published writings. At the age of seventy-seven Mr. Harris made his home in New York City, and was still alert with pen and brain.

HARTE, Francis Bret, b. Albany, N. Y., 25 Aug., 1839. He lost his father in childhood, and, after receiving a common school education, went to Sonora, Cal., where he taught for a while. He afterwards worked in a mine and in a printing-office, was an express agent, and finally formed an editorial connection with "The Golden Era" of San Francisco. In 1864 he was made secretary of the U. S. Branch Mint, and became editor of "The Californian," in which weekly he published his "Condensed Novels." In 1868 he began to edit the newly founded "Overland Monthly," and contributed to its second number his story "The Luck of Roaring Camp." The humorous poem "Plain Talk from Truthful James" appeared in the same magazine in 1870. His fame spreading, he removed to the Atlantic coast in 1871; was appointed U. S. consul at Crefeld, Germany, in 1878, and at Glasgow, Scotland, in 1880. After holding the latter office five years, he made his home in England, near London. Among his works are "Condensed Novels," 1867; "Poems," 1871; "The Luck of Roaring Camp, and Other Sketches," 1871; "East and West Poems," 1871; "Stories of the Sierras," 1872; "Poetical Works," 1873; "Echoes of the Foothills," poems, 1874; "Tales of the Argonauts," 1875; "Thankful Blossom," 1876; "Drift from Two Shores," 1878; "In the Carquinez Woods," 1883; "By Shore and Sedge," 1885; "Maruja," novel, 1885; "Snowbound at Eagle's," 1886; "The Queen of the Pirate Isle," for children, 1887; "A Phyllis of the Sierras," 1887; "A Waif of the Plains," 1890; "In a Hollow of the Hills," 1895; "Three Partners," 1897. D. Camberley, Eng., 6 May, 1902.

HASTINGS, Thomas, musician and hymn-writer, b. Washington, Conn., 1784; d. New York, N. Y., 1872. Widely known as composer, lecturer, teacher, and writer in the interest of sacred music. Distinguished with Dr. Lowell Mason as a founder of the prevailing psalmody of America. From 1842 till his death, Dr. Hastings made New York City the centre of his labors, being associated with many churches of the metropolis, and a constant contributor to the periodic press.

HAWKES, Clarence, b. Goshen, Mass., 1869. Known as the "Blind Poet of New England." An industrious writer of short stories, poems, and sketches, and also a lecturer. Among his publications are "Pebbles and Shells," verse, 1895; "Idyls of Old New England," 1897; "The Hope of the World, and Other Poems," 1900.

HAWTHORNE, Hildegarde, b. New York, N. Y., 18—. A daughter of Julian Hawthorne. By her occasional poems and sketches she has proved that a literary heritage can descend to the third generation.

HAWTHORNE, Julian, novelist, b. Boston, Mass., 22 June, 1846. Son of Nathaniel Hawthorne, and brother of Rose Hawthorne Lathrop. He spent a number of years in Europe before and after his graduation at Harvard, beginning life as a civil engineer. Since 1882 he has lived chiefly in New York City and its vicinage. His "Saxon Studies" were published in "The Contemporary Review" and afterwards in a volume. His works include "Garth," 1875; "Archibald Malmaison," 1878; "Nathaniel Hawthorne and His Wife," 1885; "Confessions and Criticisms," 1887; and many other volumes in various departments of literature.

HAWTHORNE, Nathaniel, romancer, b. Salem, Mass., 4 July, 1804; d. Plymouth, N. H., 19 May, 1864. The most imaginative and eminent of American romancers in the 19th century left no volume of poetry, and it appears not to have been recalled, until very recently, that anything in verse-form had appeared from his pen. Geo. Parsons Lathrop, however, before his own death, in 1898, chanced upon a copy of the religious illustrated gift-book, in the style of the "Annuals" of that day, "Scenes in the Life of our Saviour: by the Poets and Painters," published under R. W. Griswold's editorship, 1845. The book contains two contributions in verse by Hawthorne, entitled "Walking on the Sea," and "The Star of Calvary." The last-named poem, composed, like Hood's "Eugene Aram" and Rossetti's "Blessed Damozel," in the measure and manner of Coleridge's "Wondrous Rime," is by far the better of the two and worth its space on p. 191.

HAY, Helen, b. New York, N. Y., 18—. Daughter of John Hay. The poetry in Miss Hay's initial volume, "Some Verses," 1898, has the quality of distinction, and was at once approved for its artistic perfection, impassioned lyrical expression, and suggestion of reserved dramatic force. (Now Mrs. Payne Whitney.)

HAY, John, diplomat and statesman, b. Salem, Ind., 8 Oct., 1838. Graduated at Brown University; admitted to the bar in 1861. He was assistant private secretary to Lincoln from the beginning of the war till the President's death, and served as his adjutant and aide-de-camp. In 186- he went to the front with Generals Hunter and Gillmore and saw active service. He won the rank of major and assistant adjutant-general, and was brevetted lieutenant colonel and colonel. He was U. S. secretary of legation at Paris, 1865–67; chargé d'affaires at Vienna, 1867–68; and secretary of legation at Madrid, 1868–70. After his return to America he joined the staff of the New York "Tribune," and was one of the ablest leader-writers that have adorned our journalism. As a diversion, he contributed some of his Pike County Ballads to that paper. He was assistant secretary of state under President Hayes, 1879–81, but it was not until 1897 that an administration gave him an opportunity, as ambassador to Great Britain, of fully utilizing his natural and trained abilities for the highest diplomatic service. In 1898 he was recalled to enter Pres. McKinley's cabinet as secretary of state, at the most important and historic stage, since the Civil War, of American events. Mr. Hay has published "Pike County Ballads, and Other Pieces," 1871; "Castilian Days," 1871; "Poems," 1890; and with J. G. Nicolay, the authoritative history of Abraham Lincoln which first appeared in "The Century Magazine," 1887. Thought to have been author of the anonymous novel "The Bread-Winners," 1883. (D. Newbury, N. H., 1 July, 1905.)

HAYES, Ednah Proctor (Clarke), b. New York, N. Y., 187–. Daughter of Col. I. Edwards Clarke, of the U. S. Bureau of Education, Washington, D. C., which city was her chief place of residence until her marriage in 1899 to Dr. Henry L. Hayes, and her removal with him to the Hawaiian Islands. Is a cousin of Edna Dean Proctor. Author of "An Opal: Verses by Ednah Proctor Clarke," 1897.

HAYES, John Russell, asst. professor of English, Swarthmore College, b. West Chester, Penn., 1866. Graduate of Swarthmore, Harvard, and University of Pennsylvania Law School. Author of "The Old Fashioned Garden, and Other Verses," 1895; "The Brandywine," 1898; "West Chester Centennial Ode," 1899; "Swarthmore Idylls," 1899.

HAYNE, Paul Hamilton, b. Charleston, S. C., 1 Jan., 1830; d. "Copse Hill," Grovetown, Ga., 6 July, 1886. He was graduated at the University of South Carolina, gave up the practice of law for literature, and edited successively, "Russell's Magazine," the Charleston "Literary Gazette" and "Evening News." He was a colonel in the Confederate army, and wrote several popular Confederate songs. The war undermining his health and destroying his home, he retired with his family to a cottage, "Copse Hill," at Grovetown, in the pine barrens near Augusta, Ga. Hayne was long our representative Southern poet, honored and beloved by his colleagues in all portions of the United States, and by not a few in the Motherland. He issued "Poems," 1855; "Sonnets and Other Poems," 1857; "Avolio, a Legend of Cos," 1859; "Legends and Lyrics," 1872; "The Mountain of the Lovers, and Other Poems," 1873. He wrote a memoir of Henry Timrod, 1873; and lives of Hugh S. Legaré and of his uncle, Robert Y. Hayne, 1878. An elegant edition of his complete poems appeared in 1882.

HAYNE, William Hamilton, b. Charleston, S. C., 1856. Son of Paul Hamilton Hayne. Received his education chiefly at home. The greater part of his life has been passed at "Copse Hill," Grovetown, the family residence near Augusta, Ga. His first published poem appeared in 1881. Author of "Sylvan Lyrics, and Other Verses," 1893, and of numerous critical articles.

HEATON, John Langdon, journalist, b. Canton, N. J., 1860. Graduated there, at St. Lawrence University, 1880. Among his writings are "Stories of Napoleon," 1895; "The Quilting Bee, and Other Poems," 1896.

HEDGE, Frederic Henry, Unitarian clergyman, b. Cambridge, Mass., 1805; d. there, 1890. Son of Prof. Levi Hedge. In 1818 he was sent to Germany, where he passed five years in study. Graduated at Harvard in 1825, and in 1857 was appointed professor of ecclesiastical history there, and later professor of German. He edited "The Christian Examiner," 1857–60, wrote the standard work, "The Prose Writers of Germany," 1848; "Martin Luther, and Other Essays," 1888; several theological works, and many hymns and translations of hymns. With Mrs. Annis Lee Wister he prepared "Metrical Translations and Poems."

HELLMAN, George Sidney, b. New York, N. Y., 1878. Son of Mrs. Frances Hellman, whose translations from Heine and other German poets have distinction. Graduated at Columbia, where he was editor of the "Literary Monthly" and managing editor of the "Spectator." In 1899, with Mr. W. A. Bradley, he established "East and West," a monthly literary magazine.

"H. H." — See *Helen Maria (Fiske) Jackson.*

HERBERT, Henry William ("Frank Forester"), b. London, Eng., 1807; died by his own hand, New York, N. Y., 1858. Son of the Dean of Manchester, and a graduate of Oxford. He came to New Jersey in the thirties, and made his living by work as a classical editor and man of letters. Edited the "American Monthly," 1833–36. Author of "Cromwell," 1837; "My Shooting Box," 1846, and many books on field sports and on historical themes. His (collected) "Poems, a Memorial Volume," was edited by Mrs. Margaret Herbert Mather, ("Morgan Herbert") and brought out in an elegant subscription edition, 1888.

HERFORD, Oliver, b. (Fairyland?) 186–. Son of the Rev. Brooke Herford. His double talent with pen and pencil, in the exercise of fancy, wit, and humor, has won him an enviable position among writers of the day. Some of his publications are: "Artful Anticks," 1888; "The Primer of Natural History," 1899; "The Bashful Earthquake," 1899.

"HERMES, Paul." — See *W. R. Thayer.*

HICKOX, Chauncey, journalist, b. Ravenna, O., 1837. A resident of Washington, D. C., since 1865.

HIGGINSON, Ella (Rhoads), b. Council Grove, Kan., 186–. She married Russell Cardon Higginson in 1882, and of late has resided in New Whatcom, Wash. Has published several books of short stories, and also a volume of verse, "When the Birds go North again," 1898.

HIGGINSON, Mary Potter (Thacher), b. Machias, Me., 1844. She was married to Col. Thomas Wentworth Higginson in 1879. She has written "Seashore and Prairie, Stories and Sketches," 1876; and, with her husband, a volume of poems, "Such as They Are," 1893.

HIGGINSON, Thomas Wentworth, b. Cambridge, Mass., 22 Dec., 1823. A descendant of the Rev. Francis Higginson, distinguished among the earliest Puritan colonists of New England. Graduating at Harvard, he was for a time engaged in teaching. He studied for the liberal ministry, and was settled over churches at Newburyport and Worcester, Mass. During this period, 1847 to 1858, he took an active part in the anti-slavery movement, and served as a soldier in the Free State campaign in Kansas. He resigned from the ministry in 1858, and thereafter engaged in literary work. From 1862 to 1864 he was colonel of the first regiment of freed slaves recruited for the Federal army, and served in the Florida and South Carolina campaigns. A few years after the war he made his permanent residence at Cambridge, Mass. Colonel Higginson labored earnestly, both as a lecturer and writer, in behalf of woman suffrage and other reform movements. He was appointed military and naval historian of Massachusetts in the Civil War in 1889. He has published books in many departments of literature, including "Outdoor Papers," 1863; "Malbone, an Oldport Romance," 1869; "Army Life in a Black Regiment," 1870; "Atlantic Essays," 1871; "The Sympathies of Religions," 1871; "Common Sense about Women," 1882; "Life of Margaret Fuller," 1884; "The Monarch of Dreams," 1887; "The Afternoon Landscape: Poems and Translations," 1888; "Concerning All of Us," 1892; and "Cheerful Yesterdays," autobiographical, 1898. As a scholar, critic, and exponent of his own early essay, "A Plea for Culture," Col. Higginson in his career has been identified with the progress of American thought and letters during the second half of the nineteenth century.

HILDRETH, Charles Lotin, b. New York, N. Y., 1857; d. 1896. A journalist of New York, who wrote for the "World," 1883, and was afterward a writer for "Belford's Magazine." Author of "Judith," a novel, 1876; "The New Symphony, and Other Stories," 1878; "The Masque of Death, and Other Poems," 1889.

HILL, Benjamin Dionysius (Father Edmund of the Heart of Mary, C. P.), b. Wottan Underwood, Buckinghamshire, Eng., 1842. Now a resident of Dunkirk, N. Y. His father was vicar of Wottan. Father Edmund was educated at Oxford and Cambridge Universities. His poetical works include "Poems Devotional and Occasional," 1877; "Passion Flowers," 1898; "Mariae Corolla: a Wreath for Our Lady," 1898.

HILL, George, b. Guilford, Conn., 1796; d. New York, N. Y., 1871. He graduated at Yale, and held several positions under the U. S. government. His "The Ruins of Athens, and Other Poems," 1834, was reissued, with additions, in 1839, as "The Ruins of Athens, Titania's Banquet, and Other Poems."

HILLHOUSE, Augustus Lucas, b. New Haven, Conn., 1792; d. near Paris, France, 1859. Brother of J. A. Hillhouse, and a graduate of Yale. His hymn, "Forgiveness of Sins a Joy Unknown to Angels," written at Paris, was published in the "Christian Spectator," 1822.

HILLHOUSE, James Abraham, b. New Haven, Conn., 1789; d. New Haven, Conn., 1841. Graduated at Yale. After engaging in mercantile pursuits for a few years, he resigned and spent the rest of his life quietly at his country home near New Haven. "Dramas, Discourses, and Other Pieces" appeared in 1839. As he was one of the earliest Americans to write a truly poetic drama, its most effective scene, which in some degree reflects the influence of Byron, is included in the present Anthology.

HIRST, Henry Beck, b. Philadelphia, Penn., 1813; d. there, 1874. A lawyer, who resided in his native city. He published a "Poetical Dictionary," 18—; "The Coming of the Mammoth, and Other Poems," 1845; "Endymion, a Tale of Greece," verse, 1848; "The Penance of Roland, a Romance of the Peine Forte et Dure, and Other Poems," 1849. He was severely criticised by Poe, who nevertheless paid tribute to his poetic qualities. A collective edition of poems has been promised under the editorship of Dr. Matthews Woods, who is of the belief that Poe found suggestions for some of his own effects in verse from the measures of the author of "The Funeral of Time" and kindred lyrics.

HOFFMAN, Charles Fenno, lawyer and journalist, b. New York, N. Y., 1806; d. Harrisburg, Penn., 1884. Studied at Columbia College, and practised law in New York. Was associate editor of the New York "American;" founded the "Knickerbocker Magazine," 1833; editor and owner of the "American Monthly;" edited the New York "Mirror" and "Literary World." In 1849 his mind became unbalanced, and the rest of his life was spent in retirement. Author of "A Winter in the West," 1835; "Wild Scenes in Forest and Prairie," 1837; "Vanderlyn," 1837; "Grayslaer," 1840. His "Poems" complete appeared in 1873.

HOLLAND, Josiah Gilbert, b. Belchertown, Mass., 24 July, 1819; d. New York, N. Y., 12 Oct., 1881. He practised medicine, and was engaged in educational work, until 1849, when he joined the editorial staff of the "Springfield (Mass.) Republican," with which paper he was associated until 1866. During this editorship his popular "Timothy Titcomb's Letters" appeared in the "Republican" and were reissued in book-form in 1858. "Bitter Sweet," 1858, "Katrina," 1867, and "The Mistress of the Manse," 1874, poems of home life, proved equal favorites with the people. His other poetical works were "The Marble Prophecy, and Other Poems," 1872; "Garnered Sheaves," a collective edition, 1873; and "The Puritan's Guest, and Other Poems." Dr. Holland was the projector of "Scribner's Monthly," afterwards the "Century Magazine," which he edited from its establishment, in 1870, until his death. Among his novels, some of which were published serially in the magazine, are: "Miss Gilbert's Career," 1860; "Arthur Bonnicastle," 1873; and "Nicholas Minturn," 1876.

HOLMES, Oliver Wendell, b. Cambridge, Mass., 29 Aug., 1809; d. Boston, 7 Oct., 1894. His father, Abiel Holmes, was pastor of the First Church, Cambridge, and author of historical and religious works. The son was educated at Andover and Harvard. His poem "Old Ironsides," in the Boston "Advertiser," saved the frigate Constitution from destruction, and was the first of note that he published; although a few other verses had crept into print. He gave up law for medicine, and in 1834 published a remarkable essay on puerperal fever, doing away with established views on the subject. In 1836, after more than two years of study in America, and three in the hospitals of Edinburgh and Paris, he took his medical degree, and in the same year published his first volume of "Poems." In 1839 he became professor of anatomy and physiology at Dartmouth. In 1840 he married Amelia Lee Jackson, and established a practice in Boston. From 1847 to 1882 he was Parkman professor of anatomy and physiology at Harvard, and then was made professor emeritus. Lowell, as editor of the "Atlantic Monthly," was one of the first to recognize his essential genius. In 1857 he began in that magazine, just founded, the series published in book-form in 1859, with the title "The Autocrat of the Breakfast-Table." "The Professor at the Breakfast-Table" followed in 1860; "The Poet at the Breakfast-Table" in 1873. The novels "Elsie Venner" and "The Guardian Angel" appeared in 1861 and 1868. Certain features of the latter were far in advance of the times, and its publication in the "Atlantic Monthly" temporarily diminished its circulation. Among his other works in prose are "Lectures on the English Poets of the Nineteenth Century," first delivered in 1852; "Soundings from the Atlantic," 1863; "Mechanism in Thought and Morals," 1871; "John Lothrop Motley," 1878; "Life of Ralph Waldo Emerson," 1884; "A Mortal Antipathy," novel, 1885; "The New Portfolio," 1886; "Our Hundred Days in Europe," 1887; "Over the Teacups," 1890. His verse includes "Urania," 1846; "Astraea," 1850; "Songs in Many Keys," 1861; "Humorous Poems," 1865; "Songs of Many Seasons," 1874; "The School-Boy," 1878; "The Iron Gate, and Other Poems," 1880; "Before the Curfew, and Other Poems," 1888. Dr. Holmes, above all others the poet and wit of Boston, — his "hub of the solar system," — held for half a century a unique position. At the Atlantic Monthly Breakfast given to him on his 70th birthday, 1879, his fellow authors of distinction, young and old, gathered to render him their tributes in speech and writing, to which his own response, "The Iron Gate," remains a model of that English poetry, half grave, half gay, in which he was without a peer — and was revered as the master by its makers on both sides of the Atlantic. Cp. "Poets of America," chap. viii. [L. C. B.]

HONEYWOOD, St. John, lawyer, b. Leicester, Mass., 1763; d. Salem, N. Y., 1798. Graduated from Yale, 1782. Studied law at Albany, and practised at Salem until his death. One of the presidential electors when John Adams succeeded Washington. His "Poems" appeared posthumously in 1801.

HOPKINSON, Joseph, lawyer, b. Philadelphia, Penn., 1770; d. Philadelphia, Penn., 1842. A distinguished lawyer, statesman, and scholar. His fame rests chiefly on his national song, "Hail, Columbia," written, to the tune of "The President's March," in 1798. Intense feeling was rife in America at that time with respect to the war then raging between France and England. The famous ode, sung first at the benefit performance of a Philadelphia actor, was composed with the object of inspiring in the hostile factions a patriotism which should transcend the bitterness of party feeling.

HORTON, George, journalist, b. Fairville, N. Y., 1859. Early removed to Michigan, and in 1878 graduated from its University. Has been engaged in journalism for some years, and at present is literary editor of the Chicago "Times-Herald." Mr. Horton was American consul-general at Athens during President Cleveland's second term. His principal works are "Songs of the Lowly," 1892; "In Unknown Seas," verse, 1895; "Aphroessa," verse, 1897; "A Fair Brigand," 1899.

HOUGHTON, George Washington Wright, b. Cambridge, Mass., 1850; d. Yonkers, N. Y., 1891. He became a resident of New York, where he was engaged for some years in editing a trade paper. His books of verse include "Songs from over the Sea," 1874; "The Legend of St. Olaf's Kirk," 1880; and "Niagara and Other Poems," 1882.

HOVEY, Richard, b. Normal, Ill., 4 May, 1864; d. New York, N. Y., 24 Feb., 1900. Graduated at Dartmouth, 1885, and studied at the General Theological Seminary, New York. He was for some time lay assistant at a New York ritualistic church, but abandoned his intention to enter the ministry, and his subsequent career was by turns that of a journalist, actor, dramatist, and English lecturer and professor. His Dartmouth Ode was accepted by his Alma Mater after a prolonged competition. Passing some years abroad, he was impressed by the methods of the latter-day French and Belgian schools, and familiarized himself with their poems and plays. He made the only translation of Maeterlinck published in this country. His original works include "The Laurel: an Ode," 1889; "Launcelot and Guenevere, a Poem in Dramas" (comprising "The Quest of Merlin," "The Marriage of Guenevere," and "The Birth of Galahad"), 1891–98, a series in which the Arthurian legends are treated in a fresh manner, with daring but imaginative innovations; "Seaward, Elegy upon the Death of Thomas William Parsons," 1893, which follows the idyllic Sicilian strain, like the elegies of Shelley, Arnold, and Swinburne, and of Roberts and Woodberry in America. In 1893, also, "Songs from Vagabondia," by Hovey and his friend, Bliss Carman, appeared, and were heartily welcomed for their blithe lyrical quality, and their zest of youth and freedom. "More Songs from Vagabondia" followed in 1896, and in 1898 Hovey's "Along the Trail," a collection of his miscellaneous poems. In the same year the last of his dramatic series mentioned heretofore ("The Birth of Galahad") showed his advance in diction and dramatic power. But his highest and most distinctive effort, in his own mind and that of his friends, was "Taliesin: A Masque," which appeared, 1896, in "Poet-Lore," and was ready in book-form at the time of his death, in the spring of 1900. This work, cast in dramatic form, is not "of the earth, earthy," and may be thought open to the gloss made by Mary Shelley upon her husband's "Witch of Atlas," as "discarding human interest;" but it is sheer poetry or nothing, the proof of an ear and a voice which it seems ill to have lost just at the moment of their completed training. Hovey, in fact, was slow to mature, and when taken off, showed more promise than at any time before. He thought very well of himself, not without reason, and felt that he had enjoyed his wanderjahr to the full, and that the serious work of his life was straight before him. He was ridding himself in a measure of certain affectations that told against him, and at last had a chance, with a University position, to utilize the fruits of a good deal of hard study and reflection, while nearing some best field for the exercise of his specific gift. That his aim was high is shown even by his failures; and in his death there is no doubt that America has lost one of her best-equipped lyrical and dramatic writers. This somewhat extended note may well be accorded to the dead singer, who, on the threshold of the new century that beckoned to him, was bidden to halt and abide with the "inheritors of unfulfilled renown." [E. C. S.]

HOWARTH, Ellen Clementine (Doran), b. Cooperstown, N. Y., 1827; d. Trenton, N. J., 1899. When a child of seven she worked in a factory. She married Joseph Howarth and lived in Trenton, N. J. Author of "The Wind Harp, and Other Poems," 1864; "Poems," 1867.

HOWE, Julia (Ward), b. New York, N. Y., 27 May, 1819. A daughter of Samuel Ward, a banker of New York, in which city she received her education under private tutors. She was married in 1843 to Dr. S. G. Howe, first superintendent of the Perkins Institute for the Blind, and made her residence in Boston. She edited with him "The Commonwealth," of that city, an anti-slavery paper, and took part as lecturer and writer in the furtherance of many public movements in behalf of female suffrage, prison reforms, and other causes. "Passion Flowers," 1854, was her first volume of poems, and was succeeded by several tragedies and books of verse. "Later Lyrics," 1866; "From Sunset Ridge, Poems New and Old," 1898; and books of travel, social science, and biography are among her writings. Her "Battle Hymn of the Republic" will last as long as the Civil War is remembered in history. It was written in 1861, after the author's observing, in the camps near Washington, the marching of the enthusiastic young soldiers to the song "John Brown's Body." Mrs. Howe's words were at once adopted and sung throughout the North.

HOWE, Mark Antony De Wolfe, b. Bristol, R. I., 1864. Educated at Lehigh and Harvard universities. Some of his works are: "Shadows," 1897; "Phillips Brooks," 1899. Editor of "The Memory of Lincoln," 1899, and an associate editor on the staff of the "Youth's Companion."

HOWELL, Elizabeth (Lloyd), b. Philadelphia, Penn., 1811; d. Wernersville, Penn., 1896. Her family were Quakers, but she became an Episcopalian on her marriage, in 1853, to Robert Howell, of Philadelphia. Her poems, some of which appeared in "The Wheatsheaf," 1852, are not numerous. The one given in this Anthology is the best known.

HOWELLS, Mildred, b. Cambridge, Mass., 187–. The younger daughter of William Dean Howells. Miss Howells as a child was introduced to the public through "A Little Girl among the Old Masters," unique drawings of her youthful impressions of early Italian art, with preface and comment by her father. She has since relied upon her own pen, as well as her pencil, for her artistic position.

HOWELLS, William Dean, novelist and poet, b. Martin's Ferry, Belmont Co., O., 1 Mar., 1837. He learned to set type at Hamilton, O., in the office of the paper his father edited. In 1858 he became one of the editors of the Columbus "Ohio State Journal." In 1860 he published "Poems of Two Friends" (with John Piatt), and a life of Abraham Lincoln. He was U. S. consul at Venice, 1861-65. His "Venetian Life," 1866, at once brought him into repute, and from the date of its appearance he has maintained his eminent position among those authors to whose steadfast and meritorious labors the advances of American literature since the Civil War are mainly due. "Italian Journeys" and a collection of his "Poems" followed in 1867. After service on the New York "Nation," he edited "The Atlantic Monthly," 1871-81; "The Editor's Study" of "Harper's Magazine," 1886-91; and "The Cosmopolitan," 1892. Among his works are "Suburban Sketches," 1868; "No Love Lost, a Poem of Travel," 1868; "Their Wedding Journey," 1871; "A Chance Acquaintance," 1873, and many subsequent novels; his first comedy, "The Parlor Car," 1876; "A Little Girl among the Old Masters" (illustrated by his daughter Mildred), 1884; "Tuscan Cities," 1885; "Poems," 1886; "Modern Italian Poets," 1887; "A Traveller from Altruria," 1894; "My Literary Passion," 1895; "Stops of Various Quills," poems, 1895; "Impressions and Experiences," autobiographical, 1896; "Landlord at Lion's Head," 1896; "A Parting and a Meeting," 1896; "A Previous Engagement," 1897. He has edited "George Fuller: His Life and Works," 1886; "Library of Universal Adventure, by Sea and Land" (with T. S. Perry), 1888; and the "Poems of George Pellew," 1892. Mr. Howells was unquestionably the founder of the latter-day natural school of American fiction, in which truth to every-day life is given precedence, while rhetoric, forced situations, and the arts of the melodramatist are sedulously avoided. But pathos, genuine feeling, human nature, and a delicate vein of very characteristic humor are at his own command. His later writings have been pervaded by a lofty spirit of humanitarianism, tinged with the sadness of a heart deeply moved by the enigma of life and the unequal distributions of sorrow and welfare. [E. C. S.]

HOWELLS, Winifred, b. Venice, Italy, 1863; d. Mass., 1889. Eldest child of William Dean Howells. She was a girl of endearing beauty and promise, gifted with insight, and exhibiting the poet's sensitiveness and reserve. A few of her lyrics have been embodied in her father's touching and exquisitely written memorial of her life and character. (Cp. the sonnet by Mrs. Moulton, p. 811.)

HOWLAND, Edward, socialist, b. Charleston, S. C., 1832; d. Camp La Logia, Topolobampo Colony, Sinaloa, Mexico, 1890. He was a graduate of Harvard, and, after many years of business and literary pursuits, became interested in the socialistic movement which culminated in establishment of a colony in the Fuerte valley, to which he removed with his wife, the well-known writer and reformer, Marie Howland, in 1888. Mr. and Mrs. Howland edited "The Credit Foncier of Sinaloa," the colony organ, at Hammonton, N. J., and in Mexico, from 1885 until his death.

HOYT, Ralph, clergyman and philanthropist, b. New York, N. Y., 1806; d. there, 1878. Entered the Protestant Episcopal ministry, 1842. Published "The Chant of Life, and Other Poems;" "Echoes of Memory and Emotion," poems, 1859; "Sketches of Life and Landscape," poems, 1852, new ed. 1873.

HUGHES, Rupert, b. Lancaster, Mo., 1872. He graduated at Adelbert College, Cleveland, O., and took a post-graduate course at Yale University. Has been on the editorial staffs of "Godey's Magazine" and "The Criterion." His boy's book, "The Lakerim Athletic Club," appeared first in the "St. Nicholas," and was published in book form in 1899.

HUNTINGTON, William Reed, D. D., b. Lowell, Mass., 1838. A Protestant Episcopal clergyman, rector of All Saints Church, Worcester, Mass., 1862-83; and of Grace Church, New York, since 1883. Author of several religious works in prose, and of "Sonnets and a Dream," 1899.

HUTCHINSON, Ellen Mackay. — See *E. M. H. Cortissoz.*

HUTCHISON, Percy Adams, Harvard University, Class of 1899.

HUTTON, Laurence, b. New York, N. Y., 8 Aug., 1843. Of Scottish descent. Began life as a merchant, but after 1870 was an active and scholarly man of letters, delighting in the society of his colleagues, and full of poetic devotion to the traditions of authors and literature. Dramatic critic of the N. Y. "Evening Mail," and edited "Literary Notes" in "Harper's Magazine." Author of "Plays and Players," 1875; the unique series of "Literary Landmarks," which began with those of London, 1885, and extended to 1898; "Artists of the Nineteenth Century," with Mrs. Waters. Editor of "The American Actor" series, 1881-82. Mr. Hutton of late years was prominent in the literary activities of his native city, and was a founder of the Authors Club, and closely associated with Edwin Booth in the organization of "The Players," and a member of the Council of the American Copyright League. In later years resided at Princeton, N. J., and gave to its University his collection of the Life and Death Masks of celebrities. (D. Princeton, N. J., 10 June, 1904.)

"IDAS." — See *John Elton Wayland.*

INGALLS, John James, b. Middleton, Mass., 1833; d. 1900. After admission to the bar, he removed to Atchison, Kan., and edited the "Atchison Champion" from 1862 to 1865. He was elected to the State Senate, 1862, and to the United States Senate, 1873, 1879, 1885.

INGHAM, John Hall, lawyer, b. Philadelphia, Penn., 1860. His poems contributed to magazines have never been published in collective form.

"**INNSLEY, Owen.**" — See *Lucy White Jennison.*

"**IRONQUILL.**" — See *Eugene Fitch Ware.*

JACKSON, Helen Maria (Fiske), "H. H.," b. Amherst, Mass., 18 Oct., 1831; d. San Francisco, Cal., 12 Aug., 1885. She was educated at Ipswich, Mass., and married at twenty-one to Captain Edward Hunt, U. S. army, who died in 1863. In 1875 she became the wife of William S. Jackson, a banker of Colorado Springs. In 1883 she received the appointment of special examiner into the condition of the Mission Indians of California, her book, "A Century of Dishonor," in behalf of the Indians, having appeared in 1881. Her novel, "Ramona," on the same subject, followed in 1884. Two other novels, "Mercy Philbrick's Choice," 1876, and "Hetty's Strange History," 1877, had been published in the "No Name" series; "Verses by H. H.," in 1870; "Sonnets and Lyrics," in 1876. She is thought to have written some if not most of the "Saxe Holm Stories," published in "Scribner's Monthly" and afterwards in two volumes.

JAMES, Alice Archer (Sewall), illustrator, b. Glendale, Ohio, 187-. Daughter of Frank Sewall, q. v. Studied art in the foreign capitals and at Washington. Author of "Ode to Girlhood, and Other Poems," 1899.

JANVIER, Margaret Thomson, "Margaret Vandegrift," b. New Orleans, La., 1845. A sister of Thomas A. Janvier. Among her books for children are: "Under the Dog-Star," 1881; "The Absent-Minded Fairy, and Other Verses," 1883; "The Dead Doll, and Other Verses," 1888. The beautiful dramatic lyric given in this volume has been refused publication in the "Century," "Atlantic," "Harper's," and other leading periodicals — on what grounds of either criticism or policy it might be difficult for a lover of genuine poetry to determine. [E. C. S.]

JENKS, Tudor, editor, b. Brooklyn, N. Y., 1857. Graduated from Yale in 1878, and from the law school of Columbia College, 1880. Practised law in New York City until 1887, when he joined the editorial staff of the "St. Nicholas Magazine." Author of "Century World's Fair Book," 1893; "Imaginotions: Truthless Tales," 1894.

JENNISON, Lucy White, "Owen Innsley," b. Newton, Mass., 1850. She is the daughter of Samuel Jennison, of Boston, in which city she received her education. She has resided in Italy for a number of years. Author of "Love Poems and Sonnets," 1882, and of many contributions to periodicals.

JEWETT, Sophie, "Ellen Burroughs," educator, b. Moravia, N. Y., 1861. Has resided chiefly in Buffalo. Since 1889 has been teaching in Wellesley College, where she is an associate professor in the department of English literature. Author of "The Pilgrim, and Other Poems," 1896.

"**JOHNSON, Benj. F., of Boone.**" — See *James Whitcomb Riley.*

JOHNSON, Charles Frederick, b. New York, N. Y., 1836. He was graduated from Yale at the age of nineteen, and is the distinguished professor of English literature at Trinity College, Hartford, Conn. He has written "Three Americans and Three Englishmen," lectures, 1886; "English Words," 1891; "What can I do for Brady, and Other Verse," 1897.

JOHNSON, Robert Underwood, b. Washington, D. C., 12 Jan., 1853. Graduated at Earlham College, Ind. Joined the staff of the "Century Magazine," 1873, and became associate editor, 1881. Edited, with Clarence C. Buel, the "Century" war series and the resulting volumes entitled "Battles and Leaders of the Civil War," 1887-88, and persuaded Gen. Grant to write his memoirs. For his services, as secretary of the American Copyright League, in behalf of the passage of the International Copyright bill of 1891, Mr. Johnson was decorated by the French and Italian governments. — "The Winter Hour, and Other Poems," 1891; "Songs of Liberty, and Other Poems," 1897.

JOHNSON, Rossiter, man of letters, b. Rochester, N. Y., 27 Jan., 1840. A graduate of the University of Rochester. He was associate editor of the Rochester "Democrat," 1864-68, and editor of the Concord, N. H., "Statesman," 1869-72. Since 1872 he has resided chiefly in New York City, where he has taken a leading part in the work and convocations of the literary guild. With John Denison Champlin and George Cary Eggleston he edited with great success the costly and unique book issued by the Authors Club, "Liber Scriptorum," 1893. Author of "Phaeton Rogers," a story for boys, 1881; "Idler and Poet," poems, 1833; "A History of the War of Secession," 1888; "Three Decades," verse, 1895. Editor of "Famous Single Poems;" "Play-Day Poems;" the series, "Little Classics," 18 vols. 1874-77; and Appleton's "Annual Cyclopædia," from 1883.

JOHNSON, Samuel, clergyman, b. Salem, Mass., 1822; d. North Andover, Mass., 1882. He was a graduate of Harvard, and became pastor of a Unitarian church at Salem, Mass. He edited, with Samuel Longfellow, "Hymns for Public and Private Devotion," 1846, and was himself a writer of religious verse, also publishing several works on Oriental theology.

JOHNSON, William Martin, physician, b. about 1771; d. Jamaica, L. I., N. Y., 1797. Specimens of his poems appeared in articles contributed by J. H. Payne to the "Democratic Review," 1838.

JORDAN, David Starr, naturalist and educator, b. Gainesville, N. Y., 1851. A graduate of Cornell University. Dr. Jordan was president of the Indiana University, 1885-91, and resigned to become president of the Leland

Stanford, Junior, University. He is the author of various scientific works; also of "The Story of the Innumerable Company, and Other Verses," 1896; "Barbara, and Other Poems," 1897.

JUDSON, Emily (Chubbuck), "Fanny Forester," b. Eaton, N. Y., 1817; d. Hamilton, N. Y., 1854. She contributed to the N. Y. "Mirror," 1844–46, and in the latter year some of her stories were collected under the title of "Alderbrook." In 1846 she became the wife of the missionary Adoniram Judson, and accompanied him to Bengal, where she lived until his death, 1850. Mrs. Judson published a number of remembered prose works, and "An Olio of Domestic Verses," 1852.

KEELER, Charles Augustus, ornithologist, b. Milwaukee, Wis., 1871. Educated at the University of California. In addition to several prose works he has published "A Light through the Storm," verse, 1894; "The Promise of the Ages," 1896; "The Siege of the Golden City," 1896; "A Season's Sowing," 1899.

KEMBLE, Frances Anne, actress, b. London, Eng., 1809; d. there, 1893. Daughter of Charles Kemble, and niece of Mrs. Siddons. Her first appearance was as Juliet, in Covent Garden, 1829. In 1832 she came to America, and was married to Pierce Butler in 1834, obtaining a divorce in 1839. Gave Shakespearean readings, 1849–68. She wrote "Francis the First," a drama, produced in 1832; "Journal of a Residence in America," 1835; "The Star of Seville," a play, 1837; "Poems," 1844 and 1859; "Records of Later Life" and "Notes on Some of Shakespeare's Plays," 1882. As a citizen of this country, Fanny Kemble may well be represented in the present collection by her stanzas, the "Lament of a Mocking Bird." See, also, "A Victorian Anthology," p. 66.

KENYON, James Benjamin, clergyman, b. Frankfort, N. Y., 1858. Entered the Methodist Episcopal ministry, 1878, and subsequently became pastor of a church at Watertown, N. Y. Some of his volumes of poetry are "In Realms of Gold," 1887; "At the Gate of Dreams," 1892; "An Oaten Pipe," 1895.

KEPPEL, Frederick, art-connoisseur, b. Tullow, Ireland, 1846. Of English parentage, and Holland Dutch extraction, being a descendant of the first Duke of Albemarle. Resided as a child in England, but later removed to New York City, where he is engaged in business.

"**KERR**, Orpheus C." — See *Robert Henry Newell*.

KEY, Francis Scott, lawyer, b. Frederick, Md., 1779; d. Washington, D. C., 1843. Educated at St. John's College, Annapolis. Began practising law at Frederick, Md., in 1801, but removed some years later to Washington, where he became district attorney. Is best known as the author of the "Star Spangled Banner," thus far at the head of American national songs. During the bombardment of Fort McHenry, Mr. Key was detained as a prisoner on board the British fleet. All night he watched the engagement with keenest anxiety. The now historic piece was written next morning, instantly printed, and sung all over the country to the air of "Anacreon in Heaven." With other patriotic and devotional songs it was published after his death in a volume of his "Poems," 1857.

KIMBALL, Hannah Parker, b. Boston, Mass., 186–. She has published three volumes of verse, "The Cup of Life," 1892; "Soul and Sense," 1896; "Victory, and Other Poems," 1897.

KIMBALL, Harriet McEwen, b. Portsmouth, N. H., 1834. She has been long devoted to charitable work, establishing a cottage hospital in her native city, and has published "Hymns," 1867; "Swallow-Flights of Song," 1874; "The Blessed Company of all Faithful People," 1879; and "Poems," complete, 1889. Miss Kimball may be termed the foremost Episcopalian writer in America of devotional poems.

KING, Edward, b. Middlefield, Mass., 1848; d. Brooklyn, N. Y., 1896. He went to Paris in 1868, as a correspondent for American journals. Author of "My Paris: French Character Sketches," 1868; "The Great South," 1875; "Echoes from the Orient," poems, 1880; "The Gentle Savage," novel, 1883; "A Venetian Lover," poems, 1887; "Joseph Zalmonah," 1893, a striking novel directed against the "sweat-shops" of the East Side of New York City; "Under the Red Flag," 189–.

KINNEY, Elizabeth Clementine (Dodge), b. New York, N. Y., 1810; d. Summit, N. J., 1889. Granddaughter of Aaron Cleveland. She contributed poetry to the "Knickerbocker Magazine," "Blackwood's," and other periodicals. In 1830 she was married to Edmund Burke Stedman of Hartford, and after his death, 1836, lived at Plainfield, N. J. She was married, 1841, to William B. Kinney, who founded the Newark, N. J., "Advertiser" and was appointed, 1851, minister to the Court of Turin. While in Europe, where she remained for fourteen years, she wrote "Felicita, a Metrical Romance," 1855. After her return to America, 1865, she published her "Poems," 1867, and "Bianca Capello, a Tragedy," 1873. At Florence, Mrs. Kinney was an intimate friend of the Brownings, and a leader in the American and English circles. She has left her "Reminiscences," which are still unpublished.

KNOWLES, Frederic Lawrence, b. Lawrence, Mass., 1869. Son of Rev. D. C. Knowles, D. D. Associated with leading houses of the Boston book-trade. Mr. Knowles has published "Practical Hints for Young Writers," 1897; "Cap and Gown, Second Series," 1897; "Golden Treasury of American Songs and

Lyrics," 1897; "A Kipling Primer," 1899, republished in England; "On Life's Stairway," verse, 1900. (D. Roxbury, Mass., 1905.)

KOOPMAN, Harry Lyman, librarian, b. Freeport, Me., 1860. Graduated at Colby College, and took M. A. degree at Harvard. He filled positions as cataloguer at various Eastern libraries until his appointment as librarian of Brown University, 1893. Author of "Orestes, and Other Poems," 1888; "Woman's Will, with Other Poems," 1888; "Morrow-Songs," 1898, and catalogues of the Brown and other libraries.

LAMAR, Mirabeau Bonaparte, b. Louisville, Ga., 1798; d. Richmond, Tex., 1859. Gen. Lamar engaged in the war for the independence of Texas, of which, as a republic, he was president from 1838 to 1841. His "Verse Memorials" appeared in 1857.

LANIER, Sidney, b. Macon, Ga., 3 Feb., 1842; d. Lynn, N. C., 7 Sept., 1881. Graduated at Oglethorpe College, Midway, Ga., 1860. He was among the earliest volunteers in the Confederate army, and toward the close of the war was taken prisoner while trying to run a blockade. The pulmonary weakness which resulted in his death is perhaps traceable to his five months of captivity at Point Lookout. After teaching school in Alabama, he studied and practised law at Macon, with his father, Robert S. Lanier. Being an excellent musician, equally devoted to the practice and theory of music, the poet was first flute in the Peabody symphony concerts of Baltimore, in which city he spent the last years of his life. His first venture in literature was "Tiger Lilies," 1867, a novel founded on army life. His poem, "Corn," in "Lippincott's Magazine," struck a new note, and two years later he was chosen to write the Centennial Ode for the exposition of 1876. He defined and illustrated his original conception of the relations between music and poetry in two courses of lectures, 1879–81, at Johns Hopkins University; and in "The Science of English Verse," his main work in prose, 1880. Among his other works are "Florida: Its Scenery, Climate, and History," 1876; "Poems," 1877; the series beginning with "The Boy's Froissart," 1878; "The English Novel, and the Principles of Its Development," 1883. His "Poems," edited by his wife, with a memoir by William Hayes Ward, were published about three years after his lamented death. Cp. "Poets of America," 449–451; also, "The Nature and Elements of Poetry," pp. 62, 196, 253, 282. [L. C. B.]

LANIGAN, George Thomas, b. St. Charles, P. Q., Canada, 1845; d. Philadelphia, Penn., 1886. Founded, with Robert Graham, the humorous Montreal "Free Lance," now "The Evening Star," and was on the staff of papers in New York and Chicago. He published "Canadian Ballads," 1864; "Fables Out of the World, by George Washington Æsop," 1878.

LARCOM, Lucy, b. Beverly, Mass., 1826; d. Boston, Mass., 1893. She was employed in the mills at Lowell, and became a literary protégé of Whittier, through contributions to his paper. Was assistant editor of "Our Young Folks" from 1866 to 1874. Among her books of verse are "Poems," 1868; "An Idyl of Work," 1875; "Wild Roses of Cape Ann," 1880; and "Poetical Works," 1885.

LARREMORE, Wilbur, lawyer, b. New York, N. Y., 1855. Editor of N. Y. "Law Journal" since 1890, and author of a volume of verse, "Mother Carey's Chickens," 1888.

LATHROP, George Parsons, b. Oahu, Hawaiian Islands, 25 Aug., 1851; d. New York, N. Y., 19 April, 1898. He received his education in New York and in Dresden, Germany. From 1875 to 1877 he was assistant editor of the "Atlantic Monthly," and filled other editorial positions. He removed to New York in 1883. The same year he was concerned in the organization of the American Copyright League, of which he was secretary for two years. Some of his published volumes are "Rose and Rooftree," verse, 1875; "A Study of Hawthorne," 1876; "Gettysburg, a Battle Ode," 1888; "Dreams and Days," verse, 1892, and several novels, including "An Echo of Passion," 1882, and "Newport," 1884.

LATHROP, Rose (Hawthorne), b. Lenox, Mass., 185–. The daughter of Nathaniel Hawthorne. Her childhood was passed in Europe, where she received her education. In 1871 she was married to George Parsons Lathrop. Besides many contributions of fiction, poetry, and literary articles to the magazines, she has published "Along the Shore," verse, 1888; "Annals of the Georgetown Convent" (with G. P. Lathrop), 1894, and "Memories of Hawthorne," 1897. In 189- Mrs. Lathrop established in New York a home for the care of destitute women suffering from cancer.

LAWTON, William Cranston, educator, b. New Bedford, Mass., 1853. Graduated at Harvard University, and afterwards studied and travelled in Europe. For some years he has been a professor in the Adelphi College, Brooklyn. A contributor of classical essays to the periodicals, and author of "Three Dramas of Euripides," 1889; "Art and Humanity in Homer," 1896; "New England Poets," 1898; "Successors of Homer," 1898; and of a volume of verse, "Folia Dispersa," 1895.

LAZARUS, Emma, b. New York, N. Y., 1849; d. there, 1887. Of Portuguese Jewish ancestry. She was educated at home, and began the composition of poetry at the age of fourteen. Her "Poems and Translations" was published in 1867, and was followed by "Admetus, and Other Poems," 1871. "Alide," a romance in prose drawn from Goethe's autobiography, appeared in 1874. "The Spagnoletto," a tragedy, 1876, received high praise from Emerson. In 1883 Miss Lazarus, influenced by the persecutions of the Jews in Russia, devoted herself to a literary crusade in behalf of her race, and her subsequent writings were chiefly connected with Jewish themes. The "Dance to Death," a drama of persecution in the twelfth century, was inspired by the Russian crisis, the results of which she witnessed during her work among the refugees in New York. Her later volumes include "Poems and Ballads of Heine," translations, 1881; and "Songs of a Semite," 1882. A complete edition of her verse, with a memoir, was published in 1888.

LEARNED, Walter, b. New London, Conn., 1847. He is connected with the Savings Bank of New London, and has published "Between Times," poems, 1889; and translated "Ten Tales from Coppée," 1890. Has edited "A Treasury of American Verse," 1898.

LEGARÉ, James Mathews, b. Charleston, N. C., 1823; d. Aiken, S. C., 1859. He was an inventor, and contributed verse and prose articles to the magazines. "Orta-Undis, and Other Poems," was published in 1847.

LEIGH, Amy. An American song-writer, resident in California. Her song "If I but Knew," has been set to music by Wilson G. Smith.

LEISER, Joseph, rabbi, b. Canandaigua, N. Y., 1873. Of East-German Jewish parentage. Graduated at the University of Chicago. In 1896 he became the rabbi of a Jewish congregation in Springfield, Ill. Author of "Before the Dawn," poems, 1898.

LELAND, Charles Godfrey, b. Philadelphia, Penn., 15 Aug., 1824. He was graduated at Princeton, and studied at German and French universities. He practised law, and engaged in literary work and journalism in his native city until 1869, after which he resided chiefly in London, giving much time to the study of life among the gypsies, Indians, Italian witches, etc. In 1880 Mr. Leland visited America and devoted four years here to the introduction of the minor arts as a branch of instruction in the public schools. Among his volumes of verse are "Meister Karl's Sketch-Book," 1851; "Hans Breitmann's Ballads," 1868; "The Music Lesson of Confucius, and Other Poems," 1871; and "Songs of the Sea and Lays of the Land," 1895. Mr. Leland has also, among other works, made a translation of Heine's "Pictures of Travel," 1855. (D. Florence, Italy, 20 March, 1903.)

LINDSEY, William, merchant, b. Fall River, Mass., 1858. Received his education in the schools of that city. Entered on a business life, 1877, removing to Boston, 1888. Author of "Apples of Istakhar," poems, 1895; "At Start and Finish," fiction, 1900.

LIPPMANN, Julie Mathilde, b. Brooklyn, N. Y., 186–. A contributor to periodicals, and author of several books for children. A volume of her collected poems is to appear.

LITCHFIELD, Grace Denio, novelist, b. New York, N. Y., 1849. The daughter of Edwin C. Litchfield. Much of her early life was spent in Europe. She became a resident of Washington, D. C., in 1888. "Mimosa Leaves," 1895, contains her collected poems. Her volumes of fiction include "The Knight of the Black Forest," 1885; and "A Hard-Won Victory," 1888. Is a sister of the author Mrs. Francese Turnbull, of Baltimore, who, with her husband, Lawrence Turnbull, established the noted lecture-courses on Poetry, at Johns Hopkins University.

LLOYD, Beatrix Demarest, b. New York, N. Y., 188–. Daughter of the late David Demarest Lloyd, the lamented journalist and playwright, and herself a young writer of short stories, plays, and verse. Miss Lloyd is a grandniece of the late Chief Justice Chase.

LODGE, George Cabot, b. Boston, Mass., 1873. Son of Henry Cabot Lodge. A graduate of Harvard, 1895. — "The Song of the Wave, and Other Poems," 1898.

LOINES, Russell Hillard, Columbia University, Class of 1894.

LONGFELLOW, Henry Wadsworth, b. Portland, Me., 27 Feb., 1807; d. Cambridge, Mass., 24 Mar., 1882. The most refined of our elder poets, and for many years the one best known to American and British readers as our pioneer of sentiment, romanticism, and artistic feeling. Son of Stephen Longfellow, whose Yorkshire ancestors emigrated about 1675. Graduated at Bowdoin, where he entered the sophomore class in 1822, with N. Hawthorne as one of his classmates. From 1826 to 1829 he studied modern languages in France, Spain, Italy, Germany. He was professor of modern languages at Bowdoin in 1829–35. In 1835 he revisited Europe for a course of study preparatory to occupying the chair of modern languages at Harvard, which he held from 1836 to 1854. In 1831 he had married Miss Mary Potter of Portland, who died in Rotterdam, 1835. In 1843 he married Miss Frances Appleton, the tragedy of whose sudden death, in 1861, cast its shadow over his remaining years. The event occurred at their home in Cambridge, Craigie House, which had been the headquarters of Washington in the siege of Boston. During Longfellow's visit to England in 1868, he received the degrees of LL. D. from Cambridge, and D. C. L. from Oxford. In 1884 his bust in marble was placed in the Poets' Corner of Westminster Abbey. Samuel Longfellow's "Life of Henry Wadsworth Longfellow," and "Final Memorials," 1886–87, were largely compiled from his brother's diaries and letters. While an undergraduate, the future American laureate published poetry in the Boston "Literary Gazette," etc.; while professor at Bowdoin, he wrote for the "North American Review;" and in 1833–34 contributed to the "New England Magazine" the papers called "The Schoolmaster," but forming the basis of "Outre-Mer, a Pilgrimage beyond the Sea," 1835. "Hyperion," a prose romance full of the spirit of youth, and charged with poetic sentiment, appeared in 1839, and "Voices of the Night" in the same year. "Ballads and Other Poems," 1841, confirmed his reputation, and almost every work that he gave to the public thereafter received a warm welcome at home and abroad. His subsequent works include "Poems on Slavery," 1842; "The Spanish Student," drama, 1843; "The Belfry of Bruges, and Other Poems," 1846; "Evangeline, a Tale of Acadie," 1847 (for years the most popular of our longer idyllic poems); "Kavanagh," tale, 1849; "The Seaside and the Fireside," 1850; "The Golden Legend," 1851; "The Song of Hiawatha," 1855; "The Courtship of Miles Standish," 1858; "Birds of Passage," 1858–63; "Tales of a Wayside Inn," 1863; "Flower de Luce," 1867; "The Divine Comedy" of Dante, translation, 1867–70; "New England Tragedies," 1868; "The Divine Tragedy," 1871; "Three Books of Song," 1872; "Aftermath," 1873; "The Hanging of the Crane," 1874; "Morituri Salutamus," "The Masque of Pandora," 1875; "Keramos, and Other Poems," 1878; "Ultima Thule," 1880; "Hermes Trismegistus," 1882; "In the Harbor," 1882. He edited the anthology, "Poets and Poetry of Europe," containing some of his own translations, 1843; and "Poems of Places," 31 vols., 1876–79. The Riverside edition of Longfellow's complete works, 11 vols., 1886, is the authoritative and definite one. For an extended review of the life and works of the poet who may be said, all in all, to have been America's untitled laureate throughout his most productive career, cp. "Poets of America," chap. vi, pp. 51, 177, 178. [L. C. B.]

LORD, William Wilberforce, clergyman, b. Madison Co., New York, 1819. Rector of an Episcopal church at Vicksburg, Miss., and more recently of a church at Cooperstown, New York. Served as chaplain in the Confederate army. Author of "Poems," 1845; "Christ in Hades," 1851; and "Andre, a Tragedy," 1856. Cp. "Poets of America," p. 123. (D. 1907.)

LORING, Frederick Wadsworth, b. Boston, Mass., 1848; d. near Wickenburg, Ar., 1871. Graduated at Harvard in 1870, and went in 1871, as correspondent of "Appleton's Journal," on a government expedition to Arizona, where he was killed by Apache Indians. Author of "Two College Friends," a novel, and of "The Boston Dip, and Other Verses." His best-known poem, "In the Old Churchyard at Fredericksburg," was based on a newspaper report that one of Shakespeare's pall-bearers, Helder by name, was buried in St. George's churchyard, Fredericksburg, Va. This report, originated during the Civil War, was investigated by Moncure D. Conway, who after several visits to Stafford Co., Va., discovered the tombstone of one Edmond Helder, a physician in another part of the county. Helder died in 1618, aged 76, and it is thought that some one may have suggested that he could have been in point of time one of Shakespeare's bearers, and thus started the legend. The stone itself bore no such record.

LOVEMAN, Robert, b. Cleveland, O., 1864. Received an academic education. Is a resident of Dalton, Ga. Author of "Poems," 1897; "A Book of Verses," 1900.

LOWELL, James Russell, b. Cambridge, Mass., 22 Feb., 1819; d. Cambridge, Aug. 12, 1891. Of cultured parents, he received the early training that such a nature needs. He entered Harvard in 1834, where he devoted himself to reading if not to study. He wrote the class poem; and after graduating from the law school, published a volume of poems, "A Year's Life," 1841. In 1844 his second book, entitled "Poems," appeared, containing the "Legend of Brittany," "Rhœcus," etc. Another volume, "Poems," was published in 1848, and "Poetical Works" in 1850. The "Biglow Papers" began to appear in 1846, and made an immediate hit. The second series came out in 1862–66. They won for him a fame that his most exquisite poems of nature had failed to bring. Even apart from his poetical works, Lowell's pen was never idle. His "Conversations on Some of the Old Poets," 1844, is a proof of his critical ability, though an early specimen. In 1855 he became a professor of modern languages and belles lettres at Harvard, and his influence in that capacity was widespread. He became editor of the "Atlantic Monthly" in 1857, a position he held four years, contributing constantly to its pages. From 1864 to 1869 he was an editor of the "North American Review," to which he contributed some literary essays of note. His prose work appeared in collected form in "Fireside Travels," 1864; "Among My Books," 1870; "My Study Windows," 1871; "Among My Books," second series, 1876. His prose style is individual and distinctive; his discrimination sure, and while he sometimes fails in construction, his trouble lies in an embarrassment of rich material. "Under the Willows, and Other Poems," appeared in 1868; "The Cathedral" in 1870; "Three Memorial Poems" in 1875–76. These last were delivered at Concord, 19 April, 1875, at Cambridge, 3 July, 1875, and Boston, 4 July, 1876. In 1877 he was appointed to the Spanish Mission by President Hayes, and in 1880 was transferred to London, where he remained until 1885. In 1887 he published "Democracy, and Other Addresses," which had been delivered in England. "Heartsease and Rue," poems, appeared in 1888; and "Political Essays" in the same year. The degree of D. C. L. was conferred on him in 1873, by Oxford; and LL. D. by Cambridge in 1874. For an extended review of the genius and writings of this representative poet, scholar, and man of letters, cp. "Poets of America," chap. ix. [B. D. L.]

LOWELL, Maria (White), b. Watertown,

Mass., 1821; d. Cambridge, Mass., 1853. She was the first wife of James Russell Lowell, to whom she was married in 1844. Her poems were published in a privately printed edition in 1853. Mrs. Lowell was beloved for her intellect and womanly charm.

LOWELL, Robert Traill Spence, brother of James Russell Lowell, b. Boston, Mass., 1816; d. Schenectady, N. Y., 1891. He studied medicine, but became an Episcopal clergyman in Bermuda, 1842. He passed three years in Newfoundland, was head master of a school in Massachusetts, and professor of Latin in Union College, Schenectady. Author of "The New Priest in Conception Bay," novel, 1858; "Fresh Hearts that Failed Three Thousand Years Ago, and Other Poems," 1860; "A Story or Two from a Dutch Town," 1878. Among his poems is the stirring "Defence of Lucknow."

LUDERS, Charles Henry, b. Philadelphia, Penn., 1858; d. there, 1891. A contributor of verse and prose to the magazines, and joint author with S. D. Smith, Jr., of "Hallo, my Fancy!" poems, 1887. A posthumous collection of his lyrics and idyls, "The Dead Nymph, and Other Poems," was published in 1892. He was a poet of unusual promise, whose memory is cherished tenderly by his surviving associates.

LUNT, George, b. Newburyport, Mass., 1803; d. Boston, Mass., 1885. He was graduated at Harvard, practised law, and with George S. Hillard edited the Boston "Courier" during the Civil War. He published "Poems," 1839; "The Age of Gold," 1843; "The Dove and the Eagle," 1851; "Lyric Poems," 1854; "Radicalism in Religion, Philosophy, and Social Life," 1858; "Origin of the Late War," 1866; "Old New England Traits," 1873; "Miscellanies, Poems, etc.," 1884.

LYTLE, William Haines, b. Cincinnati, O., 1826; fell at the battle of Chickamauga, Tenn., 1863. He was an officer in the Mexican and Civil wars, and by gallant conduct gained the rank of brigadier-general of volunteers. An edition of his poems, with memoir by W. H. Venable, appeared in 1894.

MACE, Frances Parker (Laughton), b. Orono, Me., 1836; d. Los Gatos, Cal., 1899. She was married, in 1855, to B. H. Mace, a prominent lawyer of Bangor, Me. Author of "Legends, Lyrics, and Sonnets," 1884; and "Under Pine and Palm," 1888.

MALONE, Walter, lawyer, b. De Soto Co., Miss., 1866. Educated at the University of Mississippi, and now a resident of New York City. He has published numerous volumes of verse, including "Songs of Dusk and Dawn," 1894; "Songs of December and June," 1896; "The Coming of the King," 1897.

MARKHAM, Edwin, educator and reformer, b. Oregon City, Ore., 23 April, 1852. A descendant of William Markham, first cousin of William Penn. His parents were early pioneers from Michigan. His father dying, the family settled in central California. Mr. Markham took the classical course at Christian College, Santa Rosa, Cal., and studied for the law, but did not practise. He was for many years superintendent and principal of various schools in California, and contributed to the advance of education in that State. In 1899 he resigned the head mastership of the Tompkins Observation School at Oakland, and took up his residence in Brooklyn, N. Y., not long after the remarkable success of his poem, "The Man with the Hoe," — suggested by J. F. Millet's painting with the same title. His poems have been collected as "The Man with the Hoe, and Other Poems," and "Lincoln, and Other Poems," 1900. For some years he has been at work upon a lyrical epic of the destiny of man here and hereafter.

MARTIN, Edward Sanford, b. "Willowbrook," Owasco Lake, N. Y., 1856. A graduate of Harvard University. He edited the N. Y. "Life" at its start in 1883. The selections in this Anthology are taken from his volume of verse, "A Little Brother of the Rich," 1888. Mr. Martin contributes to "Harper's Weekly" a special department entitled "This Busy World."

MASON, Agnes Louisa (Carter), b. New York, N. Y., 18—. Now a resident of Montclair, N. J. Daughter of Walter Carter, the publisher. She was married to Frank G. Mason in 1896. Mrs. Mason began to write when a young girl, and has published a volume of verse, "The White Nun."

MASON, Caroline Atherton (Briggs), b. Marblehead, Mass., 1823; d. 1890. Popularly known as the author of "Do They Miss Me at Home" and "The King's Quest." Published "Utterance, a Collection of Home Poems," 1852; "Lost Ring and Other Poems," 1891.

MASON, Mary Augusta, b. Windsor, N. Y., 18—. Educated at Windsor and Binghamton academies. Adopted daughter of Mr. and Mrs. Charles M. Dickinson, of Binghamton, N. Y. A contributor of verse and prose to the magazines, and author of "With the Seasons," poems, 1897. — Cp. *C. M. Dickinson.*

MATHEWS, Albert, "Paul Siegvolk," b. New York, N. Y., 1820. A cousin of the late dramatic poet, Cornelius Mathews. Graduated at Yale in 1842. He practised law in New York City, where he was prominent in literary circles; he published "Walter Ashwood; a Love Story," 1860; "A Bundle of Papers," 1879; "Ruminations, and Other Essays," 1893. (D. Lake Mohonk, N. Y., 1903.)

MATHEWS, Cornelius, lawyer, b. Portchester, N. Y., 1817; d. New York, N. Y., 1889. He graduated at the University of New York, and followed his profession in that city. "Behemoth: a Legend of the Mound-Builders," 1839, "Puffer Hopkins," 1841, "Poems on Man," 1843, and several dramas which were produced, were among his more important literary efforts.

MATTHEWS, (James) Brander, b. New Orleans, La., 21 Feb., 1852. Graduated from Columbia University, 1871, and from its law school, 1873, receiving also its degree of A. M., 1874. He was admitted to the N. Y. bar, but has devoted himself to letters and the drama, and is an authority on French dramatic literature. In 1892 he became a member of the Faculty at Columbia, and is one of its professors in literature. A founder of the Authors Club, and of the Dunlap Society, and prominent in the organization of the American Copyright League. Has for some years been active with his pen in the defence and maintenance of the national quality in American literature. Prof. Matthews is the author of many works of criticism, fiction, and of plays, but has written little in verse-form. His novels have to do with real life. His comedy "Peter Stuyvesant," written in collaboration with Bronson Howard, was produced in New York, 1899. He is an accomplished bibliophile, and on the alert with respect to the rights and traditions of the literary profession.

McCABE, William Gordon, b. near Richmond, Va., 4 Aug., 1841; graduated at the University of Virginia. He was a captain of artillery in the Confederate army, and in 1888 became head master of the celebrated University School at Petersburg, Va., now removed to Richmond. Author of "The Defence of Petersburg, Campaign of 1864–65," 1876; a Latin grammar, and several lyrics very popular in the Civil War. Mr. McCabe has enjoyed the intimate friendship of Tennyson, and has been a welcome member of the literary groups of England and America, among whom he is distinguished as a scholar, wit, and raconteur.

McGAFFEY, Ernest, lawyer, b. London, O., 1861. Now a resident of Chicago, Ill., where he practises his profession. Besides being identified as an author, Mr. McGaffey has standing as a sportsman, and celebrant of the gun and rod. "Poems of Gun and Rod," 1892; "Poems," 1895.

McLELLAN, Isaac, b. Portland, Me., 1806; d. Greenport, L. I., 1899. A lawyer and sportsman, who published "The Fall of the Indian," 1830; "The Year and Other Poems," 1832; "Poems of the Rod and Gun," 1883. "New England's Dead" has long been a school-reader classic.

McMASTER, Guy Humphreys, jurist, b. Clyde, N. Y., 1829; d. Bath, N. Y., 1887. A graduate of Hamilton College. In 1864 he was elected judge of Steuben Co., N. Y., and in 1884 surrogate of the same county. The unique, masterly, sonorous "Carmen Bellicosum" ("The Old Continentals") appeared in the "Knickerbocker Magazine," 1849. He wrote a few other poems, "A History of Steuben County," and a series of letters from abroad to the Steuben "Courier."

MELLEN, Grenville, lawyer, b. Biddeford, Me., 1799; d. New York, N. Y., 1841. Followed his profession at Portland and North Yarmouth, Me. The last part of his life was passed in New York. Wrote "The Martyr's Triumph, Buried Valley, and Other Poems," 1833, and several prose volumes.

MELVILLE, Herman, romancer, b. New York, N. Y., 1 Aug., 1819; d. there, 28 Sept., 1891. He was descended from Major Thomas Melville, one of the participants in the Boston "tea-party," and the original of Dr. Holmes's "Last Leaf." Mr. Melville early embraced a seafaring life, and gained, as a sailor before the mast, the experiences which are more or less realistically portrayed in his romances of adventure. The first and most successful, "Typee," 1846, was followed by "Omoo," 1847; "White Jacket," 1850; and "Moby Dick," 1851. On returning from his voyages, he resided for several years at Pittsfield, Mass., engaged in literary pursuits. In 1860 he removed to New York. His poetical works include "Battle-Pieces, and Aspects of the War," 1866, and two privately printed booklets containing his later poems. Melville now holds his station, both in Great Britain and America, as one of the most original romancers that this country has produced. His leading books, "Typee," "Omoo," "Moby Dick," and "White Jacket," were reprinted in a four volume edition, with an Introduction by Arthur Stedman, in 1892.

MERCER, Margaret, b. Annapolis, Md., 1791; d. 1846. She was a daughter of John Mercer, governor of Maryland. A writer of religious verse. Was engaged in teaching school for the greater part of her life.

MEREDITH, William Tuckey, b. Philadelphia, Penn., 1839. An officer of the U. S. army, who served under Farragut in the battle of Mobile Bay, and became his secretary. Afterwards a banker in New York City. He published a novel, "Not of Her Father's Race," 1891.

MERINGTON, Marguerite, b. Stoke Newington, London, England, 18—. A well-known and successful playwright of New York City, and writer of occasional short stories.

MERRILL, Charles Edmund, Jr., Yale University, Class of 1898.

MESSINGER, Robert Hinckley, b. Boston, Mass., 1811; d. Stamford, Conn., 1874. He lived in New York, and contributed short pieces to "The American" of that city.

MIFFLIN, Lloyd, b. Columbia, Penn., 1846. Son of J. Houston Mifflin, the portrait painter, and himself an artist. He was obliged to abandon painting in 1877, on account of failing health, and afterwards devoted himself to literary work. Always a resident of Columbia. Besides general contributions to the periodicals he has published the following volumes of poems: "The Hills," 1895; "At the Gates of

Song," 1897; "The Slopes of Helicon, and Other Poems," 1898; "Echoes of Greek Idyls," 1899; and "The Fields of Dawn," 1900.

MILLER, Alice (Duer), sister of Caroline Duer (q. v.), b. near Fort Wadsworth, Staten Island, N. Y., 187–. In 1899 she was married to Henry Wise Miller, and her present residence is Costa Rica, Central America. Mrs. Miller is the joint author with her sister of "Poems by Caroline and Alice Duer," 1896.

MILLER, Cincinnatus Hiner (Joaquin), b. Wabash District, Ind., 10 Nov., 1841. When about thirteen he removed to Willamette Valley, Oregon. After a brief experience in a California gold mine he returned, in 1860, to Oregon, studied law, was admitted to the bar, edited the Eugene "Democratic Register," and practised law in Canyon City. He wrote a defence of the Mexican brigand, Joaquin Murietta, and adopted his first name for a pseudonym. From 1866 to 1870 he was judge of Grant Co., Oregon. He visited England and other parts of Europe in 1870, and in the following year published his first volume of verse, "Songs of the Sierras." In 1887, after some years of journalistic work in Washington, D. C., he removed to Oakland, Cal. In 1898 he visited the Klondike. His picturesque home is on the heights behind Fruitvale, overlooking San Francisco Bay. Among his works are "Songs of the Sunlands," 1873; "The Ship of the Desert," "The Ships in the Desert," "Songs of the Desert," 1875; "The Baroness of New York," novel, 1877; "Songs of Italy," 1878; "Shadows of Shasta," 1881; "The Danites in the Sierras," 1881, a novel, dramatized and successfully produced as "The Danites;" "Memorie and Rime," 1884; "Songs of the Mexican Seas," 1887; "Songs of the Soul," 1896. A collective edition of his poems was issued in California, in 1897.

"**MILLER**, Joaquin." — See *C. H. Miller*.

MILLER, Katherine (Wise), b. Spezia, Italy, 18—. Daughter of the late Commodore Henry A. Wise, U. S. N. (author of "Los Gringos," "Capt. Brand," etc.), and wife of Commodore J. W. Miller of the naval reserve. Her poem, "Stevenson's Birthday," is based on an actual occurrence.

MITCHELL, Langdon Elwyn, b. Philadelphia, Penn., 1862. Son of Dr. S. Weir Mitchell. Received his education at Berlin and Heidelberg, Germany, and studied for several years at the Harvard law school. He passed the bar examination in New York City. His first book of verse, "Sylvian, a Tragedy, and Poems," 1885, was issued over the pen name of "John Philip Varley." His "Poems" appeared in 1894. Mr. Mitchell has made a study of dramatic construction. "Becky Sharp," his successful dramatization of Thackeray's "Vanity Fair," was produced at the Fifth Avenue Theatre, New York, by Mrs. Fiske, in 1899.

MITCHELL, Silas Weir, b. Philadelphia, Penn., 15 Feb., 1829. He was graduated at Jefferson Medical College in 1850. Dr. Mitchell has published numerous technical and popular medical works of importance. His volume of short stories, "Hepzibah Guinness," 1880, was followed by "In War Time," 1884; "Roland Blake," 1886; "Characteristics," 1893; "Hugh Wynne, Free Quaker," 1897; "The Adventures of François," 1898; "The Autobiography of a Quack," 1899. His first volume of verse, "The Hill of Stones, and Other Poems," appeared in 1882, his collected poems to date in 1896, and "The Wager and Other Poems," 1900. It is interesting to note that Dr. Mitchell, by seniority of years, leads the authors of the "Second Lyrical Period" (p. 311), although almost the first lyric by which he won the critical public was the delightful bit of "patrician verse," "A Decanter of Madeira," composed in 1886. His son, Langdon Elwyn, by a pleasant coincidence, and by transmission of the poetic gift, is the first-named author in the closing division of this Anthology.

MITCHELL, Walter, clergyman, b. Nantucket, Mass., 1826. He was graduated at Harvard, entered the Episcopal ministry, and presided over several churches in the East. Was editorially connected with "The Churchman," contributed to other periodicals, in verse and prose, and is the author of the well-known polemic novel, "Bryan Maurice," and of a volume of poems.

MONROE, Harriet, b. Chicago, Ill., 186–. Graduated at the Visitation Academy, Georgetown, D. C. She has always resided at Chicago, where she wrote the text of the cantata for the opening of the Chicago Auditorium, 1889. Miss Munroe having been appointed to write the "Columbian Ode" on the occasion of the dedicatory ceremonies of the World's Columbian Exposition, her ode was read before a vast gathering on the 400th anniversary, — 21 Oct., 1892 — of the discovery of America. It was published the following year. Author of "Valeria, and Other Poems," 1891; "John Wellborn Root, a Memoir," 1896; and of many reviews and sketches.

MONTGOMERY, George Edgar, b. New York, N. Y., 1855; d. there, 1898. Studied at the College of the City of New York, and at Paris. Always a resident of New York. Was for some time dramatic critic of the N. Y. "Times," and correspondent for various papers. His writings in prose and verse have not been collected.

MOODY, William Vaughn, educator, b. Spencer, Ind., 1869. Graduated at Harvard, 1893. Instructor in English and rhetoric (1895–1901) and assistant professor and professor of English literature (1901–1907) at the University of Chicago. Author of "The Masque of Judgment," drama, 1900; "Poems," 1901; "The Fire-Bringer," 1904. Editor of the "Cambridge" Milton.

MOORE, Charles Leonard, lawyer, b. Philadelphia, Penn., 1854. Was U. S. consular agent at San Antonio, Brazil, 1878-79. His poetical works are "Atlas," 1881; "Poems Antique and Modern," 1883; "Book of Day Dreams," 1888; "Banquet of Palacios," 1889; "Odes," 1896.

MOORE, Clement Clarke, educator, b. New York, N. Y., 1779; d. Newport, R. I., 1863. Professor of Oriental languages at the New York General Theological Seminary from 1821 until his death. His famous poem, "A Visit from St. Nicholas," written for his children, Christmas, 1822, was sent without his knowledge to the Troy "Sentinel," where it appeared anonymously Dec. 23, 1823. A collection of his verse was published in 1844.

MORGRIDGE, Harriet Sampson, b. Chesterville, Me, 18—. Miss Morgridge's occasional verse is often written in a quaint and original vein.

MORRIS, George Pope, journalist, b. Philadelphia, Penn., 1802; d. New York, N. Y., 1864. Removed to New York at an early age, where he became a prominent figure in literary circles. In 1823 he established with Samuel Woodworth the "Mirror," which he edited until 1844. Two years later he founded the "Home Journal," with N. P. Willis as coeditor, and was connected with this periodical for the remainder of his life. His drama of the Revolution, "Briar Cliff," was produced with success. His best-known song is "Woodman, Spare that Tree!" Others are almost as popular. A volume of his prose sketches was published in 1836, and a collective edition of "Poems" in 1860.

MORRIS, Gouverneur, Yale University, Class of 1898.

MORRIS, Harrison Smith, b. Philadelphia, Penn., 1856. Always a resident of that city, where he received his education in the grammar schools, supplementing it by reading and study. He was engaged in business and literary work until 1893, when his activity and learning in art matters brought him the appointment of managing director of the Penn. Acad. of the Fine Arts. In 1899 he became editor of the new "Lippincott's Magazine." Author of "Tales from Ten Poets," 1893; "Tales from Shakespeare," continuing the work of Charles and Mary Lamb, 1893; "Madonna, and Other Poems," 1894. Editor of "In the Yule Log Glow," 1892.

MORSE, James Herbert, educator and critic, b. Hubbardstown, Mass., 1841. Graduated at Harvard. He established the Morse and Rogers Collegiate School in New York City, and is a frequent contributor, in verse and prose, to periodical literature. Author of "Summer-Haven Songs," 1886. Mr. Morse is a leading member of the Authors Club, and of the Council of the American Copyright League.

MOULTON, Ellen Louise (Chandler), b. Pomfret, Conn., 1835. She was educated at a seminary in Troy, N. Y., wrote for publication in girlhood, and was married, at twenty, to the Boston publisher, William Moulton. She became the Boston literary correspondent of the N. Y. "Tribune," in which for years her letters and reports were conspicuous. Mrs. Moulton has visited Europe frequently, and was the literary executor of the English poet Philip Bourke Marston, whose poems she edited, with a feeling preface. Her works include "This, That, and the Other," stories, essays, and poems, 1854; "Juno Clifford," novel, 1855; "Poems," 1877; "Swallow-Flights, and Other Poems," 1878; "Random Rambles," 1881; "Some Women's Hearts," 1888; "In the Garden of Dreams, Lyrics and Sonnets," 1890; "At the Wind's Will," 1900. This last volume contains the following tribute to Miss Howells, which, because of the late publication of the book, could not be inserted on its rightful page in this Anthology.

THE CLOSED GATE

But life is short; so gently close the gate.
WINIFRED HOWELLS.

Thus wrote she when the heart in her was high,
And her brief tale of youth seemed just begun.
Like some white flower that shivers in the sun
She heard from far the low winds prophesy —
Blowing across the grave where she must lie —
Had strange prevision of the victory won
In the swift race that Life with Death should run,
And, hand in hand with Life, saw Death draw nigh.
Beyond this world the hostile surges foam:
Our eyes are dim with tears and cannot see
In what fair paths her feet our coming wait,
What stars rise for her in her far new home.
We but conjecture all she yet may be,
While on the Joy she was, we close the gate.

MUHLENBERG, William Augustus, Episcopal clergyman, b. Philadelphia, Penn., 1796; d. New York, N. Y., 1877. Graduated at the University of Pennsylvania. He was rector of the Church of the Holy Communion in New York from 1843 until his death. "I would not live alway" is the best known of his hymns.

MUNGER, Robert Louis, Yale University, Class of 1897.

MUNKITTRICK, Richard Kendall, b. Manchester, England, 1853. Came to America in childhood, and received education at private academies. A resident of Summit, N. J. On editorial staff of "Puck," 1881-89. Some of his contributions in prose and verse to the periodicals have been published as "Farming," 1891; "The Moon Prince, and Other Nabobs," 1893; "The Acrobatic Muse," 1897; etc.

NASON, Emma (Huntington), b. Hallowell, Me., 1845. She lives in Augusta, Me., and has written "White Sails," verse, 1888; "The Tower, with Legends and Lyrics," 1895.

NEAL, John, b. Portland, Me., 1793; d. Portland, Me., 1876. After admission to the bar at Baltimore, Md., 1819, he spent several years in legal practice and in mercantile pursuits before he began his literary career. "Randolph" and "Seventy-Six," the most notable of his fiction, followed the production of several novels, some poems, and some historcial work. In 1824 he went abroad, where, under the guise of an Englishman, he appeared in "Blackwood's Magazine" and other British quarterlies, to correct prevailing opinion of social and political conditions in the United States. He is said to have been one of the first Americans to write on American topics in England, an originator of the woman's suffrage movement, among the first to establish a gymnasium in this country, and one of the earliest to encourage Poe's talents. "Wandering Recollections of a Somewhat Busy Life," 1869, was his last volume.

NEGRO SPIRITUALS. — The editor has thought it well to represent the most characteristic folk-songs which this country has produced by a few of those "universal" among the colored population of the Southern States. They have the tunes and words, the essential melody and import that constitute original "themes." The text is chiefly that adopted for Stedman and Hutchinson's "Library of American Literature" from the collection edited by W. F. Allen, E. P. Ware, and Lucy McKim Garrison, 1867, and from the Hampton "Cabin and Plantation Songs" arranged by T. P. Fenner, 1875. Colonel Higginson's article entitled "Negro Spirituals" can be found in the "Atlantic Monthly," 1867.

NESMITH, James Ernest, artist, b. Mass., 1856; d. 1898. Mr. Nesmith resided in Lowell, Mass., and published "Monadnoc, and Other Sketches in Verse," 1888; "Philoctetes, and Other Poems and Sonnets," 1894. His poetry is refined and scholarly, with a thoughtful undertone, the second collection containing some vigorous "Later Sonnets."

NEWELL, Robert Henry, "Orpheus C. Kerr," b. New York, N. Y., 1836. He was on the staff of the N. Y. "Mercury," 1858–62, and of the N. Y. "World," 1869–74. Edited "Hearth and Home," 1874–76, and published "The Orpheus C. Kerr Papers," a famous satirical series during and after the Civil War, 1862–68; "The Palace Beautiful, and Other Poems," 1865; "The Cloven Foot," story, 1870; several other romances, and "Studies in Stanzas," 1882. A resident of Brooklyn, N. Y., where he died 1901.

NORTON, Andrews, Unitarian clergyman, b. Hingham, Mass., 1786; d. Newport, R. I., 1853. He was graduated at Harvard, and was professor of sacred literature in that institution from 1819 to 1830. Besides numerous theological works, he was the author of several cherished hymns and of other poems.

O'BRIEN, Fitz-James, b. Limerick, Ireland, 1828; d. Cumberland, Md., 1862. Was educated at Dublin University, came to America in 1852, and lived in New York City till 1861, when he enlisted in the United States army; a year later he was fatally wounded. The facts that his literary career was chiefly in America, and that he gave his life for this country, eminently warrant his representation here. He was a frequent contributor to "Harper's Magazine." His story "The Diamond Lens" appeared in an early number of "The Atlantic Monthly." His most successful play was "A Gentleman from Ireland," produced at Wallack's Theatre. "The Poems and Stories of Fitz-James O'Brien; Edited, with a Sketch of the Author, by William Winter," appeared in 1881; and a collection of his stories in 1887.

"OCCIDENTE, Maria del." — See *Maria Gowen Brooks.*

O'CONNOR, Joseph, journalist, b. Tribes Hill, N. Y., 1841. Graduated at the University of Rochester. Entered journalism in 1870, and became editor of the Rochester "Post-Express" in 1886. His "Poems" were published in 1895.

O'CONNOR, Michael, brother of the preceding, b. Eastchester, N. Y., 1837; d. Potomac Station, Va., 28 Dec., 1862. Sergeant of volunteers in the Civil War.

O'HARA, Theodore, soldier, b. Danville, Ky., 1820; d. near Guerryton, Ala., 1867. He served in the U. S. army during the Mexican War, and in the Confederate army during the Civil War, and at one time practised law in Washington. His oft-quoted poem, "The Bivouac of the Dead," commemorates the Kentuckians who fell at Buena Vista.

O'REILLY, John Boyle, b. Dowth Castle, Co. Meath, Ireland, 28 June, 1844; d. Hull, Mass., 10 Aug., 1890. Son of the master of Nettleville Institute at Dowth Castle. He did some journalistic work in Drogheda, near his birthplace, but was sent to England as an agent of the Fenian society. He was arrested and condemned to death, but his sentence was commuted, and he was sent to Australia. After a year of penal servitude he escaped in a boat, was rescued by an American whaler, and landed at Philadelphia, Penn., 1869. He became editor and joint owner of the Boston "Pilot," and published "Songs of the Southern Seas," 1873; "Songs, Legends, and Ballads," 1878; "Moondyne," novel, 1879; "Statues in the Block," poems, 1881; "In Bohemia," 1886; "The Ethics of Boxing," 1888; "Stories and Sketches," 1888. At the time of his death he was preparing a work on Ireland. In 1896 a statue of Mr. O'Reilly by Daniel French was unveiled in Boston. Below the statue, which is fourteen feet tall, is a group of symbolic figures.

"O'REILLY, Miles." — See *Charles Graham Halpine.*

OSBORNE, (Samuel) Duffield, novelist, b. Brooklyn, N. Y., 1858. He graduated from Columbia College, taking the degrees of A. B. in 1879, LL. B. in 1881, and A. M. in 1882. Has contributed extensively to magazines. His books, "The Spell of Ashtaroth," 1888, and "The Robe of Nessus," 1890, are historical romances.

OSGOOD, Frances Sargent (Locke), b. Boston, Mass., 1811; d. Hingham, Mass., 1850. When a child she contributed verses to Lydia Maria Child's "Juvenile Miscellany." In 1834 the artist S. S. Osgood won her heart while painting her portrait. Soon after their marriage they went to London, and while there she published "A Wreath of Wild Flowers from New England," poems. Her play, "The Happy Release, or the Triumphs of Love," written at Sheridan Knowles's request, was accepted but never produced. During a residence in New York she formed a friendship with Poe, and her influence over him lasted till his death. Her "Poetry of Flowers" appeared in 1841, her "Poems," 1846, and "The Floral Offering," 1847.

OSGOOD, Kate Putnam, b. Fryeburg, Me., 1841. Sister of the late publisher, James R. Osgood. She has spent a number of years in Europe, and lives in Boston, Mass. Her poem "Driving Home the Cows" appeared in "Harper's Monthly," 1865.

PAGE, Thomas Nelson, b. Oakland, Va., 23 Apr., 1853. He was educated at the Washington and Lee University, and graduated in law at the University of Virginia. Practised law at Richmond from 1875 to 1893, when he removed to Washington, D. C. Some of this leading Southern novelist's books of fiction are "In Ole Virginia," 1887; "Two Little Confederates," 1888; "On New-found River," 1891; "Red Rock," 1899. He has also published "The Old South: Essays, Social and Political," 1892; and, with A. C. Gordon, "Befo' de War," verse, 1888.

PAINE, Albert Bigelow, b. New Bedford, Mass., 1861. Early removed to Illinois, where he was educated in the public schools. Engaged in business in the West until the success of his contributions of fiction and verse led him to make his home in New York. Joined the staff of "St. Nicholas," 1899. Author of "Rhymes by Two Friends," with W. A. White, 1893; "The Arkansaw Bear," fiction, 1898; "The Bread Line," fiction, 1900; etc.

PALFREY, Sarah Hammond, "E. Foxton," b. Massachusetts, 1823. Daughter of John Gorham Palfrey, the historian. Her verse includes "Prémices," 1855; "Sir Pavon and St. Pavon," 1867; "The Chapel and Other Poems," 1880; "The Blossoming Red and Other Poems," 1886. In fiction she has published "Hermann, or Young Knighthood," 1866; "Katherine Morse, or First Love and Best," 1867.

PALMER, John Williamson, physician, b. Baltimore, Md., 1825. Early in life he practised his profession in San Francisco. Resided in New York after 1870, and engaged in general literary work; was editorially connected with the "Century Dictionary." His ballad "Stonewall Jackson's Way" was written at Oakland, Md., on the 17 Sept., 1862, while the battle of Antietem was in progress. Collected poems are published in "For Charlie's Sake, and Other Ballads and Lyrics," 1901. (D. 1906.)

PALMER, Ray, Cong. clergyman, b. Little Compton, R. I., 1808; d. Newark, N. J., 1887. Pastor at Bath, Me., and Albany, N. Y. His hymn "My Faith Looks up to Thee" has been translated into twenty languages. He published several volumes of hymns. His complete poetical works appeared in 1876.

PARADISE, Caroline Wilder (Fellowes), b. East Orange, N. J., 186–. She was married, in 1890, to the Rev. Frank Ilsey Paradise, of Boston, Mass. Her poetry is uncollected.

PARKER, Theodore, the eminent Unitarian clergyman and abolitionist, b. Lexington, Mass., 1810; d. Florence, Italy, 1860. The poem "Jesus," given in the Anthology, is taken from his lecture, "Mistakes about Jesus." His complete works, edited by Frances Power Cobbe, appeared in London, 1863–65, and a Boston edition in 1870. Among his biographers are Weiss and Frothingham.

PARSONS, Thomas William, b. Boston, Mass., 18 Aug., 1819; d. Scituate, Mass., 3 Sept., 1892. He received his education at the Boston Latin School and at home. Visited Europe in 1836, and pursued in Italy the studies which culminated in his metrical translation of the first ten cantos of Dante's "Inferno," 1843, reissued in extended form in 1867 and 1893. He studied dentistry, and practised in Boston and London, residing in the former city after 1872. Dr. Parsons's noble lyric "Lines on a Bust of Dante" first appeared in the Boston "Advertiser and Patriot," 1841. His books of original poetry are "The Magnolia, and Other Poems," 1867; "The Old House at Sudbury," 1870; "The Shadow of the Obelisk, and Other Poems," 1872; and "Poems," definitive edition, 1893. Cp. "Poets of America," p. 55.

"PAUL, John." — See *Charles Henry Webb.*

PAULDING, James Kirke, early novelist, b. Pleasant Valley, N. Y., 1779; d. Hyde Park, N. Y., 1860. Associated with Washington and William Irving in the publication of "Salmagundi," 1807–08. Secretary of the navy under President Van Buren, 1837–41. His works, chiefly fiction, include "The Diverting History of John Bull and Brother Jonathan," 1812; "The Backwoodsman," a poem, 1818; "Königsmarke," 1823; "The Dutchman's Fireside," 1831; "The Puritan and His Daughter," 1849; "Letters on Slavery," 1835; "Life of George Washington," 1854.

PAYNE, John Howard, actor and dramatist, b. New York, N. Y., 9 June, 1791; d. Tunis, Africa, 9 April, 1852. Entered Union College, which he left for his first appearance on the stage at New York in 1809. He had already gained attention as the editor of a juvenile paper, the "Thespian Mirror." Was successful as an actor in America and England. His best-known plays are "Brutus" and "Charles II." The song "Home, Sweet Home" is contained in Payne's opera "Clari, the Maid of Milan," produced at Covent Garden Theatre in 1823. He was U. S. consul at Tunis from 1841 until his death. In 1883 his remains were removed, under the supervision of John Worthington, U. S. consul at Malta, and at the expense of W. W. Corcoran, to Washington, D. C., and were interred in the Oak Hill Cemetery.

PAYNE, William Morton, educator and critic, b. Newburyport, Mass., 1858. He assisted Dr. Poole in the Chicago Public Library, 1874–76, and since 1876 has been a professor in the high schools of that city. Became associate editor of "The Dial," 1892, and is its leading reviewer. Author of "Our New Education," 1884; "Little Leaders," 1895; and translator of Norwegian classics. Mr. Payne is an authority upon modern Scandinavian literature, and prominent among American scholars and critics.

PEABODY, Josephine Preston, b. New York, N. Y., 187–. Resident in Cambridge, Mass. Instructor in English Literature, Wellesley College, 1901–03. Author of "The Wayfarers," 1898; "Marlowe," 1901; "The Singing Leaves," etc. (In 1906 m. Lionel Marks.)

PEABODY, William Oliver Bourne, D. D., b. Exeter, N. H., 1799; d. Springfield, Mass., 1847. Graduated at Harvard. Pastor of the Unitarian Church at Springfield, 1820–47. Edited "The Springfield Collection of Hymns," 1833; wrote the report on "Birds of the Commonwealth," 1839. A prominent contributor to the "North American Review" and "Christian Examiner." The selection from Dr. Peabody relates to a passage in which Thomas Hope's Anastasius laments the death of his child Alexander. His "Literary Remains" appeared in 1850. Dr. Peabody's twin brother, Oliver William Bourne Peabody, wrote an eloquent lyric, "Hymn to the Stars," which may be found in "A Library of American Literature," vol. v.

PECK, Harry Thurston, L. H. D., educator and critic, b. Stamford, Conn., 1856. He graduated at Columbia, and afterward became professor of Latin in that university. Since 1895 he has been the American editor of "The Bookman," and is also literary editor of the New York "Commercial Advertiser." Author of "The Semitic Theory of Creation," 1886; "Latin Pronunciation," 1890; "The Personal Equation," essays, 1897; "What is Good English, and Other Essays," 1899; "Greystone and Porphyry," verse, 1900. Editor of "The International Cyclopædia," 1892, and of classical text-books and reference works.

PECK, Samuel Minturn, b. Tuscaloosa, Ala., 1854. Graduated at the University of Alabama, and afterwards studied medicine in New York. A resident of his native town, where he divides his time between literature and farming. His published volumes are "Caps and Bells," 1886; "Rings and Love-knots," 1892; "Rhymes and Roses," 1895; "Fair Women of To-day," 1898.

PELLEW, George, b. Cowes, Isle of Wight, England, 1859; d. New York, N. Y., 1892. He was a grandson of John Jay. Graduated at Harvard, 1880, and at the Harvard law school, 1883. Although admitted to the bar, he devoted himself to literary work. A trip to Ireland resulted in his book "In Cabin and Castle," 1888, commended by John Morley. Also author of "Women and the Commonwealth," 1888; "John Jay," in "American Statesmen" series, 1890; "Poems," edited by W. D. Howells, 1892.

PERCIVAL, James Gates, geologist, b. Berlin, Conn., 15 Sept., 1795; d. Hazel Green, Wis., 2 May, 1856. He was graduated at Yale, and practised as a physician at Charleston and in the U. S. recruiting service. Began the study of geology at New Haven in 1827, and prepared state reports on the geological conditions of Connecticut and Wisconsin. His first volume of poems, "Prometheus," appeared in 1820. "Poetical Works," 1859, contains his miscellaneous poems and tragedies. Cp. "Poets of America," p. 38.

"PERCY, Florence." — See *E. A. (Chase) (Akers) Allen.*

PERRY, Lilla Cabot, b. Mass., 185–. Wife of Thomas Sargeant Perry. Author of "English Literature in the Eighteenth Century," etc. A resident of Boston. She has published a volume of poems, "Impressions," 1898.

PERRY, Nora, b. Dudley, Mass., 183–; d. there, 1896. Her early life was passed in Providence, R. I. She was Boston correspondent of the Chicago "Tribune," and later of the Providence "Journal." Among her writings are: "After the Ball, and Other Poems," 1875; "Her Lover's Friend, and Other Poems," 1879; "A Book of Love Stories," 1881; "For a Woman," novel, 1885; "New Songs and Ballads," 1886; "Legends and Lyrics," 1890; and numerous stories for girls.

PETERSON, Arthur, b. Philadelphia, Penn., 1851. Son of Henry Peterson. Entering the navy as a paymaster, Mr. Peterson has served on many cruises since 1877. His poems have been published as follows: "Songs of New Sweden," 1887; "Penekyn's Pilgrimage," 1894; and "Collected Poems," 1900.

PETERSON, Frederick, physician, b. Faribault, Minn., 1859. A graduate of the University of Buffalo, and instructor in mental and nervous diseases at Columbia University. Author of "Poems and Swedish Translations," 1883, and "In the Shade of Ygdrasil," 1893.

PETERSON, Henry, publisher, b. Philadelphia, Penn., 1818; d. 1891. For twenty years assistant editor of the Philadelphia "Saturday Evening Post." He published "Poems," 1863 and 1883; "The Modern Job, and Other Poems," 1869; "Faire-Mount," poem, 1874; "Confessions of a Minister," 1874; "Bessie's Lovers," 1877; "Cæsar, a Dramatic Study," 1879. His drama "Helen, or 100 Years Ago," was produced in 1876. The "Ode for Decoration Day," from which an extract is given on pp. 180, 181, was one of the earliest poems of its class and is memorable for the line, "Foes for a day and brothers for all time."

PHELPS, Charles Henry, b. Stockton, Cal., 1853, but belongs to the distinguished Phelps family of Eastern Massachusetts. Educated at the University of California and the Harvard law school. He practised law in San Francisco, edited "The Californian" (afterwards "Overland Monthly"), 1880–82; and published "Californian Verses," 1882. Is still an occasional writer for the "Atlantic Monthly" and other magazines. Now a leading member of the New York bar, and an authority on copyright law.

PIATT, John James, b. James Mill, now Milton, Ind., 1 March, 1835. He studied at Kenyon College, and became private secretary to G. D. Prentice, of the Louisville "Journal." During the Civil War he was in the Treasury Department, Washington, having gained the friendship of Mr. Chase. In 1871 he became librarian of the House of Representatives at Washington, and in 1882, U. S. consul at Cork, Ireland, where he remained till 1894. With W. D. Howells he wrote "Poems of Two Friends," 1860 (now "rare" and valuable as a "first book" of each author); and with Mrs. Piatt, "The Nests at Washington, and Other Poems," 1864, and "The Children Out of Doors," 1884. He has also published "Poems in Sunshine and Firelight," 1866; "Western Windows, and Other Poems," 1869; "Landmarks, and Other Poems," 1871; "Poems of House and Home," 1879; "Idyls and Lyrics of the Ohio Valley," 1884, 1888, 1893; "At the Holy Well," 1887; "A Book of Gold, and Other Sonnets," 1889; "Little New-World Idyls, and Other Poems," 1893; "Pencilled Fly-Leaves," and "A Return to Paradise" in prose. He has edited "The Union of American Poetry and Art." Mr. Piatt is a representative poet of the middle West. His wife was Sallie Bryan, of Kentucky, and the two, like the Stoddards, often receive the appellation, once bestowed upon the Brownings, of "the wedded poets." Cp. "Poets of America," p. 453.

PIATT, Sarah Morgan (Bryan), b. Lexington, Ky., 1836. She studied at the Henry female college of New Castle, Ky., and published her first verses in the Louisville "Journal." In 1861 she was married to John J. Piatt. Her works include "A Woman's Poems," 1871; "A Voyage to the Fortunate Isles," 1874; "That New World, and Other Poems," 1876; "Poems in Company with Children," 1877; "Dramatic Persons and Moods," 1880; "An Irish Garland," 1884; "Child-World Ballads," 1887; "The Witch in the Glass, and Other Poems," 1889; "An Enchanted Castle," 1893. For volumes issued in collaboration with her husband, see *Piatt, J. J.* Mrs. Piatt's verse has met with high favor both here and in Great Britain.

PIERPONT, John, Unitarian clergyman, b. Litchfield, Conn., 1785, thus antedating Bryant; d. Medford, Conn., 1866. Graduated at Yale, 1804. Occupied himself successively with teaching, business, and the law. Entered the Unitarian ministry in 1819, and was for twenty-six years pastor of the Hollis Street Church, Boston. Becoming embroiled with his congregation on account of his sympathy with the abolition and temperance movements, he resigned his charge in 1845. Preached for a time at Troy, N. Y., and at Medford, Mass. Volunteered at the age of seventy-six as chaplain in the Civil War, but was soon afterward, in consideration of his infirmities, transferred to the Treasury Department, where he retained a clerkship until his death. Author of "Airs of Palestine, and Other Poems," 1816 and 1840; and "Poems," 1845.

PIKE, Albert, lawyer, b. Boston, Mass., 1809; d. Washington, D. C., 1891. Studied at Harvard. In 1831 he made Western explorations. Edited the "Arkansas Advocate." He was an officer in the Mexican War, and afterwards as a Confederate general led Indians to battle in the Civil War. His nobly planned and classical "Hymns to the Gods," first published in "Blackwood's Magazine," 1839, were included in "Nugae," privately printed, 1854. General Pike rose to be at the head of Freemasonry in America. His "Morals and Dogma of Freemasonry" appeared in 1870. Editions of his "Poems" were issued in 1873 and 1881.

PINKNEY, Edward Coate, b. London, England, 1802; d. Baltimore, Md., 1828. Son of William Pinkney, American minister to Great Britain. Entered the U. S. navy in 1816, resigning in 1824. Practised law at Baltimore, but without success, and fell into an early decline. His "Poems," a tiny volume containing some exquisite songs, was published in 1825.

POE, Edgar Allan, b. Boston, Mass., 19 Jan., 1809; d. Baltimore, Md., 7 Oct., 1849. In 1811, on the death of both his parents in the same week, Poe was received into the family of Mr. and Mrs. Allan, at Richmond, Va. He was sent to a small private school, and, being a child of great beauty and precocious talents, won his way in all hearts. He had a talent for declamation, probably inherited from his parents, who were actors by profession, and he often recited before company. In 1815 he was taken abroad with the family, and put to school near London. In 1820 the Allans returned to Richmond, where he was set to his studies under a new master. He was an acknowledged leader among his schoolmates, and in 1824 became lieutenant of the Richmond Junior Volunteers. He was usually at the head of his classes, learning without effort, and constantly writing verses, sometimes in Latin. In athletics he was foremost of the boys, renowned especially for his feats of swimming. He entered, 1826, the University of Virginia, where his scholarship was satisfactory, but where a fondness for excitants seems to have taken hold of him never to relinquish its grasp. Mr. Allan refused to honor his debts, but started him in a commercial career. The prospect was not attractive to the young man, and he ran away to Boston, enlisting in the army, 1827, under the alias "Edgar Perry." He seems to have devoted his spare time to literature, and in the summer of the war published a pamphlet entitled "Tamerlane and Other Poems, by a Bostonian." In 1829 his second publication appeared, "Al Aaraaf, Tamerlane, and Minor Poems," under his own name. In 1830 he entered West Point, but within the next year brought about his own expulsion. At the same time, in 1831, obtaining subscriptions from his mates, he issued a volume of "Poems." After the death of his patroness, Mrs. Allan, and the remarriage of her husband, Poe had no hope of further assistance from the latter. He went to Baltimore, living with his aunt, Mrs. Clemm. His first bit of good fortune was in 1833, when the "Saturday Visitor" awarded him a prize of $100 for the "MS. Found in a Bottle." In 1835 T. W. White, the editor of "The Southern Literary Messenger," gave him some remunerative employment. In 1836 he married his cousin Virginia Clemm, a girl of thirteen. In 1837 he went to New York, and in the next year the "Narrative of Arthur Gordon Pym" was brought out. He then removed to Philadelphia, contributed to many periodicals, and published "The Conchologist's First Book." Shifting to New York again, he became associate editor of Burton's "Gentleman's Magazine," 1839. His connection with the paper lasted one year. His stories were collected, 1840, under the title "Tales of the Arabesque and Grotesque," and in 1843 "The Prose Romances of Edgar A. Poe" appeared, and met with favor. He continued to contribute to the periodicals, notably a succession of critical and personal sketches of contemporary American authors, and had intervals of energy and hopefulness, alternating with attacks of inebriation and despondency. In 1845 a volume of "Tales" and "The Raven and Other Poems" appeared. The "Raven" was copied everywhere, and Poe suddenly found himself the most talked-of writer of the day. He seems never to have abandoned the hope of publishing a magazine of his own. In 1846 he moved to a cottage at Fordham with his wife, who was dangerously ill with consumption, and in January of the next year she died. In 1848 "Eureka; a Prose Poem" was published. In the summer of 1849 he revisited Richmond, where he lectured with success, was socially well received, and regained his vagrant hopefulness. He left in September, starting north, but did not get beyond Baltimore. There he was taken to the Washington Hospital in a stupor, and died after four days of delirium. From that time the world has mourned the untimely end of a man of genius, who struggled ineffectually against the recurrent habits that destroyed him. His work, for all its charm and its wonder, is the uneven and unfulfilled suggestion of what might have been. Rufus Wilmot Griswold, whom the poet made his literary executor, promptly brought together his "Tales, Poems, and Essays" in three volumes, 1850; and a fourth volume, containing "Arthur Gordon Pym and Miscellanies," was added in 1856. Since then Poe's writings have been repeatedly translated into French, German, Italian, etc., and many editions in English have been published. The definitive edition in ten volumes, edited and rearranged by Stedman and Woodberry, with memoir, bibliography, critical introductions, and variorum text of the poems, appeared in 1894–95. From the present condensed note, most important details of an exceptional career are necessarily absent. For an inclusive and critical review of the most famous Southern poet, essayist, and romancer, cp. "Poets of America," chap. vii. [B. D. L.]

POLLOCK, Edward, b. Philadelphia, Penn., 1823; d. San Francisco, Cal., 1858. When a child he worked in a cotton factory, and at fourteen became a sign-painter's apprentice. In 1852 he went to California, where he was admitted to the bar. He wrote for the "San Francisco Pioneer," and in 1876 his poems were collected posthumously.

PRATT, Anna Maria, b. Chelsea, Mass., 18—. For some years engaged in teaching. A resident of Cleveland, Ohio. Has written chiefly for children's periodicals. Author of "Little Rhymes for Little People," 1896.

PRENTICE, George Denison, journalist, b. Preston, Conn., 1802; d. Louisville, Ky., 1870. After a brief experience as editor in Connecticut he removed to Kentucky, assuming charge of the Louisville "Journal," which he edited until his death. "Prenticeana, or Wit and Humor," appeared in 1860. A volume of his "Poems" was brought out in 1876.

PRESTON, Margaret (Junkin), b. Philadelphia, Penn., 1820; d. Baltimore, Md., 1897. Her father, Rev. Dr. Junkin, was founder of Lafayette College. In 1848 he was made president of Washington and Lee University, Lexington, Va., which place became the daughter's home. She had written considerably when, in 1857, she was married to Col. John T. L. Preston. Her books of verse include "Beechenbrook, a Rhyme of the War," 1866; "Old Songs and New," 1870; "Cartoons," 1875; "For Love's Sake," 1887; and "Colonial Ballads, Sonnets, and Other Verse," 1887. Among her other works are "The Young Ruler's Question;" "Silverwood," a novel; and "A Handful of Monographs."

PROCTOR, Edna Dean, b. Henniker, N. H., 1838. She has made her home in Concord, N. H., Brooklyn, N. Y., and South Framingham, Mass., spending much time in Europe. Author of "Poems," 1866; "A Russian Journey," 1872; "The Song of the Ancient People," 1892.

PROUDFIT, David Law, b. Newburgh, N. Y., 1842; d. New York, N. Y., 1897. He enlisted in the U. S. army at the outbreak of the Civil War, and became a major. Afterwards in business in New York City. He was induced to adopt a pseudonym, "Peleg Arkwright," which he later discarded. Author of "Love among the Gamins," 1877; "The Man from the West," "Mask and Domino," poems, 1888.

PULLEN, Elisabeth (Jones), (Elisabeth Cavazza), b. Portland, Me., 18—. Daughter of Charles Jones, a merchant of that city, where she has always resided. She was first married to Nino Cavazza, an Italian gentleman. Her second husband is Stanley T. Pullen, a journalist and financier of Portland. For several years Mrs. Pullen was a staff writer for the "Literary World" of Boston. Her contributions of verse and prose to the periodicals have been not numerous, but of a very high order. Her metrical satires, "Algernon in London" and "Algernon the Footstool-Bearer," published in the Portland "Transcript" some years ago, attracted wide attention. Some of her short stories were issued as "Don Finimondone: Italian Sketches," 1892.

PULLEN, Eugene Henry, b. Baltimore, Md., 1832; d. Brooklyn, 1899. He was vice-president of the "National Bank of the Republic" of New York, president of the "American Bankers' Association," 1895-96. His "Now I lay me down to Sleep," p. 470, was published many years before Eugene Field's poem, p. 527, on the same theme.

RANDALL, James Ryder, journalist, b. Baltimore, Md., 1839. He was a student at Georgetown College, D. C.; was afterwards connected with the New Orleans "Sunday Delta." At Poydras College, La., he composed, in 1861, the battle-hymn "Maryland, My Maryland!" In 1866 Mr. Randall became editor-in-chief of the Augusta, Ga., "Constitutionalist," and more recently was a member of the staff of the Baltimore "American." Later he was a press correspondent at Washington and Augusta. His poems, appearing in periodicals and compilations, are uncollected. (D. 1908.)

RANDOLPH, Anson Davies Fitz, publisher, b. Woodbridge, N. J., 1820; d. Westhampton, L. I., N. Y., 1896. He conducted a publishing house in New York, over his own name, from 1851 to his death. "Hopefully Waiting, and Other Verses," 1867 (enlarged edition, 1885), is a collection of his religious poetry. Its title-poem is widely familiar.

RANKIN, Jeremiah Eames, educator, b. Thornton, N. H., 1828. He graduated at Middlebury College, and entered the Congregational ministry. He became president of Howard University, Washington, in 1889. Some of Dr. Rankin's hymns have found place in the religious collections. Beside his prose volumes, he is the author of "Auld Scotch Mither, and Other Poems," 1873; "Ingleside Rhaims," 1887; "Broken Cadences," 1889; "Hymns Pro Patria," 1889; and "German-English Lyrics," 1897. Stanzas of Dr. Rankin's charming little lyric "The Babie" have been wrongly but not unnaturally attributed by collectors to the pen of Hugh Miller, the Scottish geologist, and the error was repeated by the present editor in the early editions of his "Victorian Anthology." For this mistake he now makes amends. The poem has been expunged from the last-named collection and now appears, on page 296 of this volume, accredited to its veritable author.

"RAYMOND, Grace." — See *Annie Raymond Stillman.*

READ, Thomas Buchanan, artist, b. Chester Co., Penn., 12 March, 1822; d. New York, N. Y., 11 May, 1872. He studied portrait painting as a specialty, and practised his art in various Eastern cities. For several years his studies were carried on at Rome, which city he revisited later in life. Mr. Read was chiefly identified with Philadelphia, where he brought out his first volume "of Poems," in 1847. Beside editing a well-known collection of verse, "The Female Poets of America," 1848, illustrated by engravings from his own portraits, he published his "Lays and Ballads," 1848; "The New Pastoral," 1855; "The Wagoner of the Alleghanies," 1862; and "A Summer Story, Sheridan's Ride, and Other Poems," 1865.

REALF, Richard, b. Framfield, near Lewes, Sussex, England, 1834; d. by his own hand, Oakland, Cal., 1878. He wrote verses when about fifteen, and won the regard of the poet Rogers, Miss Mitford, Miss Martineau, — and of Lady Byron, who made him steward on one of her estates. His first volume of poems, "Guesses at the Beautiful," London, 1852, was edited by Thackeray's nephew Charles de la Pryme. In 1854 he emigrated to Kansas, and, removing to New York, was an assistant at the Five Points House of Industry, 1855-56. He seconded the plans of John Brown, and just before the outbreak at Harper's Ferry went to Europe to give lectures in behalf of the anti-slavery movement. He enlisted in the Union army, and was commended for gallantry at Chickamauga and elsewhere. A posthumous edition of his poems, with a memoir by his loyal friend and executor, Colonel Richard J. Hinton, appeared in 1899.

REESE, Lizette Woodworth, b. Waverly, Md., 186–. Early removed to Baltimore, which place has since been her residence. Author of

"A Branch of May," 1887; "A Handful of Lavender," 1891; "A Quiet Road," 1896. Miss Reese's poetry is of a rare quality, — artistic, natural, beautiful with the old-time atmosphere and associations, and at times rising to a noble classicism, of which the lines "To a Town Poet," p. 611, afford a fine example.

RICE, Wallace, "Cecil de Groot," b. Hamilton, Canada, 1859, of American parentage. Educated at Harvard, Class of 1883. Since 1890 has been engaged in critical as well as creative literary work: "Under the Stars, and Other Songs of the Sea" (Barrett Eastman, collaborator), 1898; "Heroic Deeds," prose and verse, 1898; "Flying Sands," verse, 1898. Later, "Ballads of Valor and Victory," (Clinton Scollard, collaborator); "Great Travellers." Also editor of "Poems," 1898, by Francis Brooks, and "Poems," by Rudyard Kipling.

RICHARDS, Laura Elizabeth, b. Boston, Mass., 185–. The daughter of Samuel G. and Julia Ward Howe. In 1871 she married Henry Richards, of Gardiner, Me., where she afterwards resided. Author of successful books for children in prose and verse, and of poems and other contributions to the magazines.

RICHARDSON, Charles Francis, b. Hallowell, Me., 1851. He graduated at Dartmouth College, where he was appointed professor of English literature in 1882, having served on the editorial staff of the "Independent" from 1872–78. His books include the valued "Primer of American Literature," 1878, enlarged, 1896; "The Cross," verse, 1879; "The Choice of Books," 1881; an important "History of American Literature," 2 vols., 1887–89; "The End of the Beginning," fiction, 1896.

RICHARDSON, George Lynde, Williams College, Class of 1888.

RILEY, James Whitcomb, "Benj. F. Johnson of Boone," b. Greenfield, Ind., 1853. His father, an attorney of Greenfield, intended that his son should follow his own profession, but the latter tired of study and joined a patent-medicine travelling wagon. After various experiences as sign-painter, actor, etc., he returned and began newspaper work on a Greenfield paper. He began contributing verse to the Indianapolis papers in 1873, and secured a position on the "Journal" of that city, where he has since resided. More recently he has given readings from his poetry in all parts of the country with more than usual success. His first book of verse in the "Hoosier" dialect, "The Old Swimmin'-Hole, and 'Leven More Poems," 1883, has been followed by a series of volumes, the humor, pathos, originality, and natural sentiment of which have particularly endeared him to his countrymen. "Afterwhiles," 1888; "Old-Fashioned Roses," 1888; "Pipes o' Pan at Zekesbury," 1889; "Rhymes of Childhood," 1890; "Flying Islands of the Night," 1891; "Neighborly Poems," 1891; "An Old Sweetheart of Mine," 1891; "Green Fields and Running Brooks," 1892; "Poems here at Home," 1893; "Armazindy," 1894; "A Child-World," 1896; "Rubaiyat of Doc Sifers," 1899. "The Boss Girl, and Other Sketches," prose, appeared in 1886.

RIVES, Amélie. — See *Princess Troubetskoy*.

ROBINSON, Annie Douglas (Green), "Marian Douglas," b. Plymouth, N. H., 1842. A writer of Bristol, N. H., who has published "Picture Poems," for children, 1872; "Peter and Polly, or Home Life in New England One Hundred Years Ago," 1876.

ROBINSON, Edwin Arlington, b. Head Tide, Me., 1869. Now a resident of New York City. Engaged in literary pursuits. His poetry has an individual cast, and is contained, thus far, in his two collections "The Torrent and the Night Before," 1896; "The Children of the Night," 1897.

ROBINSON, Lucy Catlin (Bull), b. Hartford, Conn., 186–. With the exception of two years in Paris, she has lived in New York since 1891. Author of "A Child's Poems," composed in her tenth year, and published with a preface by her mother. This unique volume gained critical attention, and was reviewed by the late Mr. Dennett, of "The Nation," as written by "One of America's Pet Marjories." In 1899 she was married to the poet Tracy Robinson of Colon, Panama, and accompanied him to the tropics. (D. Colon, Panama, 1903.)

ROBINSON, Tracy, b. Clarendon, N. Y., 1833. He was educated at Rochester University, and was an official of railways in Tennessee and Louisiana until 1861, when he became connected with the Panama railroad, and removed to Colon, Panama. He has published "Song of the Palm and Other Poems," 1889, and contributed poems to the New York magazines.

ROCHE, James Jeffrey, b. Queen's Co., Ireland, 1847. His early life was passed in Prince Edward Island and at St. Dunstan's College. He edited the Boston "Pilot," 1890–1904, and published "Songs and Satires," 1887; "Life of John Boyle O'Reilly," 1891; "Ballads of Blue Water," 1895; "The Vase and Other Bric-a-Brac," 1900. (D. 3 April, 1908.)

ROGÉ, Madame. — See *Charlotte (Fiske) Bates*.

ROGERS, Robert Cameron, b. Buffalo, N. Y., 1862. Son of the late Sherman S. Rogers, a noted lawyer of Buffalo. Graduated at Yale, and afterwards resided in his native city, and at Santa Barbara, Cal., engaged in literary work. Author of two books of fiction, "Will o' the Wasp: a Sea Yarn of the War of 1812," and "Old Dorset: Chronicles of a New York Country Side." His poems have been collected and published as "The Wind in the

Clearing, and Other Poems," 1895; "For the King, and Other Poems," 1899.

ROLLINS, Alice Marland (Wellington), b. Boston, Mass., 1847; d. Lawrence Park, Bronxville, N. Y., 1897. She received instruction from her father, Ambrose Wellington, visited Europe, and in 1876 was married to Daniel M. Rollins, of New York City. She wrote "The Ring of Amethyst," poems, 1878; "The Story of a Ranch," 1885; "Uncle Tom's Tenement," 1888, and several books of travel, and was an efficient and favorite member of the N. Y. literary circles.

ROONEY, John Jerome, broker, b. Binghamton, N. Y., 1866. Educated at Mt. St. Mary's College. He has devoted much time to journalistic work. His spirited poems relating to the phases and incidents of the Spanish-American war are a feature of its literature.

ROSENBERG, James Naumburg, Columbia University, Class of 1895.

ROSENFELD, Morris, b. Boksha, Poland, 1861. Born of humble parents, he received the education that is given to Jewish boys of like origin. Some years ago, he came to this country, and supported himself in the sweat-shops of New York City. Although well-read in German and English literature, he is master only of his native tongue — Yiddish. Mr. Rosenfeld was first known in literary circles by his "Songs from the Ghetto," translated by Leo Wiener, 1898. These songs, at once spontaneous, simple, and pathetic, are fraught with the desolation and despair of life in the Jewish slums. The poem included in this Anthology was the first written in English by its author.

RUNKLE, Bertha Brooks, b. Berkeley Heights, N. J., 18—. Daughter of the distinguished critic and journalist, Mrs. Lucia Gilbert Runkle. Her serial romance, "The Helmet of Navarre," appeared in "The Century Magazine," 1900.

RUSSELL, Irwin, b. Port Gibson, Miss., 1853; d. New Orleans, La., 1879. Among Southern writers he was one of the first to introduce the negro character to metrical literature. After his early death, his verse was collected, and published as "Poems," 1888.

RYAN, Abram Joseph, "Father Ryan," b. Norfolk, Va., 1839; d. Louisville, Ky., 1886. He was a Catholic priest and chaplain in the Confederate army, editor of several religious periodicals, and pastor of a church in Mobile, Ala. The title-piece of his volume, "The Conquered Banner, and Other Poems," 1880, was written soon after Lee's surrender. He also published "Poems, Patriotic, Religious, and Miscellaneous," 1880, and "A Crown for Our Queen," 1882. He died before completing his "Life of Christ."

"**RYAN**, Father." — See *Abram Joseph Ryan.*

SALTUS, Francis Saltus, b. New York, N. Y., 1849; d. Tarrytown, N. Y., 1889. Educated in his native city and at the Roblot Institution, Paris. He was an extensive traveller and mastered many languages. His first volume of verse, "Honey and Gall," was published in 1873. A posthumous edition of his metrical works, in four volumes, was edited by his father, Francis H. Saltus. He left many writings which have not yet seen the light, among which is said to be a noteworthy life of Donizetti.

SANBORN, Franklin Benjamin, b. Hampton Falls, N. H., 1831. A graduate of Harvard, 1855. The next year he was elected secretary of the Mass. state Kansas committee. In 1866 he began his continued service as literary correspondent of the Springfield "Republican," chiefly from Boston and Concord. Mr. Sanborn has been closely identified with, and often the inaugurator of, various social and political reforms. He was one of the founders of the American Social Science Association and of the Concord School of Philosophy. He has written biographies of Thoreau, Emerson, Alcott, Dr. Earle, and John Brown, and with the latter was closely associated at historic periods of his career. The first two lines of the sonnet "Ariana," given in this Anthology, were written by A. B. Alcott, at whose request Mr. Sanborn perfected the tribute to his own wife.

SANDS, Robert Charles, journalist, b. Flatbush, L. I., 1799; d. Hoboken, N. J., 1832. Graduating from Columbia, 1815, he took up the study of law and was admitted to the bar, but practised only a few years. From early boyhood devoted to literature, both as a reader and writer, Mr. Sands had connections with several distinguished authors. He was co-editor with W. C. Bryant of the N. Y. "Review," 1825-27, and issued with Bryant and Verplanck the "Talisman," 1828-30. He was on the staff of the N. Y. "Commercial Advertiser" from 1827 until his death. His life of Paul Jones was published in 1831, and a posthumous edition of his collected "Writings," with a memoir by G. C. Verplanck, in 1834. Mr. Sands was cut down in the early prime of a notable career.

SANGSTER, Margaret Elizabeth (Munson), journalist, b. New Rochelle, N. Y., 1838. Editor of "Harper's Bazar," 1889-99. Formerly associate editor of the New York "Hearth and Home," "Christian at Work," and "Christian Intelligencer;" editor of "Harper's Young People," 1882-89. She has published "Poems of the Household," 1882; "Home Fairies and Heart Flowers," 1887; "Hours with Girls," and several other volumes of verse and juvenile books.

SANTAYANA, George, b. Madrid, Spain, 1863, of Spanish parentage. He graduated from Harvard in 1886, and has since been connected with that university as assistant professor of philosophy. His writings include "Sonnets and Other Poems," 1894; "The Sense of Beauty," 1896; "Lucifer, a Theological Tragedy," 1899; "Interpretations of Poetry and Religion," 1900.

SARGENT, Epes, author of the song "A Life on the Ocean Wave," b. Gloucester, Mass., 1813; d. Boston, Mass., 1880. He was one of the editors of the New York "Mirror," and editor for several years of the Boston "Evening Transcript." His play "The Bride of Genoa," 1836, was performed with success and followed by three others: "Velasco," 1837; "Change Makes Change," and "The Priestess." He published "Wealth and Worth," a novel, 1840; a "Life of Henry Clay," 1843, and a memoir of Benjamin Franklin; "Songs of the Sea," poems, 1847; "Antic Adventures by Sea and Land," 1857; and several works on spiritualism. He compiled a "Cyclopædia of English and American Poetry," published after his death.

SARGENT, John Osborne, lawyer, b. Gloucester, Mass., 1811; d. New York, N. Y., 1891. Brother of Epes Sargent. Graduating from Harvard in 1830, he studied law and was admitted to the Suffolk bar in 1833. In 1841, after several years of journalism as well, he became a member of the bar of the Supreme Court of the United States. During his practice in Washington he was one of the managers of "The Republic." Mr. Sargent edited some of the English poets, with biographies. It was his purpose to make translations of all the Odes of Horace; and though he did not live to complete this work, his "Horatian Echoes," 1893, issued posthumously, with an introduction by O. W. Holmes, contains the majority of the Odes.

SAVAGE, Minot Judson, liberal Unitarian clergyman, b. Norridgewock, Me., 1841; educated at Bowdoin College and Bangor theological seminary. After some years of mission work in California, he was pastor, for twenty-two years, of the Church of the Unity, Boston, Mass., where his liberal preaching soon gathered a large congregation, and is now pastor of the Church of the Messiah, New York. Besides many books on religious and social themes, he has written "Bluffton, a Story of Today," 1878; "Poems," 1882; "Life beyond Death," 1899.

SAVAGE, Philip Henry, b. North Brookfield, Mass., 1868; d. Mass., 1899. Son of the Rev. Minot Judson Savage. Graduated at Harvard University. His "First Poems and Fragments" appeared in 1895, and was followed by "Poems," in 1898. He died, with fortitude, almost at the outset of what promised to be an enviable career.

SAXTON, Andrew Bice, b. Middlefield, N. Y., 1856. Graduated at Hartwick Seminary, N. Y. Was occupied as a farmer and teacher until 1890, when he accepted an editorial position on "The Herald" of Oneonta, N. Y.

SCHUYLER, Montgomery, journalist, b. Ithaca, N. Y., 1843. Son of the Rev. Anthony Schuyler, of Orange, N. J. Studied at Hobart College. He was connected with the N. Y. "World" from 1865 to 1883, and more or less with "Harper's Weekly," when he joined the editorial staff of the N. Y. "Times." He is engaged in preparing "A History of Architecture in the United States."

SCOLLARD, Clinton, b. Clinton, N. Y., 18 Sept., 1860. Graduated at Hamilton College, and took graduate courses at Harvard, and at Cambridge, England. He was professor of English literature at Hamilton College from 1888 to 1896, Clinton being his permanent residence. Author of "With Reed and Lyre," 1886; "Old and New World Lyrics," 1888; "Giovo and Giulia," 1891; "Songs of Sunrise Lands," 1892; "Pictures in Songs," 1894; "The Hills of Song," 1895; "Skenandoa," 1896; "A Boy's Book of Rhyme," 1896; and two prose works, "Under Summer Skies," 1892; "On Sunny Shores," 1893.

SCOTT, Mary McNeil. — See *M. McN. Fenollosa.*

SCUDDER, Eliza, b. Barnstable, Mass., 1821; d. Weston, Mass., 1896. She was a daughter of Elisha Gage Scudder. The volume of her "Hymns and Sonnets," 1880, was reissued in 1896 with an introduction by her cousin, Horace E. Scudder.

SEARING, Laura Catherine (Redden), "Howard Glyndon," b. Somerset Co., Md., 1840. She lost her speech and hearing at the age of ten, yet has done much journalistic work. In 1876 she was married to Edward W. Searing, of New York City, and in 1886 removed with him to California. Author of "Idyls of Battle," 1864; "Sounds from Secret Chambers," 1873.

SEARS, Edmund Hamilton, b. Sandisfield, Mass., 1810; d. Weston, Mass., 1876. Pastor of several Unitarian churches, and editor of "The Monthly Religious Magazine." He published "Christian Lyrics," 1860; "Sermons and Songs of the Christian Life," 1875; "That Glorious Song of Old," etc.

SEWALL, Alice Archer. — See *A. A. (S.) James.*

SEWALL, Frank, b. Bath, Me., 1837. Graduated at Bowdoin. A Swedenborgian minister living in Washington, D. C. Author of "Moody Mike, or the Power of Love," 1869; "Angelo, the Circus Boy," 1879; "The New Ethics," 1881; "Carducci and the Classic Realism," 1892; and a translation of Carducci's poems, 1892.

SEWALL, Harriet (Winslow), b. Portland, Me., 1819; d. Wellesley, Mass., 1889. She was twice married, in 1848 to Charles List, of Philadelphia, and in 1857 to Samuel E. Sewall, of Boston, and afterwards resided in the last-named city. Her "Poems" were published in 1889, with a memoir by Ednah D. Cheney.

SHAW, John, physician, b. Annapolis, Md., 1778; d. on a voyage to the Bahamas, 1809. Took his degree in medicine in Philadelphia, and practised later at Baltimore. His "Poems," 1810, were collected by his friends and published after his death. The book is now very "rare."

SHEPHERD, Nathaniel Graham, journalist, b. New York, N. Y., 1835; d. there, 1869. During the Civil War he was for some time a war correspondent for the New York "Tribune." Author of several stirring poems of army life.

SHERMAN, Frank Dempster, educator, b. Peekskill, N. Y., 6 May, 1860. He graduated at Columbia, and took a graduate course at Harvard. He became a fellow of Columbia in 1887, and was instructor in architecture there until his appointment as adjunct professor. Though best known by his metrical work, he has done much literary reviewing. Author of "Madrigals and Catches," 1887; "Lyrics for a Lute," 1890; "Little-Folk Lyrics," 1892, enlarged edition, 1897. Joint author, with John Kendrick Bangs, of "New Waggings of Old Tales. By Two Wags," 1887.

SHINN, Milicent Washburn, b. Washington Township, Alameda Co., Cal., 1858. She graduated at the University of California, and in 1882 assumed the editorship of the new "Overland Monthly," which she held until 1894. Besides her work of an editorial nature Miss Shinn has been a leading contributor to the magazines. Of late she has been engaged in the psychological study of children. Her investigations have met with both scientific and literary recognition and have brought her the degree of Ph. D. m. c. l., from her own university.

SICKLES, David Banks, diplomat, b. New York, N. Y., 1837. Engaged in newspaper work, and was a correspondent in the Civil War. He was United States minister to Siam from 1876 to 1881. He has lectured extensively on Oriental subjects, and is the author of "Leaves of the Lotus," 1896; "The Land of the Lotus," 1899, and of much miscellaneous prose and verse.

"SIEGVOLK, Paul." — See *Albert Mathews.*

SIGOURNEY, Lydia (Huntley), educator and philanthropist, b. Norwich, Conn., 1 Sept., 1791; d. Hartford, Conn., 10 June, 1865. A pioneer among American women in literature and in advocacy of the higher education for women. She taught for two years in Norwich, and afterward established her famous select school for young ladies at Hartford in 1814. She was married in 1819 to Charles Sigourney. Among her fifty-three volumes of prose and verse are "Moral Pieces in Prose and Verse," 1815; "Traits of the Aborigines," 1822; "Poems by the Author of Moral Pieces," 1827; "Poetry for Children," 1823; "Zinzendorff, and Other Poems," 1836; "Pocahontas, and Other Poems," 1841; "Water Drops, a Plea for Temperance," 1847; "Post Meridian," 1854; "The Daily Counsellor," poems, 1858; "The Man of Uz, and Other Poems," 1862; "Letters of Life," issued posthumously, 1866.

SILL, Edward Rowland, b. Windsor, Conn., 1841; d. Cleveland, O., 1887. He was graduated at Yale in 1861, and after teaching several years at Cuyahoga Falls, O., was professor of English literature at the University of California, 1874–82. He wrote "Hermione, and Other Poems," 186–; "The Hermitage, and Later Poems," 1867; "The Venus of Milo, and other Poems," a posthumous volume, 1888; and a posthumous collection of "The Prose of Edward Rowland Sill: Being Essays in Literature and Education, and Friendly Letters," 1900. Sill was a man of rare temperament and insight, and those who knew him have never ceased to regret his loss.

SIMMS, William Gilmore, novelist, b. Charleston, S. C., 1806; d. there, 1870. Published "Lyrical and Other Poems," 1826. Became editor and owner of the Charleston "City Gazette." His best-known poem is "Atalantis, a Tale of the Sea," 1832. Among his colonial, Revolutionary, and frontier novels are "Yemassee," "The Partisan," 1835; "Castle Dismal," 1845; "The Wigwam and the Cabin, or Tales of the South," 1845–46. Wrote biographies of Marion, Greene, Capt. John Smith, Chevalier Bayard. "A History of South Carolina" appeared in 1840; "Areytos, or Songs and Ballads of the South," in 1846; and his selected works in 19 vols., 1859. He wrote a number of dramas for the stage.

SMITH, Elizabeth Oakes (Prince), b. Cumberland, Me., 1806; d. 1893. Her later years were spent in New York, N. Y., and Hollywood, S. C. Wife of the journalist and satirist Seba Smith. She advocated woman's rights, and was the earliest woman lecturer in America. Author of "The Sinless Child and Other Poems," 1841; "Old New York, or Jacob Leisler," a tragedy, etc. Her children assumed the name of Oaksmith.

SMITH, Harry Bache, librettist, b. Buffalo, N. Y., 1860. He wrote dramatic and literary criticisms for the newspaper press until he turned his attention to dramatic authorship. "The Begum," his first opera, was produced in 1887. Of the many others "Robin Hood" appeared in 1891, and "Rob Roy" in 1893. His miscellaneous poems were published as "Lyrics and Sonnets," 1894.

SMITH, Mary ("May") Louise Riley, b. Brighton, N. Y., 1842. After her marriage to Albert Smith she removed to New York City. She has published "A Gift of Gentians, and Other Verses," 1882; "The Inn of Rest," 1888; "Cradle and Armchair," poems, 1893; "Sometime, and Other Poems," 1897.

SMITH, Samuel Francis, Baptist clergyman, b. Boston, Mass., 1808; d. Bridgeport, Conn., 1895. He wrote "America," "The Morning Light is Breaking," 1832, and many other hymns; "Knights and Sea Kings;" "Mythology and Early Greek History," and "Poor Boys Who Became Great," for the young. He edited "Lyric Years" and "The Psalmist," 1843; "Rock of Ages," 1866.

SPALDING, John Lancaster, Catholic bishop of Peoria, Ill., b. Lebanon, Ky., 1840. He is actively interested in education and literature. Author of a "Life of Archbishop Spalding," his uncle, 1872; "Essays and Reviews," 1876; "America, and Other Poems," 1885; "The Poet's Praise," 1891; "Education and the Higher Life," 1891; "Things of the Mind," 1894; "Songs, Chiefly from the German," 1896. Bishop Spalding is one of the most refined and imaginative of latter-day meditative poets.

SPALDING, Susan (Marr), b. Bath, Me., 18—. She was educated at a young ladies' seminary. Her parents' death occasioned her removal to the home of relatives in New York, where she married a gentleman of that city. A few years later she made Philadelphia her permanent residence. Author of "The Wings of Icarus, and Other Poems," 1892.

SPINGARN, Joel Elias, Columbia University, Class of 1895.

SPOFFORD, Harriet Elizabeth (Prescott), b. Calais, Me., 1835. She studied at Pinkerton Academy, Derry, N. H. Her father becoming an invalid, she added to her family's scanty income by writing stories for periodicals. Her first story of unusual merit was "In a Cellar," "Atlantic Monthly," 1859. Since her marriage to Richard S. Spofford, she has lived on Deer Island, in the Merrimac River, near Newburyport, Mass. Her works include "Sir Rohan's Ghost," 1859; "The Amber Gods, and Other Stories," 1863, which gave her an instant reputation; "Azarian," an episode, 1864; "New England Legends," 1871; "The Thief in the Night," 1872; "Marquis of Carabas," poems, 1882; "Ballads about Authors," 1887; "In Titian's Garden, and Other Poems," 1897.

SPRAGUE, Charles, b. Boston, Mass., 1791; d. there, 1875. From 1824 to 1865 he was cashier of the Globe Bank in Boston. Mr. Sprague was a pioneer among the early American poets, and was greatly honored by his own generation. Author of "The Winged Worshippers," "Curiosity," "The Family Meeting," and other poems included in a collected edition of "Poetical and Prose Writings," 1841 (revised eds. 1850–76).

STANTON, Frank Lebby, journalist, b. Charleston, S. C., 1857. A resident of Atlanta, Ga., and a member of the staff of the "Atlanta Constitution." Author of "Songs of the Soil," 1894; "Comes One with a Song," 1899. His lyrics are familar to all newspaper readers, and are widely popular.

STARR, Hattie, composer, b. Rome, N. Y., 18—. She married the late Chas. L. Harris, an actor. Miss Starr is the composer, as well as the verse-maker, of many popular songs. Her "Little Alabama Coon" is perhaps the most notable example of the so-called "coon-songs," a typical class of attempts to revive for the end of the century something of the melody and charm belonging to the earlier songs of the South.

STEBBINS, Mary Elizabeth (Moore) (Hewitt), b. Malden, Mass., 1818; was married to James L. Hewitt, and in 1829 removed to New York. She wrote a "Memorial of F. S. Osgood;" "Songs of Our Lord, and Other Poems," 1845; "Heroines of History;" "Poems Sacred, Passionate, and Legendary." Her poem "Harold the Valiant" appeared closely upon the date of Longfellow's "Skeleton in Armor," with which it has points of resemblance. The present editor has been unable to determine which lyric has the right of chronological precedence.

STEDMAN, Edmund Clarence, b. Hartford, Conn., 8 Oct., 1833. (Son of Mrs. E. C. Kinney, q. v.) He entered Yale at the age of fifteen, and took first prize for his poem on "Westminster Abbey," but was suspended for irregularities at the end of his sophomore year. In 1871, he was restored to his class (that of '53) and given the degree of M. A. Edited the Norwich "Tribune" and Winsted "Herald," 1852–55, but in the latter year went to New York. After a temporary connection with Greeley's "Tribune" — where he first printed his "Tribune Lyrics" ("Osawatomie Brown," "The Diamond Wedding," etc.) — he joined the staff of the N. Y. "World" in 1860, and was its war correspondent, 1861-63. For a time he served in Washington under Lincoln's attorney general, Edward Bates. In 1864 he aided in the construction and financiering of the first section of the first Pacific Railway. This led him into Wall Street, and, desiring to have time and means for strictly literary work, he there remained from 1864; becoming, 1869, an active member of the Stock Exchange, and holding his seat until 1900. Among his works are "Poems Lyric and Idyllic," 1860; "Alice of Monmouth," 1863; "The Blameless Prince," 1869; "Victorian Poets," 1875 (London 1876); "Hawthorne, and Other Poems," 1877; "Lyrics and Idylls" (London), 1879; "Poems, Household Edition," 1884; "Poets of America," 1885; "The Nature and Elements of Poetry" (lectures forming the initial course of the Turnbull Chair of Poetry, Johns Hopkins Univ.), 1892; "Poems Now First Collected," 1897; "Complete Poems," 1908. From 1866 he worked for international copyright, and he became president of the American Copyright League in 1891. He re-delivered his lectures on poetry at the University of Pennsylvania, and at Columbia University, and received from

Columbia the degree of L. H. D. In 1894 Yale gave him the degree of LL. D., and he wrote the "Commencement Ode," set to imposing music by Prof. Parker and sung at Yale on stated occasions. He edited "A Library of American Literature," with Ellen M. Hutchinson, 1888–89; "The Works of Edgar Allan Poe," with G. E. Woodberry, 1895; "A Victorian Anthology," 1895. The present Anthology completes a critical series begun in "Victorian Poets." (D. 18 January, 1908.) [L. C. B.]

STEIN, Evaleen, b. LaFayette, Ind., 18—, where she still resides. Besides poetic contributions to various periodicals and her children's stories of old Provence, Miss Stein has published "One Way to the Woods," 1897, a collection of lyrics showing a very genuine gift.

"**STERNE, STUART.**"—See *Gertrude Bloede.*

STETSON, Charlotte (Perkins), socialist, b. Hartford, Conn., 186–. Great-granddaughter of Lyman Beecher. Much of her time has been given to lecturing on various reforms. Mrs. Stetson received the gold medal of the Alameda Country Trades and Labor Union for an essay on "The Labor Movement," and is the author of "Woman and Economics." "In this our World," verse, was published in 1893.

STETSON, Grace Ellery Channing.—See *Mrs. Channing-Stetson.*

STILLMAN, Annie Raymond, "**Grace Raymond**," b. Charleston, S. C., 1855. Descended from Elias Badeau, one of the Huguenot settlers in New Rochelle. Resided at Charleston until 1892, when she removed to Birmingham, Ala. Author of "How They Kept the Faith: a Tale of the Huguenots of Languedoc," 1889, and of occasional poems and sketches.

STOCKARD, Henry Jerome, educator, b. North Carolina, 1858. Graduated from the University of North Carolina, where he was afterwards associate professor. Later he was professor at Fredericksburg College. His "Fugitive Lines" appeared in 1897.

STODDARD, Charles Warren, b. Rochester, N. Y., 1843. When a boy he received encouragement from Bret Harte, who edited his first book of verse. Some of his life since 1864 has been spent in the Hawaiian Islands. From 1873 to 1878 he visited many countries as correspondent of the San Francisco "Chronicle." He was professor of English literature at Notre Dame College, Ind., and is now a lecturer on English literature at the Catholic University, Washington, D. C. Author of "Poems," 1867; "South Sea Idyls," 1873; "Summer Cruising in the South Seas," 1874; "Mashallah!" 1880; "The Lepers of Molokai," 1885. The first selection from Mr. Stoddard's verse, p. 445, is a poem delivered on the reception by the Bohemian Club of a royal mummy from the tombs of Egypt.

STODDARD, Elizabeth Drew (Barstow), b. Mattapoisett, Mass., 6 May, 1823. Her father was connected with shipping interests. Mrs. Stoddard was educated at a young ladies' seminary. She was married to Richard Henry Stoddard, the poet, in 1851, and since then has resided in New York City. She began to contribute poems to the periodicals a few years after her marriage. In 1862 the first of her highly original novels, "The Morgesons," appeared, followed by "Two Men," 1865, and "Temple House," 1867. They were reissued in 1888, with an introduction by the editor of this work. Her collected "Poems" were published in 1895. A series of articles giving her recollections of "Literary Folk as They Came and Went, with Ourselves," appeared in the "Saturday Evening Post" of Philadelphia, 1900. (D. New York, N. Y., 1 Aug., 1902.)

STODDARD, Lavinia (Stone), b. Guilford, Conn., 1787; d. Blakely, Ala., 1820. She was the wife of Dr. William Stoddard, and with him conducted an academy at Troy, N. Y. Her poem "The Soul's Defiance" is the best-known of her writings.

STODDARD, Richard Henry, poet and journalist, b. Hingham, Mass., 2 July, 1825. His father was a sea-captain, and was lost at sea; his mother removed to New York in 1835, and there re-married. The son obtained his education at the public schools of that city, and sought work in an iron foundry, which he continued until 1849, supplementing his earlier studies by reading the best authors, and more particularly poetry. He made friends with Bayard Taylor, just after the publication of the latter's "Views Afoot." Mrs. Caroline Kirkland was then editing the "Union Magazine," and going abroad in 1847, she left the magazine in Mr. Taylor's charge, and recommended Mr. Stoddard to him. Stoddard's first poem appeared in this magazine, and in 1849 he issued a small volume of verse, "Footprints," the edition of which was afterwards suppressed. Failing health having obliged him to give up his occupation at the foundry, he devoted himself altogether to literary work. He became a contributor to the "Knickerbocker" and other leading magazines; and his second volume, "Poems," was published in 1852, containing "Leonatus," "The Witch's Whelp," and other poems, which brought him into much favor. He had become acquainted with Read, Boker, and other prominent authors of Philadelphia, Boston, and New York, and visited Hawthorne at Concord, with James T. Fields and Edwin P. Whipple, in the summer of 1852. In 1852, also, he married Miss Elizabeth Barstow, of Mattapoisett, Mass. The following year, with the assistance of Hawthorne, he obtained a position in the New York custom-house, which he held until 1870, having found that the literary market of that time gave returns that needed supplementing by another means of support. The poems contained in "Songs of Summer," 1857, had appeared in "Putnam's

Monthly" and other periodicals, and this book marked a new phase in American poetry, wholly devoted as it was to beauty and feeling, and not to didactics or reform. Mr. Stoddard was literary editor of the N. Y. "World" from 1860 to 1870. "The King's Bell," a narrative poem, appeared in 1863, as also the grandly phrased "Abraham Lincoln: a Horatian Ode," 1865; and these confirmed his reputation. They were followed by "The Book of the East," 1867. From 1859 to 1861 the Stoddards and Taylors occupied the same house in New York, and in the former year their long friendship with the editor of the present work began. In 1872, Stoddard became editor of "The Aldine," a New York literary journal, which he managed for several years. From 1880 to the present time he has been literary editor of the N. Y. "Mail and Express." His studies in early and recent English poetry, which have made him a leading authority on this subject, have taken shape in several volumes. "The Loves and Heroines of the Poets," 1861, is of biographical, critical, and descriptive character. He edited "Melodies and Madrigals, mostly from the Old English Poets," 1865, and selections from "The Late English Poets," 1865. More recently he has edited, with W. J. Linton, "English Verse," in five volumes, 1883; and a volume of his essays, chiefly concerning modern English poets, has been published as "Under the Evening Lamp," 1892. Mr. Stoddard also edited the enlarged edition of Griswold's "Poets and Poetry of America" and "Female Poets of America," 1872–73, and wrote a Memoir of Poe for the reissue of Griswold's edition of the "Select Works," 1880. He prepared the monographs on Bryant, Irving, Shelley, and other authors, and edited the "Bric-a-Brac" series, in ten volumes, 1874–76. A collective edition of his "Poems" appeared in 1880. His later poetry is mostly contained in "The Lion's Cub, with Other Verse," 1890. He delivered, before the Army of the Potomac, at Springfield, Mass., a poem entitled "The Victories of Peace" in 1878, and the same year recited his poem "History," before the Phi Beta Kappa Society at Harvard. Mr. Stoddard was the guest of the Authors Club, assisted by members of the Century Association, at New York, at a brilliant dinner given in his honor on March 26, 1897. His voice was as lyrical, and his touch as fine and strong as ever, despite the years that weighed upon him. The poem of "The Witch's Whelp," p. 279, was written as a companion piece to, and at the same time with, Bayard Taylor's "Ariel," p. 271. Cp. "Poets of America," pp. 57, 58, 403, and "The Nature and Elements of Poetry," p. 252. (D. New York, N. Y., 12 May, 1903.)

STORY, William Wetmore, sculptor, b. Salem, Mass., 12 Feb., 1819; d. Vallombrosa, near Florence, Italy, 7 Oct., 1895. He was a son of Justice Joseph Story, of the U. S. Supreme Court. Graduating at Harvard, and entering the bar, he was occupied with legal work until 1848, preparing several volumes of law books; but in that year he abandoned his profession, and thereafter making his residence in Rome, devoted himself to sculpture, in which art he gained a leading position. Mr. Story's "Poems" appeared in 1847, and was followed by numerous volumes of poetry, fiction, and essays. Among his poems "Cleopatra" is perhaps the best known. His books include "Life and Letters of Joseph Story," 1851; "Roba di Roma," prose, 1862; "Graffiti d' Italia," poems, 1868; "Nero: an Historical Play," 1875; "He and She; or a Poet's Portfolio," 1883; "Fiammetta," a novel, 1885; "Poems," 1886; "Conversations in a Studio," 1890; and "Excursions in Art and Letters," essays, 1891.

STOWE, Mrs. Harriet Elizabeth Beecher, b. Litchfield, Conn., 14 June, 1812; d. Hartford, Conn., 1 July, 1896. Before removing to Cincinnati with her father, Lyman Beecher, in 1832, she studied and taught in her sister Catherine's school at Hartford. In 1836 she was married to the Rev. Calvin E. Stowe, of Lane Seminary. Having strong anti-slavery opinions, they received fugitives in their home, and were close observers of slavery in the Southern States. In 1849 Mrs. Stowe published "The Mayflower, or Short Sketches of the Descendants of the Pilgrims." "Uncle Tom's Cabin, or Life Among the Lowly," first appeared, as a serial, in the Washington "National Era," in 1851; in 1852 it was issued in book-form, and by the end of the year, it is said, its sale on both sides of the water had amounted to more than a million copies. "A Key to Uncle Tom's Cabin" and "A Peep for Children into Uncle Tom's Cabin" appeared in 1853. After her first visit to Europe, where she was received with great distinction, she published, with her husband, two volumes of travel, "Sunny Memories of Foreign Lands," 1854. Among later works by this world-famous woman are "Dred, a Tale of the Great Dismal Swamp," 1856; "The Minister's Wooing," 1859; "The Pearl of Orr's Island," 1862; "Agnes of Sorrento," 1862; "Religious Poems," 1865; "Men of our Times," 1868; "Lady Byron Vindicated, a History of the Byron Controversy," 1869; "Pink and White Tyranny," 1871; "Palmetto Leaves," 1873; "Footsteps of the Master," 1876; "Poganuc People," 1878; "A Dog's Mission," 1881.

STREET, Alfred Billings, b. Poughkeepsie, N. Y., 1811; d. Albany, N. Y., 1881. For thirty-three years librarian of New York State. Author of "The Burning of Schenectady, and Other Poems," 1842; "Drawings and Tintings," poems, 1844; "Fugitive Poems," 1846; "Frontenac, or the Atotarho of the Iroquois, a Metrical Romance," celebrating the expedition of Frontenac, governor-general of Canada, against the Iroquois; London and New York, 1849; "Forest Pictures in the Adirondacks," 1865.

SUTPHEN, William Gilbert van Tassel,

b. Philadelphia, Penn., 1861. Since graduating at Princeton he has been engaged in editorial work, residing at Morristown, N. J. Author of fugitive poems and sketches, and of "The Golficide," 1898; "The Golfer's Alphabet," 1898.

SWIFT, Frances Dorr. — See *F. D. S. Tatnall.*

TABB, John Banister, b. Amelia Co., Va., 1845. A Catholic priest, instructor in English literature in St. Charles College, Ellicott City, Md. He served as captain's mate on a blockade-runner in the Civil War; was ordained in 1884, and has published "Poems," 1894; "Lyrics," 1897; "An Octave to Mary." A revised edition of his poems is soon to appear. Father Tabb's lyrics are marked by exquisite beauty, point, and finish, and have won him a deserved reputation.

TAPPAN, William Bingham, b. Beverly, Mass., 1794; d. West Needham, Mass., 1849. Was engaged for a large part of his life as a general agent of the American Sunday School Union in Cincinnati and Boston. Several volumes of his poems were published, largely devotional in character.

TASSIN, Algernon, Harvard University, Class of 1892.

TATNALL, Frances Dorr (Swift), b. Newark, N. J., 187–. Since 1889 she has been a resident of Wilmington, Del., where she was married, in 1897, to H. L. Tatnall, Jr. Her song "Art Thou the Same" was set to music by her mother.

TAYLOR, Bayard, b. Kennett Square, Penn., 11 Jan., 1825; d. Berlin, Germany, 19 Dec., 1878. It is impossible to give an adequate account in condensed form of this nomadic and eventful life, with its constantly shifting background. Reared in a little Quaker town, his two great ambitions as a child, both destined to be realized, were to become a poet and to travel. He was seven years old when he wrote his first verse, and the first published poem appeared in the "Saturday Evening Post," 1841, a "Soliloquy of a Young Poet." "Ximen; or the Battle of the Sierra Morena, and Other Poems, by James Bayard Taylor," appeared in 1844. The restless desire for travel overcame him in this year, and he went to Europe, where he tramped about for nearly two years on foot and in the face of great privation. He afterwards published "Views Afoot; or Europe seen with Knapsack and Staff," which brought him ample reward for his endurance. In 1848 he became chief of the literary department of the New York "Tribune." His reputation began, and increased, and he found many friends and plenty to do. His vivacity and humor as well as his genius won the public heart. In 1849 he sailed to California, where he spent five months, sharing the hardships of the gold-diggers. The record of his journey appeared under the title "Eldorado," etc. In July he read "The American Legend" before the Phi Beta Kappa Society at Cambridge, where it was received with marked favor. In October he married Miss Mary Agnew, whom he had loved since childhood. She was incurably ill, and died two months after their marriage. He sailed for Europe in 1851, and shortly after his departure "A Book of Romances, Lyrics, and Songs" was published. He journeyed into the East, and his letters to the "Tribune" brought fame to him at home. During his life he published many books of travel, and was in constant demand in the lecture halls. In 1856 he broke down from overwork, and in July sailed again for Europe with his brother and sisters. He was everywhere received with distinction, but especially in Germany. Here he met Miss Marie Hansen, daughter of the astronomer, Prof. Hansen, and they were married in Gotha, 1857. In 1859 he was able to establish his well-known home, "Cedarcroft," in a broad-acred tract within his native town. But his life was a series of long travellings and trips abroad, letters and other contributions to the press, and innumerable lecture tours. The amount of work that he produced, in spite of this constant change and activity, seems almost incredible, but much of his prose was done with facile speed. His novels and poetry, however, were the result of careful and critical labor. His position in the literary world was enviable, and his friends were the most cultured men the country has produced. In 1862 he became secretary to the legation in Russia. The year following he published a novel, "Hannah Thurston," which was followed by "John Godfrey's Fortunes," 1864, and "The Story of Kennett," 1866. In 1870 his translation of Goethe's "Faust" appeared, and nearly the entire first edition was sold in one day. His other poetical work includes "Rhymes of Travel, Ballads, and Poems," 1848; "Poems of the Orient," 1854; "Poems of Bayard Taylor," 1864; "Poems," 1865; "Picture of St. John," 1866; "The Masque of the Gods," 1872; "Lars, a Pastoral of Norway," 1873; "The Prophet," 1874; "Prince Deukalion," 1878. In 1878 he went to Germany as United States minister, eagerly intending, also, to complete his researches for a "Life of Goethe," which he had long projected, and was above all others fitted to write. But he soon fell ill, and suffered great pain, which he bore with courage for many days until his death. His widow has devoted herself to the re-editing of his "Works," and also wrote with H. E. Scudder his "Life and Letters," 1884. For an account of Taylor and his time, cp. "Poets of America," chap. xi. [B. D. L.]

TAYLOR, Charles Edward, Trinity College, Class of 1892.

TAYLOR, Joseph Russell, educator, b. Circleville, O., 1868. His poems have not yet been collected.

THAXTER, Mrs. Celia (Laighton), b. Portsmouth, N. H., 1836; d. Appledore Island,

N. H., 29 June, 1894. Her father was keeper of the lighthouse on the Isles of Shoals, where much of her life was spent, both before and after her marriage to Levi Lincoln Thaxter, the Browning scholar. Her works include "Among the Isles of Shoals," 1873, papers published in "The Atlantic Monthly;" "Poems," 1874, with later enlarged editions; "Drift-Weed," 1878; "Poems for Children," 1883; "The Cruise of the Mystery, and Other Poems," 1886; "The Yule Log," 1889; "An Island Garden," 1894; "Letters," and "Stories and Poems for Children," 1895. Mrs. Thaxter was something of an artist, and chiefly illustrated her own books in water-color for friends and collectors.

THAYER, Stephen Henry, b. New Ipswich, N. H., Dec., 1839. He attended Appleton Academy, N. H., and after removing to Tarrytown, N. Y., became a banker in New York City. He has published "Songs of Sleepy Hollow," 1886, and is a frequent contributor of verse and critical essays to the current press.

THAYER, William Roscoe, historian, b. Boston, Mass., 1859. He graduated at Harvard University, and was for several years instructor there in English. Editor of "The Harvard Graduates' Magazine" since its foundation, in 1892. His volumes of verse include "The Confession of Hermes, and Other Poems," 1884; "Hesper," an American drama, 1888; "Poems, New and Old," 1894. Mr. Thayer has made modern Italy the field of his important historical works and studies.

THOMAS, Charles Edward, Yale University, Class of 1897.

THOMAS, Edith Matilda, b. Chatham, O., 12 Aug., 1854. She had written but little for publication when in 1881 she met Mrs. Helen Jackson. The latter showed a keen interest in Miss Thomas's poetical work, and encouraged her to write for the public. Her poems, by turns strong and delicate, and always exquisitely finished, at once came into favor. As a prose writer, her sketches of nature, bird life, etc., have been of high order, and touched with a quality all her own, while other essays reveal the sympathy for the antique, — the classicism that has so refined and chastened the beauty of her verse. Her place is secure among the truest living poets of our English tongue. Since 1888 she has lived in New York City. Among her best-known volumes in prose are "The Round Year," 1886; "Children of the Seasons" series, 1888; "Babes of the Year," 1888; "Babes of the Nation," 1889; "Heaven and Earth," 1889. Her poems are contained chiefly in "A New Year's Mask," 1885; "Lyrics and Sonnets," 1887; "The Inverted Torch," 1890; "Fair Shadow Land," 1893; "In Sunshine Land," 1894; "In the Young World," 1895; "A Winter Swallow, and other Verse," 1896.

THOMAS, Frederick William, lawyer and journalist, b. Providence, R. I., 1808; d. Washington, D. C., 1866. He grew up in Charleston, S. C., and removed to Cincinnati, O., where he published "The Emigrant," poem, 1833; the novels, "Clinton Bradshaw," 1835; "East and West," 1836; "Howard Pinckney," 1840; "The Beechen Tree, and Other Poems," 1840; "Sketches of Character," 1849; "John Randolph of Roanoke," 1853.

THOMPSON, James Maurice, b. Fairfield, Ind., 9 Sept., 1844. His early life was passed in Kentucky and Georgia. He served in the Confederate army, and after the war practised law at Crawfordsville, Ind. From 1885 to 1889 he was state geologist of Indiana. In 1890 he joined the literary staff of the N. Y. "Independent." Among his writings are "Hoosier Mosaics," 1875; "A Tallahassee Girl," novel, 1882; "Songs of Fair Weather," 1883; "Byways and Bird-notes," 1885; "Sylvan Secrets in Bird-Songs and Brooks," 1887; "The Story of Louisiana," 1888; "Poems," 1892; "The Ocala Boy," 1895; "Lincoln's Grave," poem. Mr. Thompson stood at the head of our poetic celebrants of forest archery, fishing, and other outdoor sports. His critical writings exhibit independence and a sense of what should characterize American literature. D. Crawfordsville, Ind., 15 Feb., 1901.

THOMPSON, John Randolph, journalist, b. Richmond, Va., 23 Oct., 1823; d. New York, N. Y., 30 April, 1873. He graduated at the University of Virginia, and studied for the law. In 1847 he assumed the editorship of the "Southern Literary Messenger," which he held until 1859, during which period he made this magazine a notable success, and promoted the interests of literature in the South. In the last years of his life he was literary editor of the New York "Evening Post." He contributed much verse to American and English periodicals, including some popular lyrics, but his poems have not been issued in book-form.

THOMPSON, Vance, b. 1862, of English parentage. After a boyhood in Pittsburgh, Penn., he graduated at Princeton and studied at German universities. Has since resided chiefly in New York, engaged as a journalist and playwright. Founded and edited "M'lle New York," an illustrated town-fortnightly. Among his plays are "In Old Japan;" "The Dresden Shepherdess;" "Floriane's Dream." Author of "Songs and Symbols," 1900; "French Portraits: Being Appreciations of the Writers of Young France," 1900.

THOMPSON, Will Henry, lawyer, b. Calhoun, Gordon Co., Ga., 1848. A brother of Maurice Thompson, and his comrade in the sports of outdoor life. Served in Confederate army through the war. Removed to Crawfordsville, Ind., in 1868, and later established there a law partnership with his brother. Became a resident of Seattle, Wash., in 1889. Noted as an orator, and the author of various poems, among which is a strong ballad, "The High Tide at Gettysburg."

THOREAU, Henry David, nonconformer and naturalist, b. Concord, Mass., 12 July, 1817; d. there, 6 May, 1862. Graduated at Harvard, 1837. He had no settled occupation, but did just enough teaching, lecturing, land-surveying, farming, and pencil-making to secure the necessities of life. He disliked society, and lived for more than two years in a hut built with his own hands, in 1845, near Walden Pond, on the property of his fellow-philosopher Emerson. In 1849 he published "A Week on the Concord and Merrimack Rivers," describing a few days spent with his brother in boating and camping out, ten years before. "Walden, or Life in the Woods," followed in 1854, and "Echoes of Harper's Ferry" in 1860. He was imprisoned for refusing to pay taxes to a State that did not condemn slavery. He observed nature closely, studied animals minutely, and struck a transcendental note in his poetry. He was a frequent contributor to "The Dial," "The Atlantic Monthly," the New York "Tribune," and other periodicals. His posthumous works were "Excursions in Field and Forest," with a memoir by Emerson, 1863; "The Maine Woods," 1864; "Cape Cod," "Letters to Various Persons," edited by Emerson, 1865; "A Yankee in Canada," 1866; "Early Spring in Massachusetts," 1881; "Summer," 1884; "Winter," 1888; "Autumn," 1892; "Works," ten vols., "Familiar Letters," 1894; "Poems of Nature," 1895. They were compiled for the most part from his diary, begun in 1835 and numbering 30 vols.

TICKNOR, Francis Orrery, physician, b. Baldwin Co., Ga., 1822; d. near Columbus, Ga., 1874. He resided near Columbus, where he practised his profession, and is remembered for several favorite poems of the Civil War. His "Poems," 1879, were edited by Paul Hamilton Hayne.

TILLEY, Lucy Evangeline, b. Chatham, O., 1859; d. Medina, O., 1890. She removed to Medina early in life. Many of her poems appeared in magazines and weekly publications. They were collected in two volumes, "Little Rhymes in Brown," 1886; and "Verses," 1892.

TILTON, Theodore, journalist and orator, b. New York, N. Y., 1835. Graduated at the College of New York. After fifteen years of editorial work on "The Independent," he founded and edited "The Golden Age." He lived abroad from 1883, and made his home in Paris. His works include "The Sexton's Tale, and Other Poems," 1867; "Tempest Tossed," story, 1873; "Swabian Stories," 1882. "The Chameleon's Dish," 1893, and "Heart's Ease," 1894, both published in London, contain his revised complete poetical works. (D. 1907.)

TIMROD, Henry, b. Charleston, S. C., 1829; d. Columbia, S. C., 1867. Son of the bookbinder, William Henry Timrod, who published a volume of verse. Slender means prevented the son from taking the full course at the University of Georgia, and he became a tutor in the family of a Carolina planter. During the Civil War he was a correspondent of the Charleston "Mercury," and assistant editor of the Columbia "South Carolinian." The death of a favorite child and the destruction wrought by Sherman's troops in Columbia broke up his little home, and after a severe struggle with poverty he fell a prey to disease. His poems, having the misfortune to appear in 1860, had attracted less attention than they deserved; but in 1873 they were republished, with a sketch of the author by Paul H. Hayne, and a revised edition has appeared, 1899.

TOOKER, Lewis Frank, b. Port Jefferson, L. I., 1855. A graduate of Yale, 1877, and long in the employ of the Century Company, New York. His poems have appeared in magazines, but are not yet collected. A ballad more effective, in diction, structure, and dramatic power, than "The Sea-Fight" will be hard to find in recent literature.

TORRENCE, Frederic Ridgely, librarian, b. Xenia, O., 1875. Educated at Miami and Princeton universities. His initial volume, "The House of a Hundred Lights," written after reading couplets from Bidpai, was published early in 1900.

TOWNSEND, George Alfred, journalist, b. Georgetown, Del., 30 Jan., 1841. He was a New York "World" and "Herald" correspondent during the Civil War, and in 1866 a correspondent in the Austro-Prussian War, and throughout his subsequent life has been a breezy and picturesque writer, chiefly from Washington, for various journals. Among his publications are "Campaigns of a Non-Combatant," 1865; "Poems," 1870; "Washington Outside and Inside," 1871; "Tales of the Chesapeake," 1880; "The Entailed Hat," novel, 1884; also lives of Garibaldi, Lincoln, and Levi P. Morton. Mr. Townsend's country home is on South Mountain, Md., where through his exertions a stately mural monument has been erected in memory of the Army Correspondents of the Civil War. An elegant "limited edition" of his poems was issued by subscription in 1898.

TOWNSEND, Mary Ashley (Van Voorhis), "Xariffa," b. Lyons, N. Y., 1832. After her marriage to Gideon Townsend she lived in New Orleans, La. She was chosen poet of the New Orleans exposition of 1884. Her works include "The Brother Clerks," 1859; "Poems," 1870; "The Captain's Story," 1874; "Xariffa's Poems," 1881; "Down the Bayou, and Other Poems," 1882; "Distaff and Spindle," sonnets, 1895. D. Galveston, Texas, 1901.

TRASK, Kate (Nichols). — See *Katrina Trask.*

TRASK, Katrina (Kate Nichols Trask), b. Brooklyn, N. Y., 18—. She was married to Spencer Trask, the banker, in 1874. Her "Under King Constantine," 1893, legends and poems, composed in finished blank verse, has passed through several editions. Mrs. Trask has also issued "Sonnets and Lyrics," 1894.

TRAUBEL, Horace Logo, b. Camden, N. J., 1858. Editorially connected with the Boston "Commonwealth" and Chicago "Unity," 1882–88. Established "The Conservator" at Camden, 1888, of which journal he has always been proprietor and editor. He was devoted to the personal welfare of Walt Whitman, assisted him in preparing the final editions of his prose and verse, and was one of his literary executors. Editor of "Camden's Compliment to Walt Whitman," 1889; "Good-bye and Hail, Walt Whitman," 1892; "In Re Walt Whitman," with R. M. Bucke and T. B. Harned, 1893.

TROUBETSKOY, Princess Amélie (Rives), b. Richmond, Va., 1863. The granddaughter of Senator William C. Rives, of Virginia, and the daughter of Alfred L. Rives, engineer, of Castle Hill, Cobham, Va. She received her education from private instructors. Was first married to John Armstrong Chanler, of New York. She was afterwards married to Prince Pierre Troubetskoy, of Russia, and has since resided chiefly at Castle Hill. The success of "A Brother to Dragons, and Other Old-Time Tales," 1888, was repeated by "The Quick or the Dead?" in the same year. Among her other works of fiction are "Virginia of Virginia," "According to St. John," and "Barbara Dering." In verse, she is the author of "Herod and Mariamne: a Drama," 1889; and of many uncollected poems.

TROWBRIDGE, John Townsend, b. Ogden, N. Y., 18 Sept., 1827. He was born on a farm, and received his education in the common schools, supplemented by a term at a classical school and by private studies. In 1847 he began writing for the press, having come to New York, and soon afterwards he removed to Boston, in the vicinity of which he subsequently resided, engaged in editorial and literary work. He became a popular writer of juvenile fiction, of which he published many volumes, and was managing editor of "Our Young Folks" from 1870 to 1873. His books of verse include "The Vagabonds, and Other Poems," 1869; "The Emigrant's Story," 1875; "A Home Idyl," 1881; and "The Lost Earl," 1888.

TRUMBULL, Annie Eliot, b. Hartford, Conn., 1857. Graduated at the High School, Hartford, in which city she has since resided. — "An Hour's Promise," 1889; "White Birches," 1893; "A Masque of Culture," play, 1893; "A Christmas Accident, and Other Stories," 1897; "Mistress Content Cradock," 1899.

TUCKER, St. George, jurist, b. Bermuda, 1752; d. Warminster, Va., 1828. Graduated from William and Mary College, 1772; lieutenant-colonel in the Revolutionary War; judge of the Court of Appeals, 1804–11. Author of numerous law treatises, "The Probationary Odes of Jonathan Pindar, Esq.," 1896; and of occasional poems.

TUCKERMAN, Henry Theodore, essayist, b. Boston, Mass., 1813; d. New York, 1871. He travelled much in Europe, and after 1845 lived in New York. Among his works are "Italian Sketch-Book," 1835; "Isabel, or Sicily," 1839; "Thoughts on the Poets," 1846; "Artist Life," 1847; "Characteristics of Literature," 1849–51; "The Optimist," 1850; "Poems," 1851; "Essays," 1857; "Art in America," 1858; "America and her Commentators," 1864; "Maga Papers about Paris," 1867; "Book of the Artists," 1867; "The Collector, Essays," 1868; "Life of John Pendleton Kennedy," 1871.

UNDERWOOD, Wilbur, b. Washington, D. C., 1876. Educated in that city, which is his residence. Author of occasional poems and of "The Burden of the Desert," 1896.

URMY, Clarence (Thomas), organist, b. San Francisco, Cal., 1858. His productions in book-form are "A Rosary of Rhyme," 1884; "A Vintage of Verse," 1897.

VALENTINE, Edward Abram Uffington, b. Bellefonte, Penn., 1870. He was educated at Haverford College, and afterwards studied law in the Old Maryland University. He gave up the law for journalism and became literary editor of the Baltimore "Evening News."

"VANDEGRIFT, Margaret." — See *Margaret Thomson Janvier*.

VAN DYKE, Henry, D. D., LL. D., b. Germantown, Penn., 1852. Graduated at Princeton, 1873; Princeton Theo. Sem., 1877; and Berlin University, 1879. Became pastor of the United Cong. Church, Newport, R. I. In 1882 was called to the pastorate of the "Brick Presbyterian Church" of New York. In 1899, he accepted the professorship of English literature at Princeton. He delivered the memorial ode on the occasion of the one hundred and fiftieth anniversary of his Alma Mater. The wide range of Dr. Van Dyke's equipment is shown by the record of his varied and felicitously written work. — "The Reality of Religion," 1884; "The Story of the Psalms," 1887; "The Poetry of Tennyson," 1890, enlarged edition, 1895; "Straight Sermons to Young Men," 1893; "Little Rivers," 1895; "The Gospel for an Age of Doubt," 1896; "The Builders, and Other Poems," 1897; "The Gospel for a World of Sin," 1899; "The Toiling of Felix, and Other Poems," 1899; "Fisherman's Luck, and Other Uncertain Things," 1899.

VAN RENSSELAER, Peyton, b. New York, N. Y., 1863. A resident of Stockbridge, Mass. His song "At Twilight" has been set to music by Ethelbert Nevin.

VAN VORST, Marie, b. New York, N. Y., 187–. A daughter of the late Hooper C. Van Vorst, first president of the Holland Society, and long a justice of the Supreme Court of

New York. For some years past she has been active with her pen, writing verse, children's stories, and special articles. Now a resident of Paris.

"VARLEY, John Philip." — See *Langdon Elwyn Mitchell.*

VENABLE, William Henry, b. near Waynesville, O., 1836. He was president of Chickering Institute, Cincinnati, 1881–86, and has published "June on the Miami, and Other Poems," 1871; "Melodies of the Heart," 1885; "The Last Flight," 1893; "Biography of William D. Gallagher," 1888; "Footprints of the Pioneers in the Ohio Valley;" "The Beginnings of Literary Culture in the Ohio Valley." He edited "Dramatic Scenes from the Best Authors," 1874.

VERY, Jones, transcendentalist, b. Salem, Mass., 28 Aug., 1813; d. there, 8 May, 1880. He made voyages with his father, a cultivated sea-captain, and had schooling in Salem and New Orleans. A graduate of Harvard in 1836, he taught Greek there for two years. His first volume of essays and poems appeared in 1839. In 1843 the Cambridge Association licensed him to preach, but he was never ordained. He was the intimate friend of Emerson and Channing, and a frequent contributor to "The Christian Register" and other Unitarian journals. His friend James Freeman Clarke edited a complete posthumous edition of his poems and essays. In 1883 Very's "Poems" were reëdited by William P. Andrews, with a memoir. The sonnet, somewhat on the Shakesperean model, was the form of expression most natural to him.

WALLACE, Lewis, soldier, lawyer, and novelist, b. Brookville, Ind., 10 Apr., 1827. Participated in the Mexican and Civil wars, gaining the rank of general in the latter. Was U. S. minister to Turkey, 1881–85. Author of "The Fair God," 1873; "Ben-Hur," 1880; "The Prince of India," 1893. Resided at Crawfordsville, Ind., where he practised law for many years, dying there 15 Feb., 1905.

WARD, Elizabeth Stuart (Phelps), b. Andover, Mass., 1844. Daughter of Prof. Austin Phelps and of Elizabeth (Stuart) Phelps, also an author. Miss Phelps was married, 1888, to Rev. Herbert D. Ward, of New York City, a man of letters (son of Dr. W. Hayes Ward), and has since lived in Newton, Mass. Among her many works are "Ellen's Idol," 1864; "The Gates Ajar," 1868, which met with success, and has been followed by "Beyond the Gates," 1883; "The Gates Between," 1887; the "Trotty" and "Gipsy" series for children; "Poetic Studies," poems, 1875; "The Story of Avis," 1877; "Songs of the Silent World," 1885, and "The Master of the Magicians," with her husband, 1890; "The Story of Jesus Christ," 1897.

WARD, Samuel, b. New York, N. Y., 1813; d. Pegli, Italy, 1884. Graduated at Columbia, and about 1862 removed to Washington. In 1871 he published "Lyrical Recreations." He was a brother of Julia Ward Howe; by turns a banker, diplomat, classicist, and expert in American Indian dialects. To the arts of a select *bon vivant* and man of the world, he diverted talents that might have gained him more than a passing distinction. His personal charm was a rare and lovable endowment.

WARD, William Hayes, archæologist, b. Abington, Mass., 1835. Graduated at Amherst, 1856, and at Andover, 1859. He was professor of Latin at Ripon College, Wis., 1860–68, and became superintending editor of the New York "Independent," 1870, in which position he has since remained. He conducted the Wolfe expedition to Babylonia, 1884–85, and wrote a pamphlet on the subject. Author of "Notes on Oriental Antiquities," and numerous archæological articles in the "Bibliotheca Sacra" and elsewhere.

WARE, Eugene Fitch, "Ironquill," lawyer, b. Hartford, Conn., 1841. Served during the Civil War, and afterwards was captain of cavalry and aid to Maj.-Gen. G. M. Dodge. He has twice been elected to the Kansas Senate. His quaint "Rhymes of Ironquill" appeared in 1885. An enlarged edition was published in 1899.

WARNER, Charles Dudley, man of letters, b. Plainfield, Mass., 12 Sept., 1829; d. Hartford, Conn., 20 Oct., 1900. This honored author, editor, and social scientist occasionally wrote verse, of which the sonnet upon an Oriental theme, p. 308, is an interesting example.

WATSON, Edward Willard, physician, b. Newport, R. I., 1843; now a resident of Philadelphia, Penn. Educated at the University of Pennsylvania and the University Medical School. Besides contributing to medical literature, Dr. Watson has published two volumes of verse: "To-day and Yesterday," 1895; "Songs of Flying Hours," 1897.

WAYLAND, John Elton, "Idas," lawyer, b. Waterbury, Conn., 1860. Graduated at Yale, 1883, and at the Columbia Law School, 1895. He was admitted to the New York bar the same year, and has since practised in that city. His poem "An Epilogue at Wallack's" appeared in the "Yale Courant" for 1882, and in W. Winter's "John Gilbert," published by the Dunlap Society, 1890.

WEBB, Charles Henry, "John Paul," b. Rouse's Point, N. Y., 1834. Went to sea in boyhood. For three years was on the staff of the N. Y. "Times," contributing notable book reviews and special articles. His "John Paul" letters were long a feature of the "Tribune." Founded "The Californian." He, like Bret Harte, was a pioneer in the literature of the Pacific Slope; and, beginning as a humorist, has produced lyrics of a true poetic vein. Author of "John Paul's Book," 1874; "Parodies,

Prose and Verse," 1876; "Vagrom Verse," 1889; "With Lead and Line along Varying Shores," 1901. (D. New York, N. Y., 1905.)

WEBSTER, Daniel, statesman, b. Salisbury (now Franklin), N. H., 18 Jan. 1782; d. Marshfield, Mass., 24 Oct., 1852. U. S. representative, 1813–17, and 1823–27. U. S. senator from Mass., with the exception of three years as secretary of state, 1827–50. A few poems, including "The Memory of the Heart," published posthumously in his "Private Correspondence," 1856, are the only examples of verse extant from the pen of Daniel Webster.

WEEDEN, Howard, b. Huntsville, Ala., 18–, of Virginia and Georgia parentage. Her father and grandfather were cotton planters; and from her mother's family, of Scottish ancestry, Miss Weeden inherited a taste for letters. — "Bandanna Ballads," 1899. (D. 1905.)

WEEKS, Robert Kelley, b. New York, N. Y., 1840; d. there, 1876. A graduate of Yale and member of the New York bar, who gave up law for literature, and published "Poems," 1866; "Episodes and Lyric Pieces," 1870.

WELBY, Amelia B. (Coppuck), b. St. Michael's, Md., 1819; d. Louisville, Ky., 1852. Her family removed to Louisville, where she was married in 1838 to George B. Welby, of that city. "Poems by Amelia" was published in 1844. An illustrated edition appeared in 1850.

WHARTON, Edith (Jones), b. New York, N. Y., 186–. Of Revolutionary ancestry. Daughter of George Frederic Jones, of N. Y., and the wife of Edward Wharton. Author, with Ogden Codman, Jr., of "The Decoration of Houses;" "The Greater Inclination," short stories, 1899; "The Touchstone," 1900.

WHICHER, George Meason, educator, b. Muscatine, Iowa, 1860. Educated at Iowa College. Professor of classical languages at the Normal College, city of New York. Editor of Greek and Latin text-books, and a contributor of essays and verse to the periodicals.

WHITE, Edward Lucas, b. Bergen, N. J., 1865. A resident of Baltimore, Md., where he is engaged in teaching Latin and Greek. His poems, hitherto uncollected, may soon be published in book-form.

WHITE, Eugene Richard, b. Buffalo, N. Y., 1872. Editor of the Niagara Falls "Gazette." He graduated at Williams in 1894. In 1898 his volume "Songs of Good Fighting" was published.

WHITING, Charles Goodrich, critic of letters and art, b. St. Albans, Vt., 1842. He grew up in Springfield, Mass., and has been connected with "The Republican" of that city since 1866, becoming in 1874 its literary editor, and also paying constant and influential attention to the progress of American art. In 1885 he wrote the poem for the unveiling of the soldiers' monument at Springfield. He has published "The Saunterer," prose and verse, 1886; "Essays on Nature."

WHITING, Lilian, journalist, b. Niagara Falls, N. Y., 185–. She has been successful in editorial work and as a newspaper correspondent, and was literary editor of the Boston "Traveller," 1883–90. Her permanent residence is Boston. Author of "The World Beautiful," 1st, 2d, 3d, series, essays, 1894–98; "After Her Death: the Story of a Summer," 1897; "From Dreamland Sent," poems, 1899; "Kate Field: a Record," 1899.

WHITMAN, Sarah Helen (Power), b. Providence, R. I., 1803; d. 1878. Widowed, 1833; betrothed to Poe, 1848. The engagement was broken, but she defended him in her monograph, "Edgar A. Poe and His Critics," 1860. Her published works include "Fairy Ballads," written with her sister, Anna M. Power; "Hours of Life and Other Poems," 1853; and "Poems," posthumous, 1878.

WHITMAN, Walt (originally Walter), b. West Hills, Huntington township, Suffolk Co., L. I., N. Y., 31 May, 1819; d. Camden, N. J., 26 March, 1892. He was descended from Connecticut, English, and Long Island Dutch forbears. His father left the ancestral farm for Brooklyn, 1823, where Walt lived until 1836, studying in the public schools and learning the printer's trade. He taught school, and edited a paper at Huntington for about a year in 1839. Until 1861 he was occupied as a printer, editor, and miscellaneous writer. Whitman had always devoted as much time as possible to the study of nature on the Long Island beaches, and to observing the throngs of people at the Brooklyn ferries and in the New York streets, when, in 1853, he began to experiment in the direction of the new forms of poetry and philosophy developed in "Leaves of Grass," 1855. His previous work had been altogether conventional. At the same time he assumed the dress of a workingman, and became conspicuous as an associate of the common people. His book created much discussion. Enlarged editions appeared in 1856 and 1861, and Whitman's verse became a "cult." It was in 1862 that he began his three years' service as a volunteer army nurse in the hospitals about Washington. This experience is set forth in "Memoranda during the War," 1875. His health failing, he secured a place in the Interior Department, 1865, from which he was dismissed by the secretary, who had read and disapproved of passages in "Leaves of Grass." This incident called out the pamphlet by W. D. O'Connor, entitled the "Good Gray Poet: A Vindication," from which Whitman's sobriquet originated. He soon obtained another clerkship in the attorney-general's office, which he held until his final breakdown from paralysis in 1873. He resided with his brother at Camden until 1883, when his own resources and the assistance of friends enabled him to secure the home in Mickle Street, Camden. Some of his best verse is contained in "Walt Whitman's Drum-Taps," 1865–66, inspired by the war and by President Lincoln's assassination. A selected edition of his "Poems," edited by W. M. Rossetti, and published in England, 1868, was the beginning of his fame in that country, and brought him letters from Tennyson and others. Enlarged editions of "Leaves of Grass" appeared in 1867, 1871, 1872. His prose volume, "Democratic Vistas," was published, 1871, and in this he took occasion to reply to his critics. In 1876, the "Centennial" edition of his works was issued by the author in two volumes. Whitman lectured in New York, Boston, and other cities, on the anniversary of Lincoln's death. A definitive edition of "Leaves of Grass" appeared in Boston, 1882, but was suppressed through the action of the attorney-general of Massachusetts, and subsequently issued in Philadelphia. "Specimen Days and Collect," 1883, was a collection of his prose works. Volumes supplementary to "Leaves of Grass" are "November Boughs," 1888, and "Good Bye, My Fancy," 1891. The final edition, "Leaves of Grass," 1892, includes these. Whitman lies in a massive tomb in Harleigh Cemetery, Camden, which he designed and built shortly before his death. Cp. "Poets of America," chap. x.

[A. S.]

WHITNEY, Hattie, b. St. Louis, Mo., 18—. Of New England descent. Her early life was passed in the country. Her present residence is in St. Louis. She has written much verse and fiction for literary publications.

WHITNEY, Helen (Hay). — See *Helen Hay.*

WHITNEY, Joseph Ernest, educator, b. Cornwall, Conn., 1858; d. Colorado Springs, Col., 1893. Graduated at Yale, where he was appointed instructor in English, 1884, resigning on account of ill-health, 1888. Joint editor with Henry S. Durand of "Elm Leaves," a collection of Yale verse, 1881. His miscellaneous writings gave evidence of his fine natural qualities, and of the high standard at which he aimed throughout his brief term of service.

WHITTIER, John Greenleaf, New England's Quaker Poet, b. East Haverhill, Mass., 17 Dec., 1807; d. Hampton Falls, N. H., 7 Sept. 1892. Having scant schooling and few books, he steeped his mind in the Bible, and in the journals of Friends. A chance knowledge of Burns's poetry had a stimulating effect upon his imagination. The poems of his boyhood were numerous, but the earliest that he saw fit to include in the complete and definitive edition of his writings (7 vols. 1888–89) are dated 1825. One of them, "The Exile's Departure," was sent by his sister Mary to the Newburyport "Free Press." Its editor, William Lloyd Garrison, accepted the poem, and gave its young author a home in his own family, enabling him to attend the Haverhill Academy. Here he paid for a winter's schooling with money earned by making slippers. Afterwards he wrote for the press, and successively edited "The American Manufacturer," Boston; "The Haverhill Gazette;" and "The New England Weekly Review," Hartford, Conn. In 1833 he published at his own expense the pamphlet "Justice and Expediency," which identified him with the anti-slavery movement. In 1836, he became a secretary of the American Anti-Slavery Society, and made, with the poem "Mogg Megone," his first appearance in book-form. "Legends of New England in Prose and Verse," pamphlet, had appeared in 1831; "Moll Pitcher," a pamphlet, in 1832. In 1837 the collection, "Poems Written during the Progress of the Abolition Question in the United States" was published without his knowledge. Frail health closed his service in the Massachusetts legislature, and also his editorship of the Philadelphia "Pennsylvania Freeman," 1837–40. He retired to the home in Amesbury, Mass., whither his mother and sister had removed. Here and in Danvers, in the same county, the rest of his life was quietly passed. He never married, but found happiness in the companionship of his sister Elizabeth, who died in 1864. The complete edition of his works includes a number of her poems. Whittier wrote for Garrison's "Liberator" and for the Washington "National Era," where also Mrs. Stowe's "Uncle Tom's Cabin" first appeared. To the "Atlantic Monthly," established in 1857, he became a favorite contributor. "Voices of Freedom," 1849, was the first comprehensive collection of his poems. It was followed by "Songs of Labor," 1850; "The Chapel of the Hermits," "A Sabbath Scene," 1853; "The Panorama," 1856; "Home Ballads," 1860; "In War Time," 1863; "National Lyrics," 1865; "Snow Bound," 1866; "The Tent on the Beach," 1867; "Among the Hills," 1868; "Ballads of New England," 1869; "Miriam and Other Poems," 1870; "The Pennsylvania Pilgrim," 1872; "Mabel Martin," 1874; "Hazel Blossoms," 1875; "Centennial Hymn," 1876; "The Vision of Echard," 1878; "The King's Missive," 1881; "The Bay of Seven Islands," 1883; "Poems of Nature," 1885; "St. Gregory's Guest, and Recent Poems," 1886; "At Sundown," 1890, dedicated to E. C. Stedman, and ending with his last poem, addressed to O. W. Holmes. His prose works are "The Stranger in Lowell," 1845; "Supernaturalism in New England," 1847; "Leaves from Margaret Smith's Journal," 1849; "Old Portraits and Modern Sketches," 1850; "Literary Recollections," 1854. He edited "John Woolman's Journal," 1873, and "The Letters of Lydia Maria Child," 1882. He compiled "Songs of Three Centuries," 1873; "Child-Life," 1871; and "Child-Life in Prose," 1873. The authoritative Life of Whittier is written by his nephew-in-law and literary executor, Samuel T. Pickard, 1894. His home in Amesbury, Mass., has been purchased by the Whittier Home Association; a club has been formed there; the house and grounds are thrown open to members on special occasions; and on the poet's birthday memorial ceremonies are held. For an extended review of Whittier's career and writings, cp. "Poets of America," chap. iv. [L. C. B.]

WILCOX, Ella Wheeler, b. Johnstown Centre, Wis., 185–. She was educated at the University of Wisconsin, and was married, 1884, to Robert M. Wilcox, of Meriden, Conn. Her home is in New York City. Among her writings are "Drops of Water," temperance poems, 1872; "Shells," 1873; "Maurine, and Other Poems," 1882; "Poems of Passion," 1883; "Mal Moulée," story, 1885; "Poems of Pleasure," 1888; "Custer, and Other Poems," 1895.

WILDE, Richard Henry, lawyer, b. Dublin, Ireland, 1789; d. New Orleans, La., 1847. Reared in poverty, but a natural poet and scholar. Prepared himself for the law and rose by his own effort to a position of eminence in letters and in public life. Lived in Italy from 1835 to 1840. Was afterward until his death a prominent lawyer in New Orleans. Author of fugitive poems, notably "My Life is Like a Summer Rose." Wrote also, as a result of his Italian studies, "Conjectures and Researches Concerning the Love, Madness, and Imprisonment of Torquato Tasso," 1842.

WILKINS, Mary Eleanor, b. Randolph, Mass., 1862. Miss Wilkins is known by her prose work rather than by her poetry, of which she has written comparatively little. Early in 1893, "Giles Corey," a poetic drama, was produced in Boston, under the auspices of The Theatre of Arts and Letters. Her well-known novels are charming realistic tales of New England, delineating the life and manners of its people.

WILKINSON, William Cleaver, D. D., b. Westford, Vt., 1833. A Baptist clergyman, formerly professor in the Rochester Theological Seminary, and professor of poetry and criticism at the University of Chicago since 1892. Among his writings are "A Free Lance in the Field of Life and Letters," 1874; "Webster, an Ode," 1882; "Poems," 1883; "Edwin Arnold as Poetizer and Paganizer," 1884; "The Epic of Saul," 1891; "A College Greek Course in English," 1893; "The Epic of Paul," 1898.

WILLARD, Emma (Hart), educator, b. New Berlin, Conn., 1787; d. Troy, N. Y., 1870. She conducted the Troy female seminary from 1821 to 1838, inaugurating many reforms in the education of women. She was the author of several prose works, and of "Poems," 1830, the latter including the well-known "Rocked in the Cradle of the Deep."

WILLIAMS, Francis Howard, b. Philadelphia, Penn., 1844. Connected with a trust company in Philadelphia, and an able contributor to various journals. Author of "The Princess Elizabeth: a Lyric Drama," 1880; "The Higher Education," comedy, 1881; "A Reformer in Ruffles," comedy, 1881; "Theodora: a Christmas Pastoral," 1882; "Master and Man," play, 1884; "Boscosel," short story in the collection, "The Septameron," 1888; "Atman: the Documents in a Strange Case," story, 1891; "Pennsylvania Poets of the Provençal Period," essay, 1893; "The Flute Player, and Other Poems," 1894.

WILLIS, Nathaniel Parker, poet and essayist, b. Portland, Me., 1806; d. "Idlewild," near Newburgh, N. Y., 1867. Won at Yale, where he was graduated, 1827, a prize for the best poem. His earliest verses appeared in the "Youth's Companion" and "Boston Recorder," both founded by his father. In 1829, he established the "American Monthly Magazine," afterwards the "New York Mirror." In 1831 he visited Europe and the East, contributing letters to the "Mirror." A rebuke from Capt. Marryat in the "Metropolitan Magazine," for reporting private interviews, led to a bloodless duel. In 1839 he published the "Corsair," to which Thackeray contributed. In 1846 he founded, with G. P. Morris, the "Home Journal," remaining associate editor till his death, at the estate on the Hudson which he purchased in 1846 and named "Idlewild." Published "Poetical Scripture Sketches," 1827; "Melanie, and Other Poems," "Lady Jane, and Other Poems," 1844; and many volumes of brilliant prose sketches, letters, travels, etc. A complete edition of his poems appeared in 1868. Cp. "Poets of America," pp. 41, 42.

WILLSON (Byron), Forceythe, b. Little Genesee, N. Y., 1837; d. Alfred, N. Y., 1867. He spent part of his childhood in Kentucky, studied at Harvard, and was on the staff of the Louisville "Courier." Author of "The Old Sergeant, and Other Poems," written during the Civil War and published in 1867. A strongly imaginative balladist, whose death was a loss to poetry.

WILSON, Alexander, ornithologist, b. Paisley, Scotland, 1766; d. Philadelphia, Penn., 1813. Emigrated to America, 1794. Followed his trades, — weaving and peddling, — taught school, and was editor of an edition of "Rees's Cyclopædia." In 1804 he began his "American Ornithology;" published seven volumes, 1808–13; the other two volumes being edited after his death by a friend. Author of "Poems," 1790 and 1791; "Watty and Meg," 1792; "The Foresters," 1805; "Poems and Literary Prose," 1876.

WILSON, Robert Burns, b. Washington Co., Penn., 1850. Early in life he became a resident of Frankfort, Ky. He studied painting, and his pictures were exhibited with success. His verse has gained him a prominent position among Western poets. Besides many uncollected poems in the magazines, he is the author of "Life and Love," 1887, and "The Shadows of the Trees," 1898.

WINTER, William, b. Gloucester, Mass., 15 July, 1836. He graduated at the Harvard Law School, and for a time studied law under Rufus Choate. In 1859 he removed to New York, and soon won respect by the standard of his work for the "Saturday Press," "Vanity Fair," "Albion," etc. With an instinct for comradeship, he was the attached friend of George Arnold, O'Brien, and others among whom his lot was cast in the struggling days of authorship, and he survived to become their loyal editor and memorialist. Since 1865 he has been the dramatic critic of the N. Y. "Tribune," and in that capacity has gained distinction for both his journal and himself, ranking with his most eminent contemporaries here and abroad, and held in intimacy and honor by the foremost actors of his time. He has indulged to the full his passion for the scenes and traditions of old England, and on many sentimental journeys thither, and his resultant books have become "little classics" on both sides of the Atlantic. Mr. Winter's home is on Staten Island, where he has associated his name with the Staten Island Academy, by founding its Arthur Winter library, in memory of a gifted and favorite child. In New York he long has held the primacy as poet and orator of festive or memorial occasions, having the stops of humor and pathos at full command in classical speech as well as in his song. Author of "The Convent, and Other Poems," 1854; "The Queen's Domain," poems, 1858; "My Witness," poems, 1871; "Thistledown," poems, 1878; "Poems," complete to date, 1880; "The Jeffersons," 1881; "Henry Irving," 1885; "The Stage-Life of Mary Anderson," 1886; "Shakespeare's England," 1886; "Wanderers," poems, 1888; "Gray Days and Gold," 1891; "Old Shrines and Ivy," 1892; "The Life and Art of Edwin Booth," 1894; "Brown Heath and Blue Bells," 1895. He has edited "Life, Stories, and the Poems of John Brougham," 1881; the poems of G. Arnold and O'Brien, and various other works of this class, besides the "Shakespearan and Miscellaneous Plays of Edwin Booth," 1899. Cp. "Poets of America," p. 440.

WINTHROP, Theodore, b. New Haven, Conn., 1828; fell at Great Bethel, Va., 1861. An early and distinguished writer of the Civil War. He was graduated at Yale, and after spending two years in Europe and several in Panama, removed to New York City, where he was admitted to the bar. In 1861 he became General Butler's secretary, and planned with him the campaign that cost him his own life. Though he published a notable article, "The March of the Seventh," in the "Atlantic Monthly," the writings which were to preserve his name and fame appeared after the close of his sorrowfully brief career, and comprise the following volumes: "Cecil Dreeme," 1861; "John Brent," 1862; "Edwin Brothertoft," 1862; "The Canoe and the Saddle," 1862; "Life in the Open Air, and Other Papers," 1863. His novels were in some degree the forerunners of a new departure in American fiction.

WOODBERRY, George Edward, poet, critic, and educator, b. Beverly, Mass., 12 May, 1855. Was fitted for college at Phillips Academy, Exeter, N. H., and graduated at Harvard, 1877. He was acting professor of rhetoric, English literature, and history, at the State University of Nebraska, 1877–78, and professor of Anglo-Saxon and rhetoric, and instructor in composition, at the same university, 1880–82. From 1878 to 1879 he was engaged on the staff of "The Nation." He resided at Beverly, occupied with literary work until his appointment, in 1891, to a professorship of English literature at Columbia. Author of "History of Wood Engraving," 1883; "The North Shore Watch: a Threnody," privately printed, 1883; "Edgar Allan Poe," in "American Men of Letters," 1885; "The North Shore Watch, and Other Poems," 1890; "Studies in Letters and Life," essays, 1890; "Heart of Man," essays, 1899; "Wild Eden," verse, 1899; "Makers of Literature," essays, 1900. Professor Woodberry has edited "Selected Poems" of Aubrey de Vere, 1895; "The Complete Poetical Works of Percy Bysshe Shelley," 4 vols., 1892; "The Works of Edgar Allan Poe," with Edmund C. Stedman, 10 vols., 1894. Is editor of the "National Studies in American Letters" series, to which he contributes "Flowers of Essex," 1900.

WOODWORTH, Samuel, journalist and writer, b. Scituate, Mass., 13 Jan., 1785; d. New York, N. Y., 9 Dec., 1842. Connected with several papers, notably with the N. Y. "Mirror," of which he was one of the founders. Author of "The Champions of Freedom," 1816, and several operettas and dramatic pieces. A collection of his poems was made in 1826 under the patronage of De Witt Clinton, but only "The Old Oaken Bucket" is now remembered.

WOOLSEY, Sarah Chauncey, "Susan Coolidge," b. Cleveland, O., about 184-. Niece of President Woolsey of Yale College. Her home was in Newport, R. I. She has published "Old Convent School in Paris;" "The New Year's Bargain," 1871; the series beginning with "What Katy Did," 1872; and many other books for young girls; "Verses," 1880; "Ballads of Romance and History," with others, 1887; "A Few More Verses." She has edited "The Autobiography and Correspondence of Mrs. Delaney," 1879; "The Diary and Letters of Frances Burney," 1880. (D. Newport, R. I., 1905.)

WOOLSEY, Theodore Dwight, scholar, b. New York, N. Y., 1801; d. New Haven, Conn., 1889. Graduated at Yale, and studied for the ministry at Princeton. He was appointed professor of Greek at Yale in 1831, and was president of the same institution from 1846 to 1871. Author of numerous classical text-books and works on political and social science. "Eros, and Other Poems" was privately printed in 1880.

WOOLSON, Constance Fenimore, novelist, b. Claremont, N. H., 1840; d. Venice, Italy, 1894. A grand-niece of James Fenimore Cooper; educated at Cleveland, O., and at a French school in New York City. From 1873 to 1879 she lived chiefly in Florida. The last years of her life were passed in Italy. In 1870 she began to contribute stories to "Harper's Monthly," and most of her prose and verse appeared in that magazine. Author of "The Old Stone House," 1873; "Castle Nowhere," "Lake-Country Sketches," 1875; "Anne," 1882; "East Angels," 1886; "Jupiter Lights," 1889; "The Front Yard, and Other Italian Stories;" "Horace Chase," 1894. No woman of rarer personal qualities, or with more decided gifts as a novelist, figured in her own generation of American writers.

WRIGHT, William Bull, physician and teacher, b. New York, N. Y., 1840; d. Atlanta, Ga., 1880. His home was in Buffalo, N. Y. Dr. Wright served in the Civil War, and was professor of ancient languages in the Buffalo normal school, 1871–78. Author of "Highland Rambles," poems, 1868; and "The Brook, and Other Poems," 1873.

"XARIFFA." — See *M. A. (Van V.) Townsend.*

YOUNG, Edward, b. Bristol, Eng., 1818. He came to the United States in 1832. His parents settled in Trenton, N. J., where he learned the watchmaker's trade. After changes of residence he removed to Lexington, Ga., which became his permanent home. His volume, "Ladye Lillian, and Other Poems," appeared in 1859.

YOUNG, William, b. Monmouth, Ill., 1847. He took a course in law, but wishing to become a dramatist, for a while went on the stage. He also made a study of the drama while living in London. His plays, "Jonquil," 1871; "The Rogue's March," 1872; "Pendragon," verse, 1881; "The Rajah," 1883; "Ganelon," verse, 1889, — were produced in Chicago and New York City. His "Wishmaker's Town," 1885 (new ed. 1898, with a preface by T. B. Aldrich), is a series of quaint and imaginative poems on one theme. His dramatic setting of Wallace's "Ben Hur" was placed on the New York stage, 1899–1900.

INDEXES

INDEX OF FIRST LINES

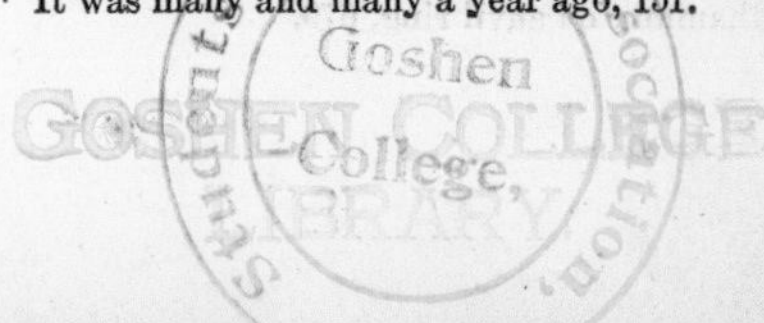

INDEX OF TITLES

INDEX OF POETS

The Riverside Press
CAMBRIDGE · MASSACHUSETTS
U · S · A

THE CRITICAL AND POETICAL WORKS

OF

EDMUND CLARENCE STEDMAN

HOUGHTON MIFFLIN COMPANY
BOSTON: 4 PARK STREET. NEW YORK: 85 FIFTH AVENUE
The Riverside Press, Cambridge